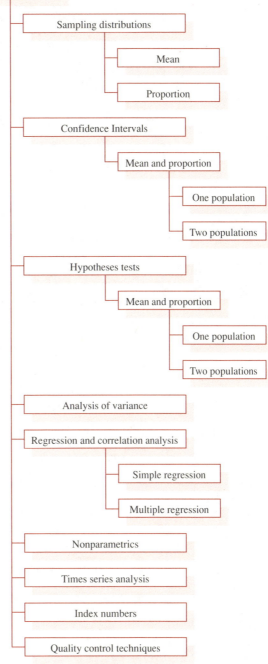

Inferential statistics

Sampling distributions

Mean

Proportion

Confidence Intervals

Mean and proportion

One population

Two populations

Hypotheses tests

Mean and proportion

One population

Two populations

Analysis of variance

Regression and correlation analysis

Simple regression

Multiple regression

Nonparametrics

Times series analysis

Index numbers

Quality control techniques

APPLIED STATISTICS
FOR BUSINESS AND ECONOMICS

○○○○

APPLIED STATISTICS
FOR BUSINESS AND ECONOMICS

OOOO

ALLEN WEBSTER
Bradley University

HOMEWOOD, IL 60430
BOSTON, MA 02116

SPONSORING EDITOR: Richard T. Hercher, Jr.
DEVELOPMENT EDITOR: James Minatel
PROJECT EDITOR: Rita McMullen
PRODUCTION MANAGER: Irene H. Sotiroff
DESIGNER: John Rokusek/Rokusek Design
COVER ILLUSTRATOR: Valerie Sinclair
ARTIST: Electronic Desktop Services
COMPOSITOR: Beacon Graphics Corporation
TYPEFACE: 10/12 Times Roman
PRINTER: R. R. Donnelley & Sons Company

Library of Congress Cataloging-in-Publication Data

Webster, Allen.
    Applied statistics for business and economics / Allen Webster.
        p.   cm.
    Includes index.
    ISBN 0-256-07314-7 ISBN 0-256-11251-7 (Instructor's Edition)
    1. Commercial statistics.   2. Economics—Statistical methods.
    I. Title.
    HF1017.W43   1992
    519.5'02433—dc20   91–26252

Printed in the United States of America

2 3 4 5 6 7 8 9 0 DOC 8 7 6 5 4 3 2

To my loving wife, Patty, who is several standard deviations above the mean, and to our "children," Corbin and Cassie

PREFACE TO THE STUDENT

This book is written with you in mind. In the past my students have voiced many reasons why they found a text difficult to read. These complaints have ranged from excessive use of mathematical symbols to overly detailed discussions and an absence of any sense of purpose or relevance. One young, budding statistician even argued that the material was difficult to read and understand because the words were too close to the page. This book is written with an attempt to avoid all the problems registered by former students—with the exception of the last one.

Since most students never read the preface, and I am not naive enough to believe this one is an exception, I will endeavor to make only one point. Specifically, statistics can be of tremendous benefit to you in your forthcoming career. In today's complex and competitive business world, it is no longer possible to make decisions on the basis of mere conjecture or what has worked in the past. Instead, it is only after deliberate consideration and scientific inquiry that well-informed and intelligent decisions can be realized. Furthermore, the need to properly *interpret* the results of all statistical tests cannot be overemphasized. It is not enough to merely "crunch numbers" and derive an answer. Without the ability to interpret that answer, its meaning and usefulness are lost.

To provide you with the necessary statistical expertise that you will most certainly require to adequately perform your job-related responsibilities, this text contains certain special features that distinguish it from others. These unique characteristics include:

A PREVIEW OF THINGS TO LOOK FOR

Each chapter begins with a short list of the most important concepts and techniques that you should be looking for as you read the chapter. By knowing in advance what you will encounter in the chapter, you can be better prepared to learn.

CHAPTER BLUEPRINT

This feature is also designed to prepare you for the coming chapter. In the blueprint, the order, flow, and dependency of all of the major topics are laid out. This should help you in organizing how the concepts relate to each other.

THREE-PART EXAMPLES

Each of the more than 115 examples in the text, which illustrate the use of statistical analysis, consists of three parts. The first is the *Statement,* which describes the problem that must be addressed. The second is a complete and coherent *Solution,* including explanations along the way. The final segment of each example offers an informative and enlightening *Statistical Interpretation* of the results. This third part is the key to understanding the meaning and use of statistics. It is here that students begin to develop their ability to interpret the answer rather than just calculating results. This adds a sense of reality and application.

QUICK CHECKS

A series of short exercises that allow you to test your comprehension before moving on to the next topic is included in each chapter. Approximately 120 mini-problems provide you with assurance as you progress through the chapter; yet they are brief enough to prevent any interruption in the flow and continuity of the material.

DECISION MAKING THROUGH PROBLEM SOLVING

Placed throughout each chapter are more than 40 short narratives taken directly from popular business and news publications that describe how statistics was actually used by a business to make decisions and solve a real world problem. These short, anecdotal sketches contain no numbers or formulas of any sort but are simply brief accounts of how a business relied on statistics to solve a dilemma. This provides you with a bridge to reality by illustrating how statistics can be applied.

FIGURES

Graphs and pictorial displays are an important part of how information is analyzed and communicated in statistics and in the business world. There are over 250 figures and graphs in the text to aid you in understanding the concepts, calculations, and their interpretations.

SOLVED PROBLEMS

Each chapter concludes with problems and elaborately worked out solutions, which demonstrate and reinforce each statistical tool covered in the chapter.

What You Should Have Learned from This Chapter

After you have studied a chapter, it is useful to reflect on the important concepts. When you review the material, this is a good place to start.

Computer Applications

Because much of the analytical work that you will be doing in your actual job will be accomplished using a computer, this text provides a brief introduction to several popular statistical programs. In a short section in each chapter, SAS, SPSS-PC, and Minitab are used to demonstrate how modern computers and software simplify statistical analysis. The input commands for one or more of the programs are shown, along with plenty of sample output.

List of Symbols and Terms and List of Formulas

Although I have endeavored to keep notation and formulas to a minimum, they are a necessary part of any statistics text. In order to help you organize and review the formulas, notation, and terminology introduced in each chapter, these lists are included for your convenience.

Chapter Exercises

An ample supply of exercises (over 950) with a varying degree of difficulty follow each chapter and provide you with an opportunity to sharpen your statistical skills. These exercises are grouped according to which type of skills they test.

You Make the Decision Many sets of Chapter Exercises begin with these exercises, which do not involve any numerical calculations but allow you to identify what particular statistical tool would be needed to solve a specific type of problem. This practice develops the much needed ability to recognize when and how statistics can be brought into play to aid in determining solutions to common problem situations.

Conceptual Questions Like the You Make the Decision exercises, these questions do not involve any numerical calculations. As the name implies, they are designed to reinforce your knowledge of key concepts introduced in the chapter.

Problems These are the meat of the Chapter Exercises. These questions involve calculations and often require interpretation, much like the Examples and Solved Problems.

Empirical Exercises A further sense of reality can be introduced through the use of empirical exercises, which offer the opportunity for you to devise and implement your own simple statistical exercises. These exercises are much like the Problems in their brevity and concise nature. However, you will acquire a more complete appreciation for a statistical study by devising a simple statistical exercise of your own and collecting the data on your own without specific guidance or direction normally provided by the Problems.

CASE APPLICATIONS   These are questions that permit you to apply the statistical tools you learned in the chapter to solve a more complex problem situation and provide an interpretation of the solution. In many instances, these tools must be applied in combination in order to devise a complete and adequate solution.

COMPUTER EXERCISES   The Chapter Exercises provide several exercises designed to be solved with the aid of computers. These exercises show how the computer can be used to solve common business problems with your choice of computer software.

In addition to this wealth of pedagogical aids, a complete set of supplementary materials is offered.

The *Student Study Guide* contains worked-out solutions to approximately one-third of the odd-numbered chapter exercises. It also contains detailed solutions to *every* Quick Check in the text. Each chapter in the *Study Guide* begins with a short overview of the corresponding text chapter. It also has short examples to reinforce the use of the definitions and formulas in the chapter. For your convenience, all of the chapter formulas are repeated here.

Three *Computer Guides* are available for use with this text. These Guides are available for SPSS-PC, SAS-PC, and Minitab, the three computer programs discussed in the text. These manuals detail in easy-to-follow steps exactly what commands should be entered to obtain the desired output. Many examples in these manuals use data and questions from the examples and solved problems in the text.

A computer data disk is also available that provides the data files referred to in the text Computer Exercises. This disk contains the data in formats for all of the computer packages cited above.

ACKNOWLEDGEMENTS

Writing a text is a major undertaking which could not be accomplished without the help of many others. I would be remiss if I did not thank the many reviewers who examined one or more of the several drafts of the manuscript for this text over the last two years. These reviewers made substantial contributions to the form and substance of the finished product:

James Baldwin
Nassau Community College
John P. Briscoe
Indiana University Southeast

Sharad Chitgopekar
Illinois State University

Rex Cutshall
Vincennes University

Kamvar Farahbod
California State University, San Bernardino

Frank Forst
Loyola University of Chicago

Donald Goldschen
University of the District of Columbia

Steve Grahm
Vincennes University

Robert J. Miller
Missouri Southern State College

William Morrow
Eastern Kentucky University

William Sanders
Clarion University

Patricia Setlick
William Rainey Harper College

Marsha Shelburn
University of South Carolina at Aiken

With the large number of examples, exercises, and other numerical computations in this text, it would be impossible for any one person to correctly calculate and record every one of them. However, a team of dedicated statisticians has a much better chance to produce an error-free text. To this end, Kamvar Farahbod and Patricia Setlick independently resolved every numerical calculation in the text. Without their superb dedication to this project, this text could not have been published. Kamvar Farahbod also solved all of the Chapter Exercises to recheck the answers and solutions.

Writing the supplements is a task unto itself, and these authors deserve a round of applause: Barbara McKinney co-authored the *Student Study Guide.* She has written a superb *Study Guide* that will be valuable to every student taking this course. She also wrote the *Test Bank and CompuTest Manual.* I have found her test questions to be very appropriate, and I hope that you will utilize this fine manual. Kilman Shin authored all of the *Computer Guides.* With his in-depth knowledge of many statistical software packages and of applied statistics, he was able to write these guides, which will be of great benefit to anyone using, or learning to use, one of these three statistical packages.

I wish to extend a special thanks to Kristin Smith, one of the many fine students we have here at Bradley University, for her ceaseless effort and diligence in helping find and eliminate errors.

Finally, the fine professionals at Richard D. Irwin, Inc. contributed their expertise to this project. Special thanks go to Richard T. Hercher, Jr., senior sponsoring editor, for signing my text. Jim Minatel, the developmental editor on this project, worked with me for over two years to bring this text and the supplements to their final form.

Allen Webster

CONTENTS IN BRIEF

CONTENTS

CHAPTER 9
HYPOTHESIS TESTING, 384

APPLIED STATISTICS
FOR BUSINESS AND ECONOMICS

CHAPTER ONE

THE ROLE OF STATISTICS

CHAPTER BLUEPRINT

This chapter introduces the concept of statistics as an organized study. You will be exposed to the general purpose of statistical analysis and the many ways in which statistics can help you find solutions to problems in your professional life.

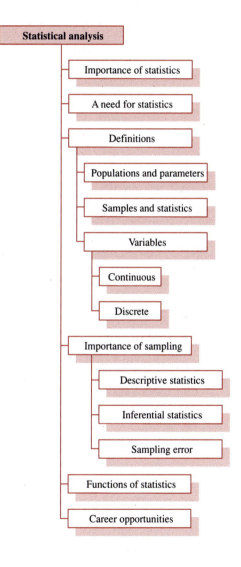

You can prove anything with statistics.
Sometimes even the truth.

1.1 INTRODUCTION

As our world grows in complexity, it becomes increasingly difficult to make informed and intelligent decisions. Often these decisions must be made with less than perfect knowledge and in the presence of considerable uncertainty. Yet solutions to these problems are essential to our well-being and even our ultimate survival. We are continually pressured by distressing economic problems such as raging inflation, a cumbersome tax system, and excessive swings in the business cycle. Our entire social and economic fabric is threatened by environmental pollution, a burdensome public debt, an ever-increasing crime rate, and unpredictable interest rates.

If these conditions seem characteristic of today's life-style, you should be reminded that problems of this nature contributed more to the downfall of ancient Rome than did the invasion of barbarian hordes from the North. Our relatively short period of success on this planet is no guarantee of future survival. Unless viable solutions to these pressing problems can be found, we may, like the ancient Romans, follow the dinosaur and the dodo bird into oblivion.

This chapter will provide a general impression of what statistics is and how it can be useful to you. This overview of the nature of statistics and the benefits it can contribute will be accomplished by examining

• Basic definitions of statistical tools.
• How sampling can be used to perform statistical analysis.
• The functions that statistics performs.
• How statistics can help you in your career.

We begin with a brief discussion of the meaningful role statistics plays in the important process of making delicate decisions.

1.2 THE IMPORTANCE OF STATISTICS

Virtually every area of serious, scientific inquiry can benefit from statistical analysis. For the economic policy maker who must advise the president and other public officials on proper, economic procedure, statistics has proven to be an invaluable tool. Decisions regarding tax rates, social programs, defense spending, and many other issues can be made intelligently only with the aid of statistical analysis. Businessmen and businesswomen, in their eternal quest for profit, find statistics essential in the decision-making process. Efforts at quality control, cost minimization, product and inventory mix, and a host of other business matters can be effectively managed by using proven statistical procedures.

For those in marketing research, statistics is of invaluable assistance in determining if a new product is likely to prove successful. Statistics is also quite useful in the evaluation of investment opportunities by financial consultants. Accountants, personnel managers, and manufacturers all find unlimited opportunities to utilize statistical analysis. Even the medical researcher, concerned about the effectiveness of a new drug, finds statistics a helpful ally.

Such applications and many others are repeatedly illustrated in this text. You will be shown how statistics can be used to improve your job performance and many aspects of your daily life.

1.3   You Will Have a Need for Statistical Literacy!

You may feel that the type of work you intend to pursue will not require statistical analysis. Or you might argue that the staff of statisticians employed by your company will perform all necessary statistical work, and that there is no need for you to master the details of statistical analysis.

Such is not the case. Even if the professional statisticians in your organization are going to perform the necessary statistical work for you, it is essential that you possess a certain level of statistical literacy. In order to determine how the statistical staff can assist you in your job performance, you must know what statistics is, what statisticians do, and how they go about doing it. When problems arise, you must be able to determine how statistics can be of help. To do so, you must have at least a nodding acquaintance with statistical procedures and be able to communicate with statisticians in the joint effort to devise adequate solutions. Once this solid familiarity with statistical analysis has been acquired, you will marvel at the limitless ways statistics can simplify your life and prove to be quite useful in the solution of common problems.

1.4   Some Basic Definitions

Every branch of scientific inquiry has its unique vocabulary. Statistics is no exception. This section examines some common terms used in statistical analysis. These definitions and expressions are essential to any comprehension of how statistical tests are carried out.

A.   Populations and Parameters

In any statistical study, the researcher is interested in a certain collection or set of observations called the **population.** If the incomes of all 121 million wage earners in the United States are of interest to an economist assisting Congress in formulating a national tax plan, then all 121 million incomes constitute the population. If a tax plan is being considered only for those incomes in excess of, say, $100,000, then those incomes above $100,000 are the population. The population is the entire collection of all observations of interest.

Population
A population is the entire collection of all observations of interest to the researcher.

If the chief executive officer (CEO) for a large manufacturing firm wishes to study the output of all the plants owned by the firm, then the output of all plants is the population.

A **parameter** is any descriptive measure of a population. Examples are the average income of all those wage earners in the United States, or the total output of all the manufacturing plants. The point to remember is that a parameter describes a population.

Parameter
A parameter is a descriptive measure of the entire population of all observations of interest to the researcher.

B. SAMPLES AND STATISTICS

Although statisticians are generally interested in some aspect of the entire population, they generally find that populations are too big to study in their entirety. Calculating the average income of all the 121 million wage earners would be an overwhelming task. Therefore, we must usually be content to study only a small portion of that population. This smaller and more manageable portion is called a **sample**. A sample is a scientifically selected subset of the population.

Sample
A sample is a representative portion of the population which is selected for study because the population is too large to examine in its entirety.

Each month the U.S. Department of Labor calculates the average income of a sample of only several thousand wage earners selected from the entire population of all 121 million workers. The average from this sample is then used as an estimate of the average income for the entire population. Samples are necessary because studying entire populations is too time-consuming and costly.

A **statistic** is any descriptive measure of a sample. The average income of those several thousand workers computed by the Department of Labor is a statistic. The statistic is to the sample what the parameter is to the population. Of importance, the statistic serves as an estimate of the parameter. Although we are really interested in the value of the parameter of the population, we most often must be resigned to only estimating it with a statistic from the sample we have selected.

Statistic
A statistic describes a sample and serves as an estimate of the corresponding population parameter.

C. VARIABLES

A **variable** is the characteristic of the sample or the population being observed. If the statistical advisor for the mayor of San Francisco is interested in the distance commuters must drive each morning, the variable is *miles driven.* In a study concerning the income of wage earners in the United States, the variable is *income.*

Variable
A variable is the characteristic of the population that is being examined in the statistical study.

A variable can be (1) quantitative or (2) qualitative. If the observations can be expressed numerically, it is a **quantitative** variable. The incomes of all the wage earners is an example of a quantitative population. Other examples include the heights of all people we might be interested in, scores students receive on the final examination in statistics, and the number of miles those commuters in San Francisco must drive each morning. In each case, the observations are measured numerically.

A **qualitative** variable is measured nonnumerically. The marital status of credit applicants, the sex of students in your statistics class, and the race, hair color, and religious preference of those San Francisco commuters are examples of qualitative variables. In every case, the observations are measured nonnumerically.

In addition, variables can be (1) continuous or (2) discrete. A **continuous** variable is one that can take on any value within a given range. No matter how close two observations might be, if the instrument of measurement is precise enough, a third observation can be found which will fall between the first two. A continuous variable generally results from measurement.

A **discrete** variable is restricted to certain values, usually whole numbers. They are often the result of enumeration or counting. The number of students in your class or the number of cars sold by General Motors are examples. In neither case will you observe fractional values.

Throughout your study of statistics you will repeatedly refer to these concepts and terms. You must be aware of the role each plays in the process of statistical analysis. It is particularly important that you be able to distinguish between a population and its parameters, and a sample and its statistics.

1.5   THE IMPORTANCE OF SAMPLING

As noted, much of a statistician's work is done with samples. Samples are made necessary because populations are often too big to study in their entirety. It is too time-consuming and costly to examine the entire population, and we must select a sample from the population, calculate the sample statistic, and use it to estimate the corresponding population parameter.

This discussion of samples leads to a distinction between the two main branches of statistical analysis: (1) descriptive statistics and (2) inferential statistics. **Descriptive statistics** is the process of collecting, organizing, and presenting data in some manner which quickly and easily describes these data. The next two chapters examine descriptive statistics and illustrate the various methods and tools which can be used to present and summarize large data sets.

Inferential statistics involves the use of a sample to draw some inference, or conclusion, about the population from which that sample was taken. When the Department of Labor uses the average income of a sample of several thousand workers to estimate the average income of all 121 million workers, it is engaging in a simple form of inferential statistics.

The accuracy of any estimate is of extreme importance. This accuracy depends in large part on the manner in which your sample was taken, and how careful you are to ensure that the sample provides a reliable image of the population. However, all too often, the sample proves not to be fully representative of the population, and **sampling error** will result. Sampling error is the difference between the sample statistic used to estimate the population parameter and the actual but unknown value of the parameter.

Sampling Error
Sampling error is the difference between the unknown population parameter and the sample statistic used to estimate the parameter.

There are at least two possible causes of sampling error. The first source of sampling error is mere chance in the sampling process. Due to the luck of the draw in selecting the sample elements, it is possible to unknowingly choose atypical elements which misrepresent the population. In the effort to estimate the population mean, for example, it is possible to select elements in the sample that are abnormally large, thereby resulting in an overestimate of the population mean. On the other hand, the luck of the draw may produce a large number of sample elements that are unusually small, causing an underestimate of the parameter. In either case, sampling error has occurred.

A more serious form of sampling error is found in **sampling bias.** Sampling bias occurs when there is some tendency in the sampling process to select certain sample elements over others. If the sampling procedure is incorrectly designed and tends to promote the selection of too many units with a particular characteristic at the expense of units without that characteristic, the sample is said to be biased. For example, the sampling process may inherently favor the selection of males to the exclusion of females, or married persons at the expense of singles.

Sampling Bias
Sampling bias is the tendency to favor the selection of certain sample elements over others.

A more thorough treatment of sampling bias is presented in a later chapter. Although sampling error can never be measured, since the parameter remains unknown, we must be aware that it is likely to occur.

1.6   THE FUNCTIONS OF STATISTICS

We have repeatedly emphasized the usefulness of statistics and the wide variety of problems that it can solve. In order to more fully illustrate the wide applicability of statistics, let us examine the various functions of statistics. **Statistics** is the science concerned with the (1) collection, (2) organization, (3) presentation, (4) analysis, and (5) interpretation of data.

Although the first step in any statistical study is the collection of the data, it is common practice in a beginning statistics course to assume that the data have already been collected for us and now lie at our disposal. Therefore, our work begins with the effort to organize and present these data in some meaningful and descriptive manner. The data must be put into some logical order which tends to quickly and readily reveal the message they contain. This procedure constitutes the process of descriptive statistics, as defined, and is discussed in the next few chapters. After the data have been organized and presented for examination, the statistician must analyze and interpret them. These procedures rely on inferential statistics and constitute a major benefit of statistical analysis by aiding in the decision-making and problem-solving process.

Given these essential functions of statistical analysis, we emphasize that the final fulfillment of statistics is that of prediction. You will find that through the application of precise statistical procedures it is possible to actually predict the future with some degree of accuracy. Any business firm faced with competitive pressures can benefit considerably from the ability to anticipate business conditions before they occur. If a firm knows what its sales are going to be at some time in the near future, management can devise more accurate and effective plans regarding current operations. If future sales are estimated with a reliable degree of accuracy, management can easily make important decisions regarding inventory levels, raw material orders, employment requirements, and virtually every other aspect of business operations.

1.7   CAREER OPPORTUNITIES IN STATISTICS

In a few short years, you will leave the relative safety of your academic environment and be thrust headlong into the competitive world of corporate America. From a practical standpoint, many of you may be interested in how you might use your background in statistics upon graduation. There is no doubt that an academic experience heavily laced with a strong quantitative foundation will greatly enhance your chances of obtaining meaningful employment and, subsequently, demonstrating job competence.

When you finally land that dream job on the fast track to corporate success, your employer is going to expect you to do two things:

1.   Solve problems.
2.   Make decisions.

With these two skills you can place yourself high in demand in the job market. If you can make incisive decisions while solving a person's problems, he or she will certainly be willing to pay you handsomely. To accomplish this requires at least a nodding acquaintance with basic statistical tools. A firm grasp of the statistical techniques contained in these pages will provide you with a foundation for an adequate statistical background.

Employers recognize that the complex problems faced in today's world require quantitative solutions. The inability to apply statistics and other related quantitative methods to the many common problems you will encounter will place you at a stark disadvantage in the job market.

Other courses of study which complement statistical analysis and markedly enhance your ability to effectively apply the statistical method include, but are not limited to, economics, finance, and accounting. The principles learned in the study of management and marketing techniques also provide a useful balance to your educational preparation.

Financial and economic analysts must often rely on their quantitative skills to devise effective solutions for difficult problems. An understanding of economic and financial principles permits you to apply statistical techniques to reach viable solutions and make decisions. Those of you aspiring to management positions, as well as accountants, the self-employed, or any other career in the industrial sector will find that a basic understanding of statistics will not only magnify your chances of obtaining a position, but will also enhance the likelihood of promotion by improving your job performance.

Those persons employed in quantitative areas working with statistical procedures often enjoy higher salaries and avoid the dreadful dead-end jobs. Furthermore, early in their careers they usually find themselves in closer contact with high-level management. This proximity to the executive elite occurs because upper management needs the information and assistance which statistically trained people can provide. In the current labor market, employers simply do not want to hire or retain the statistically illiterate.

Fortune magazine recently described the problem Nike, a maker of athletic shoes, was having in deciding which type of color design was preferred among its customers. There was some confusion on the part of upper management regarding which of two competing fashions would attract more consumer interest.

A sample of over 1,000 die-hard runners was carefully selected. The runners were given the opportunity to express their preferences. From this information, management was able to determine that the population of consumers displayed an overwhelming preference for one design over the other. On this basis, the decision was made as to which design to manufacture and market.

Whether your career aspirations tend toward private industry, public service with the government, or any other source of gainful livelihood, you will be much better served by your academic experience if you acquire a solid background in the fundamentals of statistical analysis.

1.8   WHAT YOU SHOULD HAVE LEARNED IN THIS CHAPTER

By now you should have some insight into the innumerable ways in which statistical analysis can be applied in the solution of common problems which you will soon face in your chosen career. It should be apparent that statistics allows you to reason, to think analytically, and devise answers to complex questions.

There is hardly a problem in life that cannot benefit from the application of statistical thought. The world that it opens to you promises extraordinary and intriguing fascination. You should approach this study of statistics with the goal of mastering the many ways in which statistics can serve you as a fascinating tool in your daily pursuits.

In the next chapter you will examine the many ways that data can be brought to life and given meaning. You will gain an understanding of the techniques used to organize and present large data sets. It is only through such a systematic presentation that essential information can be derived from the data.

LIST OF SYMBOLS AND TERMS

Population The entire set of all observations in a study.
Parameter Any descriptive measure of the characteristics of a population.
Sample Any subset or portion of the population selected to represent the population.
Statistic Any descriptive measure of a sample.
Variable The characteristic of the population or sample being observed.
Descriptive statistics The process of collecting, organizing, and presenting a data set.
Inferential statistic The use of sample data to draw inferences or conclusions about the population.
Sample error The difference between the sample statistic which serves as an estimate of the unknown population parameter and the parameter itself.

CHAPTER EXERCISES

1. The production director for the Ford Motor plant in Cleveland must report to her superior on the average number of days the employees at the plant are absent from work. However, the plant employs well over 2,000 workers, and the production director does not have enough time to examine the personnel records of all the employees. As her assistant, you must decide how she can obtain the necessary information. What advice do you offer?

2. Describe in your own words how statistics can be used to solve problems in various disciplines and occupations.

3. What specific occupation do you plan to pursue after graduation? If you are uncertain, choose the area in which you are most interested. Discuss in some detail, using specific examples, the types of problems that may arise and the decisions you will have to make in which statistical analysis may prove helpful.

4. In what manner will you use the services of the professional statistician in your organization once you find employment? Why is it unlikely that you will escape the need for a basic understanding of statistics?

5. Describe in your own words the difference between a population and a sample; between a parameter and a statistic.

6. What is the difference between a quantitative variable and a qualitative variable? Give examples.

7. Distinguish between a continuous variable and a discrete valuable. Give examples of each.

8. A recent report in *Fortune* magazine revealed that the Japanese may soon control as much as 35 percent of auto sales in the United States. This compares with 28 percent in the late 1980s, and is up from only 8 percent in 1970. Does this information contain descriptive statistics, inferential statistics, or both? Explain.

9. What is the difference between descriptive statistics and inferential statistics? Which do you feel constitutes a higher form of statistical analysis and why?

10. To what uses or functions can statistics be put? How do you think each might be used to solve real-world business problems? Give examples of specific problems that might arise and explain how statistics could be used to develop solutions and answers.

11. Select any population which might interest you. Identify quantitative and qualitative variables of that population which could be selected for study.

12. If statisticians are actually interested in populations, why do they generally work with samples?

13. Are the following variables discrete or continuous?
    a. Number of courses students at your school are taking this semester.
    b. Number of passes caught by Tim Brown, wide receiver for the L. A. Raiders.
    c. The weights of Tim Brown's teammates.
    d. Weight of the contents of cereal boxes.
    e. Number of books you read last year.

14. Define sampling error and explain what causes it.

15. A poll taken in the 1988 presidential race was reported in *Fortune* magazine, showing that 40 percent of the respondents preferred Michael Dukakis, 52 percent preferred George Bush, and the rest were undecided. This poll was intended to represent what population? What factors might cause the poll to vary from actual conditions?

16. The president of a fraternity on campus wishes to take a sample of the opinion of the 112 members regarding desired rush activities for the fall term.
    a. What is the population?
    b. How might a sample best be taken?
17. Viewers of the long-running TV daytime drama "All My Children" are to be sampled by the show's producer to learn their feeling about plans to kill off a popular character. What problems might arise in this effort? What would you recommend and why?
18. General Mills is concerned about the weight of the net contents of the boxes of Cheerios coming off the production line in its Detroit plant. The box advertises 36 ounces, and if less is actually contained in the box, General Mills could be charged with false advertising. As a newly hired member of the General Mills management team, you suggest that a sample of the boxes be opened and their contents weighed. The vice president of the quality control division asks what kind of sample should be taken. How do you respond?
19. Since production is down at the General Mills plant, it is possible to actually open up all the boxes produced during the most recent production period. Such a process would avoid sampling error and produce more accurate results. Since the population of all boxes is not too large, is sampling necessary?

EMPIRICAL EXERCISES

20. From the popular press, such as newspapers and weekly news magazines, locate articles containing instances in which samples were taken or should have been taken in order to solve a problem and make a decision. Why was it necessary or advisable to take each sample?
21. From the popular press, find articles that communicate facts or knowledge in the form of statistical information. In what way is this information useful, and how might it be used to make decisions and solve problems?

DESCRIBING DATA SETS

A PREVIEW OF THINGS TO LOOK FOR

1 The various ways in which data can be organized to quickly provide a visual impression of their meaning.

2 The use of frequency tables, histograms, and other visual aids, such as pie charts, line charts, ogives, and bar charts to organize a data set.

3 How contingency tables can be constructed to show detailed meaning of a data set.

4 How to properly determine class intervals and midpoints.

5 The development of stem-and-leaf designs to aid in data organization and presentation.

CHAPTER BLUEPRINT

This chapter presents illustrations and examples of the many ways in which a large data set can be organized and managed in such a way as to provide a quick visual interpretation of the message the data convey. These statistical tools allow us to describe a set of raw data in a concise, easy-to-read manner.

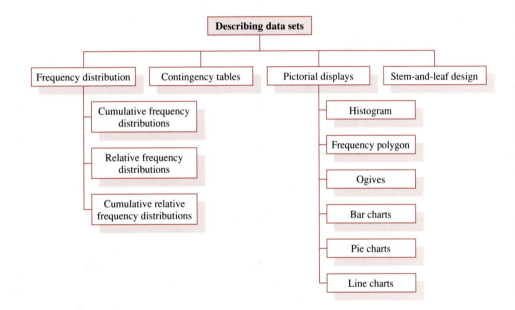

Statistics show that only 20% of the people
in the U.S. die in good health.

Bum Phillips: *Former head coach of the Houston Oilers*

2.1   INTRODUCTION

Almost every statistical effort begins with the process of collecting the necessary
data and thereby forming the data set which will be used in the study. For our general purposes, we will adopt the convenient assumption that this often rather tedious task has already been completed for us and the data lie at our disposal.

This collection of raw data in itself reveals very little. It is extremely difficult to
determine the true meaning of a bunch of numbers which have simply been recorded
on a piece of paper. It remains for us to organize and describe these data in a concise, meaningful manner. In order to determine their significance, we must organize
the data into some form so that, at a mere glance, we can get an idea as to what the
data are trying to tell us.

Statistical tools that are particularly useful in achieving this purpose include

- Frequency tables which place all the data in specific classes.
- Various pictorial displays that can provide a handy visual representation of
  the data.
- Contingency tables and stem-and-leaf designs which also allow presentation of a
  large data set in a concise, discernible form.

2.2   METHODS OF ORGANIZING DATA

Several basic tools can be used to describe and summarize a large data set. The simplest, and perhaps least useful, is an **ordered array.** Assume that the IQ scores of
five valedictorians from Podunk University are 75, 73, 91, 83, and 80. An ordered
array merely lists these observations in ascending or descending order. The five values might thus appear as 73, 75, 80, 83, 91. The ordered array provides some organization to the data set. For example, it can now readily be seen that the two extreme
values are 73 and 91. However, the usefulness of an ordered array is limited. Better
techniques are needed to describe our data set. The rest of this section examines
some common methods of organizing a large collection of data, thereby making it
possible to comprehend the information it contains.

A.   FREQUENCY DISTRIBUTIONS

As the resident statistician for Pigs & People Airline, you have been asked by the
chairman of the board to collect and organize data regarding flight operations. You
are primarily interested in the daily values for two variables: (1) number of passen-

gers and (2) number of miles flown. You are able to obtain these data from daily flight records for the past 50 days, and you have recorded this information in Table 2-1 and Table 2-2. However, in this form it is unlikely that the chairman could gain any useful knowledge regarding operations. The data you have collected are not organized in any way, and would appear to the chairman to be nothing more than a series of numbers jotted down on a piece of paper. It is difficult to gain any information or perception from them in this crude form. The same is true for data on miles flown, rounded to the nearest tenth, and displayed in Table 2-2. Some organized manner of presenting the data must be devised to more easily and quickly provide the user with an impression of the information they contain.

By reviewing the two data sets in their raw form, it is difficult for the chairman to acquire any useful information or impression from the numbers that you have collected. The chairman could more easily acquire some understanding of the significance of these numbers if you could present them in a more systematic, organized manner. There are several ways to organize your presentation. We will first examine the manner in which a frequency distribution can be used to bring organization to your data set.

TABLE 2-1   Raw Data on the Number of Passengers for P & P Airlines

68	71	77	83	79
72	74	57	67	69
50	60	70	66	76
70	84	59	75	94
65	72	85	79	71
83	84	74	82	97
77	73	78	93	95
78	81	79	90	83
80	84	91	101	86
93	92	102	80	69

TABLE 2-2   Raw Data on Miles Flown for P & P Airlines

569.3	420.4	468.5	443.9	403.7
519.7	518.7	445.3	459.0	373.4
493.7	505.7	453.7	397.1	463.9
618.3	493.3	477.0	380.0	423.7
391.0	553.5	513.7	330.0	419.8
370.7	544.1	470.0	361.9	483.8
405.7	550.6	504.6	343.3	497.9
453.3	604.3	473.3	393.3	478.4
437.9	320.4	473.3	359.3	568.2
450.0	413.4	469.3	383.7	469.1

A **frequency distribution** (or frequency table) will provide some order to your data by dividing them into classes and recording the number of observations in each class. You might then provide the chairman with a frequency table like that in Table 2-3 for the daily number of passengers over the last 50 days.

TABLE 2-3   Frequency Distribution for Passengers

Class (passengers)	Tally	Frequency (days)
50 to 59	|||	3
60 to 69	||||| ||	7
70 to 79	||||| ||||| ||||| |||	**18**
80 to 89	||||| ||||| ||	12
90 to 99	||||| |||	8
100 to 109	||	2
		50

It can now easily be seen that on 18 of the 50 days examined, between 70 and 79 passengers flew on P & P Airlines. On all but three days, P & P flew at least 60 people. The daily passenger list never exceeded 109. With a mere glance, the chairman can detect patterns which were not apparent from the raw data. These patterns are useful in making decisions and solving problems that might arise.

Notice that each class has a **lower boundary** and an **upper boundary.** The exact limits of these boundaries are quite important. It is essential that class boundaries do not overlap. Boundaries such as

50 to 60
60 to 70
70 to 80
. . .

are confusing. For example, in which class should 60 be recorded? Similarly, complications would arise if the boundaries were specified as

51 to 59
61 to 69
71 to 79
. . .

In this instance, there is no class containing the observation 60. Furthermore, since *passengers* is a discrete variable, values such as 59.9 pose no problem since it is not possible to have fractional values.

On the other hand, *miles flown* is a continuous variable since it is possible to fly a fraction of a mile. The boundaries for the frequency table of miles flown must account for this. It would be improper to set the boundaries as

300 to 349
350 to 399
400 to 449

since it is unclear in which class observations such as 349.9 or 399.7 should be tallied. The frequency distribution for miles flown might instead appear as Table 2-4.

TABLE 2-4   Frequency Distribution for Miles Flown (in 100's)

Class (miles)	Tally	Frequency (days)
300 and under 350	|||	3
350 and under 400	||||| ||||	9
400 and under 450	||||| ||||	9
450 and under 500	||||| ||||| ||||| ||	17
500 and under 550	||||| |	6
550 and under 600	||||	4
600 and under 650	||	2
		50

Again, the chairman can now detect a pattern to flight operations which is not apparent from the raw data in Table 2-2. For example, P & P never flew over 650 miles on any of the 50 days examined. They flew between 450 and 500 miles more often than any other single distance. On 26 of the 50 days examined, total mileage was between 400 and 500 miles.

The **number of classes** in a frequency table is somewhat arbitrary. In general, your table should have between 5 and 20 classes. Too few classes would not reveal any details about the data; too many would prove as confusing as the list of raw data itself.

A simple rule you can follow to approximate the number of classes states that the number of classes, c, is

$$2^c \geq n \qquad\qquad (2.1)$$

where n is the number of observations. The number of classes is the power to which 2 is raised so that the result is equal to or greater than the number of observations. In our example for P & P, we have $n = 50$ observations. Thus,

$$2^c \geq 50 .$$

Solving for c, which can easily be done on a hand calculator, we find $2^6 = 64$, which exceeds n. This rule suggests that there should be six classes in the frequency table.

This rule should not be taken as the final determining factor. For convenience, more classes or fewer classes may be used.

QUICK CHECK 2.2.1

OOOO   A data set has 150 observations. How many classes should be in the frequency table?

Answer: About eight.

B. CLASS INTERVALS AND MIDPOINTS

The **class interval** is the range of values found within a class. It is determined by subtracting the lower (or upper) boundary of one class from the lower (or upper) boundary of the next class. The interval of the first class in Table 2-3 is thus $60 - 50 = 10$.

It is desirable to make all class intervals of equal size in a frequency distribution. Doing so facilitates the statistical interpretation of any subsequent uses to which the data may be put. In some cases, however, equal class sizes may not always be possible. It may be necessary to use open-ended intervals which do not cite a lower boundary for the first class or an upper boundary for the last class. The last class in Table 2-4 might be stated as "600 and up."

For the purpose of constructing the frequency table, the class interval can be determined by the following expression:

$$\text{CI} = \frac{\text{Largest value} - \text{smallest value}}{\text{Number of desired classes}} \tag{2.2}$$

Since you decided on six classes for your report in the table on data for passengers, the class interval was originally set by

$$\text{CI} = \frac{102 - 50}{6} = 8.7$$

Since 8.7 is an awkward number, the results can be slightly adjusted up or down to facilitate construction of the frequency table. For convenience, the interval of 10 was selected in forming Table 2-3.

TABLE 2-5   Frequency Distribution for
Passengers

Class	Frequency	Midpoint
50 to 59	3	54.5
60 to 69	7	64.5
70 to 79	18	74.5
80 to 89	12	84.5
90 to 99	8	94.5
100 to 109	2	104.5

It is often necessary to determine a **class midpoint.** This is done by calculating the average of the boundaries for a class by adding the upper and lower boundaries and dividing by 2. Thus, the midpoint for the first class in Table 2-3 is $50 + 59/2 = 54.5$. The remaining midpoints are shown in Table 2-5.

QUICK CHECK 2.2.2

○○○○

A data set contains 100 observations, the largest of which is 212 and the smallest of which is 42. Suppose you desire a frequency table with seven classes. (a) What is the class interval? (b) What is the midpoint of the first class?

Answer: (a) 24.29. You may decide to round up to 25 for the sake of convenience. (b) If the first class is set with boundaries of 40 and 65, the midpoint is 52.5.

C.   CUMULATIVE FREQUENCY DISTRIBUTIONS

Often, we may want to determine the number of observations that are greater than or less than some amount. This is done through the use of a **less-than cumulative frequency distribution** or a **more-than cumulative frequency distribution.** These cumulative frequencies tables can easily be constructed from their respective frequency tables.

A less-than cumulative frequency distribution for a particular class is found by adding the frequency in that class to those in all previous classes. Table 2-6 shows a less-than cumulative frequency distribution for the data set on passengers. The frequencies from Table 2-3 are repeated in Table 2-6. It can be seen that at no time did the number of passengers fall below 50. On only three days did fewer than 60 passengers fly P & P. On 10 days, fewer than 70 passengers flew on P & P. The chairman can now easily see that, on 40 of the 50 days, less than 90 passengers flew the airways of P & P.

On the other hand, the values for a more-than cumulative frequency distribution are found by subtracting frequencies of previous classes. This is reflected in Table 2-7. Again, using Table 2–3, we find that on all 50 days at least 50 passengers boarded

TABLE 2-6   Less-Than Cumulative Frequency
Distribution for Number of Passengers

Class (passengers)	Frequency (days)	Cumulative Frequency (days)
Less than 50	0	0
Less than 60	3	3
Less than 70	7	10
Less than 80	18	28
Less than 90	12	40
Less than 100	8	48
Less than 110	2	50

P & P Airlines. Since less than 60 passengers bought tickets on only three of the 50 days, then on the remaining 47 days 60 or more people flew P & P. Table 2-7 also tells the chairman that on 22 days at least 80 passengers flew the airline. Similar information can be obtained from Table 2-7.

TABLE 2-7   More-Than Cumulative Frequency
Distribution for the Number of Passengers

Class (passengers)	Frequency (days)	Cumulative Frequency (days)
50 or more	3	50
60 or more	7	47
70 or more	18	40
80 or more	12	22
90 or more	8	10
100 or more	2	2
110 or more	0	0

D.   RELATIVE FREQUENCY DISTRIBUTIONS

A **relative frequency distribution** expresses the frequency within a class as a percentage of the total number of observations in the sample. This allows us to make statements regarding the number of observations in a single class relative to the entire sample. Using the data from Table 2-3 on passengers, we can compute a relative frequency distribution by dividing each frequency by the sample size 50. See Table 2-8.

TABLE 2-8   Relative Frequency Distribution for Passengers

Class (passengers)	Frequency (days)	Relative Frequency (%)
50 to 59	3	3/50 = 6
60 to 69	7	7/50 = 14
70 to 79	18	18/50 = 36
80 to 89	12	12/50 = 24
90 to 99	8	8/50 = 16
100 to 109	2	2/50 = 4
	50	100

In this fashion we can see, for example, that on 36 percent of the days sampled, between 70 and 79 passengers embarked on a journey using P & P Airlines as their preferred means of travel. Furthermore, 60 percent of the time, P & P served between 70 and 89 airborne travelers.

E. CUMULATIVE RELATIVE FREQUENCY DISTRIBUTION

As the name suggests, a **cumulative relative frequency distribution** expresses the cumulative frequency of each class relative to the entire sample. The cumulative process can be based on a more-than or less-than principle. A less-than cumulative relative frequency distribution is shown in Table 2-9. It is left as a simple exercise for the student to illustrate a more-than table.

TABLE 2-9   Less-Than Cumulative Relative Frequency Distribution for Passengers

Class (passengers)	Frequency (days)	Cumulative Frequency	Cum. Relative Frequency (%)
Less than 50	0	0	0/50 = 0
Less than 60	3	3	3/50 = 6
Less than 70	7	10	10/50 = 20
Less than 80	18	28	28/50 = 56
Less than 90	12	40	40/50 = 80
Less than 100	8	48	48/50 = 96
Less than 110	2	50	50/50 = 100

The last column provides the information in which we are interested. Through simple examination, it can be seen that, for example, 80 percent of the time less than 90 passengers boarded P & P airplanes.

In a conversation with George Krimski, assistant plant manager at the Ford Motor Company truck plant in Louisville, Kentucky, it was learned that the plant was having difficulty with inventory control. Office workers often found that certain supplies that were infrequently used were missing when they were needed. Because their use was sporadic, it was difficult to maintain accurate records on their inventory. Deciding when to order additional supplies was haphazard at best.

Mr. Krimski revealed that the use of a frequency table to maintain a computerized record of how often employees requisitioned these supplies made it much easier to control inventories and prevent shortages. Decisions regarding new orders became routine, and operations were performed more smoothly. The manner in which frequency tables can be computerized is described later in this chapter.

F.   CONTINGENCY TABLES

Notice that the data sets above involved only one variable, the number of passengers or the number of miles flown. What could we do if we wanted to examine two variables simultaneously in order to gain a more complete picture of P & P's flight operations? Perhaps we might desire to categorize by age levels the number of flights typically taken by passengers.

This problem can be handled by using **contingency tables,** which indicate the number of observations for both variables which fall jointly in each category. If we obtained data relating to age and frequency of flying, we could present this information in the form of a contingency table, such as Table 2-10.

TABLE 2-10   P & P's Contingency Table for Age and Flights

	Number of Flights per Year			
Age	**1–2**	**3–5**	**Over 5**	**Total**
0 to less than 10	1 (0.02)	1 (0.02)	2 (0.04)	4 (0.08)
10 to less than 40	2 (0.04)	**8** (0.16)	10 (0.20)	20 (0.40)
40 to less than 65	1 (0.02)	6 (0.12)	15 (0.30)	22 (0.44)
65 and over	1 (0.02)	2 (0.04)	1 (0.02)	4 (0.08)
Total	5 (0.10)	17 (0.34)	28 (0.56)	50 (1.00)

Since we have four age categories and three flight categories, there are 12 **cells.** Each of the 50 people in our sample will fall into one of these 12 joint categories.

○○○○   DECISION MAKING THROUGH PROBLEM SOLVING   ○○○○
ILLUSTRATION 2.2

Maintaining a firm control over spending is a difficult chore for most businesses. A recent article in *Nation's Business* discussed the problem a small manufacturing firm had in trying to allocate funds for research and development (R & D) purposes. The firm was simultaneously funding several different R & D projects. The company had to decide several times each quarter how much each project was to receive.

To help make these crucial decisions, the firm set up a contingency table which showed how much money was allocated to each project. There were four projects, and the amount allocated to each project every quarter was placed in one of five categories ($10,000 to $20,000; $20,000 to $30,000; etc.), giving a total of 20 cells in the table. This allowed management to quickly compare the amount committed to each project and made it easier to decide future disbursements.

The percentage within each cell is shown in parentheses. For example, 8 of the 50 passengers, or 16 percent, between the ages of 10 and 40 fly between three and five times a year. Contingency tables are also called cross-tabulations or cross-tabs.

From the table, we can determine if and how the two characteristics are related. It may be seen in the last column, for example, that most of the passengers come from the second and third age categories. As shown, 40 percent and 44 percent of the passengers in the sample were in these age groups, respectively. It can also be determined that people in the 40 to less than 65 age group flew over five times a year more often than any other frequency.

We could display the information contained in each cell on the basis of sex. Thus, of the eight people in the second age category who fly between three and five times a year, six might be males and the other two females. The entry in that cell could then appear as 6, 2 (0.16). This could be done for all 12 cells if we felt information of this nature would prove useful in making business decisions designed to better serve our customers.

As you can imagine, we could develop a rather descriptive profile of our typical passenger. Such information would be of considerable value in marketing our service to those people who currently identify with the type of service we offer. Additionally, if we wished to alter our marketing approach to appeal to a different type of customer, the contingency table could again serve as an effective decision-making tool. Further applications and uses of the table are illustrated in the chapter dealing with chi-square distributions.

2.3   PICTORIAL DISPLAYS

Pictorial displays are useful in describing data. By examining the display, the researcher can gain a meaningful understanding of the story the data set is trying to tell.

A **histogram** is a useful and common means of displaying data. It places the classes of a frequency distribution on the horizontal axis and the frequencies on the vertical axis. The area in each rectangular bar is proportional to the frequency in that class. In Figure 2-1, the histogram reveals details and patterns not clearly illustrated by the raw data. The relative, as well as the absolute, frequency of each class is readily discernible.

FIGURE 2-1   Histograms for P & P's Passengers

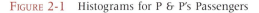
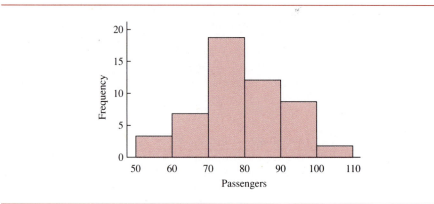

A **frequency polygon** expresses the distribution of the data by means of a single line determined by the midpoints of the classes. See Figure 2-2. It is common practice to extend the ends of the frequency polygon to the horizontal axis at those points that would be the midpoints of the next class at each end.

FIGURE 2-2   Frequency Polygon for P & P's Passengers

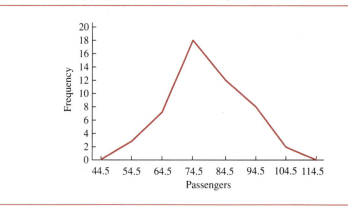

The information shown in a less-than cumulative frequency distribution and a more-than cumulative frequency distribution can also be displayed pictorially. Such a graph is called an **ogive** and is shown in Figure 2-3. The less-than ogive shows, for

FIGURE 2-3   Ogives for Passengers Data

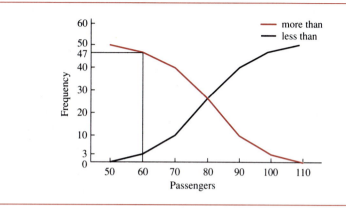

example, that on 3 days less than 60 passengers flew P & P Airlines, and the more-than ogive reveals that on 47 days more than 59 (60 or more) travelers bought tickets.

A **bar chart** presents the data in a manner similar to a histogram. The main difference is that the bar chart need not show frequencies on the axis, but may express the data in absolute amounts or even percentages. Also, the bars may be presented horizontally or vertically. See Figure 2-4. It is possible to show more than one value at a time on a bar chart. Figure 2-5 displays the revenues and costs for P & P Airlines. Figure 2-6 provides further examples of the use of bar charts.

FIGURE 2-4   Bar Charts

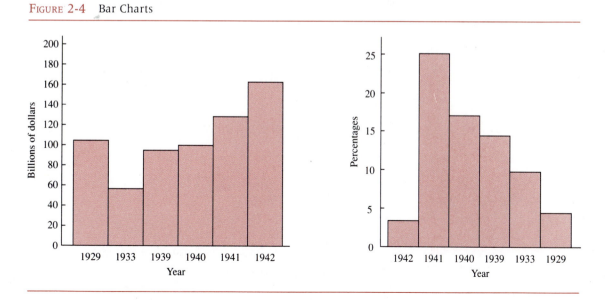

FIGURE 2-5   P & P Performance

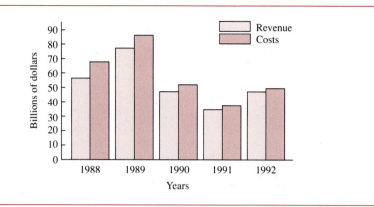

FIGURE 2-6

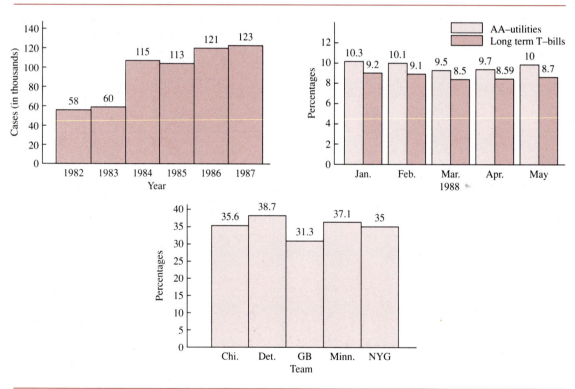

Figure 2-7 contains **stacked bar charts,** which provide a different look at the use of these displays.

A **pie chart** presents the data in the form of a circle. The "slices" represent the absolute or relative (percentages) proportions. Pie charts are quite useful for dis-

FIGURE 2-7

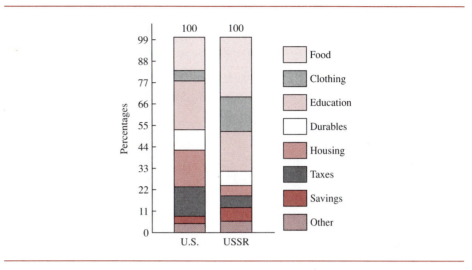

playing relative differences among observations, and they are particularly appropriate for illustrating percentage differences. A pie chart is formed by marking off a portion of the "pie" corresponding to each characteristic being displayed. Characteristics of the nation's work force taken from a recent edition of *The Wall Street Journal* are displayed in Figure 2-8(A). It can be seen that 48 percent of all workers in the United States never take work home, whereas 13 percent do so every day. Other characteristics are equally apparent. Figure 2.8(B) shows that 57.4 percent of the nation's workers drive from one suburb to another when commuting to and from work, but only 24.8 percent drive between suburb and city.

FIGURE 2-8 Pie Charts

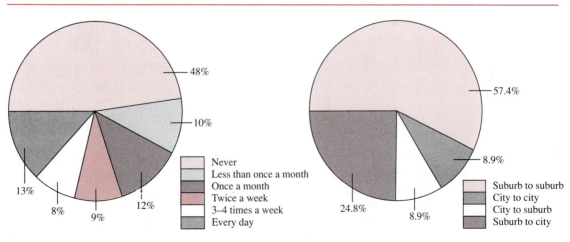

Still another handy display is the **line chart.** Since much of the business and economic data we work with is measured over time, a line chart is useful because it permits us to express units of time on the horizontal axis. A line chart for the unemployment rate in the United States is shown in Figure 2-9.

FIGURE 2-9

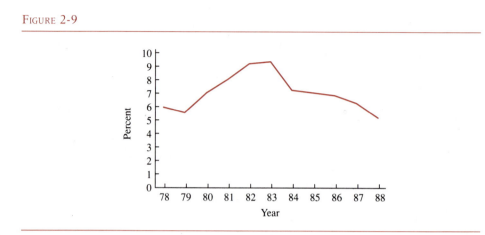

Financial data are often displayed with the aid of a **high-low-close** chart. As the name suggests, it displays the highest value, the lowest value, and the closing value for a selected variable during a given time period. Perhaps the most well-recognized example is the Dow Jones averages found daily in *The Wall Street Journal (WSJ).* Figure 2-10 is just such a display, based on the following data from the *WSJ* for the Dow-Jones index on 15 utilities for five days:

	High	Low	Close
June 9	181.07	178.17	178.88
10	180.65	178.28	179.11
13	180.24	178.17	179.35
14	182.79	179.82	181.37
15	182.14	179.53	181.31

Sometimes called *ticks and tabs,* the upper end of the vertical line, or tick, marks off the highest value that the index reached on that day; the lower end of the tick indicates the lowest value of the day. The closing value is shown by the little tab in between. Similar presentations could be made for commodities and currencies traded on the world's organized exchanges.

By now you should be convinced that organizing a raw data set in some systematic form can quickly lend meaning and clarity which otherwise goes undetected.

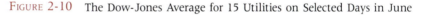

○○○○   **DECISION MAKING THROUGH PROBLEM SOLVING**   ○○○○
ILLUSTRATION 2.3

According to a recent article in *The Wall Street Journal*, Tramco is a subsidiary of B. F. Goodrich which specializes in aircraft maintenance. Since Goodrich is known mostly for producing automobile and truck tires, it was having a difficult time keeping its employees informed about the progress it was making with Tramco in the aircraft maintenance area. However, upper management determined that it was important to keep the workers informed so that they felt they were part of the "corporate family."

To accomplish this mission of communicating with the employees, the *WSJ* stated that "a series of pie charts was posted on employee bulletin boards, lunch room counters and even restroom walls" showing such things as sources of revenues, cost allocations, and productivity gains. The charts were easy to read and required little time or statistical expertise. They communicated at a glance the information management wanted to share with the workers.

FIGURE 2-10   The Dow-Jones Average for 15 Utilities on Selected Days in June

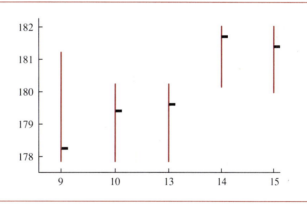

2.4   STEM-AND-LEAF DESIGNS

John Tukey, a noted statistician, devised the stem-and-leaf design as an alternative to a histogram. Like other descriptive measures, the stem-and-leaf design provides a quick visual impression of the number of observations in a class.

Each observation in the data set is divided into two parts; a *stem* and a *leaf*. Although there is considerable flexibility in the procedure to be followed, it is often convenient to identify all but the last digit of an observation as the stem. The last digit is then identified as the leaf.

Given the data 68, 71, 77, 83, and 79 in the first row of Table 2-1 for passengers, the stem-and-leaf values for each are shown in Table 2-11 with the stem on the left side of a vertical line and the leaf on the right.

TABLE 2-11   Stem-and-Leaf Design for Passenger Data

Stem	Leaf
6	8
7	1, 7, 9
8	3

The stems must be placed in an ordered array from lowest to highest. It is also often desirable to place the values in the leaf in an ordered array. If the data set contains fractional observations, it might be advantageous to use as the stem all the digits to the left of the decimal point, while those on the right become the leaf. The six observations 29.5, 28.7, 27.8, 29.3, 28.3, and 26.0 would appear as

Stem	Leaf
26	0
27	8
28	3, 7
29	3, 5

However, the precise design can be adjusted to fit any particular data set and is limited only by the needs and imagination of the researcher. The complete stem-and-leaf design for the data on passengers in Table 2-1 is presented in Table 2-12.

TABLE 2-12   Stem-and-Leaf Design for Passenger Data

Stem	Leaf
5	0, 7, 9
6	0, 5, 6, 7, 8, 9, 9
7	0, 0, 1, 1, 2, 2, 3, 4, 4, 5, 6, 7, 7, 8, 8, 9, 9, 9
8	0, 0, 1, 2, 3, 3, 3, 4, 4, 4, 5, 6
9	0, 1, 2, 3, 3, 4, 5, 7
10	1, 2

Now it is apparent that not only are there three observations in the 50s, but their individual values of 50, 57, and 59 are easily seen. We can further discern that the observations range from a low of 50 to a high of 102. As you can see, the stem-and-leaf design is similar to a histogram, but offers the advantage of retaining the values of the original observations. However, a histogram provides considerable convenience if a large number of observations is involved or if there is a desire to reveal relative frequencies or alter class boundaries.

In some instances, it may prove convenient to round off the observations. Figures such as $88.12, $73.53, $98.53, and $109.12 might be rounded to $88, $74, $99, and $109, yielding

Stem	Leaf
7	4
8	8
9	9
10	9

2.5 SOLVED PROBLEMS

1. **Middle East Uses Oil Revenues to Buy the United States** In many financial circles there was considerable concern over the acquisitions of Western assets by Middle East oil sheiks during the 1980s. In 1988, *U.S. News and World Report* described the purchase by Saudi Arabia of half-interest in Texaco's refinery and service station operations. Kuwait bought 22 percent of giant British Petroleum for $5.5 billion. By 1987, six Persian Gulf nations—Saudi Arabia, Kuwait, Bahrain, Oman, Qatar, and the United Arab Emirates—owned $330 billion in Western assets.

   The U.S. Treasury Department collected data on the various acquisitions by several Arab countries during the 1980s. The figures shown here are in billions of dollars and represent 42 single purchases of Western interests by Arab governments.

5.5	3.9	5.3	8.9	3.9
1.9	1.8	2.1	3.5	7.3
2.8	2.7	5.1	4.2	
7.3	4.7	9.3	8.2	
10.9	3.2	2.8	9.7	
8.7	4.8	8.3	8.2	
1.5	9.2	1.9	6.2	
5.3	1.5	2.7	4.7	
4.1	3.9	4.2	5.3	
10.1	6.1	5.7	6.2	

Statisticians at the Treasury Department set up a frequency table to facilitate the interpretation of the data. The number of classes is

$$2^c \geq 42 \qquad \text{where } c = 6$$

The class interval is

$$CI = \frac{\text{Highest} - \text{lowest}}{\text{Number of classes}}$$
$$= \frac{10.9 - 1.5}{6}$$
$$= 1.6$$

Rounding the interval down to 1.5, we could construct Table 2-13.

TABLE 2-13   Western Assets Purchased by Persian Gulf Nations

Class	Tally	Frequency
1.5 and under 3.0	||||| |||||	10
3.0 and under 4.5	||||| |||	8
4.5 and under 6.0	||||| ||||	9
6.0 and under 7.5	|||||	5
7.5 and under 9.0	|||||	5
9.0 and under 10.5	||||	4
10.5 and under 12.0			1

This table requires seven classes in order to tally all observations. If we wished to strictly retain six classes, the interval would have to be increased slightly. Such flexibility is permissible.

A less-than cumulative frequency distribution is formed by adding the frequency in any given class and all those above it as illustrated in Table 2-14. Table 2-15 shows how a

TABLE 2-14   Less-Than Cumulative Frequency Distribution

Class	Frequency	Cumulative Frequency
Less than 1.5	0	0
Less than 3.0	10	10
Less than 4.5	8	18
Less than 6.0	9	27
Less than 7.5	5	32
Less than 9.0	5	37
Less than 10.5	4	41
Less than 12.0	1	42
	42	

TABLE 2-15   More-Than Cumulative Frequency Distribution

Class	Frequency	Cumulative Frequency
1.5 or more	10	42
3.0 or more	8	32
4.5 or more	9	24
6.0 or more	5	15
7.5 or more	5	10
9.0 or more	4	5
10.5 or more	1	1
12.0 or more	0	0
	42	

more-than cumulative frequency distribution can be constructed by adding the frequency of any class to all those below it. A relative frequency distribution for Middle East purchases of Western assets is shown in Table 2-16. A less-than cumulative relative frequency distribution and a more-than cumulative relative frequency distribution are shown in Table 2-17 and Table 2-18, respectively. Finally, the data could also be summarized and presented in a stem-and-leaf design as shown in Table 2-19.

TABLE 2-16   Relative Frequency Distribution

Class	Frequency	Relative Frequency (%)
1.5 up to 3.0	10	10/42 = 23.8
3.0 up to 4.5	8	8/42 = 19.0
4.5 up to 6.0	9	9/42 = 21.4
6.0 up to 7.5	5	5/42 = 11.9
7.5 up to 9.0	5	5/42 = 11.9
9.0 up to 10.5	4	4/42 = 9.5
10.5 up to 12.0	1	1/42 = 2.4
	42	1.00

TABLE 2-17   Less-Than Cumulative Relative Frequency

Class	Frequency	Cumulative Frequency	Cumulative Relative Frequency (%)
Less than 1.5	0	0	0/42 = 0.0
Less than 3.0	10	10	10/42 = 23.8
Less than 4.5	8	18	18/42 = 42.9
Less than 6.0	9	27	27/42 = 64.3
Less than 7.5	5	32	32/42 = 76.2
Less than 9.0	5	37	37/42 = 88.1
Less than 10.5	4	41	41/42 = 97.6
Less than 12.0	1	42	42/42 = 100

TABLE 2-18   More-Than Cumulative Relative Frequency

Class	Frequency	Cumulative Frequency	Cumulative Relative Frequency (%)
1.5 or more	10	42	42/42 = 1.00
3.0 or more	8	32	32/42 = 76.2
4.5 or more	9	24	24/42 = 57.1
6.0 or more	5	15	15/42 = 35.7
7.5 or more	5	10	10/42 = 23.8
9.0 or more	4	5	5/42 = 11.9
10.5 or more	1	1	1/42 = 2.4
12.0 or more	0	0	0/42 = 0

TABLE 2-19   Stem-and-Leaf Design for Middle East
Acquisitions

Stem	Leaf
1	5, 5, 8, 9, 9
2	1, 7, 7, 8, 8
3	2, 5, 9, 9, 9
4	1, 2, 2, 7, 7, 8
5	1, 3, 3, 3, 5, 7
6	1, 2, 2
7	3, 3
8	2, 2, 3, 7, 9
9	2, 3, 7
10	1, 9

Various pictorial displays could also be used to further illustrate and describe the data. Using these tools, one can provide a clear and definite characterization of the data. The message they convey can easily be determined.

2.6   WHAT YOU SHOULD HAVE LEARNED FROM THIS CHAPTER

The point we are trying to grasp in this entire chapter is the need to express the raw data in some form which instantly gives meaning to the researcher. The collection of raw data itself is of little value.

As you have seen, several techniques can be used to convey the message that the data contain. Mastery of these techniques is essential to effectively use the tools of statistical analysis.

After reading this chapter and working the problems, you should have a clear idea of how frequency tables and pictorial displays can be used to describe data. You should also know how to determine the number of classes in a frequency table, as well as the proper methods to calculate class intervals and midpoints. The uses of stem-and-leaf designs and contingency tables should also be evident after you have solved the problems at the end of this chapter.

2.7   COMPUTER APPLICATIONS

Most of the visual displays presented in this chapter can be generated quickly with the many computer programs available to the statistician or researcher. By relying on the power and efficiency of the computer, the statistician can greatly simplify his or her task of managing large data sets.

At the end of each chapter is a section describing the procedure by which you can perform on the computer the statistical exercises discussed in that chapter. Three popular computer packages will be featured: SAS-PC, SPSS-PC, and Minitab. Complete programs which must be input into the computer are provided for all three packages. Every keystroke necessary for the programs is specified. The resulting printouts are also shown, accompanied by a discussion explaining each printout.

In this section we will demonstrate the application of certain computer programs to the process of describing data. The examination and interpretation of the computer printouts are provided.

For the raw data on P & P's passengers in Table 2-1, the SAS program produces the printout below.

INPUT

```
DATA;
TITLE "P & P PASSENGER DATA"
INPUT PASS;
CARDS;
  68
  72
  50
  70
   :
   .

remaining observations go here
   :
   .
  83
  86
  69
PROC CHART;
   VBAR PASS / MIDPOINTS = 54.5 64.5 74.5 84.5 94.5
                      104.5;
```

The TITLE line is optional and prints out at the top of the page. The resulting printout would appear as

SAS OUTPUT I

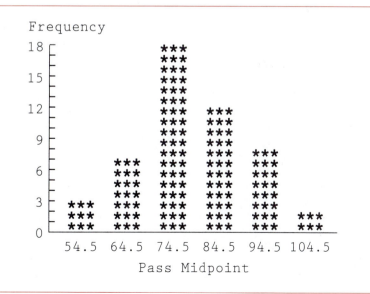

If

```
PROC CHART;
   HBAR PASS;
```

appears in the program, a horizontal bar chart will result.

To illustrate pie charts and contingency tables, assume that we have collected data on the ages and class levels of 30 students at State University. The data might appear as

Observation	Age	Sophomore
1	19	Freshman
2	22	Sophomore
3	27	Junior
4	18	Junior
5	22	Senior
⋮	⋮	⋮
30	20	Sophomore

The corresponding SAS program would be

INPUT

```
DATA;
INPUT AGE $CLASS;
CARDS;
    19   FR
    22   SO
    27   JU
     :    :
     .    .
    20   SO
PROC CHART;
   PIE CLASS;
PROC FREQ;
    TABLES AGE;
    TABLES AGE * CLASS;
```

This SAS program produces the printout shown here.

SAS OUTPUT II

(a)

SAS
Freq pie chart of class

(c) TABLE OF AGE BY CLASS

AGE FREQUENCY PERCENT ROW CT COL PCT	FR	JU	SO	SR	TOTAL
18	4 13.33 100.00 50.00	0 0.00 0.00 0.00	0 0.00 0.00 0.00	0 0.00 0.00 0.00	4 13.33
19	3 10.00 75.00 37.50	0 0.00 0.00 0.00	1 3.33 25.00 10.00	0 0.00 0.00 0.00	4 13.33
20	1 3.33 16.67 12.50	0 0.00 0.00 0.00	5 16.67 83.33 100.00	0 0.00 0.00 0.00	6 20.00
21	0 0.00 0.00 0.00	0 0.00 0.00 0.00	2 6.67 100.00 20.00	0 0.00 0.00 0.00	2 6.67
22	0 0.00 0.00 0.00	1 3.33 25.00 20.00	2 6.67 50.00 20.00	1 3.33 25.00 14.29	4 13.33
23	0 0.00 0.00 0.00	3 10.00 60.00 60.00	0 0.00 0.00 0.00	2 6.67 40.00 28.57	5 16.67
24	0 0.00 0.00 0.00	1 3.33 25.00 20.00	0 0.00 0.00 0.00	3 10.00 75.00 42.86	4 13.33
26	0 0.00 0.00 0.00	0 0.00 0.00 0.00	0 0.00 0.00 0.00	1 3.33 100.00 14.29	1 3.33
TOTAL	8 26.67	5 16.67	10 33.33	7 23.33	30 100.00

(b)

AGE	FREQUENCY	PERCENT	CUMULATIVE FREQUENCY	CUMULATIVE FREQUENCY
18	4	13.3	4	13.3
19	4	13.3	8	26.7
20	6	20.0	14	46.7
21	2	6.7	16	53.3
22	4	13.3	20	66.7
23	5	16.7	25	83.3
24	4	13.3	29	96.7
26	1	3.3	30	100.0

The pie chart shows, for example, that out of the 30 students, 5, or 16.67 percent, are juniors. The program

```
PROC FREQ;
    TABLES AGE;
```

generates the first table showing the frequency, percentage, cumulative frequency, and cumulative percentage for each age group.

The request for TABLES AGE*CLASS; produces the given contingency table. The four numbers in each cell show the frequency, percent of the total number of observations falling in that cell, the row percentage, and the column percentage. For example, in the cell for 19-year-old sophomores, the first number shows that there was only one 19-year-old who was a sophomore. This represented 3.33 percent of the 30 students in the sample. There were a total of four 19-year-olds, and one of them, or 25 percent, fell in the sophomore class. There were a total of 10 sophomores, and only one, or 10 percent, was 19 years old.

If the statistician is using SPSS-PC, the program for the bar chart is written as

INPUT

```
TITLE  P & P PASSENGER DATA
DATA LIST FREE/PASS.
BEGIN DATA.
68
72
50
70
 :
 .
83
86
69
END DATA.
FREQUENCIES  VARIABLES = PASS/BARCHART.
```

The DATA LIST command identifies the data as free form and provides a name for it. The printout looks much like the one above for SAS and is therefore not repeated here.

Finally, Minitab, another popular statistics program, can also be used to produce the desired results. It generates a printout quite similar to those already shown.

LIST OF SYMBOLS AND TERMS

Ordered array The arrangement of a data set from the highest observation to the lowest, or from the lowest to the highest.

Frequency distribution A tabular arrangement of data into classes into which each observation is grouped.

Frequency table Same as a frequency distribution.

Class interval Range of values within a class in a frequency table.

Class midpoint The average of the upper and lower boundaries of a class in a frequency table.

Cumulative frequency distribution (CFD) A frequency table that shows the number of observations that are either (1) equal to or less than the upper boundary of each class (less-than CFD), or (2) at least equal to the lower boundary of each class (more-than CFD).

Relative frequency distribution Shows the percentage of observation in each class relative to the whole.

Contingency table Records the number of observations that simultaneously meet two distinct characteristics.

Histogram A pictorial display that depicts the information in a frequency table.

Frequency polygon Expresses the distribution of a data set by means of a single line determined by the midpoints of the classes in a frequency table.

Ogives Similar to a frequency polygon, except it applies to a cumulative frequency table.

LIST OF FORMULAS

$$2^c \geq n \tag{2.1}$$

Calculates the approximate number of classes in a frequency table.

$$CI = \frac{\text{Largest value} - \text{smallest value}}{\text{Number of desired classes}} \tag{2.2}$$

Used to calculate the proper class interval for a frequency table.

CHAPTER EXERCISES

YOU MAKE THE DECISION

1. Annually, *Fortune* magazine publishes the Fortune 500, which lists the 500 largest corporations in the world on the basis of sales. The Securities and Exchange Commission (SEC) wants to analyze the sales records for these firms, but finds the listings too cumbersome and bewildering. As the assistant to the director of management operations, you must decide how to arrange all these data so that your analysts can gain some insight into and appreciation for the patterns and significance of the sales data.

2. In your position as chief credit officer for a large department store chain, you must decide how to arrange data regarding credit trends of your customers. Information has been collected on the marital status (married, divorced, single, widowed) and type of credit card used most (VISA, Mastercard, Carte Blanc, and American Express). How can you display the data in a form which will quickly convey meaning?

3. As a new staff member for a major computer company in New York, you are in charge of preparing a report detailing the recent success of your firm to investors who are not highly familiar with statistical concepts. Decide which techniques you might use to accomplish your objective.

CONCEPTUAL QUESTIONS

4. Why is it necessary to organize data in some systematic manner after they are collected? Why not just leave them in their raw form in order to preserve their integrity and not violate their true meaning?

5. Define and give examples of the methods of organizing data listed here. What are the advantages of each?
   a. Frequency distribution.
   b. Cumulative frequency distribution.
   c. Relative frequency distribution.
   d. Pie chart.
   e. Histogram.

6. What is the relationship between a frequency polygon and an ogive?

7. How will the class limits of a frequency distribution be affected if you are working with continuous data as opposed to discrete data?
8. Distinguish between less-than and more-than cumulative frequency distributions. Present a brief example of each.
9. Briefly discuss the rules that must be followed in setting class intervals and boundaries for a frequency distribution. What consideration(s) must be given if you are working with continuous data?

PROBLEMS

10. A particular data set has 100 observations. Approximately how many classes should the frequency distribution contain?
11. If the data set in Problem 10 has 53 as its lowest value and 190 as its highest value, what class boundaries would you advise? Construct the entire set of class boundaries for (a) discrete data and (b) continuous data. Are the intervals that you selected the only possibilities? How might they vary?
12. Bill Bissey, vice president of Bank One in Indianapolis has control over the approval of loans for local business development. Over the past five years the largest loan was $1.2 million, and the smallest was $10,000. He wishes to construct a frequency table with 10 classes. What would the boundaries of the classes be? What would the class interval be?
13. Mr. Bissey also maintains records on personal savings accounts. Of the 40 new accounts opened last month, the current balances are

$ 179.80	$ 890.00	$ 712.10	$ 415.00
112.17	1200.00	293.00	602.02
1150.00	1482.00	579.00	1312.52
100.00	695.15	287.00	1175.00
1009.10	952.51	1112.52	783.00
1212.43	510.52	1394.05	1390.00
470.53	783.00	1101.00	666.66
780.00	793.10	501.01	1555.10
352.00	937.01	711.11	1422.03
1595.10	217.00	1202.00	1273.01

Construct a frequency table with seven classes. Are you working with continous data or discrete data? Explain.
14. Using the data from Problem 13, construct and interpret a relative frequency table, a cumulative frequency table, and a cumulative relative frequency table.
15. Using the data from Problem 13, construct a histogram and a frequency polygon.
16. Using the data from Problem 13, construct a bar chart showing the percentages in each class.
17. Your company is considering a proposal to use a new type of carpeting in the luxury automobiles that you manufacture. In a test of durability, 100 pieces of the carpet are subjected to wear tests, the results of which are tabulated here.

Wear Test for Best-Made Carpet (in hours)

53.7	40.9	35.9	47.3	52.7	52.1	47.3	44.1	49.5	41.1
51.7	38.3	54.5	46.5	54.4	49.1	48.9	49.7	48.2	40.1
44.5	35.8	36.3	49.9	43.3	56.4	38.9	51.2	43.7	39.7
54.1	52.2	40.1	37.4	38.9	52.9	36.1	53.9	35.9	45.3
36.7	35.9	42.5	36.9	36.9	54.2	39.9	38.2	41.5	46.0
35.0	35.2	45.0	52.5	39.2	41.2	40.2	41.7	44.5	51.9
52.0	37.3	47.5	50.0	40.7	42.5	44.2	43.9	45.8	52.3
51.1	38.7	50.3	44.4	41.1	43.5	46.7	46.2	51.3	54.0
35.5	42.8	52.8	37.9	43.1	44.7	48.9	48.2	51.7	54.3
38.2	49.3	52.8	50.7	47.3	49.7	49.9	50.2	54.1	51.3

Your boss does not have time to review a bunch of numbers to figure out what they mean. You must therefore develop a frequency distribution to reveal their meaning. Since your boss is a tyrant, be prepared to defend your choice for the number of classes and the class interval.

18. Using the data from Problem 17, construct a
   a. Stem-and-leaf design.
   b. Cumulative frequency distribution.
   c. Relative frequency distribution.
   d. Cumulative relative frequency distribution.

19. *Fortune* magazine recently provided a listing of the incomes of chief executive officers of some of the largest U.S. corporations. The annual salaries, in thousands of dollars, were

1380	1380	889	1030	1050	1180
997	1201	920	783	709	883
842	900	1000	950	970	990
1273	753	1350	1290	815	1250
712	850	797	1153	1080	1300

   a. Construct the stem-and-leaf design.
   b. Develop a frequency distribution. Use seven classes. In what way could the stem-and-leaf design be of help in determining class boundaries?
   c. Construct the corresponding histogram.
   d. Illustrate and interpret the relative frequency distribution.
   e. Construct more-than and less-than cumulative frequency distributions.

20. As a private economic consultant you find it necessary to faithfully read *The Wall Street Journal* to remain current in your professional field. A recent report in *WSJ* showed the following data for percentages of executives in 42 top U.S. corporations suffering from drug abuse problems.

5.9	8.8	14.3	8.3	9.1	5.1	15.3
17.5	17.3	15.0	9.3	9.9	7.0	16.7
10.3	11.5	17.0	8.5	7.2	13.7	16.3
12.7	8.7	6.5	6.8	13.4	5.5	15.2
8.4	9.8	7.3	10.0	11.0	13.2	16.3
9.1	12.3	8.5	16.0	10.2	11.7	14.2

    a. Construct a stem-and-leaf design.
    b. Construct the corresponding histogram.
    c. Construct the frequency distribution and find the class midpoints.
    d. Construct the relative frequency distribution.
    e. Construct the frequency polygon.
    f. Construct a more-than cumulative frequency distribution and its corresponding ogive.

21.   *U.S. News and World Report* published figures on the number of crimes during a recent week in the New York City subway system. They were as follows: murders 3, rapes 5, muggings 23, assults 17, robberies 7. Construct a bar chart displaying this crime spree.

22.   A recent study in *Business Week* showing percentage increases in capital spending in three selected months for both current dollars and inflation-adjusted constant dollars reported these amounts:

	Current Dollars (%)	Constant Dollars (%)
November 1987	6.2	1.9
March 1988	8.3	4.4
May 1988	9.9	5.3

Construct a bar chart for these data.

23.   These data regarding where Americans spend their vacations were recently published in *Travel and Leisure:* city 31%; ocean 26%; lake 5%; mountains 10%; state and national parks 6%; small rural town 22%. As director of the tourist board for your state, it is your job to present these data in a pie chart.

24.   The Bureau of Land Management of the U.S. Department of the Interior administers a program to locate homes for our nation's wild mustangs, which freely graze on public land. However, this adopt-a-horse effort has been heavily criticized. Government figures show that 100 horses were sold in each of the first four months of 1988. After eight months the status of the horses is as follows:

	January	February	March	April
Died of thirst	12	10	3	7
Starved	5	17	5	10
Euthanized	27	22	42	18
Died of disease	42	36	21	53
Living	14	15	29	12

As a statistician retained by a group of concerned citizens, evaluate the BLM's performance using

a. A stacked bar chart.

b. Pie charts for March and April.

25. In a recent issue of *U.S. News and World Report*, changes in Italy's GNP from 1981 to 1988 were reported as

$$0.17\% \quad -0.52\% \quad -0.20\% \quad 2.8\% \quad 2.3\% \quad 2.8\% \quad 2.74\% \quad 2.7\%$$

Construct a bar chart showing these changes.

26. At a recent NCAA convention, representatives addressed important issues concerning the limitations on the number of scholarships which can be offered in several sports. Here is a listing of the current limits and the proposed changes under consideration.

Sport	Current Limit	Proposed Limit
Basketball	13	15
1-A Football	95	90
1-AA Football	70	65
Baseball	13	12
Fencing	5	4
Lacrosse	14	12

Construct a bar chart illustrating these limits. Construct pie charts doing the same. Can you cite any comparative advantages or disadvantages of the bar chart as compared to the pie charts?

27. The U.S. Department of Commerce has reported net U.S. international investment—the level of U.S. investments abroad minus foreign investment in the U.S.—of the following amounts (in billions of dollars):

1980	106.3	1984	3.6	1988	−577.5
1981	141.1	1985	−111.9	1989	−736.5
1982	137.0	1986	−263.6	1990	−886.5
1983	89.6	1987	−420.5	1991	−1000.0

Construct a bar graph to illustrate these figures and interpret its meaning.

28. Big Al, the local loan shark, currently has 120 outstanding accounts payable. Big Al's accountant informs him that of the 25 accounts in the $0 to $4,999 range, 10 are due, 5 are overdue, and the rest are delinquent, placing the debtor in danger of being visited by Big Al's enforcer. Of the 37 in the $5,000 to $9,999 range, 15 are due, 10 are overdue, and the rest are delinquent. There are 39 in the $10,000 to $14,999 that show 11 are due, 10 are overdue, and the rest are delinquent. Of the remaining accounts, in the $15,000 and up range, 5 are due, 7 are overdue, and the rest are delinquent. Big Al wants to see a contingency table for these accounts. Interpret their significance by citing a few of the statistics you feel are most important and revealing.

29. Construct a frequency table for the advertising budgets of top U.S. corporations. These figures are in thousands of dollars.

51.02	99.99	73.99	79.99	80.00
63.09	71.11	58.73	61.11	72.14
83.21	50.00	70.00	60.00	65.72
69.99	57.03	92.29	60.00	89.49
81.00	82.22	59.99	89.99	90.00
79.82	77.77	89.89	80.00	69.99

Put five classes in the table, with intervals of $10, and begin with $50 as the lower boundary of the first class.

30. Construct a stem-and-leaf design for the data in Problem 29.

31. These closing prices of randomly selected stocks listed on the NYSE were taken from *The Wall Street Journal:*

20 1/8	22 1/8	18 3/4	24 5/8
19 3/8	18 1/2	21 1/8	20 1/8
25 3/4	25 3/8	18 7/8	22 5/8
17 1/4	19 5/8	21 7/8	21 7/8
18 7/8	17 1/2	18 1/8	22 1/2
19 3/8	25 7/8	21 1/2	20 1/4

a. How many classes should the frequency table contain?
b. What is the proper class interval?
c. Construct the frequency table.

32. Typical weather patterns are shown for the following cities:

	Percentages of Days That Are		
	Sunny	**Snowy**	**Rainy**
Tallahassee, FL	78	0	22
Kansas City, KS	53	31	16
Toledo, OH	49	27	24
Buffalo, NY	47	42	11

Construct a stacked bar chart and pie charts to display these values.

33. Monthly sales for Luggit Hardware last year were (in hundreds of dollars)

Jan. 42	April 51	July 63	Oct. 58
Feb. 57	May 53	Aug. 79	Nov. 62
March 49	June 54	Sept. 69	Dec. 70

Construct a line chart for these data.

34. Total points scored by the teams in the western division of the American Football Conference of the NFL in 1989, along with their number of first downs were

	Points	First Downs
San Diego Chargers	253	264
Kansas City Chiefs	273	265
Los Angeles Raiders	301	300
Denver Broncos	379	331
Seattle Seahawks	371	301

Form the corresponding line chart and interpret it.

35. According to *Football Digest,* the number of fumbles by each team from Problem 34 and the number of fumbles caused by the defense of each team in 1990 were

	By	Caused By
San Diego Chargers	12	6
Kansas City Chiefs	4	12
Los Angeles Raiders	10	8
Denver Broncos	9	5
Seattle Seahawks	9	8

Develop a stacked bar chart and a line chart for these figures. What conclusion can you draw from them?

36. The Dow-Jones averages for 30 industrial stocks reported the following values in June of 1988. Construct a high-low-close chart based on these data.

	High	Low	Close
June 9	2119.31	2081.79	2093.35
10	2123.58	2084.82	2101.71
13	2144.15	2084.64	2099.40
14	2148.12	2111.13	2124.47

37. Each spring, *Fortune* magazine reports the 500 largest U.S. industrial corporations ranked on the basis of sales. In 1988, the largest firm, General Motors, had sales of $101,781.9 million, and the 500th largest firm was M. A. Hanna, which had sales of $459.4 million. Determine how many classes should be formed if you wished to construct a frequency table.

38. What is the class interval for the frequency table from Problem 37?

39. Refer to Problem 37. If the lower boundary of the first class was set at $450 million, what values would the remaining boundaries take. Illustrate by constructing the entire table.

40. The observations listed are times (in minutes) that 30 students took to complete their first statistics test.

42.3	67.7	53.3	63.9	70.1
70.0	52.6	61.9	41.7	39.2
37.2	63.2	45.7	38.9	68.3
69.2	39.2	42.7	52.4	52.5
41.9	58.9	69.1	68.3	64.9
39.2	45.5	55.5	61.2	69.8

Determine the appropriate number of classes.

41. What should the class interval be for Problem 40?
42. Construct the frequency table based on data in Problem 40. Tally the observations and record the frequency in each class.
43. Construct a more-than cumulative frequency distribution from the data in Problem 40.
44. Construct a less-than cumulative frequency distribution from Problem 40.
45. Construct a relative frequency distribution from Problem 40.
46. Construct a more-than cumulative relative frequency distribution from Problem 40.
47. Construct a histogram from the data on students' times from Problem 40.
48. Construct a frequency polygon for Problem 40.
49. Construct a more-than ogive for Problem 40.
50. The U.S. Travel Data Center for *Better Homes and Gardens* reported the following numbers of people who took vacations last summer based on the structure of family members. Numbers are in millions of adults.

	Adults with Children	**Adults w/o Children**
Weekend trips	59	45
Non-week-end		
short trips	30	21
Long trips	39	31

Construct a single bar chart illustrating these values.

51. Present the information in Problem 50 with a stacked bar chart.
52. The Bureau of Labor Statistics in the U.S. Department of Labor produced a report in a 1988 edition of *Newsweek* which revealed certain economic trends. It showed that in 1969 the percentages of families in the lower, middle, and upper social classes were 32 percent, 58 percent, and 10 percent, respectively. In 1986, the figures were 29 percent, 53 percent, and 18 percent. Construct pie charts for these data. What conclusion concerning the mobility between social classes do the charts suggest?
53. *Billboard Magazine* recently reported earnings figures for major record companies. Columbia Records earned $178 million with hits by George Michael, Janet Jackson, Billy Joel, Barbara Streisand, and Madonna. Paula Abdul, Whitesnake, Fleetwood Mac, and U2 earned Warner Communications $214 million. The Mercury label received $160 million with hits by Bon Jovi, Def Leppard, and, believe it or not, Vladimir Horowitz. RCA took in $75 million from releases by Grateful Dead and The Judds. The Pet Shop Boys, David

Bowie, Bob Seger, and Natalie Cole collected $40 million for Capital Records. MCA received $30 million from performances by Tiffany, Elton John, and Reba McEntire. Summarize this information with a pie chart.

54. Unemployment rates over the last 15 months were reported by the U.S. Department of Labor as 4.3, 4.7, 5.4, 5.5, 5.5, 5.6, 5.7, 5.3, 5.7, 6.1, 6.5, 7.2, 7.0, 7.1, and 6.8 percent. Construct a stem-and-leaf design.

EMPIRICAL EXERCISES

55. Survey 40 people (20 males and 20 females) about how they feel about the economic policies of the U.S. president. Use the following categories: excellent, above average, average, below average, and poor. Construct a histogram so that it shows the differences in opinion within each category between males and females.

56. From the financial pages of *The Wall Street Journal* (or any newspaper reporting the activities on the New York Stock Exchange), collect the closing prices on 50 to 100 randomly selected stocks. Report the results in a frequency table, showing the cumulative frequency and the relative frequency for each class. Justify your choice of interval size and number of classes. Interpret your results. Assuming the stocks you chose were representative of the trading that day on the NYSE, what conclusions might you be able to derive?

57. Construct a histogram based on the data from Problem 56. Illustrate how an ogive can be used to further analyze your findings.

CASE APPLICATIONS

58. The U.S. Department of Commerce is responsible for maintaining national data on a wide variety of business and economic series. Your job is to help compile and organize much of these data. Your supervisor has assigned you the task of explaining trends in the monthly unemployment rate for the past three years, starting with the most recently available figure.

   The information must display in a direct and obvious manner what trends and developments have occurred in the U.S. unemployment rate over the past several months. How will you provide your supervisor with a quick and convenient impression of the recent behavior in this important labor statistic? Give illustrated examples.

59. Mort Greenbaum has just developed a new processing method for his company's product. Tests indicate that it will increase output dramatically. The results of these tests, shown tabulated, are to be presented at the next board of directors meeting. Greenbaum feels that a clear and forceful presentation of the potential savings is necessary if the board is to "buy off" on the new method. How would you advise Greenbaum to make that presentation? That is, what devices might he employ?

Daily Output in Older Plants (12 plants)

Operating Time (hours)	Current Rate (units)	Potential Rate (units)
8	212	254
16	390	468
24	512	614

Daily Output in Modernized Plants (10 plants)

Operating Time (hours)	Current Rate (units)	Potential Rate (units)
8	323	387
16	553	663
24	811	973

COMPUTER EXERCISES

1. Access the file REVENUE in your data bank. It consists of 100 observations (REV) for the monthly revenue figures (in hundreds) of Trimtex, a manufacturer of diet products. The worst month for sales was last January, when total sales revenues were only $21.2 ($21,200). However, just last month, sales reached an all-time high of $47.2.

    The CEO wishes to analyze the company's performance and requests that your department prepare revenue figures for a presentation at a forthcoming meeting of the board of directors. Use the data in REVENUE to construct a frequency table. Analyze and interpret your printout and provide a brief report to the CEO outlining the presentation you would make at the board meeting.

2. Access the file AUTO in your data bank. It contains values for the percentages of defective automobiles produced during each day of the week. The district supervisor feels that more defective cars are produced on Monday and Friday than on any other days. Your boss feels that certain visual aids, such as pie charts and bar charts, might improve production efficiency. Provide him with these statistical tools, along with an interpretation of your printout. Present a brief report speculating on the action that might be taken to correct the problem.

3. Access the file STUDENT, which contains 50 observations for the grade point average rounded to the nearest one-half, and the years of undergraduate schooling, ranging from 1 to 4. GPAs include the values of 2.0, 2.5, 3.0, 3.5, 3.5, 4.0. Obtain a contingency table for these data and analyze the results. The dean of instruction at State University wishes to implement a study program directed at those classes with lower GPAs. Write a brief report to the dean explaining which class(es) might benefit from such a program.

CHAPTER THREE

MEASURES OF CENTRAL TENDENCY AND DISPERSION

CHAPTER BLUEPRINT

This chapter illustrates the manner in which an entire data set can be characterized and described with only a few numbers. It will be shown how measures of central tendency and measures of dispersion can be quite useful in the study of statistical analysis.

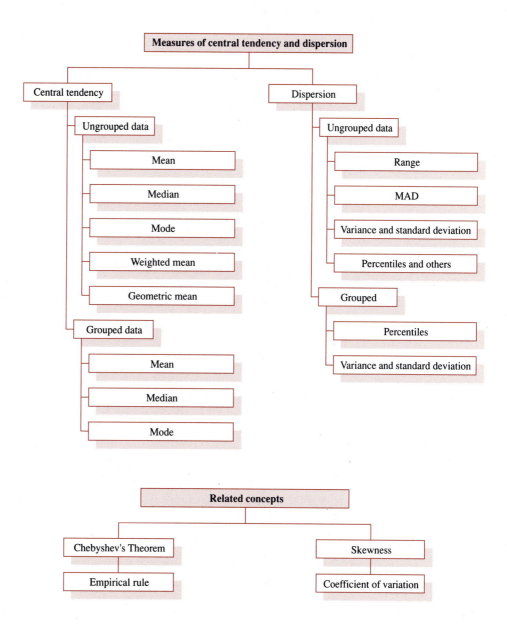

Statistics show that most people
live in heavily populated areas.

3.1 INTRODUCTION

Data, like students, often tend to congregate around certain favorite gathering spots. Students seem to flock together in all sorts of places, such as football games, popular bars and other likely watering holes, frat houses, and, on rare occasions, even the library. In similar fashion, numbers also seem to enjoy each other's company, so they too are prone to collect around some central point. This central location is most often referred to as simply the *average*. The purpose of this chapter is, in part, to determine various ways in which the average of a data set can be calculated. These averages are referred to as **measures of central tendency.** In addition, we will also fully explore ways in which we can judge the extent to which the individual observations in a data set are spread out around their center point. These valuations of spread are called **measures of dispersion.** A measure of central tendency locates the center, or average, of a data set. A measure of dispersion indicates the tendency for the individual observations to deviate from that center point. We can calculate these important measures for raw, ungrouped data or for data that have already been grouped into classes within a frequency table. These objectives can best be achieved by examining the

- Mean, median, and mode of grouped and ungrouped data.
- Mean absolute deviation.
- Variance and standard deviation for grouped and ungrouped data.
- Quartiles, deciles, and percentiles for grouped and ungrouped data.

It might be easier to first compute the measures of central tendency for ungrouped data.

3.2 MEASURES OF CENTRAL TENDENCY FOR UNGROUPED DATA

There are three common methods of identifying the center of a data set around which the data are located. They are the **mean**, the **median**, and the **mode**. Although all three values are used to determine the center, or central point of a data set, their precise determination can vary, depending on your definition of center. However, in each case we are locating that point around which all the numbers in the data set seem to be grouped.

A. MEAN

The mean is the measure of central tendency most commonly thought of as the average. If you want to compute the mean of your last 10 exams in your statistics course, you simply add them up and divide by 10. The mean of a population, μ (pronounced mu), containing N observations is calculated as

$$\mu = \frac{X_1 + X_2 + X_3 + \cdots + X_N}{N} = \frac{\sum\limits_{i=1}^{N} X_i}{N} \qquad (3.1)$$

The Greek letter capital sigma (Σ) is used as a summation sign, telling you to sum up all of the observations. That is, add up all the X_i's where the values for i run from 1, the first observation, to N, the last observation. For the purpose of simplicity, the notational subscripts and superscripts will be dropped, and the summation sign will be used by itself as simply Σ. Remember! The mean of the population is a parameter.

Arithmetic Mean
Arithmetic mean is the measure of central tendency normally thought of as the average.

Suppose the population was too large and it would prove too time-consuming to add up all the observations. Your only alternative might be to take a sample and calculate its mean. Recall from Chapter 1 that the mean of a sample, $\overline{X}$, is a statistic. It is found as follows:

$$\overline{X} = \frac{X_1 + X_2 + X_3 + \cdots + X_n}{n} = \frac{\Sigma X_i}{n} \qquad (3.2)$$

Remember also that the size of the population is denoted by N, whereas n symbolizes the number in a sample.

EXAMPLE 3-1 The Mean of a Population

Denny is rightfully worried about his grade in statistics. He scored the following grades on all five tests given this semester: $63, 59, 71, 41, 32$. His professor has warned Denny that any grade below 60 is failing. Calculate and interpret Denny's mean grade.

SOLUTION:
Denny's rather disappointing average can be calculated as

$$\mu = \frac{\Sigma X_i}{N} = \frac{63 + 59 + 71 + 41 + 32}{5} = \frac{266}{5} = 53.2$$

STATISTICAL INTERPRETATION:
Since all five grades were used in the calculation, 53.2 is the mean of the population and is therefore a parameter. Obviously, he's in trouble!

B. MEDIAN

The median is sometimes referred to as the *positional average,* because it is that value that lies exactly in the middle of the data set after the values have been placed into an ordered array. One-half of the observations will be *above* the median, and one-half will be *below* the median. Before the median can be calculated, the observations must be put into an ordered array.

> **Median**
> The median is the middle observation after the data have been put into an ordered array.

In a data set with an odd number of observations, this middle position is found as follows:

$$\text{Median position} = \frac{N + 1}{2} \qquad (3.3)$$

In Denny's unfortunate case we calculate his median grade by first putting the values in an ordered array in either ascending or descending order. Thus, we have

$$32, 41, 59, 63, 71$$

The *position* of the median grade is determined as $(N + 1)/2 = (5 + 1)/2 = 3$. The median is then 59, which is located in the third position after the data have been placed into the ordered array.

If there is an even number of observations, the median is the average of the two middle values. Assume a sixth test was given and Denny scored another 63 on it. The ordered array would appear as

$$32, 41, \mathbf{59, 63}, 63, 71$$

The median position is then $(N + 1)/2 = (6 + 1)/2 = 3.5$—that is, the third and one-half position. The median is then that value halfway between the third and fourth observations, and is therefore

$$\frac{59 + 63}{2} = 61$$

This means that half of his test grades were below 61 and half were above 61.

C. MODE

The mode is that observation which occurs with the greatest frequency. Given Denny's six grades, the modal grade is 63 because it occurred more often than any other grade. If still another test was given and Denny managed another 41 on it, the data set is said to be *bimodal* because both 41 and 63 occurred with equal frequency.

Mode
The mode is that observation which occurs most often.

If all the observations occur with equal frequency, the data set has no mode. For example, with Denny's first five tests of 32, 41, 59, 63, and 71, there is no modal grade.

D. THE WEIGHTED MEAN

In our discussion of the mean, we assumed that each observation was equally important. However, in certain cases you might want to give some observations greater weight. For example, if your statistics professor threatens to count the final exam twice as much as the other tests when determining your final grade, then the score you get on the final must be given twice as much weight. That is, it must be counted twice in figuring your grade. This is exactly what the weighted mean does. The proper procedure necessary to accomplish this is given by Formula (3.4).

$$\overline{X}_W = \frac{\Sigma XW}{\Sigma W}$$ (3.4)

---

where $\overline{X}_W$ is the weighted mean
        X is the individual observations
        W is the weight assigned to each observation

Assume you scored 89, 92, and 79 on the hour exams, and a 94 on the final exam. We can reflect these scores and their respective weights with Table 3-1. Formula (3.4) then yields

$$\overline{X}_W = \frac{\Sigma XW}{\Sigma W} = \frac{448}{5} = 89.6$$

TABLE 3-1   Calculation of the Weighted Mean

Grade (X)	Weight (W)	XW
89	1	89
92	1	92
79	1	79
94	2	188
	5	448

This approach is the same as adding the score on the final exam twice in computing the average.

$$\overline{X}_W = \frac{89 + 92 + 79 + 94 + 94}{5} = 89.6$$

Weighted Mean
The weighted mean takes into consideration the relative importance of the observations.

EXAMPLE 3-2 Calculation of the Weighted Mean

Paul the Plumber sells five types of drain cleaner. Each type, along with the profit per can and the number of cans sold, is shown in the table.

Cleaner	Profit per Can (X)	Sales Volume in Cans (W)	XW
Glunk Out	$ 2.00	3	$ 6.00
Bubble Up	3.50	7	24.50
Dream Drain	5.00	15	75.00
Clear More	7.50	12	90.00
Main Drain	6.00	15	90.00
	$24.00	52	$285.50

You can calculate the simple arithmetic mean of Paul's profit as $24/5 = $4.80 per can.

SOLUTION:

However, this is probably not a good estimate of Paul's average profit, since he sells more of some types than he does of others. In order to get a financial statement more representative of his true business performance, Paul must give more weight to the more popular types of cleaner. The proper calculation would therefore be the weighted mean. The proper measure of weight would be the amounts sold. The weighted mean is then

$$\overline{X}_W = \frac{\Sigma XW}{\Sigma W} = \frac{\$285.50}{52} = \$5.49 \text{ per can}$$

STATISTICAL INTERPRETATION:

The weighted mean is higher than the simple arithmetic mean because Paul sells more of those types of cleaner with a higher profit margin.

E. THE GEOMETRIC MEAN

The geometric mean can be used to show percentage changes in a series of positive numbers. As such, it has wide application in business and economics, since we are often interested in determining the percentage change in sales, gross national product, or any of the many economic series with which we must often work.

> **Geometric Mean**
> The geometric mean provides an accurate measure of the average percentage change in a series of numbers.

The geometric mean (GM) is found by taking the nth root of the product of n numbers. Thus,

$$GM = \sqrt[n]{X_1 X_2 X_3 \cdots X_n} \qquad (3.5A)$$

Most handheld calculators can compute the nth root of any number. However, if you find this difficult, an alternative to Formula (3.5A) is

$$\log GM = \frac{1}{n}(\log X_1 + \log X_2 + \log X_3 + \cdots + \log X_n) \qquad (3.5B)$$

The geometric mean of 5, 6, 8, and 12 by (3.5A) is

$$GM = \sqrt[4]{5 \times 6 \times 8 \times 12} = \sqrt[4]{2880} = 7.33$$

By (3.5B), it is

$$\log GM = (1/4)(\log 5 + \log 6 + \log 8 + \log 12)$$
$$= (1/4)(0.7 + 0.778 + 0.903 + 1.079)$$
$$= (1/4)(3.46)$$
$$= 0.865$$

Taking the antilog of 0.865 to determine GM yields 7.33. The arithmetic mean is $5 + 6 + 8 + 12/4 = 7.75$.

The geometric mean is most often used to calculate the average percentage growth rate over time of some given series. To illustrate its application in a business setting, consider the revenue figures in Example 3-3 for White-Knuckle Airlines, P & P's main competitor, over the past five years.

○○○○   **DECISION MAKING THROUGH PROBLEM SOLVING**   ○○○○
                                ILLUSTRATION 3.1

Warren Buffett, the noted financier and multibillionaire, described his record of success and failure in a recent issue of *Fortune* magazine. In reference to his successes,
Mr. Buffett noted that he had amassed considerable wealth in Berkshire Hathaway, a
textile manufacture he acquired in 1965. The stock originally sold for $12 a share. By
1990, it was priced at $7,450 per share!

    In 1990, it was necessary for the courts to decide how much tax Mr. Buffett owed
on the basis of the annual increase in his holdings. The courts calculated this average
increase on the basis of a simple arithmetic mean. In his typically shrewd manner,
Mr. Buffett demonstrated the logic of using a geometric mean to compute percentage
increases. The resulting geometric mean increase was less than the arithmetic mean
(as it always is) determined by the courts, thereby reducing Mr. Buffett's total tax bite.

EXAMPLE 3-3   The Geometric Mean

The CEO for White-Knuckle Airlines wishes to determine the average growth rate
in revenue based on the figures in the table.

Revenues for White-Knuckle Airlines

(1) Year	(2) Revenue	(3) Percentage of Previous Year
1992	$50,000	— —
1993	55,000	55/50 = 1.10
1994	66,000	66/55 = 1.20
1995	60,000	60/66 = 0.91
1996	78,000	78/60 = 1.30

SOLUTION:

It is first necessary to determine what percentage each year's revenue is of the previous year. In other words, the revenue in 1993 is what percentage of the revenue in
1992? This is found by dividing revenues in 1993 by those in 1992. The result 1.10
reveals that 1993 revenues are 110 percent of revenues in 1992. Percentages for the
three remaining years are also calculated. Taking the geometric mean of these percentages gives

$$\text{GM} = \sqrt[4]{(1.10)(1.2)(0.91)(1.3)} = 1.1179$$

Subtracting 1 in order to convert to an average annual increase yields 0.1179, or an
11.79 percent average increase over the five-year period.

Using logs from (3.5B) produces

$$\log GM = (1/4)(\log 1.1 + \log 1.2 + \log 0.91 + \log 1.3)$$
$$= (1/4)(0.041 + 0.079 + (-0.04) + 0.114)$$
$$= 0.0485$$

Taking the antilog of 0.0485 yields

$$GM = 1.1179$$

providing an average increase each year over the five-year period of 11.79 percent. The simple arithmetic average is

$$\overline{X} = \frac{1.1 + 1.2 + 0.91 + 1.3}{4} = \frac{4.51}{4} = 1.1275$$

or a 12.75 percent average change. We divide by 4 since there were four changes over the five-year period.

However, if an average increase of 12.75 percent based on the simple arithmetic average is applied to the series starting with $50,000, the results are

$$\$50,000 \times 1.1275 = \$56,375$$
$$\$56,375 \times 1.1275 = \$63,563$$
$$\$63,563 \times 1.1275 = \$71,667$$
$$\$71,667 \times 1.1275 = \$80,805$$

Since $80,805 exceeds the $78,000 White-Knuckle Airlines actually earned, the 12.75 percent increase is obviously too high. On the other hand, if the geometric mean growth rate of 11.79 percent is used, we get

$$\$50,000 \times 1.1179 = \$55,895$$
$$\$55,895 \times 1.1179 = \$62,485$$
$$\$62,485 \times 1.1179 = \$69,852$$
$$\$69,852 \times 1.1179 = \$78,088 \approx \$78,000$$

This gives us a value of $78,088, which is much closer to the actual revenue figure of $78,000.

STATISTICAL INTERPRETATION:

The geometric mean will always be less than the arithmetic mean except in the rare case in which all the annual increases are the same, in which case the two means are equal.

3.3   MEASURES OF CENTRAL TENDENCY FOR GROUPED DATA

If the data have been grouped into classes in a frequency table, it is impossible to determine the mean by the method just discussed since the individual values are not given. An alternative approach must be found. The assumption is made that the observations in each class are equal to the class midpoint. Although this may be a rather heroic assumption, it probably all balances out since it is likely that some of the observations exceed the midpoint while others fall below it. Thus, on the average, the assumption is not all that illogical. It should be kept in mind, however, that computations made using grouped data are only approximations.

A.   MEAN

Given this assumption, we must take into consideration the frequency and midpoints of each class when computing the mean using grouped data. Formula (3.6) does just that.

$$\overline{X}_g = \frac{\Sigma fM}{n} = \frac{\Sigma fM}{\Sigma f} \tag{3.6}$$

where f is the frequency or number of observations in each class
        M is the midpoint of each class
        n is the sample size and equals the combined frequencies in all classes.

TABLE 3-2 Frequency Distribution for Passengers

(1) Class (passengers)	(2) Frequency (f) (days)	(3) M	(4) fM
50 to 59	3	54.5	163.5
60 to 69	7	64.5	451.5
70 to 79	18	74.5	1341.0
80 to 89	12	84.5	1014.0
90 to 99	8	94.5	756.0
100 to 109	2	104.5	208.0
	50		3935.0

The frequency table for Pigs & People Airlines that we developed in Chapter 2 is repeated in Table 3-2 for your convenience, along with the midpoints for each class, which, as you remember, are determined by averaging the upper and lower boundaries.

Using Formula (3.6), we can see that P & P flew a daily average of 78.7 passengers.

$$\overline{X}_g = \frac{\Sigma fM}{n} = \frac{3935}{50} = 78.7$$

B. MEDIAN

If the data have been recorded in a frequency table, they cannot be placed in an ordered array in order to calculate the median. As an illustration, the frequency table for P & P Airlines is given in Table 3-3.

TABLE 3-3 Frequency Distribution for Passengers

Class	f	Cumulative Frequency
50 to 59	3	3
60 to 69	7	10
70 to 79	18	28
80 to 89	12	40
90 to 99	8	48
100 to 109	2	50

We must first find the median class of the frequency distribution. The **median class** is that class whose cumulative frequency is greater than or equal to $n/2$.

Since n is 50, we need to locate the first class with a cumulative frequency of 25 or more. The third class has a cumulative frequency of 28 and is therefore the median class. The median can then be determined as

$$\text{Median} = L_{md} + \left[\frac{n/2 - F}{f_{md}}\right](C) \qquad (3.7)$$

where L_{md} is the lower boundary of median class (70)
           F is the cumulative frequency of the class *preceding* the median class (10)
           f_{md} is the frequency of the median class (18)
           C is the class interval of the median class (10)

Using Formula (3.7), we obtain the median:

$$\text{Median} = 70 + \left[\frac{50/2 - 10}{18}\right]10 = 78.33$$

We can then conclude that on 25 days—one half of the 50 days surveyed—less than 78.33 passengers flew on P & P Airlines, and on the other 25 days more than 78.33 passengers flew the friendly skies of P & P.

C. MODE

Since by definition the mode is the observation that occurs most often, it will be found in the class with the highest frequency. This class with the largest frequency is called the **modal class.** To estimate the mode in the case of grouped data, we use Formula (3.8).

$$\text{Mode} = L_{mo} + \left[\frac{D_a}{D_b + D_a}\right](C) \qquad (3.8)$$

where L_{mo} is the lower boundary of the modal class
           D_a is the difference between the frequency of the modal class and the class preceding it
           D_b is the difference between the frequency of the modal and the class after it
           C is the class interval of the modal class

From Table 3-3 the mode is

$$\text{Mode} = 70 + \left[\frac{18 - 7}{(18 - 12) + (18 - 7)}\right](10) = 76.47$$

To summarize much of what we have done, consider the following example.

EXAMPLE 3-4 Central Tendencies with Grouped Data

In a recent issue of *Fortune,* 30 companies out of the 500 largest U.S. corporations reported revenues in millions of dollars, as shown in the frequency table.

Revenues of 30 U.S. Corporations (in millions of dollars)

Class	f	M	F	fM
20 up to 30	5	25	5	125
30 up to 40	2	35	7	70
40 up to 50	4	45	11	180
50 up to 60	8	55	19	440
60 up to 70	7	65		455
70 up to 80	2	75		150
80 up to 90	1	85		85
90 up to 100	1	95		95
	30			1,600

As an economic analyst for a large Wall Street brokerage firm, you must report to your office manager before the end of the day's trading on the New York Stock Exchange the following statistics for these revenue figures: (a) the mean, (b) the median, and (c) the mode.

SOLUTION:

a. The mean can be calculated from Formula (3.6):

$$\overline{X}_g = \frac{\Sigma fM}{\Sigma f} = \frac{1,600}{30} = \$53.33 \text{ million}$$

b. The median is found from Formula (3.7):

$$\text{Median} = L_{md} + \left[\frac{n/2 - F}{f_{md}}\right](C)$$

$$= 50 + \left[\frac{15 - 11}{8}\right](10)$$

$$= \$55 \text{ million}$$

c. According to Formula (3.7), the mode is

$$\text{Mode} = L_{mo} + \left[\frac{D_a}{D_b + D_a}\right](C)$$

$$= 50 + \frac{4}{5}(10)$$

$$= \$58 \text{ million}$$

STATISTICAL INTERPRETATION:

The values shown serve as estimates of central tendencies for the revenue data. Your manager can now gain insight into the nature of the earnings of these firms. Although all three are representative of the center point, your manager may prefer one of them. It will be shown in the next two sections how and why one central measure may be more desirable than others.

3.4   COMPARING THE MEAN, MEDIAN, AND MODE

The mean is the most common measure of central tendency and enjoys the advantage of being easily understood in general conversation. It is also rather easily determined for both grouped and ungrouped data. Furthermore, the mean lends itself handily to further algebraic manipulation and interpretation. Unfortunately the mean is affected by extreme values, or *outliers,* and, unlike the median, can be drastically biased by observations which lie significantly above or below it.

For example, for the data $4, 5, 6, 7, 8$, the mean and the median are both 6 and represent an excellent measure of the data's center point. If the last observation were 80 instead of 8, the mean becomes 20.4 but the median is still 6. Since the median is not affected by this extreme value, it is probably a better reflection of the data set's true center.

The mode is also less affected by a few atypical observations. If we had $4, 6, 6, 7, 8$, the mode remains 6 even if the last value were 80. However, if there is no mode, or if the data set is bimodal, its use can be confusing.

3.5   SELECTING THE APPROPRIATE MEASURE OF CENTRAL TENDENCY

In many cases all three averages will give nearly the same results, so it often doesn't matter which you cite. However, the opportunity sometimes exists to influence the impression generated by calculations by choosing to report one average instead of another. Judicious selection of your reporting statistics can often prove beneficial.

For example, presume you work as a production manager for Novelties, Inc. marketing electric forks to wealthy residents of Beverly Hills, California, who can't find anything else on which to spend their money. The number of forks produced each day over the past 10 days is 142, 153, 116, 101, 97, 106, 103, 99, 100, and 106. Upon arriving at the plant on Rodeo Drive one morning, your statistician frantically approaches you with the news that several people have called demanding production figures. Your boss wants to know if production quotas are being met, while the IRS needs a figure upon which to base tax assessments. You calculate the true averages you might report as

$$\text{Mean} = 112.3 \text{ forks}$$

$$\text{Median} = 104.5 \text{ forks}$$

$$\text{Mode} = 106 \text{ forks}$$

Recognizing that the elevated production levels of the first two days will inflate the mean, since it is affected by extreme values, you are not surprised to find the mean is the highest of the three measures.

You report an average production level of 112.3 to your regional manager and bask in his praise for maintaining exemplary standards of efficiency. At the same time, you tell the IRS the average production level was only 104.5 forks in order to minimize your taxes. In neither case did you really lie.

Later that day, the shipping department wants to know how many empty crates to prepare. They will not accept fractional units because you can't ship part of a fork, so you tell them the average over the past 10 days has been 106.

3.6   MEASURES OF DISPERSION FOR UNGROUPED DATA

In our efforts to describe a set of numbers, we have seen that it is useful to locate the center of that data set. However, identifying a measure of central tendency is not always sufficient. It often proves to be helpful if we can also cite the extent to which the individual observations are spread out around that center point.

Take the three rather small, but, for our purposes, sufficient, data sets shown here:

Data Set 1	Data Set 2	Data Set 3
0, 10	4, 6	5, 5

As you can plainly see, all three average exactly five. Are we then to conclude that the data sets are similar? Of course not. However, if we were told only what the averages were without seeing the observations in each data set, we might presume a similarity.

To provide a more complete description of the data sets, we need a measure of how spread out the observations are from that mean of 5. A **measure of dispersion** indicates to what degree the individual observations are dispersed or spread out around their mean. The observations in the first data set are quite spread out and away from their mean of 5, whereas the observations in the second data set are very close to their mean. The first data set has a greater measure of dispersion. The third data set, on the other hand, has no dispersion at all. Envision a data set with 1,000 observations. Wouldn't a measure of dispersion prove useful in telling you something about the nature of the data set? You can see then how a measure of dispersion can be used to further describe a data set and give the statistician an idea as to the nature of the observations which have been collected for analysis.

This section presents various measures of distribution which prove beneficial in our effort to describe a set of numbers.

A. RANGE

A simple, but not particularly useful, measure of dispersion is the range. The **range** is the difference between the highest observation and the lowest observation. Its advantage is that it is easy to calculate and at least gives some impression as to the makeup of the data set. Its disadvantage is that it takes only two of the, perhaps, hundreds of observations in the data set into consideration in its calculation. The rest of the observations are ignored.

B. MEAN ABSOLUTE DEVIATION

It might seem to the untrained mind that a practical approach to measuring the dispersion in a data set is to simply calculate the average amount by which the observations vary from the mean. This is called the **average deviation** (AD). It requires that we subtract the mean from each of the observations and then average the differences. That is,

$$AD = \frac{\Sigma(X_i - \overline{X})}{n} \tag{3.9}$$

Let's see what happens if we try it. Professor Willie Doezoff, a long-time resident of the statistics department, gave a quiz to his introductory statistics class last week. Eight of the brightest students scored 73, 82, 64, 61, 63, 68, 52, and 73. The average is $\overline{X} = 67$, and is used to calculate the average deviation in the manner shown in Table 3-4. Wait a minute! The result is an average deviation of 0. This happens be-

TABLE 3-4 Grades for Professor Doezoff's Stat Class

X_i	$X_i - \overline{X}$
73	$73 - 67 = 6$
82	$82 - 67 = 15$
64	$64 - 67 = -3$
61	$61 - 67 = -6$
63	$63 - 67 = -4$
68	$68 - 67 = 1$
52	$52 - 67 = -15$
73	$73 - 67 = 6$
	$0 = \Sigma(X_i - \overline{X})$

TABLE 3-5 Grades for Professor Doezoff's Stat Class

X_i	$X_i - \overline{X}$	$|X_i - \overline{X}|$
73	6	6
82	15	15
64	−3	3
61	−6	6
63	−4	4
68	1	1
52	−15	15
73	6	6
	0	$56 = \Sigma|X_i - \overline{X}|$

cause the pluses and minuses canceled each other out. The average deviation of a data set is *always* zero.

A solution to this enigma is the **mean absolute deviation** (MAD). As shown in Table 3-5, MAD takes the absolute value of the differences, so the negatives do not cancel out the positives. Thus,

$$\text{MAD} = \frac{\Sigma|X_i - \overline{X}|}{n} \tag{3.10}$$

$$= \frac{56}{8}$$

$$= 7$$

The resulting value of 7 serves as an indication of the amount by which the individual observations are dispersed around their mean of 67: the higher the MAD the more the dispersion.

MAD is a "quick and dirty" method of measuring the amount of deviation in a data set. However, its use is limited because absolute values do not lend themselves to further mathematical manipulation. Much of the calculation loses its meaning when absolute values are applied. A more suitable method which does not suffer from this handicap is desired. The answer lies in the variance and the standard deviation.

C. VARIANCE AND THE STANDARD DEVIATION FOR A POPULATION

This improved method of measuring dispersion can be achieved by examining the two most important measures of dispersion: the variance and the standard deviation. The standard deviation is the square root of the variance. We will always calculate them by first finding the variance and taking its square root to get the standard deviation. Remember, as measures of dispersion, they measure the tendency for the individual observations to deviate from their mean.

The **variance** is the mean of the squared deviations from the mean. What does that mean in English? It means that (1) you find the amount by which each observation deviates from the mean, (2) square those deviations, and (3) find the average of those squared deviations. You then have the mean of the squared deviations from the mean.

Variance
Variance is the mean of the squared deviations of the observations from their mean. It is an important measure of dispersion.

The variance for a population, σ^2 (read sigma squared) is

$$\sigma^2 = \frac{(X_1 - \mu)^2 + (X_2 - \mu)^2 + (X_3 - \mu)^2 + \cdots + (X_N - \mu)^2}{N}$$

$$= \frac{\Sigma(X_i - \mu)^2}{N}$$

(3.11)

where $X_1, X_2, X_3, \ldots, X_N$ are the individual observations
        μ is the population mean
        N is the number of observations

The standard deviation σ is

$$\sigma = \sqrt{\sigma^2} \tag{3.12}$$

Notice that since we are working with a population the mean is μ, not $\overline{X}$ as it is for a sample, and the number of observations is N, not n as it is for a sample.

> **Standard Deviation**
> Standard deviation is the square root of the variance. It is an important measure of the dispersion of the data.

To illustrate, Chuckie Chadwell sells five different insurance policies out of the trunk of his 1973 Plymouth. Their respective monthly premiums are $110, $145, $125, $95, and $150. The average premium is

$$\mu = \frac{110 + 145 + 125 + 95 + 150}{5} = \$125$$

The variance is found by:

1. Subtracting the mean of 125 from each of the five observations.
2. Squaring these deviations from the mean.
3. Taking the average of these squared deviations.

Following these three steps yields

$$\sigma^2 = \frac{(110 - 125)^2 + (145 - 125)^2 + (125 - 125)^2 + (95 - 125)^2 + (150 - 125)^2}{5}$$

$$= 430$$

Despite the importance and common usage of the variance, it presents two problems. To begin with, it is a rather large number relative to the observations themselves. As you can see, it is several times greater than even the largest observation. Due to its sheer size, the variance therefore often becomes difficult to work with.

An even more distressing problem results from the fact that since the deviations are squared, the variance is always expressed in terms of the original data squared. In Chuckie's case, since he squared the deviations from the mean, it becomes 430 dollars squared—a unit of measure which makes no sense. If you are originally working with, for example, work experience measured in years, the variance is expressed in years squared. In most instances, the variance is expressed in terms that have no logical meaning or interpretation.

However, both complications can be solved in a flash. Just find the standard deviation σ by taking the square root of the variance:

$$\sigma = \sqrt{430} = 20.74 \text{ dollars}$$

As easy as that, both problems are solved. You now have a much smaller number which is easier to work with, and, more importantly, it is now expressed in dollars since you took the square root of dollars squared.

The concept of the standard deviation is often quite important in business and economics. For example, in finance the standard deviation is used as a measure of the risk associated with various investment opportunities. By using the standard deviation to measure the variability in rates of return offered by different investments, the financial analyst can gauge the level of risk carried by each financial asset. Generally, the higher the standard deviation of the rate of return of a particular investment, the greater the degree of risk.

EXAMPLE 3-5 Variance and Standard Deviation of a Population

Markus Boggs is manager of Nest Egg Investments, a financial planning firm that assists individuals in setting up their personal portfolios. Recently, Markus was interested in the rates of return over the past five years of two different mutual funds. Megabucks, Inc. showed rates of return over the five-year period of 12, 10, 13, 9, and 11 percent, while Dynamics Corporation yielded 13, 12, 14, 10, and 6 percent. A client approached Boggs and expressed an interest in one of these mutual funds. Which one should Boggs choose for his client?

SOLUTION:

Notice that both funds offer an average return of 11 percent. (In Example 3-14, we will examine the effects of eliminating this coincidental occurrence.) Since both offer the same return on the average, the safer investment is the one with the smaller degree of risk as measured by the standard deviation. Boggs calculates the variance and takes its square root to get the standard deviation for each stock. For Megabucks, it becomes

$$\sigma^2 = \frac{(12 - 11)^2 + (10 - 11)^2 + (13 - 11)^2 + (9 - 11)^2 + (11 - 11)^2}{5}$$

$$= 2$$

The standard deviation is

$$\sigma = \sqrt{2} = 1.41\%$$

For Dynamics,

$$\sigma^2 = \frac{(13 - 11)^2 + (12 - 11)^2 + (14 - 11)^2 + (10 - 11)^2 + (6 - 11)^2}{5}$$

$$= 8$$

The standard deviation is therefore

$$\sigma = \sqrt{8} = 2.83\%$$

STATISTICAL INTERPRETATION:

Since Megabucks exhibits less variability in its returns and offers the same rate of return on the average as does Dynamics, Megabucks represents the safer of the two investments and is therefore the preferred investment opportunity.

D. VARIANCE AND STANDARD DEVIATION FOR A SAMPLE

Make note! The previous examples relate to the variance and standard deviation for a *population*. The symbols σ^2 and σ are Greek letters typical of parameters.

Seldom do we calculate parameters. In most cases, we will instead estimate them by taking a sample and computing the corresponding statistics. With that in mind, this section examines the way in which we can calculate these important measures of dispersion as they relate to samples.

The variance and standard deviation for a sample still represent measures of dispersion around the mean. They are calculated quite similarly to those for a population. The sample variance s^2 is

$$s^2 = \frac{\Sigma(X_i - \overline{X})^2}{n - 1} \qquad (3.13)$$

and the sample standard deviation is

$$s = \sqrt{s^2} \qquad (3.14)$$

Notice that the mean in Formula (3.13) is expressed as $\overline{X}$, and not μ, since we are working with samples. Furthermore, you divide by $n - 1$ rather than N because you have $n - 1$ *degrees of freedom*, or $df = n - 1$. The number of degrees of freedom in any statistical operation is equal to the number of observations minus any constraints placed on the data. A constraint is any value which must be computed from the observations.

For example, assume you are to choose $n = 4$ numbers which must average to $\overline{X} = 10$. Under these conditions, you are free to pick any three numbers you want—say your hat size, your age, and your IQ. Once those first three numbers are chosen, however, the fourth is predetermined if they are to average $\overline{X} = 10$. As Formula (3.13) illustrates, the variance uses the value for $\overline{X}$ which functions as a constraint and thereby reduces the degrees of freedom by 1. Hence, we divide by the number of observations, n, minus 1.

Another reason we divide by $n - 1$ is that a sample is generally a little less dispersed than the population from which it was taken. There is therefore a tendency for the sample standard deviation s to be a little less than the population standard deviation σ. This is unfortunate. Remember, we are trying to use the value of s as an estimation of σ. However, s will consistently underestimate σ. We must offset this condition by artificially inflating s by dividing by a slightly smaller number, $n - 1$, rather than n.

To illustrate the technique of determining these measures of dispersion for a sample, consider another problem Boggs has regarding efforts to help his clients make investment decisions.

EXAMPLE 3-6 Variance and Standard Deviation for a Sample

Mr. Boggs wishes to determine the stability of the price of a particular stock. He decides to base his judgment regarding stability on the standard deviation of the stock's daily closing price. Checking the financial pages, Boggs learns that the stock has been traded on the exchange for quite some time and there are many closing prices dating back several months. Rather than using all these prices, Boggs decides to simplify his arithmetic and select a random sample of $n = 7$ days. (Although 7 is probably too small a sample, it will serve our purposes for the moment.) He notes the closing prices of

$$\$87, \$120, \$54, \$92, \$73, \$80, \text{ and } \$63$$

SOLUTION:

Then, $\overline{X} = \$81.29$ and

$$s^2 = \frac{\Sigma(X_i - \overline{X})^2}{n - 1}$$

$$= (87 - 81.29)^2 + (120 - 81.29)^2 + (54 - 81.29)^2$$

$$+ \frac{(92 - 81.29)^2 + (73 - 81.29)^2 + (80 - 81.29)^2 + (63 - 81.29)^2}{7 - 1}$$

$$s^2 = 465.9 \text{ dollars squared}$$

$$s = \sqrt{465.9} = 21.58 \text{ dollars}$$

STATISTICAL INTERPRETATION:

Boggs has estimated the mean closing price of the stock to be $81.29, with a tendency to vary above and below that price by $21.58. A further explanation of the use and interpretation of the standard deviation is offered later in this chapter. However, keep in mind that Boggs can always interpret the standard deviation of $21.58 as a measure of the tendency of the closing prices to fluctuate around their mean of $81.29.

3.7   SHORTCUT METHOD FOR VARIANCE AND STANDARD DEVIATION

Although the procedure for calculating the variance and the standard deviation based on Formulas (3.13) and (3.14) provides the correct answer, it entails a good deal of arithmetic. The formulas are somewhat cumbersome and mathematically disagreeable. They are given only to better illustrate conceptually what a measure of dispersion is.

A more convenient method for actually calculating the variance and standard deviation for a population is

$$\sigma^2 = \frac{\Sigma X^2}{N} - \left[\frac{\Sigma X}{N}\right]^2 \qquad (3.15)$$

and

$$\sigma = \sqrt{\sigma^2} \qquad (3.16)$$

Since we usually do not calculate parameters, let's move on to a discussion of the proper way to compute the variance and standard deviation for a sample, using the more convenient formulas

$$s^2 = \frac{\Sigma X^2 - n\overline{X}^2}{n - 1} \qquad (3.17)$$

and

$$s = \sqrt{s^2} \qquad (3.18)$$

EXAMPLE 3-7 Shortcut Method for Sample Measures of Dispersion

Let's have Boggs repeat the exercise of measuring the variation in stock prices by using this simplified shortcut approach. The seven prices selected in the sample were $87, $120, $54, $92, $73, $80, and $63, yielding $\overline{X} = \$81.29$.

SOLUTION:

Then, using (3.17), we have

X	X^2
87	7,569
120	14,400
54	2,916
92	8,464
73	5,329
80	6,400
63	3,969
$\Sigma X = 569$	$\Sigma X^2 = 49,047$

$$s^2 = \frac{\Sigma X^2 - n\overline{X}^2}{n - 1}$$

$$s^2 = \frac{49,047 - 7(81.29)^2}{7 - 1} = 465.9 \text{ dollars squared}$$

$$s = \sqrt{465.9} = 21.58 \text{ dollars}$$

STATISTICAL INTERPRETATION:

This approach requires less arithmetic and gives Boggs the same answer as the more involved procedure using Formulas (3.13) and (3.14).

Remember, Formulas (3.13) and (3.14) are given only to illustrate the concept of a measure of dispersion, or to use if you have just a few observations. In most cases you will find the shortcut approach using Formulas (3.17) and (3.18) much easier.

3.8   OTHER MEASURES OF DISPERSION

Although the variance and the standard deviation are the most useful measures of dispersion in statistical analysis, there are other ways in which the dispersion of a data set might be measured. These additional measures of dispersion, which often prove to be quite serviceable, are **quartiles, deciles,** and **percentiles**.

Every data set has three quartiles which divide it into four equal parts. As seen in Figure 3-1, if the horizontal line can be thought of as a data set arranged in an ordered array, three quartiles can be identified which produce four separate parts or subsets of equal size in the data set.

The first quartile is that value below which at most 25 percent of the observations fall and above which the remaining 75 percent can be found. The second quartile is

FIGURE 3-1

Three Quartiles Produce Four Equal Subsets

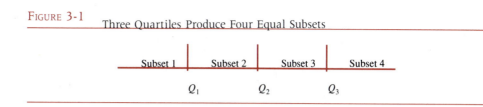

right in the middle. One-half the observations are below it and one-half the observations are above it. In this sense, it is the same as the median. The third quartile is that value below which at most 75 percent of the observations are located and above which the remaining 25 percent can be found.

The determination of quartiles is often useful. Many graduate schools, for example, will admit only those students in the top 25 percent (first quartile) of their applicants. Corporations often wish to single out those plants whose poor production records place them in the bottom quartile in order to identify certain trouble spots in need of remedial treatment. With only a little imagination, it is possible to envision numerous instances in which the determination of quartiles might prove beneficial.

Deciles separate a data set into 10 equal subsets, and percentiles produce 100 parts. The first decile is that observation below which at most 10 percent of the observations are found while the remaining 90 percent are located above it. The first percentile is that value below which at most 1 percent of the observations are located, and the rest are above it. A similar interpretation can be applied to the rest of the deciles and percentiles. Each data set has 9 deciles and 99 percentiles.

A percentile and its location in an ordered array are identified by means of subscripts. For example, the 15th percentile is indicated as P_{15}, and its location in the ordered array is L_{15}.

To illustrate the calculation of percentiles, assume that we have the observations for the number of shares for 50 stocks traded on the New York Stock Exchange as shown in Table 3-6. Notice that the data have been placed in an ordered array. The location of the Pth percentile is found as

$$Lp = (n + 1)\frac{P}{100} \qquad (3.19)$$

where L is the location in the ordered array of the desired percentile
          n is the number of observations
          P is the desired percentile

Assume that we wish to calculate the 25th percentile, P_{25}, for the stocks in Table 3-6. We must first find its location in the ordered array.

$$L_{25} = (50 + 1)\frac{25}{100}$$

$$= 12.75$$

The resulting value of 12.75 tells us that the 25th percentile is located 75 percent of the way between the 12th observation of 20 and the 13th observation of 21, or $P_{25} = 20.75$.

TABLE 3-6   Numbers of Shares Traded on the NYSE (in 100's)

3	10	19	27	34	38	48	56	67	74
4	12	**20**	29	34	39	48	59	67	74
7	14	**21**	31	36	43	52	62	69	76
9	15	25	31	37	45	53	63	72	79
10	17	27	34	38	47	56	64	73	80

If we were to calculate the 35th percentile, we find

$$L_{35} = (50 + 1)\frac{35}{100}$$

$$= 17.85$$

The 35th percentile is 85 percent of the way between the 17th observation of 29 and the 18th observation of 31, or $P_{35} = 29 + (0.85)(31 - 29) = 30.7$. Thus, 35 percent of the observations are below 30.7, and the remaining 65 percent are above 30.7.

Returning to deciles and quartiles for a moment, note that the first decile is equal to P_{10}, that the second decile is equal to P_{20}, and so on. Additionally, the first quartile is the same as P_{25}, the second quartile equals P_{50}, and P_{75} locates the third quartile. With that in mind, the calculation of deciles and quartiles simply becomes a matter of determining the appropriate percentiles according to the rules that we have just established.

EXAMPLE 3-8   Calculating Quartiles

As the financial analyst for a large investment firm in New York, you must determine which stocks in Table 3-6 should be designated as potential "gainers" based on how active they are in the market. You decide to single out those stocks above the third quartile (P_{75}).

SOLUTION:

The third quartile is

$$L_{75} = (n + 1)\frac{75}{100}$$

$$= (50 + 1)\frac{75}{100}$$

$$= 38.25$$

The third quartile is then 25 percent of the way between the 38th and 39th observations. Thus, $62 + (0.25)(63 - 62) = 62.25$, or 6,225 shares since the data were originally expressed in hundreds of shares.

STATISTICAL INTERPRETATION:

Of the 50 stocks cited, 75 percent of them traded less than 6,225 shares, and the remaining 25 percent were so active as to trade more than 6,225 shares. You report to your boss that any stocks trading more than 6,225 shares are sufficiently active to warrant attention. There are 12 stocks in this group.

Your superiors, however, are not at all happy with your report. They contend that you should have been more exclusive in your selection. The number of choices must be reduced. You therefore decide that the only stocks to be assigned to this privileged status are those in the top two deciles. That is, those in the upper 20 percent in terms of activity. You must then find P_{80}, since the ordered array is from lowest to highest.

EXAMPLE 3-9 Calculating Deciles

The procedure for locating the 80th percentile must be followed.

SOLUTION:

Given that there are 50 observations, we have

$$L_{80} = (50 + 1)\frac{80}{100}$$

$$= 40.80$$

The 80th percentile is 80 percent of the way between the 40th observation of 64 and the 41st observation, which is 67. Thus, $P_{80} = 64 + (0.80)(67 - 64) = 66.4$.

STATISTICAL INTERPRETATION:

Of the 50 possible investments, 80 percent traded less than 6,640 shares, and the rest, those trading more than 6,640 shares, are singled out as preferred investment opportunities. Only nine stocks fall into this category.

A unique measure of dispersion is the **interquartile range** (IQR). The IQR is the difference between the first quartile and the third quartile. That is, $P_{75} - P_{25}$.

One-half of the observations lie within this range. It consists of the middle 50 percent of the observations in that it cuts off the lower 25 percent and the upper 25 percent of the data points. As a result, the IQR provides a measure of dispersion that is not heavily influenced by a few extreme observations. The interquartile range is illustrated in Figure 3-2.

FIGURE 3-2   The Interquartile Range

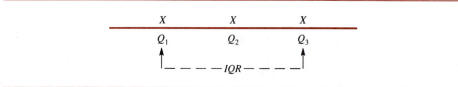

3.9   MEASURES OF DISPERSION WITH GROUPED DATA

If the observations for volume of stock trading on the NYSE in Table 3-6 were grouped into a frequency distribution, the individual observations would be unavailable and an ordered array could not be formed. The procedure described above to determine a particular percentile using ungrouped data would not be appropriate. An alternative method must be found.

A.   PERCENTILES WITH GROUPED DATA

When data are grouped, it is not necessary to determine the location of a percentile. Instead, the desired percentile can be calculated directed from the frequency table. Given the data in Table 3-6, the cumulative frequency distribution in Table 3-7 can be constructed.

TABLE 3-7   Frequency Distribution for Trading Volume of 50 Stocks

Class	Frequency	Cumulative Frequency
3–13	7	7
14–24	6	13
25–35	9	22
36–46	7	29
47–57	7	36
58–68	6	42
69–79	7	49
80–89	1	50
	50	

If we sought, for example, P_{70}, we wish to determine that value below which at most 70 percent of the observations fell. Seventy percent of 50 is 35 observations. Since the cumulative frequency of the fourth class is only 29, the 35th observation is in the 47–57 class. Given the 29 observations in the first four classes, to reach 35 we need an additional six of the seven observations in the 47–57 class. That is, we need 6/7 of the observations in the fifth class. It is also necessary to consider the lower boundary of the class containing the desired percentile (47 in our case) and the class interval of 11. Then P_{70} is

$$P_{70} = 47 + \frac{6}{7}(11) = 56.4$$

Since the use of grouped data results only in an approximation, an examination of Table 3-4 reveals that this method provides the acceptable alternative that we seek.

EXAMPLE 3-10 Finding Deciles and Quartiles with Grouped Data

In order to obtain a more complete division of the level of stock activity, the director of financial services for your investment firm requires that you calculate all three quartiles (P_{25}, P_{50}, P_{75}) as well as the first decile (P_{10}) and last decile (P_{90}) for the 50 stocks displayed in Table 3-7.

SOLUTION:
For the first quartile you seek that value that lies above 25 percent of the 50 observations. Twenty-five percent of 50 is 12.5, which requires that you round up to 13 observations. Since only seven observations are in the first class, the first quartile is located in the 14–24 class, that is, the second class. Along with the seven observations in the first class, you need an additional six from the second class to obtain the full 13. Thus, you must take all six of those in the second class.

$$P_{25} = 14 + \frac{6}{6}(11) = 25 \qquad (\text{or } 2,500 \text{ shares})$$

Although this observation does not appear in the second class, since grouped data result only in approximations, it serves as your estimate of the first quartile. The second quartile, P_{50}, is above 25 of the observations (50 percent of the 50 observations). Along with the 22 observations in the first three classes, you must also include 3 of the 7 observations in the fourth class. Thus,

$$P_{50} = 36 + \frac{3}{7}(11) = 40.7 \qquad (\text{or } 4,070 \text{ shares})$$

Similarly, the third quartile includes 38 observations.

$$P_{75} = 58 + \frac{2}{6}(11) = 61.7 \qquad (6,170 \text{ shares})$$

The first decile, P_{10}, and ninth decile, P_{90}, require 5 (10 percent of 50) and 45 (90 percent of 50) observations, respectively.

$$P_{10} = 3 + \frac{5}{7}(11) = 10.9 \qquad (1{,}090 \text{ shares})$$

$$P_{90} = 69 + \frac{3}{7}(11) = 73.7 \qquad (7{,}370 \text{ shares})$$

STATISTICAL INTERPRETATION:

You can now give the director a more complete breakdown of the activity level of the stocks under examination. Twenty-five percent of the stocks sold less than 2,500 shares, 50 percent sold less than 4,070 shares, and 75 percent sold less than 6,170 shares. In addition, the deciles reveal that 10 percent sold less than 1,090 shares and 90 percent sold less than 7,310 shares. If investment decisions are to be made on the basis of activity levels, this division provides a foundation on which to base these decisions.

B.   VARIANCE AND STANDARD DEVIATION WITH GROUPED DATA

As you might expect, calculating the variance and standard deviation for grouped data involves formulas different from those used with ungrouped data. Specifically,

$$s^2 = \frac{\Sigma f M^2 - n\overline{X}^2}{n - 1} \qquad (3.20)$$

and

$$s = \sqrt{s^2} \qquad (3.21)$$

where f is the class frequency
        M is the class midpoint
        n is the number of observations

EXAMPLE 3-11 Measures of Dispersion for Grouped Data

Using the data from P & P Airlines as our model, assume we want to determine how dispersed the numbers of passengers are. We need such an estimate in order to make decisions regarding the type of flights to offer, the times to schedule them, and the size of the planes which would maximize efficiency. There might be numerous decisions which depend on the degree of dispersion exhibited by our data. The frequency table for P & P appeared as

Class (passengers)	f (days)	M	fM	M^2	fM^2
50–58	2	54	108	2916	5,832
59–67	5	63	315	3969	19,845
68–76	14	72	1008	5184	72,576
77–85	18	81	1458	6561	118,098
86–94	7	90	630	8100	56,700
95–103	4	99	396	9801	39,204
	$n = 50$		$\Sigma fM = 3915$		$\Sigma fM^2 = 312{,}255$

SOLUTION:

Given that we calculated $\overline{X}_g = 78.3$ in an earlier example as

$$\overline{X}_g = \frac{\Sigma fM}{n} = \frac{3915}{50} = 78.3$$

Formula (3.20) gives us

$$s^2 = \frac{\Sigma fM^2 - n\overline{X}^2}{n-1}$$

$$s^2 = \frac{312{,}255 - 50(78.3)^2}{49} = 116.54 \text{ passengers squared}$$

$$s = \sqrt{116.54} = 10.80 \text{ passengers}$$

STATISTICAL INTERPRETATION:

Daily numbers of passengers for P & P average 78.3 and tend to vary from that mean by 10.8 passengers.

3.10 COMMON USES FOR THE STANDARD DEVIATION

As we have emphasized, the standard deviation is useful in describing a data set by measuring the extent to which the individual observations are spread out around their mean. There are at least two additional applications for the standard deviation. The first one involves Chebyshev's Theorem and applies to *any* distribution of observations, while the second is appropriate only if the distribution meets specific conditions of normality.

A.   CHEBYSHEV'S THEOREM

Chebyshev's Theorem (sometimes spelled Tchebysheff's Theorem) was formulated by the Russian mathematician P. L. Chebyshev (1821–1894). It states that for *any* data set, at least $1 - 1/K^2$ percent of the observations lie within K standard deviations of the mean, where K is any number greater than 1. Chebyshev's Theorem is expressed as

$$1 - \left[\frac{1}{K^2} \right] \qquad\qquad (3.22)$$

Thus, if we form an interval from K = three standard deviations above the mean to three standard deviations below the mean, then at least

$$1 - \frac{1}{3^2} = 88.89\%$$

of all the observations will be within that interval.

EXAMPLE 3-12 Chebyshev's Theorem Applied to Pigs and People Airline
Passengers for P & P averaged 78.3 per day with, as we saw in Example 3-11, a standard deviation of 10.8. In order to schedule times for a new route P & P opened, management wants to know how often the number of passengers is within K = two standard deviations of the mean, and what that interval is.

SOLUTION:
If we move two standard deviations $(2 \times 10.8) = 21.6$ passengers above and below the mean of 78.3, we would have an interval of $(78.3 - 21.6) = 56.7$ to $(78.3 + 21.6) = 99.9$ passengers. We can then be certain that at least

$$1 - \frac{1}{2^2} = 75\%$$

of the time, the number of daily passenger was between 56 and 99 passengers.

STATISTICAL INTERPRETATION:
On at least 75 percent of the days (that is, 75 percent of 50 equals 37 days), the number of passengers was between 56 and 99. This provides the management of P & P with valuable information regarding how many passengers to prepare for in flight operations.

B.   THE NORMAL DISTRIBUTION AND THE EMPIRICAL RULE

More importantly, the standard deviation can be used to draw certain conclusions if the data set in question is *normally distributed*. The concept of a normal distribution is commonly encountered in statistical analysis and is of considerable importance. Thus, it would prove fruitful to gain an early understanding of what a normal distribution entails.

A much more thorough discussion of the normal distribution is presented in later chapters. However, this early introduction to this all-important concept will allow us to demonstrate a practical use for the standard deviation and set the basis for the more thorough investigation which is to come. A **normal distribution** is a distribution of continuous (not discrete) data which produces a bell-shaped, symmetrical curve like that shown in Figure 3-3.

FIGURE 3-3   A Normal Distribution

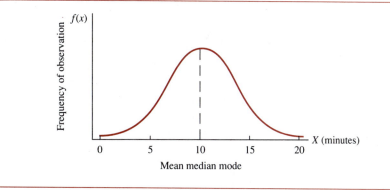

Mean median mode

Assume that we have a large number of observations for the time, in minutes, that it takes skiers to complete a particular run. If we graph the frequency with which each observation occurs, it will take the shape of Figure 3-3. You will notice that those observations at each extreme occur relatively infrequently, but those observations closer to the middle occur with increasing frequency, thereby producing the bell-shaped, symmetrical curve. The modal observation (10 in our case) is the one occurring with the greatest frequency and is therefore at the peak of the distribution. In a normal distribution, the mean, median, and mode are all equal.

Of importance, one-half of the observations are above the mean and one-half are below it. This means that one-half of the area under the curve is to the left of the mean, and one-half of the area under the curve is to the right of the mean.

To illustrate how the standard deviation applies to this principle of the normal distribution, assume 1,000 skiers slalom down the bunny slope at Vail. The times for all skiers happen to be normally distributed with a mean of exactly $\mu = 10$ minutes and a standard deviation of $\sigma = 2$ minutes. The **Empirical Rule** tells us that if we include all observations within one standard deviation of the mean (that is, one standard deviation above the mean and one standard deviation below the mean) we will encompass 68.8 percent of all the observations. That is, no matter what the mean is and no matter what the standard deviation is, we can be certain that 68.8 percent of the observations lie within one standard deviation of the mean if the observations are normally distributed.

Since the skiers averaged 10 minutes to complete the run, moving one standard deviation (that is, 2 minutes) above and below this mean of 10 produces a range of 8 to 12 minutes. Thus, according to the Empirical Rule, 688 (68.8 percent of the 1,000) skiers took between 8 and 12 minutes to get down the mountain.

Of course, if we move more than one standard deviation above and below the mean, we will encompass a larger percentage of the observations. The Empirical Rule specifies that

68.8 percent of the observations lie within plus or minus one standard deviation of the mean.
95.5 percent of the observations lie within plus or minus two standard deviations of the mean.
99.7 percent of the observations lie within plus or minus three standard deviations of the mean.

Given the skiers' times, one standard deviation (two minutes) above and below the mean of 10 yields a range of 8 to 12 minutes. Two standard deviations (four minutes) above and below the mean of 10 yields a range of 6 to 14 minutes. Three standard deviations (six minutes) yields a range of 4 to 16 minutes. This is shown in Figure 3-4.

FIGURE 3-4   Normally Distributed Times of 1,000 Skiers

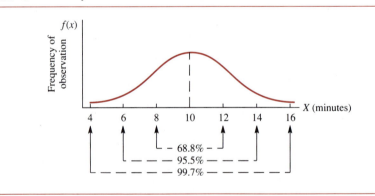

According to the Empirical Rule, 997 of the 1,000 skiers took between 4 minutes and 16 minutes to complete the run. Thus, only 3 of the 1,000 skiers were either very good skiers and took less than 4 minutes or were lousy skiers and took more than 16 minutes. An observation more than three standard deviations from the mean (above or below it) is a rarity and happens less than 1 percent of the time if the data are normally distributed.

It should be noted that the Empirical Rule also applies to sample data. Thus, for example, $\overline{X} \pm 2s$ produces a range which includes 95.5 percent of all the observations in the sample. It is also important to remember that the Empirical Rule reveals the total area under the normal curve that is found within a given range. Thus, not only did 68.8 percent of all the skiers take between 8 and 12 minutes to get safely down the mountain, but, in addition, 68.8 percent of all the area under the normal curve lies within that same 8 to 12 minute range.

If the observations are highly dispersed, the bell-shaped curve will be flattened and spread out. Assume a second group of skiers also averaged 10 minutes slushing over the moguls, but had a standard deviation of 4 minutes. The times of the second group are more dispersed than those of the first. The faster ski times were farther below 10, and the slower ski times were farther above 10 than the first group. This greater dispersion would be reflected in the normal distribution curve which is more spread out, as shown in Figure 3-5.

FIGURE 3-5   Two Normal Distributions with Equal Means but Different Standard Deviations

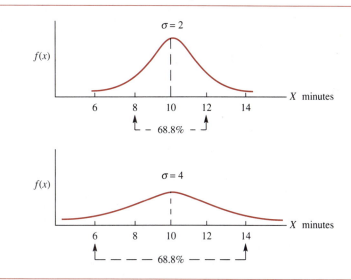

Notice that both distributions are centered at the mean of $\mu = 10$ minutes, but the one with the greater distribution of $\sigma = 4$ minutes is more spread out than the set of observations with less dispersion. To encompass 68.8 percent of the observations in this more dispersed group, it is necessary to include all those within the interval from 6 to 14.

C. SKEWNESS

Not all distributions are normal. Some are **skewed** left or right. In Figure 3-6, we find distribution curves for people's weights. In Figure 3-6(a), the distribution is said to be skewed right. It would seem that a few of the heavier people at the upper end of the weight scale (perhaps some larger males) pulled the tail of the distribution to the right. In a second distribution of weights shown in Figure 3-6(b), a few diminutive females pull the distribution toward the lower end, causing it to be skewed left.

FIGURE 3-6   Skewed Distributions of People's Weights

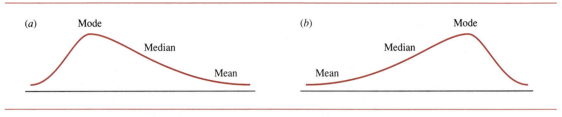

In both cases, the mode is, by definition, that observation occurring with the greatest frequency. It is therefore at the peak of the distribution. However, as we noted earlier, by its very nature, the mean is most affected by extreme observations. Therefore, it is pulled in the direction of the skewness more than is the median, which takes up residence somewhere between the mean and the mode.

These conditions of skewness are important and can be measured by the **Pearsonian coefficient of skewness.**

$$P = \frac{3(\overline{X} - \text{median})}{s} \qquad\qquad (3.23)$$

If $P < 0$, the data are skewed left; if $P > 0$, they are skewed right; if $P = 0$, they are normally distributed.

EXAMPLE 3-13 Skewness for P & P Passengers
Recall that, using data from P & P's passenger list, we calculated $\overline{X} = 78.3, s = 10.8$, and the median $= 77.9$. Given this information, the CEO for P & P can plainly see that the data are skewed right, since the mean exceeds the median. In addition, he also wants a measure of the extent or degree of skewness.

SOLUTION:
We have

$$P = \frac{3(78.3 - 77.9)}{10.8} = 0.11$$

STATISTICAL INTERPRETATION:
Since $P > 0$, the data for P & P are, as presumed, skewed right. The extent to which they are skewed is reflected in the value of the Pearsonian coefficient. If we were to graph the data, they would appear as in Figure 3-6(A).

D.   COEFFICIENT OF VARIATION

As we have emphasized, an important use of the standard deviation is to serve as a measure of dispersion. However, certain limitations apply. When considering two or more distributions with significantly different means, or that are measured in different units, it is dangerous to draw conclusions regarding dispersion merely on the basis of the standard deviation. It is like violating the old adage about comparing apples and oranges.

We must therefore often turn to the **coefficient of variation** (CV), which serves as a *relative* measure of dispersion. The coefficient of variation assesses the degree of dispersion of a data set relative to its mean. It is computed by dividing the standard deviation of a distribution by its mean and multiplying by 100.

$$CV = \frac{s}{\bar{X}}(100) \qquad\qquad (3.24)$$

EXAMPLE 3-14 The Coefficient of Variation

In Example 3-6, Markus Boggs computed the average price of a certain stock to be $81.29 with a standard deviation of $21.58. Assume that a second stock has recorded the following closing prices: $147, $120, $115, $110, $100, $73, and $105. He wishes to compare the variation in the prices of these two stocks.

SOLUTION:

Markus calculates the standard deviation of the second stock as follows:

X	X^2
147	21,609
120	14,400
115	13,225
110	12,100
100	10,000
73	5,329
105	11,025
770	87,688

$$\overline{X} = \frac{770}{7} = \$110$$

$$s^2 = \frac{\Sigma X^2 - n\overline{X}^2}{n-1}$$

$$= \frac{87{,}688 - 7(110)^2}{6}$$

$$= 498$$

$$s = \sqrt{498}$$

$$= \$22.30 > \$21.58$$

Since the second stock has a higher standard deviation, Markus might be inclined to conclude that it exhibits a greater degree of dispersion. However, that decision would belie the true nature of the two data sets. He should notice that the second data set also has a larger mean and that, in general, he is working with larger numbers in the second data set. No wonder the standard deviation is larger. A more accurate depiction of the comparable degree of dispersion can be formed by relating each standard deviation to its mean as shown in Formula (3.22). This produces the coefficient of variation. For the first stock, we have

$$CV = \frac{21.58}{81.29}(100) = 26.55$$

while the second stock yields

$$CV = \frac{22.3}{110}(100) = 20.27$$

STATISTICAL INTERPRETATION:
Despite the larger standard deviation of the second stock, its prices, relative to their mean, deviate less than do the prices of the first stock relative to their mean. Markus can therefore conclude that the price of the second stock is less volatile than the first in a relative sense.

Furthermore, since the coefficient of variation is expressed as a percentage, it can be used to compare measures of dispersion expressed in different units. If you wished to compare the variation in sales revenue measured in dollars with labor inputs measured in numbers of employees, the coefficient of variation should be used.

3.11   A SUMMARY OF THE MORE IMPORTANT CONCEPTS

Figure 3-7 provides a summary of the more important measures of central tendency. Figure 3-8 displays the more significant measures of dispersion. You will frequently encounter these tools in the remainder of your study of statistical analysis.

FIGURE 3-7 Important Measures of Central Tendency

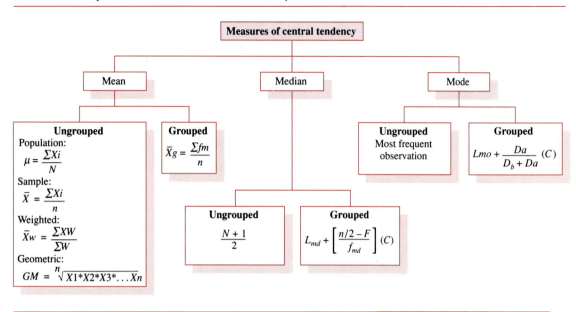

FIGURE 3-8 Important Measures of Dispersion

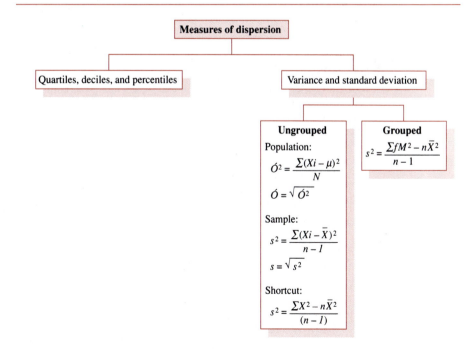

3.12 SOLVED PROBLEMS

1. **Is the NFL Losing Its Offensive Punch?** In 1988, Pete Rozelle, commissioner of the National Football League, became concerned that the games were not attracting as many fans because teams were scoring fewer touchdowns. This lack of offense made the game less exciting and didn't promote spectator interest. As part of his investigation into this matter, Rozelle closely examined the number of touchdowns scored by all 14 teams in the National Football Conference of the NFL for 1987. *Football Digest,* which publishes many of the official statistics for the NFL, recorded the number of touchdowns by NFL teams. The teams, listed alphabetically, and their number of touchdowns are shown here.

Atlanta 24	L.A. Rams 38	St. Louis 46
Chicago 42	Minnesota 42	San Francisco 59
Dallas 38	New Orleans 46	Tampa Bay 33
Detroit 27	N.Y. Giants 32	Washington 47
Green Bay 28	Philadelphia 40	

a. In order to compare these data to previous years, Rozelle calculated the mean number of touchdowns by adding all 14 numbers and dividing by 14. Treating these data as a sample, he found

$$\overline{X} = \frac{\Sigma X}{n} = \frac{542}{14} = 38.71 \text{ touchdowns per team}$$

b. The median requires that the data be put into an ordered array.

$$24, 27, 28, 32, 33, 38, 38, 40, 42, 42, 46, 46, 47, 59, \text{etc.}$$

The median position is

$$\text{Median position} = \frac{n + 1}{2} = \frac{15}{2} = 7.5$$

The median is the value found by averaging the numbers in the seventh and eighth positions. Thus, the median is

$$\frac{38 + 40}{2} = 39$$

c. The data set actually has three modes: 38, 42, and 46. Commissioner Rozelle's purpose was to fully examine the 1987 figures of the teams and thereby permit a comparison with previous years to determine if there had been any reduction in the level of performance over time. In this regard, Rozelle calculated the variance and standard deviation.

d. Treating the data as a sample, this was done as follows:

$$s^2 = \frac{\Sigma(X_i - \overline{X})^2}{n - 1}$$

$$= \frac{(24 - 38.71)^2 + (27 - 38.71)^2 + \cdots + (59 - 38.71)^2}{14 - 1}$$

$$s^2 = 87.83$$

$$s = 9.3 \text{ touchdowns}$$

e. By the shortcut method, which is desirable for larger data sets, the variance becomes

$$s^2 = \frac{\Sigma X^2 - n\bar{X}^2}{n - 1}$$

Then

X	X^2
24	576
27	729
28	784
32	1,024
33	1,089
38	1,444
38	1,444
40	1,600
42	1,764
42	1,764
46	2,116
46	2,116
47	2,209
59	3,481
	22,140

$$s^2 = \frac{22{,}140 - 14(38.72)^2}{14 - 1} = 89.35$$

$$s = \sqrt{89.35} = 9.45 \text{ touchdowns}$$

The difference is due to rounding.

f. If these data were seen as the population, the commissioner had

$$\sigma^2 = \frac{\Sigma X^2}{N} - \left[\frac{\Sigma X}{N}\right]^2 = \frac{22{,}140}{14} - \left[\frac{542}{14}\right]^2$$

$$= 82.63$$

$$\sigma = 9.09$$

g. The third quartile and the first decile were found from the ordered array as

$$L_{75} = (n + 1)\frac{75}{100}$$

$$= 11.25$$

Then, $P_{75} = 46$. This means that at most 75 percent of the teams scored less than 46 touchdowns (TDs). This number could easily be compared with the third quartile (75th percentile) from previous years to determine any trend in scoring patterns. The first decile (10th percentile) is

$$L_{10} = (n + 1)\frac{10}{100}$$

$$= 1.5$$

Then $P_{10} = 24 + (0.5)(27 - 24) = 25.5$. Thus, at most 10 percent of the teams scored less than 25 TDs.

Data analysis performed in this manner can provide information regarding movements and trends in tendency of teams to display offensive power. On the basis of such information, rules committees in the past have enacted certain rules changes designed to aid the offensive teams and promote interest on the part of the general public.

2. **A Change in Career Choices for College Grads** In the past few years, there has been an unmistakable shift in career preferences of college graduates. Through the mid-1980s, many Masters of Business Administration (MBAs) were drawn to Wall Street in search of megasalaries and guaranteed positions on the fast track of corporate life. However, an article in a summer issue of *Fortune* magazine in 1988 stated that "from Cambridge to Palo Alto there has been a sharp decline in the number of graduates signing on with investment banks and brokerage houses." Only 11 percent of Harvard's 1988 MBA class entered the field of investment banking, compared with 30 percent the previous year. Admission to law schools across the nation rose 19 percent in 1988. When asked why this marked increase in law school enrollment, Thomas Jackson, dean of the University of Virginia Law School, replied, "It's partly because of the popularity of the TV program 'L.A. Law' and partly due to a change in personal motivational factors." When MBAs for 11 top schools were asked to determine the order of importance of their personal and career concerns, they listed such things as family, health, ethics, and leisure at or near the top of the list. Money and power came in seventh and ninth, respectively.

In search of what *Fortune* called the New Grail, 88 students from several MBA programs in the Midwest were asked to name the minimum starting salaries they were willing to accept. The results are shown in Table 3-8.

TABLE 3-8   Minimum Starting Salaries for MBAs (in 1,000's)

Class	f	M	fM	F	M^2	fM^2
15 to 20	5	17.5	87.5	5	306.25	1,531.25
20 to 25	8	22.5	180.0	13	506.25	4,050.00
25 to 30	7	27.5	192.5	20	756.25	5,293.75
30 to 35	10	32.5	325.0	30	1,056.25	10,562.50
35 to 40	12	37.5	450.0	42	1,406.25	16,875.00
40 to 45	15	42.5	637.5	57	1,806.25	27,093.75
45 to 50	12	47.5	570.0	69	2,256.25	27,075.00
50 to 55	10	52.5	525.0	79	2,756.25	27,562.50
55 to 60	2	57.5	115.0	81	3,306.25	6,612.50
60 & up	7	62.5	437.5	88	3,906.25	27,343.75
	88		3520			154,000.00

The Graduate Management Admission Council (GMAC), which administers the standardized test for applicants to MBA programs, analyzed this information.

a. The mean was calculated as

$$\overline{X}_g = \frac{\Sigma fM}{n} = \frac{3,520}{88} = 40 \text{ or } \$40,000$$

b. The GMAC calculated the median as

$$M = L_{md} + \left[\frac{n/2 - F}{f_{md}}\right](C)$$

$$= 40 + \frac{88/2 - 42}{15}(5)$$

$$= 40.67 \text{ or } \$40,670$$

c. The mode is

$$\text{Mode} = L_{mo} + \left[\frac{D_a}{D_b + D_a}\right](C)$$

$$= 40 + \frac{3}{6}(5)$$

$$= 42.5 \text{ or } \$42,500$$

The GMAC concluded that the center point for minimum average acceptable salaries by these MBA graduates is between \$40,000 and \$42,500. Any of the three measures of central tendency could be cited as the average.

d. In addition to the central tendency, the GMAC was interested in the degree of dispersion around the mean.

$$s^2 = \frac{\Sigma f M^2 - n\overline{X}^2}{n - 1}$$

$$= \frac{154,000 - (88)(40)^2}{87}$$

$$= 151.72$$

$$s = \sqrt{151.72} = 12.32 \text{ or } \$12,320$$

The GMAC interpreted this analysis by concluding that the minimum average acceptable salaries of MBA graduates was \$40,000, with a tendency for the salaries to deviate above and below \$40,000 by about \$12,320.

e. Information of this nature is of benefit, for example, to those businesses that wish to hire MBA graduates. If a particularly prestigious firm wished to hire only those graduates in the top 25 percent of their class, it might wish to determine the minimum salary it must offer.

Assuming class rank determines salary, the firm would have to calculate the proper percentile. Since the data are grouped into a frequency distribution from lowest to highest, the firm would calculate the 75th percentile. Seventy-five percent of 88 is 66. Since there are only 57 observations through the first six classes, the firm must take an additional 9 of the 12 observations in the seventh class.

$$P_{75} = 45 + \frac{9}{12}(5)$$

$$= 48.75 \text{ or } \$48,750$$

The firm should expect to pay at least \$48,750 to attract a graduate of that caliber. If it wished to hire only the top 10 percent of the graduating MBAs, it would have to pay

$$P_{90} = 55 + \frac{1}{2}(5)$$

$$= 57.5 \text{ or } \$57,500$$

3. **The Average Growth Rate in GNP** *The Federal Reserve Bulletin,* which is a monthly publication by the Federal Reserve Board containing a wealth of economic and financial data, reports the level of GNP in the United States for the first quarter of 1987 through the first quarter of 1988, as measured in billions of current dollars, is 4,377.7, 4,445.1, 4,524.0, 4,607.4, and 4,660.9. The U.S. Department of Commerce, as well as a host of other agencies, will often compute the average growth rate for GNP.

Since the geometric mean is most appropriate for calculating growth rates over time, it is used here.

Time	GNP	Percentage of Previous Year
1987-I	4377.7	
1987-II	4445.1	1.0154
1987-III	4524.0	1.0177
1987-IV	4607.4	1.0184
1989-I	4660.9	1.0116

$$GM = \sqrt[4]{(1.0154)(1.0177)(1.0184)(1.0116)}$$

$$= 1.01577 - 1 = 1.577\%$$

Over that period there was a little more than 1.5 percent increase in GNP per quarter.

4. **A Career Choice: To Play or Not to Play** In 1988, the Professional Golf Association published the incomes of the top golfers from around the world who played in at least one sanctioned tournament during the year. The earnings appeared normally distributed. They averaged \$26,700, with a standard deviation of \$7,500. A student at a major midwestern university was on the university's golf team while completing his MBA. The student's coach encouraged him to consider a career as a professional golfer based on the student's considerable talents on the links. Discounting the obvious advantage of playing golf for a living, and concentrating solely on the monetary rewards, the student had a career choice to make. Assuming he could market his MBA for the salaries cited in Problem 2, the student compared his relative potential for economic gain if he were to become a professional golfer.

FIGURE 3-9   A Normal Distribution

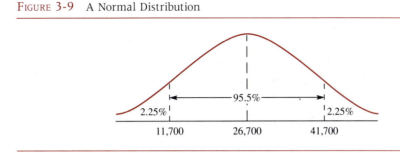

He began by estimating his chances of making $40,000, which is the average salary of an MBA as noted in Problem 2, on the professional golf tour. Given that the professional golfers' incomes appeared normally distributed, this budding Arnie Palmer applied the Empirical Rule. Using Figure 3-9 to aid in his decision, the student reasoned that if golfers average $26,700 with a standard deviation of $7,500, he would have to be approximately two standard deviations ($7,500 $\times$ 2 = $15,000) above the mean of $26,700 to equal his starting salary as an MBA. That is, $26,700 + $15,000 = $41,700, which is close to the $40,000 MBAs earn.

Since 95.5 percent of all observations fall within two standard deviations of the mean—a range of ($26,700 − 15,000 =) $11,700 to (26,700 + 15,000 =) $41,700—he reasoned that the remaining 4.5 percent are either below $11,700 or above $41,700. Since the normal curve is symmetrical, one-half of that 4.5 percent, or 2.25 percent of the golfers earn more than $41,700. He therefore concluded that his chances of earning more money on the professional golf tour than he could receive selling his services as an MBA were slim indeed.

On a personal note, despite the logic of his conclusion, the student spurned the MBA market and has decided to devote five years to the professional tour. If he fails to make it as a professional golfer after that length of time, he figures he could always fall back on the MBA.

3.13   WHAT YOU SHOULD HAVE LEARNED IN THIS CHAPTER

According to this chapter, there are many ways in which we can characterize a data set. Its center point, or central tendency, and the extent to which the observations are spread out above and below that center point are two of the more important and fundamental concepts in statistical analysis.

By now you should know the difference between measures of central tendency such as the mean, the median, the mode, the geometric mean, and the weighted mean. An understanding of the measures of dispersions, including the variance, the standard deviation, and the coefficient of variation, is also critical. You should have a conceptual understanding of measures of central tendency and measures of dispersion.

You must know what a normal distribution is and how it relates to Chebyshev's Theorem and the Empirical Rule. If you don't, you'll have a difficult time mastering the rest of the material.

With the knowledge of the measures of central tendency and dispersion, we can understand the meaning and message of the data more fully.

3.14   COMPUTER APPLICATIONS

The analysis discussed throughout this chapter can be greatly facilitated through the use of computers. If large data sets are involved, a computer becomes essential. Many programs and computer packages can be used to obtain the desired results.

The computer programs and resulting printouts for SAS, SPSS-PC, and Minitab, three of the most popular packages, are presented and discussed in this section. The student can readily see that once the data have been entered, it is a relatively simple matter to obtain any measure of central tendency or measure of dispersion desired.

If in examining Denny's test grades in Example 3-1 we had collected 20 test scores, 20 quiz scores, and 15 grades on homework problems, our data set on Denny might appear as follows:

Observation	Test	Quizzes	Homework
1	63	8	15
2	59	10	5
3	71	5	16
4	41	12	9
5	32	12	17
6	54	6	16
7	69	18	6
8	78	6	15
9	62	18	14
10	63	18	4
11	72	5	19
12	82	14	14
13	45	15	12
14	65	2	12
15	56	18	14
16	68	14	.
17	65	2	.
18	87	15	.
19	55	19	.
20	65	12	.

The dots are necessary in many computer programs to indicate missing data. We would write a simple SAS program as follows:

INPUT

```
DATA    DENNY;
INPUT   TESTS QUIZZES HOME;
CARDS;
63   8   15
59   10   5
—    —    —
—    —    —
remaining observations go here
—    —    —
—    —    —
55   19   —
65   12   —
TITLE "DESCRIPTIVE STATISTICS FOR DENNY'S GRADES"
PROC MEANS;
```

The TITLE line is optional and used only to label the computer results. The data set is called DENNY, and the INPUT line lists the variables in the order in which they were entered into the computer. The resulting printout is

SAS OUTPUT FOR DESCRIPTIVE STATISTICS ON DENNY'S PERFORMANCE

DESCRIPTIVE STATISTICS FOR DENNY'S GRADE PERFORMANCE

VARIABLE	N	MEAN	STANDARD DEVIATION	MINIMUM VALUE	MAXIMUM VALUE	STD ERROR OF MEAN	SUM	VARIANCE	C.V.
TESTS	20	62.600	13.291	32.000	87.000	2.972	1252.000	176.673	21.233
QUIZZES	20	11.450	5.633	2.000	19.000	1.259	229.000	31.734	49.199
HOME	15	12.533	4.549	4.000	19.000	1.174	188.000	20.695	36.297

The first two columns list the variables and the number of observations for each one. The mean and the standard deviation appear in the third and fourth columns. The last two columns report the variance and the coefficient of variation. The standard error of the mean will be discussed in a future chapter.

The next program demonstrates how to use SPSS-PC to get the measures of descriptive statistics for Denny's grades. The necessary input is as follows:

INPUT

```
TITLE "DESCRIPTIVE STATISTICS FOR DENNY'S GRADES".
DATA LIST FREE  /  TESTS  QUIZZES   HOME.
BEGIN DATA.
63 8 15
59 10 5
|   |   |
|   |   |
|   |   |
|   |   |
  rest of data lines go here
|   |   |
|   |   |
|   |
|   |   .
65 12  .
END DATA.
DESCRIPTIVE VARIABLES = TESTS QUIZZES HOME
    /STATISTICS = MEAN STDDEV MIN MAX SEMEAN VARIANCE.
```

The printout resulting from this program appears as

SPSS-PC OUTPUT

```
NUMBER OF VALID OBSERVATIONS =       20
VARIABLE    MEAN     STD DEV      MIN       MAX      N

TESTS      62.60    13.2918     32.000    87.000    20
QUIZZES    11.45     6.6333      2.000    19.000    20
HOME       12.53     4.5492      4.000    19.000    15
```

Minitab provides the following results for the same data.

MINITAB PRINTOUT FOR DESCRIPTIVE STATISTICS

	N	MEAN	MEDIAN	TRMEAN	STDEV	SEMEAN
TESTS	20	62.76	65.00	54.33	14.33	2.972
QUIZZES	20	11.53	14.00	10.22	11.53	1.259
HOME	15	18.12	14.00	21.93	18.12	1.175

TRMEAN is a 5 percent trimmed mean. After the data are placed in an ordered array, the smallest 5 percent and the largest 5 percent of the values are trimmed off and the remaining 90 percent are averaged. This is to minimize the distortion effects of outliers. SEMEAN is the standard error of the mean. The standard deviation (STDEV) and the first and third quartiles (Q1 & Q2) are also given.

LIST OF SYMBOLS AND TERMS

μ	Mean of the population
$\overline{X}$	Mean of the sample
$\overline{X}_W$	Weighted mean
GM	Geometric mean
$\overline{X}_g$	Mean for grouped data
MAD	Mean absolute deviation
σ^2	Variance of the population
σ	Standard deviation of the population
s^2	Variance of a sample
s	Standard deviation of a sample
df	Degrees of freedom
CV	Coefficient of variation

LIST OF FORMULAS

$$\mu = \frac{X_1 + X_2 + X_3 + \cdots + X_N}{N} = \frac{\Sigma X_i}{N} \tag{3.1}$$

Used to compute the mean of the population

$$\overline{X} = \frac{X_1 + X_2 + X_3 + \cdots + X_n}{n} = \frac{\Sigma X_i}{n} \tag{3.2}$$

Used to compute the mean of the sample

$$\text{Median position} = \frac{N + 1}{2} \tag{3.3}$$

Used to calculate the median position of ungrouped data that have been arranged into an ordered array

$$\overline{X}_W = \frac{\Sigma XW}{\Sigma W} \tag{3.4}$$

Used to compute the weighted mean of any set of observations

$$GM = \sqrt[n]{X_1 X_2 X_3 \cdots X_n} \tag{3.5A}$$

Used to calculate the geometric mean for any series of positive numbers

$$\log GM = \frac{1}{n}(\log X_1 + \log X_2 + \log X_3 + \cdots + \log X_n) \tag{3.5B}$$

An alternate method for calculating the geometric mean

$$\overline{X}_g = \frac{\Sigma fM}{n} = \frac{\Sigma fM}{\Sigma f} \tag{3.6}$$

Used to calculate the mean of data grouped into a frequency table

$$\text{Median} = L_{md} + \left[\frac{n/2 - F}{f_{md}}\right](C) \tag{3.7}$$

Used to calculate the median for grouped data

$$\text{Mode} = L_{mo} + \left[\frac{D_a}{D_b + D_a}\right](C) \tag{3.8}$$

Used to calculate the mode for grouped data

$$\text{AD} = \frac{\Sigma(X_i - \overline{X})}{n} \tag{3.9}$$

Used to calculate the average deviation of a set of observations from their mean

$$\text{MAD} = \frac{\Sigma|X_i - \overline{X}|}{n} \tag{3.10}$$

Used to calculate the mean absolute deviation of ungrouped data

$$\sigma^2 = \frac{(X_1 - \mu)^2 + (X_2 - \mu)^2 + (X_3 - \mu)^2 + \cdots + (X_N - \mu)^2}{N}$$
$$= \frac{\Sigma(X_i - \mu)^2}{N} \tag{3.11}$$

Used to calculate the variance of the population for ungrouped data

$$\sigma = \sqrt{\sigma^2} \tag{3.12}$$

Used to calculate the standard deviation of the population for ungrouped data

$$s^2 = \frac{\Sigma(X_i - \overline{X})^2}{n - 1} \tag{3.13}$$

Used to calculate the variance of a sample for ungrouped data

$$s = \sqrt{s^2} \tag{3.14}$$

Used to calculate the standard deviation of a sample for ungrouped data

$$\sigma^2 = \frac{\Sigma X^2}{N} - \left[\frac{\Sigma X}{N}\right]^2 \tag{3.15}$$

Shortcut method used to calculate the variance of a population for ungrouped data

$$\sigma = \sqrt{\sigma^2} \tag{3.16}$$

Shortcut method used to calculate the standard deviation of a population for ungrouped data

$$s^2 = \frac{\Sigma X^2 - n\overline{X}^2}{n - 1} \tag{3.17}$$

Shortcut method used to calculate the variance of a sample for ungrouped data

$$s = \sqrt{s^2} \qquad (3.18)$$

Shortcut method used to calculate the standard deviation of a sample for ungrouped data

$$L_p = (n + 1)\frac{P}{100} \qquad (3.19)$$

Used to find the position of a given percentile in ungrouped data

$$s^2 = \frac{\Sigma f M^2 - n\overline{X}^2}{n - 1} \qquad (3.20)$$

Used to calculate the variance of a sample for grouped data

$$s = \sqrt{s^2} \qquad (3.21)$$

Used to calculate the standard deviation of a sample for grouped data

$$1 - \left[\frac{1}{K^2}\right] \qquad (3.22)$$

According to Chebyshev's Theorem, determines the minimum percentage of the observations within K standard deviations of the mean for any data set.

$$P = \frac{3(\overline{X} - \text{median})}{s} \qquad (3.23)$$

Used to calculate the Pearsonian coefficient of skewness for a set of sample data

$$CV = \frac{s}{\overline{X}}(100) \qquad (3.24)$$

Used to calculate the coefficient of variation of a set for sample data

CHAPTER EXERCISES

YOU MAKE THE DECISION

1. Paula Hopkins is director of personnel at Chase Manhattan Bank in New York. She has collected the balances of over 500 customers' checking accounts, but finds all the data confusing and unmanageable. Help her decide how she might acquire some understanding of the data in a concise and meaningful manner.

2. Brokers for Merril Lynch have rates of return over the past several years for four different stocks. All seem to be paying about the same average return over the time period. The brokers must now decide how to identify those stocks which offer less risk as investment opportunities?

3. In preparation for an upcoming bargaining session with management, a local union representative for the United Auto Workers is trying to decide how data on wage rates for 350 union members might be used to analyze pay scales and to determine what workers typically receive and what differences in wage levels might prevail. What techniques would you suggest?

4. The CEO for a small electronics firm recently introduced a revolutionary electric relay component which he hopes will grow in popularity. He now has the problem of deciding how to measure its average growth in sales over the past several years. What would you suggest?

5. The chief financial officer for a manufacturing firm in the Midwest must decide what percentage of the parts produced by her firm have weights within a certain range. It is known that the parts average 34.6 ounces, with a standard deviation of 12.1 ounces. What advice might you offer if it is also known that the weights are normally distributed? If it is not known whether the weights are normally distributed?

CONCEPTUAL QUESTIONS

6. Define and give examples of a measure of central tendency and a measure of dispersion.

7. Under what conditions would you prefer the median to the mean as a measure of central tendency? Explain.

8. Professor Doezoff transfers from the statistics department to the economics department. The dean alleges this transfer will lower the average IQ of both departments. What assumption is he making about the IQ levels in each department as well as that of Professor Doezoff?

PROBLEMS

9. A sample of nine workers at the Colonial Canning Company in Claremont, California, were asked how far they drive to work each day. Their responses, in miles, were 17, 12, 9, 22, 14, 19, 12, 15, and 18.
    a. What is the range of the miles driven?
    b. Compute and interpret the mean, median, and mode.
    c. Compute and interpret the variance and standard deviation.

10. The Snowflake markets ski boots in San Luis Obispo, California. Of the last 100 pairs sold, 4 were size 9, 33 were size 9 1/2, 26 were size 10, 29 were size 10 1/2, and 8 were size 13. Comment on the use of the mean, median, and mode as measures of central tendency and the use of each in making decisions regarding sizes to hold in inventory. Calculate each measure.

11. Are the observations in Problem 9 normal, skewed right, or skewed left? Explain. Draw the distribution, label the axes, and show the placement of the three measures of central tendency.

12. The football coach for State University recorded the yardage gained (or lost) on the first down by his offense in last Saturday's game. The values were

$$7, 12, -5, 4, 0, -7, 2, -3$$

Calculate the mean, median, and mode.

13. Interest rates (in percent) on a certain AAA corporate bond over the last 12 months were

| 5.0 | 5.7 | 5.2 | 4.7 | 5.0 | 5.1 |
| 5.2 | 6.3 | 6.7 | 6.5 | 6.1 | 6.0 |

    a. Calculate the mean, median, and modal interest rates.
    b. Are the observations normally distributed? How can you tell?

14. Another corporate bond paid interest rates (in percent) of

4.5	5.1	5.5	6.2	4.5	3.4
6.5	6.1	6.4	5.9	5.8	5.7

Is the average interest rate paid by this bond higher than that paid by the one in the previous problem?

15. Alan Munday manufactures a paint sealant for automobiles in the Denver area. He uses four different chemicals in the production process. In order to make a unit of his product, Munday must use 2 gallons of calcimine which costs $2.50 per gallon, 1/2 gallon of kalsolite at $1.25 per gallon, 1 gallon of binder costing $0.75 per gallon, and 3 gallons of drying oil at $2.00 per gallon. The rest of the mixture is water at a nominal cost. Calculate the average cost of a unit of the sealant.

16. During the early 1980s, gross national product was as indicated (in billions):

Year	GNP
1981	1,915
1982	2,050
1983	2,229
1984	2,423
1985	2,581

   a. Calculate the average annual percentage increase in GNP over that period.
   b. If in 1991, GNP is 3,000, what will it be in 1995 if it continues to increase at the rate you have calculated?

17. In 1988, Carl Icahn initiated a proxy fight to take over Texaco, Inc., which the management of Texaco insisted was tantamount to greenmail. In this effort, Icahn proposed to offer $60 per share to all stockholders willing to sell to him. During the week just prior to the offer, Texaco stock on the New York Stock Exchange closed at

$$49.5 \quad 52.25 \quad 47.5 \quad 51 \quad 48$$

   a. What are the mean, median, and modal closing prices?
   b. What was the average percentage change over the week?

18. As owner of a prospering advertising agency in Chicago, George Kay earns $110,000 a year. His seven newest employees make $15,000, $21,000, $18,500, $17,900, $21,200, $15,900, and $22,500. Which measure of central tendency do you think is the best indication of the average of all eight incomes? Calculate the average.

19. The Noah Fence Company sells four types of fencing to local suburbanites. Grade A costs Noah $5.00 per running foot to install, grade B costs $3.50, grade C costs $2.50, and grade D costs $2.00. Yesterday, Noah installed 100 yards of A, 150 yards of B, 75 yards of C, and 200 yards of D. What was Noah's average installation cost per foot?

20. A recent account of investment opportunities surveyed by *Fortune* magazine revealed that typical investments in stocks yielded a 7.2 percent return, money held in bonds provided an 8.1 percent yield, funds placed in real estate generated a 3.7 percent yield, and assets held in the form of cash yielded a 5.5 percent return in a savings or money market account.

John Wise, according to *Fortune,* holds 40 percent of his wealth in stocks, 40 percent in bonds, and the rest in cash. Lars Holton maintains a portfolio consisting of 34 percent stocks, 10 percent real estate, 16 percent cash, and 40 percent bonds. Which investor has the higher average rate of return?

21. A sample of weekly sales receipts for Pig-In-A-Poke Bar-B-Q are, in hundreds of dollars,

43.3, 54.2, 34.8, 42.9, 49.2, 29.5, and 28.6

An advertising program designed to even out sales is implemented. A subsequent sample of sales proves to be

45.5, 39.5, 35.7, 36.7, 42.6, 42.14

Did the advertising campaign achieve its goal of smoothing weekly sales?

22. From the money he won in the state lottery, Lucky Louie purchased one $10,000 corporate bond, a $5,000 federal security, and deposited $7,000 and $8,000, respectively, in two money market accounts. The four investments yield returns of 12, 7, 8, and 9 percent, respectively. What is Lucky's average rate of return?

23. As a telephone operator, Tom Bell must meet certain efficiency standards requiring him to handle an average of at least 50 calls per hour over the course of his 10-hour work day. Tom's supervisor recorded the number of calls Tom responded to each hour during yesterday's shift.

52	47	57	43	52
48	50	44	59	53

Does it appear that Tom is meeting the efficiency criterion?

24. Six years ago you entered your local Paine-Webber brokerage office with $1,000 to invest in mutual funds, demanding at least a 15 percent average rate of return. Over the years, your investment was valued at the amounts shown. Did you get the return you wanted?

Year	Value
1989	1000
1990	1150
1991	1290
1992	1570
1993	2041
1994	2350

25. Bill Karl purchased 20 shares of stock at $15 each, 50 shares at $20, 100 shares at $30, and 75 shares at $35.
  a. What is the total amount of his investment?
  b. What is the average price per share?

26. Below is the frequency table for the number of state legislators elected by voters in each of the nation's 50 state capitals.

Legislators (people)	Frequency (states)
60–69	8
70–79	11
80–89	9
90–99	10
100–109	5
110–119	7

   a. Calculate the average number of legislators in our state capitals.
   b. How consistent are state constitutions in providing for similar numbers of legislators?
   c. Calculate the three quartiles for legislators.

27. Using the data from the previous problem, calculate the
   a. median number of legislators.
   b. modal number of legislators.

28. Janna Vice uses two different machines to produce paper chutes for Kodak copiers. A sample of the chutes from the first machine measured 12.2, 11.9, 11.8, 12.1, 11.9, 12.4, 11.3, and 12.3 inches. Chutes made with the second machine measured 12.2, 11.9, 11.5, 12.1, 12.2, 11.9, and 11.8 inches. Janna must use that machine which has the greater consistency in sizes of the chutes. Which machine should she use?

29. Helen Highwater is director of personnel services for a large bank in Chicago. She must hire a secretary based on his or her typing efficiency. One candidate for the job typed a manuscript six times with the following number of mistakes: 5, 6, 2, 1, 2, 0. Another candidate typed the same manuscript six times with 3, 4, 5, 3, 4, and 5 mistakes. Which candidate should Helen hire?

30. A sample of the number of health and safety violations each month at Acme, Inc. revealed the following numbers:

$$5, 4\ 6, 3, 7, 5, 8, 5, 9, 10$$

Calculate the mean, the median, and the mode.

31. The following sample data have been obtained for the number of daily customers at Rosie's Flower Shoppe:

$$34, 45, 23, 34, 26, 32, 31, 41$$

Calculate the variance, the standard deviation, and the interquartile range.

32. The following is a sample of the earnings per share, in dollars, for stocks listed on the New York Stock Exchange:

$$1.12, 1.43, 2.17, -1.19, 2.87, -1.49$$

   a. Calculate the variance and the standard deviation.
   b. Interpret the standard deviation.

33. A sample of the daily number of newspapers sold by the *Kansas City Star* (in hundreds) is shown for the last 50 days. Construct a frequency table with five classes and compute
     a. the mean.
     b. the median.
     c. the variance and the standard deviation.

615	778	500	712	742	615	663	783	715	555
635	597	573	753	687	579	689	643	701	595
643	783	599	654	792	537	673	678	743	687
693	711	749	553	543	640	683	772	559	642
743	782	692	593	718	622	590	672	778	735

34. For the following sample of 24 daily observations for the number of miles, rounded to the nearest one-tenth, driven by Ronnie Roadrunner on his job as a traveling salesman,

100.3	122.7	93.4	112.0	129.7	101.3
117.7	98.9	127.3	119.1	120.1	97.3
121.9	130.7	115.3	105.5	99.4	109.1
101.1	125.7	122.3	98.1	97.2	95.3

     construct a frequency table with six classes and calculate the
     a. mean.
     b. median.
     c. variance and standard deviation.

35. The number of hours worked each week by Ronnie over the past two months are

                    52 48 37 54 48 15 42 12

     Assuming these are sample data, calculate the
     a. mean.
     b. median.
     c. mode.
     d. Which is probably a better measure of the center point?

36. Using Ronnie's work hours from the previous problem, calculate and interpret the
     a. range.
     b. variance.
     c. standard deviation.
     d. mean absolute deviation. What is the drawback of MAD?
     e. first quartile.
     f. 25th percentile.
     g. interquartile range.

37. Data on the frequency of absenteeism in a plant owned by Novell Electronics are shown in the table. Management retains your statistical expertise to analyze their employees' behavior as compared with national norms. Studies show that the average number of days per year that employees are absent across the nation for similar plants is about 27. Help Novell evaluate and discern the meaning of the figures. Calculate the mean, median, and mode, and comment.

Days Absent per Year	Frequency
0–10	4
11–21	10
22–32	12
33–43	15
44–54	10
55–65	5
66 and over	4
	60

38. The disc jockeys on KAYS claim they play more songs each hour than their crosstown rivals on KROC. Over the last 24 hours, data on the number of songs played for both stations were collected and tabulated. Use the data to prepare a report comparing the two stations. Your finished report is to be submitted to the Federal Communications Commission and contains references to measures of central tendency and measures of dispersion.

Number of Hits per Hour	KAYS	KROC
5–10	2	4
11–16	4	5
17–22	6	7
23–28	8	5
29–34	2	2
35–40	2	1

39. In the table is a recent sample of 86 firms in *Fortune*'s 500 showing the number of robotic manufacturing units each firm currently uses in its plants across the nation.

Number of Robotic Units	Number of Firms
10 and under 20	3
20 and under 30	8
30 and under 40	9
40 and under 50	6
50 and under 60	12
60 and under 70	15
70 and under 80	10
80 and under 90	11
90 and under 100	12

a. Calculate the measures of central tendency.
b. Calculate the variance and standard deviation.

40. A report in a recent issue of *Fortune* magazine described the increased use of fax machines in daily business activity. It stated that certain financial offices tend to fax documents on the average of "15 to 20 times each day." As office director, Pam Whiting is concerned about the rising costs associated with the fax machine in her office. The results of a sample of the number of times her office faxes documents each day over a 66-day period are tabulated.
   a. Calculate the mean, median, and mode, and comment on whether Pam has cause for such concern.
   b. Compute the variance and standard deviation to obtain a measure of the dispersion in the daily use of the fax.

Class (number of documents)	Frequency (number of days)
0 and under 5	3
5 and under 10	7
10 and under 15	12
15 and under 20	10
20 and under 25	19
25 and under 30	15

41. *The Wall Street Journal* described a dispute between management and the local labor union regarding the efficiency and productivity of the workers. Management argued that it was taking the employees more than 20 minutes to complete a certain job task. If 85 employees are timed, yielding the results tabulated, is management correct based on this sample? Compute all three measures of central tendency.

Class (number of minutes)	Frequency (number of employees)
5 and under 7	2
7 and under 9	8
9 and under 11	10
11 and under 13	15
13 and under 15	17
15 and under 17	14
17 and under 19	7
19 and under 21	9
21 and under 23	3

42. Management from the previous problem is also worried that employees' performance is too erratic; there is too much variation in the amount of time it takes the workers to complete the task. Identify and compute the statistic that would address management's concern.

43. Using the data from the two previous problems, compute the interquartile range.

44. *Forbes* magazine presented an article about a British financial and investment consortium that was buying up racehorses in Lexington, Kentucky. Concern within the consortium focused on the depressed nature of racetracks around the country, and the fact that betting at racetracks is down to a 20-year low of only $13.9 billion. The winnings of 88 thoroughbreds are classified here. The consortium wants an average of $100,000 for each horse it owns.

   a. Do these data suggest the consortium is obtaining that goal? Calculate all three measures of central tendency and comment.

   b. Calculate the proper measure of variation in the horses' earnings.

Winnings (1,000's)	Number of Horses
10 and under 30	8
30 and under 50	7
50 and under 70	12
70 and under 90	15
90 and under 110	18
110 and under 130	19
130 and under 150	9

45. Closing prices for 42 randomly selected stocks on the New York Stock Exchange are classified in the table. If you wanted to reflect an "up" market showing the highest possible average closing prices, would you use the mean, the median, or the mode?

Class (closing prices)	Frequency (number of stocks)
$0 and under 10	2
10 and under 20	0
20 and under 30	4
30 and under 40	7
40 and under 50	9
50 and under 60	7
60 and under 70	6
70 and under 80	4
80 and under 90	2
90 and under 100	1

46. Using the data from the previous problem, calculate the variance and the standard deviation.

47. Given the following nine tests scores for Professor Pundit's economics class, compute the Pearsonian coefficient of skewness. Assume these represent sample data.

80 83 87 85 90 86 84 82 88

48.   Unionists at a Ford Motor Company plant in Toledo argue that, in violation of the labor agreement, production line workers average a lower hourly wage with greater variability than do office workers. A sample of $n = 10$ is taken from each class of workers, yielding the following values. Do they support the unionists' charge?

Workers	Production Workers	Office Workers
1	12.15	15.12
2	18.17	18.42
3	19.42	17.12
4	15.17	16.92
5	18.63	18.15
6	16.42	15.81
7	15.49	19.12
8	18.73	19.15
9	19.12	18.73
10	18.36	19.66

49.   Three firms producing microchips in Sunnyvale, California, report the following values for the number of employees, average daily output, and standard deviation in daily output over the past 100 days.

Firm	Employees	Output	Standard Deviation
1	95	110	27
2	63	253	32
3	87	312	134

a.   Which firm seems to be most consistent in its level of output?
b.   Assuming the data for all three firms are normally distributed, use the Empirical Rule to determine the range of output for each firm on approximately 68 of the 100 days; on 95 of the 100 days.
c.   Which firm had the highest average level of output per employee? What was that average?

50.   Linemen on the UCLA football team averaged 257 pounds, with a standard deviation of 32 pounds. Their counterparts on the Notre Dame squad averaged 242 pounds, with a standard deviation of 35 pounds.
a.   Which team is most consistent in weight?
b.   Which probably has the larger player(s) if you assume normality in distribution of weights?

51.   In a recent Olympic diving meet, the U.S. diver and the East German diver received the performance marks shown from the six judges.

	Judges					
	Bulgaria	**Britain**	**E. Germany**	**USA**	**USSR**	**France**
U.S. diver	3.2	8.2	6.4	7.0	7.3	6.7
East German diver	7.6	5.5	8.5	6.5	6.5	5.8

a. In Olympic competition, the highest and lowest marks are disregarded in calculating the mean score. Why?

b. Calculate each diver's mean score before and after the extreme marks are thrown out.

c. In the event of ties, the diver with the most consistent performance wins. Which diver would win given that the extreme scores are discarded?

52. An investment broker finds two promising stocks. The first yields an average return of 10 percent with a standard deviation of 1.2 percent. The second yields a 20 percent average rate of return with a standard deviation of 5 percent. The rate of return tends to follow a normal distribution. Using the coefficient of variation as a measure of risk, he advises his more conservative client to invest in the first. Would you agree? Explain.

53. Manly Bankford works as a stockbroker for E. F. Hutton. His records show that the rates of return (in percent) on two securities for 10 selected months were

Security 1	5.6	7.2	6.3	6.3	7.1
	8.2	7.9	5.3	6.2	6.2
Security 2	7.5	7.3	6.2	8.3	8.2
	8.0	8.1	7.3	5.9	5.3

a. Which security might be better for those clients interested in a higher return?

b. Which security should Manly advise to those clients who prefer less risk?

54. The price-earning ratios for 30 different stocks trading on the New York Stock Exchange (NYSE) are shown here.

4.8	5.2	7.6	5.7	6.2	6.6	7.5	8.0	9.0	7.7
3.7	7.3	6.7	7.7	8.2	9.2	8.3	7.3	8.2	6.5
5.4	9.3	10.0	7.3	8.2	9.7	8.4	4.7	7.4	8.3

a. Calculate the mean and standard deviation.

b. According to Chebyshev's Theorem, at least how many price-earnings ratios lie within two standard deviations of the mean?

c. How many actually do lie within two standard deviations of the mean?

55. The local mechanic at Vinney's Auto Shop and Charm School tells you that the repairs on your car will cost $714.12. Industry data show that the average bill for repairs similar to yours is $615, with a standard deviation of $31. What might you conclude about Vinney's rates if you assume that repairs are normally distributed?

56. Given here is the frequency table of monthly sales in dollars for skydiving equipment in the southern California market (figures are in hundreds).

Class (in $100's)	Number of Months
5 and under 10	5
10 and under 15	7
15 and under 20	9
20 and under 15	10
25 and under 30	8
30 and under 35	3
35 and under 40	2

a. You are chief statistician for the Bounce Twice Parachute Company, and your manager requests a breakdown on the frequency of sales. He is interested in that value below which at most 60 percent of the observations fell along with a complete quartile breakdown.

b. In addition, you feel that it would be useful to determine the values of the 10th and 90th percentiles.

57. Recently, *Fortune* printed an article on baby-boomers who at a relatively young age had become CEOs for major U.S. corporations. This information is summarized here. Compute the mean, median, and modal ages of the corporate moguls.

CEO	Corporation	Age
William Beasley III	Lone Star Technologies	41
Christie Hefner	Playboy Enterprises	35
Joe "Rod" Canion	Compaq Computer	43
Jeffrey H. Coors	Adolph Coors Company	43
Richard Sharp	Circuit City Stores	41
Jim Manzi	Lotus Development	36

58. The figures shown here are daily high and low temperatures for selected cities around the world in the month of August. Calculate the mean, median, and modal values for the

a. high.

b. low.

	High	Low
Athens	97	73
Beirut	88	75
Cleveland	93	73
Fargo	88	67
Kansas City	99	75
Hong Kong	81	79
Syndney	61	50
Juneau	62	51
Moscow	68	57
Rome	91	63

59. The accompanying table displays incomes of stockbrokers who work at the Paine-Webber office in San Jose, California. Compute the mean, median, and modal income levels.

Class (in $1,000's)	Frequency
40 and under 60	3
60 and under 80	5
80 and under 100	10
100 and under 120	12
120 and under 140	17
140 and under 160	21
160 and under 180	19
180 and under 200	10
200 and under 220	5
220 and under 240	8

60. Grade point averages for a sample of 50 students at Ohio State University are shown here. Determine the number of classes using the proper class interval for a frequency. Construct the table and compute the mean, median, and mode.

3.72	1.97	2.22	0.59	4.00
1.47	4.00	3.99	1.83	1.75
2.77	3.01	1.97	2.87	2.52
3.01	1.29	2.57	3.31	0.97
0.57	2.01	3.40	0.59	3.34
1.52	3.59	1.09	1.55	3.20
3.44	3.88	0.59	2.57	3.32
3.54	3.01	2.89	2.79	2.23
3.45	1.11	0.88	3.88	1.19
2.09	1.09	1.55	3.42	2.02

61. *Fortune* reported the earnings of the 500 largest U.S. industrial corporations based on total sales in 1988. The earnings of the 34 largest are shown here. Figures are in billions of dollars.

General Motors 102	Philip Morris 22	Dow 13
Exxon 76	Shell Oil 21	Kodak 13
Ford Motors 72	Amoco 20	McDonnell Douglas 13
IBM 54	United Technologies 17	Rockwell 12
Mobil Oil 51	Occidental Oil 17	Allied Signal 12
GE 39	Procter & Gamble 17	Pepsico 12
Texaco 34	Atlantic Richfield 16	Lockheed 11
AT&T 34	Nabisco 16	Kraft 11
Du Pont 30	Boeing 15	Phillips 11
Chrysler 26	Tenneco 15	Westinghouse 11
Chevron 26	BP America 15	Xerox 10
		Goodyear 10

Compute the
a.   range.
b.   three quartiles.
c.   first and last deciles.

62.   Provide a list of firms in the interquartile range given the data in the previous problem.

63.   From the two previous problems, calculate and interpret the variance and standard deviation of the top 20 firms in the *Fortune* 500 list assuming that the list constitutes a
a.   population.
b.   sample.

64.   A sample of 100 closing prices on the NYSE resulted in the table shown. Prices are rounded to the nearest dollar. Calculate the variance and standard deviation.

Class	Frequency
20 and under 25	2
25 and under 30	8
30 and under 35	9
35 and under 40	19
40 and under 45	26
45 and under 50	20
50 and under 55	16

65.   A data set of size $n = 5,000$ not known to be normal has a mean of 500 and a standard deviation of 25. At least how many observations are within the range 450 to 550?

66.   A data set that is known to be normal contains $n = 10,000$ observations and has a mean of 52.5 and a standard deviation of 5.5.
a.   How many observations are within the interval 47 and 58?
b.   How many observations are within the interval of 41.5 and 63.5?
c.   How many observations are either below 36 or above 69?

67.   If the distribution of data is normal in the previous problem, what percentage of the observations
a.   lie between the mean and one standard deviation above the mean? Draw a graph to illustrate.
b.   lie between the mean and one standard deviation below the mean? Draw a graph to illustrate.
c.   are either more than one standard deviation above the mean or less than one standard deviation below the mean? Draw a graph to illustrate.

68.   A sample of $n = 1,000$ of 36-ounce boxes of Kellogg's Rice Krispies is selected off the production line. The net weights of the contents are normally distributed and average 37 ounces with a standard deviation of 2 ounces. The CEO for Kellogg's insists that at least 75 percent of all boxes coming off the production line are within 0.5 ounce of the net weight specified on the box (36 ounces in this case). Does this sample tend to support the CEO's statement? Draw a graph to illustrate.

EMPIRICAL EXERCISES

69. Select 100 stocks at random from the financial pages of the daily newspaper. Construct a frequency table for the closing prices of these stocks, and compute the mean and standard deviation for these prices.

70. From Standard & Poor's or Moody's manuals obtain data for the number of shares of common stock outstanding for 30 to 100 firms. Prepare a frequency distribution table for these data. Calculate the mean, median, and modal number of shares outstanding.

71. Using the data from Problem 69, calculate and interpret the variance and the standard deviation. How do the three quartiles compare with the mean, median, and mode calculated in Problem 69?

72. Collect net income figures for the 10 largest and 10 smallest firms on *Fortune's* 500 list. You can find the list in an April issue, probably Number 9 for the current year. Compare the amount of dispersion in net income for the largest firms with that exhibited by the smallest firms. What are your conclusions regarding this comparison, and how might you theorize an explanation for your findings?

CASE APPLICATIONS

73. John White is a stockbroker for Paine-Webber. One of his biggest clients expresses an interest in investing approximately $100,000 in the market. Three stocks interest him, but he wishes to invest his money in only one of them. Since he is risk-averse, he wants to invest in the stock that has the lowest risk (lowest variability in returns). As his broker, John is given the following information to help his client make the right decision.

| | Returns | | |
Year	Stock A (%)	Stock B (%)	Stock C (%)
1983	15	17	19
1984	28	20	13
1985	17	20	16
1986	15	19	22
1987	25	15	25

In which stock should he invest?

74. George Kay lives in Peoria, where recent increases in property tax assessments have many residents alarmed. In an attempt to fight city hall, Mr. Kay and several of his neighbors collect data on tax assessments for several cities throughout the Midwest. They find that the mean assessment is $512 with a standard deviation of $56. It appears that the data are normally distributed.

Mr. Kay became especially upset to learn that his tax assessment for the coming year is $652. The mayor of Peoria promises that he will reduce the average Peoria tax burden. His goal is to reduce taxes in the city so that the average amount paid does not exceed one standard deviation above the mean, based on the Midwest data in Mr. Kay's study.

Mr. Kay retains a professional statistician to seek the answers to some questions. Of importance to Mr. Kay is the amount by which his taxes must come down if they are to meet the pledge offered by the mayor. Furthermore, should he be alarmed by the current tax assessment? What factors other than those presented here must be considered?

75. The quantitative analysis group for Paine-Webber conducted a survey of 50 of their offices throughout the world. They wanted to analyze office performance in terms of the number of clients each was able to generate, and the ability of each office to retain client loyalty.

Arble Jackson has just been hired by the group as a new statistical analyst. He is responsible for preparing the data for presentation to upper management. The board of directors for Paine-Webber is interested in prioritizing financial assistance to local offices. Those offices with an exemplary record of performance in terms of obtaining and retaining clients will be eligible to receive expansion funds from the home office.

Jackson's job, therefore, is to prepare and analyze the following data for the 50 offices with the intent to establish standards to which each local office's performance can be compared. Again, the board is concerned primarily with client production and retention.

Number of Clients for 50 Paine-Webber Offices

117	122	98	97	155
92	212	115	213	250
83	293	265	217	220
150	173	342	178	150
212	315	162	183	163
342	392	352	211	214
279	215	291	143	184
283	143	173	194	243
307	357	233	165	219
99	293	315	183	210

COMPUTER EXERCISES

Access the file SALES in your data bank. It contains 20 observations for monthly sales figures in dollars for each of the three sales regions for a large manufacturing firm. The company CEO wishes to compare the sales results of each region to determine which region is performing best. Examine the results of your computer printout and write a brief report responding to each of the following questions the CEO has.

a. Which region has the highest average monthly sales?
b. Which region seems to be reporting the most consistent level of sales?
c. What were the total sales for each region?
d. What are the total sales for the company?
e. Which region had the highest single monthly sales figure, and how much was it?
f. Explain the reason for the difference between the standard deviation and the coefficient of variation.

CHAPTER FOUR

PRINCIPLES OF PROBABILITY

A PREVIEW OF THINGS TO LOOK FOR

1 Fundamental definitions for experiments, outcomes, and sets.

2 How events can be mutually exclusive and dependent.

3 The three basic approaches to the study of probability: the relative frequency approach, the subjective approach, and the classical approach.

4 The two rules of probability: the Rule of Multiplication and the Rule of Addition.

5 The importance of unions and intersections.

6 How probability trees can be used to determine the probability of specific events.

7 The many uses of probability tables.

8 The manner in which conditional probability can be used to determine the likelihood of certain events.

9 How Bayes' Rule applies to conditional probability.

10 How counting techniques provide answers to many questions often encountered in the business world.

CHAPTER BLUEPRINT

This chapter examines ways in which the probability or likelihood of specific events can be calculated. By being able to determine the likelihood of future events, we can greatly reduce the risk associated with the decision-making process and enhance our chances of making more intelligent decisions. Those business managers who are able to estimate the course of future events are much more likely to survive and prosper in the competitive environment of the business world.

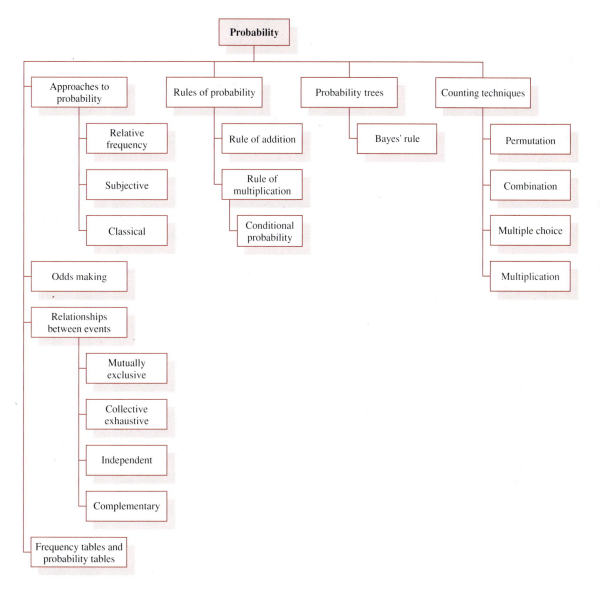

> Statistics show that marriage is the
> leading cause of divorce —
> Groucho Marx

4.1   INTRODUCTION

Regardless of your chosen profession, one thing is certain. You will find it necessary to make decisions. More often than not, you will have to do so under conditions of uncertainty and with less than full knowledge of the surrounding conditions or the ultimate consequences. For example, investors must decide whether to invest in a particular stock based on their expectations regarding future returns. In deciding whether to market a new product, entrepreneurs face uncertainty as to the likelihood of its success. In addition, a manager of a retail outlet must decide on current inventory levels without knowing future sales, while market research groups for major corporations must often proceed with advertising plans without full knowledge of their impact. In each instance, as with most business matters, decisions must often be made without all the relevant information.

Any effort to reduce the level of uncertainty in the decision-making process will greatly increase the likelihood that more intelligent and well-informed decisions will be made. It is the purpose of this chapter to illustrate the ways in which the likelihood or probability of uncertain events can be measured. By improving our ability to judge the occurrence of future events, we are able to minimize the risk and perilous speculation associated with the decision-making process.

4.2   EXPERIMENTS, OUTCOMES, AND SETS

Statisticians often take samples for the purpose of gaining knowledge regarding the world around them. On the basis of these samples, they can frequently estimate the probability that specific events will occur. This insight will aid in the decision-making process. **Probability** is the numerical likelihood of the occurrence of an uncertain event. The probability of an event is measured by values between 0 and 1. The more likely the event is to occur, the closer to 1 will be its assigned probability. The probability of a certainty is 1. The probability of an impossibility is 0. We could write this as

$$P(\text{certain event}) = 1$$

$$P(\text{impossible event}) = 0$$

The probability that the sun will rise tomorrow is very high—quite close to 1. The probability you will pass this course without studying is, at the other extreme, close to zero. In this regard, the **first property** of probability states that the probabil-

---

---

ity that some uncertain event will occur is between 0 and 1. If E_i is any given event, then it can be said that

$$0 \leq P(E_i) \leq 1$$

Probability
Probability is the numerical likelihood, measured between 0 and 1, that an uncertain event will occur.

The process that produces the event is called an experiment. An **experiment** is any well-defined action which leads to a single, well-defined result. That result is called the **outcome**. Rolling a die (one-half of a pair of dice) is an experiment. It is a well-defined action that leads to a well-defined result or outcome. That well-defined outcome is a number from 1 to 6. An experiment might consist of examining a product to determine if it meets certain manufacturing specifications. The outcome is either (1) it is defective or (2) it is not defective.

A **set** is any collection of objects. The students in your statistics class are a set. The seven continents are a set, as are the molecules of air in the Goodyear blimp. The objects in a set are its **elements** or **members**. There are 50 elements in the set of all U.S. states. There is an infinite number of elements in the set of all positive integers.

The set of all possible outcomes for an experiment is the **sample space.** The sample space for rolling a die is

$$SS = (1, 2, 3, 4, 5, 6)$$

while the sample space for the experiment of flipping a coin is

$$SS = (heads, tails)$$

In the case of the coin flip, either a head or a tail must occur. The occurrence of either a head or a tail is a certainty. Since the probability of a certainty is equal to 1, the probability that a head or a tail occurs equals 1. That is,

$$P(\text{head or tail}) = 1$$

In all instances, the probability that one of the events in the sample space will occur is equal to 1. There are no other possibilities. Thus, the **second property** of probability states that if E_i is an event representing some element in a sample space, then

$$\Sigma P(E_i) = 1$$

To summarize,

Properties of Probability

The first property is

$$0 \leq P(E_i) \leq 1$$

The second property is

$$\Sigma P(E_i) = 1$$

4.3   APPROACHES TO PROBABILITY

History is filled with references to the principles of probability. In the 1600s, Jacob Bernoulli (1654–1705), a member of a Swiss family of mathematicians, set forth many of the basic laws of modern probability. Thomas Bayes (1702–1761) and Joseph Lagrange (1736–1813) were also among the early pioneers of probability theory. Early accounts suggest that probability theory has its origins in ancient forms of gambling and games of chance. Gerolamo Cardan (1501–1576) stated that almost 2,000 years ago Roman soldiers originated many of our present-day gambling games just to pass the time between their campaigns to subjugate most of the civilized world.

Today we find probability theory occupies a prominent position in many business matters. Insurance and actuarial practices are firmly based on the principles of probability theory. The life insurance rates we pay depend on mortality tables, which are based on the probabilities of death at specific ages. Other forms of insurance rates such as property and auto insurance are similarly determined. Probability also plays a role in estimating the number of defective units in the manufacturing process, the likelihood of receiving payments on accounts receivable, and the potential sales of a new product. Even professional odds-makers for sporting events must have a firm understanding of probability theory.

Despite the widespread application of the principles of probability, there are only three generally accepted ways to approach probability: (1) the relative frequency (or posterior) approach, (2) the subjective approach, and (3) the classical (or a priori) approach. This section examines each in turn.

○○○○ **DECISION MAKING THROUGH PROBLEM SOLVING** ○○○○
ILLUSTRATION 4-2

A story in the *San Francisco Chronicle* told of the problem that city officials faced in deciding what risk passengers on their fabled cable cars suffered as a result of drug abuse by those transit employees who operated these colorful modes of travel. Officials wanted to determine how likely it was that an employee under the influence of an illegal drug would be placed in charge of one of the cable cars.

    Using the relative frequency approach based on previous incidents of drug abuse discovered among transit drivers, the city's administrators determined the probability that any driver might be using illicit drugs during working hours. This provided them with a clear picture of the dangers tourists and residents alike encounter in their sojourn around the city by the bay.

A. THE RELATIVE FREQUENCY APPROACH

The relative frequency approach uses past data that have been empirically observed. It notes the frequency with which some event has occurred in the past and estimates the probability of its reoccurrence on the basis of these historic data. The probability of an event based on the relative frequency approach is determined by

$$P(E) = \frac{\text{Number of times the event has occurred in the past}}{\text{Total number of observations}} \qquad (4.1)$$

For example, assume that during the last calendar year there were 50 births at a local hospital. Thirty-two of the little new arrivals were baby girls. The relative frequency approach reveals that the probability that the next birth (or any randomly selected birth) is a female is determined as

$$P(\text{female}) = \frac{\text{Number of females born last year}}{\text{Total number of births}}$$

$$= \frac{32}{50}$$

EXAMPLE 4-1 Relative Frequency Probability

John Dough, megatycoon, is considering a purchase of 500 shares of ABC, Inc. on the New York Stock Exchange. He wishes to determine the probability that (1) its price will decline in today's trading, (2) its price will rise in today's trading, and (3) its price will remain unchanged. As his highly paid statistician, you must determine these probabilities.

SOLUTION:

You quickly recognize this as a standard case of relative frequency probability. By inspecting the records from NYSE trading over the past 100 days, you learn that the price declined 20 of those days, rose 50 of those days, and remained unchanged for the rest.

The probability of the event the price will decrease, $P(D)$, in today's trading is

$$P(D) = \frac{\text{Number of times event has occurred}}{\text{Total number of observations}}$$

$$= \frac{\text{Number of times the price has declined}}{\text{Total number of observations}}$$

$$= \frac{20}{100}$$

$$= 0.20 = 20\%$$

The probability that the price will rise, $P(R)$, in today's trading is

$$P(R) = \frac{50}{100}$$

$$= 0.50 = 50\%$$

The probability that the price will remained unchanged, $P(U)$, is

$$P(U) = \frac{30}{100}$$

$$= 0.30 = 30\%$$

STATISTICAL INTERPRETATION:

The probability that the price will fall is 20%, and the probability that it will rise is 50%. There is a 1 out of 5 chance that it will fall and a 1 out of 2 chance that it will rise. Notice that, in accordance with the second property of probability, the probabilities of all three events sum to one since one of the three events must occur.

A common problem with the relative frequency approach results when estimates are made with an insufficient number of observations. For example, assume that both flights you booked on an airline last year were late in arriving at their destinations. You therefore conclude that the flight you are to take next month on the same airline will also be late. Although such inferences are common, there is not sufficient data to draw such a conclusion, and basing decisions on such inferences must be avoided.

B.   THE SUBJECTIVE APPROACH

In many instances past data are not available. It is therefore not possible to calculate probability from previous performance. The only alternative is to estimate probability on the basis of our best judgment. This **subjective approach** requires the assignment of the probability of some event on the basis of the best available evidence. In many instances, this may be nothing more than an educated guess. The subjective approach is used when we want to assign probability to an event that has never occurred. The probability that a woman will be elected president of the United States is an example. Since there are no past data to rely on, we must examine our opinions and beliefs to obtain a subjective estimation.

C. THE CLASSICAL APPROACH

Of the three methods of assessing probability, the **classical approach** is the one most often associated with gambling and games of chance. The classical probability of an event E is determined as

$$P(E) = \frac{\text{Number of ways the event can occur}}{\text{Total number of possible outcomes}} \qquad (4.2)$$

Even without a discussion of classical probability, you may be aware that the probability of getting a head in the single flip of a fair coin is 1/2. This can be illustrated using Formula (4.2) as

$$P(\text{head}) = \frac{\text{Number of ways the event can occur}}{\text{Total number of possible outcomes}}$$

$$= \frac{1}{2}$$

There is only one way that the event can occur (you get a head), and only two possible outcomes (a head or a tail). In similar fashion, the probability of rolling a 3 with a six-sided die is

$$P(3) = \frac{\text{Number of ways the event can occur}}{\text{Total number of possible outcomes}}$$

$$= \frac{1}{6}$$

There is only one way that the event can occur (you roll a 3), and six possible outcomes.

Classical probability involves the determination of the probability of some event in an a priori (before the fact) manner. Thus, *before* drawing a card from a deck of 52 cards, it can be determined that the probability of drawing an ace is

$$P(\text{ace}) = \frac{\text{Number of ways the event can occur}}{\text{Total number of possible outcomes}}$$

$$= \frac{4}{52}$$

Consider this example of classical probability. A machine produces 10 percent
defective parts. One out of every 10 parts, on the average, is defective. The probability that the next part produced is defective is 1/10, or 10 percent. A note of warning:
This is not to suggest that of every 10 parts produced, one is defective. The rate of
defective parts is merely an average. Since we are assigning probability in an a priori
fashion, the failure rate is not to be taken as a regularly recurring event. This is true
of the experiment with the die. Although the probability of rolling a 3 is 1/6, this is
not to suggest that of every six rolls, one is a 3. Instead, the implication is that if the
die is rolled a large number of times (technically, an infinite number), one-sixth of
the rolls produces a 3.

EXAMPLE 4-2 The Probability of Winning at Craps

Craps is a game of chance played with two dice. The rules of at least one version of
the game (there are several possible variations) state that you immediately win if you
roll a 7 or 11 the first time. If you roll anything other than a 7 or 11, you must roll
that number again (which is called your *mark* or *point*) before rolling either a 7 or 11.
If you roll a 7 or 11 before rolling your mark, you lose.

a.   What is the probability of winning a game of craps on the first roll?
b.   If your mark is a 6, are you more likely to win or lose the game?

SOLUTION:

The sample space of all possible outcomes is the sum of the two dice. These outcomes and the ways in which they can occur are shown here.

		Outcome of first die					
		1	**2**	**3**	**4**	**5**	**6**
Outcome of	**1**	2	3	4	5	6	7
second die	**2**	3	4	5	6	7	8
	3	4	5	6	7	8	9
	4	5	6	7	8	9	10
	5	6	7	8	9	10	11
	6	7	8	9	10	11	12

a. There are 36 possible outcomes. Only eight of these produce a 7 or 11, which result in a win. Thus,

$$P(\text{win on first roll}) = \frac{8}{36}$$

b. If you roll a 6, the probability of repeating that roll is

$$P(6) = \frac{5}{36}$$

STATISTICAL INTERPRETATION:
Since 8/36 is more than 5/36, you are more likely to lose by rolling craps than you are to win by rolling your mark of 6.

QUICK CHECK 4.3.1

○○○○   Of 75 people who apply for a job, 20 are not high school graduates. If one person is selected at random, what is the probability that he or she is not a high school graduate?
Answer: 0.267

QUICK CHECK 4.3.2

What approach to probability did you use to find the answer to Quick Check 4.3.1?
Answer: The classical approach

QUICK CHECK 4.3.3

What approach would you use to determine the probability that the water supply for the entire eastern seaboard will dry up? Why is that approach the proper one?
Answer: The subjective approach is the appropriate one because this event has never occurred.

QUICK CHECK 4.3.4

Over the past 200 working days, Sam has been sick 120 days. What is the probability that he will be sick today? What approach did you use to determine this?
Answer: 120/200 = 0.60 or 60%. The relative frequency approach.

4.4   THE PRACTICE OF ODDS-MAKING

If the odds that some event E will occur are estimated to be 3 to 1, written 3:1, then the probability it will occur can be figured as

$$P(E) = \frac{3}{3 + 1}$$

$$= 0.75$$

The odds against its occurrence are 1:3, and the probability it will not occur is

$$P(\text{not occur}) = \frac{1}{3 + 1}$$

$$= 0.25$$

In general, if the odds of an event occurring are set at $A:B$, the probability of its occurrence is

$$P(E) = \frac{A}{A + B} \tag{4.3}$$

Professional gamblers and Las Vegas odds-makers rely on the principles of probability in establishing betting odds on sporting events. If the odds that the Des Moines Bonecrushers will win the big game Sunday are set at 10:1, this means that *if* betting was fair, as the "player" you must put up $10 to win $1. If you bet on the Bonecrushers and they win, you get $1. If they lose, you must give up $10. A bet of $1 against the Des Moines team will win you $10 if they lose the game.

However, professional gamblers don't gamble. They always set the **betting** odds to ensure that they win. If the odds that a team will win are estimated to be 10:1, yielding a probability of

$$P(\text{win}) = \frac{10}{10 + 1}$$

$$= 0.91$$

the betting odds will be set at some level greater than 10:1, say 11:1 or 12:1. In this effort to ensure that they win, odds-makers will set the odds at levels slightly worse (higher) from the standpoint of the player than what actual probabilities would dictate. Thus, you can't really calculate the probability of winning from the established betting odds, since the professional gamblers will shrewdly add some unknown amount to the actual probability.

Business Week reported that banks expecting the interest rate to rise outnumbered "those not expecting a rise by three to one." If these odds are correct, the probability of selecting one bank at random which predicts an increase in the interest rate is $3/(3 + 1) = 0.75$.

QUICK CHECK 4.4.1

○○○○

In southern California, the odds that it will rain on any given day were given by a local radio station as 1 out of 37. What is the probability it will rain today?

Answer: 0.0263

4.5   Relationships between Events

Comprehension of the principles of probability requires that we examine the manner in which events are related to each other. Two events are said to be **mutually exclusive** if the occurrence of one event precludes the occurrence of the other. That is, if one event happens, the other cannot.

Mutually Exclusive Events
Events that cannot occur jointly are mutually exclusive events.

A classic example of mutually exclusive events is flipping a head and a tail in a single coin flip. If the head occurs, the tail cannot. Other examples include rolling a 3 or a 5 with a single roll of a die, rolling a 3 or an even number, drawing from a 52-card deck one card that is a queen or an ace, or drawing a 10 or a face card. In each of these cases, if one of the events occurred the other could not. On the other hand, drawing a queen or a heart are not mutually exclusive events, since it is possible to draw both with one card by getting the queen of hearts. The same is true for rolling a 3 or an odd number. These are not mutually exclusive events since both a 3 and an odd number can occur on the same roll. (In fact, if the 3 occurs, the odd number must occur, since a 3 is always odd.)

Collectively exhaustive events are those events that consist of all possible outcomes of an experiment. The collectively exhaustive events of rolling a die are 1, 2, 3, 4, 5, and 6. The collectively exhaustive events for an experiment constitute its sample space.

Collectively Exhaustive Events
The set of all possible outcomes of an experiment constitutes the collectively exhaustive events.

The combined probability of collectively exhaustive events is equal to 1, since it is a certainty that one of these collectively exhaustive events will occur. That is, if you roll a die you are certain that a 1 or 2 or 3 or 4 or 5 or 6 must occur. Thus,

$$P(1 \text{ or } 2 \text{ or } 3 \text{ or } 4 \text{ or } 5 \text{ or } 6) = 1$$

We can cite many instances in which the occurrence of one event has no effect on the occurrence of a second event. The outcomes of (1) a coin flip and (2) rolling a die have no bearing on each other. The result of the coin flip in no way influences the outcome observed when the die is rolled. Events of this nature are said to be **independent events.** Since the result of drawing a card from a deck has no impact on whether it rains tomorrow, the result of the draw is independent of tomorrow's weather.

> **Independent Events**
> Two events are independent if the occurrence of one event has no effect on the probability that the second will occur.

Are the results of drawing two cards from a deck independent events? That is, does the outcome of the first draw affect the probability of the second outcome? It depends on whether the first card is replaced before the second is drawn. Let the first event be drawing a queen and the second event be drawing an ace. According to the classical approach, the probability of drawing a queen on the first draw is

$$P(Q) = \frac{4}{52}$$

The probability of drawing an ace on the second draw depends on whether the first card is replaced before the second is drawn. Assume that a queen, or any card other than an ace, was drawn the first time. If that card is held out of the deck on the second draw, the probability of drawing an ace is

$$P(A) = \frac{4}{51}$$

since 4 of the remaining 51 cards are aces. If the first card is returned to the deck before the second is drawn, the probability of an ace on the second draw is

$$P(A) = \frac{4}{52}$$

We can therefore say that when drawing from a finite set, such as a deck of cards, two events are independent if and only if the drawing is done **with replacement.** However, if the first element is not replaced before the second is drawn, the two events are dependent.

Complementary events are events such that if one event does not occur, the other must. If event A is rolling an even number with a die (2, 4, or 6), the complement is rolling an odd number (1, 3, or 5). If you do not get an even number, you must get an odd number. The complement of A is written $\overline{A}$, and is referred to as "not A."

Of course, complementary events are also collectively exhaustive, because if A does not occur $\overline{A}$ must occur. Thus,

$$P(A) + P(\overline{A}) = 1$$

and

$$P(A) = 1 - P(\overline{A})$$

> **Complementary Events**
> Two events are complementary if the failure of one to occur means the other must occur. Complementary events are collectively exhaustive.

4.6   Unions, Intersections, and Venn Diagrams

As you recall, we defined a set as any collection of objects. It is often useful to isolate the manner in which sets can be related to each other. Assume we have identified two sets A and B. Each contains numerous elements. It is entirely possible for some elements to be in both sets. For example, assume set A consists of all the students in your statistics class, and set B consists of all students at your university or college who are majoring in economics. Those elements (students) that are in both sets are the economics majors in your statistics class. These students constitute what is called the intersection of A and B. The **intersection** of A and B, written $A \cap B$ and read as "A intersection B," consists of those elements that are common to both A and B.

A Venn diagram is a useful tool to portray the relationship between sets. Developed by John Venn (1834–1923), an English mathematician, this pictorial display is shown in Figure 4-1. The two sets, A and B, can be seen in the diagram. The overlapping area contains elements that are in both sets and constitutes $A \cap B$. These are the students that are in both set A (in your class) and set B (economics majors). For an element to be considered in $A \cap B$ it must be in both A and B.

Intersection of A and B
The set of all elements in *both* A and B is called the intersection of A and B.

Figure 4-1   A Venn Diagram

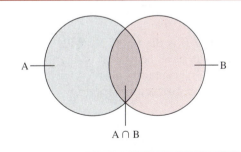

$A \cap B$

A student in your statistics class who is not an economics major is not in $A \cap B$. Similarly, economics majors who are not in your statistics class are not $A \cap B$. Given $A \cap B$, the events A and B are called **joint events.** Both must occur before the event $A \cap B$ is satisfied.

The **union** of A and B, written $A \cup B$ and read as "A union B," consists of those elements that are in either A or B or both. As seen in Figure 4-1, all students who are in your class (set A), regardless of their major, and all economics majors (set B), regardless of whether they are in your class, are elements in $A \cup B$.

The Union of A and B
The set of all elements that are in A or B is called the union of A and B.

For an element to be in $A \cup B$, it need only be in set A or set B or both.

EXAMPLE 4-3   Unions and Intersections

Given a deck of 52 cards, set A is all hearts and set B is all kings. Identify $A \cup B$ and $A \cap B$.

SOLUTION:

The two sets are shown in the Venn diagram. You can see in Figure 4-2 that the jack of spades, 2 of clubs, 10 of diamonds, and all other cards that are not hearts or kings are not in either set A or set B.

FIGURE 4-2   A Venn Diagram for a Deck of Cards

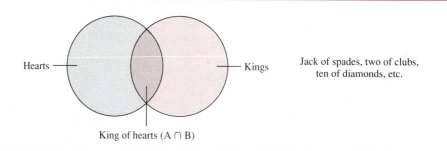

$A \cup B$ is the set of all cards that are in either set A or set B (i.e., A or B) and consists of all hearts (including the king) and all kings (including the heart).

$A \cap B$ contains only those elements that are in both A and B; those elements that are both hearts and kings. Of course, there is only one such element—the king of hearts.

STATISTICAL INTERPRETATION:

The event $A \cup B$ is satisfied if either a king or a heart is drawn from the deck. The joint event $A \cap B$ is satisfied only if the king of hearts is drawn.

4.7   FREQUENCY TABLES AND PROBABILITY TABLES

The use of frequency tables and probability tables provides handy devices to summarize data which can be used to compute probabilities. Consider the data set collected by Helen Highwater, Sales Director for E-Z-C Eye Care Center. Ms.

Highwater noted the style and size of frames for eyeglasses for the last 100 sales. The results are shown in Table 4-1.

TABLE 4-1   Frequency Table for Sales for E-Z-C Eye Care Center

Size	Frame Style			Total
	Plastic	Wire	Composite	
Large	12	8	5	25
Medium	23	31	1	55
Small	6	6	8	20
Total	41	45	14	100

The table contains nine "cells," three across the top for the style and three down the side for the size. The totals for each category are shown across the bottom and down the last column. According to the table, 25 of the last 100 frames were the large size. A total of 45 wire frames were sold. The values down the right margin show the totals for each size category, while those across the bottom margin reveal totals for each style.

A figure in a cell indicates the number of observations that fit both categories. For example, the first cell shows that 12 of the 100 frames were large, plastic frames. Of the 41 plastic frames, 12 were large. Of the 25 large frames, 12 were plastic. The value in a cell shows the joint frequency of style and size. Consider how difficult it would be to convey all this information without the use of the table.

A probability table can be constructed from the frequency table, and is shown in Table 4-2.

TABLE 4-2   A Probability Table for Sales for E-Z-C Eye Care Center

Size	Frame Style			Total
	Plastic	Wire	Composite	
Large	$12/100 = 0.12$	$8/100 = 0.08$	$5/100 = 0.05$	$25/100 = 0.25$
Medium	$23/100 = 0.23$	$31/100 = 0.31$	$1/100 = 0.01$	$55/100 = 0.55$
Small	$6/100 = 0.06$	$6/100 = 0.06$	$8/100 = 0.08$	$20/100 = 0.20$
Total	$41/100 = 0.41$	$45/100 = 0.45$	$14/100 = 0.14$	1.00

Each value in the frequency table is divided by the total number of observations to form a probability table. It can readily be seen that 12 percent of the sales were of large, plastic frames. Further, 25 percent of all sales were of the large size.

The value in a cell in a probability table is the **joint probability** of the two events, in our case, size and style (size ∩ style). The probability that a medium, wire frame will be sold is 31 percent.

Joint Probability

The probability that two events will occur simultaneously is called the joint probability.

The values across the bottom margin and down the last column (right-hand margin) show the **marginal probabilities.** The marginal probability of large frames is 25 percent, while that of a wire frame is 45 percent.

Marginal Probability

The probability of the occurrence of a single event is called the marginal probability.

Conditional probability is another important aspect of probability theory which we will examine in the next section.

4.8 TWO RULES OF PROBABILITY

The earlier discussion of intersections and unions suggests that we have an interest in calculating the probability of events such as "*A* and *B*," and "*A* or *B*." This can be done by using the two basic rules of probability.

The **Rule of Multiplication** is used to determine the probability of the joint events *A* and *B*. The **Rule of Addition** is used to determine the probability of *A* or *B*. Although it is a little more involved than that, it is important to remember that (1) if *or* is used we add, and (2) if *and* is used we multiply. To more fully explain, to find the probability of *A* and *B* (*A* ∩ *B*), the Rule of Multiplication states that

1. If *A* and *B* are independent events, we must multiply the probability of event *A* with that of event *B*.
2. If *A* and *B* are dependent events, we must multiply the probability of event *A* with the probability that event *B* will occur, given event *A* has already occurred.

This prerequisite that event *A* has already occurred is based on the principles of conditional probability, and asks for the likelihood that event *B* will occur under the condition that event *A* has already occurred. A thorough examination of conditional probability will be presented in this chapter.

To find the probability of A or B ($A \cup B$), the Rule of Addition states that

1. If A and B are mutually exclusive events, we must add the probability of event A to that of event B.
2. If A and B are not mutually exclusive events, we must add the probability of event A to that of event B and subtract the joint probability of A and B.

While this may be a lot to digest at this point, just remember the general rule that for *and* we multiply, and for *or* we add.

The remainder of this section examines these important rules of probability and illustrates how they can be used to solve many common business problems. Let's begin with the Rule of Multiplication, and this principle referred to earlier as conditional probability.

A.   THE RULE OF MULTIPLICATION AND CONDITIONAL PROBABILITY

We often want to determine the probability of some event given the fact that some other event has already occurred. This is called **conditional probability.**

> **Conditional Probability**
> The probability that event A will occur given that, or on the condition that, event B has already occurred is called conditional probability.

The notation for conditional probability is

$$P(A|B)$$

and is read as "the probability of A given B". (The "|" does not imply division.) For example, if a card was drawn from a deck, the probability that it is a jack is

$$P(J) = \frac{4}{52}$$

However, if you were told that the card drawn was a face card, you would want to revise that probability. The question now becomes, "What is the probability the card drawn is a jack, given (on the condition that) it is a face card?" This is stated as $P(J|F)$. Since there are 12 face cards in the deck, 4 of which are jacks, we find

$$P(J|F) = \frac{4}{12}$$

which differs from $P(J) = 4/52$.

In general, conditional probability can be computed as

$$P(A|B) = \frac{P(A \text{ and } B)}{P(B)} \qquad (4.4)$$

Conditional probability can be taken from a probability table. Return to the illustration of the E-Z-C Eye Care Center. Presume that Ms. Highwater wanted to calculate the probability that a frame was large given that it was plastic. This is stated as

$$P(L|P) = \frac{P(L \text{ and } P)}{P(P)}$$

The value $P(L \text{ and } P)$ is the probability of the joint event large and plastic. This is found in the first cell of Table 4-2 to be 0.12. Since 41 percent of all the frames were plastic, as shown by the marginal probability in the first column in Table 4-2, we have

$$P(L|P) = \frac{0.12}{0.41}$$

$$= 0.29$$

Thus, while the probability that a frame was large is $P(L) = 0.25$, the probability that a frame was large given that it was plastic is $P(L|P) = 0.29$.

We will return to our discussion of conditional probability shortly. For the moment, we have the necessary groundwork required to examine the Multiplication Rule. Recall that the Multiplication Rule is used to find the probability of the joint event A and B. The rule requires that we multiply the probabilities of the two events. Accordingly, if A and B are independent events,

$$P(A \text{ and } B) = P(A) \times P(B) \qquad (4.5)$$

For example, consider the probability of drawing a king from a deck and rolling a 5 with a die. These are two independent events since what was drawn from the deck has no bearing on whether a 5 is rolled. Then

$$P(K \text{ and } 5) = P(K) \times P(5)$$

$$= \frac{4}{52} \times \frac{1}{6}$$

$$= \frac{4}{312}$$

However, if A and B are *dependent* events, Formula (4.5) is inappropriate. Instead, if A and B are dependent, we have

$$P(A \text{ and } B) = P(A) \times P(B|A) \qquad (4.6)$$

Notice that the last term, $P(B|A)$, involves conditional probability. Formula (4.6) tells us to multiply the probability of A by the probability of B given that A has already occurred. After all, if A and B are *dependent* events, then by definition the occurrence of A does have a bearing on the probability of event B, and it is necessary to take event A into consideration when determining the probability of event B.

As an example of the joint probability of two dependent events, let's explore the probability of drawing two cards from a deck, the first of which is an ace and the second of which is a king. Drawing is done without replacement, so the probability of the second draw depends on what was drawn the first time. Then,

$$P(A \text{ and } K) = P(A) \times P(K|A)$$

$$= \frac{4}{52} \times \frac{4}{51}$$

$$= \frac{16}{2652}$$

The $P(K|A)$ is 4/51 since, given an ace was drawn on the first draw, 4 of the remaining 51 cards are kings. If the first card was replaced before the second was drawn, then the events ace and king would be independent (since what was drawn the first time would have no effect on what was drawn the second time) and, as Formula (4.5) for independent events illustrates, we would have

$$P(A \text{ and } K) = P(A) \times P(K)$$

$$= \frac{4}{52} \times \frac{4}{52}$$

$$= \frac{16}{2704} \neq \frac{16}{2652}$$

Assume Ms. Highwater wishes to compute the probability of selling glasses that have a large plastic frame. Size and style are dependent, since the percentage of large frames that are plastic is different than that of the small or medium frames that are plastic. That is, of the 25 large frames, 12, or 48 percent, were plastic. But, of the 55 medium frames, 23, or 42 percent, were plastic. Thus, since the probability a frame is plastic varies depending on size, we must consider whether a frame is large in determining the probability it is plastic. Therefore Ms. Highwater requires

$$P(L \text{ and } P) = P(L) \times P(P|L)$$

$$= \frac{25}{100} \times \frac{12}{25}$$

$$= \frac{12}{100}$$

Of the 100 glasses, 25 are large. Thus, $P(L) = 25/100$. Of the 25 large frames, 12 are plastic. Thus, $P(P|L) = 12/25$.

Consider the following case. Of 200 people in a survey, 120 are men and 80 are women. Of the 120 men, 40 own stock in a U.S. corporation, while 20 of the women are stockholders. Thus, we have

120 men, 40 of whom own stock

80 women, 20 of whom own stock

Determine the probability of selecting one person at random who is a man and owns stock. This task will require the use of conditional probability.

$$P(\text{M and S}) = P(\text{M}) \times P(\text{S}|\text{M})$$

$$= \frac{120}{200} \times \frac{40}{120}$$

$$= \frac{40}{200}$$

The $P(\text{M})$ is 120/200 since 120 of the 200 people are men. The $P(\text{S}|\text{M})$ is 40/120 because it asks for the probability of stock ownership given that we have only the 120 men.

The statement $P(\text{S}|\text{M})$ must be used because the probability of owning stock depends on gender since a different (higher) proportion of men own stock than do women. If, by pure coincidence, 60 of the 120 men and 40 of the 80 women owned stock, then, regardless of gender, $P(\text{S}|\text{M}) = P(\text{S}|\text{W}) = P(\text{S}) = 0.5$. Gender and ownership of stock would then be independent events, and $P(\text{S})$ could have been used in place of $P(\text{S}|\text{M})$.

B. RULE OF ADDITION

The Rule of Addition is used when we seek the probability of A or B. That is, for *or* we must add. The rule is written as

$$P(A \text{ or } B) = P(A) + P(B) - P(A \text{ and } B) \qquad (4.7)$$

It states that we must add the probability of the two separate events and subtract the probability of the joint event A and B.

However, if A and B are mutually exclusive events, their joint probability is zero. By definition they cannot jointly occur and $P(A \text{ and } B) = 0$. Therefore, for mutually exclusive events the rule reduces to

$$P(A \text{ or } B) = P(A) + P(B) \qquad (4.8)$$

For example, assume that we wish to find the probability of drawing either an ace or a heart in a single draw from a deck of cards. That is, we seek $P(A \text{ or } H)$. (There are 13 hearts in a deck of 52 cards.) Then

$$P(A \text{ or } H) = P(A) + P(H) - P(A \text{ and } H)$$

$$= \frac{4}{52} + \frac{13}{52} - \frac{1}{52}$$

$$= \frac{16}{52}$$

The joint event A and H occurs only if the ace of hearts is drawn, the probability of which is 1/52. It is necessary to subtract $P(A \text{ and } H)$ because the probability of drawing the ace of hearts was included twice—once when we computed the probability of all 4 aces, and once when we computed the probability of all 13 hearts. Since there is only one ace of hearts, we need to deduct the probability of the joint event in order to avoid **double counting**—that is, counting the ace of hearts twice.

Double Counting
Counting a single event twice is referred to as double counting.

Now consider a case in which the two events are mutually exclusive. Assume we want to find the probability of drawing either a heart or a diamond. These events are mutually exclusive because you cannot draw both a heart and a diamond on the same draw, and the joint probability of H and D is zero. Thus, Formula (4.8) yields

$$P(H \text{ or } D) = P(H) + P(D)$$

$$= \frac{13}{52} + \frac{13}{52}$$

$$= \frac{26}{52}$$

$$= \frac{1}{2}$$

This should come as no surprise since one-half of the cards are red.

Returning to the E-Z-C Eye Care Center data, we can now find the probability of selling glasses that have either a large frame or a small frame: $P(L \text{ or } S)$. Since *or* is involved, we must add. Further, since large and small are mutually exclusive, we do not have to worry about double counting. Thus,

$$P(L \text{ or } S) = P(L) + P(S)$$

$$= \frac{25}{100} + \frac{20}{100}$$

$$= \frac{45}{100}$$

The probability of selling glasses that have either a large frame or a plastic frame does require conditional probability since large and plastic are not mutually exclusive.

$$P(\text{L or P}) = P(\text{L}) + P(\text{P}) - P(\text{L and P})$$

$$= \frac{25}{100} + \frac{41}{100} - \frac{12}{100}$$

$$= \frac{54}{100}$$

Twenty-five of the 100 frames are large, 41 of the 100 frames are plastic, and earlier we calculated the probability of L and P to be 12/100.

QUICK CHECK 4.8.1

What is the probability of picking a card and getting a face card or a 10?

Answer: 16/52

QUICK CHECK 4.8.2

What is the probability of rolling a die and getting a 3 or an odd number?

Answer: 3/6

The two rules of probability are summarized in Figure 4-3, and remind us to add when we use *or* and multiply when we use *and*.

FIGURE 4-3   The Addition Rule and the Multiplication Rule

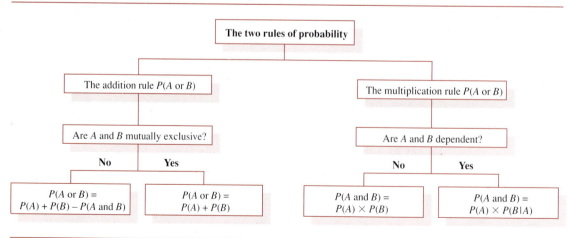

C.   A COUPLE OF HELPFUL HINTS

To find the probabilities of certain events, it is often useful to ask yourself two pertinent questions:

1.   In how many ways can the event happen?
2.   What are the contents of the set from which you are drawing?

Consider the following problem you face as a new manager for the Jesse James State Bank. The bank president has just hired 10 of his relatives to work at the bank as auditors. However, only four are qualified to serve in that capacity. You must select 3 of the 10 new employees at random to assist you in auditing the bank's records. What is the probability that two of the three you select are qualified to serve as auditors?

To summarize:

Ten new employees.
Four are qualified.
Three out of 10 are selected at random.
What is the probability that two of the three are qualified?

Helpful Hint 1
Determine in how many ways the event can occur.

You must begin by asking yourself the first question, "How can the event happen?" That is, of the three employees selected, how could two be qualified? There are three possibilities:

1.   The first was not qualified, and the other two were.
2.   The second was not qualified, and the other two were.
3.   The third was not qualified, and the other two were.

If one of these three possibilities occurs, then the event "two of the three are qualified" has occurred.

Since you must find three people to help with the audit, you cannot put the first one back before choosing the next. Drawing is therefore done without replacement, and the events are dependent.

The first way the event can happen is that the first person selected is not qualified, and the second is qualified given that the first was not, and the third is qualified given that the first was not and the second was. That is,

$$P(\overline{Q}_1 \text{ and } Q_2 \text{ and } Q_3) = P(\overline{Q}_1) \times P(Q_2|\overline{Q}_1) \times P(Q_3|\overline{Q}_1 \text{ and } Q_2)$$

where $\overline{Q}_1$ is the first person and not qualified
Q_2 is the second person and is qualified
Q_3 is the third person and is qualified.

Helpful Hint 2
In calculating the probability of drawing some element, you must ask what the set you are drawing from contains.

To determine these probabilities, you must ask another helpful question: "What does the set I am drawing from contain?" There are 10 people in the set, of whom 4 are qualified and 6 are not. Then

$$P(\overline{Q}_1) = \frac{6}{10}$$

After drawing the first person, "what does the set you are drawing from contain now?" If the first one drawn was not qualified, there are now nine people, of whom four are qualified, and five are not. Then

$$P(Q_2|\overline{Q}_1) = \frac{4}{9}$$

Now "what does the set contain?" If the first was not qualified and the second was, there are now eight people, of whom three are qualified and five are not. Then

$$P(Q_3|\overline{Q}_1 \text{ and } Q_2) = \frac{3}{8}$$

Therefore, the first way in which the event can happen is

$$P(\overline{Q}_1 \text{ and } Q_2 \text{ and } Q_3) = \frac{6}{10} \times \frac{4}{9} \times \frac{3}{8} = \frac{72}{720}$$

Notice that we multiply the three values since the statement contains *and*.

The second way the event could happen is

$$P(Q_1 \text{ and } \overline{Q}_2 \text{ and } Q_3) = P(Q_1) \times P(\overline{Q}_2|Q_1) \times P(Q_3|Q_1 \text{ and } \overline{Q}_2)$$

$$= \frac{4}{10} \times \frac{6}{9} \times \frac{3}{8}$$

$$= \frac{72}{720}$$

With the first draw, four of the 10 are qualified. For the second draw, the set contains nine people, six of whom are not qualified. For the third draw, the set contains eight people, three of whom are qualified.

Similarly, for the third way in which you can get two out of three who are qualified, we have

$$P(Q_1 \text{ and } Q_2 \text{ and } \overline{Q}_3) = P(Q_1) \times P(Q_2|Q_1) \times P(\overline{Q}_3|Q_1 \text{ and } Q_2)$$

$$= \frac{4}{10} \times \frac{3}{9} \times \frac{6}{8}$$

$$= \frac{72}{720}$$

Since the event can happen the first way or the second way or the third way, we must add the three probabilities.

$$P(2 \text{ of the 3 are qualified}) = \frac{72}{720} + \frac{72}{720} + \frac{72}{720}$$

$$= \frac{216}{720}$$

In each case it was helpful, even necessary, to consider what the set contained in order to calculate the probability.

D. FURTHER ILLUSTRATIONS OF THE TWO RULES OF PROBABILITY

The next four examples illustrate the two rules of probability, beginning with the Rule of Multiplication for independent events.

EXAMPLE 4-4 Cleaning Up—The Probability of Independent Events

Business Week described Procter & Gamble's efforts to compare Tide, their best-selling laundry detergent, to Surf, produced by Lever Brothers. P&G surveyed shoppers in a large mall in Cincinnati, Ohio, to determine their preferences. For notational purposes, assume that T_1 means "Tide was preferred by the first shopper" and S_2 means "Surf was preferred by the second shopper."

Industry reports reveal that Tide has 20 percent of the market, and Surf enjoys a 5 percent market share. Assuming these market shares translate into probabilities, P&G executives wanted to know, if two shoppers are selected at random, what is the probability that

a. Both preferred Tide: $P(T_1 \text{ and } T_2)$.
b. Both preferred Surf: $P(S_1 \text{ and } S_2)$.
c. The first preferred Tide and the second preferred Surf: $P(T_1 \text{ and } S_2)$.
d. The first preferred Surf and the second preferred Tide: $P(S_1 \text{ and } T_2)$.
e. One shopper preferred one detergent and the other shopper preferred the other detergent: $P(T_1 \text{ and } S_2)$ or $P(S_1 \text{ and } T_2)$.

SOLUTION:
Since it may be presumed that the preference of one shopper had no effect or influence on the second, the two events are independent. Using Formula (4.5), we have

a. $P(T_1 \text{ and } T_2) = P(T_1) \times P(T_2)$

$$= (0.20) \times (0.20)$$

$$= 0.04$$

b. $P(S_1 \text{ and } S_2) = P(S_1) \times P(S_2)$

$$= (0.05) \times (0.05)$$

$$= 0.0025$$

   c. $P(T_1 \text{ and } S_2) = P(T_1) \times P(S_2)$

$$= (0.20) \times (0.05)$$

$$= 0.01$$

   d. $P(S_1 \text{ and } T_2) = P(S_1) \times P(T_2)$

$$= (0.05) \times (0.20)$$

$$= 0.01$$

   e.   Each detergent is preferred by one shopper. You must ask yourself, "How can
        the event occur?" This would occur if $(T_1 \text{ and } S_2)$ or if $(S_1 \text{ and } T_2)$. Since the
        event can happen the first way or the second way, you must add the two
        probabilities.

$$P(\text{each is preferred}) = P(T_1 \text{ and } S_2) + P(S_1 \text{ and } T_2)$$

$$= 0.01 + 0.01$$

$$= 0.02$$

STATISTICAL INTERPRETATION:
Since the joint events are independent, the probability of the second event does not
require consideration of the first event, and the element of conditional probability is
not needed.

   This next example considers the case in which the joint events are dependent.
This circumstance will require conditional probability.

EXAMPLE 4-5 Getting Credit — Joint Dependent Events

In order to obtain a profile on her customers and better understand their needs, the
credit manager at Dollar-Wise Department Store collected data on the last 100 customers to enter the store. Of the 60 men (M) in the group, 40 had a credit card (C)
for the store. Of the 40 women (W), 30 had credit cards. While none of the men
currently have a positive credit balance (B), 10 of the women presently report a
positive balance in their credit account. The credit manager wants to determine the
probability that if a customer is selected at random, that customer

   a.   Is a man with a credit card.
   b.   Is a woman with a card.
   c.   Is a woman without a card.
   d.   Is a woman with a balance.
   e.   Has a card with a positive balance.
   f.   Is a man with a balance.

SOLUTION:

$a.$ $P(\text{M and C}) = P(\text{M}) \times P(C|M)$

$$= \frac{60}{100} \times \frac{40}{60}$$

$$= \frac{40}{100}$$

$P(C|M)$ is 40/60 since it asks for the probability that the customer owns a credit card given we have only the 60 men.

These two events are dependent because a different proportion of men own cards than do women. Thus, the probability that a customer holds a credit card depends on whether "it is given" that the customer is a man or a woman. Hence, the conditional probability $P(C|M)$ must be used. If the same percentage of men and women had credit cards, then conditional probability would not be necessary. For example, assume that 6 of the 60 men had cards and 4 of the 40 women had cards. Then, regardless of gender, $P(C|M) = P(C|W) = P(C) = 0.1$. Card ownership would be independent of gender, and $P(C)$ could be used in this problem instead of $P(C|M)$.

$b.$ $P(\text{W and C}) = P(\text{W}) \times P(C|W)$

$$= \frac{40}{100} \times \frac{30}{40}$$

$$= \frac{30}{100}$$

This problem requires the statement for conditional probability for the same reason that the first one did. The proportion of women who have cards is different from the proportion of men who do. Therefore, in determining the probability of a card, you must consider gender. Thus, $P(C|W)$, not merely $P(C)$, is required. Furthermore, $P(C|W) = 30/40$ since it asks for the probability a card is owned "given only the 40 women."

$c.$ $P(\text{W and } \overline{\text{C}}) = P(\text{W}) \times P(\overline{C}|W)$

$$= \frac{40}{100} \times \frac{10}{40}$$

$$= \frac{10}{100}$$

$P(\overline{C}|W) = 10/40$, because 10 of the 40 women do not have cards.

d. $P(\text{W and B}) = P(\text{W}) \times P(\text{B}|\text{W})$

$$= \frac{40}{100} \times \frac{10}{40}$$

$$= \frac{10}{100}$$

e. $P(\text{C and B}) = P(\text{C}) \times P(\text{B}|\text{C})$

$$= \frac{70}{100} \times \frac{10}{70}$$

$$= \frac{10}{100}$$

f. $P(\text{M and B}) = P(\text{M}) \times P(\text{B}|\text{M})$

$$= \frac{60}{100} \times 0$$

$$= 0$$

This should come as no surprise since none of the men have positive balances.

STATISTICAL INTERPRETATION:

The statement for conditional probability must be used in these problems because the joint events are dependent. This dependence was due to the fact that a difference existed between the proportion of men who had cards and the proportion of women who did. Thus, in determining the probability of a card, gender had to be considered.

These next two examples illustrate the Rule of Addition, beginning with events that are not mutually exclusive. This first example returns to the credit data for Dollar-Wise Department Store.

QUICK CHECK 4.8.3

○○○○   What is the probability that you toss a coin and get a head, then roll a die and get a 3?

Answer: 1/12

QUICK CHECK 4.8.4

What is the probability that you pick a king from a deck and roll a 9 with two dice?

Answer: 16/1872

EXAMPLE 4-6 The Probability of Events That Are Not Mutually Exclusive

Recall that of the 60 men, 40 had cards and none had a positive balance; of the 40 women, 30 had cards and 10 of those had a positive balance. The credit manager now wants to determine the probability that the customer selected at random is

a. $P(M \text{ or } C)$.
b. $P(W \text{ or } C)$.
c. $P(W \text{ or } B)$.
d. $P(C \text{ or } B)$.

SOLUTION:

a. $P(M \text{ or } C) = P(M) + P(C) - P(M \text{ and } C)$

$$= \frac{60}{100} + \frac{70}{100} - \frac{40}{100}$$

$$= \frac{90}{100}$$

$P(M \text{ and } C)$ was determined to be 40/100 in the previous example. It must be subtracted to prevent (M and C) from being included twice, once when we took the $P(M)$ and once when we took $P(C)$. Failure to do so would result in double counting.

b. $P(W \text{ or } C) = P(W) + P(C) - P(W \text{ and } C)$

$$= \frac{40}{100} + \frac{70}{100} - \frac{30}{100}$$

$$= \frac{80}{100}$$

c. $P(W \text{ or } B) = P(W) + P(B) - P(W \text{ and } B)$

$$= \frac{40}{100} + \frac{10}{100} - \frac{10}{100}$$

$$= \frac{40}{100}$$

Compare this one to $P(M \text{ or } B)$, which is mutually exclusive since no man had a balance. If M occurred, B could not. If B occurred, M could not. Then

$$P(M \text{ or } B) = P(M) + P(B) + 0$$

$$= \frac{60}{100} + \frac{10}{100}$$

$$= \frac{70}{200}$$

d. $P(C \text{ or } B) = P(C) + P(B) - P(C \text{ and } B)$

$$= \frac{70}{100} + \frac{10}{100} - \frac{10}{100}$$

$$= \frac{70}{100}$$

STATISTICAL INTERPRETATION:

In these cases the two events were not mutually exclusive. It was necessary to subtract the probability of the joint events to avoid double counting.

The case of mutually exclusive events is considered in this next example.

EXAMPLE 4-7 Winning Big (MACs)—Mutually Exclusive Events

A noted neighborhood hamburger emporium frequented by the students at the local university recently ran a promotional contest. With each purchase of a Big Mac, the customer was given a coupon allowing him or her the opportunity to win a prize. Of the 500 coupons given out,

100 were good for a free ticket to that week's football game (F).
50 could be redeemed at a local clothing store for a gift certificate (C).
20 provided for a free tank of gas at a local service station (G).
10 could be exchanged for another Big Mac (M).

The manager of the McDonald's wanted to know the probability of winning

a. F or C.
b. G or M.
c. Anything other than a Big Mac.
d. Anything.
e. Nothing.

SOLUTION:
Since no coupon would permit winning more than one prize, the events are mutually exclusive.

a. $P(\text{F or C}) = P(\text{F}) + P(\text{C})$

$$= \frac{100}{500} + \frac{50}{500}$$

$$= \frac{150}{500}$$

Since F and C are mutually exclusive, $P(\text{F and C}) = 0$, and it not necessary to subtract to avoid double counting.

b. $P(\text{G or M}) = P(\text{G}) + P(\text{M})$

$$= \frac{20}{500} + \frac{10}{500}$$

$$= \frac{30}{500}$$

c. $P(\text{F or C or G}) = P(\text{F}) + P(\text{C}) + P(\text{G})$

$$= \frac{100}{500} + \frac{50}{500} + \frac{20}{500}$$

$$= \frac{170}{500}$$

d. $P(\text{anything}) = P(\text{F or C or G or M})$

$$= P(\text{F}) \text{ or } P(\text{C}) \text{ or } P(\text{G}) \text{ or } P(\text{M})$$

$$= \frac{100}{500} + \frac{50}{500} + \frac{20}{500} + \frac{10}{500}$$

$$= \frac{180}{500}$$

e. $P(\text{nothing}) = 1 - P(\text{anything})$

$$= 1 - \frac{180}{500}$$

$$= \frac{320}{500}$$

STATISTICAL INTERPRETATION:
Since the events were mutually exclusive, double counting was not a problem, and it was not necessary to subtract the probability of the joint events.

Example 4-8 provides further application of the rules of probability by considering the random selection of two choices from a set.

EXAMPLE 4-8 Democracy in Action

A check of voter registration records in one precinct in Peoria County, Illinois, reveals that there are 512 registered voters. Of those, 309 are Democrats and 150 are Republicans. The rest are registered Independent or as a third party. Of the 512 voters, 323 are men and 189 are women.

Two registered voters must be selected at random to serve as poll watchers. The county registrar must determine the composition of these poll watchers in hopes of ensuring equal representation by sex and party affiliation. Using the subscripts 1 and 2 to indicate the first and second selection, respectively, the registrar wishes to know the probability that

a. Both are Democrats; $P(D_1 \text{ and } D_2)$.
b. Both are Republicans; $P(R_1 \text{ and } R_2)$.
c. The first is a Democrat and the second is a Republican; $P(D_1 \text{ and } R_2)$.
d. The first is a Republican and the second is a Democrat; $P(R_1 \text{ and } D_2)$.
e. Both are women; $P(W_1 \text{ and } W_2)$.
f. Both are men; $P(M_1 \text{ and } M_2)$.
g. One is a man and one is a woman.

Since two people are to be selected to serve as poll watchers, it is impossible to replace the first person before the second is chosen. Drawing must be done without replacement. Therefore, the two events are dependent.

SOLUTION:

a. $P(D_1 \text{ and } D_2) = P(D_1) \times P(D_2 | D_1)$

$$= \frac{309}{512} \times \frac{308}{511}$$

$$= \frac{95{,}172}{261{,}632}$$

$$= 36.4\%$$

Since 309 of the 512 voters are Democrats, the probability of choosing a Democrat as the first poll watcher is $P(D_1) = 309/512$. Given that the first was a Democrat, 308 of the remaining 511 voters are Democrat. Thus, $P(D_2 | D_1) = 308/511$.

b. $P(R_1 \text{ and } R_2) = P(R_1) \times P(R_2 | R_1)$

$$= \frac{150}{512} \times \frac{149}{511}$$

$$= \frac{22{,}350}{261{,}632}$$

$$= 8.5\%$$

Of the 512 voters, 150 are Republicans. The probability of selecting a Republican as the first poll watcher is 150/512. Given that the first was a Republican, 149 of the remaining 511 voters are Republican.

c. $P(D_1 \text{ and } R_2) = P(D_1) \times P(R_2|D_1)$

$$= \frac{309}{512} \times \frac{150}{511} = \frac{46,350}{261,632} = 17.7\%$$

d. $P(R_1 \text{ and } D_2) = P(R_1) \times P(D_2|R_1)$

$$= \frac{150}{512} \times \frac{309}{511} = \frac{46.350}{261,632} = 17.7\%$$

which is the same as the previous problem, since both result in one voter from each party.

e. $P(W_1 \text{ and } W_2) = P(W_1) \times P(W_2|W_1)$

$$= \frac{189}{512} \times \frac{188}{511} = \frac{35,532}{261,632} = 13.6$$

f. $P(M_1 \text{ and } M_2) = P(M_1) \times P(M_2|M_1)$

$$= \frac{323}{512} \times \frac{322}{511} = \frac{104,006}{261,632} = 39.8\%$$

g. One man and one woman can occur as either $P(M_1 \text{ and } W_2)$ or $P(W_1 \text{ and } M_2)$ Thus,

$$P(M_1 \text{ and } W_2) = P(M_1) \times P(W_2)$$

$$= \frac{323}{512} \times \frac{189}{511} = \frac{61,047}{261,632}$$

$$= 23.3\%$$

$$P(W_1 \text{ and } M_2) = P(W_1) \times P(M_2)$$

$$= \frac{189}{512} \times \frac{323}{511}$$

$$= 23.3\%$$

Since one of each gender can occur either the first way or the second way, we must add the probabilities of each. Thus, 23.3 percent + 23.3 percent = 46.6 percent.

STATISTICAL INTERPRETATION:

It would seem that equal representation is unlikely. There is a 36 percent chance that both poll watchers will be Democrats, and only an 8.5 percent chance that both are Republicans. There is an almost 40 percent chance that both are men, but only a 13.6 percent chance that both are women. There is a 40 percent + 13.6 percent = 53.6 percent chance that either both will be men or both will be women, but only a 46.6 percent chance that one of each gender will be selected.

In 1990, MCA Entertainment, Inc. entered negotiations to purchase Hanna-Barbera, the creator of Yogi Bear, The Flintstones, and other Saturday morning staples. In order to decide on an offer price, MCA had to determine the chances that these residents of Jellystone Park, Bedrock, and similar fanciful neighborhoods would find a home on network television, in amusement theme parks, and movie houses across the nation.

The likelihood that these cartoon characters would become gainfully employed was determined by using the rules of probability, and thereby offered MCA an estimate of the earnings potential of their investment.

QUICK CHECK 4.8.7
○○○○   An urn contains four red and eight green marbles. If two are selected without replacement, what is the probability that the first is red and the second is green?
Answer: 32/132

4.9   PROBABILITY TREES

When it is necessary to find the probabilities of several joint events, it is often useful to construct a probability tree. A **probability tree** or **tree diagram** shows all the probabilities associated with an entire set of specific events. Once the tree has been constructed, we can "pick" from it any of the probabilities we desire. Consider the following illustration.

All major manufacturing firms maintain quality control departments whose main function is to ensure that their products meet certain production specifications. It is their responsibility to minimize the production of defective units and to ensure that defects do not leave the plant. Figure 4-4 provides a tree diagram for a firm that suffers a rate of defect of 10 percent. That is, 10 percent of the units produced at the plant do not meet the minimum specifications. The probability of a defective unit is 10 percent, and the probability of a nondefective unit is therefore 90 percent. Then $P(D) = 0.10$ and $P(\overline{D}) = 0.90$. Two units are selected at random off the assembly line, and it is noted whether each is defective.

We start at the left end of the tree. The only two possible outcomes of the first selection, defective and not defective, are shown along with their associated probabilities as branches emanating from the origin. The unit drawn may be either defective, with a probability of 0.10, or not defective, with a probability of 0.90. By following a certain sequence of branches, we can arrive at one of the four possible events, A, B, C, or D. For example, event B is derived if the first is defective and the second is not, the probability of which is 0.09.

FIGURE 4-4   Probability Tree for a Production Process

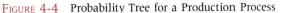

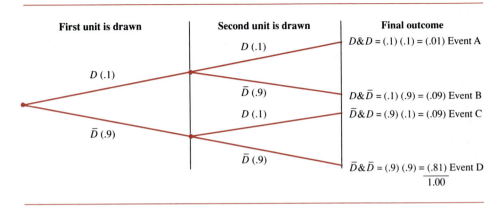

Now, by merely examining the tree, it is possible to determine the probability of any of the final outcomes. Assume the plant manager wishes to select two nondefective units. Then the only outcome that will please him is $\bar{D}_1$ and $\bar{D}_2$, or event D, the probability of which is 0.81. The event of selecting two units, only one of which is defective, is satisfied if either event B or event C occurs, the probability of which is $0.09 + 0.09 = 0.18$.

Note that the joint probabilities of all four events must sum to 1, since they constitute collectively exhaustive events.

The tree shown in Figure 4-4 is for independent events, but trees are equally useful if the events are dependent. Figure 4-5 reflects the outcomes of picking two cards from a deck without replacement and noting whether they are kings.

FIGURE 4-5   A Tree for Dependent Events

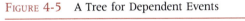

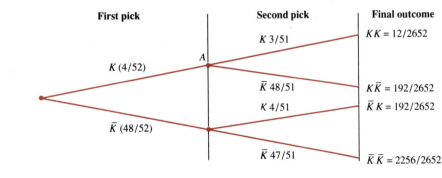

Starting at the left end of the diagram, we see it is possible to draw a king, $P(K) = 4/52$, or not a king, $P(\bar{K}) = 48/52$. If a king were drawn the first time, we move to point A. There it is again possible to draw a king or not a king. Since drawing is done without replacement, we have $P(K) = 3/51$ and $P(\bar{K}) = 48/51$. Thus, for example, $P(K_1 \text{ and } K_2) = 12/2652$ and $P(\bar{K}_1 \text{ and } K_2) = 192/2652$.

4.10 BAYES' RULE AND CONDITIONAL PROBABILITY

In our earlier discussion of conditional probability, we found the probability of drawing a jack from a deck to be 4/52. This was the a priori probability of that event. The **a priori** probability is the probability estimate before the event occurs, and may be subject to change after further study.

A Priori Probability

The probability measure before any additional information is obtained is called a priori probability. It may be revised if further relevant information is revealed.

After it was learned that the card was a face card, we had

$$P(J \mid F) = \frac{4}{12}$$

This revised probability is posterior probability. **Posterior probabilities** are conditional probabilities based on additional information.

Posterior Probability

The probability measure which has been revised on the condition that some known event has occurred is called posterior probability.

To more fully understand conditional probability, consider the following situation. The Occupational Health and Safety Administration (OSHA) has found that 15 percent of all employees working at construction sites are injured on the job. OSHA has also determined that 20 percent of all construction workers are on jobs classified as dangerous. Accident reports filed by construction firms show that 10 percent of all employees are on dangerous jobs and are injured. This is *not* to say that 10 percent of all employees on dangerous jobs are injured. It says that of all employees, 10 percent are on dangerous jobs and are injured. Thus,

$$P \text{ (injured)} = 0.15$$

$$P \text{ (dangerous)} = 0.20$$

$$P \text{ (dangerous and injured)} = 0.10$$

This information is summarized in a probability table (Table 4-3). The three values with an asterisk are given by the information above. The rest are determined by the fact that the events must sum to 100 percent.

TABLE 4-3 Probability Table for OSHA Data

	Injured	Not injured	Total
Dangerous	0.10*	0.10	0.20*
Not dangerous	0.05	0.75	0.80
Total	0.15*	0.85	1.00

Given this information, the foreman at a construction site wishes to know the probability that a worker is injured. Since OSHA records show that 15 percent of all construction workers are injured, the relative frequency approach reveals that the probability of injury is $P(I) = 15$ percent. Assume that the same foreman now wants to know the probability that a worker is injured if he is working on a job classified as dangerous. That is, he wishes to determine $P(I|D)$. Since he seeks the probability of injury given, or on the condition, that the worker is on a dangerous job, the conditional probability formula is necessary. We noted earlier that the general formula for conditional probability states

$$P(A|B) = \frac{P(A \text{ and } B)}{P(B)}$$

Applying this to our construction site example gives

$$P(I|D) = \frac{P(I \text{ and } D)}{P(D)}$$

$$= \frac{0.10}{0.20}$$

$$= 0.50$$

Thus, while the probability of injury is 15 percent, the probability of injury on the condition that the worker is on a dangerous job is 50 percent.

QUICK CHECK 4.10.1

○○○○   Of 1,000 18-year-olds, 800 are high school graduates, 600 are employed, and 400 of the graduates have jobs. If a graduate is selected at random, what is the probability that he or she is employed?

Answer: 0.5

Using this principle of conditional probability as a focal point, the Reverend Thomas Bayes (1702–1761) reasoned that given $P(A)$ and $P(B|A)$ it was possible to determine $P(A|B)$. To illustrate, Jack and Jill sell insurance in the family business. Jack sells 80 percent of the policies, and Jill sells the rest. Of the 80 percent sold by Jack, 10 percent of the policyholders file a claim within one year. The comparable figure for Jill is 25 percent. To summarize:

$$P(\text{Jack}) = 0.80$$

$$P(\text{Jill}) = 0.20$$

$$P(\text{claim} | \text{Jack}) = 0.10$$

$$P(\text{claim} | \text{Jill}) = 0.25$$

A client announces his intention to file a claim. What is the probability Jack sold him the policy? That is, find $P(\text{Jack}|\text{claim})$. According to the formula for conditional probability,

$$P(\text{Jack} | \text{claim}) = \frac{P(\text{Jack and claim})}{P(\text{claim})}$$

Applying the Rule of Multiplication to the numerator gives us

$$P(\text{Jack} | \text{claim}) = \frac{P(\text{Jack}) \times P(\text{claim} | \text{Jack})}{P(\text{claim})}$$

Hence,

$$P(\text{Jack} | \text{claim}) = \frac{(0.8)\,(0.10)}{P(\text{claim})}$$

However, we are still left without $P(\text{claim})$. It is here that Bayes' Rule must be applied. Ask yourself the question, "How can the event 'claim' occur?" A claim can occur because (1) Jack sold the policy and the client wishes to file, or because (2) Jill sold the policy and the client wishes to file. That is, of the 80 percent of the claims sold by Jack, 10 percent will file, or of the 20 percent of the claims sold by Jill, 25 percent will file. Thus,

$$P(\text{claim}) = P(\text{Jack}) \times P(\text{claim} | \text{Jack}) + P(\text{Jill}) \times P(\text{claim} | \text{Jill})$$

$$= (0.8)\,(0.10) + (0.20)\,(0.25) = 0.13$$

In a more general sense, where A and $\overline{A}$ are the events A and not A, respectively, the probability of some event B is

$$P(B) = P(A) \times P(B|A) + P(\overline{A}) \times P(B|\overline{A}) \qquad (4.9)$$

We must now note Bayes' Rule, which states that

$$P(A|B) = \frac{P(A) \times P(B|A)}{P(B)} \qquad (4.10)$$

Using (4.9) in the denominator, we have

$$P(A|B) = \frac{P(A) \times P(B|A)}{P(A) \times P(B|A) + P(\overline{A}) \times P(B|\overline{A})}$$

Returning to our example of Jack's insurance claims, we have

$$P(\text{Jack}|\text{claim}) = \frac{P(\text{Jack}) \times P(\text{claim}|\text{Jack})}{P(\text{claim})}$$

Applying (4.9) to the denominator results in

$$P(\text{Jack}|\text{claim}) = \frac{P(\text{Jack}) \times P(\text{claim}|\text{Jack})}{P(\text{claim}) = P(\text{Jack}) \times P(\text{claim}|\text{Jack}) + P(\text{Jill}) \times P(\text{claim}|\text{Jill})}$$

Thus,

$$P(\text{Jack}|\text{claim}) = \frac{(0.8)(0.10)}{0.13}$$

$$= 0.62$$

The probability that Jack sold the policy, given that the holder wishes to file a claim is $P(\text{Jack}|\text{claim}) = 62\%$. This compares with the probability that Jack sold any given policy as $P(\text{Jack}) = 80$ percent.

EXAMPLE 4.9 Bayes' Rule: How to Keep Your Batteries Charged

In their effort to stem the tide of foreign imports, American automobile manufacturers have taken steps to improve the quality and reliability of their cars. *Automobile News,* a trade publication widely read within the industry, described a procedure at a GM plant producing Delco car batteries, which was designed to detect and eliminate defective products. The plant uses two separate work shifts, one during the morning (8:00 A.M. to 4:30 P.M.) and one in the evening (5:00 P.M. to midnight) to produce the batteries.

The quality control department regularly tests samples of these batteries after they have set dormant for at least six months, to determine if they would hold a charge. The morning shift produces 65 percent of all the batteries, the evening shift the other 35 percent. Previous examinations by the QC department have revealed that 5 percent of the batteries produced by the morning shift are defective, while the evening shift has a defective rate of 8 percent.

During spot checks, the plant manager selects one battery and tests it himself. The last battery checked was found to be defective. The manager wanted to know which shift was more likely to have produced that defective battery.

SOLUTION:

It might seem that the evening shift is more likely to have produced that battery since its rate of defect is higher. However, given that the battery was found to be defective, we must compare $P(M|D)$ to $P(E|D)$, where M is morning shift, E is evening shift, and D is defective. The information given can be summarized as

$$P(M) = 0.65 \qquad P(D|M) = 0.05$$
$$P(E) = 0.35 \qquad P(D|E) = 0.08$$

Given the information, we can make the following comparison:

$$P(M|D) = \frac{P(M \text{ and } D)}{P(D)} = \frac{P(M) \times P(D|M)}{P(M)P(D|M) + P(E)P(D|E)}$$

$$= \frac{(0.65)(0.05)}{(0.65)(0.05)(0.35)(0.08)}$$

$$= \frac{0.0325}{0.0605}$$

$$= 54\%$$

$$P(E|D) = \frac{P(E \text{ and } D)}{P(D)} = \frac{P(E) \times P(D|E)}{0.0605}$$

$$= \frac{(0.35)(0.08)}{0.0605}$$

$$= 46\%$$

STATISTICAL INTERPRETATION:

Despite the higher defective rate of the evening shift, the morning shift is more likely to have produced that defective battery, or any other battery found to be defective. If the plant wishes to reduce the number of defects, it should, perhaps, concentrate on the morning shift.

Applications for conditional probability are common occurrences in the business world, since new discoveries and additional information is constantly coming to light. This newfound knowledge can then be used to determine the probability of specific events.

4.11   COUNTING TECHNIQUES

It seems that almost every adult has a credit card. It is un-American to go through life without being in debt. Although at birth each of us is given a name, later in life we are more likely to be identified by our credit card number. Some VISA cards, for example, have 13 digits which singles out the holder of that card as the only individual responsible for items charged on that card. Why so many digits? Even if every person on the face of this earth, all 5 billion of us, had a VISA card, we would still need only 10 digits on our credit cards. The extra digits are to prevent billing mistakes. There are 10 trillion possible 13-digit VISA account numbers, but only 65 million of us have VISA cards. Therefore, it is extremely unlikely that someone will accidentally record an incorrect account number. The probability that a particular 13-digit account number can be mistakenly recorded at random is 0.000000000000001.

Determining the total number of possible VISA cards that can be issued requires the use of counting techniques. Counting techniques are useful in determining how many smaller groups can be formed from all the elements found in a larger group. For example, suppose we have the set consisting of the first five letters of the alphabet, A, B, C, D, and E. How many subsets of size 3 might we be able to get from the five elements? We could list them and then count them. Taking any three out of the five, we could get

$A\ B\ C$	$A\ D\ E$
$A\ B\ D$	$B\ C\ D$
$A\ B\ E$	$B\ C\ E$
$A\ C\ D$	$B\ D\ E$
$A\ C\ E$	$C\ D\ E$

There is a total of 10 different arrangements of these five letters taken three at a time. As you might imagine, as the number of possible choices increases, it becomes much more difficult to make a complete list. If all 26 letters were used, the list would include 400 trillion trillion possible arrangements. Luckily, there is a better way to determine the number of subsets that can be obtained from any set of objects. This preferred method is based on **counting techniques** which determine the number of subsets or arrangements that can be taken from a set.

Counting Techniques
Methods to determine how many subsets can be obtained from a set of objects are called counting techniques.

We will examine four counting techniques: (1) permutations, (2) combinations, (3) multiple-choice arrangements, and (4) the multiplication method. Let's look at permutations and combinations first. The important distinction between permutations and combinations is that with permutations, order makes a difference, whereas with combinations, order does not make a difference. For instance, in arrangements *A B C* and *A C B* the elements are the same. The only difference is the order in which they are arranged. Since order makes a difference with permutations, *A B C* and *A C B* constitute two different permutations; that is, *A B C* is not the same as *A C B*. However, with combinations, order does not make a difference. Thus, arrangements *A B C* and *A C B* are the same and generate only one combination. Since the two arrangements contain the same elements, and differ only in terms of the order in which they are arranged, they are merely two orderings of the same combination. Also note that for permutations and combinations, duplication is not allowed: arrangements such as *A A B*, *A B B*, and *A C A* are not permitted.

A. PERMUTATIONS

Given just the three letters, *A*, *B*, and *C*, how many permutations of size 3 can we get. **Permutations** are arrangements in which order makes a difference. The list of permutations of all three elements is

$$
\begin{array}{ll}
A\,B\,C & \quad B\,C\,A \\
A\,C\,B & \quad C\,A\,B \\
B\,A\,C & \quad C\,B\,A
\end{array}
$$

Notice that six different permutations are obtained by simply reordering the elements. Since with permutation, order makes a difference, a different ordering yields a different permutation.

Permutation
A set of items in which both composition and order are important is a permutation.

In the likely event that the number of elements is too large to permit a complete listing, we can use Formula (4.11) to determine the number of possible permutations. This formula, which gives the number of permutations of *n* elements taken *r* at a time is

$$
{}_nP_r = \frac{n!}{(n-r)!} \tag{4.11}
$$

where the expression $n!$ (read n factorial) is the product of all numbers 1 through n. Thus, $4! = 1 \times 2 \times 3 \times 4 = 24$. By definition, $0! = 1$. In the case of the three letters taken three at a time, we have

$$_3P_3 = \frac{3!}{(3-3)!} = \frac{1 \times 2 \times 3}{0!} = 6$$

Given the first five letters of the alphabet, if we wished to determine the number of permutations of five elements taken three at a time, it becomes

$$_5P_3 = \frac{5!}{(5-3)!} = \frac{1 \times 2 \times 3 \times 4 \times 5}{1 \times 2} = 60$$

Suppose 10 contestants enter the hog-judging competition at the state fair. Three hogs will be selected from the 10 and awarded a blue ribbon for first place, a red ribbon for second, and a white ribbon for third place. The order of selection matters since the first hog selected gets the prize blue ribbon, and the second- and third-place finishers get only red and white ribbons. Since order is important, we are dealing with permutations. How many possible arrangements of first-, second-, and third-place finishers are there in the field of 10 hogs?

$$_{10}P_3 = \frac{10!}{(10-3)!} = \frac{1 \times 2 \times 3 \times 4 \times 5 \times 6 \times 7 \times 8 \times 9 \times 10}{1 \times 2 \times 3 \times 4 \times 5 \times 6 \times 7}$$
$$= 720$$

There are 720 ways in which first-, second-, and third-place finishers might be selected by the hog judges from the list of 10 competitors. Given that each hog has an equal likelihood of being selected for each of three places, there is a probability of only 1/720 that any three hogs will finish in a specific order.

QUICK CHECK 4.11.1

○○○○   A consumer is asked to rank his preference of five brands of soda. How many different rankings can result?

Answer: 120

B.   COMBINATIONS

Assume for the moment that the three hogs at the fair are selected as winners, and each is given a ribbon with no distinction among first-, second-, and third-place finishes. In this event, order of selection is not important. We are then working with **combinations**.

> **Combination**
> The set of items in which only composition is important (i.e., order makes no difference) is called a combination.

The total number of possible combinations of n elements selected r at a time is

$$_nC_r = \frac{n!}{r!\,(n-r)!} \tag{4.12}$$

In the case of the 10 hogs, 3 of which are selected as winners with no distinction made as to the order in which they finished the competition, we have

$$_{10}C_3 = \frac{10!}{3!\,(10-3)!} = \frac{1 \times 2 \times 3 \times 4 \times 5 \times 6 \times 7 \times 8 \times 9 \times 10}{(1 \times 2 \times 3) \times (1 \times 2 \times 3 \times 4 \times 5 \times 6 \times 7)}$$

$$= \frac{8 \times 9 \times 10}{1 \times 2 \times 3}$$

$$= 120$$

There are 120 ways in which 3 hogs out of the 10 can be singled out as worthy of recognition.

EXAMPLE 4-10 A Distinction between Combinations and Permutations

The CEO for Dow Chemical Company must select 5 people from a list of 15 young executives to serve as examples of outstanding managerial talent. Each executive is to receive a monetary reward. The first one selected will get the highest bonus, the second one selected will get the second highest, and so on.

The CEO must also select a 5-member committee from a group of 15 corporate planners that will determine the site for a new chemical plant Dow plans to build. The CEO wonders how many subsets she can get in each case.

SOLUTION:

Since the order in which the young executives is selected determines how large their bonus is, the CEO is working with permutations.

$$_{15}P_5 = \frac{15!}{(15-5)!} = 360,360$$

There are 360,360 possible different permutations of the 15 executives who will receive a bonus in their pay checks next pay period.

In the case of the selection of the corporate planners, all five members of the planning committee will serve jointly in the effort to select a construction site.

There is no distinction made among the duties of the committee members. There-fore, the order in which they are selected is of no consequence.

$$_{15}C_5 = \frac{15!}{5!\,(15-5)!} = 3{,}003$$

There are only 3,003 committees of size five which can be selected from the 15-member board if order of selection is not of any importance.

STATISTICAL INTERPRETATION:
Given any set of conditions involving the selection of r items from a list of n items, where $r \leq n$, the number of possible permutations will exceed the number of combinations, since merely rearranging the r elements produces a new permutation.

QUICK CHECK 4.11.2
○○○○   How many groups of five students can be drawn from a total of seven students in which order does not count?
Answer: 21

QUICK CHECK 4.11.3
The president of the company must select four of her six vice presidents to handle problems when they arise. How many different arrangements of vice presidents can the president devise?
Answer: 15

EXAMPLE 4-11 How Counting Techniques Can Be Used To Determine Probability

The CEO for Dow prefers Houston, Texas, as the site for the chemical plant to be built. Seven of the 15 members of the board of directors agree with the CEO, but the remaining eight prefer other locations. What is the probability that of the five selected for the committee all agree with the CEO?

SOLUTION:
As we have seen, there are 3,003 possible different committees. If all five must be selected from the seven who agree with the CEO, there are

$$_{7}C_5 = \frac{7!}{5!\,(7-5)!} = 21$$

possible committees that will produce all five members who prefer Houston. The number of ways in which the event all five prefer Houston can occur is 21. The total number of outcomes (all possible committees) is 3,003.

Thus,

$$P(\text{all agree with CEO}) = \frac{\text{Number of ways the event can happen}}{\text{Total number of outcomes}}$$

$$= \frac{_7C_5}{_{15}C_5}$$

$$= \frac{21}{3{,}003} = 0.00699$$

or, where $P(A_i)$ is probability the ith person selected agrees with the CEO, we have

$$P(\text{all agree}) = P(A_1) \times P(A_2|A_1) \times P(A_3|A_2 \text{ and } A_1)$$
$$\times P(A_4|A_3 \text{ and } A_2 \text{ and } A_3) \times P(A_5|A_4 \text{ and } A_3 \text{ and } A_2 \text{ and } A_1)$$

$$= \frac{7}{15} \times \frac{6}{14} \times \frac{5}{13} \times \frac{4}{12} \times \frac{3}{11} = 0.00699$$

STATISTICAL INTERPRETATION:

Obviously, electing a committee which unanimously supports the CEO is unlikely.

EXAMPLE 4-12   The Probability That Four of the Five Selected Agree with the CEO

Dow's CEO wishes to determine the probability that four of the five selected for the committee prefer Houston.

SOLUTION:

Recall that our first Helpful Hint discussed earlier suggested that we ask, "How can the event occur?" Four of the five would agree if the last one selected did not agree, and the first four did agree; or if the fourth one selected did not agree, and the rest did; or if the third one selected did not agree and the rest did; or if the second one selected did not agree and the rest did; or if the first one selected did not agree and the rest did.

Where $P(A_i)$ is the probability the ith person agrees with the CEO, the probability that the last one did not agree and the rest did is found as

$$P(\text{first 4 agree}) = P(A_1) \times P(A_2|A_1) \times P(A_3|A_2 \text{ and } A_1)$$
$$\times P(A_4|A_3 \text{ and } A_2 \text{ and } A_1)$$
$$\times P(\overline{A_5}|A_4 \text{ and } A_3 \text{ and } A_2 \text{ and } A_1)$$

$$= \frac{7}{15} \times \frac{6}{14} \times \frac{5}{13} \times \frac{4}{12} \times \frac{8}{11}$$

$$= \frac{6{,}720}{360{,}360}$$

P(the fourth does not agree and the rest agree)

$$= P(A_1) \times P(A_2|A_1) \times P(A_3|A_2 \text{ and } A_1) \times P(\overline{A_4}|A_3 \text{ and } A_2 \text{ and } A_1)$$
$$\times P(A_5|\overline{A_4} \text{ and } A_3 \text{ and } A_2 \text{ and } A_1)$$

$$= \frac{7}{15} \times \frac{6}{14} \times \frac{5}{13} \times \frac{8}{12} \times \frac{4}{11}$$

$$= \frac{6{,}720}{360{,}360}$$

which is the same as P(first 4 agree).

P(the third does not agree and the rest do)

$$= P(A_1) \times P(A_2|A_1) \times P(\overline{A_3}|A_2 \text{ and } A_1)$$
$$\times P(A_4|\overline{A_3} \text{ and } A_2 \text{ and } A_1) \times P(A_5|A_4 \text{ and } \overline{A_3} \text{ and } A_2 \text{ and } A_1)$$

$$= \frac{7}{15} \times \frac{6}{14} \times \frac{8}{13} \times \frac{5}{12} \times \frac{4}{11}$$

$$= \frac{6{,}720}{360{,}360}$$

which is also the same as above.

We could continue with this tedious procedure and then add all five ways in which four could agree, or we could merely calculate

$$\frac{6{,}720}{360{,}360} \times 5 = \frac{33{,}600}{360{,}360} = 0.0932$$

Or, the same results can be obtained as

$$P(4 \text{ out of 5 agree}) = \frac{\text{Probability of choosing 4 who agree and one who does not}}{\text{Total number of ways to draw 5}}$$

$$= \frac{{}_7C_4 \times {}_8C_1}{{}_{15}C_5}$$

$$= \frac{35 \times 8}{3{,}003}$$

$$= 0.0932$$

Since 7 agree with the CEO, the number of ways in which you can pick 4 of those 7 is ${}_7C_4 = 35$. There are ${}_8C_1 = 8$ ways in which you can choose 1 of the 8 who do not agree, and 3,003 total possible committees of 5 from the 15 members on the board of directors.

The probability of selecting four who agree with the CEO (0.0932) is greater than selecting a committee in which all five agree (0.00699).

C.   MULTIPLE-CHOICE ARRANGEMENT

The **multiple-choice arrangement** is a counting technique in which order makes a difference. It is distinguished from both a permutation and a combination by the fact that duplication is allowed. That is, in the case of multiple-choice arrangements, the same element can be used more than once. The number of multiple-choice arrangements of n items taken r at a time is

$$_nM_r = n^r \qquad\qquad (4.13)$$

To illustrate, assume that you must choose three universities from a list of five different universities in which your three teenagers will enroll this fall. The order in which the schools are chosen is important because it determines which student goes to which school. Also, since two or more can go to the same school, duplication is allowed. The total number of selections of three schools out of the five is

$$_5M_3 = 5^3 = 125$$

There are 125 different possible arrangements in which the three students can choose among the five schools.

QUICK CHECK 4.11.4

○○○○   A car dealer has three types of cars from which two customers will pick one. How many different sales can the dealer make?
Answer: 9

QUICK CHECK 4.11.5

Another dealer has two different types of cars from which three customers will make a selection. How many different sales can this dealer make?
Answer: 8

D.   MULTIPLICATION METHOD

The **multiplication method** is appropriate when choices must be made from two or more distinct groups. It there are m possible selections in one group and n possible selections in a second group, the total number of arrangements is $m \times n$.

As your dear old grandmother's birthday approaches, you are to select a gift for her consisting of flowers and a birthday card. A store offers an assortment of m = three different kinds of flowers and n = five different types of cards. If you choose one kind of flowers and one type of card, the total number of possible gifts is $m \times n = 3 \times 5 = 15$. The key to identifying the multiplication method is to recognize that the selections are made from two or more distinct groups. Notice that the flowers and the card are to be chosen from two different sets.

4.12 SOLVED PROBLEMS

1. **The Acceptability of Star Wars** In 1988 there were 56 Democrats in the U.S. Senate, 21 of whom supported the president's Strategic Defense Initiative (Star Wars). Twenty-nine of the 39 Republicans supported SDI. The remaining five senators, of whom three supported SDI, were neither Republican or Democrat. Two senators were to be chosen at random to serve in an advisory capacity regarding national defense matters. Find the following probabilities:

    a. The probability both favor SDI is

    $$P(F_1 \text{ and } F_2) = P(F_1) \times P(F_2 | F_1)$$

    $$= \frac{53}{100} \times \frac{52}{99} = \frac{2,756}{9,900}$$

    Since the two senators are chosen to serve on a committee, selection is done without replacement. Therefore, the two events F_1 and F_2 are dependent and require the statement $P(F_2 | F_1)$, not just $P(F_2)$.

    b. The probability the first favors SDI and the second does not is

    $$P(F_1 \text{ and } \overline{F}_2) = P(F_1) \times P(\overline{F}_2 | F_1)$$

    $$= \frac{53}{100} \times \frac{47}{99} = \frac{2,491}{9,900}$$

    This statement imposes the restriction of order in that the first favors SDI and the second does not. Compare it to the next case.

    c. The probability only one senator favors SDI.
    This statement does not impose any restriction of order on selection. The event can be satisfied if the first favors SDI and the second does not, or if the first does not and the second does. In either case, one of the two senators favors SDI and one does not.

    $$P(\text{only one of the two chosen favors SDI}) = P(F_1 \text{ and } \overline{F}_2) \text{ or } P(\overline{F}_1 \text{ and } F_2)$$

    $$P(F_1 \text{ and } \overline{F}_2) = P(F_1) \times P(\overline{F}_2 | F_1)$$

    $$= \frac{53}{100} \times \frac{47}{99} = \frac{2,491}{9,900}$$

or

$$P(\overline{F}_1 \text{ and } F_2) = P(\overline{F}_1) \times P(F_2|\overline{F}_1)$$

$$= \frac{47}{100} \times \frac{53}{99} = \frac{2{,}491}{9{,}900}$$

Therefore,

$$P(\text{only one of two favors}) = \frac{2{,}491}{9{,}900} + \frac{2{,}491}{9{,}900} = \frac{4{,}982}{9{,}900}$$

d. The probability both are Republicans who favor SDI is

$$P[(R \text{ and } F)_1 \text{ and } (R \text{ and } F)_2] = P(R \text{ and } F)_1 \times P[(R \text{ and } F)_2|(R \text{ and } F)_1]$$

$$= P(R_1) \times P(F_1|R_1)$$

$$\times P[(R_2) \times (F_2|R_2)|(R \text{ and } F)_1]$$

$$= \left[\frac{39}{100} \times \frac{29}{39}\right] \times \left[\frac{38}{99} \times \frac{28}{38}\right]$$

$$= 0.082 \text{ or } 8.2\%$$

Or the simplified way is to recognize that of the 100 senators, 29 are Republicans who favor SDI. Thus, $P(RF_1) = 29/100$. On the second draw, 28 of the remaining 99 senators are Republicans favorable to SDI. The $P(RF_2) = 28/99$. Then

$$P(R \text{ and } F)_1 \times P[(R \text{ and } F)_2|(R \text{ and } F)_1]$$

$$= \frac{29}{100} \times \frac{28}{99}$$

$$= 0.082$$

e. If only one senator is selected at random, the probability he or she

1. Is a Republican who favors SDI is

$$P(R \text{ and } F) = P(R) \times P(F|R)$$

$$= \frac{39}{100} \times \frac{29}{39} = 0.29$$

Or, merely recognizing that 29 of the 100 senators are Republicans favorable to SDI,

$$P(R \text{ and } F) = \frac{29}{100} = 0.29$$

2. Is a Republican or favors SDI is

$$P(\text{R or F}) = P(\text{R}) + P(\text{F}) - P(\text{R and F})$$

$$= \frac{39}{100} + \frac{53}{100} - \frac{29}{100}$$

$$= \frac{63}{100}$$

3. Is either a Democrat or does not support SDI is

$$P(\text{D or } \overline{\text{F}}) = P(\text{D}) + P(\overline{\text{F}}) - P(\text{D and } \overline{\text{F}})$$

$$= P(\text{D}) + P(\overline{\text{F}}) - [P(\text{D}) \times P(\overline{\text{F}} | \text{D})]$$

$$= \frac{56}{100} + \frac{47}{100} - \left[\frac{56}{100} \times \frac{35}{56}\right]$$

$$= \frac{56}{100} + \frac{47}{100} - \frac{35}{100}$$

$$= \frac{68}{100}$$

f. The president of the United States wishes to determine the probability of choosing five senators, all of whom favored SDI.

$$P(5 \text{ favor}) = P(\text{F}_1 \text{ and F}_2 \text{ and F}_3 \text{ and F}_4 \text{ and F}_5)$$

$$= \frac{53}{100} \times \frac{52}{99} \times \frac{51}{98} \times \frac{50}{97} \times \frac{49}{96}$$

$$= \frac{344,362,200}{9,034,502,400}$$

$$= 0.038$$

Or,

$$P(5 \text{ favor}) = \frac{_{53}C_5}{_{100}C_5}$$

$$= \frac{2,869,685}{75,287,520}$$

$$= 0.038$$

Here, $_{53}C_5$ is the number of ways the event all five favor can occur—that is, the number of ways the president can pick 5 of the 53 senators who support SDI; and $_{100}C_5$ is the number of total possible outcomes—the number of ways the president can pick 5 out of the 100 senators.

g. The president wished to know the probability of choosing five senators, four of whom supported SDI:

$$P(4 \text{ out of 5 favor}) = P(F_1 \text{ and } F_2 \text{ and } F_3 \text{ and } F_4 \text{ and } \overline{F}_5) = \frac{53}{100} \times \frac{52}{99} \times \frac{51}{98} \times \frac{50}{97} \times \frac{47}{96}$$

$$= \frac{330,306,600}{9,034,502,400}$$

$$= 0.037$$

$$+ P(F_1 \text{ and } F_2 \text{ and } F_3 \text{ and } \overline{F}_4 \text{ and } F_5) = \frac{53}{100} \times \frac{52}{99} \times \frac{51}{98} \times \frac{47}{97} \times \frac{50}{96}$$

$$= 0.037$$

$$+ P(F_1 \text{ and } F_2 \text{ and } \overline{F}_3 \text{ and } F_4 \text{ and } F_5) = \frac{53}{100} \times \frac{52}{99} \times \frac{47}{98} \times \frac{51}{97} \times \frac{50}{96}$$

$$= 0.037$$

$$+ P(F_1 \text{ and } \overline{F}_2 \text{ and } F_3 \text{ and } F_4 \text{ and } F_5) = \frac{53}{100} \times \frac{47}{99} \times \frac{52}{98} \times \frac{51}{97} \times \frac{50}{96}$$

$$= 0.037$$

$$+ P(\overline{F}_1 \text{ and } F_2 \text{ and } F_3 \text{ and } F_4 \text{ and } F_5) = \frac{47}{100} \times \frac{53}{99} \times \frac{52}{98} \times \frac{51}{97} \times \frac{50}{96}$$

$$= 0.037$$

Thus, $0.037 \times 5 = 0.185$

Or,

$$P(4 \text{ out of 5 favor}) = \frac{\text{Number of ways to draw 1 who does not favor and 4 who favor}}{\text{Number of ways to draw 5}}$$

$$= \frac{_{47}C_1 \times _{53}C_4}{_{100}C_5} = 0.185$$

where $_{47}C_1$ is the number of ways to draw 1 out of the 47 senators who do not favor SDI, and $_{53}C_4$ is the number of ways to draw 4 from the 53 who favor SDI.

2. **The Effectiveness of State Lotteries** In 1988, 23 states were operating lotteries. James Thompson, governor of Illinois, requested a study to analyze the impact of a state lottery. Data seemed to suggest that those states with less than 1.5 million people were less likely to enjoy high revenues from the lottery game, while those with populations above that level were more likely to earn at least the $30 million. The data were first summarized for the governor's attention in a frequency table (Table 4-4), broken down on the basis of both population and level of earnings. The corresponding probability table is shown in Table 4-5.

It can be seen from Table 4-5, for example, that only 4 percent of the states with populations less than 1.5 million earned more than $30 million, while 65 percent of the

TABLE 4-4   Frequency Table for State Lotteries

	Lottery Earnings		
Population	**More than $30 million**	**Less than $30 million**	**Total**
More than 1.5 million people	15	2	17
Less than 1.5 million people	1	5	6
Total	16	7	23

TABLE 4-5   Probability Table for Lotteries

	Lottery Earnings		
Population	**More than $30 million**	**Less than $30 million**	**Total**
More than 1.5 million people	0.65	0.09	0.74
Less than 1.5 million people	0.04	0.22	0.26
Total	0.69	0.31	1.00

larger states earned revenues in excess of that amount. Only 31 percent of all states earned less than the $30 million level.

A probability tree produces the same results and appears as Figure 4-6.

FIGURE 4-6   A Probability Tree

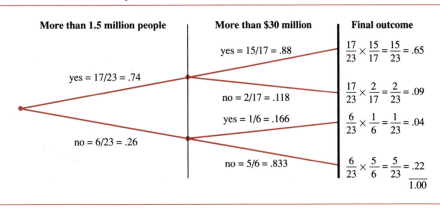

Conditional probabilities can also be determined from either the probability table or the tree. The probability of any randomly selected state having more than 1.5 million people is

$$P(\text{more than } 1.5) = \frac{17}{23} = 74\%$$

However, if you are given the additional information that the state earns more than $30 million on the lottery, you would wish to reverse your statement as to the probability that its population is in excess of 1.5 million. The probability that its population is more than 1.5 million given, that is, on the condition, that it earns in excess of $30 million can be calculated using Formula (4.7) for conditional probability as

$$P(\text{more than } 1.5 \mid \text{more than } \$30) = \frac{P(\text{more than } 1.5 \text{ and more than } \$30)}{P(\text{more than } \$30)}$$

$$= \frac{\begin{array}{c} P(\text{more than } 1.5) \\ \times P(\text{more than } 30 \mid \text{more than } 1.5) \end{array}}{P(\text{more than } 30)}$$

$$= \frac{17/23 \times 15/17}{16/23}$$

$$= 0.94$$

Or, it can be read directly form Table 4-4 as $15/16 = 0.94$. This example also illustrates Bayes' Rule.

3. **Winning at Churchill Downs** Thoroughbred racing at Churchill Downs permits a type of betting called trifecta waging. To win the trifecta, the bettor must pick the first three horses in order of finish as win, place, and show. If there are nine horses in the first race

   a. What is the probability of winning the trifecta if all horses have an equal likelihood of winning?

   $$P(\text{picking three winners in order of finish}) = (1/9)(1/8)(1/7) = 1/504$$

   b. How many possible trifecta finishes are there?

   $$_9P_3 = \frac{9!}{(9 \times 3)!} = 504$$

   Notice that the probability of winning reflects the number of possible trifecta finishes.

   c. Another type of betting at many race tracks requires the bettor to pick the first three horses in any order. How many possible finishes of this type are there?

   $$_9C_3 = \frac{9!}{3!(9 \times 3)!} = 84$$

4.13   WHAT YOU SHOULD HAVE LEARNED IN THIS CHAPTER

This chapter has provided a survey of the basic principles and rules of probability theory. You should now be able to determine the probability of single events such as drawing a king from a deck. You should also know how to calculate the probability of several mutually exclusive and several nonmutually exclusive events which require the two rules of addition. The rules of multiplication for dependent events and independent events should also be within your grasp. In short, you should have mastered the four primary rules of probability based on Formulas (4.5), (4.6), (4.7), and (4.8). By working the chapter problems which follow, the proper use of these rules should become more apparent and rather natural. It will be clear to you when to add and when to multiply.

The distinctions among the four counting techniques should be equally evident, as well as the techniques for conditional probability and Bayes' Rule. The construction of probability tables and probability trees also provides useful tools you should now be equipped to use.

In the following chapters you will rely on your understanding of the principles of probability to comprehend entire distributions of data and to determine the likelihood of certain events. You will investigate the manner in which these rules of probability can be used to make decisions and reach conclusions in common situations in the business world.

LIST OF SYMBOLS AND TERMS

Probability The numerical likelihood of the occurrence of some uncertain event.
Experiment Any well-defined action leading to a well-defined result. Example: drawing a card from a deck.
Outcome The well-defined result of an experiment. Example: a king.
Mutually Exclusive Events Events that cannot jointly occur. Example: rolling a die once and getting a six and an odd number.
Collectively Exhaustive Events The entire set of all possible outcomes of an experiment.
Independent Events Two or more events such that the occurrence of one has no influence on the occurrence of another.
Complementary Events Events such that if one does not occur the other must.
Permutations Arrangements in which order makes a difference and duplication is not allowed.
Combinations Arrangements in which order does not make a difference and duplication is not allowed.

LIST OF FORMULAS

$$P(E) = \frac{\text{Number of times the event has occurred in the past}}{\text{Total number of observations}} \tag{4.1}$$

Used to determine the probability of a single event under the relative frequency approach.

$$P(E) = \frac{\text{Number of ways the event can occur}}{\text{Total number of possible outcomes}} \tag{4.2}$$

Used to determine the probability of a single event under the classical approach.

$$P(E) = \frac{A}{A + B} \tag{4.3}$$

Determines the probability associated with given odds.

$$P(A \mid B) = \frac{P(A \text{ and } B)}{P(B)} \tag{4.4}$$

Used to determine conditional probability.

$$P(A \text{ and } B) = P(A) \times P(B) \tag{4.5}$$

Used to calculate the probability that both A and B occur under the condition that the two events are independent of each other.

$$P(A \text{ and } B) = P(A) \times P(B \mid A) \tag{4.6}$$

Used when the two events are dependent.

$$P(A \text{ or } B) = P(A) + P(B) - P(A \text{ and } B) \tag{4.7}$$

Used to determine the probability that either A or B will occur, given that A and B are not mutually exclusive.

$$P(A \text{ or } B) = P(A) + P(B) \tag{4.8}$$

Used to determine the probability that either A or B will occur given that A and B are mutually exclusive.

$$P(B) = P(A) \times P(B \mid A) + P(\overline{A}) \times P(B \mid \overline{A}) \tag{4.9}$$

Used in conjunction with conditional probability.

$$P(A \mid B) = \frac{P(A) \times P(B \mid A)}{P(B)} \tag{4.10}$$

Used for Bayes' Rule.

$$_nP_r = \frac{n!}{(n - r)!} \tag{4.11}$$

Provides the number of permutation of n elements taken r at a time.

$$_nC_r = \frac{n!}{r!\,(n - r)!} \tag{4.12}$$

Provides the number of combinations of n elements taken r at a time.

$$_nM_r = n^r \tag{4.13}$$

Provides the number of multiple-choice arrangements of n items taken r at a time.

CHAPTER EXERCISES

CONCEPTUAL QUESTIONS

1. Clearly distinguish in your own words among the features of the three approaches to probability. Under what circumstances would each type be more appropriate than the others?
2. Which approach to probability would be most appropriate under each of the following conditions?
    a. Rolling a die and noting the outcome.
    b. Trying to determine if the price of gold would rise or fall.
    c. Determining the likelihood that you will pass this course.
    d. Estimating the likelihood that your company's sales will increase next year given the government's economic forecast.
    e. A professional gambler or odds-maker establishing the odds on the winner of a prizefight.
3. What is the sample space assigned to the experiment of drawing a card from a deck and noting the
    a. suit?
    b. color?
4. What is the sample space in the experiment of observing the behavior of the price of a certain stock on the NYSE?
5. What is the relationship between probability and odds? How do professional gamblers ensure that they will win?
6. Define each of the following and provide business-related examples:
    a. Complementary events.
    b. Collectively exhaustive events.
    c. A union of events.
    d. An intersection of events.

PROBLEMS

7. What is the probability that
    a. you will be elected president of the United States in the next election?
    b. somebody will be elected president in the next election?
8. The odds that a new product offered by Tupperware will be successful are 5:1. What is the probability it will prove to be a success?
9. If the probability a certain boxer will win a prizefight is 80 percent,
    a. what betting odds will be set by the odds-makers?
    b. if you bet $12 on the boxer and he wins, how much do you get?
    c. if you bet $1 he will lose, how much will you win if he does lose?
10. What is the probability of
    a. rolling a die and getting a 3?
    b. rolling a die and getting an odd number?
    c. drawing a heart from a deck?
    d. drawing a jack from a deck?

11. Quick-Think, Inc., offers two types of computers: (1) the standard model and (2) the deluxe model. Each can be purchased with an optional hard drive. Construct a Venn diagram to show
   a. the standard models and the deluxe models.
   b. the standard models and those models with a hard drive.
   c. the standard models, the deluxe models, and those models without a hard drive.

12. What is the probability of
   a. rolling a die and getting either a 6 or an odd number and drawing a heart from a deck of cards?
   b. rolling a die and getting either a 6 or an even number and drawing a heart from a deck?
   c. flipping a coin twice and getting two heads and drawing a king from a deck?

13. Why is the probability of rolling a die and getting a 6 or an even number equal to the probability of getting an even number, while the probability of drawing a king or a spade is not equal to the probability of drawing a spade? That is, why is $P(6 \text{ or even}) = P(\text{even})$ while $P(\text{king or spade}) \neq P(\text{spade})$?

14. Prove $P(6 \text{ or even}) = P(\text{even})$.

15. In the Parker Brother's game of Monopoly, there are 40 spaces around the board. Four are railroads, 3 are chances, and 22 are pieces of real estate. Of the 16 chance cards you draw from in the event you land on one of the 3 chance squares, 8 are bad, 6 are good, and the other 2 depend on circumstances. If you have equal probability of landing on any square, what is the probability of landing on
   a. a real estate space?
   b. a railroad or a chance?
   c. chance and drawing a good card?

16. While playing the Monopoly game described in the preceding problem, you need to roll a 9 to win. What is the probability you do so?

17. *Forbes* magazine recently reported a survey of 50 U.S. corporations. It was shown that 32 use net present value (NPV) to make investment decisions. The rest use the internal rate of return (IRR) criterion. Of the 32 who use NPV, 27 always maximize stockholders' wealth. Of those using IRR, seven manage to always maximize stockholders' wealth. If you are to select a firm at random, what is the probability it
   a. uses NPV or maximizes wealth?
   b. uses IRR or does not maximize wealth?
   c. uses IRR and maximizes wealth?
   d. uses NPV or IRR?
   e. uses NPV and does not maximize wealth?
   f. uses NPV or does not maximize wealth?

18. Construct a probability table for the *Forbes* data on NPV and IRR in Problem 17. Circle the answers to parts (c) and (e) of Problem 17.

19. Given the information in Problems 17 and 18, use the rules of conditional probability to determine the probability that
   a. a firm will maximize stockholders' wealth if it uses the NPV method.
   b. a firm will maximize stockholders' wealth if it uses IRR.
   c. a firm that maximizes wealth uses NPV.

20. Many efforts have been made to use daily news events to explain the behavior of the stock market. Data were collected on daily changes in the Dow-Jones index and the major new item of the day for the 22 trading days in January 1989. Of the 12 days on which the index rose, the major new story was favorable 6 days, unfavorable on 2 days, and neutral on

4 days. Of the 10 days in which the index fell, news was good 4 days, bad twice, and neutral the rest. Find the probability that on any given day
a. the index rose and the news was good.
b. the index rose and the news was bad.
c. the index rose or the news was bad.
d. the index fell or the news was bad.
e. the index fell and the news was good.

21. Applying the principle of conditional probability, use the data from Problem 20 to calculate the probability that
a. bad news makes the market fall.
b. good news makes the market rise.
c. bad news makes the market rise.
d. good news makes the market fall.

22. From your answers to Problem 21, would it appear that the market rises in response to good news and falls in response to bad news?

23. Construct a probability table for the data in Problem 20.

24. Construct a probability tree for the data in Problem 20.

25. The Federal Savings and Loan Insurance Corporation (FSLIC) has found that 7 percent of the heads of households who have a home mortgage with a savings and loan association are currently unemployed. It has also found that 12 percent of all borrowers default on their loans and that 60 percent of all unemployed persons default. What is the probability that a borrower
a. is unemployed and will default?
b. is unemployed or will default?

26. The American Express Company found that 25 percent of the people in a recent survey owned an AE card and that 12 percent of the people surveyed had taken a trip to Europe. In addition, 6 percent of those in the survey had an AE card and went to Europe. The Quantitative Analysis Division of AE in Miami, Florida, wished to determine
a. the probability a person selected at random either had a card or went to Europe.
b. the percentage of people who, given they had a card, went to Europe.
c. what percentage of the people who had been to Europe had a card.

27. Mark buys three different stocks. The probability the first will rise in value is 1/3, the probability the second will rise is 3/4, and the probability the third will rise is 1/10. Determine the probability that
a. all will rise in value.
b. none will rise.
c. one will rise.
d. two will rise.
e. at least two will rise.
f. at least one will rise.

28. From a list of 12 growth stocks and 17 income stocks, an analyst must pick 2 for his client. What is the probability that
a. both are growth stocks?
b. the first is a growth stock and the second is an income stock?
c. one is a growth stock and the other is an income stock?

29. Recent figures released by the U.S. government reveal that on any given day the probability the dollar will fall against foreign currencies is 60 percent, the probability of a rise in

domestic interest rates is 35 percent, and the probability the dollar will fall if interest rates have gone up is 30 percent. Find

    a. the probability that on any given day picked at random, the dollar falls and interest rates rise.

    b. the probability that the dollar falls or interest rises.

30. In Problem 29, how can you prove that a drop in the dollar and a rise in the interest rates are not mutually exclusive events?

31. Given the information in Problem 29, what is the probability that if the dollar falls interest rates will rise?

32. *Fortune* magazine found that 10 percent of those workers in upper-level corporate executive positions were women and that 3 percent of those in the upper level were women with MBA degrees. The board of directors of a large corporation, whose executive profile fits this description, wishes to select one of their executive women at random. How likely is it that they will select an MBA?

33. Refer to Problem 32. It is also known that 25 percent of corporate executives hold MBAs. What is the probability of selecting a woman from among their MBAs?

34. Racetracks in Kentucky recently instituted the Pick-6 form of betting in which anyone feeling lucky can pick the winners of the first six races. If you pick your horses at random, what is the probability of walking away the big winner if there are 10 horses in the first race, 12 in the second, 8 in the third, 9 in the fourth, 10 in the fifth, and 8 in the sixth?

35. Refer to Problem 34. State regulations require that if no one wins Pick-6 for the day, the track declares as winner anyone who picked five winners out of the first six races. What is the probability of picking five winners if picks are random?

36. A major credit card company surveyed 1,000 people to determine if age made a difference in the use of credit in making major purchases. Based on the results shown in the table,

	Used credit	Not used credit	Total
Under 30	312	102	414
Over 30	280	306	586
	592	408	1,000

    a. what is the probability that a person who is under 30 uses credit?

    b. what is the probability that a person who is over 30 does not use credit?

    c. is the use of credit independent of age?

37. At a university fund-raising event, students pay $1 for the chance to throw a pie in the face of their "favorite" professor chosen from among those faculty who have volunteered for this hazardous duty. The student flips a coin twice. If the results are the same both times (two heads or two tails), the student's chosen target flips the same coin three times. If the professor does not get the same results all three times, the student hits the professor with the pie. However, if the student does not get the same results on both of his flips, and the professor does get the same results on his three flips (three heads or three tails), the professor gets to hit the student. Who is more likely to get hit with the pie, the student or the professor?

38. From Problem 37, what is the probability nobody gets hit with a pie?

39. Develop a probability tree for the E-Z-C Eye Care Center of Table 4-1. Note that the probability a frame is large and plastic is the joint probability found in the first cell of Table 4-2 and on the first sequence of branches on your tree.

40. Given the data in Problem 39, find the probability that, of those frames that are large, one can be selected that is wire. Where can this value be found on the tree you constructed in Problem 39?

41. Biggie Burger offers their burgers with a selection of five different condiments: mustard, pickle, ketchup, onion, and tomatoes. How many different burgers can you buy?

42. Your sweetie has changed his/her phone number. You know only the first three digits, but not the last four. What is the probability your sweetie will answer if you dial at random?

43. Auto license plates in Kentucky consist of three letters followed by three numbers. How many different license plates can be made?

44. Randy Rusty, owner of Rusty Used Cars, has eight cars with power steering, four with power windows, and three with sun roofs. How many different option packages can you choose from?

45. Studies by the National Education Association show that 30 percent of the nation's teachers leave the profession within 10 years. Furthermore, of those who leave, 60 percent have an advanced degree, while of those who do not leave, 20 percent have an advanced degree. Mr. Chips, the students' favorite teacher, just got his advanced degree. What is the probability he will leave the students behind and take a different job?

46. Seven people are on the Board of Governors of the Federal Reserve System. Four are Republican appointees, three are Democratic. How many committees can be formed of
    a. three Republican appointees and two Democrats?
    b. four people, of which no more than two are Democratic appointees?

47. Unable to find a date for your fifth high school reunion, you decide to check out the personal data files at Mother's, a video matchmaking service in San Bernardino. You have narrowed the prospects to 12 interesting possibilities, 7 of which have expressed an interest in your personal data file. You are going to further narrow your choices to only five candidates. How many groups of possible dates can you get if you want
    a. all five to consist of those who have expressed an interest in your data file?
    b. four who have expressed an interest in your file?
    c. at least three of the five to have expressed an interest in your file?

48. A certain manufacturing process is known to produce 10 percent defective units. A firm using the process has two plants, one in Chicago and one in Houston. The firm has found that there is a 20 percent chance the unit came from Chicago if it is defective and a 10 percent chance it came from Chicago if it is not defective. It has also determined that the same values for Houston are 5 percent and 15 percent, respectively. If management wants to select one unit at random to favorably impress potential customers, should it select a unit from Houston or Chicago?

49. A combat tactical team has 15 members. Five are demolition experts, and the other 10 are small-weapons specialists. In picking a squad of eight, the team's sergeant wants to be relatively certain that five of the eight are small-weapons specialists. Can he feel secure in that position?

50. Silent Servant, Inc. markets candy and other snacks in vending machines on college campuses throughout the Midwest. A new machine they were considering displayed a panel containing the numbers 1 through 9 and the letters A through G. After inserting the proper coins, customers selected one number and one letter to identify their choice. Will this machine serve Silent Servant's needs if they wish to offer 50 different treats for customers' selection?

51. The president must select 5 members from a list of 12 senators, of whom 7 support him and 5 oppose him. If he picks at random, what is the probability that a majority of the committee support the president?

52. The Botany Club at the local university is offering faculty the opportunity to choose from 10 types of trees. The faculty can then, at no cost, take the trees home and plant them. Professor Dozeoff is to select four trees, one for each side of his house. If due to sun exposure and other weather conditions, it makes a difference where he plants each tree, how many different sets of trees can be planted?

53. The Botany Club has 20 members. They are going to select a president, a vice president, a secretary, and a treasurer. How many different groups of officers are there?

54. Telephone numbers at the university have one prefix followed by four digits, such as 677-XXXX. The university has 10,001 phones to install. Will it have enough numbers to assign a different one to each phone?

55. Records for ABC, Inc. show that 60 percent of all sales are to former customers. Seventy percent of the time these former customers buy on credit. New customers buy on credit only 20 percent of the time. If customer buys on credit,
   a. what is the probability that customer is a new customer?
   b. what is the probability that customer is a former customer?

56. Patricia Pugh sells mobile telephones offering five styles, four colors, and seven service options. How many different phones can Ms. Pugh offer her customers?

57. *Entrepreneur* magazine carried an article describing how a new business could avoid bad-debt losses by calculating the probability a customer would default on a debt. Assume that of 100 customers, 20 are delinquent in payment (D), 12 are written off as bad debts (B) this month, and the rest have paid (P) their bills. You select three customers at random without replacement. If the selections can be indicated as, for example, B_1, D_2, P_3, meaning that the first was a bad debt, the second was deliquent, and the third was paid, what is the probability of
   a. D_1, D_2, D_3?
   b. B_1, D_2, D_3?
   c. P_1, B_2, P_3?
   d. D_1, P_2, P_3?

EMPIRICAL EXERCISES

58. Flip a coin 100 times (or 5 coins 20 times to reduce the amount of time involved). According to the classical approach to probability, how many heads should you get? How many did you get? Explain any difference that might result.

59. What would happen to the proportion of heads if you flipped the coin 200 times? Explain.

CASE APPLICATIONS

60. Rita Davis is manager of a plant in Toledo which manufactures glass products. She has recently been concerned about sagging productivity levels. The home office in Corning, Pennsylvania, has instructed her to take actions to reverse the slide in worker output. In this effort Ms. Davis has contacted Emerson Company, an educational reinforcement firm which specializes in the training and retraining of production line workers.

   Emerson has outlined two training programs for Davis's workers. However, Davis is unable to determine which plan would be more beneficial to her firm. Their first plan would cost Davis $5,000 to administer, while the second would require an outlay of $7,500. In her effort to select the more useful training program, Davis has learned that of all workers trained by Emerson, 80 percent showed improved productivity. This still does not answer the question as to which plan she should choose. She also is able to determine that given a worker showed improvement, there was a 60 percent chance he took the first training program and an 80 percent chance he took the second. Also, if no improvement was shown, there was a 20 percent chance he took the first training program and a 50 percent chance he took the second. Davis also figures that each 10 percent improvement in productivity will increase plant revenues by $1,000. On this basis, Davis hires you as a statistical consultant to assist them in determining which training plan is preferable. How do you respond?

61. A recent issue of *Fortune* magazine addressed the attempts by Dow Chemical to identify those employees with superior managerial potential. It seems that Dow administers a test to those employees who might have executive capabilities. Past evidence shows that 70 percent of the people are of managerial quality. Kyle Rogers, who is the director of personnel relations for the southern branch of Dow, has determined that the test correctly identifies a good manager only 80 percent of the time, and 10 percent of the time it incorrectly identifies someone as worthy of consideration for a management position who later proves to lack any managerial talent. Rogers recently administered the test to two people. One passed the test, and one did not. Rogers wonders how to interpret these results given that the test is not perfect. He had always felt that the person who failed the test had exhibited the qualities Dow seeks in its managers, and he therefore feels that, despite the test results, this person should be promoted and given a broader range of responsibilities. Rogers wishes to determine the probability that each of the people tested does possess management skills.

CHAPTER FIVE

PROBABILITY DISTRIBUTIONS

A PREVIEW OF THINGS TO LOOK FOR

1 Description of a probability distribution.

2 The difference between a discrete and a continuous probability distribution.

3 The various types of probability distributions and when to use each one.

4 How to calculate the mean and variance of a probability distribution.

5 Techniques used to evaluate queuing systems.

6 The use of lot acceptance in reducing the rate of defects.

CHAPTER BLUEPRINT

In this chapter we will examine the many ways in which probability distributions can be used to solve common business problems. Both discrete and continuous variables are examined. It should be quite obvious after reading this chapter that probability distributions have many applications in the business world, and can be quite useful in solving numerous business problems.

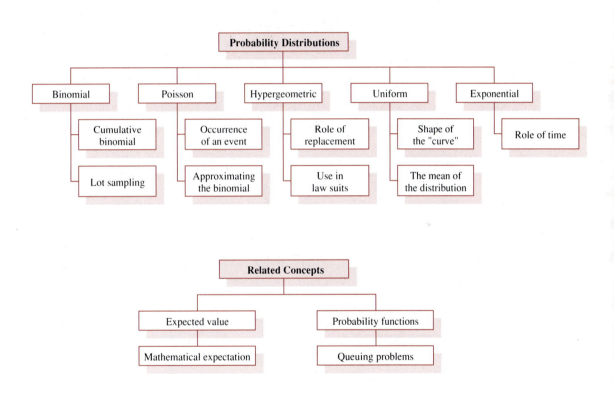

○○○○
○○○
○○
○

Statistics show the worse the haircut
the slower it grows out

5.1   INTRODUCTION

In the previous chapter we examined the concepts of probability theory. Our main objective was to determine how to calculate the probability of a single event or the probability of compound events. In this chapter we will define random variables and use the laws of probability to discuss the manner in which they relate to experiments. It will be shown how the entire set of events or outcomes for an experiment can be easily represented and expressed as a random variable.

A **random variable** is a variable whose value is the result of a random event. The experiment of flipping a coin and noting the outcome is an example. The specific outcome of a single flip, either a head or a tail, is an observation. In a more general sense, *the outcome of the flip* is the random variable. The value of the random variable (either a head or a tail in this case) is the result of chance.

Random Variable
A variable whose outcome occurs by chance is called a random variable. Number of units sold, daily levels of output, and the height of customers are examples.

Probability distributions are based on the outcomes of random variables. This chapter examines several different types of probability distributions including

- Binomial distributions.
- Poisson distributions.
- Hypergeometric distributions.
- Uniform distributions.
- Exponential distributions.

A **probability distribution** is a display of all possible outcomes of an experiment, along with the probabilities of each outcome. We found in the previous chapter that the probability of flipping a coin three times and getting (1) no heads is 1/8, (2) one head is 3/8, (3) two heads is 3/8, and (4) three heads is 1/8. The probability distribution is shown in Table 5-1. Notice that the probability distribution lists all possible outcomes, along with the probability associated with each outcome. Notice also that the probabilities of all possible outcomes sum to 1.

The same information in Table 5-1 can also be shown graphically as in Figure 5-1.

TABLE 5-1   Probability Distribution for Flipping Heads

Outcome (heads)	Probability
0	1/8
1	3/8
2	3/8
3	1/8
	1

FIGURE 5-1   Probability Distribution for Flipping Heads

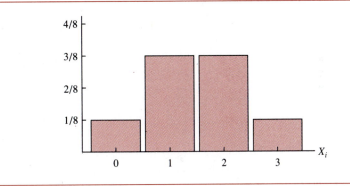

Probability Distribution
A probability distribution is a list of all possible outcomes of an experiment and the probabilities associated with each outcome as presented in the form of a table, a graph, or a formula.

The probability that the random variable X can take on some specific value, x_i, is written

$$P(X = x_i)$$

Thus, the probability that three flips of a coin result in two heads is

$$P(X = 2) = 3/8$$

Note that

$$0 \leq P(X = x_i) \leq 1 \quad \text{and} \quad \Sigma P(X = x_i) = 1$$

As a further illustration, a **uniform probability distribution** is a distribution in which the probabilities of all outcomes are the same. The experiment of rolling a die is an example. The probabilities of all possible outcomes (numbers 1 to 6) are all 1/6. The number that actually occurs in a single role is an observation, while *the outcome of the role* is a random variable and can take any value from 1 to 6. Figure 5-2 provides an illustration. Notice that all possible outcomes have the same probability of occurrence and therefore constitute a uniform probability distribution.

FIGURE 5-2   A Uniform Probability Distribution

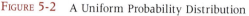

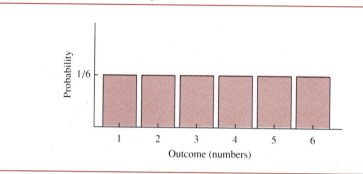

At this point it would prove advantageous to distinguish between (1) discrete probability distributions and (2) continuous probability distributions. As we noted in a previous chapter, variables can be discrete or continuous. An analogy can be made to probability distributions. The variable in a discrete probability distribution can take only certain values, usually whole numbers. It is most often the result of counting or enumeration. Flipping a coin several times and counting the number of heads or randomly selecting classes of students and noting the number of finance majors in each class are examples. In each case, fractional values are not observed. The use of a discrete random variable leads to the formation of a discrete probability distribution.

Discrete Probability Distribution
In a discrete probability distribution, the random variable can take only a distinct number of values. The number of customers, the number of units sold, or the number of errors in a printed advertisement are examples.

The variable in a continuous probability distribution can take any value within a given range. There are no gaps in the observations because no matter how close two observations might be, a third can be found which will fall between the first two.

A continuous probability distribution is usually the result of measurement. Daily measurements of snow fall at Vail, Colorado, and the mean time between failures (MTBF) of a new computer chip as measured in hours of operation are examples. If our instrument of measurement is precise enough, we could virtually get an infinite number of possible observations. The use of a continuous random variable leads to the formation of a continuous probability distribution.

Continuous Probability Distribution
A continuous probability distribution uses a random variable that can take an infinite number of values if the instrument used to take the measurement is precise enough.

Before our examination of several types of probability distributions, a word of explanation is in order. Monetary units such as the dollar cannot be broken down into a continuous and infinite number of divisions. The dollar, for example, can be subdivided only 100 times (cents). Measures smaller than 1 cent are generally not practical. However, despite the inability to achieve infinite subdivision, probability distributions dealing with monetary units are generally thought of as continuous probability distributions and will be treated as such hereafter. With that, let us begin our discussion of probability distributions, starting with discrete distributions.

5.2   THE MEAN AND VARIANCE OF DISCRETE RANDOM VARIABLES

Just as we found the mean of a data set back in Chapter 3, we can also find the mean of a probability distribution. The mean of a probability distribution is called the **expected value** of the random variable. The expected value of a random variable X is written $E(X)$ and is found by multiplying each possible outcome by its probability and then summing the results. Since the expected value is a mean, it can also be expressed as μ. Thus, we have for the expected value of a random variable X the expression

$$\mu = E(X) = \Sigma[(x_i)P(x_i)] \tag{5.1}$$

where x_i are the individual outcomes. The expected value of the experiment of rolling a die is

$$\mu = E(X) = [1 \times 1/6] + [2 \times 1/6] + [3 \times 1/6] + [4 \times 1/6]$$
$$+ [5 \times 1/6] + [6 \times 1/6]$$
$$= 3.5$$

Each outcome, the numbers 1 through 6, is multiplied by its respective probability and the results are summed. In this case, all the probabilities are equal since we are dealing with a uniform probability distribution.

Does this answer suggest that if we roll a die we can expect a 3.5 to appear? Hardly. It means that if we average the results from rolling a die many times (technically, an infinite number), we will get 3.5. In practice, the larger the number of rolls, the closer the mean is to 3.5.

Expected Value
The expected value of a discrete random variable is the weighted mean of all possible outcomes, in which the weights are the respective probabilities of those outcomes.

The variance of a probability distribution is conceptually the same as that variance we calculated in Chapter 3. It is the mean of the squared deviations from the mean. The variance σ^2 may be written as

$$\sigma^2 = \Sigma[(x_i - \mu)^2 P(x_i)] \qquad\qquad (5.2)$$

or

$$\sigma^2 = \Sigma[(x_i^2)P(x_i)] - \mu^2 \qquad\qquad (5.3)$$

For the experiment of rolling the die, with $\mu = 3.5$, Formula (5.2) produces

$$\sigma^2 = \Sigma[(x_i - \mu)^2 P(x_i)]$$
$$= (1 - 3.5)^2(1/6) + (2 - 3.5)^2(1/6)$$
$$+ (3 - 3.5)^2(1/6) + (4 - 3.5)^2(1/6)$$
$$+ (5 - 3.5)^2(1/6) + (6 - 3.5)^2(1/6)$$
$$= 2.92$$

Formula (5.3) yields the same results.

$$\sigma^2 = \Sigma[(x_i^2) \cdot P(x_i)] - \mu^2$$
$$= 1^2(1/6) + 2^2(1/6) + 3^2(1/6) + 4^2(1/6)$$
$$+ 5^2(1/6) + 6^2(1/6) - (3.5)^2$$
$$= 15.17 - (3.5)^2$$
$$= 2.92$$

EXAMPLE 5-1 A Probability Distribution

The investment firm of Loosit and Lye employs 20 investment analysts. Every morning each analyst is assigned up to five stocks to evaluate. The assignments that were made this morning were

Outcome (x_i) (number of stocks)	Frequency of x_i (number of analysts)
1	4
2	2
3	3
4	5
5	6
	20

a. Mr. Loosit wished to develop a probability distribution for the random variable of the number of stocks assigned to the analysts this morning.

SOLUTION:

The probability distribution must show each possible outcome, the number of stocks assigned to each broker, x_i, and the probability associated with each outcome. The value the random variable can take is some number 1 through 5. Thus, the probability distribution appears as

Number of Stocks (x_i)	Frequency	$P(X = x_i)$
1	4	4/20 = 0.20
2	2	2/20 = 0.10
3	3	3/20 = 0.15
4	5	5/20 = 0.25
5	6	6/20 = 0.30
		1.00

Or, the probability distribution might be expressed as

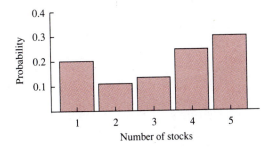

STATISTICAL INTERPRETATION:
If any analyst is picked at random, the probability that he or she will have five stocks to evaluate today is greater than any other single number. Only 10 percent of the analysts have two stocks to analyze before the day is over.

b. Mr. Lye determines the mean and variance for the probability distribution of the number of stocks assigned each analyst in the firm.

SOLUTION:
The mean becomes

$$\mu = \Sigma[(x_i)P(x_i)]$$

$$= (1 \times 4/20) + (2 \times 2/20) + (3 \times 3/20) + (4 \times 5/20)$$

$$+ (5 \times 6/20)$$

$$= 3.35 \text{ stocks}$$

Formula (5.2) is used to calculate the variance as

$$\sigma^2 = \Sigma[(x_i - \mu)^2 P(x_i)]$$

$$= (1 - 3.35)^2(4/20) + (2 - 3.35)^2(2/20)$$

$$+ (3 - 3.35)^2(3/20) + (4 - 3.35)^2(5/20)$$

$$+ (5 - 3.35)^2(6/20)$$

$$= 2.23$$

Formula (5.3) results in

$$\sigma^2 = \Sigma[(x_i^2)P(x_i)] - \mu^2$$

$$= 1^2(4/20) + 2^2(2/20) + 3^2(3/20) + 4^2(5/20)$$

$$+ 5^2(6/20) - (3.35)^2$$

$$= 13.45 - (3.35)^2$$

$$= 2.23$$

STATISTICAL INTERPRETATION:
The brokers are assigned an average of 3.35 stocks to evaluate and analyze. The variance of 2.23 carries the usual interpretation. It is a measure of the dispersion around the mean of 3.35.

QUICK CHECK 5.2.1

OOOO

Over the last 100 business days, Harry has had 20 customers on 30 of those days, 25 customers on 20 days, 35 customers on 30 days, 40 customers on 10 days, and 45 customers on 10 days. How many customers might he expect today, and what is the variance in the number of customers?

Answer: $E(X) = 30$ customers, $\sigma^2 = 75$

○○○○   **DECISION MAKING THROUGH PROBLEM SOLVING**   ○○○○
ILLUSTRATION 5-1

According to the stockbrokers working in the Paine Webber brokerage office in San Jose, California, it was the common practice of the office manager to calculate the typical number of accounts each broker in the office might expect to manage on a regular basis. This was done much like the circumstance depicted in Example 5-1. Although the actual numbers were quite different from those used for illustration in the example, the purpose was to measure brokers' workloads and aid in decisions regarding the assignment of new "walk-in" accounts.

The next three sections treat different types of discrete probability distributions which have a wide application to problems often encountered. Specifically, we will examine (1) binomial distributions, (2) Poisson distributions, and (3) hypergeometric distributions.

5.3 THE BINOMIAL DISTRIBUTION

The experiment with the coin flip discussed above has only two possible outcomes: (1) head or (2) tail. The probability of each is known and constant from one trial (flip) to the next. In addition, the experiment can be repeated many times, yielding a large number of trials.

Experiments of this type follow a **binomial distribution.** Based on the Bernoulli process, named for Jacob Bernoulli (1654–1705), a member of a family of Swiss mathematicians, a binomial distribution must fit certain conditions:

1. There must be only two possible outcomes. One is identified as a success, the other as a failure. However, you are warned not to attach any connotation of "good" or "bad" to these terms. They are quite objective, and a "success" does not necessarily imply a desirable outcome.
2. The probability of a success, π, remains constant from one trial to the next, as does the probability of a failure, $1 - \pi$.
3. The probability of a success in one trial is totally independent of any other trial.
4. The experiment can be repeated many times.

It should be apparent why the coin flip fits the requirements for a binomial distribution:

1. There are only two possible outcomes, and we can call a tail a success.
2. The probability of a success remains constant at $\pi = 0.5$ for all flips.
3. The probability of a success on any flip is not affected by the results of any other flip.
4. A coin may be flipped many times.

Many business-related examples can also be cited. Labor unions often want to know how many workers (1) are interested in joining a union as opposed to those who (2) are not interested. Bankers may survey economic experts as to whether they feel interest rates (1) will go up or (2) not go up. Marketing personnel want to know if a person (1) does or (2) does not prefer a certain product. The application of the binomial distribution to business settings is almost unlimited.

A Binomial Distribution
Each trial in a binomial distribution results in one of only two mutually exclusive outcomes, one of which is identified as a success and the other as a failure. The probability of each remains constant from one trial to the next.

If we know the probability that any given trial will result in a success, it is possible to estimate how many successes there will be in a given number of trials. For example, if the probability that any single worker is interested in joining a union is known, then, the probability that any given number of workers in the labor force would be interested in joining can be estimated. The probability that out of n number of workers, a given number x would be interested in joining is

$$
P(x) = \frac{n!}{x!\,(n-x)!}\,\pi^x(1-\pi)^{n-x}
$$
$$
= \,_nC_x(\pi)^x(1-\pi)^{n-x}
$$

(5.4)

Although the formula looks rather formidable, do not despair. Probabilities for different values of π, x, and n have been calculated for you and tabulated in Table B in the back of the book. You need only learn how to read the table. Consider the following situation. A credit manager for American Express has found that $\pi = 10\%$ of their card users do not pay the full amount of indebtedness during any given month. She wants to determine the probability that of $n = 20$ accounts randomly selected, $x = 5$ of them are not paid. This can be written as $P(X = 5\,|\,n = 20, \pi = 0.10)$, which is read as "the probability of five successes given that there are 20 trials and the probability of a success on any one trial is 10 percent."
Does this set of circumstances fit the conditions for a binomial distribution?

There are only two possible outcomes. Either the account (1) is or (2) is not paid in full. We can assign the identity of a success to an account which is not paid, and a failure to one that is.
The probability of a success remains constant at $\pi = 0.10$ from one trial (account) to the next.

The probability one person pays off his or her account is independent of
whether someone else pays.

Last, there are many different accounts available for examination.

Clearly, the binomial distribution applies, and we can use it to solve the credit manager's problem.

The probability that 5 accounts out of the 20 sampled remain unpaid can be calculated by using Formula (5.4). Where $n = 20$, $X = 5$, and $\pi = 0.10$, we have

$$_{20}C_5(0.10)^5(0.90)^{20-5} = (15504)(0.00001)(0.2058911) = 0.0319$$

If the probability that any one account is not paid in full is $\pi = 0.10$, then there is
a 3.19 percent chance that exactly 5 of 20 accounts selected at random will retain a
positive balance.

This information is more readily attained through the use of Table B. Notice that
the first two columns in the table show possible values for n and X. Locate the value
of 20 for n since there are 20 trails (accounts) in our experiment. Since the credit
manager seeks the probability $X = 5$ successes (unpaid accounts), locate the row
containing probability values for $X = 5$. Proceed across that row until you find the
column headed by $\pi = 0.10$. There you will find the value 0.0319, the answer to the
credit manager's question.

Consider this second example of binomial distribution. Sales personnel for Widgets, Inc. make a sale to 15 percent of the customers on whom they call. If a member
of the sales staff calls on 15 customers today, what is the probability he or she will
sell exactly two widgets? Given $\pi = 0.15$, $n = 15$, and $X = 2$, locate the value for
$n = 15$, then the row pertaining to $X = 2$. In that row headed by the column
$\pi = 0.15$, you will find $P(X = 2 | n = 15, \pi = 0.15) = 0.2856$. There is a 28.56 percent chance that exactly 2 sales will be made out of 15 sales calls.

EXAMPLE 5-2 Summer Jobs and Some Are Not

According to the *Journal of Higher Education*, 40 percent of all high school graduates work during the summer to earn money for college tuition for the upcoming fall
term. If 18 graduates are selected at random, what is the probability that (a) 12 have
summer jobs, (b) none work, (c) all work?

SOLUTION:

a. Locate the value for $n = 18$ and the column headed by $\pi = 0.40$. The row
corresponding to $X = 12$ yields a value of 0.0145. There is a 1.45 percent
probability that 12 of the 18 graduates have taken summer jobs to earn tuition
money.

b. Given $n = 18$ and $\pi = 0.40$, the probability that none work is shown in the
table to be $P(X = 0) = 0.0001$.

c. $P(X = 18 | n = 18, \pi = 0.4) = 0.0000$.

STATISTICAL INTERPRETATION:

It is highly unlikely that either none or all of the students work.

○○○○   DECISION MAKING THROUGH PROBLEM SOLVING   ○○○○
ILLUSTRATION 5-2

Business applications of the binomial distribution are almost limitless. A recent issue of *Fortune* carried a news story about a rather interesting manner in which the binomial distribution played a role in uncovering the "great Florida oil scam." It seems Stephen L. Smith was running a phony oil-drilling business in his home town of Winter Haven, Florida. Although he owned no oil wells, Smith told prospective investors that he could produce at least a 60 percent return on their money. He then defrauded "bankers, grandmothers, people with whom he double-dated at Winter Haven High School," and many others out of vast sums of money. He kept the scam alive by recycling money from new investors into dividends for existing ones, with a fat cut for himself.

His downfall was precipitated by his extraordinary record of "success." He reported only 6 dry holes out of the last 120. Given the probability that a well is either (1) a dry hole or (2) a producer, Fred Meyer, an experienced land assessor and friend of one of Smith's investors, knew that it was extremely unlikely that anyone could be so lucky. Further investigation revealed that Smith was a con artist. By the time he was caught, Smith had amassed a fortune of $74 million and bilked some 700 investors out of $130 million.

The next example has a slight twist to it. Assume that the probability of making a sale for Widgets, Inc. is $\pi = 60\%$. What is the probability that 2 of the 15 customers will buy. Direct use of the table is prohibited since values for π only go up to 0.50. We must therefore make a slight transformation of the data. If the probability of a sale is 0.60, the probability of not selling on any single visit is 0.40. Thus, instead of finding the probability of selling 2 widgets out of 15 trials with $\pi = 0.6$, we find the probability of not selling 13 out of 15 trials with $\pi = 0.4$. This is done by locating values for n and X of 15 and 13, respectively. The answer 0.0003 is then found in the column headed by $\pi = 0.40$. In the event that $\pi > 0.5$, we must find the complement of the event, which will ensure that π becomes less than 0.5.

EXAMPLE 5-3 Herman's Transformation

Records show that the firm's computer is up and running 80 percent of the time. Herman, the firm's resident computer jock, examines the computer nine times. What is the probability that it is functional three times?

SOLUTION:

This problem calls for $n = 9$, $X = 3$, and $\pi = 0.80$. That is, $P(X = 3 \mid n = 9, \pi = 0.80)$. However, since Table B has values for π only up to 0.50, we must find the probability of $n = 6$ successes $(9 - 3)$ if $\pi = 0.20$ $(1.00 - 0.80)$. Thus, $P(X = 6 \mid n = 9, \pi = 0.20)$ is 0.0028. There is less than a 1 percent chance that the computer will be running exactly three of the nine times Herman inspects it.

STATISTICAL INTERPRETATION:

When the value for π exceeds 0.50, it is necessary to adjust the level of X and π.

A. Cumulative Binomial Probability

In our Widgets, Inc. example we found the probability of selling exactly two widgets out of 15 sales calls to be 0.2856 if the probability of sale on any single call was $\pi = 15\%$. Suppose, instead, we were interested in the probability of selling at most two widgets (two or less) from those 15 calls. This event would be satisfied if we sold zero widgets or one widget or two widgets. The presence of the *or* reveals the need to add the respective probabilities of each of these three sales levels. This procedure involves **cumulative binomial probability.**

Cumulative Binomial Probability
Cumulative binomial probability measures the probability of some event over a range of values.

Cumulative binomial probabilities can be found in Table C, which shows the probability that the random variable is equal to or less than some value. To illustrate the use of the table, locate values for $n = 15$, $X = 2$, and $\pi = 0.15$. Given these values, we find $P(X \le 2) = 0.6042$. Thus, the probability of selling two or fewer widgets is 60.42 percent.

Since the event of selling not more than two widgets can be satisfied over a range of values (zero, one, or two widgets), this problem involves cumulative binomial probability. If, as in our earlier example, the event is satisfied by only one value, such as selling exactly two widgets, we are dealing with a binomial distribution.

Example 5-4 Identifying Defects

A common business application of the binomial distribution is determining the probability of selecting a certain number of defective units. *Nation's Business* described the process by which Jerrico, Inc., the holding company for several national restaurant chains, including Long John Silver Seafood Shoppe, classifies shipments of food products. A shipment of chicken planks comes in boxes of 20. It is Jerrico's policy to classify a shipment as "acceptable" if no more than two boxes (two or fewer) are spoiled. It is assumed that the probability that any box is spoiled is independent of any other box.

If a shipment of 20 boxes of chicken planks is received, what is the probability that the shipment will be accepted if the probability that any randomly selected box is spoiled is 10 percent.

Solution:

Since 10 percent of the boxes are spoiled, $\pi = 0.10$. That is, 10 percent of the boxes are "successes" (spoiled). In Table C, locate the values for $n = 20$ and $\pi = 0.10$. The value corresponding to X of 2 shows the cumulative probability that the number of boxes that are spoiled is 2 or less to be 0.6769. Thus, $P(X \le 2) = 0.6769$. There is a 67.69 percent chance that two or fewer boxes will be spoiled and the shipment will be accepted.

STATISTICAL INTERPRETATION:

Although the exact numbers used by Jerrico have been changed for the sake of simplicity in this illustration, it can be seen how a business might find a useful purpose for the binomial distribution.

Earlier, the managers at Widgets, Inc. wanted to find the probability that no more than 2 sales would be made: $P(X \leq 2 | n = 15, \pi = 0.15)$. Now suppose they are interested in determining the likelihood that 2 or more sales are made: $P(X \geq 2 | n = 15, \pi = 0.15)$. Table C provides only those probabilities for random variables that are equal to or less than some amount. Now the Widget manager wants to ascertain the probability that the value of the random variable is equal to or greater than some amount.

This is accomplished by using the rule of complements:

$$P(A) = 1 - P(\overline{A})$$

Thus,

$$P(X \geq 2) = 1.00 - P(X \leq 1)$$

$$= 1.00 - 0.3186$$

$$= 0.6814$$

Instead of finding the probability of 2 or more successes, find the complement of 1 or less, and subtract from 1.00.

B.   MEAN AND VARIANCE OF A BINOMIAL DISTRIBUTION

The mean and variance for a binomial distribution are calculated as

$$\mu = n\pi \qquad (5.5)$$

and

$$\sigma^2 = n\pi(1 - \pi) \qquad (5.6)$$

where n is the number of trials and π is the probability of a success on any given trial. Thus, we would expect that on the average there are $n\pi$ successes out of n trials. Sales personnel for Widgets, Inc., who make 15 calls, with a probability of a sale on any call of 0.15, should average $\mu = 15(0.15) = 2.25$ sales for every 15 sales calls. If a salesperson makes 15 calls a day for many days, he or she will average, over the long run, 2.25 sales per day. The variance in the number of daily sales is

$$\sigma^2 = 15(0.15)(0.85)$$

$$= 1.91 \text{ widgets squared}$$

$$\sigma = 1.38 \text{ widgets}$$

C. LOT ACCEPTANCE SAMPLING

A common application of the binomial distribution relates to the decision whether to accept a shipment (lot) of goods from the manufacturer. This decision is based on how many defective goods may be in the shipment. Firms will generally return an entire shipment of goods if there is evidence that more than a certain number is defective.

CompStat, Ltd., a major producer of computer chips, has a 5 percent defect rate for their microprocessor chip. An important customer of CompStat orders 500 chips, from which a sample of 12 chips is to be selected. If more than 2 of the sample chips are defective, the entire lot of 500 will be returned to CompStat. What is the probability the lot is returned?

It will be returned if the number of defects is 3 or more; that is, if $3 \leq X \leq 12$. In this case it is easier to use the rule of complements, which says the probability of returning the lot is 1 minus probability of acceptance.

The lot will be accepted only if two or fewer chips are defective.

$$P(\text{accepted}) = P(X = 0) + P(X = 1) + P(X = 2)$$

Since $\pi = 0.05$ and $n = 12$, Table B reveals

$$P(\text{accepted}) = P(X = 0) = 0.5404$$
$$P(X = 1) = 0.3413$$
$$P(X = 2) = \underline{0.0988}$$
$$0.9805$$

The 0.9805 can also be found in Table C, where the values are already summed for you. Then,

$$P(\text{returned}) = 1 - P(\text{accepted})$$
$$= 1 - 0.9805$$
$$= 0.0195$$
$$= 1.95\%$$

If CompStat suffers a 10 percent defective rate ($\pi = .10$), the results are

$$P(\text{accepted}) = P(X = 0) = 0.2824$$
$$P(X = 1) = 0.3766$$
$$P(X = 2) = \underline{0.2301}$$
$$0.8891$$

$$P(\text{returned}) = 1 - 0.8891$$
$$= 0.1109$$
$$= 11.09\%$$

Further, if $\pi = 0.15$, $P(\text{accepted}) = 73.58$ percent and $P(\text{returned}) = 26.42$ percent.

If several such probabilities are calculated for different values of π, an **acceptance probability function** can be developed, as shown in Figure 5-3.

FIGURE 5-3   Acceptance Probability Function

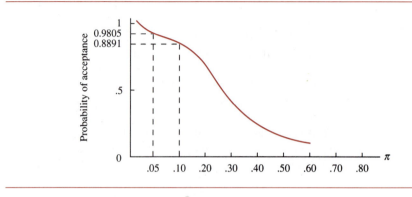

The acceptance probability function shows the probability of accepting a shipment for different defect rates. It aids a firm in deciding what acceptances standards to set as measured against the costs of retaining a shipment with a given number of defective units.

EXAMPLE 5-5 Trading with the Soviet Union

As relations with the Soviet Union have continued to improve, international trade between the USSR and the United States has increased. In response, *Izvestia,* the official Soviet government newspaper, sent 5,000 letters to Western business leaders soliciting advertisements from Western firms. Past data show that 20 percent of such ads contain typographical errors or errors due to translations from the Cyrillic alphabet.

1. If you were to examine 10 such advertisements, what is the probability you would find

a. $X = 3$ errors?
b. $X = 8$ errors?
c.   Between 2 to 5 errors (inclusive)?
d.   More than 2 errors?
e.   At least 7 errors?
f.   At most 7 errors?
g.   No more than 3 errors?

SOLUTION:

Since an advertisement either does or does not contain an error, and it may be assumed that the other characteristics of a Bernoulli trial are present, the binomial solution is called for.

a. $P(X = 3) = {}_{10}C_3(0.20)^3(0.80)^{10-3}$

$$= 120(0.008)\,(0.2097)$$

$$= 0.2013$$

b. $P(X = 8) = {}_{10}C_8(0.20)^8(0.80)^2 = 0.0001$

Table B yields these same results.

c. $P(2 \le X \le 5)$

$$= P(X = 2) + P(X = 3) + P(X = 4) + P(X = 5)$$

$$= 0.3020 + 0.2013 + 0.0881 + 0.0264 = 0.6178$$

Table B yields these same results, or Table C may be used:

$$P(X \le 5) - P(X \le 1) = 0.9936 - 0.3758 = 0.6178$$

d. $P(X > 2) = 1 - P(X \le 2)$

$$= 1 - 0.6778$$

$$= 0.3222$$

e. $P(X \ge 7) = 1 - P(X \le 6)$

$$= 1 - 0.9991$$

$$= 0.0009$$

f. $P(X \le 7) = 0.9999$

g. $P(X \le 3) = 0.8791$

2. If 100 advertisements were examined, how many errors would you expect to find? What dispersion in the number of errors might you find if you examined many sets of 100 advertisements?

SOLUTION:

$$\mu = n\pi = (100)\,(0.20) = 20 \text{ errors}$$

$$\sigma^2 = n\pi(1 - \pi)$$

$$= 100(0.2)\,(0.8) = 16 \text{ errors squared}$$

$$\sigma = \sqrt{16} = 4 \text{ errors}$$

STATISTICAL INTERPRETATION:

These answers can be verified by consulting Tables B and C and the proper formulas for the mean and standard deviation.

D. THE SHAPE OF THE BINOMIAL DISTRIBUTION

If $\pi = 0.5$, the binomial distribution will be perfectly symmetrical and can be illustrated as Figure 5-4(a). If $\pi < 0.5$, the curve will be skewed right. That skewness will increase as π decreases [Figure 5-4(b)]. If $\pi > 0.5$, the distribution will be skewed left, and the degree of skewness will increase as π approaches 1 [Figure 5-4(c)].

Holding π constant, as n increase, the binomial distribution will approach normality. Compare Figures 5-4(b) and 5-4(d). Notice that π is held constant, but Figure 5-4(d) displays a distribution closer to normality (less skewed) since n is larger.

FIGURE 5-4   Probability Mass Functions

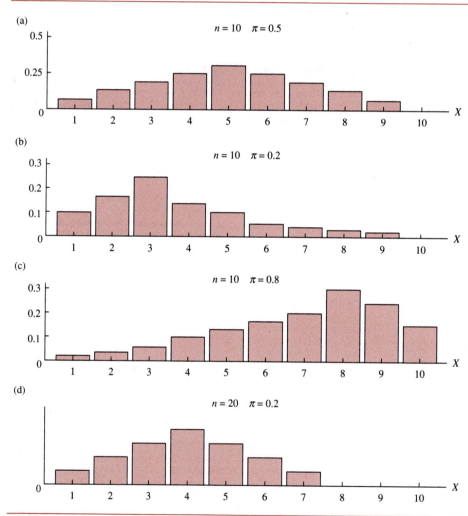

QUICK CHECK 5.3.1

○○○○ What is the probability of drawing five cards from a deck and getting (a) exactly three spades, (b) at most two spades, (c) at least three spades? Use the proper tables to obtain the answers.

Answer: (a) 0.0879, (b) 0.8965, (c) 0.1035

QUICK CHECK 5.3.2

If, on many occasions, you drew five cards from a deck and counted the number of spades each time, what would be the mean and standard deviation of the number of spades?

Answer: $\mu = 1.25$ spades, $\sigma = 0.968$ spades.

5.4 THE POISSON DISTRIBUTION

A discrete random variable which is highly useful in measuring the relative frequency of an event over some unit of time or space is the **Poisson distribution.** It is often used to describe the number of arrivals of customers per hour, the number of industrial accidents each month, the number of defective electrical connections per mile of wiring in a city's power system, or the number of machines that break down and are awaiting repair. In each of these cases, the random variable (customers, accidents, defects, machines) is measured per unit of time or space (distance).

> **Poisson Distribution**
> Developed by the French mathematician Simeon Poisson (1781–1840), the Poisson distribution measures the probability of a random event over some interval of time or space.

Two assumptions are necessary for the application of the Poisson distribution:

1. The probability of the occurrence of the event is constant for any two intervals of time or space.
2. The occurrence of the event in any interval is independent of the occurrence in any other interval.

Given these assumptions, the Poisson probability function can be expressed as

$$P(x) = \frac{\mu^x e^{-\mu}}{x!} \tag{5.7}$$

where x is the number of times the event occurs
         μ is the mean number of occurrence per unit of time or space
         $e = 2.71828$ is the base of the natural logarithm system

Suppose we are interested in the probability that exactly five customers will arrive during the next hour (or any given hour) of business. Simple observation over the past 80 hours has shown that 800 customers have entered our business. Thus, $\mu = 10$ per hour.

$$P(5) = \frac{(10)^5 \times 2.71828^{-10}}{5!} = 0.0378$$

Since this formula is a little awkward, probabilities for selected values are given in Table D. Go across the top of the table until you find $\mu = 10$. Go down that column to the row where $x = 5$. There you will find 0.0378. There is a 3.78 percent chance that exactly five customers will enter the store during the next 60 minutes.

A local paving company obtained a contract with the county to maintain roads servicing a large urban center. The roads recently paved by this company revealed an average of two defects per mile after being used for one year. If the county retains this paving company, what is the probability of one defect in any given mile of road after carrying traffic for one year?

$$P(1) = \frac{2^1 \times 2.71828^{-2}}{1!} = 0.2707$$

or 27.1 percent. To use Table D, find the column where $\mu = 2$ and the row where $x = 1$. There you will find the value 0.2707.

The Poisson distribution is also useful as an approximation for binomial probabilities. This approximation is often necessary if the number of trials is large, since binomial tables for large values of n are often not available. The approximation process is permitted only if n is large and π is small. As a rule of thumb, the approximation is reasonably accurate if $n \geq 20$ and $\pi \leq 0.10$. If π is large, simply reverse your definition of a success and a failure so that π becomes small.

As an illustration, assume that industry records show that 10 percent of employees steal from their employers. The personnel manager of a firm in that industry wishes to determine the probability that from a sample of 20 employees, 3 have illegally taken company property. Then, using Table B for the binomial distribution, we find

$$P(3) = {}_{20}C_3(0.10)^3(0.90)^{20-3}$$

$$= 0.1901$$

This could be approximated by the Poisson distribution by letting

$$\mu = n\pi = (20)(0.10)$$

$$= 2.0$$

and $x = 3$. Table D reveals a probability of 0.1804, a difference of 0.0097. For larger values of n and/or smaller values of π, the approximation may be even closer.

○○○○　　　　**DECISION MAKING THROUGH PROBLEM SOLVING**　　　○○○○
ILLUSTRATION 5-3

Industry Weekly published the results of efforts by BioTech, a medical research center in Atlanta, to establish a company policy to deal with defective merchandise that had been returned by the firm's clients. BioTech knew that 6 percent of a particular chemical compound failed market specifications. The firm shipped this chemical in units of 50 containers. Using a Poisson distribution, BioTech was able to conclude that, given the chemical's price, the firm could absorb the financial loss associated with a policy which would allow clients to return the merchandise if three or more of the containers were defective. Based on a Poisson distribution, BioTech concluded that the probability that three or more would not meet specifications was small enough not to cause a financial burden.

Assume the personnel manager had a sample of 100 employees and wanted to know the probability that 3 were stealing from the company. Since the binomial table does not contain values for n in excess of 20, the Poisson approximation is required. Given,

$$\mu = n\pi = (100)(0.1) = 10$$

and

$$x = 3.$$

Table D yields a value of 0.0076. There is less than a 1 percent chance that exactly three employees are stealing.

QUICK CHECK 5.4.1
○○○○　　　Tennis players arrive at the courts at the average rate of 12 per hour. Assuming a Poisson distribution, what is the probability that exactly three will arrive in (a) the next hour, (b) the next minute?
Answer: (a) 0.0018 (b) 0.0011

QUICK CHECK 5.4.2
The probability of a success on a single trial is 0.30. Out of 50 trials, what is the probability there will be exactly 8 successes?
Answer: 0.0194

5.5　THE HYPERGEOMETRIC DISTRIBUTION

As we learned earlier, the binomial distribution is appropriate only if the probability of a success remains constant for each trial. This will occur if the sampling is done from an infinite (or very large) population. However, if the population is rather small, or the sample contains a large portion of the population, the probability of a success will vary between trials. For example, the probability of choosing a female from a group of 30 people consisting of 10 females and 20 males is 10/30. The probability of selecting a female without replacement on the second draw is either 9/29, if F_1 or 10/29 if M_1. In neither case is $P(F_2) = P(F_1) = 10/30$.

If the probability of a success is not constant, the **hypergeometric distribution** is particularly useful. The probability function for the hypergeometric distribution is

$$P(x) = \frac{{}_rC_x \, {}_{N-r}C_{n-x}}{{}_NC_n} \qquad (5.8)$$

where N is the population size
        r is the number in the population identified as a success
        n is the sample size
        x is the number in the sample identified as a success

The Hypergeometric Distribution
If a sample is selected without replacement from a known finite population and contains a relatively large proportion of the population, such that the probability of a success is measurably altered from one selection to the next, the hypergeometric distribution should be used.

Assume a racing stable has $N = 10$ horses, $r = 4$ of them have a contagious disease. What is the probability of selecting a sample of $n = 3$ in which there are $x = 2$ diseased horses?

$$P(X = 2) = \frac{{}_4C_2 \, {}_{10-4}C_{3-2}}{{}_{10}C_3}$$

$$= \frac{6 \times 6}{120}$$

$$= 0.30$$

There is a 30 percent probability of selecting three racehorses, two of which are ill.

Note the subtle yet crucial distinction between this example with the horses and the previous case dealing with Soviet typesetting errors. Why is the problem concerning diseased racehorses a hypergeometric distribution, while the typesetting problem involves the binomial distribution? In both cases there are only two possible outcomes: the horses are either (1) diseased or (2) not diseased, while the Soviet advertisements either (1) do or (2) do not contain errors. How can we distinguish the two distributions?

The distinction lies in the population size, especially as it relates to the size of the sample. In the case of the Soviet advertisement, you were told that of *all* past advertisements, 20 percent contained an error. Attention was then focused on only

10 of all those advertisements. In examining the newspaper advertisement, the probability of an error remained virtually constant since the population was so large compared with $n = 10$. However, regarding the horses, a sample of 3 was selected from a population of only $N = 10$ horses. Thus, the probability of a success was significantly altered each time an observation (horse) was chosen for the sample.

EXAMPLE 5-6 Use of the Hypergeometric to Examine Discrimination

In a recent case in Johnson District Court in Kansas City, three women brought suit against a local utility company charging sex discrimination. Of nine people who were eligible for promotion, four were women. Three of the nine were actually chosen for promotions. Only one of those promoted was a woman. The other three eligible women sued the utility. A major consideration in the case hinged on the probability that out of the three people promoted, no more than one woman could be chosen by chance. That is, if gender was not a factor, what is the probability that no more than one of the three promotions would go to a woman?

SOLUTION:

An economic consultant specializing in legal matters was called in by the defense attorney to address the charges. The economist calculated the probability that, in the absence of discrimination, only one of the women would be promoted. This calculation was based on

   $N = 9$: the number of people eligible for promotion.
   $r = 4$: the number in the population identified as successes (women).
   $n = 3$: the number in the sample (those chosen for promotion).
   $x \leq 1$: the number of successes (women) in the sample.

The probability that no more than one woman was promoted is $P(X = 0) + P(X = 1)$.

$$P(X = 1) = \frac{_4C_1\,_5C_2}{_9C_3} = \frac{4 \times 10}{84} = 0.4762$$

$$P(X = 0) = \frac{_4C_0\,_5C_3}{_9C_3} = \frac{1 \times 10}{84} = 0.1190$$

Thus, $P(X \leq 1) = 0.4762 + 0.1190 = 0.5952$.

STATISTICAL INTERPRETATION:

There was almost a 60 percent probability that without any consideration given to gender, no more than one woman would be promoted. On the basis of these findings, as well as other evidence presented in the case, the court ruled that there was not sufficient evidence of discrimination.

QUICK CHECK 5.5.1
○○○○
Of five cars on the lot, three have bad transmissions. What is the probability that if you select two cars, both have faulty transmissions?

Answer: 0.30

5.6 MATHEMATICAL EXPECTATION

As we have already seen, many of the rules of probability have their roots firmly implanted in humans' early lascivious efforts to develop games of chance. All of today's casino games are built on the principles of probability and are designed to ensure that the house, that is, the casino itself, has a bettor's edge and is therefore assured of winning more often than it loses.

When games of chance are being considered, the term **mathematical expectation** is used to describe the expected value of the payoff. According to Formula (5.1), the expected value of a random variable, $E(X)$, is $E(X) = \Sigma[P(x_i)x_i]$.

Suppose someone offers you the bet of flipping a coin three times. If you get all heads, you win $20, while two heads (and one tail) wins you $10. If you get one head (and two tails), you lose $12, and all tails causes you to lose $20. Should you take this bet?

The probability of three heads is 1/8.

$$H_1 \text{ and } H_2 \text{ and } H_3 = 1/2 \times 1/2 \times 1/2 = 1/8$$

The probability of two heads is 3/8.

$$H_1 \text{ and } H_2 \text{ and } T_3 = 1/2 \times 1/2 \times 1/2 = 1/8$$
$$H_1 \text{ and } T_2 \text{ and } H_3 = 1/2 \times 1/2 \times 1/2 = 1/8$$
$$T_1 \text{ and } H_2 \text{ and } H_3 = 1/2 \times 1/2 \times 1/2 = \underline{1/8}$$
$$3/8$$

The probability of one head is 3/8.

$$H_1 \text{ and } T_2 \text{ and } T_3 = 1/2 \times 1/2 \times 1/2 = 1/8$$
$$T_1 \text{ and } H_2 \text{ and } T_3 = 1/2 \times 1/2 \times 1/2 = 1/8$$
$$T_1 \text{ and } T_2 \text{ and } H_3 = 1/2 \times 1/2 \times 1/2 = \underline{1/8}$$
$$3/8$$

the probability of no heads is 1/8.

$$T_1 \text{ and } T_2 \text{ and } T_3 = 1/2 \times 1/2 \times 1/2 = 1/8$$

The details of this wager are outlined in Table 5-2.

TABLE 5-2   Mathematical Expectation

Event	Probability $[P(x_i)]$	Payoff (x_i)
3 heads	1/8	$20.00
2 heads	3/8	10.00
1 head	3/8	−12.00
0 heads	1/8	−20.00

The expected value of the payoff, that is, the amount you might expect to win, is

$$E(X) = (1/8)(20) + (3/8)(10) - (3/8)(12) - (1/8)(20)$$
$$= 2.5 + 3.75 - 4.5 - 2.5$$
$$= -0.75$$

This game has a negative expected value. Does this mean if you play the game, you must lose? No. You can win as much as $20. It means that if you play the game many times, you will, on the average, lose 75 cents for each time you have played. The **expected value** is the average amount you will win (or lose in this case) if you play the game often enough. Given the rules of this game, if you play a large number of times (theoretically, an infinite number of times) you will suffer a net loss.

EXAMPLE 5-7 Expected Value How to Win Your Own Caribbean Island

Gambling houses (or casinos) are poorly named. They don't gamble. All games of chance are constructed so as to have a negative expected value for the players, or gamblers, and a positive expected value from the standpoint of the house.

A popular gambling game on Barbados, an island in the West Indies, is called Two-fers. You are allowed to draw two cards without replacement. If you get two cards of the same suit you win $15 American. If you draw anything else, you lose the $5 you must put up to play the game. Should you play the game?

SOLUTION:
Where H is heart, C is clubs, D is diamonds, and S is spades, the probability of winning is

$$P(\text{winning}) = (H_1 \text{ and } H_2) \text{ or } (C_1 \text{ and } C_2) \text{ or } (D_1 \text{ and } D_2) \text{ or } (S_1 \text{ and } S_2)$$
$$= \left[\frac{13}{52} \times \frac{12}{51}\right] + \left[\frac{13}{52} \times \frac{12}{51}\right] + \left[\frac{13}{52} \times \frac{12}{51}\right] + \left[\frac{13}{52} \times \frac{12}{51}\right]$$
$$= 0.2353$$

The probability of losing is

$$P(\text{losing}) = 1 - 0.2353 = 0.7647$$

The expected value of the game is

$$E(X) = 0.2353(15.00) + 0.7647(-5.00)$$
$$= 3.53 - 3.82$$
$$= -0.29$$

STATISTICAL INTERPRETATION:
Should you play the game? Only if you feel lucky. Sometimes you win and sometimes you lose. But if you play the game often enough, you will lose an average of 29 cents every time you play the game. Or, if enough people play the game only once, which is what the casino is assuming will happen, the house will win an average of 29 cents for every gambler who tried his or her luck.

The fact that gambling games are rigged to favor the house is why casinos in Las Vegas can afford to pay outrageous sums to headline entertainers to sing a few songs to the now destitute gamblers who were tempted by lady luck.

QUICK CHECK 5.6.1

○○○○   You pay $5 to roll a die once. You will receive $1.50 for each dot that appears. Should you play the game?

Answer: The expected value is $5.25 > $5. On the average you will win.

5.7 UNIFORM DISTRIBUTION

At the beginning of this chapter the concept of a probability distribution was introduced with a uniform distribution. A more complete discussion of this important distribution is presented in this section. A **uniform distribution** is one in which every possible outcome has an equal chance of occurring. Figure 5-5 shows a uniform distribution in which all outcomes over the distribution's entire range of possibilities from its minimum of *a* to its maximum of *b* are equally likely.

FIGURE 5-5   A Uniform Distribution

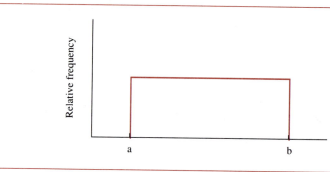

Uniform Distribution
The probabilities in a uniform distribution are the same for all possible outcomes.

The mean of a uniform distribution is halfway between its two end points. Thus,

$$\mu = \frac{a + b}{2}$$

(5.9)

The total area under the curve, as is the case with all continuous probability distributions, must equal 1, or 100%. Since the area is height times width, the height is

$$\text{Height} = \frac{\text{Area}}{\text{Width}}$$

and, therefore,

$$\text{Height} = \frac{1}{b - a} \qquad\qquad (5.10)$$

where $b - a$ is the width or range of the distribution.

Suppose the contents of the 16-ounce cans of fruit produced by Del Monte range anywhere from 14.5 ounces to 17.5 ounces and fit a uniform distribution. This is displayed in Figure 5-6. The mean is

$$\mu = \frac{14.5 + 17.5}{2} = 16 \text{ ounces}$$

FIGURE 5-6   A Uniform Distribution of Canned Products

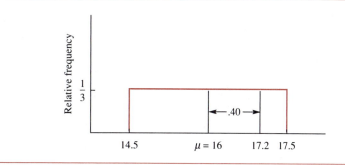

and the height is

$$\text{Height} = \frac{1}{17.5 - 14.5}$$

$$= 1/3$$

Assume Del Monte wanted to find the probability a single can weighed between 16 and 17.2 ounces. This value is provided by the area within that range as shown in Figure 5-6 and can be determined in two ways. The first method relies on the fact that area is height times width, and is calculated as $(1/3)(17.2 - 16) = 0.40$. There is a 40 percent probability that a can selected at random contains between 16 and 17.2 ounces.

The second method determines the probability a single observation will fall between two values X_1 and X_2 as

$$P(X_1 < X < X_2) = \frac{X_2 - X_1}{\text{Range}} \qquad (5.11)$$

For the Del Monte can, it becomes

$$P(16 < X < 17.2) = \frac{17.2 - 16}{17.5 - 14.5}$$

$$= 0.40$$

EXAMPLE 5-8 The Uniform Distribution and Fertilizer

Dow Chemical produces nonorganic lawn fertilizer for homeowners who fertilize their grass so they can mow it more often. One type of fertilizer is sold in bags with uniformly distributed weights with a mean weight of 25 pounds and a range of 2.4 pounds. Harry Homeowner needs 23 pounds to fertilize his lawn, but he is hesitant to buy only one bag since they deviate from 25 pounds over a range of 2.4 pounds. He is also curious about the probability of buying a bag with more than 25.5 pounds.

SOLUTION:

If the bags average 25 pounds over a range of 2.4 pounds, then one-half of that range, or 1.2 pounds, must be below 25 and the other half is above 25 pounds. Therefore the lowest weight is $25 - 1.2 = 23.8$ pounds, and the highest weight is $25 + 1.2 = 26.2$ pounds, as seen in the figure. The probability of selecting a single bag that contains between 25.5 and 26.2 pounds is

$$P(25.5 < X < 26.2) = \frac{26.2 - 25.5}{2.4} = 0.2917$$

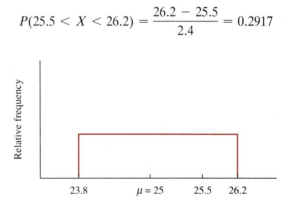

STATISTICAL INTERPRETATION:

Harry need not worry. The lightest bag he could buy is 23.8 pounds. He will definitely get at least the 23 pounds he needs for his lawn. In addition, the probability of selecting a bag with more than 25.5 pounds is 29.17 percent.

The standard deviation of a uniform distribution is difficult to show graphically, but is found as

$$\sigma = \frac{b - a}{\sqrt{12}} \qquad (5.12)$$

where b is the upper end point and a is the lower end point of the distribution.

QUICK CHECK 5.7.1

OOOO   A random variable with a uniform distribution has a mean of 40 and a lowest observation of 32. What is the probability an observation is between 42 and 47?

Answer: 0.3125

5.8   THE EXPONENTIAL DISTRIBUTION

The Poisson distribution is a discrete probability distribution which measures the number of occurrences of some event over time or space. It describes, for example, the number of customers who might arrive during some given period. The **exponential distribution** measures the passage of time between those occurrences. Thus, while the Poisson distribution describes arrival rates of units (people, trucks, telephone calls, etc.) within some time period, the exponential distribution estimates the lapse of time between arrivals. It can measure the time lapse as (1) the time that passes between two successive arrivals or (2) the amount of time that it takes to complete one action, such as serving one customer, loading one truck, or handling one call.

> **Exponential Distribution**
> Problems dealing with the lapse of time can often be approached by using the exponential distribution.

Exponential probability distributions are depicted as in Figure 5-7 by a steadily decreasing function which shows that the larger the value of the random variable, as measured in units of elapsed time, the less likely it is to occur. One-half of an hour is more likely to occur than is one hour, since one-half an hour must always lapse before a full hour can pass.

FIGURE 5-7   An Exponential Probability Function

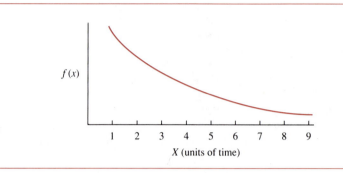

If the arrival process is Poisson-distributed, then the lapse of time between arrivals is exponentially distributed. Let μ be the mean number of arrivals in a given time period, and let μ^* be the mean lapse of time between arrivals. Then,

$$\mu^* = \frac{1}{\mu} \tag{5.13}$$

For example, if an average of four trucks arrive every hour at the loading dock ($\mu = 4$), then, on the average, one truck arrives every 0.25 hour. That is,

$$\mu^* = \frac{1}{4} = 0.25 \text{ hour}$$

A.   DETERMINING PROBABILITIES

Based on the relationship between Poisson and exponential distributions, it is possible to determine the probability that a specified time period will lapse given knowledge of the average arrival rate. The probability that no more than t units of time elapse between successive occurrences is

$$P(0 < X < t) = 1 - e^{-\mu t} \tag{5.14}$$

where μ is the mean rate of occurrence
$e = 2.71828$ is the base of the natural logarithm system

To illustrate the exponential distribution and the manner in which it relates to the Poisson, consider the following example. Trucks arrive at a loading dock at the mean rate of 1.5 per hour. What is the probability that no more than 2 hours will lapse between the arrivals of two successive trucks?

$$P(0 < X < 2) = 1 - e^{-1.5(2)}$$

$$= 1 - e^{-3}$$

The value for e^{-3} can be found from Table D, as it was for the Poisson. The trick is to set $x = 0$ and ignore the negative sign for μ. Thus, with the value of 3 for the exponent and $x = 0$, we find $e^{-3} = 0.0498$. Then

$$P(0 < X < 2) = 1 - 0.0498 = 95.02\%$$

The probability that a second truck will arrive within 2 hours of the first one is 95.02 percent.

EXAMPLE 5-9 Exponential Distribution for Cross-City Taxi

Cross-City schedules the arrival of their taxicabs at the local airport in a Poisson distribution with an average arrival rate of 12 per hour. You have just landed at the airport and must get into town to close a big business deal. What is the probability you will have to wait no more than 5 minutes to get a cab?

SOLUTION:
Assuming the worst, that the last cab just left, you seek

$$P(0 < X < 5 \text{ minutes})$$

Since μ is stated in terms of 12 per hour, it must be transformed to minutes to conform to the problem, which specified a time period of 5 minutes. Thus, $\mu = 12/60 = 0.2$ per minute.

$$P(0 < X < 5) = 1 - e^{-\mu t}$$

$$= 1 - e^{-(0.2)(5)}$$

$$= 1 - e^{-1}$$

$$= 1 - 0.3679$$

$$= 0.6321$$

STATISTICAL INTERPRETATION:
There is a 63.21 percent chance a cab will come by within 5 minutes.

It is necessary to ensure that the unit of time in which μ is expressed coincides with the time unit as stated in the problem. Instead of adjusting μ from 12 per hour to 0.2 per minute, it is possible to adjust the time period in the problem from 5 minutes to 1/12 hour. Then we would have

$$P(0 < X < 1/12) = 1 - e^{-(12)(1/12)}$$

$$= 1 - e^{-1}$$

which is equivalent to Example 5-9.

This concept can be approached from a slightly different angle. Assume that the average time it takes to service one customer is 5 minutes. Find the probability that it takes no longer than 10 minutes to service a customer. Notice that the information is given as time elapsed to perform one task (serve one customer) rather than the lapse of time between occurrences (such as the arrival of cabs). In such a case as this, it is necessary to restate the given information in terms of a single unit of time. Instead of expressing it as "the average time to serve one customer is 5 minutes," it must be stated as "one-fifth of a customer per minute." Therefore, the average rate of occurrence is $\mu = 1/5$ per minute. The probability that no more than 10 minutes will lapse for that occurrence is

$$P(0 < X < 10) = 1 - e^{-\mu t}$$
$$= 1 - e^{-(1/5)(10)}$$
$$= 1 - e^{-2}$$
$$= 1 - 0.1353$$
$$= 0.8647$$

There is an 86 percent chance you can service the customer within 10 minutes.

EXAMPLE 5-10 Exponential Distribution for the Completion of a Task

Faced by mounting competition from foreign imports, Markov Manufacturing sets a goal of completing a project on the average of every four days. After establishing a production plan to accomplish this goal, Markov finds that foreign operations can complete the project in 1.2 days. How likely is it that Markov can match this competition?

SOLUTION:

Since the data are expressed as time elapsed (four days) to perform one task (a project), it is necessary to restate the information as one-fourth of a project per day. Thus, μ becomes 1/4 per day. Then

$$P(0 < X < 1.2) = 1 - e^{-(0.25)(1.2)}$$
$$= 1 - e^{-0.3}$$
$$= 1 - 0.7408$$
$$= 0.2592$$

STATISTICAL INTERPRETATION:

There is only a 25.92 percent chance that Markov can complete the project within 1.2 days. Or, the results can be interpreted as only 25.92 percent of these projects Markov undertakes can be completed in 1.2 days.

Example 5-11 offers still a slightly different look at the exponential distribution.

EXAMPLE 5-11 Exponential Distribution and MTBF

Transistors produced by Bell Laboratories have a mean life of 25 hours. That is, the mean time between failures (MTBF) is 25 hours. As purchasing agent for your firm, you acquire 1,000 of these transistors.

a. What is the probability a single transistor will last more than 30 hours?
b. How many of them will last at most 20 hours?

SOLUTION:

a. If MTBF is 25 hours, then each hour you will use 1/25 of a transistor. Thus, $\mu = 1/25$ per hour. Then,

$$P(0 < X < 30) = 1 - e^{-(1/25)(30)}$$
$$= 1 - e^{-1.2}$$
$$= 1 - 0.3012$$
$$P(X > 30) = 1 - P(X < 30)$$
$$= 1 - 0.3012$$
$$= 0.6988$$

b. $$P(0 < X < 20) = 1 - e^{-(1/25)(20)}$$
$$= 1 - e^{-0.8}$$
$$= 1 - 0.4493$$
$$= 0.5507$$

There is a 55.07 percent probability that any transistor will last no longer than 20 hours. Then, of the 1,000 transistors you acquired, $1,000(0.5507) = 550.7$ of them will last at most 20 hours.

STATISTICAL INTERPRETATION:

There is a 30.12 percent chance that any given transistor will last more than 30 hours before failure. More than one-half of the units you bought, or 55.07 percent of them, will last at most 20 hours.

B. QUEUING PROBLEMS

The exponential distribution has a very common and useful application in business in the evaluation of waiting lines, or queues. Many business operations involve lines. Customers queue up for service, telephone calls come into a switchboard, trucks arrive at the loading dock, and machines break down and must be repaired. All of these situations and many others that commonly occur in business matters constitute queuing problems which must be effectively dealt with if the business is to operate efficiently.

Businesses strive to evaluate and improve their queuing systems. For example, businesses often want to determine the probability the queuing system is empty, or the likelihood that a given number of units are present. Exponential and Poisson distributions can be quite helpful in that effort.

The following discussion pertains to the simplest type of queuing system in which there is only one queue, or line, and only one point where a unit may receive service. Although a complete analysis of queuing principles cannot be presented here, even this brief examination will prove the importance of an efficient queuing system to business operations. Letting Λ (the Greek letter capital lambda) be the average rate at which units arrive for service per unit of time, and μ the average number of units that can be serviced in that same time unit, a queuing system can be evaluated on the basis of the following criteria:

$$P_0 = 1 - \frac{\Lambda}{\mu} \qquad (5.15)$$

where P_0 is the probability the system is idle; that is, there are no units in the system;

$$P_n = \left[\frac{\Lambda}{\mu} \right]^n (P_0) \qquad (5.16)$$

where P_n is the probability n units are in the system;

$$L = \frac{\Lambda}{\mu - \Lambda} \qquad (5.17)$$

where L is the average number of units in the system (those waiting for service plus the one receiving the service);

$$W = \frac{1}{\mu - \Lambda} \qquad (5.18)$$

where W is the average time a unit spends in the system waiting for service and receiving that service (waiting time plus service time);

$$L_q = \frac{\Lambda^2}{\mu(\mu - \Lambda)} \qquad (5.19)$$

where L_q is the average number of units waiting for service

$$W_q = \frac{\Lambda}{\mu(\mu - \Lambda)} \qquad (5.20)$$

where W_q is the average time spent in the queue waiting for service to begin.

Notice, for example that L and L_q differ in that the latter does not include the unit currently receiving service, but counts only those lined up behind it waiting for service.

EXAMPLE 5-12 A Queuing System for Minute-Mart

Minute-Mart, a popular convenience store selling smaller food items and offering fast service, became aware that during heavy traffic periods such as the noon hour and the hour following 5:00 P.M. when people left work, a queue sometimes formed at the cash register. Management felt that this delay posed a threat to the speedy service which attracted many customers. An investigation was ordered, which revealed that during these busy hours an average of 72 customers per hour entered the store. It took 35 seconds on the average to handle a customer who had queued up with his or her purchases. Minute-Mart wondered about the impact on business of this queuing system.

SOLUTION:

$$\Lambda = 72/\text{hour or } 1.2 \text{ per minute}$$

$$\mu = \frac{60}{35} = 1.7 \text{ per minute}$$

Note that Λ and μ must be expressed in the same time period. Then

a. The probability nobody is at the register is

$$P_0 = 1 - \frac{1.2}{1.7} = 0.2941$$

b. The probability that someone must wait is the probability there are two or more in line (if there is only one person in line, he is not waiting for service, he is receiving it)

$$P(\text{someone must wait}) = P(n \geq 2)$$

$$P(n \geq 2) = 1 - [P(n = 0) + P(n = 1)]$$

$$P_0 = 0.2941$$

$$P_1 = \left[\frac{\Lambda}{\mu}\right]^1 P_0$$

$$= \frac{1.2}{1.7}(0.2941) = 0.2076$$

$$P(n \geq 2) = 1 - (0.2941 + 0.2076) = 0.4983$$

c. The average amount of time spent in the system (time between when customer approaches the cash register line with his selections and time he leaves store) is

$$W = \frac{1}{\mu - \Lambda} = 2 \text{ minutes}$$

d. The average amount of time spent waiting for service (from the time when customer approaches the cash register with his selections to the time he begins to have his items checked) is

$$W_g = \frac{1.2}{\mu(\mu - \Lambda)} = 1.41 \text{ minutes}$$

STATISTICAL INTERPRETATION:

On the basis of the above evaluation, management must decide, for example, if waiting two minutes is too discouraging to customers seeking fast, convenient service. The other criteria of queuing evalution not calculated in this example might also prove revealing.

With only a little thought it should become apparent that queuing problems are common in assembly line manufacturing, customer relations, and most other aspects of business procedures.

5.9 SOLVED PROBLEMS

1. **The Impact of Television on Study Habits** In a national survey, the National Education Association asked 1,000 school-age children how many hours of TV per day they watched on weekdays. The results were

Number of Children	Hours of TV
20	0
53	1
89	2
155	3
315	4
253	5
115	6
1000	

a. Construct a probability distribution displaying the above information.

SOLUTION:

Outcome (hours of TV)	Frequency (number of children)	Probability
0	20	$20/1000 = 0.020$
1	53	$53/1000 = 0.053$
2	89	$89/1000 = 0.089$
3	155	$155/1000 = 0.155$
4	315	$315/1000 = 0.315$
5	253	$253/1000 = 0.253$
6	115	$115/1000 = 0.115$
		1.000

The probability distribution appears graphically as

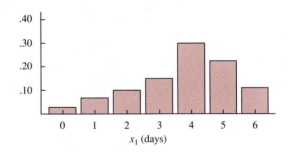

b. Is the variable continuous or discrete?

SOLUTION:
Although measurements of time are often continuous, in this case it is a discrete variable since the children responded only in units of whole hours and were apparently not given the opportunity to cite fractional units such as 3.5 hours or 4 hours and 15 minutes.

c. If one child were chosen at random, how many hours of TV would you expect him or her to watch?

SOLUTION:
This is determined by calculating the mean, or expected value, of the probability distribution.

$$\mu = E(X) = \Sigma[(x_i)P(x_i)]$$

$$= 0(0.02) + 1(0.053) + 2(0.089) + 3(0.155) + 4(0.315)$$

$$+ 5(0.253) + 6(0.115)$$

$$= 3.91 \text{ hours}$$

d. While the average time spent in front of the tube was 3.91 hours each day, not all 1,000 children watched TV for 3.91 hours. There was some variation above and below 3.91 hours. How would you measure that variation?

SOLUTION:
The variance and standard deviation would serve as a measure of dispersion. Using Formula (5.2), we have

$$\sigma^2 = \Sigma[(x_i - \mu)^2 P(x_i)]$$

$$= (0 - 3.91)^2(0.02) + (1 - 3.91)^2(0.053)$$

$$+ (2 - 3.91)^2(0.089) + (3 - 3.91)^2(0.155)$$

$$+ (4 - 3.91)^2(0.315) + (5 - 3.91)^2(0.253)$$

$$+ (6 - 3.91)^2(0.115)$$

$$= 2.013 \text{ days squared}$$

The standard deviation is $\sigma = \sqrt{2.013} = 1.42$ days.

2. **Survival Rates of Children** St. Jude's Children's Hospital in Miami, Florida, recently reported that only 40 percent of the children who suffer a particular accident survive. In March of 1989, St. Jude's had nine children who were hospitalized by the type of injury in question. As part of the effort to coordinate medical facilities, the hospital staff had to arrive at several difficult decisions.

a. What is the probability that all nine will survive? Since children either (1) survive or (2) do not survive, binomial probability is appropriate.

SOLUTION:

$$_nC_x\pi^x(1 - \pi)^{n-x}$$

$$_9C_9(0.4)^9(0.6)^0 = 0.0002621$$

The answer can be obtained from Table B.

b. Hospital facilities are currently capable of treating no more than five such cases on a long-term basis. Should the hospital consider borrowing necessary equipment from nearby hospitals or expanding in-house capabilities in anticipation that existing facilities will be overburdened?

SOLUTION:

$$P(X > 5) = P(X = 6) + P(X = 7) + P(X = 8) + P(X = 9)$$

$$= 0.0993 + 0.0743 + 0.0212 + 0.0035 + 0.0003$$

$$= 0.0993$$

Or $P(X > 5) = 1 - P(X \leq 5)$. From Table C, $P(X \leq 5) = 0.9006$. Then

$$P(X > 5) = 1 - P(X \leq 5)$$

$$= 1 - 0.9006$$

$$= 0.0994$$

The probability that six or more will need long-term treatment, creating a shortage in existing care facilities, is 9.94 percent. The decision to increase treatment capabilities would be made by hospital officials on this basis.

c. How many of the nine children might the medical staff expect to survive?

SOLUTION:

$$\mu = n\pi = (9)(0.40) = 3.6 \text{ children}$$

Three or four of the nine can be expected to survive.

d. If only 10 percent normally survive, how many can we expect to survive if 50 children are admitted?

SOLUTION:

Since π is relatively low and n is large, the Poisson distribution will more likely result in a more accurate approximation.

$$\mu = n\pi$$

$$= (50)(0.10)$$

$$= 5$$

3. **St. Jude's Emergency Room Facilities** St. Jude's has also reported that an average of 7.2 patients arrive in the emergency room each hour. The hospital administrator wants to know the probability that (1) exactly 10 patients arrive in any given hour, and (2) the probability the number of arrivals will exceed emergency room capacity, which is set for 15 patients.

SOLUTION:

Since the problem deals with the random occurrence of an event (arrival) over some interval of time or space (time, in this case), it requires a Poisson solution.

$$P(X = 10) = \frac{\mu^x e^{-\mu}}{x!}$$

$$= \frac{(7.2^{10})(2.71828^{-7.2})}{10!} = ?$$

From Table D, this is found to be 0.0770.

$$P(X > 15) = P(X = 16) + P(X = 17) + P(X = 18)\ldots$$

From Table D, we find

$$P(X = 16) = 0.0019$$

$$P(X = 17) = 0.0008$$

$$P(X = 18) = 0.0003$$

$$P(X = 19) = 0.0001$$

$$P(X = 20) = \underline{0.0000}$$

$$.0031$$

4. **In the Swim at Pismo** Lifeguards at Pismo Beach must pass a swimming test before being hired, which requires, in part, that the applicant swim from one point to another in
less than a stipulated time. Seven of the 22 applicants currently seeking a position can
qualify. The beach patrol at Pismo needs to hire three more lifguards. If 5 are selected at
random from the 22 applicants and are given a chance to pass the swim test, what is the
probability the beach patrol will fulfill its personnel requirements?

SOLUTION:
Either the applicant (1) can or (2) cannot pass the swim test. It might appear that this
problem entails a binomial distribution. However, such is not the case. This is a hypergeometric distribution because a population of only $N = 22$ applicants is being considered.
The sample of $n = 5$ is a significant portion of the 22 would-be lifeguards which make up
the population. Therefore, the probability of a success is not constant from one trial to
the next. If the $n = 5$ were selected from all potential lifeguards in California, and not
just these specific 22, then the binomial approach would be proper. However, in this case
we have

$N = 22$: number in population.
$r = 7$: number of successes (those who can pass the test) in the population.
$n = 5$: sample size.
$x = 3$: number of successes in the sample of 5 who can pass the swimming test.

Then

$$P(x) = \frac{{_r}C_x \; {_{N-r}}C_{n-x}}{{_N}C_n}$$

$$P(3) = \frac{{_7}C_3 \; {_{15}}C_2}{{_{22}}C_5} = \frac{35 \times 105}{26,334} = 13.96\%$$

5. **Piping Petroleum** Texaco, Inc. maintains a large oil field in western Kansas which moves
the petroleum by pipeline to a distribution center just outside of Norman, Oklahoma.
The rate at which the lines will move the oil is uniformly distributed between 30 and
35 barrels per minute.

Earl Coleman, the Midwest manager for Texaco, has been under pressure from his immediate superior, Bud Lester, to provide a full accounting of the Midwest operations.

a. Lester wants to know the average number of barrels moved per hour and any deviation in that average that might be expected. Thirty to 35 barrels per minute is 1,800 to 2,100 barrels per hour. Thus, Lester is told

$$\mu = \frac{a + b}{2} = \frac{1,800 + 2,100}{2} = 1,950 \text{ barrels per hour}$$

and

$$\sigma = \frac{2,100 - 1,800}{\sqrt{12}} = 86.61 \text{ barrels per hour}$$

b. Lester is worried that a production quota calling for the delivery of at least 1,900 barrels may not reach their destination within the next hour. How worried should he be?

$$P(X_1 < X < X_2) = \frac{X_2 - X_1}{\text{Range}}$$

$$P(1,900 < X < 2,100) = \frac{2,100 - 1,900}{300}$$

$$= 0.6667$$

There is a 66.67 percent probability that at least 1,900 barrels will be delivered.

6. **MTBF—Failure Rates for TV Tubes** A major manufacturer of TV tubes has learned that the average life of their product is 14.2 years, with an exponential distribution in mean time between failures. A potential customer with considerable buying power has a few questions before it agrees to a purchase contract.

a. The customer wants to know what percentage of the tubes will last more than 15 years.

$$P(X > 15) = 1 - P(X \le 15)$$

$$P(0 < X < 15) = 1 - e^{-\mu t}$$

We must determine μ, which is the mean number of occurrences per time period. The time period in question is stated in terms of years. If a tube fails on the average every 14.2 years, there will occur an average of $1/14.2 = 0.07$ failures each year. Thus, $\mu = 0.07$.

$$P(0 < X < 15) = 1 - e^{-(0.07)(15)}$$

$$= 1 - e^{-1.1}$$

$$= 1 - 0.3329 \quad \text{(using Table D)}$$

$$= 0.6671$$

$$P(X > 15) = 1 - 0.6671 = 0.3329$$

Then 33.29 percent of the tubes will last longer than 15 years.

b. The customer also wants to know the probability that at most 20 years will lapse between two consecutive failures.

$$P(0 < X < 20) = 1 - e^{-(0.07)(20)}$$

$$= 1 - e^{-1.4}$$

$$= 1 - 0.2466 \qquad \text{(using Table D)}$$

$$= 0.7534$$

5.10   WHAT YOU SHOULD HAVE LEARNED FROM THIS CHAPTER

The material in this chapter illustrates how different types of probability distributions can be used to provide answers to a variety of questions. The application of both discrete and continuous probability distributions is common practice under many different circumstances.

Proper use of these statistical tools is possible, however, only if you are certain as to when you must use one type of probability distribution in preference to another. Distinguishing between the binomial distribution and the hypergeometric is particularly difficult and requires special attention. It should also be remembered that the normal distribution, which is explored in the next chapter, is perhaps the most common distribution and is used throughout the rest of your study of statistics. A full understanding of its role in statistical analysis is essential. The Poisson distribution often proves its value in making many business decisions. No well-schooled business manager can do without a comprehension of its contribution to decision making.

5.11   COMPUTER APPLICATIONS

As is the case with most statistical procedures, our work can be greatly facilitated through the use of the computer. In this section we will again examine how computers can be used in our statistical pursuits.

MINITAB

The Minitab program also allows calculations of many of the statistics presented in this chapter. To determine binomial probabilities for the Widgets problem, at the MTB> prompt, enter

```
MTB > PDF;
SUBc>  Binomial   N = 15  p = .15.
```

It will give the probabilities of obtaining the specific number of successes as indicated. If cumulative probabilities are desired, enter

```
MTB> CDF;
Subc> Binomial   N = 15   p = .15.
```

The printout will reveal the probability of obtaining at least the number of successes as indicated.

It is possible to request from Minitab the probability of only a specified number of successes. Suppose, for example, you wanted to know the probability of at least 2 successes in the Widgets sales case where there were 15 trials, and the probability of a success on any single trial was 0.15. Simply enter

```
MTB> CDF 2;
Subc> Binomial n = 15   p = .15.
```

Minitab will respond with 0.6042.
The Poisson distribution is performed similarly.

```
MTB > PDF;
Subc > Poisson   mu = 10
```

It gives the probability of exactly a given number of occurrences.

```
MTB > CDF;
Subc > Poisson   mu = 10.
```

It reveals the probability of at least a certain number of occurrences.

Minitab does exponential distribution slightly differently. Suppose we wished to calculate the probability of catching the Cross-City taxi in Example 5-9. The average arrival rate was 12 per hour or 0.2 per minute. We wanted the probability that we wouldn't have to wait more than 5 minutes. Enter

```
MTB> CDF 5;      (since waiting time was not to exceed five minutes)
SUBC> Expo 5.
```

The 5 in the SUBC statement is the time lapse between occurrences. That is, if 0.2 cab = 1/5 cab comes each minute, it will be 5 minutes for one cab to come.
Minitab gives $P(0 < X < t)$, not $P(X > t)$.

List of Symbols and Terms

π: Probability of a success
μ^*:   Mean lapse of time between occurrences as per exponential distribution
P_0:   The probability a queue is empty
L: Average number of units in a queue
W: Average time in a queue
L_q: Average number of units in queue waiting for service
W_q: Average time waiting in queue for service

List of Formulas

$$\mu = E(X) = \Sigma[(x_i)P(x_i)] \qquad (5.1)$$

Mean of a probability distribution.

$$\sigma^2 = \Sigma[(x_i - \mu)^2 P(x_i)] \qquad (5.2)$$

$$\sigma^2 = \Sigma[(x_i^2)P(x_i)] - \mu^2 \qquad (5.3)$$

Both (5.2) and (5.3) are used to find the variance of a probability distribution.

$$P(x) = {}_nC_x(\pi)^x(1 - \pi)^{n-x} \qquad (5.4)$$

Probability of x successes in a Bernoulli (binomial) trial.

$$\mu = n\pi \qquad (5.5)$$

Mean of a binomial probability distribution.

$$\sigma^2 = n\pi(1 - \pi) \qquad (5.6)$$

Variance of a binomial distribution.

$$P(x) = \frac{\mu^x e^{-\mu}}{x!} \qquad (5.7)$$

Probability of x successes in a Poisson probability distribution.

$$P(x) = \frac{{}_rC_x \; {}_{N-r}C_{n-x}}{{}_NC_n} \qquad (5.8)$$

Probability of x successes in a hypergeometric probability distribution.

$$\mu = \frac{a + b}{2} \qquad (5.9)$$

Mean of a uniform probability distribution.

$$\text{Height} = \frac{1}{b - a} \qquad (5.10)$$

Height of a uniform probability distribution.

$$P(X_1 < X < X_2) = \frac{X_2 - X_1}{\text{Range}} \qquad (5.11)$$

Determines probability that single observation falls between two values in a uniform distribution.

$$\sigma = \frac{b - a}{\sqrt{12}} \qquad (5.12)$$

Standard deviation of a uniform distribution.

$$\mu^* = \frac{1}{\mu} \qquad (5.13)$$

Describes relationship between mean arrival rate μ as per Poisson distribution, and mean lapse of time μ^* as per exponential distribution.

$$P(0 < X < t) = 1 - e^{-\mu t} \qquad (5.14)$$

Determines probability of elapsed time between two successive occurrences.

$$P_0 = 1 - \frac{\Lambda}{\mu} \tag{5.15}$$

The probability a queue is empty.

$$P_n = \left[\frac{\Lambda}{\mu}\right]^n P_0 \tag{5.16}$$

The probability n units are in a queuing system.

$$L = \frac{\Lambda}{\mu - \Lambda} \tag{5.17}$$

Average number of units in a queuing system.

$$W = \frac{1}{\mu - \Lambda} \tag{5.18}$$

Average time spent in queuing system.

$$L_q = \frac{\Lambda^2}{\mu(\mu - \Lambda)} \tag{5.19}$$

Average number of units in queuing system waiting for service.

$$W_q = \frac{\Lambda}{\mu(\mu - \Lambda)} \tag{5.20}$$

Average time spent waiting for service in a queue.

CHAPTER EXERCISES

PROBLEMS

1. A study by a local Ferrari dealer revealing the sales levels at his dealership provides the following data:

Number of cars sold per week	Relative frequency
0	0.05
1	0.12
2	0.17
3	0.08
4	0.12
5	0.20
6	0.07
7	0.02
8	0.07
9	0.02
10	0.03
11	0.05

a. If the cars sell for a mean price of $120,000 what is the average weekly revenue the dealer might expect?

b. Determine and interpret the variance and standard deviation of the number of cars sold each week.

2. Of 52 Wal-Mart stores in the Southeast, the number of managers and assistant managers in each store are shown in the accompanying table

Number of managers and assistants	Number of stores
2	10
3	12
4	16
5	14

Construct a probability distribution showing the relative distribution of managers and the cumulative probability distribution for managers.

3. Charter Bus Company offers intercity transportation to surrounding locations. One particular run carries passengers as shown by the probability distribution.

Number of passengers	Relative frequency
20	0.2
25	0.3
30	0.15
35	0.10
40	0.25

a. Costs are fixed at $200 per trip regardless of the number of passengers. If CBC wants to average a profit of $100 for each run, how much should they charge per passenger?

b. What variation in revenue will result if they charge the amount specified in part (a)?

4. A recent article in *Forbes* suggested that a $1,000 investment in gold stocks might lead to the following results:

Gain or loss in dollars	Relative frequency
−500	0.2
−100	0.3
100	0.2
500	0.2
700	0.1

An investment of $1,000 in a mutual fund could produce the following:

Gain or loss	Relative frequency
−200	0.1
50	0.6
100	0.3

    a. If you were to invest $1,000 what return might you expect to earn from each investment?

    b. Using the coefficient of variation as a measure of risk, which investment is safer?

5. As a broker for Paine Webber you often place limit orders at a particular price for your clients. If the stock's market price drops to that specified in the limit order, the sale is automatically finalized. If the price does not drop, the sale is canceled. Anytime a sale is made you receive $100. Earlier today you placed three limit orders, but you do not yet know the results. The probability the market price of the first stock will drop sufficiently to allow its sale is 0.3. The probability the price of the second stock will fall to the limit price is 0.2. There is a 0.7 probability the third stock order will execute. Assume the sales are independent events.

    a. Prepare a probability distribution showing the results of the sales.

    b. How much money might you expect to make from the limit orders?

6. Experience has shown that the probabilities that the customer will buy certain amounts of a given product are

Units purchased	Probability
0	0.5
1	0.1
2	0.2
3	0.2

If the salesperson earns a 10 percent commission and the products sell for $110, how much does the salesperson earn per sales call on the average? What variation occurs in that income?

7. A survey of 1,000 independent businesses is taken to determine if they favor or do not favor higher tariffs on imported goods. Do the results fit a binomial distribution?

8. The CEO for a large industrial firm learns that only 20 percent of her employees are qualified to perform an important task. If she must select 15 employees at random, what is the probability

    a. five are qualified?

    b. at most five are qualified?

    c. at least five are qualified?

    d. between three and six inclusive are qualified?

9. *Automobile News* announced that 40 percent of all domestic cars suffered repair bills in excess of $200 during their first year of service. If Acme Cabs purchases 10 cars, what is the probability
   a. two will experience repair bills in excess of $200?
   b. at least two will do so?
   c. at most two will do so?

10. According to the Securities Exchange Commission, discount brokers make a sale of over $1,000 for every 10 clients they contact. What is the probability a broker will sell to exactly five clients if he contacts
    a. 10 clients?
    b. 12 clients?
    c. 20 clients?

11. Seventy-five percent of Texaco's stockholders preferred current management in a hostile takeover led by Carl Icahn. If eight were contacted at random, what is the probability that
    a. five would prefer current management?
    b. two would do so?
    c. all would do so?
    d. none would do so?

12. Given the information in Problem 11, calculate the mean number of stockholders who prefer present management. Calculate the variance.

13. A tropical fish store has found that only 65 percent of the fish it orders survive shipment. If it orders 20 fish, what is the probability
    a. 5 die?
    b. 7 die?
    c. 2 die?

14. An article in *The Wall Street Journal* stated that 40 percent of the nation's top CEOs had cellular phones installed in their personal cars. Radio Shack is devising plans to market a new type of cellular phone. If they selected 20 top CEOs at random, what is the probability that
    a. at most four have phones?
    b. between 5 and 10 inclusive have phones?
    c. at least nine have phones?

15. Records show that only 10 percent of the people who take a new drug suffer side effects. If the drug is administered to 15 people, what is the probability that no more than 7 suffer side effects?

16. In violation of the Federal Aviation Authority regulations, many airlines overbook passengers, realizing that some will cancel at the last minute. Mid-West air uses planes that hold only 12 passengers. Their records show that 10 percent of the passengers who make reservations fail to appear at flight time. If Mid-West books 15 reservations for its flights, what is the probability that on any given flight
    a. one person will not have a seat?
    b. at least one person will not have a seat?
    c. there will be one empty seat?
    d. there will be at least one empty seat?

17. Records kept by the American Medical Association show that only 30 percent of adult males get an annual medical exam each year. Dr. Hart, the local cardiologist, consults the records of seven of his patients. What is the probability he will find
    a. all seven have exams?
    b. none have exams?

     c. between two and four inclusive have exams?

     d. between one and three inclusive have exams?

18. Given the conditions for Dr. Hart in Problem 17, what is the probability that out of seven patients

     a. four have not had an exam?

     b. two to four inclusive have not had an exam?

     c. at least five have not?

     d. less than three have not?

19. A local bank claims that 80 percent of the people in the town have an account with them. Of 20 people selected at random nine had accounts. If the bank's claim is correct, what is the probability of this occurring? What conclusion can you draw?

20. A manufacturer regulates operations to produce 10 percent defective units. If the defective rate is less than that, the manufacturer feels that resources allocated to quality control are excessive, and the cost of reducing the rate of defective units is greater than the benefit derived from doing so. If the rate exceeds 10 percent, production standards are not being met. If a sample of 15 units is selected, what number of defects is most likely to occur if $\pi = 0.10$?

21. Seventy percent of the population will be involved in serious auto accidents in their lifetimes. If 10 people are selected at random

     a. what is the probability three are in accidents?

     b. how many of the 10 would you expect to be in an accident?

     c. what is the standard deviation in the number of victims?

22. Assume 100 people are sampled to determine if they have been in an auto accident (see Problem 21). Using Chebyshev's theorem, within what interval would you expect the successes to fall 75 percent of the time? Interpret your answer.

23. *Business Week* reported that 80 percent of the population thinks congressional salaries are too high. If 15 people are chosen to form a committee to decide by majority vote whether these salaries should be raised, what is the probability the vote will be to not increase them?

24. Nicholas Brady, Treasury secretary in 1988, supported a $3.5 billion short-term loan to Mexico. Only 30 percent of those in Congress agreed. If 10 members of Congress are selected at random what is the probability

     a. four will support the loan?

     b. all will support it?

     c. none will oppose it?

     d. at least five will oppose it?

     e. at most seven will oppose it?

     f. no more than three will oppose it?

     g. between two and seven inclusive will support it?

     h. between two and seven inclusive will oppose it?

25. There are five possible answers for 100 multiple-choice questions on your exam. If you failed to study and had to guess at random on each one, what score would you expect to get?

26. The Occupational Safety and Health Administration says that 10 percent of all workers in the shipping industry are injured. Using the Poisson distribution, what is the probability five will be injured out of a sample of $n = 73$?

27. If Acme Shipping (see above problem) has enough money to pay the hospital bills for three employees, what is the probability they will not have sufficient funds on hand to take care of employee hospitalization if they employ 100 people?

28. Retail outlets for Goodyear Tire Company will accept shipments from the production center in Akron, Ohio, if the rate of defects is 20 percent or less. Goodyear's overall rate of defect

is 10 percent. The retail outlet in Beaver Falls, Idaho, receives a typical shipment from Akron. Ten of these tires received are selected as a sample out of the shipment and tested for defects. What is the probability the shipment will be accepted?

29. A producer suffers a 30 percent defective rate. Your company buys from this producer and wants to keep the probability of accepting a shipment as close to 10 percent as possible. In a shipment from which a sample of 20 is selected, what is the maximum number of defects you can tolerate?

30. Airplanes arrive at Chicago's O'Hare airport at the average rate of 5.2 per minute. Air traffic controllers can safely handle a maximum of seven airplanes per minute. What is the probability airport safety is jeopardized?

31. Cars at a local fast-food restaurant pull up to the drive-in window at the rate of 6.2 per minute during the rush period. The manager wants to know the probability that
    a. four will arrive in the next minute?
    b. at most four will arrive in the next minute?
    c. at least four will arrive in the next minute?

32. A production line generates an average of 7.8 units per day. Lisa Lawing, the production supervisor, has contracted to deliver 16 units to an important customer. What is the probability she can do so?

33. The chance that any given taxicab in New York will be involved in an accident is 0.02. If a particular cab company has 75 cabs on the street, what is the probability that exactly 4 will be in an accident?

34. Each year 87 claims are filed against your insurance firm. What is the probability five will be filed in any given month?

35. Trucks arrive for loading at the rate of 9.3 per hour on the average. The dock foreman knows that if six or fewer trucks arrive, only one loading dock is necessary. If more than six arrive, a second dock must be opened. Should he open a second dock?

36. The Alaska oil pipeline has been found to have 0.04 weld faults per mile. What is the probability that over a 10-mile length there are no faults?

37. In the production of reinforcement bars used in construction, industry standards result in an average of 1.8 defects per 100 bars. What is the probability of two defects in 100 bars?

38. Given the conditions in the preceding problem, you refuse to accept a set of 100 bars unless they measure up to industry standards (1.8 defects per 100). If you want about a 10 percent chance of incorrectly rejecting a set of 100 bars when they actually do meet industry standards, how many defects should you allow before rejection?

39. Temps, Ltd. dispatched nine temporary day workers to the Bank of America in San Francisco. Only six of them are actually qualified to do the job to which they might be assigned. The accounting department selects five of the nine employees. What is the probability
    a. all five are qualified?
    b. four are qualified?
    c. at least three are qualified?

40. The president must select a committee of 5 from 12 senators, of whom four are Democrats and the rest Republicans. What is the probability
    a. all are Republicans?
    b. three are Democrats?
    c. two are Republicans?
    d. at least four are Republicans?
    e. a majority are Republicans?

41. Sam Johnson, the fourth-generation scion of the Johnson Wax fortune, has long been an advocate of private family ownership of the Johnson corporation. In 1989, *Business Week* described his efforts to sell to the public $26.7 million worth of his empire. A stock offering was made to 14 nonfamily investors. Eight of the 14 had worked with Sam's father and grandfather. If 6 of the 14 are to buy stock in the Johnson business, what is the probability that
    a. five had done business with Sam's father?
    b. all but two had done business with Sam's father?
    c. four had never associated with Sam's father?

42. The board of directors for ABC, Inc. consists of four economists, three accountants, and five engineers. What is the probability that a committee of two economists, two accountants, and three engineers can be selected?

43. Computers Unlimited markets five types of printers, four types of computers, and six types of monitors. What is the probability that you select at random and get three printers, two computers, and no monitors?

44. Janet Powell is the chief accountant for a large clothing store in a major shopping mall. She completes the payrolls for all 11 employees, but seven contain errors. Janet's boss, Martha Holt, has become displeased with her work lately and selects five payroll records to examine. It is found that three contain errors. Janet defends herself by arguing that the 3 errors were all that she made out of the 11 records. Is this a good argument?

45. The weights contained in boxes of cereal are uniformly distributed with a mean of 35 ounces and a range of 3.4 ounces.
    a. What are the smallest and largest weights in the boxes?
    b. What is the probability that a single box contains between 32 and 33 ounces?

46. Over the past 20 years Fred has driven to work in San Francisco every day. The quickest he has made the trip is 63 minutes. The longest it has ever taken him is 110 minutes. If driving times are uniformly distributed
    a. what is Fred's average time spent in traffic?
    b. what is the probability he can make it within 1.5 hours?

47. In 1989 the average price of jet fuel was 53.5 cents per gallon according to the *Airline Monitor,* an airline industry trade publication which quotes weekly figures. Over the year it hit a high of 59.5 and appeared to be uniformly distributed. In how many weeks did the price exceed 56 cents?

48. In the effort to reduce costs, Wendy's International Inc., a popular fast-food restaurant, examined the tendency for its automatic processors to determine the weights of hamburger in their quarter-pound burgers. It was found that the weights ranged from 3.2 ounces to 4.9 ounces. A uniform distribution was assumed. What percentage of the burgers are more than one-quarter of a pound?

49. Industrial lighting fixtures made by General Electric have an average life of 3,600 hours, which follows a Poisson distribution.
    a. What percentage of them last more than 4,320 hours?
    b. What percentage of them last more than 165 days? (assume a 24-hour day)

50. Davies Repair and Fixit takes an average of eight hours to complete a certain type of job. Find the probability that it will not take longer than 12 hours this time. Times appear to be of a Poisson distribution.

51. Ralph's Repair and Fixit can complete four jobs in 1 hour. What is the probability that it will take less than 15 minutes to complete one such job? Times are Poisson distributed.

52. The drive-in teller window at the Jesse James First National Bank in Kansas City has enough space to accommodate three cars. Cars arrive at an average rate of 10 per hour. It takes an average of 5 minutes to service one customer.
    a. Does the bank have enough space to accommodate the traffic it might expect to face?
    b. What is the probability exactly three cars will be at the bank?
    c. Evaluate all other aspects of the bank's queuing system based on the proper criteria.

EMPIRICAL EXERCISES

53. Select a discrete variable of interest to you regarding your fellow students (number of brothers and sisters each has, number of dates each week or month, classification such as freshman, sophomore, etc.). Take a sample of students and construct a probability distribution displaying your results. Compute and interpret the mean and variance of the probability distribution. [*Note:* Select a variable that has a discrete value with a limited number of observations (perhaps between 5 and 10) to keep your results manageable.]

54. A national education forum of college administrators designed to study our nation's institutions of higher education revealed that 22 percent of undergraduates are married. If the estimate of 22 percent is accurate and assuming your campus is typical, how many would you expect to be married? How many in your sample were married? What can you conclude regarding the marital status of students on your campus, compared with the national norm?

55. Use the data from Problem 54 and assume a normality in the distribution of married students. Find the probability that the proportion of married students will differ from the national norm of 22 percent by more than those in your sample. On this basis, what can you conclude about the marital habits on your campus compared with the rest of the nation?

56. Over a specified time rate, observe the arrival of customers at a local fast-food chain, the student cafeteria, bookstore, or other business at which traffic can be counted. Determine μ, the average arrival rate per time period. Choose some number of arrivals which conforms to your data. What is the probability that number of arrivals will be observed during a given time period? Why would you want to take a sample at different times of the day?

57. Data compiled by the Institute of Health and Life Insurance show the mean height of adult males to be 70.5 inches, with a standard deviation of 4.2 inches. Determine the height of one adult male of your choice. What is the probability his height will be greater than 70.5 inches? What percentage of adult males are taller than your selection? Assume a normal distribution of heights.

CASE APPLICATIONS

58. Reprint, Inc. manufactures copiers used to duplicate important documents. Walter Waxman, CEO for Reprint, takes great care to maintain high quality standards. Mr. Waxman argues that no more than 5 percent of the machines his company makes are defective. Baltimore Ramsey, who owns a large real estate agency in Hoboken, recently ordered 15 copiers from Reprint. Three of them proved defective. Mr. Ramsey wrote a letter of complaint to Mr. Waxman, demanding a refund of all his money. Ramsey argued that out of 15 copiers no more than one should be defective. Three defects certainly disproved Reprint's claim of a 5% defective rate. As a mid-level manager for Reprint, Mr. Waxman has instructed you to draft a reply to Ramsey. How would you respond?

59. Officials for the California Highway Patrol have become concerned over the increasing incidence of accidents on the freeway system in and around the Los Angeles area. Captain Kisner at the CHP post in Oxnard has been collecting statistics on accidents for the past several months. One intersection in particular is a cause for concern. The captain's data show that over the past 150 days there have been 90 accidents, 15 of which caused at least one fatality.

Under Kisner's direction, the Oxnard post has contacted the California Highway Authority requesting that immediate action be taken to reduce the danger of fatal accidents at that intersection. Citing a lack of public funds as reason for the absence of any corrective action, the Highway Authority insists that certain proof be forthcoming before resources are provided to correct one intersection.

After constant urging on the part of Captain Kisner, the highway authorities finally agree to investigate the threat to public life and limb at the intersection in question. They tell the captain that they can designate two people to observe traffic patterns for one day. If there are more than two accidents, the California Highway Authority promises to take constructive action. Captain Kisner is thankful for the attention, but feels the matter is too important to be decided on the basis of one day's observation. He proposes instead that data be collected over the next 30 days. If there is more than one accident involving a fatality, the highway authorities should decide what steps should be taken.

A statistical consultant is called in to evaluate the two proposals. If you were that consultant, how would you compare the likelihood that each plan would cause the authorities to pursue a policy to reduce accidents at that intersection.

60. Baxter Laboratories tests bacterial cultures for hospitals in a major urban area. Last Wednesday, Baxter received 20 such cultures for testing from several different medical centers. Tests showed that of the 20, 8 contained some form of contagious bacteria. The results were to be reported the next day to the respective hospitals.

However, Ruth Michell, a new medical technician at Baxter, mixed up the results of the tests. The University Hospital submitted five cultures for testing, but Baxter is now unsure how many of those were contagious. The staff at University Hospital is understandably upset by the confusion. The director at Baxter apologizes for the complication, but assures University Hospital that if they submitted only 5 of the 20 cultures, the chance that any of the 5 would prove to be contagious is quite small. Dr. Hasper at University Hospital is not comforted by this assurance, and tries desperately to determine the probability that any of her five cultures might exhibit contagious bacteria. As the resident statistician for University, how can you help?

COMPUTER EXERCISES

1. Using your selected computer package, compute solved problem 2, parts (a), (b), (d), and (e).
2. Complete solved problems 3, 5, and 7.
3. Many of the chapter problems can also be worked on the computer, to test your understanding of how the computer can be used to assist in solving statistical problems.

CHAPTER SIX

THE NORMAL DISTRIBUTION

A PREVIEW OF THINGS TO LOOK FOR

1   The nature of a normal distribution.

2   Numerous applications of a normal distribution in business settings.

3   Manner in which the standard deviation affects the shape of the normal distribution.

4   How the Empirical Rule relates to the normal distribution.

5   Use of the conversion formula.

6   How the normal distribution can be used to approximate the binomial distribution.

The normal distribution is perhaps the most important and certainly the most commonly used distribution in statistical analysis. This chapter examines the many ways in which this important distribution can be applied in the solution of many common business problems and emphasizes its use in conjunction with other statistical tools throughout this text. An insight and understanding of the normal distribution is crucial to the comprehension of many of the concepts that you will study in forthcoming chapters.

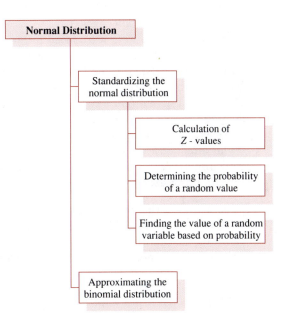

239

> ◯◯◯◯ Statistics show that if you drop a piece of bread,
> ◯◯◯   it does always land buttered side down.
> ◯◯
> ◯

6.1   INTRODUCTION

Of all the probability distributions we will examine, none is more important than the normal distribution. This importance stems in part from the fact that the normal distribution can serve as an approximation of other probability distributions, such as the binomial distribution. However, the normal distribution proves of even greater value in its ability to function as the very foundation for more advanced statistical analysis. With the aid and support of the vantage provided by the normal distribution, it becomes possible to command a level of statistical inference that otherwise could not be achieved.

In Chapter 3 you were introduced to the basic nature of the normal distribution. There you learned about its characteristic bell-shaped symmetry, as well as the manner in which it related to the Empirical Rule. At this time, you should be reminded that the normal distribution is a continuous (not discrete) distribution. It is used to reflect the distribution of variables such as heights, weights, distances, and other measurements that are infinitely divisible. Such continuous variables, you will recall, are generally the result of measurement.

Our attention then turns to this important statistical tool. We will, in the effort to acquire a working understanding of the many ways in which the normal distribution can prove useful, examine

- The nature of the normal distribution.
- The manner in which the normal distribution can be standardized.
- How the normal distribution can be used to determine probabilities.
- The many common business problems that the normal distribution can address.

We begin with a brief review of the basic nature of the normal distribution as we earlier presented it in Chapter 3.

6.2   THE GENERAL NATURE OF THE NORMAL DISTRIBUTION

The normal distribution is a unique arrangement of values in that, if they are graphed, the curve takes a distinct bell-shaped and symmetrical form. Consider for a moment the case recently presented in *Fortune* magazine in which Tops Wear, a large clothing manufacturer, wished to study the distribution in peoples' heights. Tops Wear recognized that the public is ever-changing in its physical size and proportions. In the effort to produce better-fitting clothing, it was felt by upper management that a thorough analysis was needed of current trends in fashion sizes. On the basis of this analysis, presume that if Tops Wear were to measure the heights of all their potential customers, they would find that these heights were normally distributed around some mean of, say, 67 inches. That is, while the heights averaged 67 inches, some people were of course taller than that, and some were shorter. This dispersion above and below the mean could be measured by the standard deviation that we calculated back in Chapter 3. Assume that the standard deviation in customers' heights is found to be 2 inches.

Of importance, however, is the fact that the heights were normally distributed. Thus, any attempt to graph these observations representing heights would produce the customary bell shape. Assume that the graph, as shown in Figure 6-1, places the individual observations on the horizontal axis, and the frequency with which each of these observations occurred on the vertical axis. If the values are indeed normal (i.e., normally distributed), then by definition of normality the extreme observations would occur relatively infrequently. That is, the particularly high observations and the particularly low observations would not occur as often as those heights closer to the mean of 67 inches.

FIGURE 6-1   A Normal Distribution of Heights for Tops Wear

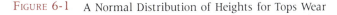

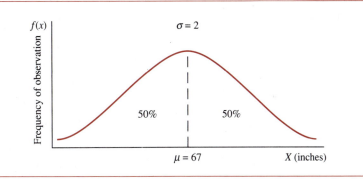

This is seen to be the case in Figure 6-1. Those values farther above 67 and those farther below 67 have a low frequency of occurrence, while the distribution rises to a peak for the mean height of 67. The spread or dispersion around the mean of 67 is seen to be 2 inches in the figure.

Recall further that in the event of a normal distribution 50 percent of the observations (heights) are above the mean and 50 percent are below the mean. Similarly, it can be concluded that of all the area under the normal curve, 50 percent of it is to the right of the mean, and 50 percent of that area is to the left of the mean. This too is shown in Figure 6-1.

This distinct distribution is not uncommon in the world around us. In many instances we will find that a set of values is normally distributed, or closely approximates normality, allowing the application of this important statistical principle.

In addition, we will find in the next chapter that under certain circumstances, the sampling process will ensure normality even if the population from which the sample is taken is *not* normal. This increases even further the prominence of the role played by normality in our statistical analysis.

A.   A Comparison of Normal Distributions

The shape and position of a normal distribution are determined entirely by two parameters: its mean μ and standard deviation σ. Figure 6-2 shows three different normal distributions for the sizes that Tops Wear might find in their study of fashion trends. The first (I) is the distribution described above which, you recall, has a mean of $\mu = 50$ and a standard deviation of $\sigma = 2$. It is centered at 50 with one-half of the observations above 50 and one-half below 50. The standard deviation of 2 indicated the degree in which the individual observations are spread out above and below 50.

Figure 6-2   Three Normal Distributions

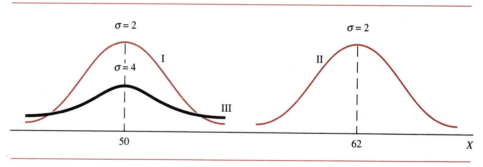

A second distribution (II) has a higher mean of $\mu = 62$, but the same standard deviation of $\sigma = 2$. It is therefore centered farther to the right directly above 62. But since it has the same degree of dispersion ($\sigma = 2$), it takes on the same shape as the first distribution.

A third distribution (III) has the same mean as the first ($\mu = 50$) and is therefore centered at the same place. However, its measure of dispersion is greater. The standard deviation is $\sigma = 4$. The observations vary above and below that mean of 50 to a greater degree than do those observations in the first distribution. As the curve illustrates, the distribution with $\sigma = 4$ is flatter and more spread out above and below the mean of 50.

B.   The Empirical Rule Revisited

Despite their differences, all three are normal distributions. They are all symmetrical and bell-shaped. Furthermore, as normally distributed data sets, the Empirical Rule that we first examined back in Chapter 3 applies to each distribution. The

Empirical Rule specifies that, regardless of the value of the mean or the standard deviation,

> 68.8 percent of all the observations lie within one standard deviation of the mean.
> 95.5 percent of all the observations lie within two standard deviations of the mean.
> 99.7 percent of all the observations lie within three standard deviations of the mean.

Figure 6-3 illustrates the Empirical Rule. Notice that for all three data sets, regardless of the value for μ or σ, the intervals contain the specified proportions. Compare the first distribution (I) to that of the third distribution (III). Since the third distribution is more highly dispersed, it is necessary to take in a wider interval in order to encompass the same proportion of the observations. For example, while the first distribution encloses 68.8 percent of all the observations within the interval 48 to 52, the third distribution can encompass this same percentage within the wider interval 46 to 54.

FIGURE 6-3 The Empirical Rule

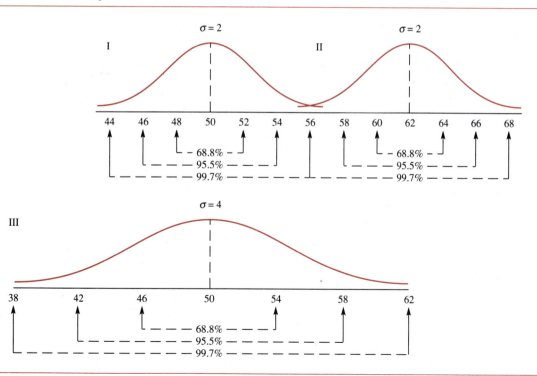

Remember that to enclose a certain percentage of all the observations within some interval means also to encompass that same percentage of all the area under the curve within that interval. Thus, while the interval 48 to 52 contains 68.8 percent of all the observations in the first distribution, that same interval also contains 68.8 percent of all the area under the normal curve.

C. THE NORMAL DEVIATE

It should be apparent from the discussion above that there can exist an infinite number of possible normal distributions, each with its own mean and standard deviation. Since we obviously cannot examine such a large number of possibilities, it is necessary to convert all these normal distributions into one standard form. This conversion to the **standard normal distribution** is done with the **conversion formula** (or Z-formula)

$$Z = \frac{X - \mu}{\sigma} \tag{6.1}$$

where Z is the **normal deviate** and X is some specified value for the random variable. After this conversion process, the mean of the distribution is 0 and the standard deviation is 1. Regardless of what the mean and standard deviation are as measured in the original units in the distribution, after the conversion formula is applied the mean is 0 and the standard deviation is 1. This is because the numerator in the conversion formula requires that you subtract the exact amount of the mean of the distribution. The distribution would appear as in Figure 6-4. Notice that the horizontal axis is now measured in units of Z and the distribution is now centered at $\mu = 0$. It is important to remember that all normal distributions can be converted into a stan-

FIGURE 6-4   A Standardized Normal Distribution

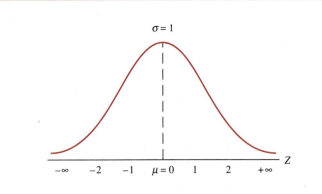

dard form. This is done by rescaling the horizontal axis from the actual units of measure to units of measure in terms of the Z-value.

Standard Normal Distribution
After any normal distribution has been standardized using the conversion formula, it will have a mean of $\mu = 0$ and a standard deviation of $\sigma = 1$.

To illustrate the conversion process, Telcom, a telephone answering service for business executives in the Chicago metropolitan area, has found that the average telephone message is 150 seconds, with a standard deviation of 15 seconds. It has also observed that the length of messages is a normally distributed variable. This distribution is shown in Figure 6-5.

FIGURE 6-5   A Standardized Normal Distribution for Telcom

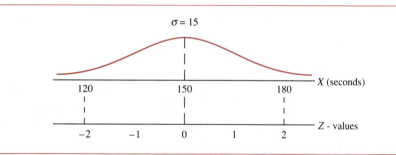

The distribution is centered at 150 seconds and is symmetrical around that point. A second axis appears below the distribution. This one is rescaled not in units of time but in units of Z's. It expresses distances along the axis in terms of Z-values. Notice that on the Z-scale the distribution is centered at the mean point of zero. This is because the numerator in the conversion formula requires that we subtract the mean of 150.

Assume a particular phone message took 180 seconds. This just happens to be two standard deviations above the mean of 150. We can measure this distance between 150 seconds and 180 seconds in two ways. We can say this point of 180 seconds is (1) 30 seconds above the mean, or we can say (2) it is two standard deviations above the mean. In either case, we find ourselves at the same point. By expressing the distance in standard deviations, we are saying that the Z-value is two standard deviations. That is, $Z = 2$. The Z-value is the number of standard deviations a given point (180 in this case) is above or below the mean. Using the conversion formula, we have

$$Z = \frac{X - \mu}{\sigma}$$

$$= \frac{180 - 150}{15}$$

$$= 2$$

The Z-value
The Z-value is the number of standard deviations a given point is from the mean after a normal distribution has been standardized.

In similar fashion, 120 seconds is two standard deviations below the mean. Thus, $Z = -2$.

6.3   CALCULATING PROBABILITIES WITH THE NORMAL DEVIATE

Standardizing a distribution in this fashion offers certain advantages. Now there is only one distribution to master rather than an infinite number. More importantly for our current purposes, the standardization process facilitates calculating the probability that the value of a random variable falls within a given range. For example, it is now possible to determine the probability that a given phone message will take between 150 and 180 seconds, or 120 and 180 seconds, or any other range of values in which we might be interested.

This probability is determined by finding the area under the normal curve between the mean μ and the value of interest X. If Telcom wants to compute the probability that any phone message will take between $\mu = 150$ and $X = 180$ seconds, they simply find the area under the curve between these two values. If they can find this relevant area, they will have found the probability.

That is, if you can find the relevant area under the normal curve, you will know the desired probability. For example, assume you are shooting at a target, of which three-fourths is painted green, and one-fourth is red. You have the same chance of hitting any one point on the target as you do of hitting any other single point. You are not aiming at the bull's-eye, just the target in general. The probability you will hit green is three-fourths. Why? Because three-fourths of its area is painted green. Area and probability can be thought of as synonymous. Since you know area, you know probability. The same can be said for the area under the curve between 150 and 180. If Telcom can find that area, they will know the desired probability.

Converting to a standard normal distribution assists in the effort to find that area. Table E provides the desired areas under a standardized normal curve. Since this table is used repeatedly in statistical analysis, it is reproduced for convenience inside the back cover. The table requires that we calculate the Z-value using the conversion formula. This Z-value then allows us to simply look up the desired area in Table E. It is essential to remember that the entries in the table give *only* that portion of the area under the curve from the mean to some value above it or below it.

The phone messages averaged 150 seconds with a standard deviation of 15 seconds. This can be written as

$$X \sim N(150, 15)$$

which means that X is a normally distributed random variable with a mean of 150 and a standard deviation of 15.

FIGURE 6-6   The Probability Any Single Phone Message Takes between 150 and 180 Seconds

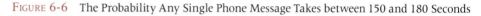

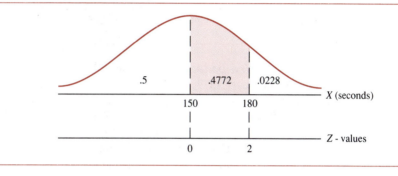

If Telcom wishes to determine the area under the curve between 150 and 180 as shown in Figure 6-6, they must calculate the Z-value for 180. Thus,

$$Z = \frac{X - \mu}{\sigma}$$

$$= \frac{180 - 150}{15}$$

$$= 2.00$$

Table E now comes into play. Notice that it provides values for Z to the nearest one-tenth down the left margin. Telcom seeks that area for a Z-value of 2.00. They must therefore move down the left margin to the value 2.0. Since they want 2.00, they must then move to the first column headed by 0.00. This is done since 2.0 + 0.00 = 2.00. Here they find the value 0.4772. This shows that 47.72 percent of the total area under the curve is found in the shaded area of Figure 6-6 between the mean of 150 and 180 seconds. If they had sought the area corresponding to a Z-value of, say 2.15, they would move down the left margin to the Z-value of 2.1, and then across that row to the sixth column headed by the value 0.05, since 2.1 + 0.05 = 2.15. There they would find the value 0.4842.

Now that Telcom has found the area of 0.4772 under the normal curve between the values 150 and 180 seconds, they arrive at two conclusions or interpretations of their findings. Telcom can conclude that

1. There is a 47.72 percent chance that any single telephone message will last between 150 and 180 seconds.
2. 47.72 percent of all messages last between 150 and 180 seconds.

Either interpretation is correct, depending on the use to which Telcom wishes to apply their findings.

The Z-Table
The Z-table gives the area under the normal curve from the mean to some specific value above or below the mean.

It must always be remembered that Table E gives the area between the mean and some value above or below the mean. If a different area is desired, an adjustment must be made. For example, if Telcom wished to determine the probability that a single call selected at random exceeded 180 seconds, $P(X > 180)$, they would first have to find the area from 150 to 180 since that is all the table will provide. Then, recognizing that in a normal distribution 50 percent of the area is above the mean of 150, Telcom would subtract from 0.5000 the area from 150 to 180 of 0.4772. The remainder, 0.5000 − 0.4772 = 0.0228, is the area above 180. That is, if 0.5000 of the total area under the curve is above the mean of 150, and 0.4772 of that area is between 150 and 180, then the rest, 0.0228, must be that area above 180. This is also illustrated in Figure 6-6.

It should come as no surprise that 0.4772 of the area under the curve is found between 150 and 180. Based on the Empirical Rule, we know that 95.5 percent of the area under the curve is within two standard deviations above and below the mean. This interval of 120 to 180 is shown in Figure 6-7. Since the curve is symmet-

FIGURE 6-7   A Review of the Empirical Rule

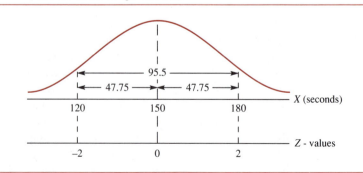

rical, one-half of the 95.5 percent, or 47.75 percent, is between 150 and 180, while the other 47.75 percent is between 120 and 150. The difference between 47.75 percent calculated in Figure 6-7 and 47.72 found in the table is due to rounding.

Using the procedure illustrated above, it is possible to find the probability that a randomly selected telephone call will fall within any desired interval. Illustrations are provided in Figure 6-8 for the various intervals that can arise.

FIGURE 6-8 Possible Intervals of Interest to Telcom

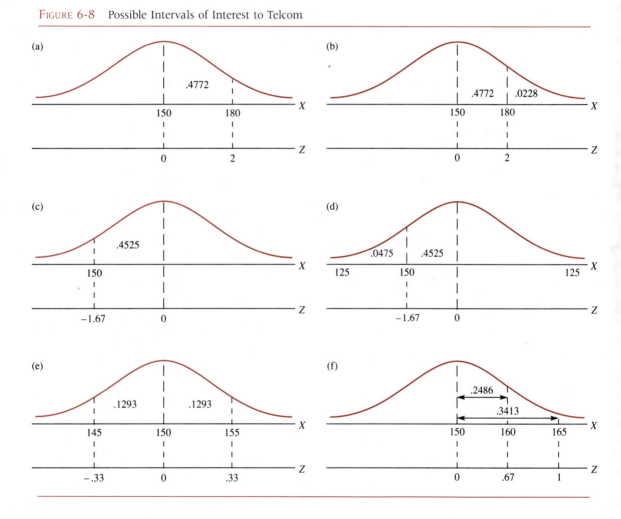

To repeat the experiment above, suppose the CEO for Telcom wants to determine the probability that a single telephone message will last between 150 and

180 seconds [see Figure 6-8(a)]. He is interested in finding $P(150 < X < 180)$. Using the conversion formula, we have

$$Z = \frac{X - \mu}{\sigma} = \frac{180 - 150}{15} = 2$$

A Z-value of 2 yields an area of 0.4772 from Table E. There is therefore a 47.72 percent chance that any phone call chosen at random will last between 150 and 180 seconds.

FIND $P(X > 180)$: SEE 6-8(b)   The area for this interval is not given in Table E since it is not an interval from the mean of 150 to some point above or below 150. Telcom must therefore adjust for this fact by subtracting from 0.5000. The area between 150 and 180 is found as

$$Z = \frac{180 - 150}{15} = 2; \quad \text{or an area of } 0.4772$$

The area above 180 is therefore $0.5000 - 0.4772 = 0.0228$.

FIND $P(125 < X < 150)$: SEE 6-8(c)

$$Z = \frac{125 - 150}{15} = 1.67$$

Although the Z-value is actually -1.67, it does not make any difference whether we are working in the right side of the curve or in the left side, since the curve is symmetrical. Thus, for the sake of convenience we can ignore the sign in cases of this nature.

A Z-value of 1.67 yields an area of 0.4525. There is a 45.25 percent chance that any single call will last between 125 and 150 seconds. Or, it can be concluded that 45.25 percent of all messages last between 125 and 150 seconds.

FIND $P(X < 125)$: SEE 6-8(d)

$$Z = \frac{125 - 150}{15} = 1.67; \quad \text{or an area of } 0.4525$$

The probability a single call will last between 125 and 150 seconds is 45.25 percent. Therefore, the probability a single call will take less than 125 seconds is $0.5000 - 0.4525 = 0.0475$. That is, 4.75 percent of all the messages last less than 125 seconds.

FIND $P(145 < X < 155)$ SEE 6-8(e)   Since Table E provides values for areas only from the mean to some point above or below it, this problem requires that we find

$P(145 < X < 150)$ and $P(150 < X < 155)$, and add them together to get the area we need.

$$Z_1 = \frac{145 - 150}{15} = 0.33; \quad \text{or an area of } 0.1293$$

$$Z_2 = \frac{155 - 150}{15} = 0.33; \quad \text{or an area of } 0.1293$$

$$P(145 < X < 155) = 0.1293 + 0.1293 = 0.2586$$

The probability a single call will last between 145 and 155 seconds is 25.86 percent.

FIND $P(160 < X < 165)$: SEE 6-8(f)   Again, we must use the Z-formula twice. First we find $P(150 < X < 165)$, which contains the area we want and some that we do not want. Then $P(150 < X < 160)$ is subtracted out to yield just the area we want.

$$Z_1 = \frac{165 - 150}{15} = 1; \quad \text{or an area of } 0.3413$$

and

$$Z_2 = \frac{160 - 150}{15} = 0.67; \quad \text{an area of } 0.2486$$

Then

$$P(160 < X < 165) = 0.3414 - 0.2486 = 0.0928$$

The probability a single call will take between 160 and 165 seconds is 9.27 percent. Or, 9.27 percent of all calls take between 160 and 165 seconds. It should be apparent that the probability associated with any interval of interest can be found in this fashion. To reinforce this idea, consider the following example.

EXAMPLE 6-1 Protecting U.S. Astronauts

Parker Seal, Inc. makes O-rings for NASA's space shuttle. The rings are designed to seal connections and joint fittings in the fuel system to prevent leaks. One type of ring must be 5 centimeters in diameter in order to fit properly. It can vary up or down by only 0.25 centimeter without causing a dangerous leak. Parker Seal claims that this ring averages 5 centimeters, with a standard deviation of 0.17 centimeter. If these figures are correct and a normal distribution in diameters is assumed, NASA officials wish to determine

a. The proportions of rings that will fit properly.
b. The proportion of rings that are defective.
c. The probability any one ring has a diameter greater than 5.3 centimeters.
d. The probability any one ring has a diameter between 4.9 and 5.2 centimeters.
e. The proportion of rings that have a diameter between 4.9 and 5.2 centimeters.
f. The probability a single ring chosen at random has a diameter between 5.3 and 5.5 centimeters.

SOLUTION:

a. Since the rings can deviate from 5 cm by 0.25 cm without causing a hazardous condition, NASA needs to know $P(4.75 < X < 5.25)$, as shown by the shaded area.

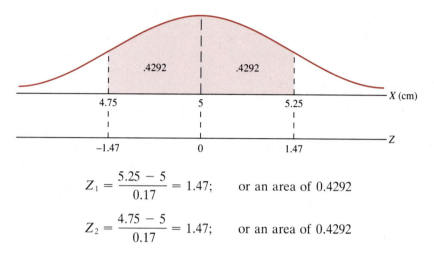

$$Z_1 = \frac{5.25 - 5}{0.17} = 1.47; \qquad \text{or an area of } 0.4292$$

$$Z_2 = \frac{4.75 - 5}{0.17} = 1.47; \qquad \text{or an area of } 0.4292$$

Thus,

$$P(4.75 < X < 5.25) = 0.4292 + 0.4292 = 0.8584$$

b. The proportion of defective rings is $P(X < 4.75) + P(X > 5.25)$.

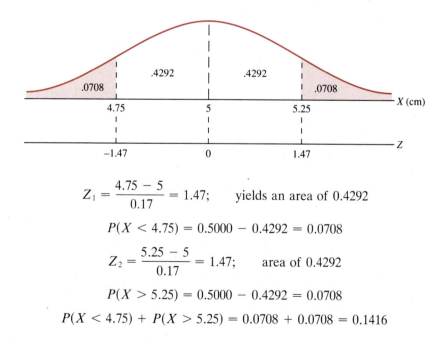

$$Z_1 = \frac{4.75 - 5}{0.17} = 1.47; \qquad \text{yields an area of } 0.4292$$

$$P(X < 4.75) = 0.5000 - 0.4292 = 0.0708$$

$$Z_2 = \frac{5.25 - 5}{0.17} = 1.47; \qquad \text{area of } 0.4292$$

$$P(X > 5.25) = 0.5000 - 0.4292 = 0.0708$$

$$P(X < 4.75) + P(X > 5.25) = 0.0708 + 0.0708 = 0.1416$$

c. $P(X > 5.3)$

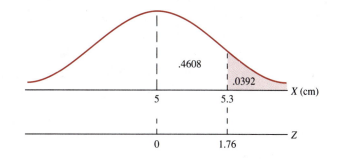

$$Z = \frac{5.3 - 5}{0.17} = 1.76; \qquad \text{yields an area of } 0.4608$$

$$P(X > 5.3) = 0.5000 - 0.4608 = 0.0392$$

d. $P(4.9 < X < 5.2)$

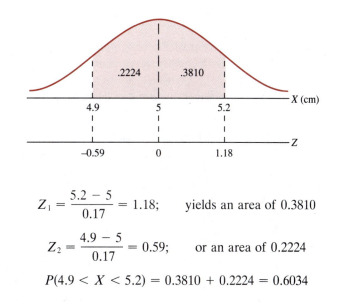

$$Z_1 = \frac{5.2 - 5}{0.17} = 1.18; \qquad \text{yields an area of } 0.3810$$

$$Z_2 = \frac{4.9 - 5}{0.17} = 0.59; \qquad \text{or an area of } 0.2224$$

$$P(4.9 < X < 5.2) = 0.3810 + 0.2224 = 0.6034$$

e. Exactly the same as part (d).

f. $P(5.3 < X < 5.5)$

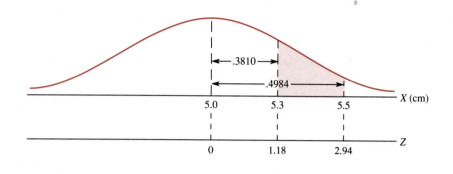

$$Z_1 = \frac{5.5 - 5}{0.17} = 2.94; \qquad \text{or an area of } 0.4984$$

$$Z_2 = \frac{5.3 - 5}{0.17} = 1.76; \qquad \text{or an area of } 0.4608$$

$$P(5.3 < X < 5.5) = 0.4984 - 0.4608 = 0.0376$$

STATISTICAL INTERPRETATION:
As an illustration, part (a) can be interpreted as

1. 85.84 percent of the rings manufactured by Parker Seal will fit properly.
2. There is an 85.84 percent chance that any ring selected at random will fit.

A similar interpretation can be derived for parts (b) through (f).

Since the Z-table gives values for Z only up to 3.99, a question may arise as to what we should do if a value for Z greater than 3.99 is encountered. Notice that as Z gets larger and approaches 3.99, the corresponding area approaches 0.5000. It is therefore the standard practice to assume an area of 0.5000 if Z exceeds 3.99.

Also note that

$$P(X < x_i) = P(X \le x_i)$$

where x_i is any value of the continuous random variable, and is represented by a point on the axis. The inclusion of the point on the axis corresponding to x_i in the interval does not increase the area because a point is a geometric tool which only shows location and has no dimensions. Therefore, the area directly above a point is zero.

○○○○   **DECISION MAKING THROUGH PROBLEM SOLVING**   ○○○○
ILLUSTRATION 6-1

As reported in *Retail Age,* Federated Department Stores, the holding company for several of the nation's largest department stores, used the concept of a normal distribution to compile a profile of the nature of payments that are received after their due date. Records seemed to suggest that late payments were normally distributed around some mean number of days. It was possible for Federated to determine what percentage of those belated payments are typically received within a given time period. On the basis of this information, Federated was able to establish policy on late charges attached to bills of those customers who waited unusually long to remit payment. It was decided that a $5 to $10 carrying charge would be added to any bill more than 10 days late.

QUICK CHECK 6.3.1

○○○○   Given $N \sim (75, 5)$, find $P(X > 82)$.
Answer: $0.5000 - 0.4192 = 0.0808$

QUICK CHECK 6.3.2

Given $N \sim (212, 32)$, find $P(X < 222)$.
Answer: $0.5000 + 0.1217 = 0.6217$

QUICK CHECK 6.3.3

Given $N \sim (45, 15)$, find $P(39 < X < 44)$.
Answer: $0.1554 - 0.0279 = 0.1275$

6.4   CALCULATING AN X-VALUE FROM A KNOWN PROBABILITY

In Section 6.3 you were asked to calculate a probability given some value of X. That is, you were given a value X for the random variable, and you wished to find the area between that value and the mean. It was demonstrated that this is a very common practice in many business matters.

However, sometimes you may know what probability you require and must determine what value for X will yield that desired probability. For example, assume the president's economic advisers propose a welfare program to aid the disadvantaged, which consists of a money payment to the nation's poorest 15 percent. The question then arises as to what income level separates the lower 15 percent of the people from the rest. In 1988, mean disposable personal income measured in 1982 dollars was $11,151, with a standard deviation of $3,550. This is shown in Figure 6-9. There is some level of income shown as "?" which separates the lowest 15 percent from the upper 85 percent.

FIGURE 6-9   Incomes of the Poorest 15 Percent

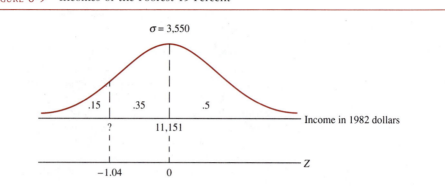

Assume incomes are normally distributed. The question then becomes, "If people who are receiving the lowest 15 percent of the nation's incomes are to be subsidized, below what level must a person's income be before he or she receive a subsidy?" That is, what level of income separates the lowest 15 percent of the population from the other 85 percent?

As shown in Figure 6-9, we know the area and seek the corresponding value for X which is shown by the question mark. In the earlier problems, we calculated a Z-value and used it to look up an area in the table. This time we have an area, and we can use Table E to look up the corresponding Z-value. Although we are interested in the value of 0.15, we must look up 0.3500 (0.5 − 0.15), since only the area from the mean to some value above or below it is given in the table. We then search out in the main body of Table E the area value of 0.3500. The closest we can get is 0.3508 which corresponds to a Z-value of 1.04. (Extrapolation can be used when a greater degree of accuracy is required.) Since

$$Z = \frac{X - \mu}{\sigma}$$

and a Z-value of 1.04 was found, we have

$$-1.04 = \frac{X - 11{,}151}{3{,}550}$$

We then solve for X and get $X = \$7{,}459$. Anyone with an income of $7,459 or less will receive the government subsidy.

Notice the negative sign for the Z-value. The algebraic sign of Z was unimportant in earlier problems because we merely used the Z-value to look up an area in Table E. However, such is not the case now. In this instance, the Z-value is used for further mathematical calculations in solving for X. Hence, its sign is of importance.

The rule of thumb to remember is, if we are working in the area to the left of the mean, the sign is always negative.

EXAMPLE 6-2 Improving Urban Fire Prevention

The Fire Prevention Act of 1988 calls for increased efforts on the part of local fire departments to reduce response time to fire calls. A group of experts impaneled by the president of the United States is attempting to identify those city fire departments whose response time is either (1) in the lowest 10 percent, or (2) who took longer than 90 percent of all fire departments in the study. Those in the first group are to serve as models for the less efficient fire units in the second group.

Data show that the mean response times for a certain class of fire departments is 12.8 minutes, with a standard deviation of 3.7 minutes.

SOLUTION:

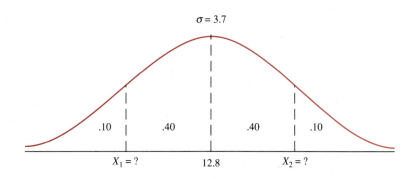

Assuming response times are normally distributed, the accompanying figure illustrates the panel's problem. It must determine two response times. The first is so short that only 10 percent of all fire units arrive at the fire within that time. The second is so long that only 10 percent of all fire units took more time. The Z-formula is used to determine each X value. To ascertain the quicker response time, we look up 0.4000 in the main body of Table E. Although we are concerned about the bottom 10 percent, we must look up 0.4000 since that is what the table is designed to reveal. The entry $0.3997 \approx 0.4000$ is the closest, yielding a Z-value of 1.28. Since we are seeking a value for X in the left tail, the Z-value is given the appropriate negative sign.

$$Z_1 = \frac{X_1 - \mu}{\sigma}$$

$$-1.28 = \frac{X_1 - 12.8}{3.7}$$

$$X_1 = 8.06 \text{ minutes}$$

and

$$Z_2 = \frac{X_2 - \mu}{\sigma}$$

$$1.28 = \frac{X_2 - 12.8}{3.7}$$

$$X_2 = 17.54 \text{ minutes}$$

The Z-value for X_2 is given a positive sign since we seek a value in the right tail greater than the mean.

STATISTICAL INTERPRETATION:
Only 10 percent of the fire departments in this classification responded to fire calls in less than 8.06 minutes. These fire units will serve as model programs for the 10 percent of fire departments whose fire runs exceeded 17.54 minutes.

QUICK CHECK 6.4.1

○○○○   Assume $N \sim (100, 35)$. Below what value of X is 60 percent of the area under the curve found?

Answer: 108.75 ($Z = 0.25$ is used)

QUICK CHECK 6.4.2

Assume $N \sim (25, 12)$. Above what value of X is 75 percent of the area under the curve found?

Answer: 16.96 ($Z = -0.67$ is used)

6.5   NORMAL APPROXIMATION TO THE BINOMIAL

We found in the previous chapter that the Poisson distribution was a useful approximation of the binomial distribution. That approximation was often necessary if the number of trials was large since the binomial table provided values only up to $n = 20$.

The normal distribution can also serve as an approximation of the binomial. However, while the Poisson distribution is appropriate when π is small (preferably, $\pi \le 0.10$), the normal distribution provides a more accurate estimate of the binomial when π is near 0.50 because the binomial approaches symmetry as π approaches 0.50.

To apply the normal distribution, we must have the mean and standard deviation in order to compute the Z-value. Formulas (5.5) and (5.6) showed that in a binomial setting the mean and standard deviation are

$$\mu = n\pi \quad \text{and} \quad \sigma = \sqrt{n\pi(1 - \pi)}$$

Consider the following example. Company records show that 40 percent of all the automobiles produced by Ford Motor Company contain at least one part imported from Japan. Suppose a production manager for Ford wanted to know the probability that out of the next 200 cars produced, 90 contained an imported part. The problem lends itself to the binomial distribution since there are only two possible outcomes: either a car (1) does or (2) does not contain an imported part. The other conditions for the binomial are also present. However, since $n = 200$ is so large, neither Table B nor Formula (5.4) provide a viable or convenient solution.

We may therefore wish to apply the normal approximation since π is close to 0.50. Thus,

$$\mu = n\pi$$
$$= 200(0.4)$$
$$= 80$$
$$\sigma = \sqrt{n\pi(1 - \pi)}$$
$$= \sqrt{200(0.4)(0.6)}$$
$$= 6.93$$

There is one slight adjustment we must make before the solution can be derived. As noted above, under a normal distribution the probability that the random variable is equal to a specific value such as 90 is zero. We must therefore treat the probability of exactly 90 parts as the interval between 89.5 parts and 90.5 parts. See Figure 6-10. Thus,

$$P(X = 90) = P(89.5 < X < 90.5)$$
$$Z_1 = \frac{X_1 - \mu}{\sigma} = \frac{90.5 - 80}{6.93}$$
$$= 1.52, \quad \text{or an area of } 0.4357$$
$$Z_2 = \frac{X_2 - \mu}{\sigma}$$
$$= \frac{89.5 - 80}{6.93}$$
$$= 1.37, \quad \text{or an area of } 0.4147$$
$$P(89.5 < X < 90.5) = 0.4357 - 0.4147 = 0.0210$$

There is a 2.1 percent chance that out of 200 cars selected at random, exactly 90 will have an imported part.

FIGURE 6-10   Frequency of Imported Parts for FMC

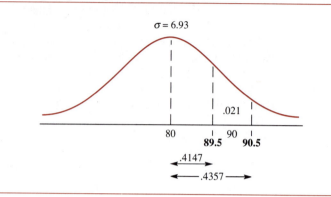

The mean income of the people at a plant is $330 per week, with a standard deviation of $102. Should you take a job there if you want a 30 percent chance of earning at least $400?

Answer: $P(X \geq 400) = 0.2451 < 0.30.$ Do not take the job.

QUICK CHECK 6.5.2

Given the data from 6.5.1, (a) what is the least income you can make and still be in the top 20 percent of the wage earners; (b) what is the most income you can make and still earn less than 80 percent of the workers?

Answer: (a) $416 (b) $244

6.6   SOLVED PROBLEMS

1. **Is the Rabbit Dead?** *Business Week* has reported that fiscal earnings for Playboy Enterprises, Inc. have shown significant reductions in the last few years. Christie Hefner, the founder's daughter, assumed the position of CEO Playboy in November 1988. Ms. Hefner has found that the mean monthly revenues for the various Playboy clubs around the nation are $1.23 million with a standard deviation of $0.65 million. Assume for the moment a normality in the distribution of monthly earnings.

    a.   If the revenues for one month were selected for any one of the clubs, what is the probability it would

1. exceed $1.3 million?

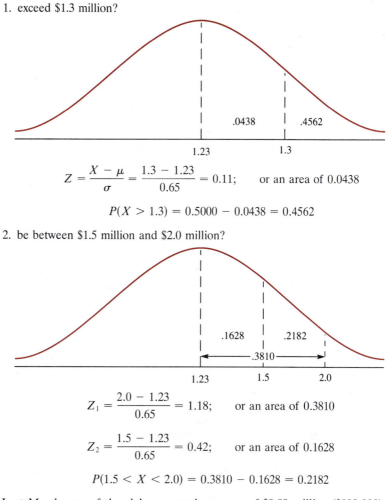

$$Z = \frac{X - \mu}{\sigma} = \frac{1.3 - 1.23}{0.65} = 0.11; \quad \text{or an area of } 0.0438$$

$$P(X > 1.3) = 0.5000 - 0.0438 = 0.4562$$

2. be between $1.5 million and $2.0 million?

$$Z_1 = \frac{2.0 - 1.23}{0.65} = 1.18; \quad \text{or an area of } 0.3810$$

$$Z_2 = \frac{1.5 - 1.23}{0.65} = 0.42; \quad \text{or an area of } 0.1628$$

$$P(1.5 < X < 2.0) = 0.3810 - 0.1628 = 0.2182$$

b. Last March, one of the clubs reported revenues of $0.89 million ($890,000). In response to Ms. Hefner's displeasure, the manager of that particular club offered the defense that revenues that low were not unusual. How would you respond to such a defense?

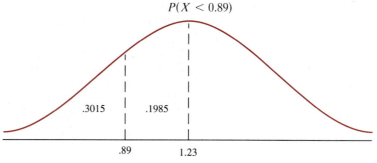

$$Z = \frac{0.89 - 1.23}{0.65} = 0.52; \quad \text{or an area of } 0.1985$$

$$P(X < 0.89) = 0.5000 - 0.1985 = 0.3015$$

This appears to be a reasonable defense. It seems that 30.15 percent of the time (almost one out of three times) clubs report monthly earnings lower than this one did in March.

c. If Ms. Hefner wishes to single out for corrective actions those clubs reporting receipts in the lowest 12 percent, what level of revenues must a club exceed without receiving this undesirable attention?

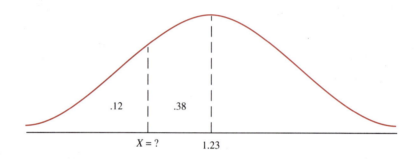

The proper Z-value is found in the table by searching for the area of 0.3800. This value is found to be 1.18 (or 1.17), which is given the proper negative sign since we are in the left-hand tail.

$$-1.18 = \frac{X - 1.23}{0.65}$$

Solving for X yields $X = 0.4630$ or $463,000.

2. **Smooth Operator** Assume that over the course of an entire year, St. Jude's Hospital admitted 50 patients who must be examined to determine if they might require surgery. What is the probability that more than one-half will require surgery? Records show that traditionally, 40 percent of their patients must submit to surgery.

   The binomial table will not provide an answer since $n > 20$, and use of the binomial formula is difficult. Therefore, an approximation is called for. Since $\pi = 0.40$ is reasonably close to 0.50, the normal approximation is best.

$$\mu = n\pi = (50)(0.40) = 20$$

$$\sigma = \sqrt{n\pi(1 - \pi)} = \sqrt{50(0.4)(0.6)} = 3.46$$

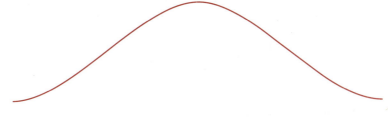

$$Z = \frac{25.5 - 20}{3.46} = 1.59; \qquad \text{or an area of } 0.4441$$

$$P(X > 25) = 0.5000 - 0.4441 = 0.0559$$

6.7   WHAT YOU SHOULD HAVE LEARNED FROM THIS CHAPTER

It should be apparent that the normal distribution is highly useful is solving many business-related problems. From a careful reading of this chapter you can now determine how the normal deviate can serve in the determination of probabilities pertaining to common business applications. Further, the use of the normal distribution as an approximation of the binomial should be clear.

6.8   COMPUTER APPLICATIONS

MINITAB

Normal probability can be approached in a number of different ways using Minitab. The commands

```
MTB > CDF;
Subc > Normal 150, 15.
```

yield a value for $P(X < 180) = 0.9772$ in a normal distribution with a mean of 150 and a standard deviation of 15. This agrees with the Telcom results presented in the chapter. In addition,

```
MTB > PDF 180;
Subc > Normal 150, 15.
```

provide $P(X = 180) = 0.0036$.

Minitab also allows you to find a value associated with a specific area under the curve. In the welfare program displayed in Figure 5-12 we wanted to find that level of income below which 15 percent of the people fell. The mean and standard deviation were $11,151 and $3,550. This is done as

```
MTB> INVCDF .15;
Subc> Normal 11151, 3550.
```

List of Symbols and Terms

Z: The normal deviate. It measures the number of standard deviations a point is above or below the mean after a normal distribution has been standardized.

List of Formulas

$$Z = \frac{X - \mu}{\sigma}$$ (6.1)

Conversion formula (or Z formula) to standardize all normal distributions.

Chapter Exercises

Conceptual Questions

1. Describe a normal distribution. What two parameters determine its location and shape?
2. Is the normal distribution a discrete or a continuous distribution? Defend your answer.
3. If two normally distributed data sets have the same mean but different standard deviations, how will the range which encompasses 68.8 percent of all the observations compare from one data set to the other? Draw the necessary figures to illustrate how the Empirical Rule can apply to both distributions.

Problems

4. Given $X \sim N(30,5)$, find the probability that
   a. $X > 32$.
   b. $X > 22$.
   c. $33 < X < 39$.
   d. $27 < X < 33$.
5. The completion time for a certain job averages 4.2 days with a standard deviation of 1.3 days. If times are normally distributed, what is the probability that the next time the job is to be done, it will take
   a. more than five days?
   b. between four and five days?
   c. less than three days?

6. Monthly Production costs for a print shop in Toledo have averaged $410 with a standard deviation of $87. The manager promises the shop owner to hold costs below $300 this month. If costs are normally distributed, can the owner believe the manager?

7. *The Journal of Mid-West Management* reviewed a study which showed that starting salaries for accounting majors averaged $22,510, with a standard deviation of $2,250. If salaries are normally distributed, what is the probability a new graduate will earn
   a. more than $21,000?
   b. less than $25,000?
   c. between $24,000 and $26,000?
   d. at least $20,000?

8. Given the information from the previous problem, what percentage of the accounting graduates earn
   a. more than $21,000?
   b. less than $25,000?
   c. between $24,000 and $26,000?
   d. at least $20,000?

9. The mean time it took all competitors to run the 100 meters was 12.92 seconds. Assuming a standard deviation of 1.3 seconds and a normal distribution in times, what percentage of the competitors finished the race in under 10.5 seconds?

10. The *San Jose Mercury News* reported that the average household telephone bill was $43.14 per month with a standard deviation of $15.12.
    a. What is the probability any single household selected at random would have a bill below $32?
    b. What percentage of the households have bills below $32?

11. The average telephone bill for a certain type of business is $215.45 with a standard deviation of $57.10. The CEO for that type of business wants to reward his branch operations by giving a bonus to any branch whose telephone bill is in the lowest 30 percent. Below what amount must a branch's bill be before getting the bonus?

12. Sales personnel for Acme Sales average $1,520 per week in sales with a standard deviation of $22. The sales manager will give a day off with pay to those on the sales force who are in the top 10 percent. Your sales this week were $2,250. Will you get the day off?

13. The city commission is considering raising property taxes to finance a new library. The commission feels they should tax only those who own homes valued in the top 40 percent. If property values can be expressed as $X \sim N$ ($62,500, $8,250), what is the highest value that can be placed on your property without being subjected to the tax?

14. Weekly production levels for a glass plant in Toledo average 2,730 pounds per employee with a standard deviation of 875 pounds. Production levels are normally distributed. What percentage of the employees produce more than 3,500 pounds per week?

15. If the glass company in the previous problem employs 1,500 people, how many of them produce
    a. more than 3,500 pounds?
    b. more than 2,730 pounds?

16. Given the data for the glass company above, within what interval will the middle 50 percent of productions lie?

17. The accounting firm of Dooit and Quick finds that the time it takes to complete an auditing process is approximately normally distributed with a mean time of 17.2 days and a standard deviation of 3.7 days. Mr. Dooit promises to start an auditing job for your firm within 20 days, but must finish the one he has just begun. How likely is it he will keep his promise?

18. Given the data from the preceding problem, if Mr. Dooit wants to be 95 percent certain of completing a job on time, how many number of days should he allow for completion?

19. According to *The Wall Street Journal,* corporate debt averages 90 percent of equity for the Fortune 500 firms. Assume it was found that the standard deviation was 25 percent and debt-to-equity ratios were normally distributed. How many of the 500 firms have a debt-to-equity ratio above 40 percent?

20. Given the data in the preceding problem, if a firm wished to avoid debt and ensure that its debt-to-equity ratio remained in the bottom 10 percent, below what level should its ratio be kept?

21. A story in *Business Week* stated that 45 percent of American businesses used memory chips and microprocessors imported exclusively from Japan. If 200 firms are selected at random, what is the probability that
    a. fifty percent use Japanese products exclusively?
    b. at least 50 percent use Japanese products exclusively?

22. *The Wall Street Journal* stated that European luxury car dealers were finding it increasingly difficult to sell their BMWs and other status symbols. Dealerships were overstocked by an average of 75 luxury units (cars). If the number of overstocked units is normally distributed with a standard deviation of 10 cars, what percentage of the dealerships are overstocked by more than 115 cars?

23. As a result of the unprovoked attack by a Klingon vessel on the Starship *Enterprise* of the United Federation, Captain James T. Kirk and his crew must consider the destructive power of the Klingon torpedos directed against them. It is known that the torpedos carry a mean destructive force of 1,000 tons of explosives, with a standard deviation of 200 tons. If Captain Kirk wants to ensure that 90 percent of the torpedos will not penetrate the *Enterprise*'s deflector shields, what tonnage level must he be prepared to defend against?

24. Daffy Doo Dry Cleaners has learned that if clothing is pressed at temperatures under 115 degrees or above 135 degrees, they are not done properly. Their Wrinkle-Free Pants Presser is found to be functioning improperly. It maintains a mean temperature of 130 degrees, with a standard deviation of 12 degrees. Assuming the temperatures are normally distributed, if 1,000 pants have been pressed, how many will have to be redone?

25. A designer for Cars-R-Us wants to construct the back seat in a new automobile so that at least 90 percent of the people who use it will have a 3-inch clearance from hip to knee. Studies show that the length of people's upper legs is normally distributed, and averages 15 inches with a standard deviation of 2.3 inches. How much room must the designer allow for in the back seat of his cars?

26. The ages of Happy Harry's customers are normally distributed with a mean of 56.6 and a standard deviation of 10.1. What is the probability that if one customer is picked at random, he or she is
    a. over 55 years old?
    b. under 60?
    c. between 55 and 60?

27. The average life of an electrically powered packaloma is 2.7 years with a standard deviation of six months. Packaloma, Inc. in Hoboken, New Jersey, has sold 10,000 packalomas with a warranty that they will be replaced if they do not last at least 2.5 years. How many packalomas will the firm have to replace?

28. Daily receipts at one of the attractions at Dollywood in Tennessee average $1,012 with a standard deviation of $312. What is the probability that today the attraction will take in more than $1,100?

29. Students taking the Graduate Management Aptitude Test averaged 812 with a standard deviation of 145. Only those in the top 20 percent can apply for a particular scholarship. Gus Genius received a 900 on the test. Can he apply?

30. The job manual for Jiffy Lube, a national auto maintenance outlet, specifies that the average time it should take to change the oil in passengers cars is 22 minutes with a standard deviation of 4.4 minutes. Marvelous Marv the Mechanic says he can complete the job in 19 minutes or less. How likely is he to fulfill this boast?

31. Response time for 911 emergency numbers in Peoria, Illinois, averages 4.8 minutes. Assume that the standard deviation is 1.2 minutes. A local resident calls claiming that the police took more than 7 minutes to show up at her door. How likely is that?

32. A particular job task requires on the average 6.2 weeks to complete, with a standard deviation of 1.5 weeks. Under a contract your firm has with a customer, it is agreed that if the job is not completed within seven weeks, you are subject to a lawsuit for the damages suffered by this customer due to your delay. You want the business, but you do not want to run more than a 30 percent chance of being sued. Should you take the job?

33. Acme Printing is given the job of providing the advertisement copy for a local business. A job such as this one averages 18.6 hours with a standard deviation of 2.2 hours. The business wants the material back in 16 hours. Will the work be done?

34. Daily receipts for a department store average $12,234 with a standard deviation of $2,345. The manager is being closely watched by the home office to determine his ability to generate revenues. The home office declares that if revenues on this particular day are less than $12,000 the manager will be fired. How likely is it he will be looking for a new job?

35. Happy Hair will hire only those hairdressers in the top 20 percent based on the amount of time it takes them to perform a task. If the mean time to perform this task is 67.5 minutes with a standard deviation of 12.5, how quickly must Harvey do the job in order to be hired?

36. Consumer test ratings for a new line of products have averaged 67.5 with a standard deviation of 23.3. Jeff Erickson has developed a new device which he wishes to market. His supervisor tells him that in order to put it into production, the device must receive a rating of at least 70. How likely is it that Jeff's project will reach the assembly line?

CASE APPLICATIONS

37. A study by professors in the College of Business at Bradley University in Peoria, Illinois, revealed that the response time to 911 emergency calls was 4.8 minutes with a standard deviation of 1.2 minutes. It was assumed that response times were normally distributed. The mayor of Peoria wanted to reduce mean response time enough so that 40 percent of all calls were answered within 3.5 minutes.

     It was estimated that the cost for patrol cars, fire units, and personnel would be $575,000 for every reduction of 30 seconds. The necessary revenue was to be raised by a property tax. However, it was felt that the tax burden should be borne only by those homes above $70,000 in assessed value. Homes averaged $45,000 in value, with a standard deviation of $15,110. It was felt that an average of an additional $96 could be raised for each home in Peoria over $70,000. There are 42,000 homes in the Peoria city limits. Based on these constraints, is the mayor's plan feasible?

SAMPLING DISTRIBUTIONS: AN INTRODUCTION TO INFERENTIAL STATISTICS

A PREVIEW OF THINGS TO LOOK FOR

1 What a sampling distribution is and how to create one.

2 How the luck of the draw can create sampling error.

3 How to calculate the mean of the sample means, and why it is equal to the mean of the population.

4 A definition and interpretation of the standard error of the sampling distribution, and why it exists.

5 Why the sampling distribution is normally distributed.

6 The impact of the sample size on the standard error.

7 The importance of the Central Limit Theorem.

8 The role of the finite population correction factor.

9 The numerous types of samples that can be taken.

CHAPTER BLUEPRINT

This chapter offers an introduction to the all-important concept of sampling and the manner in which samples are used to draw inferences about the population.

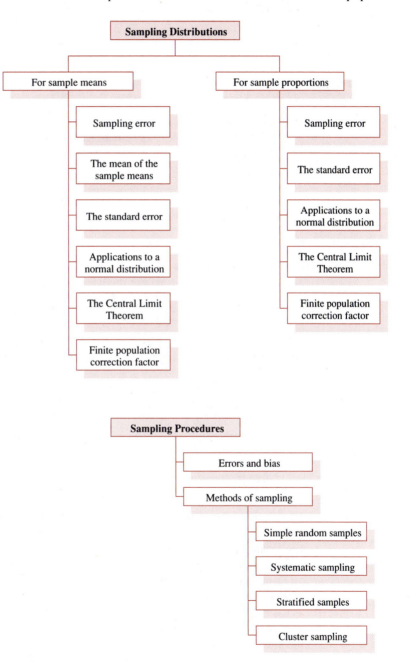

> Statistics show that you can never
> beat a man at his own game

7.1 INTRODUCTION

Populations are usually too large to study in their entirety. It is necessary to select a representative sample of a more manageable size. This sample is then used to draw conclusions about the population in which we are interested. For instance, we may calculate the sample mean, which is the statistic $\overline{X}$, and use it as an estimate of the population mean μ. The statistic is used as an **estimator** of the parameter. By relying on a sample to draw some conclusion, or inference, about the population, we are engaging in **Inferential Statistics.**

> **Inferential Statistics**
> Inferential statistics involves the use of a statistic to form a conclusion, or inference, about the corresponding parameter.

This inferential process is extremely important in many statistical analyses. In the following chapters dealing with estimation and hypothesis testing, inferential statistics proves essential.

However, the value of the statistic depends on the sample taken. From any given population of size N, it is possible to get many different samples of size n. Each sample may well have a different mean. In fact, it is possible to get an entire distribution of different $\overline{X}$'s from the various possible samples.

7.2 SAMPLING DISTRIBUTIONS

In a study of the firms on the Fortune 500 list of the nation's largest businesses, we might want to take a sample of, say, $n = 50$. From this sample we could calculate the mean rate of return $\overline{X}$ for these 50 firms. This sample mean would then serve as an estimate of μ, the population mean rate of return for all 500 firms.

From this list of 500 firms, it would be possible to get many different samples of size 50. Specifically, we could get $_{500}C_{50}$ different samples of size $n = 50$. Since $_{500}C_{50}$ is a rather large number, let us assume for the sake of simplicity in our discussion that we have a population of $N = 4$ incomes for four college students. These incomes are $100, $200, $300, and $400. The mean income can be calculated as $\mu = 250. However, to make matters even simpler, we may feel that calculating the mean of four observations requires too much effort. As an alternative, we decide to select a sample of $n = 2$ observations in order to estimate the "unknown" μ. We would then randomly select one sample from the $_4C_2 = 6$ possible samples. These six different samples and their means are shown in Table 7-1.

With the exception of the third and fourth samples, each sample has a different mean. Assuming each sample is equally likely to be chosen, the probability of selecting a sample that yields an $\overline{X}$ of 150 is

$$P(\overline{X} = 150) = \frac{1}{_NC_n} = \frac{1}{6}$$

Since $\mu = 250$, the probability of randomly selecting a sample which will yield an accurate estimate of μ is only

$$P(\overline{X} = 250) = \frac{2}{6}$$

Four of the six samples will result in some error in the estimation process. This **sampling error** is the difference between μ and the sample mean we use to estimate it. This difference occurs due to the mere chance that some extreme observations may be chosen for the sample. If chance dictates that a few extremely large observations are drawn for the sample, the sample mean will overestimate μ. For example, if by chance we happen to pick sample 5 in Table 7-1, our estimate of μ is $\overline{X} = 300$, which is greater than the actual value for the population mean. If, on the other hand, chance dictates that a few extremely small observations are drawn for the sample, the sample mean will underestimate μ. Samples 1 and 2 in Table 7-1 produce an underestimate of the population mean.

Sampling Error
The difference between the population parameter and the sample statistic used to estimate the parameter is called sampling error.

TABLE 7-1 All Possible Samples of Size $n = 2$ from a
Population of $N = 4$ Incomes

Sample	Sample elements X_i	Sample means $\overline{X}$
1	100, 200	150
2	100, 300	200
3	100, 400	250
4	200, 300	250
5	200, 400	300
6	300, 400	350

Due just to the luck of the draw, we may select a sample of $n = 2$ consisting of $100 and $300. The resulting mean of $\overline{X} = \$200$ produces a sampling error of $250 − $200 = $50. Of course, we can never really calculate the size of the sampling error since the population mean remains unknown. However, we must be aware that some sampling error is likely to occur.

With a population of only $N = 4$, we can list every possible sample mean shown in Table 7-1, along with its respective probability. Such a listing is called a **sampling distribution,** and is shown in Table 7-2. This sampling distribution is shown graphically as a histogram in Figure 7-1.

Sampling Distribution
A list of all possible values for a statistic and the probability associated with each value is called a sampling distribution.

TABLE 7-2   Sampling Distribution for Samples of Size $n = 2$ from a Population of $N = 4$ Incomes

Sample mean $\overline{X}$	Number of samples yielding $\overline{X}$	Probability $P(\overline{X})$
150	1	1/6
200	1	1/6
250	2	2/6
300	1	1/6
350	1	1/6
		1

FIGURE 7-1   Sampling Distribution for Samples of Size $n = 2$ from a Population of $N = 4$ Incomes

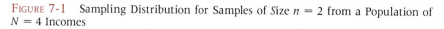
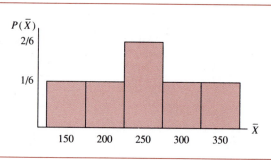

A.   THE MEAN OF THE SAMPLE MEANS

As illustrated above, the sampling distribution for the sample means is merely a listing of the six $\overline{X}$'s. Like any other list of numbers, these sample means have a mean. It is called the "mean of the sample means," or the **grand mean.** The mean of the sample means is calculated in the usual fashion: the individual observations (sample means) are summed, and the result is divided by the number of observations (samples). Using the symbol $\overline{\overline{X}}$ for the mean of the sample means, we have

$$\overline{\overline{X}} = \frac{\Sigma \overline{X}}{K} \qquad\qquad (7.1)$$

where K is the number of samples. Given the example above for the four incomes, it becomes

$$\overline{\overline{X}} = \frac{150 + 200 + 250 + 250 + 300 + 350}{6}$$

$$= 250$$

Grand Mean
The grand mean is the mean of all possible sample means.

Notice that the mean of the sample means equals the population mean of $\mu = 250$. This is no coincidence. The grand mean will always equal the population mean. If we were to take every possible sample of size n from a population and calculate each sample mean, the mean of those sample means would equal the population mean. The expected value of the sample means equals the population mean. Thus,

$$E(\overline{X}) = \mu$$

Be careful not to confuse n, the number of observations in a single sample, with K, the number of possible samples. In the example of the four incomes that we have been working with, the sample size is $n = 2$, while the number of possible samples is $_4C_2 = K = 6$.

EXAMPLE 7-1   A Sampling Distribution for Your Test Scores

Your statistics professor has given five tests this semester. You scored 70, 75, 65, 80, and 95 for a mean of $\mu = 77$. He decides to determine your grade by randomly selecting a sample of three test scores. Construct the sampling distribution for this process. What observations might you make?

SOLUTION:

There are $_5C_3 = 10$ possible samples.

Sample number	Sample elements X_i	Sample mean $\overline{X}$	Sample number	Sample elements X_i	Sample mean $\overline{X}$
1	70, 75, 65	70.0	6	70, 80, 95	81.7
2	70, 75, 80	75.0	7	75, 65, 80	73.3
3	70, 75, 95	80.0	8	75, 65, 95	78.3
4	70, 65, 80	71.7	9	75, 80, 95	83.3
5	70, 65, 95	76.7	10	65, 80, 95	80.0

The sampling distribution is

$\overline{X}$	$P(\overline{X})$
70.0	1/10
71.7	1/10
73.3	1/10
75.0	1/10
76.7	1/10
78.3	1/10
80.0	2/10
81.7	1/10
83.3	1/10
	1.00

STATISTICAL INTERPRETATION:

Since your average score was $\mu = 77$, 5 of the 10 possible samples will produce a sample mean $\overline{X}$ in excess of the mean of all five test scores, while the other 5 samples will underestimate it.

Remember that the sampling distribution of the sample means is nothing more than a set of numbers. Like any set of numbers, these sample means have a mean.

B. THE STANDARD ERROR OF THE SAMPLING DISTRIBUTION

The sample means also have a variance. This variance in the distribution of all the sample means is like any other variance. It measures the dispersion of the individual observations (sample means) around their mean (the grand mean). Furthermore, this variance is calculated like any other variance. It is the mean of the squared deviations from the mean. It can be found by

1. Determining the amount by which each of the observations (sample means) differs from their mean (the grand mean).

2. Squaring those deviations.
3. Averaging the squared deviations by dividing by the number of sample means, K.

Thus, where $\sigma_{\bar{x}}^2$ is the variance of the sampling distribution of sample means, we find

$$\sigma_{\bar{x}}^2 = \frac{\Sigma(\bar{X} - \overline{\overline{X}})^2}{K} \qquad (7.2)$$

Given the four incomes above,

$$\sigma_{\bar{x}}^2 = \frac{\begin{array}{c}(150 - 250)^2 + (200 - 250)^2 + (250 - 250)^2 + (250 - 250)^2 \\ + (300 - 250)^2 + (350 - 250)^2\end{array}}{6}$$

$$= 4{,}167 \text{ dollars squared}$$

If we were to take the square root of the variance in the distribution of these sample means, we would have the **standard error of the sampling distribution, $\sigma_{\bar{x}}$.** Thus,

$$\sigma_{\bar{x}} = \sqrt{\sigma_{\bar{x}}^2} \qquad (7.3)$$

$$= \sqrt{4{,}167}$$
$$= 64.55 \text{ dollars}$$

This standard error of the sampling distribution of sample means is a measure of the dispersion of the sample means around μ. It is analogous to the standard deviation that we calculated in Chapter 3. In Chapter 3, the standard deviation measured the dispersion of a set of individual observations around their mean. Here, the standard error of the sampling distribution of sample means (or, simply, standard error) measures the dispersion of a set of sample means around the grand mean.

The principle is the same in both cases. However, we seem to find ourselves working with too many "standard deviations"! There is the standard deviation of an entire population, σ, the standard deviation of a single sample, s, and now we have a measure for the standard deviation of an entire set of sample means. This might tend to get a little baffling. So to minimize the confusion factor, let's call the standard deviation of a set of sample means the "standard error of the sampling distribution of sample means," or just standard error for short.

There is an even better reason for using the term *standard error*. The difference between $\overline{X}$ and μ is called the *sampling error*. Since $\sigma_{\bar{x}}$ measures the dispersion in the sample means around μ, it is a measure of the sampling error we will typically experience in our effort to estimate μ. Thus, $\sigma_{\bar{x}}$, the standard error of the sampling distribution of sample means, measures the tendency to suffer sampling error in our estimate of μ.

Standard Error
The standard error is the measure of the variation of the sample means around the grand mean. As such, it measures the tendency to suffer sampling error in the effort to estimate the parameter.

EXAMPLE 7-2 The Standard Error

Your professor promises to give you an A if you can compute the standard error of the sampling distribution from Example 7-1.

SOLUTION:

$$\mu = \overline{\overline{X}} = \frac{\Sigma \overline{X}}{K} = 77$$

$$\sigma_{\bar{x}}^2 = \frac{\Sigma(\overline{X} - \overline{\overline{X}})^2}{K}$$

$$= \frac{(70 - 77)^2 + (75 - 77)^2 + (80 - 77)^2 + (71.7 - 77)^2 + (76.7 - 77)^2 + \cdots + (80 - 77)^2}{10}$$

$$= 17.6 \text{ points squared}$$

$$\sigma_{\bar{x}} = \sqrt{17.6} = 4.20 \text{ points}$$

STATISTICAL INTERPRETATION:
All 10 possible sample means averaged 77. That is, $\overline{\overline{X}} = \mu = 77$. There was a tendency for the sample means to vary from that 77 by 4.20 points.

Formulas (7.2) and (7.3) require a good deal of arithmetic and are awkward and cumbersome to use. A close approximation of the variance and standard error can be found much more easily with

---

$$\sigma_{\bar{x}}^2 = \frac{\sigma^2}{n} \qquad\qquad\qquad (7.4)$$

---

and

$$\sigma_{\bar{x}} = \frac{\sigma}{\sqrt{n}} \qquad\qquad (7.5)$$

where σ^2 is the population variance. This, of course, presumes that the population variance is known.

C. THE STANDARD ERROR AND NORMALITY

If the data in a population are normally distributed, then the sampling distribution of the sample means will also be normal. That is, if all possible samples of some given size are taken from a normally distributed population, and the means of all those samples are calculated, those sample means will be normally distributed.

Assume that we have incomes for several thousand students which average $500 and that these incomes are normally distributed. If all samples of size n are selected from that normal population of student incomes, then the sampling distribution of the sample means will also be normal. This is displayed in Figure 7-2. The individual observations in the population, X_i, are measured on the axis in Figure 7-2(a), while the various sample means, $\bar{X}$'s, are measured on the axis of Figure 7-2(b).

FIGURE 7-2   A Normal Population and Its Sampling Distribution

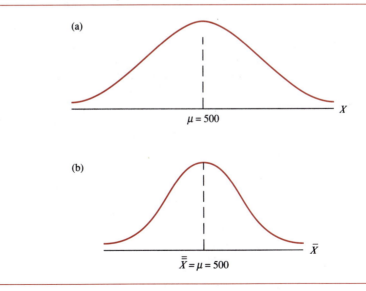

Furthermore, since the standard error of the sample means is found as

$$\sigma_{\bar{x}} = \frac{\sigma}{\sqrt{n}}$$

then

$$\sigma_{\bar{x}} < \sigma$$

The $\bar{X}$'s are less dispersed than the original data. That is, $\sigma_{\bar{x}}$, the standard error of the sampling distribution of the $\bar{X}$'s, is smaller than the standard deviation of the original population, σ. This is reflected by the shapes of the normal curves in Figure 7-2. In Figure 7-2(b), the $\bar{X}$'s are more closely clustered around their mean than are the individual observations in Figure 7-2(a).

Notice also that since the population of all the students' incomes averages $\mu = \$500$, then the mean of all the sample means, $\bar{\bar{X}}$, is also equal to 500. Both distributions in Figure 7-2 are centered at 500.

D.   THE IMPACT OF SAMPLE SIZE ON THE STANDARD ERROR

Given a population of $N = 100$, do you think you would get a more accurate esti-mate of the population mean with a sample of $n = 10$ or a larger sample of $n = 90$? Unquestionably, a more exact estimate is more likely with a larger sample. It seems only logical that a larger sample will tend to result in a smaller error. This assump-tion can be verified by

$$\sigma_{\bar{x}} = \frac{\sigma}{\sqrt{n}}$$

Based on simple arithmetic, it can be seen that as n goes up, $\sigma_{\bar{x}}$ must go down. Re-turn for a moment to our example of the four students' incomes. When samples of size $n = 2$ were taken, sample means ranged from a low of 150 to a high of 350. This distribution is repeated in Table 7-3, along with the distribution of all sample means of $n = 3$. With $n = 3$, possible sample means have a narrower range around

TABLE 7-3   A Comparison of Distributions with Different Sample Sizes

$X \mid n = 2$	$\bar{X}$	$X \mid n = 3$	$\bar{X}$
100, 200	150	100, 200, 300	200
100, 300	200	100, 200, 400	233
100, 400	250	100, 300, 400	266
200, 300	250	200, 300, 400	300
200, 400	300		
300, 400	350		

$\mu = 250$. If $n = 2$, it is possible to select a sample which varies from $\mu = 250$ by as much as \$100. This happens if the first sample with a mean of \$150 is chosen or if the last sample with a mean of \$350 is chosen. However, if $n = 3$, the largest sampling error that can occur is only \$50, one-half of the error you might suffer if $n = 2$. The first sample and the last sample have means of \$200 and \$300 respectively. Each differs from the population mean by only \$50.

This is further supported by Figure 7-3. If $n = 2$, the sampling distribution is illustrated in Figure 7-3(a). The distribution in Figure 7-3(b) that results when $n = 3$ displays less dispersion around the mean of \$250. As n increases, the spread in the sampling distribution, which is measured by the standard error, will decrease. Therefore, there is less chance for a larger error.

FIGURE 7-3   A Comparison of Distributions with Different Sample Sizes

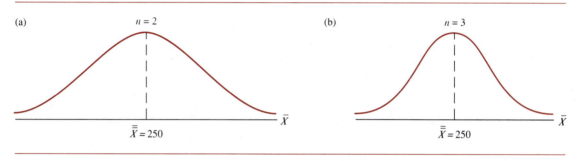

(a) $n = 2$ (b) $n = 3$

$\bar{\bar{X}} = 250$ $\bar{\bar{X}} = 250$

QUICK CHECK 7.2.1

○○○○   Given the years of work experience for four employees of 10, 7, 12, 8, calculate the (a) sampling distribution and (b) grand mean.

Answer:

(a)

X	$\bar{X}$
10, 7	8.5
10, 12	11.0
10, 8	9.0
7, 12	9.5
7, 8	7.5
12, 8	10.0

(b) $\bar{\bar{X}} = \mu = 55.5/6 = 9.25$

7.3   THE CENTRAL LIMIT THEOREM

As noted earlier, a sampling distribution of sample means is normally distributed if it is taken from a normal population. However, in many instances the population is not normally distributed. In such a case we must rely on the **Central Limit Theorem.** This crucial proposition states that for any population, whether it is normal or not, the sampling distribution will approach normality provided the sample size is "large."

Even if the population is not normally distributed, or if we have no knowledge of its distribution, the Central Limit Theorem allows us to conclude that the sampling distribution will be normally distributed if the sample size is sufficiently large. It is generally accepted that a sample size of at least $n = 30$ is large enough to conclude that the Central Limit Theorem will ensure a normal distribution in the sampling process regardless of the distribution of the original population. This is a very important consideration. If we can depend on the fact that sample means are normally distributed, we can then use the normal deviate Z that we encountered in the previous chapter. Our ability to rely on the Z conversion formula offers a vital salvation when no other solution is viable.

In a more formal sense, the Central Limit Theorem states that, for any distribution, as n gets larger, the sampling distribution will approach a normal distribution with $\overline{\overline{X}} = \mu$ and $\sigma_{\bar{x}} = \sigma/\sqrt{n}$. This means that even if the population is not normally distributed, the distribution of sample means will be normal if $n \geq 30$, and we can continue to use the Z conversion formula in our calculations.

Central Limit Theorem
As n gets larger, the sampling distribution will approach a normal distribution with $\overline{\overline{X}} = \mu$ and $\sigma_{\bar{x}} = \sigma/\sqrt{n}$.

Figure 7-4 illustrates how the distribution of sample means approaches normality as n gets bigger. Notice that as we move from n_1 to n_5, the sample sizes increase, and each curve is more bell-shaped than the previous one.

Assuming that n_5 is at least 30, it can be seen that the distribution of sample means is normal. Further, since $n_5 > n_4$, not only is the distribution normal where $n = n_5$, but the sample means are more closely clustered around the grand mean. This is because the standard error is smaller as n gets bigger, as we illustrated in Figure 7-3.

This Central Limit Theorem is a very important statement in statistical analysis. It allows us to apply the useful and advantageous principles of normality in the sampling process even when the distribution of the population is unknown. The Central Limit Theorem assures us that if we sample from a nonnormal population, we will achieve approximately the same results as we would if the population were normally distributed, provided $n \geq 30$.

FIGURE 7-4   Impact of the Central Limit Theorem Where $n_1 < n_2 < n_3 < n_4 < n_5$

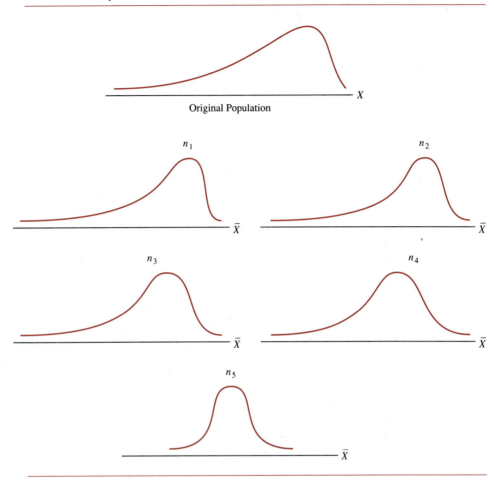

7.4   THE FINITE POPULATION CORRECTION FACTOR

The Central Limit Theorem and the assumption of a normal distribution in the sample means apply only if sampling is done with replacement or from an infinite population. If sampling is performed from a finite population, and drawing is done without replacement, the sampling process is slightly altered because selection of the sample elements is not an independent event. The probability of choosing a given element on any draw depends on previous selections if drawing is done without replacement. The probability of selecting a king from a deck of cards on the second draw depends on whether a king was drawn the first time.

In order to adjust for this modification in probabilities, the **finite population correction** factor (FPC) must be used in calculating the standard error. Specifically, we find that if drawing is done without replacement from a finite population the variance is

$$\sigma_{\bar{x}}^2 = \left[\frac{\sigma^2}{n}\right]\left[\frac{N-n}{N-1}\right] \qquad (7.6)$$

and the standard error becomes

$$\sigma_{\bar{x}} = \left[\frac{\sigma}{\sqrt{n}}\right]\sqrt{\frac{N-n}{N-1}} \qquad (7.7)$$

where

$$\frac{N-n}{N-1}$$

is the FPC. This expression accounts for the fact that N is finite, and thereby provides a more accurate statement of the variation in the sampling distribution.

If n is small relative to N, however, the FPC approaches 1. That is, if the sample size is relatively small compared with the population, Formula (7.6) yields a value for the FPC close to 1. Since there is no sense in multiplying by 1, the FPC is used only if n is large relative to N. The general rule of thumb is to use the FPC only if n is more than 10 percent of N.

EXAMPLE 7-3 Using the FPC

The U.S. Bureau of Census wishes to estimate the birthrates per 100,000 people in the nation's 100 largest cities. It is known that the standard deviation in the birthrates for these 100 urban centers is 12 births per 100,000 people.

a. Calculate the variance and standard error of the sampling distribution of $n = 8$ cities.
b. Calculate the variance and standard error of the sampling distribution of $n = 15$ cities.

SOLUTION:

a. Since n is less than 10 percent of N, the FPC is not required. The variance and standard error are

$$\sigma_{\bar{x}}^2 = \frac{\sigma^2}{n} = \frac{12^2}{8} = 18$$

and

$$\sigma_{\bar{x}} = \frac{\sigma}{\sqrt{n}}$$

$$= \frac{12}{\sqrt{8}}$$

$$= 4.24 = \sqrt{18}$$

b. Since n is more than 10 percent of N, the FPC is required.

$$\sigma_{\bar{x}}^2 = \left[\frac{\sigma^2}{n}\right]\left[\frac{N-n}{N-1}\right]$$

$$= \left[\frac{12^2}{15}\right]\left[\frac{100-15}{99}\right]$$

$$= 8.24$$

$$\sigma_{\bar{x}} = \left[\frac{\sigma}{\sqrt{n}}\right]\sqrt{\frac{N-n}{N-1}}$$

$$= \left[\frac{12}{\sqrt{15}}\right]\sqrt{\frac{100-15}{99}}$$

$$= 2.87 = \sqrt{8.24}$$

Statistical Interpretation:
Not surprisingly, the larger sample has a smaller standard error and will tend to re-sult in less sampling error in estimating the birthrates in the 100 cities.

Just as a comparison, if we were to calculate the standard error when $n = 15$ without using the FPC, we would have

$$\sigma_{\bar{x}} = \frac{\sigma}{\sqrt{n}} = \frac{12}{\sqrt{15}} = 3.1$$

This compares with $\sigma_{\bar{x}} = 2.87$ when the FPC was used. The value 2.87 is a more accurate statement of the sampling distribution since it incorporated the FPC.

Quick Check 7.4.1

◯◯◯◯ From a population of 200 observations, a sample of $n = 50$ is selected. Calculate the standard error if the population standard deviation equals 22.

Answer: 2.7

7.5 USING THE SAMPLING DISTRIBUTION

The importance of the foregoing discussion can only be recognized if we recall that many decisions are made on the basis of sample results. A business manager may sample her product to determine if certain production specifications are being met. A government official will take a sample of residents to decide if a certain tax plan or welfare program will produce the desired results. Academicians often sample students to ascertain the impact of instructional efforts.

Generally speaking, samples have a very direct and consequential impact on decisions that are made. Therefore, any conclusion we can draw or knowledge we have regarding a sample is quite important. An extremely common and quite useful application of a sampling distribution is to determine the probability that a sample mean will fall within a given range. Given that the sampling distribution will be normally distributed because (1) the sample is taken from a normal population, or (2) $n \geq 30$ and the Central Limit Theorem ensures normality in the sampling process, the normal deviate may be used to gain information necessary in decision making.

In the previous chapter we determined the probability of selecting one observation that would fall within a given range. Recall that Telcom recorded telephone messages for their customers. These messages averaged 150 seconds with a standard deviation of 15 seconds. Telcom wished to determine the probability that one single call lasted between 150 and 155 seconds.

This was done using the conversion formula, or Z-formula,

$$Z = \frac{X - \mu}{\sigma}$$

in which X is a single observation of interest and σ is the population standard deviation.

Although such information is extremely useful in making business decisions regarding the number of operators who must be on duty or the type of equipment that might be needed, its application is somewhat restricted. This restriction results from the fact that the conversion formula, as expressed above, applies to only one observation X.

However, many business decisions depend on an entire sample, not just one observation. In this case the conversion formula must be altered to account for the fact that we are interested not in one observation X but in the mean of several observations, $\overline{X}$. Therefore, when sampling is done, the conversion formula becomes

$$Z = \frac{\overline{X} - \mu}{\sigma_{\bar{x}}} \qquad (7.8)$$

The observation of interest in the numerator is now $\overline{X}$, not X. Also, the denominator is not the population standard deviation σ, but the standard error of the sampling distribution, $\sigma_{\bar{x}} = \sigma/\sqrt{n}$. Formula (7.8) differs from the conversion formula employed in Chapter 6 in that Formula (7.8) is used when we have taken a sample. This distinction must always be kept in mind.

In the previous chapter, samples were not taken and the value of interest was a single observation (one phone call). The Z-formula was used to convert all normal distributions of X-values to a single standard form.

Despite the differences in the symbols shown in Formula (7.8) the Z-formula has the same purpose as before: it is used to convert all normal distributions (of $\bar{X}$'s in this case) to a standard form.

Instead of determining the probability of the duration of a single call, we now have the tools to calculate the probability that the mean of a sample of several phone calls will last a certain length of time. As an illustration of this newly found ability, let us determine the probability that the mean duration of a sample of $n = 35$ calls is between 150 and 155 seconds.

In the previous chapter Telcom wanted to know the probability that one call would take between 150 and 155 seconds. That is, $P(150 < X < 155)$. Given that the calls averaged 150 seconds with a standard deviation of 15 seconds this was determined as

$$Z = \frac{X - \mu}{\sigma}$$

$$= \frac{155 - 150}{15} = 0.33; \qquad \text{or an area of } 0.1293$$

The probability one call would take between 150 and 155 seconds of an operator's time was 12.93 percent. This is shown in Figure 7-5(a).

FIGURE 7-5   Comparing a Single Observation and the Mean of a Sample of Observations

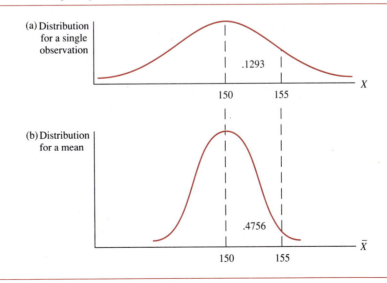

Compare Figure 7-5(b). Here Telcom wants to know the probability that a sample of $n = 35$ calls will have a mean between 150 and 155 seconds. That is, $P(150 < \overline{X} < 155)$. Since $n > 1$ and we are taking a sample, Formula (7.8) must be used. Then

$$Z = \frac{\overline{X} - \mu}{\sigma_{\bar{x}}} = \frac{\overline{X} - \mu}{\sigma/\sqrt{n}}$$

$$= \frac{155 - 150}{15/\sqrt{35}}$$

$$= 1.97; \quad \text{or an area of } 0.4756$$

While the probability that a single call will last between 150 and 155 seconds is 12.93 percent, the probability that a sample of 35 calls will have a mean duration within that range is 47.56 percent. The reason for this difference is that, you will recall, the sampling distribution is less dispersed than the original population. In Figure 7-5(a) a relatively small portion of the area under the curve is found between 150 and 155 seconds. But in the less dispersed distribution of sample means in Figure 7-5(b), a much larger portion on the total area under the curve is clustered within that narrow range.

It is possible to determine the probability that a sample mean will fall within any specified range. To illustrate this, consider Example 7-4.

EXAMPLE 7-4 Sampling Distribution for Telcom

Telcom plans to install new equipment which will improve the efficiency of their operations. However, before they can decide if such an investment would be cost-effective, they must determine the probability that the mean of a sample of $n = 35$

a. Is between 145 and 150.
b. Is greater than 145.
c. Is less than 155.
d. Is between 145 and 155.
e. Is greater than 155.

SOLUTION:
a. $P(145 < \overline{X} < 150)$

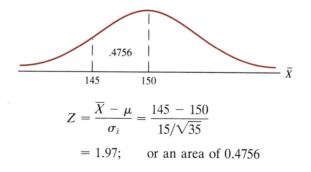

$$Z = \frac{\overline{X} - \mu}{\sigma_{\bar{x}}} = \frac{145 - 150}{15/\sqrt{35}}$$

$$= 1.97; \quad \text{or an area of } 0.4756$$

b. $P(\overline{X} > 145) = 0.4756 + 0.5 = 0.9756$

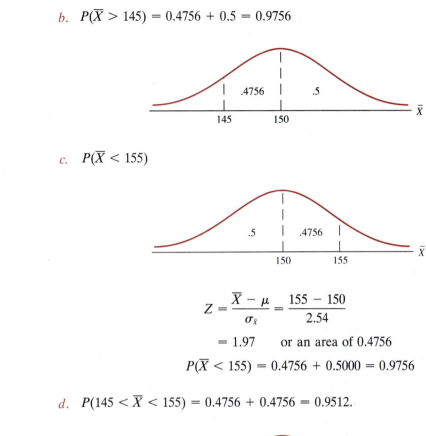

c. $P(\overline{X} < 155)$

$$Z = \frac{\overline{X} - \mu}{\sigma_{\bar{x}}} = \frac{155 - 150}{2.54}$$

$$= 1.97 \quad \text{or an area of } 0.4756$$

$$P(\overline{X} < 155) = 0.4756 + 0.5000 = 0.9756$$

d. $P(145 < \overline{X} < 155) = 0.4756 + 0.4756 = 0.9512.$

e. $P(\overline{X} > 155) = 0.5000 - 0.4756 = 0.0244.$

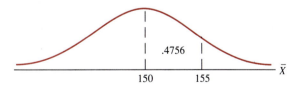

STATISTICAL INTERPRETATION:
On the basis of this profile of their business, Telcom can make a more intelligent decision regarding the need of the new equipment.

By being able to predict the likelihood that a certain statistic will fall within a given range, decision making becomes more precise and scientific. Less is left to chance and guesswork. Consider the following example.

EXAMPLE 7-5 Attention, K mart Shoppers

When J. E. Antonini became CEO for K mart in 1987, he expressed concern that Wal-Mart, his main competitor, was gaining an increasing share of the discount market. *Fortune* described Antonini's efforts to upgrade K mart performance. He ordered all store managers to survey their local customers' buying preference and income patterns.

The manager of a store in Detroit, K mart's home office, was told by the city government that average income in Detroit was $26,500, with a standard deviation of $8,750. The Detroit manager picked a sample of $n = 100$ customers and found a mean income of $\overline{X} = 24,510$. These 100 customers were surveyed regarding their buying preferences. However, due to the difference in the sample mean of $24,510 and the reported population mean of $26,500, the manager was concerned that the sample did not really represent the population. He questioned how likely it would be to get a sample with a mean of $24,510 from a population with a mean income of $26,500.

SOLUTION:

The manager is questioning the likelihood of getting a sample mean as low or lower than $24,510 if the population mean is indeed $26,500. That is, since $\overline{X} < \mu$, the manager is really asking how likely it is to get $\overline{X} \le 24,510$ if the sample came from a population with $\mu = \$26,500$.

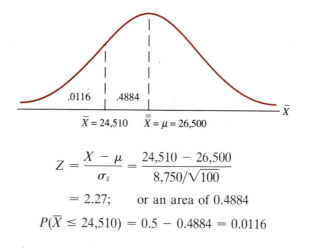

$$Z = \frac{X - \mu}{\sigma_{\overline{x}}} = \frac{24,510 - 26,500}{8,750/\sqrt{100}}$$

$$= 2.27; \quad \text{or an area of } 0.4884$$

$$P(\overline{X} \le 24,510) = 0.5 - 0.4884 = 0.0116$$

STATISTICAL INTERPRETATION:

If $\mu = \$26,500$ the probability of selecting a sample with a mean of $24,510 or less is 1.16 percent. It appears unlikely that the sample came from a population with a mean income of $26,500. Either (1) the sample is not representative of Detroit's population due to sample bias, or (2) the government is wrong in its statement that $\mu = \$26,500$. A third interpretation might suggest that K mart shoppers are a sub-population of Detroit with a mean income less than $26,500. In any event, it is unlikely that this sample came from a population with a mean income of $\mu = \$26,500$.

Consider Example 7-6 as an illustration of still another way in which sampling distribution can be used in making decisions.

EXAMPLE 7-6 The Stock Market Panic

According to a story in *Business Week,* Yargo Panic (pronounced PAN-eesh) fled Hungary to start BSE Pharmaceutical Inc. in California. Congressional hearings on AIDS research uncovered the fact that BSE had encouraged doctors to use a drug not approved by the FDA. BSE's stock fell dramatically, but Panic assured investors its daily price had averaged $22.10 with a standard deviation of $9.80. A sample of $n = 50$ days revealed a mean price of $20.40. What might this tell you regarding BSE's market performance?

SOLUTION:
Since $\overline{X} = \$20.40$ is less than Panic's claim of $\mu = \$22.10$, you want to determine the probability a sample could yield an $\overline{X}$ as low or lower than $20.40 if μ was indeed $22.10; $P(\overline{X} \le 20.40)$.

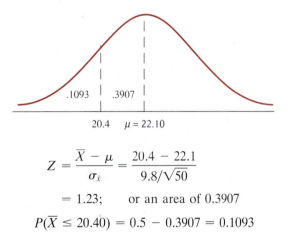

$$Z = \frac{\overline{X} - \mu}{\sigma_{\bar{x}}} = \frac{20.4 - 22.1}{9.8/\sqrt{50}}$$

$$= 1.23; \quad \text{or an area of } 0.3907$$

$$P(\overline{X} \le 20.40) = 0.5 - 0.3907 = 0.1093$$

STATISTICAL INTERPRETATION:
There is only about an 11 percent chance that if the average price of the stock has held at $22.10, a sample of size 50 could yield an $\overline{X}$ of just $20.40 or less. It might be concluded that

1. The sample was biased. Perhaps a second sample might be selected, taking precautions to ensure it is representative.
2. The value of $22.10 overstates the true mean. Panic was wrong, and the reason a lower $\overline{X}$ was found is because $\mu < \$22.10$.

○○○○   **DECISION MAKING THROUGH PROBLEM SOLVING**   ○○○○
                            ILLUSTRATION 7-1

According to a spokesman for the Del Monte Canning Company in Monterey, California, it is a standard practice for the firm to apply the principles of a sampling distribution as discussed here. It is essential that their canning operations meet certain
specifications. For example, automatic fillers on the production line must be set to in-
sure that the 36-ounce cans of Del Monte peaches maintain a net weight of about
36 ounces on the average. Amounts less than this can result in complaints by consumers and legal action by the Federal Trade Commission, while fills of more than
36 ounces produce unnecessary costs.

   The Del Monte spokesman explained that staff personnel will regularly select a
sample of several cans ($n > 30$) directly off the production line. These cans are
opened and the contents are weighed. They then compute the probability that the resulting sample mean could occur if the automatic fillers were indeed putting an average of 36 ounces in the cans as they pass through the production process. If this
probability is too low, the staff concludes that the automatic fillers are not working properly, and the production line must be shut down to allow the necessary
adjustments.

The sampling error can also be examined using sampling distributions. There are
many instances in which we may want to determine the probability of suffering an
error in excess of some tolerable level.

EXAMPLE 7-7 The Probability of Error

Batex manufactures telephone dialing systems for Bell Laboratories which average
3.2 inches in length with a standard deviation of 1.1 inches. If a sample of $n = 64$
systems is selected, what is the probability the sampling error will exceed 0.20 inch
in length?

SOLUTION:

A sampling error of at least 0.20 inch requires that the mean length of the 64 dialing
units randomly selected for the sample deviates from the population mean of 3.2 by
at least 0.20. That is, the mean length of the 64 units is less than 3.0 inches or more
than 3.4 inches. Therefore, Batex seeks the probability that the mean length of dialing units is less than 3.0 or more than 3.4 inches.

   Batex must therefore calculate two Z-values. The first yields the probability that
the sample mean of 64 units is greater than 3.4. However, the Z-table will only provide areas from the mean of 3.2 up to some chosen value of interest. They must
therefore calculate the area from the mean of 3.2 up to 3.4, and then subtract that
area from 0.5 to obtain the value that they want.

   This is done by

$$Z_1 = \frac{\overline{X} - \mu}{\sigma_{\bar{x}}} = \frac{3.4 - 3.2}{1.1/\sqrt{64}}$$

$$= 1.45; \quad \text{or an area of } 0.4265$$

Therefore,

$$P(\overline{X} > 3.4) = 0.5 - 0.4265 = 0.0735$$

See the accompanying figure.

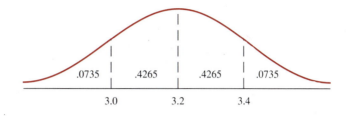

Similarly, the probability that the sample mean is less than 3.0 is found by determining the area from 3.2 down to 3.0 and subtracting from 0.5.

$$Z_2 = \frac{\overline{X} - \mu}{\sigma_{\bar{x}}} = \frac{3.0 - 3.2}{1.1/\sqrt{64}}$$

$$= 1.45; \quad \text{or an area of } 0.4265$$

Therefore,

$$P(\overline{X} < 3.0) = 0.5 - 0.4265 = 0.0735$$

Then

$$P(\overline{X} < 3.0) + P(\overline{X} > 3.4) = 0.0735 + 0.0735 = 0.1470$$

STATISTICAL INTERPRETATION:
We can be fairly certain that the sampling error will not exceed 0.2 inch if a sample of 64 is taken. There is only a 14.7 percent probability that $\overline{X}$ would differ from μ by more than 0.20 inch.

Often the population mean is unknown. The conversion formula cannot be used in its usual manner since μ is used in the numerator. However, the concept of normality is still useful. Consider Example 7-8.

EXAMPLE 7-8 Buying the American Way

The standard deviation of the purchases of consumers at a particular store is $18. A random sample of 100 customers is selected.

a. What is the standard error of the sampling distribution?
b. What is the probability the sample mean exceeds the population mean by more than $5?

SOLUTION:

a.

$$\sigma_{\bar{x}} = \frac{\sigma}{\sqrt{n}} = \frac{18}{\sqrt{100}} = \$1.80$$

b.   Since the difference between $\overline{X}$ and μ is set at $\overline{X} - \mu = 5$, we have

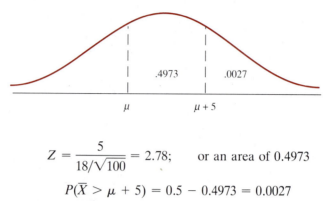

$$Z = \frac{5}{18/\sqrt{100}} = 2.78; \qquad \text{or an area of } 0.4973$$

$$P(\overline{X} > \mu + 5) = 0.5 - 0.4973 = 0.0027$$

STATISTICAL INTERPRETATION:

There is only a 0.27 percent probability that a sample of 100 will yield an $\overline{X}$ which overestimates μ by more than $5.

QUICK CHECK 7.5.1

○○○○

From a population with a mean of 53 and a standard deviation of 18, a sample of $n = 49$ is taken. What is the probability the sample mean will exceed 55?

Answer: 0.2177

QUICK CHECK 7.5.2

Temperatures in Tallahassee average 87 with a standard deviation of 37. If a sample of $n = 100$ days is selected, what is the probability the sampling error will exceed 5 degrees?

Answer: 0.1770

7.6   THE SAMPLING DISTRIBUTIONS FOR PROPORTIONS

In the preceding discussion our attention has focused on the sample means and their distribution. Our interest has been in some variable which might be measured and averaged. However, many instances arise in which our concern is only whether a particular observation (1) does or (2) does not fit a certain characteristic. A politician wants to know if a voter (1) is or (2) is not going to vote for him. A businesswoman wants to know if a customer (1) is or (2) is not going to buy. A doctor is interested in whether a drug (1) does or (2) does not aid his patient.

In all of these instances there are only two possible outcomes for each observation: a success or a failure. This situation is obviously related to the problems in the previous chapter dealing with binomial distribution. Those problems concerned efforts to determine the probability that a certain number of observations met a particular characteristic. Here we are interested not in the number, or count, of observations, but the percentage or proportion of observations that meet the characteristic. The politician wants to know not how many people are going to vote for him, but what percentage of the people will do so. Thus, instead of sample means, we are dealing with sample proportions.

Given a large population of scuba divers, we could take a sample of n divers to determine who (1) could and (2) could not pass safety tests. Those who could do so would be identified as a success. We could then note the proportion of successes in the sample. Note that $_N C_n$ samples could be selected. Each would have its own proportion of successes. An entire distribution of sample proportions could be obtained. If a sample proportion is designated as p, the mean of all the sample proportions is $\bar{p}$.

Before we go any further, perhaps a word of caution is in order regarding symbols. Do not confuse $X, \bar{X}, \bar{\bar{X}}, p,$ and $\bar{p}$.

X is a single observation.
$\bar{X}$ is the mean of one sample.
$\bar{\bar{X}}$ is the mean of all the sample means and pertains to the entire sampling distribution (of means).
p is the proportion of successes of one sample.
$\bar{p}$ is the mean of all sample proportions and, like $\bar{\bar{X}}$, pertains to the entire sampling distribution (of proportions).

If S denotes the number of successes in a sample, then

$$p = \frac{S}{n} \tag{7.9}$$

Assume the politician surveys 1,000 voters and finds that only 350 are going to vote for him. Then

$$p = \frac{350}{1000} = 0.35$$

A different sample of $n = 1,000$ voters may yield a different p. The mean of the sample proportions, $\bar{p}$, will equal π, the population proportion. The analogy can be drawn from our discussion of the sampling distribution of sample means in which $\bar{\bar{X}} = \mu$. The standard error of the proportion is

$$\sigma_p = \sqrt{\frac{\pi(1 - \pi)}{n}} \tag{7.10}$$

As the sample size increases, the Central Limit Theorem applies to the distribution for proportions just as it does to the distribution for means. Specifically, the distribution of sample proportions will approach normality as long as $n > 50$ and both $n\pi$ and $n(1 - \pi)$ are greater than 5. Larger samples of 50 are needed for sampling proportions than the $n = 30$ that was necessary for distributions of sample means. This is because the sampling distribution of proportions only approximates a normal distribution, and therefore a larger sample is necessary to retain accuracy and validity. Furthermore, if sampling is done without replacement from a finite population and $n > 0.10N$, then the finite population correction factor is needed, and we have

$$\sigma_p = \sqrt{\frac{\pi(1 - \pi)}{n}} \sqrt{\frac{N - n}{N - 1}} \qquad (7.11)$$

With this discussion as a foundation, we are ready to examine distributions of sample proportions. Assume a doctor administers a drug to $N = 5$ patients. The results for each patient are, respectively, dies, lives, lives, dies, dies. We have D_1, L_2, L_3, D_4, D_5. All possible samples of size $n = 2$ are taken, and the proportion of successes (lives) are recorded in Table 7-4. From the population it can be seen that the proportion of successes is $\pi = 2/5 = 40$ percent. Also,

$$\bar{p} = \frac{\Sigma p}{K} = \frac{4}{10} = 0.40$$

which equals the population proportion. That is, the mean of all the sample proportions equals the population proportion. In addition,

$$\sigma_p = \sqrt{\frac{\pi(1 - \pi)}{n}} \sqrt{\frac{N - n}{N - 1}}$$

$$= \sqrt{\frac{(0.4)(0.6)}{2}} \sqrt{\frac{5 - 2}{5 - 1}}$$

$$= 0.30$$

Now suppose the doctor gives the drug to many patients, $\pi = 45$ percent of whom live. If a sample of 80 patients is selected, what is the probability more than 40 lived? Since $n > 50$ and both $n\pi$ and $n(1 - \pi)$ exceed 5, we may approximate the answer using the normal distribution and the Z-formula. For proportions the formula becomes

$$Z = \frac{p - \pi}{\sigma_p} \qquad (7.12)$$

TABLE 7-4   A Distribution of Sample Proportions

Sample		Proportion of successes (p)
D_1	L_2	0.5
D_1	L_3	0.5
D_1	D_4	0.0
D_1	D_5	0.0
L_2	L_3	1.0
L_2	D_4	0.5
L_2	D_5	0.5
L_3	D_4	0.5
L_3	D_5	0.5
D_4	D_5	0.0
		4.0

As was the case when the formula was used for sampling means, the numerator contains the relevant statistic p and the parameter π (instead of $\overline{X}$ and μ). The denominator consists of the standard error. Despite the differences in the symbols, the Z-formula has the same purpose as before: it is used to convert all normal distributions (of proportions) to a standard form.

The doctor wants to determine the probability that if $\pi = 0.45$ and $n = 80$, there were at least 40 of the 80 who lived. That is, the proportion of successes was at least 50 percent; $P(p \geq 0.5)$.

$$Z = \frac{p - \pi}{\sigma_p} = \frac{p - \pi}{\sqrt{(\pi)(1 - \pi)/n}}$$

$$= \frac{0.5 - 0.45}{\sqrt{(0.45)(0.55)/80}}$$

$$Z = 0.89; \quad \text{or an area of } 0.3133$$

Figure 7-6 provides an illustration. Thus,

$$P(p \geq 0.5) = 0.5 - 0.3133 = 0.1867$$

FIGURE 7-6   The Proportion of Patients Who Survived

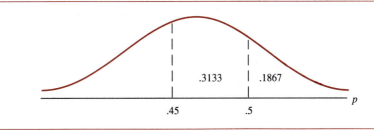

.3133   .1867

.45   .5

○○○○   DECISION MAKING THROUGH PROBLEM SOLVING   ○○○○
                        ILLUSTRATION 7-2

A report in an in-house publication by Head Sports Equipment detailed the manner in
which their quality control engineers ensured adherence to certain production specifications in the manufacture of their ski boots. Recognizing that no one is perfect,
Head expected 3 percent of the boots to suffer a particular malfunction. To establish
if an amount in excess of that limit failed their strict tests, Head statisticians randomly selected about 125 boots off the production line and determined the percentage
that were deemed defective. Using the test described above, they then calculated the
probability of getting a percentage of defects that high or higher if the production process was indeed generating only a 3 percent defective rate. If the likelihood of obtaining a sample defect rate over that range was too small (less than 5 percent), it was
concluded that the 3 percent limit was not being maintained. Technicians were ordered to locate the cause for the poor manufacturing performance.

EXAMPLE 7-9 The Probability of Getting Rich

Marry-Mate sells a popular product designed to make you more attractive to members of the opposite sex. Company records show that 75 percent of all potential customers contacted by mail purchase the device. Charlie sends out 200 letters offering
to sell the recipients the product. Charlie must sell at least 160 of them to make
enough commission to take his vacation to Cancun, Mexico. What is the probability
he will do so?

SOLUTION:

Charlie must have at least 160 out of 200 successes. Therefore,

$$p = \frac{S}{n} = \frac{160}{200} = 0.8$$

and he must determine $P(p \geq 0.8)$. Since $\pi = 0.75$ and $n = 200$, we have

$$Z = \frac{p - \pi}{\sigma_p} = \frac{p - \pi}{\sqrt{\pi(1 - \pi)/n}}$$

$$= \frac{0.8 - 0.75}{\sqrt{(0.75)(0.25)/200}}$$

$$= 1.63; \quad \text{or an area of } 0.4484$$

$$P(p \geq 0.8) = 0.5 - 0.4484 = 0.0516$$

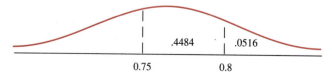

Statistical Interpretation:

Charlie might as well not pack a bag. There is only a 5.16 percent probability he is going to Cancun.

Quick Check 7.6.1

○○○○

Records show that 15 percent of a company's products shipped through the mail are damaged. If 500 are shipped, what is the probability more than 70 are damaged?

Answer: 0.7357

7.7   An Examination of Sampling Procedures

In our work thus far, the importance of taking a sample has been amply demonstrated. Without the ability to select a sample representative of the population, most of the statistical tools we commonly use in the decision-making process would not be available. It is only through the use of samples that inferential statistics allows us to draw conclusions regarding the population in which we are interested.

It should therefore come as no great shock to learn that considerable attention has been devoted to the efforts to construct reliable and scientific methods by which dependable samples can be selected. After all, the conclusions upon which our samples are based are no better than the samples themselves. We begin our review of sampling procedures with a brief discussion of the hazards associated with the sampling procedure: sampling error and bias.

A.   Sampling Error and Bias

The nature of sampling error is revealed in our earlier discussion of sampling distributions. To the extent that our samples are not representative of the population, we will suffer from sampling error. An unrepresentative sample will produce an erroneous estimate of the parameter and result in sampling error. Sampling error is the difference between the sample statistic and the population parameter we are trying to estimate.

Due to the debilitating nature of sampling error which undermines our aspirations to discover the true character of the world around us, you might well ask what might cause this error. There are two basic sources of sampling error. The first is something we all have had the misfortune to experience—plain bad luck. Just due to the luck of the draw, our sample might contain elements that are not characteristic of the population. Fate may dictate that certain selections in the sample are atypically larger than most of those in the population, which would result in an overestimation of the parameter, or perhaps many of the sample elements tend to be smaller than what are typically found in the population, in which case an underestimation would result. In either event, we are at the mercy of circumstance and can only hope that the sampling error is minimized. Assuming that we take our sample in accordance with established procedures, which will be discussed shortly, we can reduce sampling error, as we have seen earlier in this chapter, only by taking a larger sample.

A second source of sampling error is sampling bias. Bias results from the tendency to favor the selection of some elements over others in the collection of our sample data. The classic example of sampling bias occurred in the 1936 presidential election. Franklin D. Roosevelt was running on the Democratic ballot against Alf Landon, the Republican candidate. A survey of voters conducted by the *Literary Digest,* which long ago ceased publication, revealed that Landon would win in a veritable landslide. When the smoke lifted after the election, the editors of *Literary Digest* tried courageously to determine how they could have been so wrong!

They soon discovered their blunder. In selecting the people for their sample, they took names from two sources: the phone book and their own subscription rolls. Remember, in 1936 the nation was suffering from the worst depression we had ever known. Most people, rightfully or wrongfully, blamed the Republicans for this economic catastrophe and steadfastly refused to vote for anyone with that party affiliation. Thus, while the vast majority of the nation was caught in the viselike grip of the Great Depression, *Literary Digest* chose people who were less affected by harsh financial conditions and could actually afford a telephone and a regular subscription to a magazine. The people used in the survey were therefore not representative of the nation as a whole. The survey, as conducted by the magazine, tended to favor in its selection those voters who were not so adamantly opposed to the Republicans. No wonder the magazine is no longer in circulation.

There are many other instances in which the selection of the sample can result in error. It is therefore wise to ensure that the collection of sample data follows a prescribed method which has proven its ability to minimize such error. Although an exhaustive examination of sampling methods is beyond the scope of this text, a brief statement focusing on proper sampling procedures is warranted at this point.

B.   SIMPLE RANDOM SAMPLE

As was just illustrated, several different samples of a given size can be selected from a population. A **simple random sample** involves a method by which each possible sample has the same likelihood or probability of being selected. Assume that a national fast-food chain wishes to randomly select 5 of the 50 states to sample consumer tastes. If the five states are chosen in such a way that any one of the $_{50}C_5 = 2,118,760$ possible samples of five states is as likely to be chosen as any other sample of five states, a simple random sample has been taken.

There are at least two generally recognized methods of choosing a random sample. Perhaps the simplest technique is to merely list the states on 50 identical pieces of paper, put them in a hat, and draw out five of them. For example, when the military draft was still in effect, the U.S. Selective Service Commission developed a lottery system to determine the order of draft eligibility. A barrel was filled with 365 Ping-Pong balls corresponding to the days of the year. After mixing them thoroughly, one ball was selected. Those eligible males born on that day were "awarded" a first priority rating in the draft system. The contents of the barrel were again mixed, and a second date was drawn. This continued until the barrel was empty. This random selection represents a simple random sampling process. In theory, it ensured fairness in that each possible ordering of birth dates had an equal chance of appearing.

The Selective Service Commission might have used a second method commonly employed to establish a random sample. This alternative approach requires a random number table. A **random number table,** which is often generated by a computer program, is formed through the repeated selection of numerical digits. Each time, all 10 digits (0–9) have an equal likelihood of being selected. If a three-digit table is preferred, the computer program might randomly select the digits 2, 7, 9, 0, 1, 3, 9, 8, 4, 2, and so on, producing a partial random number table such as

Number	Priority
279	First
013	Second
984	Third
2..	. . .
. . .	. . .

The commission could then list each day of the year, and identify it with a three-digit number such as

Number	Date
001	Jan 1
002	Jan 2
003	Jan 3
004	Jan 4
.	.
.	.
.	.
279	Oct 6
.	.
.	.
.	.
365	Dec 31

Given the partial random number table above, the 279th day of the year (October 6) would be assigned the first priority, January 13 the second priority, and so on. If a number exceeding 365, such as the 984, is encountered, it is simply skipped and we move to the next entry in the table.

EXAMPLE 7-10 The Use of a Random Sample

Ralph Noah, president and founder of the Noah Fence Company, is planning a new marketing program which he hopes will increase sales. A random sample of past customers is required to implement the program. Mr. Noah does not enjoy the advantages of an adequate statistical background and must rely upon you, his newly hired marketing specialist, to correctly take a sample. He does realize, however, that the sample must be representative of the population if sampling error is to be minimized. Mr. Noah also expects a complete explanation and justification for your approach.

SOLUTION:

There have been more than 1,000 customers over the past three years, the period selected for the study. Your sample is selected by obtaining a list of these customers from company records and consecutively assigning each customer an identification number. A table of random numbers is then used to select a sample of the desired size.

STATISTICAL INTERPRETATION:

You explain to Mr. Noah that this technique produces a sample with the same likelihood of selection from the population as any other sample of that size. Given the randomness of this selection, it is reasonable to assume that it is representative of the population.

C. SYSTEMATIC SAMPLING

A **systematic sample** is formed by selecting every ith item from the population. If i is set equal to 10, a systematic sample consists of every tenth observation in the population. The population must be ordered or listed in a random fashion.

The first selection must be randomly determined, and if $i = 10$, it will be somewhere within the first 10 observations. The exact starting point can be identified by either selecting a number between 1 and 10 drawn from a hat, or by using a table of random numbers. In any event, every tenth observation thereafter is selected.

The process of systematic sampling is advantageous in that it doesn't require a highly skilled expert to count to 10 and record the outcome. In addition, the method permits flexibility in that i can be set to 10, 100, 1,000, or any other desired number. Determination of the proper value for i is also quite easy. If we wish to select a sample of size 100 from a population of 1,000, i must be 10.

The primary danger that must be avoided is the occurrence of a pattern in the ordering of the population. For example, listing the population alphabetically assumes a random distribution throughout the alphabet.

D. STRATIFIED SAMPLING

The U.S. Department of Agriculture recently became interested in the impact of drought conditions on the production of wheat. Of particular concern was the rate of bankruptcies causing farmers to lose their land. It was felt that an account of the production levels by farmers in Kansas, Oklahoma, Nebraska, and South Dakota, the four states hardest hit by the drought, might prove useful in devising a relief program. The department decided that a sample of this year's harvest should be taken for several hundred farmers from each state.

However, it was noted that the number of farmers was quite different in each state. If a simple random sample was taken from all four states as a whole, it might very well include proportionately too few farmers from some states and too many from others. This would result in a nonrepresentative sample which would increase the sampling error.

The Department of Agriculture decided to take a stratified sample by dividing all the farmers into subgroups or strata (hence the term *stratified sampling*). In this case, the logical subgroups would be the four states in question. The proportion of farmers included in the sample from each state would be set equal to those proportions of all farmers in each state. If Kansas farmers made up 30 percent of all the farmers in all four states, then 30 percent of the farmers in the sample would be randomly selected from Kansas.

A **stratified sample** is taken by forcing the proportions of the sample from each strata to conform to the pattern of the population. It is commonly employed when the population is heterogeneous, or dissimilar, yet certain homogeneous subgroups can be isolated. In this manner the researcher can increase accuracy beyond that obtained by a simple random sample of similar size.

Example 7-11 Use of a Stratified Sample

Mr. Noah is impressed with the convenience and ease of sampling. However, he feels that the behavior of his customers may depend upon whether they are home owners or renters. Records show that 75 percent of those doing business with the Noah Fence Company own their own home. He questions you about this potential problem. How do you respond?

Solution:

You suggest to your employer that a stratified sample be taken which reflects this proportion in customers' tendency for home ownership. Thus, 75 percent of the sample taken will consist of home owners. The rest will be those who pay rent.

Statistical Interpretation:

A stratified sample is designed to capture the same proportions of certain homogeneous substrata in the sample as found in the population. Given Mr. Noah's concern about the impact of ownership on buying habits, a stratified sample is called for and should prove more representative of the population.

E. Cluster Sampling

As still another alternative technique, cluster sampling offers certain advantages over other methods. It consists of dividing the entire population into clusters, or groups, and then selecting a sample of these clusters. All observations in those selected clusters are included in the sample. To illustrate, consider the following example. The U.S. Department of Agriculture, in its study of drought conditions, might decide that a cluster sample is preferable. A cluster sample is taken by identifying the counties in each state as clusters. A sample of these counties (clusters) is then chosen randomly by using a table of random numbers or some other generally accepted means. All farmers in the counties selected in this manner are included in the sample. This procedure is often easier and quicker than simple random sampling or stratified sampling. For example, if it is necessary to travel to each farm in the sample to observe the effects of the drought, it is easier to visit several farmers in the same county.

It is also possible to combine stratified sampling with cluster sampling. In our agricultural example, it might be wise to select for our sample a number of counties from each state proportional to the total number of counties in all four states.

Certain problems can arise in the use of cluster sampling. If an abnormally large (or small) percentage of the farmers in a selected cluster tend to use irrigation to enhance crop yields, the sample results may be biased.

EXAMPLE 7-12 Use of Cluster Sampling

Although Noah agrees that a sample can provide valuable information about the buying habits of his customers, he still feels that sampling will involve too much time sorting through old records. He demands that you devise a method which will prove quicker, less costly, and will still produce a representative sample.

SOLUTION:

You explain to Mr. Noah that it is possible to identify each month over the three-year study period as a cluster. A random sample of the clusters could be easily selected. It is then necessary to locate, organize, and examine only those records from the months comprising the sample, not all 36 months over the entire three-year period.

STATISTICAL INTERPRETATION:

A cluster sample can often simplify the sampling process to an even greater extent. This results in a further reduction in the cost and time associated with sample taking.

This discussion is in no way a complete account of sampling methods or the problems that can arise in the process of searching for a representative sample which can be used to draw statistical inferences. A study of sampling techniques constitutes an entire course in and of itself and is beyond the confines and scope of this text. However, due to the importance of the sampling process, even the beginning student should be aware of sampling fundamentals.

7.8 SOLVED PROBLEMS

1. **A Call to Arms** Arms International markets their product worldwide. Since much of their business is done over the telephone, it is important to minimize any delay customers may experience in trying to contact Arms' sales personnel. The CEO for Arms found

that six calls entered their switchboard this morning. Due to insufficient staffing, the delays each caller experienced, in minutes, in reaching the sales office were 20, 12, 17, 15, 18, and 15.

a. If the CEO were to select a sample of two calls, how many samples would there be in the sampling distribution?

SOLUTION:

$$_N C_n = {}_6 C_2 = 15$$

b. Compute the population standard deviation. You will use it in part (e).

$$\sigma^2 = \frac{\Sigma(X_i - \mu)^2}{N} = \frac{38.83}{6} = 6.47$$

$$\sigma = 2.54$$

c. Construct the sampling distribution.

SOLUTION:

Sample	X	$\bar{X}$	Sample	X	$\bar{X}$
1	20, 12	16.0	9	12, 15	13.5
2	20, 17	18.5	10	17, 15	16.0
3	20, 15	17.5	11	17, 18	17.5
4	20, 18	19.0	12	17, 15	16.0
5	20, 15	17.5	13	15, 18	16.5
6	12, 17	14.5	14	15, 15	15.0
7	12, 15	13.5	15	18, 15	16.5
8	12, 18	15.0			

The sampling distribution would then appear as

$\bar{X}$	$P(\bar{X})$
13.5	2/15
14.5	1/15
15.0	2/15
16.0	3/15
16.5	2/15
17.5	3/15
18.5	1/15
19.0	1/15
	1

d. What is the probability (1) the two longest delays are selected as the sample, and (2) the 17-minute delay is included in the sample.

SOLUTION:

The two longest delays, 20 and 18, can be selected in only one of the 15 possible samples:

$$P(2 \text{ longest}) = \frac{1}{15}$$

$$P(17 \text{ is in sample}) = \frac{5}{15}$$

e. What is the mean and standard error of the sampling distribution? How does the mean of the sampling distribution compare with the mean of the population?

SOLUTION:

$$\overline{\overline{X}} = \frac{\Sigma \overline{X}}{K} = \frac{242.5}{15} = 16.167 = \mu$$

The standard error can be found in two ways. Using Formula (7.2), we find

$$\sigma_{\bar{x}}^2 = \frac{\Sigma(\overline{X} - \overline{\overline{X}})^2}{K} = \frac{38.83}{15} = 2.59$$

$$\sigma_{\bar{x}} = \sqrt{2.59} = 1.609$$

Using Formula (7.7), which is simpler but provides only an approximation, yields

$$\sigma_{\bar{x}} = \frac{\sigma}{\sqrt{n}} \sqrt{\frac{N - n}{N - 1}} = \frac{2.54}{\sqrt{2}} \sqrt{\frac{6 - 2}{6 - 1}} = 1.612$$

f. Interpret $\sigma_{\bar{x}}$.

SOLUTION:

The standard error of the sampling distribution of sample means is a measure of dispersion in the 15 sample means in the distribution. It measures the tendency to suffer sampling error on our estimates of μ.

2. **Greed and LBOs** *Fortune* reported that the impact of leveraged buyouts is difficult to detect. In 1988 the average value of Fortune 500 firms who were bought out was $3.51 billion with a standard deviation of $1.92 billion.

   a. If a sample of $n = 64$ firms is taken, what is the probability the sample mean will exceed $3.65 billion?

SOLUTION:

$$Z = \frac{\overline{X} - \mu}{\sigma_{\bar{x}}} = \frac{\overline{X} - \mu}{\sigma/\sqrt{n}} = \frac{3.65 - 3.51}{1.92/\sqrt{64}}$$

$$= 0.58; \quad area = 0.2190$$

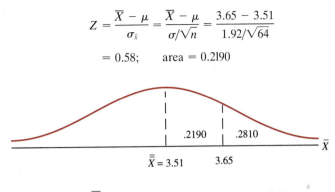

.2190 | .2810

$\overline{X} = 3.51$ 3.65

$$P(\overline{X} > 3.65) = 0.5000 - 0.2190 = 0.2810$$

b. What percentage of all possible samples of size 64 would yield an $\overline{X} > 3.65$?

SOLUTION:

0.2810

c. If you took a sample of $n = 64$ and got an $\overline{X} = 3.90$, what might you conclude?

SOLUTION:

The question is really asking, "How likely is it that you could get an $\overline{X}$ equal to or greater than 3.90?" It is "greater than" since $\overline{X} > \mu$.

$$Z = \frac{\overline{X} - \mu}{\sigma_{\bar{x}}} = \frac{3.90 - 3.51}{0.24}$$

$$= 1.63; \quad area = 0.4484$$

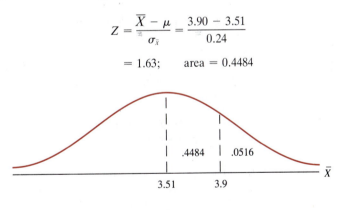

.4484 | .0516

3.51   3.9

$$P(\overline{X} \geq 3.90) = 0.5 - 0.4484 = 0.0516$$

Since there is only a 5.16 percent chance of selecting a sample that yields an $\overline{X}$ greater than 3.9, you might conclude that your sample was biased or *Fortune's* data are wrong and $\mu > 3.51$. The only other explanation is that a rarity has occurred in that you selected a unique sample that would exist in only 5.16 percent of the cases.

d. If *Fortune's* data are correct, how likely is it that if you take a sample of $n = 100$ firms, your sampling error will exceed $500 million?

SOLUTION:

Since $500 million is $0.5 billion, any value outside the range of $3.51 \pm 0.5 = 3.01$ to 4.01 would constitute an error in excess of the stipulated amount.

$$P(\text{error} > 0.5) = 1 - P(3.01 < \overline{X} < 4.01)$$

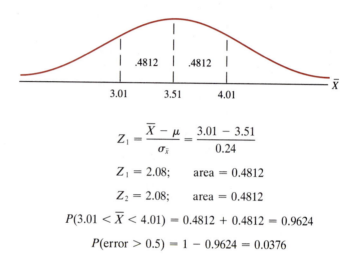

$$Z_1 = \frac{\overline{X} - \mu}{\sigma_{\bar{x}}} = \frac{3.01 - 3.51}{0.24}$$

$$Z_1 = 2.08; \quad \text{area} = 0.4812$$

$$Z_2 = 2.08; \quad \text{area} = 0.4812$$

$$P(3.01 < \overline{X} < 4.01) = 0.4812 + 0.4812 = 0.9624$$

$$P(\text{error} > 0.5) = 1 - 0.9624 = 0.0376$$

3. **Protecting the Taxpayer** Government officials in Washington have recently expressed concern regarding overruns on military contracts. These unplanned expenditures have been costing American taxpayers billions of dollars every year. The president impanels a committee of experts to estimate the average amount each contract costs the government over and above the amount agreed upon. The committee has already determined that the standard deviation in overruns is $17.5 billion, and that they appear to be normally distributed.

a. If a sample of 25 contracts is selected, how likely is it the sample will overestimate the population mean by more than $10 billion?

SOLUTION:

Since we are told the distribution of overruns is normal, a large sample is not required to apply the normal deviate. Thus,

$$Z = \frac{\overline{X} - \mu}{17.5/\sqrt{25}}$$

$$Z = \frac{10}{17.5/\sqrt{25}} = 2.86; \quad \text{or an area of } 0.4979$$

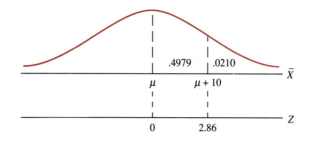

$$P(\overline{X} > \mu + 10) = P(Z > 2.86) = 0.5000 - 0.4979 = 0.0021$$

b.   The president will accept an error of $5 billion in the estimate of μ. How likely is he to receive an estimate from the committee within the specified range?

SOLUTION:

$$Z = \frac{\overline{X} - \mu}{\sigma_{\bar{x}}}$$

$$Z = \frac{5}{17.5/\sqrt{25}} = 1.43; \qquad \text{or an area of } 0.4236$$

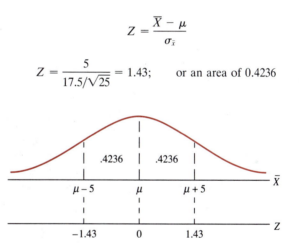

The probability that $\overline{X}$ will be within $5 billion of μ is 0.8472.

4. **A Square Deal and a Round Ball** As NCAA investigations probe deeper into college sports, one official has estimated that 70 percent of collegiate basketball programs have violated NCAA rules.

a.   If 32 out of 40 programs examined are found to have committed at least one infraction, what might be concluded about the official's estimate?

SOLUTION:

The proportion of violators in the sample is $p = S/n = 32/40 = 0.8$. The question then becomes, "If 70 percent of all programs are in violation, what is the probability a sample of 40 could yield a proportion of 80 percent or more?" We seek $P(p \geq 0.8)$ since $p > \pi$.

$$Z = \frac{p - \pi}{\sigma_p} = \frac{p - \pi}{\sqrt{\pi(1 - \pi)/n}}$$

$$Z = \frac{0.8 - 0.7}{\sqrt{(0.7)(0.3)/40}} = 1.38; \qquad \text{area} = 0.4162$$

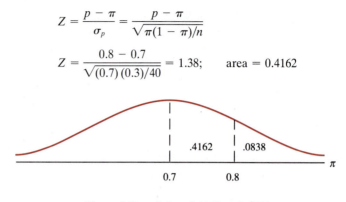

$$P(p \geq 0.8) = 0.5 - 0.4162 = 0.0838$$

Since the likelihood of finding a sample proportion like the one above ($p \geq 0.80$) is so low, it might suggest that $\pi > 0.70$.

7.9   WHAT YOU SHOULD HAVE LEARNED FROM THIS CHAPTER

This chapter has illustrated how a sampling distribution can be formed by selecting all possible samples of size n from a population. The fact that different samples will likely lead to different results and thereby affect the sampling error should be apparent by now. You should also be aware of how to determine the probability that sample results will fall within a given range, and how those results impact on any conclusions you might reach. The material in this chapter also focused on how sampling can assist you in making difficult decisions. Working the problems should strengthen your understanding of how sampling can be useful in many business situations.

Various extensions such as the finite population correction factor and the Central Limit Theorem were also examined. The importance of "large" samples, and how their use, in the absence of foreknowledge regarding the distribution of the population, directs the Central Limit Theorem to allow application of the normal deviate.

In the next chapter we will see what can be done if $n < 30$, and the population is known to be normal. The all-important practice of estimation will be examined using what we have learned about sampling distributions. The process of inferential statistics is more fully explored, and the manner in which it can assist the business decision maker is illustrated.

7.10   COMPUTER APPLICATIONS

Many of the types of problems worked on the computer in the last chapter can also be applied to the material covered in the present chapter. The commands that are entered are virtually the same. Interpretation of the printouts is based on the intent and nature of the problem. Z-values are found in much the same way with the same commands as those shown in the previous chapter. This is true for normal values because they apply to both sample means and proportions.

In addition to the computer techniques described in the last chapter, Minitab will also provide a random sample of observations. A command of

```
MTB > RANDOM 30 C1
```

produces 30 random numbers with a mean of 0 and a standard deviation of 1 of column 1.

```
MTB > PRINT C1
```

prints out those numbers.
Specifications can be added, such as

```
MTB > RANDOM 30 C1;
SUBC > NORMAL 100 5.
```

Column 1 will then contain 30 random observations with a normal distribution with $\mu = 100$ and $\sigma = 5$. Other distributions such as binomial, exponential, and several others can also be requested.

LIST OF SYMBOLS AND TERMS

Grand Mean The mean of the sample means.
K The number of samples in a sampling distribution.

LIST OF FORMULAS

$$\overline{\overline{X}} = \frac{\Sigma \overline{X}}{K} \tag{7.1}$$

Calculate the mean of the sample means or the grand mean.

$$\sigma_{\overline{x}}^2 = \frac{\Sigma(\overline{X} - \overline{\overline{X}})^2}{K} \tag{7.2}$$

and

$$\sigma_{\overline{x}}^2 = \frac{\sigma^2}{n} \tag{7.4}$$

Formulas (7.2) and (7.4) calculate the variance of a sampling distribution.

$$\sigma_{\overline{x}} = \sqrt{\sigma_{\overline{x}}^2} \tag{7.3}$$

$$\sigma_{\overline{x}} = \frac{\sigma}{\sqrt{n}} \tag{7.5}$$

Formulas (7.3) and (7.5) calculate the standard error of the sampling distribution.

$$\sigma_{\bar{x}}^2 = \left[\frac{\sigma^2}{n}\right]\left[\frac{N-n}{N-1}\right]$$

(7.6)

The variance of the sampling distribution using the FPC.

$$\sigma_{\bar{x}} = \left[\frac{\sigma}{\sqrt{n}}\right]\sqrt{\frac{N-n}{N-1}}$$

(7.7)

The standard error using the FPC.

$$Z = \frac{\bar{X} - \mu}{\sigma_{\bar{x}}}$$

(7.8)

Conversion formula to standardize a sampling distribution.

$$p = \frac{S}{n}$$

(7.9)

The sample proportion.

$$\sigma_p = \sqrt{\frac{\pi(1-\pi)}{n}}$$

(7.10)

The standard error of the sampling distribution of sample proportions.

$$\sigma_p = \sqrt{\frac{\pi(1-\pi)}{n}}\sqrt{\frac{N-n}{N-1}}$$

(7.11)

The standard error of proportions if the FPC is required.

$$Z = \frac{p - \pi}{\sigma_p}$$

(7.12)

The normal deviate for sample proportions.

CHAPTER EXERCISES

CONCEPTUAL QUESTIONS

1. If a sample is taken in which $n < 30$, what problem might we have in working with it?
2. If several samples of a given size are taken from a population, what would influence the variability of those sample means? What happens to that variability as n increases?
3. From a single population, two sampling distributions are formed by taking all possible samples of a given size to get sampling distribution A, and all possible samples of a different size to get sampling distribution B. These distributions are graphed here. Which distribution contains the larger sample size? How can you tell?

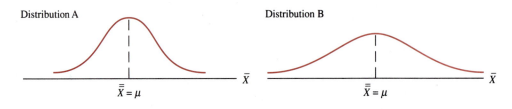

Distribution A

$\bar{\bar{X}} = \mu$

Distribution B

$\bar{\bar{X}} = \mu$

PROBLEMS

4. A population of the ages of five people consists of 20, 45, 27, 32, and 38.
   a. Calculate and interpret σ.
   b. Set $n = 2$ and develop the sampling distribution.
   c. Calculate and interpret $\sigma_{\bar{x}}$. How does it relate to σ?
   d. Calculate and interpret μ.
   e. Calculate and interpret $\bar{\bar{X}}$. How does it compare with μ?
5. Using the data in Problem 4, set $n = 3$ and
   a. develop the sampling distribution.
   b. calculate $\bar{X}$ and $\sigma_{\bar{x}}$. How do they differ from the values in Problem 4, and why?
6. A sample of $n = 50$ is taken from a large population with a mean of 2.7 and a standard deviation of 1.1. What are the mean and standard error of the sampling distribution of sample means?
7. A sampling distribution with $n = 10$ has a mean of $\bar{\bar{X}} = 105$ and a standard error of 10.2. What are the mean and standard deviation of the population?
8. From a large population with mean 75 and standard deviation of 10, samples of $n = 40$ are taken. Illustrate graphically the sampling distribution. What is its mean and standard error? If samples of $n = 80$ are taken, how would the sampling distribution compare with that obtained when $n = 40$? Graphically compare the two distributions of sample means.
9. The mean capacity of oil tankers used to ship petroleum from the Middle East is 500 million barrels, with a standard deviation of 170 million barrels. If a sample of size 50 is selected, what is the probability its mean will exceed 450 barrels?
10. Jim Sears manufactures farm equipment. His work requires the use of steel bars which must have a mean length of at least 50 inches. The bars can be purchased from a supplier in Kansas City whose bars average only 47 inches with a standard deviation of 12 inches, or from a supplier in Dallas whose bars average 49 inches with a standard deviation of 3.6 inches. If Sears is to buy 81 bars, should he use the supplier in Kansas City or Dallas?
11. According to *Business Week*, the average years of experience of airline pilots is 25.2. Assume a standard deviation of 12 years. This year you must make 36 business flights. You hope the average length of experience for the pilots of your flights is over 30. How likely is it that $\bar{X} > 30$?
12. The mean weight of cement bags used in a construction job is 40 pounds with a standard deviation of 22 pounds. Weights are normally distributed.
    a. If one bag is selected at random, what is the probability its weight will exceed 43 pounds?
    b. If a sample of $n = 64$ is taken, what is the probability the mean weight will exceed 43?
    c. Why does taking a sample decrease your answer?
13. *The Wall Street Journal* described the problem PepsiCo, makers of soft drinks, had with ensuring that the proper amount of fluid was in each bottle. The quality control department decided to examine the bottling plant in Cleveland to ensure production standards were being met, by taking a sample of containers, designed to hold 67.7 ounces, to determine if $\bar{X}$ was close to 67.7 ounces as stated on the container. The manager of the plant felt certain that he was, on the average, filling the containers to the correct amount. He therefore wants to maximize the probability that $\bar{X}$ is close to 67.7. Should he insist that a very large sample be taken, or would it be to his benefit to make the sample smaller?
14. The mean expenditures for Christmas gifts for a family of four was $612 in 1988 according to *USA Today.* Assuming a standard deviation of $150 and a normal distribution
    a. what is the probability a single family of four spent over $600 for Christmas?
    b. what is the probability 100 families spent over $600 on the average?
    c. what is the probability 200 families spent over $600 on the average?

15. The average hourly wage of members of the Teamsters union was $38.10 in 1988 with a standard deviation of $4.30. Wages are normally distributed. If a sample of 25 members of the Teamsters is selected, what is the probability $\overline{X}$ will be less than $40?

16. The mean wage of teachers in the Baltimore school system was $17.12 in 1988 with a standard deviation of $2.20. If a sample of 100 teachers is selected, what is the probability the sample mean will be less than $17.50?

17. Why was it necessary to specify normality in wages in Problem 15, but no mention of normality was required to work Problem 16?

18. Incomes for production line workers in Chicago average $21.15 per hour with a standard deviation of $5.15. These incomes are skewed left. Describe the sampling distribution of incomes for sample size 100. Draw the distributions for both the original population and the sampling distribution.

19. If the sample size in Problem 18 was 64, how would the sampling distributions compare? Graph both.

20. A local mechanic charges $110 on the average to complete a certain repair. Records show a standard deviation of $21.50 in billings. A customer recently complained that his bill of $115.50 was excessive. After considerable haggling, the mechanic agrees to refund the money if a sample of 36 similar jobs revealed a mean billing less than the customer's bill. Do you think the mechanic was wise in offering this settlement?

21. A manufacturing process produces units that average 10 inches in length with a standard deviation of 3.2 inches. If only those units between 9.5 and 10.5 inches can be used, how many out of a sample of 100 must be thrown away?

22. The average parking fine paid by students at college was $10.15 with a standard deviation of $4.80. If a sample of 144 students' fines is averaged, what is the probability the mean will be between $10.15 and $11?

23. Assume from Problem 22, that a sample of 64 is taken. Without working the problem, explain what would happen to your answer and why.

24. Assume from Problem 22 the standard deviation of the population is $5.80 instead of $4.80 and $n = 144$. Without working the problem, explain what would happen to your answer and why?

25. The standard deviation of commute times into the city is 10.2 minutes. It takes 37.2 minutes on the average.
   a. If you commuted into the city 70 times over the past 12 weeks, what is the probability your average commute time was less than 35 minutes?
   b. If you must get into the city within 35 minutes this morning, what is the probability you will make it? What assumption do you now have to make regarding times?

26. The manager of a mutual fund claims that his fund has averaged 10.2 percent per year with a standard deviation of 3.5 percent for his clients over the past several years. If a sample of 90 investors reported a mean rate of return of 9.6 percent, are you inclined to believe the fund manager?

27. Workers in a production plant are allowed 3.7 hours to complete a job process. The union argues this is not enough time since the average completion time is 4.3 hours with a standard deviation of 1.2 hours. A sample of 40 recent completions averaged 3.92 hours. Do you agree with the union?

28. Fifty drug dealers were arrested in Miami. The police argue that the average time dealers serve in jail is only 4.2 months, with a standard deviation of 1.7 months. Thirty-five of the dealers spent an average of 4.6 months in jail. Are the police correct in their assessment of the mean length of time served?

29. The mayor in a town of 650 people thinks that the average income is $42,550, with a standard deviation of $15,900. A random sample of 200 people yields an average income of $41,000. How likely is this if the mayor is correct?

30. Given the data in Problem 29, what would you conclude about the mayor's impression of incomes in his town if a sample of 250 yielded a mean of $41,000?

31. The standard deviation in the amount of time it takes to train a worker to perform a task is 40 minutes. A random sample of 64 workers is taken.
   a. What is the probability the sample mean will exceed the population mean by more than 5 minutes?
   b. What is the probability the sample mean is more than 8 minutes less than the population mean?

32. A random sample of 81 purchases at a local department store was taken to estimate mean of all purchases. It is known that the population standard deviation is $25.
   a. What is the probability the sample mean will not overstate the population mean by more than $4?
   b. What is the probability the sample mean will understate the population mean by more than $1?

33. Given the conditions in the preceding problem.
   a. Answer parts (a) and (b) if a sample of 100 is taken?
   b. Why does a larger sample have that effect?

34. Given the condition in Problem 32.
   a. Answer parts (a) and (b) if $\sigma = 30$ instead of 25 ($n = 81$).
   b. Why does a larger standard deviation in the population have that effect?

35. The standard deviation of the population of rents paid by social security recipients is $97. A sample of 100 recipients is chosen.
   a. The probability is 15 percent that $\overline{X}$ exceeds the population mean by how much?
   b. The probability is 20 percent that $\overline{X}$ is below the population by how much?

36. The standard deviation for a population of driving speeds is 10.3 miles per hour. A sample of $n = 49$ speeds is selected.
   a. The probability is 10 percent that $\overline{X}$ exceeds μ by how much?
   b. The probability is 40 percent that $\overline{X}$ is below μ by how much?

37. Jack maintains company records on monthly production hours for drilling equipment. To minimize repairs, the company wishes to avoid excessive use of the equipment. The standard deviation in usage for a certain piece of equipment is 450 hours. Jack wants to estimate the mean usage time per month.
   a. What is the minimum sample size Jack must take to ensure that the probability the sample mean exceeds the population mean by less than 75 hours is 40 percent?
   b. What is the minimum sample size Jack must take to ensure that the probability the sample mean differs from the population by less than 50 hours is 90 percent?

38. An article in *The Wall Street Journal* discussed a problem Allied Chemical was having with production specifications. Allied put liquid chemicals in barrels averaging 55 gallons with a standard deviation of 3.7 gallons. The barrels were usually sold in lots of 100. Customers are concerned they are not getting the proper amounts due to the variation of 3.7 gallons. Find the probability that if 100 barrels are sold the sampling error is less than 1 gallon per barrel.

39. To protect the public, the Interstate Commerce Commission regulates the number of hours long-haul truck drivers can work. The ICC insists that drivers for trucking firms average no more than 35 hours per week. The AAA Trucking Company tells the ICC that the standard deviation in the driving time of their drivers is 8.3 hours, but they will not release

the mean driving time, which is 35.6 hours. If the ICC takes a sample of 40 drivers, what is the probability the sampling error will be sufficient to prevent the ICC from learning that AAA has violated the maximum requirement of 35 hours?

40. Over-The-Road Transit, AAA's main competitor (see previous problem) does not know the mean driving time of its drivers. They do know the standard deviation is 7.3 hours. If a sample of $n = 64$ drivers is chosen to estimate μ, what is the probability the error will not exceed 1.2 hours?

41. Purina Dog Chow is packaged in 10-pound sacks with a standard deviation of 1.5 pounds. To test the automatic fillers, a sample of 200 bags is randomly selected from the assembly line, yielding a mean of 9.7 pounds. If Purina does not want to risk more than a 10 percent probability of underfilling bags by the amount, should they readjust the machines?

42. National figures show that 32 percent of all students fail their first statistics test. If 100 students are selected at random, what is the probability more than 40 fail?

43. It is known that an industrial process produces 12 percent defective units. If you purchase 80 units, what is the probability less than 15 percent are defective?

44. It is known that an industrial process produces 12 percent defective units. If you purchase 80 units, what is the probability less than 15 will be defective?

45. A producer of VCRs advertises that 28 percent of the VCRs sold on the market are their brand. Of 150 recent sales, exactly 40 were produced by this company. How do you feel about the company's claim?

46. Your production process requires that 85 percent of the raw materials you purchase must be free of impurities. Last week, 143 of the 196 units of raw materials you purchased were contaminated. Did you violate production specifications?

47. The maker of a new computer proves to you that you will experience only 9 percent downtime for repairs and maintenance with their new model. A check of your current hardware reveals that out of the last 90 hours, 12 hours were downtime. Is the new computer more reliable than your current model?

48. Five cards are laid out on a table face down. Your friend claims he has ESP. You select 200 cards at random without revealing your choice to your friend. Out of the 200 attempts, he correctly identifies 54 cards. Do you believe your friend has ESP?

49. A corporation is going to float a new stock issue. Law requires that current stockholders be given the first opportunity to buy any new issue. Management feels that 45 percent of current stockholders will want to make a purchase. A random sample of 130 stockholders is selected, 63 of whom express a desire to buy.
     a. What is the standard error of the sample proportion?
     b. What is the mean of the sampling distribution of sample proportions?
     c. What is the probability of obtaining the results described in the problem if $\pi = 0.45$?

50. Sears has determined that 17 percent of all purchases made during the Christmas season are returned. If a store sells 150 video games, what is the probability that at most 20 percent will be returned?

51. Without working the problem, explain what would happen to the answer in the previous problem if n increased to 200. Why?

EMPIRICAL EXERCISES

52. National data show that 22 percent of all college students are married. Take a sample to determine if the students on your campus are representative of the national norm. Your sample should be at least how large? How likely is it that you could get the results you did if the national data are correct, assuming your campus is representative of the national norm?

53. These same national data report that the average age of undergraduates has risen significantly in the past 10 years. It currently stands at 23.3 years, with a standard deviation of 5.2 years. Take a sample of students on your campus. Do they appear to be typical? How likely is it that you could get these results if the national data are correct and your campus is representative?

CASE APPLICATIONS

54. During the past school year it has come to light that the county school districts in Kentucky are deficient in their use of funds. A state official claims that the county school boards have spent an average of $110,500 more than allotted by the state government. Some counties have been particularly wasteful, while others have tried to minimize excess expenditures. The standard deviation in overspending is said to be $35,000.

   The governor orders a study of the financial condition for all school boards in the state. An official sympathetic to the county system hopes to take a sample of 50 counties for the pilot study. The methodology to be employed in the study will be perfected and then applied to all counties. The official is basing his proposal in the hope of taking a sample and obtaining a mean of no more than $90,000 in overspending. However, the sample mean is $145,700. This causes considerable question regarding the estimate that all systems average $110,500 in excess spending. Given this uncertainty about the population mean, the governor begins to question the likelihood that any sample of size 50 could be obtained in which the sample error was less than $20,000.

   How might the principles of a normal distribution be used to aid the governor in his quest for answers?

55. Doctors at the Regional Medical Center use two drugs to treat a certain ailment. Benicite has a cure rate of 90 percent. However, 15 percent of the patients suffer side effects from the drug. Maycine cures 80 percent of the patients to whom it is administered, and has a side-effect rate of 10 percent. A drug is administered to 150 patients. Of those, 138 show significant signs of improvement, while 21 suffer side effects. However, hospital records fail to indicate which drug was given to the patients.

   A group of hospital examiners is due to visit RMC, and the medical staff must determine which of the two drugs was the one administered to the patients. In addition, a third drug with a cure rate and side-effect rate of 85 percent and 12 percent, respectively, was given to 200 other patients. The examiners will select a sample of 50 of those patients to test the effectiveness of the drug. The drug will be approved for general use only if 8 or less of the 50 patients report no side effects.

   How might the medical staff use the forms of statistical analysis presented in this chapter to determine which drug, Benicite or Maycin, was more likely to be the one given to the 150 patients, and to predict if the third drug might be approved?

CHAPTER EIGHT

ESTIMATING WITH CONFIDENCE INTERVALS

This chapter shows you how to determine confidence intervals for parameters. Confidence intervals are extremely useful in making many business-related decisions. You will learn how to construct intervals for both population means and population proportions under a variety of conditions. The many ways in which this statistical tool can be applied to the business setting will become obvious as you work through the chapter.

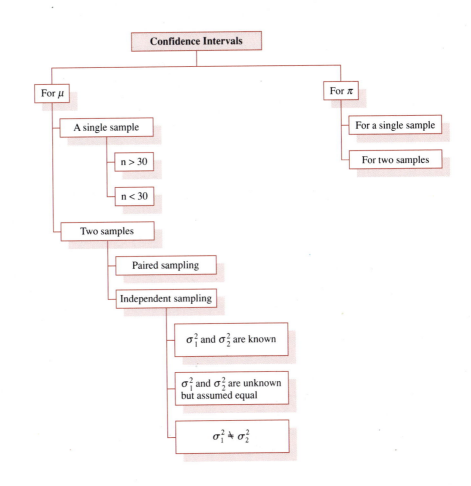

> ○○○○
> ○○○
> ○○   Statistics show that
> ○   you can never afford
>   the one you want.

8.1   INTRODUCTION

By now you should be well aware that populations are generally too large to study in their entirety. Their size requires that we select samples, which are then used to draw inferences about the populations. If a manager of a retail store wished to know the mean expenditure by her customers last year, she would find it difficult to calculate the average of the hundreds or perhaps thousands of customers who shopped in her store. It would prove much easier to use an estimate of the population mean by calculating the mean of a representative sample.

There are at least two types of estimators commonly used for this purpose: a point estimate and an interval estimate. A **point estimate** uses a statistic to estimate the parameter at a single value or point. The store manager may select a sample of $n = 500$ customers and find $\overline{X} = \$37.10$. This value serves as the point estimate for the population mean.

An **interval estimate** specifies a range within which the unknown parameter may lie. The manager may decide the population mean lies somewhere between \$35 and \$38. Such an interval is often accompanied by a statement as to the level of confidence which can be placed in its accuracy. It is therefore called a **confidence interval.**

> **Estimates**
> A point estimate uses a single number or value to pinpoint an estimate of the parameter. A confidence interval denotes a **range** within which the parameter might be found and the level of confidence that the interval does contain the parameter.

Actually there are three levels of confidence commonly associated with confidence intervals: 99, 95, and 90 percent. There is nothing magical about these three values. We could calculate an 82 percent confidence interval if we so desired. These three levels of confidence, called **confidence coefficients,** are simply conventional.

> **Confidence Coefficient**
> The confidence coefficient is the probability that a stated interval contains the unknown parameter.

The manager referred to above might, for example, be 95 percent confident that the population mean is between $35 and $38.

Interval estimates enjoy certain advantages over point estimates. Due to sampling error, $\overline{X}$ will likely not equal μ. However, we have no way of knowing how large the sampling error is. Intervals are therefore used to account for this unknown discrepancy.

Confidence intervals can be constructed under a wide variety of conditions. We will focus our attention on

Intervals for the population mean for both one-sample and two-sample cases.
Intervals for the population proportion for both one- and two-sample cases.

We begin with a discussion of what a confidence interval is and how to interpret it.

A. THE PRINCIPLE OF A CONFIDENCE INTERVAL

A confidence interval has a **lower confidence limit** (LCL) and an **upper confidence limit** (UCL). As we will see shortly, these two limits are found by calculating the point estimate, adding a certain amount to it to get the UCL, and subtracting the same amount from it to get the LCL. The determination of that amount is the subject of this chapter.

The Central Limit Theorem assures us that 95 percent of all sample means lie within 1.96 standard errors ($\pm 1.96\ \sigma_{\bar{x}}$) of μ. Therefore, 95 percent of all the sample means will produce the interval. $\overline{X} \pm 1.96\ \sigma_{\bar{x}}$ which will contain μ. This principle is illustrated in Figure 8-1. If we wish to be 95 percent confident that the parameter is within the interval, we must add 1.96 $\sigma_{\bar{x}}$ to the sample mean to get the UCL and subtract 1.96 $\sigma_{\bar{x}}$ from the sample mean to get the LCL. This 95 percent, called the **confidence coefficient,** affects the width of the interval and the probability that the interval contains μ.

FIGURE 8-1 A 95 Percent Confidence Limit

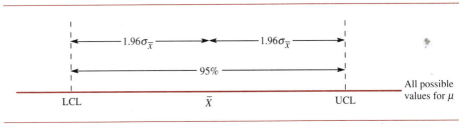

Perhaps our work is so critical that we feel it necessary to be more than 95 percent confident of our findings. In the case of medical research in which lives are at risk, or if our decisions have significant economic consequences, we may desire a higher level of confidence.

We can elevate the level of confidence, given any sample size, only by increasing the width of the interval. If we wish to be 99 percent confident the interval contains the parameter, we must construct a wider interval. Figure 8-2 illustrates how a 99 percent confidence interval must encompass a wider interval along the axis.

FIGURE 8-2   Comparing Interval Widths

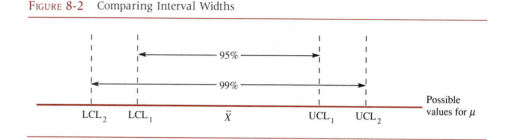

However, there is a trade-off involved. Although we are now more confident the interval contains the true value of the parameter, the confidence interval is now wider and less precise. This larger interval encompasses a wider range of possible values for the unknown parameter and fails to "pinpoint" its actual value as closely as does the narrower interval. This issue of precision will be dealt with in detail later in the chapter.

B.   THE INTERPRETATION OF CONFIDENCE INTERVALS

A confidence interval can be interpreted in two different ways. Consider, for example, the $35 to $38 interval cited by the retail manager for customers' mean expenditures last year. She attached a 95 percent level of significance to that interval. The first interpretation which she can apply to this interval is

Interpretation 1:
She is 95 percent confident that the population mean is between $35 and $38.

This is *not* to say that "there is a 95 percent probability that μ is between $35 and $38." This is a common misinterpretation of a confidence interval, and it is entirely inaccurate. The population mean either (1) is or (2) is not within that interval. Thus the probability that μ is between $35 and $38 is either 1 or 0; it is not 95 percent. The 95 percent probability is assigned to our level of confidence that μ is within that range. It is not assigned to the probability that μ is contained in the interval.

The second interpretation of a confidence interval is based on the realization that each effort to calculate an interval will produce slightly different results. Assume you select a sample of size n from a population and find an $\overline{X} = 50$. If you were to select a second sample of the same size from the same population, would you again get an $\overline{X} = 50$? Most likely not! Due to variation in the sampling error, each sample will yield a different mean. In the same way, each attempt to construct a confidence interval will yield slightly different results. A second 95 percent confidence interval may produce, for example, an interval of \$35.10 to \$38.10. Each sample will produce a slightly different interval because each sample has a slightly different mean. The second interpretation of a confidence interval thus states

Interpretation 2:
If many confidence intervals are constructed, 95 percent of them will include the unknown parameter.

This assumes, of course, they are all 95 percent confidence intervals. A similar interpretation can be applied to intervals with other confidence levels.

8.2 CONFIDENCE INTERVAL FOR THE POPULATION MEAN—LARGE SAMPLES

Perhaps the most common use of confidence intervals is to provide an estimate of the population mean. There are many instances in which a typical business situation dictates the need to estimate some population mean. A variety of circumstances exists under which a confidence interval can be used to produce that estimate. We will examine cases involving (1) a known population variance, (2) an unknown variance, and (3) a nonnormal population. Actually, we will find very little difference in the procedures used under each of these sets of conditions, as long as the sample size is large ($n > 30$).

A. A KNOWN POPULATION VARIANCE

Presume we have a population with an unknown mean but a known variance. This may seem somewhat unrealistic. If we know the variance, chances are we would know the mean. However, there are times when past experience and familiarity with a population may reveal its variance, but the mean remains a mystery. In any event, this assumption presents a logical starting point for our discussion of confidence intervals. We will abandon the assumption of a known population variance shortly.

Consider a producer who wishes to estimate his mean daily output. Previous experience provides the producer with some knowledge regarding the variance, yet the mean is unknown. He decides to calculate a confidence interval for the mean.

Recall that a confidence interval consists of an upper confidence limit (UCL) and a lower confidence limit (LCL). Using the point estimator $\overline{X}$ as a starting point, the producer will add a certain amount to get the UCL and subtract that same amount to determine the LCL. The question is, how much should be added and subtracted? This depends on how precise the producer wishes to be. Assume he wants to be 95 percent confident that the interval contains the true population mean. We know from our work in previous chapters that the sampling distribution of $\overline{X}$'s will be normally distributed if

1. The population is known to be normal.

                           or

2. The sample size is greater than 30.

Although we will assume for the time being that the populations in question are normally distributed, this assumption will shortly be abandoned in order to illustrate the computation of confidence intervals under conditions of both normal and non-normal populations. However, in doing so we will find that it makes no difference in our analysis as long as the sample exceeds 30. In either case, normality is ensured (1) if the population is normal or (2) if the sample is large, the Central Limit Theorem ensures a normal distribution of sample means. Thus, the normal deviate Z may be used.

Figure 8-3 illustrates the producer's objective. He must identify an LCL and a UCL which will encompass 95 percent of the possible values for μ along the axis. Further, the normal deviate

$$Z = \frac{\overline{X} - \mu}{\sigma_{\bar{x}}}$$

can be rewritten algebraically as

$$
\begin{aligned}
\mu &= \overline{X} \pm Z\sigma_{\bar{x}} \\
&= \overline{X} \pm Z\frac{\sigma}{\sqrt{n}}
\end{aligned}
\qquad (8.1\text{A})
$$

The Z-value carries both a plus and a minus sign since $Z\sigma_{\bar{x}}$ is added to and subtracted from the sample mean.

FIGURE 8-3   A 95 Percent Confidence Interval for Mean Daily Output

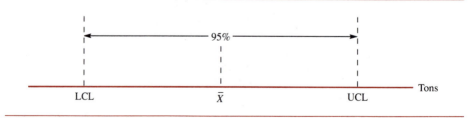

To express Formula (8.1A) in terms of a confidence interval, it can be rewritten as

$$\text{C.I. for } \mu = \overline{X} \pm Z\sigma_{\bar{x}}$$

$$= \overline{X} \pm Z\frac{\sigma}{\sqrt{n}} \qquad (8.1B)$$

In his effort to construct a 95 percent confidence interval for the mean daily output level, the producer selects a sample of $n = 100$ and calculates an $\overline{X} = 112$ tons of output. Past experience has shown that the population standard deviation in output is $\sigma = 50$ tons. Formula (8.1B) yields

$$\text{C.I. for } \mu = 112 \pm Z\frac{50}{\sqrt{100}}$$

The producer still needs a value for Z, which will be taken from the Z-table. Figure 8-4 will aid in that regard. If a 95 percent level of confidence is desired, it is necessary to divide the 0.95 by 2 because the Z-table we are using gives values from the mean to some point above (UCL) or below (LCL) it. That is, the Z-table will not give the entire value from the LCL to the UCL. It contains values only from $\overline{X}$ to the UCL or from $\overline{X}$ to the LCL. We must then search the main body of the Z-table for the area 0.4750. Once located, it can be seen that the corresponding Z-value is 1.96. The producer can now complete his answer.

$$\text{C.I. for } \mu = \overline{X} \pm Z\frac{\sigma}{\sqrt{n}}$$

$$= 112 \pm (1.96)\frac{50}{\sqrt{100}}$$

$$102.2 \le \mu \le 121.8 \text{ tons}$$

Figure 8-4 A 95 Percent Confidence Interval for the Mean Daily Output

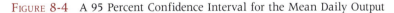

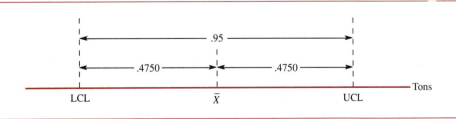

The producer can draw two inferences about the population from his sample, each based on one of the two interpretations of a confidence interval discussed above:

1. He can be 95 percent confident that the mean daily output lies between 102.2 and 121.8 tons.
2. Ninety-five percent of all confidence intervals formed in this manner will include the true value for μ.

With reference to this second interpretation, consider the following: If the producer would repeat the experiment, would he get the same answer for the interval? No, because he would likely get a different value for $\overline{X}$. However, he can be certain that 95 percent of all the confidence intervals he might construct in this manner would include μ.

EXAMPLE 8-1 Estimating Market Values

The director of marketing services for a Chicago-based manufacturer wants to analyze the market value of business firms of a similar size. Market value is defined as the number of common shares outstanding times share price as listed on an organized exchange. A sample of 600 firms revealed a mean market value of $850 million. Assuming values are normally distributed and the population standard deviation is $200 million, construct a 95 percent confidence interval for the mean market value of all firms of this size.

SOLUTION:

The point estimate is $\overline{X}$ = $850 million. Since the level of confidence is 95 percent, the figure illustrates that the appropriate area is 0.95/2 = 0.4750.

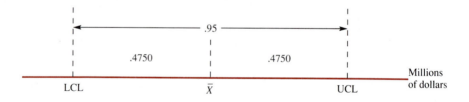

A Z-value of 1.96 is called for.

$$\text{C.I. for } \mu = \overline{X} \pm Z\sigma_{\bar{x}}$$

$$= 850 \pm (1.96)\frac{200}{\sqrt{600}}$$

$$= 850 \pm 15.99$$

$$\$834.01 \le \mu \le \$865.99$$

STATISTICAL INTERPRETATION:

The director can be 95 percent confident that the mean market value is between $834.01 million and $865.99 million. Also, 95 percent of all confidence intervals constructed in this manner will contain the true value for μ.

Consider the following example using a different level of confidence.

EXAMPLE 8-2 The Mean Completion Time for a Process: A Quality Control Example

You have just graduated with a degree in business and have obtained a position with the manufacturing firm in the previous example. The director of marketing services has asked you to estimate the mean time required to complete a particular phase of the manufacturing process. A sample of 600 processes yielded a mean of 7.2 days. Assume times are normally distributed with a standard deviation of $\sigma = 1.9$ days, and calculate a 90 percent confidence interval for the mean completion time for the process.

SOLUTION:

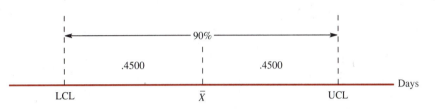

As shown in the figure, when the 90 percent confidence level is divided by 2, the appropriate area is 0.4500. Again, this division is carried out solely because the table we use gives only those areas from the mean to some value above it (UCL) or some value below it (LCL). The table will not give the Z-value for the 90 percent of the area from the LCL to the UCL.

As you look in the Z-table for 0.4500, you find that the closest values are 0.4495 ($Z = 1.64$) and 0.4505 ($Z = 1.65$). Either Z-value is appropriate. If a greater degree of accuracy is desired, you may wish to interpolate and use a Z-value of 1.645. Your answer will differ very little regardless of which Z-value you use. The most conservative approach is to use 1.65, which is the practice we will follow here.

$$\text{C.I. for } \mu = \overline{X} \pm Z\sigma_{\bar{x}}$$

$$= 7.2 \pm (1.65)\frac{1.9}{\sqrt{600}}$$

$$= 7.2 \pm 0.128$$

$$7.072 \le \mu \le 7.328 \text{ days}$$

STATISTICAL INTERPRETATION:

You can now inform the director that you are 90 percent confident that the mean time required to complete the manufacturing phase is between 7.072 days and 7.328 days.

As we noted earlier, a higher level of confidence requires a wider, less precise interval. This next example computes a 99 percent confidence interval for the mean completion time for the production process, and compares the results to those obtained from the 90 percent confidence interval in the previous example.

EXAMPLE 8-3 A Comparison of Intervals

The director now wants to be 99 percent confident that the interval contains the true parameter for the mean completion time for the process under examination. She therefore instructs you to construct a 99 percent interval for μ.

SOLUTION:

$$\text{C.I. for } \mu = \overline{X} \pm Z\sigma_{\bar{x}}$$

$$= 7.2 \pm Z\frac{1.9}{\sqrt{600}}$$

When 0.99 is divided by 2, the resulting value of 0.4950 yields a Z-value of 2.58. Thus,

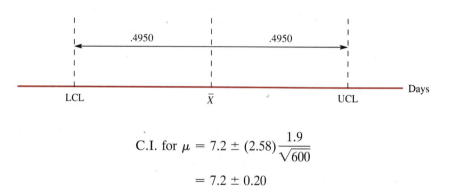

$$\text{C.I. for } \mu = 7.2 \pm (2.58)\frac{1.9}{\sqrt{600}}$$

$$= 7.2 \pm 0.20$$

$$7.00 \le \mu \le 7.40$$

STATISTICAL INTERPRETATION:

The 99 percent confidence interval of 7.00 to 7.40 is indeed wider than the 90 percent confidence interval of 7.072 to 7.328 found in the previous example. Again, this happens because given our sample size of 600, if we desire a greater level of confidence that the interval contains μ, the interval must be wider. This is reflected in the figure.

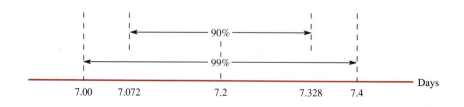

○○○○   **Decision Making through Problem Solving**
Illustration 8-1

The Economist reported that Alan Greenspan, chairman of the Federal Reserve System, wanted to measure the "volatility in America's financial institutions." The intent was to implement "circuit-breakers" which would temporarily halt trading on the New York Stock Exchange and the Chicago Mercantile Exchange if the Dow-Jones index changed by a certain amount.

To determine what that critical amount should be, it was necessary to approximate the typical daily movement in the index. An estimate of the mean change in the Dow-Jones was obtained by taking a sample of the last 550 business days. Given this sample, a confidence interval of 236.8 to 278.2 points was formed for the mean daily fluctuation in the Dow-Jones. (The article didn't indicate which level of confidence was used.) It was concluded that a change of 250 points or more should signal market instability, necessitating a temporary cessation in trading.

Quick Check 8.2.1

○○○○   If the sample mean is 42.5, construct a 90 percent confidence interval for the population mean if $n = 81$ and $\sigma = 15.3$.

Answer: $39.7 \leq \mu \leq 45.31$

Quick Check 8.2.2

Given the information in 8.2.1, construct a 99 percent confidence interval. Why is it different?

Answer: $38.11 \leq \mu \leq 46.89$. The interval must be wider since the confidence is greater.

Quick Check 8.2.3

A sample of 100 observations reveals a mean of 16.3. What is the 95 percent confidence interval if $\sigma = 3.7$?

Answer: $15.57 \leq \mu \leq 17.03$

Quick Check 8.2.4

Construct the 95 percent confidence interval given the information in 8.2.3 if $\sigma = 5.7$. Explain the difference.

Answer: $15.18 \leq \mu \leq 17.42$. The interval must be wider since the data are more dispersed.

B.   The Probability of Error—The Alpha Value

In formulating a confidence interval, there is always a chance that you will be wrong and the interval will not contain the actual but unknown population mean. If the interval carries a 95 percent level of confidence, there is a 5 percent chance (100 percent − 95 percent) that μ is not within the specified interval. That is, if there is a 95 percent probability that the interval includes μ, then there is 5 percent chance that it does not. This likelihood that the interval does not contain the population mean is called the probability of error, and is designated as the **alpha value** (α-value).

Alpha Value
The alpha value is the probability that the specified interval does not contain the unknown value for the parameter.

Figure 8-5 illustrates how a 95 percent confidence interval results in a 5 percent probability that the interval does not contain the parameter. Since 95 percent of all sample means are within $\pm 1.96\ \sigma_{\bar{x}}$ of μ, and will produce an interval containing μ, the remaining 5 percent will produce an interval that fails to encompass μ. There is a 5 percent chance that the interval is in error. The interval carries a probability of error—an α-value—of 5 percent. A 99 percent confidence interval carries an α-value of 1 percent, while a 90 percent confidence interval has an α-value of 10 percent.

FIGURE 8-5   A 5 Percent Probability of Error

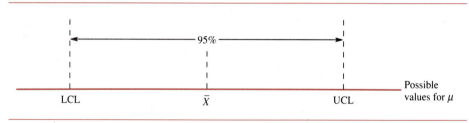

C.   CONFIDENCE INTERVALS WITH σ UNKNOWN

In the examples above we assumed the population standard deviation was known. In the likely event the population standard deviation is not available, it is necessary to estimate it by using s, the sample standard deviation in its place. The sample standard deviation can always be calculated from the sample as we did in Chapter 3. In this event, the estimator becomes

$$\text{C.I. for } \mu = \overline{X} \pm Z\frac{s}{\sqrt{n}} \tag{8.2}$$

Notice that we have merely substituted s in the formula for the unknown σ. This approach is valid only if normality in the sampling distribution is ensured because (1) n is large or (2) the population from which the sample is taken is known to be normal.

In 1989 the Federal Housing Administration (FHA) estimated the mean mortgage rate for savings and loan institutions (S&Ls) across the nation. A sample of 100 S&Ls was taken under the assumption that rates were normally distributed. A mean and standard deviation of $\overline{X} = 10.3$ percent and $s = 2.1$ percent were calculated. The FHA wanted to be extremely confident of their findings and chose $\alpha = 0.01$, as displayed in Figure 8-6.

FIGURE 8-6 A Confidence Interval for Home Mortgage Rates in 1989

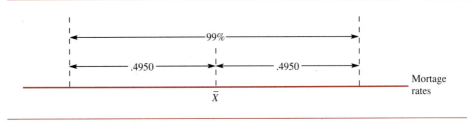

The α-value of 0.01 requires a 99 percent confidence interval, which, when divided by 2, yields 0.4950. From the Z-table, we find a Z-value of 2.58. Then

$$\text{C.I. for } \mu = \overline{X} \pm Z \frac{s}{\sqrt{n}}$$

$$= 10.3 \pm (2.58)\frac{2.1}{\sqrt{100}}$$

$$= 10.3 \pm 0.542$$

$$9.758\% \leq \mu \leq 10.842\%$$

The FHA has estimated that the mean mortgage rate for S&Ls is between 9.758 percent and 10.842 percent, with a probability of error of only 1 percent.

EXAMPLE 8-4 Estimating Purchasing Power

John Dreiling owns an auto dealership for expensive imports in Los Angeles. He has just asked you, his newly hired statistical assistant, to prepare a confidence interval for the mean income of L.A. residents. Dreiling warns that there can be only a 10 percent probability that you are wrong. A sample of 400 potential customers reveals a mean income of $275,000 with a standard deviation of $75,500. How do you respond? Assume incomes are normally distributed.

SOLUTION:

The solution is simple. An α-value of 10 percent (a confidence interval of 90 percent) is shown in the figure. The value of $0.90/2 = 0.4500$ calls for a Z of 1.65.

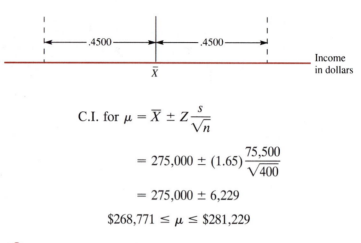

$$\text{C.I. for } \mu = \overline{X} \pm Z \frac{s}{\sqrt{n}}$$

$$= 275,000 \pm (1.65) \frac{75,500}{\sqrt{400}}$$

$$= 275,000 \pm 6,229$$

$$\$268,771 \leq \mu \leq \$281,229$$

STATISTICAL INTERPRETATION:

You can tell J. D. that you are 90 percent confident that the mean income of potential L.A. customers is between \$268,771 and \$281,229.

As you can clearly tell, knowledge of the population standard deviation is not a requirement, provided $n > 30$. In its absence we simply substituted the sample standard deviation, which can always be calculated from the sample. All this assumes that (1) large samples ($n > 30$) are taken or (2) the population is normal. The procedure that must be followed if these conditions are absent will be discussed shortly.

D. SAMPLING NONNORMAL POPULATIONS

In each instance above, we assumed that the populations were normally distributed with regard to the parameter under examination. The objection may be raised that this, too, is a rather unrealistic assumption. How did we know in the previous example concerning Dreiling's auto dealership that incomes were normal?

In the interest of realism, we will dispense with the assumption of a normal population. We find that it makes absolutely no difference whether the population is normal. As long as $n > 30$, the Central Limit Theorem will ensure normality in the sampling distribution. Thus, the distribution of $\overline{X}$'s will be normally distributed. The procedure is identical to that described above for normal populations.

In 1989 a consumer advocacy group headed by Ralph Nader tested the impurities in city drinking water. Of 300 cities across the nation, tap water was found to contain contaminates at the mean rate of 0.03 particles per gallon (ppg). National data revealed a standard deviation of 0.009 ppg. Contamination levels are not known to be normally distributed. The advocacy group wants a 99 percent confidence interval for the national mean contamination level.

Since σ is known, it should be used in the calculation. A 99 percent confidence interval requires a Z-value of 2.58.

$$\text{C.I. for } \mu = \overline{X} \pm Z\frac{\sigma}{\sqrt{n}}$$

$$= 0.03 \pm (2.58)\frac{0.009}{\sqrt{300}}$$

$$= 0.03 \pm 0.0013$$

$$0.0287 \leq \mu \leq 0.0313$$

Mr. Nader can be 99 percent certain the stated interval does contain the national mean level of contaminates. Despite the lack of knowledge regarding the distribution of contamination at the population level, the normal deviate Z can be used since the Central Limit Theorem ensures normality in the sampling distribution given that $n > 30$.

EXAMPLE 8-5 Where There's Smoke There's Tobacco

Walter Raleigh owns an exclusive pipe and tobacco shop in the downtown civic center of Durham, North Carolina. Inventory records suggest a particular tobacco blend is quite popular. Data indicate that, on the average, shops like Walt's across the Southeast sell an average of 12.2 pounds per day of that blend. Curious as to how his sales compare with this average, Walt takes a sample of his sales over 200 days and finds a mean of 14.3 pounds, with a standard deviation of 2.7 pounds. Walt does not know if daily sales are normally distributed. What does a 90 percent confidence interval reveal about Walt's average sales compared with other tobacco shops?

SOLUTION:
Since $0.90/2 = 0.4500$, a Z-value of 1.65 is required.

$$\text{C.I. for } \mu = \overline{X} \pm Z\frac{s}{\sqrt{n}}$$

$$= 14.3 \pm (1.65)\frac{2.7}{\sqrt{200}}$$

$$= 14.3 \pm 0.315$$

$$13.99 \leq \mu \leq 14.62$$

STATISTICAL INTERPRETATION:
Walt can be 90 percent confident his average is between 13.99 pounds and 14.62 pounds. He can be at least 90 percent confident his mean exceeds the average of other shops in the Southeast.

Does this mean there is a 90 percent probability his average exceeds that of similar tobacco shops in the Southeast? *No!* Either his average (1) does or (2) does not exceed the average of other stores. The probability his mean exceeds other stores' is either (1) 1 or (2) 0. If this logic eludes you, reread the section earlier in this chapter dealing with the interpretation of confidence intervals.

8.3 CONFIDENCE INTERVALS FOR THE POPULATION MEAN—SMALL SAMPLES

So far we have examined estimating techniques for the population mean under a variety of conditions. At times σ was known, while at other times this assumption was relaxed. We calculated confidence intervals under the assumption of a normally distributed population as well as under the condition that the population's distribution was unknown.

However, all cases had one common circumstance: a large sample ($n > 30$) was selected. In many applications we may find that a large sample is impractical or perhaps even impossible to obtain. A classic example involves the efforts by insurance companies to test the crash resistance of automobiles. Purposely destroying 30 or more vehicles can get a bit expensive. In testing a new drug, a medical researcher may not be able to find 30 or more people to whom the drug has been administered or who are willing to assume the role of human guinea pig. Many other such cases may be cited in which a large sample is not available.

In the event a small sample ($n < 30$) must be taken, the normal distribution may not be appropriate. Specifically, when (1) the sample is small and (2) σ is unknown, the Z-distribution will not apply. Instead, if the population is known to be normal, an alternative distribution, called **Student's *t*-distribution** (or simply the *t*-distribution) must be used. The Student's *t*-distribution was developed in 1908 by William S. Gosset (1876–1937), who worked as a brewmaster for Guinness Breweries in Dublin, Ireland. Guinness would not allow any of its employees to publish their research. When Gosset, who liked to "toy with numbers for pure relaxation," first reported on the *t*-distribution he published under the pseudonym "Student" in order to protect his job. Hence, the term Student's *t*-distribution.

Like the Z-distribution, the *t*-distribution has a mean of zero, is symmetrical about the mean, and ranges from $-\infty$ to $+\infty$. However, while the Z-distribution has a variance of $\sigma^2 = 1$, the variance of the *t*-distribution is greater than 1. As a result, the *t*-distribution is flatter and more dispersed than the Z-distribution (see Figure 8-7).

Actually the *t*-distribution is an entire family of distributions with different variances. The variance of the *t*-distribution depends on the degrees of freedom (d.f.), which is equal to $n - 1$.

The variance can be written as

$$\sigma^2 = \frac{n - 1}{n - 3} \tag{8.3}$$

Figure 8-7   A Comparison of the Z-Distribution and the t-Distribution

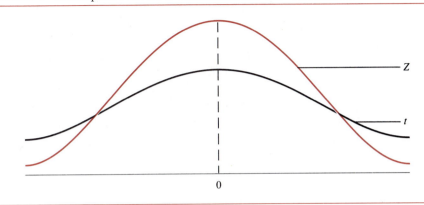

As n increases, the variance approaches 1. When $n > 30$, the t-distribution will, like the Z-distribution, have a variance of 1 (or very close to it). This explains why the Z-distribution can be used for large samples. Figure 8-8 demonstrates the impact of larger sample sizes on the t-distribution.

Figure 8-8   A Family of t-Distributions

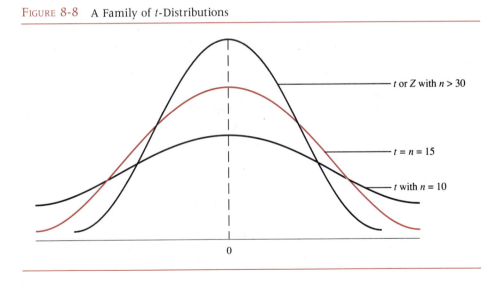

It is important to remember that the t-distribution is used when (1) the population is assumed to be normal, (2) a small sample is taken, and (3) σ is unknown. As we shall see shortly, for any given set of conditions the t-distribution will produce a wider interval than would the Z-distribution if it were used. This additional width is necessary since some accuracy is lost because σ is unknown and must be estimated.

The t-statistic is calculated like the Z-statistic.

$$t = \frac{\overline{X} - \mu}{s_{\bar{x}}}$$ (8.4)

Rewriting (8.4) algebraically to express it as a confidence interval for μ, we have

$$\text{C.I. for } \mu = \overline{X} \pm (t)(s_{\bar{x}})$$

$$= \overline{X} \pm t\frac{s}{\sqrt{n}}$$ (8.5)

The proper t-value can be found from Table F in the appendix. To illustrate, assume you want a 95 percent confidence interval and have a sample of 20 observations. Since $n = 20$, the degrees of freedom are d.f. $= n - 1 = 19$. Move down the first column in Table F under "d.f." to 19. Move across that row to the column headed by a confidence level of 0.95 for two-tailed tests. (Ignore the two rows concerning one-tailed tests. They will be dealt with in the next chapter.) The resulting entry of 2.093 is the proper t-value for a 95 percent confidence interval with a sample size of 20 (d.f. $= 19$).

Consider the following problem taken from a news story in *The Wall Street Journal*. A construction firm was charged with inflating the expense vouchers it files in conjunction with construction contracts with the federal government. The contract states that a certain type of job should average $1,150. In the interest of time, the directors of only 12 government agencies were called on to enter court testimony regarding the firm's vouchers. If a mean of $1,275 and a standard deviation of $235 are discovered from testimony, would a 95 percent confidence interval support the firm's legal case? Assume voucher amounts are normal.

A 95 percent level of confidence with d.f. $= 12 - 1 = 11$ yields from Table F a t-value of 2.201. Then

$$\text{C.I. for } \mu = \overline{X} \pm t\frac{s}{\sqrt{n}}$$

$$= 1275 \pm (2.201)\frac{235}{\sqrt{12}}$$

$$= 1275 \pm 149.49$$

$$\$1,125.51 \leq \mu \leq \$1,424.49$$

The court can be 95 percent confident that the mean voucher was between $1,125 and $1,424. Since this interval contains the $1,150 amount agreed upon, it would seem to strengthen the firm's defense.

EXAMPLE 8-6 UAW v. FMC

The labor agreement between the United Auto Workers and Ford Motor Company required that the mean output for a particular production section be held at 112 units per month per employee. Disagreement arose between UAW and FMC as to whether this standard was being maintained. It was decided to take a sample of workers' productivity levels to determine if production guides were being met. Due to the cost involved, only 20 workers were tested, yielding a mean of 102 units. Assume a standard deviation of 8.5 units was found and output levels can be assumed to be normally distributed. Does a 90 percent confidence interval tend to suggest a violation of the labor contract?

SOLUTION:

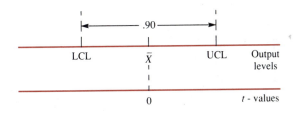

With a 90 percent level of confidence and $n - 1 = 19$ d.f., Table F yields a t-value of 1.729.

$$\text{C.I. for } \mu = \overline{X} \pm t\frac{s}{\sqrt{n}}$$

$$= 102 \pm (1.729)\frac{8.5}{\sqrt{20}}$$

$$= 102 \pm 3.27$$

$$98.73 \leq \mu \leq 105.27$$

The mean output level of 112 units specified in the labor contract is not in the confidence interval.

STATISTICAL INTERPRETATION:

There is a 90 percent level of confidence that the contract is being violated.

Obviously, deciding whether to use a t-test or a Z-test is crucial. Figure 8-9 will aid in selecting the proper test statistic. Remember that the t-distribution should be used when all three of these conditions are present: (1) the population is normal, (2) a small sample is taken, and (3) σ is unknown.

FIGURE 8-9   Selecting the Proper Test Statistic for μ

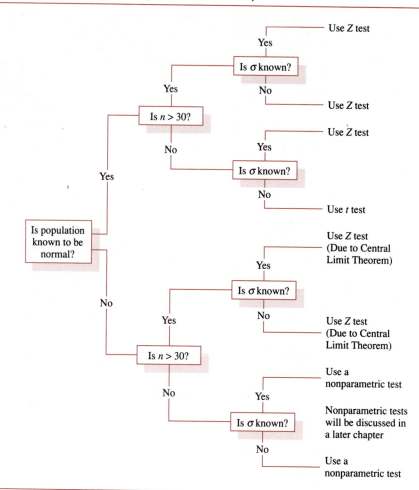

QUICK CHECK 8.3.1

○○○○

A sample of 20 people drove an average of 27.3 miles to and from work each day, with a standard deviation of 8.3 miles. What is the 90 percent confidence interval for the mean driving distance for the population? Assume distances are normally distributed.

Answer: $24.08 \leq \mu \leq 30.52$

Quick Check 8.3.2

○○○○   Seventeen employees at ABC, Inc. averaged 8.3 sick days last year, with a
standard deviation of 1.2 days. Assuming sick days are normally distributed,
what is the 98 percent confidence interval for sick days for all of ABC's
employees?

Answer: $7.55 \leq \mu \leq 9.05$

Quick Check 8.3.3

If the population standard deviation in 8.3.2 were 1.2 days, what is the
98 percent confidence interval?

Answer: $7.62 \leq \mu \leq 8.98$ by the Z-test since σ is known.

8.4   Estimating the Difference between Two Normal Population Means

There are numerous occasions in which a comparison of two separate populations is
crucial. Many business decisions depend on the comparative durability of two products, the relative dependability of two manufacturing processes, or the variation in
the effectiveness of two advertising schemes. Two sampling methods can be used to
compare two populations: (1) paired (dependent) sampling and (2) independent
sampling.

A.   Paired Sampling

Also called matched pairs, **paired sampling** involves a procedure in which several
pairs of observations are matched up as closely as possible in terms of relevant characteristics. Both sets of observations are different in only one respect or "treatment." Any subsequent difference in the two groups is attributed to that treatment.

> **Paired Samples**
> Matched pairs are two observations which are as similar as possible to each
> other. They differ in only one relevant aspect.

Assume a medical researcher wishes to test the effects of new drugs on patients'
blood pressure levels. Twenty people in one group are paired off as closely as possible with 20 people in a second group in terms of weight, age, sex, levels of activity,
cholesterol, and any other factor which might impact on blood pressure. We then
have 20 pairs of "identical twins." One group is given one new drug, and the other
group receives the other drug. No one except the researcher knows which group gets
which medication. Any subsequent differences, good or bad, in the twins' blood pressures is attributed to the drugs since we have "corrected" for all other relevant

factors affecting pressure such as age and sex. This correction was accomplished by matching up pairs of observations (twins) that are identical in terms of these other relevant factors.

Another method of using paired samples involves the examination of the same observations before and after treatment. It is a common practice in industry to test employees before and after a training program. We then have a "before" test score and an "after" test score for each observation (employee). Any change in the score can be attributed to the training. The researcher should be cautioned that some bias may affect the sampling because the employees may resent being tested or may remember their answers from the first test and try to be consistent in their responses.

This before-and-after sampling procedure is not possible with our blood pressure study since the same people could not be given both drugs. It would be possible to test, however, the relative effects of one drug against not taking the drug by measuring the same person's blood pressure before and after taking the drug.

Paired sampling has certain advantages in that smaller samples will often lead to more accurate results, since by controlling for the other relevant factors the researcher does not have to rely on the use of large samples to reduce sampling error.

To illustrate, asssume that we have test scores for 10 employees before and after they are given additional on the job training. The scores are shown in Table 8-1. Assume further that we want to use the differences between the before and after scores of these $n = 10$ employees to estimate the mean difference in scores for all employees who might be given the same training. Let d_i be the difference between any matched pair. The mean of the differences between all pairs is then

$$\bar{d} = \frac{\Sigma d_i}{n} \tag{8.6}$$

$$= \frac{-5}{10}$$

$$= -0.5$$

The variance of these differences is

$$s_{\bar{d}}^2 = \frac{\Sigma d_i^2 - n\bar{d}^2}{n - 1} \tag{8.7}$$

$$= \frac{7.38 - 10(-0.5)^2}{9}$$

$$= 0.54$$

TABLE 8-1   Before and After Test Scores

Employee	Score before OJT	Score after OJT	d_i	d_i^2
1	9.0	9.2	−0.2	0.04
2	7.3	8.2	−0.9	0.81
3	6.7	8.5	−1.8	3.24
4	5.3	4.9	0.4	0.16
5	8.7	8.9	−0.2	0.04
6	6.3	5.8	0.5	0.25
7	7.9	8.2	−0.3	0.09
8	7.3	7.8	−0.5	0.25
9	8.0	9.5	−1.5	2.25
10	7.5	8.0	−0.5	0.25
	74.0	79.0	−5.0	7.38

The standard deviation of these differences is

$$s_d = \sqrt{0.54} = 0.73$$

Since $n < 30$ and the standard deviation of the differences in scores, σ_d, is unknown, use of the t-statistic is required. If n had been greater than 30 or σ_d was known, the Z-statistic could have been used. Furthermore, it must be assumed that the d-values are normally distributed. The distribution of the raw scores themselves is immaterial, but the d-values must be normal.

Then, for a 90 percent confidence level and $n - 1 = 9$ d.f., a confidence interval for the mean of the difference in scores before and after training is

$$\text{C.I. for } \mu_d = \bar{d} \pm t \frac{s_d}{\sqrt{n}} \qquad (8.8)$$

$$= -0.5 \pm (1.833) \frac{0.73}{\sqrt{10}}$$

$$-0.92 \le \mu_d \le -0.08$$

Since the before test scores had the lower mean, this interval tells us that we can be 90 percent confident that the mean of the after test scores will exceed that of the before test scores by 0.08 to 0.92 points. Or, equivalently, before test scores will display a mean lower than that of after test scores between −0.92 and −0.08.

The question of whether to use paired samples or independent sampling may arise. If the same observations are used before and after some treatment (such as the training program discussed here), paired samples is the prescribed approach. Or, if two nearly identical samples have been matched up, such as in the blood pressure example, paired samples are assumed.

In addition, recall that paired sampling is done to correct for relevant factors such as, in the blood pressure case, age, and sex. That is, factors other than the medication we wish to test may influence test results. We correct for these other influential factors by matching observations between samples. If this matching process is beneficial, it will produce a narrower, more precise interval than that which would result in the absence of pairing. This is because matching observations reduces any variance in results due to these other influential factors, since pairing tends to cancel their influence.

On the other hand, presume for the moment (contrary to all medical evidence) that age and sex are not relevant factors in determining blood pressure. Trying to correct for these irrelevant factors through pairing, when correction is not warranted, will likely increase interval width and reduce precision, because pairing reduces the number of degrees of freedom. With pairing, d.f. $= n - 1$. As we will see, independent samples produce d.f. $> n - 1$. Therefore, if pairing is to prove beneficial, it must reduce the variance sufficiently to compensate for the loss of degrees of freedom.

If it appears paired sampling is called for, but some question remains, proceed in the following manner: compute the interval on the basis of paired samples. Then reconstruct the interval by using independent sampling. If the paired sampling does not reduce the interval, the correction brought about by pairing was insufficient to offset the lesser degrees of freedom, and the independent sampling methods discussed below should be used.

QUICK CHECK 8.4.1
○○○○ $\Sigma d_i = 40$, $n = 15$, $\Sigma d_i^2 = 415$. Calculate a 95 percent confidence interval
                for μ_d.
                Answer: $0.073 \leq \mu_d \leq 5.27$

QUICK CHECK 8.4.2
                $\Sigma d_i = 8$, $\Sigma d_i^2 = 24$, $n = 5$. Calculate a 90 percent confidence interval for μ_d.
                Answer: $0.01 \leq \mu_d \leq 3.19$

B.   INDEPENDENT SAMPLING

Many situations will arise in which it is desirable to select two totally independent samples from two different populations. Perhaps a manufacturer wishes to compare the customer loyalty of one of its products to that of the product of its competitor. Comparing the performance of two groups of employees may require independent sampling. When independent samples are taken, no effort is made to match observations in one sample with those in another.

Independent Sampling
Independent samples are two random samples selected from two distinct populations.

Two independent samples, unlike paired samples, need not be of the same size. Furthermore, a researcher may face several different sets of conditions in the process of selecting independent samples. Each is examined in turn.

1.   INDEPENDENT SAMPLES—KNOWN VARIANCES   Insurance companies often charge different auto premiums to men than they do women. This difference is based on the contention that there exists a disparity in risk based on gender. Both life and auto insurance premiums are therefore higher for men. (Recent legislation has curtailed insurance companies' right to charge higher auto rates to male drivers unless individual driving records warrant such discriminatory treatment.)

In the effort to determine rate structures, insurance companies compare the risk factors associated with insuring males to that associated with insuring females. The point estimate of the difference between the mean risk level is $\overline{X}_1 - \overline{X}_2$, where $\overline{X}_1$ is the risk level for males and X_2 is that of females. Thus, $\overline{X}_1 - \overline{X}_2$ serves as an estimate of $\mu_1 - \mu_2$.

If a sample of men and a sample of women are compared, there will likely be a difference between the two sample means. If two more samples are selected, the difference between the two sample means will probably not be the same as was the difference between the first two samples. This variation in the differences between two sample means is measured by the **standard error of the sampling distribution of the differences between two sample means.** The standard error of the sampling distribution of the differences (as it is called for short) is an important concept and must be mastered.

Standard Error of the Sampling Distribution of the Differences between Two Sample Means
This statistic measures the variation in the differences between pairs of sample means.

If the population variances are known, the standard error of the sampling distribution of the differences between the two sample means can be measured as

$$\sigma_{\bar{x}_1-\bar{x}_2} = \sqrt{\frac{\sigma_1^2}{n_1} + \frac{\sigma_2^2}{n_2}} \qquad (8.9)$$

where σ_1^2 and σ_2^2 are the variances of the two populations
           n_1 and n_2 are the two sample sizes (which do not have to be equal)
The confidence interval for the difference between μ_1 and μ_2 is

$$\text{C.I. for } \mu_1 - \mu_2 = (\bar{X}_1 - \bar{X}_2) \pm Z\sigma_{\bar{x}_1-\bar{x}_2} \qquad (8.10)$$

An article in *Nation's Business* described a test conducted by Allied Chemical Company to compare the effectiveness of two types of chemical fertilizers. Fifty acres were planted with each type. The increases in yields per acre of wheat averaged $\bar{X}_1 = 14.2$ bushels for fertilizer 1 and $\bar{X}_2 = 17.5$ bushels for fertilizer 2. The variances for both fertilizers were known to be $\sigma_1^2 = 3.7$ and $\sigma_2^2 = 4.2$. Figure 8-10 displays this condition for a 99 percent confidence interval.

FIGURE 8-10   Difference in Mean Yields

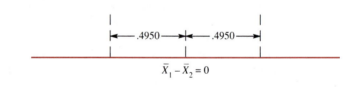

Since

$$\sigma_{\bar{x}_1-\bar{x}_2} = \sqrt{\frac{\sigma_1^2}{n_1} + \frac{\sigma_2^2}{n_2}}$$

$$= 0.397$$

we have

$$\text{C.I. for } \mu_1 - \mu_2 = (\bar{X}_1 - \bar{X}_2) \pm Z\sigma_{\bar{x}_1-\bar{x}_2}$$

$$= (14.2 - 17.5) \pm (2.58)(0.397)$$

$$-4.32 \le \mu_1 - \mu_2 \le -2.28$$

Since subtracting the mean of fertilizer 2 from that of fertilizer 1 produced negative values, Allied can be 99 percent confident that the first fertilizer increases per acre yields by 2.28 to 4.32 bushels less than the second type.

EXAMPLE 8-7 The Mean Cost of Mortgages

In 1989, *Banker's News* reported that mortgage rates in the South were higher than those in the Midwest. A survey of 100 banks in southern states and 123 banks in Kansas and the four surrounding states revealed mean rates of 11.75 percent and 10.53 percent, respectively. Assume the variances were 2.5 percent and 3.0 percent. As a corporate executive, you must decide where to open a new company headquarters. A consideration in this decision is employees' housing costs. You want to form a 92 percent confidence interval for the difference between mean mortgage rates in the South and in the Midwest.

SOLUTION:

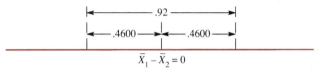

An area of 0.4600 yields a Z-value of 1.75 from the table. Then

$$\text{C.I. for } \mu_1 - \mu_2 = (\overline{X}_1 - \overline{X}_2) \pm Z\sigma_{\bar{x}_1-\bar{x}_2}$$

$$= (11.75 - 10.53) \pm 1.75 \sqrt{\frac{2.5}{100} + \frac{3.0}{123}}$$

$$= 1.22 \pm 0.389$$

$$0.83 \le \mu_1 - \mu_2 \le 1.61$$

STATISTICAL INTERPRETATION:

You can be 92 percent confident that average rates in the South exceed those in the Midwest by an amount between 0.83 percent and 1.61 percent.

QUICK CHECK 8.4.3

○○○○

Two machines produce snow tires with normally distributed diameters and variances of $\sigma_1^2 = 85.1$ inches and $\sigma_2^2 = 72.3$ inches. Independent samples of $n_1 = n_2 = 100$ are taken, yielding $\overline{X}_1 = 37.3$ inches and $\overline{X}_2 = 35.2$ inches. Develop a 90 percent confidence interval for the difference between the mean diameters of tires produced by these two machines.

Answer: $0.04 \le \mu_1 - \mu_2 \le 4.16$

QUICK CHECK 8.4.4

Without calculating the interval, would a 95 percent level of confidence require a larger or smaller interval than that from Quick Check 8.4.3?

Answer: Larger, if you are to be more confident of your findings.

2. INDEPENDENT SAMPLES—VARIANCES UNKNOWN BUT ASSUMED EQUAL   As you might expect, if population variances are unknown they must be estimated with sample variances. If small samples are taken, the t-statistic must be used and the assumption of normally distributed populations is made. Furthermore, in the previous example the known population variances were not equal. Assume for the moment that the population variances are unknown but presumed to be equal. You may question the logic of presuming the equality of two variances if we do not even know what they are. However, a classic example of this situation can be found in many assembly-line techniques of production. Automatic fillers are often used for product containers such as cans, bottles, boxes, and other packaged products. When the fillers are adjusted periodically to ensure proper operation, it is assumed that the mean fill level changes, but the variance of the fills remains the same. If samples are taken before and after the adjustment, the mean will differ but the variances in those fills remains constant. (A method is presented in Chapter 10 to test equality of variances.)

It is assumed that the population of fills before the adjustment and the population of fills after the adjustment have the same variance. However, due to sampling error, if a sample is taken from each population, the sample variances will likely differ from each other as well as from the variance common to both populations. But since the populations have a common variance, the data from both samples can be pooled to obtain a single estimate of σ^2. This is done by computing the weighted average of the two sample variances, where the weights are the degrees of freedom for each sample. This **pooled estimate** of the common population variance, s_p^2, is

$$s_p^2 = \frac{s_1^2(n_1 - 1) + s_2^2(n_2 - 1)}{n_1 + n_2 - 2} \qquad (8.11)$$

The confidence interval for the difference between the two population means is

$$\text{C.I. for } \mu_1 - \mu_2 = (\bar{X}_1 - \bar{X}_2) \pm (t)(s_p)\sqrt{\frac{1}{n_1} + \frac{1}{n_2}} \qquad (8.12)$$

A vending machine in the student cafeteria dispenses drinks into paper cups. A sample of 15 cups yields a mean of 15.3 ounces with a variance of 3.5 ounces. After adjusting the machine, a sample of 10 cups produces an average of 17.1 ounces with a variance of 3.9 ounces. If σ^2 is assumed to be constant before and after the adjustment, construct a 95 percent confidence interval for the difference in mean fills. Assume the amounts dispensed are normally distributed. The degrees of freedom for this test is $n_1 + n_2 - 2$.

Then

$$s_p^2 = \frac{3.5(14) + 3.9(9)}{15 + 10 - 2}$$

$$= 3.66$$

$$s_p = \sqrt{3.66} = 1.91$$

With $\alpha = 0.05$ (a 95 percent level of confidence) and $n_1 + n_2 - 2 = 23$ d.f., the t-table reveals a value of 2.069.

$$\text{C.I. for } \mu_1 - \mu_2 = (15.3 - 17.1) \pm (2.069)(1.91) \sqrt{\frac{1}{15} + \frac{1}{10}}$$

$$= -1.8 \pm 1.61$$

$$-3.41 \le \mu_1 - \mu_2 \le -0.19$$

We can be 95 percent confident that the adjustment increased the mean fill level between 0.19 ounce and 3.41 ounces.

EXAMPLE 8-8 A Difference in Means: Common Variance

Wage negotiations between your firm and the union representing your workers are about to collapse. There is considerable disagreement about the mean wage level of workers in the plant in Atlanta and the plant in Newport News, Virginia. Wages were set by the old labor agreement reached three years ago and are based strictly on seniority. Since wages are closely controlled by the labor contract, it is assumed that the variation in wages is the same at both plants and that the wages are normally distributed. However, due to differing patterns of seniority between the two plants, it is felt that there is a difference between the mean wage levels.

Management's head labor negotiator wants you to develop a 98 percent confidence interval for the difference between the mean wage levels.

SOLUTION:

Samples of workers taken from each plant reveal the following information.

Atlanta Plant	Newport News Plant
$n_A = 23$	$n_N = 19$
$\overline{X}_A = \$17.53$ per hour	$\overline{X}_N = \$15.50$
$s_A^2 = \$92.10$	$s_N^2 = \$87.10$

Then

$$s_p^2 = \frac{92.10(22) + 87.1(18)}{23 + 19 - 2}$$

$$= 89.85$$

$$s_p = 9.48$$

Given $\alpha = 0.02$ and d.f. $= 23 + 19 - 2 = 40$, Table F reveals a t-value of 2.423.

$$\text{C.I. for } \mu_1 - \mu_2 = (17.53 - 15.5) \pm 2.423(9.48)\sqrt{\frac{1}{23} + \frac{1}{19}}$$

$$= 2.03 \pm 7.12$$

$$-5.09 \le \mu_1 - \mu_2 \le 9.15$$

STATISTICAL INTERPRETATION:

You can be 98 percent confident that the difference in the two mean wage levels is between these values. Since this interval contains $0, the conclusion that no difference exists is possible.

QUICK CHECK 8.4.5

OOOO

A business owns two restaurants in separate locations. Daily receipts at both are normally distributed, and it is assumed that $\sigma_1^2 = \sigma_2^2$. Samples of 15 days' receipts from each restaurant yielded $\overline{X}_1 = \$17,515$ with $s_1^2 = \$1,515$ and $\overline{X}_2 = \$16,912$ with $s_2^2 = \$1,412$. Construct a 99 percent confidence interval for $\mu_1 - \mu_2$.

Answer: $\$565 \le \mu_1 - \mu_2 \le \$641$

---

3. INDEPENDENT SAMPLES — $\sigma_1^2 \ne \sigma_2^2$ In many cases the population variances are unequal or there is no evidence to assume an equality. In this event, none of the procedures described above directly apply because the distribution of differences between sample means does not fit a t-distribution with $n_1 + n_2 - 2$ d.f. In fact, no exact distribution has been found which adequately describes this sampling process, and only approximations have been developed. One such approximation has been proposed using the t-statistic with d.f. slightly altered. In the event $\sigma_1^2 \ne \sigma_2^2$, d.f. can be found as

$$\text{d.f.} = \frac{(s_1^2/n_1 + s_2^2/n_2)^2}{(s_1^2/n_1)^2/(n_1 - 1) + (s_2^2/n_2)^2/(n_2 - 1)} \qquad (8.13)$$

Since d.f. is calculated in this altered manner, the t-statistic is symbolized as t'. The confidence interval is then calculated as

$$\text{C.I. for } \mu_1 - \mu_2 = (\overline{X}_1 - \overline{X}_2) \pm t'\sqrt{\frac{s_1^2}{n_1} + \frac{s_2^2}{n_2}} \qquad (8.14)$$

The Wall Street Journal described two training programs used by IBM. Twelve executives who were given the first type of training scored a mean of 73.5 on an achievement test. Although the news article did not report the standard deviation for these 12 employees, let us assume that the variance in test scores for this group was 100.2 points. Fifteen executives to whom the second training program was administered scored an average of 79.8. Assume a variance of 121.3 for this second group. Develop a 95 percent confidence interval for the difference in the mean scores of all executives entered in these programs.

$$\text{d.f.} = \frac{(100.2/12 + 121.3/15)^2}{(100.2/12)^2/11 + (121.3/15)^2/14}$$

$$= 24.55$$

If d.f. is fractional, round down to the next lowest whole integer. Thus, d.f. = 24. A 95 percent confidence interval with 24 degrees of freedom calls for a t'-value of 2.064.

$$\text{C.I. for } \mu_1 - \mu_2 = (\overline{X}_1 - \overline{X}_2) \pm t' \sqrt{\frac{s_1^2}{n_1} + \frac{s_2^2}{n_2}}$$

$$= (73.5 - 79.8) \pm 2.064 \sqrt{\frac{100.2}{12} + \frac{121.3}{15}}$$

$$= -6.3 \pm 8.36$$

$$-14.66 \leq \mu_1 - \mu_2 \leq 2.06$$

Since the interval contains zero, there is no strong evidence that there exists a difference in the effectiveness of the training programs.

EXAMPLE 8-9 Rubber Baby Buggy Bumpers

Acme, Ltd. sells two types of rubber baby buggy bumpers. Wear tests for durability revealed that 13 of type 1 lasted an average of 11.3 weeks with a standard deviation of 3.5 weeks, while 10 of type 2 lasted an average of 7.5 weeks with a standard deviation of 2.7 weeks. Type 1 costs more to manufacture, and the CEO of Acme doesn't want to use it unless it averages at least eight weeks longer than type 2. The CEO will tolerate a probability of error of only 2 percent. There is no evidence to suggest that variances in wear for the two products are equal.

SOLUTION:

$$\overline{X}_1 = 11.3 \qquad \overline{X}_2 = 7.5$$

$$n_1 = 13 \qquad n_2 = 10$$

$$s_1 = 3.5 \qquad s_2 = 2.7$$

$$\text{d.f.} = \frac{(s_1^2/n_1 + s_2^2/n_2)^2}{(s_1^2/n_1)^2/(n_1 - 1) + (s_2^2/n_2)^2/(n_2 - 1)}$$

$$= \frac{[(3.5)^2/13 + (2.7)^2/10]^2}{\dfrac{[(3.5)^2/13]^2}{12} + \dfrac{[(2.7)^2/10]^2}{9}}$$

$$= 20.99 \approx 20$$

A 98 percent confidence interval ($\alpha = 0.02$) with 20 d.f. requires a t'-value of 2.528.

$$\text{C.I. for } \mu_1 - \mu_2 = (11.3 - 7.5) \pm 2.528 \sqrt{\frac{(3.5)^2}{13} + \frac{(2.7)^2}{10}}$$

$$= 3.8 \pm 3.3$$

$$0.5 \leq \mu_1 - \mu_2 \leq 7.1 \text{ weeks}$$

STATISTICAL INTERPRETATION:

Since the required eight-week difference is not in the interval, the CEO can be 98 percent confident he does not want to use type 1.

QUICK CHECK 8.4.6

OOOO

Samples of sizes $n_1 = 10$ and $n_2 = 8$ are taken from two normal populations with unequal variances. The results are $\overline{X}_1 = 50.3$, $s_1^2 = 80.0$, $\overline{X}_2 = 41.1$, $s_2^2 = 75.1$. Calculate a 90 percent confidence interval for $\mu_1 - \mu_2$.

Answer: $1.89 \leq \mu_1 - \mu_2 \leq 16.51$

QUICK CHECK 8.4.7

Why is it suggested that you round down in the calculation of d.f.?

Answer: Fewer degrees of freedom produce a wider, more conservative answer.

The checksheet should help you organize the various two-sample tests for normal populations.

In addition to the checksheet, three further points should be noted:

1. If both n_1 and n_2 are greater than 30, the Z-statistic can be used in the above cases.
2. If the populations are not normal and large samples are taken, the Z-test can be used regardless of whether the population variances are known.
3. If the populations are not known to be normal and small samples are taken, certain nonparametric tests discussed in a later chapter must be used.

Checksheet for Confidence Intervals for $\mu_1 - \mu_2$ for Normal Populations

Condition	Test	
1. Paired sampling n_1 or $n_2 < 30$	$\bar{d} = \dfrac{\Sigma d_i}{n}$	(8.6)
	$s_d^2 = \dfrac{\Sigma d_i^2 - n\bar{d}^2}{n-1}$	(8.7)
	C.I. for $\mu_d = \bar{d} \pm t\dfrac{s_d}{\sqrt{n}}$	(8.8)
2. Independent sampling A. σ_1 and σ_2 known regardless of sample sizes	$\sigma_{\bar{x}_1 - \bar{x}_2} = \sqrt{\dfrac{\sigma_1^2}{n_1} + \dfrac{\sigma_2^2}{n_2}}$	(8.9)
	C.I. for $\mu_1 - \mu_2 = (\bar{X}_1 - \bar{X}_2) \pm Z\sigma_{\bar{x}_1 - \bar{x}_2}$	(8.10)
B. $\sigma_1 = \sigma_2$ Variances unknown n_1 or $n_2 < 30$	$s_p^2 = \dfrac{s_1^2(n_1 - 1) + s_2^2(n_2 - 1)}{n_1 + n_2 - 2}$	(8.11)
	C.I. for $\mu_1 - \mu_2 = (\bar{X}_1 - \bar{X}_2) \pm (t)s_p \sqrt{\dfrac{1}{n_1} + \dfrac{1}{n_2}}$	(8.12)
C. $\sigma_1 \neq \sigma_2$ Variances unknown n_1 or $n_2 < 30$	d.f. $= \dfrac{(s_1^2/n_1 + s_2^2/n_2)^2}{(s_1^2/n_1)^2/(n_1 - 1) + (s_2^2/n_2)^2/(n_2 - 1)}$	(8.13)
	C.I. for $\mu_1 - \mu_2 = (\bar{X}_1 - \bar{X}_2) \pm t' \sqrt{\dfrac{s_1^2}{n_1} + \dfrac{s_2^2}{n_2}}$	(8.14)

Figure 8-11 on page 350 should lend further assistance in deciding on the appropriate test.

8.5 CONFIDENCE INTERVALS FOR POPULATION PROPORTIONS

Decisions often depend on parameters that are binary—that is, parameters with only two possible categories into which responses may fall. In this event, the parameter of concern is the population proportion. A firm may want to know what proportion of its customers pay on credit as opposed to those who use cash. Corporations are often interested in what percentage of their products are defective as opposed to that percentage which is not defective, or what proportion of their employees quit after one year in contrast to that proportion who do not quit after one year. In each of these instances, there are only two possible outcomes. Concern is therefore focused on that proportion of responses that fall into one of these two outcomes.

FIGURE 8-11   Selecting the Proper Test Statistic for $\mu_1 - \mu_2$

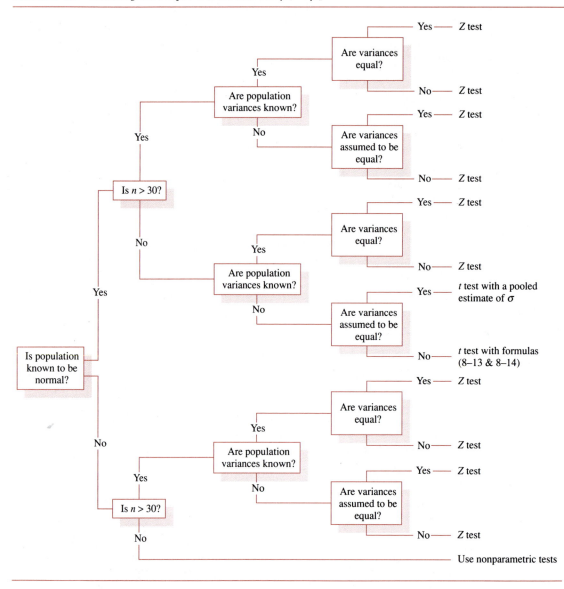

A.   CONFIDENCE INTERVALS FOR A SINGLE PROPORTION π

In the previous chapter we found that if $n\pi$ and $n(1 - \pi)$ are both greater than 5, the distribution of sample proportions will be normal. The stipulation was also made that n should be greater than 50. The sampling distribution of sample proportions will have a mean equal to the population proportion π and a standard error of

$$\sigma_p = \sqrt{\frac{\pi(1 - \pi)}{n}} \qquad\qquad (8.15)$$

However, Formula (8.15) requires π, the parameter we must estimate. Therefore, the sample proportion p is used as an estimator for π.

Formula (8.15) becomes

$$s_p = \sqrt{\frac{p(1 - p)}{n}} \qquad\qquad (8.16)$$

The confidence interval is then

$$\text{C.I. for } \pi = p \pm Z s_p \qquad\qquad (8.17)$$

The manager of a TV station must determine what percentage of households in the city have more than one TV set. A random sample of 500 homes reveals that 275 have two or more sets. What is the 90 percent confidence interval for the proportion of all homes with two or more sets? Given these data, $p = 275/500 = 0.55$, and

$$s_p = \sqrt{\frac{(0.55)(0.45)}{500}}$$

$$= 0.022$$

Table E yields a Z of 1.65 for a 90 percent confidence interval.

$$\text{C.I. for } \pi = 0.55 \pm (1.65)(0.022)$$

$$= 0.55 \pm 0.036$$

$$0.514 \leq \pi \leq 0.586$$

The manager can be 90 percent confident that between 51.4 percent and 58.6 percent of the homes in the city have more than one TV.

EXAMPLE 8-10 Headhunters in Paradise

Executive search firms specialize in helping corporations locate and secure top-level management talent. Called "headhunters," these firms are responsible for the placement of many of the nation's top CEOs. *Business Week* recently reported on the "efforts by headhunters to place executives in a heavenly corporate setting." A source was quoted in the story as saying that "1 out of every 4 CEOs is an outsider—an executive with less than 5 years at the company he runs." If, in a sample of 350 U.S. corporations, 77 have outsider CEOs, would a 99 percent confidence interval support the quote?

SOLUTION:

$$p = \frac{77}{350} = 0.22$$

$$s_p = \sqrt{\frac{(0.22)(0.78)}{350}} = 0.022$$

C.I. for $\pi = p \pm Zs_p$

$$= 0.22 \pm (2.58)(0.022)$$

$$0.163 \leq \pi \leq 0.277$$

STATISTICAL INTERPRETATION:
We are confident at the 99 percent level that between 16.3 percent and 27.7 percent of U.S. corporations have outside CEOs. The quote is supported by these findings since 25 percent is contained within the interval.

B. CONFIDENCE INTERVALS FOR THE DIFFERENCE BETWEEN TWO PROPORTIONS

Many occasions often arise in which we must compare the proportions of two different populations. Firms continually examine the proportions of defective products produced by different methods. Medical researchers are concerned about the proportion of men who suffer heart attacks as opposed to the percentage of women. In general, many business matters are determined by the estimation of the relative proportions of two populations.

The pattern by which this is done should be familiar to you by now. The standard error of the difference between two sample proportions ($p_1 - p_2$) is estimated by

$$s_{p_1-p_2} = \sqrt{\frac{p_1(1 - p_1)}{n_1} + \frac{p_2(1 - p_2)}{n_2}} \qquad (8.18)$$

$s_{p_1-p_2}$ recognizes that if several samples were taken from each population and the differences were calculated, ($p_1 - p_2$) would vary. Formula (8.18) accounts for that variation. The confidence interval is

○○○○ **DECISION MAKING THROUGH PROBLEM SOLVING** ○○○○
ILLUSTRATION 8-4

No election year is complete without voters' opinion polls taken by every candidate from president to dogcatcher to determine what percentage of the voters favor his or her candidacy. In the Bush-Dukakis race for president in 1987, a poll taken by the Bush organization revealed that the populace favored their candidate over Dukakis by a 57 percent to 41 percent ratio, with the rest undecided. A poll taken by the Democratic election committee, however, resulted in a 49 percent to 45 percent edge for Dukakis. What might have accounted for these disparities?

$$\text{C.I. for } \pi_1 - \pi_2 = p_1 - p_2 \pm (Z)s_{p_1-p_2} \qquad (8.19)$$

A firm conducts a study to determine if absenteeism of day workers is different from those employees who work the night shift. A comparison is made of 150 workers from each shift. The results show that 37 day workers have been absent at least five times over the past year, while 52 night workers have missed at least five times. What does this reveal about the tendency for absenteeism among the workers? Calculate a 90 percent confidence interval for the difference in the proportion of workers on the two shifts who missed five times or more.

$$p_1 = \frac{37}{150} = 0.25, \qquad p_2 = \frac{52}{150} = 0.35$$

$$s_{p_1-p_2} = \sqrt{\frac{(0.25)(0.75)}{150} + \frac{(0.35)(0.65)}{150}}$$

$$= 0.0526$$

$$\text{C.I. for } \pi_1 - \pi_2 = (p_1 - p_2) \pm (Z)s_{p_1-p_2}$$

$$= (0.25 - 0.35) \pm (1.65)(0.0526)$$

$$= -0.10 \pm 0.087$$

$$-18.7\% \leq \pi_1 - \pi_2 \leq -1.3\%$$

Since the proportion of night workers who were absent five times or more (p_2) was subtracted from the proportion of day workers who were absent, the firm can be 90 percent certain that the proportion of night workers absent five or more times is between 1.3 percent and 18.7 percent higher than that for day workers.

○○○○   **DECISION MAKING THROUGH PROBLEM SOLVING**   ○○○○
                                ILLUSTRATION 8-5

In the eternal battle of the television network ratings, a poll was taken by the Harris Organization to compare the popularity of "The Cosby Show," an NBC staple, with that of "The Simpsons" shown on the Fox Network. To obtain a complete viewer profile, Harris broke down the market on the basis of several demographic factors, including, for example, gender. Thus, two distinct market groups were formed. A comparison of the percentage of males, as opposed to females, who preferred Bart and his lovely family of misfits could then be made.

QUICK CHECK 8.5.1
○○○○
A sample of 200 cars randomly selected by the California Highway Patrol revealed that only 23 were obeying the speed limit. What is the 95 percent confidence interval for the proportion of all cars obeying the speed limit?
Answer: $0.07 \leq \pi \leq 0.16$

QUICK CHECK 8.5.2

A sample of 175 trucks found that 38 were obeying the speed limit. Use the data from Exercise 8.5.1 to develop a 90 percent confidence interval for the difference between the proportion of trucks and the proportion of cars that obey the legal limit.
Answer: $0.038 \leq \pi_T - \pi_C \leq 0.166$

8.6   CONTROLLING THE INTERVAL WIDTH

In working through some of the problems encountered thus far in this chapter, you may have become somewhat alarmed by the width of the interval. Some concern might be caused by the fact that the interval was too wide and failed to localize the parameter with sufficient precision. Narrowing the interval will, of course, provide the researcher with a more exact estimation of the parameter's value. There are two common methods of narrowing the interval. Both, however, entail a cost of some kind. These procedures to achieve a more precise interval are (1) decreasing the level of confidence, and (2) increasing the sample size.

A.   ADJUSTING THE LEVEL OF CONFIDENCE

By the mere nature of confidence intervals, accepting a lower level of confidence in the interval will generate a more precise, narrower interval. In Example 8-10 we found that the proportion of "outsiders" who were CEOs for the company they ran was estimated to be between 16.3 percent and 27.7 percent. This might be considered a rather wide interval, but it permitted a level of confidence of 99 percent.

If we were willing to accept a 10 percent probability of error, by constructing a 90 percent interval, we would have

$$\text{C.I. for } \mu = 0.22 \pm (1.65)(0.022)$$

$$= 0.22 \pm 0.036$$

$$0.184 \leq \mu \leq 0.256$$

The effect of decreasing the level of confidence from 99 percent to 90 percent is shown in Figure 8-12.

Figure 8-12   Comparing 99 Percent and 90 Percent Confidence Intervals

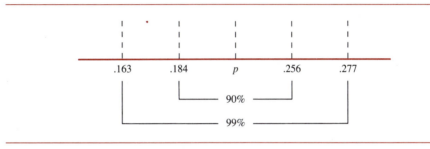

The estimate now places π between 18.4 percent and 25.6 percent. This is certainly a narrower interval, but the aforementioned cost is a loss of confidence in the interval and a marked increase in the probability of error. It is up to the researcher, based on how critical his or her work is, to determine what probability of error can be tolerated. A trade-off must be made.

B.   Adjusting the Sample Size

Another common method of generating a narrower interval is to take a larger sample. It has been repeatedly emphasized that large samples will reduce the expected error and are more likely to produce an estimate closer to the true value of the parameter. Therefore, you can retain a given level of confidence and still reduce the width of the interval.

Return again to Example 8-10. In a sample of $n = 350$, 22 percent of the CEOs were outsiders. The 99 percent confidence interval was 16.3 percent to 27.7 percent. In order to narrow the interval and yet retain the 99 percent level of confidence, it is necessary to increase the sample size. Assume that in a sample of $n = 700$, 22 percent are found to be outsiders. The sample proportion of 22 percent is held constant to ensure that the only factor we change is sample size. The 99 percent confidence interval is then

$$s_p = \sqrt{\frac{(0.22)(0.78)}{700}} = 0.0157$$

$$\text{C.I. for } \pi = 0.22 \pm (2.58)(0.0157)$$

$$= 0.22 \pm 0.041$$

$$0.179 \le \pi \le 0.261$$

The results of increasing the size of the sample are shown in Figure 8-13. Notice that the larger sample size produced a smaller standard error, s_p, and 99 percent of the sample proportions are within a smaller interval around π. The 99 percent confidence interval is therefore contained within a narrower range.

FIGURE 8-13   Comparing Sample Sizes

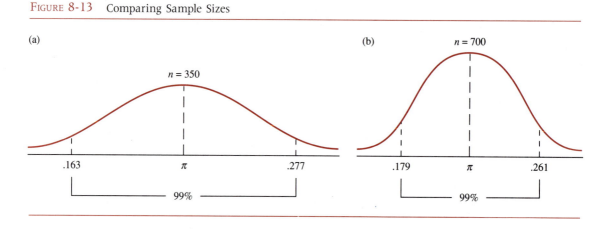

There is again, however, a cost associated with producing this more precise interval in the form of the time and expenses required to collect a larger sample. This additional cost must be judged against the higher degree of precision.

8.7   DETERMINING THE SAMPLE SIZE

The size of the sample has an important impact on the probability of error and the precision of the estimate, as well as other important factors associated with the research effort. Determination of the appropriate sample size is crucial. Given any desired confidence level, two factors are particularly instrumental in influencing the necessary sample size: (1) the variability of the population, σ^2, and (2) size of the error that can be tolerated. While the first factor is beyond the control of the researcher, the size of the tolerable error should be examined at this point.

The extent of error a researcher can tolerate depends on how critical the work must be. Some tasks are extremely delicate and require exacting results. For example, vital medical procedures upon which lives may depend or the production of machine parts which must meet precise measurements can tolerate only a small error. In other instances, larger errors may be of lesser consequence.

Presume that in manufacturing a part for compact disk players an error of 2 centimeters (cm) in diameter will cause no problem. Any error in excess of 2 cm will, however, result in a defective disk player. If the part can vary above and below some desired mean diameter by 2 cm, an interval of 4 cm is allowed. Any given interval is twice the tolerable error. See Figure 8-14 for an illustration.

Tolerable Error
The confidence interval can extend above and below the mean by the amount of the tolerable error.

The remainder of this section considers the determination of the proper sample size under various conditions.

FIGURE 8-14   The Tolerable Error Is One-Half the Interval

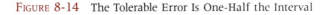

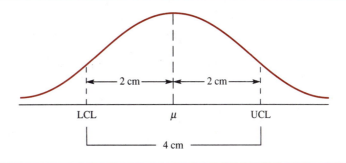

A.   SAMPLE SIZE FOR μ

Recall that the normal deviate Z can be expressed as

$$Z = \frac{\overline{X} - \mu}{\sigma_{\bar{x}}} = \frac{\overline{X} - \mu}{\sigma/\sqrt{n}}$$

This can be rewritten algebraically as

$$n = \frac{Z^2 \sigma^2}{(\overline{X} - \mu)^2} \qquad (8.20)$$

where the difference between the sample mean and the population mean $(\overline{X} - \mu)$ is the error. In the example above for the compact disk players with a tolerable error of 2 cm, Formula (8.20) would be written as

$$n = \frac{Z^2 \sigma^2}{(2)^2}$$

The value of Z depends on the level of confidence required. This leaves only σ^2 to be determined in order to calculate the proper sample size. In the likely event σ^2 is unknown, it can be estimated with a **pilot sample** of any reasonable size $(n > 30)$. The variance calculated from this preliminary sample can then be used in For-mula (8.20).

As an example, the mayor of a small town in Wisconsin wants to know the mean income of residents in his town. He wants to be 95 percent confident that the inter-val estimate is not in error by more than $1,500. It is known (or is estimated by a pilot sample) that the standard deviation in incomes is $15,500. How large should the sample be? A 95 percent confidence interval calls for a Z-value of 1.96. Thus,

$$n = \frac{(1.96)^2(15,500)^2}{(1,500)^2} = 410.2 \approx 411$$

The mayor should select a sample of 411 people. From this sample, a 95 percent confidence interval for the mean income of the town's residents can then be calcu-lated and produce an estimate with an error not greater than $1,500.

B. SAMPLE SIZE FOR $\mu_1 - \mu_2$

The procedure just examined can be adapted to deal with a comparison of the means of two populations. The correct sample size is found by

$$n = \frac{Z^2(\sigma_1^2 + \sigma_2^2)}{(\text{error})^2} \qquad (8.21)$$

An economist at the University of Texas at Arlington has been asked by the Texas Economic Planning Commission to develop a 99 percent confidence interval for the difference between the mean length of service by public employees and that of workers in the private sector. The commission desires an interval width of three years. Pilot samples yield variances of 15 years and 21 years, respectively. How large should the samples taken from each population be?

Since the interval is to be 3 years, the error is one-half of that, or 1.5 years. Then

$$n = \frac{(2.58)^2(15 + 21)}{(1.5)^2}$$

$$= 106.5, \text{ or } 107$$

Thus, 107 employees should be selected from the public sector and 107 should be selected from the private sector in order to make the comparison.

QUICK CHECK 8.7.1

○○○○ A motel chain wants to determine a confidence interval for the daily mean occupancy of its rooms. It wants an interval of five rooms and a 99 percent confidence level. How large should the sample be if $\sigma^2 = 40$ rooms per day?

Answer: $n = 43$ days

QUICK CHECK 8.7.2

What would happen to the required number of days if the population was less variable? Say, $\sigma^2 = 30$?

Answer: n decreases; $n = 32$

QUICK CHECK 8.7.3

A trucking firm uses two different routes to deliver goods. The firm wants to construct a 90 percent confidence interval for the difference in mean delivery times. The interval is to be 1 hour. How large should the samples be if $\sigma_1^2 = 3.2$ and $\sigma_2^2 = 2.5$?

Answer: 62

C. SAMPLE SIZE FOR π

In the previous chapter we found that

$$Z = \frac{p - \pi}{\sigma_p}$$

where

$$\sigma_p = \sqrt{\frac{\pi(1 - \pi)}{n}}$$

This can be rewritten to produce an expression for sample size,

$$n = \frac{Z^2 \pi(1 - \pi)}{(p - \pi)^2} \qquad (8.22)$$

where $(p - \pi)$ is the difference between the sample proportion and the population proportion, and is therefore the error.

Formula (8.22) requires a value for π. However, π is the parameter we wish to estimate and is unknown. This problem can be handled in one of two ways. A pilot sample can be taken to obtain a preliminary value for π as was done in our efforts to determine the proper sample size for the mean. Another method entails merely setting $\pi = 0.5$ for the purpose of determining sample size. This approach is often preferred because it is very "safe" or conservative in that it will ensure the largest possible sample size given any desired level of confidence and error. This larger sample results from the fact that the numerator of Formula (8.22), which contains $\pi(1 - \pi)$, will be maximized (thus, n will be maximized) if $\pi = 1 - \pi = 0.5$.

There is no value other than 0.5 which you could assign to π that would make $\pi(1 - \pi)$ larger. If $\pi = 0.5$, then $\pi(1 - \pi) = 0.25$. Any value other than 0.5 would result in $\pi(1 - \pi) < 0.25$. Thus, n would be smaller.

Wally Simpleton is running for governor. He wants to estimate within 1 percentage point the proportion of people who will vote for him. He also wants to be 95 percent confident of his findings. How large should the sample size be?

$$n = \frac{(1.96)^2(0.5)(0.5)}{(0.01)^2}$$

$$= 9,604 \text{ voters}$$

D.   SAMPLE SIZE FOR $\pi_1 - \pi_2$

In deciding on the correct sample size to estimate the difference between two population proportions, the procedure to follow is shown above. Specifically,

$$n = \frac{Z^2[\pi_1(1 - \pi_1) + \pi_2(1 - \pi_2)]}{(\text{error})^2} \qquad (8.23)$$

Hobart Doolittle, Wally Simpleton's opponent in the governor's race, wants to develop a confidence interval with a width of 3 percentage points and a 99 percent level of confidence for the difference between the proportion of men and the proportion of women who favor his candidacy. How large should the samples be? A pilot sample for men and women revealed $p_m = 0.40$ and $p_w = 0.30$. If the interval width is 0.03, the error is $0.03/2 = 0.015$.

$$n = \frac{(2.58)^2[(0.4)(0.6) + (0.3)(0.7)]}{(0.015)^2}$$

$$= 13,312 \text{ men and } 13,312 \text{ women}$$

QUICK CHECK 8.7.4

OOOO   A banker wants to estimate the percentage of people who respond favorably to a new TV advertising campaign. The interval width is to be 5 percent with a 90 percent level of confidence. Determine n. A pilot sample estimated π at 0.85.

Answer: 556 people

QUICK CHECK 8.7.5

A manufacturer wants to estimate the difference in the proportions of blacks and whites who have used his product. The interval is to carry a 99 percent level of confidence and a width of 8 percent. No pilot samples were taken. How large should the samples be?

Answer: 2,081 blacks and 2,081 whites

8.8 PROPERTIES OF GOOD ESTIMATORS

A distinction should be drawn between an estimator and an estimate. An **estimator** is the rule or procedure, usually expressed as a formula, that is used to derive the **estimate**. For example,

$$\overline{X} = \frac{\Sigma X_i}{n}$$

is the estimator for the population mean. If the value of the estimator $\overline{X}$ is found to be, say, 10, then it is said that 10 is the estimate of μ.

Estimators and Estimates
An estimator is the process by which the estimate is obtained.

To perform reliably, estimators must be (1) unbiased, (2) efficient, (3) consistent, and (4) sufficient. Each property is discussed in turn in this section.

A. AN UNBIASED ESTIMATOR

As we saw in the previous chapter, it is possible to construct a sampling distribution by selecting all possible samples of a given size from a population. An estimator is unbiased if the mean of the statistic computed from all these samples equals the corresponding parameter.

Let θ (Greek letter *theta*) be the parameter we are trying to estimate by $\hat{\theta}$ (read "theta hat"). Then $\hat{\theta}$ is an unbiased estimator if its mean, or expected value, $E(\hat{\theta})$, equals θ. That is,

$$E(\hat{\theta}) = \theta$$

To cite a specific example, $\overline{X}$ is an unbiased estimator of μ because the mean of the sampling distribution of sample means, $\overline{X}$, equals μ. Thus,

$$E(\overline{X}) = \overline{\overline{X}} = \mu$$

Unbiased Estimator
An estimator is unbiased if the mean of the sampling distribution equals the corresponding parameter.

Figure 8-15 illustrates how the mean of a sampling distribution must equal the corresponding parameter to ensure an unbiased estimator.

Here, $\hat{\theta}_1$ is an unbiased estimator of θ since its distribution is centered over θ. Thus, $E(\hat{\theta}_1) = \theta$. If many different samples were taken, yielding many different values for $\hat{\theta}_1$, their mean would equal θ. Conversely, if many samples were taken and

FIGURE 8-15   Distributions for Biased and Unbiased Estimators

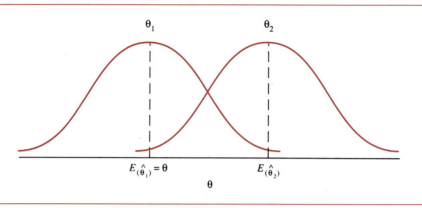

$\hat{\theta}_2$ was calculated each time, their mean would exceed θ. Thus, $\hat{\theta}_2$ is a biased (upward) estimator of θ. The measure of bias is the difference between the mean of $\hat{\theta}_2$ and θ. Note that

$$E(\hat{\theta}_1) - \theta = 0$$

while

$$E(\hat{\theta}_2) - \theta \neq 0$$

B.   AN EFFICIENT ESTIMATOR

Let $\hat{\theta}_1$ and $\hat{\theta}_2$ be two unbiased estimators of θ. Then $\hat{\theta}_1$ is a more efficient estimator if, in repeated sampling with a given sample size, its variance is less than that of $\hat{\theta}_2$. It is only logical that an estimator with a smaller variance will more closely estimate the parameter. Consider Figure 8-16, which shows the sampling distributions with a

FIGURE 8-16   The Variance of Estimators

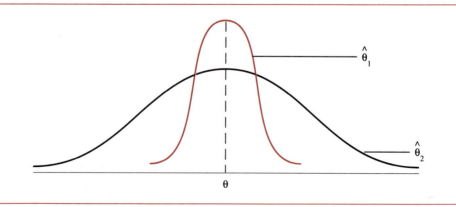

given sample size of two statistics, $\hat{\theta}_1$ and $\hat{\theta}_2$. Both $\hat{\theta}_1$ and $\hat{\theta}_2$ are unbiased estimators of θ because their sampling distributions are centered above θ, and

$$E(\hat{\theta}_1) = E(\hat{\theta}_2) = \theta$$

However, the variance of the sampling distribution of $\hat{\theta}_1$ is less than that of $\hat{\theta}_2$. Possible values for $\hat{\theta}_2$ are more dispersed. Any estimate of θ using $\hat{\theta}_2$ is likely to produce a larger sampling error than an estimate of θ using $\hat{\theta}_1$.

An Efficient Estimator
Given any unbiased estimators, the most efficient estimator is the one with the smallest variance.

Compare the mean and the median as estimators of μ. It may be noted that

$$\text{Variance } (\overline{X}) = \frac{\sigma^2}{n} \tag{8.24}$$

and

$$\text{Variance (median)} = \frac{\pi}{2} \times \frac{\sigma^2}{n} \tag{8.25}$$

$$= 1.57 \times \frac{\sigma^2}{n}$$

$$= 1.57[\text{Variance } (\overline{X})]$$

The variance of the median is 1.57 times greater than the variance of the mean. Thus, the mean is a more efficient estimator of μ than is the median.

C. A CONSISTENT ESTIMATOR

An estimator is consistent if, as n increases, the estimator approaches the value of the parameter.

Consistent Estimator
An estimate is consistent if, as n increases, the value of the statistic approaches the parameter.

For an estimate to be consistent, it must be unbiased and its variance must approach zero as n increases. The variance of the sampling distribution of the sample means, $\sigma_{\bar{x}}^2$, is σ^2/n. As n gets larger, $\sigma_{\bar{x}}^2$ will approach zero. Therefore, it can be said that $\bar{X}$ is a consistent estimator of μ.

If a statistic is not a consistent estimator, taking a larger sample to improve your estimate will prove fruitless.

D. A Sufficient Estimator

An estimator is sufficient if it uses all relevant information about the parameter contained in the sample.

> **Sufficient Estimator**
> An estimator is sufficient if no other estimator could provide more information about the parameter.

If an estimator is sufficient, nothing can be gained by using any other estimator.

This discussion of estimator properties is by no means a complete account. It does, however, provide a sufficient foundation for an examination of estimating parameters by constructing confidence intervals.

8.9   Solved Problems

1. **Speed Kills** A February 1989 issue of *Fortune* details efforts by companies to increase the rate at which they can develop, produce, and market their products. A survey of 50 companies by Kaiser Associates, a Vienna, Virginia, consulting firm, found that almost all firms placed emphasis on "time-based strategy," as the new approach is called. The attraction to TBS, as one CEO put it, comes from the fact that "speed kills the competition."

    a. General Electric became concerned about the length of time it took to deliver custom-made circuit breaker panels. The Akron, Ohio, plant felt it averaged about three weeks to deliver a panel after receiving the order. If the last 100 orders averaged 3.4 weeks with a standard deviation of 1.1 weeks, is the estimate of 3 weeks confirmed at the 98 percent level?

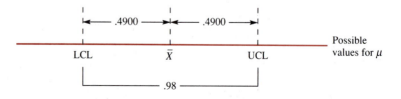

Since $0.98/2 = 0.4900$ yields a Z-value of 2.33, we have

$$\text{C.I. for } \mu = \bar{X} \pm Zs_{\bar{x}}$$

$$= 3.4 \pm (2.33)\frac{1.1}{\sqrt{100}}$$

$$3.14 \leq \mu \leq 3.66$$

There is a 98 percent level of confidence that it actually takes a little longer than three weeks. If σ were known, it should have been used in the calculations.

b. After placing more emphasis on time-based strategy, the Akron plant felt they had reduced delivery time to the point that there were 18 days difference between the mean delivery time before and after TBS. Is this claim justified if samples revealed the following?

Before TBS	After TBS
$n_b = 100$ delivery times	$n_a = 120$ delivery times
$\bar{X}_b = 23.2$ days	$\bar{X}_a = 3.2$ days
$s_b = 7.1$ days	$s_a = 0.91$ day

Construct a confidence interval for the difference in mean delivery times that carries a probability of error of $\alpha = 0.05$. A 95 percent confidence interval requires a Z-value of 1.96.

$$\text{C.I. for } \mu_b - \mu_a = (\bar{X}_b - \bar{X}_a) \pm Z \sqrt{\frac{s_b^2}{n_b} + \frac{s_a^2}{n_a}}$$

$$= (23.2 - 3.2) \pm 1.96 \sqrt{\frac{(7.1)^2}{100} + \frac{(0.91)^2}{120}}$$

$$= 20 \pm 1.4$$

$$18.6 \leq \mu_b - \mu_a \leq 21.4$$

There is a 95 percent level of confidence that TBS reduced mean delivery time by more than 18 days.

c. In a sample of $n = 12$ design projects, AT&T took an average of 2.3 years to design and develop a new phone. The design times for the 12 projects had a standard deviation of 1.5 years. If we assume a normal distribution in design times, what is the 90 percent confidence interval for mean times?

$$\text{C.I. for } \mu = \bar{X} \pm ts_{\bar{x}}$$

$$= 2.3 \pm (1.796)\frac{1.5}{\sqrt{12}}$$

$$= 2.3 \pm 0.779$$

$$1.52 \leq \mu \leq 3.079 \text{ years}$$

d.   If the assumption of normality in part (c) could not be supported, how would the test be performed? It would be necessary to use nonparametric tests since $n < 30$.

e.   After TBS, AT&T took a second sample of $n = 15$ design projects and found $\overline{X} = 1.1$ years and $s = 0.47$ year. What is the confidence interval for the difference between mean completion times?

Set $\alpha = 0.10$. Assume a normality in the population of times. We have a normal population, small samples, and population variances are unknown and not assumed equal. Figure 8-11 shows how to use Formulas (8.13) and (8.14), where subscripts b and a stand for before TBS and after TBS:

$$\text{d.f.} = \frac{(s_b^2/n_b + s_a^2/n_a)^2}{(s_b^2/n_b)^2/(n_b - 1) + (s_a^2/n_a)^2/(n_a - 1)}$$

$$= \frac{[(1.5)^2/12 + (0.47)^2/15]^2}{[(1.5)^2/12]^2/11 + [(0.47)^2/15]^2/14}$$

$$= 12$$

With 12 d.f. and a confidence level of 90 percent ($\alpha = 0.10$), $t' = 1.782$.

$$\text{C.I. for } \mu_b - \mu_a = (\overline{X}_b - \overline{X}_a) \pm 1.782 \sqrt{\frac{s_b^2}{n_b} + \frac{s_a^2}{n_a}}$$

$$= (2.3 - 1.1) \pm (1.782)(0.45)$$

$$= 1.2 \pm 0.80$$

$$0.4 \leq \mu_1 - \mu_2 \leq 2 \text{ years}$$

f.   If the population variances were assumed to be equal before and after TBS, what would the interval from (e) be? Figure 8-11 directs us to use a pooled estimate of the common σ^2.

$$s_p^2 = \frac{s_b^2(n_b - 1) + s_a^2(n_a - 1)}{n_b + n_a - 2}$$

$$= 1.11$$

$$s_p = 1.05$$

There are $12 + 15 - 2 = 25$ d.f.

$$\text{C.I. for } \mu_b - \mu_a = \overline{X}_b - \overline{X}_a \pm (t)s_p \sqrt{\frac{1}{n_b} + \frac{1}{n_a}}$$

$$= 2.3 - 1.1 \pm (1.708)(1.05)(0.39)$$

$$= 1.2 \pm 0.7$$

$$0.5 \leq \mu_b - \mu_a \leq 1.9$$

2.   **Speed Killed the Noyd** Tom Monaghan, CEO of Domino's Pizza, is a true sports buff. In addition to owning the Detroit Tigers baseball team, he jogs over 6 miles every day, and

every Monday he takes his managers along with him. The company is organized along the lines of a professional sports league with regional divisions competing against each other in terms of overall performance, including delivery times. Monaghan has built Domino's into the nation's second largest pizza chain, behind Pizza Hut, by offering a $3 discount to customers on any pizza that takes more than 30 minutes to arrive. "Our whole business is built on speed," he claims.

a. Monaghan is interested in the proportion of pizzas that fail the 30-minute test, thereby requiring a discount. Assume that in a sample of 780 deliveries, 54 are late. Monaghan wants a confidence interval that has only a 4 percent probability of error for the proportion of all deliveries that cost him $3.

$$p = \frac{54}{780} = 0.069$$

$$s_p = \sqrt{\frac{p(1 - p)}{n}} = 0.0091$$

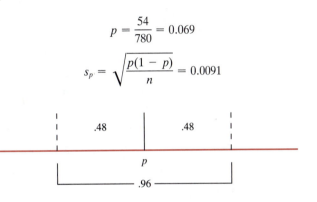

C.I. for $\pi = p \pm Zs_p$

$$= 0.069 \pm (2.05)(0.0091)$$

$$0.05 \leq \pi \leq 0.09$$

b. If in the competition among regions, a sample of 500 deliveries by the southern region revealed that 45 were late, and 612 deliveries by the northeastern region revealed that 67 were late, what is the 99 percent confidence interval for the difference in the two population proportions of late deliveries?

$$p_S = \frac{45}{500} = 0.09 \qquad p_N = \frac{67}{612} = 0.109$$

$$s_{p_S - p_N} = \sqrt{\frac{p_S(1 - p_S)}{n_S} + \frac{p_N(1 - p_N)}{n_N}}$$

$$= \sqrt{\frac{(0.09)(0.91)}{500} + \frac{(0.109)(0.891)}{612}}$$

$$= 0.018$$

C.I. for $\pi_S - \pi_N = (p_S - p_N) \pm (Z)s_{p_S - p_N}$

$$= (0.09 - 0.109) \pm (2.58)(0.018)$$

$$-0.065 \leq \pi_S - \pi_N \leq 0.027$$

3. **Sizes and Slices** *a.* If Domino's wants a 99 percent confidence interval for the mean delivery time that is not in error by more than 1.5 minutes, how large should the sample be if a pilot sample estimates the standard deviation at 6 minutes?

$$n = \frac{Z^2\sigma^2}{(\text{error})^2} = \frac{(2.58)^2(6)^2}{(1.5)^2} = 107$$

b. If a 95 percent confidence interval for the proportion of all late deliveries is to be constructed which provides an estimate within 1 percent, how large should the sample be?

$$n = \frac{Z^2\pi(1 - \pi)}{(p - \pi)^2} = \frac{(1.96)^2(0.5)(0.5)}{(0.01)^2}$$

$$= 9{,}604 \text{ deliveries}$$

c. Domino's wants a 99 percent confidence interval for the difference in mean delivery times between region 1 and region 2. If the interval is to be held to 5 minutes and $\sigma_1^2 = 64$ and $\sigma_2^2 = 100$, how large should the sample be?

$$n = \frac{Z^2(\sigma_1^2 + \sigma_2^2)}{(\text{error})^2} = \frac{(2.58)^2(64 + 100)}{(2.5)^2}$$

$$= 175$$

d. Finally, Domino's wishes to develop a 90 percent confidence interval of 5 percent in width for the difference in the proportion of late deliveries between region 1 and region 2. π_1 and π_2 are estimated with pilot samples at 0.10 and 0.14.

$$n = \frac{Z^2[\pi_1(1 - \pi_1) + \pi_2(1 - \pi_2)]}{(\text{error})^2}$$

$$= \frac{(1.65)^2[(0.1)(0.9) + (0.14)(0.86)]}{(0.025)^2}$$

$$= 917$$

8.10 WHAT YOU SHOULD HAVE LEARNED FROM THIS CHAPTER

This chapter has provided an introduction to statistical inference in the form of interval estimation. The idea of a confidence level and its counterpart, the probability of error, α, were also presented. The interpretation of a confidence interval is a critical point which you must comprehend in order to fully understand much of the material you will soon encounter.

The t-distribution was introduced along with an explanation of when and how it should be used. You should have a clear idea of when to use the Z-test and when to use the t-test.

This idea of inference will be continued in the next two chapters with a discussion of hypothesis testing. Many of the principles you learned in this chapter will apply to tests of hypotheses about population means and proportions. Combining the material on confidence intervals with that dealing with hypothesis testing provides a set of useful techniques to estimate parameters and gain a helpful insight into the nature of a population.

8.11 COMPUTER APPLICATIONS

Confidence intervals can be easily calculated with modern computer packages. This section examines the methods by which the intervals can be determined on the computer.

MINITAB

Calculating a confidence interval with Minitab requires a few simple commands. If a large sample is used, the necessary commands are

```
SET C1
  data go here

END

ZINT (level of confidence)(standard deviation) confidence interval
```

Assume a sample of $n = 39$ yields a mean of 73.31 and a standard deviation of 15.45. If a 90 percent confidence interval is desired, the last command becomes

```
ZINT 90 15.45 C1
```

The resulting printout is shown in Minitab 1

MINITAB 1

	N	Mean	STDEV	SE Mean	95.0 Percent C.I.
CI	39	73.31	15.45	2.516	(68.38, 78.24)

If a small sample of $n = 22$ with a mean of 53.73 and a standard deviation of 10.2 is entered in column 2, a 95 percent confidence interval is obtained with the command

```
TINT 95 C2
```

Notice that the standard deviation is not specified for a small sample.

Minitab is also well designed to provide a confidence interval for the difference between two means. Twenty-two observations are entered in column 3 of our Minitab data base. They are paired with the 22 observations in column 2, and the difference in means is to be estimated. This is done by placing the differences in the observations in column 4 and basing the interval on that column. A 99 percent confidence interval for the difference between the means of column 2 and column 3 is obtained by

```
LET C4 = C2-C3

TINT 99 C4
```

If the samples are not paired, the process is entirely different. A 95 percent pooled, two-sample test between column 2 and column 3 is done with the commands

```
TWOSAMPLE T 95 C2 C3;

POOLED.
```

A 90 percent two sample test that is not pooled requires the command

```
TWOSAMPLE T 90 C2 C3
```

Confidence intervals for proportions require certain steps beyond the scope of this text. The remaining packages, SAS and SPSS-PC, do not readily lend themselves to the calculation of confidence intervals.

LIST OF SYMBOLS AND TERMS

Point Estimator: A single number used to estimate a parameter.
Interval Estimator: A range within which the parameter is thought to lie, accompanied by a statement of the probability that the parameter is within the range.
Confidence Interval: Same as an interval estimator.
Alpha: The probability of error. The probability the interval does not contain the parameter.

LIST OF FORMULAS

$$\text{C.I. for } \mu = \overline{X} \pm Z\sigma_{\bar{x}} \tag{8.1}$$

Used if population variance is known.

$$\text{C.I. for } \mu = \overline{X} \pm Zs_{\bar{x}} \tag{8.2}$$

Used if population variance is unknown.

$$\sigma^2 = \frac{n-1}{n-3} \tag{8.3}$$

The variance of the t-distribution.

$$\text{C.I. for } \mu = \overline{X} \pm (t)(s_{\bar{x}}) \tag{8.5}$$

Used when $n < 30$ and population variance is unknown.

$$s_d^2 = \frac{\Sigma d_i^2 - n\overline{d}^2}{n-1} \tag{8.7}$$

Variance for matched pairs.

$$\text{C.I. for } \mu_d = \overline{d} \pm t\frac{s_d}{\sqrt{n}} \tag{8.8}$$

Used for matched pairs estimation.

$$\sigma_{\bar{x}_1-\bar{x}_2} = \sqrt{\frac{\sigma_1^2}{n_1} + \frac{\sigma_2^2}{n_2}} \qquad (8.9)$$

The standard error of the difference between two sample means.

$$\text{C.I. for } \mu_1 - \mu_2 = (\bar{X}_1 - \bar{X}_2) \pm Z\sigma_{\bar{x}_1-\bar{x}_2} \qquad (8.10)$$

Provides confidence interval for difference between two means.

$$s_p^2 = \frac{s_1^2(n_1 - 1) + s_2^2(n_2 - 1)}{n_1 + n_2 - 2} \qquad (8.11)$$

Estimates the common variance of two populations.

$$\text{C.I. for } \mu_1 - \mu_2 = (\bar{X}_1 - \bar{X}_2) \pm (t)(s_p)\sqrt{\frac{1}{n_1} + \frac{1}{n_2}} \qquad (8.12)$$

Provides confidence interval for difference between the means of two populations with a common variance.

$$\text{d.f.} = \frac{(s_1^2/n_1 + s_2^2/n_2)^2}{(s_1^2/n_1)^2/(n_1 - 1) + (s_2^2/n_2)^2/(n_2 - 1)} \qquad (8.13)$$

Calculates the degrees of freedom for a *t*-test when two populations with unequal variances are involved.

$$\text{C.I. for } \mu_1 - \mu_2 = (\bar{X}_1 - \bar{X}_2) \pm t'\sqrt{\frac{s_1^2}{n_1} + \frac{s_2^2}{n_2}} \qquad (8.14)$$

Complements Formula (8.13).

$$\sigma_p = \sqrt{\frac{\pi(1 - \pi)}{n}} \qquad (8.15)$$

Standard error of sampling distribution of proportions.

$$\text{C.I. for } \pi = p \pm Zs_p \qquad (8.17)$$

Confidence interval for proportions.

$$s_{p_1-p_2} = \sqrt{\frac{p_1(1 - p_1)}{n_1} + \frac{p_2(1 - p_2)}{n_2}} \qquad (8.18)$$

Standard error of the difference between two sample proportions.

$$\text{C.I. for } \pi_1 - \pi_2 = (p_1 - p_2) \pm (Z)s_{p_1-p_2} \qquad (8.19)$$

Confidence interval for the difference between two proportions.

$$n = \frac{Z^2\sigma^2}{(\bar{X} - \mu)^2} \qquad (8.20)$$

Determines sample size to estimate μ.

$$n = \frac{Z^2(\sigma_1^2 + \sigma_2^2)}{(\text{error})^2} \qquad (8.21)$$

Determines sample size to estimate $\mu_1 - \mu_2$.

$$n = \frac{Z^2 \pi (1 - \pi)}{(p - \pi)^2} \qquad (8.22)$$

Determines sample size to estimate π.

$$n = \frac{Z^2 [\pi_1 (1 - \pi_1) + \pi_2 (1 - \pi_2)]}{(\text{error})^2} \qquad (8.23)$$

Determines sample size to estimate $\pi_1 - \pi_2$.

CHAPTER EXERCISES

YOU MAKE THE DECISION

1. A 95 percent confidence interval is constructed yielding a lower confidence limit of 62 and an upper confidence limit of 69. Can you conclude from this that there is a 95 percent probability the parameter is between 62 and 69? Explain.
2. Why is the median a less efficient estimator than the mean?
3. Jose has a thriving business in Acapulco selling authentic plastic Inca relics to American tourists. He selects $n = 60$ days to estimate his daily profit. However, Jose does not know whether the population of daily profits is normally distributed, and is uncertain how to proceed. What should he do?
4. The supervisor instructs Mary Martin to construct a 99 percent confidence interval for weekly output. Upon receipt of the results, the supervisor then tells Freddie Frost to repeat the effort using the same sample size. Freddie's results differ from Mary's. The supervisor is convinced that either Mary or Freddie is wrong. They must persuade the supervisor otherwise. How can they do this?
5. Martha calculates a 95 percent confidence interval for the mean number of customers who are delinquent in paying their bills. However, the resulting interval is too wide and lacking in precision. If she does not want to increase the α-value, what can she do?

PROBLEMS

6. As a quality control expert, you want to estimate the mean thickness of optical lenses produced by your firm. A sample of 120 lenses reveals a mean of 0.52 millimeter (mm). The population standard deviation is known to be 0.17 mm. You feel that you can risk a probability of error of only 1 percent. Construct the appropriate confidence interval.
7. How would the previous problem change if σ was unknown and the sample standard deviation was 0.17 mm? Calculate the interval.
8. A random sample of 50 automobile owners in an Atlanta suburb showed that the average age of the automobiles was 4.2 years with a standard deviation of 2.1 years. What is the 90 percent confidence interval for the mean age of all autos?
9. A sample of 2,200 marketing majors taken by *U.S. News & World Report* in 1989 had a mean starting salary of $22,951. If the standard deviation was $7,200, what is the 98 percent confidence interval for the mean starting salary of all marketing majors?

10. John, a marketing major, constructed the confidence interval for the previous problem. He concluded there was a 98 percent chance that his starting salary would be within that interval. Is this interpretation correct? How should he interpret the interval?

11. In a survey of 6,000 people, *U.S. News & World Report* found that, in his or her lifetime, the average American spends six months sitting at stoplights. Taking this as the sample mean, and assuming the standard deviation is 2.2 months, what is the 90 percent confidence interval for the population mean?

12. *Automobile News,* a trade publication for the auto industry, published a story in 1989 regarding employee absenteeism. It claimed workers were missing an average of 4.0 days of work per month. A sample of 200 employees finds a mean of 3.8 days and a standard deviation of 1.91 days. With an α-value of 0.02, does a confidence interval support the news story?

13. If a section chief for the auto industry claimed that 200 of his employees selected at random averaged only 2.5 days off the job per month, would you believe him? (See previous problem.)

14. *The Journal of Retail Management* reported that a sample of 600 shoppers spent an average of 1.79 hours in a shopping mall per visit. The standard deviation was 0.83 hour. What is the interval estimate of the average number of hours all shoppers spend in the mall? Set $\alpha = 0.10$.

15. Your product requires that a certain component used in its manufacture average 15.2 grams. If you purchase 100 components from a supplier and find $\overline{X} = 14.8$ grams with $s = 3.2$ grams, what would a confidence interval tell you about the advisability of continuing to buy from this supplier? Your product is very delicate, and you feel you can tolerate only a 1 percent probability of error.

16. If, given the conditions in the previous problem, the sample had yielded a mean of 14.1 grams, what would you conclude?

17. Wally wants to buy his wife a brand new septic tank for her birthday. Being a careful shopper, he examines over 40 different models and finds a mean price of $712 with a standard deviation of $215. What is the 95 percent confidence interval for the mean price of all septic tanks?

18. A manufacturer of snow skis wants to estimate the mean number of ski trips taken by avid skiers. A sample of 1,100 skiers yields $\overline{X} = 15.3$ trips per season, with $s = 5.1$ trips. What is the 99 percent confidence interval for the population mean?

19. Consider the data in the previous problem:
    a. Without working the problem, explain what would happen to the interval if the level of confidence were decreased to 90 percent.
    b. Work the problem with $\alpha = 0.10$ and show how the answer supports your response to part (a).

20. Consider Problem 18.
    a. Without working the problem, explain what would happen to the interval if the sample size were decreased to 500 and the 99 percent confidence level was retained? Why would this occur? Draw a distribution of the sample means to illustrate.
    b. Construct the interval.

21. Consider Problem 18. Without working the problem, explain what would happen to the interval if $n = 1,100$, $\alpha = 0.01$, but the sample proved to be less varied by reporting $s = 2.1$. Draw a distribution of the sample means to illustrate. Calculate the interval.

22. A researcher found that a sample of 100 with $\overline{X} = 50.3$ and $s = 10.1$ generated a confidence interval of 48.3204 to 52.2796. What level of confidence can be attributed to this interval?

23. The weights of 25 packages shipped through United Parcel had a mean of 3.7 pounds and a standard deviation of 1.2 pounds. Find the 95 percent confidence interval for the mean weight of all packages. Package weights are known to be normally distributed.

24. A sample of 12 donations by political action committees to congressional campaign funds were recorded, in thousands of dollars, as 12.1, 8.3, 15.7, 9.35, 14.3, 12.9, 13.2, 9.73, 16.9, 15.5, 14.3, and 12.8. Calculate the 90 percent confidence interval for the mean donation by PACs. Donations are assumed to be normal.

25. The earnings per share for 10 industrial stocks listed on the Dow-Jones were $1.90, $2.15, $2.01, $0.89, $1.53, $1.89, $2.12, $2.05, $1.75, and $2.22. Calculate a 99 percent confidence interval for the EPS of all the industrials listed in the DJIA. What assumption must you make?

26. In 1989 *Business Week* reported on an FBI "sting" operation that uncovered a multimillion dollar cheating scandal in the Chicago Board of Trade. Over a two-year period, 37 violations of BOT rulings involving $410.5 million were discovered. Assume these violations had a $3.3 million standard deviation. Calculate the confidence interval for all such violations. Set $\alpha = 0.03$.

27. Dr. Bottoms, the local proctologist, found that the average age of 75 of his patients was 47.3 with a standard deviation of 10.9 years. Calculate the 99 percent confidence interval for the mean age of all his patients under the assumption that the ages are not normally distributed.

28. *The Wall Street Journal* reported on an effort by Subaru of America to test two possible assembly processes. Twelve experienced workers were asked to assemble a transmission using each method. The times, in hours, were

Worker	Method 1	Method 2	Worker	Method 1	Method 2
1	1.2	1.1	7	1.9	1.7
2	1.9	1.5	8	1.6	1.7
3	2.3	2.1	9	1.3	1.5
4	2.1	2.2	10	1.2	1.2
5	1.5	1.4	11	2.2	1.7
6	1.7	1.3	12	1.8	1.3

a. Develop a 95 percent confidence interval to determine which method might be faster.
b. What assumption must be made?

29. The Kansas City Traffic Division of Public Safety designated eight drivers to negotiate a driving course for city auto traffic under two separate traffic patterns. Each driver then rated on a scale of 1 to 10 the ease of maneuvering through each pattern. Given the ratings shown here, construct a 90 percent confidence interval for the difference in ratings. What assumption must be made?

Driver	Pattern 1	Pattern 2	Driver	Pattern 1	Pattern 2
1	5	6	5	7	7
2	6	8	6	6	7
3	4	3	7	5	8
4	4	6	8	8	8

30. A researcher for the U.S. Forestry Service split 12 logs in half. Each of the logs in one set was treated with an experimental chemical to improve resistance to fires. The other 12 splits were left untreated. Fire-resistance ratings between 1 and 10 were assigned to each split as shown here. Calculate the 90 percent confidence interval for the mean difference in ratings. Ratings are known to be normal.

	Resistance Ratings			Resistance Ratings	
Split	Treated	Untreated	Split	Treated	Untreated
1	8	4	7	9	6
2	7	5	8	6	5
3	8	6	9	7	7
4	6	5	10	8	7
5	9	6	11	8	6
6	5	4	12	9	6

31. The Forestry Service also wants a 95 percent confidence interval for the mean value of all treated logs given the data in the previous problem.

32. A large public accounting firm hired an industrial psychologist to measure the job satisfaction of its senior partners. Seventeen partners were given a test to measure satisfaction and scored an average of 83.2 out of a possible 100. From previous studies the firm knows that the test scores are normal and the variance for all its partners is 120. What is the 90 percent confidence interval for the mean score?

33. In response to an effort in 1989 to raise the pay for members of Congress and other federal workers, the Bureau of Labor Statistics of the U.S. Department of Labor released the figures shown here for six key professions in the public and private sectors. Assuming normality in salary levels and that these six salaries are representative, compute the 90 percent confidence interval for the mean difference in salaries between public and private positions. Assume paired observations.

Occupation	Private	Public
Accountant	$ 67,950	$45,244
Attorney	110,489	64,026
Buyer	22,071	16,732
Chemist	65,526	46,448
Computer programmer	22,356	16,737
Engineer	85,725	65,862

34. Using the data from the previous problem, construct the 90 percent confidence interval under the condition of independent sampling with equal variances. Does it appear that paired sampling is the appropriate procedure?

35. A national discount chain bases its decision on whether to open a retail outlet on per capita income. A survey of two rural communities revealed the data, in thousands of dollars, shown here. Calculate a 90 percent confidence interval for the difference between incomes

of these two communities. There is no evidence that population variances are equal, and incomes are assumed to be normally distributed.

Pikeville	Hazard
$n = 25$	$n = 20$
$\overline{X} = 8.525$	$\overline{X} = 8.97$
$s = 1.301$	$s = 1.4$

36. When manufactured under one process, a sample of $n = 12$ floppy disks used by personal computers had a mean life of 4,020 hours with a standard deviation of 720 hours. When a different process was used, the mean life of $n = 12$ was 5,219 hours with a standard deviation of 1,050 hours. The manufacturer felt that the different processes did not change the variance in life. Calculate a confidence interval for the difference in mean lifetime if times are normally distributed. Set $\alpha = 0.05$.

37. Work the previous problem under the assumption that population variances are not equal.

38. *Barron's* reported in 1989 that a labor dispute between the United Steel Workers and Republic Steel centered on the difference in mean wages of two groups of workers. The labor contract specified that the lower-paid group must earn, on the average, no more than $5.50 less than the higher-paid group. Samples of size $n_1 = n_2 = 25$ revealed means of $\overline{X}_1 = \$37.10$ and $\overline{X}_2 = \$28.80$. It was previously determined that $\sigma_1 = \$6.20$ and $\sigma_2 = \$5.51$. Does it appear the labor contract is being violated? Determine the appropriate confidence interval with a 10 percent probability of error. Assume incomes are normally distributed.

39. Given the information from the previous problem, if it could not be assumed that incomes were normally distributed, what must be done to calculate a confidence interval?

40. A manufacturer produces widgets using two different assembly lines. Over a 50-day period, line 1 averaged 220 widgets per day, with a standard deviation of 31 widgets. Comparable figures for line 2 were 197 and 33 over a 56-day period. What is the 99 percent confidence interval for the difference in mean output?

41. Pierre owns a fur salon in Beverly Hills. He wishes to compare the mean profit per sale for his two most popular furs. Ten recent sales of Minkus Plushus averaged $997 in profit with a standard deviation of $210. Twelve sales of Domesticus Catus averaged $1,222 with a standard deviation of $232. If Pierre assumes variances are equal and profits are normally distributed, what is the 90 percent confidence interval for the difference in mean profits per sale?

42. If Pierre could not make the assumption of equal variances, what interval is obtained? (See the previous problem.)

43. After their August sale, a wine store in Covina, California, tried to calculate the mean daily sales of two types of wine. Their Don Perion sold an average of 22.2 bottles per day with a standard deviation of 2.2 bottles, while Vino Ordinaire sold an average of 27.8 bottles and had a standard deviation of 3.9 bottles. There is no evidence to suggest variances of daily sales are the same for the two wines. It is assumed daily sales are normally distributed. The store manager wants a 90 percent confidence interval for the difference in mean daily sales. Data were collected over a 20-day period for both wines.

44. *The Wall Street Journal* carried a story about the effects on the sale of Audi luxury cars of reports of "sudden acceleration." Audi owners were reporting that their cars were, with no apparent cause, suddenly accelerating beyond control. Sales dropped from a daily average of 205.1 cars per day in June of 1985 to just 63.7 per day in June 1989. If daily variances were

4,928.04 and 767.3 for 1985 and 1989, respectively, what is the 95 percent confidence interval for the difference in mean daily sales for the two years? Figure 20 business days in June of both years. What assumption must you make?

45. The dean of a small southern college has just hired a new graduate to assist with evaluation studies within the college. The assistant's first task is to prepare a report on student's study habits. Eight students are randomly selected, who willingly reveal the time spent studying and at leisure each day. The dean wants a 95 percent confidence interval for the difference in mean times of these two pursuits.

Student	Hours at Leisure	Hours Studying
1	6	3
2	2	6
3	10	1
4	8	3
5	5	2
6	7	3
7	8	5
8	9	1

46. Biologists at Florida State University want to compare the mean length of lobsters in the Gulf of Mexico with those off the Atlantic Coast. Concern over pollution in the Gulf and its effects on lobster growth and reproduction prompted the study. Ten lobsters were caught in both locales, and the lengths in inches are shown here. They now want to compute the confidence interval for the difference in mean length. Set $\alpha = 0.01$. Assume lengths are normally distributed.

Lobster	Gulf	Atlantic
1	5.2	5.5
2	6.7	6.3
3	4.3	7.2
4	7.7	6.5
5	4.5	5.9
6	5.9	4.5
7	7.3	8.3
8	8.1	6.4
9	6.5	5.5
10	5.9	5.7

On the basis of these data can it be concluded that a difference exists in the size of lobsters in the Gulf and in the Atlantic?

47. Billy the bat boy wonders about the difference in batting averages in the National and American leagues. Twenty-one players in each league are randomly sampled, yielding the following information: $\bar{X}_N = 232.1$, $s_N = 42.5$, $\bar{X}_A = 212.2$, and $s_A = 39.7$. Billy computes the 95 percent confidence interval for the mean difference. What answer should he get if he assumes variances in both leagues are equal?

48. Death Ray Video plans to market a new video game. Currently, they have narrowed their choice to "Repel the Invaders" and "Destroy the Martians." The final decision will rest on comparable popularity based on the number of plays each game gets. Ten of the "Repel" units are installed in arcades throughout the marketing area. Thirty days later the games are checked, and it is learned that the 10 units averaged 241.3 plays with a standard deviation of 67.3 plays. Comparable figures for 12 "Destroy" units are 253.1 and 79.2 plays. If Death Ray will decide which game to choose based on average plays, would a 99 percent confidence interval for the mean difference in plays aid in their decision? Assume plays of different video games have a common variance and are normal.

49. The Jesse James First National Bank has hired you as a statistical consultant to analyze operation of its automatic teller machines. Transactions at two machines at different locations reveal daily volumes in the amounts shown. Does a 95 percent confidence interval suggest location influences the level of transactions? Assume equal variances.

Machine 1	Machine 2
n = 15 days	n = 17 days
$\overline{X}$ = \$4,810/day	$\overline{X}$ = \$5,250/day
s = \$1,205/day	s = \$1,395/day

50. According to *Police Gazette*, police in Newport News, Virginia, studied crime trends in urban centers compared with suburban areas. Over a 12-week period they found urban centers reported 21.2 crimes per 5,000 people with a standard deviation among weeks of 5.6 crimes. Suburban areas reported 3.4 crimes per 5,000 people with a standard deviation of 1.2 crimes. Would a 90 percent confidence interval suggest area may affect crime rates? There is nothing to suggest that variances in weekly rates are the same in both localities.

51. The U.S. Department of Agriculture tested two growth hormones on cattle at the Kansas University Agricultural Experiment Station in Lawrence, Kansas. Eight cattle were given each hormone and compared with separate control groups. The cattle were paired as closely as possible with respect to relevant factors affecting growth. The resulting increases in weights, as measured in pounds, are shown here. What do 90 percent confidence intervals reveal about the relative effects of the hormones on cattle growth?

Increases in Weights (pounds) over Three-Week Period

Untreated Cattle	Cattle Receiving Hormone 1	Untreated Cattle	Cattle Receiving Hormone 2
15.2	19.3	13.3	17.3
17.3	15.6	13.7	17.8
13.1	17.3	14.9	19.4
10.5	12.5	10.8	14.0
12.3	13.2	12.5	16.3
10.7	12.7	11.7	15.2
14.3	13.7	13.5	17.6
13.5	15.6	16.3	21.0

52. Considering the data for hormone 2 in the preceding problem, does controlling for growth factors by matching observations improve the precision of the estimate?

53. *Fortune* reported that banks in San Francisco have increased the intensity of competition for depositors. Much of this increased rivalry is between domestic banks and foreign-held banks. A survey of 10 domestic and 10 foreign controlled banks resulted in the data shown here:

	Domestic	Foreign
Sample size	10	10
Average number of depositors (1,000s)	42.1	37.8
Standard deviation in depositor (1,000s)	10.7	11.2

What is the 98 percent confidence interval for the difference in average depositors? Assume variances are unequal.

54. The personnel director at a large manufacturing plant in Miami, Florida, has been asked by the plant manager to investigate reports of excessive overtime. A sample of 15 employees reveals a mean of 52.3 hours overtime per employee for the month of August with a standard deviation of 33.2 hours. In comparison, a similar plant in Norfolk, Virginia, showed that 15 randomly selected employees had a mean of only 37.2 hours with a standard deviation of 29.9 hours for August. The personnel director recommends that the Miami plant be reprimanded for such high overtime expenses, based on the fact that it reports more than 12 hours of overtime per employee in excess of the Norfolk plant. What would a 90 percent confidence interval suggest? Assume variances are equal.

55. In an effort to reduce insider trading, the Securities and Exchange Commission requested information regarding the proportion of bank holding companies whose officers hold more than 50 percent of their outstanding stock. Of 200 companies selected at random, 79 reported that insiders held a majority of their stock. What is the 90 percent confidence interval for the proportion of all bank holding companies whose officers hold at least 50 percent of their stock?

56. A report by NBC News in 1989 stated that 84 percent of those on welfare in Chicago were unwed mothers. A sample of 512 welfare recipients revealed that 422 were unwed mothers. Based on these figures, would a 95 percent confidence interval support the statement by NBC News?

57. In a survey done through her daily advice column, Ann Landers found that 86 percent of the 46,121 respondents said they would not have children next time if they had the chance to reconsider. Assuming these respondents are a representative sample of the U.S. population (which is probably a heroic assumption), what is the 99 percent confidence interval for the proportion of all people in the nation who would choose not to have children?

58. If only 100 people had responded to the survey in the preceding problem, what would the confidence interval be? Retain $p = 0.86$.

59. *The Miami Herald* reported in 1988 that of 200 traffic accidents in southern Florida, selected at random, alcohol was identified as a probable cause in 134 of them. Use a 90 percent confidence interval to estimate the proportion of all accidents involving alcohol.

60. A researcher for the Federal Aviation Administration was quoted in a February issue of *The Washington Post* as saying that of 112 airline accidents, "73 involved some type of structural problem with the aircraft." If these figures are representative, what is the confidence interval for the proportion of accidents involving such a structural defect? Set $\alpha = 0.01$.

61. United Airlines surveyed 93 passengers on a flight from Cincinnati to Atlanta. Sixty-four said they would like to have been on a later flight had space been available. United had decided that if more than 50 percent of the passengers expressed interest in departures later in the day, they would consider making such flights available. Given the results of the survey, does a 90 percent confidence interval suggest they should do so?

62. After several revelations in 1988 and 1989 regarding insider trading, misappropriation of corporate funds, and other improper financial behavior, there arose a public outcry against such abuses. The Washington-based Institute for Ethical Behavior argued that "at least 20% of all dealings on organized securities exchanges involving institutional traders are characterized by certain improprieties." A survey of 150 such transactions revealed that 27 fit that description. Does a 95 percent confidence interval support the institute's claim?

63. *The Wall Street Journal* reported efforts by Nestlé, the world's largest food company, to introduce a new product. Management decided to use the Chicago area as a test market. If more than 30 percent of the people expressed a desire for the product, they would consider marketing it in a wider area. Of 820 people tested, 215 expressed a positive reaction. Would a 90 percent confidence interval for the proportion of all consumers who prefer the product encourage management to continue with their marketing plans?

64. A study by the National Association of Manufacturers in 1989 revealed that 681 out of 955 graduates of private universities received job offers from the employer they most preferred, while 464 out of 867 public college graduates received similar offers. Construct a 99 percent confidence interval for the difference between public and private college graduates who are given the opportunity to work for the employer they most prefer.

65. Allstate Insurance surveyed 112 male drivers and 98 female drivers. Results showed that 17 of the males and 12 of the females had received traffic tickets in the past 12 months.
    a. Find the 90 percent confidence interval for the proportion of drivers who have received tickets in the past year.
    b. Find the 90 percent confidence interval for the difference in the proportions of male and female drivers who have received tickets.

66. VISA questioned 367 females and 351 males regarding their buying habits. Of the women surveyed, 276 said they regularly use credit to make purchases within 50 miles of their home, while 201 males made the same claim. Set $\alpha = 0.07$ and calculate the confidence interval for the difference in the proportion of females and males who use credit within a 50-mile radius of their home.

67. A study was conducted by researchers at the University of Virginia on socialization patterns of college students. They found that of 1,112 college women, only 69 would have been willing to trade "dating the opposite sex" for a perfect grade point average, while 41 of the 977 men surveyed would have made the trade. What is the confidence interval for the difference between the proportion of women and men willing to give up dating in exchange for all As? Set $\alpha = 0.04$.

68. *The Wall Street Journal* presented details of a study by the Foundation for Fair Taxation. When asked, "If taxes must be raised, would you prefer an increase in income taxes, or some other form of taxation?" 17 percent of the 686 self-employed people said they preferred an increase in the income tax. Only 12 percent of 1,055 employees responded similarly when given this option. What is the 98 percent confidence interval for the

difference in the proportions of self-employed and employees who prefer the income tax as a method of raising needed government revenue?

69.   Recently the physical fitness craze has swept corporate America. According to an article in *Fortune,* Ford Motor Company has decided to provide additional recreational facilities for their executives if it can be shown that daily exercise reduces the risk of heart attacks by 10 percent or more. To aid in their decision, 87 executives who exercise regularly were monitored over several years. Ten subsequently suffer heart attacks. Of 132 executives of similar age and physical condition who did not exercise, 28 had heart attacks over the same period of time. What impact would a 90 percent confidence interval have on Ford's decision?

70.   According to *Time,* sociologists at Penn State found that 87 percent of the 627 children surveyed from broken homes failed to attend college, and 46 percent of the 795 children from two-parent homes did not go to college. The Florida Education Association has lobbied the state government to develop programs to encourage educational pursuits by students from single-parent homes. How might the FEA use a confidence interval of the difference between the proportion of students in each group who attend college as a persuasive tool in their argument? Set $\alpha = 0.10$.

71.   Drexel Industries instituted the use of a new training program for entry-level managers. In order to compare its success with that of the previous training method, data are collected which show that 40 of the 63 managers trained under the new method stayed with the company at least three years, while 54 of the 69 managers trained under the old method remained at least three years. Does a 95 percent confidence interval suggest a preferred method of training to promote employee retention?

72.   A manufacturer of computer printers wishes to estimate the mean life of their print wheels. The estimate is to be within 2 hours of the mean and exhibit a 90 percent level of confidence. If a pilot sample reveals a standard deviation of 25 hours, how large should the sample be?

73.   *Business Week* carried a story about efforts by the 12 member countries of the Common Market to curtail a growing wave of mergers thought to be "economically undesirable to international interests." A sample is to be selected to estimate the mean size of firms (as measured in corporate net worth) involved in mergers. If the interval is to be $5.2 million and carry a level of confidence of 95 percent, how large should the sample be if the standard deviation of corporate net worth is deemed to be $21.7 million?

74.   The U.S. Immigration and Naturalization Service is attempting to study immigration trends in the nation. Concern is focused on mean weekly immigration rates of Latin America as opposed to the rest of the world. If the interval width is to be 30 people, and pilot samples show that variances in weekly levels of immigration are 32 and 17 immigrants, how many weeks of data should be collected? Set $\alpha = 0.01$.

75.   One of the Big-6 accounting firms wants to estimate the mean number of auditing errors per job by the staff in its two largest offices. The number of errors is not to exceed 5, and the level of confidence is 97 percent. If the standard deviations in errors per job are 12 and 17.1, how many jobs should be selected for the sample?

76.   A survey of violence in schools is designed to estimate the percentage of male students who were threatened with violence on school grounds over the past year. The tolerable error is set at 1 percent, and the level of confidence is to be 99 percent. What is the proper sample size?

77.   The same survey as the one mentioned in the previous problem also wanted to determine within 1 percent at 99 percent confidence the difference in the proportion of male and female students threatened with violence. How large should the samples be?

78. *U.S. News & World Report* described how financial analysts want to estimate the percentage of issues on the New York Stock Exchange that reported an increase in value last month with that percentage recording an increase one year earlier. If the error is set at 3 percent and a 95 percent level of confidence is desired, how large should the samples be? Assume pilot samples revealed percentages of 60 percent and 52 percent.

EMPIRICAL EXERCISES

79. Select a random sample of at least 30 from among the students on your campus, or in your dorm, sorority, fraternity, or similar identifiable population. Designate some characteristic of interest such as grade point average, number of dates per week or month, height, age, or other variable that can be easily ascertained. Collect the data. Select a value for α and calculate the confidence interval. Submit your results along with their interpretation and the raw data you collected.

80. Select a random sample of at least 50 people. Identify a binary characteristic that has only two possible outcomes, such as married or single, in-state student or out-of-state student. Collect the data. Select a value for α and calculate the confidence interval for the proportion of successes. Submit your results along with the interpretation and raw data you collected. Explain why the characteristic of age or height would not work for this exercise.

81. From the list of Fortune 500 companies (which can be found in one of the March or April issues) select a random sample of firms, using the table of random numbers found in the appendix. Calculate a confidence interval for the mean level of sales or some other variable reported in the list. Interpret your findings.

82. Identify two separate populations and a characteristic of each which can be measured. Collect at least 30 observations from each population and compute a confidence interval for the difference in the two means.

83. Perform the previous exercise using a binary characteristic and compute the confidence interval for the difference between the two proportions.

CASE APPLICATIONS

84. A dispute has arisen between Dave Williams and Mid-Town Manufacturing, the firm Dave has been working for over the past three years. Dave has charged MTM with discrimination based on his salary level as compared with that of other MTM employees with similar backgrounds. Dave feels that the reason he has not received raises in his hourly wage is due to a personal dislike on the part of his immediate supervisor. He has therefore filed charges in his local court demanding fair and equitable treatment.

Both sides in the case have collected the necessary data and information to substantiate their position before the court. The judge who is to hear the case has already been provided with information that Dave's starting salary was $9.12 per hour. After three years he is now earning $12.17. The judge has requested that a sample of workers comparable to Dave be selected and their earning figures be submitted to the court. A sample of 56 employees who have worked for MTM for approximately the same length of time and whose experience prior to employment was similar to Dave's are earning, on the average, $14.75 with a standard deviation of $3.41. In addition, 47 percent of them have received an increase in rank since starting at MTM. Dave's supervisor has never considered him for a rank increase despite the fact that an objective employee rating system has shown Dave's work evaluation to be at least comparable to other employees.

Use the tools learned in this chapter, and previous material, to evaluate the strength of each case. Do you feel Dave has been the subject of discriminatory treatment?

85. Newt Dimswitch owns a small construction company in Redondo Beach, California. He often uses more than one construction crew, and has had a difficult time maintaining records on profit levels, cost controls, and other variables that are necessary in making business decisions. Newt somehow feels that the use of one of his construction crews is not proving as profitable as other crews when sent out on a job. To make some kind of intelligent estimate of profit levels, Newt collects cost data for the crew in question for the last nine jobs it completed. Completion times, in hours, for these jobs were 79, 83, 64, 77, 75, 81, 65, 73, and 92. Newt must pay his crew a total of $112 per hour while it is on the job. This crew has brought in revenues (in 100's) on these nine jobs of $112, 117, 109, 115, 93, 111, 83, 89, and 110.

Newt compared these figures to a more experienced crew, which receives an average pay of $121 per hour. On its last eight jobs, it took 83, 52, 79, 65, 59, 69, 73, and 71 hours to complete the jobs. Revenues (in 100's) on these jobs were 142, 137, 121, 132, 92, 101, 112, and 119.

Now that Newt has these data, he isn't sure what to do with them. He heard something about how confidence intervals could be used to make estimates. How could you help poor Newt decide if the less experienced crew is as profitable?

86. *Fortune* published its findings regarding the 10 most admired corporations in the United States. This ranking is based on corporate reputation among peer companies as to earnings, growth, product innovation, operating goals, and other factors contained in the *Fortune* survey. The companies and their earnings per share (EPS) for two consecutive years are shown here.

Rank	Corporation	EPS 1	EPS 2
1	Merck (pharmaceuticals)	6.68	4.92
2	Rubbermaid (rubber products)	1.15	2.10
3	3M (scientific/photographic equip.)	4.02	3.15
4	Philip Morris (tobacco)	7.75	6.15
5	Wal-Mart (retailing)	3.27	2.53
6	Exxon (oil refining)	3.43	3.17
7	Pepsico (beverages)	2.26	2.19
8	Boeing (aerospace)	3.10	4.12
9	Herman Miller (furniture)	3.43	4.97
10	Shell Oil (refining)	2.55	3.52

The CEO for Financial Corporation of America, which topped *Fortune's* least admired list (rank of 305), wondered if there was any noticeable difference in the mean EPS from one year to the next for these 10 firms.

HYPOTHESIS TESTING

A PREVIEW OF THINGS TO LOOK FOR

1 The principle of a hypothesis test.

2 Why hypotheses can never be "accepted."

3 How a decision rule can be established.

4 The difference between a one-tailed test and a two-tailed test.

5 The alternative method of testing a hypothesis.

6 Type I and Type II errors.

7 Operating characteristic curves and power curves.

8 The effect of the sample size on the standard error.

9 How confidence intervals can be used to test hypotheses.

CHAPTER BLUEPRINT

Many occasions arise in which it is desirable to test the validity of an assumption or conjecture that you might have regarding some condition affecting your business. An inference may be made regarding some unknown feature of the population, such as its mean. This inference, called the hypothesis, must then be tested to determine the likelihood that it could be true. This chapter examines the numerous circumstances under which hypotheses can be tested.

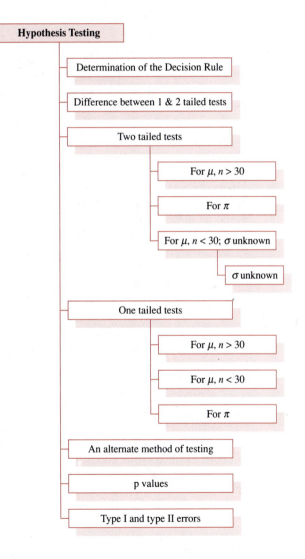

There are lies, damn lies and statistics
Disraeli: Former British Prime Minister

9.1   INTRODUCTION

As we have noted many times, our purpose in taking a sample is to draw some conclusion, or inference, about the population. It is actually the population and its parameter that we are interested in, not the sample or its statistic. The only reason we must settle for examining samples is because populations are often too large and costly to study.

Upon collecting the sample data, we want to determine what they are telling us about the population. We may assume, or hypothesize, that the average IQ of all students at Podunk University is $\mu = 115$. If we were to take a sample and find $\overline{X}$ to be 116, could we conclude that our hypothesis that $\mu = 115$ is incorrect? After all, 115 is not 116! Of course, we couldn't. Although 116 is not 115, it is awfully close. It would be quite possible to select a sample with a mean of $\overline{X} = 116$ from a population with a mean of $\mu = 115$. This small difference could easily be explained by sampling error. Due to the luck of the draw, we might just happen to choose for our sample a few of the students who were a little more intelligent on the average than the rest. This would have the effect of slightly inflating the sample mean above that of the population. It would in no way suggest that the population mean was not 115.

On the other hand, if the sample mean turned out to be as high as, for example, 150, it would be difficult to explain this large difference merely on the basis of sampling error. We might have to conclude that the difference between what we thought the population mean was ($\mu = 115$) and what our sample suggests it to be ($\overline{X} = 150$) is a "significant difference"—a difference which cannot be explained by sampling error. A result as high as $\overline{X} = 150$ might suggest that the reason we observed such a high sample mean is because the population from which the sample was taken has a mean in excess of our hypothesized value of 115.

There are numerous conditions under which hypotheses can be tested. We will examine several of these circumstances, including

- Two-tailed and one-tailed tests.
- Tests for the population mean and for the population proportion.
- Tests using both large samples and small samples.

○○○○   DECISION MAKING THROUGH PROBLEM SOLVING   ○○○○
                        ILLUSTRATION 9-1

A realtor in Atlanta was told by the chamber of commerce that the average selling price for houses in the city was $89,500. With rising interest rates, conditions had become so bad that the realtor was contemplating the possibility of a career change. Her decision was based partly on the average selling price of houses in the local market. If it was as low as the chamber of commerce reported, she decided she would change her career path.

   She took a sample of over 100 houses which were sold during the past two years and found a sample mean of slightly over $112,000. She felt that it was highly unlikely that a sample mean that large could result if the average selling price of all houses in the Atlanta area was as low as that noted by the chamber of commerce. A second sample produced a mean selling price close to the first. After a few statistical tests, the realtor concluded that the information obtained from the chamber of commerce was inaccurate. When last heard from, she was still successfully pursuing a career in the real estate field.

9.2   THE PRINCIPLE OF HYPOTHESIS TESTING

In order to perform hypotheses tests, we must make some inference, or educated guess, about the population. This inference will serve as our hypothesis. A sample is then taken to see if that hypothesis might be correct. The hypothesis we are testing is called the **null hypothesis** (H_0). The null is tested against the **alternative hypothesis** (H_A). Then, on the basis of our sample findings, we either reject the null hypothesis in favor of the alternative, or we do not reject the null and assume that our original estimation of the population parameter could indeed be correct. The failure to reject the null hypothesis does not imply that the null is true. It simply means that the sample evidence is insufficient to lead to a rejection of the null.

> **Hypothesis Testing**
> The **null** hypothesis is the hypothesis being tested. It is either rejected or not rejected on the basis of the sample information. The **alternative** hypothesis is specified as another choice if the null is rejected.

Our set of hypotheses for the IQs of students at PU mentioned above is

$$H_0: \mu = 115$$

$$H_A: \mu \neq 115$$

○○○○   **DECISION MAKING THROUGH PROBLEM SOLVING**   ○○○○
ILLUSTRATION 9-2

All manufacturing processes that involve filling containers with predetermined amounts of a product must follow certain procedures to ensure that the proper levels are being placed in the containers. Any deviation from the amount specified on the container can result in substantial penalties to the manufacturer.

It is therefore common practice for these firms to continually run tests to decide whether the containers have the proper amount of contents. A manufacturer may, for example, sell 16-ounce cans of soft drinks. On a routine basis, the firm must sample cans taken off the assembly line. If the mean weight of the contents of this sample differs "significantly" from 16 ounces, it is necessary to adjust the fill process.

If (1) the IQs of PU students are normally distributed or (2) a large sample is taken, then we are assured that the sampling distribution of sample means is normally distributed around the population mean. As our earlier study of sampling distributions revealed, this population mean is also equal to the mean of the sampling distribution (or the grand mean), $\overline{\overline{X}}$. This is shown in Figure 9-1.

FIGURE 9-1   Hypothesized Values for IQs

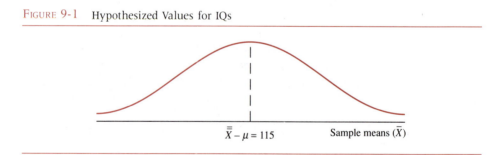

$$\overline{\overline{X}} - \mu = 115 \qquad \text{Sample means } (\overline{X})$$

A.   WE NEVER "ACCEPT" THE NULL HYPOTHESIS

It is often argued that our only two choices are to (1) "reject" or (2) "not reject" the null hypothesis. It is never possible to prove beyond any doubt that the null is correct, so it is never possible to "accept" it as such. If we were to hypothesize that μ is 115, and then actually found an $\overline{X}$ exactly equal to 115, it would still not *prove* that μ is 115. It could well be that μ is actually 113, and our sample just happened to contain a few of the larger observations. Thus, even a sample mean which is exactly equal to our hypothesized value does not conclusively prove that the hypothesis is correct.

B.   THE LEVEL OF SIGNIFICANCE AND A TYPE I ERROR

Each hypothesis is tested at a chosen level of significance. As with confidence intervals, common levels of significance, called α-values, are 1, 5, and 10 percent. However, other values for α can be selected to fit the needs of the researcher. Seldom will the α-value exceed 10 percent.

In deciding whether to reject a hypothesis, there are two types of mistakes that we can make. A **Type I error** occurs if we reject a null hypothesis that is true. It will be shown later in this chapter that the level of significance, or α-value, used for the test is the probability of committing a Type I error.

On the other hand, we might fail to reject a null hypothesis that is false. This is called a **Type II error**. The probability of committing a Type II error is called β.

Type I and Type II Errors
Rejecting the null hypothesis when it is true is a Type I error. Failing to reject the null hypothesis when it is false is a Type II error.

9.3   DETERMINATION OF THE DECISION RULE

Given our set of hypotheses as stated above, we must now determine a **decision rule** which will tell us whether to reject the null hypothesis. This decision rule specifies a value for $\overline{X}$ which is too far from the hypothesized value of μ to attribute the difference to sampling error. In this manner, the decision rule identifies critical values for our sample mean $\overline{X}_c$ which are too far above 115 or too far below 115 to allow us to retain our assumption that $\mu = 115$.

Decision Rule
The decision rule is a statement that we follow in determining whether to reject the null hypothesis. It specifies the critical value for the sample findings.

If we decide to test the null hypothesis at the 5 percent level of significance (the 95 percent level of confidence), we must find critical values for the sample mean above and below the hypothesized value of $\mu = 115$ that cut off 95 percent of the area under the normal curve. The remaining 5 percent is evenly divided in the two tails, as shown in Figure 9-2. There is a 95 percent chance that if the population mean really is 115, a sample will yield a mean between the critical values shown in Figure 9-2.

FIGURE 9-2   A 95 Percent Hypothesis Test

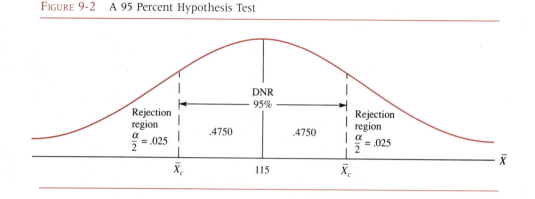

Values for $\overline{X}$ within this 95 percent range are close enough to the hypothesized value of 115 to attribute the difference to sampling error. This difference is said to be *statistically insignificant* at the 5 percent level and can be explained merely by chance variation in the sample. Thus, we do not reject (DNR) the null hypothesis.

Sample findings for $\overline{X}$ beyond those critical values in either tail are too far above or too far below 115 to attribute the difference to sampling error. The difference is said to be *statistically significant* at the 5 percent level. If μ does equal 115, it is unlikely that a sample could be taken which would produce a mean either significantly below 115 or significantly above 115. In fact, there is only a 5 percent chance that a population with a mean of 115 could produce an $\overline{X}$ that would fall in either rejection region.

A rejection region is found in both tails because if the sample findings for $\overline{X}$ are too far above or too far below 115, the null hypothesis must be rejected. Either way, the population mean is probably not equal to 115. These all-important critical values are found by the formula

$$\overline{X}_c = \mu_H \pm Zs_{\bar{x}} \qquad (9.1)$$

where μ_H is the hypothesized value for the population mean.
$s_{\bar{x}} = s/\sqrt{n}$ is the standard error of the sampling distribution.

The Z-value is found in the Z-table. However, since the table gives only the area under the curve from μ to some value above or below it, the 95 percent must be divided by 2. The resulting area of 0.4750 shown in Figure 9-2 is then found in the Z-table, and the corresponding value of Z is seen to be 1.96.

Notice that we add $Zs_{\bar{x}}$ to μ_H to get the upper value for $\overline{X}_c$ and subtract $Zs_{\bar{x}}$ from μ_H to get the lower value of $\overline{X}_c$. Then if our sample mean exceeds the upper value for $\overline{X}_c$ or is less than the lower value for $\overline{X}_c$, it would fall in one of the rejection regions and must be considered significantly different from 115. The difference between μ_H and $\overline{X}$ could not be explained on the basis of sampling error, and we must therefore reject the null hypothesis that $\mu = 115$.

Formula (9.1) is used to determine the critical values for $\overline{X}$. These critical values are then used to form a decision rule upon which the hypothesis will either be rejected or not rejected. For example, assume for the moment that under the hypothesis H_0: $\mu = 115$, we let $s_{\bar{x}}$ be 5, and we test the hypothesis at the 95 percent level of confidence. Then $0.95/2 = 0.4750$, which yields a Z-value from the table of 1.96. Formula (9.1) becomes

$$\overline{X}_c = \mu_H + Zs_{\bar{x}}$$

$$\overline{X}_c = 115 \pm 1.96(5)$$

$$= 115 \pm 9.8$$

$$105.2\text{-------------}124.8$$

The lower and upper values for $\overline{X}_c$ are 105.2 and 124.8, respectively. If the sample mean is found to be below 105.2 or above 124.8, it falls in one of the rejection regions and is said to be significantly different from 115. The difference would be statistically significant at the 5 percent level, and cannot be explained away on the basis of sampling error. The null that $\mu = 115$ is therefore rejected. However, if the sample mean is found to be between 105.2 and 124.8, it is close enough to the hypothesized value for μ of 115 that we feel the difference is due merely to sampling error. That is, there is a 95 percent probability of drawing a sample with a mean anywhere between 105.2 and 124.8 from a population with a mean of $\mu = 115$. Thus, if the sample mean is indeed within this range, we cannot reject the null hypothesis that $\mu = 115$. The decision rule (DR) can then be stated as:

Decision Rule
Do not reject the null if $\overline{X}$ is greater than 105.2 or less than 124.8. That is, $105.2 < \overline{X} < 124.8$. Reject the null if $\overline{X} < 105.2$ or if $\overline{X} > 124.8$.

In the unlikely event that the population standard deviation σ is known, Formula (9.1) becomes

$$\overline{X}_c = \mu_H \pm Z\sigma_{\bar{x}} \qquad (9.2)$$

where $\sigma_{\bar{x}} = \sigma/\sqrt{n}$.

9.4 DIFFERENCE BETWEEN A ONE-TAILED AND A TWO-TAILED TEST

When a set of hypotheses is expressed as

$$H_0: \mu = 115$$

$$H_A: \mu \neq 115$$

the hypothesis test is a **two-tailed test.** Since we are saying $\mu = 115$, we can reject it if our sample findings are either too high or too low. Either way, μ is not 115. That is why there are rejection regions in both tails of Figure 9-2.

However, in many cases, we may be interested in only one extreme or the other. For example, we might say that on the average it takes "three or more days" to ship fresh seafood to a restaurant in Kansas City. We didn't specify how many days, only that it was three or more. This is a **one-tailed test** because the statement can be rejected *only* if our sample findings suggest that it takes significantly *less* than three days. A finding of five days, or eight days, or anything more than three days would support, not refute, the hypothesis. Thus, there is a rejection region in only the left-hand tail. This is illustrated in Figure 9-3(a).

FIGURE 9-3   A One-Tailed Test

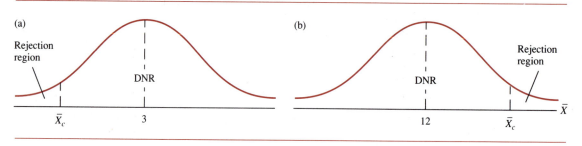

On the other hand, a production manager might feel that "on the average the completion of a certain task requires 12 hours or less." This is also a one-tailed-test, which will result in the rejection of the null hypothesis only if the sample findings suggest that it takes significantly *more* than 12 hours. Findings less than 12 support the hypothesis that μ is 12 or less, and would not lead to its rejection. Thus, a critical value for the sample mean significantly above 12 marks off the rejection region, as shown in Figure 9-3(b).

With a two-tailed test, the set of hypotheses is easily determined. It is always stated as

$$H_0: \mu = h$$

$$H_A: \mu \neq h$$

where h is some specific hypothesized value such as 115. However, with a one-tailed test the set of hypotheses might appear as

$$H_0: \mu \leq h$$

$$H_A: \mu > h$$

or

$$H_0: \mu \geq h$$

$$H_A: \mu < h$$

It is essential to determine which set of hypothesis is correct. The way in which this decision is made will be illustrated later in this chapter. Right now, let us more fully explore the practice of hypothesis testing in the case of a two-tailed test. We will more closely examine one-tailed tests shortly.

9.5 A Two-Tailed Hypothesis Test for the Population Mean—Large Sample

There are almost an infinite number of instances in which we may want to test a hypothesis about the value of the population mean. An auditor may wish to examine the average number of errors made in her accounts payable vouchers. A trucking firm may wonder about the average weight of last month's shipments. There may be some concern on the part of government officials as to the average income of tax-payers in a particular congressional district. In essence, a large number of business decisions are based on the population mean. If evidence regarding this parameter can be gathered, those decisions are more reliable and are likely to produce more favorable outcomes.

For our purposes, let us propose a case in which the manufacturer of Coco Crunchy Crispies, a new breakfast food, is concerned about the average weight of cereal it is putting into its boxes. The boxes proclaim a net weight of 36 ounces, and Coco Crunchy Crispies does not want to be guilty of false advertising. Since Coco Crunchy Crispies claims that $\mu = 36$ ounces, the set of hypotheses would appear as

$$H_0: \mu = 36$$

$$H_A: \mu \neq 36$$

Assume that management wants to test its hypothesis at the 5 percent level of significance. It must then use Formula (9.1) to calculate the critical values for $\overline{X}$ above and below 36 that mark off 95 percent of the area under the curve. A sample of $n = 100$ boxes is randomly selected and the contents are weighted, yielding a mean of $\overline{X} = 37.6$ ounces and a standard deviation of $s = 3$ ounces. The Z-value is found by first dividing the 95 percent level of confidence by 2 because the Z-table will give only those values from the mean to some point above the mean or some point below the mean. The resulting value of $0.95/2 = 0.4750$ is then found in the Z-table, and the corresponding Z-value of 1.96 is used. Furthermore, $s_{\bar{x}}$ is $s/\sqrt{n} = 3/\sqrt{100} = 0.3$. Then

$$\bar{X}_c = \mu_H \pm Z s_{\bar{x}}$$

$$= 36 \pm (1.96)(0.3)$$

$$= 36 \pm 0.588$$

35.41------------36.59

The critical values for $\bar{X}$ are 35.41 ounces and 36.59 ounces. If the sample mean is within that interval, the difference is small enough to be explained away on the basis of sampling error. However, if the sample mean is below 35.41 or above 36.59, the difference is significant at the 5 percent level and cannot be explained away on the basis of sampling error. There is only a 5 percent chance that if μ really is 36, a sample of $n = 100$ could be taken which would yield a mean below 35.41 or above 36.59. The decision rule is stated as

Decision Rule

Do not reject the null if $35.41 < \bar{X} < 36.59$. Reject the null if $\bar{X} < 35.41$ or $\bar{X} > 36.59$.

Figure 9-4 demonstrates the rejection regions under the normal curve.

FIGURE 9-4   Weights for Coco Crunchy Crispies

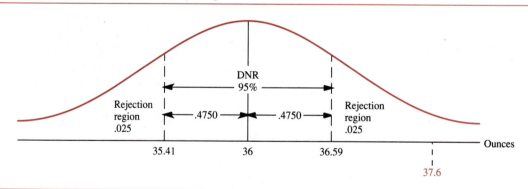

Since the sample mean was found to be 37.6, the null must be rejected. It is unlikely that $\mu = 36$. There is only a 2.5 percent probability that a sample of $n = 100$ would yield a mean greater than 36.59 if μ really was 36.

Instead, it is reasonable to conclude that the reason such a high sample mean was obtained is that μ is greater than 36, and the center of the true distribution of population weights is located somewhere to the right of 36.

The process of hypothesis testing is very exact and must be carried out in a precise manner. By reexamining the discussion above, you can see that there were basically four steps we carried out to complete the test. First, we had to determine the hypotheses. This required that we decide if it is a one-tailed or two-tailed test. Second, we had to calculate the critical value for the sample statistic. This was done using Formula (9.1). Third, we had to formulate the decision rule based on the critical value. Last, it was necessary to draw the proper conclusion or inference in accord with the decision rule. These four steps can be summarized as follows:

Step 1. Formulate the hypothesis.
Step 2. Calculate the critical value.
Step 3. Determine the decision rule.
Step 4. State the conclusion of the test regarding rejection of the null, and any interpretations which might be derived from that conclusion.

In the following examples, note the manner in which these four steps are followed.

EXAMPLE 9-1 Hypothesis Test of the Population Mean: A Two-Tailed Test

The Noah Fence Company feels that the average number of days required to complete a job is $\mu = 27$. Fifty jobs are randomly selected in order to test this assertion. The mean is found to be $\bar{X} = 25.3$ days, with a standard deviation of $s = 2.1$ days. Mr. Noah wishes to test the hypothesis at the 1 percent level of significance (99 percent of confidence). State the set of hypotheses and run the test.

SOLUTION:
Given Mr. Noah's statement that the average time required was 27 days, the set of hypotheses is stated as

$$H_0: \mu = 27$$

$$H_A: \mu \neq 27$$

This is a two-tailed test since the null can be rejected if sample findings are significantly above or below 27. A rejection region appears in both tails of the distribution.

The Z-value is found by first dividing the level of confidence by 2. Thus, $0.99/2 = 0.4950$ yields a Z of 2.58. Furthermore, $s_{\bar{x}} = s/\sqrt{n} = 2.1/\sqrt{50} = 0.297$. Then

$$\bar{X}_c = \mu_H \pm Z s_{\bar{x}}$$

$$= 27 \pm (2.58)(0.297)$$

$$= 27 \pm 0.77$$

$$26.23\text{-------}27.77$$

Decision Rule

Do not reject H_0 if $\overline{X}$ is between 26.23 and 27.77. Reject H_0 if $\overline{X}$ is less than 26.23 or greater than 27.77.

The conditions of the test and the manner in which the decision rule applies is illustrated in the figure.

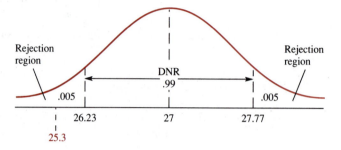

STATISTICAL INTERPRETATION:

An $\overline{X}$ of 25.3 is in the lower rejection region, too far below the μ_H of 27 to attribute the difference to sampling error. There is only a 0.005 chance that a sample of 50 could yield an $\overline{X}$ less than 26.23 if μ was indeed 27. Thus, 25.3 is significantly different from 27, forcing Noah to conclude that μ is probably not 27, but less than that. He must reject the null hypothesis.

Another example may help to further illustrate the process of hypothesis testing.

EXAMPLE 9-2 Hypothesis Test of the Population Mean: Two-Tailed Test

The Square Wheel Tire Company has determined that their tires must average 36 inches in diameter in order to fit most car models. A random sample of 100 tires revealed a mean of 36.4 inches with a standard deviation of 2.1 inches. Do you think management has anything to worry about?

This problem should be approached by testing the hypothesis that $\mu = 36$ at, say, the 1 percent level.

SOLUTION:

Z is $0.99/2 = 0.4950$, which from the table yields a Z-value of 2.58, and $s_{\bar{x}} = s/\sqrt{n} = 2.1/\sqrt{100} = 0.21$. The hypotheses are

$$H_0: \mu = 36$$

$$H_A: \mu \neq 36$$

Then

$$\overline{X}_c = \mu_H \pm Zs_{\bar{x}}$$

$$= 36 \pm (2.58)(0.21)$$

$$= 36 \pm (0.542)$$

$$35.458\text{---------}36.542$$

Decision Rule

Do not reject H_0: $\mu = 36$ if $\overline{X}$ is between 35.458 and 36.542. Reject H_0: $\mu = 36$ if $\overline{X}$ is less than 35.458 or greater than 36.542.

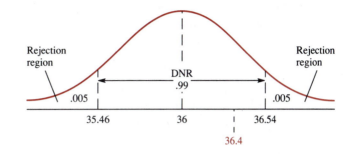

STATISTICAL INTERPRETATION:

Since the $\overline{X}$ of 36.4 falls in the DNR region, the null hypothesis that $\mu = 36$ is not rejected. The difference between 36 and 36.4 is attributed to chance variation in the sampling process. There is 99 percent probability that a population with a mean of $\mu = 36$ could produce a sample of size 100 with a mean between 35.46 and 36.54.

QUICK CHECK 9.5.1

○○○○

ABC, Inc. hypothesizes that the mean earnings of its sales staff is $72,500 annually. A sample of 42 sales personnel yielded a mean of $71,220 with a standard deviation of $5,900.

a. State the hypotheses.
b. Determine the decision rule at the 90 percent level.
c. Test the hypothesis and state the results.

Answer:
a. H_0: $\mu = \$72,500$ H_A: $\mu \neq \$72,500$
b. Do not reject the null if $\$70,998 < \overline{X} < \$74,002$.
    Reject the null if $\overline{X} < \$70,998$ or $\overline{X} > \$74,002$
c. Since $\overline{X} = \$71,220$, the null is not rejected.

QUICK CHECK 9.5.2

XYZ, Inc. feels that their mean weekly sales revenue is $750. A sample of 200 weeks reveals a standard deviation of $112 with a mean of $722.50.

a. State the hypotheses.
b. Determine the decision rule at the 5 percent level of significance.
c. Test the hypothesis if the sample mean is $722.50.

Answer:
a. H_0: $\mu = \$750$ H_A: $\mu \neq \$750$
b. Do not reject the null if $\$734.48 < \overline{X} < \$765.52$. Reject the null if $\overline{X} < \$734.48$ or if $\overline{X} > \$765.52$.
c. Since $\overline{X} = \$722.50$, reject the null.

9.6   A Two-Tailed Hypothesis Test for a Population Proportion—Large Samples

There will often arise instances in which researchers are interested in the proportion of a population that fits some characteristic. The concern is not with the average of the population but instead with what percentage of it meets or fails to meet a certain specification. For example, Square Wheel may not be concerned with the average diameter of the tires but is instead interested in that proportion that is not 36 inches. Remember, with a proportion, the observations either (1) do or (2) do not meet some specification. In measuring the tires we do not record their diameters in inches. We only make note of whether they differ from 36 inches. The exact diameter is of no interest to us. If Square Wheel was concerned about what proportion of the tires are defective, they could sample 100 tires and simply count all those that do not measure 36 inches. Recall from Chapter 8 that the sample proportion p is X/n, where X is the number of successes.

They might feel that 20 percent of the tires they manufacture fail to meet the 36-inch specification. That is, they assume that the population proportion π is 20 percent. The set of hypotheses is

$$H_0: \pi = 0.20$$

$$H_A: \pi \neq 0.20$$

We are then looking for some critical value for the sample proportion, p_c, which is too far above or too far below 20 percent to attribute the difference to chance variation in the luck of the draw in the sample of 100 tires.

If we wish to test the hypothesis at the 5 percent level of significance, we must find critical values for p that mark off 95 percent of the area under the curve, leaving the remaining 5 percent evenly divided in the two tails. These critical values are found from the formula

$$p_c = \pi_H \pm Z\sigma_p \tag{9.3}$$

where σ_p is the standard error of the proportion, and measures how far a typical sample proportion p will deviate from the population proportion π. It is found by

$$\sigma_p = \sqrt{\frac{\pi_H(1 - \pi_H)}{n}} \tag{9.4}$$

You will remember that this approach differs from the calculation of σ_p when computing confidence intervals in the previous chapter. At that time we had no knowledge of the population proportion, and we had to estimate it by using the sample proportion p.

Now, given the hypothesized value for π of 0.20, Formula (9.4) produces

$$\sigma_p = \sqrt{\frac{(0.20)\,(0.80)}{100}} = 0.04$$

Then the critical values for the sample proportion are

$$p_c = \pi_H \pm Z\sigma_p$$
$$= 0.20 \pm (1.96)\,(0.04)$$
$$= 0.20 \pm 0.078$$
$$0.122\text{---------}0.278$$

Decision Rule

Do not reject the null if the sample proportion p is between 0.122 and 0.278. Reject the null if p is less than 0.122 or if p is greater than 0.278.

Figure 9-5 illustrates these findings.

FIGURE 9-5   Critical Values for the Sample Proportion

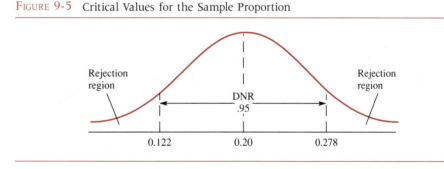

Any value for p, the sample proportion, between 12.2 percent and 27.8 percent is considered close enough to the hypothesized population proportion of 20 percent to be explained by sampling error. There is a 95 percent probability that if a sample of $n = 100$ is taken from a population with a proportion of $\pi = 0.20$, the sample proportion will be between 12.2 percent and 27.8 percent.

However, there is only a 5 percent probability that the sampling error could be so large as to produce a sample proportion outside that range if $\pi = 0.20$.

If our sample of 100 tires contained 22 that differ from the 36-inch limit, the sample proportion is $p = X/n = 22/100 = 22$ percent, which is within the tolerable range. We therefore do not reject the null hypothesis.

EXAMPLE 9-3 Hypothesis Test for Population Proportion:
A Two-Tailed Test

Roscoe, head chef at the Squat and Gobble Cafe, feels that 37 percent of his noon customers order the luncheon special. Of the 50 customers he randomly selects, 21 selected the special for their noon dining enjoyment. Roscoe wants to test his hypothesis at the 1 percent level of significance.

SOLUTION:
His hypotheses are

$$H_0: \pi = 0.37$$

$$H_A: \pi \neq 0.37$$

A 99 percent test requires the determination of upper and lower values for p which leave the remaining 1 percent evenly divided in the two tails. The Z-value is found in the usual fashion. The confidence level of 0.99 is divided by 2 to yield 0.4950, which, from the Z-table, results in a value of 2.58. From Formula (9.4), we find

$$\sigma_p = \sqrt{\frac{\pi_H(1 - \pi_H)}{n}}$$

$$= \sqrt{\frac{(0.37)(1 - 0.37)}{50}}$$

$$= 0.068$$

Then

$$p_c = \pi_H \pm Z\sigma_p$$

$$= 0.37 \pm (2.58)(0.068)$$

$$= 0.37 \pm 0.175$$

$$0.195\text{---------}0.545$$

The figure aids in forming the decision rule.

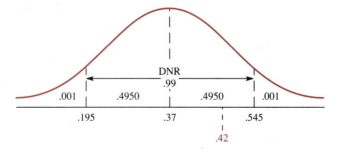

Decision Rule

Do not reject the null hypothesis that $\pi = 37$ percent if p is between 19.5 percent and 54.5 percent. Reject the null if p is less than 19.5 percent or more than 54.5 percent.

The sample proportion is $X/n = 21/50 = 0.42$.

STATISTICAL INTERPRETATION:

There is a 99 percent chance that if $\pi = 37$ percent, a sample of size 50 could yield a proportion between 19.5 percent and 54.5 percent. Since our sample proportion was 42 percent, we do not reject the null.

Another example in which we do reject the null will further illustrate the test for π.

EXAMPLE 9-4 Hypothesis Test for Population Proportion: Two-Tailed Test

Mom's Home Cookin', Squat and Gobble's main competitor, claims that 70 percent of the customers are able to dine for less than $5. Mom wishes to test this claim at the 92 percent level of confidence.

SOLUTION:

The hypotheses are

$$H_0: \pi = 0.70$$

$$H_A: \pi \neq 0.70$$

Since $0.92/2 = 0.4600$, a Z-value of 1.75 is obtained from the table. If a sample of $n = 110$ is taken, we have

$$\sigma_p = \sqrt{\frac{(0.70)(0.30)}{110}}$$

$$= 0.044$$

Then,

$$p_c = \pi_H \pm Z\sigma_p$$

$$p_c = 0.7 \pm (1.75)(0.044)$$

$$= 0.7 \pm 0.077$$

$$0.623\text{------------}0.777$$

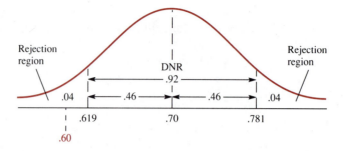

Decision Rule

Do not reject the null hypothesis that $\pi = 70$ percent if p is between 62.3 percent and 77.7 percent. Reject null if p is greater than 77.7 percent or less than 62.3 percent.

A random sample of 110 patrons revealed that 66 paid less than \$5 for lunch. Thus, $p = X/n = 66/110 = 0.60$.

STATISTICAL INTERPRETATION:

Our example shows that if $\pi = 0.70$, there is only an 8 percent chance of taking a sample of size 110 and getting a sample proportion outside the 62.3 percent to 77.7 percent range. Since our sample proportion of $66/110 = 0.60$ is outside that range, we must reject the null. Mom has underestimated the cost of her meals.

QUICK CHECK 9.6.1

○○○○

Apex Company hypothesizes that 15 percent of the goods they produce by a new method are defective. A sample of 132 reveals 22 defects. Set α at 0.10.

a. State the hypotheses.
b. Determine the decision rule.
c. Test the hypothesis.

Answer:

a. $H_0: \pi = 0.15$ $H_A: \pi \neq 0.15$
b. Do not reject if p, the sample proportion, is between 0.10 and 0.20. Reject the null if p is below 0.10 or above 0.20.
c. Since $p = 0.17$, do not reject.

QUICK CHECK 9.6.2

Honest John claims that 70 percent of car buyers buy new cars. Of 400 sampled, 310 bought new. Set α at 5 percent.

a. State the hypotheses.
b. Determine the decision rule.
c. Test the hypothesis.

Answer:

a. $H_0: \pi = 0.70$ $H_A: \pi \neq 0.70$
b. Do not reject if $0.66 < p < 0.74$. Reject the null if $p < 0.66$ or $p > 0.74$.
c. Since $p = 0.78$, reject the null.

9.7 A TWO-TAILED HYPOTHESIS TEST FOR THE POPULATION MEAN— SMALL SAMPLES

The preceding discussion dealt with hypothesis tests for population means and proportions using large samples ($n > 30$). However, there are many situations in which a large sample is not practical. We often find that a small sample is the only way to complete the test. In such a situation it may be necessary to use Student's t-test introduced in the previous chapter. Specifically, given a small sample, the t-test must be employed if the population is normal and σ is unknown. As we saw in Chapter 8, determining when to use the t-test can be somewhat bewildering. Table 9-1 may prove useful in making that decision. It repeats much of the information contained in Table 8-9.

TABLE 9-1 When to Use a t-Test

For a small sample
   If the population is known to be normal
      Use a t-test if σ is unknown
      Use a Z-test if σ is known
   If the population is not known to be normal
      Use a nonparametric test whether or not σ is known
Use a t-test only if all of the following conditions hold:
   $n < 30$
   The population is known to be normal
   σ is unknown

A. WHEN σ IS UNKNOWN

As we noted during our discussion of confidence intervals, the t-distribution produces a wider interval than does a similar Z-test. This wider interval is needed when working with samples of less than 30 since the use of small samples tends to increase the size of the standard error. Other than the use of the t-distribution in place of the Z-distribution, the hypothesis test for μ is exactly the same as with large samples. The t-value, based on n-1 degrees of freedom and the desired level of confidence, is found in the t-table. It is then used in place of the Z-value in the formulas shown above.

EXAMPLE 9-5 Hogs and Kisses: Two-Tailed Test for the Population Mean (small sample)

The residents of Hogs Breath, Kentucky, will sell a herd of pigs only when their average weight reaches 220 pounds. Zeke Ziffel, a long-time resident of Hogs Breath, is getting married next week, and he needs some hard cash for his honeymoon to Butcher's Hollow. Zeke selects 12 pigs out of his herd and weighs them. The mean and standard deviation are 217 pounds and 26 pounds, respectively. Should

Zeke sell? Let $\alpha = 0.05$. Zeke assumes that the population of weights is normally distributed.

SOLUTION:

Zeke sets his hypothesis as

$$H_0: \mu = 220$$

$$H_A: \mu \neq 220$$

With a 95 percent level of confidence and d.f. $= 12 - 1 = 11$, the t-value is found from the table to be 2.201. Also, $s_{\bar{x}} = s/\sqrt{n} = 26/\sqrt{12} = 7.51$. Thus,

$$\overline{X}_c = \mu_H + ts_{\bar{x}}$$

$$= 220 \pm (2.201)(7.51)$$

$$= 220 \pm 16.53$$

$$203.47\text{-------------}236.53$$

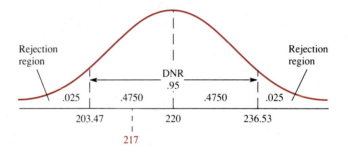

Decision Rule

Do not reject the null hypothesis that $\mu = 220$ if the sample mean is between 203.47 pounds and 236.53 pounds. Reject the null if the sample mean is below 203.47 pounds or above 236.53 pounds.

STATISTICAL INTERPRETATION:

Since the sample mean was 217 pounds, we should not reject the null that $\mu = 220$, and advise Zeke to take the little piggies to market.

B.   IF σ IS KNOWN

As noted above, if the population standard deviation is known, it should be used in place of the sample standard deviation s. If σ is known, however, even a small sample allows the use of the Z-distribution. Thus, since $\sigma_{\bar{x}} = \sigma/\sqrt{n}$, we may use

$$\overline{X}_c = \mu_H \pm Z \frac{\sigma}{\sqrt{n}}$$

even if $n < 30$. That is, if σ is given, the Z-distribution applies regardless of sample size if the population is normal. This is true because, since we do not have to estimate σ, the standard error will be less and we do not need the wider interval produced by the t-distribution.

EXAMPLE 9-6 More Hogs and Kisses: Two-Tailed Test for the Population Mean (small sample with σ given)

If in the above example Zeke had somehow known that the standard deviation of all of his pigs' weights was $\sigma = 26$ pounds, and not just the 12 he sampled, the hypothesis test could use the Z-distribution. If α remains 0.05, we proceed as follows.

SOLUTION:

$$H_0: \mu = 220$$

$$H_A: \mu \neq 220$$

$$\overline{X}_c = \mu_H \pm Z\sigma_{\bar{x}}$$

$$= 220 \pm (1.96)\,(7.51)$$

$$= 220 \pm 14.72$$

$$205.28\text{--------------}234.72$$

Decision Rule
Do not reject H_0 if the sample mean is between 205.28 pounds and 234.72 pounds. Reject H_0 if the sample mean is less than 205.28 or more than 234.72.

STATISTICAL INTERPRETATION:
Since $\overline{X} = 217$ pounds, we do not reject the null that $\mu = 220$ and ship the livestock to market.

Note: Since Z was less than t, the same test using the Z-distribution resulted in a narrower interval (205.28 to 234.72) than in Example 9-5 using the t-distribution (203.47 to 236.53).

You must remember to determine if the population standard deviation is given. If so, use a Z-test regardless of sample size, providing the population is normal. If the population standard deviation is not given, you must estimate it with the sample standard deviation and then resort to the wider interval provided by the t-test if $n < 30$.

We will not conduct a small-sample test for the population proportion because the complexities which arise are beyond the scope of this material.

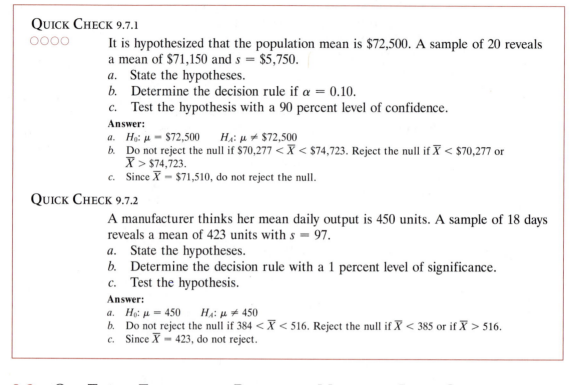

It is hypothesized that the population mean is $72,500. A sample of 20 reveals a mean of $71,150 and $s = \$5,750$.
a. State the hypotheses.
b. Determine the decision rule if $\alpha = 0.10$.
c. Test the hypothesis with a 90 percent level of confidence.
Answer:
a. H_0: $\mu = \$72,500$ H_A: $\mu \neq \$72,500$
b. Do not reject the null if $\$70,277 < \overline{X} < \$74,723$. Reject the null if $\overline{X} < \$70,277$ or $\overline{X} > \$74,723$.
c. Since $\overline{X} = \$71,510$, do not reject the null.

A manufacturer thinks her mean daily output is 450 units. A sample of 18 days reveals a mean of 423 units with $s = 97$.
a. State the hypotheses.
b. Determine the decision rule with a 1 percent level of significance.
c. Test the hypothesis.
Answer:
a. H_0: $\mu = 450$ H_A: $\mu \neq 450$
b. Do not reject the null if $384 < \overline{X} < 516$. Reject the null if $\overline{X} < 385$ or if $\overline{X} > 516$.
c. Since $\overline{X} = 423$, do not reject.

9.8 ONE-TAILED TESTS FOR THE POPULATION MEAN WITH LARGE SAMPLES

All the examples illustrated above were two-tailed tests. We wanted to test the hypothesis that the population mean or proportion was exactly *equal to some specific value*. Sample findings significantly *above or below* that amount resulted in the rejection of the null hypothesis. Thus, there were rejection regions in both tails of the curve.

However, with just a little thought, you could probably envision many instances in which we might be concerned with only one extreme or the other. For example, assume that instead of wanting to test the hypothesis that the average weight of their cereal boxes was equal to exactly 36 ounces, Coco Crunchy Crispies wanted to ensure that $\mu \geq 36$. In this case they would be working with a one-tailed test. The problem would involve a rejection region in only one tail. Deciding which tail should contain the rejection region is somewhat tricky, so the next section is particularly important.

A. DETERMINATION OF HYPOTHESES IN A ONE-TAILED TEST

A two-tailed test involves only one standard set of hypotheses:

$$H_0: \mu = h$$

$$H_A: \mu \neq h$$

where h is some hypothesized value for the population mean, such as 36 ounces. However, a one-tailed test, as we noted earlier in this chapter, can result in either of two different sets of hypotheses:

$$H_0: \mu \leq h$$

$$H_A: \mu > h$$

or

$$H_0: \mu \geq h$$

$$H_A: \mu < h$$

Determining which set of hypotheses is correct is crucial. First of all, note that the equal sign appears in the null hypothesis in both sets. This is because the null hypothesis traditionally tests the implication of "no difference." That is, the null implies that the actual parametric value does not differ significantly from its hypothesized value.

Another explanation as to why the null will contain the equal sign is based on the realization that it is the null, not the alternative hypothesis, being tested. Moreover, it is being tested at a specific level of significance, say, 5 percent. You cannot test the ambiguous statement $\mu > h$ at a specific significance level. The statement $\mu > h$ is ambiguous because it does not say how much greater μ is, nor does it make any claim regarding the precise value of μ. Therefore, in order to test the null at a specific level of significance, it must contain the precision provided by the equal sign.

To identify the proper set of hypotheses, we must pay close attention to the statement in the problem. For example, assume that management for Coco Crunchy Crispies claims that the cereal boxes contain an average of more than 36 ounces. Carefully interpreted, this means $\mu > 36$. Since this statement does *not* contain the equal sign, it must be the *alternative* hypothesis, and the null is $\mu \leq 36$. Thus, the set of hypotheses is

$$H_0: \mu \leq 36$$

$$H_A: \mu > 36$$

On the other hand, had Coco Crunchy Crispies stated that the boxes contained a mean of 36 or more, a strict interpretation would be written as $\mu \geq 36$ and *would* contain the equal sign. It must therefore be the *null* hypothesis and the set of hypotheses would appear as

$$H_0: \mu \geq 36$$

$$H_A: \mu < 36$$

Remember, if a strict interpretation of the statement in the problem contains the equal sign, it is treated as the null hypothesis. If it does not, it is taken as the alternative.

The logic behind this interpretation is based on the realization, as noted above, that the null is to be tested at a specific α-level. It is therefore necessary to provide the null with the precision and specificity conferred by the equal sign.

Once the correct set of hypotheses has been identified, it is then necessary to determine in which tail the rejection region is to be located. To do so, you must ask yourself the question, "What will cause the rejection of the null?" Consider the first set of hypotheses above, which appeared as

$$H_0: \mu \leq 36$$

$$H_A: \mu > 36$$

Written in this manner, the null allows for small values for the mean. It clearly states that the mean is equal to or *less than* 36. Small values less than 36 will therefore support, not refute, the null hypothesis. Findings to the left of 36 will tend to confirm the null that μ is equal to or less than 36. Thus, it is only values significantly *above* 36 that tend to result in the rejection of the null hypothesis. The rejection region is therefore found only in the upper, or right, tail of the distribution. This right-tailed test is shown in Figure 9-6.

FIGURE 9-6   A Right-Tailed Test

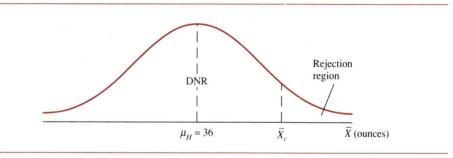

The critical value for the sample mean which is identified as significantly different from the hypothesized μ marks off the rejection region in the right tail. The formula for this critical value in a right-tailed test is

$$\overline{X}_c = \mu_H + Zs_{\bar{x}} \tag{9.5}$$

Notice that it adds some amount to the hypothesized value for the population mean, thereby producing a rejection region in the right tail.

Conversely, presume that Coco Crunchy Crispies made the statement that the mean was 36 or more. This is written as $\mu \geq 36$ and contains the equal sign. It will therefore serve as the null hypothesis. The set of hypotheses appears as

$$H_0: \mu \geq 36$$

$$H_A: \mu < 36$$

To determine which tail contains the rejection region, you must again ask yourself the all-important question, "What would cause the rejection of the null?" As stated here, the null allows for large values for the mean. It clearly states that the mean is equal to or greater than 36. Large values for the sample mean greater than 36 will therefore support, not refute, the null hypothesis. Thus, it is only values significantly below 36 that will cause a rejection of the null. The rejection region is therefore found only in the lower, or left, tail of the distribution. This left-tailed test is demonstrated in Figure 9-7.

FIGURE 9-7   A Left-Tailed Test

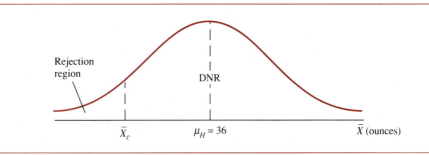

The critical value for the sample mean which is identified as significantly different from the hypothesized μ marks off the rejection region in the left tail. The formula for this critical value in a left-tailed test is

$$\overline{X}_c = \mu_H - Zs_{\bar{x}} \tag{9.6}$$

Notice that it subtracts some amount from the hypothesized value for the population mean, thereby producing a rejection region in the left tail.

The point to remember is that the null must contain the equal sign. You then have only to determine whether significantly large or significantly small values would result in the rejection of the null. The rejection region is then placed in that tail. In the event that you forget this reasoning, remember one simple rule: the rejection region will appear in the tail indicated by the inequality sign in the *alternative* hypothesis.

Assume, for example, that the proper set of hypotheses is determined to be

$$H_0: \mu \geq h$$

$$H_A: \mu < h$$

Since the null allows large values for the mean (it says the mean is equal to or greater than some amount h), only significantly small values will result in the rejection of the null hypothesis. The rejection region will be found in the left tail. Notice that the inequality sign in the alternative hypothesis calls for small values (it "points" to the left).

If, on the other hand, the appropriate set of hypotheses is found to be

$$H_0: \mu \le h$$

$$H_A: \mu > h$$

the null would permit small values for the mean (it says that the mean is equal to or less than some amount h). Only significantly large values would result in the rejection of the null. The rejection region would be found in the right tail. Notice that the inequality sign in the alternative hypothesis calls for large values (it "points" to the right).

This simple rule of observing the inequality sign in the alternative hypothesis is followed because it will result in a "strong" test. It is strong in the sense that a rejection of the null can take place only after it has been proved wrong beyond any reasonable doubt. The analogy is often made that the null is like a person on trial. Before the prisoner is convicted (or the null rejected), guilt must be firmly established.

The strength inherent in this test can be illustrated with a simple example. If an employer claimed the mean number of days his employees missed work was 10 or more (i.e., $\mu \ge 10$), the proper set of hypotheses would be

$$H_0: \mu \ge 10$$

$$H_A: \mu < 10$$

Remember the rule about the equal sign appearing in the null. The inequality sign in the alternative then calls for a left-tailed test as shown in Figure 9-8. Formula (9.6) would be used, resulting in a critical value for the sample mean significantly less than 10 before the null of $\mu \ge 10$ would be rejected. That is, an $\overline{X}$ of, say, 9.9 or 9.8, although less than the hypothesized value of 10, would not be low enough to cause

FIGURE 9-8   A Left-Tailed Test

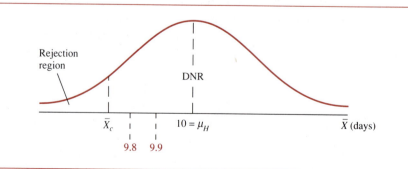

rejection. Before the null of $\mu \geq 10$ can be rejected, not only must the sampling findings be less than 10, but they must be *significantly less* than 10.

As another illustration of a one-tailed test, consider a manufacturer of batteries who has developed a new and improved method of production which he feels will extend the mean life of his product beyond the current 150 hours. If he were to test the hypothesis of life extension, would he use a two-tailed test or a one-tailed test? If he decided on a one-tailed test, should it be left-tailed or right-tailed? You must keep in mind that the producer is assuming (hypothesizing) that under this improved production method the mean life now exceeds 150 hours. That is, $\mu > 150$. Expressed in this manner, the statement does not contain the equal sign. It must therefore be the alternative hypothesis in a one-tailed test. The set of hypotheses, which produce a right-tailed test, is

$$H_0: \mu \leq 150$$

$$H_A: \mu > 150$$

B. FINDING THE CORRECT VALUE FOR Z FOR A ONE-TAILED TEST

As we have seen, the correct value for Z is obtained in a two-tailed test by dividing the level of confidence by 2 and then looking up that area in the main body of the Z-table. The corresponding Z-value is then used in the calculations. Thus, if a 95 percent level of confidence is used, $0.4750 (= 0.95/2)$ is located in the Z-table. The appropriate Z-value is seen to be 1.96.

However, in a one-tailed test, as illustrated in Figure 9-9, the entire value for alpha is located in only one tail. Remember, the Z-table gives the area under the curve from the mean to some value above or below it. Therefore, the proper area for a one-tailed test is found by subtracting the α-value from 0.50. In Figure 9-9(a), a left-tailed test with a 95 percent level of confidence $(\alpha = 0.05)$ is shown. Then, $0.5 - 0.05 = 0.4500$, which from the Z-table yields a value of 1.65. Figure 9-9(b) shows the Z-value if you wanted a right-tailed test at the 99 percent level of confidence. Since α would be 0.01, the Z-value is found by first subtracting 0.01 from 0.50. The result of 0.4900 is located in the Z-table to get the proper Z-value of 2.33.

FIGURE 9-9   A One-Tailed Test

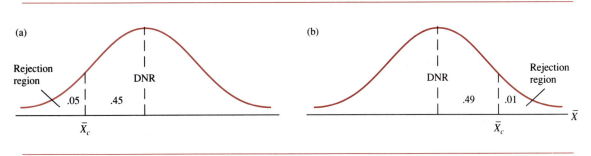

In summary, remember that, in conducting a one-tailed test:

1. If a strict interpretation of the statement contains the equal sign, it becomes the null hypothesis; if it does not contain the equal sign, it is the alternative.
2. The tail containing the rejection region is shown by the inequality sign in the alternative hypothesis.
3. The proper Z-value is found by subtracting the α-value from 0.50 and finding the result in the Z-table.

Formula (9.5) or (9.6) is then used to compute the single value for $\overline{X}_c$. Example 9-7 should help to clarify the matter.

EXAMPLE 9-7 Hypothesis Test for Population Mean: One-Tailed Test

The accounting firm of Smith, Smith, Smith, and Jones advertises that on the average it takes less than five days to complete customers' tax returns. Sixty-four returns are examined, showing a mean of 4.7 days with a standard deviation of 1.2 days. State the hypotheses and test at the 0.05 level.

SOLUTION:

Since the statement "less than five days" is written $\mu < 5$ and does not contain the equal sign, it is the alternative hypothesis. Therefore,

$$H_0: \mu \geq 5$$

$$H_A: \mu < 5$$

The null permits large sample findings. It states that the population mean is equal to or greater than 5. It can therefore be rejected only if significantly small sample findings result. A left-tailed test is required. After all, note that the inequality sign in the alternative hypothesis "points" to the left.

By the way, notice that the null hypothesis and the claim by the accounting firm are not the same. The firm states that the mean is less than five days, while the null states that the mean is equal to or more than five. The Z-value is $0.50 - 0.05 = 0.4500$, which yields a value of 1.65 from the Z-table. Formula (9.6) yields

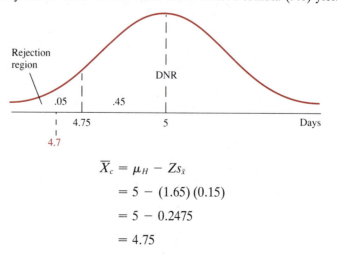

$$\overline{X}_c = \mu_H - Zs_{\bar{x}}$$

$$= 5 - (1.65)(0.15)$$

$$= 5 - 0.2475$$

$$= 4.75$$

Decision Rule
Do not reject the null if the sample mean exceeds 4.75 days. Reject the null if the sample mean is less than 4.75 days.

STATISTICAL INTERPRETATION:
Our example shows that if $\mu = 5$ or more, there is only a 5 percent chance that a sample of 64 returns would yield an $\overline{X}$ less than 4.75 days. Since the sample mean was $\overline{X} = 4.70$, we reject the null of $\mu \geq 5$. It is too unlikely that a population with a mean of 5 or more could produce a sample with a mean of 4.70. We can conclude with 95 percent certainty that the firm's claim that the average completion time for a tax return is less than five days is correct.

EXAMPLE 9-8 Hypothesis Test for Population Mean: One-Tailed Test

Honest John claims that the owners of his used cars can drive an average of at least 10,000 miles without major repairs. In order to determine how honest Honest John is, you select 100 customers and find they drove an average of 9,112 miles without repairs, with $s = 207$. If you want to be 99 percent certain Honest John isn't lying, how could you test his claim?

SOLUTION:
An average of at least 10,000 is written $\mu \geq 10,000$ and contains the equal sign. Therefore, it becomes the null hypothesis. The null hypothesis and John's claim are synonymous.

$$H_0: \mu \geq 10,000$$

$$H_A: \mu < 10,000$$

A left-tailed test is called for as indicated by the inequality sign in the alternative hypothesis. Z is $0.5 - 0.01 = 0.4900$. The 0.4900 specifies a value for Z of 2.33.
Using Formula (9.6), we have

$$\overline{X}_c = \mu_H - Zs_{\overline{x}}$$

$$= 10,000 - (2.33)(20.7)$$

$$= 10,000 - 48.23$$

$$= 9,952 \text{ miles}$$

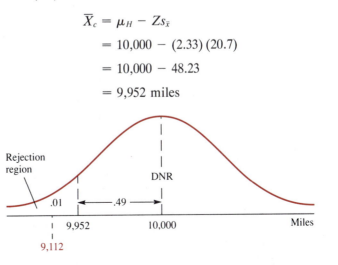

Decision Rule

Do not reject the null if the sample mean exceeds 9,952 miles. Reject the null if the sample mean is less than 9,952.

STATISTICAL INTERPRETATION:

Since our $\overline{X} = 9{,}112$, we reject the null and John's claim that μ is at least 10,000, and decide that Honest John isn't so honest after all.

Compare this case with one in which Honest John's claim is slightly altered.

EXAMPLE 9-9 Hypothesis Test of Population Mean: One-Tailed Test

Instead of claiming his customers can drive at least 10,000 miles, suppose Honest John claims that they can average more than 10,000 miles. This statement is expressed as $\mu > 10{,}000$, which must be taken as the alternative hypothesis. The alternative hypothesis and John's claim are synonymous.

SOLUTION:

Therefore,

$$H_0: \mu \le 10{,}000$$

$$H_A: \mu > 10{,}000$$

and a right-tailed test must be made. We will use the same findings from the previous example in which $n = 100$, $\overline{X} = 9{,}112$, $s = 207$, and $\alpha = 0.01$. Since we are working in the right tail, Formula (9.5) is used because it requires that we add $Zs_{\bar{x}}$ to μ_H.

$$\overline{X}_c = \mu_H + Zs_{\bar{x}}$$

$$= 10{,}000 + (2.33)(20.7)$$

$$= 10{,}000 + 48.23$$

$$= 10{,}048 \text{ miles}$$

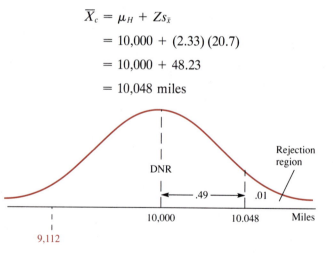

Decision Rule

Do not reject the null if the sample mean is less than 10,048 miles. Reject the null if the sample mean exceeds 10,048.

STATISTICAL INTERPRETATION:

Since $\overline{X} = 9{,}112$, we do not reject the null that $\mu \le 10{,}000$. We reject Honest John's claim of $\mu > 10{,}000$ and still buy our cars elsewhere.

QUICK CHECK 9.8.1

○○○○   If drivers for Acme Trucking average more than 3,000 miles per week during
            the year, they will get a Christmas bonus. Over the past 35 weeks, John has
            averaged 3,209 miles with a standard deviation of 712. Set $\alpha = 0.05$.
            a.   State the hypotheses.
            b.   Determine the decision rule.
            c.   Test the hypothesis.
            Answer:
            a. H_0: $\mu \leq 3,000$ H_A: $\mu > 3,000$
            b.   Do not reject if $\overline{X} < 3,199$. Reject if $\overline{X} > 3,199$.
            c.   Since $\overline{X} = 3,209$, reject null and give John the bonus.

QUICK CHECK 9.8.2

            A buyer complains that she is getting less than the promised 30 units per
            container from her supplier. A sample of 57 containers yields a mean of
            28.2 units with $s = 3.9$. Set $\alpha = 0.01$.
            a.   State the hypotheses.
            b.   Determine the decision rule.
            c.   Test the hypothesis.
            Answer:
            a. H_0: $\mu \geq 30$ H_A: $\mu < 30$
            b.   Do not reject if $\overline{X} > 28.8$. Reject if $\overline{X} < 28.8$.
            c.   Since $\overline{X} = 28.2$, reject null.

9.9   ONE-TAILED TESTS FOR THE MEAN WITH SMALL SAMPLES

There are many instances in which a large sample of 30 or more is impractical or,
perhaps, even impossible. In these cases, as with two-tailed tests, if the population
is known to be normal and the population standard deviation is unknown, Student's
t-test must be used. The formula for $\overline{X}_c$ becomes

$$\overline{X}_c = \mu_H + t s_{\bar{x}} \tag{9.7}$$

for right-tailed tests, and

$$\overline{X}_c = \mu_H - t s_{\bar{x}} \tag{9.8}$$

for left-tailed tests.

EXAMPLE 9-10 A One-Tailed Test with a Small Sample

The Rancid Meat Packing Company fears that the average weight of their shipments exceeds 30 pounds. This is undesirable because anything over that requires additional shipping costs. To determine the average weight of their shipments, 25 orders are selected at random. The sample mean is 32.1 pounds with a standard deviation of 3.1 pounds. State the hypotheses for Rancid and run the test with $\alpha = 0.05$.

SOLUTION:

Since "exceed 30 pounds" is written as $\mu > 30$, it is the alternative hypothesis since it does not contain the equal sign. Then

$$H_0: \mu \leq 30$$

$$H_A: \mu > 30$$

A right-tailed test is called for. With $n - 1 = 24$ degrees of freedom and $\alpha = 0.05$ for a one-tailed test, the t-value is found in the table to be $t = 1.711$. Formula (9.7) results in

$$\overline{X}_c = \mu_H + ts_{\bar{x}}$$

$$= 30 + (1.711)(0.62)$$

$$= 30 + 1.06$$

$$= 31.06$$

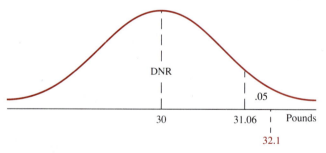

Decision Rule

Do not reject the null if the sample mean is less than 31.06. Reject the null if the sample mean exceeds 31.06.

STATISTICAL INTERPRETATION:

Since our sample mean was 32.1, we must conclude that it is significantly greater than 30 and cannot be explained merely on the basis of the nature of our particular sample. There is only a 5 percent chance that if $\mu \leq 30$, a sample of 25 orders could produce a mean in excess of 31.06 pounds. Therefore, μ is probably greater than 30, and we reject the null that $\mu \leq 30$. Rancid should take steps to reduce the size of their shipments to avoid excessive shipping costs.

In all the above instances, if the population standard deviation is known, the Z-test can be used to replace the t-test, as was the case with two-tailed tests.

9.10 ONE-TAILED TESTS FOR PROPORTIONS—LARGE SAMPLES

By now the process of hypothesis testing should be somewhat familiar. The test for population proportions follows the pattern established above. So with little discussion, let's work a problem or two dealing with proportions.

In the case of proportions the formulas for the critical value for the sample proportion are

$$p_c = \pi_H + Z(\sigma_p) \qquad (9.9)$$

for right-hand tailed tests, and

$$p_c = \pi_H - Z(\sigma_p) \qquad (9.10)$$

for left-hand tailed tests, where π_H is the hypothesized population proportion. Formula (9.4), you are reminded, tells us that

$$\sigma_p = \sqrt{\frac{\pi_H(1 - \pi_H)}{n}}$$

EXAMPLE 9-11 Hypothesis Test for Proportions

The manager of KAYS-TV in Hays, Kansas, has told his board of directors that at least 40 percent of all viewers tune into their local 5:00 evening news show. If the board of directors finds that in a sample of 250 viewers contacted by telephone, 97 of them are watching the news program, what conclusion can the board draw regarding the station's popularity? $\alpha = 0.01$.

SOLUTION:

Since "at least 40 percent" is written "$\pi \geq 0.40$" and contains the equal sign, it must be taken as the null. Thus,

$$H_0: \pi \geq 0.40$$

$$H_A: \pi < 0.40$$

produces a left-hand tailed test. As was the case with one-tailed tests for the population mean, the Z-value is found by subtracting the α from 0.50. Thus, we have

0.50 − 0.01 = 0.4900, which yields a Z-value of 2.33. The accompanying figure provides an illustration. Using Formula (9.10) gives

$$p_c = \pi_H - Z\sigma_p$$

$$= 0.4 - (2.33)(0.031)$$

$$= 0.4 - 0.072$$

$$= 0.328$$

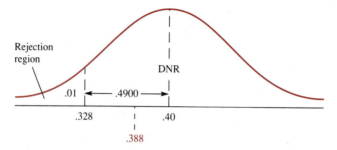

Decision Rule
Do not reject the null if the sample proportion exceeds 32.8 percent. Reject the null if the sample proportion is less than 32.8 percent.

STATISTICAL INTERPRETATION:
Since our sample proportions is 97/250 = 38.8 percent, we will not reject the null, and assume that the station manager is correct.

EXAMPLE 9-12 One-Tailed Hypothesis Test for Proportions
In 1990, a contract dispute between the National Football League and the Players' Association arose regarding the retirement system. The NFL agreed to a settlement only if it could be shown that less than 60 percent of the players retired with five years or less playing time in their careers.

In a sample of 220 players who had retired over the past seven years, 136 had played five years or less before retirement. Based on these findings, should the NFL sign the contract if they want to be 98 percent certain of the findings? ($\alpha = 0.02$)

SOLUTION:
"Less than 60 percent" means $\pi < 0.60$. Thus,

$$H_0: \pi \geq 0.60$$

$$H_A: \pi < 0.60$$

produces a left-tailed test. The Z-value is 0.50 − 0.02 = 0.4800. When 0.4800 is located in the Z-table, the corresponding value for Z is 2.05. Furthermore,

$$\sigma_p = \sqrt{\frac{\pi_H(1 - \pi_H)}{n}}$$

$$= \sqrt{\frac{(0.6)\,(0.4)}{220}}$$

$$= 0.03$$

Then

$$p_c = \pi_H - Z\sigma_p$$

$$= 0.6 - (2.05)\,(0.03)$$

$$= 0.6 - 0.06$$

$$= 0.54$$

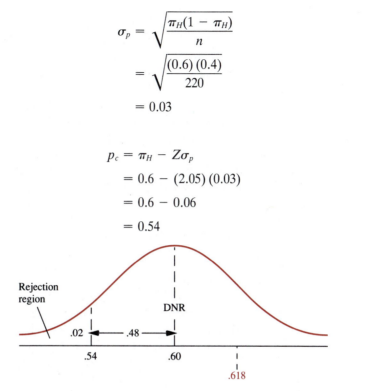

Decision Rule

Do not reject the null if the sample proportion exceeds 54 percent. Reject the null if the sample proportion is less than 54 percent.

STATISTICAL INTERPRETATION:

Since our sample proportion is $p = X/n = 136/220 = 61.8$ percent, it is well within the DNR region. The NFL should not reject the null that $\pi \geq 0.60$ and will therefore not sign the contract.

QUICK CHECK 9.10.1

○○○○

Acme, Inc. fears that more than 20 percent of its management trainees quit within one year of completing the training program. Of the past 55 trainees, 12 have quit within 12 months. Set $\alpha = 0.10$.

a.   State the hypotheses.

b.   Determine the decision rule.

c.   Test the hypothesis.

Answer:

a. $H_0: \pi \leq 0.20$ $H_A: \pi > 0.20$

b.   Do not reject if $p < 0.27$. Reject the null if $p > 0.27$.

c.   Since $p = 0.22$, do not reject.

9.11 AN OPTIONAL METHOD OF HYPOTHESIS TESTING

In testing for the population mean or population proportion, a critical value is calculated for the sample mean or the sample proportion. This critical value for the sample statistic is regarded as significantly different from the hypothesized value for the population parameter. Of importance, all the measurements are expressed in the same units. If the original data are measured in feet, for example, then the entire problem is worked in feet. The critical values for the sample mean or the sample proportion, as well as the hypotheses, are stated in the same units. If, as in Example 9-10, the hypothesized value for the population mean is measured in pounds, the critical value for the sample mean is stated in pounds. Whatever standard is used to calibrate the original data, this same standard is used throughout the problem. In Example 9-7 the mean completion time for tax returns by Smith, Smith, Smith, and Jones was expressed as five days. Thus, the critical value for the sample mean was 4.75 days. The actual sample mean was found to be 4.70 days. In all instances the "measuring rod" was expressed in the same units as the original claim of the accounting firm—days.

An optional method of testing hypotheses can be proposed. This alternative procedure involves comparing the Z-value that can be calculated from the sample findings, called a Z_{test}, with a critical Z_c-value taken from the Z-table. This approach will yield the same results as the method of hypothesis testing examined above. However, it involves an entirely different process.

An Alternative Method of Testing Hypotheses
The method discussed earlier involves comparing the actual sample mean $\overline{X}$ to a critical value $\overline{X}_c$. This proposal entails a comparison of the Z_{test} value calculated on the basis of the sample findings to a critical value for Z obtained from the Z-table.

The Z-value which is to be calculated on the basis of sample findings is

$$Z_{\text{test}} = \frac{\overline{X} - \mu_H}{s_{\bar{x}}} \qquad (9.11)$$

In Example 9-7, the accounting firm of Smith, Smith, Smith, and Jones hypothesized that it took an average of five days to complete tax returns. $\overline{X}$ was found to be 4.7 days, s was 1.2 days, and $n = 64$. As shown in Figure 9-10, the critical value for the sample mean was 4.75 days. Since $\overline{X} = 4.70$ days < 4.75 days, the null was rejected. Notice that the axis is measuring the units in terms of days.

FIGURE 9-10   Comparing Hypothesis Tests

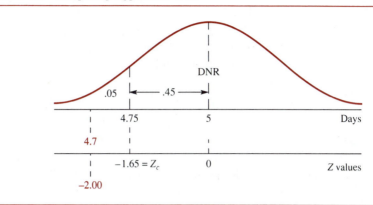

However, it is possible to recalibrate the axis in terms of Z units. The mean is set at $Z = 0$ under the assumption that there is no significant difference between the true mean and the null hypothesis.

Using Formula (9.11), we can calculate a test value for Z which is compared with the Z-value taken from the table. The value taken from the Z-table is based on a selected level of significance chosen by the researcher. If this Z_{test}-value falls in a rejection region, the null hypothesis is rejected.

Given the data for Smith, Smith, Smith, and Jones, the test value for Z becomes

$$Z_{test} = \frac{\overline{X} - \mu_H}{s_{\bar{x}}}$$

$$= \frac{4.7 - 5}{0.15} = -2.00$$

We must now determine a critical value for Z which will be taken from the Z-table. We want a value for Z that leaves $\alpha = 5$ percent of the area under the normal curve in the left tail. Since the table provides areas only from the mean to some value above it or below it, we must subtract 0.05 from 0.50. The resulting value of 0.4500 yields a critical Z of -1.65, as shown in Figure 9-10. It is a negative 1.65 because we are to the left of the mean.

If the sample findings produce a Z_{test} less than -1.65, it will be in the rejection region. Thus, the decision rule is

Decision Rule
Do not reject if $Z_{test} > -1.65$. Reject if $Z_{test} < -1.65$.

Since the test statistic of -2.00 is less than -1.65, the null is rejected just as it was the first time.

Another illustration of this alternative method can be provided by comparing the results of its use to those obtained in Example 9-8 for Honest John.

EXAMPLE 9-13 An Optional Method for Testing a Hypothesis:
A One-Tailed Test

Honest John claimed that customers could drive "at least 10,000 miles" without major repairs. A sample of $n = 100$ customers revealed a mean of 9,112 miles and a standard deviation of 207 miles.

SOLUTION:

His hypotheses were

$$H_0: \mu \geq 10,000$$

$$H_A: \mu < 10,000$$

and the critical value for $\overline{X}_c$ was 9,952 miles. In contrast, this optional method reveals

$$Z_{test} = \frac{\overline{X} - \mu_H}{s_{\bar{x}}}$$

$$= \frac{9,112 - 10,000}{20.7}$$

$$= -42.9$$

Since α was set at 0.01, the Z-value from the table is $0.05 - 0.01 = 0.4900$, which reveals a $Z_c = -2.33$. Again, the Z-value carries a negative sign because we are in the left tail.

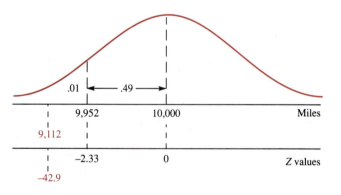

Decision Rule

Do not reject the null if the Z_{test} exceeds -2.33. Reject the null if the Z_{test} is less than -2.33.

STATISTICAL INTERPRETATION:

Since $-42.9 < -2.33$, we reject the null just as we did the first time.

Now try a right-tail test as patterned from Example 9-9 in which Honest John advertised that his customers could drive "more than 10,000" miles without major repairs.

EXAMPLE 9-14 An Optional Method for Testing a Hypothesis: A One-Tailed Test

From Example 9-9 the hypotheses were

$$H_0: \mu \leq 10{,}000$$

$$H_A: \mu > 10{,}000$$

The critical value was found to be $\overline{X}_c = 10{,}048$ miles. Since α was 0.01, the Z_c-value from the table is $+2.33$.

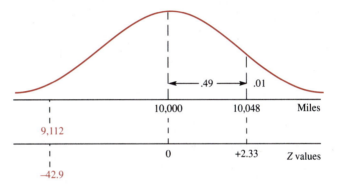

SOLUTION:
The test statistic is

$$Z_{\text{test}} = \frac{\overline{X} - \mu_H}{S_{\overline{x}}}$$

$$= \frac{9{,}112 - 10{,}000}{20.7}$$

$$= -42.9$$

Decision Rule

Do not reject the null if Z_{test} is less than 2.33. Reject the null if Z_{test} exceeds 2.33.

STATISTICAL INTERPRETATION:

Since $-42.9 < 2.33$, we do not reject the null that $\mu \leq 10{,}000$, and we dispute Honest John's claim that customers can drive more than 10,000 miles without repair. This, of course, is the same result we found in Example 9-9.

Using this alternative method to conduct a two-tailed test follows a similar pattern. For the purpose of comparison, the following illustration is based on Example 9-1, dealing with the Noah Fence Company.

EXAMPLE 9-15 An Optional Method of Testing a Hypothesis:
A Two-Tailed Test

In Example 9-1 Noah hypothesized that the average completion time for his jobs was 27 days. The sample mean for $n = 50$ jobs was 25.3 days, and $s = 2.1$. The hypotheses were specified as

$$H_0: \mu = 27$$

$$H_A: \mu \neq 27$$

The values for $\overline{X}_c$ were calculated to be 26.70 and 27.58. The decision rule specified that the null should be rejected if the sample mean was less than 26.70 or greater than 27.58.

Based on a 95 percent level of confidence, this alternative method specifies a critical Z-value taken from the table to be $0.95/2 = 0.4750$, which calls for $Z_c = \pm 1.96$.

SOLUTION:

Under the alternative method of testing the null hypothesis, the decision rule is written as

Decision Rule

Do not reject the null if Z_{test} is between -1.96 and $+1.96$. Reject the null if Z_{test} is below -1.96 or above $+1.96$.

The Z_{test} value is

$$Z_{test} = \frac{X - \mu_H}{s_{\bar{x}}}$$

$$= \frac{25.3 - 27}{0.297}$$

$$= -5.72$$

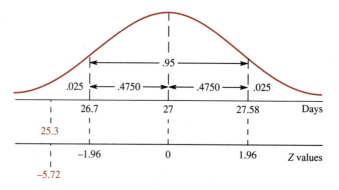

STATISTICAL INTERPRETATION:

Since Z_{test} -5.72 is less than -1.96, we are in the lower rejection region and reach the same conclusion as in Example 9-1. Noah's hypothesis that $\mu = 27$ is rejected.

Tests for proportions and those involving small samples can be adjusted accordingly to account for this alternative method.

As you can see, this optional method yields the same results. However, it is argued here that it is less desirable than the first method illustrated because the first method allows the researcher to work in the same familiar, common terms and units as the original data, such as days, pounds, or miles. The optional method, on the other hand, requires use of the more abstract Z units, which are somewhat vague and less easily understood.

However, we must master both methods because each is used in the examination of different statistical tests. The first method is required in the calculation of β, which is the probability of a Type II error. This issue will be explored shortly. The alternative method, on the other hand, is essential in the determination of p-values, a concept we now examine.

QUICK CHECK 9.11.1

○○○○   Use the optional method to test the hypothesis in Quick Check 9.8.1.

Answer: Do not reject the null if $Z_{\text{test}} < 1.65$. Reject if $Z_{\text{test}} > 1.65$. $Z_{\text{test}} = 1.74$. Therefore reject the null.

QUICK CHECK 9.11.2

Use the optional method to test the hypothesis in Quick Check 9.5.1.

Answer: Do not reject the null if $-1.65 < Z_{\text{test}} > 1.65$. Otherwise, reject the null. $Z_{\text{test}} = -1.41$. Therefore do not reject.

A.   CALCULATION AND INTERPRETATION OF p-VALUES

The alternative method to hypothesis testing is worthy of attention because it facilitates the reporting of p-values. These p-values are of growing importance, owing to the increased use of computers in business and the fact that many computer packages report these p-values.

The p-value is a probability measure. More specifically, it is the probability that the sample mean will be at least as extreme (either as high or as low) as the one you actually got, if the hypothesized value for μ is indeed true. The p-value measures the likelihood that, if the population mean does equal the hypothesized value, the sample findings will be at least as extreme as those actually reported by your sample. Thus, under the condition that the null hypothesis is true, the p-value measures the probability that the sample findings will be (1) at least as high or (2) at least as low as those actually reported by your sample. Perhaps more important, the p-value is the smallest value for α at which you can reject the null hypothesis.

---

p-value
The p-value is the smallest level of significance at which the null hypothesis can be rejected.

The following discussion illustrates the manner in which these *p*-values can be calculated. In a 1989 article appearing in *The Wall Street Journal,* Denton James, an employee for Opus, Inc., which specializes in the sale of gold bullion to investors, described his efforts to examine the average monthly income Opus employees received by participating in their employee stock option plan (ESOP). Denton felt that the average monthly receipt from the plan was at least $100 ($\mu \geq 100$). Assume that he tested this claim at the 5 percent level.

The proper set of hypotheses would be

$$H_0: \mu \geq 100$$

$$H_A: \mu < 100$$

Assume further that a sample of 100 employees revealed a mean of $91.64, with a standard deviation of $40. The alternative method of testing hypotheses must be completed before we can calculate the *p*-value. We have

$$Z_{test} = \frac{\overline{X} - \mu_H}{s_{\bar{x}}}$$

$$= \frac{91.64 - 100}{4}$$

$$= -2.09$$

With α set at 0.05, the decision rule becomes

Decision Rule
Do not reject the null if Z_{test} exceeds -1.65. Reject the null if Z_{test} is less than -1.65.

Figure 9-11 illustrates.

Since $-2.09 < -1.65$, it would appear unlikely that the mean monthly income from the ESOP is at least $100, and we reject the null that $\mu \geq 100$. With the hypothesis test completed, it is possible to calculate the corresponding *p*-value. Consider Example 9-16.

FIGURE 9-11   An Alternative Hypothesis Test

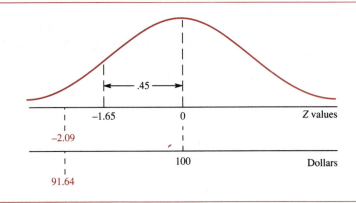

EXAMPLE 9-16 *p*-Values for Hypothesis Testing: One-Tailed Test

Upon the rejection of James's hypothesis, he wishes to determine the associated *p*-value. This *p*-value will tell James the probability of obtaining a sample mean as low or lower than the \$91.64 he actually got if the null hypothesis that $\mu \geq 100$ were indeed true.

SOLUTION:

From the Z-table it can be seen that the area from the mean ($Z = 0$) to the Z_{test} value of -2.09 is 0.4817. The figure illustrates that the area below -2.09 is therefore $0.5 - 0.4817 = 0.0183$. Thus, if the mean interest income is indeed \$100, the probability of getting sample results which will produce a Z-value of -2.09 or less is only 1.83 percent. This value of 1.83 percent is the *p*-value associated with James's test.

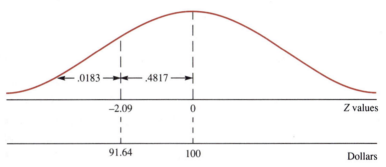

STATISTICAL INTERPRETATION:

Given the sample results of $Z_{\text{test}} = -2.09$, it is therefore unlikely that $\mu \geq \$100$. There is only a 1.83 percent chance that if the null were true and $\mu \geq 100$, sample findings would generate a Z_{test} of -2.09 or lower.

Furthermore, since by definition the *p*-value is the lowest level of significance at which the null hypothesis can be rejected, we can conclude that the null will be rejected at all levels of significance above 1.83 percent. It would be rejected if α was set equal to 5 percent, but it would not be rejected if it were tested at the 1 percent level of significance. If any α-value less than 1.83 percent is selected, the Z_{test} of -2.09 will fall in the DNR region.

To prove that the null would not be rejected at any α-value below 1.83 percent, let us test James's hypothesis at the 1 percent level. A left-tailed test with a level of significance of 1 percent carries a critical Z-value of -2.33 as Figure 9-12 demonstrates. The decision rule is

Decision Rule
Do not reject if $Z_{\text{test}} > -2.33$. Reject if $Z_{\text{test}} < -2.33$.

The Z_{test} value of -2.09 produced by James's sample is now in the DNR region. If an α-value is selected that is less than the *p*-value, the null is not rejected. If any α-value less than 1.83 percent is chosen, it *automatically* puts Z_{test} of -2.09 in the DNR region. The *p*-value is the lowest level of significance at which the null will be rejected.

FIGURE 9-12   If α Is Less than the p-Value

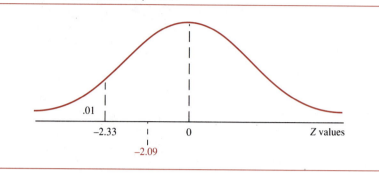

If James alters his estimation of the income available from the ESOP to "the average income is \$100," the test becomes a two-tailed test centered at \$100. The p-value for a two-sided test is twice that for a comparable one-sided test, because a two-sided test has a rejection region in both tails and we must divide the α-value by 2 to determine the area in each tail.

EXAMPLE 9-17 p-Values for Hypothesis Testing: Two-Tailed Test

James respecifies his claim as noted above and requests a test of the hypothesis and the appropriate p-value.

SOLUTION:

The hypotheses become

$$H_0: \mu = 100$$

$$H_A: \mu \neq 100$$

Given the same sample results as before, we find

$$Z_{\text{test}} = \frac{91.64 - 100}{4}$$

$$= -2.09$$

The p-value is the probability that $Z < -2.09$ plus the probability that $Z > +2.09$. The p-value is $(0.0183)(2) = 0.0366$, since α is divided by 2 to get the area in the rejection regions. Holding α constant at 0.05, the critical Z-values are $0.95/2 = 0.4750$, which from the table yields $Z = \pm 1.96$.

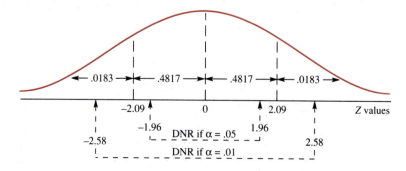

Decision Rule
Reject H_0: $\mu = 100$ if Z_{test} is less than -1.96 or more than ± 1.96. Do not reject the null if the Z_{test} is between -1.96 and $+1.96$.

STATISTICAL INTERPRETATION:
Given the findings above, at the 5 percent level we reject the null that $\mu = 100$. The chance of getting a Z_{test} as extreme as ± 2.09 is 0.0366 if μ does equal \$100. Thus, 3.66 percent is the lowest value at which you can reject the null. Since α was set at 5 percent > 3.66 percent, we reject the null. We would not reject the null if the test was performed at any level of significance below 3.66, such as 1 percent. Notice that the use of $\alpha = 0.01$ produces critical Z-values of ± 2.58 and thereby automatically places the Z_{test} of -2.09 in the DNR region.

In addition to the fact that p-values are commonly reported by most computer programs these days, there is another reason why they are important. If a researcher merely reports that a null hypothesis was either rejected or not rejected at a particular level of significance of, say, 5 percent, he or she restricts anyone who wishes to use these findings to that significance level. Nothing is revealed about the status of the null hypothesis at other levels of significance.

However, by reporting the p-value, additional information is conveyed. Remember, the p-value is the smallest value for α at which you can reject the null hypothesis given your sample findings. Thus, since $p = 1.83$ percent in Example 9-16, the null of H_0: $\mu \geq 100$ would not have been rejected if the test had been conducted at the 1 percent level since 1 percent < 1.8 percent. The same is true for Example 9-17.

QUICK CHECK 9.11.3
○○○○   Determine the p-value associated with Quick Check 9.11.1.
Answer: $p = 0.0409$

QUICK CHECK 9.11.4
          Determine the p-value associated with Quick Check 9.11.2.
Answer: $p = 0.1586$

9.12   TYPE I AND TYPE II ERRORS

We noted earlier that in testing a hypothesis we run the risk of committing two types of mistakes. A **Type I error** occurs if we reject a true hypothesis. On the other hand, the failure to reject a false hypothesis is called a **Type II error**.

It can be shown that the α-value for a test is the probability of committing a Type I error. That is, $P(\text{Type I error}) = \alpha$. For example, the hypothesis by the Noah Fence Company was

$$H_0: \mu = 27$$

$$H_A: \mu \neq 27$$

An α-value of 5 percent produced rejection regions as shown in Figure 9-13 of those areas below 26.70 days and above 27.58 days.

FIGURE 9-13   Type I Error

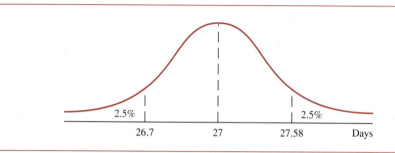

This means that if μ really is 27, there is still a probability of 5 percent (the value of α) that a sample could be selected at random which would yield a mean falling within one of the rejection regions. This would cause us to reject the true null of $\mu = 27$. This would constitute a Type I error. Thus, the probability of a Type I error is equal to α.

A.   CALCULATING β (THE PROBABILITY OF A TYPE II ERROR)

Once the α-value is specified, the β-value is fixed for any given sample size. This is not to suggest, however, that like the α-value there is only one β-value.

In fact, since a Type II error occurs when we fail to reject a false null hypothesis, there is a different β-value for each true value of the population mean. If we assume $\mu = 10,000$ and it is really 11,000, we get one β-value. If it is really 12,000, we get a different β-value, and so on, for any true value of μ.

This is perhaps best illustrated with a one-tailed test. In Example 9-9, Honest John hypothesized

$$H_0: \mu \leq 10,000 \text{ miles}$$

$$H_A: \mu > 10,000 \text{ miles}$$

with $n = 100$, $s = 207$, and $\alpha = 0.01$.

The test of the hypothesis concluded that we would not reject $\mu \leq 10,000$ if $\overline{X}$ was found to be less than $\overline{X}_c = 10,048$.

Decision Rule
Do not reject if $\overline{X} < 10,084$. Reject if $\overline{X} > 10,048$.

The question then becomes, if the null hypothesis is false and the population mean is greater than 10,000, what is the probability of not rejecting the null and thereby committing a Type II error? We would not reject the false null if our sample produced a mean less than 10,048. We must then determine the probability of getting a sample mean less than 10,048.

The answer depends on what μ really is. If the population mean is one amount, the probability $\overline{X} < 10,048$ will be a certain level. If the population mean is some other amount, the probability $\overline{X} < 10,048$ will be different. Thus, the probability the sample mean will be in the DNR region depends on what the true value for μ really is. If the true population mean is 10,020, for example, we want to find the probability of getting a sample mean less than the critical value of $\overline{X}_c = 10,048$, which would cause us to not reject the false hypothesis of $\mu \leq 10,000$. The process is illustrated in Figure 9-14. Figure 9-14(a) demonstrates the distribution under the assumption that $\mu = 10,000$. Since α was set at 1 percent, the critical value of $\overline{X}_c = 10,048$ cuts off 1 percent of the right tail. However, if the true but unknown mean is actually 10,020, the distribution would appear as in Figure 9-14(b).

FIGURE 9-14   Calculating β

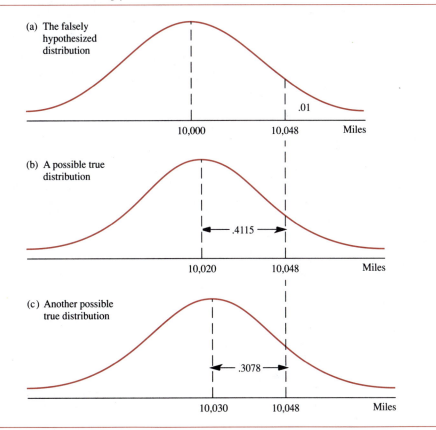

We must then find the probability of taking a sample with a mean less than 10,048, which would cause us to not reject the false null, if the population mean is actually $\mu = 10,020$. If the true mean is 10,020, the distribution would look like Figure 9-14(b). The probability of finding a sample mean less than the critical value of 10,048 is that area to the left of $\overline{X}_c = 10,048$. That is, if the distribution is centered at 10,020, then the probability of not rejecting the false null of $\mu \le 10,000$ is that area below 10,048 in (b). We must find the area from 10,020 to 10,048 in (b), which is then added to 0.5.

We simply calculate the probability $10,020 < \overline{X} < 10,048$ if $\mu = 10,020$. Using the Z formula,

$$Z = \frac{\overline{X} - \mu_H}{s_{\bar{x}}}$$

$$= \frac{10,048 - 10,020}{207/\sqrt{100}}$$

$$= 1.35, \text{ or an area of } 0.4115$$

There is therefore a 91.15 percent $(0.5 + 0.4115)$ chance that if $\mu = 10,020$, we can still take a sample yielding an $\overline{X}$ less than 10,048, which will cause us to not reject the false hypothesis that $\mu \le 10,000$. That is, $\beta = 91.15$ percent.

It can be seen that an actual value for μ other than 10,020 would result in a different β. There is a different β-value for each true value of μ.

If $\mu = 10,030$, as shown in 9-14(c), the probability of a Type II error = $P(\overline{X} < 10,048)$. Then,

$$Z = \frac{10,048 - 10,030}{207/\sqrt{100}}$$

$$= 0.87, \text{ or an area of } 0.3078.$$

Thus, β is 0.8078, or 80.78 percent. Notice that, since the difference between the hypothesized value of μ of 10,000 and the actual value of 10,030 is greater than in (b), the probability of a Type II error is less. The greater the difference between the falsely hypothesized mean and the true value of the mean, the easier it is to distinguish one from the other, and the less likely we are to commit a Type II error. Thus, the greater the difference between the true value for μ and the hypothesized value, the lower β will be.

The **power** of a test is $1 - \beta$. It represents the probability of correctly rejecting a false hypothesis. This is more fully explored in the next section.

B. SELECTING AN α-VALUE

When conducting a hypothesis test, you can select the α-value, or level of significance, you prefer. This selection should be done with a purpose in mind. Specifically, if a Type I error might prove to be more costly than a Type II error, you would want to minimize the probability of committing a Type I error. Since the probability of a Type I error is equal to the α-value of a test, this means you should choose a low

α-value, say, 1 percent. Certainly, an α-value of no more than 5 percent should be used. On the other hand, if a Type II error may prove to be more costly, a higher α-value such as 10 percent might be called for.

For example, Coco Crunchy Crispies wanted to put 36 ounces in their cereal boxes. If their hypothesis test that $\mu = 36$ resulted in a rejection of the null, they had to shut down the entire production line and readjust the automatic fillers. If shutting down the production line when μ is 36 (a type I error) is an extremely costly mistake, we would want to minimize the probability of doing so by choosing a low value for α such as 1 percent. However, if continuing to run the production line when μ is not 36 (a Type II error) is the more harmful mistake, then we should choose a higher α-value. The choice for our α-value depends largely on which error, Type I or Type II, we most want to avoid.

QUICK CHECK 9.12.1

OOOO

Bob has hypothesized that the population mean is equal to or greater than 17. A sample of 50 reveals a standard deviation of 4.2, and α is set at 5 percent. If the unknown mean is actually 15.2, what is the probability Bob will commit a Type II error?

Answer: 0.0823

9.13   THE OPERATING CHARACTERISTIC CURVE AND THE POWER CURVE

As we noted, when the null is false there are an infinite number of β-values. There is a different β-value for each possible true value for μ. If we were to calculate the β-value for several possible true values of μ, it would be possible to construct an **operating characteristic curve** for the β-values. Figure 9-15 does this for the Honest John case.

FIGURE 9-15   Operating Characteristic Curve for H_0: $\mu = 10,000$

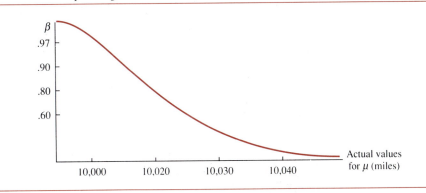

> **Operating Characteristic Curve**
> An operating characteristic curve shows the various probabilities of
> committing a Type II error for different true values of the population mean.

As you can see, the further the actual μ is from the hypothesized value of 10,000,
the lower the β-value and the less the probability of committing a Type II error. If
μ is 10,020, the probability of a Type II error is 0.9115. If μ is actually 10,030, we are
even less likely to confuse it with a value of 10,000, and the probability of not rejecting H_0: $\mu = 10,000$ is only 0.8078, as shown by the computations and Figure 9-16.

$$Z = \frac{\overline{X} - \mu_H}{s_{\bar{x}}}$$

$$Z = \frac{10,000 - 10,030}{207/\sqrt{100}}$$

$$= 0.87, \text{ or an area of } 0.3078$$

FIGURE 9-16   Calculating β

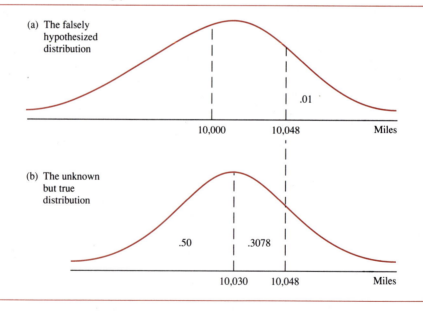

In most cases the probability of not rejecting a false hypothesis is larger than the
probability of rejecting a true hypothesis. That is, $\beta > \alpha$. This is why we can say
that a decision based on a rejected hypothesis is more conclusive and reliable than a
decision based on a hypothesis which is not rejected.

Of course, given several β-values, we can easily calculate the several corresponding power values since **power** $= 1 - \beta$. A power curve such as that in Figure 9-17 can then be drawn. Given these curves, you can then estimate the power and β-values for any possible value of μ.

FIGURE 9-17   A Power Curve

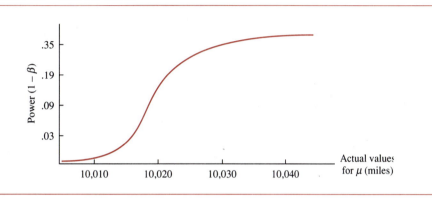

9.14   EFFECT OF SAMPLE SIZE ON β

We have already seen that an increase in sample size will reduce $\sigma_{\bar{x}}$, the standard error of the sampling distribution. This fact can be expanded to β-values. As more information becomes available from a larger sample and α is held constant, the probability, β, of committing a Type II error will decrease. That is, for a given α-value, the chances of making a Type II error will go down as the sample size goes up.

9.15   CHOOSING THE CORRECT TEST

There are many decisions to be made in conducting a hypothesis test. You must determine if a Z-test or a t-test is appropriate. Then it is essential that the proper formula be used to complete the test. Figure 9-18 will assist in making many of these decisions.

9.16   USING CONFIDENCE INTERVALS TO TEST HYPOTHESES

In the previous chapter we examined confidence intervals and the manner in which they can be used to solve many business-related problems. Our study of inferential statistics was broadened to include hypothesis tests in this chapter. The impression was given that these two powerful tools of statistical analysis were separate and

FIGURE 9-18   Selecting the Proper Test Procedure for a Normal Population (The procedures shown here are for two-tailed tests. The proper adjustments must be made if a one-tailed test is desired.)

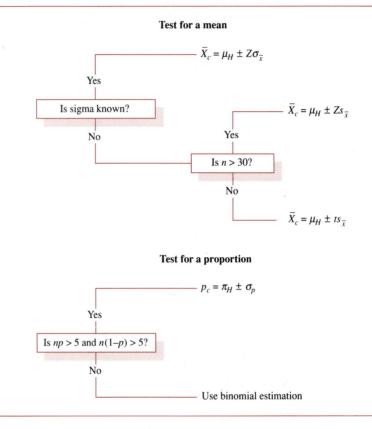

Test for a mean

$$\bar{X}_c = \mu_H \pm Z\sigma_{\bar{x}}$$

Yes

Is sigma known?

No

$$\bar{X}_c = \mu_H \pm Zs_{\bar{x}}$$

Yes

Is $n > 30$?

No

$$\bar{X}_c = \mu_H \pm ts_{\bar{x}}$$

Test for a proportion

$$p_c = \pi_H \pm \sigma_p$$

Yes

Is $np > 5$ and $n(1-p) > 5$?

No

Use binomial estimation

distinct concepts, and that each was used under a special set of circumstances. Indeed this is true. Confidence intervals are used to form an estimate of an unknown parameter, usually μ or π. Given the results of the interval, we then have more complete knowledge about the world in which we live and work. The hypothesis test, on the other hand, allows us to test some preconceived idea about the value of a parameter.

It may then surprise you to learn that we can use a confidence interval to test a hypothesis. Although each tool has its unique place in statistical analysis, and the proper time when each is to be used should not be confused, it is helpful to recognize the interaction between confidence intervals and hypothesis tests.

For example, suppose you hypothesize that the mean number of Western tourists crossing the border into Hungary each hour is 1,120. You wish to test the hypothesis that

$$H_0: \mu = 1,120$$

$$H_A: \mu \neq 1,120$$

If a confidence interval formed on the basis of sample data contains the hypothesized value of 1,120, the null hypothesis is not rejected. If the interval does not contain 1,120, the null is rejected.

Consider our earlier example in which Coco Crunchy Crispies wanted to test the hypothesis that the mean weight of the cereal in their boxes was 36 ounces.

$$H_0: \mu = 36$$
$$H_A: \mu \neq 36$$

A sample of $n = 100$ boxes revealed a mean of $\overline{X} = 37.6$ ounces and a standard deviation of $s = 3$ ounces. Testing at the 5 percent level required a Z of 1.96. Critical values for $\overline{X}$ used in the hypothesis test were

$$\overline{X}_c = \mu_H \pm Z s_{\overline{x}}$$
$$= 36 \pm (1.96)(0.3)$$
$$35.41\text{--------------}36.59$$

Decision Rule

Do not reject if $35.41 < \overline{X} < 36.59$. Reject otherwise.

Since the sample produced a mean of $\overline{X} = 37.6$, the null was rejected.

This same hypothesis can be tested by forming a confidence interval. Recall from Chapter 8 that a confidence interval is

$$\text{C.I. for } \mu = \overline{X} \pm Z s_{\overline{x}}$$
$$= 37.6 \pm (1.96)(0.3)$$
$$37.01\text{--------------}38.19$$

Since the interval does not contain the hypothesized value of 36, the null is rejected.

A similar interaction exists between confidence intervals and hypothesis tests for the population proportion.

9.17 SOLVED PROBLEMS

1. **America's Richest Man** *U.S. News & World Report* carried an article about the success Wal-Mart has had. It is now the nation's largest retail chain, growing from a single discount store in tiny Rogers, Arkansas, to 1,300 stores in 25 states. This success has earned Sam Walton, founder and largest shareholder, the title of America's richest man. Annual sales revenues are estimated to average $15 million per store.

   a. If a sample of 120 stores is randomly selected and a mean sales revenue of $15.39 million is found with a standard deviation of $2.9 million, is the hypothesis that $\mu = \$15$ million supported at the 10 percent level of significance?

$$H_0: \mu = 15$$
$$H_A: \mu \neq 15$$

$$\overline{X}_c = 15 \pm (1.65)\frac{2.9}{\sqrt{120}}$$

$$14.56\text{--------------}15.44$$

Decision Rule

Do not reject null if $14.56 < \overline{X} < 15.44$. Reject null if $\overline{X} < 14.56$ or if $\overline{X} > 15.44$.
Conclusion: Do not reject.

b.   Calculate the *p*-value associated with the findings.

$$Z_{test} = \frac{15.39 - 15}{2.9/\sqrt{120}} = 1.47, \text{ or an area of } 0.4292$$

$$p\text{-value} = 0.5 - 0.4292 = 0.0708(2) = 0.1416$$

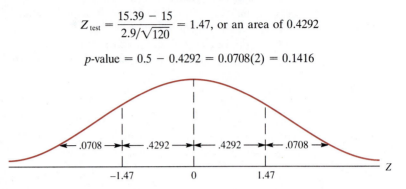

The null will be rejected only at levels of significance above 14.16 percent.

c.   If μ is actually \$14.8 million, what is the probability of a Type II error?

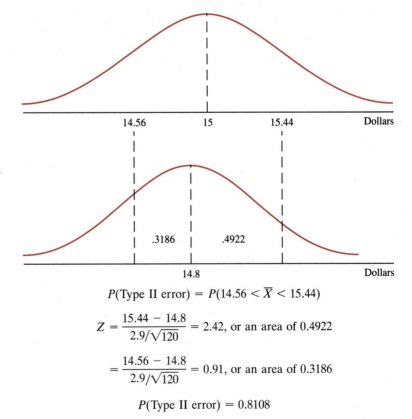

$$P(\text{Type II error}) = P(14.56 < \overline{X} < 15.44)$$

$$Z = \frac{15.44 - 14.8}{2.9/\sqrt{120}} = 2.42, \text{ or an area of } 0.4922$$

$$= \frac{14.56 - 14.8}{2.9/\sqrt{120}} = 0.91, \text{ or an area of } 0.3186$$

$$P(\text{Type II error}) = 0.8108$$

2.   **America's Richest Man—Revisited** Given the conditions described in the preceding problem, recalculate parts (a), (b), and (c) if the estimate of sales revenues had been expressed as "revenues do not exceed \$15 million per store."
   a. $H_0: \mu \leq 15$

   $H_A: \mu > 15$

$$\overline{X}_c = 15 + (1.28)\frac{2.9}{\sqrt{120}}$$

$$= 15.34$$

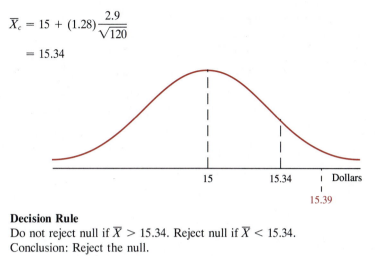

15   15.34   Dollars

15.39

Decision Rule
Do not reject null if $\overline{X} > 15.34$. Reject null if $\overline{X} < 15.34$.
Conclusion: Reject the null.

b.

$$Z_{\text{test}} = \frac{15.39 - 15}{2.9/\sqrt{120}} = 1.47, \text{ or an area of } 0.4292$$

$$p\text{-value} = 0.5 - 0.4292 = 0.0708$$

.4292   .0708

0   1.47   Dollars

c.

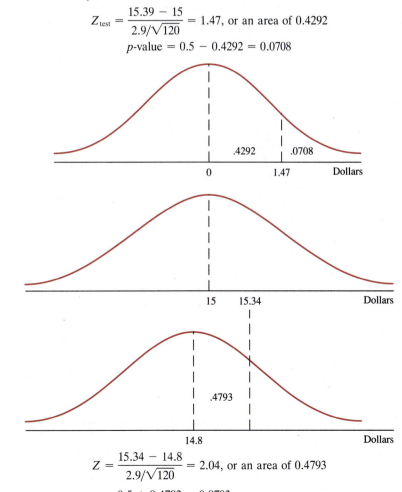

15   15.34   Dollars

.4793

14.8   Dollars

$$Z = \frac{15.34 - 14.8}{2.9/\sqrt{120}} = 2.04, \text{ or an area of } 0.4793$$

$$p = 0.5 + 0.4793 = 0.9793$$

3. **Tagging Salmon** The U.S. Fish and Wildlife Service tagged salmon spawning in the Hood River near Seattle to determine migration patterns. The service felt that 40 percent of the fish returned there each year.

a. If a sample of 2,022 revealed 822 had been tagged the previous year, is the service's hypothesis supported at the 5 percent level?

$$H_0: \pi = 0.40$$

$$H_A: \pi \neq 0.40$$

$$p_c = 0.4 \pm 1.96 \sqrt{\frac{(0.4)(0.6)}{2,022}}$$

$$0.38 \text{---------------} 0.42$$

Decision Rule

Do not reject if $0.38 < p < 0.42$

Conclusion: $822/2,022 = 0.41$. Do not reject.

b. Calculate the p-value associated with the findings.

$$Z = \frac{0.41 - 0.4}{\sqrt{\frac{(0.4)(0.6)}{2,022}}} = 0.92, \text{ or an area of } 0.3212$$

$$p = (0.5 - 0.3212)(2) = 0.3576$$

The null can be rejected only at levels of significance equal to or greater than 0.3576.

c. Calculate the probability of a Type II error if the true proportion is 0.38.

$$P(\text{Type II error}) = P(0.38 < p < 0.42)$$

$$Z = \frac{0.42 - 0.38}{\sqrt{(0.4)(0.6)/2,022}} = 3.67, \text{ or an area of } 0.5$$

$$P(\text{Type II error}) = 0.5$$

4. **Tagging More Fish** From the preceding problem, if the service hypothesized that more than 40 percent of the fish returned each year, what are your responses to parts (a), (b), and (c)?

a.
$$H_0: \pi \leq 0.40$$

$$H_A: \pi > 0.40$$

$$p_c = 0.4 + 1.65 \sqrt{\frac{(0.4)(0.6)}{2,022}} = 0.42$$

Decision Rule
Do not reject if $p < 0.42$. Reject null if $p > 0.42$.
Conclusion: Do not reject.

b.
$$Z = \frac{0.41 - 0.40}{\sqrt{(0.4)(0.6)/2,022}} = 0.92, \text{ or an area of } 0.3212$$

$$p = 0.5 - 0.3212 = 0.1788$$

c.

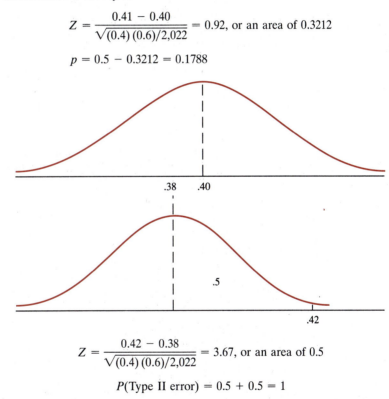

$$Z = \frac{0.42 - 0.38}{\sqrt{(0.4)(0.6)/2,022}} = 3.67, \text{ or an area of } 0.5$$

$$P(\text{Type II error}) = 0.5 + 0.5 = 1$$

If the true proportion is 0.38, it is almost a certainty that the null will mistakenly not be rejected.

9.18 WHAT YOU SHOULD HAVE LEARNED FROM THIS CHAPTER

The material provides the necessary information to formulate and test hypotheses regarding parameters. You should now have the skills to distinguish between a one-tailed test and a two-tailed test, and to determine if a Z-test or a t-test should be used. Noting the difference between a test for a mean and for a proportion is also crucial. In addition, calculating p-values and the probability of a Type II error, as well as their interpretation, should also be a part of your statistical expertise.

9.19 COMPUTER APPLICATIONS

In contrast to the method of testing a hypothesis about a population mean as discussed in the chapter, when the test is performed on the computer the researcher does not specify an α-value, because most computer programs print out a p-value, which allows determination of the level of significance. Nevertheless, before running the test you should select a level of significance on which to base your ultimate decision to reject or not reject the null hypothesis. Your criterion for the decision should not be based on the results. Only Minitab lends itself to testing a hypothesis about a single population.

The proper use of Minitab to test a hypothesis depends on whether a Z-test or a t-test is to be conducted. If a large sample is used or if the population standard is known, the Z-statistic is called for. In this event the commands are

```
READ C1
    data go here in column one
END
ZTEST hypothesized mean    standard deviation C1
```

Assume a sample of $n = 45$ produced a mean of 53.4 and a standard deviation of 7.03. Since $n > 30$, a Z-test can be used. To conduct a two-tailed test for the hypothesis that the population mean equals 55.5, the last command shown above would be

```
ZTEST 55.5 7.03 C1
```

The resulting printout is revealed in Minitab 1.

Notice that the p-value of 0.045 indicates that the hypothesis that the population mean equals 55.5 is rejected at the 5 percent level but not at the 1 percent level. If a one-tailed test is desired, a subcommand must be added. A left-tailed test is specified as

```
ZTEST 55.5 7.03 C1;
ALTE −1.
```

while a right-tailed test requires

```
ZTEST 55.5 7.03 C1;
ALTE 1.
```

Notice that the left-tailed test requires a negative sign, -1. The p-value is, as expected, one-half that in the two-tailed test and suggests that the null be rejected for level of significance above 2.3 percent.

If the sample size is small and the population standard deviation is not known, a t-test must be performed. Assume a sample of $n = 20$ is entered in column 2 of a Minitab worksheet and yields a mean of 32.35. A t-test involves replacing the ZTEST in the above set of

MINITAB 1

```
MTB > DESC C1

              N      MEAN    MEDIAN    TRMEAN    STDEV    SEMEAN
C1           45     53.40     52.00     53.34     7.03     1.05

            MIN       MAX        Q1        Q3
C1        41.00     68.00     47.00     58.50

MTB > ZTEST 55.5 7.03 C1

TEST OF MU = 55.500 VS MU N.E. 55.500
THE ASSUMED SIGMA = 7.03

              N      MEAN     STDEV   SE MEAN        Z    P VALUE
C1           45    53.400     7.030     1.048    -2.00      0.045

MTB > ZTEST 55.5 7.03 C1;
SUBC> ALTE -1.

TEST OF MU = 55.500 VS MU L.T. 55.500
THE ASSUMED SIGMA = 7.03

              N      MEAN     STDEV   SE MEAN        Z    P VALUE
C1           45    53.400     7.030     1.048    -2.00      0.023
```

commands with a TTEST command. If the hypothesis that the population mean equals 30 is to be tested, the command becomes

```
TTEST 30 C2
```

Notice that no value for the standard deviation is specified.

If a one-tailed test is performed, the appropriate subcommand as described above must be entered. A right-tailed test is called for by

```
TEST 30 C2;
ALTE 1.
```

LIST OF SYMBOLS AND TERMS

$\overline{X}_c$ The critical value for the sample mean which is compared with the actual sample mean in deciding whether to reject the null.

p_c The critical value for the sample proportion which is compared with the actual sample proportion in deciding whether to reject the null.

α The level of significance in a hypothesis test and the probability of a Type I error, i.e., of rejecting a true H_0.

β The probability of a Type II error, i.e., not rejecting a false H_0.

Power of a test Probability of correctly rejecting a false hypothesis. Power $= 1 - \beta$

$$\overline{X}_c = \mu_H \pm Zs_{\bar{x}} \tag{9.1}$$

Used to calculate the upper and lower critical values for the sample mean in a two-tailed hypothesis test of μ (large sample).

$$\overline{X}_c = \mu_H \pm Z\sigma_{\bar{x}} \tag{9.2}$$

Used to calculate the upper and lower critical values for the sample mean in a two-tailed hypothesis test of μ when σ is known (large sample).

$$p_c = \pi_H \pm Z\sigma_p \tag{9.3}$$

Used to calculate the upper and lower critical values for the sample proportion in a two-tailed hypothesis test of π (large sample).

$$\sigma_p = \sqrt{\frac{\pi_H(1 - \pi_H)}{n}} \tag{9.4}$$

Used to calculate the standard error of the proportion in a hypothesis test for π.

$$\overline{X}_c = \mu_H + Zs_{\bar{x}} \tag{9.5}$$

Used to calculate the critical value for the sample mean in a right-tailed test for μ (large sample).

$$\overline{X}_c = \mu_H - Zs_{\bar{x}} \tag{9.6}$$

Used to calculate the critical value for the sample mean in a left-tailed test for μ (large sample).

$$\overline{X}_c = \mu_H + ts_{\bar{x}} \tag{9.7}$$

Used to calculate the critical value for the sample mean in a right-tailed test for μ (small sample).

$$\overline{X}_c = \mu_H - ts_{\bar{x}} \tag{9.8}$$

Used to calculate the critical value for the sample mean in a left-tailed test for μ (small sample).

$$p_c = \pi_H + Z(\sigma_p) \tag{9.9}$$

Used to calculate the critical value for the sample proportion in a right-tailed test.

$$p_c = \pi_H - Z(\sigma_p) \tag{9.10}$$

Used to calculate the critical value for the sample proportion in a left-tailed test.

$$Z_{\text{test}} = \frac{\overline{X} - \mu_H}{s_{\bar{x}}} \tag{9.11}$$

Used to calculate a test Z-statistic in an optional test for μ.

CHAPTER EXERCISES

YOU MAKE THE DECISION

1. Ralph Root works in the garden center at the local K mart. In the effort to estimate the mean growth rate of the pansies they sell, Ralph is at a loss in trying to explain the role of the critical value in a hypothesis test. Help poor Ralph out.

CONCEPTUAL QUESTIONS

2. What does it mean for a sample finding to "differ significantly" from the hypothesized value?
3. What is meant by a Type I error? How does it affect the critical value of a test?
4. Describe the effect of an increase in the sample size on the
   a. probability of a Type I error.
   b. critical values.
   Illustrate your answer with the proper graphical work.
5. What is a Type II error, and what is its relationship to a Type I error? Is $P(\text{Type I}) + P(\text{Type II}) = 1$?
6. Why does an extremely low p-value mean that the null hypothesis will likely be rejected?
7. What impact will the sample standard deviation have on the critical values of a test?

PROBLEMS

In problems requiring a hypothesis test, clearly formulate all four steps of the test as cited in the chapter.

8. A candy distributor claims that her packages average 16 ounces of candy. A sample of 500 packages yields a mean of 15.75 ounces with a standard deviation of 3.4 ounces. Set $\alpha = 0.05$ and test the hypothesis.
9. In 1989, *The Wall Street Journal* discussed the strike at Eastern Airlines. Management argued that the unionists were getting paid an average hourly wage of $18.98. Is management supported at the 10 percent level if a sample of 250 employees average $18.10 with a standard deviation of $3.15?
10. A labor-management contract calls for an average daily output of 50 units. A sample of 150 days reveals a mean of 47.3 with a standard deviation of 5.7 units. Set $\alpha = 5$ percent and determine if this contract provision is fulfilled.
11. The Colonial Canning Company of Claremont, California, uses a machine to fill their 18-ounce cans of cumquats. If the machine performs improperly, it is readjusted. A sample of 50 cans is found to have a mean of 18.9 ounces with a standard deviation of 4.7 ounces. Should the machine be readjusted? Set $\alpha = 5$ percent.
12. From the previous problem, if a sample of 500 cans was taken, yielding the same mean and standard deviation as the smaller sample, should the machine be readjusted?
13. Since the two previous problems yield conflicting results, which do you believe? Why?
14. A *Fortune* article discussing the rising trend for employees to sue their companies for failure to meet promises regarding proposed health benefits concluded the average lawsuit was for $115,000. Forty-two suits averaged $114,412. Assume a standard deviation of $14,000. Is the hypothesis supported at the 7 percent level?

15. In the effort to defend his company from an age discrimination suit, Charles Peck found that a sample of 75 employees averaged 47.2 years of age with a standard deviation of 6.3. The American Civil Liberties Union threatened to file suit unless Peck's employees averaged 48.2, which was the mean for other companies in the industry. At the 5 percent level, should the ACLU initiate the suit?

16. A drug under consideration by the Federal Drug Administration must reduce blood pressure in cardiac patients by 13 points before it will be accepted for general use. In a test on 51 patients it lowered pressure by an average of 12.2 points with a standard deviation of 2.3 points. At the 1 percent level, should the FDA approve the drug?

17. *Auto Weekly* carried a claim by Toyota, Inc. that their cars averaged 38 mpg on the highway and 32 mpg in the city. Tests on 73 cars showed mileage in the city was 31.7 mpg with a standard deviation of 5.7 mpg, while highway mileage was 35.2 mpg with a standard deviation of 2.1 mpg. At the 5 percent level, what does this say about Toyota's advertising?

18. Members of the Strain and Sweat Health Club are distressed by a decision by the owner to limit racketball court reservations to an unacceptable time restriction. They claim that the average set of games lasts two hours. From 27 recent sets a mean of 1.82 hours is found with a standard deviation of 0.32 hour. The manager agrees to remove the time limit if members are correct in their assertion. Set $\alpha = 2$ percent. What should the manager do?

19. *Sports Illustrated* discussed the problems TV networks were having telecasting professional football games, due to variations in the amount of time it takes to play a game. Games that took additional time due to high scoring or numerous time-outs often ran into the time slot for the next program, while games that required less time left the networks with time gaps to fill. NBC decided to test the hypothesis that they should allot exactly 3.1 hours for a game. To test this hypothesis, times for 12 games were selected. The results, in hours, are shown here. If $\alpha = 1$ percent, what should NBC do?

Times (in hours) for 12 Professional
Football Games on NBC in 1989

2.91	3.19	3.05
3.21	3.09	3.19
3.12	2.98	3.17
2.93	2.95	3.14

20. The Santa Clara, California, police department has found that traffic officers should write an average of 27 traffic tickets per month. If an officer writes more than that, he is likely too zealous in the performance of his duties. If fewer tickets are handed out, the officer may not be doing a thorough job. To evaluate his officers, the police chief noted the number of tickets written by 15 officers. The results are shown here. At the 5 percent level, does it appear the police force is performing satisfactorily?

28	34	30
31	29	33
22	32	38
26	25	31
25	24	31

21. Mel's Mexicana Cafe offers diners a choice of chili dishes with a range of cayenne pepper including Sissy, He-Man, Stove Pipe, and Inferno. The recipe for Inferno calls for an average of at least five cayenne peppers in each bowl. A sample of 50 bowls revealed a mean of 4.7 peppers with a standard deviation of 0.27. At the 5 percent level, does it appear that Mel's high standards are being maintained?

22. A company policy at State Farm Insurance is to restrict the proportion of claims settled in favor of the insured to 25 percent. Of the past 1,122 policies, 242 fully compensated the insured. If $\alpha = 0.10$, is the policy being observed?

23. Due to grade inflation in which professors have been giving too many high grades, the dean insists that each professor fail 30 percent of his or her students. In a sample of 315 recent students, Professor Nodoze failed 112 students. Is the professor fulfilling the dean's requirement? Set $\alpha = 0.05$.

24. Given the dean's stipulation in the previous problem, the faculty argues that it unduly restricts their grading authority. The dean therefore relaxes his requirement by stating that the faculty must fail an average of 30 percent of the students. The failure rates for eight faculty are

$$0.27, 0.31, 0.32, 0.25, 0.33, 0.25, 0.26, 0.31$$

Is the dean going to be happy with these data? Set $\alpha = 0.01$.

25. A weight-reduction plan stipulates that 75 percent of the people placed on the plan should lose between 5 percent and 12 percent of their body weight within the first six weeks. If more than 75 percent lose the stipulated amount, the diet is too severe. If fewer than 75 percent of the participants lose the required amount, the diet is too lax. Of 450 people surveyed, 347 lost an amount within the tolerable range. At the 5 percent level, what does this say about the diet?

26. *Fortune* stated that RJR-Nabisco tries to ensure that 20 percent of its employees receive annual promotions, while 80 percent must wait at least another year. If this percentage is not observed, the promotion process is revised. Should this revision be undertaken if 157 out of a sample of 655 employees received promotions this year? Set $\alpha = 5$ percent.

27. The manager for the Whatchaneed market feels that 50 percent of his customers spend less than $10 during any visit to the store. Many of his pricing decisions are based on this assumption. He decides to test this assumption by sampling 50 customers whose total bills are shown here. What do these data reveal about the manager's pricing decisions? Set $\alpha = 5$ percent.

Total Bills in Dollars

18.17	21.12	4.12	8.73	8.42
7.17	17.18	27.18	2.17	7.12
2.08	6.12	2.17	6.42	9.17
4.17	2.12	8.15	12.18	2.63
18.02	9.99	3.02	8.84	21.22
8.73	10.00	0.65	17.17	18.42
4.12	5.12	11.12	11.17	4.82
8.15	5.12	3.32	17.89	5.55
5.15	12.12	4.83	11.12	11.11
17.15	18.17	10.12	8.92	17.83

28. Brach's Candies mixes their jelly bean candy so that 20 percent of the bags contain at least five colors of beans. Quality control examines 400 bags and finds that 87 contain more than five colors. At the 1 percent level, is this quality feature being met?

29. Biggie Burger claims that their deluxe special has at least 0.25 pound of beef. A sample of 100 burgers had a mean of 0.237 pound with a standard deviation of 0.04 pound. Is Biggie Burger guilty of false advertising at the 95 percent level of confidence?

30. Minit-Mart, a nationwide convenience store chain, stated in *The Wall Street Journal* that they will not open a store in any location unless median income in the neighborhood is at least $12,000. A survey of 200 families in a given neighborhood produces a mean income of $11,852 with a standard deviation of $1,517. Should they open the store if all other criteria for a desirable location are met? Set $\alpha = 1$ percent.

31. A tire manufacturer has been making snow tires in Akron, Ohio, for over 40 years. His best tire has averaged 52,500 miles with a standard deviation of 7,075 miles. A new tread design is thought to add additional wear to the tires. Sixty tires with the new design are tested, revealing a mean of 54,112 miles with a standard deviation of 7,912 miles. At the 5 percent level, can it be said that the new tread adds to tire wear? (Note: In addition to the sample standard deviation of 7,912, it happens that the population standard deviation of 7,075 is also known. Which one should be used in the calculations? Why?)

32. In a *Fortune* article concerning R. J. Reynolds' leveraged buyout (LBO) of Nabisco in an attempt to diversify out of the tobacco industry, it was alleged that each bondholder suffered a paper loss of over $43,000. If a sample of 343 bondholders has a mean of $45,912 with a standard deviation of $17,112, is the article correct with 90 percent confidence?

33. Industrial espionage is a growing problem. *Business Week* reported that former employees of Du Pont demanded that the chemical firm pay a ransom of $10 million, or competitors would be given the company's secret for making Lycra, the popular fiber used in underwear, bathing suits, and other clothing. It has been estimated that corporate extortion cost companies an average of more than $3.5 million. If 75 cases of this nature are examined and found to average $3.71 million with a standard deviation of $1.21 million, is that estimate supported at the 10 percent level?

34. When Eastern Airlines filed for protection from creditors under Chapter 11 bankruptcy laws in 1989, it became evident that many of the nation's major corporations were in financial trouble. During a Senate subcommittee hearing, Senator Kennedy estimated that corporations seeking relief from creditors' pressures were, on the average, more than $2.2 billion in debt. A check of 17 recent Chapter 11 filings revealed that the corporations involved were $2.43 in debt, with a standard deviation of $0.9 billion. Is Kennedy's claim supported at the 10 percent level?

35. Dow Chemical Company has developed a new process to reduce water contamination in the production of its chemical products. A spokesperson for the company claims to have evidence that impurities are less than 52 parts per million (ppm). A sample of 100 gallons is tested, and a mean of 49.7 ppm is found, with a standard deviation of 8.9 ppm. At the 5 percent level, is the spokesperson's claim upheld?

36. The director of management for Devlon, a manufacturer of picnic tables and picnic supplies, is considering the purchase of a machine used in the production of family picnic tables which will comfortably seat only four people. All those tables currently on the market seat more than four and sell at a price considerably higher than Devlon envisions for its new model. Devlon is assured by the machine's manufacturer that the average U.S. family does not exceed 3.8 members. Devlon wants to be certain of this before it makes the purchase. A sample of 1,000 families reveals a mean of 4.1 members, with a standard deviation of 1.1 members. At the 1 percent level, should Devlon buy the machine?

37. A new production control assistant is hired by Wong's Cookie Factory. He has promised to increase production to a least 17,000 cookies a day. If he does not, he has promised to quit. After 90 days on the job, output has averaged 16,714.3 cookies, with a standard deviation of 8,012 cookies. At the 10 percent level, must he now resign as the new assistant in production control?

38. Pat Daily entertains college students on spring break at Sloppy Joe's in Key West. His popularity is spreading, and Pat claims that more than 750 partygoers crowd into Sloppy Joe's each night to watch him perform. Over a two-week period (12 days since Pat doesn't perform on Mondays), the patrons at this famous gathering spot averaged 822.3, with a standard deviation of 79.7. At the 1 percent level, does it appear that Pat's claim to fame is accurate?

39. A production process for your firm must fill bottles of pure Bavarian spring water with at least 16.2 ounces. Otherwise, the process is discontinued while adjustments are made. As the resident statistician for the firm, you have been charged with the responsibility of determining if the process is working properly. You take a sample of 24 bottles and find a mean weight of 15.7 ounces and a standard deviation of 3.7 ounces. Should you order that the process be shut down for adjustments? Your superior will not accept anything less than 99 percent confidence.

40. Referring to the previous problem, production standards also specify that no more than 12 percent of the bottles can be improperly sealed. If this standard is not met, the process is again in danger of being shut down while adjustments are made. If 35 out of 225 bottles selected for examination prove to be improperly capped, should you shut down the assembly lines? Remember, your boss wants $\alpha = 1$ percent.

41. A study by the registrar's office at a major university claims that more than 22 percent of all college students will have to repeat at least one course during their college careers. Of 912 students selected at random, 203 faced the nightmare of repeating one or more courses. Do these statistics support the registrar's claim? Set $\alpha = 5$ percent.

42. A recent report in *Fortune* magazine stated that more than 65 percent of college graduates quit their first job within two years. A study by two management professors at the University of Colorado found that 352 out of 488 recent graduates surveyed held their first job for less than two years. At the 3 percent level, do these findings support the *Fortune* study?

43. The Environmental Protection Agency has set pollution control standards for foreign-made automobiles which must be met if the autos are to be imported. Friendly Fred is considering the possibility of purchasing a franchise to sell the Marxian Delight, a new Bulgarian import. His only remaining obstacle is to determine if at least 85 percent of the cars pass EPA requirements. Of 378 Delights inspected, 287 meet antipollution standards. Should Fred buy the Bulgarian franchise? Fred is very conservative, so set $\alpha = 1$ percent.

44. As a new management trainee for 3M company, your boss has asked you to determine if shipments in the plant are being sent out on time. Like many assignments in the real world, this one is a little indefinite, and you are left wondering exactly what your boss meant. You decide to test the hypothesis that at least 95 percent of all shipments meet the time requirements. To be safe, you set $\alpha = 1$ percent. You then take a sample of 112 shipments and find that 104 of them went out on time. What do you tell your boss?

45. Your boss from the previous problem now tells you that he wants to know if 85 percent of the shipments are on time. You therefore take another sample of 175 shipments and learn that 157 of them went out within the time limitations. Retaining an $\alpha = 1$ percent, what do you now tell the boss?

46. Your firm has determined in the past that exactly 53 percent of the people in your marketing area prefer your product. Several thousand dollars are spent on an advertising program to increase your market share. Afterwards, a sample of 622 reveals that 348 prefer your product. At the 4 percent level of significance, was the money well spent?

47. You have been working for an advertising firm in Chicago for five years. Now you are thinking of starting your own company, but you are worried about losing many of your clients. You decide to go it alone only if at least 30 percent of those accounts you now handle will leave with you and follow you to your new business. As a test, you find that 14 out of 54 accounts you sample express their desire to go with you if you leave the company. At the 7 percent level, should you start your own firm?

48. As a franchised outlet for Tandy computers, you have been trying to stock as many of the laptop 1400 models as you possibly can. You obtained an agreement with the parent company in Fort Worth, Texas, that 25 percent of the shipments you order will contain at least 10 percent of the 1400 model. Of the past 42 shipments received by your store, 12 have included at least 10 percent of the laptops. At the 5 percent level, is the agreement being met?

49. Your position as Marketing Representative for Wakco Wheels, a manufacturer of toy cars and trucks for children under five, requires that you test the durability of your product. Your company claims that the Richard Petty Rapid Roller will endure at least 200 pounds of pressure per square inch without breaking. You test 100 of these models and find a mean breaking point of 195 pounds, with a standard deviation of 22.2 pounds.
    a. At the 5 percent level of significance, is your company's claim supported?
    b. If the claim is true, what is the probability of getting a Z_{test} value as low or lower than that obtained by the sample?

50. A supplier for Ralph's Tanning Parlor and Quickie Car Wash Emporium insists that no more than 33 percent of Ralph's customers spend less than $20 on the average per visit. Of 80 customers polled randomly, 29 spend less than $20.
    a. At the 1 percent level, is the supplier correct?
    b. What is the lowest α-value at which the supplier would be deemed wrong?

51. Weight Watchers claims that those people who use their program lose an average of 42 pounds. A sample of 400 determined dieters lost an average of 43.17 pounds, with a standard deviation of 8.7 pounds.
    a. Is the claim supported at the 5 percent level?
    b. What is the lowest α-value at which the claim could be rejected?

52. Hilda Radner owns a publishing company in Palo Alto, California. Business has improved recently, and Hilda thinks that daily revenues are higher than the $500 they were last year. A sample of 256 days reveals a mean of $520 and a standard deviation of $80.70.
    a. At the 1 percent level of significance, is Hilda correct?
    b. If mean revenues are actually $507, what is the probability of committing a Type II error? Draw the proper normal curves to illustrate.

53. You have recently been promoted to district manager of your electronics firm in Vero Beach. Your first assignment is to determine if the mean number of weekly unpaid accounts has dropped from the previous mean of 17.2. A sample of 55 weeks shows a mean of 16.4 and a standard deviation of 5.5
    a. At the 5 percent level, what can you conclude?
    b. If the mean is actually 15, what is the probability of a Type II error? Draw the proper normal curves to illustrate.

EMPIRICAL EXERCISES

54. Identify some characteristic about the student body in your university, college, or dorm, such as mean distance in miles from their hometowns to the campus, their mean grade point averages, proportion who live off-campus, or any other measurable characteristic.
    a. Develop a set of hypotheses about the mean or proportion of that characteristic.
    b. Select a random sample from the student body or dorm residents.
    c. Select a value for α.
    d. Calculate $\overline{X}$ and the sample standard deviation.
    e. Calculate $\overline{X}_c$.
    f. State the decision rule.
    g. Announce and interpret your conclusion regarding H_0.

55. Develop a hypothesis about the mean or proportion of some national economic measure, such as the mean monthly unemployment rate over the past several years or the proportion of stocks on the New York Stock Exchange with a closing price higher than the previous day.
    a. Select α.
    b. Using the *Federal Reserve Bulletin,* the *Survey of Current Business, The Wall Street Journal,* or some other business publication, take a random sample of your population.
    c. Calculate $\overline{X}_c, \overline{X}$, and s.
    d. State the decision rule.
    e. Announce and interpret your conclusion regarding H_0.

56. Identify a population of interest.
    a. Select a characteristic about that population you wish to investigate.
    b. Develop a hypothesis about the mean or proportion of the population.
    c. Select a value for α.
    d. Take a random sample of $n > 30$ and record your findings.
    e. Calculate $\overline{X}, \overline{X}_c$, and the sample standard deviation.
    f. State the decision rule.
    g. Announce and interpret your conclusion regarding H_0.

CASE APPLICATIONS

57. Vickie Hickie is an ambitious mid-level manager for Sudso, International, a detergent manufacturer in Cincinnati. Over the past year or two, competition from other manufacturers has been a growing problem, and Sudso faces increased pressure from disgruntled stockholders. Vickie's immediate supervisor has announced at a divisional meeting that the top brass of Sudso is demanding improved performance from all plant operations.

    The main problems in Vickie's division seem to focus on production levels and the frequency with which the division fails to meet production quotas. Management insists that daily production averages at least 1,700 pounds of soap. This level of production must be packaged and delivered to customers on order. Management also becomes upset if production units fail to meet quota arrangements more than 10 percent of the time. However, Vickie's supervisor does not want failure rates to fall below 10 percent since it entails significantly higher costs to reduce rates. If top management will accept 10 percent, both Vickie and her supervisor will too.

To impress her supervisor, Vickie has taken a sample of production performance for 200 days. She learned that output averaged 1,659 pounds with a standard deviation of 212 pounds. In only 17 cases did they fail to meet the production quota assigned to them.

How might Vickie use this sample information to determine if she and her supervisor should be satisfied with their plant's performance?

58. Vickie's supervisor wants to double-check average production figures before forwarding them to the home office in Hoboken. He collects output figures for several days and finds them to be, in hundreds of pounds,

16.15	17.76
17.82	17.89
17.79	17.98
16.82	18.52
18.12	15.12
10.66	15.73

Do you feel he should be pleased with these figures? How do they compare with those found by Vickie's sample? How might you account for any differences between his findings and Vickie's?

59. An article in *U.S. News & World Report* discussed at length the appreciation in home resale values over the past year. Several mortgage bankers became somewhat concerned about inflated prices and their impact on business. Presented below are the 14 metro areas with the highest percentage increase in sales value in the nation.

Metro Areas with the Biggest
Percentage Increases in Resale Values
of Homes during 1986

	Change (%)	
	1985	1986
Providence	18.4	37.3
Hartford	13.3	29.5
Albany	14.3	22.6
New York	29.6	19.9
Detroit	7.9	16.2
Buffalo	8.9	16.0
Boston	38.2	15.9
Memphis	−3.1	11.4
Philadelphia	16.5	11.3
Akron	6.8	9.9
Kansas City	0.3	9.4
Orange County	6.9	9.2
St. Louis	6.5	9.1
Los Angeles	4.7	8.6

Note: Figures represent the median sales price of existing single-family homes. *U.S. News & World Report.* Basic Data: National Association of Realtors.

John Pfister, a vice president with Chicago Title & Trust Company, was heard to say, "This may be the last hurrah of the first-time buyer." His concern was based on a study which suggests that price rises in excess of 16 percent are likely to force new buyers out of the market. Do you think Pfister might be correct?

COMPUTER EXERCISES

1. Complete Problem 19 by using a computer.
2. Given the data shown here, test the hypothesis that they are sample data taken from a population with a mean
   a. equal to 50.
   b. greater than 50.

   56 54 52 63 69 68 62 67 25 24 29 23 36 45 54 58 65 69 25 52
   65 63 45 87 78 52 45 49 87 74 75 56 25 41 25 45 78 45 78.

3. Access the file REVENUE in your data base. It consists of 100 observations for monthly revenues, in thousands, for Trimtex. Test the hypothesis that Trimtex's monthly revenues are
   a. equal to $30,000.
   b. greater than $30,000.

CHAPTER 10

TESTS OF TWO POPULATIONS

A PREVIEW OF THINGS TO LOOK FOR

1 The role of the critical difference in hypothesis testing.

2 Calculation of the standard error of the difference between two means.

3 How to tests means when the difference is not based on zero.

4 Differences in test procedures when the variances are (1) assumed equal but remain unknown, (2) are not equal, and (3) are under paired sampling.

Many business problems require the comparison of two populations in order to make the correct decision. This chapter discusses the situations in which such a comparison can be made. Illustrations are provided showing the circumstances in which it is essential to compare two populations, and the proper manner in which these comparisons can be made.

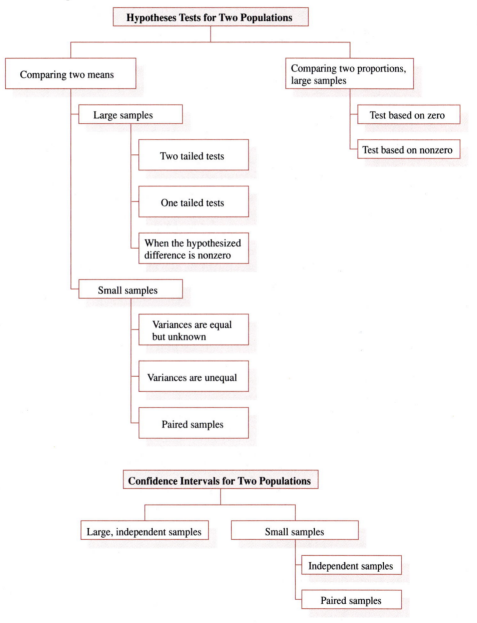

> Statistics show that nothing is ever as bad as it seems
> or as good as it sounds.

10.1   INTRODUCTION

Countless business decisions focus on the differences that might exist between two populations. Therefore, many statistical procedures have been developed which are designed to test for the difference between two population means or two population proportions.

Is there a significant difference between the average durability of ski boots made by North Slope and those made by Head? Do workers in one plant produce more per week, on the average, than workers in another plant? Is the proportion of residents in one area who prefer trade restrictions on Japanese imports different from the proportion in another area? All these are important questions which can be approached using tests that involve two populations.

To explore the application of statistical analysis to tests involving two populations, we will examine the

Difference between two means using large samples with two-tailed tests and with one-tailed tests.

Difference between two means using small samples when population variances are known and when they are unknown, and when paired samples are used.

Difference between two proportions.

Use of confidence intervals in testing hypotheses.

10.2   DIFFERENCES BETWEEN TWO MEANS—LARGE SAMPLES

In testing the difference between two means, the question becomes, "Is there a significant difference between μ_1 and μ_2?" where μ_1 and μ_2 are the means of the first and second populations, respectively. It must be recognized that there are two separate and distinct populations we wish to compare.

In making this comparison, the null hypothesis is stated so as to express no difference in the means. Thus, we have

$$H_0: \mu_1 = \mu_2$$

$$H_A: \mu_1 \neq \mu_2$$

or, the equivalent,

$$H_0: \mu_1 - \mu_2 = 0$$

$$H_A: \mu_1 - \mu_2 \neq 0$$

The process of testing the hypothesis of the difference between two population means involves the selection of two samples, one from each population. The difference between the two sample means $(\overline{X}_1 - \overline{X}_2)$ is taken as the estimate of $\mu_1 - \mu_2$. In some instances the samples must be taken independently of each other, while in other cases paired sampling is used. Each technique will be discussed in turn.

Of course, there will almost certainly be a difference between $\overline{X}_1$ and $\overline{X}_2$. Even if two samples were taken from the same population, they would likely yield different means due to sampling error. The question, therefore, is not, "Is there a difference between $\overline{X}_1$ and $\overline{X}_2$?" but, "Is the difference significant in that it suggests that the samples came from dissimilar populations, or can the difference be explained merely on the basis of sampling error?" The objective is to find a **critical difference** between $\overline{X}_1$ and $\overline{X}_2$—that is, a difference that is too large to attribute to sampling error.

The Critical Difference
A difference between two sample means that is too large to be attributed to the luck of the draw. It is instead concluded that the sample means differ by such a large amount because they came from dissimilar populations with unequal means.

Provided the population variances are known, the critical difference can be found as

$$d_c = \pm Z\sigma_{\bar{x}_1-\bar{x}_2} \tag{10.1}$$

where $\sigma_{\bar{x}_1-\bar{x}_2}$ is the **standard error of the difference between the two sample means.** This standard error recognizes that if samples were drawn from two populations, the differences in those sample means would not always be the same. The standard error is designed to capture that variation in the difference between two sample means.

> **The Standard Error of the Difference between Two Sample Means**
> If on several occasions samples are taken from each of two populations, the differences in these pairs of sample means would vary. The standard error measures this variation.

This standard error is

$$\sigma_{\bar{x}_1 - \bar{x}_2} = \sqrt{\frac{\sigma_1^2}{n_1} + \frac{\sigma_2^2}{n_2}} \qquad\qquad (10.2)$$

where σ_1^2 and σ_2^2 are the two population variances
n_1 and n_2 are the two sample sizes

The actual difference between the sample means, which is $d_a = \overline{X}_1 - \overline{X}_2$, is then compared with the critical difference found from Formula (10.1).

Figure 10-1 aids in the interpretation of the hypothesis test. In the two previous chapters, we found that a test at the 95 percent level of confidence calls for a Z-value of 1.96. Given that both sample sizes are greater than 30, the Central Limit Theorem will ensure a normal distribution in these sample means. Then, if the null hypothesis is true and $\mu_1 = \mu_2$, we will find that 95 percent of the time the differences between the two sample means, $\overline{X}_1 - \overline{X}_2$, will not differ from zero by more than 1.96 standard errors. That is, the difference between the two sample means will be less than 1.96 standard errors 95 percent of the time. This value of 1.96 standard errors is the critical difference d_c, which is compared to the actual difference between the two sample means and is found by Formula (10.1).

FIGURE 10-1   A Two-Tailed Test of the Difference between Two Means

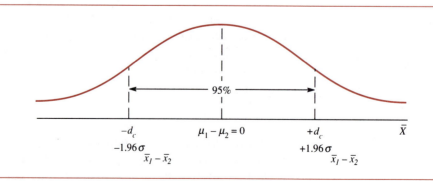

If the null is true, there is only a 5 percent probability that the actual difference between the sample means will be greater than d_c. Thus, if the difference between $\overline{X}_1$ and $\overline{X}_2$ exceeds d_c, the null is rejected. The difference is considered significant and cannot be explained merely by sampling error. It is instead assumed that the samples came from dissimilar populations—that is, populations with unequal means. We therefore reject the null hypothesis that $\mu_1 = \mu_2$. If the actual difference is so small as to fall within the critical range, that is $-d_c < d_a < +d_c$, then we cannot reject the null hypothesis that the samples came from populations with equal means. This insignificant difference in sample means is simply attributed to sampling error.

EXAMPLE 10-1 A Penny Saved

The Federal Deposit Insurance Corporation wants to compare the mean level of savings accounts in commercial banks in Virginia with those in Maryland. Samples of 230 banks in Virginia and 302 banks in Maryland reveal means of $\overline{X}_v = \$1,512$ and $\overline{X}_m = \$1,317$, respectively. It is known that the standard deviations in accounts for each state are $\sigma_v = \$517$ and $\sigma_m = \$485$. Test the hypothesis that there is no difference in mean savings at the 5 percent level.

SOLUTION:
The hypotheses are

$$H_0: \mu_v = \mu_m$$

$$H_A: \mu_v \neq \mu_m$$

The null hypothesis states that there is no difference in the mean savings held by people in Virginia and in Maryland. We must now find that critical difference which is too large to be explained away on the basis of sampling error. As demonstrated in Chapters 8 and 9, if $\alpha = 0.05$, a two-tailed test calls for a Z-value of 1.96.

$$d_c = \pm Z\sigma_{\bar{x}_1 - \bar{x}_2}$$

$$= \pm 1.96 \sqrt{\frac{(517)^2}{230} + \frac{(485)^2}{302}}$$

$$= \pm 86.35$$

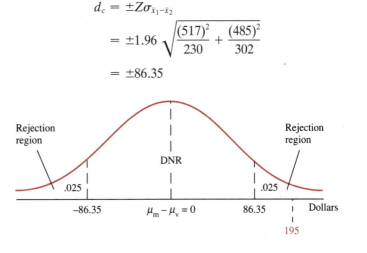

Decision Rule

Do not reject null if $-86.35 < d_a < 86.35$. Reject null if $d_a < -86.35$ or $d_a > 86.35$.

STATISTICAL INTERPRETATION:

There is a 95 percent change that if the mean levels of savings are the same in both states, sample means taken from the populations would not differ by more than $86.35. Or, stated differently, if the mean levels of savings are the same in both states, there is only a 5 percent chance that samples taken from each population would have means that differ by more than $86.35. Since $d_a = 1,512 - 1,317 = 195 > 86.35$, we must reject the null that the population means are equal. There is only a 5 percent probability that if the two populations means were equal, two samples could be taken whose means would differ by more than $86.35. The probability that you could find two random samples which differed by $195 when the population means were equal is too small. The evidence suggests that the mean level of savings is greater in Virginia.

Notice from the above example that the same four-step procedure is used here as in the hypothesis tests with only one population:

1. Formulate the hypotheses.
2. Calculate the critical value(s) and draw a graph marking off the rejection region(s).
3. Determine the decision rule.
4. State the conclusion and interpretation.

In the likely event that the population variances are unknown, a slight adjustment must be made. The sample variances are used as estimates, and the standard error of the difference between sample means is estimated as

$$
s_{\bar{x}_1 - \bar{x}_2} = \sqrt{\frac{s_1^2}{n_1} + \frac{s_2^2}{n_2}} \qquad (10.3)
$$

where s_1^2 and s_2^2 are the two sample variances. Formula (10.1) becomes

$$
d_c = \pm Z s_{\bar{x}_1 - \bar{x}_2} \qquad (10.4)
$$

EXAMPLE 10-2 How to Get a Charge out of Life:
A Quality Control Example

Two different procedures are used to produce battery packs for laptop computers. A major electronics firm tested the packs produced by each method to determine the number of hours they would last before final failure. The $n_1 = 150$ packs produced by the first method exhibited a mean life of $\overline{X}_1 = 812$ hours, while the $n_2 = 200$ packs produced by the second method reported a mean of $\overline{X}_2 = 789$ hours before failing. Although the population variances are unknown, the use of large samples permits their safe approximation with the sample variances. The tests revealed $s_1^2 = 85{,}512$ and $s_2^2 = 74{,}402$. The electronics firm wants to know if there is a difference in the mean time before failure of the two battery packs. It is willing to accept a 10 percent probability of a Type I error.

SOLUTION:
The hypotheses are

$$H_0: \mu_1 = \mu_2$$

$$H_A: \mu_1 \neq \mu_2$$

The firm must find critical values that cut off 5 percent of the area under the curve in each tail. As noted in earlier chapters, a 90 percent test requires a Z-value of 1.65. Thus,

$$d_c = \pm Z \sqrt{\frac{s_1^2}{n_1} + \frac{s_2^2}{n_2}}$$

$$= \pm 1.65 \sqrt{\frac{85{,}512}{150} + \frac{74{,}402}{200}}$$

$$= \pm 50.64$$

Decision Rule
Do not reject null if $-50.64 < d_a < 50.64$. Reject null if $d_a < -50.64$ or $d_a > 50.64$.

This is shown in the following graph.

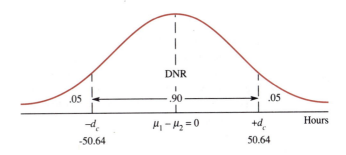

STATISTICAL INTERPRETATION:
Given the variances of 85,512 and 74,402, if the battery packs have the same mean life, there is only a 10 percent chance that the means of samples of the sizes taken from each population could differ by as much as 50.64 hours. Since $d_a = 812 - 789 = 23$ is within the tolerable range of the do not reject (DNR) region, this insignificant difference of 23 is attributed to sampling error. There is a 95 percent probability that two samples taken from populations with equal means could produce

sample means that differ by as much as 50.64 hours. Since $\overline{X}_1 - \overline{X}_2 = 23$, we can be 90 percent certain that $\mu_1 = \mu_2$. It is reasonably probable that if the two types of packs have the same mean life, sample means that differ by only 23 could be found. There is not sufficient evidence to conclude that there is a difference in the mean life of the two types of packs.

A. ONE-TAILED HYPOTHESIS TESTS

It is also possible to use a one-tailed test to conduct a hypothesis test for the difference between two means. The set of hypotheses is either

$$H_0\colon \mu_1 \geq \mu_2$$

$$H_A\colon \mu_1 < \mu_2$$

yielding a left-tailed test, or

$$H_0\colon \mu_1 \leq \mu_2$$

$$H_A\colon \mu_1 > \mu_2$$

yielding a right-tailed test.

As with single-population tests, the problem statement must be closely examined to determine which set of hypotheses is correct. Be sure that the equality sign appears in the null. The rejection region appears in the tail indicated by the inequality sign in the alternative hypothesis.

Carl Weathers, a marketing representative for Mid-South Sales feels that his mean weekly sales are at least as much in Florida as they are in Alabama. He wishes to test this hypothesis. Since "at least as much" is written $\mu_F \geq \mu_A$ and contains the equal sign, it is the null hypothesis. The complete set of hypotheses becomes

$$H_0\colon \mu_F \geq \mu_A$$

$$H_A\colon \mu_F < \mu_A$$

To determine which tail contains the rejection region, you must again ask yourself the same question as was the case with single-population tests: "What would cause the rejection of the null?" The null allows for mean sales in Florida to exceed those in Alabama. We can reject the null if and only if our samples suggest that sales in Florida are significantly less than those in Alabama. That is, $\overline{X}_F < \overline{X}_A$, and the difference between $\overline{X}_F$ and $\overline{X}_A$ yields a *negative* number: $\overline{X}_F - \overline{X}_A < 0$. This places the rejection in the *left* tail. This is confirmed by examining the inequality sign in the alternative hypothesis.

Assume Carl felt that sales in Florida did not exceed those in Alabama and that therefore the hypotheses had been stated differently:

$$H_0\colon \mu_F \leq \mu_A$$

$$H_A\colon \mu_F > \mu_A$$

Now the null hypothesis permits Florida sales to be less than those in Alabama. It could be rejected if and only if our samples suggest that Florida sales are significantly more than those in Alabama. That is, $\overline{X}_F > \overline{X}_A$, by a significant amount, and the difference between $\overline{X}_F$ and $\overline{X}_A$ yields a *positive* number: $\overline{X}_F - \overline{X}_A > 0$. This places the rejection region in the *right* tail as indicated by the inequality sign in the alternative hypothesis. Given our present left-tailed test for Carl, the critical difference is

$$d_c = -Z\sigma_{\bar{x}_1 - \bar{x}_2} \tag{10.5}$$

or, if population variances are unknown,

$$d_c = -Zs_{\bar{x}_1 - \bar{x}_2} \tag{10.6}$$

If a right-tailed test were to be conducted, the critical value is

$$d_c = Z\sigma_{\bar{x}_1 - \bar{x}_2} \tag{10.7}$$

or, if population variances are unknown,

$$d_c = Zs_{\bar{x}_1 - \bar{x}_2} \tag{10.8}$$

EXAMPLE 10-3 Surf's Up!!!

Doug Warren and his wife B. J. own a successful surfboard manufacturing firm in Kansas. There is some question about the average length of time it takes to produce their two most popular models. B. J. argues that it takes longer to produce the Boogie Board than it does to produce the Super Surfer. Doug disagrees. They decide to test B. J.'s argument at the 5 percent level. Production records show that 90 of the Boogie Boards took an average of 140.2 hours with a standard deviation of 22.7 hours, while 110 of the Super Surfer required a mean of 131.7 hours, with a standard deviation of 23.9 hours.

SOLUTION:

Since B. J. insists that $\mu_B > \mu_S$, the hypotheses are

$$H_0: \mu_B \leq \mu_S$$
$$H_A: \mu_B > \mu_S$$

and call for a right-tailed test.

Again, as was the case with single population tests, the Z-value for a one-tailed test is found by subtracting α from 0.5. The resulting area of $0.5 - 0.05 = 0.45$ yields a corresponding Z-value of 1.65. The extrapolated value of 1.645 should be used if more accuracy is required. However, for simplicity's sake, we will use 1.65. The critical value becomes

$$d_c = Zs_{\bar{x}_1 - \bar{x}_2}$$

$$= 1.65 \sqrt{\frac{(22.7)^2}{90} + \frac{(23.9)^2}{110}}$$

$$= 5.45$$

The accompanying figure provides an illustration. Notice that the full amount of α is located in the right tail since this is a one-tailed test.

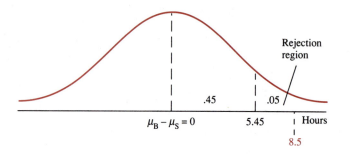

Decision Rule
Do not reject null if $\bar{X}_B - \bar{X}_S = d_a < 5.45$. Reject null if $d_a > 5.45$.

STATISTICAL INTERPRETATION:
Given the standard deviations of 22.7 and 23.9, there is only a 5 percent chance that if both boards require the same mean production time, a sample of 90 Boogie Boards could produce a mean that exceeded that of 110 Super Surfers by as much as 5.45. Since $d_a = 140.2 - 131.7 = 8.5$, the null is rejected and B. J.'s argument is supported. It is unlikely that $\mu_B \leq \mu_S$, since the sample of Boogie Boards exceeded that of the Super Surfers by more than 5.45.

B. WHEN THE HYPOTHESIZED DIFFERENCE IS NOT ZERO

It is a common occurrence to presume not only that two means are not equal, but that the difference is more than some specified amount. For instance, assume that in the example above, B. J. did not merely argue that the mean finishing time for Boogie Boards exceeded that of Super Surfers, but that the difference was more than 7 hours. In essence, she was arguing that $\mu_B > (\mu_S + 7)$, or, restated, $\mu_B - \mu_S > 7$. The hypotheses then become

$$H_0\!: \mu_B \leq \mu_S + 7$$

$$H_A\!: \mu_B > \mu_S + 7$$

The critical difference must be adjusted to allow for the additional 7 hours.

$$d_c = Z \sqrt{\frac{s_B^2}{n_B} + \frac{s_S^2}{n_S}} + 7$$

$$= 12.45 \text{ hours}$$

The decision rule is then based on a critical value of 12.45 hours.

Decision Rule
Do not reject if $\overline{X}_B - \overline{X}_S = d_a < 12.45$. Reject if $d_a > 12.45$.

Since $d_a = 8.5$, as Figure 10-2(a) shows, the null is not rejected, and B. J.'s claim
that μ_B exceeds μ_S by more than 7 is refuted. If B. J. had stated that μ_B exceeds μ_S
by at least 7 hours, the hypotheses would be

$$H_0: \mu_B \geq \mu_S + 7$$

$$H_A: \mu_B < \mu_S + 7$$

This left-tailed test results in

$$d_c = -Z \sqrt{\frac{s_1^2}{n_1} + \frac{s_2^2}{n_2}} + 7$$

$$= -12.45$$

This left-tailed test is shown in Figure 10-2(b).

FIGURE 10-2   A One-Tailed Test

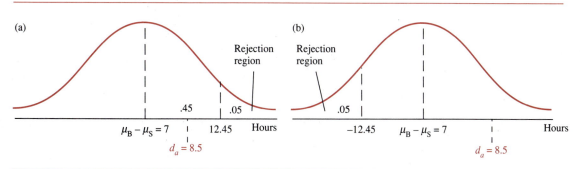

QUICK CHECK 10.2.1

○○○○ If $\overline{X}_1 = 50.3$, $s_1 = 7.2$, $n_1 = 200$, $\overline{X}_2 = 54.7$, $s_2 = 8.7$, $n_2 = 200$, and $\alpha = 0.10$, test the hypothesis that there is no difference in the population means by
a. stating the hypothesis.
b. determining the critical values.
c. stating the decision rule.
d. stating the conclusion.

Answer: a. $H_0: \mu_1 = \mu_2$ $H_A: \mu_1 \neq \mu_2$
b. ±1.32
c. Do not reject if $-1.32 < d_a < 1.32$. Reject if $d_a < -1.32$ or $d_a > 1.32$.
d. $d_a = -4.4 < -1.32$. Reject the null.

QUICK CHECK 10.2.2

Given the data from 10.2.1, it is thought that μ_2 is greater than μ_1. Test this claim using the same four steps.

Answer: a. $H_0: \mu_1 \geq \mu_2$ $H_A: \mu_1 < \mu_2$
b. -1.02
c. Do not reject if $d_a > -1.02$. Reject null if $d_a < -1.02$.
d. $d_a = -4.4 < -1.02$. Reject the null. The claim is supported. *Note:* Since the statement is "μ_2 is greater than μ_1," the hypotheses could be written as $H_0: \mu^2 \leq \mu_1$, $H_a: \mu_2 > \mu_1$, producing a right-tailed test. Then μ_1 must be subtracted from μ_2 to get d_a, and the signs would be reversed. However, it is customary to always put μ_1 first.

QUICK CHECK 10.2.3

Given the data from 10.2.1, it is suggested that μ_2 exceeds μ_1 and the difference is more than 2. Run the appropriate hypothesis test, using the four-step procedure.

Answer: a. $H_0: \mu_1 \geq \mu_2 - 2$ $H_A: \mu_1 < \mu_2 - 2$
b. -3.02
c. Do not reject if $d_a > -3.02$. Reject if $d_a < -3.02$.
d. Since $d_a = -4.4$, reject null.

10.3   DIFFERENCE BETWEEN TWO MEANS—SMALL SAMPLES

If the population is known to be normal, and the population variances are known, the methods described above are appropriate even if small samples are taken. However, if the populations are known to be normal, but the variances are unknown, Student's t must be used if $n_1 < 30$ or $n_2 < 30$. In the application of the t-statistic, we must distinguish between (1) a situation in which the unknown variances are assumed to be equal and (2) the case when this assumption is not made. This is the same distinction made in Chapter 8 in our discussion of confidence intervals. Each is examined in turn. Both require the assumption of normal populations.

A. EQUAL BUT UNKNOWN VARIANCES

The rationale for this premise was established in Chapter 8. It was noted, for example, that adjustments in certain manufacturing processes or assembly-line techniques of production may alter the mean but leave the variance unchanged. In this
instance, the assumption of equal variances before and after the adjustment is not
unreasonable.

If there is evidence that leads to the belief that the two populations under comparison have equal variances, it is desirable to develop an estimate of this common
variance. This estimate is based on pooled data from both samples. Again, this procedure is analogous to that used in the formation of confidence intervals in Chapter 8.

When small samples are taken from normal populations in the presence of unknown but equal variances, the proper t-test used to calculate the critical difference is

$$d_c = \pm t \sqrt{\frac{s_p^2}{n_1} + \frac{s_p^2}{n_2}} \qquad (10.9)$$

where

$$s_p^2 = \frac{s_1^2(n_1 - 1) + s_2^2(n_2 - 1)}{n_1 + n_2 - 2} \qquad (10.10)$$

Formula (10.10) is the estimator for the variance common to both populations. You
will note by the numerator that it is the weighted mean of the two sample variances,
in which the weights are the sample sizes, minus 1. The t-test is conducted with
d.f. $= n_1 + n_2 - 2$.

A local insurance agency wishes to compare the average damage from similar accidents to two models of automobiles. Nine of the first model are subjected to a controlled collision. The mean damage is $\overline{X}_1 = \$330$, with a standard deviation of
$s_1 = \$97$. Seven of the second model are involved in the same type of collision with
a resulting mean damage of $\overline{X}_2 = \$313$ and $s_2 = \$83$. At the 10 percent level of significance, does there appear to be a difference in the autos' crash resistance? It is
assumed damages for both cars are normally distributed with equal variances.

The hypotheses are

$$H_0: \mu_1 = \mu_2$$

$$H_A: \mu_1 \neq \mu_2$$

The common variance is estimated as

$$s_p^2 = \frac{97^2(9 - 1) + 83^2(7 - 1)}{9 + 7 - 2} = 8,329$$

With $n_1 + n_2 - 2 = 14$ d.f. and $\alpha = 0.10$, the t-value from the table is 1.761.

$$d_c = \pm t \sqrt{\frac{s_p^2}{n_1} + \frac{s_p^2}{n_2}}$$

$$= \pm 1.761 \sqrt{\frac{8,329}{9} + \frac{8,329}{7}}$$

$$= \pm 80.99$$

Decision Rule
Do not reject the null if $-80.99 < d_a < 80.99$. Reject the null if $d_a < -80.99$ or $d_a > 80.99$.

As shown in Figure 10-3, $d_a = 330 - 313 = 17$. The agency would conclude that there is no significant difference in the damages to the two types of automobiles.

FIGURE 10-3   The Mean Damage to Autos

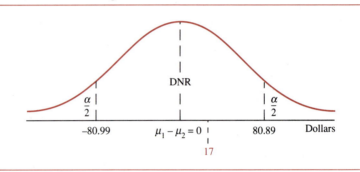

EXAMPLE 10-4 **The Yen to Play Golf**
According to an article in *Business Week* on the growing worldwide popularity of golf, it was stated that greens fees in Japan can top \$79, and memberships in golf clubs exceed \$2,000,000. Yet facilities are crowded, delaying progress of the game. Since the Japanese businessman often works 15 or more hours a day, any loss of time due to delay is crucial. To compare playing times at two exclusive clubs, one Japanese executive notes that $n_1 = 12$ games played at one club averaged $\overline{X}_1 = 6.4$ hours with a standard deviation of $s_1 = 2.7$ hours. In addition, $n_2 = 10$ games at a second club averaged $\overline{X}_2 = 5.9$ hours with $s_2 = 2.1$ hours. The executive feels that the mean playing time at the first club exceeds that of the second. Is he correct at the 5 percent level of significance? It is assumed the playing times are normally distributed with equal variances.

SOLUTION:

$$H_0: \mu_1 \leq \mu_2$$
$$H_A: \mu_1 > \mu_2$$
$$s_p^2 = \frac{2.7^2(12 - 1) + 2.1^2(10 - 1)}{12 + 10 - 2}$$
$$= 5.99$$

With d.f. $= 12 + 10 - 2 = 20$ and $\alpha = 0.05$, t is 2.086.

$$d_c = +1.725 \sqrt{\frac{5.99}{12} + \frac{5.99}{10}}$$

$$= 1.81 \text{ hours}$$

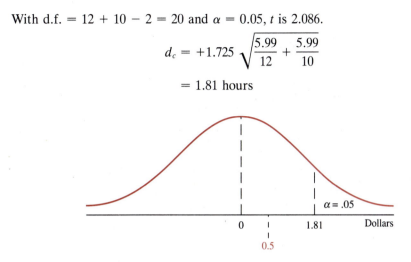

Decision Rule
Do not reject if $d_a < 1.81$. Reject if $d_a > 1.81$.

STATISTICAL INTERPRETATION:
If the null is true, there is only a 5 percent probability that samples of sizes 12 and 10, respectively, could be taken in which the mean of the first exceeded that of the second by 1.81, given the standard deviations cited above. Since $d_a = 6.4 - 5.9 = 0.5 < 1.81$, we do not reject the null. Evidence suggests that playing times at the first club do not significantly exceed those at the second. The executive's claim is not supported.

QUICK CHECK 10.3.1

○○○○

If $\overline{X}_1 = 291$, $n_1 = 10$, $s_1 = 92$, $\overline{X}_2 = 301$, $n_2 = 10$, and $s_2 = 101$, test the hypothesis that there is no significant difference in the population means at the 10 percent level, assuming populations are normal with equal variances. Perform all four steps of a hypothesis test.

Answer: a. $H_0: \mu_1 = \mu_2$ $H_A: \mu_1 \neq \mu_2$
  b. ± 74.91
  c. Do not reject if $-74.91 < d_a < 74.91$. Reject if $d_a < -74.91$ or $d_a > 74.91$.
  d. Since $d_a = 291 - 301 = -10$, do not reject null.

QUICK CHECK 10.3.2

$\overline{X}_1 = 93$, $n_1 = 8$, $s_1 = 20$, $\overline{X}_2 = 129$, $n_2 = 9$, and $s_2 = 24$. It is thought $\mu_2 > \mu_1$. Test the appropriate hypothesis assuming normal distributions and equal variances. Set $\alpha = 0.01$. Perform all four steps of a hypothesis test.

Answer: a. $H_0: \mu_1 \geq \mu_2$ $H_A: \mu_1 < \mu_2$
  b. -28.01
  c. Do not reject if $d_a > -28.01$. Reject null if $d_a < -28.01$.
  d. $d_a = 93 - 129 = -36 < 31.82$. Therefore, reject null.

B.   UNEQUAL VARIANCES

In many instances the variances of the two populations are not equal. A test will be presented in a later chapter which is designed to examine whether equal variances exist. In the absence of this equality, the pooled method just discussed is not appropriate.

In fact, if the two population variances are not assumed to be equal, the proper statistic does not fit a typical t-distribution. This is exactly the same problem we encountered when constructing confidence intervals under similar circumstances. It will be dealt with here in exactly the same manner. You will recall in our discussion of confidence interval that it was necessary to calculate the degrees of freedom for this slightly modified t-statistic, which we signified as t'. The formula we used then to determine the degrees of freedom was

$$\text{d.f.} = \frac{[s_1^2/n_1 + s_2^2/n_2]^2}{(s_1^2/n_1)^2/(n_1 - 1) + (s_2^2/n_2)^2/(n_2 - 1)} \qquad (10.11)$$

If Formula (10.11) does not yield an integer (whole number), it should always be rounded down to the nearest integer. (For example, even 12.9 should be rounded down to 12.) The appropriate t-value, t', can then be found in the t-table based on the degrees of freedom found by Formula (10.11). The critical difference which is too large to be explained on the basis of sampling error is then

$$d_c = \pm t' \sqrt{\frac{s_1^2}{n_1} + \frac{s_2^2}{n_2}} \qquad (10.12)$$

Notice that Formula (10.12) does not involve pooling data, as did Formula (10.9). Also, Formula (10.12) pertains to a two-tailed test. If a one-tailed test is desired, the appropriate positive or negative sign is used.

Consider the following example taken from the monthly publication *Florida Today* published by the Florida state government in Tallahassee. The Florida Education Association wishes to determine if there is a difference in the mean expenditures per pupil of urban high schools and those in rural areas. Fifteen high schools of each type are randomly selected. The statistics for urban (U) and rural (R) schools were

$$\overline{X}_U = \$6{,}012 \qquad \overline{X}_R = \$5{,}832$$

$$s_U = \quad \$602 \qquad s_R = \quad \$497$$

Then,

$$H_0: \mu_U = \mu_R$$

$$H_A: \mu_U \neq \mu_R$$

$$\text{d.f.} = \frac{\{(602)^2/15 + (497)^2/15\}^2}{[(602)^2/15]^2/(15-1) + [(497)^2/15]^2/(15-1)}$$

$$= 27.03 \approx 27$$

If the hypothesis is tested at the 10 percent level of significance, the t-table reveals a t' of 1.703. Then

$$d_c = \pm 1.703 \sqrt{\frac{(602)^2}{15} + \frac{(497)^2}{15}}$$

$$= \pm\$343$$

FIGURE 10-4   Educational Expenditures in Florida

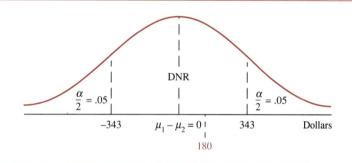

As portrayed in Figure 10-4, the decision rule is,

Decision Rule
If $-343 < d_a < 343$, do not reject the null. If $d_a < -343$ or $d_a > 343$, reject the null.

Since $d_a = 6{,}012 - 5{,}832 = 180$, we do not reject the null and assume that there is no significant difference between mean expenditures by the high schools. Example 10-5 illustrates a one-tailed test.

EXAMPLE 10-5   Something's Fishy in Florida

Florida Today also reported that environmental statisticians for the Florida Fish and Game Commission undertook a study to determine if there was any difference in the mean tonnage of shrimp taken by those boats using drag nets compared to boats using bottom nets. Drag nets have traditionally been used in the Gulf of Mexico, and it has been widely held that this method produces larger catches. The commission's study furnished the following data from observing 12 boats using each type of netting system during the study conducted in the summer of 1989:

Drag Nets	Bottom Nets
$\overline{X}_1 = 3.2$ tons	$\overline{X}_2 = 2.87$ tons
$s_1 = 0.34$ ton	$s_2 = 0.41$ ton

There is no reason to believe variances are equal, but the populations appear to be normally distributed. The test was conducted at the 5 percent level.

SOLUTION:

Since only 12 boats were in each sample and the population variances are unknown, Student's t must be used. However, the t-value must be adjusted according to Formulas (10.11) and (10.12) because the variances are not assumed equal.

Furthermore, since it was assumed that $\mu_1 > \mu_2$, we have

$$H_0: \mu_1 \leq \mu_2$$

$$H_A: \mu_1 > \mu_2$$

A right-tailed test is called for, and the degrees of freedom are found as

$$\text{d.f.} = \frac{\{(0.34)^2/12 + (0.41)^2/12\}^2}{[(0.34)^2/12]^2/11 + [(0.41)^2/12]^2/11}$$

$$= 21.27, \text{ or } 21 \text{ degrees of freedom}$$

Since $\alpha = 0.05$, $t' = 1.721$.

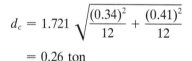

$$d_c = 1.721 \sqrt{\frac{(0.34)^2}{12} + \frac{(0.41)^2}{12}}$$

$$= 0.26 \text{ ton}$$

The following figure aids in forming the decision rule and the interpretation.

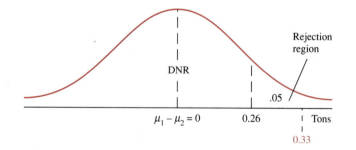

Decision Rule

Do not reject if $d_a < 0.26$. Reject if $d_a > 0.26$.

STATISTICAL INTERPRETATION:
There is only a 5 percent chance that if the null is true, samples of the given sizes will result in means such that $\overline{X}_1$ could exceed $\overline{X}_2$ by 0.26 or more. Since $d_a = 3.2 - 2.87 = 0.33$, reject the null and conclude that there appears to be evidence to suggest that drag nets are more effective. The value of 0.33 is too large to occur under any reasonable (95 percent) conditions if the null were true.

QUICK CHECK 10.3.3

○○○○

If a sample of $n_1 = 12$ reports a mean and standard deviation of $\overline{X}_1 = 8.12$ and $s_1 = 1.02$, and a second sample of $n_2 = 10$ has $\overline{X}_2 = 9.73$ and $s_2 = 0.97$, does there appear to be any difference in the two population means at the 10 percent level? Assume variances are not known to be equal. Respond by

a. stating the hypotheses.
b. determining the d.f. and t'.
c. stating the decision rule.
d. drawing your conclusion.

Answer: a. $H_0: \mu_1 = \mu_2$ $H_A: \mu_1 \neq \mu_2$
b. d.f. = 19, $t' = 1.729$
c. Do not reject if $-0.70 < d_a < 0.70$. Reject if $d_a < -0.70$ or $d_a > 0.70$.
d. $d_a = 8.12 - 9.73 = -1.61 < -0.70$. Reject the null.

C. PAIRED SAMPLING

The principles and conditions pertaining to paired sampling were established in our previous chapter dealing with confidence intervals. It was demonstrated that numerous occasions arise in which we may match observations in one sample with an equal number of observations in a second sample on a one-to-one basis. The following discussion will provide an illustration.

The economic analysis divisions for several state governments around the country are studying the economic impact of state-regulated horse racing at selected sites. Many of them have been considering the relative merits of racing horses on turf (grass) as opposed to dirt tracks. A good deal of track revenue will be affected by this decision which depends, in part, on the impact that the track surface has on racing times. To make a comparison, seven horses are timed in competitive races on each type of track. The results are reported in Table 10-1, along with necessary computations. The times are in minutes. Notice that the observations are paired, since the same observations (horses) were taken under two different circumstances (tracks). As we did with confidence intervals in Chapter 8, the objective is to perform the test on the mean of the differences between the observations, $\overline{d}_a$, where

$$\overline{d}_a = \frac{\Sigma d_i}{n} \qquad (10.13)$$

TABLE 10-1   Race Times* in the 10 Furlong

Horse	Time on Dirt Track	Time on Turf Track	Difference in Times (d_i)	d_i^2
Take Your Chances	1.82	1.73	0.09	0.0081
Meatball	1.91	1.87	0.04	0.0016
Cross Your Fingers	1.87	1.82	0.05	0.0025
Jockey's Folly	1.73	1.67	0.06	0.0036
Nose Knows	1.59	1.63	−0.04	0.0016
Boogaloo	1.67	1.72	−0.05	0.0025
My Mare	1.76	1.65	0.11	0.0121
			0.26	0.0320

*When track conditions were rated "good."

The critical mean difference is

$$\bar{d}_c = \pm t \frac{s_d}{\sqrt{n}} \tag{10.14}$$

where s_d is the standard error of the difference between race times, and is computed as

$$s_d = \sqrt{\frac{\Sigma d_i^2 - n(\bar{d}_a)^2}{n - 1}} \tag{10.15}$$

Given that the tracks want to determine if there is any difference in the race times, a two-tailed test is required. Thus, where D is dirt tracks and T is turf tracks, we have

$$H_0: \mu_D = \mu_T$$

$$H_A: \mu_D \neq \mu_T$$

$$\bar{d}_a = \frac{\Sigma d_i}{n}$$

$$= \frac{0.26}{7}$$

$$= 0.037$$

In the 1991 survey of professional incomes by *U.S. News and World Report* referred to earlier, a comparison was provided of entry-level salaries for various occupations in different areas of the nation. Some of the results of that survey are shown here.

	New England Area	**Pacific Area**
Accountant	$22,800	$26,700
Computer operator	20,300	20,700
Customer service	19,700	20,900
Financial analysts	28,300	29,100
Programmer	28,300	32,400
Purchasing agent	26,700	26,500
System analyst	35,800	38,200

Using information of this nature, it is possible to determine if salaries differ in these two regions of the country by pairing the different professions across regions as shown here.

If $\alpha = 0.10$ and there are $n - 1 = 6$ degrees of freedom, the *t*-value from the table is 1.943. Then

$$s_d = \sqrt{\frac{0.0320 - 7(0.037)^2}{7 - 1}}$$

$$= 0.0611$$

Then

$$\bar{d}_c = \pm 1.943 \left(\frac{0.0611}{\sqrt{7}} \right)$$

$$= \pm 0.0449$$

Decision Rule
Do not reject if $-0.0449 < \bar{d}_a < 0.0449$. Reject if $\bar{d}_a < -0.0449$ or $\bar{d}_a > 0.0449$.

Since $\bar{d}_a = 0.037$, we conclude that the track surface has no effect on race times.

EXAMPLE 10-6 Pairing Pups

K-9 Kennel Chow is attempting to establish itself as a leader in the dog food market. In its effort to gain a pawhold in the industry, statisticians in the marketing division for K-9 conducted a comparison test against another popular brand. The purpose of the test was to demonstrate that the more expensive dog food sold by the competitor would not promote growth and weight gain any more than would the product sold by K-9 Kennel.

The test, which was reported in *Dog Breeders Journal,* involved the selection of eight different breeds of dogs (ranging from cocker spaniels to Irish wolfhounds), which were fed exclusively K-9 Kennel dog food. Eight more of the same breeds of similar ages were fed the competitor's food. As you can see, the dogs in each group were paired according to breed and age. Each pair was weighed at the start of the test period and after four months. The weight gains are shown here for each breed.

Weight Gain (in pounds)

Breed	K-9 Kennel	Competitor's Brand	d_i	d_i^2
1	3.2	3.4	−0.2	0.04
2	4.7	4.2	0.5	0.25
3	4.2	4.3	−0.1	0.01
4	5.7	5.9	−0.2	0.04
5	3.1	3.5	−0.4	0.16
6	5.4	5.1	0.3	0.09
7	4.3	4.3	0.0	0.00
8	5.5	5.7	−0.2	0.04
			−0.3	0.63

SOLUTION:

To test the hypothesis that there is no difference in mean weight gains, we have

$$H_0: \mu_{K\text{-}9} = \mu_{\text{competitor}}$$

$$H_A: \mu_{K\text{-}9} \neq \mu_{\text{competitor}}$$

$$\bar{d}_a = \frac{-0.3}{8} = -0.0375 \text{ pound}$$

$$s_d = \sqrt{\frac{0.63 - 8(-0.0375)^2}{8 - 1}}$$

$$= 0.297$$

If α is set at 10 percent with $n - 1 = 7$ degrees of freedom, the t-value from the table is 1.895. The critical mean difference is

$$\bar{d}_c = \pm t \frac{s_d}{\sqrt{n}}$$

$$= \pm 1.895 \left(\frac{0.297}{\sqrt{8}} \right)$$

$$= \pm 0.199 \text{ pound}$$

Decision Rule

Do not reject null if $-0.199 < \bar{d}_a < 0.199$. Reject null if $\bar{d}_a < -0.199$ or $\bar{d}_a > 0.199$.

STATISTICAL INTERPRETATION:

Do not reject null since $\bar{d}_a = -0.0375$. Evidence suggests that there is not a significant difference between the weight gain provided by K-9 Kennel and the more expensive product.

Many different types of tests can be conducted which involve the comparison of two populations. Chart 10-1 will aid in determining the proper test procedure for hypotheses involving two populations.

CHART 10-1 Test Procedure for Hypotheses Involving Two Populations

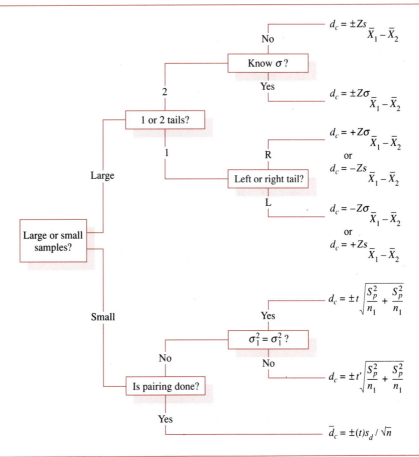

10.4   A TEST FOR THE DIFFERENCE BETWEEN TWO PROPORTIONS—LARGE SAMPLES

A problem often arises in the business world requiring the comparison of two different population proportions: for example, the proportion of defects produced by one method compared to that produced by a second, or the proportion of bad debts in one firm compared to that in another.

A.   BASING THE TEST ON ZERO

Most often, any test regarding two population proportions is based on a difference of zero. That is, the null specifies that the difference between π_1 and π_2 is zero. A two-tailed test would be written as

$$H_0: \pi_1 = \pi_2$$

$$H_A: \pi_1 \neq \pi_2$$

The implication is that the two populations may have a common proportion π. Under this condition, it is possible to combine the sample data to derive an estimate of that common proportion. The estimate $\hat{\pi}$ (anything under a "hat" is being estimated) is the weighted average of the two sample proportions, where the weights are the sample sizes. If p_1 and p_2 are the sample proportions,

$$\hat{\pi} = \frac{n_1 p_1 + n_2 p_2}{n_1 + n_2} \tag{10.16}$$

This has the effect of giving more weight to the larger sample. For computational purposes, it might prove more convenient to reduce Formula (10.16) to

$$\hat{\pi} = \frac{X_1 + X_2}{n_1 + n_2} \tag{10.17}$$

where X_1 and X_2 are the numbers of successes in the two samples.

The standard error of the difference between the two sample proportions is

$$S_{p_1-p_2} = \sqrt{\frac{\hat{\pi}(1-\hat{\pi})}{n_1} + \frac{\hat{\pi}(1-\hat{\pi})}{n_2}} \qquad (10.18)$$

The standard error recognizes that different samples would give different proportions, and Formula (10.18) accounts for that variation.

The critical difference between the sample proportions which is judged too large to be explained by sampling error is

$$d_c = \pm Z s_{p_1-p_2} \qquad (10.19)$$

As a term project, a marketing major at a state university wants to determine if there is any difference in the proportion of men who respond favorably to a certain advertisement and the proportion of women who do so. Out of 875 men, 412 report a positive impression. Of the 910 women surveyed, only 309 are receptive. The data are summarized in Table 10-2. If the marketing student tests for equality in population proportions, she has

$$H_0: \pi_M = \pi_W$$

$$H_A: \pi_M \neq \pi_W$$

$$\hat{\pi} = \frac{412 + 309}{875 + 910}$$

$$= 0.40$$

$$S_{p_M-p_W} = \sqrt{\frac{(0.4)(0.6)}{875} + \frac{(0.4)(0.6)}{910}}$$

$$= 0.0232$$

If she conducts the test at the 10 percent level of significance, what should her findings be? At $\alpha = 0.10$, $Z = 1.65$.

$$d_c = \pm 1.65(0.0232)$$

$$= \pm 0.0383$$

TABLE 10-2   Comparing Opinions of an Advertisement

Men	Women
$n_M = 875$	$n_W = 910$
$X_M = 412$	$X_W = 309$
$p_M = 412/875 = 0.47$	$p_W = 309/910 = 0.34$

Decision Rule
Do not reject if $-0.0383 < \bar{d}_a < 0.0383$. Reject null if $\bar{d}_a < -0.0383$ or $\bar{d}_a > 0.0383$.

The results are confirmed in Figure 10-5. If the null is true, there is only a 10 percent probability that samples of this size could produce proportions which differ by more than 3.83 percent.

FIGURE 10-5   The Impact of Advertisements

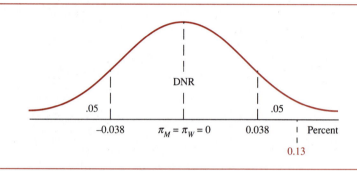

Since $d_a = 0.47 - 0.34 = 0.13$, she should reject the null. As seen in the area in the right tail of Figure 10-5, if the two population proportions are equal, there is only a 5 percent chance that samples could be taken in which the proportion of men who favor the advertisement exceeds that of women by 3.8 percent. It is concluded that men and women perceive the advertisement differently. Specifically, men are more likely to perceive it favorably.

Assume for a moment that the student had reason to believe that men might prefer the advertisement more than women. She would then specify that $\pi_M > \pi_W$. A one-tailed test would be run based on

$$H_0: \pi_M \leq \pi_W$$

$$H_A: \pi_M > \pi_W$$

A right-tailed test is required.

$$d_c = +1.28(0.0232)$$

$$= 0.0297$$

Figure 10-6 shows that the decision rule can be stated as

Decision Rule
Do not reject if $d_a < 0.0297$. Reject null if $d_a > 0.0297$.

Since the actual difference between the sample proportions is $0.13 > 0.0297$, the null should be rejected. The evidence suggests that a greater percentage of men prefer the advertisement.

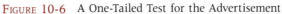

FIGURE 10-6   A One-Tailed Test for the Advertisement

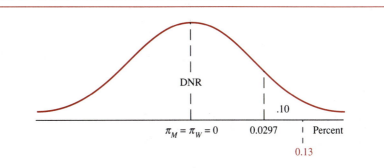

B.   BASING THE TEST ON A NONZERO VALUE

Now assume that the marketing student thought not only that men would be more likely to prefer the advertisement ($\pi_M > \pi_W$) but that the proportion of men who prefer it exceeds that of women by some specific amount, say 15 percent. That is, $\pi_M > \pi_W + 0.15$. This is a one-tailed test, but with different hypotheses than those cited above. Specifically,

$$H_0: \pi_M \leq \pi_W + 0.15$$

$$H_A: \pi_M > \pi_W + 0.15$$

Unlike the previous tests the student performed, the specification is not zero. Therefore, it is not hypothesized that any difference in population proportions is based on zero nor that a common proportion exists. With no common proportion, pooling is not permitted, and Formulas (10.17) and (10.18) do not apply. Instead, the individual sample proportions must be used to estimate the standard error. That is,

$$s_{p_1 - p_2} = \sqrt{\frac{p_1 q_1}{n_1} + \frac{p_2 q_2}{n_2}} \qquad (10.20)$$

where p_1 is the proportion of successes in the first sample
   q_1 is the proportion of failures and is found as $1 - p_1$.

In the case of our marketing student,

$$
\begin{aligned}
s_{p_M - p_W} &= \sqrt{\frac{p_M q_M}{n_M} + \frac{p_W q_W}{n_W}} \\
&= \sqrt{\frac{(0.47)(0.53)}{875} + \frac{(0.34)(0.66)}{910}} \\
&= 0.02305
\end{aligned}
$$

The critical difference must now allow for the additional 15 percent hypothesized to exist, and is therefore written as

$$d_c = +Zs_{p_M - p_W} + 0.15$$

If an α-value of 0.10 is retained, the marketing major would have

$$= +1.28(0.02305) + 0.15$$

$$= +0.1795$$

Decision Rule
Do not reject if $d_a < 0.1795$. Reject if $d_a > 0.1795$.

Since $d_a = 0.13$, she would not reject the null and would conclude that the proportion of men who prefer the advertisement does not exceed that of women by more than 3 percent. Figure 10-7 illustrates.

FIGURE 10-7   A Comparison of Advertising Preferences

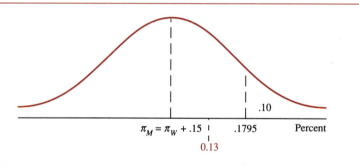

QUICK CHECK 10.4.1
○○○○

A manufacturer claims that compared with his closest competitor, fewer of his employees are union members. Of 318 of his employees, 117 are unionists. From a sample of 255 of the competitor's labor force, 109 are union members. Perform a hypothesis test by

a.   stating the hypotheses.
b.   calculating the critical value.
c.   determining the decision rule.
d.   drawing the conclusion.

Set $\alpha = 0.05$.

Answer: a. $H_0: \pi_1 \geq \pi_2$ $H_A: \pi_1 < \pi_2$
        b. -0.068
        c.   Do not reject if $d_a > -0.068$. Reject if $d_a < -0.068$.
        d. $d_a = 0.37 - 0.43 = -0.06 < -0.068$. DNR. Manufacturer is wrong.

10.5   Confidence Intervals for Two Populations

Although confidence intervals and tests of hypotheses are different procedures, it is
actually possible to use confidence intervals to test hypotheses. This is true whether
we are working with one sample, as in the previous chapter, or with two samples, as
in this chapter.

For example, recall that in the last chapter Coco Crunchy Crispies tested the hypothesis that the mean weight of their cereal boxes was 36 ounces. It is possible to
test the mean weight by constructing a confidence interval. If the interval contains
36, the null would not be rejected. If the interval did not contain the hypothesized
value of 36, the null would be rejected.

Similarly, with two-sample tests we hypothesize that $\mu_1 = \mu_2$, or, alternatively,
$\mu_1 - \mu_2 = 0$. If the corresponding confidence interval contains zero, the null is
not rejected.

We will now examine the manner in which confidence intervals for two samples
can be devised. Attention will focus on confidence intervals for

1. Large, independent samples.
2. Small, independent samples.
3. Paired samples.

A.   Confidence Intervals for Large, Independent Samples

In a one-sample test we used the sample mean as our point estimate of the unknown
population mean. Since in a two-sample test our interest lies in the difference in two
population means, the point estimate is the difference between the two sample
means $\overline{X}_1 - \overline{X}_2$.

In Example 10-1 we tested the hypothesis that the mean level of deposits in banks
in Virginia was equal to that in Maryland. That hypothesis, you recall, was rejected.

A confidence interval for the two-sample test would begin with the point estimate, which is provided by the difference in the sample means in the two states. It
makes no difference which state is identified as sample 1 and which is sample 2. It

may be more convenient to set the higher mean as $\overline{X}_1$ since that would generate a positive number.

The confidence coefficient is then added to and subtracted from the point estimate. This coefficient is found by multiplying Z (or t) by the standard error, which is found according to Formula (10.2). Thus, the confidence interval is calculated as

$$\text{C.I. for } \mu_1 - \mu_2 = (\overline{X}_1 - \overline{X}_2) \pm Z \sqrt{\frac{\sigma_1^2}{n_1} + \frac{\sigma_1^2}{n_2}} \qquad (10.21)$$

The data for the comparison of deposit levels were

$$\overline{X}_V = \$1{,}317 \quad \sigma_V = \$517 \quad n_V = 230$$

$$\overline{X}_M = \$1{,}512 \quad \sigma_M = \$485 \quad n_M = 302$$

The α-value of 0.05 called for a Z-value of 1.96.

Then, using Virginia as sample 1,

$$\text{C.I. for } \mu_1 - \mu_2 = (1{,}512 - 1{,}317) \pm 1.96 \sqrt{\frac{(517)^2}{230} + \frac{(485)^2}{302}}$$

$$= 195 \pm 86.35$$

$$108.65 \le \mu_1 - \mu_2 \le 281.35$$

As in Chapter 8, two interpretations of the confidence interval are possible:

1. We can be 95 percent confident that our point estimate of $195 of the difference in the mean deposit level between the two states is within $86.35 of the true unknown mean.
2. We can be 95 percent confident that the true difference between the mean deposit levels in the two states is between $108.65 and $281.35.

Recall that the hypothesis $\mu_V = \mu_M$ was rejected. This decision is supported by the fact that the confidence interval does not contain zero.

If the population standard deviations are not known, the standard error is estimated using the sample variances. Then

$$\text{C.I. for } \mu_1 - \mu_2 = (\overline{X}_1 - \overline{X}_2) \pm Z \sqrt{\frac{s_1^2}{n_1} + \frac{s_1^2}{n_2}} \qquad (10.22)$$

EXAMPLE 10-7 Mean Life Expectancies

Health care economists for the Liberty Life Company alluded to earlier in this chapter conducted a test to compare the mean ages at which smokers and nonsmokers die. The ages at which 300 smokers and 400 nonsmokers who had died within the past three months were collected from insurance records. The mean ages at death were $\overline{X}_S = 68.1$ and $\overline{X}_N = 77.3$ for smokers and nonsmokers, respectively. The standard deviations of ages for all people in these groups were not known. However, the standard deviations of the samples were computed to be $s_S = 8.2$ and $s_N = 5.3$. A 99 percent confidence interval is desired.

Solution:

$$\text{C.I. for } \mu_1 - \mu_2 = (77.3 - 68.1) \pm 2.58 \sqrt{\frac{(5.3)^2}{400} + \frac{(8.2)^2}{300}}$$

$$9.2 \pm 1.4$$

$$7.8 \leq \mu_1 - \mu_2 \leq 10.6$$

Statistical Interpretation:

We can be 99 percent confident that our point estimate of 9.2 years for the difference between the mean life expectancy of smokers and nonsmokers is within 1.4 years of the actual mean difference. Also, we can be 99 percent certain that the true difference between the mean life expectancy of these two groups of people is between 7.8 and 10.6 years.

B. Confidence Interval with Two Small, Independent Samples

By now you should be aware that the use of small samples without the knowledge of the population variance requires a *t*-test. Furthermore, if we assume that the two population variances are equal, we can pool data from the two samples to compute s_p^2, the estimate of the variance common to both populations. This is done with Formula (10.10).

Then

$$\text{C.I. for } \mu_1 - \mu_2 = (\overline{X}_1 - \overline{X}_2) \pm t \sqrt{\frac{s_p^2}{n_1} + \frac{s_p^2}{n_2}} \qquad (10.23)$$

The *t*-value carries $n_1 + n_2 - 2$ degrees of freedom.

Example 10-8 Mean Interest Rates

The Economist, a weekly British publication, measured the mean interest rates of 7 Western countries and 11 Eastern nations. The values were reported as

$$\overline{X}_W = 17.5\% \qquad s_W = 3.2\%$$

$$\overline{X}_E = 15.3\% \qquad s_E = 2.9\%$$

Calculate a 90 percent confidence interval for the difference between the mean interest rates in Eastern and Western countries throughout the world.

SOLUTION:

$$s_p^2 = \frac{s_W^2(n_W - 1) + s_E^2(n_E - 1)}{n_W + n_E - 2}$$

$$= \frac{(3.2)^2(7 - 1) + (2.9)^2(11 - 1)}{7 + 11 - 2}$$

$$= 9.09$$

With $\alpha = 0.10$, and $n_W + n_E - 2 = 16$ d.f., the proper t-value is 1.746. Then

$$\text{C.I. for } \mu_1 - \mu_2 = (17.5 - 15.3) \pm 1.746 \sqrt{\frac{9.09}{7} + \frac{9.09}{11}}$$

$$2.2 \pm 2.55$$

$$-0.35 \leq \mu_1 - \mu_2 \leq 4.75$$

STATISTICAL INTERPRETATION:

We can be 90 percent certain that our point estimate of 2.2 percent for the difference between the mean interest rates of Eastern and Western countries is within 2.55 percent of the actual mean difference.

Also, we can be 90 percent confident that the true mean difference in interest rates is between −0.35 percent and 4.75 percent.

This example assumed that the variances in the two populations were equal. If that assumption cannot be made, then the t-value must be replaced by the t'-value. This procedure was described earlier in this chapter in our discussion of hypothesis testing.

C. PAIRED SAMPLES

Confidence intervals can also be calculated when paired samples are taken by using the formula

$$\text{C.I. for } \mu_1 - \mu_2 = \bar{d}_a \pm t\frac{s_d}{\sqrt{n}} \qquad (10.24)$$

Using the data in Table 10-1 for race times of horses, we have

$$\text{C.I. for } \mu_1 - \mu_2 = 0.037 \pm 1.943\frac{0.0611}{\sqrt{7}}$$

$$-0.008 \leq \mu_1 - \mu_2 \leq 0.0819$$

The usual interpretations apply.

10.6   SOLVED PROBLEMS

1. **The Yuppies' Work Ethic** An April 1991 issue of *Fortune* carried a story about workaholic baby boomers, ages 25 to 43, who have corporate managerial jobs. The article compared the work life of these young executives who had placed themselves on the fast corporate track with workers who committed less time to their jobs. While those in the success-oriented mode often reported 70, 80, or even 90 hours on the job each week, about 60 was typical. The data were gathered from interviews of corporate employees. Letting group 1 be the fast-trackers and group 2 be those who spent less time on the job, assume the interviews revealed the following statistics regarding weekly work schedules:

Group 1	Group 2
$\overline{X}_1 = 62.5$ hours	$\overline{X}_2 = 39.7$ hours
$s_1 = 23.7$ hours	$s_2 = 8.9$ hours
$n_1 = 175$	$n_2 = 168$

a. At the 10 percent level of significance, does there appear to be a difference in the mean number of hours per week devoted to the job by the two groups?

Since we seek to determine if there is any difference, a two-tailed test is to be made.

$$H_0: \mu_1 = \mu_2$$

$$H_A: \mu_1 \neq \mu_2$$

The sample standard deviations must be used to estimate the standard error of the difference between means because the corresponding parameters are unknown.

$$s_{x_1-x_2} = \sqrt{\frac{s_1^2}{n_1} + \frac{s_2^2}{n_2}}$$

$$= \sqrt{\frac{(23.7)^2}{175} + \frac{(8.9)^2}{168}}$$

$$= 1.92 \text{ hours}$$

Then

$$d_c = \pm 1.65(1.92)$$

$$= \pm 3.17 \text{ hours}$$

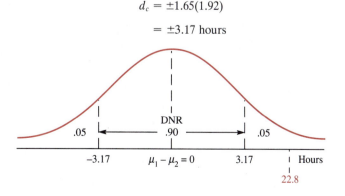

Decision Rule
Do not reject if $-3.17 < d_a < 3.17$. Reject if $d_a < -3.17$ or $d_a > 3.17$.

Conclusion: Since $d_a = 62.5 - 39.7 = 22.8$ hours, reject the null and conclude that there is a significant difference in mean work weeks.

b. Perhaps you wanted to determine if those in the first group worked longer hours on the average than those in the second. This is expressed as $\mu_1 > \mu_2$, and becomes the alternative hypothesis (it does not contain the equal sign). It calls for a right-tailed test.

$$H_0: \mu_1 \leq \mu_2$$

$$H_A: \mu_1 > \mu_2$$

Then, if $\alpha = 0.10$,

$$d_c = Zs_{\bar{x}_1-\bar{x}_2}$$

$$= 1.28(1.92)$$

$$= 2.46 \text{ hours}$$

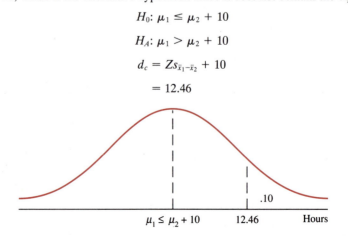

Decision Rule
Do not reject if $d_a < 2.46$. Reject null if $d_a > 2.46$.

Conclusion: Since $d_a = 22.8 > 2.46$, reject null. Evidence suggests mean of first group exceeds that of second.

c. A third approach to this comparison is to test the hypothesis that μ_1 exceeds μ_2 by some specific (nonzero) amount, such as 10 hours. Then, the statement becomes $\mu_1 > \mu_2 + 10$, which is the alternative hypothesis since it does not contain the equal sign.

$$H_0: \mu_1 \leq \mu_2 + 10$$

$$H_A: \mu_1 > \mu_2 + 10$$

$$d_c = Zs_{\bar{x}_1-\bar{x}_2} + 10$$

$$= 12.46$$

Decision Rule
Do not reject null if $d_a < 12.46$. Reject null if $d_a > 12.46$.

Conclusion: Since $d_a = 22.8$, reject null. Evidence suggests mean of first group exceeds that of second by more than 10.

2. **Inflation and Market Power** Many economic studies focus on industries in which a good deal of market power is concentrated in the hands of just a few firms. It is feared that powerful firms in such highly concentrated industries will dominate the market to their own selfish advantage. Firms in nine concentrated industries were paired with firms in an equal number of industries in which economic power was more dispersed. Industries in each group were matched with respect to foreign competition, cost structures, and all other factors which can affect industry prices. The average price increases in percentages in each industry are shown here. Does it appear at the 5 percent level that concentrated industries exhibit more pronounced inflationary pressures than do less concentrated industries?

Industry Pairings	Concentrated Industries (%)	Less Concentrated Industries (%)	d_i (%)	d_i^2 (%)
1	3.7	3.2	0.5	0.25
2	4.1	3.7	0.4	0.16
3	2.1	2.6	−0.5	0.25
4	−0.9	0.1	−1.0	1.00
5	4.6	4.1	0.5	0.25
6	5.2	4.8	0.4	0.16
7	6.7	5.2	1.5	2.25
8	3.8	3.9	−0.1	0.01
9	4.9	4.6	0.3	0.09
			2.0	4.42

$$H_0: \mu_1 - \mu_2 \le 0$$

$$H_A: \mu_1 - \mu_2 > 0$$

$$\bar{d}_a = \frac{\Sigma d_i}{n}$$

$$= \frac{2}{9}$$

$$= 0.22$$

$$s_d = \sqrt{\frac{\Sigma d_i^2 - n(\bar{d}_a)^2}{n - 1}}$$

$$= \sqrt{\frac{4.42 - 9(0.22)^2}{8}}$$

$$= 0.706$$

With $\alpha = 0.05$ and d.f. $= n - 1 = 8$,

$$\bar{d}_c = +t\frac{s_d}{\sqrt{n}}$$

$$= 1.860\left(\frac{0.706}{\sqrt{9}}\right)$$

$$= 0.438$$

Decision Rule
Do not reject if $\bar{d}_a < 0.438$. Reject if $\bar{d}_a > 0.438$.

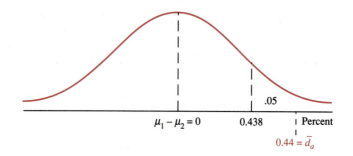

Conclusion: Do not reject the null. Evidence suggests that the mean price rise is higher in concentrated industries.

3. **Small-Sample t-Tests** A drilling company tests two drill bits by sinking wells to a maximum of 112 feet and recording the number of hours the procedure took. The first bit was used in 12 cases, resulting in a mean time of $\overline{X}_1 = 27.3$ hours and $s_1 = 8.7$ hours. Ten wells were dug with the second bit, producing an $\overline{X}_2 = 31.7$ hours and $s_2 = 8.3$ hours.
   a. Does it appear that one bit is more effective than the other? Set $\alpha = 0.10$. No evidence suggests variances are equal.

$$H_0: \mu_1 = \mu_2$$

$$H_A: \mu_1 \neq \mu_2$$

$$\text{d.f.} = \frac{[s_1^2/n_1 + s_2^2/n_2]^2}{\dfrac{(s_1^2/n_1)^2}{(n_1 - 1)} + \dfrac{(s_2^2/n_2)^2}{(n_2 - 1)}}$$

$$= \frac{[(8.7)^2/12 + (8.3)2/10]^2}{\dfrac{[(8.7)^2/12]^2}{11} + \dfrac{[(8.3)^2/10]^2}{9}} = \frac{174.15}{8.89}$$

$$= 19.78$$

$$\approx 19$$

With d.f. $= 19$, and $\alpha = 0.10$,

$$d_c = \pm t' \sqrt{\frac{s_1^2}{n_1} + \frac{s_2^2}{n_2}}$$

$$= \pm 1.729 \sqrt{\frac{(8.7)^2}{12} + \frac{(8.3)^2}{10}}$$

$$= \pm 6.28$$

Decision Rule
Do not reject if $-6.28 < d_a < 6.28$. Reject if $d_a < -6.28$ or $d_a > 6.28$.

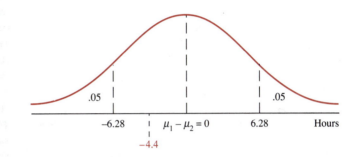

Conclusion: $d_a = -4.4$. Do not reject. Mean times of two bits are similar.

b. All the wells were dug with the same drilling team and in the same soil. If for these reasons, or any others that might be cited, the drilling company felt drilling times had equal variances, how would the test differ from part (a)? (Remember, a procedure will be given in the next chapter which tests for equal variances.) Equal variances allow the pooling of sample data.

$$s_p^2 = \frac{s_1^2(n_1 - 1) + s_2^2(n_2 - 1)}{n_1 + n_2 - 2}$$

$$= \frac{(8.7)^2(12 - 1) + (8.3)^2(10 - 1)}{12 + 10 - 2}$$

$$= 72.63 \text{ hours squared}$$

$$d_c = \pm t \sqrt{\frac{s_p^2}{n_1} + \frac{s_p^2}{n_2}}$$

$$= \pm 1.725 \sqrt{\frac{72.63}{12} + \frac{72.63}{10}}$$

$$= \pm 6.29$$

Decision Rule

Do not reject if $-6.29 \le d_a \le 6.29$. Reject if $d_a < -6.29$ or $d_a > 6.29$.

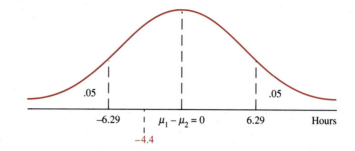

Conclusion: $d_a = -4.4$. Do not reject.

4. **The Credit Crunch** A study in *Retail Management* revealed that 131 of 468 women who made retail purchases did so using a particular credit card, while 57 of 237 men used the same card.

   a. Is there evidence to suggest a difference in the proportion of women and men who use that card? Let $\alpha = 0.05$.

$$H_0: \pi_W = \pi_M$$

$$H_A: \pi_W \ne \pi_M$$

$$\hat{\pi} = \frac{X_1 + X_2}{n_1 + n_2}$$

$$= \frac{131 + 57}{468 + 237}$$

$$= 0.27$$

$$s_{p_1-p_2} = \sqrt{\frac{\hat{\pi}(1 - \hat{\pi})}{n_1} + \frac{\hat{\pi}(1 - \hat{\pi})}{n_2}}$$

$$= \sqrt{\frac{(0.27)(0.73)}{468} + \frac{(0.27)(0.73)}{237}}$$

$$= 0.035$$

$$d_c = \pm Z s_{p_1-p_2}$$

$$= \pm 1.96(0.035)$$

$$= \pm 0.069$$

Decision Rule

Do not reject if $-0.069 < d_a < 0.069$. Reject if $d_a < -0.069$ or $d_a > 0.069$.

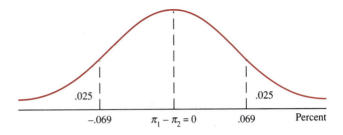

Conclusion: Since $d_a = 0.28 - 0.24 = 0.04$, do not reject the null hypothesis that the two proportions are equal.

b. Suppose it was hypothesized that $\pi_w > \pi_M$.

$$H_0: \pi_w \leq \pi_M$$

$$H_A: \pi_w > \pi_M$$

$$d_c = +1.65(0.035)$$

$$= 0.058$$

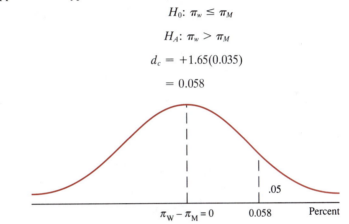

Decision Rule

Do not reject if $d_a < 0.058$. Reject null if $d_a > 0.058$.

Conclusion: $d_a = 0.04$. Do not reject null. There is no evidence to suggest a difference.

c. Suppose it was hypothesized that the proportion of women was at least as great as that of men ($\pi_w \geq \pi_M$).

$$H_0: \pi_w \geq \pi_M$$

$$H_A: \pi_w < \pi_M$$

$$d_c = -1.65(0.035)$$

$$= -0.058$$

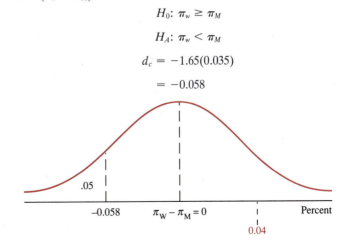

Decision Rule

Do not reject if $d_a > -0.058$. Reject if $d_a < -0.058$.

Conclusion: Since $d_a = 0.04$, do not reject. There is no evidence to suggest a difference.

d. Suppose it was hypothesized that the proportion of women exceeds the proportion of men by more than 1.5 percent ($\pi_w > \pi_M + 0.015$).

$$H_0: \pi_W - \pi_M \leq 0.015$$

$$H_A: \pi_W - \pi_M > 0.015$$

$$d_c = 1.65(0.035) + 0.015$$

$$= 0.07$$

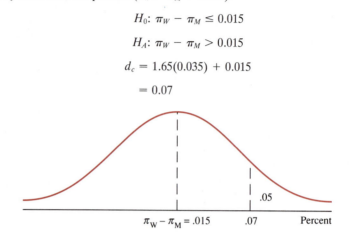

Decision Rule

Do not reject if $d_a < 0.07$. Reject if $d_a > 0.07$.

Conclusion: Do not reject null. There is no evidence to suggest a difference.

10.7 WHAT YOU SHOULD HAVE LEARNED FROM THIS CHAPTER

This chapter has provided still another tool in your statistical depository. This additional inferential device permits the comparison of two populations. It should be apparent that such a comparison is often essential in making business decisions. Every business manager in any position requiring discretionary action, no matter how incidental the consequences might be, is always faced with a choice regarding the relative merits of alternatives.

The material contained in this chapter illustrates the manner in which the results of comparisons can be used to draw important business conclusions. These comparisons extend to both population means and proportions. You should understand how to conduct these statistical tests for large and small samples.

10.8 COMPUTER APPLICATIONS

Considering the number of business decisions which depend upon the comparison of two populations, it is not surprising that many computer packages have been designed to handle such conditions. The three packages we have been examining offer no exceptions. Each is equipped to provide the decision maker with the information that he or she requires to identify the optimal policy action. In this section we will examine each in turn.

A. MINITAB

To compare large samples, the data are entered (we will assume in the first two columns) and the command

```
MTB> TWOSAMPLE T C1 C2
```

is given. If you enter TWOSAMPLE Z C1 C2, identical printouts appear, since t and Z produce the same results with large samples. Notice that the Minitab printout Minitab 1 provides a confidence interval for the difference between the two means (a process we did not cover in this chapter). Of present interest, the last line tests the hypothesis of equal means. The small t-value of 0.86 indicates that the results obtained here are quite possible if the null is correct. The p-value of 0.39 means that this is the lowest value for α at which we can reject the null. The null cannot be rejected at the 10 percent level, for example. At any of the generally used values for α (0.10, 0.05, or 0.01), the null is not rejected. We can safely conclude that the population means are equal.

MINITAB 1

```
TTEST mu C1 = mu C2 (US NE): T = 0.86   P = 0.39
```

If the samples are small, you must decide if pooled data are to be used. If pooled data are used because the variances are assumed equal, the commands are

```
MTB> TWOSAMPLE T C1 C2;
SUBC> POOLED.
```

The printout is shown in Minitab 1. If pooled data are not assumed, simply omit the subcommand POOLED.

B. SAS

In contrast to Minitab, SAS requires that the data for the variable being tested be listed in a single column. A second column is used to identify in which of the two groups each observation is to be placed. Given the description of the test in the section on Minitab, assume that we have 35 observations for production levels in each sample. Perhaps one sample is for day-shift workers and the other for night-shift workers. The SAS program must be written as

```
DATA;
INPUT PRODUCTION SHIFT;
CARDS;
45 D
52 D
...
...
rest of data for day shift go here
53 N
47 N
...
rest of data for night shift go here
PROC TTEST;
CLASS SHIFT;
```

PROC TTEST first determines if the assumption of equal variances is feasible. It then performs the appropriate hypothesis test. The CLASS statement identifies the variable that divides the data into the two groups you wish to compare.

SAS 1

```
TTEST PROCEDURE
VARIABLE PRODUCTION
Group    N          Mean                    Std Dev                 Std Error
  D      35
  N      35
Variances      T              DF             Prob >|T|
unequal      10.51            68               0.3913
Equal        10.51            68               0.3913
For Ho: variances are equal, F¹ = 0.5386
```

To interpret the output shown in SAS 1, first examine the last line headed by For Ho: Variances are equal, and note the value of PROB>F' = . If this value is greater than 0.10, proceed with the assumptions of equal variances. If the value is less than 0.10, the assumption of unequal variances is made. Examine the two lines directly above this and select the appropriate one. The T-values, degrees of freedom, and Prob values are given. The decision regarding rejection of the hypothesis is based on the value of the Prob. For example, in SAS 1, PROB $> F' = 0.5386 > 0.10$. We then assume equal variances, and the line EQUAL is read. (Actually, it makes no difference since both lines are the same. In most cases this will not occur.) The lowest value for which the null can be rejected is 39.13 percent. Thus, at any acceptable level for α, the null is not rejected.

C. SPSS-PC

For a description of the test, browse through the discussions on Minitab and SAS. To run the test described in the section on SAS the SPSS-PC command is

```
T-TEST GROUPS=SHIFT(1,2)/VARIABLES=PROD.
```

LIST OF FORMULAS

$$d_c = \pm Z\sigma_{\bar{x}_1-\bar{x}_2} \tag{10.1}$$

Used to determine the critical differences in a two-tailed test with large samples.

$$\sigma_{\bar{x}_1-\bar{x}_2} = \sqrt{\frac{\sigma_1^2}{n_1} + \frac{\sigma_2^2}{n_2}} \tag{10.2}$$

The standard error of the difference between the two means.

$$s_{\bar{x}_1-\bar{x}_2} = \sqrt{\frac{s_1^2}{n_1} + \frac{s_2^2}{n_2}} \tag{10.3}$$

An estimator of the difference between the sample means. Used when population variances are unknown.

$$d_c = \pm Z s_{\bar{x}_1 - \bar{x}_2} \tag{10.4}$$

Used in conjunction with (10.3) to determine the critical differences in a two-tailed test.

$$d_c = -Z \sigma_{\bar{x}_1 - \bar{x}_2} \tag{10.5}$$

Used to calculate the critical difference in a left-tailed test when population variances are known.

$$d_c = -Z s_{\bar{x}_1 - \bar{x}_2} \tag{10.6}$$

Used in place of (10.5) if population variances are unknown.

$$d_c = Z \sigma_{\bar{x}_1 - \bar{x}_2} \tag{10.7}$$

Used to calculate the critical difference in a right-tailed test when population variances are known.

$$d_c = Z s_{\bar{x}_1 - \bar{x}_2} \tag{10.8}$$

Used in place of (10.7) if population variances are unknown.

$$d_c = \pm t \sqrt{\frac{s_p^2}{n_1} + \frac{s_p^2}{n_2}} \tag{10.9}$$

Calculates the critical difference between two means using small samples and unknown but equal variances.

$$s_p^2 = \frac{s_1^2(n_1 - 1) + s_2^2(n_2 - 1)}{n_1 + n_2 - 2} \tag{10.10}$$

The estimator for the common variance of the populations.

$$\text{d.f.} = \frac{[s_1^2/n_1 + s_2^2/n_2]^2}{(s_1^2/n_1)^2/(n_1 - 1) + (s_2^2/n_2)^2/(n_2 - 1)} \tag{10.11}$$

Calculates the degrees of freedom for t' when comparing with normal populations with unequal variances using small samples.

$$d_c = \pm t' \sqrt{\frac{s_1^2}{n_1} + \frac{s_2^2}{n_2}} \tag{10.12}$$

Used in conjunction with (10.11).

$$\bar{d}_a = \frac{\Sigma d_i}{n} \tag{10.13}$$

Determines the mean difference in paired observations.

$$\bar{d}_c = \pm t \frac{s_d}{\sqrt{n}} \tag{10.14}$$

Determines the critical mean differences in paired observations.

$$s_d = \sqrt{\frac{\Sigma d_i^2 - n(\bar{d}_a)^2}{n-1}} \qquad (10.15)$$

Calculates the standard deviation in differences in paired observations.

$$\hat{\pi} = \frac{n_1 p_1 + n_2 p_2}{n_1 + n_2} \qquad (10.16)$$

Estimates common population proportions.

$$\hat{\pi} = \frac{X_1 + X_2}{n_1 + n_2} \qquad (10.17)$$

Computationally equivalent to (10.16).

$$s_{p_1-p_2} = \sqrt{\frac{\hat{\pi}(1-\hat{\pi})}{n_1} + \frac{\hat{\pi}(1-\hat{\pi})}{n_2}} \qquad (10.18)$$

Calculates the standard error in the differences between two sampling proportions.

$$d_c = \pm Z s_{p_1-p_2} \qquad (10.19)$$

Determines critical difference between proportions.

$$s_{p_1-p_2} = \sqrt{\frac{p_1 q_1}{n_1} + \frac{p_2 q_2}{n_2}} \qquad (10.20)$$

Calculates the standard error in the differences between two sample proportions when pooling is not allowed.

$$\text{C.I. for } \mu_1 - \mu_2 = (\bar{X}_1 - \bar{X}_2) \pm Z \sqrt{\frac{\sigma_1^2}{n_1} + \frac{\sigma_1^2}{n_2}} \qquad (10.21)$$

Calculates the confidence interval for the difference between two means with large samples when population variances are known.

$$\text{C.I. for } \mu_1 - \mu_2 = (\bar{X}_1 - \bar{X}_2) \pm Z \sqrt{\frac{s_1^2}{n_1} + \frac{s_1^2}{n_2}} \qquad (10.22)$$

Used to calculate the confidence interval for the difference between two means with large samples when the population variances are unknown.

$$\text{C.I. for } \mu_1 - \mu_2 = (\bar{X}_1 - \bar{X}_2) \pm t \sqrt{\frac{s_p^2}{n_1} + \frac{s_p^2}{n_2}} \qquad (10.23)$$

Used to calculate the confidence interval for the difference between two means for independent, small samples.

$$\text{C.I. for } \mu_1 - \mu_2 = \bar{d}_a \pm t \frac{s_d}{\sqrt{n}} \qquad (10.24)$$

Used to calculate the confidence interval for the difference between two means using paired samples.

CHAPTER EXERCISES

CONCEPTUAL QUESTIONS

1. What is the purpose of the $\sigma_{\bar{x}_1-\bar{x}_2}$, the standard error of the difference between two sample means?
2. What happens to the critical difference of a right-tailed test as population variances increase? Why?
3. What is the formula for the standard error of the difference between the two sample means, and what is the purpose of this statistic?

PROBLEMS

4. An accountant for a large corporation in the Midwest must decide whether to select AT&T or Sprint to handle the firm's long-distance telephone service. Data are collected for many calls, using both services and are reported here.

	AT&T	Sprint
Number of calls	145	102
Mean cost	$4.07	$3.89
Standard deviation	$0.97	$0.85

If these data suggest that there is a significant difference in the mean cost, additional consideration such as reliability will be given to determine which service should be selected. At the 5 percent level, does it appear further analysis will be necessary?

5. Past records show that the mean time lapse from the time an order is placed with firm 1 to the time the shipment is received is 7.3 days, with a standard deviation of 2.1 days. For firm 2, corresponding figures were 8.9 and 2.7 days. These data were based on samples of $n_1 = 73$ and $n_2 = 52$. Your supervisor has charged you with the responsibility of choosing a supplier based on any difference that may exist in this time lag. At the 10 percent level, what is your decision?

6. In an article on business travel, *U.S. News and World Report* stated that the mean cost for one national hotel chain was $45.12 per night, and a second chain was $42.62 per night. Assume these statistics are based on samples of 82 and 97, respectively, and that population variances for each chain are known to be $9.48 and $8.29, respectively. You must determine which chain of hotels your company will use. At the 1 percent level, what is your decision if it is based solely on any difference in cost that may exist?

7. Assume the sample sizes in the previous problem are $n_1 = 182$ and $n_2 = 197$.
   a. Without working the problem, explain what would happen to the critical difference with these larger samples. Why does it happen?
   b. Work the problem with these larger samples and see if you were right?

8. A winery in California was experiencing a problem with evaporation during bottling. Two processing methods revealed a mean loss of 2.2 ounces and 2.7 ounces per bottle, using $n_1 = 55$ and $n_2 = 62$ bottles. It is known from industry standards that variances in evaporation losses are 0.81 ounce and 0.98 ounce, respectively. At the 8 percent level of significance, which method would you advise if the decision is made on the basis of any existing difference in mean evaporation rates?

9. A recent issue of *Business Week* discussed efforts by a major car company to determine if one type of vehicle was withstanding the wear and tear of daily use more than was a second type. A finance major who has just graduated from a local university was hired to determine if any difference exists in mean life. She collects data on the mean number of months a vehicle is in service before the first major repair is necessary, and finds the following information: vehicle 1: $\overline{X}_1 = 27.3$ months, $s_1 = 7.8$ months, and $n_1 = 82$ vehicles; vehicle 2: $\overline{X}_2 = 33.3$ months, $s_2 = 10.4$ months, and $n_2 = 73$ vehicles. At the 2 percent level, does there appear to be a difference?

10. Your business is critically dependent on rapid delivery of printed material from one location to another in the financial district of New York City. One delivery service took a mean of 0.21 hour to deliver 45 documents, with a standard deviation of 0.07 hour. A second delivery service required a mean of 0.29 hour for the delivery of 39 documents, with a standard deviation of 0.09 hour. Can you conclude at the 5 percent level that there is any difference in mean delivery time?

11. In the battle of the bulge, diet experts examined the caloric content of different types of junk food. The mean number of calories in 100 four-ounce servings of potato chips was 612, with a standard deviation of 97 calories. One hundred 4-ounce servings of pretzels contained a mean of 402 calories, with a standard deviation of 67. Is there a difference in the caloric count of these snacks? Set $\alpha = 0.10$.

12. The National Education Association studied the effect of kindergarten on childrens' performances on standardized tests by the time they reached the second grade. The test was administered to 1,000 second graders, 600 of whom had completed kindergarten. The mean score for the kindergarten graduates was 79.3 out of a possible 99, with a standard deviation of 27.3. Those children who did not attend kindergarten scored a mean of 68.3 with a standard deviation of 31.2. Do these data present sufficient evidence to suggest a difference in test performance at the 5 percent level?

13. *U.S. News and World Report* carried an article concerning drug-related murders in the nation's capital. A sample of 112 days in 1987 revealed an average of three homicides per day in a particular section of the capital. In a sample of 200 days in 1988 that mean increased to 4.2. If the respective standard deviations were 1.9 and 2.2 murders, do these data suggest that the incidence of homicides increased in 1988? Set $\alpha = 0.05$.

14. *The Wall Street Journal* reported that Ford Motor Company became interested in the mean salaries of its executives stationed overseas as opposed to those based stateside. The mean salary for 87 executives posted abroad was $78,010, with a standard deviation of $15,700. The same number of executives placed in domestic service revealed a mean and standard deviation of $69,410 and $10,012. At the 3 percent level of significance, does there seem to be a difference?

15. Alex Trotman, head of global operations for Ford Motor Company, has always alleged that foreign-based executives received higher pay. At the 10 percent level, do the data from the previous problem support his contention?

16. *The Wall Street Journal* also reported that concern has been raised regarding the environment in which beef cattle are kept prior to slaughter. Supposedly, stress-free surroundings promote growth and quality of the meat. A beef grower in northern California even advertises that he "treats his cattle to a spectacular seaside view" before preparing them for the meat counter at the local grocery store. Assume 50 cattle raised in this vacation-like setting gain an average of 112 pounds with $s = 32.3$ pounds over a given time period. During the same time, 50 cows with a view of the slaughterhouse gain 105.7 pounds on the average with $s = 28.7$ pounds. At the 10 percent level, can the claim that a pleasant environment promotes weight gain be supported?

17. The popularity of video games sparked interest among arcade owners regarding the relative merits of different types of amusement. A sample of 40 "flipper and bumper" games yielded a mean weekly revenue of $280, with a standard deviation of $81. A like number of electronic games produced mean weekly revenues of $297 with $s = \$72$. At the 1 percent level, do these data suggest a difference in the ability to generate revenue?

18. Several Christmases ago a portion of Santa Claus's elves unionized. Since that time Santa has wondered if there was any difference in mean productivity of unionized elves and nonunionized elves. A sample of 150 unionized elves reported a mean output of 27.3 toys per week per elf, with a standard deviation of 8.7 toys. A sample of 132 nonunionized elves revealed a mean of 29.7 toys per week per elf, with $s = 10.7$. Can Santa conclude at the 10 percent level that there is a difference in mean productivity levels?

19. A study by the National Health Institute revealed that 500 women in a sample exercised an average of 6.4 hours per week with $s = 3.7$ hours. Five hundred men reported a mean exercise time of 5.1 hours with $s = 2.1$ hours. Can the NHI conclude at the 5 percent level that women exercise more than men on the average?

20. A large textile firm uses two trucking companies, Apex and Omega, to deliver products to its customers. The CEO for the textile firm has long felt that Apex provides shorter delivery times. As a new management trainee, you have been told by the CEO to compare delivery times. You find that 50 deliveries by Apex took a mean of 40.7 hours with a standard deviation of 10.3 hours. Fifty deliveries by Omega required a mean of 42.5 hours with a standard deviation of 9.7 hours. Do these data support the CEO's suspicions? Set α at 0.01.

21. While serving as a summer intern for a major insurance company, a management major at the local university performed a study to measure the mean life expectancy of alcoholics as opposed to those who do not drink excessively. The company felt that insurance costs were affected by the shorter life-span of heavy drinkers.

    The mean age at death for 100 alcoholics was found to be 63.7 years with $s = 17.7$, while 100 moderate and nondrinkers lived an average of 75.2 years with $s = 8.7$. At the 5 percent level, do these data suggest that the company should expect to pay earlier benefits for alcoholics?

22. A pricing experiment was conducted by a national chain of stereo equipment outlets. For one weekend, the price of their top compact disk players was raised by 4 percent in 35 stores and lowered by a like amount in 35 other randomly selected stores. Changes in sales revenue were noted in each case. In those stores raising their price, revenues on the CD players increased by an average of $842, with $s = \$217$. The mean increase in revenues in those stores lowering prices was $817, with $s = \$202$. The marketing manager for the firm has always felt that an increase in price would raise revenues more than would a decrease (a concept economists call elasticity of demand). Do these data suggest the manager is correct? Set $\alpha = 1$ percent.

23. A controversial theory in finance holds that stocks traded on the organized exchanges always increase more on Fridays than on Mondays due to the timing of Treasury auctions. As his senior project, a finance major at a large university randomly selects 302 stocks trading on the New York Stock Exchange on Friday and finds the average price change to be 0.375 point, with a standard deviation of 0.075. The 412 stocks randomly selected on Monday's trading yielded a mean price change of -0.25 point, with a standard deviation of 0.05. At the 1 percent level, do these data support this theory?

24. Lynne Hampton has just graduated with a bachelor's degree in marketing and has obtained a position with a large sportswear manufacturer. The firm produces two types of shoes: Jolly Joggers and Weinee Walkers. The marketing director feels that weekly sales revenues from the Jolly Joggers are more than $50 in excess of what the Weinee Walkers generate.

Hampton has been given the task of determining if this is true. She collects the data shown here and sets $\alpha = 5$ percent. What should her conclusion be?

	Jolly Joggers	Weinee Walkers
Mean weekly revenues	$X_J = \$8,940$	$X_W = \$7,405$
Standard deviation	$s_J = \$3,050$	$s_W = \$2,912$
Number of weeks	$n_J = 50$	$n_W = 50$

25. As a new analyst in the financial analysis division of a Florida-based firm making jet skis, you must determine if the firm should concentrate its efforts on supplying customers on the West Coast or those in Florida. The decision will rest in part on which market is paying the higher price. The CEO feels that the average price on the West Coast is more than $15 above what the firm can receive from Florida customers. Test the CEO's assumption at the 5 percent level, using the following data:

	West Coast Orders	Florida Orders
Number of orders	37	41
Mean price	$418.10	$397.20
Standard deviation	$73.00	$62.10

26. In the effort to reduce the cost of fuel, your firm tests the gas mileage for two different types of vehicles. Seven vehicles of type 1 yield a mean of 23.7 mpg with $s = 9.2$ mpg. Nine of type 2 have a mean of 26.2 mpg and $s = 8.5$ mpg. Mileage is normally distributed, and there is evidence to suggest that population variances are equal. At the 5 percent level, does it appear that a difference exist in the mean gas mileage of the two types of vehicles?

27. Six economists working for the government are asked to predict inflation rates for the upcoming year. Eight economists who work for private concerns are given the same task. The six government economists report rates of 4.2 percent, 5.1 percent, 3.9 percent, 4.7 percent, 4.9 percent, and 5.8 percent. The eight privately employed economists forecast rates of 5.7 percent, 6.1 percent, 5.2 percent, 4.9 percent, 4.6 percent, 4.5 percent, 5.2 percent, and 5.5 percent. At the 10 percent level, does there appear to be a difference in the forecasts of the two groups of economists?

28. Many economic impact studies have been done to determine the effect of labor unions on wage rates. To address this important issue, an economist examines 10 union shops where a mean wage rate of $22.07 and $s = \$8.12$ are found. Twelve nonunion shops reveal a mean of $24.17 and $s = \$9.07$. With $\alpha = 0.01$ and using a two-tailed test, should your shop unionize to get larger wage increases? Assume $\sigma_1 = \sigma_2$.

29. *The Wall Street Journal* reported that a food distributor in the Midwest examined the effects of two sales programs on per capita milk consumption. Ten cities were treated to extensive TV advertising, and the subsequent increase in mean daily consumption of 0.25 gallon and a standard deviation of 0.09 gallon was recorded. Twelve other cities were saturated with newspaper advertisements. There resulted an increase of 0.02 gallon in mean consumption

per capita, with $s = 0.02$ gallon. The distributor felt that TV advertising would be more effective in increasing consumption levels. At the 10 percent level, does this appear to be true? Assume that $\sigma_1 = \sigma_2$.

30. B. F. Skinner, a noted behavioral theorist, has long espoused the use of positive reinforcement in shaping work attitudes. Emery Air Freight was one of the first to use Skinner's behavioral modification techniques. Assume employees in 12 Emery offices using Skinner's principles are given work attitude tests and report a mean score of 79.3 and a standard deviation of 10.7. Employees in 15 offices not using these principles score a mean of 71.5 with $s = 11.2$. If $\alpha = 0.05$, do these data support Skinner's theories? Assume $\sigma_1 = \sigma_2$.

31. Sports enthusiasts often agree that the total points of both teams in a professional basketball game exceed that of both teams in a college game. Using these scores from the 1989 playoff games, do these data support this claim at the 5 percent level? Assume $\sigma_1 = \sigma_2$.

College				Total Points
Illinois	89	Syracuse	86	175
Duke	85	Georgetown	77	162
Seton Hall	84	UNLV	61	145
Michigan	102	Virginia	65	167
Duke	87	Minnesota	70	157
Oklahoma	124	LA Tech	81	205
Virginia	86	Oklahoma	80	166
Michigan	92	N. Carolina	87	179
Michigan	80	Seton Hall	79	159

Professional				Total Points
Boston	115	New York	111	226
Philly	135	San Antonio	122	257
Detroit	112	New Jersey	96	208
Utah	114	Dallas	105	209
Utah	112	Denver	90	202
Chicago	118	Portland	113	221
Milwaukee	113	Cleveland	105	218
Atlanta	115	New York	108	223

32. An auditor randomly selects the accounting records for 10 firms in a certain industry and finds a mean earnings per share (EPS) of $8.12 and a standard deviation of $2.17. Fifteen firms in a second industry report a mean EPS of $9.17 and $s = \$2.83$. There is no reason to believe that $\sigma_1 = \sigma_2$. At the 10 percent level, does there appear to be a difference in the mean EPS of these two industries?

33. Many European countries use a value added tax (VAT), which is a tax on the value added to a good at each stage of production. Eight countries using a consumption-type VAT reported a mean per capita weekly revenue of $1,142 with $s = \$312$. Ten countries using a gross-income-type VAT reported a mean per capita weekly tax take of $1,372 with $s = \$502$. If $\alpha = 0.05$ and $\sigma_1 \neq \sigma_2$, which type of VAT would you choose to maximize tax revenue?

34. The impact of different pay methods on productivity and workers' levels of satisfaction has always been of interest to labor economists. *Fortune* reported that a sporting goods company experimented with the effects of two methods of payment on employee morale in an Ohio plant. Fourteen workers paid a fixed salary were given a test measuring morale and scored a mean of 79.7 with $s = 8.2$. Twelve workers paid on a commission achieved a mean of 72.7 with $s = 5.1$. Set $\alpha = 0.10$ and assume $\sigma_1 \neq \sigma_2$. What can be concluded regarding the relative merits of the two pay systems?

35. The chief financial officer (CFO) for a Fortune 500 firm must decide if debt financing or equity financing would prove less costly. She examines recent market transactions for firms similar to hers and finds that 17 firms using bonds (debt financing) experienced a mean cost of 17.3 percent with $s = 3.7$ percent, and 10 recent stock issues (equity financing) resulted in figures of 22.7 percent and 4.7 percent, respectively. Which method should she suggest to the board of directors if $\alpha = 0.05$ and the population variances in costs are assumed to be unequal?

36. Economists often interpret an increase in national savings rates as an indication that consumers lack confidence in the economy. The mean saving levels at nine Boston area banks in 1989 was 6.7 percent of disposal income with $s = 1.6$ percent. In 1990 a second independent sample of 10 banks revealed values of 9.2 percent and $s = 1.6$, respectively. Does this represent a significant increase in the saving rate, suggesting that consumers are losing confidence? Set $\alpha = 0.05$ and $\sigma_1 = \sigma_2$.

37. A study designed to compare capital investment levels in Japanese industries with that in U.S. industries was reported in *Business Week*. A mean investment level of 24.4 percent of capital assets with a standard deviation of 4.7 percent was found for 15 Japanese industries. Twelve U.S. industries reported figures of 17.7 percent and 8.2 percent. If $\alpha = 0.10$ and $\sigma_{US} \neq \sigma_J$, do these data support the claim that U.S. industries invest at least as high a percentage of capital assets as do Japanese industries?

38. In 1989 a wave of political and economic reform swept through Eastern Europe. Hungarian and Polish leaders even began to speak of economic success in terms of profit measures. The industrial minister of Poland called for the closure of any plant experiencing a "significant drop in returns." If a Polish steel mill had mean weekly output over a 10-week period of 897 tons with $s = 142$ tons in 1989, and in 1990, reported figures of 812 tons with $s = 117$ for a randomly selected 12-week period, do these data suggest a significant reduction in output? Assume $\alpha = 0.10$ and $\sigma_{89} = \sigma_{90}$.

39. As a newly hired staff member in the financial division of a major manufacturer of video games, you must compare failure rates of two types of games. Ten "Blast the Enemy" videos played for a mean of 1,012.3 hours before failure, with $s = 110$ hours. Eleven "Crush the Crusaders" videos lasted an average of 1,217.4 hours without a failure and had a standard deviation of 92 hours before the failure. Your superiors want a report regarding any difference that might exist in the reliability of the two games. At the 10 percent level, and assuming $\sigma_B \neq \sigma_C$, what do you tell them?

40. Private placement involves the sale of security issue directly to a group of investors or a single large investor such as an insurance company or pension fund. A public offering is the sale of the issue to the general public. A recent study by the American Finance Institute showed that of 17 large private offerings, the mean was $27.5 million and $s = \$5.1$ million. Ten large public offerings averaged $22.2 million with $s = \$8.7$ million. Is there evidence to suggest at the 10 percent level that there is a significant difference in private and public offerings? Assume $\sigma_1 \neq \sigma_2$.

41. The CEOs for seven different Fortune 500 firms are asked to rate the desirability under a given set of circumstances of using private placement as opposed to public offerings in the flotation of a new stock issue. A rating scale of 0 to 10 is established and the results are shown here.

	Rating for	
CEO	Private	Public
1	7	8
2	6	7
3	5	7
4	8	7
5	7	6
6	6	6
7	5	6

Does there appear to be a difference in preference between private and public offerings at the 5 percent level?

42. Businesses spend huge sums of money to train their employees to make them more productive. Your firm tests the output level of 10 employees before training and after an extensive training program. The results are shown here measured in units per hour. As director of management operations, you must determine if the training tends to increase output. Set $\alpha = 0.10$.

	Output	
Employee	After Training	Before Training
1	40	31
2	42	35
3	53	42
4	47	49
5	45	37
6	45	32
7	57	41
8	42	31
9	47	30
10	49	31

43. Snow White buys her seven dwarfs new shovels for Christmas. The amounts that each dwarf could dig in their mine with the old shovels and the new shovels are shown here. At the 10 percent level, did Snow White's gift to her seven little buddies improve output?

	Daily Output in Tons	
Dwarf	Old Shovels	New Shovels
Doc	1.7	1.9
Happy	1.4	1.5
Grumpy	2.1	2.2
Bashful	1.9	2.0
Sleepy	2.2	2.2
Dopey	1.4	1.5
Sneezy	1.9	1.8

44. In finance, an efficient market is defined as one that allocates funds to the most productive use. A considerable body of literature exists which is designed to determine if securities markets are indeed efficient. *Business Week* recently surveyed financial analysts. Of 110 analysts who work for private manufacturing firms in the effort to sell their firms' securities, 42 felt markets were efficient, while 31 of 75 analysts who work for brokerage houses who assist in these sales agreed that markets were efficient. At the 5 percent level, does there appear to be a difference in the proportion of these two types of analysts who accept the concept of market efficiency?

45. Of 220 Republicans·in Congress who were surveyed by the *Washington Post*, 183 supported an increase in the minimum wage. Of 302 Democrats, 275 did so. Set $\alpha = 0.01$. Do the data suggest a difference in the proportion of Democrats and Republicans who favor a hike in the minimum wage?

46. As part of her senior project, a marketing major at North Texas State University in Denton, Texas, surveyed 100 men and 100 women at a local shopping mall regarding their buying habits. Of the men, 79 said they had used a credit card to make a purchase over $10 in the past month, while 84 of the women admitted to this type of purchase. The student was attempting to refute the notion that women are more likely to use credit. At the 5 percent level, did she do so?

47. A term paper by a computer science major at Ohio State University, entitled "Your Chip Is about To Come In," examined the quality of computer chips manufactured by two companies. Of 453 chips made by company 1, 54 proved defective. Of 317 made by company 2, 43 proved defective. If $\alpha = 0.10$, is there evidence to suggest that one firm maintains stricter quality control than the other?

48. For many years the *Cincinnati Inquirer* has held claim to being the leading newspaper in southern Ohio and northern Kentucky. To illustrate its influential position, the paper polled a random sample of 802 readers regarding their knowledge of a specific tax issue facing the city, and found that 112 were aware of the problem. After one month in which the issue was given considerable attention in the paper, a second independent random sample was taken, which revealed that 136 of 693 readers felt they had an awareness of the circumstances surrounding the tax proposal. The *Inquirer* argued that this proved its power to inform people. At the 5 percent level, do you agree?

49. Net present value (NPV), which is calculated by subtracting the initial investment from the present value of cash inflows, is often used as a criterion in making a decision regarding investment projects. If the NPV is greater than zero, the project should be accepted. Of 500 projects that were evaluated by your firm last year, 389 reported positive NPVs. This year 278 of 402 projects had NPVs greater than zero. Does this suggest that there is a difference in the proportion of potentially profitable investment opportunities in these two years? Set $\alpha = 0.02$.

50. Denny Dimwit, a securities analyst for Your Bottom Dollar, Inc. has always felt that convertible bonds are more likely to be overvalued than are income bonds. Of 312 convertible bonds examined last year, Denny found 202 to be overvalued, while 102 of the 205 income bonds proved to be overvalued. Do these data support Denny's assumption? Set $\alpha = 0.10$.

51. Mary Metz uses the PDQ Delivery Service to transport important shipments. However, PDQ has failed to deliver on time with increasing frequency. In a sample of 97 shipments Mary randomly selects from last year's operations, 42 were delivered late. Mary decides to give her business to Getitthere Deliveries if their record is better than PDQ's. Of 73 deliveries last year, Getitthere was late 22 times. At the 5 percent level, should Mary change delivery services?

52. Charge Rite Batteries claims that the proportion of their products meeting minimum industry standards is more than 5 percent in excess of that of their nearest competitor, Lite Rite. Of 400 Charge Rite batteries, 309 meet these minimum standards, while 218 of 317 Lite Rite batteries do. At the 5 percent level, is Charge Rite right?

53. As a marketing specialist for Federated department stores, you have been asked by your supervisor to prepare a 95 percent confidence interval for the difference in the mean revenues of stores in the South and those in the Midwest. In this effort, 75 stores in the South that you select at random report mean daily revenues of $1,125 with a standard deviation of $213, while 83 stores in the Midwest yield values of $1,282 and $298. Produce the interval and the proper interpretation.

54. Barry Byte, a recent graduate in the computer science department of a large state university, has just obtained a position with a manufacturing firm in Chicago. Barry has been told to prepare a report on the performance of the employees in the computer analysis division of his firm. Part of that report consists of a 90 percent confidence interval for the difference in the mean efficiency ratings of the employees in his firm with that of employees in a competitor's firm. The data reveal that 35 employees in Barry's firm had a mean rating of 78 with a standard deviation of 12. A mean of 71 was reported for 45 employees in the other firm, with a standard deviation of 15. What is the interval Barry seeks, and how can Barry interpret the results of that interval?

55. Larry Ledger must compare the use of one type of spreadsheet used in his firm to that of a second type used elsewhere. Ten of the spreadsheets used in his firm reveal an average of 2.3 errors with a standard deviation of 1.2 errors. Fifteen of the other spreadsheets report a mean of 3.1 errors and a standard deviation of 0.9 errors. Help Larry develop a 99 percent confidence interval for the difference in the mean number of errors. Larry assumes that the population variance in the number of errors is the same for both types of spreadsheets.

56. An economist for the International Monetary Fund wishes to construct a 90 percent confidence interval for the difference in the mean rates of inflation in debtor nations and in creditor nations. Eight debtor nations report a mean rate of inflation of 5.23 percent with a standard deviation of 1.23 percent. Twelve debtor nations display a mean rate of inflation of 7.88 percent with a standard deviation of 2.22 percent. If equal variances is assumed, what is the proper interval?

57. Larry Ledger, from a previous problem, wishes to compare the use of two different spreadsheets by having seven employees work with each spreadsheet and then noting any difference in mean number of errors that are committed. Shown here are the results of that comparison.

	Number of Errors	
Employee	**Spread Sheet 1**	**Spread Sheet 2**
Joe	3	4
Clyde	4	2
Homer	2	7
Bart	7	3
Moe	5	2
Larry	3	1
Curly	2	5

Develop a 95 percent confidence interval for the difference in the mean number of errors.

58. Is there a difference in the proportion of men and women on your campus who favor
    a. abortion on demand?
    b. stiffer gun control legislation?
    c. the death penalty?
59. Is there a difference in the price of stocks traded on the New York Stock Exchange and those traded on the American Stock Exchange?
60. Is there a difference in the price of stocks traded on the organized exchanges and those traded over-the-counter?
61. Using Standard and Poor's Industrial manuals, is there a difference in the
    a. proportion of firms in the automobile and automobile parts industry that have recently merged with another firm and the proportion of firms in the petroleum industry that have done so?
    b. mean earnings of firms in the two industries cited in part (a)?

62. Tel-Tronics produces component parts for FAX machines used through most of the nation. Recently, production standards have suffered, as the firm's rapid growth has brought certain quality control problems. The Tel-Tronics plant in Kansas City has recently instituted a new production system designed to ensure that production standards are met. However, L. L. Budd, the firm's long-time president and CEO is doubtful of the system's success.

    As an economist and financial analyst in the statistical division of the firm, you must evaluate the system. Production records prior to the introduction of the system show that on 150 days selected at random, total output was 7,800 units with a daily standard deviation in output of 21 units. In addition, 936 of those units were defective. During a 95-day period in which the new production system was in operation, total output was 4,980 units with a daily standard deviation of 17 units. Furthermore, 747 of the 4,980 units were defective. What would you conclude regarding the worth of the new production system?

63. Al Hogan started a computer repair franchise operation in 1987. Since then Hogan's business has grown at an unexpected rate, and he now has the luxury of facing the many problems which often accompany rapid growth. One such problem is deciding which type of personal computer disk drive system has the best record of reliability. Al is currently considering drive systems from Drive-Right, Inc. and Compu-Drive, Ltd. Each company produces two types of drives. Al tests each system and records the number of hours of use before drive failure. The results are shown here.

Drive-Right		Compu-Drive	
Accu-Drive	Drive-Exact	Reli-Drive	Precise-Drive
67	32	25	35
52	47	31	37
58	31	45	35
69	41	41	39
59	41	35	42

Drive-Right		Compu-Drive	
Accu-Drive	**Drive-Exact**	**Reli-Drive**	**Precise-Drive**
48	42	37	45
54	31	36	41
62	43	39	45

Al will choose one system from each company to service in his franchise locations. However, of the two selected, one will be featured as his stores' primary system. The determination in each case will rest on which drive system has the best performance record and goes the longest time without failure. Although Al is a whiz at statistical analysis, he does not have the time to make these decisions. How can you help?

COMPUTER EXERCISES

1. Solve Problem 27 on the computer.
2. Solve Problem 57 on the computer.
3. Access the file PE from your data bank. It contains 40 obervations for the price/earnings ratios for firms on the New York Stock Exchange and a like number for firms cited in a 1989 issue of *Business Week* as "up and coming." Is there a difference in the mean P/E ratios?

TESTS OF VARIANCES AND ANALYSIS OF VARIANCE

A PREVIEW OF THINGS TO LOOK FOR

1   How to use chi-square to test the hypothesis regarding a population variance.

2   How to use an *F*-test to test the hypothesis regarding the difference between two population variances.

3   How to develop a confidence interval for a population variance.

4   The three types of variation in an analysis of variance test.

5   The principle behind analysis of variance.

6   The importance of treatment effects.

7   How to create an analysis of variance table.

8   How to use blocking to improve the results of an analysis of variance test.

CHAPTER BLUEPRINT

This chapter concentrates on the use of analysis of variance tests to compare the means of more than two populations. We will also examine the use of chi-square to test the variance of populations.

Tests of Variance

- Chi-square
- The F-test

Tests of Means

- One-way ANOVA
  - Tests for the difference between pairs
    - Balanced design
      - The Tukey method
      - The least significant difference
    - Unbalanced design
      - The least significant difference
- Two-way ANOVA
  - The use of blocking

Statistics show that money really
can buy happiness after all.

11.1 INTRODUCTION

Tests presented in earlier chapters centered on the estimation of population means and proportions. Techniques to estimate these parameters, or to compare two means or two proportions, were demonstrated.

However, there are many instances in which decision makers are interested not only in the mean of a distribution but also in the degree of dispersion around that mean. This degree of dispersion is, of course, measured by the variance σ^2. For example, a manufacturing process is designed to produce parts for automobile transmissions that are 15 centimeters (cm) in length. If the part varies from that 15 cm by 1 or 2 cm, it may not fit. To test their quality control procedures, the manufacturer selects 100 parts and finds a sample mean very close to 15 cm. It would appear that the production standards are being met. That's the good news. However, that mean of 15 may have been obtained by 50 parts with a length of 10 cm and 50 parts 20 cm in length. Despite the mean of 15, all of the parts are defective. That's the bad news. Obviously, the variance is an important consideration in determining production performance. When a business firm specifies the production standard for the mean dimension of some product, it also stipulates the tolerable variance in that dimension. The specifications for the transmission part might then read "a mean of 15 cm, with a variance of 0.89." A production manual used by workers at the Ford assembly plant in Kansas City states that "the mean diameter of the carburetor intake passage must be 10.5 millimeters, with a variation of no more than 0.315 millimeters."

Given the importance of the variance in maintaining production standards, it should come as no great surprise that tests have been developed to estimate the variance of a distribution. The test for the value of a single variance is based on a continuous distribution known as the chi-square distribution.

> **Chi-Square**
> We can use chi-square to test a hypothesis about the variance of a population. The chi-square distribution introduced in this chapter allows us to draw conclusions regarding the variability of a population.

Furthermore, the comparison of the variances of two populations can be made using another statistical technique based on an *F*-distribution. In earlier chapters we

OOOO **DECISION MAKING THROUGH PROBLEM SOLVING** OOOO
ILLUSTRATION 11-1

The Wall Street Journal recently carried a story about Rupert Murdoch, the Australian-born publisher who has built a worldwide media empire by borrowing funds from banks throughout the world. As the *WSJ* stated it, he now "faces the perils of leverage, and must make difficult decisions regarding repayment." Much of that debt occurred during a recent period of expansion in the acquisition and formation of three new ventures including *TV Guide,* Sky Lab, and the Fox television network, which is experiencing certain difficulties despite the successes of Bart Simpson and his family of misfits.

The article stated that Murdoch would have to compare the relative debt positions of each of these three new aspects of his far-flung enterprise. This comparison could well involve the use of ANOVA to compare the mean levels of debt acquired in each of Murdoch's three new ventures.

noted that certain tests require the assumption of equal variances. In Chapter 8, for example, when the confidence interval for the difference between two population means was developed using pooled data, it was necessary to assume that the variances of the two populations were equal in order to pool the sample data. You were promised at that time that a test for the equality of variances would be presented. True to this pledge, we will examine the *F*-distribution in this chapter.

F-distribution
The *F*-distribution is used to test the equality of population variances.

The *F*-distribution is not only useful in the comparison of variances, but it also forms the cornerstone for an important statistical tool referred to as analysis of variance (ANOVA).

ANOVA is an extremely versatile technique which allows the comparison of two or more population means. While previous tests permitted us to compare only two means, ANOVA provides additional flexibility by enabling the decision maker to compare two or more means.

ANOVA
Analysis of variance is used to test hypotheses regarding population means.

11.2 TESTING THE VARIANCE OF A NORMALLY DISTRIBUTED POPULATION: CHI-SQUARE (χ^2)

The production specifications for Head tennis rackets require that the Graphite Edge model be made to a length of 27 inches. The length may not have a variance in excess of 0.71 inch squared. The statistical analysis division for Head recognizes that χ^2 can be useful in testing the variance.

Actually, the χ^2-distribution is, like the t-distribution, an entire family of distributions. There is a different distribution for each degree of freedom, where d.f. $= n - 1$. Figure 11-1 shows the various distributions for different degrees of freedom. Each represents a distribution for chi-square if many samples of a given size are selected. The first is the distribution of χ^2-values if many samples of size $n = 2$ (d.f. $= 2 - 1 = 1$) were taken. The second is the distribution of χ^2-values if many samples of size $n = 4$ (d.f. $= 4 - 1 = 3$) were taken, and so on.

FIGURE 11-1   Various Chi-Square Distributions

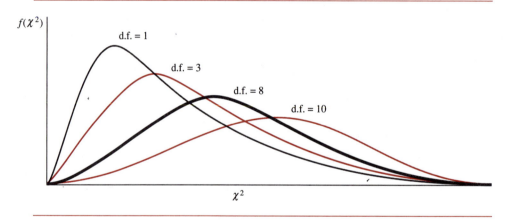

Notice that as n goes up, the distribution of χ^2-values becomes increasingly symmetrical. For d.f. > 30 the distribution is close to normal, and the appropriate Z-values may be used. If $n = \infty$ the chi-square distribution and the normal distribution are identical.

In order to test the hypothesis about a population variance, a sample variance s^2 must be determined. Recall that every different sample that could be selected would yield its own variance, and an entire distribution of sample variances is possible. It is necessary to standardize this distribution of potential sample variances for much the same reason that we used the Z-distribution to standardize values of $\overline{X}$ when testing hypotheses about the population mean. By doing so we then have only one standard form of the distribution to analyze. While the Z-distribution was used to standardize sample means, the chi-square distribution is used for variances. This standardized χ^2-value is

$$\chi^2 = \frac{(n-1)s^2}{\sigma^2} \qquad\qquad (11.1)$$

where n is the sample size
       s^2 is the sample variance
       σ^2 is the hypothesized population variance

Table H provides the critical values for χ^2 just as Table E did for the critical values of Z.

A. HYPOTHESIS TESTS FOR A VARIANCE

The case mentioned above for Head tennis rackets will serve to demonstrate how chi-square can be used to test for variances. The production specifications stipulated that the variance in length "may not exceed 0.71 inches squared." The null hypothesis is therefore written as $\sigma^2 \le 0.71$. Thus, the set of hypotheses involved in the test is

$$H_0\colon \sigma^2 \le 0.71$$

$$H_a\colon \sigma^2 > 0.71$$

which requires a right-tailed test.

To test the hypothesis, the production manager selects 25 rackets and finds $s^2 = 0.81$ inches squared. If a 90 percent level of confidence is desired (α is set at 10 percent), can it be concluded that the production specification is being met?

Figure 11-2 illustrates the problem. A value for χ^2 will be calculated using Formula (11.1). If it exceeds the critical value for chi-square, χ_c^2, as found in Table H, the null is rejected. If Formula (11.1) yields a value less than the critical χ^2 from the table, we do not reject the null. This critical value for χ^2 is found in Table H by

FIGURE 11-2   Quality Control for Head Tennis Rackets

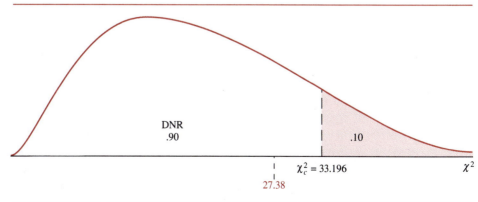

DNR
.90

.10

$\chi_c^2 = 33.196$

χ^2

27.38

moving down the left column to d.f. $= 25 - 1 = 24$ and across to the column headed by the value 0.10. There the critical value for χ^2 is seen to be 33.196. The decision rule can then be stated as follows:

Decision Rule
Do not reject the null if $\chi^2 < 33.196$. Reject null if $\chi^2 > 33.196$.

Using Formula (11.1), we have

$$\chi^2 = \frac{(25 - 1)(0.81)}{0.71}$$

$$= 27.38$$

Since $27.38 < 33.196$, the null is not rejected. There is not sufficient evidence to suggest that the variance in the length of the racket exceeds the prescribed limit of 0.71 inches squared, and the production manager therefore assumes that production standards are being met.

It should be emphasized that Table H gives only the values for the area under the curve *above* the critical value of χ^2. The shaded area in Figure 11-2 above the critical value of $\chi^2 = 33.1963$ is 10 percent of the total area under the curve.

Figure 11-3 shows other areas of possible interest. If d.f. $= 24$, suppose Head wanted to determine that value for χ^2 above which 20 percent of the area can be found. Figure 11-3(a) shows this to be 29.553. If we sought that value above which 90 percent of the area lies (and, hence, below which 10 percent can be found), we move down the first column for degrees of freedom to d.f. $= 24$ and across to the next column headed by the value 0.90. There the value of 15.659 is found.

FIGURE 11-3   Other Areas of Possible Interest for Head

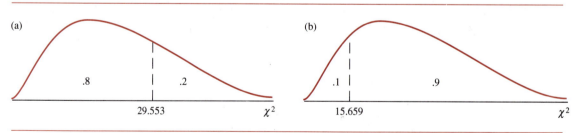

EXAMPLE 11-1   Relief in a Bottle: A Case of Quality Control

Many packaged products are sold under the guarantee that the mean weight of the packages is a specified amount, with the additional warranty that the variance in those weights does not exceed a particular limit.

A recent article in *Business Week* on marketing strategies described efforts by Procter & Gamble to expand sales of many of its over-the-counter drugs such as Pepto-Bismol and NyQuil. Much of this effort centered on "performance claims" regarding product quality. It is highly likely that some of these claims focused on the net weight of the contents.

Presume that P&G told its customers that the variance in the weights of its bottles of Pepto-Bismol is less than 1.2 ounces squared. As a marketing representative for P&G, you select 25 bottles and find a variance of 1.7. At the 10 percent level of significance, is P&G maintaining its pledge of product consistency?

SOLUTION:
The statement "less than 1.2 ounces squared" is written $\sigma^2 < 1.2$. Since it does not contain the equal sign, it is treated as the alternative hypothesis. The test involves the hypotheses

$$H_0: \sigma^2 \geq 1.2$$

$$H_a: \sigma^2 < 1.2$$

Since this is a left-tailed test with α equal to 0.10, it requires a value for chi-square that cuts off 10 percent of the area in the left tail of the curve. However, as noted above, Table H gives only those areas above, that is, to the right, of the chi-square value. Therefore, as shown in the accompanying figure, we must find in Table H the value 0.90 (= $1.0 - 0.10$). By moving down the first column in Table H, to d.f. = $25 - 1 = 24$ and across to the column headed by 0.90, the critical chi-square of 15.659 is located.

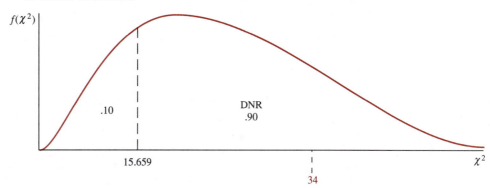

Decision Rule
Do not reject the null if $\chi^2 > 15.659$. Reject the null if $\chi^2 < 15.659$. Chi-square is calculated as

$$\chi^2 = \frac{(n-1)\, s^2}{\sigma^2}$$

$$= \frac{(24)\, 1.7}{1.2}$$

$$= 34$$

STATISTICAL INTERPRETATION:
Since 34 > 15.659, you do not reject the null that $\sigma^2 \geq 1.2$. The evidence suggests that variability in product weights exceed the maximum allowance.

In most instances, decision makers are concerned when the variance in production standards is too large. Executives for Head tennis rackets and P&G would not become distressed if production was so uniform that the variances were less than allowable tolerances. It is when production controls become too relaxed, resulting in large variations in the product, that concern arises.

However, there are conditions under which deviation in the variance either up or down might cause some anxiety. This is particularly true in cases dealing with inventory management. Firms wish to maintain inventories of raw materials within a rather narrow range. If inventories are too high, the firms have too much capital invested in unnecessary materials. Conversely, a dangerously low level may mean that production must be interrupted due to inventory depletion. Thus, wide fluctuations in inventories one way or the other must be avoided. The next example illustrates this problem.

EXAMPLE 11-2 How to Get into Hot Water

Hot Tubs, Inc. manufactures jacuzzis and jacuzzi products. Hot Tubs' top line model jacuzzi, the Buns Warmer, is equipped with a remote-controlled miniature television for the truly self-indulgent. Bill "Bubbles" Bailey, owner of Hot Tubs, Inc., wants to keep the variance in weekly inventories of these small-size TVs at $\sigma^2 = 75$ units squared. He takes a sample of 30 weeks and finds $s^2 = 71$. At the $\alpha = 10$ percent level, is Bubbles achieving his inventory goal?

SOLUTION:

Since Bubbles wants $\sigma^2 = 75$, he has a two-tailed test. The hypotheses are

$$H_0: \sigma^2 = 75$$

$$H_a: \sigma^2 \neq 75$$

With a two-tailed test, one-half of the α-value must be in each tail as shown in the accompanying figure. There are two critical values for χ^2 which must be found in Table H. These chi-square values taken from the table isolate 5 percent of the area under the curve in each tail. The proper value for the upper χ^2 leaves 5 percent of the area under the curve to the right. It is found by moving down the first column to d.f. $= n - 1 = 29$ and across to the column headed 0.05. There you find $\chi^2 = 42.557$. The lower value must leave 5 percent of the area in the left tail, with the remaining 95 percent to the right. Keeping in mind that the table only provides values for areas to the right of the χ^2, we must find that entry that corresponds to 95 percent. The entry in the 0.95 column is 17.708.

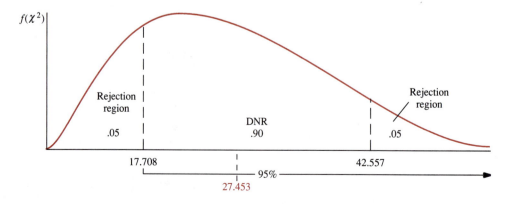

Decision Rule

Do not reject the null if $17.708 < \chi^2 < 42.557$. Reject if $\chi^2 < 17.708$ or if $\chi^2 > 42.557$.

$$\chi^2 = \frac{(n-1)s^2}{\sigma^2}$$

$$= \frac{(30-1)71}{75}$$

$$= 27.453$$

QUICK CHECK 11.2.1

OOOO

A sample of $n = 24$ yields $s^2 = 17.3$. At the 5 percent level, does this indicate that σ^2 exceeds 19.2? State the

a. hypotheses.
b. decision rule.
c. conclusion.

Answer: a. $H_0: \sigma^2 \le 19.2$ $H_a: \sigma^2 > 19.2$
b. Do not reject the null if $\chi^2 < 35.172$; reject if $\chi^2 > 35.172$.
c. Since $\chi^2 = 20.724$, DNR

QUICK CHECK 11.2.2

A sample of $n = 17$ produces an $s^2 = 101$. At the 10 percent level, can you conclude that $\sigma^2 = 97$? State the

a. hypotheses.
b. decision rule.
c. conclusion.

Answer: a. $H_0: \sigma^2 = 97$ $H_a \ne 97$
b. Do not reject the null if $7.962 < \chi^2 < 26.296$; reject if $\chi^2 < 7.962$ or $\chi^2 > 26.296$.
c. Since $\chi^2 = 16.66$, do not reject the null.

QUICK CHECK 11.2.3

A sample of $n = 29$ reported a variance of 22.7. At the 10 percent level, does this indicate that σ^2 is less than 37.2? State the

a. hypotheses.
b. decision rule.
c. conclusion.

Answer: a. $H_0: \sigma^2 \ge 37.2$ $H_a: \sigma^2 < 37.2$
b. Do not reject H_0 if $\chi^2 > 18.939$; reject if $\chi^2 < 18.939$.
c. Since $\chi^2 = 17.086$, reject the null.

B. **CONFIDENCE INTERVAL FOR THE VARIANCE OF A NORMAL POPULATION**

Regardless of whether the null hypothesis is rejected, the decision maker often has need to develop a confidence interval for σ^2 which will serve as an estimate of the unknown population variance. The confidence interval for a population variance can be calculated as

$$\frac{(n-1)s^2}{\chi_U^2} < \sigma^2 < \frac{(n-1)s^2}{\chi_L^2} \qquad (11.2)$$

where χ_U^2 is the upper χ^2-value taken from the table
           χ_L^2 is the lower χ^2-value taken from the table

In Example 11-2 Bubbles did not reject H_0: $\sigma^2 = 75$ units squared. The sample data suggest that the population variance could be 75. However, this represents only a point estimate of σ^2. Bubbles may prefer an interval estimate of the variance. Given the data from the example, that estimate becomes

$$\frac{(30-1)(71)}{42.557} < \sigma^2 < \frac{(30-1)(71)}{17.708}$$

$$48.382 < \sigma^2 < 116.275$$

Bubbles can be 90 percent confident that the weekly variance in inventory levels of the TVs falls within that range. Ninety percent of all confidence intervals constructed in this manner will contain the actual σ^2.

11.3   COMPARING THE VARIANCES OF TWO NORMAL POPULATIONS

Several of the statistical tests discussed in earlier chapters required the assumption of equal population variances. At the time you were asked to blindly accept this equality, with the promise that at a later time you would be shown how to test for it. That time has come. This section demonstrates how to determine if the assumption of equal variances is reasonable. This test is based on the F-distribution, which was developed by Sir Ronald A. Fisher (1890–1962) in 1924.

In comparing the variances of two populations, a sample is taken from each population. The sample variances serve as estimates of their respective population variances. An F-distribution is then formed by the ratio of these two sample variances. The F-ratio is

$$F = \frac{s_1^2}{s_2^2} \qquad (11.3)$$

where s_1^2 is the larger of the two sample variances
           s_2^2 is the smaller of the two sample variances

When testing the hypothesis that two population variances are equal, it is essential that the F-ratio be manipulated to ensure that the larger sample variance is placed in the numerator, while the smaller of the two sample variances goes in the denominator. This will ensure that the F-value is greater than 1, and results in only *one* rejection region located in the right tail. By manipulating the F-ratio to ensure that it is greater than 1, any rejection region that otherwise might have appeared in the left tail is now irrelevant. Only one-half as much of the area under the F-distribution is accessible as a rejection region. Therefore, it is necessary to divide the α-value by 2 and place the rejection region in only the right tail equal to $\alpha/2$.

The α-Value

When controlling the F-ratio to ensure that the larger sample variance is on top, we must divide the α-value by 2. The null hypothesis that H_0: $\sigma_1^2 = \sigma_2^2$ is a two-tailed test. But by ensuring that $F > 1$, we are conducting the two-tailed test in only the right tail. Therefore, α must be divided by 2.

This customary practice of dividing α by 2 facilitates the test for equal variances. However, this custom is discontinued when using ANOVA to test for the equality of means. We will find in the section dealing with ANOVA that dividing α by 2 is not necessary.

Assume for the sake of illustration that in a given situation the variance of the first sample exceeds that of the second. Then s_1^2 is placed in the numerator. The more s_1^2 exceeds s_2^2, the larger will be the F-ratio and the less likely it is that $\sigma_1^2 = \sigma_2^2$. That is, if s_1^2 is significantly greater than s_2^2, then it may be concluded that (1) the F-ratio is large, and (2) σ_1^2 is probably greater than σ_2^2.

By identifying some critically large value for F where s_1^2 is significantly larger than s_2^2, we can designate an F-value above which the hypothesis that $\sigma_1^2 = \sigma_2^2$ must be rejected. If F gets significantly large because s_1^2 exceeds s_2^2 by such a large amount, we must recognize the likelihood that $\sigma_1^2 > \sigma_2^2$.

To illustrate this procedure, let us return to one of the problems in a previous chapter which required the assumption of equal variances. In Chapter 10, we tested the hypothesis regarding the mean damage to two types of automobiles. This test was based on the assumption that the variances in the damage were equal. Let us now test to see if that assumption was correct. We must test the hypothesis that

$$H_0: \sigma_1^2 = \sigma_2^2$$

$$H_a: \sigma_1^2 \neq \sigma_2^2$$

The relevant statistics for the problem from Chapter 10 are repeated here.

	Autos	
	Type 1	**Type 2**
Sample size	9	7
Standard deviation in damages	$97	$83
Variance in damages	9,409	6,889

Ensuring that the larger sample variance is in the numerator, the F-ratio becomes

$$F = \frac{9,409}{6,889}$$

$$= 1.37$$

We must now determine if $F = 1.37$ exceeds some critical value which would indicate that the difference between the sample variances is too great to be explained merely on the basis of sampling error. If $F = 1.37$ is greater than the critical F-value, then we must conclude that s_1^2 exceeds s_2^2 by a statistically significant amount, and the null hypothesis must be rejected. This critical value for F is taken from Table G. Suppose an α-value of 10 percent is originally set. As noted earlier, we must divide this α by 2. Thus, we will use that portion of Table G which pertains to an α-value of 5 percent. In addition, the F-value carries 2 degrees of freedom which must be identified: one for the numerator, which is equal to $n_1 - 1$, and one for the denominator, which is $n_2 - 1$. Notational convenience allows us to express the critical F-values as $F_{\alpha/2, n_1-1, n_2-2}$. In our present example, the degrees of freedom are $9 - 1 = 8$, and $7 - 1 = 6$. The critical F-value which we must find in Table G is therefore $F_{0.05, 8, 6}$. To do so, locate that portion of the table pertaining to an α-value of 5 percent. Move across the top row for the degrees of freedom for the numerator of 8, and down that column to the degrees of freedom for the denominator of 6. There you will find the critical F-value of 4.15, which marks off 5 percent of the area under the F-distribution in the right tail. Figure 11-4 illustrates. From this procedure we can conclude that if our F-value exceeds 4.15 it is unlikely that $\sigma_1^2 = \sigma_2^2$. There is only a 5 percent chance that if the two population variances are equal we could get two sample variances which would produce an F-value in excess of 4.15.

FIGURE 11-4   The F-Distribution for Auto Damages

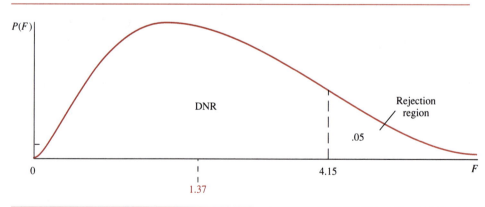

Decision Rule
Do not reject the null if $F < 4.15$. Reject the null if $F > 4.15$.

Since $F = 1.37$, we do not reject the null and assume that the two population variances are equal. This allows us to proceed with the test of mean damages to the autos using pooled data just as we did in Chapter 10.

11.4 ONE-WAY ANOVA: THE COMPLETELY RANDOMIZED DESIGN

In Chapter 10 we were able to test the hypothesis regarding the equality of two populations' means. Unfortunately, these tests were restricted in their application to a comparison of only two populations. Many business decisions, however, require the comparison of more than two populations. It is here that analysis of variance (ANOVA) proves to be useful.

ANOVA is designed specifically to test if two or more populations have the same mean. Even though the purpose of ANOVA is to test for differences in population means, it involves an examination of the variances in the samples used in the study, hence the term *analysis of variance*. More specifically, the procedure can be used to determine if a particular "treatment" when applied to a population will have a significant impact on its mean. The use of ANOVA originated in agriculture; hence, the term *treatment* is used as in treating various parcels of land with different fertilizers and noting any discrepancies in mean crop yields. However, today the word *treatment* is used quite broadly to refer to the treatment of customers to different advertising displays and noting any subsequent differences in mean purchases, to the treatment of three groups of employees to three different types of training programs and observing any differences that occur in mean levels of productivity, or any situation in which a comparison of means is desired.

In the case of subjecting three different groups of employees to different training programs, the employees are referred to as the **experimental units** and the training methods are the **treatments**. These three types of training programs constitute three **levels** of the **factor** *type of training*. That is, the factor is the general category under study, in this case training. The various levels of that factor are the treatments.

Factor
A general type or category of treatments is a factor. The different treatments constitute different levels of that factor.

Perhaps the most common application of ANOVA is the *completely randomized design* (CRD). It is referred to as completely randomized because sample observations are randomly selected and subjected to the different treatments.

For example, assume that Apex Manufacturing randomly chooses 10 of its employees to complete a particular type of training program. Ten more employees are also randomly selected who will be trained by a different training method, while a third randomly selected group will be trained in still a different manner. It is referred to as a completely randomized design because the employees (experimental units) are randomly assigned to the different training programs (treatments). There is no effort to "match up" training programs with specific employees.

> **Completely Randomized Design**
> The experimental units are assigned randomly to the various treatments. Each unit randomly chosen for the study has an equal chance of being assigned to any treatment.

The manner in which treatments are selected determines whether we are using a **fixed-effects model** or a **random-effects model.** The model described above for the employees' training program is a fixed-effects model. The three training programs were chosen, or fixed, prior to conducting the study. We know which three programs we want to test from the outset of the study. The conclusions from the study are applicable only to the three programs included in the study.

> **Fixed-Effects Model**
> Specific treatments are chosen or fixed in advance of the study.

In contrast, suppose Apex Manufacturing had no specific interest in these three particular training programs, but instead wanted to know if training programs in general had different effects on employee performance. These three training programs used in the study are seen as only a sample of all training programs which might be used by the firm. It doesn't matter which three training methods we use in the study to make the comparison. We are interested in whether training in general is effective. Any conclusions from the study are seen as applicable to the entire population of all training programs. This procedure would produce a random-effects model.

> **Random-Effects Model**
> The levels (treatments) used in the study are chosen randomly from a population of possible levels.

A more thorough study of random-effects models is beyond the scope of this text. Our attention in this chapter will focus on fixed-effects models.

Three assumptions are essential for the application of ANOVA:

1. All the populations involved are normal.
2. All the populations have the same variance.
3. The samples are independently chosen.

If the number of treatments is designated as c, the set of hypotheses to test is

$$H_0: \mu_1 = \mu_2 = \mu_3 \cdots = \mu_c$$

$$H_a: \text{Not all means are equal}$$

The letter c is used for the number of treatments because in an ANOVA table, which we will devise shortly, each treatment is specified in its own column.

You might argue that it would be possible to test the equality of several means by using several two-sample t-tests as we did in Chapter 10. However, certain complications arise which render this approach ineffective. For example, if a manufacturer wishes to compare the mean daily output for three plants, he might test all three of the following sets of hypotheses:

$$H_0: \mu_1 = \mu_2$$

$$H_a: \mu_1 \neq \mu_2$$

and

$$H_0: \mu_1 = \mu_3$$

$$H_a: \mu_1 \neq \mu_3$$

and

$$H_0: \mu_2 = \mu_3$$

$$H_a: \mu_2 \neq \mu_3$$

If the null is not rejected in each of the tests, he might conclude that all three means are equal.

At least two problems emerge which prevent this approach. First, as the number of populations (plants) increases, the number of required tests rises markedly. If there are four plants the manufacturer wants to compare, the number of individual tests doubles from 3 to $_4C_2 = 6$ tests. The second problem is perhaps even more disturbing. It arises due to a compounding of the α-value, which is the probability of a Type I error. If the tests are to be conducted at the 5 percent level, and if there are three populations requiring three separate hypotheses tests, the probability of a Type I error is far in excess of 5 percent. It can be calculated as

$$P(\text{Type I}) = [1 - (1 - 0.05)(1 - 0.05)(1 - 0.05)]$$

$$= 1 - (0.95)^3$$

$$= 0.1426$$

While we wanted to test at the 5 percent level, the need to make three tests increased the probability of the Type I error beyond acceptable limits.

A.   AN ILLUSTRATION OF ANOVA

The management director for a large industrial firm wants to determine if three different training programs have different effects on employees' productivity levels. These programs are the treatments that ANOVA can evaluate. Fourteen employees are randomly selected and assigned to one of the three programs. Upon completion of the training, each employee is given a test to determine his or her proficiency. Four employees were placed in the first training program, and five in each of the other two. Each of these three groups will be treated as separate samples and used to draw inferences about the populations of employees that might enter into the respective training programs. The employees' test scores after training are shown in Table 11-1, along with a few basic calculations.

TABLE 11-1   Employee Test Scores

	Treatments		
	Program 1	**Program 2**	**Program 3**
	85	80	82
	72	84	80
	83	81	85
	80	78	90
	**	82	88
Column means	$\overline{X}_1 = 80$	$\overline{X}_2 = 81$	$\overline{X}_3 = 85$

There are 15 cells in the table; 14 with entries and one empty cell in the first treatment. A cell is identified as X_{ij}, where i is the row and j is the column. X_{32} is the entry in the third row and second column. It is seen to be 81. X_{51} is the empty cell. Note that each cell is the score for a single, individual employee. This fact will provide an important distinction later on in our discussion. The mean is calculated for each treatment, along with the grand mean of $\overline{\overline{X}}$ for all 14 observations. To obtain the grand mean, let r_j be the number of observations in the jth treatment (sample). If there are c treatments, the grand mean is

$$\overline{\overline{X}} = \frac{\sum_{j=1}^{c} r_j \overline{X}_j}{n} \qquad (11.4A)$$

$$\overline{\overline{X}} = \frac{r_1 \overline{X}_1 + r_2 \overline{X}_2 + r_3 \overline{X}_3}{n}$$

$$= \frac{4(80) + 5(81) + 5(85)}{14}$$

$$= 82.14$$

The letter r is used to denote the number of observations (or rows) in any given sample (column) because the observations are recorded in rows as shown in Table 11-1. That is, the second observations in each of the treatments are seen in the second row to be 72, 84, and 80, respectively.

In our example there are $c = 3$ treatments (samples), so j runs from 1 to 3 in Formula (11.4); $r = 4$ for the first treatment (sample) and $r = 5$ for the two remaining treatments (samples). If each sample has the same number of observations, the grand mean is simply the mean of the column means:

$$\overline{\overline{X}} = \frac{\sum_{j=1}^{c} \overline{X}_j}{c} \qquad (11.4B)$$

ANOVA is based on a comparison of the amount of variation in each of the treatments. If the variation from one treatment to the next is significantly high, it can be concluded that the treatments are having dissimilar effects on the populations. In Table 11-1 we can identify three types, or sources, of variation. Note that the first variation is the sum of the other two.

1. There is variation among the total number of all 14 observations. Not all 14 employees scored the same on the test. This is called the **total variation.**
2. There is variation between the different treatments (samples). Employees in program 1 did not score the same as those in programs 2 or 3. This is called **between-sample variation.**
3. There is variation within any one given treatment (sample). Not all employees in the first sample, for instance, scored the same. This is called **within-sample variation.**

It is by comparing these different sources of variation that ANOVA can be used to test for the equality in means of different populations. Any difference that the treatments may have in employee productivity will be detected by a comparison of these forms of variation.

B.   THE PRINCIPLE BEHIND ANOVA

To determine if the different treatments have different effects on their respective populations, a comparison is made between the variation within samples (W/S) and the variation between samples (B/S). The variation in scores within any given sample can be caused by a variety of factors: native ability of employees in that sample, personal motivation, individual efforts and skill, blind luck, and a host of other random circumstances. The treatment itself will not produce any variation in the observations within any sample because all observations in that sample receive the same treatment.

It is a different matter with the variation between samples. The variation in scores between samples (from one sample to the next) can be caused by the same random factors as the variation within a sample (motivation, skill, luck, etc.), plus any additional influence that the different treatments may have. There can be a *treatment effect* between samples because each sample gets a different treatment.

Treatment Effect
Since different samples get different treatments, variation between samples can be caused by the different treatment effects.

If a treatment effect exists, it can then be detected by comparing between-sample and within-sample variation. If the variation between samples is significantly greater than the variation within samples, a strong treatment effect is present. This difference between variation between samples and variation within samples is precisely what ANOVA measures. ANOVA is a ratio of the variation between samples to the variation within samples. If the different treatments are having different effects, the variation between samples will rise, causing the ratio to increase. This ratio is based on the *F*-ratio introduced in the previous section.

The *F*-Ratio as Used in ANOVA
The *F*-ratio is a ratio of the variation between samples to the variation within samples.

The variation between samples can be caused in part by different treatments. Variation within a given sample can be caused only by random factors such as the luck, skill, and motivation of the employees. Such variation is independent of the treatment (since all observations within a sample get the same treatment) and is the result only of **randomized sampling error** within the sample.

The *F*-Ratio
When population means are different, a treatment effect is present, and the deviations between samples will be large compared with the error deviation within a sample. Thus, the *F*-value, which is a ratio of the treatment variation to the error variation, will rise.

The total variation is equal to the variation caused by the different treatments plus the variation caused by the random error elements within treatments such as skill, luck, and motivation. That is,

$$\text{Total variation} = \text{Treatment variation} + \text{Error variation}$$

C. THE SUMS OF SQUARES

Recognition of these three sources of variation allows us to *partition the sums of squares*, a procedure necessary for ANOVA. Each of the three types of variation gives rise to a sum of squares. There is the (1) total sum of squares (*SST*), (2) the treatment sum of squares (*SSTR*), and (3) the error sum of squares (*SSE*). As you might expect,

$$SST = SSTR + SSE$$

This illustrates that *SST* can be partitioned into its two component parts: *SSTR* and *SSE*.

These sums of squares can be used to test the equality of population means. Recall from Chapter 3 that the variance is calculated as

$$s^2 = \frac{\Sigma(X_i - \overline{X})^2}{n - 1} \tag{11.5}$$

The numerator is the sum of the squares of the deviations from the mean. In this manner, the sum of squares is used to measure variation. The denominator is the number of degrees of freedom. This equation serves as a pattern which can be applied to the sums of squares in ANOVA.

Let X_{ij} be the *i*th observation in the *j*th sample. For example, X_{21} is the second observation in the first sample. In Table 11-1, $X_{21} = 72$, $X_{32} = 81$, $X_{43} = 90$, and so on. Then,

$$SST = \sum_{i=1}^{r} \sum_{j=1}^{c} (X_{ij} - \overline{\overline{X}})^2 \tag{11.6}$$

The grand mean is subtracted from each of the 14 observations. The differences are squared and summed. As shown by the double summation sign in Formula (11.6), this is done across all rows and across all columns. Hereafter, the notation for the summation signs is dropped in the interest of simplicity.
Using the data in Table 11-1, we have

$$
\begin{aligned}
SST &= (85 - 82.14)^2 + (72 - 82.14)^2 + (83 - 82.14)^2 \\
&\quad + (80 - 82.14)^2 + (80 - 82.14)^2 + (84 - 82.14)^2 \\
&\quad + \cdots (90 - 82.14)^2 + (88 - 82.14)^2 \\
&= 251.7
\end{aligned}
$$

Also,

$$SSTR = \Sigma r_j(\overline{X}_j - \overline{\overline{X}})^2 \qquad\qquad (11.7)$$

The number of observations, or rows, in each treatment, r_j, is multiplied by the squared differences between the mean for each treatment, $\overline{X}_j$, and the grand mean. The results are summed for all treatments. Formula (11.7) tells us to multiply the number of rows in the jth column (remember, j denotes a column) by the squared deviation of the mean of that column from the grand mean.
Table 11-1 yields

$$SSTR = 4(80 - 82.14)^2 + 5(81 - 82.14)^2 + 5(85 - 82.14)^2$$
$$= 65.7$$

and

$$SSE = \Sigma\Sigma(X_{ij} - \overline{X}_j)^2 \qquad\qquad (11.8)$$

The mean of a treatment, $\overline{X}_j$, is subtracted from each observation in that treatment. The differences are squared and summed. This is done for all treatments, and the results are summed.
Using the data in Table 11-1 again, we have

$$SSE = (85 - 80)^2 + (72 - 80)^2 + (83 - 80)^2 + (80 - 80)^2$$

for the first treatment

$$+ (80 - 81)^2 + (84 - 81)^2 + (81 - 81)^2 + (78 - 81)^2 + (82 - 81)^2$$

for the second treatment

$$+ (82 - 85)^2 + (80 - 85)^2 + (85 - 85)^2 + (90 - 85)^2 + (88 - 85)^2$$

for the third treatment

$$= 186.0$$

A quick check of all these calculations can be done as

$$SST = SSTR + SSE$$
$$251.7 = 65.7 + 186.0$$

If you trust your arithmetic, you can find SSE as simply

$$SSE = SST - SSTR = 251.7 - 65.7 = 186.0$$

D.   The Mean Sums of Squares

As Formula (11.5) for the variance tells us, after we have obtained the sums of squares, each one is divided by its degrees of freedom. A sum of squares divided by its degrees of freedom results in a *mean sum of squares*. That is, if we average a sum of squares over its degrees of freedom, we get a mean sum of squares.

Recall from an earlier chapter, we defined the degrees of freedom as the total number of observations in the data set minus any "constraints" which might apply. A constraint was any value that was computed from the data set.

In that regard, notice that in calculating *SST*, we used the entire data set of n observations to calculate one value. That one value was the grand mean $\overline{\overline{X}}$, which represents one constraint. Therefore, *SST* carries $n - 1$ degrees of freedom.

The calculation of *SSTR* involved the use of the $c = 3$ sample means from which the grand mean can be computed. The sample means are therefore seen as individual data points and the grand mean is taken as a restraint. *SSTR* then has $c - 1$ degrees of freedom.

Finally, we calculated *SSE* above by noting the deviation of the $n = 14$ observations from the $c = 3$ sample means. Thus, *SSE* has $n - c$ degrees of freedom.

Note that

$$\text{d.f. for } SST = \text{d.f. for } SSTR + \text{d.f. for } SSE$$

$$n - 1 = c - 1 + n - c$$

Since, as noted above, a sum of squares divided by its degrees of freedom produces a mean sum of squares, we find the total mean square, or mean square of the total deviation, *MST*, as

$$MST = \frac{SST}{n - 1} \tag{11.9}$$

the treatment mean square (*MSTR*) as

$$MSTR = \frac{SSTR}{c - 1} \tag{11.10}$$

and the error mean square (*MSE*) as

$$MSE = \frac{SSE}{n - c} \tag{11.11}$$

Using our data from Table 11-1, we have

$$MST = \frac{SST}{n-1}$$

$$= \frac{251.7}{14-1}$$

$$= 19.4$$

$$MSTR = \frac{SSTR}{c-1}$$

$$= \frac{65.7}{3-1}$$

$$= 32.9$$

$$MSE = \frac{SSE}{n-c}$$

$$= \frac{186.0}{14-3}$$

$$= 16.9$$

These three mean squares are patterned after Formula (11.5). They are sums of squares divided by their degrees of freedom, and as such they are measures of variances. It is the ratio of the last two, $MSTR$ and MSE, that is used as the basis of ANOVA to test the hypothesis regarding the equality of means. As noted above, this ratio fits the F-distribution, and is expressed as

$$F = \frac{MSTR}{MSE} \qquad (11.12)$$

In our case it becomes

$$F = \frac{32.9}{16.9}$$

$$= 1.94$$

$MSTR$ measures the variation between treatments. If the treatments are having different effects, $MSTR$ will reflect this by increasing. The F-ratio itself will then increase. Thus, if the F-ratio becomes "significantly" large because $MSTR$ exceeds MSE by such a great amount, we must recognize that treatment effects probably exist. It is likely that the different treatments are having different effects on the means of their respective populations, and the null hypothesis that $\mu_1 = \mu_2 = \mu_3$ must be rejected.

The critical value for F that is deemed significantly large can be found in Table G as before. Assume that the management director wishes to test the following hypothesis at the 5 percent level:

$$H_0: \mu_1 = \mu_2 = \mu_3$$

$$H_a: \text{Not all means are equal}$$

Since $MSTR$ has $c - 1 = 3 - 1 = 2$ degrees of freedom and MSE has $n - c = 14 - 3 = 11$ degrees of freedom, the critical F-value is found from the table to be $F_{.05, 2, 11} = 3.98$. The 2 is listed before the 11 in the statement of the degrees of freedom because $MSTR$ is in the numerator.

The decision rule, depicted in Figure 11-5, is

Decision Rule
Do not reject the null if $F < 3.98$. Reject the null if $F > 3.98$.

FIGURE 11-5   A Test of the Effects of Different Training Programs

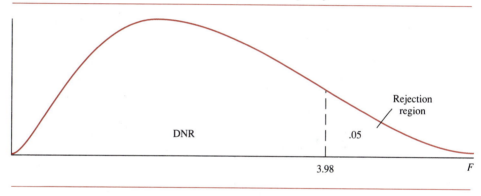

Since the F-value was calculated to be $1.94 < 3.98$, the director should not reject the null. She can be 95 percent confident that the mean test scores are the same for all three training programs. There is no significant treatment effect associated with any of the programs.

E.   AN ANOVA TABLE

It is customary to summarize the ANOVA calculations in a table. The general form of the ANOVA table is shown in Table 11-2(A), while Table 11-2(B) contains the specific values pertaining to the training program example.

Notice that the relevant sources of variation are listed. SS is the sums of squares, and MS is the mean squares. Of course, d.f. is the degrees of freedom, and the F-value of 1.94 is shown in the extreme right column. Example 11-3 provides a more concise illustration of ANOVA.

TABLE 11-2   An ANOVA Table Summarizing ANOVA Calculations

A. The Generalized ANOVA Table

Source of Variation	SS	d.f.	MS	F-value
Between samples (treatment)	SSTR	$c-1$	$SSTR/(c-1)$	MSTR/MSE
Within samples (error)	SSE	$n-c$	$SSE/(n-c)$	
Total variation	SST	$n-1$		

B. ANOVA Table for Employee Training Programs

Source of Variation	SS	d.f.	MS	F-value
Between samples (treatment)	65.7	2	32.9	1.94
Within samples (error)	186.0	11	16.9	
Total variation	251.7	13		

H_0: $\mu_1 = \mu_2 = \mu_3$
H_a: Not all means are equal
Decision Rule: Do not reject if $F < 3.98$. Reject if $F > 3.98$.
Conclusion: Since $F = 1.94 < 3.98$, do not reject the null.

EXAMPLE 11-3 Games People Play

Robert Shade is vice president for marketing at First City Bank in Atlanta. Recent promotional efforts to attract new depositors involve certain games and prizes at the bank's four branch locations. Shade is convinced that different types of promotional games would appeal to different income groups. People at one income level might prefer gifts, while another income group might be more attracted by free trips to favorite vacation spots. Shade decides to use size of deposits as a proxy measure for income. He wants to determine if there is a difference in the mean level of deposits in the four branches.

SOLUTION:

Seven deposits are randomly selected from each branch and are displayed here rounded to the nearest \$100. There are $c = 4$ treatments (samples) and $r_j = 7$ observations in each treatment. The total number of observations is $n = rc = 28$.

Deposit	Branch 1	Branch 2	Branch 3	Branch 4
1	1.3	1.9	3.6	5.1
2	1.5	1.9	4.2	4.9
3	0.9	2.1	4.5	5.6
4	1.0	2.4	4.8	4.8
5	1.9	2.1	3.9	3.8
6	1.5	3.1	4.1	5.1
7	2.1	2.5	5.1	4.8
ΣX_j	10.2	16.0	30.2	34.1
$\overline{X}_j$	1.46	2.29	4.31	4.87

$$\overline{\overline{X}} = \frac{r_1\overline{X}_1 + r_2\overline{X}_2 + r_3\overline{X}_3 + r_4\overline{X}_4}{28}$$

$$= \frac{\overline{X}_1 + \overline{X}_2 + \overline{X}_3 + \overline{X}_4}{4}$$

$$= 3.23$$

Shade wants to test the hypothesis at the 5 percent level that

$$H_0: \mu_1 = \mu_2 = \mu_3 = \mu_4$$

H_a: Not all means are equal

Using Formulas (10.6) to (10.8), he would have

$$SST = \Sigma\Sigma(X_{ij} - \overline{\overline{X}})^2$$

$$= (1.3 - 3.23)^2 + (1.5 - 3.23)^2 + (0.9 - 3.23)^2$$
$$+ \cdots + (4.8 - 3.23)^2$$

$$= 61.00$$

$$SSTR = \Sigma r_j(\overline{X}_j - \overline{\overline{X}})^2$$

$$= 7(1.46 - 3.23)^2 + 7(2.29 - 3.23)^2$$
$$+ 7(4.31 - 3.23)^2 + 7(4.87 - 3.23)^2$$

$$= 55.33$$

$$SSE = \Sigma\Sigma(X_{ij} - \overline{X}_j)^2$$

$$
\begin{aligned}
&= (1.3 - 1.46)^2 + \cdots + (2.1 - 1.46)^2 &&\text{for the first treatment}\\
&+ (1.9 - 2.29)^2 + \cdots + (2.5 - 2.29)^2 &&\text{for the second treatment}\\
&+ (3.6 - 4.31)^2 + \cdots + (5.1 - 4.31)^2 &&\text{for the third treatment}\\
&+ (5.1 - 4.87)^2 + \cdots + (4.8 - 4.87)^2 &&\text{for the fourth treatment}
\end{aligned}
$$

$$= 5.67$$

Formulas (11.10) and (11.11) for the mean squares yield

$$MSTR = \frac{55.33}{3}$$

$$= 18.44$$

$$MSE = \frac{5.67}{24}$$

$$= 0.236$$

Then the F-ratio is

$$F = \frac{MSTR}{MSE}$$

$$= \frac{18.44}{0.236}$$

$$= 78.14$$

Shade must use 3 and 24 degrees of freedom, since d.f. for $SSTR = 3$ and d.f. for $SSE = 24$. If he wants an α of 5 percent, he finds from Table G that $F_{0.05, 3, 24} = 3.01$. The ANOVA table summarizes these figures as

Source of Variation	SS	d.f.	MS	F-value
Between samples (treatment)	55.33	3	18.44	78.14
Within samples (error)	5.67	24	0.236	
Total variation	61.00	27		

H_0: $\mu_1 = \mu_2 = \mu_3 = \mu_4$
H_a: Not all means are equal
Decision Rule: Do not reject if $F < 3.01$. Reject if $F > 3.01$.
Conclusion: Since $F = 78.14 > 3.01$, reject the null.

The test is demonstrated in the following figure.

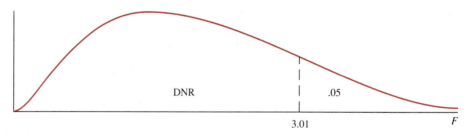

STATISTICAL INTERPRETATION:
Since $F = 78.14$, Shade must reject the null. He can be 95 percent confident that the mean deposits at all the branch banks are not equal. If he feels that different income groups are attracted by different types of promotional games, he should devise alternative schemes for each branch to entice new depositors.

11.5 TESTS FOR DIFFERENCES BETWEEN INDIVIDUAL PAIRS

As you can see from the discussion above, ANOVA tells us whether all means are equal. However, when the null hypothesis is rejected, ANOVA does not reveal which mean(s) is (are) different from the rest. We must use other statistical tests to make this determination. These tests rely on a pairwise comparison of all possible pairs of means. If the absolute value (ignoring signs) of the difference between any two sample means is greater than some standard, it is seen as a significant difference, and it is concluded that the respective population means are different.

The determination of this standard can be achieved by a variety of statistical procedures including Tukey's (Too'Key) method, the least significant difference (LSD), and the Scheffé (Shey-fay') approach.

A. TEST FOR BALANCED DESIGNS

Both the Tukey method and the first of two LSD methods shown here are used if there is an equal number of observations in each sample. Such ANOVA designs are said to be *balanced*. If the design is unbalanced in that the samples are of different sizes, the Scheffé method, or an alternative LSD approach to be illustrated shortly, must be used.

ANOVA Designs

In a balanced ANOVA design, each sample has the same number of observations. If one or more samples have a different number of observations, the design is said to be unbalanced.

In Example 11-3, Mr. Shade found that not all four of his branch banks had the same deposit levels. The next logical step is to determine which ones are different. Since there is an equal number of observations in all four samples ($r = 7$), either the Tukey method, developed by J. W. Tukey in 1953, or the first LSD approach can be used

THE TUKEY APPROACH   Tukey's method requires the calculation of the Tukey criterion, T as shown in Formula (11.13).

$$T = q_{\alpha, c, n-c} \sqrt{\frac{MSE}{r}} \qquad (11.13)$$

---

where q is a **studentized range distribution** with c and $n - c$ degrees of freedom. Recall that c is the number of samples or treatments (columns), and n is the total number of observations in all samples combined. These values are 4 and 28 in Shade's branch banking problem.

The Studentized Range Distribution

The studentized range distribution is a probability distribution with c and $n - c$ degrees of freedom.

Table L gives the critical values for q with $\alpha = 0.01$ and $\alpha = 0.05$. If α is set at 0.05, Shade wants the value for $q_{0.05, 4, 24}$. From that portion of Table L for values with $\alpha = 0.05$, move across the top row for the first degrees of freedom of 4 and down that column to the second degrees of freedom of 24. There you will find the value 3.90. Then

$$T = 3.90\sqrt{\frac{0.236}{7}}$$

$$= 0.716$$

This Tukey standard criterion of 0.716 is then compared with the absolute difference between each pairwise comparison of sample means. If any pair of sample means has an absolute difference greater than the T-value of 0.716, it can be concluded at the 5 percent level that their respective populations means are not equal. The difference between the sample means is too great to conclude that they came from similar populations. There is only a 5 percent chance that populations with equal means could yield samples of these sizes with means that differ by more than 0.716.

$$|\bar{X}_1 - \bar{X}_2| = |1.46 - 2.29| = 0.83 > 0.716$$

$$|\bar{X}_1 - \bar{X}_3| = |1.46 - 4.31| = 2.85 > 0.716$$

$$|\bar{X}_1 - \bar{X}_4| = |1.46 - 4.87| = 3.41 > 0.716$$

$$|\bar{X}_2 - \bar{X}_3| = |2.29 - 4.31| = 2.02 > 0.716$$

$$|\bar{X}_2 - \bar{X}_4| = |2.29 - 4.87| = 2.58 > 0.716$$

$$|\bar{X}_3 - \bar{X}_4| = |4.31 - 4.87| = 0.56 < 0.716$$

In comparing the absolute values of each pairwise difference in sample means to $T = 0.716$, Shade can be 95 percent confident that only branches 3 and 4 have equal mean deposit levels. All the other differences exceed the T-criterion.

LEAST SIGNIFICANT DIFFERENCE   The least significant difference approach is quite similar to the Tukey method. It compares the LSD criterion to the absolute difference in sample means. If the design is balanced, the LSD criterion is

$$LSD = \sqrt{\frac{2(MSE)F_{\alpha, 1, n-c}}{r}} \qquad (11.14)$$

Note that in using the LSD approach, F has 1 and $n - c$ degrees of freedom. In Shade's case this is 1 and $n - c = 28 - 4 = 24$ degrees of freedom. From the F-table, $F_{0.05, 1, 24} = 4.26$. Then

$$LSD = \sqrt{\frac{2(0.236)4.26}{7}}$$

$$= 0.536$$

In comparing the *LSD* of 0.536 with each of the absolute differences figured above, Shade finds that all values, including the last one, suggest different population means. The LSD approach is more conservative in that given any set of conditions, the *LSD* criterion will be less than the Tukey value.

With either method, what may appear to be inconsistencies may arise. Assume for the sake of simplicity that there are only three populations under study requiring three pairwise comparisons:

$$|\bar{X}_1 - \bar{X}_2|, \quad |\bar{X}_1 - \bar{X}_3|, \quad \text{and} \quad |\bar{X}_2 - \bar{X}_3|$$

You may find that 1 does not differ significantly from 2, and that 2 does not differ significantly from 3, but that 1 does differ significantly from 3. This may seem contradictory. According to the rule of transitivity, if 1 equals 2 and 2 equals 3, then 1 must equal 3. However, pairwise comparisons do not involve equalities. In comparing the three populations, we are merely examining statistical evidence to determine if it is sufficiently strong to reject the null. To conclude that 1 does not differ significantly from 2 simply means that we have insufficient evidence to conclude that they are different. If we conclude, as we did here, that 1 does differ from 3, it can be assumed that evidence comparing these two samples was stronger.

B.   DENOTING SIGNIFICANT DIFFERENCES

After identifying those means that differ significantly, it is sometimes desirable to denote the results in a concise manner. This can be done with *common underscoring*. We simply list the means and draw connecting lines under those means that are not significantly different.

In Shade's case, he found that only samples 3 and 4 did not differ significantly. He could use common underscoring to indicate these results by first listing the means of the "groups" (in this case, banks) in an ordered array. The ordered array is usually, but not always, arranged from lowest to highest. Shade would have

Group	1	2	3	4
Mean	1.46	2.29	4.31	4.87

The connecting line drawn under the mean deposits for groups 3 and 4 indicates that these banks did not differ significantly in their mean deposit level. That is, since they did not display a significant difference, they are adjoined with a common line. Groups 1 and 2 are not adjoined with any other groups since they did display a significant difference.

As another example, assume five group means are compared, and the results are shown here.

Group	Mean
1	5.1
2	17.8
3	9.0
4	16.5
5	4.1

The ordered array and common underscoring might appear as

Group	5	1	3	4	2
Mean	4.1	5.1	9	16.5	17.8

It can readily be seen that groups 5 and 1 were not significantly different from each other, groups 4 and 2 did not differ significantly, and group 3 differed significantly from the other four.

C. TESTS FOR UNBALANCED DESIGNS

If the design is unbalanced, the Tukey approach and the LSD method do not apply. Instead, an alternate LSD approach can be used. To compare the jth and kth samples, the equation for LSD becomes

$$LSD_{j,k} = \sqrt{\left[\frac{1}{r_j} + \frac{1}{r_k}\right](MSE)F_{\alpha,1,n-c}} \qquad (11.15)$$

where r_j is the number of observations in the jth sample and r_k is the number of observations in the kth sample. The LSD value will be different for each pair of pairwise comparisons since the number of observations is not the same in every sample.

The Scheffé criterion can be calculated for unbalanced designs as

$$S = xy \qquad (11.16)$$

where

$$x = \sqrt{(c - 1)F_{\alpha,c-1,n-c}} \qquad (11.17)$$

and

$$y = \sqrt{\left[\frac{1}{r_j} + \frac{1}{r_k}\right]MSE} \qquad (11.18)$$

EXAMPLE 11-4 The Daniel Boone Syndrome

As more Americans seek escape from urban pressures, the burden on our national parks has shown a marked increase with the rise in weekend campers. *Outdoor World* recently reported that the Yosemite National Park in California's high Sierras hired an economic consultant to study the financial position of the Park.

Part of his effort required the comparison of Park revenues from various sources, including camping fees, fishing licences, and canoe rentals. Displayed here are the data for several randomly selected visitors. Determine if there is a difference in the mean revenues the Park receives from these three activities.

Visitor	Camping	Fishing	Canoeing
1	$47.00	$30.00	$19.00
2	32.00	18.00	25.00
3	35.00	27.00	20.00
4	25.00	35.00	22.00
5	38.00	**	25.00
6	35.00	**	**
$\overline{X}_j$	$35.33	$27.50	$22.20

SOLUTION:

Assuming α is set at 5 percent, then $F_{\alpha, c-1, n-c} = F_{0.05, 2, 12} = 3.89$. The ANOVA table would appear as

Source of Variation	SS	d.f.	MS	F-value
Between samples (treatment)	480.6	2	240.3	6.48
Within samples (error)	445.1	12	37.1	
Total variation	925.7	14		

$H_0: \mu_1 = \mu_2 = \mu_3$
$H_a:$ Not all means are equal
Decision Rule: Do not reject if $F < 3.89$. Reject if $F > 3.89$.
Conclusion: Reject null since $F = 6.48 > 3.89$.

Since the null hypothesis that mean revenues from all three activities is rejected, the consultant would want to use pairwise comparisons to determine which ones differed from the rest:

$$|\overline{X}_1 - \overline{X}_2| = |35.33 - 27.50| = 7.83$$

$$|\overline{X}_1 - \overline{X}_3| = |35.33 - 22.20| = 13.13$$

$$|\overline{X}_2 - \overline{X}_3| = |27.50 - 22.20| = 5.30$$

If α is 5 percent, $F_{0.05, 1, n-c} = F_{0.05, 1, 15-3} = 4.75$. The comparison for the first (camping) and the second (fishing) activities using LSD is

$$LSD_{1,2} = \sqrt{\left[\frac{1}{6} + \frac{1}{4}\right](37.1)(4.75)}$$

$$= 8.57$$

Since the difference between the sample mean revenues for camping and fishing of 7.83 is less than the LSD criterion of 8.57, it can be concluded with 95 percent confidence that there is no difference in the mean revenues generated by these two activities. A comparison of camping and canoeing reveals

$$LSD_{1,3} = \sqrt{\left[\frac{1}{6} + \frac{1}{5}\right](37.1)(4.75)}$$

$$= 8.04$$

Since $|\overline{X}_1 - \overline{X}_3| = 13.13 > 8.04$, the data suggest that these two activities do generate different mean revenues. The last comparison of fishing and canoeing produces

$$LSD_{2,3} = \sqrt{\left[\frac{1}{4} + \frac{1}{5}\right](37.1)(4.75)}$$

$$= 8.91$$

Since $|\overline{X}_2 - \overline{X}_3| = 5.3 < 8.91$, fishing and canoeing are considered to augment Park coffers by the same mean amount.

Using the Scheffé method generates the same results. The calculations shown here compare camping and fishing as an example.

$$S_{1,2} = xy$$

$$x = \sqrt{2(3.89)}$$

$$= 2.79$$

$$y = \sqrt{\left[\frac{1}{6} + \frac{1}{4}\right](37.1)}$$

$$= 3.93$$

$$S = (2.79)(3.93)$$

$$= 10.96$$

Since $S = 10.96 > 7.83$, the Scheffé method leads to the conclusion that camping and fishing do not generate different mean revenues. The other comparisons can be made in similar fashion using Scheffé.

STATISTICAL INTERPRETATION:

It can be concluded at the 5 percent level of significance that only camping and canoeing produce different mean revenues.

The Park can now use the information provided by this statistical study to make business and financial decisions that should assist in relieving the strain on the resources used to provide an outdoor experience for modern-day urbanites.

11.6 TWO-WAY ANOVA: THE RANDOMIZED BLOCK DESIGN

With one-way ANOVA, concern must focus on only one factor at a time, such as the mean deposits in branch banks or revenues of park activities. However, there are many situations in the business world in which numerous factors must be considered in order to gain a more precise measure of the treatment's impact. For example, businesses often want to compare the mean productivity of different types of machines. The machine's output may be affected, however, by the skill of the person operating it. Consideration must therefore be given to (1) the machine's capabilities, which is the business's primary concern, as well as (2) the operator's experience, which may affect the machine's capabilities. When we want to incorporate two elements, we must rely on **two-way ANOVA.**

To illustrate, a large accounting firm is trying to select an office-integrated computer system from three models currently under consideration. The final choice will depend on the systems' productivity. Five operators are selected at random to operate each system. It is important to realize that each operator will perform on all three systems. However, the firm realizes that the level of experience the employees have in operating computers may affect the outcome of the test. There is therefore a need to account for the impact of experience in determining the relative merits of the computer systems. The resulting levels of output measured in units per hour are recorded in Table 11-3. A higher coded value for experience indicates more years of training.

TABLE 11-3   Output Levels for Computer Systems

Experience Level	Systems (Treatments)			
	1	2	3	$\bar{X}_i$
1	27	21	25	24.33
2	31	33	35	33.00
3	42	39	39	40.00
4	38	41	37	38.67
5	45	46	45	45.33
$\bar{X}_j$	36.5	36.0	36.2	

$\bar{\bar{X}} = 36.27$

Within any given sample (system) there will occur variation in output due to operator experience, proficiency, state of health at the time, and other random error factors. In one-way ANOVA we identified this as error variation. If any of these random factors associated with the operators materially affect the level of output, the accounting firm must correct for them. The firm may feel that an operator's years of experience would significantly affect his or her productivity. However, the firm is interested in the productivity of the computer systems, not that of their employees. It must therefore adjust for employee productivity by eliminating the effect of operator variability in order to get a more accurate, uncontaminated measure of system quality.

This is done by **blocking** the observations (operators) into homogeneous groups based on years of experience. Operators with the same experience level are put into the same groups or blocks. The purpose of blocking is to decrease the variation in the error term within a treatment (system). The computer system is the treatment under examination, and the experience level is the block.

> **Blocking**
> The purpose of blocking is to correct for and eliminate any variation in the observations (of computer output in our present case) due to difference in blocks (experience levels in our case).

If blocking is done effectively and is based on a factor, such as experience, which truly does affect productivity, a purer measure of system quality is obtained. However, if the factor selected for blocking does not affect productivity, such as a worker's social security number, hair color, or sex, the results can be quite misleading. It is important to determine if blocking is done correctly, and if the factor upon which blocking is based does have an impact.

The process of blocking assumes that the block effects and treatment effects are **additive**. That is, a treatment effect is the same from one block to the next. Any given computer system must affect the productivity of each block (experience level) to the same degree.

> **The Additive Feature**
> Each treatment effect is the same for all blocks.

However, if operators with a particular level of experience work more effectively on one system, while another block interacts better with a different system, the block and treatment effects are said to be **interactive**. For example, operators with experience level 2 may work more effectively with system 3 computers, but find system 1 computers are awkward and retard productivity. On the other hand, operators with experience level 4 may find just the opposite. If inconsistencies of this nature exist, block and treatment effects are said to interact.

The Interaction Feature
If different treatments affect the blocks differently, they are said to interact.

If interaction exists, certain adjustments, which are discussed briefly in the next section, must be made in our analysis.

Given our current example, it is not possible to detect interaction, because it is necessary to have more than one observation in each cell to do so. Since we set up a design experiment in which there was only one operator for each system, and we have only one observation in each cell, we cannot test for interaction. Therefore, let us continue with our discussion of two-way ANOVA under the assumption that interaction is not present.

With two-way ANOVA, the total sum of squares is partitioned into three parts: the treatment sum of squares (*SSTR*), the error sum of squares (*SSE*), and the block sum of squares (*SSBL*). Thus,

$$SST = SSTR + SSE + SSBL$$

SST and *SSTR* are calculated in the same manner as in one-way ANOVA. However, *SSE* is subdivided into a measure for *SSE* and *SSBL*, where

$$SSBL = \Sigma c_i (\overline{X}_i - \overline{\overline{X}})^2 \tag{11.19}$$

The number of treatments in each block, c_i, is multiplied by the squared difference between the mean for each block, $\overline{X}_i$, and the grand mean. The results are then summed for all blocks. The symbol c_i is used to indicate the number of treatments in a block (row) because the treatments are recorded columns.

From Table 11-3,

$$SSBL = 3(24.33 - 36.27)^2 + 3(33 - 36.27)^2 + 3(40 - 36.27)^2$$
$$+ 3(38.67 - 36.27)^2 + 3(45.33 - 36.27)^2$$
$$= 765.04$$

Formulas (11.6) and (11.7) yield

$$SST = 806.93 \qquad \text{and} \qquad SSTR = 0.93$$

SSE is calculated as

$$SSE = SST - SSTR - SSBL \tag{11.20}$$

$$= 806.93 - 0.93 - 765.04$$
$$= 40.96$$

Where there are r blocks and c treatments, there are $n = rc$ observations. The degrees of freedom for each of the sums of squares for the values in Formula (11.20) are

$$SSE = SST - SSTR - SSBL$$
$$(r-1)(c-1) = (n-1) - (c-1) - (r-1)$$
$$(5-1)(3-1) = (15-1) - (3-1) - (5-1)$$
$$8 = 14 - 2 - 4$$

The mean square total and the mean square treatment are, as before, the sum of their squares divided by their degrees of freedom. Thus,

$$\text{Mean square total} = MST = \frac{SST}{n-1}$$

$$= \frac{806.93}{14}$$

$$= 57.64$$

$$\text{Mean square treatment} = MSTR = \frac{SSTR}{c-1}$$

$$= \frac{0.93}{2}$$

$$= 0.47$$

In two-way ANOVA,

$$\text{Mean square error} = MSE = \frac{SSE}{(r-1)(c-1)} \qquad (11.21)$$

$$= \frac{40.96}{8}$$

$$= 5.1$$

$$\text{Mean square block} = MSBL = \frac{SSBL}{r-1} \qquad (11.22)$$

$$= \frac{765.04}{4}$$

$$= 191.26$$

TABLE 11-4   Two-Way ANOVA for the Computer Systems

Source of Variation	SS	d.f.	MS	F-value
Between samples (treatment)	0.93	2	0.47	0.09
Between blocks	765.04	4	191.26	37.50
Within samples (error)	40.96	8	5.10	
Total variation	806.93	14		

These calculations are summarized in Table 11-4. The F-values are calculated in the same manner as in one-way ANOVA:

$$F = \frac{MSTR}{MSE}$$

$$= \frac{0.47}{5.1}$$

$$= 0.09$$

$$F = \frac{MSBL}{MSE}$$

$$= \frac{191.26}{5.1}$$

$$= 37.50$$

Notice that two F-values are computed—one using MSTR and one for MSBL. The F-value for MSBL is calculated in order to determine if blocking was done effectively. Recall that if blocking is based on a factor that does not affect operator productivity, the results can be misleading. The accounting firm must therefore test to see if there is a significant difference between block (row) means. If there is no significant difference between mean levels of output based on experience blocks (rows), then experience is not a critical factor. In this event, two-way ANOVA should be abandoned, and a return to one-way ANOVA with no distinction between experience levels is called for. At the 5 percent level, the critical F-value for MSBL with 4 and 8 degrees of freedom is found from Table G to be $F_{0.05, 4, 8} = 3.84$. The degrees of freedom of 4 and 8 are used because the F-ratio for blocks uses MSBL with $r - 1 = 4$ degrees of freedom and MSE with $(r - 1)(c - 1) = 8$ degrees of freedom.

The accounting firm must first test the hypothesis that the mean level of output for each experience level is the same. If it is, then experience is not a factor in determining output, and blocking on it would prove useless at best. If the mean levels of output of the different experience levels are not the same, then the accounting firm must block on experience in order to correct for its impact and thereby obtain a more accurate measure of the differences in computer system quality. The hypothesis to test is

$$H_0: \mu_1 = \mu_2 = \mu_3 = \mu_4 = \mu_5$$

H_a: Not all row means are equal

where μ_i are the mean levels of output for each experience level.

Decision Rule

Do not reject the null if $F < 3.84$. Reject the null if $F < 3.84$.

Since $F = 37.50$, the null should be rejected, and the firm should conclude that experience levels have an effect on rates of output. It must correct for experience by using two-way ANOVA.

The firm is now ready to test the hypothesis in which it was originally interested. Is there a difference in the mean output of the computer systems (treatments)? If the α-value of 5 percent is retained, the $F_{\alpha, (c-1), (r-1)(c-1)} = F_{0.05, 2, 8} = 4.46$ is found from the table. The degrees of freedom of 2 and 8 are used because the F-ratio for the treatments uses $MSTR$ with 2 degrees of freedom and MSE with 8 degrees of freedom. The set of hypotheses is

$$H_0: \mu_1 = \mu_2 = \mu_3$$

$$H_a: \text{Not all column means are equal}$$

where μ_i are the column means for the three computer systems.

Decision Rule

Do not reject the null if $F < 4.46$. Reject the null if $F > 4.46$.

Table 11-4 reveals that $F = 0.09 < 4.46$. The null is not rejected, and the firm concludes that the mean output levels of the three computer systems do not differ once a correction has been made for experience. Employees of different experience levels perform equally well on all machines. It doesn't matter which computer system they buy.

Example 11-5 provides a more concise illustration of two-way ANOVA.

EXAMPLE 11-5 Supervising Supervisors: Two-Way ANOVA

A recent issue of *Fortune* magazine described efforts by a major electronics firm to develop a system in which employees would be given the opportunity to evaluate the performance of their supervisors and other managerial personnel. Assume five employees are selected at random and asked to evaluate four of their managers on a scale of 10 to 50. The results, along with row and column means, might appear as in the accompanying table.

Employee	Manager (Treatment) 1	2	3	4	$\bar{X}_i$
1	31	35	46	38	37.50
2	29	32	45	36	35.50
3	13	17	35	20	21.25
4	28	38	52	39	39.25
5	14	20	40	20	23.50
$\bar{X}_j$	23	28.4	43.6	30.6	
$\bar{\bar{X}} = 31.4$					

The management director for the electronics firm wants to know if there is a difference in the mean ratings of the four managers.

SOLUTION:
He decides to use one-way ANOVA to test the means.

$$SST = \Sigma\Sigma(X_{ij} - \overline{\overline{X}})^2$$
$$= (31 - 31.4)^2 + (29 - 31.4)^2 + \cdots + (39 - 31.4)^2$$
$$+ (20 - 31.4)^2$$
$$= 2344.8$$

$$SSTR = \Sigma r_j(\overline{X}_j - \overline{\overline{X}})^2$$
$$= 5(23 - 31.4)^2 + 5(28.4 - 31.4)^2 + 5(43.6 - 31.4)^2$$
$$+ 5(30.6 - 31.4)^2$$
$$= 1145.2$$

$$SSE = \Sigma\Sigma(X_{ij} - \overline{X}_j)^2$$
$$= (31 - 23)^2 + (29 - 23)^2 + \cdots + (35 - 28.4)^2$$
$$+ \cdots + (46 - 43.6)^2 + \cdots + (38 - 30.6)^2 + \cdots + (20 - 30.6)^2$$
$$= 1199.6$$

If the director wishes to test the hypothesis at the 1 percent level, Table G reveals that $F_{0.01, 3, 16} = 5.29$. The one-way table shown here summarizes the director's calculations.

Source of Variation	SS	d.f.	MS	F-value
Between samples (treatment)	1,145.2	3	381.7	5.09
Within samples (error)	1,199.6	16	75.0	
Total variation	2,344.8	19		

$H_0: \mu_1 = \mu_2 = \mu_3 = \mu_4$
H_a: Not all means are equal
Decision Rule: Do not reject the null if $F < 5.29$. Reject the null if $F > 5.29$.
Conclusion: The F-ratio of 5.09 is less than the critical value of 5.29, and the director therefore does not reject the null and concludes with 99 percent confidence that there is no significant difference in the mean ratings of the four managers.

However, soon after completing the analysis, the director realizes that certain differences in the employees performing the evaluations might affect the outcome. The employees' work attitudes, recent contact with management, pay grade, or a variety of other factors could materially affect their rating of the managers. The director decides to correct for all of these factors by blocking on the five employees. Each employee is seen as a block since each may have had different experiences with management which might affect his or her evaluation reports.

Although *SST* and *SSTR* are left unaffected by the use of two-way ANOVA, *SSBL* and *SSE* must be calculated.

$$SSBL = \Sigma c_i (X_i - \overline{\overline{X}})^2$$

$$= 4(37.5 - 31.4)^2 + 4(35.5 - 31.4)^2$$
$$+ 4(21.25 - 31.4)^2 + 4(39 - 31.4)^2$$
$$+ 4(23.5 - 31.4)^2$$

$$= 1124.3$$

$$SSE = SST - SSTR - SSBL$$

$$= 2344.8 - 1145.2 - 1124.3$$

$$= 75.3$$

The two-way table becomes

Source of Variation	SS	d.f.	MS	F-value
Between samples (treatment)	1,145.2	3	381.73	60.79
Between blocks	1,124.3	4	281.08	44.76
Within samples (error)	75.3	12	6.28	
Total variation	2,344.8	19		

The director can now determine if there is a significant difference in the mean ratings given by each of the five employees (rows), which would require blocking on the employees. The hypotheses are

$$H_0: \mu_1 = \mu_2 = \mu_3 = \mu_4 = \mu_5$$

$$H_a: \text{Not all row means are equal}$$

If $\alpha = 1$ percent is retained, the proper *F*-value is $F_{0.01, 4, 12} = 5.41$. The *F*-value associated with the test on blocks is shown in the ANOVA table to be $44.76 > 5.41$. The null is rejected, and it is determined at the 99 percent level of confidence that the mean ratings by the five employees (rows) are different and blocking is required.

The director can now test his primary hypothesis regarding the mean ratings of the four managers (columns). The hypotheses are

$$H_0: \mu_1 = \mu_2 = \mu_3 = \mu_4$$

$$H_a: \text{Not all column means are equal}$$

The *F*-value of $F_{0.01, 3, 12} = 5.95$ is less than 60.79. The null hypothesis must be rejected. The director can be 99 percent certain that not all managers have the same evaluation ratings even after correcting for employee bias.

STATISTICAL INTERPRETATION:
By including a blocking factor, the director was able to detect a significant difference in the mean rating of the managers by the five employees. Without the blocking

factor, the variation in the ratings due to the blocks (differences in employee attitudes) was included in the error factor SSE. This had the effect of increasing SSE and MSE. The F-value would therefore be lower since $F = MSTR/MSE$. As the F-value goes down, there is a greater likelihood of not rejecting the null.

However, with the two-way ANOVA, the MSE is subdivided into variation due to blocks ($MSBL$) and variation due to error within samples (MSE).

Now that the director knows that not all managers' ratings are the same, he can use Tukey's method or LSD to determine which are different. In applying these tools to a two-way test, certain changes must be made in the degrees of freedom associated with the Tukey method. Rather than explore that involved adjustment, the LSD method can be used with two-way ANOVA.

11.7 A POTPOURRI

To this point we have explored both one-way and two-way ANOVA, along with ways to determine which means are different. There are, however, certain related elements we have not fully examined. Although a thorough inspection of all the aspects of ANOVA is beyond the scope of this text, we will touch upon a few of the more important remaining concepts in this section.

A. INTERACTION

We noted that it is possible for block and treatment effects to interact. Interaction occurs when treatments impact on different blocks in a dissimilar fashion. If the difference in the mean effects of treatments on one block is not the same as the difference in the mean effects on other blocks, blocks and treatments are said to be interactive.

Return for a moment to our comparison of the three computer systems. For interaction *not* to occur, each computer system must increase (or decrease) the productivity of all five experience levels to the same extent. There must be a consistency in the mean impact on blocks from one treatment to the next. If there is no interaction, then the experience level which works best with one system must work best with all systems. As an example, for the sake of simplicity, assume that only two experience levels are involved. The necessary consistency in the mean impact of treatments is shown in Table 11-5.

TABLE 11-5   Absence of Interaction

Blocks (experience)	Treatments (computer systems)		
	1	2	3
1	$\mu_{11} = 30$	$\mu_{12} = 40$	$\mu_{13} = 45$
2	$\mu_{21} = 20$	$\mu_{22} = 30$	$\mu_{23} = 35$

μ_{ij} is the mean output of several operators with i experience on system j. $\mu_{12} = 40$ tells us that several operators with level of experience 1 averaged an output of 40 using system 2. Interaction does not exist in Table 11-5 because the mean impact of the three systems is the same for both blocks. For experience level 1, the difference in mean output between system 1 and system 2 is 10 (= 40 − 30). This is also true for experience level 2. The difference in mean output is also 10 (= 30 − 20). This conformity holds when comparing systems 2 and 3. For both experience levels the increase in productivity is 5 units.

If μ_{23} was 36 instead of 35, interaction would exist. In moving from system 2 to system 3, the first experience level would show an increase of 5 while the second would show an increase of 6. This inconsistency is evidence of interaction.

Interaction

Interaction occurs if, in moving from one treatment to another, the mean impact on different blocks is not the same.

In this discussion it was emphasized that the entry in any cell of Table 11-5 was the mean output of several operators. In our original example this was not the case. We kept it simple by assuming only one operator in each cell. In such a situation it is not possible to detect the presence of interaction. Interaction can be detected only if the *mean* effect on blocks differs between treatments.

It should further be noted that it is not permissible to use the mean data entries in Table 11-5 in the same manner as we did those for individual observations in Table 11-3 to compute *SST*, *SSE*, and *SSTR*. *All* the observations in a cell must be used when computing the sums of squares, not just their mean.

B. TWO-FACTOR ANOVA

So far our analysis has centered on one-factor designs in which our intent was to compare the effects of a single treatment. Even in the case of two-way ANOVA, the blocking variable was not viewed as a treatment factor, but was introduced as a control variable to correct for extraneous variation.

It is not difficult, however, to envision instances in which businesses may be interested in the impact of two or more factors. In this event, **two-factor ANOVA** is used.

A manufacturer wishes to examine the effects on costs of production of (1) the type of raw materials and (2) the structure of the assembly line used in the production process. Three types of raw materials and four assembly-line configurations can be used to produce their product. There are then two factors the firm is interested in analyzing: materials and assembly-line configuration. The first factor has three levels, and the second factor has four levels.

Do not confuse two-way ANOVA with two-factor ANOVA. Two-way ANOVA, which involves blocking, is done to eliminate variability from the error sum of squares due to an incidental force which the researcher does not wish to measure. It is called *two-way* because each observation is classified according to two criteria: a treatment (factor) and a block. *Two-factor* ANOVA is used to simultaneously examine the effects of two factors of interest.

11.8   SOLVED PROBLEMS

1. **On the Road Again** In the March issue of *Bicycling,* a magazine for the two-wheeled enthusiast, the unique problem faced by women in finding bikes that fit their body structure was explored. Women generally have shorter torsos and arms, relative to their height, than do men. This creates a difficulty in finding bike frames that provide a comfortable ride for women.

   Manufacturers are continuing to address this problem by designing models more compatible with a woman's body. Schwinn offers a frame with a shorter wheel base of 40.1 inches. Consistency and uniformity in the measurements are a major concern.

   a. Suppose Sally Spokes, director of quality maintenance for Schwinn, selects 29 bikes and finds a variance in wheel base of 32.7 inches squared. If Ms. Spokes must ensure that variation does not exceed 27 inches squared, does this sample suggest that production standards are being met? Set $\alpha = 5$ percent.

   The hypothesis to be tested is based on the requirement that variation "does not exceed" 27 inches squared. This statement is written as $\sigma^2 \leq 27$, which contains the equal sign and is therefore the null. Thus,

$$H_0: \sigma^2 \leq 27$$

$$H_a: \sigma^2 > 27$$

   Given the inequality sign in the alternative hypothesis, a right-tailed test is called for, as shown by the figure. Formula (11.1) states

$$\chi^2 = \frac{(n-1)(s^2)}{\sigma^2}$$

$$= \frac{(29-1)(32.7)}{27}$$

$$= 33.91$$

   The critical χ^2-value is found in Table H by moving down the first column to d.f. $= n - 1 = 28$, and across to the column headed by 0.05. There the entry 41.337 is found.

   Decision Rule
   Do not reject if $\chi^2 < 41.337$. Reject if $\chi^2 > 41.337$.

   Since $\chi^2 = 33.91$, Ms. Spokes does not reject the null, and concludes with 95 percent confidence that production standards are being met.

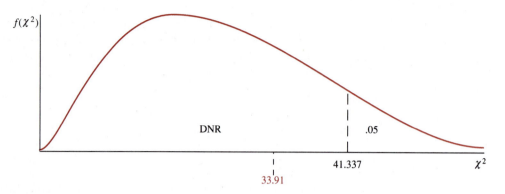

b. Assume that Ms. Spokes's instructions were that variation is kept "below 27 inches squared." The statement is then written $\sigma^2 < 27$, and the hypotheses are

$$H_0: \sigma^2 \geq 27$$

$$H_a: \sigma^2 < 27$$

requiring a left-tailed test. Assuming the same α is retained, then 5 percent of the area under the curve must be positioned in the left tail. Since Table H only gives entries for areas to the right of the χ^2, Ms. Spokes must locate that value associated with 95 percent. With d.f. $= 28$, she moves across that row to the column headed by 0.95 where the critical value of 16.928 is seen.

Decision Rule
Do not reject if $\chi^2 > 16.928$. Reject if $\chi^2 < 16.928$.

See the following figure.

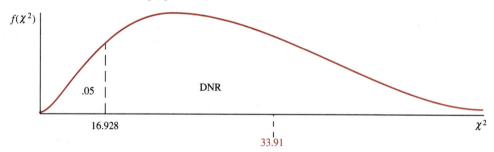

Here, χ^2 was determined to be 33.91. Ms. Spokes must not reject the null that $\sigma^2 \geq 27$. This means production standards are not being met. Corrective action must be taken.

You may wonder why the same sample findings of $s^2 = 32.7$ resulted in conflicting conclusions in parts a and b. Production standards in b required that $\sigma^2 < 27$. This is a stricter requirement than that imposed in part a, which stated that the variance only had to be less than or equal to 27. The rather high sample findings of $s^2 = 32.7$ were just in violation of the more stringent requirement in part b, but barely met that specified in part a. This illustrates the importance of properly specifying the hypothesis before testing begins.

c. Due to the inconsistencies of the previous two tests, Ms. Spokes requests that her production manager, Wallace Wheeler, develop a 90 percent confidence interval for the variance in the wheel base. To compute the interval, Wally uses Formula (10.2):

$$\frac{(n-1)s^2}{\chi_U^2} < \sigma^2 < \frac{(n-1)s^2}{\chi_L^2}$$

A 90 percent confidence interval leaves 5 percent of the area in each tail as shown in the figure. The upper χ^2-value is found in the column headed by 0.05 to be 41.337. The lower χ^2 can be located in the column under 0.95. It is 16.928.

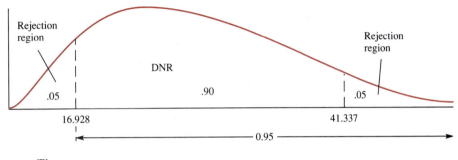

Then

$$\frac{(29-1)(32.7)}{41.337} < \sigma^2 < \frac{(29-1)(32.7)}{16.928}$$

$$22.15 < \sigma^2 < 54.09$$

Wally can be 90 percent confident that the variance in wheel base is between 22.15 and 54.09 inches, squared.

2. **Wages of Working Women** The March 1989 issue of *Woman's Day* reported that many women are reassessing their family/career options in favor of remaining in the home and placing greater emphasis on child care. A major consideration in this decision is the income brought home by the working wife.

An economist for the federal government assisting in a study on day care centers must test the hypothesis that the mean income of women with children in the home is equal to that of women with no children at home. She plans to use pooled data. This requires that the variances in incomes is the same for both groups. To test the hypothesis of equal variances, she selects 10 working women from each group. The sample variances prove to be 365 dollars squared for the women with children and 452 dollars squared for women who do not support children. Can pooled data be used?

Since pooled data requires that $\sigma_1^2 = \sigma_2^2$, the economist must test

$$H_0: \sigma_1^2 = \sigma_2^2$$

$$H_a: \sigma_1^2 \neq \sigma_2^2$$

She decides to use an α of 5 percent. The *F*-test which must be used is specified as a ratio of sample variances, and is "managed" so that the higher variance is placed in the numerator. This ensures that $F > 1$, nullifying any involvement with the lower tail, and produces a rejection region in only the upper tail. Since one tail has been excluded, the stated α must be divided by 2, yielding $0.05/2 = 0.025$ as shown in the figure. The critical F-value is based on d.f. of $n_1 - 1$ and $n_2 - 1 = 9$. From Table G, $F_{0.025,9,9} = 4.03$.

Decision Rule
Do not reject if $F < 4.03$. Reject if $F > 4.03$.

The ratio of sample variances is

$$F = \frac{452}{365}$$

$$= 1.24 < 4.03$$

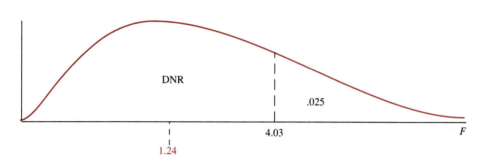

The economist can be 95 percent confident that the variances in incomes of the two groups of working women do not differ, and pooled data can be used to test the hypothesis of equal incomes.

3. **Fleecing the Motorist** In January of 1989, *Consumers' Research* published the results of a survey on U.S. driving habits. The data contained gasoline taxes per household for all 50 states. Six states are randomly chosen from the four regions of the country to determine if there is any difference in the annual mean gasoline tax within the regions. The results are shown here rounded to the nearest dollar.

		Region (treatment)		
State	**North (1)**	**South (2)**	**West (3)**	**Midwest (4)**
1	$293	$121	$114	$136
2	280	116	176	164
3	283	223	224	117
4	242	238	183	153
5	268	118	159	152
6	184	222	149	108
$\overline{X}_j$	258.3	173.0	167.5	138.3
$\overline{\overline{X}} = 184.3$				

An economist wanted to test at the 5 percent level the hypothesis that on the average residents in all four regions pay the same amount in federal gasoline taxes. Formula (11.6) states that

$$SST = \Sigma\Sigma(X_{ij} - \overline{\overline{X}})^2$$

$$= (293 - 184.3)^2 + \cdots + (108 - 184.3)^2$$

$$= 83,515$$

SSTR is found from Formula (11.7).

$$SSTR = \Sigma r_j(\overline{X}_j - \overline{\overline{X}})^2$$

$$= 6(258.3 - 184.3)^2 + \cdots + 6(138.3 - 184.3)^2$$

$$= 48,023$$

From Formula (11.8), *SSE* is

$$SSE = \Sigma\Sigma(X_{ij} - X_j)^2$$

$$= (293 - 258.3)^2 + \cdots + (108 - 138.3)^2$$

$$= 35,492$$

Formulas (11.10) and (11.11) produce

$$MSTR = \frac{SSTR}{c - 1}$$

$$= \frac{48,023}{4 - 1}$$

$$= 16,008$$

$$MSE = \frac{SSE}{n - c}$$

$$= \frac{35,492}{24 - 4}$$

$$= 1,775$$

If α is set at 5 percent, $F_{0.05, 3, 20} = 3.10$ as seen here. The hypothesis is $H_0: \mu_1 = \mu_2 = \mu_3 = \mu_4$.

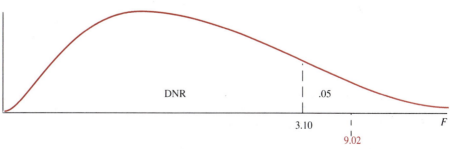

The ANOVA table is

Source of Variation	SS	d.f.	MS	F-value
Between samples (treatment)	48,023	3	16,008	9.02
Within samples (error)	35,492	20	1,775	
Total variation	83,515	23		

$H_0: \mu_1 = \mu_2 = \mu_3 = \mu_4$
H_a: Not all means are equal
Decision Rule: Do not reject the null if $F < 3.10$. Reject if $F > 3.10$.
Conclusion: Reject the null.

It can be concluded at the 95 percent level of confidence that the mean tax bite is not the same in all four regions.

4. **Who Gets Bitten the Hardest** To formulate an effective tax system, the government must now determine which regions pay more and which pay less. Using both Tukey's method and the LSD approach, the computations would proceed as shown here.

It is first necessary to find the absolute differences in the sample means of the taxes paid in each pair of the four regions.

$$|\overline{X}_1 - \overline{X}_2| = |258.3 - 173.0| = 85.3$$

$$|\overline{X}_1 - \overline{X}_3| = |258.3 - 167.5| = 90.8$$

$$|\overline{X}_1 - \overline{X}_4| = |258.3 - 138.3| = 120.0$$

$$|\overline{X}_2 - \overline{X}_3| = |173.0 - 167.5| = 5.5$$

$$|\overline{X}_2 - \overline{X}_4| = |173.0 - 138.3| = 34.7$$

$$|\overline{X}_3 - \overline{X}_4| = |167.5 - 138.3| = 29.2$$

Tukey's criterion is

$$T = q_{\alpha, c, n-c} \sqrt{\frac{MSE}{r}}$$

If α is set at 5 percent, $q_{0.05, 4, 20} = 3.96$,

$$T = 3.96 \sqrt{\frac{1,775}{6}}$$

$$= 68.11$$

Any absolute difference between the sample means greater than 68.11 is significant and suggests that their respective populations' means are different. There is only a 5 percent chance that two populations could have the same mean and generate samples of these sizes with means in excess of 68.11. Comparing 68.11 to the six pairs of sample means above, it can be seen that population 1 (North) has a mean different from the other three; μ_1 is assumed to be higher since $\overline{X}_1$ is significantly higher than the rest.

Using the LSD method, we have

$$LSD = \sqrt{\frac{2(MSE)F_{\alpha,1,n-c}}{r}}$$

$F_{0.05,1,20} = 4.35$. Then

$$LSD = \sqrt{\frac{2(1,775)(4.35)}{6}}$$

$$= 50.73$$

The *LSD* criterion is compared with the absolute differences in sample means above. Any differences greater than 50.73 are significant. Again, it is seen that those motorists in the North endure the heaviest tax burden.

5. **Acme, Ltd.** As a Production Supervisor for Acme, Ltd., Melvin Moore wishes to compare production levels of Acme's four plants. The weekly levels in tons are collected over a given seven-week period including the four weeks in August and the first three in September. The results are shown in the table.

| | Plant (treatment) | | | | |
Week	1	2	3	4	$\overline{X}_i$
1	42.7	38.3	42.9	30.1	38.5
2	47.3	35.1	38.2	37.5	39.5
3	57.3	42.7	49.9	47.8	49.4
4	63.1	58.2	59.3	53.9	58.6
5	49.2	32.7	45.7	33.8	40.4
6	51.2	30.1	48.3	38.7	42.1
7	48.0	31.1	45.2	39.7	41.0
$\overline{X}_j$	51.3	38.3	47.1	40.2	
$\overline{\overline{X}} = 44.23$					

Melvin conducts a one-way ANOVA and finds a significant difference in mean output levels. However, before submitting his report to higher management, Melvin comes to an important realization. The seven weeks were not picked randomly for each plant. Data for the same seven weeks were used for all four plants. Perhaps he should block on weeks to eliminate any variation due to the time period. Since the same weeks were recorded for each plant, blocking on weeks is possible.

SST and *SSTR* are calculated in the same fashion as in Solved Problem 4, and are found to be 2,276.1 and 761.4, respectively. In addition,

$$SSBL = \Sigma c_i (X_i - \overline{\overline{X}})^2$$

$$= 4(38.5 - 44.23)^2 + 4(39.5 - 44.23)^2$$

$$+ \cdots + 4(41 - 44.23)^2$$

$$= 1,276.6$$

$$SSE = SST - SSTR - SSBL$$

$$= 238.1$$

$$MSTR = \frac{SSTR}{c - 1}$$

$$= \frac{761.4}{4 - 1}$$

$$= 253.8$$

$$MSBL = \frac{SSBL}{r - 1}$$

$$= \frac{1,276.6}{7 - 1}$$

$$= 212.8$$

$$MSE = \frac{SSE}{(r - 1)(c - 1)}$$

$$= \frac{238.1}{(7 - 1)(4 - 1)}$$

$$= 13.2$$

These calculations are summarized in the two-way ANOVA table:

Source of Variation	SS	d.f.	MS	F-value
Between samples (treatment)	761.4	3	253.8	19.23
Between blocks	1,276.6	6	212.8	16.12
Within samples (error)	238.1	18	13.2	
Total variation	2,276.1	27		

Melvin must first determine if blocking on weeks is effective. He set α at 5 percent. The F-value for blocks is $MSBL/MSE$, and since $MSLB$ has $r - 1 = 6$ d.f. and MSE has $(r - 1)(c - 1) = 18$ d.f., $F_{0.05, 6, 18} = 2.66$ is found to be the critical F-value. Since $F = 16.12 > 2.66$, it is concluded that the mean output between weeks is different. Blocking is therefore necessary to correct for variation from one week to the next. Melvin should continue with his two-way test.

He can now test the primary hypothesis on mean plant output levels.

$$H_0: \mu_1 = \mu_2 = \mu_3 = \mu_4 = \mu_5 = \mu_6 = \mu_7$$

H_a: Not all means are equal

The F-value for treatments has $c - 1 = 3$ and $(r - 1)(c - 1) = 18$ d.f. $F_{0.05, 3, 18} = 3.16 < 19.23$. The hypothesis is rejected, and Melvin concludes that there is some difference in plant output levels on the average. LSD can now be used to determine which ones are different.

11.9 WHAT YOU SHOULD HAVE LEARNED FROM THIS CHAPTER

The uses and applicability of ANOVA should now be apparent. You should be aware of the manner in which ANOVA can be used to make business decisions. It is essential that you be able to identify those situations requiring two-way ANOVA, and to understand how pairwise comparisons can be used to isolate those population means that are different from the rest. If you are still uncertain about the use of any of these techniques, you should review the pertinent material in the chapter.

You should also be aware of the importance of testing for equal variances and the relationship that test has with those performed in earlier chapters concerning two-population hypotheses. The many ways in which chi-square is used in business situations should also be evident.

11.10 COMPUTER APPLICATIONS

After reading through all the computations associated with ANOVA in this chapter, it doesn't take a rocket scientist to determine that the analysis requires a good deal of time-consuming arithmetic. Without computers, extensive ANOVA work would be almost impossible. This section reveals the ways in which the work can be greatly simplified by using the computer. Each of the three packages we have been examining is discussed here.

A. MINITAB

Use of Minitab to complete an ANOVA study is quite easy. The data must be entered in columns based on treatments in much the same manner as the tables in this chapter. The AOVONEWAY command is then given to execute one-way ANOVA. The data for Mr. Shade's branch banks in Example 11-3 provide an illustration. The Minitab program would require the READ command to enter the data for the four branches in the first four columns. The input would appear as

```
MTB > READ C1 - C4
DATA > 1.3 1.9 3.6 5.1
DATA > 1.5 1.9 4.2 4.9
        rest of data go here
DATA > END
MTB NOTE A COMPARISON OF BANK DEPOSIT LEVELS
MTB > AOVONEWAY C1 - C4
```

The NOTE statement is optional. The last command of AOVONEWAY specifies the columns of data to be used for the ANOVA study, and produces the appropriate printout shown in Minitab 1.

The first part of the printout displays the ANOVA table.

All the values we calculated are shown, including the F-value of 78.09, which differs slightly from our value of 78.14 due to rounding. The p-value of 0.000 is also shown. Recall how we defined the p-value in earlier chapters. It is the probability of obtaining a test statistic as extreme or more so than the one actually obtained (in this case an F-value of 78.09) if the null is true. This means that the probability of calculating an F of 78.09 or higher if all four

MINITAB 1

```
ANALYSIS OF VARIANCE
SOURCE        DF        SS          MS          F           P
FACTOR        3         55.333      18.444      78.09       0.000
ERROR         24        5.669       0.236
TOTAL         27        61.001
```

banks did have the same mean deposit levels is virtually zero. It is highly unlikely that H_0: $\mu_1 = \mu_2 = \mu_3 = \mu_4$.

Minitab reports a POOLED STDEV of 0.4860 which recognizes that one of the assumptions of ANOVA is that all populations have the same variance. This POOLED STDEV is the estimate of the square root of that common variance. It is $\sqrt{MSE}$.

Two-way ANOVA requires that the data be entered in a very precise order. All the observations are put in the same column. The next two columns identify the blocks and treatments for each observation. Let us use the data from Table 11-3 concerning the comparison of computer systems as the illustration. *All* 15 observations are entered into column 1. The second column indicates which of the five blocks (rows) the observation belongs in, while the third column specifies one of the three treatments (columns) for the observation. The TWOWAY command is then given to obtain the desired output. Examine the Minitab input shown here and compare it to Table 11-3 to determine exactly how the data must be entered.

```
MTB > NAME C1 'OBSER' C2 'BLK' C3 'TRT'
MTB > READ C1 - C3
DATA > 27 1 1
DATA > 31 2 1
DATA > 42 3 1
        more data
DATA > 41 4 2
DATA > 45 5 3
DATA END
MTB > TWOWAY C1 C2 C3
```

The NAME command is optional and merely aids in identifying the three types of data. The first observation of 27 is in the first block (row) and the first treatment (column). It is therefore followed by a 1 and a 1. The next observation of 31 is in the second block and the first treatment. It is followed by a 2 and a 1. The remaining data are entered accordingly. The TWOWAY command follows.

B. SAS

An SAS program for one-way ANOVA requires that all the observations be entered in a single column. A second column identifies the treatment to which each observation belongs. The program for the study of Shade's branch banks in Example 11-3 would appear as

```
DATA;
INPUT DEPOSITS BRANCH;
CARDS
1.3 1
1.5 1
0.9 1
```

```
    more data
1.9 2
1.9 2
    more data
5.1 4
    more data
4.8 4
PROC ANOVA;
  CLASSES BRANCH;
  MODEL DEPOSITS = BRANCH;
```

The first deposit of 1.3 is in the first treatment (branch). It is therefore followed by a 1. The two observations of 1.9 are in the second treatment, so they are both followed by a 2. The remaining data are entered in similar fashion until the last observation of 4.8, which is in the fourth treatment, is reported.

The PROC ANOVA command includes a CLASSES statement which identifies the name of the treatments into which the data are divided. In this case, it is BRANCH. The MODEL statement follows, containing the name of the observations and then the name of the treatment as identified in the INPUT statement.

Caution: PROC ANOVA works only with balanced data. If unbalanced data are used as in Table 11-1, PROC GLM must be used.

The execution of two-way ANOVA requires that the data be entered in the same manner as with Minitab (see above). The program would be stated as

```
DATA;
INPUT OBS TRT BLK;
CARDS;
 the data go here
PROC ANOVA;
  CLASSES TRT BLK;
  MODEL OBS = TRT BLK;
```

The printouts look much like the one shown above.

C. SPSS-PC

The SPSS-PC program to complete the ANOVA study for Shade's branch banks is

```
DATA LIST FREE / BRANCH DEPOSIT.
ONEWAY BRANCH BY DEPOSIT(1,4).
BEGIN DATA.
1 1.3
2 1.5
...
...
...
7 2.1
1 1.9
....
...
...
7 4.8
END DATA.
```

The ONEWAY statement says that DEPOSIT has a value ranging from a low of 1 to a high of 4.

List of Formulas

$$X^2 = \frac{(n-1)s^2}{\sigma^2} \tag{11.1}$$

Calculates chi-square for the test of the variance of a normal population.

$$\frac{(n-1)s^2}{\chi_U^2} < \sigma^2 < \frac{(n-1)s^2}{\chi_L^2} \tag{11.2}$$

Calculates the confidence interval for the variance of a normal population.

$$F = \frac{s_1^2}{s_2^2} \tag{11.3}$$

F-ratio used when testing if two population variances are equal.

$$\overline{\overline{X}} = \frac{\sum_{j=1}^{c} r_j \overline{X}_j}{n} \tag{11.4A}$$

Grand mean for all observations in an ANOVA test.

$$\overline{\overline{X}} = \frac{\sum_{j=1}^{c} \overline{X}_j}{c} \tag{11.4B}$$

Grand mean for all observations in an ANOVA test when using a balanced design.

$$SST = \sum_{i=1}^{r}\sum_{j=1}^{c}(X_{ij} - \overline{\overline{X}})^2 \tag{11.6}$$

Total sum of squares.

$$SSTR = \Sigma r_j (\overline{X}_j - \overline{\overline{X}})^2 \qquad (11.7)$$

$$SSE = \Sigma\Sigma(X_{ij} - \overline{X}_j)^2 \qquad (11.8)$$

Error sum of squares.

$$MST = \frac{SST}{n-1} \qquad (11.9)$$

Total mean squares.

$$MSTR = \frac{SSTR}{c-1} \qquad (11.10)$$

Treatment mean squares.

$$MSE = \frac{SSE}{n-c} \qquad (11.11)$$

Error mean squares.

$$F = \frac{MSTR}{MSE} \qquad (11.12)$$

F-ratio for test of means.

$$T = q_{\alpha,c,n-c}\sqrt{\frac{MSE}{r}} \qquad (11.13)$$

Tukey criterion for pairwise comparisons.

$$LSD = \sqrt{\frac{2(MSE)F_{\alpha,1,n-c}}{r}} \qquad (11.14)$$

LSD **criterion for pairwise comparisons for balanced designs.**

$$LSD_{j,k} = \sqrt{\left[\frac{1}{r_j} + \frac{1}{r_k}\right](MSE)F_{\alpha,1,n-c}} \qquad (11.15)$$

LSD **criterion for pairwise comparisons for unbalanced designs.**

$$S = xy \qquad (11.16)$$

$$x = \sqrt{(c-1)F_{\alpha,c-1,n-c}} \qquad (11.17)$$

$$y = \sqrt{\left[\frac{1}{r_j} + \frac{1}{r_k}\right]MSE} \qquad (11.18)$$

Formulas (11.16) through (11.18) calculate Scheffé criterion for unbalanced designs.

$$SSBL = \Sigma c_i(\overline{X}_i - \overline{\overline{X}})^2 \qquad (11.19)$$

Block sum of squares.

$$SSE = SST - SSTR - SSBL \qquad (11.20)$$

Error sum of squares for two-way ANOVA.

$$MSE = \frac{SSE}{(r-1)(c-1)} \qquad (11.21)$$

Mean sum of squares for two-way ANOVA.

$$MSBL = \frac{SSBL}{r - 1} \qquad (11.22)$$

Mean square block.

CHAPTER EXERCISES

YOU MAKE THE DECISION

1. You have just been hired by a manufacturing firm in the Midwest. Your new supervisor wants to compare the mean durability of products produced by six plants owned by your firm. You suggest the use of ANOVA to make that comparison. The supervisor questions you regarding the nature of ANOVA and how it works. Provide a detailed response, including the role played by the F-ratio, and why a large value for the ratio will call for a rejection of the null hypothesis.

2. The supervisor from the previous problem also wants to know the difference between two-way ANOVA and two-factor ANOVA.

3. What is the difference in the use of the chi-square distribution and the F-distribution in measuring poulation variances?

PROBLEMS

4. Cunningham Hardware in Milwaukee, Wisconsin, purchases bolts of all sizes and shapes from a manufacturer who claims that the variance in the length of their largest toggle bolt will not exceed 0.21 inches squared. If Richie, the store owner's son, selects 22 toggle bolts and finds a variance of 0.27 inches squared, is the manufacturer's claim supported at the 5 percent level? Specify the hypothesis being tested, the decision rule, and the conclusion. Draw a graph illustrating the problem.

5. Tommy Hawk has recently graduated from a business college with a degree in marketing and has obtained a position at Teed Off, Inc. in the quality control division. His primary responsibility is to ensure that the standard deviation in the weight of the golf balls Teed Off produces does not exceed 1.9 grams. If it does, Tommy is empowered to shut down the assembly line and make the necessary adjustments.

    A sample of 25 balls revealed a standard deviation in weight of 2.7 grams. At the 1 percent level, should Tommy order a shutdown of the production process? Draw a graph, and cite the hypothesis and decision rule.

6. Referring to the previous problem, if shutting down an assembly line when corrections are not necessary is extremely costly, while continuing to operate under the incorrect assumption that production standards are being met is not as expensive, does Tommy want most to avoid a Type I error or a Type II error? Would he be better off with an α-value of 1 percent or 5 percent? Draw a graph to illustrate.

7. Many state usury laws designed to regulate interest rates that lenders can charge place restrictions on variations in such rates. To prevent discrimination against borrowers, one law states that the standard deviation in rates cannot exceed 0.50 percent during any six-month period. The state banking commission randomly selects eight loans made by the Loan-2-U State Bank and found the following rates: 6.2, 8.9, 7.3, 6.8, 7.9, 8.1, 7.5, and 6.9 percent. At the 5 percent level, is the bank violating state usury laws?

8. The decision by Texaco, Inc. whether to purchase an oil lease in Kansas was detailed in an article in a 1989 issue of *Business Week*. In the decision-making process, consideration was given to consistency in daily production levels of crude oil. Management of Texaco said they wouldn't buy the lease if the standard deviation in daily output was less than 112 barrels. If over a 10-day period, the standard deviation proved to be 97.5 barrels, should Texaco buy the lease? Set $\alpha = 0.10$. State the hypothesis and the decision rule, and draw a graph illustrating the problem.

9. According to *Fortune* (April 10, 1989), top managers for PepsiCo made around $125,000 a year in salary, and it was thought the standard deviation did not exceed $22,000. If 10 top-level managers revealed a standard deviation of $25,700, does the assumption regarding the $22,000 seem valid at the 5 percent level?

10. Owners of fast-food franchises can make a six-figure income. However, there is often considerable inconsistency in such incomes. One popular chain (Burger King) reported that their owners averaged over $113,000, but showed a standard deviation of $34,000. The chain claimed that they had taken action to produce more consistency in earnings. Can this be believed if you take a sample of 14 franchise operations and find a standard deviation in incomes of $32,500. Set $\alpha = 0.10$.

11. The fast-food chain from the previous problem disputes the results of your sample. They claim that the standard deviation is actually $24,000, and their sample of 20 franchises which yielded a standard deviation of $31,300 proves this at the 10 percent level. Do you agree? State the hypotheses and the decision rule. Draw a graph to illustrate.

12. Develop a 90 percent confidence interval for the variance in incomes using the data in the previous problem.

13. A national supplier of computer software is concerned about uniformity of service. It uses two different mailing services, Emery and Federal Express, and is interested in learning if there is a difference in the variance of delivery times. A sample of 21 deliveries by Emery had a standard deviation of 1.2 days, while 16 Federal Express deliveries reported a standard deviation of 0.9 days. At the 10 percent level, does there appear to be a difference in the variability of delivery times? State the hypotheses and the decision rule. Draw a graph to illustrate.

14. A large manufacturer of sports equipment has hired you as a marketing representative in the Northeast sales division to assist in the selection of a supplier of ski boot bindings. A major consideration is consistency in the amount of pressure that must be applied before the bindings release. If 12 bindings from supplier 1 yield a mean of 3.7 pounds per square inch (psi) with a standard deviation of 1.9 psi, while 21 bindings from a second supplier report a mean of 4.1 psi with a standard deviation of 2.1 psi, does there appear to be a difference in the variance in release pressure between these two types of bindings? Set $\alpha = 0.02$.

15. Your supervisor has made you responsible for choosing new fax machines for your firm's use in their offices worldwide. You must consider several factors, including the variability in the transmission time. Two models are similar in many important respects. However, one costs more than the other. A comparison of the variability in the time it takes to transmit a document is made by selecting 10 of the first type of fax machine and transmitting the same document. The standard deviation in transmission time is 2.7 minutes. Sixteen of the second type of fax machine are tested similarly, yielding a standard deviation of 3.4 minutes. At the 10 percent level, which machine should you buy?

16. A principal theory in financial analysis holds that the smaller the deviation in an asset's returns, the less the risk associated with that asset. This is so a smaller deviation will ensure that actual returns are closer to the expected return. A stockbroker seeks a low-risk investment for one of his clients. The selection has been narrowed to two securities, and sample returns for each are taken. The first security reports returns of 5.2, 7.3, 6.9, 6.5, 7.9, 4.1, 4.5, and 7.7 percent. The second security yields 6.3, 6.9, 5.7, 6.2, 6.4, 6.8, 5.8, 6.5,

and 6.1 percent. Which security should be selected at the 10 percent level? (Note: Both securities coincidentally have the same mean return of 6.26 percent. Otherwise, the coefficient of variation and not the standard deviation must be used in comparing risk factors.)

17. Uniformity in net weight of packaged products is extremely crucial in assembly-line operations. Tid-Bits, Inc. sells jars of pickled herring. Data collected by the quality control division last month suggested that the standard deviation in net weight had exceeded the limit of 2.5 ounces. However, recent adjustments have been made in the filling process, and the vice president of marketing services feels the standard deviation now does not exceed the 2.5 mark. A sample of 12 jars reveals a standard deviation of 2.9 ounces. At the 1 percent level, does it appear the VP is correct?

18. Tid-Bit (from the previous problem) is having continual difficulty maintaining production standards of consistency in fills. The chief of accounting and acquisitions has decided to purchase a set of new fillers. However, she wants to be 90 percent certain that the standard deviation in fills is less than the 2.5-ounce limitation. Fifteen jars are filled using the new system, and a standard deviation of 2.2 ounces is found. Does it appear that this new system will provide the consistency in fills that the firm desires?

19. In their relentless quest for an adequate filling system, Tid-Bits tests two machines. Robo-Fill is used to fill 20 jars and yields a standard deviation in fills of 1.9 ounces. Twenty-one jars are also filled using Automat-Fill. The standard deviation is 2.1 ounces. If Tid-Bits is to select one of these systems on the basis of consistency in fills, which should it choose? Set $\alpha = 0.10$.

20. Tensions between workers and management in a small electrical firm outside Chicago were discussed in a recent issue of *Fortune*. To combat unionization efforts, the company collected data on 16 firms that had a union structure and found the standard deviation in the length of electrical wire made to certain specifications to be 3.7 inches. Fifteen firms in which no union existed revealed a standard deviation of 2.4 inches. Management claimed that this was evidence that unionization often leads to failure to maintain standards. At the 10 percent level, do these statistics support management's claim?

21. Historically, a primary objective of labor unions has been wage leveling—the reduction in the range of wages received by workers in general. A recent study reported that 10 heavily unionized industries exhibited a standard deviation in wage rates of (rounded to the nearest dollar) $17, while 8 industries in which unions were weak or virtually nonexistent reported a standard deviation of $19. Does it appear that unions are achieving their objective? Set $\alpha = 0.01$.

22. A marketing major at the University of Akron performed an experiment at a local shopping mall to assess consumer preferences of product color. Several consumers are shown the same product in different colors and, after a series of questions, are asked to rate the product. The results are shown here. At the 10 percent level, can the student conclude that there is a difference in the mean ratings of product based on color?

Consumer	Red	Blue	White
1	40	38	38
2	52	54	50
3	47	43	41
4	49	42	38
5	52	50	42
6	46	41	38
7	—	50	—

23. A recent study by the American Assembly of Collegiate Schools of Business compared starting salaries of new graduates in several fields. A portion of their results is depicted in the table. At the 5 percent level, does there appear to be a difference in the mean salaries (in thousands of dollars) of graduates in different fields? (CIS is computer information systems, and QM is quantitative methods.)

	Field of Study			
Graduate	**Finance**	**Marketing**	**CIS**	**QM**
1	23.2	22.1	23.3	22.2
2	24.7	19.2	22.1	22.1
3	24.2	21.3	23.4	23.2
4	22.9	19.8	24.2	21.7
5	25.2	17.2	23.1	20.2
6	23.7	18.3	22.7	22.7
7	24.2	17.2	22.8	21.8

24. Considering your results from the previous problem, use Tukey's method to determine which means are different. Do you get the same results with the LSD approach? Keep $\alpha = 0.05$. Summarize the results with common underscoring.

25. A medical supply firm wishes to compare the mean daily output of its three plants in Toledo, Ohio, Ottumwa, Iowa, and Crab Apple Cove, Maine. Data were collected for each site and are listed here. At the 10 percent level, is there a difference in the means? The figures are in units of output.

Toledo: 10, 12, 15, 18, 9, 17, 15, 12, 18
Ottumwa: 15, 17, 18, 12, 13, 11, 12, 11, 12
Crab Apple Cove: 12, 17, 15, 15, 18, 12, 13, 14, 14

26. According to an article in *Fortune,* smaller manufacturing companies are having increasing difficulty receiving orders from their suppliers within a reasonable time. As the economy heats up and production capacity is strained, orders tend to backlog. As a production supervisor for Novelties, Inc., you wish to test mean delivery time in days for orders you place with three different suppliers of an important component of your firm's deluxe whoopie cushion. Delivery times are shown here. At the 5 percent level, is there a difference in mean times?

Supplier 1: 5, 6, 6, 5, 6, 6, 7
Supplier 2: 5, 4, 5, 5, 6, 5, 4
Supplier 3: 4, 5, 2, 6, 5, 2, 4

27. Given the results from the previous problem, which supplier(s) would you recommend? Which one(s) would you recommend be avoided? Set $\alpha = 0.01$. Summarize the results with common underscoring.

28. A discussion in a fall 1989 issue of *American Agriculture* drew attention to concern about the effect of different food grain supplements on the growth rates of commercially raised chickens. At Charlie's Chicken Ranch, a test was performed in which 18 chickens were evenly divided into three groups, and each group was fed a particular supplement. The

resulting increases in growth over a six-week period as measured in pounds is shown here. At the 10 percent level, does there appear to be evidence indicating which supplement Charlie should use in the future?

Chicken	Supplement		
	Grow-Big	Cluckers Choice	Cock of the Walk
1	2.2	3.7	3.8
2	2.4	2.1	4.1
3	2.7	3.2	3.9
4	3.8	2.9	2.7
5	3.2	3.9	4.1
6	3.9	3.8	3.2

29. There are many aspects to consider in developing marketing strategy. Store location is a major concern. PDQ, a convenience chain throughout the Southeast, reported the results in an in-house publication of a survey of weekly revenues from stores with urban, suburban, and rural locations. The data, which have been somewhat simplified for our purposes, are shown here. Can any conclusions be reached regarding prime locations for stores? Determine which location(s) if any are better. Set $\alpha = 0.05$. Display the results with common underscoring.

Store	Location		
	Urban	Suburban	Rural
1	789	612	718
2	762	655	655
3	722	725	725
4	745	609	645
5	802	632	622

30. A recent issue of *Bicycling* discussed the use of computer-coded programs in the development of a training regimen. One such computer-based program tested several cyclists who were in superior physical condition and concluded that, to be most beneficial, extended workouts should be done at 60 to 70 percent of the individual's maximum heart rate (approximately 220 beats per minute minus the person's age). More intense workouts of a shorter duration should reach 80 to 90 percent of that maximum.

Three training programs were devised to determine optimal training techniques. Assume five individuals were placed in each program, and at the end of six weeks final heart rates were monitored. The data, as recorded here, represent percentages of recommended maximum rates. At the 5 percent level, does there appear to be a difference in the mean maximum rates?

	Training Program		
Cyclist	**1**	**2**	**3**
1	0.62	0.68	0.72
2	0.73	0.52	0.69
3	0.59	0.59	0.73
4	0.82	0.63	0.74
5	0.79	0.61	0.68

31. Complete the calculations from the previous problem, setting $\alpha = 0.10$. Draw graphs for the F-distributions in each case which show a comparison of the tests for each α-value.

32. *Business Week* quoted John F. Akers, CEO of IBM, as saying that he felt it was unlikely that in the near future, IBM's annual growth in sales of 6.1 percent could keep pace with the overall industry's growth of 9.2 percent. This lag in receipts was due in part to IBM's reliance on mainframes, the market for which has fallen to third behind PCs and minicomputers in world sales.

Quarterly data for percentage increase in sales for five periods have been collected for each of the three hardware markets. The results are

Mainframes: 3.2, 4.8, 4.1, 4.2, 3.9
PCs: 8.7, 9.2, 9.3, 8.3, 8.9
Minicomputers: 9.1, 9.4, 8.7, 9.5, 9.9

Do these data show any significant difference in mean increase in sales at the 1 percent level?

33. *USA Today* printed a story about the use of private detectives for the purpose of uncovering any facts which might make a firm less desirable from the standpoint of a merger or acquisition. "M & A work," says J. B. Kroll, head of Kroll and Associates, a New York–based detective firm, "accounts for at least 20 percent of the $50 million Kroll should gross this year." The petrochemical industry along with banking, computers, and electronics are particularly fertile industries for M & A business.

Assume that six firms in each industry are randomly surveyed to determine the amounts involved in the takeover bids, and the results are shown here. Can it be concluded at the 5 percent level that any differences exist in mean tender offers among these industries? Values are in millions of dollars.

Tender Offer	**Petrochemicals**	**Banking**	**Computers**	**Electronics**
1	919.3	842.7	647.3	743.7
2	874.2	1,144.7	873.2	747.3
3	832.7	942.3	714.4	812.5
4	732.9	747.1	652.8	643.7
5	893.2	812.7	855.6	682.1
6	1,321.4	855.6	642.1	632.1

34. Using the data in the previous problem, if you were the financial consultant for Sam Spade Investigations, which industries would you advise Sam to specialize in and which would you suggest he avoid? Summarize the results with common underscoring. Use both the Tukey approach and the LSD method and compare your results with common underscoring. Set $\alpha = 0.05$.

35. As director of advertising for your firm, you wish to compare the effectiveness of various advertising formats. Three advertisements are shown to several shoppers, who subsequently rate them on a scale of 10 to 50. The results are shown here. Which advertisement(s) would you choose, if any, over the others for mass distribution? Set $\alpha = 0.10$. Summarize the results with common underscoring.

	Advertisements		
Shopper	**1**	**2**	**3**
1	45	40	30
2	40	30	35
3	35	30	30
4	35	35	30
5	40	40	35
6	35	25	30
7	30	25	30

36. An informal survey of students' dating habits was taken at a state university. The results, which record the number of dates per month, are shown here. At the 5 percent level, does there appear to be any difference by class in frequency of dates? If so, use both the Tukey approach and LSD to determine which are different. Summarize the results with common underscoring.

	Class			
Student	**Fr**	**So**	**Ju**	**Sr**
1	2	2	3	4
2	2	0	5	2
3	1	2	6	5
4	2	6	4	3
5	0	4	3	3
6	3	4	6	4

37. As the wave of hostile takeovers reached a frenzy in the late 1980s, many corporations reported the use of "poison pills" to make themselves less attractive to other firms looking for prospective acquisitions. The pills were actions taken to discourage a takeover, and included debt-retirement plans, stock-option policies, and golden parachutes for retiring executives, all of which were unfavorable to the acquiring firm. An informal study designed to measure the comparable effects of these three actions recorded changes in stock prices of several firms that used them. The data are shown here. At the 5 percent level, does it appear some pills are more effective at lowering firms' stock prices?

Firm	Debt Retirement Plans	Stock Options	Golden Parachutes
1	−1.55	−2.10	0.20
2	−2.54	−3.20	−1.10
3	−3.55	−1.47	1.55
4	−2.10	1.01	−1.25
5	1.50	−3.55	2.10
6	−2.17	−2.99	1.20

38. Using data from the previous problem, which pill(s) would you recommend to your board of directors if they desired to reduce stock prices to make your firm less attractive. Set $\alpha = 0.05$. Display the appropriate common underscoring.

39. The American Travel Association (ATA) provides data for domestic travel agencies who aid tourists in arranging trips abroad. In 1989 the ATA published their findings of a study to compare costs of typical trips abroad for two weeks. Data are for two travelers with accommodations listed as "moderate." They include hotel, airfare, one meal per day, and a few incidentals. Set $\alpha = 0.01$. If you were manager of a travel agency, how might you use these data to advise travelers? Data are in thousands of dollars (at December 1989 exchange rates). Which cities, if any, are more expensive? Use both LSD and Scheffé methods.

Trips	Tokyo	Moscow	Paris
1	5.92	3.12	3.89
2	6.23	3.55	4.10
3	6.74	4.01	4.50
4	5.30	5.21	3.09
5	4.51	3.22	
6		4.10	

40. As a recent graduate with a degree in marketing, you have just landed a big job with a major cosmetics firm in New York. You must assist in the analysis of the effectiveness of three advertising displays. Five consumers are randomly selected. Each is shown an advertisement and asked to rate it. The results are shown here. Your supervisor is unsure how to proceed, but your vast knowledge of statistical analysis based on your college course work tells you that two-way ANOVA is appropriate since each consumer (block) rated all three displays (treatments). Is there a significant difference in consumers' attitudes. Set $\alpha = 0.01$.

Consumer	Display 1	2	3
1	50	45	45
2	45	30	35
3	30	25	20
4	45	35	40
5	40	30	35

41. Debits and Credits, Inc., an accounting firm in Rocky Top, Tennessee, has a policy of evaluating each new employee by having him or her complete several accounting statements and compiling any errors. You and two other new members of the firms, Seymore Nuesbaum and Gretchen Nordick, must fill out six statements. They are examined by a senior partner in the firm, and the errors each of you made are displayed in the table. Does it appear that one of you might be either more or less efficient in your accounting skills? Set $\alpha = 0.05$. If so, which one? It is decided to block on each statement to account for any differences in difficulty that may exist.

	Numbers of Errors		
Statement	You	Seymore	Gretchen
1	2	2	3
2	1	3	4
3	0	1	4
4	4	6	5
5	2	3	4
6	1	4	3

42. Current negotiations between union and management focus on the effect on worker output of methods of payment. A large firm has five plants. In each one, workers are paid by commission, straight salary, or a bonus plan. Three workers are randomly selected out of all plants, with each paid by a different method. Their daily output measured in units is shown here. It is thought necessary to block on plants, correcting for any differences that might exist in mean plant output.

   Based on these data, which payment plan would you suggest to management if the objective was to maximize output? Set $\alpha = 0.05$.

	Payment Method		
Plant	Commission	Salary	Bonus
1	25	25	37
2	35	25	50
3	20	22	30
4	30	20	40
5	25	25	35

43. A coal company in West Virginia plans to test the mean production of three mines. Four work crews will work in each mine and record in tons the resulting output of coal. Since each crew will work in each mine, two-way ANOVA will be used by blocking on crews. As the new management supervisor, you must determine if any difference exists in productivity of the mines. Let $\alpha = 0.01$. Reflect which mines are more productive with common underscoring.

Crew	Mine 1	Mine 2	Mine 3
1	42.7	54.1	56.9
2	47.1	59.2	59.2
3	32.1	53.1	58.7
4	29.2	41.1	49.2

44. Curly, Moe, and Larry are selling electric forks door to door. Each goes into four neighborhoods independently and delivers his own sales pitch. The numbers of forks sold are recorded here. At the 5 percent level, does it appear one of the salesmen has a brighter future than the others. If so, which one? Since each salesman called on all neighborhoods, test to see if blocking should be used.

Neighborhood	Curly	Moe	Larry
1	15	12	19
2	27	25	12
3	24	29	30
4	32	31	29

45. The National Health Institute surveyed 1,060 adults to determine how they spend their leisure time. The data have been broken down by age groups and condensed to only 16 observations for computational purposes. Does there appear to be any difference in the mean time spent at the different pursuits. The observations are hours per week. Test to determine if blocking should be used. Set $\alpha = 0.05$.

Respondents (by age)	Pursuit			
	TV	Read	Sports	Quality Time with Family
15–18	35	12	10	6
19–25	22	13	12	8
26–35	25	15	8	15
36 and up	27	20	5	20

46. A national firm marketing tanning lotion randomly selects five people to test three tanning formulas. Each lotion is applied to different parts of the body on all test subjects. After a designated time in the sun, the tanning factor is measured using a scale developed by a noted dermatologist.

	Tanning Formulas		
Test Subjects	Tan Your Hide	Burn Not	Tanfastic
1	3	4	5
2	5	4	4
3	4	3	4
4	4	5	3
5	3	2	4

Set $\alpha = 0.01$ and determine if any formula promotes tanning more than the others. If so, identify which ones. Given the test subjects' differences in natural tanning ability, test to determine if blocking is needed.

47. A taxicab company is attempting to construct a route system which will minimize the time spent driving to certain locations. Four routes are under revision. You are hired as a statistical consultant to assist. Five cabbies drive each of the routes and record their times in minutes. At the 5 percent level can you identify which route(s) is (are) quicker? Should you block on driver? Which route(s) would you advise the company to use?

	Route			
Cabbie	1	2	3	4
1	12	15	17	13
2	18	18	18	17
3	10	11	15	9
4	13	12	12	15
5	18	14	12	15

EMPIRICAL EXERCISES

48. Is there a significant difference between the mean grade point average of freshmen, sophomores, juniors, and seniors at your college or university?

49. Some financial theories allege that trading on organized stock exchanges is always heavier on Fridays than during the rest of the week. Obtain figures for trading volume on an exchange for each day of the past few weeks. Does it appear that a difference exists?

50. In the past, economists have noticed a trend for unemployment rates to differ for June, December, and February. They increase in June when students are out of school for the summer, go down in December because of temporary sales help hired to handle the Christmas rush, and rise again in February. Obtain unemployment rates for these months over the past several years from *Survey of Current Business,* the *Federal Reserve Bulletin,* or some other easily accessible source, and test this hypothesis. Based on your data, does it appear that this trend exists?

CASE APPLICATIONS

51. John S. Mill recently received a research-oriented master's degree in economics and for the last 18 months has been working with the Central Intelligence Agency as an economic

analyst. His current project is to search for identifying characteristics which might serve as predictors of future political turmoil within a foreign country. Once those factors have been isolated, countries exhibiting such tendencies will be targeted for further study and analysis.

John's economic background has taught him that nations with high unemployment and other unfavorable economic conditions are often more likely to suffer political unrest. The Data Analysis Division of the CIA provides John with unemployment figures and inflation rates for several countries in four areas worldwide. These values are shown here with the unemployment rate first and the rate of inflation second. Thus, an entry such as 17.5% and 20.2% means the country had an unemployment rate of 17.5 percent and an inflation rate of 20.2 percent.

Country	Middle East	Eastern Europe	Far East	Central America
1	17.5% & 20.2%	10.2% & 8.2%	18.1% & 9.7%	27.8% & 50.2%
2	16.1% & 10.2%	8.4% & 7.3%	30.2% & 17.5%	39.7% & 40.3%
3	12.5% & 8.7%	7.2% & 6.3%	25.3% & 21.2%	37.8% & 47.3%
4	15.2% & 17.1%	7.5% & 5.3%	19.7% & 10.2%	42.1% & 80.7%
5	22.3% & 18.7%	9.2% & 6.1%	21.3% & —	37.0% & 38.9%
6	18.3% & 23.7%	10.7% & —	22.0% & —	48.0% & 73.1%
7	19.2% & —	17.1% & —	24.1% & —	38.7% & 63.2%

The agency has budgeted $1.7 million for the acquisition of additional intelligence-gathering equipment over the next several months. John must prepare a report indicating roughly how these funds should be allocated. How can John use these data in the decision-making process regarding proper allocation of the money? John's superiors have warned him that, at all costs, he must avoid rejecting the hypothesis of no significant differences in these countries if indeed none exists.

COMPUTER EXERCISES

1. Access the file PRICE from your data base. It consists of 20 observations for the price/earnings ratios taken from the 1989 Fortune 500 listings for firms in four industries: electronics, petroleum refining, computers, and aerospace. As an investment analyst, if an important client of yours was looking for an industry in which to purchase stock and sought companies with high P/E ratios, which industries would you tell him or her to consider and which should be avoided? Is this one-way or two-way ANOVA? Why?

2. Access the file CORP from your data base. It contains ratings by 35 randomly selected industrial leaders of the measure of social responsibility of firms in six industries. The data were graciously provided by a Ph.D. candidate in marketing at the University of Kansas. Each business leader was asked to rate six industries on a scale from 1 to 5 (with 1 being the best) on their social awareness of concerns ranging from pollution to price gouging. What conclusions can you draw? Write a report detailing your analysis and findings. Is this one-way or two-way ANOVA? Why?

3. Access the file SALES from your data base. It contains 20 observations for monthly sales figures for three sales regions of a firm. Does there appear to be a difference in mean sales among the three regions?

CHAPTER TWELVE

SIMPLE REGRESSION AND CORRELATION ANALYSIS

CHAPTER BLUEPRINT

This chapter examines two of the most important tools of statistical analysis: regression and correlation analysis. These highly useful techniques illustrate the manner in which relationships between two variables can be analyzed and used to predict future events.

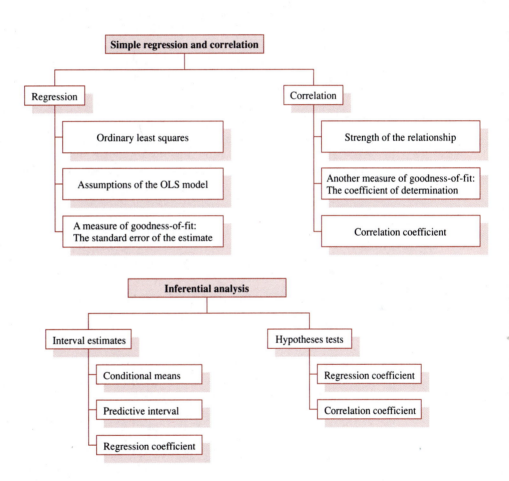

> "Don't give me no statistics here. Look at the facts."
> Archie Bunker to Meathead

12.1 INTRODUCTION

Of all the statistical techniques which you have so diligently mastered so far in this text, none is more important than regression and correlation analysis. Many empirical studies rely quite heavily on these statistical tools. They are perhaps the most commonly used forms of statistical analysis, and are invaluable when making a large number of business and economic decisions. Regression and correlation often prove vital in identifying the nature of the relationship among many of the business and economic variables that decision makers work with on a daily basis. It is difficult to overemphasize the importance of regression and correlation analysis and the extent to which they can be used to solve problems and make business decisions.

Regression and correlation analysis recognize that there is a determinable and quantifiable relationship between two or more variables. That is, one variable depends on another and can be determined by it, or we can say that one variable is a function of another. This can be stated as

$$Y = f(X) \qquad\qquad (12.1)$$

which is read "Y is a function of X," and states that Y depends on X in some manner. Since Y depends on X, it is the **dependent variable** and X is the **independent variable.**

> **Dependent and Independent Variables**
> The dependent variable is a function of the independent variable.

Regression analysis was first developed by the English scientist Sir Francis Galton (1822–1911). His earliest experiments with regression began with an attempt to analyze hereditary tendencies of sweet peas. Encouraged by the results, Sir Francis extended his study to include the hereditary patterns in the heights of adult humans. He found that children of parents who were unusually tall or unusually short would tend to "regress" back toward the average height of the adult population. With this humble introduction, the use of regression analysis has exploded into one of the most powerful statistical tools available.

Determining which is the dependent variable and which is the independent variable is crucial. This determination depends on common logic and what the statisti-

A graduate student in the health sciences at a private university in Illinois was asked by a local medical association to assist in estimating the demand for hospital beds in the area. The association wished to obtain some idea as to the number of patients who might require medical services in the future. As part of her effort, the student formulated a regression model using total population as an independent variable which could explain the number of hospital patients. For this effort, the student was given $1,500, which she used to complete her graduate studies.

cian is trying to investigate. For example, the dean of the College of Business is concerned about students' GPAs and the amount of time they spend studying. Data are gathered to examine this relationship. It is only logical to presume that more hours spent studying will result in higher GPAs and that longer periods of study can explain higher GPAs. Thus, GPAs are the dependent variable and study time is the independent variable.

Consider this common example of the distinction between the dependent and the independent variables which is often encountered in the business world. A firm's sales depend, at least in part, on the amount of advertising that it does. Sales is seen as the dependent variable and is a function of the independent variable, *advertising*. In this manner, advertising can be used to predict and forecast sales. The dependent variable Y is also referred to as the **regressand** or the **explained** variable, while the independent variable X is called the **regressor** or the **explanatory** variable.

Regression and correlation are actually two different but closely related concepts. **Regression** is a quantitative expression of the basic nature of the relationship between the dependent and independent variables. For example, given a simple regression model with one independent variable, the regression model will determine if both variables tend to move in the same direction (both increase or both decrease simultaneous) or opposite directions (one goes up while the other goes down). It will also reveal the amount by which Y will change given a 1-unit change in the independent variable.

Correlation, on the other hand, determines the strength of that relationship. That is, while regression describes the basic nature of the relationship between the two variables, correlation measures how strong that relationship is.

Regression and Correlation
Regression determines if X and Y exhibit a positive relationship in that both increase or decrease together, or if the relationship is negative in that they move in opposite directions. It will also determine the magnitude of the change in Y given a change in X. Correlation measures how strong the relationship is between X and Y.

We should distinguish between simple and multiple regression. **Simple** regression
holds that the dependent variable Y is a function of only one independent variable, as
indicated in Formula (12.1). It is sometimes called **bivariate** analysis because only
two variables are involved—one dependent and one independent.

Multiple regression involves two or more independent variables. If Y is said to depend on three independent variables, we can write $Y = f(X_1, X_2, X_3)$. A model containing k independent variables can be expressed as

$$Y = f(X_1, X_2, \ldots, X_k) \qquad (12.2)$$

where $X_1, X_2, \ldots, X_k$ are independent variables used to explain Y.

It is also important to distinguish between linear and curvilinear regression. **Linear** regression attempts to depict the relationship between X and Y by a straight line.
This procedure is based on the contention that a change in X is accompanied by a
systematic change in Y which can be represented by a line. **Curvilinear** regression is
used if the relationship can better be described by a curve.

The nature of linear regression, as well as the manner in which it differs from
curvilinear regression, can perhaps be best illustrated by the scatter diagrams in Figure 12-1. **Scatter diagrams** plot the paired observations of X and Y on a graph. Customarily, the dependent variable is placed on the vertical axis, while the independent
variable is on the horizontal axis. Assume the director of marketing for a large retail
chain collects data on sales levels and advertising expenditures for her company over
the last several months. Her intent is to use advertising expenditures to explain the
levels of sales for her firm. If these data were plotted in a scatter diagram using sales
as the dependent variable, several possible patterns might emerge. For example, the
pattern in Figure 12-1(a) suggests that as advertising increases, sales go up. This is
the logical assumption that the director might make before collecting her data, and
indicates that a positive, or direct, linear relationship exists between advertising and
sales. However, after plotting the data, the director might find, to her surprise, an
inverse, or indirect, linear relationship as shown by Figure 12-1(b). Here the data
suggest that as advertising expenditures are increased, sales actually go down. This

FIGURE 12-1   Linear and Curvilinear Relationships

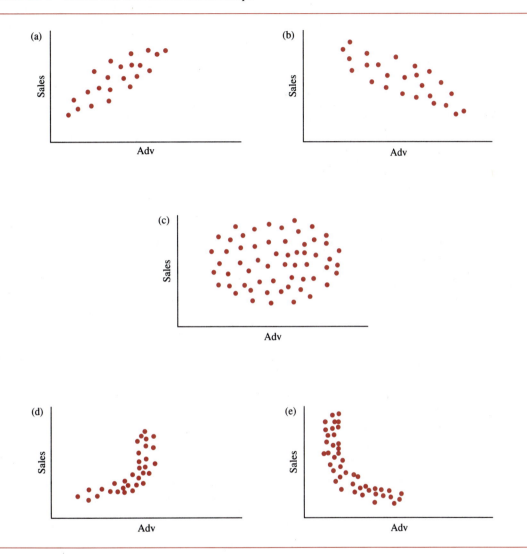

would suggest, of course, that funds spent on advertising might be used more effectively elsewhere.

On the other hand, it is difficult to observe any distinct relationship between advertising and sales in the scatter diagram in Figure 12-1(c). The pattern here suggests that no relationship exists between the two variables.

Figures 12-1(d) and 12-1(e) indicate curvilinear relationsips. Notice that the pattern in the scatter diagram seems to take on a nonlinear or curved shape.

The objective of regression analysis is to develop a line which passes through the scatter diagram and best represents the data points. Our interest throughout most of this chapter will focus primarily on **simple linear regression.**

Linear and Curvilinear Relationships
If X and Y are related in a linear manner, then, as X changes, Y changes by a constant amount. If a curvilinear relationship exists, Y will change by a constant rate as X changes.

12.2   THE MECHANICS OF A STRAIGHT LINE

Since we are going to explain the relationship between X and Y on the basis of a straight line, we need to review a few facts about the formula for a straight line. A straight line can be expressed by the formula

$$Y = b_0 + b_1 X \qquad (12.3)$$

where b_0 is the vertical intercept and b_1 is the slope of the line. If we were to find, for example, that $b_0 = 5$ and $b_1 = 2$, we would have

$$Y = 5 + 2X \qquad (12.4)$$

Figure 12-2 shows that the vertical intercept is 5. It represents the value of Y when $X = 0$. The slope of a line indicates the change in Y that occurs for every 1-unit change in X. It is found as the rise divided by the run. The rise is the vertical

FIGURE 12-2   A Linear Relationship

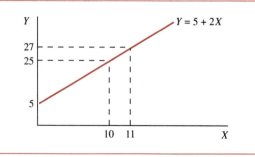

change, or change in the Y-variable since Y is measured on the vertical axis. The run is a 1-unit change in the value of the X-variable measured on the horizontal axis.

Given Formula (12.4), if $X = 10$, Y would equal 25. If X increases by 1 unit to 11, Y becomes 27. That is, Y goes up by 2. The slope is then

$$b_1 = \text{Slope} = \frac{\text{Vertical change}}{\text{Horizontal change}} = \frac{2}{1} = 2$$

It can be seen that for every 1-unit increase in X, Y goes up by 2 units.

The slope can be positive, as here, or negative if $b_1 < 0$. If the slope is negative, the line is downward-sloping, as in Figure 12-3(a), indicating that X and Y move in opposite directions. If b_1 is 0, the line has a slope of zero and is horizontal. This suggests that there is no relationship between X and Y, since Y remains constant even if X changes. Figure 12-3(b) shows that as X changes from X_1 to X_2, the value of Y does not change.

Slope

If a line has a slope of 3, a 1-unit change in X will be associated with a 3-unit change in the Y-variable.

FIGURE 12-3   Other Potential Linear Relationships

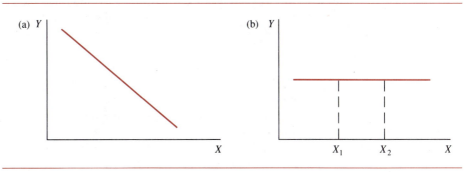

12.3   THE BASIC OBJECTIVE OF REGRESSION ANALYSIS

Relationships between variables are either **deterministic** or **stochastic** (random). An example of a deterministic relationship can be expressed by a mathematical model, or formula, which converts speed in miles per hour (mph) into kilometers per hour (kph). Since 1 mile equals approximately 1.6 kilometers, this model is 1 mph = 1.6 kph. Thus, a speed of 5 mph = 5(1.6)kph = 8.0 kph. This is a deterministic model because there is no error (except for rounding) in the determination of the rate of speed in kph. Given any value for mph, we can determine kph exactly. When mph equals 5, kph is always 8.

Unfortunately, few relationships in the business world are so exact or so easily determined. In using advertising to determine sales, for example, there is almost always some variation in the relationship. When advertising is some given amount, X_i, sales will take on some value. However, the next time advertising equals that same amount X_i, sales could very well be some other value. The dependent variable (sales) demonstrates some degree of randomness. A model of this nature is said to be stochastic, due to the presence of random variation. A model which reflects that variation is

$$Y = \underbrace{\beta_0 + \beta_1(X)}_{\begin{pmatrix}\text{deterministic}\\\text{component}\end{pmatrix}} + \underbrace{\varepsilon_i}_{\begin{pmatrix}\text{random}\\\text{component}\end{pmatrix}} \qquad (12.5)$$

Formula (12.5) represents the population (or true) relationship in which we regress Y on X. Since Formula (12.5) pertains to a population, β_0 and β_1 are parameters. The vertical intercept of the line used to reflect the relationship at the population level between X and Y is represented by β_0, while β_1 is the slope. The value ε (Greek letter epsilon) is a random error term designed to capture variation above and below the regression line due to all other factors not included in the model. For example, in addition to advertising, sales are also probably influenced by the level of competition, location, relative prices, and other factors. The random component ε_i may be positive or negative, depending on whether a value of Y, given any X value, lies above or below the regression line. It is also called the *disturbance* term since it "disturbs" the otherwise deterministic relationship between X and Y.

Deterministic and Stochastic Models
A deterministic mathematical model is expressed as $Y = \beta_0 + \beta_1X$. Given any value for X, the value of Y can be determined with precision. A stochastic model contains one or more random components that lead to errors in efforts to predict, and is written as $Y = \beta_0 + \beta_1X + \varepsilon$.

To illustrate, assume that a computer manufacturer wishes to examine the relationship between the number of hard-disk drives produced and the total cost. The firm's head financial analyst and statistician collects data over a five-day period for the number of drives produced and the corresponding costs. Although a sample of only five observations is most likely insufficient, it will serve the purposes of illustration. The data are displayed in Table 12-1. These data are then plotted in a scatter diagram shown in Figure 12-4. If a line is drawn through the middle of the scatter, some observations fall above it while others fall below it. Few, if any, relationships in the real world are perfectly linear. Therefore, not all the observations will fall di-

FIGURE 12-4   A Scatter Diagram for Production Data

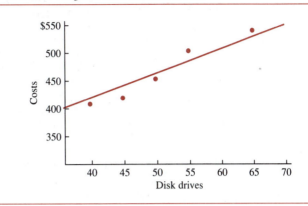

TABLE 12-1   Production Data for
Computer Hardware

Day	Number of Drives	Cost
1	50	$450
2	40	380
3	65	540
4	55	500
5	45	420

rectly on the regression line. There will likely be some variation above and below it. This deviation above and below the line is reflected in Formula (12.5) by ε.

It should be emphasized that the true population regression line will, like most parameters, remain unknown. The best that we can do is estimate it by using the sample model illustrated by Formula (12.6A).

$$Y = b_0 + b_1 X + e \qquad (12.6A)$$

The values b_0 and b_1 are estimates for the population parameters β_0 and β_1. They are called, respectively, the **regression constant** and the **regression coefficient.** The last term, e, is the error component, which is necessary because not all observations for X and Y fall exactly on a straight line. Since some of the observations fall above the line and others fall below it, e is a random variable. However, it is assumed, as emphasized later in this chapter, that the error term will have a mean value of zero and a variance of some amount we will call σ^2.

The model expressed by Formula (12.6A) is then used to estimate the relationship between X and Y, resulting in the regression line

$$\hat{Y} = b_0 + b_1 X \qquad \text{(12.6B)}$$

where $\hat{Y}$ (pronounced "Y-hat") is the estimated value for the dependent variable and is represented by a point *on* the regression line.

12.4   ORDINARY LEAST SQUARES (THE LINE OF BEST FIT)

In order to gain a better understanding of regression analysis, let us return to our scatter diagram for data on the computer disk drives discussed above. It is our desire to determine a line through the middle of the scatter which best defines or represents these data points. This regression line must depict the relationship between the dependent and independent variables with accuracy and precision, and must fit these data points better than any other line we might be able to draw. We are looking for the *line of best fit*. It is not possible to simply eyeball the exact placement of the line, as might have been suggested above.

Notice in Figure 12-5 that all the lines appear to fit the dispersion of the data portrayed by the scatter diagram. Each line seems a likely choice for the line of best fit. It is impossible to determine by mere inspection which line actually provides the most exact measure of the relationship between X and Y. This illustrates the need for a much more accurate procedure of determining our line of best fit.

FIGURE 12-5   Possible Lines of Fit

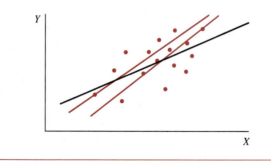

This more precise method is called **ordinary least squares** (OLS). To aid in the illustration of OLS, the scatter diagram for the computer disk drives is repeated in Figure 12-6.

It is called OLS because it results in a line which minimizes the squared vertical distances from each observation point to the line itself. To understand the meaning

FIGURE 12-6   Ordinary Least Squares

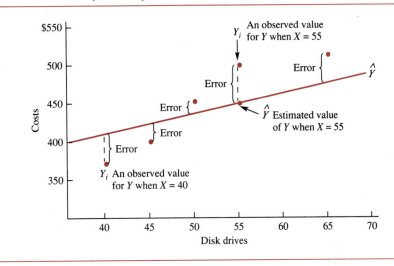

of OLS, you must remember that, as illustrated in Figure 12-6, Y_i is an actual, observed value for the Y-variable, and $\hat{Y}$ is a value on the line predicted by the equation. We then calculate the vertical difference between Y_i and $\hat{Y}$, $Y_i - \hat{Y}$. That difference is then squared to yield $(Y_i - \hat{Y})^2$. This is done for all five values of Y_i. All five squared differences are summed and expressed as

$$\Sigma(Y_i - \hat{Y})^2 = \text{min} \qquad (12.7)$$

where min is a number smaller than what you would get if you summed these squared vertical deviations between the actual data points and any other line. Hence, the term *least squares* is used.

The difference $Y_i - \hat{Y}$ is called the **residual** or error. It is the difference between what Y actually is, Y_i, and what we predicted it to be using our regression model, $\hat{Y}$. This difference between actual values, Y_i, and what we predicted them to be using our regression model, $\hat{Y}$, is, of course, our error. OLS will minimize the sum of the squared errors.

> **Ordinary Least Squares**
> The OLS method of determining the line of best fit minimizes the sum of the squared errors.

It can be shown by means of differential calculus that this sum of the squared errors will indeed be minimized by calculating the **sums of squares and cross-**

products. The proof of this statement, which is omitted here, can be found in calculus books or more advanced statistics texts.

We can calculate the sums of squares of X (SSx), the sums of squares of Y(SSy), and the sums of the cross-products ($SSxy$) as

$$
\begin{aligned}
SSx &= \Sigma(X_i - \overline{X})^2 \\
&= \Sigma X^2 - \frac{(\Sigma X)^2}{n}
\end{aligned}
\tag{12.8}
$$

$$
\begin{aligned}
SSy &= \Sigma(Y_i - \overline{Y})^2 \\
&= \Sigma Y^2 - \frac{(\Sigma Y)^2}{n}
\end{aligned}
\tag{12.9}
$$

and

$$
\begin{aligned}
SSxy &= \Sigma(X_i - \overline{X})(Y_i - \overline{Y}) \\
&= \Sigma XY - \frac{(\Sigma X)(\Sigma Y)}{n}
\end{aligned}
\tag{12.10}
$$

These formulas illustrate that the OLS line is indeed based on the deviations of the observations from their means. Furthermore, the formula for SSx, for example, is the same as that used to calculate the standard deviation in Chapter 3.

Given the sums of squares and cross-products, it is then a simple matter to calculate the intercept and regression coefficient as

$$
b_1 = \frac{SSxy}{SSx}
\tag{12.11}
$$

and

$$
b_0 = \overline{Y} - b_1\overline{X}
\tag{12.12}
$$

A word of caution: These calculations are extremely sensitive to rounding. This is particularly true for the calculation of the coefficient of determination, which is demonstrated later in this chapter. You are therefore advised in the interest of accuracy to carry out your calculations to five or six decimal places.

12.5 AN EXAMPLE USING OLS

The management of Hop Scotch Airlines, the world's smallest air carrier, assumes a direct relationship between advertising expenditures and the number of passengers who choose to fly Hop Scotch. To determine if this relationship does exist and, if so, what its exact nature might be, the statisticians employed by Hop Scotch set out to use OLS procedures to determine the regression model.

Monthly values for advertising expenditures and numbers of passengers are collected for the $n = 15$ most recent months. The data are shown in Table 12-2, along with other calculations necessary to compute the regression model. You will note that *passengers* is labeled as the Y-variable since it is assumed to depend on advertising.

TABLE 12-2   Regression Data for Hop Scotch Airlines

Observation (months)	Advertising (in $1,000's) ($X$)	Passengers (in 1,000's) (Y)	XY	X^2	Y^2
1	10	15	150	100	225
2	12	17	204	144	289
3	8	13	104	64	169
4	17	23	391	289	529
5	10	16	160	100	256
6	15	21	315	225	441
7	10	14	140	100	196
8	14	20	280	196	400
9	19	24	456	361	576
10	10	17	170	100	289
11	11	16	176	121	256
12	13	18	234	169	324
13	16	23	368	256	529
14	10	15	150	100	225
15	12	16	192	144	256
	187	268	3,490	2,469	4,960

With this simple set of data, and the subsequent computations for XY, X^2, and Y^2, it is an easy task to determine the regression model by calculating values for the regression constant and the regression coefficient in the regression line $\hat{Y} = b_0 + b_1 X$. It is first necessary to compute the sums of squares and cross-products.

$$SSx = \Sigma X^2 - \frac{(\Sigma X)^2}{n}$$

$$= 2,469 - \frac{(187)^2}{15}$$

$$= 137.7333333$$

$$SSy = \Sigma Y^2 - \frac{(\Sigma Y)^2}{n}$$

$$= 4,960 - \frac{(268)^2}{15}$$

$$= 171.733333$$

$$SSxy = \Sigma XY - \frac{(\Sigma X)(\Sigma Y)}{n}$$

$$= 3,490 - \frac{(187)(268)}{15}$$

$$= 148.933333$$

Example 12-1 demonstrates the use of the regression procedure and the manner in which the regression line is calculated.

EXAMPLE 12-1 Regression Model for Hop Scotch Airlines

In order to make decisions regarding allocations for the advertising budget, the accounting department for Hop Scotch Airlines must determine the nature of the relationship between advertising expenditures and the number of passengers. The senior accountant recognizes that regression analysis would be of invaluable assistance.

SOLUTION:
From Formulas (12.11) and (12.12), the values for b_0 and b_1 can be determined as

$$b_1 = \frac{SSxy}{SSx}$$

$$= \frac{148.933333}{137.733333}$$

$$= 1.0813166 \text{ or } 1.08$$

$$b_0 = \bar{Y} - b_1 \bar{X}$$

$$= 17.86667 - (1.0813)(12.46667)$$

$$= 4.3865 \text{ or } 4.4$$

The regression equation is therefore

$$\hat{Y} = 4.40 + 1.08X$$

STATISTICAL INTERPRETATION:
The model tells us that if, for example, $10,000 is spent on advertising ($X = 10$), then

$$\hat{Y} = 4.40 + 1.08(10)$$

$$= 15.2$$

By multiplying 15.2 by 1,000 since the Y-values were originally expressed in thousands, we predict on the basis of our model that 15,200 brave souls will choose to fly Hop Scotch when $10,000 is spent on advertising.

Remember the meaning of b_1, the regression coefficient. It indicates by how much Y will change for every 1-unit change in the X-variable. In our case, since $b_1 = 1.08$, for every additional $1,000 (which is 1 unit since X is measured in thousands) that Hop Scotch spends on advertising, 1,080 more passengers will choose the friendly skies of Hop Scotch. Again, this value of 1,080 requires that we multiply the b_1 coefficient by 1,000. This is displayed in Example 12-2.

EXAMPLE 12-2 Impact of a Change in Advertising on Passengers

The director of advertising for Hop Scotch wishes to determine how a change in the amount spent on advertising will affect the number of passengers. Hop Scotch is currently spending $10,000 on advertising and is considering spending an additional $1,000. The final decision depends on the passenger response predicted by the advertising department if this additional $1,000 is spent.

SOLUTION:
Given that

$$\hat{Y} = 4.40 + 1.08X$$

the expenditure of $10,000 ($X = 10$) is associated with 15,200 passengers. That is,

$$\hat{Y} = 4.40 + 1.08(10)$$

$$= 15.2$$

If advertising is increased by 1 unit to $11,000, the estimate of total passengers becomes

$$\hat{Y} = 4.40 + 1.08(11)$$

$$= 16.28 \text{ or } 16,280 \text{ passengers}$$

STATISTICAL INTERPRETATION:
If X is increased from 10 to 11, the predicted number of passengers is 16,280. This is exactly 1,080 more than the 15,200 passengers predicted to fly if $X = 10$. Such information is useful in determining if an increase in the advertising budget is justified.

As you can see, the regression model can be used to predict or forecast the value for the dependent variable. Given any amount in Hop Scotch's advertising budget, we can easily determine an estimate for the number of passengers who fly Hop Scotch.

Another word of caution: This is not to imply that an increase in *X causes* an increase in *Y*. Although it may appear that additional advertising caused more people to purchase tickets on Hop Scotch, we can only conclude that *X* and *Y* move together. There is no evidence of a cause-and-effect relationship. The simultaneous increase in *X* and *Y* may have been caused by an unknown third variable excluded from the study. It is a common misconception to assume that there exists a cause-and-effect relationship between the two variables. This matter will be dealt with again later in this chapter.

As you might well imagine, as the number of observations increases, it becomes quite difficult to calculate the regression model by hand. The use of computers becomes essential. Display 12-1 provides a portion of the output from a computer run using SPSS-PC to derive the regression model for Hop Scotch. Notice that the intercept (constant) and slope coefficients are found under the column headed by B to be 4.38625 and 1.08132. The other statistics reported in the printout will be discussed throughout this chapter.

DISPLAY 12-1   Coefficients for Hop Scotch

```
Equation Number 1     Dependent Variable..   PASS
Variable(s) Entered on Step Number
   1..    ADV
Multiple R              .96838
R Square                .93776
Adjusted R Square       .93297
Standard Error          .90678
          * * * *   M U L T I P L E   R E G R E S S I O N   * * * *
Equation Number 1    Dependent Variable..   PASS
-------------------- Variables in the Equation --------------------
Variable              B        SE B       Beta         T    Sig T
ADV              1.08132      .07726     .96838    13.995    .0000
(Constant)       4.38625      .99128                 4.425    .0007
End Block Number     1    All requested variables entered.
```

Let us continue with our discussion of the problem Hop Scotch is having in determining the exact nature of the relationship between passengers and advertising. The chief executive officer for Hop Scotch is concerned not only with how much money to budget for advertising purposes, but he must also decide how those funds are to be allocated. The airline often buys advertising space in the magazines *Executive Weekly* and *Fisherman's Delight*. Previous market research has shown that people who read *Executive Weekly* fall into substantially higher income brackets than those who subscribe to *Fisherman's Delight*. Therefore, the CEO is curious about the impact that a person's income has on the frequency of flying. Data are gathered for 10 passengers on their annual income levels, measured in thousands of dollars, and

TABLE 12-3   Data on Income and Flights for Hop Scotch Airlines

Passenger	Flights (Y)	Income (X)	XY	X²
1	5	30	150	900
2	4	27	108	729
3	7	38	266	1,444
4	10	48	480	2,304
5	11	59	649	3,481
6	8	54	432	2,916
7	9	42	378	1,764
8	11	63	693	3,969
9	8	52	416	2,704
10	9	47	423	2,209
	82	460	3,995	22,420

the number of flights they took during the most recent 12-month period. Since the CEO is concerned about the effect of income on flights, income takes on the role of the independent variable, and the number of flights is seen as the dependent variable. The values appear in Table 12-3. Given these data, the CEO wishes to determine the nature of the relationship between income and the tendency of people to use air service in their travel plans. He feels that this information would be useful in making a variety of decisions regarding advertising efforts and marketing policies.

EXAMPLE 12-3 The Relationship between Income and Flights

The CEO feels that the number of flights people take depends in some manner upon their income. Flights is therefore seen as the dependent variable, while income assumes the role of the independent variable. Simple regression analysis can provide the CEO with the precise knowledge he desires regarding the relationship between these two variables.

SOLUTION:

The sums of squares and cross-products are

$$SSx = \Sigma X^2 - \frac{(\Sigma X)^2}{n}$$

$$= 22{,}420 - \frac{(460)^2}{10}$$

$$= 1{,}260$$

$$SSxy = \Sigma XY - \frac{(\Sigma X)(\Sigma Y)}{n}$$

$$= 3{,}995 - \frac{(460)(82)}{10}$$

$$= 223$$

Then

$$b_1 = \frac{SSxy}{SSx}$$

$$= \frac{223}{1,260}$$

$$= 0.177$$

$$b_0 = \overline{Y} - b_1 \overline{X}$$

$$= 8.2 - (0.177)(46)$$

$$= 0.058$$

The regression equation is

$$\hat{Y} = 0.058 + 0.177X$$

STATISTICAL INTERPRETATION:

The regression coefficient of 0.177 tells the CEO that there is a positive relationship between income and the frequency of flying. As income goes up, the number of flights will increase. It is further apparent that a 1-unit increase in income of $1,000 is associated with a 0.177 increase in the number of flights. For each additional $1,000 in income, the passengers will book 0.177 more flights. The CEO's decision becomes clear. If he wishes to get the most for his advertising dollar, he should place his advertisements in *Executive Weekly* since, as noted above, people with higher incomes tend to read it more often.

To further illustrate the power of regression analysis, consider the plight of the director of personnel for Hop Scotch. In the belief that a physical fitness program for the employees at Hop Scotch will reduce absenteeism due to illness, the director has implemented an exercise program for all interested workers. However, she has had a difficult time proving its worth to higher management. They seem to feel that it is just a waste of time and money and has done little to improve employee performance. In an effort to prove that the exercise program does indeed reduce the number of days employees miss work due to illness, the director examines the records of 50 employees. She obtains figures on the number of hours each employee has been attending the exercise programs and the number of sick days for each of these workers.

The director's assertion is that illness will be reduced as exercise increases. That is, exercise impacts on illness. Therefore, the number of sick days is the dependent variable. The employee records provide these data:

$$n = 50 \qquad \Sigma XY = 1,080$$

$$\Sigma X = 180$$

$$\Sigma Y = 450 \qquad \Sigma X^2 = 5,340$$

With this information the director is able to use regression analysis to examine the relationship between illness and exercise.

EXAMPLE 12-4 The Relationship between Exercise and Sick Days

Under the realization that any linear relationship that may exist between hours in the exercise program and sick days can be identified through regression analysis, the director of personnel calculates and interprets the regression model.

SOLUTION:

Compute the constant term and the regression coefficient:

$$SSx = 5{,}340 - \frac{(180)^2}{50}$$

$$= 4{,}692$$

$$SSxy = 1{,}080 - \frac{(180)(450)}{50}$$

$$= -540$$

Therefore,

$$b_1 = \frac{-540}{4{,}692}$$

$$= -0.1151$$

$$b_0 = 9 - (-0.1151)(3.6)$$

$$= 9.4$$

The regression model is therefore

$$\hat{Y} = 9.4 - 0.1151X$$

STATISTICAL INTERPRETATION:

It would appear that the personnel director and her exercise program are vindicated. The negative sign on the regression coefficient testifies to the claim that as the employees spend more time in the exercise program, the number of days lost to illness decreases. Specifically, if one additional hour is devoted to physical exercise, the number of sick days will decrease by 0.1151 days.

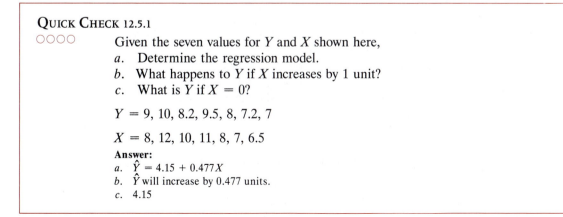

QUICK CHECK 12.5.1

○○○○

Given the seven values for Y and X shown here,

a. Determine the regression model.
b. What happens to Y if X increases by 1 unit?
c. What is Y if $X = 0$?

$Y = 9, 10, 8.2, 9.5, 8, 7.2, 7$

$X = 8, 12, 10, 11, 8, 7, 6.5$

Answer:

a. $\hat{Y} = 4.15 + 0.477X$
b. $\hat{Y}$ will increase by 0.477 units.
c. 4.15

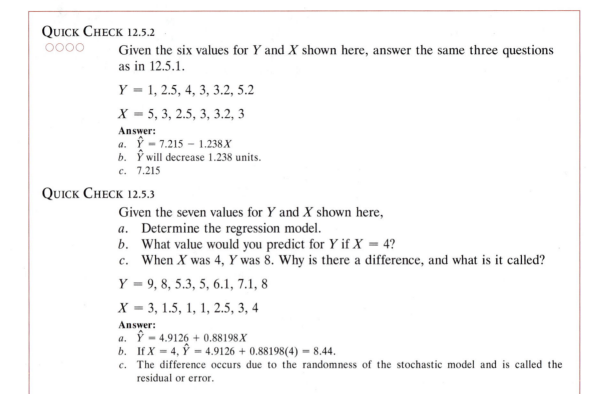

QUICK CHECK 12.5.2

OOOO   Given the six values for Y and X shown here, answer the same three questions
as in 12.5.1.

$Y = 1, 2.5, 4, 3, 3.2, 5.2$

$X = 5, 3, 2.5, 3, 3.2, 3$

Answer:
a. $\hat{Y} = 7.215 - 1.238X$
b. $\hat{Y}$ will decrease 1.238 units.
c.   7.215

QUICK CHECK 12.5.3

Given the seven values for Y and X shown here,
a.   Determine the regression model.
b.   What value would you predict for Y if $X = 4$?
c.   When X was 4, Y was 8. Why is there a difference, and what is it called?

$Y = 9, 8, 5.3, 5, 6.1, 7.1, 8$

$X = 3, 1.5, 1, 1, 2.5, 3, 4$

Answer:
a. $\hat{Y} = 4.9126 + 0.88198X$
b.   If $X = 4$, $\hat{Y} = 4.9126 + 0.88198(4) = 8.44$.
c.   The difference occurs due to the randomness of the stochastic model and is called the
residual or error.

A.   THE Y-VALUES ARE ASSUMED TO BE NORMALLY DISTRIBUTED

By examining the data in Table 12-2, we can arrive at a very logical and reasonable
conclusion. Specifically, given the same value for X on several occasions, we can see
that it is associated with different Y-values each time. In months 1, 5, 7, 10, and 14,
Hop Scotch spent $10,000 for advertising. However, in each case the corresponding
number of passengers varied. Even though the same amount was spent on advertising
each time, the number of passengers on each occasion was 15,000, 16,000, 14,000,
17,000, and 15,000. Is this a reasonable expectation? Of course it is. If Hop Scotch
repeatedly spent the same amount for advertising, there is absolutely no reason to expect the number of passengers to be the same each time. The value of the dependent
variable Y will vary even if the value for X remains fixed. Since Y is different almost
every time, the best our regression model can do is estimate the *average* value for Y
given any X-value. Regression analysis is based on the assumption that a linear relationship exists between X and the mean value of Y, $E(Y)$. The regression line can be
written $E(Y) = \beta_0 + \beta_1 X$. A point on the line denotes the average value for Y given
any X-value. For this reason, the regression line is often referred to as a *mean line*.

The point to remember is that for any value of X which may occur several times, we could very well get a different Y-value each time. In fact, an entire distribution of different Y-values will result. Regression analysis assumes that this distribution of Y-values is normal. Thus, is X was set equal to 10 many times, many different values of Y would result. If these values were graphed, they would appear as a normal distribution. This distribution is centered at the mean of these Y-values, as illustrated in Figure 12-7.

FIGURE 12-7   The Normal Distribution of Y-Values for a Given Single Value of X ($X = 10$)

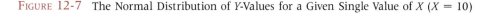
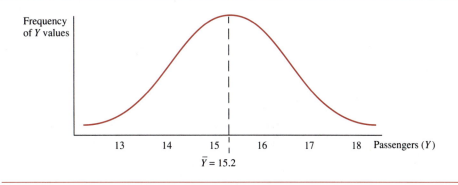

This mean value of Y can be calculated by our regression equation. If X is set equal to 10, our estimate of the number of passengers is

$$\hat{Y} = b_0 + b_1X$$

$$= 4.4 + 1.08(10)$$

$$= 15.2$$

or 15,200 since the data for passengers were expressed in thousands.

This suggests that if the airline spends $10,000 each month on advertising for several months, the number of passengers, although perhaps different each month, will average 15,200.

This normal distribution of Y-values exists for all values of X. Thus, if $X = 11$ on many separate occasions, there would occur an entire distribution of Y-values which would be normally distributed and centered at

$$\hat{Y} = 4.40 + 1.08(11)$$

$$= 16.28 \text{ or } 16,280 \text{ passengers}$$

The distribution of Y-values that results when $X = 11$ on many occasions is seen in Figure 12-8.

FIGURE 12-8   The Normal Distribution of Y-Values Where $X = 11$

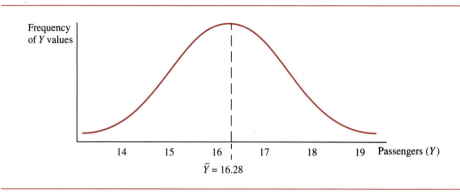

When estimating the true, but unknown, population regression line $\hat{Y} = \beta_0 + \beta_1 X$ with our sample regression line $\hat{Y} = b_0 + b_1 X$, we are trying to find that line which passes through the means of the various distributions of Y-values for each X-value.

This is shown in Figure 12-9. However, we must turn the distribution of Y-values on its side since Y is measured on the vertical axis in Figure 12-9. Notice that for each value of X there is a distribution of Y-values. This is true where $X = 10$, $X = 11$, $X = 12$, or any other value. The regression line then passes through the mean of each of those distributions.

FIGURE 12-9   The Normal Distributions of Y-Values for the Various Values of X

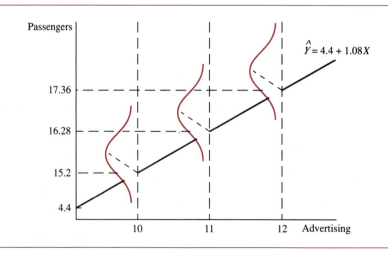

Each distribution of Y-values is normal and, like any distribution of numbers, has a variance of σ^2 and a standard deviation of σ. The important point to note here is that this variance is assumed to be the same for each distribution of Y-values regardless of the X-value. That is, the variance of Y-values when $X = 10$ is the same as the variance of Y-values when $X = 11$ (or anything else).

12.6   ASSUMPTIONS OF OLS

As you can see, the basic mechanics of regression analysis are fairly simple. We need only recognize that we are describing the relationship between X and Y on the basis of a straight line. We calculate values for the intercept and the slope of the regression line using Formulas (12.11) and (12.12). The resulting model can then be used to predict values of the dependent variable given any value for the independent variable.

However, there is really more than this to regression analysis. To gain a more complete picture of the nature of this important and useful statistical tool, it is necessary to examine the basic assumptions which underlie the OLS model. These fundamental suppositions do much to clarify and more fully depict the principle of regression analysis and to describe the conceptual framework upon which regression analysis is built. So although we have already made at least veiled reference to some of these principles, a much more detailed examination is called for.

You are again reminded that Y_i is an actual value for Y that has occurred in the past and is represented by a data point in the scatter diagram somewhere above or below the regression line. Additionally, $\hat{Y}$ is a value for Y predicted to occur on the basis of our regression model, and it is represented by a point on the line. It is the difference between these two values, $Y_i - \hat{Y}$, which constitutes our error.

With this in mind, recall that the OLS procedure will produce a model in which the sum of the errors is zero. That is, given any value for X, the actual data point Y_i will sometimes be above the regression line ($Y_i > \hat{Y}$). This causes us to underestimate the value for the dependent variable, and the error term $Y_i - \hat{Y}$ will be positive. At other times Y_i will be below our regression line and we will overestimate Y, producing a negative error. Therefore, the errors cancel out and will average to zero. Thus,

$$\Sigma(Y_i - \hat{Y}) = 0$$

Furthermore, OLS will minimize the sum of the squared errors. This is the whole idea behind OLS. If we square each error to remove the negative sign and sum these squared errors, the resulting number will be smaller than the number we would get with any other line. We can therefore say

$$\Sigma(Y_i - \hat{Y})^2 = \min$$

In addition, there are certain assumptions upon which the OLS model is built.

Assumption 1
The error term is a random variable and is normally distributed.

As we noted earlier, the repeated occurrence of any value for X (say $X = 10$) will be associated with many different values for Y_i. These values are normally distributed around the regression line. Since our error is the difference between Y_i and $\hat{Y}$, the error itself is normally distributed.

Assumption 2
Any two errors are independent of each other.

OLS further assumes that the error we experience when $X = 10$ is totally independent of the error suffered when X is equal to any other value.

Unfortunately, this assumption is often violated when using time-series data. **Time-series data** consist of the collection of a data series over time. If we were to select the prime interest rate as our data series and collect data on it for the past 12 months, we would be working with time-series data since its values over time (one year) were specified.

Why does the use of time-series data often result in the violation of Assumption 2? Many time series move in cyclical fashion. They are abnormally high for a period of time, then drop to levels somewhat below their mean level. If we try to forecast such a variable, we are likely to overestimate it when it is abnormally low and underestimate it when it is abnormally high.

This is shown in Figure 12-10. If the variable is above its mean level, we are likely to underestimate it in our forecast attempt. Then our error $Y_i - \hat{Y}$ will be positive, as for January in Figure 12-10.

FIGURE 12-10   Dependency of Errors: Autocorrelation

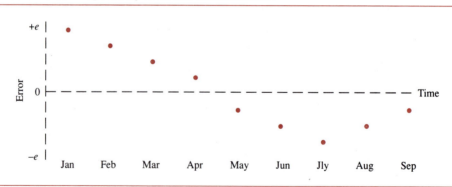

Since the variable follows a cyclical pattern, it will probably still be abnormally high in February. This results in another underestimate and another positive error. That is, given one positive error, there is a greater than 50 percent probability that the next error will be positive. Thus, the errors are *not* independent and Assumption 2 is violated. This continues until the variable drops below its average or typical level such as in the month of May. At this point there is a tendency to repeatedly overestimate the value of Y, thereby resulting in a series of negative errors. Again, the errors are not independent. A negative error was likely to be followed by another negative error.

An inspection of the error terms can be quite revealing. Any detectable pattern, such as several positive errors followed by several negative, or alternating positive-negative errors, is a sign the errors are not independent of each other. To the extent that this occurs and Assumption 2 is violated, the regression model is said to suffer from autocorrelation. **Autocorrelation,** also called **serial correlation,** occurs if errors are not independent. In the presence of autocorrelation, our regression model is less reliable.

Assumption 3
All errors have the same variance.

We specified earlier that the errors are normally dispersed above and below the regression line. The OLS procedure assumes that the variance of these Y-values where $X = 10$ is the same as it is where X is equal to any other value. Notice from Figure 12-11 that the variance in the error terms is the same at all three income levels, I_1, I_2, and I_3. In all three cases, the dispersion in the Y-values is the same, as seen by the shapes of the normal curves. This assumed condition of equal variance in errors is known as **homoscedasticity.**

FIGURE 12-11   Equality of Variance in the Error Term

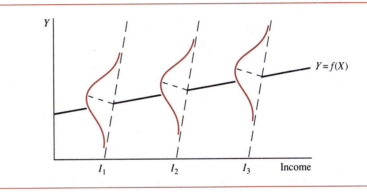

This third assumption is, however, often violated when using cross-sectional data. **Cross-sectional data** would consist, for example, of observations for various levels of consumption by residents in Kansas City in the month of July. Since the data were collected at a single point in time (July), they do not constitute time-series data. Moreover, given that the data set includes a large group of people and thus cuts across different sections of the economic strata, encompassing lower-, middle-, and upper-class income groups, they are considered cross-sectional data.

Traditional economic theory holds that wealthy individuals exhibit a different behavior pattern in their consumption expenditures than do the less fortunate. This economic principle can be used to explain how Assumption 3 can be violated. Specifically, the variation in the expenditures among the wealthy exceeds that of people in lower income brackets. Thus, the variance in consumption will increase as income goes up. This is shown in Figure 12-12. The variance in consumption patterns

FIGURE 12-12   Heteroscedasticity in Error Terms

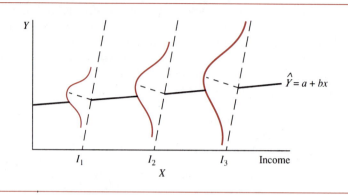

becomes greater at higher income levels, where $I_1 < I_2 < I_3$. Notice that at I_3 the spread in the errors above and below the regression is greater than at I_1. When Assumption 3 is violated, the model is said to suffer from **heteroscedasticity**. To the extent that heteroscedasticity occurs, the regression model is less reliable. The presence of heteroscedasticity will often introduce an element of bias into the model, thereby casting doubt on the values of b_0 and b_1.

Assumption 4
The means of the Y-values all lie on a straight line.

Given some value for X, X_i, there will occur a normal distribution of Y-values. This distribution of Y-values has a mean. The same is true if X is set equal to any other value. OLS assumes that these two means, as well as all others that might be observed, lie on a straight line. This is referred to as the *assumption of linearity,* and can be expressed as

$$\mu_{y|x} = \beta_0 + \beta_1 X_i$$

where $\mu_{y|x}$ is the mean of the population of Y-values for any given value of X.

These assumptions form the basis for regression analysis. It is upon them that the foundation of OLS is built. A complete comprehension of regression analysis is not possible without an understanding of these assumptions. However, these conditions represent the ideal situation. It is unlikely all of them are ever fully valid in single regression. We will examine ways to test for the validity of these conditions and learn corrective steps to take if a problem is indicated.

12.7   THE STANDARD ERROR OF THE ESTIMATE: A MEASURE OF GOODNESS-OF-FIT

The regression line, as we have already noted, is often called the line of best fit. It fits, or depicts, the relationship between X and Y better than any other line. However, just because it provides the best fit, there is no guarantee that it is any good. We would like to be able to measure just how good our best fit is.

Actually, there are at least two such measures of goodness-of-fit: (1) the standard error of the estimate and (2) the coefficient of determination. We will defer discussion of the latter concept until we examine correlation analysis later in the chapter. We embark on a description of the standard error of the estimate at this point.

The **standard error of the estimate,** *Se*, is a measure of the average amount by which the actual observations for *Y* vary around the regression line. It gauges the variation of the data points above and below the regression line. As a measure of the dispersion of the *Y*-values around the regression line, it reflects our tendency to depart from the actual value of *Y* when using our regression model for prediction purposes. In that sense, it is a measure of the average amount of our error.

FIGURE 12-13   Possible Scatter Diagrams

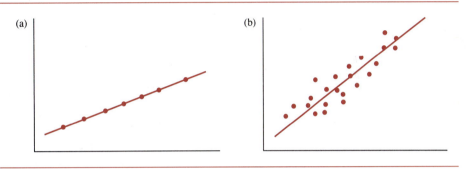

If all the data points fell on a perfectly straight line as in Figure 12-13(a), our regression line would pass through each one. In this rather fortunate case we would suffer no error in our forecasts, and the standard error of the estimate would be zero. However, data are seldom that cooperative. There is going to be some scatter in the data, as in Figure 12-13(b). The standard error of the estimate measures this average variation of the data points around the regression line we use to estimate *Y* and thus provides a measure of the error we will suffer in that estimation. Formula (12.13) illustrates this principle. Notice that the numerator reflects the difference between Y_i, the actual values for *Y*, and our estimate $\hat{Y}$.

$$Se = \sqrt{\frac{\Sigma(Y_i - \hat{Y})^2}{n - 2}} \qquad (12.13)$$

However, Formula (12.13) is computationally inconvenient. It is necessary to develop an easier method of hand calculation. Recall that σ^2 is the variance of the regression errors. One of the basic assumptions of the OLS model is that this variance in the errors around the regression line is the same for all values of *X*. The smaller the value for σ^2, the less is the dispersion of the data points around the line.

Since σ^2 is a parameter, it will likely remain unknown, and it is necessary to estimate its value with our sample data. An unbiased estimate of σ^2 is the mean square error (*MSE*). In our previous chapter on ANOVA, we learned that the *MSE* is the error sum of squares (*SSE*) divided by the degrees of freedom. In the context of regression analysis, *SSE* is

$$SSE = SSy - \frac{(SSxy)^2}{SSx} \qquad (12.14)$$

In a simple regression model, two constraints are placed on our data set since we must estimate two parameters, β_0 and β_1. There are, therefore, $n - 2$ degrees of freedom. *MSE* is

$$MSE = \frac{SSE}{n - 2} \qquad (12.15)$$

The standard error of the estimate is then

$$Se = \sqrt{MSE} \qquad (12.16)$$

Example 12-5 demonstrates the calculation of *Se* using our data set for Hop Scotch.

EXAMPLE 12-5 The Standard Error of the Estimate for Hop Scotch Airlines

After the accounting department for Hop Scotch calculates the regression model (Example 12-1), the division of marketing questions how accurate the model is in forecasting numbers of passengers. The division of marketing needs a precise estimate of passengers in order to compare how competitive they are with the rest of the industry.

The head of the marketing division feels that the standard error of the estimate will serve nicely as a measure of the closeness or precision of their estimate of the numbers of passengers which is obtained by using the regression model.

SOLUTION:
Using the data in Table 12-2 we have

$$SSE = SSy - \frac{(SSxy)^2}{SSx}$$

$$= 171.73333 - \frac{(148.9333)^2}{137.73333}$$

$$= 10.6893$$

$$MSE = \frac{10.6893}{15 - 2}$$

$$= 0.82226$$

$$Se = \sqrt{0.82226}$$

$$= 0.90678 \text{ or } 0.907$$

STATISTICAL INTERPRETATION:

For the statistical interpretation of Se, continue reading.

The standard error of the estimate is quite similar to the standard deviation of a single variable that we examined in Chapter 3. If we were to collect data on the incomes for $n = 100$ people, we could easily calculate the standard deviation. This would provide us with a measure of dispersion of the income data around their mean.

In regression analysis we have two variables, X and Y. The standard error of the estimate is thus a measure of the dispersion of the Y-values around their mean, given any specific X-value.

Since the standard error of the estimate is similar to the standard deviation for a single variable, it can be interpreted similarly. Recall that the Empirical Rule states that if the data are normally distributed an interval of one standard deviation above the mean and one standard deviation below the mean will encompass 68.8 percent of all the observations; an interval of two standard deviations on each side of the mean contains 95.5 percent of the observations; and three standard deviations on each side of the mean encompass 99.7 percent of the observations.

The same thing can be said for the standard error of the estimate. Where $X = 10$,

$$\hat{Y} = 4.4 + 1.08(10)$$

$$= 15.2$$

Remember, this value of 15.2 is the estimate of the mean value we would get for Y if we set X equal to 10 many times. To illustrate the meaning of the standard error of the estimate, locate the points that are one Se (that is, 0.907) above and below the mean value of 15.2. These points are 14.29 (15.2 − 0.907) and 16.11 (15.2 + 0.907). Draw lines through each point parallel to the regression line as in Figure 12-14. Approximately 68.8 percent of the data points will fall within these lines, and the remaining 31.2 percent of the observations will be outside this interval. In our case, 68.8 percent of the time that $10,000 is spent on advertising, the number of passengers will be between 14,290 and 16,110. The remaining 31.2 percent of time, the number of passengers will exceed 16,110 or be less than 14,290.

Given our interpretation of Se, it follows that the more dispersed the original data are, the larger Se will be. As indicated by the scatter diagrams in Figure 12-15, the data for Figure 12-15(a) are much more dispersed than those in Figure 12-15(b). The Se for Figure 12-15(a) would therefore be larger. After all, if you are to encompass 68.8 percent of the observations within one Se of the regression line, the interval must be wider if the data are more spread out.

FIGURE 12-14   Standard Error of the Estimate

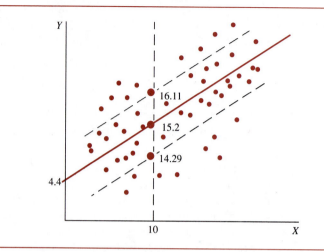

FIGURE 12-15   A Comparison of the Standard Error of the Estimate

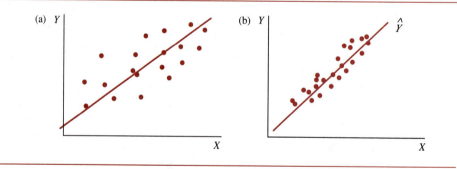

QUICK CHECK 12.7.1

OOOO

Given the values for Y and X, calculate and interpret the standard error of the estimate.

$Y = 5, 6.3, 8, 7.5, 9, 8.1, 8, 8.5, 10$

$X = 2.6, 3.9, 5, 4.9, 5.2, 5, 5.5, 5, 6$

Answer: The model is $\hat{Y} = 1.1386 + 1.39565X$; $Se = 0.50543$. (Your answer may differ slightly due to rounding.) It states that given any value for X, 68.8 percent of the observations for Y will fall within 0.50543 units of $1.1386 + 1.39565X$.

QUICK CHECK 12.7.2

○○○○ Using the values for X and Y below, determine within what interval 95.5 percent of the observations for Y will fall if $X = 4$.

$Y = 5, 4.5, 5.5, 6.2, 7.6, 5.5, 7$

$X = 1.9, 1.5, 3, 3.8, 4.5, 4, 4$

Answer: $\hat{Y} = 3.211 + 0.829X$; $Se = 0.6042$; the interval is 5.319 to 7.735.

12.8 CORRELATION ANALYSIS

Our regression model has given us a clear perception of the relationship between advertising expenditures by Hop Scotch Airlines and the number of courageous travelers who queue up at the Hop Scotch ticket counter. It is now evident that since the regression coefficient b_1 is positive, there is a direct relationship between advertising dollars and passengers. This means that as more money flows into the advertising budget, more ticket buyers select Hop Scotch. Or, conversely, a decrease in advertising expenditures is accompanied by a reduction in passenger traffic. The two variables move together. To be more precise, since $b_1 = 1.08$, for every 1-unit increase in advertising, the number of passengers increases by 1.08 units. That is, for every additional $1,000 in the advertising budget, 1,080 more passengers buy Hop Scotch tickets. However, you are again reminded that our findings do not allow us to conclude that advertising *causes* ticket sales to rise. Even though there may appear to be a cause-and-effect relationship, we can only conclude that advertising and passengers are correlated or related in a some given manner. The true cause of this relationship may lie in some third variable which influences both advertising and ticket sales.

Now that we have a general understanding of the basic nature of the relationship between advertising and number of passengers, it is beneficial to measure the strength of that relationship. This is the job of correlation analysis. This measure of strength is provided by the coefficient of determination. The **coefficient of determination** is one of the measures of goodness-of-fit we mentioned earlier along with the standard error of the estimate Se.

A. THE COEFFICIENT OF DETERMINATION

To understand correlation analysis, we must consider the **total deviation** of Y. This important concept is the amount by which the individual Y-values vary from their mean $\overline{Y}$— that is, $Y_i - \overline{Y}$.

Total Deviation
The total deviation is the amount by which an actual value of Y, Y_i, differs from $\overline{Y}$, the mean of all the values for the dependent variable.

Using month 13 as an example, the data from Table 12-2 show 23,000 people flew on Hop Scotch ($Y_i = 23$). Since the mean value for the number of passengers is

$$\overline{Y} = \frac{\Sigma Y_i}{n}$$

$$= \frac{268}{15}$$

$$= 17.87$$

the total deviation for the thirteenth month is $23 - 17.87 = 5.13$. This is shown in Figure 12-16. The value for Y_i of 23 lies 5.13 above the horizontal line representing $\overline{Y}$ of 17.87. This total deviation between Y_i and $\overline{Y}$ can be broken down into two types. The **explained deviation** is that portion of the total deviation that is explained by our model. It is the difference between what our model predicts, $\hat{Y}$, and the mean value for Y—that is, $\hat{Y} - \overline{Y}$. In this manner, the explained deviation measures the amount of the total difference between Y_i and $\overline{Y}$ that is explained by the regression model.

FIGURE 12-16   Deviations for Hop Scotch Airlines

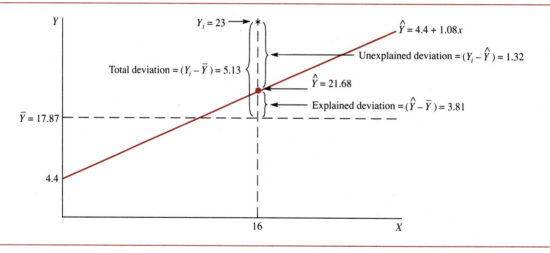

Since $X = 16$ in the thirteenth month, $\hat{Y} = 4.4 + 1.08(16) = 21.68$. The explained deviation is therefore

$$\hat{Y} - \overline{Y} = 21.68 - 17.87$$

$$= 3.81$$

Of that total deviation of 5.13 for the thirteenth month, our model explains 3.81.

The rest of the total deviation remains unexplained. The **unexplained deviation** is that portion of the total deviation of Y_i from $\overline{Y}$ not explained by our model. It is the additional deviation from $\overline{Y}$ over and above what our model is able to account for. It is found as the difference between what Y actually was (Y_i) and what our model predicted ($\hat{Y}$), that is, $Y_i - \hat{Y}$. You will recognize this value as our error.

Explained and Unexplained Deviation
The explained deviation is the difference between the value predicted by the model ($\hat{Y}$) and the mean value of $Y(\overline{Y})$: $\hat{Y} - \overline{Y}$. The unexplained deviation is the difference between the actual value of Y (Y_i) and that value predicted by the model ($\hat{Y}$): $Y_i - \hat{Y}$.

Notice that had we tried to predict Y merely on the basis of $\overline{Y}$, our error would have been $Y_i = \overline{Y} = 23 - 17.87 = 5.13$. Our regression model, on the other hand, forecasts a value for Y of

$$\hat{Y} = 4.4 + 1.08(16)$$

$$= 21.68$$

Using our regression model, our error is only $Y_i - \hat{Y} = 23 - 21.68 = 1.32$. We are closer to the actual value for passengers when we use our model than we would be if we just took the average value for Y as our prediction. Our model does have some value as an explanatory tool.

Just how much value it has is measured by the coefficient of determination. An examination of this important statistical concept requires that we calculate the sums of squares. In that regard, notice that the

Total deviation = Explained deviation + Unexplained deviation

That is,

$$(Y_i - \overline{Y}) = (\hat{Y} - \overline{Y}) + (Y_i - \hat{Y}) \qquad (12.17)$$

If we were to find each of these three types of deviations for all 15 observations (months), square them, and sum each of them, we would have the sums of squares. Thus, the total sum of squares is

$$\Sigma(Y_i - \overline{Y})^2 = SST \qquad (12.18)$$

The regression sum of squares is

$$\Sigma(\hat{Y} - \overline{Y})^2 = SSR \qquad (12.19)$$

This regression sum of squares is also called the explained deviation, since it is the regression model that is doing the explaining.

The error sum of squares is

$$\Sigma(Y_i - \hat{Y})^2 = SSE \qquad (12.20)$$

The error sum of squares is also called the unexplained deviation since that portion of the total deviation left unexplained is our error.

The squaring process is necessary to prevent negative errors from offsetting the positive errors and leaving us with nothing but zeros to work with.

Now recall what we set out to do. We want to measure how closely our line fits the data. We want a measure of how well our model explains changes in the dependent variable. Stop and think. How could we use SST, SSR, and SSE to measure the explanatory power of our model? That is, how could we measure to what extent our model explains changes in Y? Keep in mind that SST is the total amount of the deviation in Y that needs to be explained, and SSR is the amount of that deviation that is explained by our model. Couldn't we then measure the explanatory power of our model with a ratio of the total variation in Y (as measured by SST) to the portion of that variation that is explained by our model (as measured by SSR)? This is exactly what the coefficient of determination does! It is a ratio of the explained deviation to the total deviation.

The **coefficient of determination**, r^2, measures that portion of the total deviation in Y that is explained by our model. In this sense, it is a measure of the explanatory power of the regression model.

$$r^2 = \frac{\text{Explained variation}}{\text{Total variation}} = \frac{SSR}{SST} \qquad (12.21)$$

In terms of our sums of squares and cross-products, it can be calculated as

$$r^2 = \frac{(SSxy)^2}{(SSx)(SSy)} \qquad (12.22)$$

The value for r^2 must be between 0 and 1 since more than 100 percent of the change in Y cannot be explained.

If $r^2 = 70$ percent, this means 70 percent of the variation in Y is explained by changes in X. Of course, the higher the r^2, the more explanatory power our model has.

Coefficient of Determination
The coefficient of determination measures the explanatory power of the regression model.

In this manner, r^2 measures the strength of the linear relationship between X and Y. Note that r^2 has meaning only for linear relationships. Two variables may exhibit a coefficient of determination of zero and still be related in a nonlinear manner.

EXAMPLE 12-6 The Coefficient of Determination for Hop Scotch Airlines

Previously the division of marketing for Hop Scotch completed the regression analysis. This gave them a good idea as to the nature of the relationship between advertising and passengers. However, the marketing director now wants to know how strong that relationship is. He is concerned with how much reliance he can place on that relationship in the decision-making process. This information can be derived through an examination of the coefficient of determination.

SOLUTION:
Given the data for Hop Scotch from Table 12-2 we have

$$r^2 = \frac{(SSxy)^2}{(SSx)(SSy)}$$

$$= \frac{(148.9333)^2}{(137.73333)(171.73333)}$$

$$= 0.93776 \text{ or } 0.94$$

Notice that all the values were carried several decimal places due to the aforementioned sensitivity of r^2 to rounding.

STATISTICAL INTERPRETATION:
The coefficient of determination reveals that 94 percent of the change in the number of passengers is explained (not caused) by changes in advertising expenditures.

As you were warned earlier, we cannot conclude that a change in X *causes* a change in Y. Correlation does not imply causation. It may be that a third factor, totally unknown to us, is causing X and Y to behave as they do. We only know that advertising and passengers are correlated.

Since $r^2 = 0.94$, our model explains 94 percent of the change in Y. The other 6 percent can be explained by some variable(s) other than advertising. This 6 percent is sometimes referred to as the **coefficient of nondetermination, k^2.**

B.   THE COEFFICIENT OF CORRELATION

In many instances we often have need to calculate the **coefficient of correlation** (or merely the correlation coefficient). Developed by Karl Pearson around the turn of the century, it is sometimes called the **Pearsonian product-moment correlation coefficient.** Designated as r, the correlation coefficient is simply the square root of the coefficient of determination.

$$r = \sqrt{r^2} = \sqrt{0.94} = 0.97 \qquad\qquad (12.23)$$

It can be seen that $-1 < r < +1$. That is, the value for r ranges between $+1$ and -1. It is given the same sign as the regression coefficient b and, therefore, reflects the slope of the regression line. If $r > 0$, b will be positive and the line will slope up. If $r < 0$, b will be negative and the regression line will be negatively sloped.

The absolute value of r indicates the strength of the relationship between X and Y, while the sign tells us whether they are related in a direct or inverse fashion. Figure 12-17 illustrates possible values for r. An r-value of $+1$ indicates perfect positive correlation, while $r = -1$ suggests perfect negative correlation. If $r = 0$, no linear relationship between X and Y is suggested.

FIGURE 12-17   Potential Values for r

Refer back to Display 12-1 on page 594, which provided a portion of the SPSS-PC printout for Hop Scotch Airlines. The correlation coefficient and the coefficient of determination are shown as Multiple R = 0.96838, and R square = 0.93776. Notice also that the standard error discussed above of 0.90678 is also displayed. The Adjusted R Square value is of little or no consequence in simple regression and will be discussed in the next chapter, dealing with multiple regression analysis.

QUICK CHECK 12.8.1

○○○○

A study involving six employees finds the following values for job performance rating (JPR) and years experience. Using these data how well does experience explain job performance?

JPR = 1.5, 4, 4.5, 5, 6.2, 7

Experience = 2.5, 3.5, 4, 4.5, 5, 5.9 years

Answer: $r^2 = 0.964$

QUICK CHECK 12.8.2

A second study related the commuting time, in hours, for shoppers to reach the local shopping center to the duration of the visit, in hours. Given the values shown here

a.   Which is the dependent variable and which is the independent?

b.   Calculate and interpret the coefficient of determination.

Commuting time: 0.5, 0.2, 0.2, 1.5, 2, 2.1, 2, 1.5

Length of visit: 1.2, 5, 5.5, 4, 3.3, 4.2, 5.1, 5

Answer:

a.   It would seem that the duration of the visit would depend on the commuting time required to reach the shopping center. If the time was long, the shopper would want to conduct as much business there as possible.

b. $r^2 = 0.00059$. Less than 1 percent of a change in length of visit is explained by a change in commuting time.

12.9   LIMITATIONS OF REGRESSION ANALYSIS

Although regression and correlation analysis often prove extremely useful in making decisions in a wide variety of business and economic matters, there are certain limitations to their application and interpretation. As already noted, regression and correlation cannot determine cause-and-effect relationships. Correlation does not imply causation. This point was dramatically made by a British statistician who "proved" that storks bring babies. He collected data on birthrates and the number of storks in London and found a very high correlation—something like $r = 0.92$. He therefore concluded that the fairy tale about storks and babies was true.

However, as you may have already suspected, that's not really the way it works. It seems that this brand of stork liked to nest in the tops of Londoners' chimneys. Therefore, where population was dense and the birthrate was high, there were many chimneys to attract this fowl—thus, the high correlation between birthrates and storks. Actually, both storks and births were *caused* by a third factor, population density, which the researcher conveniently ignored. Remember, correlation does not mean causation.

Additionally, you must be careful not to use your regression model to predict Y on the basis of values for X outside the range of your original data set. Notice that the values for X in the Hop Scotch data set range from a low of 8 to a high of 19. We have isolated the relationship between X and Y only for that range of X-values. We have no idea what the relationship is outside that range. For all we know, it might appear as shown in Figure 12-18. As you can see, for values outside our range of 8 to 19, the X-Y relationship is entirely different than what we might expect given our sample.

FIGURE 12-18   A Possible X-Y Relationship

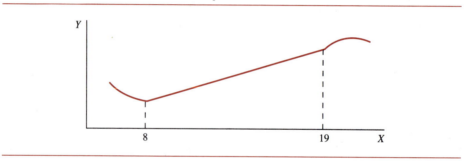

Another failing of regression and correlation analysis becomes apparent when two obviously unrelated variables seem to exhibit some relationship. Assume that for some reason you wish to examine the correlation between the number of elephants born in the Kansas City Zoo and the tonnage of sea trout caught by sports fishermen in the Gulf off Tallahassee, Florida. Lo and behold, you find an $r = 0.91$. Would you conclude that there is a relationship? Such a conclusion is obviously bizarre. Despite the r-value, pure logic tells us that there is not really any relationship between these two variables. You have merely uncovered **spurious correlation,** which is correlation that occurs just by chance. There is no substitute for common sense in regression and correlation analysis.

12.10   INTERVAL ESTIMATION IN REGRESSION ANALYSIS

One of the basic purposes in conducting regression analysis is to forecast and predict values for the dependent variable. As we have seen, once the regression equation has been determined, it is a very simple matter to develop a point estimate for the dependent variable by substituting a given value for X into the equation and solving for Y.

In addition, the researcher may be interested in interval estimates. We have already seen that they are often preferable to mere point estimates. There are at least two such interval estimates commonly associated with regression procedures.

The first one is an interval estimate for the mean value of Y given any X-value. That is, we may want to estimate the *population* mean for *all* Y-values (not just the $n = 15$ in our sample) when X is equal to some given value. We may be interested in the *average* number of passengers in *all* months in which we spend \$10,000 on advertising (i.e., $X = 10$). This is called the **conditional mean.**

A second important confidence interval seeks to estimate a *single value* of Y given that X is set equal to a specific amount. This estimate is referred to as a **predictive interval.** Thus, while the conditional mean is an estimate of the average value of Y in all months in which X is equal to a specified amount, the predictive interval estimates Y in any single month in which X is set equal to a given amount.

A. THE CONDITIONAL MEAN FOR Y

Suppose we wanted to develop an interval estimate for the conditional mean of Y, $\mu_{y|x}$. This is the population mean for all Y-values under the condition that X is equal to a specific value. Recall that if we let X equal some given amount (say $X = 10$) many times, we will get many different values of Y. The interval we are calculating here is an estimate of the mean of all of those many Y-values. That is, it is an interval estimate for the mean value of Y on the condition that X is set equal to 10 many times.

Actually, the confidence interval for the conditional mean value of Y has two possible interpretations just as did those confidence intervals we constructed back in Chapter 8. Assume that we are calculating, for example, a 95 percent confidence interval.

First Interpretation
As noted above, if we let X equal the same amount many times we will get many different Y-values. We can then be 95 percent confident that the mean of those Y-values ($\mu_{y|x}$) will fall within the specified interval.

Second Interpretation
If we were to take many different samples of X and Y values and construct confidence intervals based on each sample, 95 percent of them would contain $\mu_{y|x}$, the true but unknown mean value of Y given $X = 10$.

To calculate this interval for the conditional mean value of Y, we must first determine S_Y, the **standard error of the conditional mean.** The standard error of the conditional mean recognizes that we use a sample to calculate b_0 and b_1 in the regression equation. Thus, b_0 and b_1 are subject to sampling error. If we were to take a different set of $n = 15$ months and determine a regression equation, we would likely get different values for b_0 and b_1. The purpose of S_Y is to account for the different values for b_0 and b_1 resulting from sampling error. It is determined by

$$S_Y = Se \sqrt{\frac{1}{n} + \frac{(X_i - \overline{X})^2}{SSx}} \qquad (12.24)$$

where Se is the standard error of the estimate
        X_i is the given value for the independent variable

The confidence interval for the conditional mean is then

$$\text{C.I. for } \mu_{y|x} = \hat{Y} \pm tS_Y \qquad (12.25)$$

in which $\hat{Y}$ is the point estimator found from our original regression equation, and the t-value is based on a selected level of confidence with $n - 2$ degrees of freedom. There are $n - 2$ degrees of freedom because we must calculate two values, b_0 and b_1, from the sample data. We therefore lose two degrees of freedom.

EXAMPLE 12-7 An Interval Estimate for the Conditional Mean of Y for Hop Scotch Airlines

Since Hop Scotch seems to spend $10,000 for advertising fairly often, the CEO requests that the quantitative analysis section of the division of marketing develop a 95 percent confidence interval for $\mu_{y|x}$ on the condition that $X = 10$. The section must estimate what the true mean for Y is if $X = 10$.

SOLUTION:
Given Formula (12.24),

$$S_Y = Se \sqrt{\frac{1}{n} + \frac{(X_i - \overline{X})^2}{SSx}}$$

The value of Se was calculated to be 0.907 in Example 12-2, and X has been set at 10.

Then using the data from Table 12-1, we have

$$S_Y = 0.907 \sqrt{\frac{1}{15} + \frac{(10 - 12.47)^2}{137.7333}}$$

$$= 0.303$$

Since

$$\hat{Y} = b_0 + b_1 X$$

$$= 4.4 + 1.08(10) = 15.2$$

Formula (12.25) gives

$$\text{C.I. } \mu_{y|x} = \hat{Y} \pm tS_Y$$
$$= 15.2 \pm t(0.303)$$

Given a 95 percent confidence level ($\alpha = 0.05$) and $n - 2 = 13$ degrees of freedom, the t-table yields $t = 2.160$. Then

$$\text{C.I. } \mu_{y|x} = 15.2 \pm (2.160)(0.303)$$
$$= 15.2 \pm 0.65$$
$$14.55 < \mu_{y|x} < 15.85$$

STATISTICAL INTERPRETATION:

Hop Scotch can be 95 percent confident that the true population mean for Y is between 14,550 passengers and 15,850 passengers for all those months in which they spend $10,000 for advertising purposes.

We could calculate the confidence intervals for $\mu_{y|x}$ at several X-values. This would give us several confidence intervals. These intervals would then form an entire **confidence band** for $\mu_{y|x}$. Notice in Figure 12-19 the band becomes wider at the extremes. This happens because regression analysis is based on averages, and the farther we get away from the center point of $\overline{X} = 12.47$, the less accurate our results. Therefore, to retain our 95 percent confidence level, the band must be wider. It is most narrow at $X = \overline{X} = 12.47$. If you were to calculate the 95 percent interval at $X = 8$, you would find it to be wider than the one we just got at $X = 10$. That is, the lower limit would be less than 14.55, and the upper limit would exceed 15.85.

FIGURE 12-19   Confidence Limits for $\mu_{y|x}$

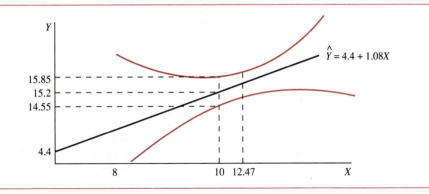

B.   THE PREDICTIVE INTERVAL FOR A SINGLE VALUE OF Y

The confidence interval constructed above is for the population mean value of all
Y-values when X is equal to a given amount many times. At other times it might be
useful to construct a confidence interval for a single value of Y that is obtained when
X is set equal to some value only once. Hop Scotch may be interested in predicting
the actual number of customers next month if they spend $10,000 on advertising.
This differs from the problem above in which the concern was with the average
value of Y if X was set equal to 10 many times.

Our interest now focuses on a prediction for a single value of Y if X is set equal to
a given amount only once. That is, instead of trying to predict the mean of many
Y-values obtained on the condition that X is set equal to 10 many times, we are now
trying to predict a single value for Y which is obtained if X is set equal to 10 only
once. Now, stop and think about this problem for a minute. Averages, by their very
nature, tend to be centered around the middle of a data set. They are therefore easier
to predict since we know about where they are. Individual values, however, are quite
scattered and are therefore much more difficult to predict. Hence, a 95 percent confidence interval for a single value of Y must be wider than that for a conditional mean.

This confidence interval for the predictive interval of Y also carries two interpretations. For the purpose of illustration, these interpretations are provided under the
assumption that the intervals we calculate are 95 percent intervals, although other
levels of confidence may of course be used.

First Interpretation
If we were to set X equal to some amount just one time, we would get one
resulting value of Y. We can be 95 percent certain that that single value of Y
falls within the specified interval.

Second Interpretation
If many samples were taken and each was used to construct a predictive
confidence interval, 95 percent of them would contain the true value for Y.

In order to calculate this predictive interval, we must first calculate the **standard
error of the forecast,** S_{y_i} (not to be confused with the standard error of the conditional mean, S_Y). This standard error of the forecast accounts for the fact that individual values are more dispersed than are means. The standard error of the forecast

reflects the sampling error inherent in S_Y, the standard error of the conditional mean, plus the additional dispersion that occurs because we are dealing with an individual value of Y. Formula (12.26) is used in its calculation.

$$S_{y_i} = Se \sqrt{1 + \frac{1}{n} + \frac{(X_i - \bar{X})^2}{SSx}} \qquad (12.26)$$

The predictive interval for a single value of Y, Y_x, is then

$$\text{C.I. for } Y_x = \hat{Y} \pm tS_{y_i} \qquad (12.27)$$

Let's now construct a 95 percent confidence interval for a single value of Y when $X = 10$ and compare it with the interval for the conditional mean constructed earlier.

EXAMPLE 12-8 The Predictive Interval for Y Given an X-Value

After receiving the interval estimate for the conditional mean from the quantitative analysis section of the division of marketing, the CEO now demands to know what the estimate is for passengers the next time they spend $X = \$10,000$ for advertising. The head of the marketing division realizes that what the CEO is asking for is the predictive interval estimate for a single value of X.

SOLUTION:

The division head therefore proceeds as follows:

$$S_{y_i} = Se \sqrt{1 + \frac{1}{15} + \frac{(10 - 12.47)^2}{137.73333}}$$

$$= 0.907 \sqrt{1.1114}$$

$$= 0.956$$

Since

$$\hat{Y} = 4.4 + 1.08(10)$$

$$= 15.2$$

we obtain

$$\text{C.I. for } Y_x = \hat{Y} \pm tS_{y_i}$$

$$= 15.2 \pm (2.160)(0.956)$$

$$= 15.2 \pm 2.065$$

$$13.14 < Y_x < 17.27$$

STATISTICAL INTERPRETATION:
We can be 95 percent certain that if in any single month $X = \$10,000$ the resulting single value of Y will be between 13,140 and 17,270 passengers.

As we promised, this interval is wider than the first because we are working with less predictable individual values. The comparison is complete in Figure 12-20.

FIGURE 12-20   Interval Estimates for $\mu_{y|x}$ and Y_x

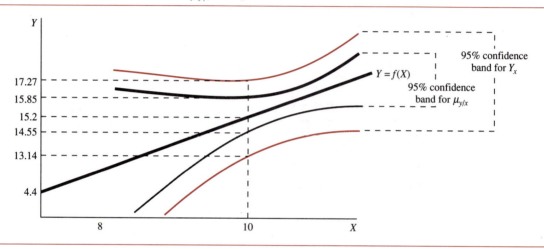

QUICK CHECK 12.10.2

◦◦◦◦   Using the data from 12.10.1, calculate the 99 percent interval for a single value of Y.

Answer: −0.557 to 15.16

C.   FACTORS INFLUENCING THE WIDTH OF THE INTERVAL

Given a level of confidence, it is preferable to minimize the width of the interval. The narrower the interval, the more accurate is our prediction of $\mu_{y|x}$ or Y_x. However, several forces are working against us in our effort to produce a narrower interval.

The first is the degree of dispersion of the original data. The more dispersed the original data are, the greater will be Se, the standard error of the estimate. Given the arithmetic in Formulas (12.24) and (12.26), a higher Se results in a wider interval.

Our sample size is a second factor in determining interval width. As we have seen in previous chapters, a large sample size results in a smaller standard error.

Again, given the arithmetic described above, a small standard error results in a small interval.

Furthermore, as we have already seen, a value for X relatively close to $\overline{X}$ will produce a small interval since regression is based on averages. Therefore, a third factor influencing interval width is how far the particular value of X that we are interested in is from $\overline{X}$.

12.11 HYPOTHESES TEST ABOUT THE POPULATION CORRELATION COEFFICIENT

Since our correlation coefficient of $r = 0.97$ is not zero, we can conclude on the basis of our sample data that there is a relationship between X and Y. However, it must be remembered that this conclusion is based on only $n = 15$ observations. Only 15 months of data were used in our study. As always, our interest is with the entire population of all X-values and all Y-values. It is therefore necessary to consider the possibility that, due to sampling error, our sample may be misleading. Although our sample data reveal a relationship, there may be no such relationship at the population level.

We must therefore consider the possibility that despite the fact our sample suggests a relationship between X and Y, it may be that no such relationship exists. Could it be that if we plotted the scatter diagram for all X, Y data points it would appear as in Figure 12-21?

FIGURE 12-21   A Possible Pattern for the Population of all Data Points for Hop Scotch Airlines

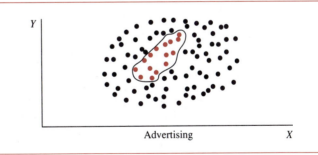

This pattern of data points reveals that the correlation is zero, and no relationship exists between X and Y. However, isn't it entirely possible that, just due to the luck of the draw, our sample might just happen to include those 15 data points enclosed in the ellipse? Indeed it is! Of all the data points in the population of X, Y-values, it is entirely possible that we might just happen to select those 15 indicated in the circle. Consider the consequences of selecting these 15 observations as the sample. A scatter diagram with these sample data would falsely suggest a positive relationship between X and Y.

The resulting problem should be obvious. Our sample has misled us. The sample correlation coefficient r would be positive, but the population correlation coefficient ρ (the Greek letter rho) would be zero. While there actually is no relationship between X and Y, our sample incorrectly reports a positive correlation. We would mistakenly conclude that a relationship did exist between X and Y.

Therefore, despite the fact that the sample correlation coefficient was not zero, it is often desirable to test the hypothesis that the population correlation coefficient *is* 0. Our hypotheses are

$$H_0: \rho = 0$$

$$H_a: \rho \neq 0$$

Although our analysis has shown that the sample correlation coefficient is not zero, the hypothesis test is done to determine if it is *significantly* different from zero. This test employs the t-statistic

$$t = \frac{r}{S_r} \tag{12.28}$$

and has $n - 2$ degrees of freedom, where S_r is the standard error of the sampling distribution of r. It recognizes that if several samples of size $n = 15$ were taken, we would get different values for r. That is, we can get many different samples from the population, each with its own r-value. If $\rho = 0$, the r-values would be distributed around ρ, ranging from -1 to $+1$ as shown in Figure 12-22. S_r is found by

$$S_r = \sqrt{\frac{1 - r^2}{n - 2}} \tag{12.29}$$

We choose a level of confidence, such as 95 percent ($\alpha = 0.05$), at which to test the null hypothesis $\rho = 0$. This choice allows us to find a critical value of t from the

FIGURE 12-22   The Distribution of the Sample Correlation Coefficient

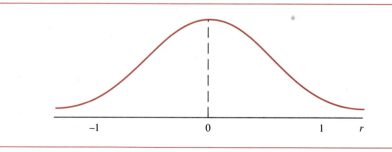

t-table. This critical value of *t* is compared with the *t* we calculated from Formula (12.28) based on our sample data.

For example, if we were to test the null at the 95 percent level of confidence, we find from the table that the critical *t*-values, given $15 - 2 = 13$ degrees of freedom, are ±2.160 as demonstrated in Figure 12-23. This means that if ρ does equal zero, 95 percent of the samples of size $n = 15$ that you could take would yield data which would provide a *t*-value between −2.160 and +2.160. There is only a 5 percent chance that if $\rho = 0$, your sample would yield a *t*-value below −2.160 or above 2.160. If in using the sample data to solve Formula (12.28), you get a *t*-value outside that range, you can be 95 percent certain that $\rho \neq 0$, thus indicating that there is a relationship between *X* and *Y* at the population level. On the other hand, if your *t*-value is between −2.160 and +2.160, you cannot reject the null hypothesis $\rho = 0$. Despite your sample results, you would not have sufficient evidence to conclude at the 95 percent level of confidence that a relationship exists between *X* and *Y*.

FIGURE 12-23   Critical *t*-Values for Testing the Hypothesis That $\rho = 0$

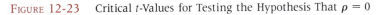
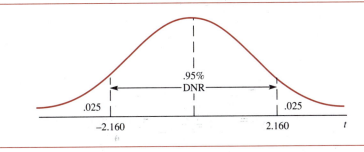

EXAMPLE 12-9 A Test of the Hypothesis That $\rho = 0$

Despite the *r*-value of 0.97 found by the marketing division, the head of the finance section for Hop Scotch is skeptical. He wants to test the hypothesis that $\rho = 0$ even though the sample collected by the marketing people strongly suggests a relationship.

SOLUTION:
If the statisticians in the finance section were to test the hypothesis that $\rho = 0$ at the 95 percent level, they would have

$$H_0: \rho = 0$$

$$H_a: \rho \neq 0$$

$$S_r = \sqrt{\frac{1 - r^2}{n - 2}}$$

$$= \sqrt{\frac{1 - 0.94}{15 - 2}}$$

$$= 0.068$$

Using Formula (12.28), we have

$$t = \frac{r}{S_r} = \frac{0.97}{0.068}$$

$$= 14.26$$

A 95 percent level of confidence carries a critical value of ± 2.160. Then the decision rule becomes

Decision Rule
Do not reject the null that $\rho = 0$ if the t-value is between -2.160 and $+2.160$. Reject $\rho = 0$ if the t-value is less than -2.160 or exceeds $+2.160$.

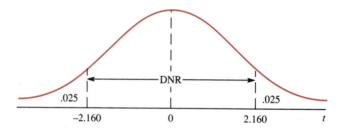

STATISTICAL INTERPRETATION:
Since $t = 14.26 > 2.160$, the head of finance can be 95 percent certain that there is a relationship between X and Y. He must reject the null that $\rho = 0$ and conclude with 95 percent certainty that there is a relationship between X and Y. This test is said to be significant at the 5 percent level.

QUICK CHECK 12.11.1

OOOO   Using the data from 12.8.1, test the hypothesis that $\rho = 0$ at the 95 percent level.

Answer: $t = 10.35 > 2.776$. Reject null that $\rho = 0$.

12.12   TESTING INFERENCES ABOUT THE POPULATION REGRESSION COEFFICIENT

Much of the work done to test inferences regarding the population correlation coefficient can also be applied to inferences concerning the population regression coefficient. The purpose and rationale are much the same. Our conclusions regarding the relationship between X and Y are based on sample data. It is possible that the implications drawn from these sample data are misleading due to sampling error. Our sample produced a nonzero regression coefficient of $b_1 = 1.08$, thereby suggesting a relationship between X and Y. However, perhaps our sample is in error and there actually exists no relationship at the population level. It is necessary to test the hypothesis that the population regression coefficient β_1 is actually zero even though b_1, the sample regression coefficient, was not zero. If it is concluded that β_1 is not zero, we can then surmise that our sample conveys the correct impression in suggesting a relationship between the dependent and independent variables.

A. HYPOTHESIS TEST FOR β_1

If the slope of the actual but unknown population regression line is zero, there is no relationship between X and Y. However, due to the luck of the draw in the sample, we might select sample data which suggest a relationship. This might happen as shown in Figure 12-24. While the population of data points shows no relationship between X and Y, and $\beta_1 = 0$, we might just happen to have selected a sample such as that represented by the $n = 15$ points circled in Figure 12-24. As you can plainly see, the sample regression would be positively sloped, $b_1 > 0$, and a relationship would be suggested by OLS. It is therefore often a wise practice to test the hypothesis that $\beta_1 = 0$ given $b_1 \neq 0$. Again, as was the case with the sample correlation coefficient, the intent is to determine if the sample regression coefficient is significantly different from zero. The test involves

$$H_0: \beta_1 = 0$$

$$H_a: \beta_1 \neq 0$$

FIGURE 12-24   A Possible Pattern of Population Data for Hop Scotch Airlines

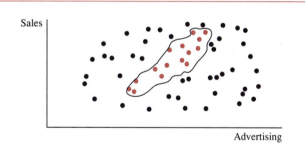

and uses a t-statistic defined as

$$t = \frac{b}{S_{b_1}} \tag{12.30}$$

where S_{b_1} is the **standard error of the regression coefficient** b_1. This standard error of the regression coefficient (not to be confused with the standard error of the estimate Se) recognizes that the regression coefficient b_1 will vary from one sample to the next. If we were to select a second sample of $n = 15$ observations and calculate the OLS model, we would likely not get a b_1-value of 1.08. Due to sampling error, the value for b_1 will vary from sample to sample. S_{b_1} measures that variation in the regression coefficient. It is calculated as

$$S_{b_1} = \frac{Se}{\sqrt{SSx}} \qquad (12.31)$$

where Se is the standard error of the estimate, which we calculated at the beginning of this chapter to be 0.907.

After deciding on the level of confidence we wish to employ, a critical value for t is obtained from the table and compared with the t-value calculated from the sample by using Formula (12.30).

EXAMPLE 12-10 A Hypothesis Test for β_1

The head of finance is tough to convince. Despite the fact that the sample regression coefficient was not zero, he now wants to perform a hypothesis test to determine if it is significantly different from zero, allowing him to conclude with some certainty that the population regression coefficient is not zero.

SOLUTION:

In running this test for Hop Scotch Airlines we specify

$$H_0: \beta_1 = 0$$

$$H_a: \beta_1 \neq 0$$

The test will be conducted at the 99 percent level of confidence in order to provide the skeptical head of the finance section with the maximum degree of assurance.

$$S_{b_1} = \frac{Se}{\sqrt{SSx}}$$

$$= \frac{0.907}{\sqrt{137.7333}}$$

$$= \frac{0.907}{11.74}$$

$$= 0.08$$

Then

$$t = \frac{b}{S_{b_1}}$$

$$= \frac{1.0813165}{0.08}$$

$$= 13.5$$

If $\alpha = 0.01$, the critical values from the t-table are ± 3.012.

Decision Rule

Do not reject H_0: $\beta_1 = 0$ if the t-value is between -3.012 and $+3.012$. Reject if the t-value is outside that range.

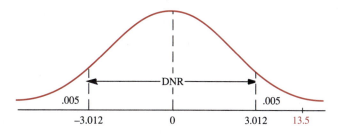

STATISTICAL INTERPRETATION:

Since $t = 13.5$, we reject H_0: $\beta_1 = 0$ and conclude that there is a relationship between X and Y. There is only a 1 percent chance that if $\beta_1 = 0$ our sample would yield a t-value outside the specified range. The t-value of 13.5 allows us to reject $\beta_1 = 0$ with a 99 percent level of confidence.

Display 12-2, which is identical to 12-1 and is repeated here for convenience, reveals the results of our SPSS-PC run. It shows under column SE B that the standard error of the regression coefficient, which we calculated using Formula (12.31), is 0.07726 and the t-value is 13.995 (which differs slightly due to rounding from the 13.5 we calculated above.) The significance of the regression coefficient is given in column Sig T. The lower this Sig T value, the "more significant" is the regression model. This Sig T value is analogous to the p-value we encountered in our discussion of hypothesis testing. It is the lowest value at which we can reject the null hypothesis that $\beta_1 = 0$. If the Sig T for ADV was, say, 0.06, then we would reject $\beta_1 = 0$ if the hypothesis was tested at $\alpha = 0.10$ (or anything above 6 percent), but we would not reject it at $\alpha = 5$ percent (or anything below 6 percent). The value shown on the printout of .0000 means that ADV is significant at any α-level we might choose.

DISPLAY 12-2   Coefficients for Hop Scotch

```
Equation Number 1    Dependent Variable..  PASS
Variable(s) Entered on Step Number
   1..    ADV
Multiple R            .96838
R Square              .93776
Adjusted R Square     .93297
Standard Error        .90678
          * * * *   M U L T I P L E   R E G R E S S I O N   * * * *
Equation Number 1    Dependent Variable..   PASS
-------------------- Variables in the Equation --------------------
Variable            B        SE B      Beta       T     Sig T
ADV            1.08132     .07726    .96838    13.995    .0000
(Constant)     4.38625     .99128              4.425     .0007
End Block Number    1    All requested variables entered.
```

QUICK CHECK 12.12.1

○○○○   Using the data from 12.7.2, test the hypothesis at the 95 percent level that the population regression coefficient = 0.

Answer: $t = 3.87 > 2.571$. Reject null.

B.   A CONFIDENCE INTERVAL FOR β_1

Since $b_1 = 1.08$ is only a point estimate of β_1, we may desire a confidence interval for the population regression coefficient. This can be accomplished via

$$\text{C.I. for } \beta_1 = b_1 \pm t S_{b_1} \qquad\qquad (12.32)$$

where the t-statistic has $n - 2$ degrees of freedom.

EXAMPLE 12-11 A Confidence Interval for β_1

Despite the fact that all of the analysis so far has found that a relationship exists between advertising and the number of passengers, the head of the finance section still insists that further tests be completed. The hypothesis test showed with 99 percent confidence that the sample regression coefficient was significantly different from zero and allowed us to conclude that the population regression coefficient was not zero. If β_1 is not zero, the head of finance wonders what it is. He therefore orders that a confidence interval for β_1 be constructed.

SOLUTION:

If we choose a 99 percent level of confidence for our test, we find

$$\text{C.I. for } \beta_1 = b_1 \pm t S_{b_1}$$

$$= 1.08 \pm (3.012)\,(0.08)$$

$$= 1.08 \pm 0.24$$

$$0.84 < \beta_1 < 1.32$$

STATISTICAL INTERPRETATION:

We can be 99 percent certain that β_1 lies between 0.84 and 1.32, thereby indicating a positive relationship between advertising and the number of passengers. Finally, the head of finance is willing to accept the fact that there is indeed a relationship between advertising and the number of passengers who choose Hop Scotch.

QUICK CHECK 12.12.2

○○○○   Using the data from 12.7.2, develop a 95 percent confidence interval for β.

Answer: 0.29 to 1.38

12.13 ANALYSIS OF VARIANCE REVISITED

The regression model presents a description of the nature of the relationship between our dependent and independent variables. We used a t-test to test the hypothesis that $\beta_1 = 0$. A similar test can be conducted with the use of analysis of variance (ANOVA) based on the F-test. The ANOVA procedure measures the amount of variation in our model. As noted earlier, there are three sources of variation in a regression model: variation explained by our regression (SSR), variation that remains unexplained due to error (SSE), and the total variation (SST), which is the sum of the first two. These can be summarized in an ANOVA table, the general form of which is shown in Table 12-4.

TABLE 12-4 A General ANOVA Table

Source of Variation	Sum of Squares	d.f.	Mean Square	F-ratio
Regression	SSR	k	$MSR = \dfrac{SSR}{k}$	$\dfrac{MSR}{MSE}$
Error	SSE	$n - k - 1$	$MSE = \dfrac{SSE}{n - k - 1}$	
Total	SST	$n - 1$		

The ratio MSR/MSE provides a measure of the accuracy of our model because it is the ratio between mean squared deviation explained by our model and the mean squared deviation left unexplained. The higher this ratio, the more explanatory power our model has. That is, a high F-value signals that our model possesses significant explanatory power. To determine what is high, our F-value must be compared with a critical value taken from Table G.

The computational formula for SSE was given by Formula (12.14). SSR can be calculated as

$$SSR = \frac{(SSxy)^2}{SSx} \tag{12.33}$$

Using our data for Hop Scotch, we have

$$SSE = SSy - \frac{(SSxy)^2}{SSx}$$

$$= 171.73333 - \frac{(148.93333)^2}{137.73333}$$

$$= 10.69$$

and

$$SSR = \frac{(148.93333)^2}{137.73333}$$

$$= 161.0441$$

SST is found as the sum of *SSR* and *SST*, as shown in Table 12-5. The *F*-value carries 1 and 13 degrees of freedom since it was formed with the mean square regression and the mean square error as seen in Table 12-5.

TABLE 12-5   The ANOVA for Hop Scotch Airlines

Source of Variation	Sum of Squares	d.f.	Mean Square	F-ratio
Regression	161.04	1	161.04	196.39
Error	10.69	13	0.82	
Total	171.73	14		

We can set $\alpha = 0.05$ to test the hypothesis that $\beta_1 = 0$. Then $F_{0.05, 1, 13} = 4.67$ produces a decision rule which states that we should reject the null if our *F*-value exceeds 4.67. Since $196.39 > 4.67$, we reject the null and conclude with 95 percent confidence that advertising has explanatory power. This is the same result obtained in our *t*-test using Formula (12.30).

Actually, in simple regression, the *F*-test and the *t*-test are analogous. Both will give the same results. The *F*-value is the square of the *t*-value. In multiple regression, the *F*-test produces a more general test to determine if any of the independent variables in the model carry explanatory power. Each variable is then tested individually with the *t*-test to determine if it is one of the significant variables.

Display 12-3 provides the ANOVA printout from our SPSS-PC computer run for Hop Scotch.

DISPLAY 12-3   ANOVA for Hop Scotch

```
Analysis of Variance
                    DF     Sum of Squares     Mean Square
Regression           1          161.04408      161.04408
Residual            13           10.68925        .82225
F =     195.85772     Signif F =   .0000
```

12.14   SOLVED PROBLEMS

1. **Lee Iacocca's Financial Inquiry** Lee Iacocca, chairman and CEO of Chrysler Corporation, expressed a concern regarding the company's high cost structure following the acquisition of AMC, and what he called "skimpy profits in the face of rising sales." In 1988

he ordered company executives to undertake a concerted study of Chrysler's cost structure as it related to reported sales. The data on K-car production shown here were collected. Company analysts used them to construct a regression model depicting the
manner in which costs depended on production and subsequent sales volume. Costs were
therefore taken as the dependent variable. Figures for costs are in units of $100,000, and
values for sales are in millions of dollars. The data are monthly values for the company as
a whole.

Month	Costs (Y)	Sales (X)
1	15.8	23
2	12.3	18
3	14.5	21
4	15.7	23
5	12.7	18
6	13.5	19
7	13.7	20
8	15.9	22
9	13.7	19
10	14.3	21

The regression model appears as

Y	X	XY	X^2	Y^2
15.8	23	363.4	529	249.64
12.3	18	221.4	324	151.29
14.5	21	304.5	441	210.25
15.7	23	361.1	529	246.49
12.7	18	228.6	324	161.29
13.5	19	256.5	361	182.25
13.7	20	274.0	400	187.69
15.9	22	349.8	484	252.81
13.7	19	260.3	361	187.69
14.3	21	300.3	441	204.49
142.1	204	2,919.9	4,194.0	2,033.89

$$SSx = \Sigma X^2 - \frac{(\Sigma X)^2}{n}$$

$$= 4,194 - \frac{(204)^2}{10}$$

$$= 32.4$$

$$SSy = \Sigma Y^2 - \frac{(\Sigma Y)^2}{n}$$

$$= 2{,}033.89 - \frac{(142.1)^2}{10}$$

$$= 14.649$$

$$SSxy = \Sigma XY - \frac{(\Sigma X)(\Sigma Y)}{n}$$

$$= 2{,}919.9 - \frac{(204)(142.1)}{10}$$

$$= 21.06$$

Then

$$b_1 = \frac{SSxy}{SSx}$$

$$= \frac{21.06}{32.4}$$

$$= 0.65$$

$$b_0 = \bar{Y} - b_1\bar{X}$$

$$= 14.21 - (0.65)(20.4)$$

$$= 0.95$$

$$\hat{Y} = 0.95 + 0.65X$$

The regression model shows that as sales increase by 1 unit, or \$1,000,000, costs will go up by 0.65 hundred thousand dollars, or \$65,000. The constant of 0.95 indicates that if the firm shuts down and sales are zero, costs will equal \$95,000. Those of you with a background in economics or finance may recognize the 0.95 hundred thousand dollars as the amount of fixed costs.

2. **Iacocca Examines the Closeness of the Relationship** Iacocca is also interested in determining the strength of the relationship between sales and costs.

$$r^2 = \frac{(SSxy)^2}{(SSx)(SSy)}$$

$$= \frac{(21.06)^2}{(32.4)(14.649)}$$

$$= 0.93$$

The coefficient of determination suggests that there is a strong positive correlation between costs and sales. In fact, 93 percent of the change in costs is explained by a change in sales.

3. **A Keynesian Consumption Function** In his famous 1936 book, *A General Theory of Employment, Interest and Money,* the noted British economist John Maynard Keynes proposed a theoretical relationship between income and personal consumption expenditures. Keynes argued that as income went up, consumption would rise by a smaller amount. This theoretical relationship has been empirically tested many times since 1936.

Milton Friedman, former professor of economics at the University of Chicago, and winner of the Nobel Prize in economics, collected extensive data on income and consumption in the United States over a long period of time. Shown here are 10 observations on annual levels of consumption and income used by Friedman in his study. Using these data, derive a consumption function under the assumption that there exists a linear relationship between consumption and income. Figures are in billions of current dollars.

Year	Income	Consumption
1950	284.8	191.0
1951	328.4	206.3
1952	345.5	216.7
1953	364.6	230.0
1954	364.8	236.5
1955	398.0	254.4
1956	419.2	266.7
1957	441.1	281.4
1958	447.3	290.1
1959	483.7	311.2

a. Since consumption depends on income, consumption is the Y, or dependent, variable. Friedman sought a consumption function in the form

$$\hat{C} = b_0 + b_1 I$$

where C is consumption and I is income.

$$\Sigma X = 3{,}877.4 \qquad \Sigma XY = 984{,}615.32 \qquad \Sigma Y^2 = 630{,}869.49$$

$$\Sigma Y = 2{,}484.3 \qquad \Sigma X^2 = 1{,}537{,}084.88$$

$$SSx = \Sigma X^2 - \frac{(\Sigma X)^2}{n}$$

$$= 1{,}537{,}084.88 - \frac{(3{,}877.4)^2}{10}$$

$$= 33{,}661.804$$

$$SSy = \Sigma Y^2 - \frac{(\Sigma Y)^2}{n}$$

$$= 630{,}869.49 - \frac{(2{,}484.3)^2}{10}$$

$$= 13{,}694.841$$

$$SSxy = \Sigma XY - \frac{(\Sigma X)(\Sigma Y)}{n}$$

$$= 984,615.32 - \frac{(3,877.4)(2,484.3)}{10}$$

$$= 21,352.838$$

$$b_1 = \frac{SSxy}{SSx}$$

$$= \frac{21,352.838}{33,661.804}$$

$$= 0.634$$

$$b_0 = \bar{Y} - b_1\bar{X}$$

$$= 248.43 - (0.634)(387.74)$$

$$= 2.603$$

Therefore,

$$\hat{C} = 2.603 + 0.63I$$

These are not the same values Friedman found because we used only a very small portion of his data set. However, our model bears out Keynes's theory. The coefficient of 0.63 shows that for every $1 (or $1,000,000,000) increase in income, consumption will increase by 63 cents (or $630,000,000). Those of you who have taken an introductory macroeconomics course will recognize 0.63 as marginal propensity to consume. The constant, or intercept term, of 2.603 is the level of consumption when income is zero. Economists often argue that this economic interpretation of the intercept term is invalid since an economic system will always generate positive income. The consumption function is therefore often graphed without the intercept, as in the figure. If $I = 345.5$, as in 1952, our model predicts

$$\hat{C} = 2.603 + 0.63(345.5) = 220.26$$

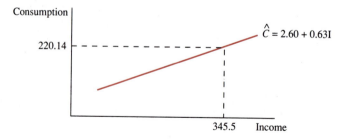

Consumption was actually 216.7 in 1952, resulting in an error of $3.56 billion.

b. The coefficient of determination is

$$r^2 = \frac{(SSxy)^2}{(SSx)(SSy)}$$

$$= \frac{(21{,}352.838)^2}{(33{,}661.804)(13{,}694.841)}$$

$$= 0.989$$

A change in income explains over 98 percent of the change in consumption. Information concerning the values of b_0, b_1, and r^2 are vital to those who advise Congress and the president on matters of national economics policy.

4. **Federal Reserve Actions to Stem Inflation** After approximately six years of continued expansion, the U.S. economy began to show signs of inflationary pressures in the fall of 1988. An article in a September issue of *The Wall Street Journal* described efforts by the Federal Reserve Board to cool these inflationary fires. This was to be done by tightening the money supply through a rise in the discount rate commercial banks must pay to borrow from the Fed. In February 1988, Manuel H. Johnson, vice-chairman of the Fed told an audience at a Cato Institute conference that Fed actions regarding the discount rate could be predicted on the basis of the federal funds rate, which is the fee banks charge each other for overnight loans. However, throughout the rest of 1988, Fed watchers argued that the federal funds rate was not serving as an adequate predictor of the changes in the discount rate. The Fed watchers argued that the poor performance of the federal funds rate as a predictor of the discount rate made it difficult for investors trying to predict the interest rate level the Fed would allow.

Shown here are values for the federal funds rate and the discount rate from mid-1987 to mid-1988. Do these data support the charges of the Fed watchers?

Federal Funds Rate (%)	Discount Rate (%)
8.0	7.5
7.5	7.5
7.0	7.0
6.5	6.5
6.0	6.0
6.0	5.5
7.0	5.5
6.0	5.5
7.0	5.5
7.5	5.5
7.0	6.0
7.5	6.5
83.0	74.5

Since Johnson argued that the federal funds rate could explain the behavior of the discount rate, the federal funds rate is seen as the independent variable.

a. The nature of the relationship between the federal funds rate and the discount rate can be examined through regression and correlation analysis.

$$\Sigma X = 83 \qquad \Sigma Y^2 = 469.25$$

$$\Sigma Y = 74.5$$

$$\Sigma XY = 518.5 \qquad \overline{Y} = 6.21$$

$$\Sigma X^2 = 579 \qquad n = 12$$

$$SSx = 4.9166667$$

$$SSy = 6.72917$$

$$SSxy = 3.20833$$

$$b_1 = 0.6525$$

$$b_0 = 1.6949$$

Therefore,

$$\hat{Y} = 1.69 + 0.653X$$

The coefficient of determination is

$$r^2 = \frac{(3.20833)^2}{(4.92)(6.73)}$$

$$= 0.3111$$

$$r = 0.56$$

The Fed watchers are correct in their criticism of the federal funds rate as a predictor of changes in the discount rate. Only 31 percent of changes in the discount rate are explained by changes in the federal funds rate.

b. A measure of goodness-of-fit which reflects the ability of the federal funds rate to predict the discount rate is the standard error of the estimate.
The standard error of the estimate is

$$SSE = SSy - \frac{(SSxy)^2}{SSx}$$

$$= 6.7292 - \frac{(3.208)^2}{4.9166}$$

$$= 4.63033$$

$$MSE = \frac{4.63033}{10}$$

$$= 0.463033$$

$$Se = \sqrt{0.463033}$$

$$= 0.6808$$

Typically, the estimate of the discount rate is in error by 0.68 of a percentage point.

c. A test of the significance of the correlation coefficient would prove useful at this point. Set the level of confidence at 95 percent. With 10 degrees of freedom the critical value for t is therefore ± 2.228.

The hypotheses are

$$H_0: \rho = 0$$

$$H_a: \rho \neq 0$$

Decision Rule

Reject H_0 if $t < -2.228$ or if $t > 2.228$. Do not reject H_0 if $-2.228 < t < 2.228$.

$$t = \frac{r}{S_r}$$

$$= \frac{r}{\sqrt{(1 - r^2)/(n - 2)}}$$

$$= \frac{0.56}{\sqrt{(1 - 0.31)/10}}$$

$$= \frac{0.56}{0.2627}$$

$$= 2.13$$

The null hypothesis cannot be rejected. Despite the sample finding of a positive relationship between federal funds rates and the discount rate, the hypothesis that there is no correlation cannot be rejected. The sample correlation coefficient is not significant at the 5 percent level.

d. A test of the significance of the sample regression coefficient of $b_1 = 0.6525424$ is also wise. The test will be conducted at the 99 percent level. With 10 degrees of freedom the critical t-value is ± 3.169.

The hypotheses are

$$H_0: \beta_1 = 0$$

$$H_a: \beta_1 \neq 0$$

Decision Rule

Reject H_0 if $t < -3.169$ or $t > 3.169$. Do not reject H_0 if $-3.169 < t < 3.169$.

The test requires

$$t = \frac{b_1}{S_{b_1}}$$

where

$$S_{b_1} = \frac{Se}{\sqrt{SSx}}$$

$$= 0.681/\sqrt{4.92} = 0.307$$

$$= \frac{0.652542}{0.307}$$

$$= 2.126$$

The hypothesis that $\beta_1 = 0$ cannot be rejected. The value for b_1 is not significantly different from zero at the 1 percent level. There is little or no confidence in the federal funds rate as a predictor of the discount rate. Investors would be unwise to rely on the federal funds rate as an indicator of what the discount rate and other interest rates will do.

5. **A Further Examination of the Discount Rate** Based on the results of Problem 4, professional bankers and investors can find little comfort in the ability of the federal funds rate to predict the discount rate. Using the regression model to develop a point estimate of the discount rate does not appear wise. To further examine the relationship between these two variables, if any exists, we can calculate interval estimates of the discount rate.

a. People employed in banking and finance would be interested in an interval estimate for the mean value of the discount rate if the federal funds rate was held constant for several months. This is, of course, an interval estimate of the conditional mean of the discount rate:

$$\text{C.I. for } \mu_{y|x} = \hat{Y} \pm tS_Y$$

and requires calculation of the standard error of the conditional mean, S_Y, and $\hat{Y}$ as the point estimator of the discount rate. Since the federal funds rate seemed to move around 7 percent quite often, it is at this rate that the confidence interval will be calculated.

To calculate S_Y and $\hat{Y}$, we have

$$S_Y = Se \sqrt{\frac{1}{n} + \frac{(X - \overline{X})^2}{SSx}}$$

$$= 0.681 \sqrt{\frac{1}{12} + \frac{(7 - 6.9167)^2}{4.92}}$$

$$= 0.1982$$

Also,

$$\hat{Y} = b_0 + b_1 X$$

$$= 1.6949 + 0.6525424(7)$$

$$= 6.2627$$

If the interval is calculated at a 95 percent level of confidence, the critical t-value is $t_{.05, n-2} = \pm 2.228$. We then have

$$\text{C.I. for } \mu_{y|x} = \hat{Y} \pm tS_Y$$

$$= 6.2627 \pm (2.228)(0.1982)$$

$$5.82 < \mu_{y|x} < 6.70$$

Bankers can be 95 percent confident that if the federal funds rate is 7 percent for several months, the mean discount rate they must pay to borrow money from the Fed will fall between 5.82 percent and 6.70 percent. Their plans and policies can be formulated according to this expectation.

b. If a banker wished to make plans for next month, he or she would be interested in what the discount rate might be in that month given that the federal funds rate was 7 percent. The banker would therefore calculate a predictive interval for next month as follows:

$$\text{C.I. for } Y_x = \hat{Y} \pm t s_{y_i}$$

and requires calculation of the standard error of the forecast, S_{y_i}. Assuming a 95 percent level of significance and a federal funds rate of 7 percent, the banker would proceed as follows:

$$S_{y_i} = Se \sqrt{1 + \frac{1}{n} + \frac{(X - \bar{X})^2}{SSx}}$$

$$= 0.70927$$

Since $\hat{Y} = 6.2627$, we have

$$\text{C.I. for } Y_x = 6.2627 \pm (2.228)(0.70927)$$

$$4.68 < Y_x < 7.85$$

The banker could formulate plans for next month's operations on the realization that he or she could be 95 percent confident that if the federal funds rate was 7 percent the discount rate would fall between 4.68 percent and 7.85 percent. This is a wider range than that found for the conditional mean of the discount rate.

It would certainly appear that Johnson's statement concerning the use of the federal funds rate to estimate or predict the discount rate is questionable. The r^2 is rather low, and the tests for significance of ρ and β_1 suggest that the hypotheses $\rho = 0$ and $\beta_1 = 0$ cannot be rejected at any acceptable levels of significance.

In all fairness, it might be argued that the federal funds rate should be lagged one month. That is, the discount rate in any month (time period t) is a function of the federal funds rate for the previous month (time period $t - 1$). This would allow the Fed time to adjust the discount rate to last month's federal funds rate since the Fed cannot respond immediately to changes in the federal funds rate. This is expressed as

$$DR_t = f(FF_{t-1})$$

where *DR* is the discount rate and *FF* is the federal funds rate. This lagged model yields

$$\hat{Y} = 0.6 + 0.8X$$

with $r^2 = 60$ percent and $Se = 0.47$. This represents a major improvement over the naive model, which does not include the lagged variable.

6. **The Effect of Productivity on Real GNP** A recent issue of *Fortune* magazine reported on the relationship between worker productivity and rates of change in the nation's level of output measured in real terms. The message was that the increase in productivity during the 1980s could serve as an explanatory factor for GNP growth. With both productivity growth and changes in GNP measured in percentages, and GNP as the dependent variable, annual data for that time period can be summarized as follows:

$$\Sigma X = 32.5 \qquad \Sigma Y^2 = 483.72$$

$$\Sigma Y = 62.2 \qquad n = 9$$

$$\Sigma XY = 255.4 \qquad \Sigma X^2 = 135.25$$

The model is

$$\hat{Y} = 0.69596273 + 1.721118X$$

indicating that if productivity increased one percentage point, real GNP will increase by 1.72 percent. The r^2 is 0.98407, and $Se = 0.35$.

For the purpose of formulating national tax policy, which some supply-side economists argue has a direct impact on worker productivity, Washington planners tested the significance of both the sample correlation coefficient and the sample regression coefficient. Each proved significant at the 10 percent level.

The same planners then requested a confidence interval for each population coefficient at the 10 percent level:

$$\text{C.I. for } \beta_1 = b_1 \pm tS_{b_1}$$

$$S_{b_1} = \frac{Se}{\sqrt{SS_x}} = 0.08275$$

$$\text{C.I. for } \beta_1 = 1.72 \pm (1.895)(0.08275)$$

$$1.56 < \beta_1 < 1.88$$

The planners can then base the formulation of national tax policy on the condition that they can be 90 percent certain that the population regression coefficient is between 1.56 and 1.88.

12.15   WHAT YOU SHOULD HAVE LEARNED FROM THIS CHAPTER

This chapter should provide you with a thorough perception of what simple linear regression is and how it can be used to make business decisions. The material in this chapter is intended to instill a proficiency in the application of OLS techniques and the principles surrounding correlations procedures. You should be able to calculate and interpret the regression model and the coefficient of determination. You should also have a sound understanding of the nature of the normal distribution of Y-values, as well as the basic assumptions that support OLS. It is also essential to possess a firm understanding of the importance of the standard error of the estimate before continuing. The problems, cases, and exercises that follow will further demonstrate the many uses and applications of regression and correlation.

In the next chapter we will examine several additional features of regression and correlation analysis, which will strengthen our ability to use OLS in solving common business problems. Tests designed to measure the significance of the regression model and the determination of confidence intervals associated with the model are explored.

12.16   COMPUTER APPLICATIONS

The advent of the modern computer has made regression and correlation much easier and more applicable in solving many of the problems commonly encountered in business situations. Without the computer the calculations required by regression and correlation analysis would likely prevent their use in many cases. This section examines the manner in which the various computer packages can be used to execute regression and correlation analysis.

Using the data for the relationship between sales and advertising for Kamikaze as the example, the SAS program calling for the regression and correlation results is

SAS Input

```
Data;
Input Adv Pass;
Cards;
10 15
12 17
 8 13
17 23
|  |
|  |
|  |
rest of data lines go here
|  |
|  |
10 15
12 16
Proc Reg;
  Model Pass = Adv;
```

As is usually the case, the variables are specified in the INPUT statement. The PROC REG; statement calls for the results of the regression package. The MODEL PASS = ADV; statement specifies the variables in the regression model. The dependent variable must be specified first, followed by an equal sign and the independent variable. The statement PROC GLM (for general linear model) can be used in place of PROC REG. The SAS output for this program is in the following display.

SAS Output

Dependent Variable: Pass

Source	DF	Sums of Squares	Mean Square	E Value
Model	1	161.044	161.044	161.04
Error	13	10.689	.822	PR > F
Corrected Total	14			0.0000

R-Square
0.93776

Parameter	Estimate	T for Ho: Parameter = 0	PR > |T|	Std Error of Estimate
Intercept	4.386	4.425	.0007	.99128
Adv	1.081	13.995	.0000	.07726

The coefficient and intercept values are shown, along with the coefficients of determination and correlation. In addition, the standard error and t-statistic are reported. The probability value in the bottom right-hand corner of the output statement of PR > |T| is 0.0000 for the independent variable, which tells us that the probability that the t-value of 13.995 has occurred by chance is virtually zero. Thus, the model is significant at the 1 percent level. The section on analysis of variance, as well as some of the other reported statistics, are discussed in other chapters.

The corresponding SPSS-PC program is also shown.

SPSS-PC Input

```
Data List Free / Adv Pass.
Begin Data.
10 15
12 17
 8 13
rest of data
10 15
12 16
End Data.
Regression Variables = Adv Pass/ Dependent = Pass
    /Method = Enter.
```

The printout provides much the same information as the SAS printout and is therefore not repeated here.

The Minitab program for a regression model is

Minitab Input

```
MTB> READ C1 AND C2
DATA> 10 15
DATA> 12 17
DATA>  8 13
DATA> |  |
      |  |
rest of data
      |  |
DATA> 12 16
DATA> END
NAME C1 = 'ADV' C2 = 'PASS'
MTB> REGRESS 'PASS' ON 1 PREDICTOR 'ADV'
```

The resulting Minitab output is

```
The regression equation is
PASS = 4.39 + 1.08 ADV
Predictor       Coef      Stdev     t-ratio        P
Constant      4.3863     0.9913        4.42    0.001
ADV          1.08132    0.07726       13.99    0.000
s = 0.9068     R-sq = 93.8%     R-sq(adj) = 93.3%
Analysis of Variance
SOURCE        DF         SS          MS        F       P
Regression    1       161.04      161.04   195.86   0.000
Error        13        10.69        0.82
Total        14       171.73
Unusual Observations
Obs.    ADV     PASS      Fit Stdev.Fit   Residual   St.Resid
 10    10.0   17.000   15.199     0.302      1.801      2.11R
R denotes an obs. with a large st. resid.
MTB >
```

Since the results are so similar to those obtained from the other packages, they should be self-explanatory.

LIST OF SYMBOLS AND TERMS

Y	Generally the dependent variable in a regression statement
X	Generally the independent variable in a regression statement
$\hat{Y}$	The estimated value for Y based on our regression model
Se	The standard error of the estimate, which measures the average amount by which the actual observations for the dependent variable vary from the regression line
$\mu_{y\|x}$	The conditional mean, which is the mean of the population of all Y-values given some specific X-value
S_Y	The standard error of the conditional mean
S_{y_i}	The standard error of the forecast
r^2	The coefficient of determination
r	The correlation coefficient
k^2	The coefficient of nondetermination
ρ	The population correlation coefficient
S_r	The standard error of the sampling distribution of the correlation coefficient
S_{b_1}	The standard error of the regression coefficient b

LIST OF FORMULAS

$$Y = b_0 + b_1 X \tag{12.3}$$

Formula for straight line which represents the linear regression model.

$$SSx = \Sigma X^2 - \frac{(\Sigma X)^2}{n} \qquad (12.8)$$

Sum of squares for X.

$$SSy = \Sigma Y^2 - \frac{(\Sigma Y)^2}{n} \qquad (12.9)$$

Sum of squares for Y.

$$SSxy = \Sigma XY - \frac{(\Sigma X)(\Sigma Y)}{n} \qquad (12.10)$$

Cross-products for X and Y.

$$b_1 = \frac{SSxy}{SSx} \qquad (12.11)$$

Computes the slope of the regression line.

$$b_0 = \overline{Y} - b_1\overline{X} \qquad (12.12)$$

Computes the intercept.

$$Se = \sqrt{\frac{\Sigma(Y_i - \hat{Y})^2}{n-2}} \qquad (12.13)$$

The standard error of the estimate measures the dispersion of the observations around the regression line. This formula is used to conceptually display the standard error of the estimate. Not used in the calculation of Se.

$$SSE = SSy - \frac{(SSxy)^2}{SSx} \qquad (12.14)$$

Error sum of squares.

$$MSE = \frac{SSE}{n-2} \qquad (12.15)$$

Mean square error.

$$Se = \sqrt{MSE} \qquad (12.16)$$

Standard error of the estimate.

$$r^2 = \frac{(SSxy)^2}{(SSx)(SSy)} \qquad (12.22)$$

The coefficient of determination measures the portion of the change in Y that is explained by a change in X.

$$S_Y = Se\sqrt{\frac{1}{n} + \frac{(X_i - \overline{X})^2}{SSx}} \qquad (12.24)$$

Used to calculate the standard error of the conditional mean.

$$\text{C.I. for } \mu_{y|x} = \hat{Y} \pm tS_Y \qquad (12.25)$$

Used to calculate the confidence interval for the conditional mean.

$$S_{y_i} = Se \sqrt{1 + \frac{1}{n} + \frac{(X_i - \overline{X})^2}{SSx}} \qquad (12.26)$$

Used to calculate the standard error of the forecast.

$$\text{C.I. for } Y_x = \hat{Y} \pm tS_{y_i} \qquad (12.27)$$

Used to calculate the predictive interval for a single value of Y given X.

$$t = \frac{r}{S_r} \qquad (12.28)$$

Used to conduct a hypothesis test about the population correlation coefficient.

$$S_r = \sqrt{\frac{1 - r^2}{n - 2}} \qquad (12.29)$$

The standard error of the sampling distribution of r measures the variation in r from one sample to the next.

$$t = \frac{b}{S_{b_1}} \qquad (12.30)$$

Used to test the hypothesis for the population regression coefficient.

$$S_{b_1} = \frac{Se}{\sqrt{SSx}} \qquad (12.31)$$

The standard error of the regression coefficient measures the variation in the coefficient from one sample to the next.

$$\text{C.I. for } \beta_1 = b_1 \pm tS_{b_1} \qquad (12.32)$$

Used to calculate the confidence interval for the population regression coefficient.

$$SSR = \frac{(SSxy)^2}{SSx} \qquad (12.33)$$

The regression sum of squares is used in various regression calculations.

CHAPTER EXERCISES

YOU MAKE THE DECISION

1. The CEO for the Acme Trucking Company is concerned about recent trends in business performance. Profits are falling, and the stockholders are calling for his resignation. He comes to you for some answers regarding this predicament. You collect data on miles driven by the firm's trucks and resulting revenues the firm earned. The CEO asks if there might be a relationship between these two important variables and to what degree miles driven might explain revenues.

   a. What do you do? How do you respond?

b. The CEO wants to know if your work will allow him to predict future revenues. How could you use your statistical results to provide an estimate of revenues in the near future?

c. Your results include the regression model

$$R\hat{e}v = 23.2 + 523.6MD$$ (where Rev is earned revenues and MD is miles driven by the firm's trucks)

with a correlation coefficient of 0.78. How would you interpret these results?

d. Your CEO feels confident in your statistical study given the fact that, he concludes, *MD* causes 78 percent of the change in *Rev*. How do you respond?

e. You tell the CEO that the regression line you have computed is a mean line and that it is the line of best fit. Having no knowledge of statistical analysis, he asks you to explain. What do you tell him?

CONCEPTUAL QUESTIONS

2. What is meant by "minimizing the sum of the errors squared" in your model for the trucking firm in Problem 1?

3. In what way might autocorrelation and heteroscedasticity present a problem in your regression model?

4. What is the difference between regression and correlation?

5. Identify the dependent and independent variables in each case:
    a. time spent working on a term paper and the grade received.
    b. height of a son and height of his father.
    c. a woman's age and the cost of her life insurance.
    d. price of a product and the number of units purchased by an individual.
    e. demand for a product and the number of consumers in the market.

PROBLEMS

6. The CEO for the Rank Cheese Company in Pine Junction, Arkansas, collected data on production levels and costs. As his highly paid statistician, you must use these data to develop a model that can predict costs of production.

Output (100's pounds)	Cost ($100's)
10	11
12	15
9	11
7	6
15	17
17	21
14	12
11	13
10	12
9	11

a. Identify the dependent and independent variables.
b. Plot a scatter diagram. Does there appear to be a relationship?
c. Develop the regression model, using OLS.
d. Plot the regression line on the scatter diagram.
e. Predict costs if Rank produces 1,100 pounds of Mozzarella. How does your prediction compare with the actual cost when output was 1,100 pounds? What accounts for the difference? How might you attempt to improve your prediction?

7. Using the data from Rank Cheese Company in Problem 6, calculate and interpret the
a. coefficient of determination.
b. correlation coefficient.

8. Rank Cheese had the following revenues for the 10 observations from Problem 6:

Revenues ($100's)

12
17
11
9
21
22
10
13
15
12

a. Develop a regression model with revenues as the dependent variable and output as the independent variable.
b. Predict profits if output is 1,100 pounds.

9. As chairman of the Federal Reserve System, Alan Greenspan has the responsibility of controlling the nation's money supply. His actions impact directly on mortgage rates people must pay to buy houses. In 1989, his staff was instructed to examine the effect of mortgage rates on the number of houses sold. A regional center in Lexington, Kentucky, gathering data for the study provided the information shown here. Housing units are in hundreds.

Year	Housing Units Sold	Mortgage Rate
1971	20	12.10
1974	17	13.50
1976	13	14.95
1978	14	13.75
1980	15	12.95
1982	14	12.50
1984	15	10.10
1986	16	9.82
1988	17	9.50

a. Determine the dependent and independent variables.
b. Assuming a linear relationship exists between these two variables, construct the regression model.

   c. Interpret the constant and the coefficient.

   d. What would be the level of units sold if the mortgage rate was 11.5 percent?

   e. What would happen to the number of units if the rate increased by 2 percentage points?

10. Compute and interpret the standard error of the estimate for the previous problem.

11. Data for the consumption of beef products as reported by the agricultural division at Florida State University are shown for 10 Florida counties. Figures are for May 1988 and are on a per-capita basis.

County	Consumption (pounds)	Price (per pound)
Dade	6.5	3.19
Taylor	6.7	2.99
Broward	6.4	3.22
Leon	6.4	3.34
Duval	6.9	2.85
Alachua	7.0	2.73
Dixie	6.5	3.04
Okaloosa	6.5	3.09
Manatee	6.3	2.88
Orange	6.4	2.91

The governor of Florida requests that state economists in Tallahassee estimate the linear demand curve for beef products.

   a. Which is the dependent variable? (*Hint:* A demand curve can be expressed with either price (P) or quantity (Q) in the dependent role. However, when, as is this case, the analysis seems to view the issue from the standpoint of the consumer rather than the producer, it is customary to argue that Q is a function of P.)

   b. Estimate the linear demand curve, using OLS.

   c. Interpret the results.

   d. What economic principle dictates that the regression coefficient should carry a negative sign?

12. Calculate the coefficients of determination and correlation for the previous problem. Interpret the results.

13. What accounts for that portion of change in quantity not explained by a change in price?

14. Calculate and interpret the standard error of the estimate for Problem 11.

15. Test the significance of the regression coefficient for Problem 11 at the 5 percent level. Interpret your results.

16. Test the significance of the sample correlation coefficient for Problem 11 at the 10 percent level. Interpret your results.

17. William Webster, former director of the Central Intelligence Agency, instructed his staff to make a study of Soviet military expenditures and the volumes of loans to the Soviet Union through Western capital markets. An article in an August 1988 edition of *Business Week* seemed to suggest such loans were facilitating Soviet military efforts. Frank Carlucci, secretary of defense at that time, argues that the article was correct in its implications regarding the strong positive relationship between expenditures and loans received by the Soviet Union. These data reflect 48 months of observations on loans (X) and military

expenditures (Y). The values are for billions of dollars. Based on these data, do regression and correlation analysis support Carlucci's fears?

$$\Sigma X = 204 \qquad \Sigma X^2 = 3012$$

$$\Sigma Y = 512 \qquad \Sigma Y^2 = 5,463.15$$

$$\Sigma XY = 2,205 \qquad n = 48$$

18. It was recently reported in *Financial Weekly* that E. F. Hutton was interested in the relationship between a person's income and the amount of money they had invested in the stock market. Fifty individuals were randomly selected on the presumption that an individual's investments in the stock market are influenced by his or her income. Using regression and correlation analysis, do these data suggest such a relationship? Data are in thousands of dollars.

   a. Identify the dependent and independent variables.
   b. Calculate and interpret the results of the regression model and the value for r^2.
   c. Are the data cross-sectional or time-series?

$$\Sigma X = 9,385 \qquad \Sigma X^2 = 3,025,553$$

$$\Sigma Y = 988.1 \qquad \Sigma Y^2 = 32,224.51$$

$$\Sigma XY = 303,471.3$$

19. Coaches in the National Football League are often concerned about the best way to improve their won-lost record. Some coaches insist that while offense may sell tickets, it's defense that wins games. Others feel that the best way to win is to emphasize the offense. In an effort to test these theories, Sam Wyche, head coach of the Cincinnati Bengals, examined the relationship between the number of wins and the number of points scored. He argued that the teams that have high-powered offenses and score many points will win more games regardless of how effective their defenses are. Data were collected for all 14 teams in the AFC in 1988. Identify the dependent and independent variables. Use regression and correlation to determine if Wyche is right.

Team	Wins	Points Scored
Cleveland	10	390
Denver	10	379
Seattle	9	371
Miami	8	362
Houston	9	345
N.Y. Jets	6	334
New England	8	320
L.A. Raiders	5	301
Indianapolis	9	300
Cincinnati	4	285
Pittsburg	8	285
Kansas City	4	273
Buffalo	7	270
San Diego	8	253

20. A principal theory in finance holds that as bond yields rise, investors take funds out of the stock market, causing it to fall, and buy debt securities (bonds). Weekly data, which use the federal funds as a proxy for bond yields, as reported by the Commerce Department in the winter of 1988 are shown.

Week	Dow Jones	Federal Funds Rate (%)
1	2,050	6.8
2	2,010	6.95
3	1,983	7.3
4	2,038	7.5
5	1,995	7.7
6	1,955	7.7
7	1,878	8.3
8	1,802	8.7

a. Assuming the federal funds rate impacts on the stock market, identify the dependent variable.

b. Do these data tend to corroborate that financial theory? In what manner and to what extent would interest rates serve as a forecasting tool for the stock market?

21. Mildred Megabucks invests in the stock market only if it is at least 30 points higher than it was last week. If the Federal Reserve Board is expecting a federal funds rate of 8.4 in week 9, will Mildred invest?

22. A popular financial theory holds that there is a direct relationship between the risk of an investment and the return it promises. A stock's risk is measured by its β-value. Shown here are the returns and β-values for 12 fictitious stocks suggested by the investment firm of Guess & Pickum. Do these data seem to support this financial theory of a direct relationship?

Stock	Return (%)	β-Value
1	5.4	1.5
2	8.9	1.9
3	2.3	1.0
4	1.5	0.5
5	3.7	1.5
6	8.2	1.8
7	5.3	1.3
8	0.5	-0.5
9	1.3	0.5
10	5.9	1.8
11	6.8	1.9
12	7.2	1.9

Investors typically view return as a function of risk. Use an interpretation of both the regression coefficient and the coefficient of correlation in your response.

23. Calculate and interpret the standard error of the estimate for Problem 22.

24. Referring to Problem 22, test the significance at the 5 percent level of the sample

a. regression coefficient.

b. correlation coefficient.

25. The *Harvard Business Review* cited a training program by Rubbermaid designed to increase worker productivity. Fifty workers spent various amounts of time in the training program, and their subsequent changes in productivity were measured. Stanley Gault, CEO for Rubbermaid, wished to examine the benefits of the training in terms of increased productivity to determine if the training costs were justified. The data shown are for time in training, measured in hours, and productivity changes, expressed in units of output per hour. Help Stanley evaluate the training program. Interpret your findings.

Sum of hours $(H) = 789$
Sum of changes in productivity $(P) = 366$
$\Sigma HP = 5,976$
$\Sigma H^2 = 14,695$
$\Sigma P^2 = 3,522$

26. The registrar's office at Podunk University used an entrance examination to estimate students' GPAs. A sample of the records of 10 students provided these results.

GPAs	Entrance Exam Score
2.20	50
2.90	30
3.30	85
3.10	92
3.40	78
2.19	45
0.09	13
3.10	40
2.00	50
3.00	90

a. If a student scored 50 on the test, what would be his or her estimated GPA?
b. Calculate and interpret the coefficients of determination and correlation.

27. In Problem 26, according to the regression model, what would be the average GPA of many students who all happen to score a 50 on the entrance exam?

28. Economic theory holds that as interest rates go down firms are able to invest more in capital equipment. Monthly figures for the interest rate and levels of new capital investment in billions of dollars are shown in the table.

Month	Interest Rate	Capital Investment
January	10.0	10
February	9.5	11
March	9.0	12
July	7.5	16
August	7.0	17
September	6.5	18
October	6.0	19
November	5.5	20
December	5.0	21

    a. Calculate the regression model.

    b. Plot the data and the regression line. Does the model support the theory that lower interest rates are associated with higher levels of investment?

    c. Calculate and plot the residuals. Does there appear to be any autocorrelation?

29. Calculate and interpret the standard error of the estimate for Problem 26.

30. Of the two sets of data in Problems 26 and 28, which requires the larger interval necessary to encompass 95.5 percent of all the data points? How large is each interval?

31. Thirty customers for Neiman-Marcus in Dallas were polled regarding the number of members in their immediate family and the dollar purchases per visit. The store wanted to know if family size might explain expenditures.

    Summation of family members $(F) = 80$

    Summation of purchase $(P) = \$1,698$

    $\Sigma FP = 3,464$

    $\Sigma F^2 = 296$

    $\Sigma P^2 = 6,366,916$

    a. Determine the dependent variable.

    b. Calculate the regression model.

    c. Interpret the parameter estimates.

    d. What is the strength of the relationship?

32. In the effort to evaluate the educational efforts of our university system, the U.S. Department of Education asked deans of MBA programs to rate on a scale of 10 to 80 the quality of education received at several of the nation's top schools. The results were reported in the *Chronicle of Higher Education.* Data were also collected on the average beginning salary for graduates of each school. Fifteen of these observations are shown here. Do the data suggest that a school's reputation has any relationship to the beginning salaries of its graduates?

School	Rating	Salary (in 1,000's)
1	25	55
2	45	100
3	47	110
4	31	65
5	33	67.5
6	52	103
7	59	120
8	43	89
9	28	60
10	61	125
11	49	100
12	20	40
13	73	150
14	69	140
15	79	160

    a. Assuming firms extend salary offers on the basis of a school's reputation, identify the dependent variable.

    b. Compute and interpret the regression equation.

    c. Compute and interpret the coefficient of determination and standard error of the estimates.

    d. Compute a confidence interval for the mean salary of many graduates from MBA schools with a rating of 50. Set $\alpha = 10$ percent.

    e. Compute a confidence interval for the salary of one graduate from a school with a 50 rating. Set $\alpha = 10$ percent.

    f. Why is your answer to part (d) narrower than the answer you got in part (e)?

33. Referring to Problem 32, set α at 10 percent and develop a confidence interval for the population regression coefficient.

34. Referring to Problem 32, set α at 5 percent and test the significance of the sample
    a. correlation coefficient.
    b. regression coefficient.

35. One hundred students are examined to determine if their entrance exam scores are good predictors of their GPAs. Results were recorded as

$$\Sigma X = 522 \qquad \Sigma XY = 17{,}325$$

$$\Sigma Y = 326 \qquad \Sigma X^2 = 28{,}854$$

$$\Sigma Y^2 = 10{,}781$$

Test scores ranged from 0 to 10, and the GPA is based on a 5-point system. The model is $\hat{Y} = 0.138831 + 0.5979251X$ and $r^2 = 0.961$.

    a. The dean of a local state university wishes to estimate the mean GPA of many students who score a 6.5 on the entrance exam. He wants to be 99 percent confident of that interval.

    b. A father of one prospective student wishes to estimate the GPA for his son who scored a 6.5 on the exam. He also wants a 99 percent confidence interval.

    c. Why is there a difference between the answers you got in parts (a) and (b)?

36. Emergency service for certain rural areas of Ohio is often a problem, especially during the winter months. The chief of the Danville Township Fire Department is concerned about response time to emergency calls. He orders an investigation to determine if distance to the call, measured in miles, can explain response time, measured in minutes. Based on 37 emergency runs, the following data were compiled.

$$\Sigma X = 234 \qquad \Sigma X^2 = 1{,}796$$

$$\Sigma Y = 831 \qquad \Sigma Y^2 = 20{,}037$$

$$\Sigma XY = 5{,}890$$

    a. What is the average response time to a call 8 miles from the fire station?

    b. How dependable is that estimate, based on the extent of the dispersion of the data points around the regression line?

37. Referring to Problem 36, at the 90 percent level of confidence what can you say about the significance of the sample
    a. regression coefficient.
    b. correlation coefficient.

38. Referring to Problem 36, with 90 percent confidence, what time interval would you predict for a call from Zeke Zipple, who lives 10 miles from the station?

39. In reference to Problem 36, with 95 percent confidence, what is the average time interval that you would predict for several calls 10 miles from the station?

40. Using the data from Problem 36, the fire chief is interested in a 95 percent confidence interval estimate of the population regression coefficient. Interpret your results for the chief.

41. Manufacturers are always trying to improve the efficiency rating of their employees. A recent report in the *Journal of Midwest Marketing* detailed the efforts of one company to improve employee performance through additional on-the-job training. Forty employees were given additional hours of OJT and the resulting net changes in their efficiency rating (as measured in efficiency points) were recorded. The results are

$$\Sigma X = 124.5 \qquad \Sigma X^2 = 475.75$$

$$\Sigma Y = 352.8 \qquad \Sigma Y^2 = 3,384$$

$$\Sigma XY = 1,246.4$$

   a. Identify the dependent variable.
   b. Provide a point estimate of the net change in efficiency for someone who spent 10 hours in OJT. Interpret your answer.

42. Referring to Problem 41, the manager of the company plans to provide all his employees with 10 hours of additional OJT if he can be 90 percent sure that it would increase efficiency rating by at least 30 points. Based on these sample results, should he proceed with his plans?

43. The manager in Problem 41 must prove to his boss that the relationship between OJT and improved performance does exist. Despite these sample results, the boss is skeptical. The manager points to the coefficient of correlation as proof of the training's benefit. However, his boss feels that this is just an aberration of the sample and that the relationship is not that strong in general. How might the manager support his defense of the OJT plan, based on the value of the sample correlation coefficient, keeping in mind that the boss is quite skeptical?

44. Upper management in Problem 41 still needs a little convincing. There is some question about the meaning of the sample regression coefficient and how it might be used to examine the effect of OJT on all the company's employees, not just the 40 included in the sample.
   a. Provide the interpretation management seeks.
   b. Provide the generalizations to the population as a whole that you feel are warranted by the sample. What statistical procedures are applicable? Set α equal to 10 percent.

45. Referring to Problem 41, the manager states in his report that "all the tests performed so far prove that OJT will cause workers to display improved efficiency ratings." Comment on his report.

46. The Love-Bush test, developed in 1968 to measure employee job satisfaction, was given to 50 employees at a food processing plant in Kansas City. The highest possible score on the test is 70, the lowest is 10. Management's intent was to determine if workers with a higher score on the test missed fewer workdays. They felt that scores on the test could explain absenteeism. Data on the 50 workers measuring workdays missed per year and raw test scores revealed

$$\Sigma X = 2,337 \qquad \Sigma XY = 52,217$$

$$\Sigma Y = 1,219 \qquad \Sigma X^2 = 119,117$$

$$\Sigma Y^2 = 34,631$$

Does it appear that an explanatory relationship exists?

47. Calculate and interpret the correlation coefficient from Problem 46.
48. Does the correlation coefficient prove significant at the 1 percent level from Problem 46?
49. Referring to Problem 46, what is the expected number of days absent if the score is 50?
50. Interpret the regression model from Problem 46.
51. How accurate does the model in Problem 46 seem to be as measured by the standard deviation of the errors around the regression line? Interpret your response.
52. The *Harvard Business Review* discussed the efforts by a trucking firm to reduce delivery time by requiring employees to study city maps and learn the road system. Study time and delivery time were both measured in hours. Fifteen employees were surveyed regarding the time they studied the map and the elapsed time of their last delivery. The results are

$$\Sigma X = 36.4 \qquad \Sigma X^2 = 90.04$$

$$\Sigma Y = 22.6 \qquad \Sigma Y^2 = 41.78$$

$$\Sigma XY = 51.37$$

   a. Is the dependent variable study time or delivery time? Explain.
   b. Compute the regression mode.
   c. Compute and interpret the correlation coefficient.

53. Based on 5 percent significance tests from the previous problem of the sample correlation and regression coefficients, what conclusion can you draw about the wisdom of continuing to require employees to study city street maps?

EMPIRICAL EXERCISES

54. *a.* Identify any two variables which you feel might be related and which pertain to your fellow students, for example, their GPA and the number of hours they normally spend studying each week.
   b. Collect these data for 10 to 20 students.
   c. Compute the regression equation and r^2.
   d. Interpret the explanatory power of your model.
   e. Estimate your value for Y given some X-value.
   f. Test the significance of the regression coefficient at the 1 percent level.
55. *a.* Cite two economic variables which economic theory tells us are related in a dependent manner (e.g., money supply and inflation rate, consumption and income).
   b. Identify which is the dependent variable and which is the independent variable.
   c. Using the *Survey of Current Business, The Federal Reserve Bulletin,* or some other source of economic data, collect 10 to 20 observation points.
   d. Plot a scatter diagram. Does there seem to be a relationship?
   e. Calculate the regression equation and r^2.
   f. Interpret your results.
   g. State clearly your conclusion regarding the validity of the economic theory which you cited in collecting your original data set.

CASE APPLICATIONS

56. John Wood works as a ranger for the Texas state police force. Lately he has noticed an alarming trend toward higher recidivism rates (repeat offenses) by criminals in several southwestern counties in Texas. Law enforcement agencies are concerned about the

escalating crime rates, and there is a growing public outcry to stem the rising tide of social disorder. Ranger Wood has been charged with the responsibility of identifying a method of predicting crime rates in anticipation of corrective action which must be taken by the Texas police force. He feels that he must therefore isolate a predictive variable which might explain crime patterns. After much consideration he finally settles on county expenditures for crime abatement, feeling that there might be a relationship between crime rates and the amount of money spent to control lawlessness. Ranger Wood therefore randomly selects 10 counties in southwest Texas and obtains monthly data for the most recent month available on the number of serious crimes in each county and the amount of money spent by the county to combat crime. The results were

County	Expenditures (1,000's)	Crimes
Maverick	10	44
Crockett	12	41
Pecos	9	47
El Paso	20	21
Loving	15	25
Jeff Davis	17	20
Midland	15	29
Coke	9	50
Dawson	7	49
Yoakum	12	47

Does it appear that Ranger Wood has uncovered a method of predicting crime rates? If Pecos County budgets $16,000 next month for law enforcement protection, what is your estimate of the number of criminal acts which might be perpetrated? The Texas legislature would like an interval estimate of county crime rates if they spend $13,000 on crime prevention in a given county. The legislators insist on 99 percent accuracy in that estimation.

COMPUTER EXERCISES

Access the file OUTPUT in your data bank. It consists of 20 observations for the monthly output levels of General Electric for the number of refrigerators produced in their Norfolk, Virginia, plant over most of 1987 and 1988. The data set also includes values for the usage of labor inputs measured in worker-hours for the same time period. Using regression and correlation analysis, determine if the amount of labor used in the production process can explain the level of output for GE. How strong is the relationship between the two variables? What happens to output as the level of labor goes up? Identify and interpret the standard error of the estimate.

CHAPTER THIRTEEN

MULTIPLE REGRESSION AND CORRELATION

Many regression models require the use of more than one independent variable to explain the values that the dependent variable may take. While the previous chapter allowed us to consider only one independent variable, this chapter incorporates other independent variables to aid in the explanation of the dependent variable.

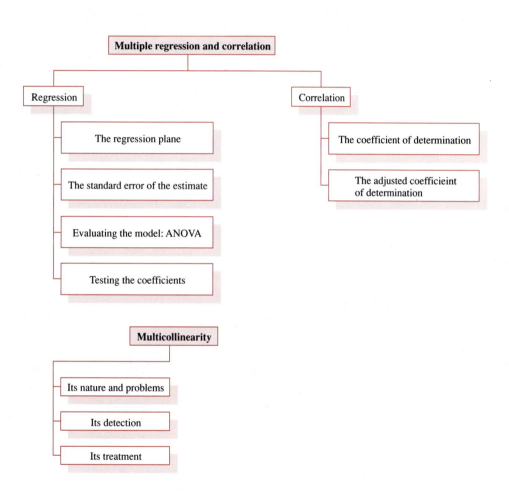

Multiple regression and correlation

Regression

The regression plane

The standard error of the estimate

Evaluating the model: ANOVA

Testing the coefficients

Correlation

The coefficient of determination

The adjusted coefficieint of determination

Multicollinearity

Its nature and problems

Its detection

Its treatment

> ○○○○
> ○○○
> ○○
> ○
> Statistics show that you can
> never go broke taking a profit.

13.1   INTRODUCTION

In the previous chapter we saw how a single independent variable could be used to predict the value for a dependent variable. We closely explored this amazing world of simple regression and correlation, and examined how to identify and measure the statistical relationship between two variables. However, simple regression limits us to only one independent variable. Consider how much more useful and explanatory the model might become if we were allowed to use more independent variables! This is precisely what multiple regression permits us to do. **Multiple regression** involves the use of two or more independent variables. The simple regression model was expressed as

$$Y = b_0 + b_1 X + e \qquad (13.1)$$

The multiple regression model is

$$Y = b_0 + b_1 X_1 + b_2 X_2 + \cdots + b_k X_k + e \qquad (13.2)$$

where k is the number of independent variables and b_i are the coefficients for the variables. In both models, e is the random error component made necessary because not all observations fall directly on the regression line. In this manner, multiple regression is a logical extension of the simple linear model developed in Chapter 12. Our principal objective is the same as with simple regression: We want to calculate b_i as an estimate of the population parameters β_i.

13.2   FORMULATION OF THE MODEL

In the previous chapter, Hop Scotch Airlines developed a simple regression model to help them predict the number of passengers they might expect and to assist in planning day-to-day operations. Their model contained only one explanatory variable, advertising. The regression equation was

$$\hat{Y} = b_0 + b_1 X$$

$$= 4.4 + 1.08 X$$

The regression coefficient of 1.08 told Hop Scotch's management that for every 1-unit ($1,000) increase in advertising, the number of passengers will increase by 1.08 units (1,080 passengers). By calculating the coefficient of determination of $r^2 = 0.94$, they found that their model explains 94 percent of the change in the number of passengers who bravely fly with Hop Scotch.

Soon after developing their model, Hop Scotch hires Ace Rickenbacker as a management consultant. Ace is to serve as a marketing and financial specialist in the effort to increase Hop Scotch's revenue. His first task is to expand the regression model, used to predict passengers, to include variables other than advertising. Ace must therefore identify other variables that might explain changes in the number of passengers. As possible candidates, Ace considers such variables as the prices of train and bus tickets, consumers' income, population, and a host of other logical alternatives. To simplify our discussion, we assume that Ace begins by adding only one variable to the model. However, the analysis can be extended to include any number of independent variables. Ace recalls that a basic premise behind the theory of demand, as preached by economists, states that income is a primary determinant of consumers' demand. He therefore feels that by incorporating a measure of consumer income, he can improve on Hop Scotch's regression model. Ace therefore settles on national income as a second possible explanatory variable. (National income per capita would likely be a much better variable. However, for the purpose of illustration and variety in our variables, we will assume Ace chooses total national income as his second variable.) His model therefore becomes

$$Y = \alpha + \beta_1 X_1 + \beta_2 X_2 + \varepsilon \qquad (13.3)$$

where Y is the number of passengers measured in units of 1,000
         X_1 is Hop Scotch's advertising expenditures measured in units of $1,000
         X_2 is national income measured in units of trillions of dollars

The sample regression model is

$$\hat{Y} = b_0 + b_1 X_1 + b_2 X_2 \qquad (13.4)$$

where the coefficients b_1 and b_2 are estimates of β_1 and β_2, respectively. Actually, b_1 and b_2 are called **partial** (or **net**) **regression coefficients** since we are working with a multiple regression model which contains more than one coefficient. However, the term *partial* is often understood given the context of multiple regression, and the expression is shortened to regression coefficient or just coefficient. The coefficients are interpreted much as they were in simple regression. The value b_1 is the amount by which Y will change for every one unit change in X_1 if X_2 is held constant. For every one unit increase in X_2, Y will change by b_2 units if X_1 is held constant.

Multiple regression involves the same assumptions cited in the previous chapter for simple regression, plus two others. The first assumption requires that the number of observations, n, exceed the number of independent variables, k, by at least 2. In multiple regression there are $k + 1$ parameters to be estimated: coefficients for the k independent variables plus the intercept term. Therefore, the degrees of freedom associated with the model are d.f. $= n - (k + 1)$. If we are to retain even one degree of freedom, n must exceed k by at least 2, so that $n - (k + 1)$ is at least 1.

The second assumption involves the relationship between the independent variables. It requires that none of the independent variables be linearly related. For example, if $X_1 = X_2 + X_3$, or perhaps $X_1 = 0.5X_2$, then a linear relationship would exist between two or more independent variables and a serious problem would arise. This problem is **multicollinearity**.

> **Multicollinearity**
> Multicollinearity exists if one of the independent variables is linearly related to any of the others.

Multicollinearity may cause the algebraic signs of the coefficients to be the opposite of what logic may dictate while greatly increasing the standard error of the coefficients. A more thorough discussion of multicollinearity follows later in this chapter.

A.   ACE'S OBJECTIVE

Ace must now devise estimates for β_1 and β_2 by determining values for b_1 and b_2. We know from the chapter on simple regression that the linear relationship between two variables can be expressed by a straight line. However, a mere line will not depict the relationship when more than two variables are involved.

If three variables are involved, as in our case with Ace's regression model, a **regression plane** is used. The presence of more than three variables requires a **hyperplane**, a concept beyond the scope of this text.

> **Regression Plane**
> The coefficients of the two independent variables are represented by the slopes of a regression plane.

Figure 13-1 illustrates a regression plane for Hop Scotch's model. The value for the dependent variable is shown on the single vertical axis. The coefficients are the slopes of the regression plane, and the intercept is shown by β_0.

The values for b_1 and b_2 in the sample regression model are found much like b_1 was found in simple regression. We want estimates of the coefficients in the equations of a plane which will minimize the sum of the squared errors $(Y_i - \hat{Y})^2$. If we

FIGURE 13-1 A Regression Plane for Hop Scotch Airlines

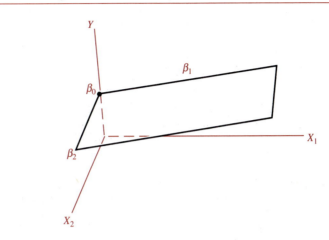

can obtain these values for b_1 and b_2, we will have developed an ordinary least-squares model which provides the best fit for our data.

B. THE NORMAL EQUATIONS

Computation of the sample coefficients is accomplished with the aid of the **normal equations.** The derivation of these normal equations requires differential calculus and is beyond the scope of this text. For those of you with knowledge of calculus, the process involves taking the partial derivatives of the sum of the errors squared with respect to all b_i and setting them equal to zero. However, for the rest of us, we will just happily accept their existence and go on from there.

For a model with two explanatory variables, the normal equations are

$$\Sigma Y - nb_0 + b_1\Sigma X_1 + b_2\Sigma X_2 \qquad (13.5)$$

$$\Sigma X_X Y = b_0\Sigma X_1 + b_1\Sigma X_1^2 + b_2\Sigma X_1 X_2 \qquad (13.6)$$

$$\Sigma X_2 Y = b_0\Sigma X_2 + b_1\Sigma X_1 X_2 + b_2\Sigma X_2^2 \qquad (13.7)$$

The solution of this system of equations requires matrix algebra and a good deal of time-consuming third-grade arithmetic. Therefore, the computations are generally done on a computer, and, for the most part, we follow this practice. However, in each instance, the hand calculations will be demonstrated in order to provide the necessary insight required to fully understand exactly what the statistic is measuring and how it can be interpreted. It is not enough to merely read the computer output. You must understand what calculations are necessary to obtain the statistics. This can be achieved only by examining the mechanics of the equations actually used to compute the statistics. The solution for the regression equation for Hop Scotch's model is shown in the chapter appendix.

C.   ACE'S SOLUTION

Since Ace has chosen national income (NI) as his second explanatory variable, he must now obtain the proper data. Recall that the original data set contained 15 observations for monthly values of (1) numbers of passengers and (2) advertising expenditures. From the *Federal Reserve Bulletin* or similar data source, Ace collects the levels of national income for those same 15 months. The complete data set would then appear as in Table 13-1.

TABLE 13-1   Multiple Regression Data for Hop Scotch Airlines

Observation (months)	Passengers (Y) (in 1,000's)	Advertising (X_1) (in $1,000)	National Income X_2 (in trillions of $)
1	15	10	2.40
2	17	12	2.72
3	13	8	2.08
4	23	17	3.68
5	16	10	2.56
6	21	15	3.36
7	14	10	2.24
8	20	14	3.20
9	24	19	3.84
10	17	10	2.72
11	16	11	2.07
12	18	13	2.33
13	23	16	2.98
14	15	10	1.94
15	16	12	2.17

With these data, Ace is now ready to compute his expanded regression model and to determine if it is an improvement over the simple model. This is the subject of the rest of this chapter.

Using a computer, Ace derives the regression model illustrated by Formula (13.8).

$$\hat{Y} = b_0 + b_1 X_1 + b_2 X_2$$

$$= 3.53 + 0.84\text{Adv} + 1.44NI$$

(13.8)

Formula (13.8) is a regression plane and represents the relationship among the three variables. The printout from an SPSS-PC computer run using the data Ace has collected is shown in Display 13-1. You may wish to examine the hand calculations in the appendix, to gain some perspective into multiple regression.

DISPLAY 13-1   A Regression Run for Hop Scotch Airlines

```
Equation Number 1    Dependent Variable..   PASS

-------------------Variables in the Equation-------------------
Variable            B         SE B       Beta        T    Sig T
NI             1.44097      .73604     .24880    1.958   .0739
ADV             .83966      .14191     .75197    5.917   .0001
(Constant)     3.52840      .99942                3.530   .0041

End Block Number   1   All requested variables entered.
```

Given the interpretation of the partial regression coefficients noted earlier, Ace can see that if advertising is increased by 1 unit and national income is held constant, the number of passengers increases by 0.84 units. Since both variables were expressed in units of 1,000, this means that if Hop Scotch spends $1,000 more (less) on advertising, assuming national income does not change, the number of passengers will increase (decrease) by 840. Furthermore, if national income goes up (down) by 1 unit ($1 trillion) and advertising is held constant, passengers will increase (decrease) by 1.44 units, or 1,440.

13.3   EVALUATING THE MODEL

Now that Ace has his model, he must determine whether it represents an improvement over the simple regression model. Several tests can be used to evaluate a multiple regression model. In this section we (1) calculate and interpret the standard error of the estimate, (2) evaluate the entire model using ANOVA and the F-test, and (3) evaluate the contribution of each independent variables with the use of t-tests. In a separate section, we examine the coefficient of multiple determination as another method of evaluating the model.

A. THE STANDARD ERROR OF THE ESTIMATE

The interpretation of the standard error of the estimate is much the same as it was with the simple regression model. It measures the dispersion of the actual values of Y around those predicted by the model, $\hat{Y}$. It is a measure of the average amount by which the actual observations vary around the regression plane. The standard error of the estimate, Se, is found much as it was in the case of simple regression. The mean square error (MSE) is found by dividing the sum of the squared errors (SSE) by the degrees of freedom.

Since $SSE = \Sigma(Y_i - \hat{Y})^2$, we have

$$MSE = \frac{\Sigma(Y_i - \hat{Y})^2}{n - k - 1} \qquad (13.9)$$

Then

$$Se = \sqrt{\frac{\Sigma(Y_i - \hat{Y})^2}{n - k - 1}} \qquad (13.10)$$

This formula requires that the predicted value of $Y(\hat{Y})$ be calculated for every observation. The error, the difference between this predicted value and the actual Y-value (Y_i), is then squared and summed for all observations. Obviously, such tedious calculations are seldom done by hand. The complete process is demonstrated in the chapter appendix to illustrate what the standard error is and what it measures. If hand calculation is necessary, Formula (13.11) provides an estimate of the standard error.

$$Se = \sqrt{\frac{\Sigma Y^2 - b_0 \Sigma Y - b_1 \Sigma X_1 Y - b_2 \Sigma X_2 Y - \cdots - b_k \Sigma X_k Y}{n - k - 1}} \qquad (13.11)$$

Table 13-2 provides much of the computation necessary for Formula (13.11). Formula (13.11) then yields

$$Se = \sqrt{\frac{4{,}960 - (3.53)(268) - (0.84)(3{,}490) - (1.44)(746.62)}{15 - 2 - 1}}$$

$$= 0.78$$

The work with Formula (13.11) and that found in the appendix provide the insight necessary to understand what the standard error of the estimate is and what it

TABLE 13-2   An Alternative Method for Calculating Se

Pass Y	Adv X_1	NI X_2	Y^2	$X_1 Y$	$X_2 Y$
15	10	2.40	225	150	36.00
17	12	2.72	289	204	46.24
13	8	2.08	169	104	27.04
23	17	3.68	529	391	84.64
16	10	2.56	256	160	40.96
21	15	3.36	441	315	70.56
14	10	2.24	196	140	31.36
20	14	3.20	400	280	64.00
24	19	3.84	576	456	92.16
17	10	2.72	289	170	46.24
16	11	2.07	256	176	33.12
18	13	2.33	324	234	41.94
23	16	2.98	529	368	68.54
15	10	1.94	225	150	29.10
16	12	2.17	256	192	34.72
268			4,960	3,490	746.62

measures. Fortunately, most computer programs are designed to report this important statistic. Display 13-2 is the printout for the SPSS-PC run. The standard error of the estimate is seen to be 0.82167.

DISPLAY 13-2   The Standard Error of the Estimate for Hop Scotch

```
Equation Number 1    Dependent Variable..    PASS

Variable(s) Entered on Step Number
    1..    NI
    2..    ADV

Multiple R           .97613
R Square             .95282
Adjusted R Square    .94496
Standard Error       .82167
```

Remember, the standard error of the estimate measures the dispersion of the actual, observed Y-values (Y_i) around the regression plane. This is illustrated in Figure 13-2. The actual Y_i-values are dispersed about the regression plane. The standard error of the estimate measures the degree of this dispersion. Of course, the less the dispersion, the smaller the Se and the more accurate the model is in prediction and forecasting.

FIGURE 13-2   The Regression Plane for Hop Scotch

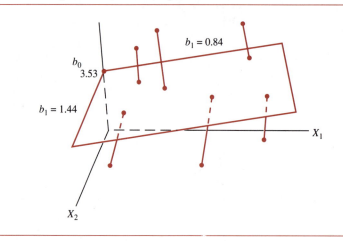

B.   EVALUATING THE MODEL AS A WHOLE

Given his regression model, one of the first questions Ace must ask himself is, "Does it have any explanatory value?" This can perhaps best be answered by performing analysis of variance (ANOVA). The ANOVA procedure will test whether any of the independent variables has a relationship with the dependent variable. If an independent variable is not related to the Y-variable, its coefficient should be zero. That is, if X_i is not related to Y, then $\beta_i = 0$. The ANOVA procedure tests the null hypothesis that all the β-values are zero against the alternative that *at least one β is not* zero. That is,

$$H_0: \beta_1 = \beta_2 = \beta_3 = \cdots = \beta_k = 0$$

$$H_a: \text{At least one } \beta \text{ is not zero}$$

If the null is not rejected, then there is no linear relationship between Y and any of the independent variables. On the other hand, if the null is rejected, then at least one independent variable is linearly related to Y.

The ANOVA process necessary to test the hypothesis was presented in Chapter 11. An ANOVA table is set up, and the F-test is used to make the determination. Table 13-3 provides the general format for an ANOVA table for multiple regression. Note its similarity to ANOVA tables you have already seen. Notice that the degrees of freedom for the regression sum of squares is equal to k, the number of independent variables in the model, while the degrees of freedom for the error sum of squares is $n - k - 1$. Each of the sums of squares is found exactly as it was for simple regression.

TABLE 13-3   A Generalized ANOVA Table

Source of Variation	SS	d.f.	MS	F-Value
Between samples (treatment)	SSR	k	$\dfrac{SSR}{k}$	$F = \dfrac{MSR}{MSE}$
Within samples (error)	SSE	$n - k - 1$	$\dfrac{SSE}{n - k - 1}$	
Total variation	SST	$n - 1$		

$$SST = \Sigma(Y_i - \overline{Y})^2 \qquad (13.12)$$

$$SSR = \Sigma(\hat{Y} - \overline{Y})^2 \qquad (13.13)$$

$$SSE = \Sigma(Y_i - \hat{Y})^2 \qquad (13.14)$$

Table 13-4 provides the results in an ANOVA table for Hop Scotch Airlines. Display 13-3 is the ANOVA table reported by SPSS-PC. Ace can then use this information to test his hypothesis.

TABLE 13-4   ANOVA Table for Hop Scotch

Source of Variation	SS	d.f.	MS	F-value
Between samples (treatment)	163.632	2	81.816	121.18
Within samples (error)	8.102	12	0.675	
Total variation	171.733	14		

DISPLAY 13-3   The ANOVA Table for Hop Scotch

```
Analysis of Variance
                DF      Sum of Squares      Mean Square
Regression       2          163.63171         81.81585
Residual        12            8.10162           .67514
F =    121.18438      Signif F =   .0000
```

To determine if the model has any explanatory power, Ace must test the hypothesis

$$H_0: \beta_1 = \beta_2 = 0$$

$$H_a: \text{At least one } \beta \text{ is not zero}$$

Since the F-ratio is MSR/MSE, the degrees of freedom needed to perform an F-test seen from Table 13-4 are 2 and 12. If Ace wants to test his hypothesis, at say, the 5 percent level, he finds from Table G that $F_{0.05, 2, 12}$ is 3.89. The decision rule for Ace's hypothesis is do not reject if $F < 3.89$; reject if $F > 3.89$. This is displayed in Figure 13-3. Ace can plainly see that $F = 121.18 > 3.89$. He will therefore reject the null hypothesis that $\beta_1 = \beta_2 = 0$. He can conclude with 95 percent confidence that a linear relationship exists between Y and at least one of the independent variables.

FIGURE 13-3   *F*-test for Ace and His Regression Model

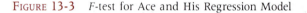

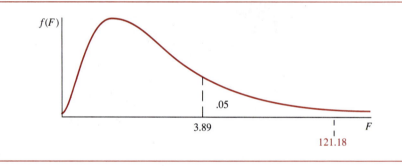

C.   TESTING INDIVIDUAL PARTIAL REGRESSION COEFFICIENTS

Ace has learned that at least one of the two independent variables has some relationship to the number of Hop Scotch passengers. The next logical step is to test each coefficient individually to determine which one (or ones) is significant.

Again notice the great similarity with testing the slope coefficient under simple regression. The procedure uses a t-distribution, since $n < 30$, and tests the hypothesis

$$H_0: \beta_i = 0$$

$$H_a: \beta_i \neq 0$$

The t-test statistic is

$$t = \frac{b_i - 0}{S_{b_i}} \tag{13.15}$$

where b_i is the individual coefficient being tested
        S_{b_i} is the standard error of b_i

S_{b_i} is used because if another sample of $n = 15$ was taken, different coefficients would result due to sampling error. That is, the coefficients would vary because the randomly selected observations in the second sample would not be the same as they were in the first sample. S_{b_i} is used to capture that variation. Like most statistics associated with multiple regression, S_{b_i} is difficult to calculate by hand. If there are only two independent variables,

$$S_{b_i} = \frac{Se}{\sqrt{\Sigma(X_i - \overline{X}_i)^2(1 - r_{12}^2)}} \quad (13.16)$$

where r_{12}^2 is the squared correlation coefficient for the two independent variables. This correlation coefficient for X_1 and X_2 is conceptually the same as the correlation coefficient for X and Y that we calculated in Chapter 12 for simple regression. Here, however, instead of measuring the correlation between the dependent and the independent variables, we are measuring the correlation between two independent variables. It is calculated as

$$r_{12} = \frac{\Sigma X_1 X_2 - (\Sigma X_1)(\Sigma X_2)/n}{\sqrt{[\Sigma X_1^2 - (\Sigma X_1)^2/n][\Sigma X_2^2 - (\Sigma X_2)^2/n]}} \cdot \quad (13.17)$$

Table 13-5 aids in the calculations. Then

$$r_{12} = \frac{525.38 - (187)(40.29)/15}{\sqrt{[2469 - (187)^2/15][113.34 - (40.29)^2/15]}}$$

$$= 0.8698$$

SPSS-PC can be used to request a correlation matrix. The results, shown in Display 13-4, reveal the correlation between NI and ADV to be 0.8698.

Ace can now test the significance of b_1, the coefficient for advertising. The hypothesis he is testing is whether advertising contributes any explanatory power to the model designed to explain Hop Scotch's passengers. The hypothesis is stated as

$$H_0: \beta_1 = 0$$

$$H_a: \beta_1 \neq 0$$

If the null is not rejected, it can be concluded that no linear relationship exists between advertising and number of passengers. This would mean that advertising offers nothing in the way of explaining the number of passengers. Ace must first

TABLE 13-5 Computations for the Correlation between Advertising
(X_1) and National Income (X_2): r_{12}

Adv X_1	NI X_2	(Adv) (NI) (X_1) (X_2)	(Adv)^2 $(X_1)^2$	(NI)^2 $(X_2)^2$
10	2.40	24.00	100	5.7600
12	2.72	32.64	144	7.3984
8	2.08	16.64	64	4.3264
17	3.68	62.56	289	13.5424
10	2.56	25.60	100	6.5536
15	3.36	50.40	225	11.2896
10	2.24	22.40	100	5.0176
14	3.20	44.80	196	10.2400
19	3.84	72.96	361	14.7456
10	2.72	27.20	100	7.3984
11	2.07	22.77	121	4.2849
13	2.33	30.29	169	5.4289
16	2.98	47.68	256	8.8804
10	1.94	19.40	100	3.7636
12	2.17	26.04	144	4.7089
187	40.29	525.38	2,469	113.3400

DISPLAY 13-4   A Correlation Matrix for Hop Scotch

```
Correlations:  PASS      ADV       NI
  PASS       1.0000    .9684**   .9029**
  ADV         .9684**  1.0000    .8698**
  NI          .9029**   .8698**  1.0000
N of cases:    15          1-tailed Signif:  * - .01  ** - .001
" . " is printed if a coefficient cannot be computed
```

calculate S_{b_i}. Again, a presentation as in Table 13-6 is helpful in obtaining S_{b_i}. Recall
that the mean value for advertising expenditures is $\overline{X}_1 = 12.467$.

$$S_{b_i} = \frac{Se}{\sqrt{\Sigma(X_1 - \overline{X}_1)^2(1 - r_{12}^2)}}$$

$$= \frac{0.8217}{\sqrt{[137.73][1 - (0.8698)^2]}}$$

$$= 0.14191$$

TABLE 13-6   Computations for Standard Error of the First Regression Coefficient b_1

Adv X_1	$X_1 - \bar{X}_1$	$(X_1 - \bar{X}_1)^2$
10	−2.467	6.0861
12	−0.467	0.2181
8	−4.467	19.9541
17	4.533	20.5481
10	−2.467	6.0861
15	2.533	6.4161
10	−2.467	6.0861
14	1.533	2.3501
19	6.533	42.6801
10	−2.467	6.0861
11	−1.467	2.1521
13	0.533	0.2841
16	3.533	12.4821
10	−2.467	6.0861
12	−0.467	0.2181
		$137.7335 = \Sigma(X_1 - \bar{X}_1)^2$

Then

$$t = \frac{b_1 - 0}{S_{b_i}}$$

$$= \frac{0.84}{0.14191}$$

$$= 5.917$$

The t-test for the hypothesis is shown in Figure 13-4.

FIGURE 13-4   A 5 Percent Test for the Significance of Advertising

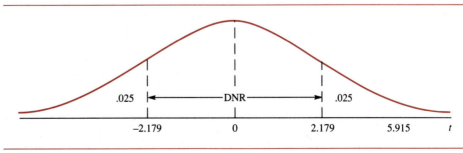

Assume Ace wishes to test at the $\alpha = 0.05$ level of significance. Recall from the ANOVA table that the number of degrees of freedom for the test is $n - k - 1 = 15 - 2 - 1 = 12$. The critical t-values taken from Table F are $t_{0.05, 12} = \pm 2.179$. It is a two-tailed test because the t-value may be significantly large or significantly small. The decision rule is

Decision Rule
Do not reject the null if $-2.179 < t < 2.179$. Reject if $t < -2.179$ or $t > 2.179$.

The value of the test statistic of 5.917 calculated from the sample data is clearly in the upper rejection region. Ace can be 95 percent confident that the null of $\beta_1 = 0$ should be rejected. Advertising does serve as an explanatory factor for Hop Scotch's passenger list.

Remember that the ability to merely read numbers on the computer printout is not sufficient to obtain a true understanding of multiple regression. Although you may never have to perform these elaborate computations by hand, you must nevertheless acquire an intuitive understanding of the nature of regression analysis. This can be done only by examining these formulas and their manipulations. Display 13-5, which is the same as Display 13-1, provides the SPSS-PC printout showing the standard error of the regression coefficient.

DISPLAY 13-5   Ace's Regression Model

```
Equation Number 1    Dependent Variable..   PASS

------------------Variables in the Equation--------------------
Variable             B        SE B       Beta         T    Sig T
NI              1.44097     .73604     .24880     1.958    .0739
ADV              .83966     .14191     .75197     5.917    .0001
(Constant)      3.52840     .99942                3.530    .0041

End Block Number   1   All requested variables entered.
```

Notice also the SIG T value of 0.0001 serves as the p-value for the test. Recall that the p-value is the lowest level of significance at which the null can be rejected. According to the printout, advertising is significant, and the null should be rejected, at any level of significance above 0.0001 (less than 1 percent). Thus, for example, the use of any of the customary levels of significance, 1, 5, or 10 percent, would result in rejection of the null, and the conclusion that advertising has a significant role to play in the explanation of passengers.

This same test for significance can also be performed for b_2, the coefficient for NI. According to the printout, NI has a p-value (SIG T) of 7.39 percent. Thus, NI should prove significant at any α-value above 7.39 percent. If we were to test at the 5 percent level, the critical t, as noted above, is ± 2.179.

Decision Rule

Do not reject if $-2.179 < t < 2.179$. Reject otherwise.

The t-value reported for NI on the printout is seen to be 1.958, which is in the do not reject region. Thus, the hypothesis that $\beta_2 = 0$ is not rejected, and it is concluded that at the 5 percent level of significance NI has no explanatory power.

However, if the test is performed at the 10 percent level, a different conclusion is reached, as seen in Figure 13-5. From Table F we find $t_{0.10, 12} = \pm 1.782$.

FIGURE 13-5   A 10 Percent Test of Significance of National Income

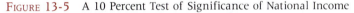

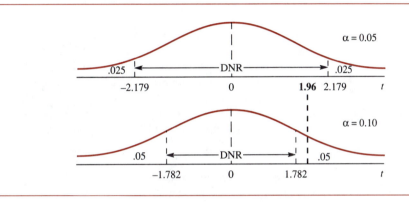

Decision Rule

Do not reject if $-1.782 < t < 1.782$. Reject otherwise.

Since $t = 1.958$, Ace must reject the null that $\beta_2 = 0$ at the 10 percent level of significance and conclude with 90 percent confidence that NI does have some explanatory linear relationship with passengers.

Our tests show that NI proves significant at the 10 percent level, but at the 5 percent level of significance the hypothesis that $\beta_2 = 0$ cannot be rejected. These results correspond with the p-value for NI, which states that the hypothesis $\beta_2 = 0$ can be rejected at any level of significance above 7.39 percent.

This demonstrates the need for the researcher to choose the value for α only after carefully considering the consequences, as discussed in Chapter 9. Different values for α can result in different conclusions.

In summary, Ace can report to Hop Scotch's management that, at the 5 percent level, advertising proves to be a significant explanatory variable for passengers, while national income does not appear significant. Of course, given the F-test performed earlier at the 5 percent level, Ace expected at least one significant variable. At the 10 percent level, both advertising and national income prove significant.

QUICK CHECK 13.3.1

○○○○ If Ace performed a 1 percent test of significance, would he find
a. the model as a whole is significant?
b. advertising is significant?

Answer:
a. $F_{0.01, 2, 12} = 6.93$. Since $F = 121.18 > 6.93$, reject null.
b. At 1 percent the critical $t = \pm 3.055$. Since $t = 5.917$, reject null. Advertising is significant at 1 percent.

13.4 MULTIPLE CORRELATION

Still another tool Ace can use to evaluate his model is the **coefficient of multiple determination.** For the sake of convenience, the term *multiple* is often assumed given the context of the discussion, and the expression is shortened to coefficient of determination as it was for the simple model. Another similarity between the simple model and a model containing two or more explanatory variables is the interpretation of the coefficient of determination. In both instances it measures the portion of the change in Y explained by all the independent variables in the model.

> **Coefficient of Determination**
> The coefficient of determination measures the strength of the relationship between Y and the independent variables.

To measure that portion of the total change in Y explained by the regression model, we use the ratio of explained variation to total variation just as we did in the case of simple regression. As we noted in Chapter 12, by *variation* we mean the variation in the observed Y-values (Y_i) from their mean ($\overline{Y}$). The variation in Y that is explained by our model is reflected by the regression sum of squares (SSR). The total variation in Y is, in turn, measured by the total sum of squares (SST). Thus,

$$R^2 = \frac{SSR}{SST} \tag{13.18}$$

Since $SST = SSR + SSE$, we also have

$$R^2 = 1 - \frac{SSE}{SST} \tag{13.19}$$

Notice that the coefficient is r^2 in the simple model and R^2 in our present discussion.

From Display 13-2, shown earlier, we see that

$$R^2 = \frac{SSR}{SST}$$

$$= \frac{163.632}{171.733}$$

$$= 0.953$$

Thus, 95.3 percent of the change in the number of passengers Hop Scotch transports is explained by changes in advertising and national income. This compares favorably to $r^2 = 0.93$ for the simple model in Chapter 12 containing only advertising. By incorporating NI as a second independent variable, we have increased the explanatory power of the model from 93 to 95.3 percent.

To avoid the need to calculate SSR and SST, we can find R^2 by

$$R^2 = \frac{n[b_0\Sigma Y + b_1\Sigma X_1 Y + b_2\Sigma X_2 Y + \cdots + b_m\Sigma X_m Y] - (\Sigma Y)^2}{n\Sigma Y^2 - (\Sigma Y)^2} \qquad (13.20)$$

$$= \frac{15[(3.53)(268) + (0.84)(3,490) + (1.44)(746.62)] - (268)^2}{(15)(4,960) - (268)^2}$$

$$= 0.957$$

The slight difference in R^2 using Formulas (13.18) and (13.20) is due to rounding. As with the simple model, we find $0 \leq R^2 \leq 1$. Of course, the higher the R^2, the more explanatory power the model has.

A.   THE ADJUSTED COEFFICIENT OF DETERMINATION

Because of its importance, R^2 is commonly reported by most computer packages. It is a quick and easy way to evaluate the regression model and to determine how well the model fits the data. Outside of the regression coefficients themselves, R^2 is perhaps the most commonly observed and closely watched statistic in regression analysis.

However, it is possible for careless, or unscrupulous, statisticians to artificially inflate R^2. An increase in R^2 can be achieved merely by adding another independent variable to the model. Even if some nonsensical variable which truly has no explanatory power is incorporated into the model, R^2 will rise. Ace could "pump up" his R^2 by adding to the model as an explanatory variable the tonnage of sea trout caught by sport fishing off the Florida coast. Now, obviously, fishing has little or nothing to do with Hop Scotch's passenger list. Yet there is probably at least a tiny bit of totally coincidental correlation, either positive or negative, between fishing and air travel. Even a minute degree of correlation will inflate R^2. By adding several of these absurd "explanatory" variables, Ace could illegitimately increase his R^2 until it approached 100 percent. A model of this nature may appear to fit the data quite well, but would produce wretched results in any attempt to predict or forecast the value for the independent variable.

It is therefore a common practice in multiple regression and correlation analysis to report the **adjusted coefficient of determination.** Symbolized as $\overline{R}^2$, and read as "R bar squared," this statistic adjusts the measure of explanatory power for the number of degrees of freedom. The degrees of freedom for SSE is $n - k - 1$. The researcher loses one degree of freedom for every additional independent variable added to the model, because each variable requires the calculation of another b_i. $\overline{R}^2$ will penalize the researcher for incorporating a variable which does not add enough explanatory power to the model to justify the loss of a degree of freedom. The value of $\overline{R}^2$ will go down. If it decreases too much, consideration must be given to excluding that variable from the model. In extreme cases, the adjusted coefficient of determination can actually become less than zero.

This adjusted coefficient is obtained by dividing SSE and SST by their respective degrees of freedom.

$$\overline{R}^2 = 1 - \frac{SSE/(n - k - 1)}{SST/(n - 1)} \qquad (13.21)$$

A more computationally convenient formula for $\overline{R}^2$ is

$$\overline{R}^2 = 1 - (1 - R^2)\frac{n - 1}{n - k - 1} \qquad (13.22)$$

Since the numerator in Formula (13.21) is the MSE, it may be said the $\overline{R}^2$ is a combination of the two measures of the performance of a regression model: the mean square error and the coefficient of determination.

By using the data from his model, Ace can determine $\overline{R}^2$ as

$$\overline{R}^2 = 1 - (1 - 0.953)\frac{15 - 1}{15 - 2 - 1}$$

$$= 0.949$$

After adjusting for the degrees of freedom, Ace's model reports a $\overline{R}^2$ of 94.9 percent.

As you might expect, most computer programs also report the adjusted coefficient of determination. Display 13-2 for SPSS-PC reveals an Adjusted R Square of 0.94496.

13.5   THE PRESENCE OF MULTICOLLINEARITY

Earlier we noted the danger of multicollinearity. This problem arises when one of the independent variables is linearly related to one or more of the other independent variables. Such a situation violates one of the conditions for multiple regression. Specifically, multicollinearity occurs if there is a high correlation between two independent variables, X_i and X_j. In Chapter 12 we discussed the correlation coefficient r for the dependent variable and the single independent variable. If this same concept is applied to two independent variables, X_i and X_j, in multiple regression, we can calculate the correlation coefficient r_{ij}. If r_{ij} is high, multicollinearity exists. What is *high?* Unfortunately, there is no answer to this critical question. There is no magic cutoff point at which the correlation is judged to be too high and multicollinearity exists. Multicollinearity is a problem of degree. Any time two or more independent variables are linearly related, some degree of multicollinearity exists. If its presence becomes too pronounced, the model is adversely affected. What is considered too high is largely a judgment call by the researcher. Some insight necessary to make that call is provided in this section.

Assume you are using regression techniques to estimate a demand curve (or demand function) for your product. Recognizing that the number of consumers impacts upon demand, you choose as explanatory variables

X_1 = all men in the market area
X_2 = all women in the market area
X_3 = total population in the market area

Obviously, X_3 is a linear combination of X_1 and X_2 ($X_3 = X_1 + X_2$). The correlation r_{13} between X_1 and X_3 and the correlation r_{23} between X_2 and X_3 are quite high. This ensures the presence of multicollinearity and creates many problems in the use of regression techniques. A discussion of some common problems follows.

A.   THE PROBLEMS OF MULTICOLLINEARITY

One of the more vexing problems of multicollinearity arises from our inability to separate the individual effects of each independent variable on Y. In the presence of multicollinearity, it is impossible to disentangle the effects of each X_i. Suppose in the model

$$\hat{Y} = 40 + 10X_1 + 8X_2$$

X_1 and X_2 showed a high degree of correlation. In this case, the coefficient of 10 for X_1 may not represent the true effect of X_1 on Y. The regression coefficients become unreliable and cannot be taken as estimates of the change in Y given a one unit change in the independent variable.

Furthermore, the standard errors of the coefficients, S_{b_i}, become inflated. If two or more samples of the same size are taken, a large variation in the coefficients would be found. In the model specified above, instead of 10 as the coefficient of X_1, a second sample may yield a coefficient of 15 or 20. If b_1 varies that much from one sample to the next, we must question its accuracy.

Multicollinearity can even cause the sign of the coefficient to be opposite that which logic would dictate. For example, if you included price as a variable in the estimation of your demand curve, you may find it takes on a positive sign. This implies that as the price of a good goes up, consumers buy more of it. This is an obvious violation of the logic behind demand theory.

B.   DETECTION OF MULTICOLLINEARITY

Perhaps the most direct way of testing for multicollinearity is to produce a **correlation matrix** for all variables in the model, as shown in Display 13-4. The value of $r_{12} = 0.8698$ for the correlation between the two independent variables indicates that NI and ADV are closely related. Although there is no predetermined value for r_{ij} which signals the onset of multicollinearity, a value of 0.8698 is probably high enough to indicate a significant problem.

Some of the guesswork can be eliminated by using a t-test to determine if the level of correlation between X_1 and X_2 differs significantly from zero. Given the nonzero relationship between X_1 and X_2 ($r_{12} = 0.8698$) in our sample, we wish to test the hypothesis that the correlation between X_1 and X_2 is zero at the population level. We will test the hypothesis that

$$H_0: \rho_{12} = 0$$

$$H_a: \rho_{12} \neq 0$$

where ρ_{12} is the population correlation coefficient between X_1 and X_2. This can be done using the techniques in Chapter 12. There it was demonstrated that

$$t = \frac{r_{12}}{S_r}$$

where

$$S_r = \sqrt{\frac{1 - r_{12}^2}{n - 2}}$$

As an illustration, the hypothesis that $\rho_{12} = 0$, where ρ_{12} is the population correlation coefficient for the two independent variables, is

$$S_r = \sqrt{\frac{1 - (0.8698)^2}{15 - 2}}$$

$$= 0.1367$$

$$t = \frac{0.8698}{0.1367}$$

$$= 6.36$$

If α is set at 5 percent, the critical $t_{0.05, 13} = 2.16$. There are $n - 2$ degrees of freedom.

Decision Rule
Do not reject if $-2.16 < t < 2.16$. Reject if $t < -2.16$ or $t > 2.16$.

Since $t = 6.36 > 2.16$, Ace can reject the null that there is no correlation between X_1 and X_2 ($\rho_{12} = 0$). Some multicollinearity does exist. This does not mean that the model is irrevocably defective. In fact, very few models would be totally free of multicollinearity. How to handle this problem is discussed shortly.

Another indication of multicollinearity can be seen by comparing the coefficients of determination between the dependent variable and each of the independent variables. We found the correlation between passengers and advertising to be $r^2 = 0.937$, while that between passengers and national income is $r^2 = 0.815$. Yet together the two independent variables revealed R^2 of only 0.957. If taken separately, the two independent variables explain 93.7 and 81.5 percent of the change in Y. But in combination they explain only 95.7 percent. Apparently there is some overlap in their explanatory power. Including the second variable of NI did little to raise the model's ability to explain the level of the passengers. Much of the information about passengers which is already provided by advertising is merely duplicated by NI. This is an indication that multicollinearity might be present.

The use of the **variance inflation factor** (VIF) is a third method of detecting multicollinearity. The VIF associated with any X-variable is found by regressing it on all the other X-variables. The resulting R^2 is then used to calculate that variable's VIF. The VIF for any X_i represents that variable's influence on multicollinearity.

Variance Inflation Factor
The VIF for any independent variable is a measure of the degree of multicollinearity contributed by that variable.

Since there are only two independent variables in Hop Scotch's model, regressing X_1 on all other independent variables (X_2) or regressing X_2 on all other independent variables (X_1) yields the same correlation coefficient ($r_{12} = 0.8698$), as shown in Table 13-6. The VIF for any given independent variable X_i is

$$\text{VIF}(X_i) = \frac{1}{1 - R_i^2} \tag{13.23}$$

where R_i^2 is the coefficient of determination obtained by regressing X_i on all other independent variables. As noted, multicollinearity produces an increase in the variation, or standard error, of the regression coefficient. VIF measures the increase in the variance of the regression coefficient over that which would occur if multicollinearity were not present.

The VIF for advertising in Ace's model is

$$\text{VIF}(X_1) = \frac{1}{1 - (0.8698)^2}$$

$$= 4.1$$

The same VIF for X_2 would be found since there are only two independent variables. The variance in b_1 and b_2 is therefore more than four times what it should be without multicollinearity in the model. If an independent variable is totally unrelated to any other independent variable, its VIF equals 1. However, in general, multicollinearity is not considered a significant problem unless the VIF of a single X_i measures at least 10, or the sum of the VIFs for all X_i is at least 10.

Other indications of multicollinearity which can be observed include large changes in coefficients or their signs when there is a small change in the number of observations. Furthermore, if the F-ratio is significant and the t-values are not, multicollinearity may be present. If the addition or deletion of a variable produces large changes in coefficients or their signs, multicollinearity may exist.

In summary, in the presence of multicollinearity we find

a. An inability to separate the net effect of individual independent variables upon Y.
b. An exaggerated standard error for the b-coefficients.
c. Algebraic signs of the coefficients that violate logic.
d. A high correlation between independent variables, and a high VIF.
e. Large changes in coefficients or their signs if the number of observations is changed by a single observation.
f. A significant F-ratio combined with insignificant t-ratios.
g. Large changes in coefficients or their signs when a variable is added or deleted.

C.   TREATING MULTICOLLINEARITY

What can be done to eliminate or mitigate the influence of multicollinearity? Perhaps the most logical solution is to drop the offending variable. If X_i and X_j are closely related, one of them can simply be excluded from the model. After all, due to overlap, the inclusion of the second variable adds little to the further explanation of Y.

In reference to Hop Scotch's model, it might be advisable to drop NI since its correlation with Y is less than that of advertising. The t-tests performed earlier also suggested that NI was not significant at the 5 percent level.

However, simply dropping one of the variables can lead to **specification bias,** in which the form of the model is in disagreement with its theoretical foundation. Multicollinearity might be avoided, for example, if income were eliminated from a functional expression for consumer demand. However, economic theory, as well as plain common sense, tells us that income should be included in any attempt to explain consumption.

Specification Bias
A misspecification of a model due to the inclusion or exclusion of certain variables which results in a violation of theoretical principles is called specification bias.

If dropping a variable is precluded due to any resulting bias, multicollinearity can often be reduced by changing the form of the variable. Perhaps dividing the original values of the offending variable by population to obtain a per-capita figure would prove beneficial. This was originally suggested in reference to NI at the outset of this chapter. Additionally, dividing certain monetary measures by a price index (such as the Consumer Price Index) and thereby obtaining a measure in "real" terms is also an effective method of eliminating multicollinearity. This, too, could be applied to NI.

It is also possible to combine two or more variables. This could be done with the model for consumer demand, which employed X_1 = men, X_2 = women, and X_3 = total population. Variables X_1 and X_2 could be added to form X_3. The model would then consist of only one explanatory variable.

In any event, we should recognize that some degree of multicollinearity exists in most regression models containing two or more independent variables. The greater the number of independent variables, the greater the likelihood of multicollinearity. However, this will not necessarily detract from the model's usefulness because the problem of multicollinearity may not be severe. Multicollinearity will cause large errors in individual coefficients, yet the combined effect of these coefficients is not drastically altered. A predictive model designed to predict the value of Y on the basis of all X_i taken in combination will still possess considerable accuracy. Only explanatory models, created to explain the contribution to the value of Y by each X_i, tend to collapse in the face of multicollinearity.

13.6   COMPARING REGRESSION COEFFICIENTS

After developing the complete model, there is often a tendency to compare regression coefficients to determine which variable exerts more influence on Y. This dangerous temptation must be avoided. For the model

$$\hat{Y} = 40 + 10X_1 + 200X_2$$

where Y is tons of output, X_1 is units of labor input, and X_2 is units of capital input, one might conclude that capital is more important than labor in determining output since it has the larger coefficient. After all, a 1-unit increase in capital, holding labor constant, results in a 200-unit increase in output. However, such a comparison is not possible. All variables are measured in totally dissimilar units; one in units of weight, another in number of people, and a third in machines.

Measuring all the variables in the same manner still does not allow us to judge relative impact of independent variables based on the size of their coefficients. Suppose a model is stated in terms of monetary units, such as

$$\hat{Y} = 50 + 10{,}000X_1 + 20X_2$$

where Y is in dollars, X_1 is in units of \$1,000 and X_2 is in cents. Despite the large coefficient for X_1, it is not possible to conclude that it is of greater impact. A \$1,000 (1 unit) increase in X_1 increases Y by 10,000 units. A \$1,000 (100,000 units) increase in X_2 will increase Y by 2,000,000 units (100,000 × 20).

Even if we express Y, X_1, and X_2 in units of \$1, we cannot compare the relative impact of X_1 and X_2 on changes in Y. Factors other than a variable's coefficient determine its total impact on Y. For example, the variance in a variable is quite important in determining its influence on Y. The variance measures how often and how much a variable changes. Thus, a variable may have a large coefficient and, every time it changes, affect Y noticeably. But if its variance is very small and it changes only once in a millennium, its overall impact on Y will be negligible.

To offset these shortcomings, we sometimes measure the response of Y to changes in the **standardized regression coefficients.** Standard regression coefficients, also called **beta coefficients** (not to be confused with the beta value β, which is the unknown coefficient at the population level), reflect the change in the mean response of Y, measured in the number of standard deviations of Y, to changes in X_i, measured in the number of standard deviations of X_i. The intended effect of calculating beta values is to make the coefficients "dimensionless."

These beta values are reported by most computer programs, and are seen in Display 13-5. A one-standard-deviation change in NI results in a 0.24880 standard deviation in Y. However, these beta coefficients suffer many of the same deficiencies as the normal coefficients. Hence, it is generally considered poor practice to reflect the importance of a variable on the basis of its beta coefficient.

13.7   AN EXPANDED MODEL

Of course, it is entirely possible that Ace may decide to include a third explanatory variable in his model. If he were to feel that, for example, the level of competition Hop Scotch encountered from other airlines might affect sales, Ace should consider including some measurement of the competitive forces in the market in his model to predict and explain sales revenues. The contribution such a measurement might provide to the model would then be examined in terms of its impact on the adjusted coefficient of determination, the standard error of the estimate, and other statistical measures presented throughout our discussion of regression and correlation analysis.

Actually, Ace may test any number of variables which he feels might add to the explanatory power of his model. It is not uncommon for a model of this nature to include several explanatory variables. The failure to include any useful explanatory variable detracts from the model's total predictive ability.

However, it is important to include only those variables which offer a definite contribution to the model's explanatory power. Including variables of little value can reduce the adjusted coefficient of determination and contribute to the problem of multicollinearity. Any model should therefore use as few variables as possible to achieve its level of explanatory power. Such a model is said to be **parsimonious**.

Parsimony
The use of as few explanatory variables as possible in the formation of a multiple regression model is known as parsimony.

13.8   STEPWISE REGRESSION

Many modern computer packages offer a procedure which allows the statistician the option of permitting the computer to select the desired independent variables from a prescribed list of possibilities. The statistician provides the data for several potential explanatory variables and then, with certain commands, instructs the computer to determine which of those variables are best-suited to formulate the complete model.

In this manner, the regression model is developed in stages and is known as **stepwise regression.** It can take the form of (1) backward elimination or (2) forward selection. Let's take a look at each in turn.

A.   BACKWARD ELIMINATION

To execute backward elimination, we calculate the entire model, using all independent variables. The t-values are then computed for all coefficients. If any prove to be insignificant, the one with a t-value closest to zero is eliminated and the model is calculated again. This continues until all remaining b_i are significantly different from zero.

B.   FORWARD SELECTION

As the name implies, forward selection is the opposite of backward elimination. First, the variable most highly correlated with Y is selected for inclusion in the model. The second step involves the selection of a second variable based on its ability to explain Y given that the first variable is already in the model. The selection of the second variable is based on its *partial coefficient of determination,* which is a variable's marginal contribution to the explanatory power of the model, given the presence of the first variable.

Assume, for example, that the first variable selected is X_5. Every possible two-variable model is computed in which one of those variables is X_5. That model which produces the highest R^2 is chosen. This process continues until all X-variables are in the model or until the addition of another variable does not result in a significant increase in R^2.

Although stepwise regression appears to be a convenient and effective method of model specification, certain precautions must be taken. The process will "mine" the data, prospecting for a statistically accurate model with the highest R^2. However, a computer cannot think or reason, and the resulting model may be statistically sound but contrary to all logical and theoretical principles, and thereby suffer from specification bias. Stepwise regression should therefore be used with extreme caution, and any model formulated in this manner should be closely scrutinized.

13.9 WHAT YOU SHOULD HAVE LEARNED FROM THIS CHAPTER

This chapter is an extension of the principles of regression and correlation analysis discussed in Chapter 12. You should understand what a multiple regression model is and why it might prove beneficial to develop one.

You should also have a grasp of the importance of multicollinearity and the practice of stepwise regression. How to interpret regression coefficients should also be clear.

Regression and correlation are important statistical tools that are widely applied.

13.10 COMPUTER APPLICATIONS

As noted, multiple regression and correlation techniques are, for the most part, accomplished with the aid of a computer package. In working through the regression model for Hop Scotch, it should be obvious that with many variables and/or observations, the computations necessary for multiple regression and correlations can be overwhelming. This section illustrates how three popular programs handle the required techniques.

A. MINITAB

After the data have been loaded into a Minitab worksheet, it is a simple matter to complete a multiple regression model. Presume Ace puts the data for passengers in column 1 of the worksheet, and columns 2 and 3 hold the values for advertising and national income, respectively. The Minitab command to regress passengers on the two independent variables is

```
MTB>REGRESS C1 on 2 C2 C3
```

The resulting printout is shown in Minitab 1. The regression equation is displayed at the top, followed by a more complete description of each variable. The coefficients (coef) are specified, along with their standard deviations and the t-values we calculated earlier. The p-values are also given. Notice that the variable NI is not significant at the 5 percent level, but is at the 10 percent level. This is exactly what we found in our previous calculations. The standard er-

Minitab 1

```
The regression equation is
C1 = 3.53 + 0.840 C2 + 1.44 C3

Predictor        Coef       Stdev    t-ratio        P        VIF
Constant       3.5284      0.9994       3.53    0.004
C2             0.8397      0.1419       5.92    0.000        4.1
C3             1.4410      0.7360       1.96    0.074        4.1

s = 0.8217     R-sq = 95.3%     R-sq(adj) = 94.5%

Analysis of Variance

SOURCE         DF          SS         MS         F        P
Regression      2     163.632     81.816    121.18    0.000
Error          12       8.102      0.675
Total          14     171.733

SOURCE         DF      SEQ SS
C2              1     161.044
C3              1       2.588
```

ror of 0.8217 is also provided. Values for R^2 and $\overline{R}^2$ follow. The ANOVA table completes the Minitab printout. All the information we so laboriously calculated by hand in the chapter is quickly obtained with Minitab.

Minitab also offers the subcommand SUBC to test for multicollinearity. The VIF can be determined as follows:

```
MTB>REGRESS C1 on 2 C2 C3;
SUBC>VIF.
```

The correlation matrix is produced by the command

```
MTB>CORR C1-C3
```

Minitab 2 displays the matrix provided by Minitab. It shows the simple correlation between each pair of variables.

Minitab 2

```
                C1          C2
C2           0.968
C3           0.903       0.870
```

B. SAS

The SAS program necessary to run the multiple regression for Hop Scotch is

```
DATA;
INPUT PASS ADV NI;
CARDS;

  data lines go here

PROC REG;
  MODEL PASS = ADV NI;
```

The subsequent printout is shown in SAS 1. The printout contains all the statistics we calculated in the chapter and is self-explanatory. For a complete discussion, see the section on Minitab. The variance inflation factors are obtained by altering the last line in the SAS program to read

```
MODEL PASS = ADV NI / VIF;
```

The correlation matrix is obtained by adding to the above program the commands

```
PROC CORR;
  VAR PASS ADV NI;
```

SAS 1

DEP VARIABLE: PASS

SOURCE	DF	SUM OF SQUARES	MEAN SQUARE	F Value	Prob > F
MODEL	2	163.6317	81.8158	121.184	0000
ERROR	12	8.1016	.6751		
C Total	14				

VARIABLE	PARAMETER ESTIMATE	STANDARD ERROR	T FOR H0: PARAMETER = 0	PROB > $|T|$
INTERCEP	3.528	.9994	3.530	.0041
NI	1.441	.7360	1.958	.0739
ADV	.839	.1419	5.917	.0001

C. SPSS-PC

The program to execute Hop Scotch's multiple regression model is

```
DATA List Free/Pass Adv NI.
Begin Data.

  data goes here

End data.
Regression Variables = Pass Adv NI/Dependent = Pass.
```

The printout looks much like those specified above.

APPENDIX

It may be beneficial to examine these hand calculations that lead to a solution for the regression equation. In so doing, you can gain an appreciation for exactly what calculations must be performed to complete a regression program and thus acquire further insight into the nature of regression analysis. The data needed to solve for the Hop Scotch equations are shown in Table 13-7.

TABLE 13-7   Computations for Hop Scotch Airlines

Y	X_1	X_2	X_1X_2	X_1^2	X_2^2	YX_1	YX_2
15	10	2.40	24.00	100	5.7600	150	36.00
17	12	2.72	32.64	144	7.3984	204	46.24
13	8	2.08	16.64	64	4.3264	104	27.04
23	17	3.68	62.56	289	13.5424	391	84.64
16	10	2.56	25.60	100	6.5536	160	40.96
21	15	3.36	50.40	225	11.2896	315	70.56
14	10	2.24	22.40	100	5.0176	140	31.36
20	14	3.20	44.80	196	10.2400	280	64.00
24	19	3.84	72.96	361	14.7456	456	92.16
17	10	2.72	27.20	100	7.3984	170	46.24
16	11	2.07	22.77	121	4.2849	176	33.12
18	13	2.33	30.29	169	5.4289	234	41.94
23	16	2.98	47.68	256	8.8804	368	68.54
15	10	1.94	19.40	100	3.7636	150	29.10
16	12	2.17	26.04	144	4.7089	192	34.72
268	187	40.29	525.38	2,469	113.3387	3,490	746.62

Using these data, Ace can then solve the system of normal equations for the intercept b_0 and coefficients b_1 and b_2. This is done by eliminating any one of them from the equations. This involves several steps, which are outlined below. For instance, suppose Ace decides to eliminate b_0. Step 1 requires that he get the coefficient of b_0 to be the same in any pair of equations. But first, let us restate the normal equations from (13.5) to (13.7).

$$\Sigma Y = nb_0 + b_1\Sigma X_1 + b_2\Sigma X_2$$

$$\Sigma X_1 Y = b_0\Sigma X_1 + b_1\Sigma X_1^2 + b_2\Sigma X_1 X_2$$

$$\Sigma X_2 Y = b_0\Sigma X_2 + b_1\Sigma X_1 X_2 + b_2\Sigma X_2^2$$

For the data in Table 13-2, these equations become

$$268 = 15b_0 + 187b_1 + 40.29b_2 \quad \boxed{1}$$

$$3{,}490 = 187b_0 + 2{,}469b_1 + 525.38b_2 \quad \boxed{2}$$

$$746.62 = 40.29b_0 + 525.38b_1 + 113.34b_2 \quad \boxed{3}$$

Step 1:   Eliminate b_0 using $\boxed{1}$ and $\boxed{2}$.
Multiply $\boxed{1}$ by 187 to obtain $\boxed{4}$ and multiply $\boxed{2}$ by 15 to obtain $\boxed{5}$. Then subtract $\boxed{5}$ from $\boxed{4}$.

$$187 \times \boxed{1} = 50{,}116 = 2{,}805b_0 + 34{,}969b_1 + 7{,}534.23b_2 \quad \boxed{4}$$

$$15 \times \boxed{2} = 52{,}350 = 2{,}805b_0 + 37{,}035b_1 + 7{,}880.7b_2 \quad \boxed{5}$$

$$\boxed{4} - \boxed{5} = -2{,}234 = -2{,}066b_1 - 346.47b_2 \quad \boxed{6}$$

Step 2:   Eliminate b_0 using $\boxed{2}$ and $\boxed{3}$ or $\boxed{1}$ and $\boxed{3}$.
Multiply $\boxed{2}$ by 40.29 to obtain $\boxed{7}$ and multiply $\boxed{3}$ by 187 to obtain $\boxed{8}$. Then subtract $\boxed{8}$ from $\boxed{7}$.

$$40.29 \times \boxed{2} = 140{,}612.1 = 7{,}534.23b_0 + 99{,}476.01b_1 + 21{,}167.5602b_2 \quad \boxed{7}$$

$$187 \times \boxed{3} = 139{,}617.94 = 7{,}534.23b_0 + 98{,}246.06b_1 + 21{,}194.58b_2 \quad \boxed{8}$$

$$\boxed{7} - \boxed{8} = 994.16 = 1{,}229.95b_1 - 27.0198b_2 \quad \boxed{9}$$

Step 3:   Use $\boxed{6}$ and $\boxed{9}$ to eliminate b_1.
Multiply $\boxed{6}$ by 1,229.95 to obtain $\boxed{10}$ and multiply $\boxed{9}$ by 2,066 to obtain $\boxed{11}$. Then add $\boxed{10}$ and $\boxed{11}$.

$$1{,}229.95 \times \boxed{6} = -2{,}747{,}708.3 = -2{,}541{,}076.7b_1 - 426{,}140.7765b_2 \quad \boxed{10}$$

$$2{,}066 \times \boxed{9} = 2{,}053{,}934.56 = 2{,}541{,}076.7b_1 - 55{,}822.9068b_2 \quad \boxed{11}$$

$$\boxed{10} + \boxed{11} = -693{,}773.74 = -481{,}963.6833b_2 \quad \boxed{12}$$

Step 4:   Obtain values for b_0, b_1, and b_2.
From $\boxed{12}$, $b_2 = 1.439473064$.
From $\boxed{6}$,

$$-2{,}234 = -2{,}066b_1 - 346.47(1.439473064)$$

$$-2{,}234 = -2{,}066b_1 - 498.7342325$$

$$b_1 = 0.839915666$$

From $\boxed{1}$,

$$268 = 15b_0 + 187(0.839915666) + 40.29(1.439473064)$$

$$b_0 = 3.529293371$$

Thus,

$$b_0 = 3.529293371 \approx 3.53$$

$$b_1 = 0.839915666 \approx 0.840$$

$$b_2 = 1.439473064 \approx 1.44$$

and

$$\hat{Y} = 3.53 + 0.84X_1 + 1.44X_2$$

Calculations for the standard error of the estimate also reveal what this statistic measures.

Pass	Adv.	NI	Predicted Y	Error	Error Squared
00	10	2.40	15.000	−0.00000	$8.00000 = \Sigma(Y_i - \hat{Y})^2$
Y_i	X_1	X_2	$\hat{Y}$	$(Y_i - \hat{Y})$	$(Y_i - \hat{Y})^2$
15	10	2.40	15.383	−0.38338	0.14698
17	12	2.72	17.524	−0.52382	0.27438
13	8	2.08	13.243	−0.24294	0.05902
23	17	3.68	23.105	−0.10547	0.01112
16	10	2.56	15.614	0.38607	0.14905
21	15	3.36	20.965	0.03497	0.00122
14	10	2.24	15.153	−1.15282	1.32900
20	14	3.20	19.895	0.10519	0.01106
24	19	3.84	25.015	−1.01536	1.03095
17	10	2.72	15.844	1.15551	1.33521
16	11	2.07	15.748	0.25248	0.06375
18	13	2.33	17.802	0.19850	0.03940
23	16	2.98	21.257	1.74287	3.03761
15	10	1.94	14.721	0.27947	0.07810
16	12	2.17	16.731	−0.73128	0.53477

$$8.10162 = \Sigma(Y_i - \hat{Y})^2$$

Then

$$Se = \sqrt{\frac{8.10162}{15 - 2 - 1}}$$

$$= 0.8217$$

LIST OF SYMBOLS AND TERMS

Se Standard error of the estimate
S_{b_i} Standard error of regression coefficient
R^2 Coefficient of (multiple) determination
$\bar{R}^2$ Adjusted coefficient of determination

Regression Plane A geometric plane with slopes that represent the values of the two independent variables in a multiple regression.
Multicollinearity The problem that arises when two or more independent variables are linearly related.
Adjusted Coefficient of Determination The coefficient of determination which has been adjusted for the degrees of freedom.
Variance Inflation Factor The measure of a variable contribution to multicollinearity.
Specification Bias The improper inclusion or exclusion of variables from the model.

$$Se = \sqrt{\frac{\Sigma Y^2 - b_0\Sigma Y - b_1\Sigma X_1 Y - b_2\Sigma X_2 Y - \cdots - b_k\Sigma X_k Y}{n - k - 1}} \qquad (13.11)$$

The standard error of the estimate measures the dispersion of the observed Y-values around the regression plane.

$$t = \frac{b_i - 0}{S_{b_i}} \qquad (13.15)$$

This tests the significance of a partial regression coefficient.

$$S_{b_i} = \frac{Se}{\sqrt{\Sigma(X_i - \bar{X}_i)^2(1 - r_2^2)}} \qquad (13.16)$$

The standard error of the regression coefficient measures the variation in the coefficients from one sample to the next.

$$r_{12} = \frac{\Sigma X_1 X_2 - (\Sigma X_1)(\Sigma X_2)/n}{\sqrt{[\Sigma X_1^2 - (\Sigma X_1)^2/n][\Sigma X_2^2 - (\Sigma X_2)^2/n]}} \qquad (13.17)$$

The correlation between independent variables is used to test for multicollinearity.

$$R^2 = \frac{n(b_0\Sigma Y + b_1\Sigma X_1 Y + b_2\Sigma X_2 Y + \cdots + b_k\Sigma X_k Y) - (\Sigma Y)^2}{n\Sigma Y^2 - (\Sigma Y)^2} \qquad (13.20)$$

The correlation coefficient measures the strength of the relationship between the dependent variable and the independent variables.

$$\bar{R}^2 = 1 - \frac{SSE(n - k - 1)}{SST/(n - 1)} \qquad (13.21)$$

The adjusted coefficient of determination accounts for the degrees of freedom in a model.

$$\bar{R}^2 = 1 - (1 - R^2)\frac{n - 1}{n - k - 1} \qquad (13.22)$$

A more convenient formula for $\bar{R}^2$.

$$VIF(X_i) = \frac{1}{1 - R_i^2} \qquad (13.23)$$

A variable's variance inflation factor measures its contribution to multicollinearity.

CHAPTER EXERCISES

YOU MAKE THE DECISION

1. An economist for the Federal Reserve Board proposed to estimate the Dow-Jones industrial average using, as explanatory variables, X_1: interest rate on AAA corporate bonds; X_2: interest rates on U.S. Treasury securities. Your advice is requested. How would you respond, and what statistical problem will likely be encountered?

CONCEPTUAL QUESTIONS

2. Given the regression equation, with t-values in parentheses,

$$\hat{Y} = 100 + 17X_1 + 80X_2$$
$$\quad\quad\quad (0.73)\quad (6.21)$$

   How might you improve this model?

3. For the equation

$$\hat{Y} = 100 - 20X_1 + 40X_2$$

   a. what is the estimated impact of X_1 on Y?
   b. what condition regarding X_2 must be observed in answering part a?

4. A demand function is expressed as

$$\hat{Q} = 10 + 12P + 8I$$

   where Q is quantity demanded, P is price, and I is consumer income. How would you respond to this equation?

PROBLEMS

5. A financial consultant for a large investment firm in Chicago regressed the price of a stock (P) on its dividend rate (D) and the expected growth rate in the dividend (G). Data from 10 observations are recorded here.

P	D	G
2.1	1.05	0.50
3.5	1.70	0.70
5.3	2.60	1.30
4.7	2.30	0.94
8.1	4.00	1.60
6.2	3.10	1.20
7.4	3.50	1.40
10.5	5.10	2.40
7.9	4.10	0.50
2.9	1.50	0.80

The regression equation is

$$\hat{P} = 0.110 + 1.92D + 0.357G$$

   a. Calculate and interpret the standard error of the estimate.
   b. Test each regression coefficient at the 5 percent level. What is the t-value for each one?
   c. Use the F-test to evaluate the entire model at $\alpha = 10$ percent.
   d. Calculate and interpret the coefficient of determination.

6. Develop the correlation matrix for Problem 5. Does there appear to be a problem with multicollinearity?

7. A model regressing consumption (C) on income (I) and wealth (W) yielded the following results:

$$R^2 = 0.86$$

$$\bar{R}^2 = 0.79$$

$$F = 17.42$$

$$\hat{C} = \underset{(0.71)}{402} + \underset{(6.21)}{0.83I} + \underset{(5.47)}{0.71W}$$

where t-values are shown in parentheses. There were 25 observations in the data set.
    a. What is the meaning of the intercept term?
    b. Are the coefficients significant at the 5 percent level?
    c. Is the model significant at the 10 percent level?

8. From the data in the previous problem, it was found that

$$r_{12} = 0.63, \qquad r_{YX_1} = 0.47, \quad \text{and} \quad r_{YX_2} = 0.53.$$

    a. Develop a correlation matrix. Does multicollinearity appear to be a problem?
    b. Test the value of the correlation coefficient between X_1 and X_2 at the 10 percent level. What conclusion can be reached regarding multicollinearity?
    c. Calculate and interpret the VIF for both X_1 and X_2.

9. A marketing major at the local university uses data from 1965 to 1990 and regresses the demand for automobiles expressed in number of cars sold on price. She finds

$$\hat{D} = 92.5 + 17.3P \qquad r^2 = 79.3$$

$$(t = 8.17)$$

    a. What does the model tell her?
    b. Does your answer in part a seem logical, and how do you explain it?

10. How might the marketing major from the previous problem improve her model?

11. A manufacturer estimates his production function as

$$\hat{Q} = 50 + 10L + 25K$$

where Q is output, L is labor in people, and K is capital.
    a. If the manufacturer employs 400 workers and uses 17 units of capital, what should output be?
    b. If labor costs \$30 and capital costs are \$57 per unit, should the manufacturer acquire more labor or more capital if he wants to increase output?

12. A field of economics referred to as human capital has often held that a person's income (I) could be determined on the basis of his or her (1) education level (E), (2) training (T), and (3) general level of health (H). Using 25 employees at a small textile firm in North Carolina, a researcher regressed income on the other three variables and got the following results.

$$\hat{I} = \underset{(3.70)}{27.2} + \underset{(6.21)}{3.7E} + \underset{(4.32)}{1.7T} + \underset{(6.79)}{3.05H}$$

$$R^2 = 0.67 \qquad F = 5.97$$

where I measured in units of $1,000, E and T are measured in years, and H is measured in terms of a scaled index of one's health: the higher the index, the better the level of health.

a. If one's education increases by two years, what happens to his or her income?

b. Is the model significant at the 5 percent level? State the hypothesis, the decision rule, and the conclusion.

c. Determine which variable(s) is (are) significant at the 10 percent level. State the hypotheses, the decision rule, and the conclusion.

d. What is the value of the adjusted coefficient of determination?

13. What does it mean if the null hypothesis in a test for a single β_i is not rejected?

14. In reference to the previous problem, if $H_0: \beta_i = 0$ is not rejected, according to the model, what will happen to Y if X_i changes by 1 unit? by 2 units?

15. Consider the following model with $n = 30$.

$$\hat{Y} = 50 + 10X_1 + 80X_2$$

$$R^2 = 0.78 \qquad S_{b_1} = 2.73 \qquad S_{b_2} = 4.71$$

Which variable(s) is (are) significant at the 5 percent level? State the hypothesis and the decision rule, and draw a conclusion.

16. Economists have long held that a community's demand for money is affected by the (1) level of income and (2) level of interest. As income goes up, people want to hold more money to facilitate their increased daily transactions. As the interest rate goes up, people choose to hold less money because of the opportunity to invest it at the higher interest rate.

An economist for the federal government regresses money demand (M) or income (I) and interest rates (r), where M is expressed in hundreds of dollars and I in thousands of dollars. The model is

$$\hat{M} = 0.44 + 5.49I + 6.4r$$

A partial ANOVA table is

Source	SS	d.f.
Between samples	93.59	2
Within samples	1.42	9

a. According to the theory of the demand for money, are the signs of the coefficients as expected? Explain.

b. Test the entire model at $\alpha = 0.01$.

17. Given the conditions in the previous problem, if the standard error for the coefficient for I is 1.37 and that of r is 43.6, determine which variable(s) is (are) significant at the 1 percent level? State the hypothesis, the decision rule, and the conclusion.

18. Considering the data from the two previous problems, what portion of the change in M is explained by the model?

19. An economic analyst for IBM wishes to forecast regional sales (S) in hundreds of dollars on the basis of the number of sales personnel (P), the number of new business starts in the region (B), and some measure of prices. As a proxy for the last variable, she uses changes in the CPI. She then collects data for 10 sales regions and derives the following model and partial ANOVA table:

$$\hat{S} = -1.01 + 0.422P + 0.091B - 1.8\text{CPI}$$

Source	SS	d.f.
Between samples	391.57	3
Within samples	31.33	6

a. Test the significance of the entire model at 1 percent. State the hypothesis, the decision rule, and the conclusion.

b. If the standard errors of the coefficients for P, B, and CPI are 0.298, 0.138, and 2.15, respectively, test each coefficient at the 10 percent level. State the hypothesis, decision rule, and conclusion in each case.

c. How can you reconcile the findings from parts a and b?

20. Given the numerous coaching changes in the National Football League in 1989, a sports enthusiast tried to build a model that would predict the number of games a team would win (W) based on net rushing yards (a team's total yards rushing minus opponent's yards rushing) (RY), net passing yards (PY), and net points (NP). She randomly selected the following teams and collected her data.

Team	W	RY	PY	NP
Bears	13	1,052	−334	80
Eagles	10	182	−454	52
Giants	10	−67	−60	55
Redskins	7	−188	697	−42
Chiefs	4	−879	697	−66
Cowboys	3	134	−55	116
Rams	10	321	545	103
49ers	13	1,134	−50	129

Her computer runs using Minitab produced the following results:

```
W = 8.82 + 0.00629 RY - 0.00080 PY - 0.0243 NP

Predictor     Coef       Stdev      t-ratio     P
Constant      8.820      1.577        5.59    0.005
RY            0.006293   0.002704     2.33    0.081
PY           -0.000803   0.002961    -0.27    0.800
NP           -0.02433    0.02458     -0.99    0.378
```

```
s = 2.769      R-sq = 60.2%     R-sq(adj) = 46.1%
Analysis of Variance


SOURCE          DF        SS        MS        F        P


Regression      3       68.836    22.945     2.99     0.159
Error           4       30.664     7.666
Total           7       99.500


                 W          RY         PY
RY            0.785
PY           -0.478      -0.602
NP            0.459       0.791      -0.599
```

Analyze the printouts and comment on any findings you feel are particularly revealing.

21. A marketing specialist wishes to study output at production plants for his firm. He takes measurements for output (O), worker-hours of labor (L), and an index for the level of technology employed in each plant (T). Output is regressed on L and T. The resulting equation is

$$\hat{Q} = -0.475 + 1.778L + 0.30275T; \qquad F = 58.03$$

with

$$\Sigma Q = 195 \qquad \Sigma QL = 678$$

$$\Sigma L = 40 \qquad \Sigma TQ = 7{,}245$$

$$\Sigma T = 428 \qquad S_{b_1} = 0.7251$$

$$\Sigma Q^2 = 3.317 \qquad S_{b_2} = 0.07374$$

$$n = 12$$

a. Test each coefficient at the 5 percent level.
b. Test each coefficient at the 10 percent level.
c. Develop a measure of the dispersion of the average amount by which the actual observations vary around the regression plane.
d. What is the coefficient of determination?

The following problems can be more easily done on a computer.

22. A management director is attempting to develop a system designed to identify what personal attributes are essential for managerial advancement. Fifteen employees who have recently been promoted are given a series of tests to determine their communication skills (X_1), ability to relate to others (X_2), and decision-making ability (X_3). Each employee's job rating (Y) is regressed on these three variables. The original raw data are

Y	X_1	X_2	X_3
80	50	72	18
75	51	74	19
84	42	79	22
62	42	71	17
92	59	85	25
75	45	73	17
63	48	75	16
69	39	73	19
68	40	71	20
87	55	80	30
92	48	83	33
82	45	80	20
74	45	75	18
80	61	75	20
62	59	70	15

    a. Develop the regression model. Evaluate it by determining if it shows a significant relationship among the dependent variable and the three independent variables.

    b. What can be said about the significance of each X_i?

23. To what cause might you attribute the insignificance of X_1 and X_3? Obtain the correlation matrix for these variables and test each pair for multicollinearity.

24. Compare your results in the previous problem to those obtained based on VIF.

25. Should the management director in the problem above use this model to identify characteristics which made an employee eligible for advancement?

26. As a class project, a team of marketing students devises a model which explains rent for student housing near their university. Rent is in dollars, SQFT is the square footage of the apartment or house, and DIST is distance in miles from house to campus.

Rent	SQFT	DIST
220	900	3.2
250	1,100	2.2
310	1,250	1.0
420	1,300	0.5
350	1,275	1.5
510	1,500	0.5
400	1,290	1.5
450	1,370	0.5
500	1,400	0.5
550	1,550	0.3
450	1,200	0.5
320	1,275	1.5

    a. Devise the model. Is it significant at the 1 percent level?

    b. Evaluate the significance of both coefficients.

    c. Are the signs appropriate? Explain.

27. Evaluate the model from the previous problems. Does it appear useful in predicting rent? Explain.

28. Is there evidence of multicollinearity in the model from the previous problem? Does it invalidate the model for predicting rent? Why or why not?

29. From the model developed above for student rents, can you conclude distance from campus is a stronger determinant of rent than is square footage? Why or why not?

30. If two apartments have the same space, but one is 2 miles closer to campus, how will its rent differ from that of the more distant dwelling?

31. In order to expand their model on students' rents, the marketing majors from the problems above devise a luxury index in which students rate the amenities of an apartment based on available comforts, such as swimming pools, tennis courts, maid service, and other luxuries to which students are traditionally accustomed. For the 12 observations above, this index measured 22, 23, 35, 40, 32, 55, 36, 41, 51, 50, 48, and 29. Incorporate the variable in your model to explain rents. Analyze and explain why you got these results. Is your model better with this additional variable? What problem are you likely encountering, and what change would you make to correct it?

32. Make the change you suggested in the previous problem and discuss your results.

33. In the past, many economists have studied the spending patterns of consumers in the economy. A famous study by Milton Friedman concludes that consumption is a function of *permanent income,* which is defined as the average level of income the consumer expects to receive well into the future. The *habit-persistence* theory of T. M. Brown argues that consumption is shaped by a consumer's most recent peak income—the highest income received in the recent past.

   To combine these two theories, an economist collected data on consumption (CONS), permanent income (PERM), and peak income (PEAK) and performed OLS to devise a model. Given these data, what did that model look like? All values are in thousands of dollars.

CONS	PERM	PEAK
12	15	17
22	28	31
15	19	21
17	19	24
19	24	27
14	17	20
20	25	29
17	21	25
15	19	22
16	20	26

   a. Evaluate the model.
   b. Would multicollinearity explain the insignificance of PEAK? How can you tell?

34. From the previous problem, run two simple models using each form of income. What can you conclude about each type of income as a predictor of consumption and the problem of multicollinearity in the multiple regression model?

35. Given the multiple regression model in Problem 33.
    a. What does the fact that b_1 and b_2 are less than 1 tell you?
    b. If PERM goes up by $1 and PEAK remains constant, by how much will CONS change?
    c. If PEAK goes up by $1 and PERM is held constant, by how much will CONS change?

36. Studies in finance have shown that the price of a share of stock (P) is directly related to the issuing company's level of debt (D) and to the dividend rate (DR), but is inversely related to the number of shares outstanding (SO). The data shown here are in dollars for P, hundreds of thousands for D, in dollars for DR, and in thousands of shares for SO.

P	D	DR	SO
52.50	12.00	2.10	100
14.25	3.40	0.69	37
35.21	7.10	1.70	68
45.21	10.40	1.81	90
17.54	4.00	0.70	32
22.00	5.10	0.88	45
37.10	8.50	1.50	78
29.12	6.70	1.20	60
46.32	10.65	1.85	95
49.30	11.34	2.00	99

    a. Devise the OLS model. Does it support the theoretical relationships expressed above? What would happen to P if
    b. D increased by $100,000?
    c. DR decreased by $0.50?
    d. SO increased by 500 shares?

37. Given the data shown, calculate the residuals for each observation. Regress Y on X_1, X_2, and the residuals. Before doing so, what should the values for Se, R^2, and $\bar{R}^2$ be? Perform the regression and see if you were right. Why did you get that value for R^2 and Se?

Y	X_1	X_2
12	25	26
23	35	36
98	87	86
65	56	54
36	23	41
65	45	52
78	69	59
21	25	36
54	65	49
25	36	24

38. The members of a national social organization at the local university got the bright idea of selling T-shirts at the campus concerts by Jimmy Buffet, a singer well known for his laid-back, tropical Caribbean theme. The shirts would cost $5.20 each plus $1.75 to imprint a picture of Buffet and the fraternity letters. They hoped to sell them for just under $10.

After a few concerts at campuses in Georgia and South Carolina, it became painfully obvious that the fraternity was having a problem judging in the market. They either found themselves with a surplus after the concert, or supply fell far short of demand. Their statistics professor suggested that they develop a model to forecast demand. From the last eight concerts, data were collected on the number of T-shirts sold or the estimate of what could have been had there been sufficient numbers (DEMAND), enrollment at the university's main campus (E), and advanced ticket sales (T). The data are shown here: E is in thousands, and T is in hundreds.

DEMAND	E	T
220	12.0	12.0
520	32.0	25.0
800	47.0	42.0
450	24.0	22.0
375	22.6	18.5
250	15.0	12.9
350	21.0	17.5
650	39.0	32.5

a. Does it appear that the model has potential to accurately predict demand?
b. What would happen to demand if E was 2,000 higher, assuming T remains constant?
c. What would happen to demand if T was 50 higher, assuming E is held steady?
39. A specialty store emphasizing fashions for the successful businessperson is trying to identify variables that can explain the level of purchases by customers. Data are collected for dollar sales each visit (S), income of customer (I) in thousands, and years of experience the customer had with his or her present employer (E). It was felt that the last variable measured how high the customer had risen on the business "success ladder" and thus reflects his or her need for fine attire.

S	I	E
630	107	12
550	95	12
320	54	6
820	141	16
450	76	10
755	130	15
750	127	14
330	55	9
1,020	174	22
655	110	13
420	127	8
545	94	11
740	125	15

After collecting the data, the store manager finds himself to be statistically illiterate has no idea what to do with them. How can you help?

40. Based on the results of the previous problem, if the manager has the opportunity to serve a customer with one more year's experience or one with $1,000 more in income, which should he accommodate?

41. Does your answer to the previous problem identify that variable which is more important in explaining sales?

42. A computer run produces the following printout with a few of the important statistics omitted. Complete the printout by providing the missing values. Identify the significant variables and their respective *p*-values.

```
Multiple R          .997
R Square            .995
Adjusted R Square
Standard Error    26.040


Analysis of Variance
                    DF     Sum of Squares     Mean Square
Regression           2        594595.268      297297.643
Residual             4          2712.446         678.111


F =                     Signif F =  .0000



Variable          B      SE B      Beta        T    Sig T


X2            -3.867     .693     -.204             .0051
X1             9.901     .342     1.060             .0000
(Constant)   957.828   55.435             17.278    .0001


End Block Number   1  All requested variables entered.



CORR VARI ALL.


Correlations:  Y        X1        X2


Y            1.000     .979**    .214
X1            .979**   1.000     .394
X2       .    .214      .394     1.000


N of cases:    7       1-tailed Signif:  * - .01  ** - .001


" * " is printed if a coefficient cannot be computed
```

43. Consider the printout from the previous problem. Perform all tests for multicollinearity. State and defend your conclusions.

EMPIRICAL EXERCISES

44. For years your teachers have told you that there is a link between studying and grades. From a survey of your fellow students willing to reveal their academic success, or lack thereof, collect data on grade point average (GPA), typical number of hours per day or week spent studying, number of earned credit hours, and any other factor you think may help explain grades. Using GPA as the dependent variable, develop a regression model based on these variables. Does it appear that the time-honored relationship between effort and grades, as well as the other variables you have chosen, does exist?

45. From Federal Reserve publications or other appropriate sources, collect data on personal consumption expenditures, the money supply, and some measure of income at the national level. Does it appear, as economic theory attests, that consumption is a function of income and the amount of liquid assets available in the economy?

46. Formulate a theoretical model using variables pertaining to your major or intended profession. If you are an economics major, a model such as that specified in Problem 45 would be appropriate. A finance major may want to investigate the relationship between stock valuation, debt levels, and dividend rates. Be sure you use a multiple regression model. Collect the necessary data to analyze the OLS model. Does it support the theoretical principles upon which the model was based?

CASE APPLICATIONS

47. John Baker owns a trucking firm which contracts with the local parts authorities in Kansas City to haul goods brought in by barge on the Missouri River. Baker picks up the cargo at the docking area every morning and delivers it throughout the city. Since the amount of cargo he is expected to haul varies considerably from one day to the next, it has been Baker's practice to hire day-workers as the need arises and to rent trucks from a local firm when his small fleet is insufficient. For some time now, Baker has wanted to devise a scheme to better estimate the volume of cargo he finds waiting for him each morning, as well as the number of workers and trucks he will need to complete the job. Baker's son, Bill, has a degree in management and took several statistics courses. Bill feels that the ability to handle cargo could best be explained by the number of day-workers hired and the number of available trucks. John fears that his money might have been wasted. It doesn't take a college degree to figure out that the amount of goods John can carry depends on the resources he has ready for use. Besides, this still leaves the problem of estimating the cargo that awaits on the dock for citywide dispersal each morning.

It is here that young Bill impresses his father. Perhaps the morning cargo could best be estimated by noting the shipping tonnage that passed through the lock upriver the previous day. Part of that tonnage will be off-loaded on Baker's dock. In addition, the amount of cargo might also depend on the number of dock workers available to unload it.

With this in mind, the younger Baker collects data for variables. Twenty days are randomly selected from the past six months. Bill records the tons transported by his father's trucking company (TT), as well as the number of day-workers (DW) and trucks (TR) employed by his father on those days. A second random sample of 15 days is taken from the same six-month period. The tonnage which passed upriver the previous day,

(*TON*), the number of dock workers (*DOCK*), and the volume of cargo off-loaded and awaiting transportation (*CARGO*) are recorded. These data are shown here:

TT	DW	TR	TON	DOCK	CARGO
52	25	7	60	7	42
47	24	6	67	8	45
37	19	5	89	13	60
68	33	9	98	15	69
59	28	8	90	13	62
63	30	8	74	11	54
74	36	10	69	10	48
55	24	7	74	11	55
36	16	5	81	12	56
49	24	7	71	11	50
71	34	9	84	13	59
65	31	9	73	12	52
60	28	8	94	14	65
60	29	9	74	12	52
42	21	5	86	13	58
69	31	9			
71	32	9			
45	22	6			
51	24	7			
47	22	5			

a. Develop the two OLS models described above and determine if Bill has assisted his father in planning for his business operations.
b. If *DOCK* = 14 and *TON* = 72, what is the amount of *CARGO* the Bakers can expect?
c. Given the values in part *b*, how many day-workers will John need if he has seven trucks?

CHAPTER FOURTEEN

DUMMY VARIABLES AND RESIDUAL ANALYSIS: EXTENSIONS OF REGRESSION AND CORRELATION

A PREVIEW OF THINGS TO LOOK FOR

1   How dummy variables can be used to incorporate qualitative measures in a regression model.

2   The ways in which residual analysis is used to evaluate a model.

3   The detection and impact of autocorrelation.

4   The role played by the Durbin-Watson statistic in residual analysis.

5   The use of logarithms and polynomials to develop curvilinear models.

CHAPTER BLUEPRINT

Chapters 12 and 13 thoroughly described the many ways in which regression and correlation can be used to develop solutions to common business problems. This chapter offers a few finishing touches to our study of regression and correlation. It explores some important features not examined earlier.

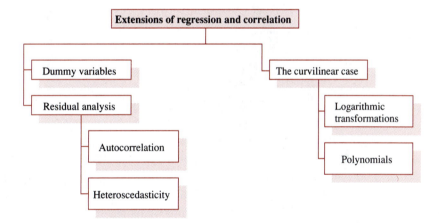

> ○○○○ Statistics show that it's often easier to do something
> ○○○   right than to explain why you did it wrong.
> ○○
> ○

14.1 INTRODUCTION

By now you should be well aware of the power and versatility of regression and correlation analysis. Throughout the last two chapters we have witnessed how these vital tools of statistical analysis can address many business problems.

However, we have not yet examined several pertinent factors related to regression and correlation. We will now explore these statistical features associated with regression and correlation, which greatly enhance the usefulness of these two powerful instruments of statistical inquiry. In addition, we will investigate ways in which regression models can be evaluated and the manner in which improvements can be implemented. Our attention will focus primarily on

- Dummy variables.
- Autocorrelation.
- Residual analysis.
- Heteroscedasticity.
- Curvilinear analysis.

14.2 DUMMY VARIABLES

In your research efforts you may find that many variables may be useful in explaining the value of the dependent variable. For example, years of education, training, and experience are instrumental in determining the level of a person's income. These variables can be easily measured numerically and readily lend themselves to statistical analysis.

However, such is not the case with many other variables which are also useful in explaining income levels. Studies have shown that sex and geography also carry considerable explanatory power. A woman with the same number of years of education and training as a man will not receive the same income. A worker in the Northeast may not earn the same as a worker in the South doing a similar job. Both gender and geography can prove to be highly useful explanatory variables in the effort to predict one's income. However, neither variable can readily be expressed numerically and cannot be directly included in a regression model. We must therefore modify the form of these nonnumeric variables so as to permit their inclusion into our model and thereby gain the additional explanatory power that they offer.

Variables which are not expressed in a direct, quantitative fashion are called **qualitative variables** or **dummy variables.** As another illustration, the sales of a firm may depend on the season. Swimwear probably sells better in the spring than it does in the fall or winter. More snow shovels are sold in December than in July. This seasonal factor can only be captured by taking into account the time of year (fall, winter, spring, or summer), a variable which cannot be measured numerically. Whether a person is married, single, or divorced may affect his or her expenditures for recreational purposes, while one's place of residence (urban, suburban, or rural) will likely impact on their tax assessment. In all these cases, the variables we wish to measure cannot readily be expressed numerically. We must use dummy variables to obtain a more complete description of the impact of these nonnumeric measures.

Dummy Variable
A variable which accounts for the qualitative nature of a variable and incorporates its explanatory power into the model is known as a dummy variable.

As the regional manager for a department store chain, you wish to study the relationship between mean expenditures by your customers and those variables you feel might explain the level of those expenditures. In addition to the logical choice of income as an explanatory variable, you feel that a customer's sex may also play a part in explaining expenditures. You therefore collect 10 observations for these three variables: expenditures in dollars, income in dollars, and sex.

But how do you encode the data for sex into the model? You cannot simply specify M or F for male and female, because these letters cannot be manipulated mathematically. The solution is found by assigning values of 0 or 1 to each observation based on sex. You might, for example, choose to record a 0 if the observation is male and a 1 if the observation is female. The reverse is equally likely. You could just as well encode a 0 if female and a 1 if male. (We will examine the effects of this alternate coding scheme shortly.)

Suppose you chose to record a 0 if the observation is male and a 1 if it is female. The complete data set for $n = 10$ observations is shown in Table 14-1, with Y in dollars and X_1 in units of $1,000. Notice that X_2 contains only values of 0 for male and 1 for female.

Using the OLS procedures discussed in the previous two chapters, the regression equation becomes

$$\hat{Y} = b_0 + b_1 X_1 + b_2 X_2$$
$$= 12.21 + 0.791 X_1 + 5.11 X_2$$
$$(0.000) \quad (0.010)$$

The p-values are shown in parentheses.

The use of a dummy variable for sex will actually produce two regression lines, one for males and one for females. These lines have the same slope but different intercepts. In other words, the equation gives two parallel regression lines that start at

TABLE 14-1   Data for Study of Customer's Expenditures

Observation	Expenditures (Y)	Income (X_1)	Sex (X_2)
1	51	40	1
2	30	25	0
3	32	27	0
4	45	32	1
5	51	45	1
6	31	29	0
7	50	42	1
8	47	38	1
9	45	30	0
10	39	29	1
11	50	41	1
12	35	23	1
13	40	36	0
14	45	42	0
15	50	48	0

different points on the vertical axis. Since we encoded a 0 for males, the equation becomes

$$\hat{Y} = b_0 + b_1 X_1 + b_2 X_2$$
$$= 12.21 + 0.791 X_1 + 5.11(0)$$
$$= 12.21 + 0.791 X_1$$

for males. This line has an intercept of 12.21 and a slope of 0.791, and is shown in Figure 14-1.

FIGURE 14-1   Regression Lines for Customer

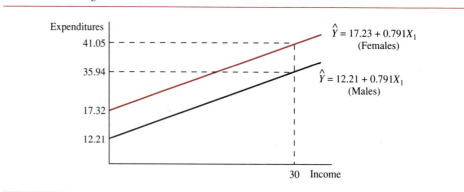

For females, the encoded value of 1 produces

$$\hat{Y} = 12.21 + 0.791X_1 + 5.11(1)$$

$$= 17.32 + 0.791X_1$$

This second line has the same slope as the line for males, but has an intercept of 17.32. Since $X_2 = 1$ for females, the intercept was determined as $b_0 + b_2 = 12.21 + 5.11 = 17.32$.

This means that for any given level of income, women customers spend $5.11 more on the average than do men. Let income equal 30 ($30,000). Then for women

$$\hat{Y} = 12.21 + 0.791(30) + 5.11(1)$$

$$= 41.05$$

and for men

$$\hat{Y} = 12.21 + 0.791(30) + 5.11(0)$$

$$= 35.94$$

The difference of $5.11 occurs because the encoded value of 0 for males cancels out the b_2 coefficient of 5.11, while the encoded value of 1 for females results in the addition of 5.11 to the equation.

The p-vlaue of 0.010 tells you that the coefficient of 5.11 for sex is significant at the 1 percent level. However, if the p-value was not given, you should test the hypothesis that it differs significantly from zero. That is,

$$H_0: \beta_2 = 0$$

$$H_a: \beta_2 \neq 0$$

Using SPSS-PC the standard error of β_2 was estimated to be

$$S_{b_2} = 1.672$$

Then

$$t = \frac{b_2}{S_{b_2}}$$

$$= \frac{5.11}{1.672}$$

$$= 3.06$$

If $\alpha = 0.05$, $t_{0.05, n-k-1} = t_{0.05, 12} = 2.179$.

Decision Rule
Do not reject if $-2.179 < t < 2.179$. Reject if $t < -2.179$ or $t > 2.179$.

The t-value of 3.06 results in a rejection of the null. It is concluded at the 95 percent level of confidence that a significant difference exists between expenditures by men and women customers.

If you had encoded the dummy valuable by assigning a 1 to a male observation and a 0 for a female observation, the results would be the same. A computer run shows the equation to be

$$\hat{Y} = 17.32 + 0.791X_1 - 5.11X_2$$

For females, we have

$$\hat{Y} = 17.32 + 0.791X_1 - 5.11(0)$$

$$= 17.32 + 0.791X_1$$

and for males

$$\hat{Y} = 17.32 + 0.791X_1 - 5.11(1)$$

$$= 12.21 + 0.791X_1$$

Encoding the dummy variables either way yields the same results.

If the data were put into a scatter diagram, they might appear as in Figure 14-2.

FIGURE 14-2   Scatter Diagram for Expenditures

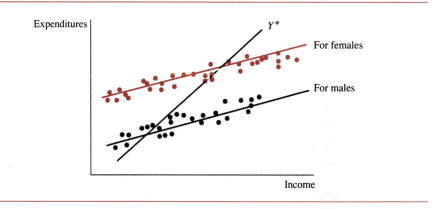

In an extreme case, there could appear two almost totally separate diagrams, one for the male observations and one for the females. If the dummy variable was ignored and only one line was fitted, its slope would be much steeper than the other two, such as the line identified as Y^*. The effect attributed to income alone by the single regression line should be partially ascribed to sex.

If a dummy variable has more than two possible responses, you cannot encode it as 0, 1, 2, 3, and so on. A variable with r possible responses will be expanded to encompass a total of $r - 1$ variables. For example, you might include a third variable in your model to study the effect of marital status on expenditures. Your possible responses might include married, single, divorced, and widowed. In addition to X_1 for income and X_2 for sex, these four possible responses require three additional variables, X_3, X_4, and X_5, to encode the data on marital status. This is done by entering only a 0 or a 1 for each variable in the following manner:

$$X_3 = 1 \qquad \text{if married}$$
$$= 0 \qquad \text{if not married}$$
$$X_4 = 1 \qquad \text{if single}$$
$$= 0 \qquad \text{if not single}$$
$$X_5 = 1 \qquad \text{if divorced}$$
$$= 0 \qquad \text{if not divorced}$$

No entry for widowed is necessary, because if $X_3 = X_4 = X_5 = 0$, the process of elimination reveals the observation to be widowed. Assume 0 is encoded for male and 1 for female in X_2. The three observations (OBS) shown here are for a (1) married male with expenditures of 30 and income of 40, (2) a divorced female with expenditures of 35 and income of 38, and (3) a widowed male with expenditures of 20 and income of 45.

OBS	Y	X_1	X_2	X_3	X_4	X_5
1	30	40	0	1	0	0
2	35	38	1	0	0	1
3	20	45	0	0	0	0

For example, in the first observation, X_2 would be 0 since the observation is male, and X_3 is 1, while both X_4 and X_5 are 0 since the observation is married.

QUICK CHECK 14.2.1

○○○○

A salesman wishes to regress sales (Y) on (1) advertising and (2) the state in which the sales were made. His territory covers Iowa, Indiana, Ohio, and Illinois.

a. How many dummy variables will he need?
b. Identify them, using X_1.
c. How would you encode an observation of 20 in sales in Iowa, 30 in Ohio, 40 in Illinois?

Answer:

a. 3
b. One possibility is X_1 = advertising, X_2 = Iowa, X_3 = Indiana, X_4 = Ohio.
c.

X_1	X_2	X_3	X_4
20	1	0	0
30	0	0	1
40	0	0	0

QUICK CHECK 14.2.2

OOOO

If the equation from 14.2.1 proved to be $Y = 20 + 40X_1 + 20X_2 + 30X_3 - 20X_4$, what would sales be

a.   in Iowa if $X_1 = 10$?

b.   in Illinois if $X_1 = 5$?

Answer: a. $S = 20 + 40(10) + 20(1) + 30(0) - 20(0) = 440$

b. $S = 20 + 40(5) + 20(0) + 30(0) - 20(0) = 220$

14.3   RESIDUAL ANALYSIS

In regression and correlation, as with other experience in life, we can learn from our mistakes. It is therefore wise to examine the residuals, or error terms, in our regression model. As noted earlier, a good regression exhibits purely random errors which are normally distributed with a mean of 0 and a variance of σ^2. If an examination of these residuals reveals conditions to the contrary, this may suggest that there are inherent problems in the model. The detection of any pattern of correlation in the error terms could suggest that some of the basic assumptions regarding the OLS model are being violated. The remainder of this chapter is devoted to an examination of error terms and to an analysis of the problems that may be detected from such an examination. We concentrate primarily on the principles of autocorrelation and heteroscedasticity.

A.   AUTOCORRELATION

One of the basic properties of the OLS model is that the errors be uncorrelated. The error in prediction that you suffer at one point in time is not linearly related to the error that you might suffer at another point. Ideally, if you were to graph your errors over time, they should appear as in Figure 14-3. There is no detectable pattern in the errors. The error terms appear to be independent and offer no indication of any relationship with each other.

FIGURE 14-3   Absence of Autocorrelation

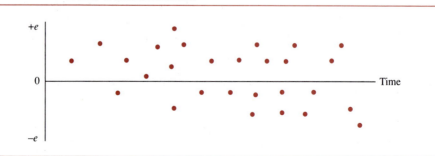

However, as noted in Chapter 12, when dealing with time-series data this condition is often violated. We find that errors can be correlated, resulting in **autocorrelation** (AC). Over time, many economic series such as unemployment, GNP, or interest rates move cyclically. If a series is unusually low (high) relative to its long run mean in one month, it is probably still low (high) in the next month. Corrections are simply not made overnight. A regression model is based on a series' long-run average. If a series is unusually low, the regression model will likely overestimate its value. This overestimate will produce a negative error since $e = Y_i - \hat{Y}$. Since the series is probably still unusually low the next time period, another negative error is to be expected. The reverse is true when the series cycles to an unusually high level. Positive errors will be generated for several successive time periods. This pattern of successive negative errors, followed by several positive errors, is evidence of autocorrelation.

Figure 14-4 illustrates autocorrelation. There is a distinct pattern in the error terms. Several successive negative errors initiate the pattern, followed by several positive errors, and, in turn, several more negative errors. (In practice, don't expect the pattern to be so obvious.)

FIGURE 14-4   Presence of Positive Autocorrelation

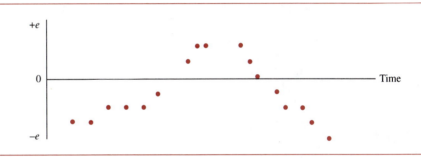

The correlation between error terms can be measured just like the correlation between any two variables in the model. The correlation between an error in one time period t and the previous time period, $t - 1$, is expressed as $\rho_{e_t, e_{t-1}}$, where the parameter ρ is the population correlation coefficient for error terms. Like all parameters, it is estimated by its corresponding statistic using the sample data. This correlation between errors at the sample level is measured by r, the same sample correlation coefficient that we have used in measuring correlation between any two variables in our model. In Figure 14-3, where AC is absent, we would estimate the correlation among error terms using $r_{e_t, e_{t-1}}$ to be zero. However, Figure 14-4 suggests that an error is likely to be followed by another error of the same sign. Thus, $r_{e_t, e_{t-1}} > 0$. There is said to be positive AC. If the errors tended to alternate in sign as in Figure 14-5, negative correlation would be present, and $r_{e_t, e_{t-1}} < 0$.

In the presence of AC, all the hypothesis tests and confidence intervals that we examined in Chapters 12 and 13 are rendered less reliable. This makes autocorrelation an extremely harmful condition.

FIGURE 14-5   Presence of Negative Autocorrelation

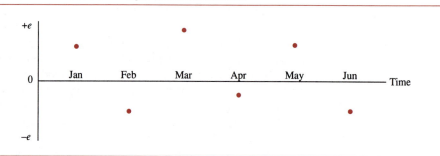

A model can be built to examine the error in your original model. If ε is the error, then the model relating the error in one time period to that in the next is

$$\varepsilon_t = \rho_{\varepsilon_{t-1}} + \mu_t \qquad\qquad (14.1)$$

where ρ is the correlation between errors in the original model, and μ is the random error term in the prediction of those errors; that is, it measures the error we suffer in trying to estimate the error in our original model. The term μ_t, often called *white noise,* occurs because errors in the original model are not perfectly correlated. There will therefore be some error in our attempt to predict the error in our original model.

Figure 14-6 also depicts error patterns which can reveal information about the model by plotting e_t against e_{t-1}.

FIGURE 14-6   Detection of Autocorrelation

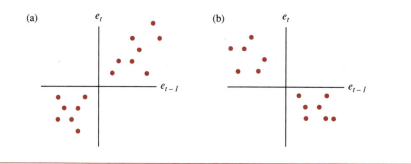

In Figure 14-6(a), positive autocorrelation is present because where e_t is positive e_{t-1} is also positive, and where e_t is negative e_{t-1} is also negative. Consecutive errors have the same sign. The error relationship is contained in the two positive quadrants of the axes. This would suggest $\rho_{e_t,e_{t-1}} > 0$.

In Figure 14-6(b) the error terms are restricted to the two negative quadrants, evidencing negative correlation. That is, e_t and e_{t-1} tend to take on opposite signs, indicating $\rho_{e_t, e_{t-1}} < 0$.

Although analyzing errors can be a means of detecting autocorrelation, it is not very reliable. Patterns are seldom as obvious as suggested here. A less fallible approach is required. This procedure is based on the Durbin-Watson statistic d. The Durbin-Watson statistic is used to test the hypothesis of no autocorrelation:

$$H_0: \rho_{e_t, e_{t-1}} = 0; \quad \text{no autocorrelation}$$

$$H_a: \rho_{e_t, e_{t-1}} \neq 0; \quad \text{autocorrelation present}$$

It is calculated as

$$d = \frac{\Sigma(e_t - e_{t-1})^2}{\Sigma(e_t)^2} \tag{14.2}$$

Using our data from the study on consumer expenditures, Table 14-2 provides the necessary calculations. Note that $0 \leq d \leq 4$. As a general rule, if d is close to 2, it is assumed that autocorrelation is not a problem. However, it is advisable to determine if the value actually found using Formula (14.2) is significant by testing the hypothesis that $\rho = 0$. Then

$$d = \frac{\Sigma(e_t - e_{t-1})^2}{\Sigma(e_t)^2}$$

$$= \frac{59.40475}{29.12203}$$

$$= 2.03$$

The critical values to which we will compare $d = 2.03$ are found using two values: the number of independent variables, k, and the number of observations, n. In our example, $k = 2$ and $n = 15$. If $\alpha = 0.05$, Table K gives $d_L = 0.95$ and $d_U = 1.54$. A simple scale can now be constructed, as in Figure 14-7, to determine if the null hypothesis of no autocorrelation is rejected or not rejected.

If $d_U < d < 4 - d_U$, there is no evidence of autocorrelation and the null is not rejected; $d < d_L$ evidences positive AC; $d > 4 - d_L$ indicates negative AC. The two inconclusive regions arise because the distribution of d depends on the characteristics

FIGURE 14-7   Durbin-Watson Statistic

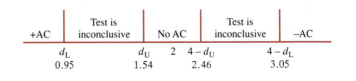

TABLE 14-2   Calculation of the Durbin-Watson Statistic

OBS	Y_i	$\hat{Y}$	e_t	$(e_t)^2$	$e_t - e_{t-1}$	$(e_t - e_{t-1})^2$
1	51	49.3359	1.66407	2.76912	*	*
2	30	30.3784	−0.37839	0.14318	−2.04246	4.1716
3	32	32.1138	−0.11380	0.01295	0.26459	0.0700
4	45	42.3943	2.60572	6.78980	2.71953	7.3958
5	51	53.6745	−2.67447	7.15280	−5.28020	27.8805
6	31	32.9815	−1.98151	3.92638	0.69296	0.4802
7	50	51.0714	−1.07135	1.14779	0.91016	0.8284
8	47	46.7328	0.26719	0.07139	1.33854	1.7917
9	45	42.5263	2.47371	6.11922	2.20652	4.8687
10	39	39.7912	−0.79115	0.62592	−3.26486	10.6593
11	50	50.2180	0.21800	0.04752	1.00915	1.01838
12	35	34.5940	0.40600	0.16483	0.18800	0.03534
13	40	39.9380	0.06200	0.00384	−0.34400	0.11834
14	45	45.1460	−0.14600	0.02132	−0.20800	0.04326
15	50	50.3540	−0.35400	0.12532	−0.20800	0.04326
				29.12203		59.40478

of the interrelationships among the independent variables. No generalization of these characteristics can be broad enough to unambiguously restrict the d-value.

The d was calculated to be 2.03, so the null is not rejected. It would appear that correlation between error terms is not a problem.

The calculations are rather tedious. They can be simplified by estimating the value for d as

$$d = 2(1 - r) \qquad (14.3)$$

where r is the correlation coefficient between e_t and e_{t-1}. Still, if the computations must be done by hand, a good deal of arithmetic is necessary. Luckily, most computer programs report the Durbin-Watson value.

QUICK CHECK 14.3.1

○○○○

In a model with $k = 3$ and $n = 30$, d is calculated to be 3.12. At the 5 percent level, is autocorrelation present? Explain.

Answer: Yes, $d_L = 1.21$; $d_U = 1.65$; $3.12 > 4 - d_L$. Negative AC is present.

QUICK CHECK 14.3.2

If $r_{e_t, e_{t-1}} = 0.75$, is AC present at the 1 percent level if $k = 4$ and $n = 35$? Explain.

Answer: $d = 2(1 - 0.75) = 0.5$; $d_L = 1.03$; $d_U = 1.51$; $0.5 < d_L$. Positive AC is present.

B. HETEROSCEDASTICITY

In addition to any absence of correlation in errors, another basic property of the OLS model is homoscedasticity. In Chapter 13 we defined homoscedasticity as a constant variation in the error terms. The variation in errors experienced when X is equal to some value, say 10, is the same as the variance in errors when X equals any other value. In Figure 14-8(a), as shown by the two normal curves, the distribution of the Y_i-values above and below the regression line is the same at $X = 10$ as it is at $X = 11$. Thus, the errors, which are represented by the difference between these Y_i-values and the regression line, are normally distributed. This indicates the presence of homoscedasticity.

FIGURE 14-8   Distribution of Errors

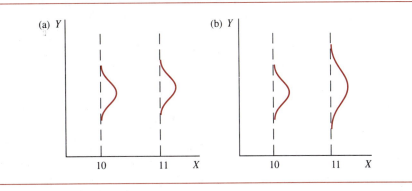

If the variance in errors is not the same for all values of X, **heteroscedasticity** occurs. Figure 14-8(b) shows that as X increases the variance in error terms becomes more pronounced. The normal curve at $X = 11$ is more spread out than the curve at $X = 10$, indicating greater dispersion in the errors.

Heteroscedasticity
The error terms do not have the same variance.

Heteroscedasticity is common with cross-sectional data. Cross-sectional data are often used, for example, in investigations of consumer spending habits. In such studies, data are collected for consumption and income across income levels which encompass the poor, the rich, and those in between. This constitutes a cross-sectional data set because it cuts across different income groups. As might be expected, the rich display a behavioral model with respect to their consumption pattern that is different from the rest of us. This difference causes a variation in error terms that evidences heteroscedasticity.

In the presence of heteroscedasticity the regression coefficients become less efficient. That is, there is an increase in the variance of the b-values. The b-value obtained with one sample differs from that obtained if a different random sample is selected. In such a case, it is difficult to place much faith in the regression coefficients.

Heteroscedasticity can often be detected by plotting the $\hat{Y}$-values against the error terms. If any pattern is displayed, heteroscedasticity is likely present. Figures 14-9(a) and 14-9(b) reveal possible patterns often encountered in the presence of heteroscedasticity. Figure 14-9(c), however, does not suggest any detectable pattern. Heteroscedasticity appears to be absent.

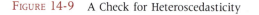

FIGURE 14-9   A Check for Heteroscedasticity

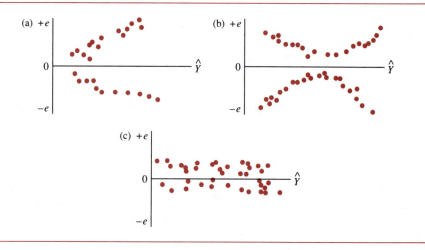

If heteroscedasticity is suspected, the use of the generalized least-squares (GLS) method is recommended. A discussion of GLS can be found in more advanced texts.

Although residual patterns are a good indication of heteroscedasticity, trying to read them is more of an art form than a scientific procedure. The patterns seldom cooperate by being as obvious as suggested above. A more concrete method of detecting heteroscedasticity is needed. The remainder of this section presents common methods of identifying the presence of heteroscedasticity.

WHITE'S TEST FOR HETEROSCEDASTICITY   In 1980, Halbert White offered such a method based on the χ^2 distribution (see Chapter 11). His approach involves several well-defined steps:

1.   Run the original regression and obtain the error term for each observation.
2.   Square the error terms to get e^2 and regress them on all independent variables, the squares of all independent variables, and the cross-products of all independent variables. If there were three independent variables X_1, X_2, and X_3, you must regress e^2 on X_1, X_2, X_3, X_1^2, X_2^2, X_3^2, $X_1 X_2$, $X_1 X_3$, and $X_2 X_3$. This regression model is called the *auxiliary model*.
3.   Compute nR^2, where n is the number of observations and R^2 is the unadjusted coefficient of determination from the auxiliary equation.

4. If $nR^2 > \chi^2_{\alpha,k}$, reject the null that error variances are equal and assume heteroscedasticity exists.

Certain precautions must be observed in carrying out step 2. Most notably for our purpose is the danger involved if dummy variables are used in the model. If X_i is a dummy variable, then X_i^2 should not be included in the auxiliary equation because X_i equals X_i^2 and perfect multicollinearity exists. In addition, the cross-product of two dummy variables is also excluded since it equals zero.

We can use the data on consumer expenditures from Table 14-1 to illustrate. The auxiliary equation would regress e^2 on X_1, X_2, X_1^2, and X_1X_2. Notice that X_2^2 is excluded since X_2 is a dummy variable. The results are

$$e^2 = -0.715 + 0.22X_1 - 5.814X_2 - 0.004X_1^2 + 0.188X_1X_2$$
$$\quad\quad\quad (0.867)\quad\;\; (0.482)\quad\;\; (0.808)\quad\quad (0.421)$$

with $R^2 = 0.121$. The p-values are reported in parentheses. Here, $nR^2 = (15)(0.121) = 1.82$, and $\chi^2_{0.05,4} = 9.488$. Since $nR^2 = 1.82 < 9.488$, we do not reject the null that the error terms have equal variances, and we conclude that heteroscedasticity does not exist.

14.4   THE CURVILINEAR CASE

Throughout our discussion, we have been assuming that the relationship between X and Y can be expressed by a straight line. That is, the relationship is linear. However, this is not always the case. Suppose we plotted our data in a scatter diagram and found results like those in Figure 14-10. A straight line $\hat{Y} = a + bX$ would produce a poor fit. The data in Figure 14-10 suggest a nonlinear (or curvilinear) exponential relationship

$$\hat{Y} = b_0 b_1^X \quad\quad\quad\quad\quad (14.4)$$

where b_0 and b_1 are constants.

FIGURE 14-10   A Nonlinear Relationship

Without the linearity we must somehow transform the data for one or both variables in order to display it as a linear model. A common method of transformation uses logarithms. This logarithmic transformation makes the data *linear in the log*. In this event, or, if for any other reason, we suspect a nonlinear relationship, a logarithmic transformation may be required.

A linear relationship assumes that for every 1-unit change in X, Y changes by a constant amount. In our Hop Scotch Airlines example, for every 1-unit increase in advertising, passengers increased by 1.08 units.

A curvilinear model assumes that Y changes by a different amount each time. Take, for example, a savings account earning a compound interest rate of 6 percent. The dollar value will increase by a larger amount each time period, since it earns 6 percent of a larger base each time. This will generate an *increasing* function, as shown in Figure 14-10. It is called an increasing function because the additions to Y increase each time. In the advent of a *decreasing* function, the additions to Y become smaller each time. We will examine each case.

A.   AN INCREASING FUNCTION

For an increasing function, the rules of logarithms allow us to express Formula (14.4) as

$$\log \hat{Y} = \log b_0 + (\log b_1)X \qquad (14.5)$$

Already it is looking like a linear expression, in which $\log b_0$ is the intercept and $\log b_1$ is the slope. The values for $\log b_0$ and $\log b_1$ are found from the equations

$$\log b_1 = \frac{n\Sigma(X \log Y) - (\Sigma X)(\Sigma \log Y)}{n\Sigma X^2 - (\Sigma X)^2} \qquad (14.6)$$

and

$$\log b_0 = \frac{\Sigma \log Y}{n} - \log b_1 \frac{\Sigma X}{n} \qquad (14.7)$$

After $\log \hat{Y}$ has been calculated, we use antilogs to get the estimate for Y. We can best illustrate this with the use of time-series data. **Time-series data** are a collection of data over a series of time periods (days, months, years, etc.). Example 14-1 illustrates.

EXAMPLE 14-1 A Nonlinear Regression Case

A common example of $\hat{Y} = b_0 b_1^X$ is found with many economic time series which tend to change by a certain percentage each time period. In this event, we are estimating a trend line based on logarithms.

Monthly sales revenues in hundreds of dollars for the Black Jack Coal Company were found to display the following values:

Revenues for Black Jack Coal Company

Month (X)	Revenues (Y)	log Y	X^2	X log Y	$(\log Y)^2$
1	31	1.4914	1	1.4914	2.2242
2	43	1.6335	4	3.2669	2.6682
3	61	1.7853	9	5.3560	3.1874
4	85	1.9294	16	7.7177	3.7227
5	118	2.0719	25	10.3594	4.2927
6	164	2.2148	36	13.2891	4.9055
7	228	2.3579	49	16.5055	5.5599
8	316	2.4997	64	19.9975	6.2484
9	444	2.6435	81	23.7911	6.9878
10	611	2.7860	100	27.8604	7.7620
55	2,101	21.4134	385	129.6349	47.5588

The CEO for Black Jack noticed that sales tended to increase by about the same percentage each month. He calculated the percentage increase to be $(43 - 31)/31 = 39$ percent. A plot of the data revealed a pattern similar to that in Figure 14-10. He therefore felt a logarithmic trend projection was called for, and has asked the quantitative analysis section to develop the regression model.

SOLUTION:
Beginning with

$$\hat{Y} = b_0 b_1^X$$

we have

$$\log \hat{Y} = \log b_0 + (\log b_1)X$$

$$\log b_1 = \frac{10(129.6349) - 55(21.4134)}{10(385) - (55)^2} = 0.1438$$

$$\log b_0 = \frac{21.4134}{10} - (0.1438)\frac{55}{10} = 1.35$$

Therefore,

$$\log \hat{Y} = 1.35 + 0.1438X$$

Taking antilogs, we obtain

$$\hat{Y} = 22.39(1.39)^X$$

It would appear that the CEO was correct. For every 1-unit increase in X, Y goes up by $1.39 - 1.00 = 0.39 = 39$ percent. An estimate of sales for the sixth time period is found by setting X equal to 6 and solving the equation

$$\hat{Y} = 22.39(1.39)^6 = 22.39(7.213) = 161.5$$

This projected value for sales closely approximates the actual sales level in the sixth time period of 164.

An estimated value for sales in the twelfth period is

$$\hat{Y} = 22.39(1.39)^{12} = 22.39(52.02) = 1,164.7$$

The 39 percent by which Y increases is the average amount by which Y increased each time period and is called the **instantaneous rate of growth.**

Notice that log Y was regressed on X. No values for log X were used. This is called a *semilog* (or *log-linear*) *model,* since logs were used for only one of the variables.

In addition, the correlation coefficient can be found from the equation

$$r = \frac{n\Sigma(X \log Y) - \Sigma X(\Sigma \log Y)}{\sqrt{[n\Sigma X^2 - (\Sigma X)^2][n\Sigma(\log Y)^2 - (\Sigma \log Y)^2]}} \qquad (14.8)$$

$$= \frac{10(129.63) - 55(21.41)}{\sqrt{[10(385) - (55)^2][10(47.56) - (21.41)^2]}}$$

$$= \frac{118.75}{119.16} = 0.99$$

$$r^2 = 0.98$$

Thus, our model is explaining 98 percent of the change in Black Jack's sales by using time as the explanatory variable.

B. A DECREASING FUNCTION

Suppose a plot of the data revealed a pattern as in Figure 14-11. Notice that Y tends to increase by a smaller amount each time. It flattens out rather than becoming steeper, as for the Black Jack Coal Company. In this instance, a semilog model which regresses Y on log X is required.

$$\hat{Y} = b_0 + b_1 \log X \qquad (14.9)$$

Figure 14-11   A Decreasing Function

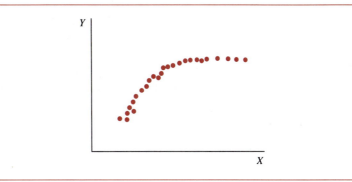

Values for b_0 and b_1 are

$$b_1 = \frac{n\Sigma(\log X)Y - (\Sigma\log X)\Sigma Y}{n\Sigma(\log X)^2 - (\Sigma\log X)^2} \qquad (14.10)$$

$$b_0 = \frac{\Sigma Y - b_1\Sigma\log X}{n} \qquad (14.11)$$

Consider the payments, in thousands of dollars, by the Noah Fence Company over a five-year period, as in Table 14-3. Unlike the case for Black Jack Coal, the time periods are given in years. They must therefore be recoded in single units to yield the X-values shown in column 2. The first year is assigned a value of 1, with each succeeding year given successive values. This recoding process is necessary since we cannot use the year 1989, for example, in our calculations. The year 1989 is not a number. Envision the need for recoding if the time periods had been given as May through September instead of 1989 through 1993. We certainly could not use the term *May* in our calculations!

Table 14-3   Payments by Noah Fence

Year	X	Payments (Y)	Log X	$(\text{Log } X)^2$	$(\text{Log } X)(Y)$	Y^2
1989	1	2.10	0.000	0.000	0.000	4.41
1990	2	2.35	0.301	0.091	0.707	5.53
1991	3	2.71	0.477	0.228	1.293	7.34
1992	4	2.80	0.602	0.362	1.686	7.84
1993	5	2.90	0.699	0.489	2.027	8.41
	15	12.86	2.079	1.170	5.713	33.53

Then

$$b_1 = \frac{(5)\,(5.713) - (2.079)\,(12.86)}{(5)\,(1.17) - (2.079)^2}$$

$$= 1.197$$

$$b_0 = \frac{12.86 - (1.197)\,(2.079)}{5}$$

$$= 2.07$$

Then

$$\hat{Y} = 2.07 + 1.197 \log X$$

A forecast for 1997, which would be time period $X = 9$, is

$$\hat{Y} = 2.07 + 1.197(\log 9)$$

Since $\log 9 = 0.954$, we have

$$\hat{Y} = 2.07 + 1.197(0.954)$$

$$= 3.21$$

The estimated level of payments in 1997 is 3.21 thousand dollars.

Furthermore,

$$r^2 = \frac{b_0 \Sigma Y + b_1 \Sigma (\log\ X) Y - n\bar{Y}^2}{\Sigma Y^2 - n\bar{Y}^2} \tag{14.12}$$

$$= \frac{(2.07)\,(12.86) + 1.197(5.713) - 5(2.572)^2}{33.53 - 5(2.572)^2}$$

$$= 0.843$$

C. OTHER POSSIBILITIES

If a plot of the data produced a pattern similar to Figure 14-12(a), the model we used for the Black Jack Coal Company, in which we regressed log Y on X, may be appropriate. If the pattern in Figure 14-12(b) is detected, then the model in which we regress Y on log X, as with the Noah Fence Company, may yield the best results. In both cases, $b_1 < 0$.

D. USING POLYNOMIAL MODELS

In many cases, the functional relationship between X and Y can be expressed by a polynomial model of some order higher than 1. For the examples cited, the appropriate model is

$$\hat{Y} = b_0 + b_1 X + b_2 X^2$$

FIGURE 14-12   Other Nonlinear Possibilities

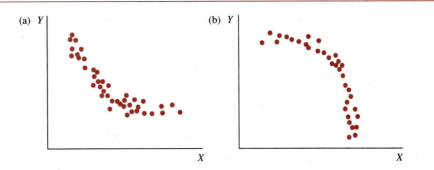

It uses as explanatory variables the values for X and X^2. It is called a *second-order polynomial* because it contains more than one variable on the right-hand side, the highest power of which is 2. The general expression for such a polynomial function is

$$Y = \beta_0 + \beta_1 X + \beta_2 X^2 + \beta_3 X^3 + \cdots + \beta_k X^k + \varepsilon \qquad (14.13)$$

Since this involves multiple regression, computations should be done on a computer. A computer run using SPSS-PC+ on the data for Black Jack Coal produced the results

$$\hat{Y} = 82.7 - 39.995 X + 9.0227 X^2$$

$$R^2 = 0.99 \qquad Se = 20.0$$

This compares with the results shown above, using the logarithmic model, of

$$\hat{Y} = 22.39(1.39)^X$$

$$r^2 = 0.98 \qquad Se = 0.004$$

It may be necessary to experiment with different functional forms in order to determine which provides the best fit. The results from different logarithmic models can be compared, along with those obtained using polynomial functions, in search of the optimal model. The use of computers makes this comparison practical.

The results of such comparisons may, however, prove inconsistent, in that one model may report a higher coefficient of determination than another (that's good) while carrying a higher standard error of the estimate (that's bad). The question then becomes, which model do you use?

The answer depends, at least in part, on the purpose for which the model is intended. If the model is to be used to explain present values of Y and to understand why it behaves as it does, the model with the higher coefficient of determination should be used. That is, if the intent is to explain, then the model with the higher explanatory value should be used.

If, on the other hand, the purpose of the model is to predict future values of Y, the model with the lower standard error of the estimate should be used. If you want to predict, you would enjoy greater success with the model that generates the lower prediction error.

However, such experimentation should be kept to a minimum. It is considered questionable, even unethical, to wildly experiment with one model and then another. You should know from the outset, given the nature of your research study, what procedure should be followed. The analogy is often made that to search blindly for the best model is similar to shooting the arrow and then drawing the target with the bull's-eye at the spot where the arrow landed.

14.5   SOLVED PROBLEMS

1. **Predicting Expenditures** The Human Resources Cabinet for the state of Virginia wished to devise a model for consumer expenditures which might aid in establishing a welfare system for the long-term unemployed. Consumption (Y) was regressed on number of family members (X_1), whether the head of household was employed (X_2), and whether children were present in the home (X_3). What would the model look like?

    Here, X_2 and X_3 were dummy variables in which $X_2 = 1$ if unemployed and 0 if employed, and $X_3 = 1$ if children were present and 0 if no children were present. The results might appear as

$$\hat{Y} = 10 + 9X_1 - 8X_2 + 7X_3$$

    Although the sizes of the coefficients are fictitious, note the negative sign of X_2. Since X_2 was coded as 1 if unemployed, we might expect $b_2 < 0$. Why? Because unemployment should tend to decrease consumption expenditures.

2. **Testing for Autocorrelation** If 50 observations were included in the data set for Problem 1, does autocorrelation exist at the 5 percent level if $d = 2.97$?

    With $k = 3$ independent variables and $n = 50$, Table K yields critical values of $d_L = 1.421$ and $d_U = 1.674$. Then

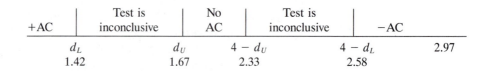

+AC	Test is inconclusive	No AC	Test is inconclusive	−AC
d_L	d_U	$4 - d_U$	$4 - d_L$	2.97
1.42	1.67	2.33	2.58	

    Yes, negative AC is suggested.

3. **A Cheeseburger in Paradise** Jose has a thriving business selling authentic plastic Aztec relics to gullible American tourists in Mexico. His accounting records show that, over the past few months, profits have been increasing and the number of hours he works each week has been going down:

Profits ($100's)	Hours
12.2	87
17.9	85
25.8	82
37.0	78
53.3	69
78.8	56
112.9	39
	21
	2

Jose wants to develop a regression model to predict profits, and another model to predict hours.

a. A graph of the data for profits reveals an increasing function, thereby suggesting a curvilinear model in which the log of profits is regressed on X. The computations appear as

Profits (Y)	X	log Y	X^2	X log Y	$(\log Y)^2$
12.2	1	1.09	1	1.09	1.18
17.9	2	1.25	4	2.51	1.57
25.8	3	1.41	9	4.23	1.99
37.0	4	1.57	16	6.27	2.46
53.3	5	1.73	25	8.63	2.98
78.8	6	1.90	36	11.38	3.60
112.9	7	2.05	49	14.37	4.20
337.9	28	10.99	140	48.48	17.99

$$\log b_1 = \frac{(7)(48.48) - (28)(10.99)}{(7)(140) - (28)^2}$$

$$= 0.16076$$

$$\log b_0 = \frac{10.99}{7} - (\log b)\frac{28}{7}$$

$$= 0.9276$$

$$\log \hat{Y} = 0.9276 + 0.16076X$$

$$\hat{Y} = 8.46(1.45)^X$$

Furthermore,

$$r = \frac{(7)\,(48.48) - (28)\,(10.99)}{\sqrt{[(7)\,(140) - (28)^2][(7)\,(17.994) - (10.99)^2]}}$$

$$= \frac{31.64}{31.86}$$

$$= 0.9932$$

The standard error is 0.0037.

The polynomial function reports as

$$\hat{Y} = 18.1 - 6.75X + 2.859X^2$$

$$R^2 = 0.997 \qquad Se = 2.77$$

b. The graph for hours produces results like those in Figure 14-12(b), requiring that we regress Y on log X.

Hours (Y)	X	log X	(log X)Y	Y^2	(log X)^2
87	1	0.00	0.00	7,569	0.00
85	2	0.30	25.59	7,225	0.09
82	3	0.48	39.12	6,724	0.23
78	4	0.60	46.96	6,084	0.36
69	5	0.70	48.23	4,761	0.49
56	6	0.78	43.58	3,136	0.61
39	7	0.85	32.96	1,521	0.71
21	8	0.90	18.96	441	0.82
2	9	0.95	1.91	4	0.91
519	45	5.56	257.31	37,465	4.22

$$b_1 = \frac{9(257.31) - (5.56)\,(519)}{9(4.22) - (5.56)^2}$$

$$= -80.64$$

$$b_0 = \frac{519 + (80.64)\,(5.56)}{9}$$

$$= 107.48$$

Then

$$\hat{Y} = 107.76 - 81.09(\log X)$$

Also,

$$r^2 = \frac{(107.48)\,(519) - (80.64)\,(257.31) - 9(57.67)^2}{37,465 - 9(57.67)^2}$$

$$= 0.677$$

$$Se = 18.5$$

The polynomial function is

$$\hat{Y} = 83.31 + 4.398X - 1.506X^2$$

$$R^2 = 0.99 \qquad Se = 1.40$$

14.6 WHAT YOU SHOULD HAVE LEARNED FROM THIS CHAPTER

The interpretation of residuals is a very revealing and highly useful procedure. It is possible to detect violations in the basic properties of the OLS model by examining the residuals generated by the model. By now you should be able to expose problems such as autocorrelation and heteroscedasticity by searching for any patterns that may appear in the residuals. You should also be able to use and interpret dummy variables to increase the range of applicability of the OLS model.

14.7 COMPUTER APPLICATIONS

Due to the brevity of this chapter, we will examine only two types of commands: those necessary to obtain the Durbin-Watson statistic and those that produce plots of residuals. In each case we assume that the data have already been entered.

A. DURBIN-WATSON STATISTIC

Minitab requires the command for regression and a subcommand for the Durbin-Watson. If you want to regress data in column 1 on two independent variables entered in columns 2 and 3, type

```
MTB>Regress C1 or 2 C2 C3:
SubC>DW.
```

SAS provides the Durbin-Watson if the option is requested in the MODEL statement as

```
PROC REG;
  MODEL Y = X1...Xm / DW;
```

Finally, the Durbin-Watson can be obtained using SPSS-PC by the commands

```
REGRESSION VARIABLES = Y X₁ X₂ X₃/
  DEPENDENT Y/METHOD ENTER/RESID DURBIN.
```

B.   PLOTS OF RESIDUALS

Minitab contains two principal plot functions.

```
MTB>PLOT C1 C2
```

plots data in column 1 against data in column 2.

```
MTB>MPLOT C1 C2 C3 C4 C1 C5
```

prints the following on the same diagram: C1 against C2; C3 against C4; C1 against C5.
SAS generates the desired diagram with

```
PROC PLOT;
  PLOT Y*X:
```

where Y and X are the two variables in which we are interested.
SCATTERGRAM Y with X instructs SPSS-PC to generate a plot.

LIST OF SYMBOLS AND TERMS

Dummy Variable A qualitative variable which is assigned a coded value of 0 or 1.
Autocorrelation Correlation between error terms in violation of the principles of OLS.
Heteroscedasticity A violation of OLS principles in which error terms do not have the same variance.

LIST OF FORMULAS

$$\varepsilon_t = \rho_{\varepsilon_{t-1}} + \mu_t \tag{14.1}$$

The regression of successive error terms to detect autocorrelation.

$$d = \frac{\Sigma(e_t - e_{t-1})^2}{\Sigma(e_t)^2} \tag{14.2}$$

The Durbin-Watson statistic measures for the presence of autocorrelation.

$$d = 2(1 - r) \tag{14.3}$$

An estimate of the Durbin-Watson statistic.

$$\hat{Y} = b_0 b_1^X \tag{14.4}$$

The functional form for an increasing function.

$$\log \hat{Y} = \log b_0 + (\log b_1)X \tag{14.5}$$

The logarithmic transformation to estimate (14.4).

$$\log b_1 = \frac{n\Sigma(X \log Y) - \Sigma X(\Sigma \log Y)}{n\Sigma X^2 - (\Sigma X)^2} \tag{14.6}$$

Used to calculate the coefficient in a nonlinear relationship.

$$\log b_0 = \frac{\Sigma \log Y}{n} - \log b_1 \frac{\Sigma X}{n} \tag{14.7}$$

Used to calculate the intercept in a nonlinear relationship for an increasing function.

$$r = \frac{n\Sigma(X \log Y) - \Sigma X(\Sigma \log Y)}{\sqrt{[n\Sigma X^2 - (\Sigma X)^2][n\Sigma(\log Y)^2 - (\Sigma \log Y)^2]}} \tag{14.8}$$

Used to calculate the correlation coefficient for a nonlinear relationship.

$$\hat{Y} = b_0 + b_1 \log X \tag{14.9}$$

The functional form for a decreasing function.

$$b_1 = \frac{n\Sigma(\log X)Y - (\Sigma \log X)\Sigma Y}{n\Sigma(\log X)^2 - (\Sigma \log X)^2} \tag{14.10}$$

Calculates the slope for a decreasing function.

$$b_0 = \frac{\Sigma Y - b_1 \Sigma \log X}{n} \tag{14.11}$$

Calculates the intercept for a decreasing function.

$$r^2 = \frac{b_0 \Sigma Y + b_1 \Sigma \log X(Y) - n\bar{Y}^2}{\Sigma Y^2 - n\bar{Y}^2} \tag{14.12}$$

Calculates the coefficient of determination for a decreasing function.

COMPUTER EXERCISES

YOU MAKE THE DECISION

1. A coal firm wants to set up a regression model to predict output (Y) which encompasses as explanatory variables hours of labor input (X_1) and whether a labor strike occurred during the time period under study (X_2). Devise the model and explain.
2. Given the model in the previous problem, should b_2 be positive or negative? Explain.
3. Wild Willie's Wennie World is testing a model to measure profits. It contains 5 explanatory variables and 25 observations. At the 1 percent level, does autocorrelation exist if the Durbin-Watson is 2.37?
4. Above what value must the Durbin-Watson be in the previous problem before negative autocorrelation is suspected?
5. Below what value must the Durbin-Watson be before positive autocorrelation is present in Problem 3?

6. Given these data, does autocorrelation exist at the 5 percent level?

Y	X₁	X₁
59	110	5
75	150	6
55	92	4
49	87	4
63	115	6
72	120	6
69	119	7
63	119	6

7. What values would you assign to dummy variables to measure a person's race if the categories included (1) white, (2) black, (3) Oriental, and (4) other.

8. In its effort to attract campaign funds, the election staff for Senator Graft is trying to code a contributor's political affiliation as 1 if Republican, 2 if Democrat, and 3 if no preference is stated. Comment on this approach. What would you advise?

9. The manager of a local accounting firm created a regression model for the length of time it takes to complete an audit. The model was

$$\hat{Y} = 17 - 1.41 X_1 + 1.73 X_2$$

where $\hat{Y}$ is time in hours
 X_1 is years of experience of auditor
 X_2 whether auditor is a CPA: 0 if yes, 1 if no

a. Interpret the coefficient for X_2.
b. Would you expect b_2 to be positive? Explain.
c. If the auditor has seven years of experience and is a CPA, how long would it take to complete the audit according to the model.
d. If another auditor also has seven years experience but is not a CPA, how long would it take to complete the audit according to the model.

10. If the dummy variable in the previous problem was 1 if CPA, 0 if not CPA, what would you expect the sign of b_2 to be? Explain.

11. A marketing representative etablishes a regression equation for units sold based on the population in the sales district and whether the district has a home office to which sales personnel report. The model proved to be

$$\hat{Y} = 78.12 + 1.01 X_1 - 17.2 X_2$$

where $\hat{Y}$ is units sold
 X_1 is population in thousands
 X_2 is 0 if district contains an office, 1 if it does not

a. Interpret $b_2 = -17.2$.
b. How would you compare the slopes and the coefficient of the two regression lines provided by this model? Compute and compare the two regression formulas.
c. Draw a graph to illustrate.

12. Considering the previous problem, if population is 17,000 in a district containing an office and 17,000 in a district without an office, what would the number of units sold in each one be? Draw a graph to illustrate.

13. Studies have shown that in states with more liberal regulations concerning the receipt of unemployment compensation, unemployment rates are higher. If a regression model for unemployment rates incorporates a dummy variable, coded 1 if regulations are liberal and 0 if otherwise, would its coefficient be greater than or less than zero according to these studies? Explain.

14. A model to predict income is to contain a dummy variable for a person's highest education level consisting of (1) high school degree, (2) undergraduate degree, (3) master's degree, (4) degree above master's. Another dummy variable for race which provides for (1) white, (2) black, and (3) other is to be included.
   a. How many dummy variables are necessary?
   b. Devise one possible coding system. Are there others? Explain.

15. An employment agency is considering a model which uses dummy variables to measure an applicant's ability to hold a job. The current proposal is to create a dummy variable to denote that the applicant has work experience, and another dummy variable to indicate that the applicant has no work experience. Comment on this approach.

16. A model to predict receipts on insurance claims by policyholders suffering a loss contains only one variable—a dummy variable coded 0 if male and 1 if female. For a male policyholder, what would $\hat{Y}$ be? What would the regression line look like?

17. The data shown were collected by Waldo's Wacky World of Wall Coverings on profit per sales (Y), square footage of area to be covered (X_1), and whether the customer is a commercial business (C), private homeowner (H), or governmental unit (G).

Observation	Profit (Y)	Area (X)	Type
1	408	1,400	H
2	817	2,200	G
3	502	1,500	C
4	315	800	C
5	782	1,000	H
6	789	1,200	G
7	604	1,100	C
8	592	900	H
9	801	1,600	G
10	732	1,400	G
11	711	1,300	H
12	612	1,100	C
13	831	1,600	G

   a. Construct the data set with the proper dummy variables. Indicate the coding system used.
   b. Solve for the regression model and interpret the results.
   c. Draw a line for each type of customer.
   d. Is autocorrelation present at the 1 percent level?

18. According to *Business Week* there appears to be a significant difference in the nature of hostile takeovers of firms, depending on the region of the country in which the firm has its home office. Use the data shown for size of firm in annual sales (1,000's) (Y),

price/earnings ratio of the firm taken over (X_1), and whether the firm's office is located in the North (N), South (S), Midwest (M), or West (W).

Observation	Size (Y)	P/E (X_1)	Location
1	120	2.02	N
2	320	3.12	S
3	502	1.17	W
4	478	0.89	N
5	389	2.89	S
6	565	2.12	W
7	317	1.29	N
8	488	1.89	S
9	532	1.98	M
10	619	2.01	M

   a. Construct the data set with the proper dummy variables. Indicate the coding system used.
   b. Solve for the regression model and interpret your results.
   c. Draw a line for each regional location.
   d. Is autocorrelation present at the 5 percent level?
19. Given the data in the previous problem, test the coefficient for each dummy variable to determine if it is significantly different from zero at the 5 percent level.
20. Use White's method to test the data in Problem 18 for heteroscedasticity at $\alpha = 0.05$.
21. The data shown were collected to explain salary levels for workers at a local plant.

Salary ($1,000's)	Years of Education	Sex
42.2	8	M
58.9	12	M
98.8	16	M
23.5	6	F
12.5	5	M
67.8	12	M
51.9	10	F
81.6	14	F
61.0	12	F

   a. Compute the regression model, using a computer.
   b. Is there evidence of sex discrimination in salary levels?
   c. Is education useful in explaining salary?
   d. Are autocorrelation and heteroscedasticity problems?
22. Twenty stores are examined to determine the effect floor space (FS) and location (L) have on profits. Location is a dummy variable, encoded with a 1 if urban and 0 if suburban. The *t*-values are given in parentheses. The results are

$$\hat{P} = 34.3 + 23.2FS - 12L$$
$$\phantom{\hat{P} = 34.3 + }(9.6) \quad (-1.6)$$

Is location important at the 5 percent level? Explain.

23.   Twenty-five other stores are surveyed to examine the effect on revenue of local population (*POP*) and type of management (*MAN*). This last variable is a dummy variable encoded with a 1 if the manager owns the store and a 0 if he or she leases it. The results are shown here. The standard errors of the regression coefficients are shown in brackets.

$$\hat{R} = 34 + 34.4POP + 71.1MAN$$
$$[27.2] \qquad [63.9]$$

Is either *POP* or *MAN* significant at the 1 percent level? Explain.

EMPIRICAL EXERCISES

24.   Are the number of class hours in which a student is enrolled this term and his or her class (freshman, sophomore, junior, or senior) good predictors of the number of hours a student spends studying each week? Obtain a sample of your fellow students to determine the usefulness of such a model.

25.   Obtain a sample of at least 30 stocks traded on the New York Stock Exchange. Does it appear that the trading volume for a stock can be predicted by (1) the difference between the high and low for the day and (2) whether the stock closed up, closed down, or remained unchanged.

CASE APPLICATIONS

26.   Holly Wood is a district manager for a chain of video stores that rents movies to the general public. The past year has seen a considerable fluctuation in revenues. Ms. Wood would like to identify those forces that explain rentals. She has collected data for 15 stores for the number of movies rented during a given week, population in hundreds within a 2-mile radius of the store, whether a movie theater is within a 2-mile radius of the store, and whether the store is located in a city (C), suburban (S), or rural (R) setting. T indicates a movie theater is within the 2-mile radius; T^1 indicates that one is not.

Observation	Movies	Population	Theater	Setting
1	407	110	T^1	C
2	809	420	T	C
3	511	150	T^1	R
4	398	101	T^1	S
5	417	112	T	R
6	540	132	T^1	S
7	718	380	T	S
8	580	155	T	R
9	798	410	T^1	C
10	884	450	T	R
11	693	312	T	S
12	782	389	T^1	R
13	619	301	T	C
14	592	289	T	S
15	667	232	T^1	S

In addition to wondering how well her model fits the data, Ms. Wood is also concerned about the presence of autocorrelation and heteroscedasticity. How can you help?

27. In a dispute among secondary teachers in Shelby County, Tennessee, charges of sex and age discrimination have been leveled at the county school board. These charges have been brought by teachers who feel their salaries do not reflect their level of experience or who believe women are paid less than men. Robert Gay, a history teacher with 17 years experience, is particularly distressed by his salary of $25,500.

The county school superintendent, alarmed by these allegations, prepares to investigate. He randomly selects 25 teachers, 10 males and 15 females, noting their years of experience, salary, and gender. The results are

Teacher	Gender	Experience (yr)	Salary (1,000's)
1	M	10	15
2	F	8	14.2
3	F	7	14
4	M	12	17.1
5	F	15	18.9
6	M	21	21
7	M	22	19.1
8	F	10	16.5
9	F	8	15.2
10	F	19	19.3
11	F	7	10.5
12	F	12	15.5
13	M	15	15.7
14	F	12	15
15	M	17	25.5
16	F	9	16
17	F	7	17.1
18	M	12	17.1
19	F	8	11
20	M	10	11.5
21	F	14	12.2
22	F	3	10
23	F	12	17
24	M	10	17
25	M	9	17

The superintendent must now respond to the teachers' charges, including that by Mr. Gay. How might he proceed? Would the standard error of the estimate be useful? How about r^2 or the slope coefficient?

28. Owners of Mighty Muscles, Inc., a health club in Hoboken, New Jersey, are trying to increase membership at the club. After reviewing operations at other health clubs in the area, Harry Hunk, the manager at Mighty Muscles, feels that there might be a relationship between the number of members in a health club and several explanatory variables, including (1) monthly dues, (2) local population, and (3) type of weight-training equipment

in the club. Three kinds of weight machines are commonly found in health clubs: MuscleUp (MU), Iron Man (IM), and Studly Dude (SD). Mr. Hunk collects data for these variables for 20 health clubs similar to Mighty Muscles. Analyze the data and determine how well the model fits the data. Interpret your findings and recommend to Harry the policy decisions he should make for the club.

Membership	Dues	Population (in 1,000's)	Equipment Type
345	$22.50	39.7	MU
387	21.00	43.3	MU
412	20.00	47.7	MU
434	20.00	48.9	SD
467	18.50	54.5	SD
490	18.00	55.7	SD
612	15.00	62.1	SD
523	17.50	56.7	IM
545	17.00	58.9	IM
567	16.50	60.0	IM
578	16.00	61.2	SD
599	15.00	63.6	SD
634	14.50	60.0	IM
656	13.00	61.0	SD
669	13.10	61.4	MU
134	30.00	23.5	MU
243	27.00	27.8	IM
259	25.50	32.1	IM
278	23.00	37.3	SD
321	24.00	35.8	SD

COMPUTER EXERCISES

1. Access the file FIRMS. It contains data on 50 firms with observations on profit levels measured in dollars, whether the firm is private, public, or quasi-public, and whether it is profit-oriented or nonprofit-oriented. Does it appear that these data can be used to explain the profitability of business concerns? Interpret your results.

2. From the results of your computer run on FIRMS in the exercise above, determine how the model might be improved. Run the program with these changes and compare the results to your first run.

3. Given the data in FIRMS, does there appear to be a problem with multicollinearity or autocorrelation?

CHAPTER 15

CHI-SQUARE AND OTHER NONPARAMETRIC TESTS

A PREVIEW OF THINGS TO LOOK FOR

1 The chi-square test and how it can be used to detect certain distributions.

2 Contingency tables in tests for independence using chi-square.

3 How the sign test can be applied in the presence of matched pairs.

4 Use of the runs test to search for randomness.

5 How two populations can be compared with the Mann-Whitney U test.

6 Using the Spearman rank correlation test on ordinally ranked data.

7 A comparison of more than two populations based on the Kruskal-Wallis test.

CHAPTER BLUEPRINT

Many of the tests performed in previous chapters required certain basic assumptions before the test could be carried out. For example, we often assumed that the population was normally distributed or that variances fit particular patterns before using some statistical tools. When those assumptions cannot be made, or essential knowledge about the population is not attainable, we have to rely on the nonparametric tests contained in this chapter.

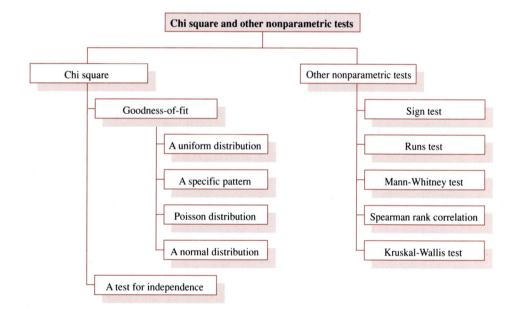

○○○○
○○○
○○
○

Statistics show that most things are
harder to get out of than in to.

15.1   INTRODUCTION

In previous chapters we presented many tests for hypotheses. Tests for both population means and population proportions were demonstrated. In some instances the sample size was greater than 30, whereas in others a small sample was used. You were introduced to tests for a single population and to tests comparing two or more populations.

However, all these test situations exhibited one common characteristic: they required certain assumptions regarding the population. For example, t-tests and F-tests required the assumption that the population was normally distributed. This condition was crucial when the sample size was small. Since such tests depend on postulates about the population and its parameters, they are called **parametric tests**.

In practice, many situations arise in which it is simply not possible to safely make any assumptions about the value of a parameter or the shape of the population distribution. Most of the tests described in earlier chapters would therefore not be applicable. We must instead use other tests which do not depend on a single type of distribution or specific parametric values. These tests are called **nonparametric** (or distribution-free) **tests**.

> **Nonparametric Tests**
> Nonparametric tests are statistical procedures that can be used to test hypotheses when no assumptions regarding parameters or population distributions are possible.

There are many different types of nonparametric tests that can be used, given a particular need; however, we examine only a few of the more common and practical nonparametric procedures. Our discussion includes

- Chi-square and the way it can be used to test for
  - Goodness-of-fit to determine if a distribution fits a certain pattern.
  - Contingency tables and tests for independence.
- The sign test to compare matched pairs.
- The runs test to test for randomness.
- The Mann-Whitney U test, which compares population distributions.
- The Kruskal-Wallis test for population means.
- The Spearman rank correlation test to measure the strength of the association between two ordinally ranked variables.

Perhaps the most widely used test is the chi-square (χ^2), introduced in Chapter 11. It will serve as the point of departure for our discussion of nonparametrics.

15.2 THE CHI-SQUARE DISTRIBUTION (χ^2)

You may recall from Chapter 11 that, like the t-distribution, there is a different chi-square distribution for each degree of freedom. Figure 15-1 shows that the fewer the degrees of freedom associated with a chi-square distribution, the more positively skewed it proves to be. As the number of degrees of freedom increases, the distribution approaches normality.

The two most common applications of chi-square are found in goodness-of-fit tests and tests for independence. Each is examined in turn.

FIGURE 15-1   The Chi-Square Distribution

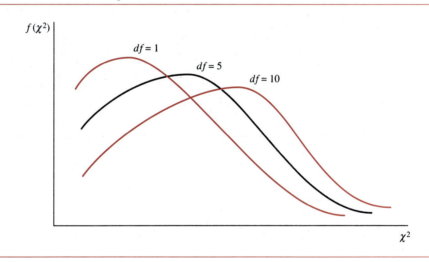

A.   GOODNESS-OF-FIT TESTS

Business decisions often require that we test some hypothesis about the unknown population distribution. Remember, the entire principle behind nonparametric tests is that we cannot automatically assume that the distribution fits a specific pattern (such as a Poisson, for example). We are therefore obliged to test any hypothesis that we might have regarding that distribution. We might, for instance, hypothesize that the population distribution is uniform and that all possible values have the same probability of occurring. The hypotheses that we would test are

H_0: The population distribution is uniform.

H_a: The population distribution is not uniform.

The goodness-of-fit test is then used to determine if the distribution of values in the population fits a particular hypothesized shape—in this case, a uniform distribution. As with all statistical tests of this nature, sample data are taken from the population and form the foundation for our findings.

Goodness-of-Fit Tests
Goodness-of-fit tests measure how closely observed sample data fit a particular hypothesized distribution. If the fit is reasonably close, it may be concluded that the hypothesized distribution exists.

If there is a large difference between what is actually observed in the sample and what you would expect to observe if the null hypothesis were correct, then it is less likely that the null is accurate. That is, the null hypothesis must be rejected when the observations obtained in the sample differ significantly from the pattern of events that is expected to occur if the hypothesized distribution does exist.

For example, if a fair die is rolled, it is reasonable to hypothesize a pattern in the outcomes such that each outcome (numbers 1 through 6) occurs approximately one-sixth of the time. However, if a significantly large or significantly small percentage of even numbers occurs, it may be concluded that the die is not properly balanced and that the hypothesis is false. That is, if the difference between the pattern of events actually observed and the pattern of events expected to occur if the null is correct proves too great to attribute to sampling error, it must be concluded that the population exhibits a distribution other than that specified in the null hypothesis.

To test the hypothesis regarding a population distribution, we must compare the difference between our expectations based on the hypothesized distribution to the actual data occurring in the sample. This is precisely what the chi-square goodness-of-fit test does. It determines if the sample observations "fit" our expectations. The test takes the form

$$\chi^2 = \sum_{i=1}^{K} \frac{(O_i - E_i)^2}{E_i} \qquad (15.1)$$

where O_i is the frequency of observed events in the sample data
        E_i is the frequency of expected events if the null is correct
        K is the number of categories or classes

The test carries $K - m - 1$ degrees of freedom, where m is the number of parameters to be estimated. The exact impact of m will become more apparent as our discussion progresses, particularly as it relates to the Poisson distribution, which follows shortly.

Notice that the numerator of Formula (15.1) measures the difference between the frequencies of the observed events and the frequencies of the expected events. When these differences are large, causing χ^2 to rise, the null should be rejected.

A TEST FOR A UNIFORM FIT   As an illustration, Chris Columbus, marketing director for Seven Seas, Inc., has the responsibility of controlling the inventory level for all four types of sailboats sold by his firm. In particular, Chris must guard against the possibility of lost sales due to inventory depletion. In the past he has ordered new boats on the premise that all four types are equally popular and the demand for each type is the same. Recently, however, inventories have become more difficult to control, and Chris feels that he should test his hypothesis regarding a uniform demand. His hypotheses are

H_0: Demand is uniform for all four types of boats.

H_a: Demand is not uniform for all four types of boats.

By assuming uniformity in demand, the null hypothesis presumes that out of a random sample of sailboats, weekend sailors would purchase an equal number of each type. To test this hypothesis, Chris selects a sample of $n = 48$ boats sold over the past several months. If demand is uniform, he can expect that $48/4 = 12$ boats of each type were sold. Table 15-1 shows this expectation, along with the number of each type that actually was sold. Chris must now determine if the numbers actually sold in each of the $K = 4$ categories are close enough to what he would expect if demand was uniform. Formula (15.1) gives

$$\chi^2 = \frac{(15 - 12)^2}{12} + \frac{(11 - 12)^2}{12} + \frac{(10 - 12)^2}{12} + \frac{(12 - 12)^2}{12}$$

$$= 1.17$$

The value 1.17 is then compared with a critical χ^2-value taken from Table H. Since there were no parameters that had to be estimated, $m = 0$ and there are $K - 1 = 3$ degrees of freedom. If Chris wanted to test at the 5 percent level, he would find, as shown in Figure 15-2, that $\chi^2_{0.05, 3} = 7.815$.

TABLE 15-1   Seven Seas Sales Record

Type of Boat	Observed Sales (O_i)	Expected Sales (E_i)
Pirates's Revenge	15	12
Jolly Roger	11	12
Bluebeard's Treasure	10	12
Ahab's Quest	12	12
	48	48

FIGURE 15-2   A Chi-Square Test for Seven Seas

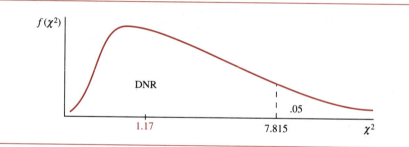

Decision Rule
Do not reject if $\chi^2 < 7.815$. Reject if $\chi^2 > 7.815$.

Since $1.17 < 7.815$, the null hypothesis that demand is uniform is not rejected. The differences between what was actually observed, O_i, and what Chris would expect to observe if demand was the same for all four types of sailboats, E_i, are not large enough to refute the null. The differences are not significant and can be attributed merely to sampling error.

A TEST FOR A FIT TO A SPECIFIC PATTERN   In our example regarding Chris's sailboats, it was assumed that the demand for all four types of sailboats was the same. The values for the expected frequencies were therefore all the same. However,

Car buyers are often warned never to buy a car made on a Friday or a Monday because worker absenteeism is higher on those days. If a survey revealed the number of defective cars to be 32, 22, 26, 19, and 30 on Monday through Friday, respectively, would it appear that the day of the week has any relationship to auto quality? Set $\alpha = 5$ percent. State the null and the decision rule, and find χ^2.

Answer: $\chi^2 = 4.53$; $\chi^2_{0.05,4} = 9.488$. Reject the null if χ^2 is greater than 9.488; do not reject otherwise. Since $\chi^2 = 4.53 < 9.488$, do not reject the null.

many instances arise in which frequencies are tested against a certain pattern in which not all expected frequencies are the same. Instead, they must be determined as

$$E_i = np_i \qquad\qquad (15.2)$$

where n is the sample size

   p_i is the probability of each category as specified in the null hypothesis

EXAMPLE 15-1 Is There Life after Debt?

Fortune magazine recently described efforts by large commerical banks to control their loan portfolios by ensuring a particular mix in the assortment of loans they give to customers. This mix is extremely important in minimizing the default rate.

The John Dillinger First National Bank in New York City tries to follow a policy of extending 60 percent of its loans to business firms, 10 percent to individuals, and 30 percent to foreign borrowers.

To determine if this policy is being followed, Jay Hoover, vice president of marketing, randomly selects 85 loans which were recently approved. He finds that 62 of those loans were extended to businesses, 10 to individuals, and 13 to foreign borrowers. At the 10 percent level, does it appear the bank's desired portfolio pattern is being preserved? Test the hypotheses that

H_0: The desired pattern is maintained: 60 percent are business loans, 10 percent are individual loans, and 30 percent are foreign loans.

H_a: The desired pattern is not maintained.

SOLUTION:
If the null hypothesis is correct, Mr. Hoover would expect 60 percent of the 85 loans in the sample to be business loans. So, for the first category, $E_i = np_i = (85)(0.60) = 51$ loans to businesses. In addition, he would expect that $(85)(0.10) =$

8.5 of the loans would be to individuals, and $(85)(0.30) = 25.5$ loans to foreign customers. The data are summarized in the table.

Type of Loan	Observed Frequencies (O_i)	Expected Frequencies (E_i)
Business	62	51
Private	10	8.5
Foreign	13	25.5
	85	85.0

The χ^2-value is

$$\chi^2 = \frac{(62-51)^2}{51} + \frac{(10-8.5)^2}{8.5} + \frac{(13-25.5)^2}{25.5}$$

$$= 8.76$$

Again, no parameters were estimated and $m = 0$. With α set at 10 percent and $K = 3$ categories or classes of loans (business, private, and foreign), there are $K - m - 1$ or $3 - 0 - 1 = 2$ degrees of freedom. Mr. Hoover finds from Table H that the critical $\chi^2_{0.10,2} = 4.605$.

Decision Rule

Do not reject the null if $\chi^2 < 4.605$. Reject the null if $\chi^2 > 4.605$.

As shown by the figure, the null should be rejected since $8.76 > 4.605$.

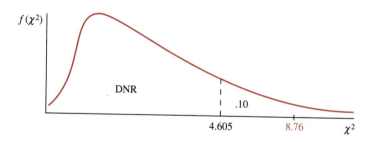

STATISTICAL INTERPRETATION:

Mr. Hoover can be 90 percent certain that the pattern of loans does not comply with bank policy. The differences between what he observed and what he would expect to observe if the desired loan pattern was achieved is too great to occur by chance. There is only a 10 percent probability that a sample of 85 randomly selected loans could produce the observed frequencies shown here if the desired pattern in the bank's loan portfolio was being maintained.

QUICK CHECK 15.2.2

In the past, sales for Acme Motors were 30 percent in new cars, 40 percent in used cars, and the rest in very used cars. After an advertising blitz, a random sample showed Acme sold 56 new cars, 63 used cars, and 39 very used cars. At the 1 percent level, does it appear there has been a change in the pattern of sales? State the χ^2, the critical χ^2, and the decision.

Answer: $\chi^2 = 3.05$; $\chi^2_{0.01, 2} = 9.21$; sales not changed.

A TEST FOR A FIT TO A POISSON DISTRIBUTION From our earlier discussion of the Poisson distribution, recall that many arrival processes fit the Poisson distribution pattern. This next example illustrates how a test can be conducted to determine if the population is Poisson.

An economic consultant is retained by O'Hare International Airfield to study traffic patterns. Flight records kept by the airport over the past several years indicate an average of 3.2 landings per minute. The consultant wants to test the hypothesis that the landings are Poisson-distributed.

H_0: Landings are Poisson-distributed.

H_a: Landings are not Poisson-distributed.

She samples the number of landings in $n = 200$ minutes. Table 15-2 displays these sample data under observed frequencies, Q_i. The table shows, for example, that in 10 of the 200 minutes sampled, there were no landings; in 23 of the 200 minutes sampled, there was only one landing, and so on. She must now determine the expected frequencies. If the null is correct, the probabilities will fit a Poisson distribution which can be found in Table D. If the average arrival rate is $\Lambda = 3.2$, Table D shows that the probability that zero landings will occur in any given time period (1 minute in this case) is 0.0408. The probability that one landing will occur is 0.1304. Probabilities for the remaining number of landings can be obtained similarly, and are

TABLE 15-2   Per Minute Arrivals at O'Hare Airport

Number of Landings	Observed Frequencies (O_i)	Poisson (p_i)	Expected Frequencies (E_i)
0	10	0.0408	8.16
1	23	0.1304	26.08
2	45	0.2087	41.74
3	49	0.2226	44.52
4	32	0.1781	35.62
5 and over	41	0.2195	43.90
	200	1.0000	200.02

shown in Table 15-2 as p_i. The expected frequencies are $E_i = np_i$. For example, the E_i for two landings is $(200)(0.2087) = 41.74$. That is, in about 41 of the 200 minutes sampled there should have been two landings if arrivals of planes are Poisson-distributed with $\Lambda = 3.2$. Actually, 45 of the 200 minutes saw the arrival of two planes.

The consultant grouped the number of landings into $K = 6$ categories (0 through 5 and over), and since the mean arrival rate was given, $m = 0$. There are therefore $K - 1 = 5$ degrees of freedom. If she wants to test the hypothesis at the 1 percent level, she finds the critical $\chi^2_{0.01,5} = 15.086$. The decision rule, displayed in Figure 15-3, is

Decision Rule
Do not reject if $\chi^2 < 15.086$. Reject if $\chi^2 > 15.086$.

FIGURE 15-3   A Test for Poisson Arrivals

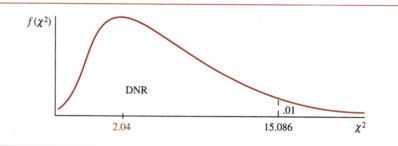

The chi-square is

$$\chi^2 = \frac{(10 - 8.16)^2}{8.16} + \frac{(23 - 26.08)^2}{26.08} + \cdots + \frac{(41 - 43.90)^2}{43.9}$$

$$= 2.04$$

Clearly, $2.04 < 15.086$, and the null should not be rejected. The consultant can be 99 percent certain that landings do fit a Poisson distribution. The unique feature of this example of a chi-square test for the hypothesis of a Poisson distribution is that the probabilities associated with the E_i values were taken directly from Table D.

Suppose the airport had not kept flight records for a long time and the mean arrival rate of 3.2 was unknown. It would then be necessary to estimate Λ from the consultant's sample data. Suppose the sample data revealed a mean of 3.7. Two important consequences develop.

1. The values for p_i must then be taken from Table D under the pretense that the mean is 3.7, not 3.2. This, of course, affects the values of E_i accordingly.
2. Since it was necessary to estimate a parameter (in this case, the mean arrival rate), $m = 1$ and the degrees of freedom equal $K - m - 1$ or $6 - 1 - 1 = 4$, not 5 as before.

○○○○   **DECISION MAKING THROUGH PROBLEM SOLVING**   ○○○○
ILLUSTRATION 15-2

Nation's Business discussed the problem PepsiCo, makers of soft drinks, had with an assembly line at a bottling plant. The plant manager had to decide whether the entire line operation had to be revised, a very costly process, or if merely changing the speed at which the current one operated was sufficient. Tests were conducted which determined that the arrival of empty bottles at the start of the production line failed to meet a Poisson distribution. This disrupted the entire production process from the start. Simple adjustments were made in bottle delivery, and the filling process continued.

Many other probability distributions, such as the binomial, can also be tested in a similar fashion. Following the Quick Check, a test is performed for a normal distribution.

QUICK CHECK 15.2.3
○○○○

The frequencies of machine failures in 150 one-hour intervals are given. The population mean is unknown. The estimate from these sample data is 1.5. At the 10 percent level, are failures Poisson with a mean of 1.5? State the χ^2, the critical χ^2, and the conclusion.

Number of machines: 0   1   2   3 4 or more
Frequency of failure: 32 51 41 18 8 = 150
Answer: $\chi^2 = 0.754$; $\chi^2_{0.10, 3} = 6.251$; do not reject null.

A TEST FOR NORMALITY   Considering the importance of the normal distribution in statistical analysis, it is fortunate that a method has been devised to test for normality. This next case demonstrates.

Specifications for the production of air tanks used in scuba diving require that the tanks be filled to a mean pressure of 600 pounds per square inch (psi). A standard deviation of 10 psi is allowed. Safety allowances permit a normal distribution in fill levels. You have just been hired by Aqua Lung, a major manufacturer of scuba equipment. Your first assignment is to determine if fill levels fit a normal distribution. Aqua Lung is certain that the mean of 600 psi and the standard deviation of 10 psi prevail. Only the nature of the distribution remains to be tested. In this effort, you measure $n = 1,000$ tanks and find the distribution shown in Table 15-3. Your hypotheses are

H_0: Fill levels are normally distributed.

H_a: Fill levels are not normally distributed.

As before, the test requires that you compare these actual observations with those you would expect to find if normality prevailed. To determine these expected

TABLE 15-3   Fill Levels for Scuba Tanks

PSI	Actual Frequency
570 and under 580	20
580 and under 590	142
590 and under 600	310
600 and under 610	370
610 and under 620	128
620 and under 630	30
	1,000

frequencies, you must calculate the probabilities that tanks selected at random would have fill levels in the intervals shown in Table 15-3. If the null is correct, and fills are normally distributed, the normal deviate Z can be used. The probability that a tank would fall in the first interval is $P(570 < X < 580)$. The problem facing you is depicted in Figure 15-4(a). You must determine the shaded area under the curve. Thus,

$$Z = \frac{X - \mu}{s}$$

$$Z_1 = \frac{570 - 600}{10}$$

$$= 3, \text{ or an area of } 0.4987$$

$$Z_2 = \frac{580 - 600}{10}$$

$$= 2, \text{ or an area of } 0.4772$$

FIGURE 15-4   Probabilities of Tank Fills

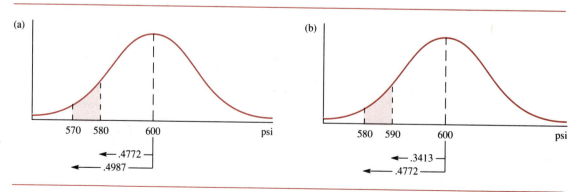

Then

$$P(570 < X < 580) = 0.4987 - 0.4772 = 0.0215$$

There is slightly more than a 2 percent chance that any tank selected at random would have a fill level between 570 and 580 psi if the mean fills are 600 psi with a standard deviation of 10 psi and are distributed normally. For the next interval, the probability that a tank selected at random would have a fill level between 580 and 590 is $P(580 < X < 590)$, and is shown in Figure 15-4(b).

$$Z_1 = \frac{580 - 600}{10}$$

$$= 2, \text{ or an area of } 0.4772$$

$$Z_2 = \frac{590 - 600}{10}$$

$$= 1, \text{ or an area of } 0.3413$$

Then

$$P(580 < X < 590) = 0.4772 - 0.3413 = 0.1359$$

The probabilities for the remaining intervals are calculated in like fashion and are shown in Table 15-4, along with the expected frequencies. The expected frequencies, as before, are $E_i = np_i$. For the first interval this becomes $(1,000)(0.0215) = 21.5$. You wish to test the hypothesis at the 5 percent level. Since both the population mean and standard deviation were given and do not have to be estimated, $m = 0$. There are $K = 6$ classes in the frequency table, so the degrees of freedom are $K - 1 = 5$. You find the critical χ^2 to be $\chi^2_{0.05,5} = 11.07$.

TABLE 15-4   Probabilities of Fill Levels

PSI	Actual Frequency (O_i)	Probabilities (p_i)	Expected Frequency (E_i)
570 and under 580	20	0.0215	21.5
580 and under 590	142	0.1359	135.9
590 and under 600	310	0.3413	341.3
600 and under 610	370	0.3413	341.3
610 and under 620	128	0.1359	135.9
620 and under 630	30	0.0215	21.5
	1,000		

Decision Rule

Do not reject the null if χ^2 is less than 11.07. Reject the null if χ^2 is greater than 11.07.

Using Formula (15.1), you find

$$\chi^2 = \frac{(20 - 21.5)^2}{21.5} + \frac{(142 - 135.9)^2}{135.9} + \cdots + \frac{(30 - 21.5)^2}{21.5}$$

$$= 9.48$$

As shown in Figure 15-5, the null should not be rejected. The differences between what were observed and what you would expect to observe if the fills were normally distributed with a mean of 600 and a standard deviation of 10 can be attributed to sampling error.

FIGURE 15-5 Chi-Square Test for Normality

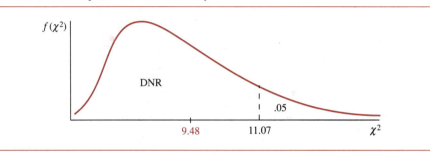

Had the mean and standard deviation not been known, it would have been necessary to estimate them from the sample data in Table 15-3. Then m would be 2, and the degrees of freedom would be $K - 2 - 1$ or $6 - 2 - 1 = 3$.

Caution: The chi-square test for goodness-of-fit is reliable only if all E_i are at least 5. Had you selected a sample of only 100 instead of 1,000 scuba tanks, the E_i for the first interval would have been $(100)(0.0125) = 1.25$ instead of 12.5. If an E_i is less than 5, we must combine adjacent classes to ensure that all categories have an $E_i \geq 5$. In the example for scuba gear, classes 1 and 2 would be combined as would classes 5 and 6. Of course, the degrees of freedom are reduced accordingly.

B. CONTINGENCY TABLES—A TEST FOR INDEPENDENCE

Notice that in all the problems so far, there was one and only one factor that captured our interest. We were concerned only with the distribution of fill levels for scuba tanks or the distribution of landing patterns at O'Hare International. In each instance our tests were designed to analyze a single feature or attribute.

However, chi-square will also permit the comparison of two attributes to determine if there is any relationship between them. Consider, for example, the efforts by a marketing specialist to determine if there is any connection between consumers' income levels and their preference for his product. Such a procedure involves the comparison of two attributes: incomes and preferences. Comparing two attributes to determine if they are independent is accomplished in the same manner as before: the difference between actual, observed frequencies and expected frequencies is analyzed.

Wilma Keeto is the director of product research at Dow Chemical. Her current project requires an examination of the effectiveness of a new insecticide that Dow plans to market. Ms. Keeto is particularly interested in whether the inclusion of a certain killing ingredient, dichlorovinyl, in the product's chemical formula produces more satisfactory results. Her most recent test involved the random selection of 100 potential customers. Seventy-five were asked to test the formula with dichlorovinyl, and 25 customers were given the same product without dichlorovinyl. Each customer then rated the product's effectiveness as "above average," "average," or "below average." The results are shown in Table 15-5, which is a **contingency table** like those introduced in Chapter 4.

TABLE 15-5   Effectiveness Ratings for Dichlorovinyl

Attribute A	Attribute B		Total
	Dichlorovinyl	No Dichlorovinyl	
Above average	20	11	31
Average	40	8	48
Below average	15	6	21
Total	75	25	100

The table has $r = 3$ rows and $c = 2$ columns. There are $rc = 6$ cells in the table. Notice, for example, that 31 customers rated the product "above average"; 20 of those used the formula containing the test ingredient dichlorovinyl.

Ms. Keeto wants to compare attribute B (whether the formula contains dichlorovinyl) to attribute A (the product's rating). Her hypotheses are

H_0: Rating and use of dichlorovinyl are independent.

H_a: Rating and use of dichlorovinyl are not independent.

If dichlorovinyl has no impact on effectiveness rating, then the percentage of users with dichlorovinyl who rated the product "above average" should equal the percentage of users without dichlorovinyl who rated the product "above average." This percentage in turn should equal that of all users who rated the product "above average."

As Table 15-5 shows, 31 percent of all 100 users rated the product "above average." Then 31 percent of the 75 who used dichlorovinyl and 31 percent of the 25 who did not use dichlorovinyl should also give this rating if no difference in effectiveness exists. These values of $(75)(0.31) = 23.3$ and $(25)(0.31) = 7.75$ give the expected frequencies E_i for each cell as shown in Table 15-6.

TABLE 15-6   Rating Frequencies

	Attribute B		
Attribute A	Dichlorovinyl	No Dichlorovinyl	Totals
Above average	$O_i = 20$ $E_i = 23.3$	$O_i = 11$ $E_i = 7.75$	31
Average	$O_i = 40$ $E_i = 36$	$O_i = 8$ $E_i = 12$	48
Below average	$O_i = 15$ $E_i = 15.8$	$O_i = 6$ $E_i = 5.25$	21
Total	75	25	100

The remaining E_i are calculated in similar fashion and displayed in Table 15-6. For example, 48 percent of the 100 users rated the product as "average." Therefore, if the null is correct, an equal percentage of the 75 users of the product containing dichlorovinyl should also rate the product "average," and 48 percent of the 25 who used the product without dichlorovinyl should record a rating of "average." The E_i are calculated as $(75)(0.48) = 36$ and $(25)(0.48) = 12$. Similarly, since 21 of the 100 users, or 21 percent, rated the product "below average," then 21 percent of the 75 who used dichlorovinyl ($E_i = 15.8$) and 21 percent of the 25 who did not use dichlorovinyl ($E_i = 5.25$) should provide a "below average" rating.

Testing the hypothesis requires a comparison of O_i and E_i over the $rc = 6$ cells using the equation

$$\chi^2 = \sum_{i=1}^{rc} \frac{(O_i - E_i)^2}{E_i} \qquad (15.3)$$

For the current problem, Wilma finds

$$\chi^2 = \frac{(20 - 23.3)^2}{23.3} + \frac{(11 - 7.75)^2}{7.75} + \frac{(40 - 36)^2}{36}$$

$$+ \frac{(8 - 12)^2}{12} + \frac{(15 - 15)^2}{15.8} + \frac{(6 - 5.25)^2}{5.25}$$

$$= 3.76$$

The test carries $(r - 1)(c - 1) = (3 - 1)(2 - 1) = 2$ degrees of freedom. If Wilma set $\alpha = 10$ percent, $\chi^2_{0.10,2} = 4.605$. As Figure 15-6 shows, the null is not rejected according to the decision rule:

Decision Rule
Do not reject the null if $\chi^2 < 4.605$. Reject if $\chi^2 > 4.605$.

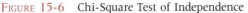

FIGURE 15-6   Chi-Square Test of Independence

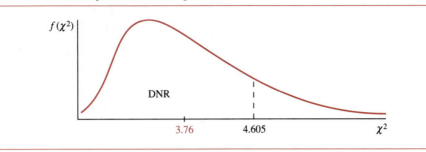

This next example provides a further illustration.

EXAMPLE 15-2 The Importance of Price

Hedonistic Auto Sales sets out to determine if there is any relationship between income of customers and the importance they attach to the price of luxury automobiles. They want to test the hypotheses that

H_0: Income and importance of price are independent.

H_a: Income and importance of price are not independent.

SOLUTION:

Customers are grouped into three income levels and asked to assign a level of significance to price in the purchase decision. Results are shown in the contingency table. Since $182/538 = 33.83$ percent of all respondents attach a "great" level of importance to price, then, if income and price are not related, we would expect 33.83 percent of those in each income bracket to respond that price was of "great" importance. Thus, the E_i are $(198)(0.3383) = 66.98$, $(191)(0.3383) = 64.62$, and $(149)(0.3383) = 50.41$.

Attribute A: Importance Level	Attribute B: Income			Total
	Low	**Medium**	**High**	**Total**
Great	$O_i = 83$ $E_i = 66.98$	$O_i = 62$ $E_i = 64.62$	$O_i = 37$ $E_i = 50.41$	182
Moderate	$O_i = 52$ $E_i = 63.32$	$O_i = 71$ $E_i = 61.06$	$O_i = 49$ $E_i = 47.64$	172
Little	$O_i = 63$ $E_i = 67.72$	$O_i = 58$ $E_i = 65.32$	$O_i = 63$ $E_i = 50.96$	184
Totals	198	191	149	538

In like fashion, $172/538 = 31.97$ of all respondents rated price moderately important. Thus, the E_i for the "moderate" category are $198(0.3197) = 63.32$, $191(0.3197) = 61.06$, and $149(0.3197) = 47.64$.

○○○○   **DECISION MAKING THROUGH PROBLEM SOLVING**   ○○○○
                       ILLUSTRATION 15-3

A recent in-house publication by State Farm Insurance Company discussed the problem State Farm was having in deciding on premium levels to charge motorists in the
suburbs of Boston. The decision was finally made on the basis of a test to determine
if there were any relationship between accident claims and the location of the suburb
in which the motorist lived.

   Using a chi-square test for independence, it was found that claims and residence
were not independent, in that some suburbs tended to report more claims than others.
Premiums were therefore based in part on the suburb in which the car owner resided.

For the "little" category, the data show $184/538 = 34.20$ percent of all customers
attached little importance to the price. Therefore, the E_i are $(198)(0.342) = 67.72$,
$(191)(0.342) = 65.32$, and $(149)(0.342) = 50.96$.
   The chi-square is

$$\chi^2 = \frac{(83 - 66.98)^2}{66.98} + \frac{(62 - 64.62)^2}{64.62} + \frac{(37 - 50.41)^2}{50.41} + \cdots$$
$$+ \frac{(63 - 50.96)^2}{50.96}$$

$$= 15.17$$

If α is set at 1 percent, and with $(r - 1)(c - 1) = (3 - 1)(3 - 1) = 4$ degrees
of freedom, $\chi^2_{0.01, 4} = 13.277$. As seen in the figure, the decision rule is

Decision Rule
Do not reject if $\chi^2 < 13.277$. Reject if $\chi^2 > 13.277$.

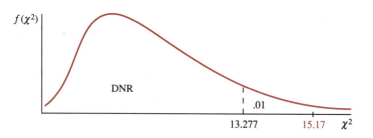

STATISTICAL INTERPRETATION:
The null hypothesis is rejected. There is only a 1 percent chance that if there is no
relationship between income and price significance, differences between O_i and E_i
would be great enough to produce a chi-square larger than 13.277.

The remainder of the chapter is devoted to different nonparametric tests. Several tests are examined to illustrate (1) when the test should be used, (2) the primary purpose and application of the test, and (3) the interpretation of the test. We explore the

Sign test.
Runs test.
Mann-Whitney U test.
Kruskal-Wallis test.
Spearman rank correlation test.

We begin with the sign test.

15.3   THE SIGN TEST

A nonparametric test commonly used to make business decisions is the **sign test.** It is most often used to test the hypothesis about the median of a population distribution, and often involves the use of matched pairs. Suppose we have before-and-after data for a sample and wish to compare these matched sets of data. We do it by subtracting the paired observations in one data set from those in the second and noting the algebraic sign that results. We have no interest in the magnitude of the difference, only whether a plus sign or a minus sign results.

The sign test is the nonparametric counterpart to the t-test for matched pairs. The t-test required the assumption that the populations were normally distributed. However, in many instances, this assumption is not possible. The sign test is useful in these cases. In addition, the sign test can also be used to test for the central location of a population distribution.

The null hypothesis states that there is no difference in the data sets. If this is true, then a plus sign and a minus sign are equally likely. The probability that either would occur is 0.50. A two-tailed test is

$$H_0: m = p$$

$$H_a: m \neq p$$

where m and p are the numbers of minus signs and plus signs, respectively. A one-tailed test is

$$H_0: m \leq p$$

$$H_a: m > p$$

or

$$H_0: m \geq p$$

$$H_a: m < p$$

Sign Test
The sign test is designed to test the hypothesis regarding the central
tendency of a population distribution.

Since there are only two possible outcomes, a minus sign and a plus sign, and
the probability of each remains constant from trial to trial, we can use the binomial
distribution.

Assume you are working as a market analyst and wish to measure the effectiveness of a promotional game on your firm's product. Prior to the promotional game,
12 retail outlets are selected and sales for the month are recorded, rounded to the
nearest $100. During the second month, the promotional game is implemented and
sales are again recorded. Table 15-7 displays these sales levels, along with the algebraic sign that results when sales in the second month are subtracted from those in
the first month. A plus sign recorded in the last column means that sales went down
during the second month.

TABLE 15-7   Sales for Twelve Retail Stores

Store	Before the Game	During the Game	Sign
1	$42	$40	+
2	57	60	−
3	38	38	0
4	49	47	+
5	63	65	−
6	36	39	−
7	48	49	−
8	58	50	+
9	47	47	0
10	51	52	−
11	83	72	+
12	27	33	−

Assume further that you want to test at the 5 percent level the hypothesis that the
promotion increased sales. If sales went up in the second month when the promotion
was in effect, then subtracting those sales from sales in the first month would produce minus signs. You would then expect the number of minus signs, m, to exceed
the number of plus signs, p. That is, $m > p$. This statement does not contain an
equal sign and is, therefore, taken as the alternative hypothesis, producing a right-
tailed test:

$$H_0: m \leq p$$

$$H_a: m > p$$

You must now ask, "What would cause the null to be rejected?" Since the null states that $m \leq p$, then either (1) a significantly large number of minus signs or (2) a significantly small number of plus signs would result in the rejection of the null. That is, the null is rejected if m is too large or if p is too small.

Table 15-7 shows 6 minus signs and 4 plus signs for a total of $n = 10$ signs. Values resulting in a zero difference are ignored. Observations 3 and 9 are therefore dropped from consideration. You must then determine the probability of six or more minus signs or four or fewer plus signs if the probabilities of both are $\pi = 0.50$. If this probability is less than the chosen α-value, the sample results are seen as significant and the null hypothesis is rejected. However, if the probability of the sample results is greater than α, the results can be attributed to sampling error, and the null is not rejected. That is, if the sample results actually observed are likely to occur, they are not interpreted as being a significant finding and the null cannot be rejected.

From the binomial table, the probability of six or more minus signs is

$$P(m \geq 6 \mid n = 10, \pi = 0.5) = 0.2051 + 0.1172 + 0.0439$$
$$+ 0.0098 + 0.0010$$
$$= 0.3770$$

Of course, if you obtained six or more minus signs, you must have obtained four or fewer plus signs. Therefore, the probability of four or fewer plus signs is also 0.3770:

$$P(p \leq 4 \mid n = 10, \pi = 0.5) = 0.2051 + 0.1172 + 0.0439$$
$$+ 0.0098 + 0.0010$$
$$= 0.3770$$

This value of 0.3770 is the probability of obtaining six or more minus signs (or four or fewer plus signs) if π, the probability of the occurrence of either sign on any trial, is 0.50. We noted that if the number of minus signs was "unusually large," it would refute the null. However, 6 is not an unusually large number. The probability of getting six or more signs is quite high at 37.7 percent. Since the probability of their occurrence is greater than an α of 5 percent, the event of six minus signs is not considered "large," and the null that $H_0: m \leq p$ is not rejected.

If the promotion were effective, there would be a large number of minus signs, and the null that $m \leq p$ would be rejected. But as we have seen, six minus signs is not an unusually large number, and the promotion cannot be considered successful.

If a test were based on the left-tailed test, the hypothesis would be

$$H_0: m \geq p$$
$$H_a: m < p$$

If m is unusually small, or p is unusually large, the null would be rejected. Assume that in an experiment with $n = 12$ trials, five minus signs and seven plus signs are observed. You would then find the probability of obtaining five or less minus signs, or the probability of seven or more plus signs. If this probability is less than the chosen α, the null is rejected.

Example 15-3 illustrates a two-tailed test. The only adjustment is that α must be divided by 2. The hypotheses are

$$H_0: m = p$$

$$H_a: m \neq p$$

The hypotheses are tested by comparing $\alpha/2$ to either (1) the probability that the sign that occurred less often could occur that many times or less, or (2) the probability that the sign that occurre. more often could occur that many times or more.

EXAMPLE 15-3 Testing Tread—A Quality Control Example

Honda tested the wear resistance of two types of tire tread on their Nighthawk motorbike. Ten bikes were randomly chosen. A tire with one type of tread was placed on the front, and the other tread was mounted on the rear. After driving the bikes a specified number of miles under set conditions, a wear rating between 0 and 40 was given to each tire. A higher rating indicated a better tire. The results are shown here. Honda's research analysts want to test the hypothesis that there is no difference in wear ratings at the 10 percent level. The hypotheses are

$$H_0: m = p$$

$$H_a: m \neq p$$

Wear Rating

Tires	Tread Type I	Tread Type II	Sign
1	32	37	−
2	27	25	+
3	21	21	0
4	13	17	−
5	25	29	−
6	38	39	−
7	17	23	−
8	29	33	−
9	32	34	−
10	34	37	−

SOLUTION:

Observation 3 is ignored because the difference is zero. There is one plus sign and eight minus signs. Honda can calculate the probability that one or fewer plus signs could occur or the probability that eight or more minus signs could occur. Focusing on the number of plus signs, we have from Table C in Appendix 1

$$P(p \leq 1 \,|\, n = 9, \pi = 0.5) = 0.0195$$

Of course, the same answer is obtained if we use the number of minus signs in the test:

$$P(m \geq 8 \,|\, n = 9, \pi = 0.5) = 1 - P(m \leq 7) = 1 - 0.9805 = 0.0195$$

Since $\alpha/2 = 0.10/2 = 0.05 > 0.0195$, the null is rejected.

STATISTICAL INTERPRETATION:

If the null is true, and $m = p$, there is only a 1.95 percent of getting one or fewer plus signs (or eight or more minus signs). There is a less than $\alpha = 5$ percent chance that the null is true. There is a difference in wear ratings. Tread type II is superior since there was a significant number of minus signs.

QUICK CHECK 15.3.1

○○○○ In measuring the effectiveness of a marketing technique, a firm finds six plus and three minus signs. If a plus sign suggests that the technique is effective, can you conclude at the 5 percent level that it is effective?

a. What are the hypotheses?
b. What questions should you ask yourself?
c. What is your response?
d. What is your conclusion?

Answer:

a. If the technique is effective, then $p > m$. Therefore, H_0: $p \leq m$; H_a: $p > m$.
b. What would cause rejection of the null?
c. Since null is $p \leq m$, a significantly large number of p signs would result in rejection.
d. $P(p \geq 6 | n = 9, \pi = 0.50) = 0.1641 + 0.0703 + 0.0176 + 0.0020 = 0.2540 > 0.05$. Do not reject null.

A. THE USE OF LARGE SAMPLES

If $n > 20$, it is permissible to use the normal approximation to the binomial. Assume that in the preceding example Honda had sampled 30 motorbikes and obtained 6 plus signs, 21 minus signs, and 3 zero differences. They would have $n = 27$ useful observations.

As we learned in Chapter 8, if the test is two-tailed with $\alpha = 0.10$ the critical Z-value is 1.65.

Decision Rule

Do not reject if $-1.65 < Z_{test} < 1.65$. Reject if $Z_{test} < -1.65$ or $Z_{test} > 1.65$.

The value for Z_{test} is

$$Z_{test} = \frac{k \pm 0.5 - 0.5n}{0.5\sqrt{n}} \qquad (15.4)$$

where k is the appropriate number of plus or minus signs and n is the sample size. If $k < n/2$, $k + 0.5$ is used. If $k > n/2$, $k - 0.5$ is used. It is necessary to adjust k by 0.5 because the binomial distribution represents discrete data, while the normal distribution applies to continuous data.

Since the Honda example is a two-tailed test, we can test either the number of plus signs or the number of minus signs. Testing the number of plus signs, we have

$$Z_{\text{test}} = \frac{6 + 0.5 - (0.5)(27)}{0.5\sqrt{27}}$$

$$= -2.69$$

Testing the number of minus signs, we find

$$Z_{\text{test}} = \frac{21 - 0.5 - (0.5)(27)}{0.5\sqrt{27}}$$

$$= 2.69$$

Since $-2.69 < -1.65$, or $2.69 > 1.65$, the null is rejected. There is a difference in the two types of tires.

B.   A ONE-SAMPLE SIGN TEST

The sign test can also be applied to a single sample. The observations in the sample are placed in one of two categories. The observations in one category are assigned plus signs; those in the other category are given minus signs. The binomial distribution is then used to determine the probability of obtaining the number of plus and minus signs recorded in the data set. If this value is less than α, the null is rejected. Example 15-4 illustrates.

EXAMPLE 15-4   Controlling Quality on the Assembly Line

Business Week reviewed efforts by a small computer firm in the San Francisco Bay area to improve its quality control measures. Records showed that 15 percent of their units were reported as defective. After changes in the production process, the firm's CEO argued that this figure had decreased ($\pi < 0.15$). You have been hired as a production analyst to determine if his claim is true.

SOLUTION:
The set of hypotheses you will test is

$$H_0: \pi \geq 0.15$$

$$H_a: \pi < 0.15$$

Of 18 units you inspect, you find that only 2 are defective. These units are assigned a plus sign. You must again ask yourself what would cause you to reject the null. Since the null says that the proportion of plus signs (defects) is at least 15 percent, a significantly smaller proportion would cause its rejection. You must therefore determine the probability that the number of plus signs could be at most 2 if the null was correct. If this probability is less than $\alpha = 0.05$, you would reject the null.

Decision Rule
Do not reject if $P(p \leq 2 \mid n = 18, \pi = .15) > 0.05$. Reject if $P(p \leq 2 \mid n = 18, \pi = .15) < 0.05$.

From the cumulative binomial table you determine that

$$P(p \leq 2 \mid n = 18, \pi = 0.15) = 0.4797 > 0.05$$

The null is not rejected.

STATISTICAL INTERPRETATION:
The CEO's claim appears invalid. There is a 47.97 percent chance that you could find 2 of the 18 units to be defective if $\pi \geq 0.15$. There is no support for the claim that $\pi < 0.15$.

This final example of a sign test more clearly illustrates how, as noted at the outset of this discussion, the sign test involves the median. Observations are simply assigned a plus or minus sign, depending on whether they are above or below some hypothesized central value. Due to the lack of knowledge regarding any symmetry in the population's distribution, the median is usually selected as that central measure.

A firm hypothesizes that median sales receipts are at least $1,000: median $\geq$ $1,000. Then if a plus sign is given to those sample observations in excess of $1,000, we have

$$H_0: \text{median} \geq \$1,000 \text{ or } p \geq m$$

$$H_a: \text{median} < \$1,000 \text{ or } p < m$$

Ask yourself, "What would cause me to reject the null?" Since the null argues that the median is greater than or equal to $1,000 ($p \geq m$), a "significantly large" number of observations less than $1,000 (minus signs) would necessitate its rejection. "Significantly large" can be interpreted as a number unlikely to occur if the null is correct.

Sample data for receipts, along with the corresponding sign in parentheses, are

$1,200 (+)	$1,420 (+)
$1,000 (0)	$1,000 (0)
$1,400 (+)	$900 (−)
$970 (−)	$1,100 (+)
$840 (−)	$1,150 (+)

There are five plus signs and three minus signs. Since, as just noted, a significantly large number of minus signs will result in a rejection of the null, you must determine $P(m \geq 3 \mid n = 8, \pi = 0.50)$, where m is the number of minus signs. The binomial table shows

$$P(m \geq 3 \mid n = 8, \pi = 0.50) = 1 - P(m \leq 2) = 1 - 0.1445 = 0.8555$$

There is an 85.55 percent chance you could get at least three out of eight minus signs if the null were correct. This is certainly not an unlikely occurrence. Three minus signs is not unusual or significantly large. The null cannot be rejected at the 5 percent level or at any acceptable α-level.

15.4 RUNS TEST

The importance of randomness in the sampling process has been repeatedly stressed throughout our discussion of statistical techniques. In the absence of randomness, many of the statistical tools upon which we rely are of little or no use. It is therefore often necessary to test for randomness in our samples. This can be accomplished using a **runs test.**

Runs Test
The runs test is a nonparametric test for randomness in the sampling process.

To complete a runs test, we assign all observations in the sample one of two symbols. A **run** consists of a sequence of one or more like symbols. If the observations are grouped into categories of, say, *A* and *B*, we might find the following sequences:

$$\underline{AA} \quad \underline{BBB} \quad \underline{A} \quad \underline{BB} \quad \underline{AAA} \quad \underline{B}$$
$$1 \qquad 2 \qquad 3 \quad 4 \qquad 5 \qquad 6$$

There are six runs, each consisting of one or more like observations.

Run
An unbroken series of one or more like symbols is called a run.

Suppose employees are selected for a training program. If selection does not depend on whether the employee is male (m) or female (f), we would expect gender to be a random event. However, if some pattern in gender is detected, we might assume randomness is absent and selection was made at least in part on the basis of a worker's gender.

A pattern can be detected by the number of runs that occur in the sample data. If there is an unusually large or unusually small number of runs, a pattern is suggested.

Assume that the gender of each employee is recorded in order of selection and proves to be

$$\underline{mmm} \quad \underline{fffff} \quad \underline{mmm}$$
$$1 \qquad 2 \qquad 3$$

Three runs occur in this sample. There are three males, followed by six females, and then three males. It would seem that the selections are not sufficiently mixed, causing a systematic pattern which implies an absence of randomness. Assume instead that the order of selection is

$$\underline{m} \; \underline{f} \; \underline{m} \; \underline{f} \; \underline{m} \; \underline{f} \; \underline{m} \; \underline{f} \; \underline{m} \quad \underline{f} \quad \underline{m} \quad \underline{f}$$
$$1 \; 2 \; 3 \;\; 4 \; 5 \;\; 6 \; 7 \;\; 8 \; 9 \;\; 10 \;\; 11 \;\; 12$$

Again, there appears to be a pattern producing an unusually large number of 12 separate runs.

Detection of a Pattern

If too few or too many runs occur, it might be assumed that randomness is absent.

The set of hypotheses to be tested is

H_0: Randomness exists in the sample.

H_a: Randomness does not exist in the sample.

To test the hypothesis, we must determine if the number of runs (r) is either too large or too small. Tables M1 and M2 show critical values for the number of runs if α is 5 percent. Since on the surface both of our examples appear nonrandom, let's take a set of selections less obvious. Suppose the selections were

$$\underline{\text{m}}\ \underline{\text{fff}}\ \underline{\text{mmm}}\ \underline{\text{ff}}\ \underline{\text{mmm}}$$
$$1\quad 2\quad\ \ 3\quad\ \ 4\quad\ \ 5$$

The selections seem more random than the other two examples in that no pattern is obvious. Let $n_1 = 7$ be the number of males and $n_2 = 5$ be the number of females. Table M1 shows the minimum critical number of runs for an α-value of 5 percent. If the number of runs is equal to or less than the value shown in Table M1, it suggests that, at the 5 percent level, there are too few runs to support the null hypothesis of randomness. Given that $n_1 = 7$ and $n_2 = 5$, the critically low value is found to be 3. Since the number of runs exceeds this minimum, there is not a significantly low number of runs to warrant rejection of the null. Table M2 provides critically high values for r. If the number of runs in a sample is equal to or greater than those values, it may be concluded that there is an extremely large number of runs, suggesting the absence of randomness. For $n_1 = 7$ and $n_2 = 5$, Table M2 reveals that the maximum number of runs is 11. If the number of runs exceeds 11, there are too many to support the hypothesis of randomness. Since the number of runs is less than 11, it is not significantly high and the null is not rejected at the 5 percent level. It would seem that our sample selection is the result of randomness.

When the sample data do not naturally fall into one of two possible categories, it is possible to use the median as a measure to bifurcate the data. Assume levels of daily output at a coal mine selected for a statistical study are, in order of selection, 31, 57, 52, 22, 24, 59, 25, 29, 27, 44, 43, 32, 40, 37, 60 tons. The median of 37 can be used as a benchmark value. Observations either fall above (A) or below (B) 37, yielding eight runs of

$$31\quad 57\ 52\quad 22\ 24\quad 59\quad 25\ 29\ 27\quad 44\ 43\quad 32\quad 40\ 60$$
$$\underline{\text{B}}\quad \underline{\text{AA}}\quad\ \underline{\text{BB}}\quad\ \underline{\text{A}}\quad\ \underline{\text{BBB}}\quad\ \underline{\text{AA}}\quad \underline{\text{B}}\quad\ \underline{\text{AA}}$$
$$1\qquad 2\qquad\ \ 3\qquad 4\qquad\ \ 5\qquad\quad 6\qquad 7\qquad 8$$

With $n_1 = 7$ for B and $n_2 = 7$ for A, Table M reveals critical values of 3 and 13 runs. Since there were eight runs, randomness is assumed and the null is not rejected.

Another application of the runs test is found in a test of randomness in the ordinary least-squares (OLS) method of regression analysis. A basic property of the OLS regression model is that the errors are random. No pattern should exist in the signs of these errors. Example 15-5 illustrates how the runs test can be used to test this condition.

EXAMPLE 15-5 Testing for Error Randomness

A marketing research firm developed a model to predict monthly sales for a new product. After 17 months, the errors were calculated and proved to have the following signs:

$$\underbrace{+\ +\ +\ +\ +\ +}_{1}\ \ \underbrace{-\ -\ -\ -\ -}_{2}\ \ \underbrace{+\ +\ +\ +}_{3}\ \ \underbrace{-\ -}_{4}$$

At the 5 percent level, does there appear to be randomness in the error terms?

SOLUTION:

There are $n_1 = 10$ plus signs, $n_2 = 7$ minus signs, and $r = 4$ runs. Tables M1 and M2 reveal the critical minimum and maximum numbers of runs, respectively, to be 5 and 14. The hypotheses are

$$H_0\text{: Randomness prevails.}$$

$$H_a\text{: Randomness does not prevail.}$$

Decision Rule
Do not reject the null if $5 < r < 14$. Reject if $r \leq 5$ or $r \geq 14$.

Since $r = 4$, the null should be rejected at the 5 percent level.

STATISTICAL INTERPRETATION:

The number of runs is significantly small. There are too few runs to support the hypothesis of randomness. The validity of the model is questionable, and the firm should examine alternatives. The low number of runs results from the fact that errors of one sign are followed by errors of like signs, an indication of positive autocorrelation.

A. LARGE-SAMPLE TESTS

If both n_1 and n_2 are greater than 20, the sampling distribution for r approximates normality. The distribution has a mean of

$$\mu_r = \frac{2n_1 n_2}{n_1 + n_2} + 1 \qquad\qquad (15.5)$$

and a standard deviation of

$$\sigma_r = \sqrt{\frac{2n_1 n_2 (2n_1 n_2 - n_1 - n_2)}{(n_1 + n_2)^2 (n_1 + n_2 - 1)}} \qquad (15.6)$$

Standardizing the distribution of runs can be accomplished by using the normal deviate:

$$Z = \frac{r - \mu_r}{\sigma_r} \qquad (15.7)$$

A sales presentation made to a group of 52 potential buyers resulted in 27 sales, 25 no-sales, and 18 runs. At the 1 percent level of significance, is the sample random?

H_0: The sample is random.

H_a: The sample is not random.

At 1 percent, the critical Z for the two-tailed test is 2.58. As shown in Figure 15-7, the decision rule is

Decision Rule
Do not reject the null if $-2.58 < Z < 2.58$. Reject the null if $Z < -2.58$ or $Z > 2.58$.

FIGURE 15-7   Testing for Randomness in Sales

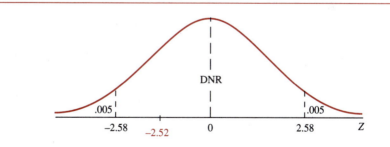
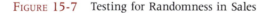

Then by Formula (15.5),

$$\mu_r = \frac{2n_1 n_2}{n_1 + n_2} + 1$$

$$= \frac{2(27)(25)}{27 + 25} + 1$$

$$= 26.96$$

> ○○○○   **DECISION MAKING THROUGH PROBLEM SOLVING**   ○○○○
>   ILLUSTRATION 15-4
>
> Ensuring that the correct amount of a product is placed in its container is a persistent
> problem in assembly-line production. A recent issue of *Industry World* described how
> Central Chemical Corporation, a small chemical and janitorial supply company in
> Kansas City, Kansas, tested the precision of their machines used to fill containers
> with cleaning fluid. A sample of 36-ounce containers was taken from the production
> line, and the contents were weighed. Overfills above 36 ounces were recorded with a
> plus sign, and underfills registered a minus sign. If the machine was properly ad-
> justed, underfills and overfills should be equally likely. A randomness should prevail
> in misfills. However, if randomness could not be verified, it was assumed that the ma-
> chine was systematically putting in too much cleaning fluid or too little fluid, result-
> ing in a small number of runs.
>   The test showed that an excessive number of underfills resulted in too few runs to
> assume misfills were random. The machine was apparently set too low and was ad-
> justed. Central Chemical now performs a runs test as a regular aspect of its general
> maintenance program.

and, by Formula (15.6),

$$\sigma_r = \sqrt{\frac{2n_1 n_2 (2n_1 n_2 - n_1 - n_2)}{(n_1 + n_2)^2 (n_1 + n_2 - 1)}}$$

$$= \sqrt{\frac{[2(27)(25)][2(27)(25) - 27 - 25)]}{(27 + 25)^2 (27 + 25 - 1)}}$$

$$= 3.56$$

The normal deviate is

$$Z = \frac{r - \mu_r}{\sigma_r}$$

$$= \frac{18 - 26.96}{3.56}$$

$$= -2.52$$

There is insufficient evidence to reject the null. It would appear that the sample is
random. There is a 99 percent probability that a random sampling process with 27
and 25 observations in the two categories, and with 18 runs, would lead to a Z between ± 2.58.

15.5   THE MANN-WHITNEY U TEST

The **Mann-Whitney U test** (or simply the U **test**) tests the equality of two population
distributions. It is based on the assumption that two random samples are independently drawn from continuous variables. In its broadest sense, the null hypothesis

states that the distributions of two populations are identical. However, the test can be tailored to examine the equality of two population means or medians. To test the equality of means, we must assume that the populations are symmetrical and have the same variance. Under these conditions the Mann-Whitney U test serves as the nonparametric alternative to the t-test, except it does not require the assumption of normality. If the assumption of symmetry is dropped, the median replaces the mean as the test statistic.

Mann-Whitney U Test
The nonparametric counterpart to the t-test for independent samples is the U test. It does not require the assumption that the differences between the two samples are normally distributed.

The data are ordinal in that they are ordered or ranked from lowest to highest. There is no effort to match pairs, as we have often done when two samples were taken. (Note that the Mann-Whitney U test is the same as the Wilcoxon rank sum test, but differs from the Wilcoxon signed-rank test. The similarity in names can be confusing.)

To illustrate the U test, suppose a pottery factory wants to compare the time it takes for clay pieces to cool after being "fired" in the oven by two different firing methods.

Twelve pieces are fired using method 1 and 10 using method 2. The number of minutes required for each piece to cool are as follows:

Method 1	27* 31 28 29 39 40 35 33 32 36 37 43
Method 2	34 24* 38 28 30 34 37 42 41 44

The observations are then ordered and ranked from lowest to highest; as shown in Table 15-8. The value 24 in method 2 is the lowest of all 22 observations and is given the rank of 1, and 27 in method 1 has a rank of 2. Ties, such as 28, are averaged over the appropriate ranks. The value 28 is the third lowest observation, and both values of 28 receive a ranking of 3.5. There is no rank of 4, since two observations were ranked as 3.5. The rankings are then summed, yielding ΣR_1 and ΣR_2.

The Mann-Whitney U-statistic for each sample is calculated from the equations

$$U_1 = n_1 n_2 + \frac{n_1(n_1 + 1)}{2} - \Sigma R_1 \qquad (15.8)$$

TABLE 15-8 Ranking Cooling Times

Method 1	Rank	Method 2	Rank
		24	1
27	2		
28	3.5	28	3.5
29	5		
		30	6
31	7		
32	8		
33	9		
		34	10.5
		34	10.5
35	12		
36	13		
37	14.5	37	14.5
		38	16
39	17		
40	18		
		41	19
		42	20
43	21		
		44	22
	$\Sigma R_1 = 130$		$\Sigma R_2 = 123$

and

$$U_2 = n_1 n_2 + \frac{n_2(n_2 + 1)}{2} - \Sigma R_2 \qquad (15.9)$$

The data in Table 15-8 yield

$$U_1 = (12)(10) + \frac{12(12 + 1)}{2} - 130$$

$$= 68$$

and

$$U_2 = (12)(10) + \frac{10(10 + 1)}{2} - 123$$

$$= 52$$

Notice that $U_1 + U_2 = n_1 n_2$ provides a quick check of your arithmetic.

If n_1 and n_2 are both at least 10, the mean and standard deviation of the sampling distribution for the U-statistic is

$$\mu_u = \frac{n_1 n_2}{2} \qquad (15.10)$$

and

$$\sigma_u = \sqrt{\frac{n_1 n_2 (n_1 + n_2 + 1)}{12}} \qquad (15.11)$$

In the present case, we find

$$\mu_u = \frac{(12)(10)}{2}$$

$$= 60$$

and

$$\sigma_u = \sqrt{\frac{(12)(10)(12 + 10 + 1)}{12}}$$

$$= 15.17$$

The distribution of the U-statistic can then be normalized by the formula

$$Z = \frac{U_i - \mu_u}{\sigma_u} \qquad (15.12)$$

where U_i is the appropriate U-value, either U_1 or U_2, depending on the nature of the test. Let's now determine which U-value is appropriate.

A.   A Two-Tailed Test

In our example of the firing ovens, the pottery factory may want to test the hypothesis that the mean cooling times of method 1 and method 2 are the same. This requires a two-tailed test with hypotheses

$$H_0: \mu_1 = \mu_2$$

$$H_a: \mu_1 \neq \mu_2$$

In a two-tailed test, either U_1 or U_2 can be used in Formula (15.12). Thus, arbitrarily using U_2, we find

$$Z = \frac{52 - 60}{15.17}$$

$$= -0.53$$

If $\alpha = 10$ percent, the decision rule, as reflected in Figure 15-8, is

Decision Rule
Do not reject if $-1.65 < Z < 1.65$. Reject if $Z < -1.65$ or $Z > 1.65$.

Since $Z = -0.53$ is in the DNR region, the pottery factory can conclude with 90 percent confidence that the mean cooling times are the same for both firing methods.

FIGURE 15-8   A Two-Tailed Test of Mean Cooling Times

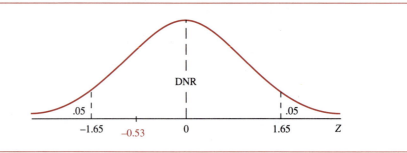

B.   **A ONE-TAILED TEST**

Suppose the factory felt that method 1 would result in a longer mean cooling time: $M_1 > M_2$. Then the hypotheses

$$H_0: M_1 \leq M_2$$

$$H_A: M_1 > M_2$$

call for a right-tailed test. If a right-tailed test is to be conducted, then the U-value in Formula (15.12) must be the higher of the two U-values. Since $U_1 = 68 > U_2 = 52$, U_1 is used to calculate the Z-value. If this were a left-tailed test, the lower U-value would be used to compute Z.

Given our right-tailed test, we have

$$Z = \frac{68 - 60}{15.17}$$

$$= 0.53$$

If $\alpha = 0.10$ is retained for this one-tail test, the decision rule, as shown in Figure 15-9, is

Decision Rule
Do not reject if $Z < 1.28$. Reject if $Z > 1.28$.

FIGURE 15-9 A One-Tailed Test for Mean Cooling Times

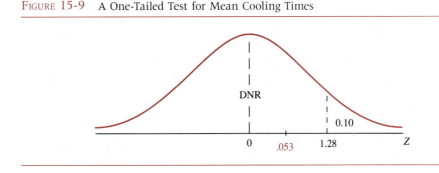

The Z-value of 0.53 is clearly in the DNR region. The pottery factory does not reject the null hypothesis that $M_1 \leq M_2$ and cannot conclude that method 2 leads to faster cooling times. Example 15-6 further illustrates the Mann-Whitney U test.

EXAMPLE 15-6 A Comparison Based on Sex

The proprietor of a local pub popular with students at the nearby university was overheard to say that, on the average, female customers spend less than do males. Challenged to support his claim by the statistics professor occupying his usual space at the end of the bar, the saloon keeper recorded the expenditures of 10 female and 10 male customers. The data were, in dollars,

Female	5.12 3.15 8.17 3.42 2.02 4.42 3.72 2.12 5.72 4.87
Male	5.83 6.49 4.45 5.12 9.02 9.73 5.42 6.43 8.79 8.89

SOLUTION:

Female	Rank	Male	Rank
2.02	1		
2.12	2		
3.15	3		
3.42	4		
3.72	5		
4.42	6		
		4.45	7
4.87	8		
5.12	9.5	5.12	9.5
		5.42	11
5.72	12	5.83	13
		6.43	14
		6.49	15
8.17	16		
		8.79	17
		8.89	18
		9.02	19
		9.73	20
	$66.5 = \Sigma R_f$		$143.5 = \Sigma R_m$

$$U_f = (10)(10) + \frac{10(10 + 1)}{2} - 66.5$$

$$= 88.5$$

$$U_m = (10)(10) + \frac{10(10 + 1)}{2} - 143.5$$

$$= 11.5$$

Since the bar owner claimed $M_f < M_m$, the hypotheses

$$H_0: M_f \geq M_m$$

$$H_a: M_f < M_m$$

produce a left-tailed test as shown in the following figure. If $\alpha = 0.10$, the critical Z is -1.28.

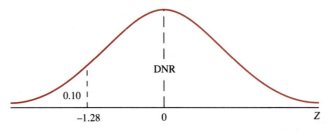

Decision Rule
Do not reject if $Z > -1.28$. Reject if $Z < -1.28$.

The mean and standard deviation of the sampling distribution for U are

$$\mu_u = \frac{(10)(10)}{2}$$

$$= 50$$

$$\sigma_u = \sqrt{\frac{(10)(10)(10 + 10 + 1)}{12}}$$

$$= 13.23$$

The left-tailed test requires that the lower U-value be used in calculating Z:

$$Z = \frac{11.5 - 50}{13.23}$$

$$= -2.91$$

STATISTICAL INTERPRETATION:
A Z of -2.91 results in rejection of the null. The owner of the bar can be 90 percent confident that his feelings regarding the comparative mean expenditures of male and female patrons are justified. There is only a 10 percent chance that a Z-value below -1.28 would result if the null were true.

QUICK CHECK 15.5.1

○○○○

Housing costs of 42 residents of Topeka, Kansas, were compared with those of 35 residents of Erie, Pennsylvania. The 77 observations were then ranked, yielding $\Sigma R_t = 1,833.5$ and $\Sigma R_e = 1,169.5$. At the 5 percent level, does it appear mean housing costs are the same in both cities? State
a. the hypotheses.
b. the Z-value.
c. the decision rule.
d. the conclusion.

Answer:
a. $H_0: M_t = M_e; M_t \neq M_e$.
b. $Z = 2$ (or -2).
c. Do not reject if $-1.96 < Z < 1.96$.
d. Reject null.

15.6 SPEARMAN RANK CORRELATION

Our earlier discussion of regression and correlation provided us with a means to measure the relationship between two variables. We learned how to calculate and interpret the Pearsonian correlation coefficient and thereby measure the strength of the relationship between two variables.

However, this approach required precise numerical values and the assumption of normality in the distribution of those values. In many instances, such numerical measurement may not be possible, and there may be no support for the assumption of normality. In such cases, the Pearsonian method cannot be used.

Nevertheless, we may still be able to systematically rank or order the observations. This ordinal ranking permits us to measure the degrees of correlation between two variables by using the **Spearman rank correlation coefficient.**

Spearman Rank Correlation
The Spearman rank correlation measures the relationship between two variables that have been ordinally ranked from lowest to highest (or highest to lowest).

Many situations in business and industry lend themselves to ordinal ranking. Last year, Amco Tech, a U.S. manufacturer of computer microchips, hired seven computer technicians. The technicians were given a test designed to measure their basic knowledge. After a year of service, their supervisor was asked to rank each technician's job performance. Tests scores and performance rankings for all seven employees are shown in Table 15-9.

TABLE 15-9   Data on Amco Tech Technicians

Technician	Test Score	Performance Ranking
J. Smith	82	4
A. Jones	73	7
D. Boone	60	6
M. Lewis	80	3
G. Clark	67	5
A. Lincoln	94	1
G. Washington	89	2

Notice that although the test score is a quantitative measure of the technician's knowledge, the performance ranking is merely an ordered list by the supervisor of which technicians he feels are doing a better job. The director of management operations therefore decides to use the Spearman rank correlation to determine if there is any relationship between test scores and job performance. The director must first develop the ranking for test scores. These rankings, along with some necessary calculations, are displayed in Table 15-10.

TABLE 15-10   Rankings of Amco Tech Technicians

Technician	Test Score	Test Rank (X)	Performance Rank (Y)	$X - Y = d_i$	$(X - Y)^2 = d_i^2$
J. Smith	82	3	4	−1	1
A. Jones	73	5	7	−2	4
D. Boone	60	7	6	1	1
M. Lewis	80	4	3	1	1
G. Clark	67	6	5	1	1
A. Lincoln	94	1	1	0	0
G. Washington	89	2	2	0	0
					$\overline{8} = \Sigma d_i^2$

The Spearman rank correlation coefficient, r_S, is then calculated using Formula (15.13).

$$r_S = 1 - \frac{6\Sigma d_i^2}{n(n^2 - 1)} \qquad (15.13)$$

where d_i is the difference between the rankings for each observation
n is the sample size

Then

$$r_S = 1 - \frac{(6)(8)}{7(7^2 - 1)}$$

$$= 0.857$$

Recalling that a correlation coefficient falls between −1 and 1, our sample suggests a rather strong, positive relationship between a technician's test score and his or her job performance rating.

We often want to test the hypothesis that the population correlation coefficient, ρ_s, is zero. That is, we want to determine the likelihood that, despite our sample findings which suggest a relationship between score and rating, there actually is no such relationship and $\rho_s = 0$.

For small samples ($n < 30$), the distribution of r_S is not normal, nor is the t-test appropriate. Instead, Table N in the appendix must be used. Critical values taken from Table N are compared with r_S to test the hypotheses

$H_0: \rho_s = 0$;   there is no relationship between the two variables.

$H_a: \rho_s \neq 0$;   there is a relationship between the two variables.

With the aid of Figure 15-10, Table N reveals that if we test the hypotheses at $\alpha = 0.10$, a sample of size $n = 7$ carries critical values of ±0.6786.

FIGURE 15-10   A Hypothesis Test for Amco Tech

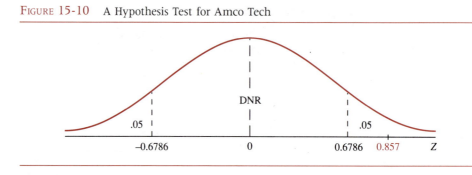

Decision Rule
Do not reject the null if $-0.6786 < r_S < 0.6786$. Reject the null if
$r_S < -0.6786$ or $r_S > 0.6786$.

The value $r_S = 0.857$ is in the right-hand rejection region. We can therefore reject
the null of $\rho_s = 0$ and conclude with 90 percent confidence that a relationship exists
between test scores and job performance rankings.
    If $n > 30$, the distribution of r_S approximates normality with a mean of zero and
a standard deviation of $1/\sqrt{n - 1}$. The Z-test is

$$Z = \frac{r_S - 0}{1/\sqrt{n - 1}} \qquad (15.14)$$
$$= r_S \sqrt{n - 1}$$

Example 15-7 demonstrates.

EXAMPLE 15-7 Hard Driving—A Quality Control Test

Amco Tech is considering whether to market a hard drive for desktop computers.
An experiment is conducted on 32 randomly selected drives to determine if a relationship exists between the number of hours a drive is tested prior to sale and the
number of times the drive fails in the process of completing a computer run. The
manager of the quality control division reasonably expects the failure rate to decrease as the number of hours a drive is tested increases. The test hours and number
of failures for all 32 drives, along with the rankings for each variable, are shown
here. For both variables, the highest observation received the first ranking, and the
lowest observation was given the thirty-second ranking.

Drive	Hours	Hours Ranking (X)	Failures	Failures Ranking (Y)	$X - Y$	$(X - Y)^2$
1	100	1.0	2	32.0	−31.0	961.00
2	99	2.5	3	30.5	−28.0	784.00
3	99	2.5	3	30.5	−28.0	784.00
4	97	4.0	4	28.5	−24.5	600.25
5	96	5.5	4	28.5	−23.0	529.00
6	96	5.5	5	27.0	−21.5	462.25
7	95	7.0	8	21.5	−14.5	210.25
8	91	8.0	6	25.5	−17.5	306.25
9	89	9.0	7	23.5	−14.5	210.25
10	88	10.5	10	17.5	− 7.0	49.00
11	88	10.5	8	21.5	−11.0	121.00
12	80	12.0	9	19.5	− 7.5	56.25
13	79	13.0	9	19.5	− 6.5	42.25
14	78	14.5	10	17.5	− 3.0	9.00
15	78	14.5	11	15.5	− 1.0	1.00
16	77	16.0	7	23.5	− 7.5	56.25
17	75	17.5	12	13.5	4.0	16.00
18	75	17.5	13	12.0	5.5	30.25
19	71	19.0	11	15.5	3.5	12.25
20	70	20.5	14	11.0	9.5	90.25
21	70	20.5	12	13.5	7.0	49.00
22	68	22.5	6	25.5	− 3.0	9.00
23	68	22.5	16	7.5	15.0	225.00
24	65	24.0	15	9.5	14.5	210.25
25	64	25.0	15	9.5	15.5	240.25
26	60	26.5	16	7.5	19.0	361.00
27	60	26.5	18	3.5	23.0	529.00
28	58	28.0	19	2.0	26.0	676.00
29	56	29.0	17	5.5	23.5	552.25
30	55	30.5	20	1.0	29.5	870.25
31	55	30.5	18	3.5	27.0	729.00
32	50	32.0	17	5.5	26.5	702.25
						10,484.00

SOLUTION:

$$r_S = 1 - \frac{6(10,484)}{32(32^2 - 1)}$$

$$= -0.922$$

Set $\alpha = 0.01$. A test of the hypothesis regarding the population correlation coefficient follows:

$$H_0: \rho_s = 0$$

$$H_a: \rho_s \neq 0$$

The critical Z-value is ±2.58. Then

$$Z = (-0.922)\sqrt{32 - 1}$$

$$= -5.14$$

As shown in the figure, the null should be rejected.

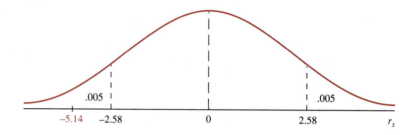

STATISTICAL INTERPRETATION:

The r_S-value of -0.922 indicates a strong, negative relationship between hours and failures. The longer a drive is tested before it is used, the fewer failures it experiences in completing the run. Amco Tech can be 99 percent certain that this relationship exists for the entire population of hard drives.

QUICK CHECK 15.6.1

○○○○   For $n = 10$, $\Sigma d_i^2 = 56.1$. At the 5 percent level of significance, does a relationship exist between the two variables?

Answer: $r_S = 0.66$; critical $r_S = \pm 0.6364$. Reject null that $\rho_S = 0$; no relationship exists.

QUICK CHECK 15.6.2

For $n = 50$, $\Sigma d_1^2 = 1153$. At the 10 percent level, does a relationship exist between the two variables?

Answer: $r_S = 0.945$; critical Z is ± 1.65; $Z = 6.62 > 1.65$. Reject null that $\rho_s = 0$.

15.7   THE KRUSKAL-WALLIS TEST

The Mann-Whitney U test serves as the nonparametric counterpart to the t-test for two independent samples, and was used to compare two populations. If we need to compare more than two populations, the **Kruskal-Wallis test** then applies as a logical extension of the Mann-Whitney test. It is used to test hypotheses regarding the distribution of three or more populations. In this capacity, the Kruskal-Wallis test functions as the nonparametric counterpart to the completely randonized design used in ANOVA tests. While the ANOVA tests depended on the assumption that all populations under comparison were normally distributed, the Kruskal-Wallis test places no such restriction on the comparison.

Kruskal-Wallis Test
This test compares three or more populations to determine if a difference exists in the distribution of the populations. It is the analogue to the F-test used in ANOVA tests.

The null hypothesis states that no difference exists in the distribution of the k populations under comparison. The hypotheses are thus

H_0: All k populations have the same distribution.

H_a: Not all k populations have the same distribution.

The test requires that the observations be ranked just as in the Mann-Whitney test.

To illustrate, assume that, as the new accounts manager for Pox Skin Ointment, you must compare the time it takes for three customers to pay for shipments of No-Flaw Face Cream, a new product offered by Pox. Several purchases are randomly selected for each customer along with the number of days each took to settle its account. The results are shown in Table 15-11. Notice that number of observations in all samples do not have to be equal.

TABLE 15-11   Number of Days to Pay Pox for Delivery

Purchase	Customer		
	1	2	3
1	28	26	22
2	19	20	17
3	13	11	16
4	28	14	15
5	29	22	29
6	22	21	
7	21		

Each observation must then be ranked from lowest to highest. As with the Mann-Whitney, ties are assigned a rank equal to the mean ranking for those observations. For example, "22 days" is the 11th observation, and it occurs three times. Thus, 22 ranks 11, 12, and 13 in the rankings. The observation 22 is therefore assigned a rank

TABLE 15-12 The Rankings for Pox

Customer 1		Customer 2		Customer 3	
Days	Rank	Days	Rank	Days	Rank
		11	1		
13	2				
		14	3		
				15	4
				16	5
				17	6
19	7				
		20	8		
21	9.5	21	9.5		
22	12	22	12	22	12
		26	14		
28	15.5				
28	15.5				
29	17.5			29	17.5
$\Sigma R_1 = 79.0$		$\Sigma R_2 = 47.5$		$\Sigma R_3 = 44.5$	

of 12, the mean of those three ranks. The rankings are then summed for all $k = 3$ samples. Table 15-12 contains the results. The Kruskal-Wallis statistic is

$$K = \frac{12}{n(n + 1)} \left[\Sigma \frac{R_i^2}{n_i} \right] - 3(n + 1) \qquad (15.15)$$

where n_i is the number of observations in the ith sample

  n is the total number of observations in all samples

  R_i is the sum of the ranks of the ith sample

If a large number of ties occurs in the rankings, the statistic must be adjusted with the following formula:

$$K' = \frac{K}{1 - [\Sigma(r_j^3 - r_j)/(n^3 - n)]} \qquad (15.16)$$

where r_j is the number of observations in the jth group of tied ranks

Since Table 15-12 contains several ties, you must use the adjusted value for the Kruskal-Wallis statistic. First you must find K from Formula (15.15).

$$K = \frac{12}{18(18 + 1)} \left[\frac{(79)^2}{7} + \frac{(47.5)^2}{6} + \frac{(44.5)^2}{5} \right] - 3(18 + 1)$$

$$= 1.39$$

To obtain the denominator for K' in Formula (15.16), note that there are four groups of tied ranks:

1. $r_j = 2$ observations at 9.5
2. $r_j = 3$ observations at 12
3. $r_j = 2$ observations at 15.5
4. $r_j = 2$ observations at 17.5

Thus,

$$\Sigma(r_j^3 - r_j) = (2^3 - 2) + (3^3 - 3) + (2^3 - 2) + (2^3 - 2)$$

$$= 42$$

Then

$$K' = \frac{1.39}{1 - \dfrac{42}{5,814}}$$

$$= 1.40$$

You can see that adjusting for ties by using K' instead of K actually makes very little difference. However, this difference will increase as the number of observations goes up, and the practice of using K' when a large number of ties occurs should be continued. It is up to the researcher to determine how many ties is required to necessitate K'.

It is now left to compare K' (or K) with a critical value. The distribution of K' (or K) is approximated by a chi-square distribution with $k - 1$ degrees of freedom. If K' (or K) exceeds the critical value for chi-square, the null is rejected. Figure 15-11

FIGURE 15-11   A Chi-Square Test for Pox

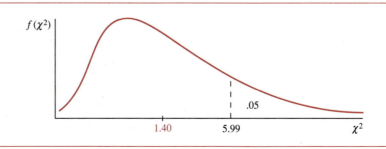

illustrates. Should you choose an α-value of 5 percent in your test for Pox, the critical chi-square value, given $3 - 1 = 2$ degrees of freedom, becomes $\chi^2_{0.05,2} = 5.99$.

Decision Rule
Do not reject if $K' < 5.99$. Reject if $K' > 5.99$.

Since $K' = 1.40 < 5.99$, do not reject the null that there is no difference in the time it takes these three customers to settle their accounts with Pox.

A. DETECTING WHICH DIFFERENCES ARE SIGNIFICANT

In the event that the null hypothesis is rejected, the next logical step is to determine which differences are statistically significant and which are due to sampling error. That is, once we have determined that not all populations have the same distribution, we must identify those populations which are significantly different. This is much like the process in which we used the Tukey methods to detect significant differences in our study of ANOVA. As with the Tukey approach, this involves a pairwise comparison of all possible pairs.

Consider the efforts by Penny Pincher, director of marketing for Homes-R-Us, a large real estate agency in San Francisco. Ms. Pincher must determine if a difference exists in the purchase price of lots in three locations within the Bay area. The values, in thousands of dollars, for several lots recently sold by Homes-R-Us are shown in Table 15-13 along with their rankings.

TABLE 15-13 Purchase Price of Housing Lots

South Bay	Rank	East Bay	Rank	Marin County	Rank
17	1				
20	2				
		23	3		
24	4				
		25	5		
26	6				
		27	7		
29	8.5	29	8.5		
		31	10		
32	11				
				41	12
				49	13
				52	14
				54	15
				55	16
				57	17
$\Sigma R_1 = 32.5$		$\Sigma R_2 = 33.5$		$\Sigma R_3 = 87$	
$n_1 = 6$		$n_2 = 5$		$n_3 = 6$	

Ms. Pincher must test the set of hypotheses:

H_0: All three areas have the same distribution.

H_a: At least one distribution is not the same.

Since there is only one tie, we will use K and not K'.

$$K = \frac{12}{17(17 + 1)} \left[\frac{(32.5)^2}{6} + \frac{(33.5)^2}{5} + \frac{(87)^2}{6} \right] - 3(17 + 1)$$

$$= 11.17$$

If $\alpha = 0.01$, $\chi^2_{0.01, 2} = 9.21$.

Decision Rule
Do not reject if $K < 9.21$. Reject if $K > 9.21$.

Ms. Pincher must reject the null and conclude that at least one region is different from the other two. She now wishes to determine which one(s) is (are) different. She begins by computing the average rank for all samples as

$$\overline{R}_i = \frac{R_i}{n_i} \tag{15.17}$$

where R_i is the sum of the ranks of the ith sample
n_i is the number of observations in the ith sample

For the first sample,

$$\overline{R}_1 = \frac{32.5}{6}$$

$$= 5.42$$

Similarly, $\overline{R}_2 = 6.7$ and $\overline{R}_3 = 14.5$. Then the absolute difference is taken for each pairwise comparison.

$$\overline{R}_1 - \overline{R}_2 = |5.42 - 6.7| = 1.28$$
$$\overline{R}_1 - \overline{R}_3 = |5.42 - 14.5| = 9.08$$
$$\overline{R}_2 - \overline{R}_3 = |6.7 - 14.5| = 7.8$$

These differences are then compared with a critical value calculated as

$$C = \sqrt{\chi^2_{\alpha, k-1} \left[\frac{n(n + 1)}{12} \right] \left[\frac{1}{n_i} + \frac{1}{n_j} \right]} \tag{15.18}$$

where n_i and n_j are the sizes of the two samples under comparison

$\chi^2_{\alpha, k-1}$ is the chi-square value used in the test of the original hypothesis (9.21 in the present case)

If the actual difference between the average ranks of two samples is greater than this critical difference C, it is considered a significant difference, and leads to the conclusion that the populations from which these samples were taken are different.

Thus, in comparing the first two samples, we find

$$C = \sqrt{9.21\left[\frac{17(18)}{12}\right]\left[\frac{1}{6} + \frac{1}{5}\right]}$$

$$= 9.28$$

Since 9.28 is greater than the actual difference between the average of the ranks of the first two samples, 1.28, it is concluded that populations 1 and 2 (South Bay and East Bay) do not have different population distributions in lot prices.

A comparison of the first and third samples yields

$$C = \sqrt{9.21\left[\frac{17(18)}{12}\right]\left[\frac{1}{6} + \frac{1}{6}\right]}$$

$$= 8.84$$

The actual difference in the average rankings of samples 1 and 3 is 9.08, which exceeds the critical value of 8.84. Thus, it is concluded that these populations differ in lot values.

Comparing samples 2 and 3 produces

$$C = \sqrt{9.21\left[\frac{17(18)}{12}\right]\left[\frac{1}{5} + \frac{1}{6}\right]}$$

$$= 9.28$$

Since the actual difference between these two samples is only 7.8, Ms. Pincher can conclude with 99 percent confidence that land values in East Bay and Marin County do not differ.

B.   THE DISTINCTION BETWEEN PARAMETRIC AND NONPARAMETRIC TESTS

It should be apparent by now that it is possible to substitute certain nonparametric tests when essential assumptions required for those statistical procedures studied in earlier chapters may not hold. In the absence of specific conditions such as a normally distributed population, these nonparametric tests may be the only appropriate course of action.

Table 15-14 compares nonparametric tests with their parametric counterparts. Where appropriate, the parametric analogue for each nonparametric test is shown. The table also indicates the assumption required by the parametric test, but is not necessary to conduct the nonparametric counterpart.

TABLE 15-14   A Comparison of Parametric and Nonparametric Tests

Nonparametric Test	Purpose	Assumption Not Required	Parametric Counterpart
Sign	Test for location of population distribution	Normal distribution of populations	t-test for matched pairs
Runs	Test for randomness		None
Mann-Whitney U test	Compare two independent samples	Difference between samples is normal	t-test for independent samples
Kruskal-Wallis test	Compare three or more samples	Sample means normally distributed	F-test with ANOVA
Spearman rank	Test for relationship between two ordinally ranked variables	Distribution of both variables is normal	Pearsonian correlation coefficient

15.8   SOLVED PROBLEMS

1. **2B or not 2B—A Quality Control Problem** According to *U.S. News and World Report,* a laboratory in Atlanta is processing snake venom for use in medical research. Five processing methods are being tested to determine which is least likely to contaminate the processed venom. If a venom solution is tested as contaminated, it is marked with the symbol "2B." Each method produces 25 vials of venom each day. The vials from each processing method are then boxed for shipment to medical research facilities.

   Assume for our purposes that scientists in the laboratory feel that the contamination is uniformly distributed, but others argue that it is binomially distributed. A statistical consultant is retained to examine defect patterns.

   a. *Is Contamination Uniform?* Output over a 100-day period is selected for each processing method, and notation is made as to which method produced the fewest contaminated vials that day. If contamination rates were uniform, the scientists would expect each method to produce the fewest contaminated vials on an equal number of days. Thus, $E_i = n/k = 100/5 = 20$. Both observed and expected frequencies are shown in the accompanying table. It shows, for example, that on 34 of the 100 days, method 1 produced the fewest contaminated vials of snake venom. The hypotheses are

   H_0: Contamination rates are uniform.

   H_a: Contamination rates are not uniform.

Processing Method	E_i	O_i	$(O_i - E_i)^2$	$(O_i - E_i)^2/E_i$
1	20	34	196	9.80
2	20	17	9	0.45
3	20	14	36	1.80
4	20	12	64	3.20
5	20	23	49	0.45
	100	100		15.70

With $K - 1 = 4$ degrees of freedom, Table H shows that a 1 percent test reveals a critical χ^2-value of $\chi^2_{0.01,4} = 13.277$. As shown in the figure, the decision rule is

Decision Rule
Do not reject if $\chi^2 < 13.277$. Reject if $\chi^2 > 13.277$.

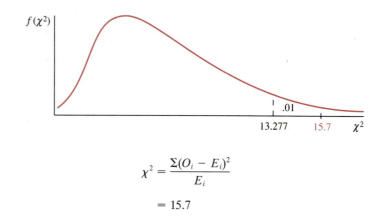

$$\chi^2 = \frac{\Sigma(O_i - E_i)^2}{E_i}$$

$$= 15.7$$

Since $15.7 > 13.277$, the null is rejected. The contamination rates do not appear to be uniform.

b. *Is Contamination Binomial?* Those scientists in the laboratory who support the idea of a binomial contamination pattern argue that 5 percent of the vials produced are contaminated. Given this 5 percent rate, the statistical consultant is to test the following hypotheses:

H_0: Contamination rates are binomial.

H_a: Contamination rates are not binomial.

The test is first applied to method 1. Each box contains $n = 25$ vials. If a binomial distribution exists in contamination rates with $\pi = 0.05$ as the scientists argued, the probability that any box contains a given number of contaminated vials, X, is found in the binomial table. For example, if $n = 25$ and $\pi = 0.05$, the probability that a box contains zero contaminated vials can be found from Table C in Appendix 1 as $P(X = 0 | n = 25, \pi = 0.05) = 0.2774$. The probability that only 1 of the 25 vials is contaminated can be found from Table C in Appendix 1 as $P(X \leq 1) - P(X \leq 0) = 0.6424 - 0.2740 = 0.3650$, and so on. Thus, the expected number of boxes out of the 100 samples that contain zero contaminated vials is $nP_i = (100)(0.2774) = 27.74$ boxes. Notice that for purposes of determining the $P(x)$ from the binomial table, $n = 25$ because there are 25 vials in each box. For determining the number of boxes with x contaminated vials, $n = 100$ because there are 100 boxes.

The values for E_i and O_i are shown in the tables. The first table shows that 31 of the 100 boxes from method 1 had zero contaminated vials.

Number of Contaminated Vials	O_i	$P(x)$	E_i
0	31	0.2774	27.74
1	32	0.3650	36.50
2	24	0.2305	23.05
3	10	0.0930	9.30
4	2	0.0269	2.69
5 or more	1	0.0071	0.71
	100		

However, some of the values for E_i are less than 5. The last three classes must be combined to correct for this. The second table is the result.

Number of Contaminated Vials	O_i	$P(x)$	E_i	$(O_i - E_i)^2/E_i$
0	31	0.2774	27.74	0.3831
1	32	0.3650	36.50	0.5548
2	24	0.2350	23.50	0.0106
3 or more	13	0.1270	12.70	0.0071
	100			0.9556

If $\alpha = 0.05$, $\chi^2_{0.05,3} = 7.815$.

Decision Rule
Do not reject if $\chi^2 < 7.815$. Reject if $\chi^2 > 7.815$.

Since $\chi^2 = 0.9556$, we do not reject the null. Contamination rates appear to be binomially distributed.

2. **The Sign Test—A Case of Quality Control** In an effort to improve their product, a firm selling bakery products asks 15 taste testers to rate their whole wheat bread between 0 and 10 before and after a slight change in the ingredients. The results are partially shown in the table.

Tester	Rating Before	Rating After	Sign
1	7	8	−
2	6	6	0
3	9	8	+
4	5	7	−
.	.	.	.
.	.	.	.
.	.	.	.
15	8	7	+

In total, eight plus signs, five minus signs, and two zero differences were recorded. The firm wants to test at the 5 percent level whether there is any difference. Thus,

$$H_0: m = p$$

$$H_a: m \neq p$$

Then

$$P(m \leq 5 \,|\, n = 13, \pi = 0.50) = 0.2905$$

The probability of getting at most five minus signs given $m = p$ is greater than $0.05/2 = 0.025$. The null is not rejected.

If the sample size had exceeded 20, the Z-test Formula (15.4) would have been used.

3. **A Mann-Whitney U Test of Means** Two advertising displays are used to aid the sales of a product. The first display resulted in daily sales of 110, 117, 82, 95, 123, 79, 92, 102, 108, and 113. The second display produced sales of 111, 85, 97, 117, 111, 89, 118, 121, and 109. Would it appear that at the 5 percent level, $\mu_1 = \mu_2$?

Display 1	Rank	Display 2	Rank
79	1	85	3
82	2	89	4
92	5	97	7
95	6	109	10
102	8	111	12.5
108	9	111	12.5
110	11	117	15.5
113	14	118	17
117	15.5	121	18
123	19		
	$90.5 = \Sigma R_1$		$99.5 = \Sigma R_2$

$$H_0: \mu_1 = \mu_2$$

$$H_a: \mu_1 \neq \mu_2$$

$$U_1 = n_1 n_2 + \frac{n_1(n_1 + 1)}{2} - \Sigma R_1$$

$$= (10)(9) + \frac{10(10 + 1)}{2} - 90.5$$

$$= 54.5$$

$$U_2 = n_1 n_2 + \frac{n_2(n_2 + 1)}{2} - \Sigma R_2$$

$$= (10)(9) + \frac{9(9 + 1)}{2} - 99.5$$

$$= 35.5$$

$$\mu_u = \frac{n_1 n_2}{2}$$

$$= 45$$

$$\sigma_u = \sqrt{\frac{n_1 n_2(n_1 + n_2 + 1)}{12}}$$

$$= 12.247$$

$$Z = \frac{U_i - \mu_u}{\sigma_u}$$

$$= \frac{54.5 - 45}{12.247}$$

$$= 0.7757$$

If α is set at 5 percent, the critical Z-value is ± 1.96.
The sample suggests that the null is not to be rejected, and that both displays have the same effect on sales.

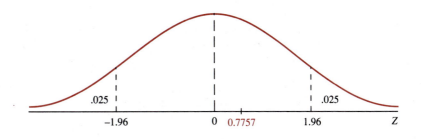

4. **Spearman Rank Correlation** A financial consultant is asked to evaluate the investment qualities of eight stocks. She uses the stock's dividend rate as reported in *The Wall Street Journal* and an index potential for growth assigned to each stock by a New York investment firm. The data are shown here and are used to determine if a relationship might exist between dividends and growth potential.

Stock	Dividend Rate (%)	Dividend Ranking (X)	Growth Index	Growth Ranking (Y)	$X - Y$	$(X - Y)^2$
1	4.20	7	40	6	1	1
2	8.12	2	20	8	−6	36
3	7.20	5	60	4	1	1
4	3.20	8	35	7	1	1
5	8.00	3	85	1	2	4
6	12.73	1	70	2	−1	1
7	7.90	4	50	5	−1	1
8	6.20	6	65	3	3	9
						54

$$r_S = 1 - \frac{6\Sigma d_i^2}{n(n^2 - 1)}$$

$$= 1 - \frac{6(54)}{8(8^2 - 1)}$$

$$= 0.357$$

If $\alpha = 0.10$, test

$$H_0: P_s = 0$$

$$H_a: P_s \neq 0$$

Table N reveals a critical value of 0.6190. Therefore, do not reject the null.

15.9   WHAT YOU SHOULD HAVE LEARNED FROM THIS CHAPTER

The statistical tools in the chapter have given you the ability to analyze data on an ordinal scale without the assumption of normality which is most often required for many of the tests presented in earlier chapters. In making business decisions, you will frequently find nonparametric analysis quite useful and, in many cases, wholly necessary.

The uses and applications of those nonparametric tests should by now be quite apparent. You should be able to recognize those situations which call for a particular test, and be skilled in the performance and interpretation of those tests.

15.10 COMPUTER APPLICATIONS

Although the principles behind nonparametric analysis associated with their use can be somewhat tedious, computers come to our aid. This section shows how computers can be used to perform nonparametric tests.

A. MINITAB

To perform chi-square tests of independence, enter the command

```
MTB > Chisq C1 C2
```

A table like Table 15-6 will result. A sign test as performed in Table 15-7 requires that the data be first entered in columns 1 and 2. Then these commands are given:

```
MTB > Let C3 = C1-C2
MTB > STEST C3;
Subc > ALTE -1.
```

For a runs test, the data must be entered as binary values of, for example, 0 for all males and 1 for females. If the observations are for algebraic signs, a 0 can be used for positive signs and a 1 for negative signs. Example 15-5 could be done by encoding 5 zeros, then 5 ones, then 4 zeros, and then 2 ones. The command MTB > RUNS C1 is then given.

A Mann-Whitney test is run with the command MTB > MANN WHITNEY C1 C2. Finally, the Spearman test is achieved by encoding the variables rankings and using MTB > CORR C1 C2.

LIST OF TERMS AND SYMBOLS

Nonparametric tests: Tests of hypothesis in which assumptions regarding population distributions and parameters are not possible.
Run: An unbroken series of one or more identical symbols.

LIST OF FORMULAS

$$\chi^2 = \sum_{i=1}^{K} \frac{(O_i - E_i)^2}{E_i} \qquad (15.1)$$

Calculates chi-square in comparison of observed and expected events.

$$E_i = np_i \qquad (15.2)$$

Calculates the expected frequencies in each category.

$$\chi^2 = \sum_{i=1}^{rc} \frac{(O_i - E_i)^2}{E_i} \qquad (15.3)$$

Chi-square for independence.

$$Z_{\text{test}} = \frac{k \pm 0.5 - 0.5n}{0.5\sqrt{n}} \qquad (15.4)$$

Calculates a Z-value for large-sample sign test.

$$\mu_r = \frac{2n_1n_2}{n_1 + n_2} + 1 \qquad (15.5)$$

The mean of the sampling distribution of the number of runs.

$$\sigma_r = \sqrt{\frac{2n_1n_2(2n_1n_2 - n_1 - n_2)}{(n_1 + n_2)^2(n_1 + n_2 - 1)}} \qquad (15.6)$$

The standard deviation for a runs test.

$$Z = \frac{r - \mu_r}{\sigma_r} \qquad (15.7)$$

The normal deviate for the distribution of runs.

$$U_1 = n_1n_2 + \frac{n_1(n_1 + 1)}{2} - \Sigma R_1 \qquad (15.8)$$

The Mann-Whitney U-statistic for the ith sample.

$$\mu_u = \frac{n_1n_2}{2} \qquad (15.10)$$

The mean of the sampling distribution of the U-statistic.

$$\sigma_u = \sqrt{\frac{n_1n_2(n_1 + n_2 + 1)}{12}} \qquad (15.11)$$

The standard deviation of the sampling distribution of the U-statistic.

$$Z = \frac{U_i - \mu_u}{\sigma_u} \qquad (15.12)$$

Normalization of the U-statistic.

$$r_S = 1 - \frac{6\Sigma d_i^2}{n(n^2 - 1)} \qquad (15.13)$$

The Spearman rank correlation coefficient.

$$Z = r_s \sqrt{n - 1} \qquad (15.14)$$

Hypothesis test for Spearman correlation when $n > 30$.

$$K = \frac{12}{n(n + 1)} \left[\Sigma \frac{R_i^2}{n_i} \right] - 3(n + 1) \qquad (15.15)$$

Determines the Kruskal-Wallis test statistic.

$$K' = \frac{K}{1 - [\Sigma(r_j^3 - r_j)/(n^3 - n)]} \tag{15.16}$$

Used if there is a large number of ties in the Kruskal-Wallis procedure.

$$\overline{R}_i = \frac{R_i}{n_i} \tag{15.17}$$

$$C = \sqrt{\chi_{\alpha, k-1}^2 \frac{n(n+1)}{12} \left[\frac{1}{n_i} + \frac{1}{n_j}\right]} \tag{15.18}$$

Both (15.17) and (15.18) are used to detect significant differences in the Kruskal-Wallis procedure.

CHAPTER EXERCISES

PROBLEMS

1. A bank in Des Moines wants to determine if the distribution of customers is uniform throughout the week. A survey finds that the numbers of customers Monday through Friday are 150, 179, 209, 79, and 252. At the 5 percent level, does it appear that a uniform distribution exists?
   a. State the hypotheses.
   b. State the decision rule.
   c. Conduct the test and make your determination.
2. The manager of the Des Moines branch bank thinks that checks with insufficient funds are Poisson distributed at her branch. She knows that the mean number of bad checks for her banking system is 3.6 per day. She collects a sample over a 95-day period and finds the data shown here.

Number of Bad Checks per Day	Frequency (days)
0	12
1	14
2	13
3	15
4	14
5	15
6 or more	12
	95

Is her hypothesis regarding the distribution correct? Set $\alpha = 0.01$.
   a. State the decision rule.
   b. Conduct your test and make your determination.

3. The dock foreman for Overland Trucking recorded the data shown here for the arrival of trucks. At the 1 percent level, does it appear a Poisson distribution exists?

Number of Arrivals per Hour	Frequency (hours)
0	10
1	11
2	14
3	15
4	12
5	14
6	12
7	9
	97

4. The frequency table shown records daily sales for 200 days. At $\alpha = 0.05$, do sales appear to be normally distributed?

Sales	Frequency
40 up to 60	7
60 up to 80	22
80 up to 100	46
100 up to 120	42
120 up to 140	42
140 up to 160	18
160 up to 180	11
180 up to 200	12

5. To determine if the rate of defects in its product is binomially distributed, a small plant in De Kalb, Illinois, took a random sample of 20 units each day for 150 days. In general, this product suffers a 5 percent defective rate. The results of the sampling process are shown here. At the 1 percent level, does it appear that defects are binomial?
    a. State the hypotheses.
    b. State the decision rule.
    c. Conduct the test and state your conclusions.

Number of Defects out of 20	Frequency (days)
0	21
1	17
2	32
3	47
4	15
5	18
	150

6. The production manager for AAA, Inc. must ensure that his product mix fits a particular quota system. He is instructed to adjust to a pattern that produces 30 percent silk goods, 20 percent wool, 10 percent cotton, and 40 percent leather. Of the last 200 units produced, 65 were silk, 45 were wool, 25 were cotton, and 65 were leather. At the 5 percent level, should he adjust the current production pattern? State the hypotheses.

7. The quality control division of ABC, Inc. has three inspectors who examine each unit produced. Each inspector either "passes" or "fails" each unit. Studies have shown that there is a 10 percent chance that a unit will fail any one inspector. The data shown represent the results of the inspection process for the last 250 units. Does it appear that the process is binomial? Set $\alpha = 0.05$.

Number of "Fails" from 3 Inspections	Number of Units
0	120
1	50
2	35
3	45
	250

8. A buyer for a large department store examines five truckloads of merchandise each hour. Each truck contains seven lots of merchandise. The buyer must decide whether to purchase each truckload. There is a 20 percent chance any truck will be accepted. Given the data shown, do acceptance levels appear to be binomial? Set $\alpha = 0.05$.

Number of Acceptances/5 Trucks	Observed Number of Acceptances
0	96
1	123
2	63
3	15
4	1
5	2

9. A retail chain has six outlets. It has been spending heavily to produce similar sales levels at all six stores. The advertising firm handling the promotional efforts claims that now each store should report equal sales. If sales are not the same, the retail chain has decided to discontinue its association with the ad agency. What decision should be made based on the data shown here? State your hypotheses. Set $\alpha = 0.01$.

Store	Sales ($100's)
1	42
2	37
3	53
4	51
5	45
6	47

10. An economic study of income levels in Washington, D.C., revealed in 1981 that of all welfare recipients, 60 percent were unemployed, 22 percent worked less than 20 hours per week, 10 percent worked between 20 and 30 hours, and the rest worked more than 30 hours. A job training program designed to increase the likelihood of employment of welfare recipients was instituted. In 1991 a survey showed that of 1,100 people on welfare, 679 were unemployed, 237 worked less than 20 hours, 121 worked between 20 and 30 hours, and the rest worked more than 30. If the job training program was designed to alter the pattern observed in 1981, should the program be retained? Set $\alpha = 0.05$.

11. Macy's department store in New York recently did a study to determine if there was any relationship between a customer's marital status and his or her dollar volume of purchases. The results are shown in the table. What is your conclusion at the 5 percent level of significance?

	Dollar Volume				
	<10	10–19	20–29	30–39	40–49
Married	32	23	15	12	14
Divorced	51	17	10	15	13
Single	21	19	29	35	39
Widowed	18	15	19	10	9

12. Many firms are trying to adjust employees' work schedules to fit their personal needs and to reduce traffic problems during the rush hour. One technique is the use of "flexi-time," which allows employees, within certain limitations, to set their own work hours. A plant in Houston surveyed their employees to determine if there was any difference among categories of workers in their preference for flexi-time. At the 1 percent level, what is your conclusion based on the data in the table?

	Preferences		
	Prefers Flexi-time	Do Not Prefer Flexi-time	No Opinion
Line workers	112	72	89
Staff	83	43	37
Management	74	22	10

13. *Runner's World* reported that a survey by Converse of people who regularly run for exercise resulted in the data shown here. The intent of the survey was to determine if the distances were independent of runners' preference for a gel-like product built into the heels of their jogging shoes. At the 1 percent level, does there appear to be any relationship? State the hypotheses.

Distance/Week (miles)	Prefer Gel	Do Not Prefer Gel	No Opinion
<3	14	5	27
3–6	18	5	17
7–10	12	8	8
10–13	17	12	5
>13	19	8	2

14. Data on years of experience and efficiency ratings for 431 employees at XYZ, Inc. are shown in the table. Can it be concluded that these attributes are independent of each other? $\alpha = 5$ percent.

	Efficiency Rating			
Experience in years	Poor	Good	Excellent	Superior
<5	14	18	12	17
5–10	18	13	27	42
11–16	16	32	24	37
17–22	24	28	21	32
>22	17	15	14	10

15. The results of a study by the American Marketing Association to determine the relationship between the importance store owners attach to advertising and the size of store they own are shown in the table. Would it seem that all store owners place the same emphasis on advertising? Set $\alpha = 0.10$. State the hypotheses.

	Advertising		
Size	Important	Not Important	No Opinion
Small	20	52	32
Medium	53	47	28
Large	67	32	25

16. A bottling company in Atlanta is interested in the effects of three methods used to sanitize glass containers. It grades containers to determine if sanitation is independent of the method. At the 10 percent level of significance, what is your conclusion based on the data in the table?

	Sanitation Grade		
Method	Acceptable	Marginal	Unacceptable
A	140	132	63
B	89	74	44
C	104	98	50

17. Eight test subjects are asked to rate a product before and after viewing a commercial for it. The ratings are shown in the table, where a rating of 10 is best. Set $\alpha = 0.10$ and use a sign test for the hypothesis that the commercial improved the product's rating. State the hypotheses.

	Ratings	
Test Subject	**Before Commercial**	**After Commercial**
1	8	9
2	7	6
3	5	6
4	5	5
5	5	4
6	7	8
7	6	7
8	6	8

18. A chemical compound is added to an oil base solution in hopes of increasing its lubricating qualities. Twenty solutions, 10 with the compound and 10 without, are compared with respect to their ability to lubricate machinery. Each is graded on a scale from 0 to 10, with 10 being the best. Based on the data in the table, does it appear that addition of the compound increases lubrication? Set $\alpha = 0.10$. State the hypotheses. What is your conclusion regarding the value of the chemical compound?

	Lubrication Grade	
Solution	**Without Compound**	**With Compound**
1	8	4
2	7	8
3	5	2
4	6	9
5	9	5
6	4	4
7	9	2
8	8	6
9	7	6
10	6	7

19. Shytel, Inc. offers communication services anywhere in the world with two satellites, the *Falcon* and the *Eagle*. Shytel's CEO thinks that the *Eagle* results in longer delays in transmission. Transmission times are shown in minutes in the table. At the 5 percent level, does it appear that the CEO is correct? State your hypotheses.

Transmission Times (minutes)

Falcon	Eagle	Sign
5.2	4.7	+
8.6	7.9	+
9.0	9.7	−
4.3	8.4	−
6.2	3.7	+
7.9	7.3	+

20. After technical adjustments to the *Falcon* (see previous problem) six transmission times were 4.2, 6.3, 8.2, 6.7, 3.2, and 6.1 minutes. Using the same data for the *Eagle* as in Problem 21, does it now seem that the CEO is correct? State your hypotheses and conclusion. Keep $\alpha = 0.05$.

21. Clyde Bloomquist has proposed a change in corporate policy concerning collection of accounts receivable. He feels it will speed the time required to obtain outstanding debts from creditors. Company records show that eight creditors took the number of days shown in the table before and after the policy change to remit funds due. Is Clyde correct? Should the policy change be retained? Set $\alpha = 0.10$. State the hypotheses.

Creditor	Before	After
1	18	12
2	27	22
3	32	31
4	23	24
5	31	28
6	36	24
7	18	16
8	35	25

22. According to an article in *Industry Weekly,* the Occupational Safety and Health Administration (OSHA) required the installation of noise-abatement equipment on machinery used in a small manufacturing plant in Chicago. Decibel measurements before and after installation on 12 machines revealed six positive values, three negative values, and three with no difference. Do the data support OSHA's contention that a reduction in the noise factor has been attained at the 10 percent level? State your hypotheses and conclusion.

23. The Bank of Houston recently restructured the queueing system in its lobby to accommodate a larger customer traffic flow per hour. Records for 16 hours before and after the restructuring revealed 10 minus values, 4 plus values, and 2 zero values. Should the new queueing system be retained because it has increased the bank's ability to serve more customers? Set $\alpha = 0.10$. State the hypotheses and conclusions.

24. Pro Max manufactures golf balls with two types of coverings. Martha Wellington, the production manager for Pro Max, insists that there is no difference between the durability factors of the coverings, even though one costs much more to manufacture. Durability tests for the coverings yielded eight minus signs, six plus signs, and three zero differences. Which covering should Martha choose? Set $\alpha = 0.10$. State your hypotheses and conclusion.

25. A retail chain with 12 outlets uses newspaper advertising one month and radio announcements the next month to promote sales. Differences in monthly revenues for the 12 stores produced seven plus signs, four minus signs, and one zero difference. Does there appear to be a difference in the effectiveness of these methods of advertising? Set $\alpha = 0.10$. State your hypotheses and conclusion.

26. Shoppers in a large mall in Dayton were randomly asked which of two brands of yogurt they preferred. Forty-two said Swedish Heaven, 31 chose Merry Melody, and 12 expressed no preference. If the local yogurt shop is to carry only one brand, which should it be? Set $\alpha = 0.10$. State the hypotheses.

27. A manufacturer uses parts from either supplier A or supplier B to make his product. A check of yesterday's output reveals that the order in which these suppliers' parts were used was

AA BBB AAA B A BB AA BB

Does it appear that the parts are being used randomly? Set $\alpha = 0.05$. State your hypotheses and conclusion.

28. Smile Bright sells toothpaste in 17-ounce containers. Management expects overfills and underfills to be random. If they are not, it is assumed something is wrong with the fill system, and the production line is shut down. Should the line be shut down if containers measured 16.8, 18.2, 17.3, 17.5, 16.3, 17.4, 16.1, 16.9, 17, 18.1, 17.3, 16.2, 17.3, and 16.8 ounces? Let $\alpha = 0.05$.

29. Sales receipts are recorded for the past 37 days. You denote those values below the median with a "B" and those above it with an "A." Counting the results, you find 18 A's and 19 B's with 10 runs. Your policy is to increase advertising if receipts are not randomly distributed. Should you increase advertising? State the hypotheses. Let $\alpha = 0.05$.

30. Acme Plumbing bids on construction jobs for city buildings. If contracts are granted by the city without regard to political consideration, Acme should witness no pattern in whether their bid is accepted or rejected. For the last 63 bids, Acme has had 32 accepted and the rest rejected, with 27 runs. At the 5 percent level, would it appear that bids are let on the basis of politics? State the hypotheses, the decision rule, and your conclusion.

31. Gladys Glucose offers vanilla- and chocolate-flavored ice cream to visitors in the park. The last 73 sales consisted of 40 vanilla and 33 chocolate with 16 runs. If sales are not random, Gladys will move her ice cream truck to the local zoo. Where should she set up business? Let $\alpha = 0.05$.

32. A large company hired 52 men and 41 women, resulting in 32 runs. If absence of randomness in the hiring process indicates discrimination, can it be alleged that the company practices sex discrimination in its hiring practices? Set $\alpha = 0.10$.

33. Over a 12-day period, Gladys Glucose sold 4, 11, 5, 7, 10, 13, 12, 5, 9, 6, 2, and 1 gallons of vanilla, and 19, 4, 6, 8, 18, 17, 17, 15, 3, 16, 14, and 0 gallons of chocolate. Using the Mann-Whitney U test, can she conclude that she sells the same amount of both flavors on the average? Set $\alpha = 0.01$.

34. The marketing director for Software, Inc. treated 15 computer disks with a solution designed to reduce wear. A second solution was used to treat 15 other disks, and all were graded on the basis of wear. Those treated with the first solution showed improved wear, measured in hours of use of 65, 73, 82, 52, 47, 51, 85, 92, 69, 77, 84, 68, 75, 74, and 89 hours. Those subjected to the second solution reported increased wear times of 73, 84, 91, 87, 90, 71, 72, 93, 99, 98, 89, 88, 79, 88, and 98 hours. At the 10 percent level, can the director conclude that there is any difference in the improved wear factors?

35. The quality control manager for a large plant in Denver gives two operations manuals to two groups of employees. Each group is then tested on operations procedures. The scores are shown in the table. The manager has always felt that manual 1 provides a better base of knowledge for new employees. Compare the mean test scores of the employees shown here and report your conclusion. State the hypotheses. Set $\alpha = 0.05$.

Employee Test Scores

Manual 1	87 97 82 97 92 90 81 89 90 88 87 89 93
Manual 2	92 79 80 73 84 93 86 88 91 82 81 84 72 74

36. Two manufacturing processes are used to make I-beams for construction of large buildings. Each I-beam is tested, and its tensile strength is recorded. Twenty-three beams made with the first process result in $\Sigma R_1 = 690$, and 27 beams made via the second process produce $\Sigma R_2 = 585$. A construction engineer argues that the first process results in beams that have at least the tensile strength demonstrated by beams made by the second process. At the 5 percent level, is he right?

37. An agricultural economist treats 50 acres of land with the chemical docide to increase crop yield. Fifty other acres are treated with mildolmine, and yields are measured. $\Sigma R_D = 2{,}125$ and $\Sigma R_M = 2{,}925$. The economist tells farmers that docide, which is a cheaper chemical, will produce a yield higher than mildolmine. At the 10 percent level, is he correct? State the hypotheses.

38. *Personnel Management* carried an article describing efforts by a manufacturing firm in Toledo to evaluate its supervisors. Employees were asked to rate their supervisors on a scale of 10 to 100. A subset of the results is shown here for three of the work areas. Determine if a difference exists in the ratings received by the supervisors. State the hypotheses, the decision rule, and your conclusion. Set α at 5 percent.

Shop	Office	Loading Dock
40	63	50
52	59	52
63	55	63
81	61	55
72	48	71
72	53	45
	49	

39. A total of 48 service calls are sampled by a local plumbing contractor to determine which of four types of plumbing fixtures produce the most problems. The results are shown here.

Fixture Model	Number of Failures
1	15
2	11
3	10
4	12

At the 1 percent level of significance, does the failure of the fixtures appear to be uniformly distributed? State your hypotheses, decision rule, and conclusion.

40. Four methods of treating steel rods are to be analyzed to determine if there is any difference in the pressure the rods can bear before breaking. The results of tests measuring the pressure in pounds before the rods bent are shown. Conduct the test complete with the hypotheses, decision rule, and conclusion. Set $\alpha = 1$ percent.

Method 1	Method 2	Method 3	Method 4
50	10	72	54
62	12	63	59
73	10	73	64
48	14	82	82
63	10	79	79

41. The-World's-Second-Best-Yogurt asks 60 people which of four new yogurt flavors they preferred. Twenty-one chose coconut-pickle, 13 chose prune with ketchup topping, 10 selected mustard à la peanut butter, and 16 expressed a partiality for essence of tuna. Does there appear to be a preference among the flavors by the customers? Set α at 10 percent. State the hypotheses and your conclusion.

42. As extra credit in her statistics course, Patty must determine if there is a difference in the average number of hours spent studying by freshmen, sophomores, juniors, and seniors at her university. Her research revealed the following:

Freshmen	Sophomores	Juniors	Seniors
20	18	22	29
29	9	19	31
10	12	21	27
17	15	31	22
15	14	42	18
23	22	22	31
27			

Help Patty earn her extra credit in statistics by stating her hypotheses and conclusion. Set $\alpha = 10$ percent.

43. As product manager of Sports Wear, Inc., Beverlee Hills must ensure that the sizes of their new line of active wear are produced according to a certain predetermined pattern. Their market research indicates that customers prefer 20 percent extra large, 30 percent large, 25 percent medium, and 25 percent small. A random sample of 145 garments reveals 32 extra large, 40 large, 41 medium, and 32 small. At the 5 percent level, does it appear that the desired proportion of sizes is being observed?

44. Ms. Hills, from the previous problem, must determine if the spending habits of various demographic groups are the same. She examines the size of typical purchases, measured in dollars, of four groups: married males (MM), married females (MF), single males (SM), and single females (SF). She finds the following information.

MM	MF	SM	SF
$50	$20	$19	$87
17	23	32	20
23	82	66	95
48	46	72	34
63	13	41	11

At the 1 percent level of significance, does it appear that a difference exists in spending habits of these four groups?

45. Seven corporate bond issues are ranked as to their investment worth by two financial analysts. The results are shown here. Using these rankings as a sample, calculate the Spearman rank correlation test to determine if there is any correlation between the rating practices of these two analysts at the 10 percent level.

Corporation	Rating of First Analyst	Rating of Second Analyst
1	4	3
2	3	4
3	1	2
4	2	5
5	7	6
6	6	1
7	5	7

46. Six truck models are rated on a scale of 1 to 10 by two companies that purchase entire fleets of trucks for industrial use. Calculate the Spearman rank coefficient to determine at the 1 percent level if the rankings are independent.

Model	Rating by First Company	Rating by Second Company
1	8	9
2	7	6
3	5	8
4	7	5
5	3	7
6	2	8

47. All 50 states are ranked by two travel agencies as to their desirability as vacation spots. The results revealed $\Sigma d^2 = 22{,}712$. Test for independence in ratings at the 10 percent level.

48. The top 10 firms on Fortune's 500 list were ranked by the AFL-CIO and by a management group on the basis of the quality of the health care system each company provides its employees. Using the results shown here, determine at the 5 percent level if there is any correlation in the rating practices of unions and management.

Firm	Union Ranking	Management Ranking
1	5	6
2	8	10
3	2	3
4	7	9
5	4	7
6	6	4
7	1	8
8	9	1
9	3	2
10	10	5

49. Seventy-three employees are ranked by two managers on the basis of their productivity levels. Calculate the Spearman rank coefficient to determine if the rankings are independent at the 1 percent level if $\Sigma d^2 = 78{,}815$.

EMPIRICAL EXERCISES

50. Is there a difference in the grade point average of freshmen, sophomores, juniors, and seniors at your university?

51. Do the number of shares traded on the New York Stock Exchange seem to be normally distributed over the five-day business week?

52. Obtain a performance rating of the president of the United States between 1 and 100 from male students, female students, male faculty, and female faculty at your university. Is there a difference in the way these groups view the manner in which the president is doing his job?

CASE APPLICATION

53. Harry Slotnik has just opened a flight school in Beaver Falls, Pennsylvania. He currently faces many problems in getting his fledgling business off the ground, and has hired you as a statistical consultant to aid in this endeavor.

   Harry's first concern focuses on the number of hours his students must spend in ground training before they are ready to take a test flight. In examining the records of 59 of his previous students, broken down into five categories, you find the following data:

Hours Spent in Ground Training before Test Flight

| Over 20 Years Old | | Over 40 Years Old | | All Other |
Men	Women	Men	Women	Students
45	58	58	22	5
89	69	87	52	10
45	78	51	61	16
54	56	87	98	3
98	78	54	65	14
98	45	52	65	12
56	85	45	47	6
85	87	96	87	2
45	58	87	54	14
65	65	89	87	8
45	54			
65	87			
87	69			
58				
65				
78				

Harry wants you to tell him if the time it takes all students in all five groups to prepare for a flight test is normally distributed? Remember the rules we developed in an earlier chapter to set up a frequency table. Select your own α-value. Harry also wonders if there is any difference in required preparation time among the five groups. Is there any difference in male and female preparation time? (You will have to ignore the observations in the category "All Other Students" since gender is unknown.)

CHAPTER SIXTEEN

TIME-SERIES ANALYSIS AND FORECASTING

CHAPTER BLUEPRINT

Many business and economic studies are based on time-series data. Such data series offer many advantages to statistical analysts who wish to examine the business world in which they live. This is particularly true in their efforts to forecast and predict events. This chapter looks at ways in which time-series data can be manipulated to reveal many secrets that would otherwise remain hidden.

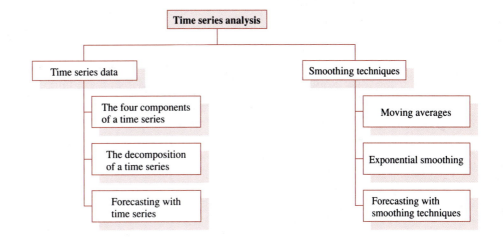

Statistics show the more you know the luckier you get.

16.1   INTRODUCTION

The importance of the ability to forecast the future with some degree of accuracy cannot be overstated. Imagine the results if you could gaze into a crystal ball and predict the future on the first Saturday in May when the Kentucky Derby is held, or just before kickoff for the next Super Bowl. Your success rate in predicting winners would no doubt skyrocket!

Such is the case in the business world. The ability to forecast and predict future events and trends greatly enhances the likelihood of success. It is therefore no wonder that businesses spend a good deal of time and effort in the pursuit of accurate forecasts of future business trends and developments.

Numerous quantitative tools can be used to develop useful forecasts. By relying on these tools, you can build your own crystal ball which can be used to peer into the future.

This chapter examines ways in which time-series data can be used to make forecasts, and how those forecasts can be used to make informed decision. We examine

- The four components of a time series.
- Two types of time-series models:
  - Additive model.
  - Multiplicative model.
- Smoothing techniques:
  - Moving average.
  - Exponential smoothing.
- The decomposition of a time series.

16.2   TIME SERIES AND THEIR COMPONENTS

Developing a forecast often starts with the collection of past data over several time periods. The resulting data set is called a **time series** because it contains observations over time. Table 16-1 shows time-series data for the U.S. gross national product. Notice that it registers data for some variable (GNP) over time.

> **A Time Series**
> A series of data for some variable or set of variables over several periods is called a time series.

TABLE 16-1   GNP
Time Series (in billions
of dollars)

Year	GNP
1985	4,014.9
1986	4,240.3
1987	4,662.8
1988	4,939.2
1989	5,403.7

The time periods can vary in length. They can be yearly, quarterly, or even daily. Time periods of only one hour may be used for highly volatile variables such as the price of a heavily traded stock on one of the organized stock exchanges.

It is our desire to use time-series data to forecast future values from past observations. One approach to this effort is to simply estimate the value in the next time period to be equal to that of the last time period. That is,

$$\hat{Y}_{t+1} = Y_t$$

where $\hat{Y}_{t+1}$ is the estimate of the value of the time series in the next time period, and Y_t is the actual value in the current time period. Referred to as the **naive method of forecasting,** this approach might be used when the data exhibit a **random walk.** Random walk movements demonstrate no trend upward or downward and typically shift direction suddenly. They can be expressed as $\hat{Y}_{t+1} = Y_t + a_t$, where a_t is some random amount, positive or negative, by which Y changes in time period t. Because it is totally random, it is virtually unpredictable. Movements in the random walk variable are analogous to an individual out for an evening stroll to nowhere in particular. When approaching an intersection, he randomly decides, perhaps by the flip of a coin, which way to turn. Such randomness is beyond prediction. The best we can do, therefore, is simply use the most recent observation as our prediction for the next value.

Naive Method of Forecasting
The naive method of forecasting uses the most recent observation for the forecast of the next observation.

Since random walk movements are not subject to accurate forecasts, we concentrate on time-series models which do lend themselves to prediction. All time series contain at least one of the following four components: (1) trend, (2) seasonal variation, (3) cyclical variation, and (4) irregular, or random, variation. The remainder of this section defines and examines each of these time-series components.

A.   SECULAR TREND

The **secular trend,** or merely trend, is the long-run behavior of the variable over an extended length of time. It reflects the general direction of the time series as upward or downward. Examples include the rising number of foreign cars sold in the United States, the increase in the volume of credit transactions over the past few years, and the downward movement in the number of people living in rural areas in the last two decades.

> **Secular Trend**
> The continuous long-term movement in a variable over an extended period of time is known as secular trend.

Some variables move smoothly over time, while others show "fit and starts" which produce a rather bumpy ride. Figure 16-1(a) shows the downward trend in agricultural employment over the last decade. There is little variation around the steadily declining trend. Figure 16-1(b), on the other hand, shows the upward secular movement in U.S. bank deposits. The data show considerable variation above and below the trend line drawn through the middle of the data.

FIGURE 16-1   Long-term Trends in U.S. Economic Activity

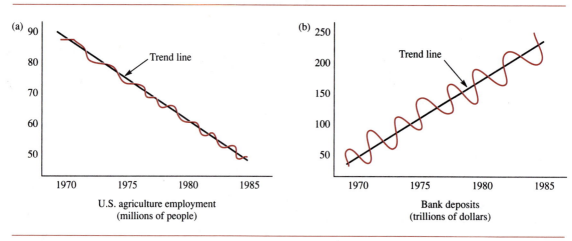

B.   THE SEASONAL COMPONENT

A lot of business activity is influenced by changing seasons of the year. For example, sales of certain seasonal goods such as Honda snowmobiles, Jantzen swimwear, and Hallmark Valentine cards would likely display a strong seasonal component. **Seasonal fluctuations** are patterns that reoccur regularly during the year.

Seasonal Fluctuations
Seasonal fluctuations are movements in the time series that reoccur each year about the same time due to the change in the seasons.

Figure 16-2 shows how each year the unemployment rate tends to go up in May when high school students enter the summer job market, and goes down in November when retail stores hire temporary help to handle the Christmas rush. Notice that no apparent trend exists in the unemployment rate.

FIGURE 16-2   Seasonal Fluctuations in Unemployment

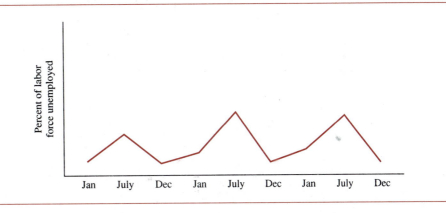

Seasonal fluctuations are regular movements of the data at roughly the same time every year. For seasonal fluctuations to be detected, the time period in which the data are reported must be less than one year. Since seasonal fluctuations occur within the year, annual data will not capture or reflect seasonal changes. Quarterly, monthly, or weekly data, for example, are necessary.

C.   CYCLICAL VARIATIONS

Many variables often exhibit a tendency to fluctuate above and below the long-term trend over a long period of time. These fluctuations are called **cyclical fluctuations** or **business cycles.** They cover much longer time periods than do seasonal variations, often encompassing three or more years in duration.

Cyclical Fluctuations
Wavelike variations in the general level of business activity over a relatively long time period are called cyclical fluctuations.

A cycle contains four phases: (1) the upswing or expansion, during which the level of business activity is accelerated and unemployment is low and production is brisk; (2) the peak, at which point the rate of economics activity has "topped out"; (3) the downturn, or contraction, when unemployment rises and activity wanes; and (4) the through, where activity is at the lowest point. A cycle runs from one phase to the next like phase and, as shown in Figure 16-3, fluctuates above and below the long-term trend in a wavelike manner.

FIGURE 16-3   Cyclical Fluctuations of Foreign Auto Imports

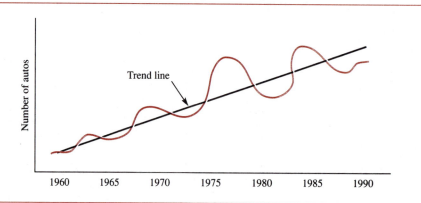

D.   IRREGULAR FLUCTUATIONS

Time series also contain **irregular**, or **random, fluctuations** caused by unusual occurrences producing movements which have no discernible pattern. These movements are, like fingerprints and snowflakes, unique and are unlikely to reoccur in similar fashion. They can be caused by events such as wars, floods, earthquakes, political elections, or oil embargoes.

16.3   TIME-SERIES MODELS

A time-series model can be expressed as some combination of these four components. The model is simply a mathematical statement of the relationship among the four components. Two types of models are commonly associated with time series: (1) the additive model and (2) the multiplicative model. The additive model is expressed as

$$Y_t = T_t + S_t + C_t + I_t$$

where Y_t is the value of the time series for time period t, and the right-hand side values are the trend, the seasonal variation, the cyclical variation, and the random or irregular variation, respectively, for the same time period. In the additive model, all values are expressed in original units, and S, C, and I are deviations around T. If we were to develop a time-series model for sales in dollars for a local retail store, we might find that $T = \$500$, $S = \$100$, $C = -\$25$, and $I = -\$10$. Sales would be

$$Y = \$500 + \$100 - \$25 - \$10$$

$$= \$565$$

Notice that the positive value for S indicates that existing seasonal influences have had a positive impact on sales. The negative cyclical value suggests that the business cycle is currently in a downswing. There was apparently some random event which had a negative impact on sales.

The additive model suffers from the somewhat unrealistic assumption that the components are independent of each other. This, however, is seldom the case in the real world. In most instances, movements in one component will have an impact on other components, thereby negating the assumption of independence. Or, perhaps even more commonly, we often find that certain forces at work in the economy simultaneously affect two or more components. Again, the assumption of independence is violated.

As a result, the multiplicative model is often preferred. It assumes that the components interact with each other and do not move independently. The multiplicative model is expressed as

$$Y_t = T_t \cdot S_t \cdot C_t \cdot I_t$$

In the multiplicative model, only T is expressed in the original units, and S, C, and I are stated in terms of percentages. For example, values for bad debts at a commercial bank might be recorded as $T = \$10$ million, $S = 1.7$, $C = 0.91$, and $I = 0.87$. Bad debts could then be computed as

$$Y = (10)(1.7)(0.91)(0.87) = \$13.46 \text{ million}$$

Since seasonal fluctuations occur within time periods of less than one year, they would not be reflected in annual data. A time series for annual data would be expressed as

$$Y_t = T_t \cdot C_t \cdot I_t$$

16.4 SMOOTHING TECHNIQUES

A primary use of time-series analysis is to forecast future values. The general behavior of the variable can often be best discussed by examining its long-term trend. However, if the time series contains too many random fluctuations or short-term seasonal changes, the trend may be somewhat obscured and difficult to observe. It is often possible to eliminate many of these confounding factors by averaging the data over several time periods. This is accomplished by the use of certain smoothing techniques which remove random fluctuations in the series, thereby providing a less obstructed view of the true behavior of the series. We examine two common methods of smoothing time series data: a moving average and exponential smoothing.

A.   MOVING AVERAGES

A **moving average** (MA) will have the effect of "smoothing out" the data, producing a movement with fewer peaks and valleys. It is computed by averaging the values in the time series over a set number of time periods. The same number of time periods is retained for each average by dropping the oldest observation and picking up the newest. Assume that the closing prices for a stock on the New York Stock Exchange for Monday through Wednesday were $20, $22, and $18, respectively. We can compute a three-period (day) moving average as

$$(20 + 22 + 18)/3 = 20$$

This value of 20 then serves as our forecast or estimate of what the closing price might be at any time in the future. If the closing on Thursday is, say, 19, the next moving average is calculated by dropping Monday's value of 20 and using Thursday's closing price of 19. Thus, the forecast becomes

$$(22 + 18 + 19)/3 = 19.67$$

The estimate figured in this manner is seen as the long-run average of the series. It is taken as the forecast for the closing price on any given day in the future.

Moving Average (MA)
A series of arithmetic averages over a given number of time periods, it is the estimate of the long-run average of the variable.

Consider the sales for Arthur Momitor's Snowmobiles, Inc. over the past 12 months as shown in Table 16-2. Both a three-month MA and a five-month MA

TABLE 16-2   Snowmobile Sales for Arthur Momitor

Month	Sales ($100)	Three-Month MA	Five-Month MA
January	52		
February	81	60.00	
March	47	64.33	59.00
April	65	54.00	63.20
May	50	62.67	56.00
June	73	56.00	58.60
July	45	59.33	55.60
August	60	51.67	61.40
September	50	63.00	55.80
October	79	58.00	59.20
November	45	62.00	
December	62		

are calculated. The first entry in the three-month MA is obtained by averaging the sales of snowmobiles in January, February, and March. The resulting value of $(52 + 81 + 47)/3 = 60$ is centered on the middle time period of February. The next entry is determined by averaging February, March, and April and centering the value of 64.33 in the middle of those three periods, which is March. The remaining entries are determined similarly.

The first entry in the five-month MA series uses values for months January through May. The average of $(52 + 51 + 47 + 65 + 50)/5 = 59$ is centered in the middle of those five time periods at March.

Moving averages have the effect of smoothing out large variations in the data. This smoothing effect is accomplished by the fact that unusually large or unusually small observations are averaged in with other values, and their impact is thereby restrained. The larger the number of time periods in a moving average, the more pronounced the smoothing affect will be. Notice that the range of values in the three-month MA is less than that in the original data and greater than the range found in the five-month MA. This tendency for the smoothing effect to increase with the number of time periods in the moving average is illustrated by Figure 16-4.

FIGURE 16-4   Comparing Moving Averages

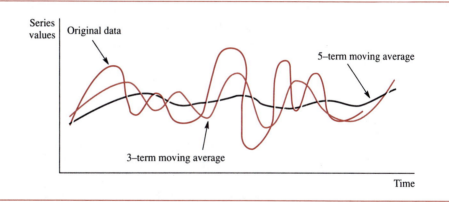

Notice that when an odd number of time periods is used in the moving average, the results can be automatically centered at the middle time period. When Arthur Momitor calculated his three-period moving average for snowmobiles, the first value, for example, could be readily centered at the middle time period of February.

However, if there is an even number of time periods in the moving average, an adjustment must be made. With an even number of time periods, there is no middle observation at which the value can be automatically centered.

Consider the quarterly sales data for Sun Shine Greeting Cards in Table 16-3. The data run from the first quarter of 1989 (89-1) to the last quarter of 1991 (91-4). A four-period (quarter) moving average is calculated. The first entry of 42.5 is obtained by averaging the data for all four quarters of 1989. However, it does not correspond to any specific time period in the original data series, but is actually set

TABLE 16-3   Sales for Sun Shine Cards ($1,000)

Time Period	Sales	Four-Quarter MA	Centered Four-Quarter MA
89-1	40		
89-2	45		
		42.50	
89-3	38		44.13
		45.75	
89-4	47		45.00
		44.25	
90-1	53		45.38
		46.50	
90-2	39		44.63
		42.75	
90-3	47		42.50
		42.25	
90-4	32		43.00
		43.75	
91-1	51		42.50
		41.25	
91-2	45		44.00
		46.75	
91-3	37		
91-4	54		

between the second and third quarters for the year. The remaining entries are similarly off-center.

It is necessary to center the moving average by taking the mean of each successive pairs of moving averages. Thus, the average of the first and second values yields

$$(42.5 + 45.75)/2 = 44.13$$

which is then centered at the third quarter. The next entry of 45.00 is obtained by averaging the second and third values, yielding

$$(45.75 + 44.25)/2 = 45.00$$

which is centered at the fourth quarter of 1989. The remaining values are likewise centered at their respective time periods.

Moving averages can be used to remove irregular and seasonal fluctuations. Each entry in the moving average is derived from four observations of quarterly data—that is, one full year's worth. Thus, the moving average "averages out" any seasonal variations that might occur within the year, effectively eliminating them and leaving only trend and cyclical variations.

In general, if the number of time periods in a moving average is sufficient to encompass a full year (12 if monthly data are used; 52 if weekly data are used), seasonal variations are averaged out and removed from the series. The data are then said to be **deseasonalized**.

As noted, the use of a larger number of time periods results in a smoother averaged series. Therefore, if the data are quite volatile, a small number of periods should be used in the forecast to avoid placing the forecast too close to the long-run average. If the data do not vary greatly from the long-run mean, a larger number of time periods should be used in forming the moving average.

The moving average method of forecasting is best used when the data show no upward or downward trend. It is a somewhat simplistic approach and finds its most common use in the decomposition of time series, a subject which receives considerable attention later in this chapter.

B.   Exponential Smoothing

As the name implies, exponential smoothing also has the effect of smoothing out a series. It also provides an effective means of prediction. **First-order exponential smoothing** is used when the data do not exhibit any trend pattern. The model contains a self-correcting mechanism which adjusts forecasts in the opposite direction of past errors. The equation is

$$F_{t+1} = \alpha A_t + (1 - \alpha)F_t \qquad (16.1)$$

where F_{t+1} is the forecast for the next time period
        A_t is the actual, observed value for the current time period
        F_t is the forecast previously made for the current time period

The term α is a "smoothing constant" which is given a value between 0 and 1. Since the data do not trend up or down but fluctuate around some long-run average, the value F_{t+1} is taken as the forecast for any future time period.

Exponential Smoothing
Exponential smoothing is a forecasting tool in which the forecast is based on a weighted average of current and past values.

As an illustration, suppose it is currently the last business day of February. Sales for Uncle Vito's Used Cars for the month have been compiled and total $110 thousand. Uncle Vito has decided to forecast sales for March. According to Formula (16.1), the March forecast, F_{t+1}, requires

1. February's actual sales, A_t.
2. The forecast for February, F_t.

However, since March is the first month in which Uncle Vito is developing his forecast, there was no forecast made for February and F_t is unknown. The general practice is to simply use the actual value of the previous time period, January in this case, for the first forecast. Uncle Vito's records show that January sales were $105 thousand. Assuming a value of 0.3 for α, the forecast for March is

$$F_{t+1} = \alpha A_t + (1 - \alpha)F_t$$

$$= \alpha A_{\text{Feb}} + (1 - \alpha)F_{\text{Feb}}$$

$$= (0.3)(110) + (0.7)(105)$$

$$= \$106.5 \text{ thousand as the forecast for sales in March}$$

As Table 16-4 reveals, Uncle Vito can plan for sales of $106.5 thousand. If actual sales in March are $107 thousand, the error is computed as $F_t - A_t = 106.5 - 107 = -0.5$. Also, $F_{\text{Apr}} = (0.3)(107) + (0.7)(106.5) = 106.65$.

TABLE 16-4   Uncle Vito's Auto Sales ($1,000)

Month	Forecast	Actual	Error $(F_t - A_t)$
January	—	105	
February	105	110	−5.0
March	106.5	107	−0.5
April	106.65	112	−5.35

Assume sales in April prove to be $112 thousand. The error of −$5.35 thousand can then be computed. It is also possible to predict sales for May:

$$F_{t+1} = \alpha A_t + (1 - \alpha)F_t$$

$$= \alpha A_{\text{Apr}} + (1 - \alpha)F_{\text{Apr}}$$

$$= (0.3)(112) + (0.7)(106.65)$$

$$= \$108.26 \text{ thousand}$$

Of course, the value selected for α is crucial. Since it is our desire to produce a forecast with the smallest possible error, the α-value which minimizes the mean square error (MSE) is identified as optimal. Trial and error often serves as the best method to determine the proper α-value. Table 16-5 contains Uncle Vito's actual

TABLE 16-5   Sales Data for Uncle Vito

Month	Actual	Forecast ($\alpha = 0.3$)	Error	Forecast ($\alpha = 0.8$)	Error
January	105				
February	110	105.00	−5.0	105.00	−5.00
March	107	106.50	−0.5	109.00	2.00
April	112	106.65	−5.35	107.40	−4.60
May	117	108.26	−8.74	111.08	−5.92
June	109	110.88	1.88	115.82	6.82
July	108	110.32	2.32	110.36	2.36
August		109.62		108.47	

sales data for the first seven months. Errors are calculated based on forecasts using α-values of 0.3 and 0.8. The *MSE* is

$$MSE = \frac{\Sigma(F_t - A_t)^2}{n - 1} \qquad (16.2)$$

For $\alpha = 0.3$, the *MSE* is

$$MSE = \frac{(-5)^2 + (-0.5)^2 + (-5.35)^2 + (-8.74)^2 + (1.88)^2 + (2.32)^2}{7 - 1}$$

$$= 23.20$$

An α of 0.8 yields

$$MSE = \frac{(-5)^2 + (2)^2 + (-4.6)^2 + (-5.92)^2 + (6.82)^2 + (2.36)^2}{7 - 1}$$

$$= 22.88$$

An α of 0.8 produces better forecasting results since it generates a smaller error factor. Other values of α may be tried to determine their impact on MSE and the accuracy of the resulting forecasts. Generally speaking, if the data are rather volatile, a lower α-value is called for. This is because smaller values for α assign less weight to more recent observations. If the data show considerable movement, the last observation may not be representative of the long-run average.

Remember, first-order exponential smoothing in the manner described here is appropriate if the data show no trend but move around some average value over the long run. If a downward or upward trend can be detected by plotting the data, second-order exponential smoothing, the mechanics of which will not be examined here, should be used.

┌───┐
│ OOOO   **DECISION MAKING THROUGH PROBLEM SOLVING**   OOOO │
│   ILLUSTRATION 16-2   │
│   │
│ In a conversation with an official of the Churchill Downs Racetrack   │
│ in Louisville, Kentucky, it was learned that the racetrack takes   │
│ great care to predict track revenues and the amount spectators wager │
│ on the races over the course of a season. Many decisions regarding   │
│ track policy and the size of potential winnings depend on how much   │
│ money the racetrack has at its disposal. The official stated that   │
│ exponential smoothing is customarily used in making these forecasts. │
└───┘

EXAMPLE 16-1 Predicting Unemployment Rates

Monthly unemployment rates for 1989 are shown here. As an analyst for the U.S. Department of Labor, you are to (1) smooth out the fluctuations using a moving average with four time periods, and (2) use an exponential smoothing model with α set at 0.4 to forecast unemployment for some future month. The data do not show any pronounced trend up or down.

January	5.4	July	5.4
February	5.1	August	5.5
March	5.0	September	5.2
April	5.2	October	5.5
May	5.3	November	5.1
June	5.3	December	5.4

SOLUTION:

Month	Rate	MA	Centered MA	F_t
January	5.4			
February	5.1			5.4
		5.175		
March	5.0		5.163	5.28
		5.150		
April	5.2		5.175	5.17
		5.200		
May	5.3		5.250	5.18
		5.300		
June	5.3		5.338	5.23
		5.375		
July	5.4		5.363	5.26
		5.350		
August	5.5		5.375	5.31
		5.400		
September	5.2		5.363	5.39
		5.325		
October	5.5		5.313	5.31
		5.300		
November	5.1			5.39
December	5.4			5.27

The first moving average of 5.175 is calculated by averaging rates for January through April. It is situated in the middle of those four months between February and March. The second entry of 5.150 is the average of the months February through May and is placed between March and April. The remaining values for MA are figured similarly. These values are then centered by averaging successive pairs of moving averages.

To forecast using exponential smoothing, you must compute all forecasted figures for February through December in order to obtain $F_{Dec} = 5.27$, which is then used in the January forecast:

$$F_{Jan} = \alpha(A_{Dec}) + (1 - \alpha)(F_{Dec})$$

$$= (0.4)(5.4) + (0.6)(5.27)$$

$$= 5.32\%$$

STATISTICAL INTERPRETATION:
The moving average method forecasts a rate of 5.313 percent. Exponential smoothing provides a forecast of 5.32 percent. This value (of 5.313 percent or 5.32 percent) is taken as the forecast for January, or for any future time period, since the data do not exhibit a trend but are thought to fluctuate around this long-term average.

Unlike moving averages, which use only a set number of time periods of data, exponential smoothing uses all past values of the time series. This is because F_{t+1} depends on A_t and F_t. Yet, F_t used A_{t-1} and F_{t-1} in its calculation, and F_{t-1} used A_{t-2} and F_{t-2}. Thus, each forecast depends on previous actual values of A_{t-n} all the way back to where the forecasts first began. The farther back in time you go, the less emphasis a value of A has on the current forecast.

QUICK CHECK 16.4.1

○○○○   Excess inventories for Mom's Apple Pies for the past 10 weeks have been 101, 122, 109, 111, 120, 117, 115, 118, 112, 117. Compute a three-week moving average and forecast excess inventories for a future week, using exponential smoothing with $\alpha = 0.2$.

Answer: Moving averages: 110.67, 114, 113.33, 116, 117.33, 116.67, 115, 115.67. $F_{t+1} = 113.69$

16.5   DECOMPOSITION OF A TIME SERIES

In this section we examine the techniques used to isolate the four components of a time series. This procedure is known as **decomposition**. Decomposition can be used to measure the degree of impact each component has on the direction of the time series itself. We begin by measuring the trend in a time series.

A. SECULAR TREND

By estimating the trend in a time series, we can remove it from the actual value and thereby determine the size of the remaining components. If the change in a time series is relatively constant, a linear trend model will likely provide a fairly accurate forecast. Since many business and economic variables display a tendency to change by a constant amount over time, a linear model is appropriate.

The most widely used method to fit a linear trend is the method of ordinary least squares discussed in Chapter 12. The main difference between the procedure discussed earlier and that presented here is that in trend analysis the independent (right-hand side) variable is time. The linear relationship can be expressed as

$$\hat{Y}_t = b_0 + b_1 t \qquad (16.3)$$

where $\hat{Y}_t$ is the estimated value of the dependent variable
  b_0 is the intercept of the trend line
  b_1 is the slope of the trend line
  t is the independent variable, X

Table 16-6 contains data for the number of housing starts in Happy Valley, California, over the past 16 years. Mayfield Construction wants to fit these time series observations, using OLS, to develop a model which can predict future housing starts.

TABLE 16-6   Housing Starts in Happy Valley (in 100's)

Year	$t(X)$	Housing Starts (Y)	XY	X^2
1977	1	7.0	7.0	1
1978	2	7.1	14.2	4
1979	3	7.9	23.7	9
1980	4	7.3	29.2	16
1981	5	8.2	41.0	25
1982	6	8.3	49.8	36
1983	7	8.1	56.7	49
1984	8	8.6	68.8	64
1985	9	8.8	79.2	81
1986	10	8.9	89.0	100
1987	11	8.7	95.7	121
1988	12	9.1	109.2	144
1989	13	9.4	122.2	169
1990	14	9.1	127.4	196
1991	15	9.5	142.5	225
1992	16	9.9	158.4	256
	136	135.9	1,214.0	1,496.0

The values for t are obtained by coding each time period starting with 1 for the first time period, 2 for the second, and so on. As we learned in Chapter 12, the sums of squares and cross-products, used to calculate the regression line, are

$$SSx = \Sigma X^2 - \frac{(\Sigma X)^2}{n} \qquad (16.4)$$

$$= 1,496 - \frac{(136)^2}{16}$$

$$= 340$$

$$SSxy = \Sigma XY = \frac{(\Sigma X)(\Sigma Y)}{n} \qquad (16.5)$$

$$= 1,214 - \frac{(136)(135.9)}{16}$$

$$= 58.85$$

The formulas for b_0 and b_1 are

$$b_1 = \frac{SSxy}{SSx} \qquad (16.6)$$

$$= \frac{58.85}{340}$$

$$= 0.173$$

$$b_0 = \bar{Y} - b_1 \bar{X} \qquad (16.7)$$

$$= 7.02$$

The equation for the trend line is

$$\hat{Y}_t = 7.02 + 0.173t$$

Figure 16-5 displays the raw data and the trend line they produce.

FIGURE 16-5   Trend Line for Housing Starts in Happy Valley

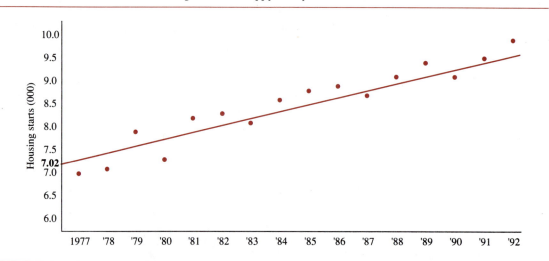

Given this equation, it is possible to predict the number of housing starts for future time periods by merely substituting the appropriate value for t. Suppose Mayfield Construction wants to forecast the housing starts for 1993. Since the value of t would be 17 in 1993, the forecast becomes

$$\hat{Y} = 7.02 + 0.173(17)$$

$$= 9.96$$

or 9,960 starts, since the data were expressed in units of 1,000.

Similarly, since 1995 would carry a t value of 19, the forecast for 1995 would be

$$\hat{Y} = 7.02 + 0.173(19)$$

$$= 10.31$$

It is estimated that there will be 1,031 housing starts in 1995.

Of course, the farther into the future a forecast is made, the less confidence you can place in its precision. Additionally, its accuracy is based on the condition that the past provides a representative picture of future trends.

EXAMPLE 16-2 Hired Killers, Inc.

Larry's Lawn Service advertises a new chemical to kill weeds. To determine the trend in the number of customers, Larry consults company records and finds the data shown here. He wishes to forecast customers for future time periods.

Time Period	$t(X)$	Customers (Y)	XY	X^2
1991 January	1	41	41	1
February	2	43	86	4
March	3	39	117	9
April	4	37	148	16
May	5	42	210	25
June	6	35	210	36
July	7	30	210	49
August	8	31	248	64
September	9	32	288	81
October	10	30	300	100
November	11	28	308	121
December	12	28	336	144
1992 January	13	29	377	169
February	14	26	364	196
	105	471	3,243	1,015

SOLUTION:

$$SSx = 1,015 - \frac{(105)^2}{14}$$

$$= 227.5$$

$$SSxy = 3,243 - \frac{(105)(471)}{14}$$

$$= -289.5$$

$$b_1 = -1.27$$

$$b_0 = \bar{Y} - b_1\bar{X}$$

$$= 33.64 - (-1.27)(7.5)$$

$$= 43.2$$

The equation for the trend line is

$$\hat{Y}_t = 43.2 - 1.27t$$

If Larry wished to forecast the number of customers his firm might get in March 1992, which would be time period 15, he would have

$$\hat{Y}_{\text{Mar}} = 43.2 - 1.27(15)$$

$$= 24.15, \text{ or } 24 \text{ customers}$$

The forecast for August is

$$\hat{Y}_{Aug} = 43.2 - 1.27(21)$$

$$= 16.53 \text{ customers}$$

STATISTICAL INTERPRETATION:

The negative coefficient for t of -1.27 tells Larry that business is trending downward at the rate of 1.27 customers each time period (month).

QUICK CHECK 16.5.1

○○○○

Industrial accidents per month at a local plant for January through October are 9, 12, 10, 14, 13, 18, 19, 17, 23, 25. Develop a trend model and forecast accidents in December.

Answer: $6.8 + 1.67t$; $\hat{Y}_{Dec} = 26.87$

B.   SEASONAL VARIATION

Many businesses experience seasonal variations in the level of their activity. Changes in weather and climate affect business conditions in agriculture and construction, as well as related industries such as farm implements and timber. Many commodities such as swimwear and snow skies are influenced by changes in the season. Artificial seasons based on social customs, including Christmas, June weddings, and May graduations, impact on business activity. Thanksgiving and Easter affect the poultry and egg industries.

Seasons do not have to be as long as those implied above. Organized stock exchanges find that trading is heavier on Friday and Mondays than it is on other weekdays. Here, the "season" is a single day.

The study of seasonal fluctuations lends much to our ability to evaluate and understand business behavior. The ultimate aim is to determine a **seasonal index** which can be used to analyze and predict business activity.

Consider the data in Table 16-7, which shows monthly profits for Vinnie's Video Village. A superficial examination reveals that profits seem to be higher during the summer months when school is out, and lower at other times of the year. This suggests the presence of seasonal factors.

The first step in developing a seasonal index is to calculate a centered moving average. Since Vinnie's profits tend to fluctuate over the course of the year, and monthly data are used, a 12-period (month) moving average is calculated. If we were to analyze activity on organized stock exchanges, we might want to use daily data and employ a five-period (for the five business days) moving average since, as noted, activity on the exchanges seems to depend on the day of the week.

The 12-month moving average and the centered moving average (CMA) are shown in Table 16-7. The calculations were done using Microstat II, a popular

TABLE 16-7   Seasonal Fluctuations in Vinnie's Profits

Time Period	(Y) Profits ($100's)	12-month MA (T · C)	Centered MA	Ratio to MA Y/CMA = S · I
1991				
January	10			
February	9			
March	11			
April	12			
May	18			
June	23	15.5833		
July	27	15.5000	15.5417	1.7373
August	26	15.6667	15.5833	1.6685
September	18	15.5833	15.6250	1.1520
October	13	15.5833	15.5833	0.8342
November	10	15.6667	15.6250	0.6400
December	10	15.8333	15.7500	0.6349
1992				
January	9	15.9167	15.8750	0.5669
February	11	16.3333	16.1250	0.6822
March	10	16.6667	16.5000	0.6061
April	12	16.8333	16.7500	0.7164
May	19	16.9167	16.8750	1.1259
June	25	17.0833	17.0000	1.4706
July	28	17.1667	17.1250	1.6350
August	31	16.9167	17.0417	1.8191
September	22	16.9167	16.9167	1.3005
October	15	16.9167	16.9167	0.8867
November	11	16.9167	16.9167	0.6502
December	12	16.9167	16.9167	0.7094
1993				
January	10	17.0000	16.9583	0.5897
February	8	17.0000	17.0000	0.4706
March	10	16.9167	16.9583	0.5897
April	12	17.0000	16.9583	0.7076
May	19	17.5833	17.2916	1.0988
June	25	18.1667	17.8750	1.3986
July	29			
August	31			
September	21			
October	16			
November	18			
December	19			

computer statistical package, and may differ slightly from hand calculations due to rounding. As noted, the moving average eliminates recurring seasonal movements as well as any random effects over the course of the year. Thus, given a multiplicative model $Y = T \cdot C \cdot S \cdot I$, the moving average eliminates S and I and contains only T and C. That is, $\text{MA} = T \cdot C$.

It is now possible to calculate the **ratio to moving average.** This is done by dividing the original series value Y by the moving average. The result produces the S and I components of the time series.

$$\frac{Y}{\text{MA}} = \frac{T \cdot C \cdot S \cdot I}{T \cdot C} = S \cdot I$$

By dividing the time-series values by the moving average, we arrive at the ratio to moving average, which contains only S and I components. The I component will be removed shortly.

To summarize, we seek to isolate and analyze the seasonal component. Strangely, we begin by eliminating S (and I) by calculating the moving average. We then restore the seasonal component by calculating the ratio to moving average. These values also appear in Table 16-7.

Ratio to Moving Average
By dividing the original time-series data by the moving average, we obtain the ratio to moving average, which contains the S and I components.

A **mean ratio to moving average** is calculated for each month as shown in Table 16-8. These mean ratios are then normalized to produce the seasonal indexes.

TABLE 16-8   Seasonal Indexes for Vinnie's Profits

Month	1991	1992	1993	Mean Ratio to MA	Seasonal Index
January		0.5669	0.5897	0.5783	0.5858
February		0.6822	0.4706	0.5764	0.5839
March		0.6061	0.5897	0.5979	0.6057
April		0.7164	0.7076	0.7120	0.7213
May		1.1259	1.0988	1.1124	1.1269
June		1.4706	1.3986	1.4346	1.4533
July	1.7373	1.6350		1.6861	1.7082
August	1.6685	1.8191		1.7438	1.7665
September	1.1520	1.3005		1.2262	1.2422
October	0.8342	0.8867		0.8605	0.8717
November	0.6400	0.6502		0.6451	0.6535
December	0.6349	0.7094		0.6721	0.6809
				11.8454	11.9999 ≈ 12

This normalization procedure is done to ensure that the seasonal indexes will sum to 12, since we used a 12-period moving average. This is accomplished by multiplying each mean by a *normalization ratio,* which is the ratio of 12 to the sum of the means. Notice in Table 16-8 that the sum of the means of the ratio to moving averages is 11.8454. The normalization ratio is then

$$\frac{12}{11.8454} = 1.01305$$

The seasonal indexes are found by multiplying each mean by 1.01305. This normalization removes the irregular component, leaving only the seasonal factor.

USES OF THE SEASONAL INDEX

1. After going to all the trouble of calculating these seasonal indexes, you will be glad to know that they are put to vital use. For example, the seasonal index for a particular month indicates *how that month performs relative to the year as a whole.* The index of 0.5858 for January tells Vinnie that profits in January are only 58.58 percent of the average for the full year. Profits are 41.42 percent $(1.000 - 0.5858)$ below the year's monthly average.
2. Perhaps more importantly, the indexes can be used to *deseasonalize data.* This has the effect of removing seasonal variation from a series to determine what the values would be in the absence of seasonal variations. It yields the average value per month that would occur if there were no seasonal changes. The deseasonalized value is found by dividing the actual value during the month by the seasonal index in that month. For example, in January 1991, the deseasonalized value is

$$\frac{10}{0.5858} = 17.07$$

In other words, if Vinnie's business was not subject to seasonal variation, profits in January 1991 would have been 17.07.

Deseasonalized values are also called **seasonally adjusted** because they tell us what the values would be once we adjust for seasonal influences. The classical example involves unemployment rates. Since unemployment is usually higher in May than most other months due to school dismissals and the influx of many teenagers into the job market, the seasonal index for May will be greater than 1. If actual unemployment in May is 7.2 percent and the index is, say, 1.103, the deseasonalized, or seasonally adjusted, rate of unemployment is $7.2/1.103 = 6.53$ percent. This is not to say that unemployment was 6.53 percent. (It was actually 7.2 percent). But when we adjust for seasonal forces which typically inflate the rate of unemployment in May, the deseasonalized rate is lower. In this manner a measure or index of seasonal variation can be used to determine if the change in some series is more or less than what might be expected given the typical seasonal behavior.

> **Deseasonalized Values**
> Deseasonalized values are obtained by dividing the actual values by their respective seasonal indexes. They reflect what the variable would be if we adjusted for seasonal influence.

3. The reverse is possible in that the seasonal index can be used to *seasonalize data* to get a better picture of what any one month might generate in profits. Assume Vinnie felt that profits might total 190 during the year. Without any seasonalization it might be argued that each month would generate $190/12 = 15.83$ in profits. However, Vinnie knows that monthly variations will occur. He could seasonalize the data to determine the extent of that monthly variation by multiplying 15.83 by the seasonal index. He knows that in January profits tend to be 58.58 percent of the yearly total. His estimate of profits for January is $(15.83)(0.5858) = 9.27$.

     Or perhaps Vinnie is working with the trend equation which, given the data is

$$Y_t = 13.85 + 0.167t$$

   The forecast for January 1994, the 37th time period is

$$\hat{Y} = 13.85 + 0.167(37)$$
$$= 20.03$$

   However, this does not account for the seasonal lows that occur in January. The value can be seasonalized by multiplying by the seasonal index for January, yielding $(20.03)(0.5858) = 11.73$, which probably more accurately reflects profits during that month.

EXAMPLE 16-3 It's a Dog-Gone Business

Marge Spaniel has owned and managed a successful breeding kennel for several years. She wishes to determine seasonal indexes for the quarterly data on revenue shown here in thousands of dollars in the first two columns of the table.

SOLUTION:

Since quarterly data are used, a four-period moving average will remove the seasonal variations.

Year-Quarter	Revenue	MA	Centered MA	Ratio to MA $Y/\text{CMA} = S \cdot I$
1991-I	24			
II	31			
		29.50		
III	21		29.8750	0.7029
		30.25		
IV	42		30.3750	1.3827
		30.50		
1992-I	27		31.0000	0.8710
		31.50		
II	32		31.3750	1.0199
		31.25		
III	25		30.3750	0.8230
		29.50		
IV	41		28.8750	1.4200
		28.25		
1993-I	20		27.3750	0.7306
		26.50		
II	27		26.2500	1.0286
		26.00		
III	18			
IV	39			

The normalization ratio is $4/3.9895 = 1.0026$.

	Ratios to Moving Average			Mean Ratio to MA	Seasonal Index
	1991	1992	1993		
I		0.8710	0.7306	0.8008	0.8029
II		1.0199	1.0286	1.0243	1.0270
III	0.7029	0.8230		0.7630	0.7650
IV	1.3827	1.4200		1.4014	1.4050
				3.9895	$3.99 \approx 4$

STATISTICAL INTERPRETATION:
Sales in the fourth quarter, for example, are 40.5 percent greater than the yearly average. The deseasonalized value for the fourth quarter of 1991 is $42/1.4050 = 29.89$.

C. CYCLICAL VARIATION

Many businesses are affected by swings in the business cycle. When the economy in general turns up, their business activity may accelerate, while an economic downturn brings on a drop in business. Some industries often exhibit movements in the opposite direction of the cycle. The entertainment industry, for example, has been known to experience countercyclical movements. Presumably, when economic conditions worsen, many people seek relief from harsh reality by escaping to the movies.

The cyclical component can be identified by first obtaining the trend and seasonal components as described earlier. The data from Example 16-3 for Ms. Spaniel will be used to illustrate. The trend line is

$$\hat{Y}_t = 28.58 + 0.0524t$$

The original data of the time series, the values predicted on the basis of this trend model, and the seasonal indexes as determined in Example 16-3 are shown in columns (2), (3), and (4) in Table 16-9. For example, the trend value for the second time period, 1991-II, is

$$\hat{Y} = 28.58 + 0.0524(2)$$

$$= 28.68$$

TABLE 16-9   Isolating the Cyclical Component

(1) Time	(2) Revenue	(3) Trend Projection	(4) Seasonal Index	(5) Statistical Norm (3) × (4)	(6) Cyclical-Irregular [(2)/(5)] (100)	(7) Cyclical Component
1991-I	24	28.63	0.8029	22.99	104.39	
-II	31	28.68	1.0270	29.45	105.26	
-III	21	28.73	0.7650	21.98	95.54	103.78
-IV	42	28.79	1.4050	40.45	103.83	105.63
1992-I	27	28.84	0.8029	23.16	116.58	108.13
-II	32	28.89	1.0270	29.67	107.85	109.90
-III	25	28.94	0.7650	22.14	112.92	105.64
-IV	41	29.00	1.4050	40.75	100.61	99.60
1993-I	20	29.05	0.8029	23.32	85.76	93.38
-II	27	29.10	1.0270	29.89	90.33	88.65
-III	18	29.15	0.7650	22.30	80.72	
-IV	39	29.21	1.4050	41.04	95.03	

The statistical norm is then calculated by multiplying the trend projection by the seasonal index. This is called the *norm* because it represents the values that would occur if only the trend and seasonal variations were present.

The cyclic and irregular components are obtained next by dividing the original data by the statistical norm which contains T and S. That is, since $Y = TSCI$,

$$\frac{Y}{TS} = \frac{TSCI}{TS} = CI$$

The results are then multiplied by 100 to express the answer in percentage form as shown in column (6). The values in column (6) contain both cyclical and irregular components. The latter is eliminated by taking a four-period moving average, leaving only the cyclical factor. This is done in column (7). The final measures in column (7) represent the actual levels in Ms. Spaniel's revenue in those time periods as a percentage of the trend.

Note that if annual data are used, they will, by definition, contain no seasonal variations. The seasonal index (as found in column (4) of Table 16-9, for example) would be unnecessary. The values of the time series would consist only of

$$Y = TCI$$

The components CI could be found directly by dividing only by the trend values:

$$\frac{Y}{T} = \frac{TCI}{T} = CI$$

D. IRREGULAR VARIATION

Having isolated the other three components of a time series, little more need be said about irregular variations. Suffice it to say that it is often possible to smooth out and effectively eliminate them by using a moving average as we did for column (7) of Table 16-9.

Table 16-10 portrays the relationship between the various forecasting tools available for our requirements. The methods in this chapter are by no means exhaustive. There are many other techniques, some considerably more sophisticated than those examined here, which can be used to provide accurate forecasts.

TABLE 16-10 Forecasting Methods

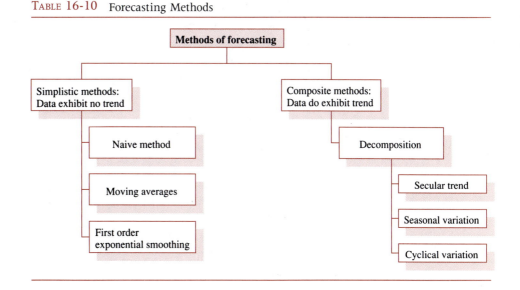

16.6 · SOLVED PROBLEMS

1. **A Smooth Rhodes**

   a. Ralph Rhodes wishes to use smoothing techniques to average out and forecast levels of capital investments his firm has made over the past several years. Both three-year and four-year moving averages are calculated. The four-year MA, since it contains an even number of terms, must subsequently be centered.

Year	Investment ($1,000) (Y)	Three-Term MA	Four-Term MA	Centered Four-Term MA
1985	73.2			
1986	68.1	71.37		
			72.50	
1987	72.8	72.27		72.33
			72.15	
1988	75.9	73.50		72.30
			72.45	
1989	71.8	72.33		71.85
			71.25	
1990	69.3	69.70		70.20
			69.15	
1991	68.0	68.27		68.91
			68.68	
1992	67.5	68.47		69.16
			69.65	
1993	69.9	70.20		70.56
			71.48	
1994	73.2	72.80		72.15
			72.83	
1995	75.3	73.80		
1996	72.9			

Using the three-term MA, 73.8 is the estimate of the long-run average around which all observations tend to fall and, as such, is the forecast for any future time period. The four-term MA produces an estimate of 72.15.

   b. Ralph also decides to forecast using exponential smoothing. Smoothing constants of $\alpha = 0.2$ and $\alpha = 0.7$ are employed. What forecasts for 1997 would Ralph get, and which is probably more accurate?

   If $\alpha = 0.2$,

$$F_{t+1} = \alpha A_t + (1 - \alpha)F_t$$

$$F_{1986} = (0.2)(73.2) + (0.8)(73.2)$$

$$= 73.2$$

$$F_{1987} = (0.2)(68.1) + (0.8)(73.2)$$

$$= 73.18$$

$$F_{1997} = (0.2)(72.9) + (0.8)(71.82)$$

$$= 72.04$$

If $\alpha = 0.7$,

$$F_{1986} = (0.7)(73.2) + (0.3)(73.2)$$
$$= 73.2$$

$$F_{1987} = (0.7)(68.1) + (0.3)(73.2)$$
$$= 69.63$$

$$F_{1988} = (0.7)(72.8) + (0.3)(69.63)$$
$$= 71.85$$

$$F_{1997} = (0.7)(72.9) + (0.3)(74.32)$$
$$= 73.33$$

Year	Actual Investment	Forecast ($\alpha = 0.2$)	Error	Forecast ($\alpha = 0.7$)	Error
1985	73.2				
1986	68.1	73.2	5.10	73.2	5.10
1987	72.8	72.18	−0.62	69.63	−3.17
1988	75.9	72.30	−3.60	71.85	4.05
1989	71.8	73.02	1.22	74.68	2.88
1990	69.3	72.78	3.48	72.67	3.37
1991	68.0	72.08	4.08	70.31	2.31
1992	67.5	71.27	3.77	68.69	1.19
1993	69.9	70.51	0.61	67.86	−2.04
1994	73.2	70.39	−2.81	69.29	−3.91
1995	75.3	70.95	−4.35	72.03	−3.27
1996	72.9	71.82	−1.08	74.32	1.42
1997		72.04		73.33	

The more accurate, reliable forecast would be the one producing the smaller *MSE*. For $\alpha = 0.2$,

$$MSE = \frac{\Sigma(F_t - A_t)^2}{n - 1}$$

$$= \frac{(5.10)^2 + (-0.62)^2 + \cdots + (-1.08)^2}{12 - 1}$$

$$= 10.20$$

For $\alpha = 0.7$,

$$MSE = \frac{(5.10)^2 + (-3.17)^2 + \cdots + (1.42)^2}{12 - 1}$$

$$= 10.10$$

The forecast values using $\alpha = 0.7$ appear more accurate on the average.

2. **A Dark Rainbow** For the past several years, business conditions for Rainbow Enterprises have been rather bleak. The CEO has collected quarterly totals of the number of employees who have been laid off over the past four years.

   a. The CEO would like to forecast the number of layoffs for the first and second quarters of 1995, using linear trend analysis.

Time	Layoffs (Y)	$t(X)$	XY	X^2
1991-I	25	1	25	1
II	27	2	54	4
III	32	3	96	9
IV	29	4	116	16
1992-I	28	5	140	25
II	32	6	192	36
III	34	7	238	49
IV	38	8	304	64
1993-I	35	9	315	81
II	37	10	370	100
III	37	11	407	121
IV	39	12	468	144
1994-I	38	13	494	169
II	42	14	588	196
III	44	15	660	225
IV	45	16	720	256
	562	136	5,187	1,496

$$SSx = \Sigma X^2 - \frac{(\Sigma X)^2}{n}$$

$$= 1,496 - \frac{(136)^2}{16}$$

$$= 340$$

$$SSxy = \Sigma XY - \frac{(\Sigma X)(\Sigma Y)}{n}$$

$$= 5,187 - \frac{(136)(562)}{16}$$

$$= 410$$

$$b_1 = \frac{410}{340}$$

$$= 1.206$$

$$b_0 = \overline{Y} - b_1 \overline{X}$$

$$= 35.13 - 1.206(8.5)$$

$$= 24.88$$

For the first quarter of 1995,

$$\hat{Y}_t = 24.88 + 1.206(17)$$

$$= 45.38$$

For the second quarter of 1995,

$$\hat{Y}_t = 24.88 + 1.206(18)$$

$$= 46.59$$

b. The CEO now wants to develop the seasonal indexes for the number of layoffs.

Time	Layoffs	Centered MA	Ratio to MA
1991-I	25		
II	27		
III	32	28.625	1.1179
IV	29	29.625	0.9789
1992-I	28	30.500	0.9180
II	32	31.875	1.0039
III	34	33.875	1.0037
IV	38	35.375	1.0742
1993-I	35	36.375	0.9622
II	37	36.875	1.0034
III	37	37.375	0.9900
IV	39	38.375	1.0163
1994-I	38	39.875	0.9530
II	42	41.500	1.0120
III	44		
IV	45		

The four-term (since quarterly data are used) MA is calculated and centered, followed by the ratio to MA. The mean ratio to MA is then determined for each quarter. Since the means sum to 4.0111, the normalization ratio is 4/4.0111 = 0.997. The seasonal indexes are obtained by multiplying each mean ratio to MA by 0.997.

	1991	1992	1993	1994	Mean	Seasonal Indexes
I		0.9180	0.9622	0.9530	0.9444	0.9416
II		1.0039	1.0034	1.0120	1.0064	1.0034
III	1.1179	1.0037	0.9900		1.0372	1.0341
IV	0.9789	1.0742	1.0163		1.0231	1.0200
					4.0111	3.9991 = 4

c. The CEO for Rainbow wants to determine layoffs if the seasonal factors are eliminated. Deseasonalized levels of layoffs for 1991-I and 1991-II are, respectively,

$$\frac{25}{0.9416} = 26.55 \text{ employees}$$

and

$$\frac{27}{1.0034} = 26.91 \text{ employees}$$

d. Rainbow executives think that general movements in the business cycle influence their need to lay off employees. They decide to calculate the cyclical components for each time period.

(1) Time Period	(2) Layoffs	(3) Trend Projection	(4) Seasonal Index	(5) Statistical Norm	(6) Cyclical- Irregular	Cyclical Component
1991-I	25	26.08	0.9416	24.56	101.80	
-II	27	27.29	1.0034	27.38	98.61	
-III	32	28.49	1.0341	29.46	108.62	100.5
-IV	29	29.70	1.0200	30.29	95.73	99.61
1992-I	28	30.90	0.9416	29.10	96.24	98.73
-II	32	32.11	1.0034	32.22	99.32	99.01
-III	34	33.32	1.0341	34.46	98.68	101.51
-IV	38	34.52	1.0200	35.21	107.92	102.55
1993-I	35	35.73	0.9416	33.64	104.03	102.01
-II	37	36.93	1.0034	37.06	99.85	100.06
-III	37	38.14	1.0341	39.44	93.81	98.15
-IV	39	39.35	1.0200	40.14	97.17	97.64
1994-I	38	40.55	0.9416	38.18	99.52	98.34
-II	42	41.76	1.0034	41.90	100.23	99.33
-III	44	42.96	1.0341	44.42	99.04	
-IV	45	44.17	1.0200	45.05	99.88	

A four-term MA is taken of the cyclical-irregular values to produce just the cyclical component in column (7). For 1991-III, the layoff of 32 employees represents 100.5 percent of the trend.

e. If layoffs in 1995-I are 46, what might Rainbow expect total layoffs for 1995 to be? Since the first quarter typically represents a period in which layoffs are only 94.16 percent of the average for the full year, quarterly layoffs based on 46 for 1995-I would be

$$\frac{46}{0.9416} = 48.85$$

For the whole year, layoffs would total (48.85)(4) = 195 employees.

f. In a final effort to control the number of necessary layoffs, Rainbow wishes to obtain deseasonalized figures for each time period. These are obtained by dividing the actual number of layoffs by the appropriate seasonal (quarterly) index. A partial listing of the results are shown.

Year-Quarter	Layoffs	Seasonal Index	Deseasonalized Layoffs
1991-I	25	0.9416	26.55
II	27	1.0034	26.91
III	32	1.0341	30.94
IV	29	1.0200	28.43
1992-I	28	0.9416	29.74

The deseasonalized values represent the number of layoffs when seasonal forces have been eliminated.

16.7 WHAT YOU SHOULD HAVE LEARNED FROM THIS CHAPTER

This chapter has provided a fundamental look at time series and the manner in which they can be used to forecast future values. It has illustrated how to identify and define the four components of a time series. It has also provided the skills to determine a moving average, as well as to forecast using exponential smoothing.

The practice and purpose of decomposition as it relates to times series should also be familiar. The manner in which time-series data can be manipulated to gain the information necessary to make business decisions should be apparent.

LIST OF FORMULAS

$$F_{t+1} = \alpha A_t + (1 - \alpha)F_t \qquad (16.1)$$

Forecasts value in a time series for the next time period using exponential smoothing.

$$MSE = \frac{\Sigma(F_t - A_t)^2}{n - 1} \qquad (16.2)$$

Calculates mean square error.

$$\hat{Y}_t = b_0 + b_1 t \qquad (16.3)$$

Estimates trend line.

$$SSx = \Sigma X^2 - \frac{(\Sigma X)^2}{n} \qquad (16.4)$$

The sums of squares for X used to compute the trend line.

$$SSxy = \Sigma XY - \frac{(\Sigma X)(\Sigma Y)}{n} \qquad (16.5)$$

The sums of the cross-products for X and Y used to compute the trend line.

$$b_1 - \frac{SSxy}{SSx} \qquad (16.6)$$

Computes slope of trend line.

$$b_0 = \overline{Y} - b_1\overline{X} \qquad (16.7)$$

Computes intercept of trend line.

CHAPTER EXERCISES

YOU MAKE THE DECISION

1. As a new business manager for Rocky's Bar and Grill, you wish to examine the trend in sales receipts for the last several months. However, receipts behave so erratically that no pattern seems evident. How might you manipulate these data so as to detect a pattern?
2. Given the conditions in the previous problem, if you were to engage in exponential smoothing, should you use a small value for α or a large value? Explain.
3. Sales at Acme, Inc., are thought to fluctuate around a long-term mean. Sometimes they exceed that mean; at other times sales are below that long-run average. What is the best method of forecasting those sales?

CONCEPTUAL QUESTIONS

4. Define: Secular trend
   Cyclical variations
   Irregular variations
   Seasonal variations
5. Which components of a time series are represented by a 12-month (or four-quarter) moving average?
6. How can you best remove the T and C components from a time series?
7. The seasonal index in January for a particular series is greater than 1. Will the seasonally adjusted value be greater than or less than the original value? Explain.
8. What does it mean to say that the seasonal index is greater than 1? less than 1?
9. What components of a time series are contained in the ratio to moving average?

PROBLEMS

10. Cars-R-US has recorded sales (in $1,000s) over the last three years of

Month	1991	1992	1993
Jan	17.2	18.1	16.3
Feb	18.7	19.2	17.3
March	19.7	20.3	18.5
April	20.2	21.5	20.3
May	21.7	22.0	21.0
June	23.1	24.7	25.0
July	24.2	23.9	22.7

Aug	25.7	26.2	25.0
Sept	21.2	22.0	21.9
Oct	19.3	18.0	17.3
Nov	22.7	19.7	21.2
Dec	19.3	17.3	16.2

a. Plot the data. Does there appear to be any trend in the data? any cyclical or seasonal variation?

b. Compute a 12-month moving average. Which component(s) do these values reflect?

11. Calculate the seasonal indexes for each month using the data for Cars-R-Us from the previous problem.

12. In Problem 10 what are the seasonally adjusted sales figures for the last six months of 1993? How do you interpret them?

13. In Problem 10 what are the deseasonalized values for the last six months of 1993? How would you interpret them?

14. In the winter of 1989–90, prices for home heating oil increased by the amounts shown. Use linear trend analysis to predict prices in March 1990. Interpret the results. How well does the model explain prices?

Month	Price
1989 Sept	$0.80
Oct	0.87
Nov	0.83
Dec	0.92
1990 Jan	1.05
Feb	1.10

15. Inventories for Bake-O-Donuts for the past two years were

Month	1990	1991
Jan	$ 87	$ 95
Feb	93	102
March	102	112
April	112	115
May	93	99
June	82	90
July	80	83
Aug	73	79
Sept	93	84
Oct	102	89
Nov	115	92
Dec	112	91

a. Use a 12-period moving average to remove seasonal variations.

b. Calculate the seasonal indexes.

c. What are the seasonally adjusted inventory levels?

16. A 1989 issue of *Business Week* reported that price/earnings ratios for Standard and Poor's 500 were as recorded here:

Year	P/E
1985	11
1986	16
1987	19
1988	14
1989	13
1990	15

a. Develop a two-period (year) moving average.

b. Forecast the price/earnings ratio for 1991.

c. Forecast the ratio for 1991 using exponential smoothing. Set α equal to 0.2 and then to 0.9. Which α-value produces the more accurate forecast?

17. According to *Business Week*, Taiwan's market share of the world's microchip industry on a quarterly basis has been as shown here in percentages:

	1989	1990	1991
I	1.1	1.4	2.5
II	1.3	1.8	2.8
III	1.6	2.1	3.1
IV	1.5	2.6	3.1

a. Use a four-period moving average to remove seasonal variations. Calculate the seasonal indexes.

b. Compute the deseasonalized market shares.

18. *Fortune* reported Dynatech's quarterly profits (in millions of dollars) as shown here.

	1989	1990	1991
I	4.2	5.9	6.5
II	3.8	5.2	7.0
III	4.9	6.3	7.5
IV	5.8	6.8	8.0

a. Graph the data. Does a cyclical component appear? Does a trend appear?

b. The CEO for Dynatech wants to achieve profits of 10.5 by the fourth quarter of 1992. Use trend analysis to determine if the goal might be reached.

c. Compute the seasonal indexes for all four quarters and the deseasonalized values.

19. Using the data from the previous problem, isolate the cyclical component.

20. Mopeds, Inc., is concerned about slumping sales. If monthly sales fall below $9,000 the Northeast regional office must be closed down. According to the figures shown here, is that likely to occur within the next five months? Figures are in thousands.

1990

J	F	M	A	M	J	J	A	S	O	N	D
18	17.3	16.9	18.1	16.8	16.3	15.1	14.5	14	14.5	14	13.1

1991

J	F	M	A	M	J	J	A	S	O	N	D
13.9	13.1	12.8	12.4	11.8	11.9	11.7	11.5	11.1	11.2	11.2	11.1

21. Using the data from the previous problem, calculate the seasonal indexes.
22. Using the data for Mopeds, Inc., what is the strength of the relationship between sales and time? Plot the trend line against the actual data.
23. From the regression model you calculated in the problem for Mopeds, Inc., what is the average monthly change in sales?
24. Recorded here are monthly ticket sales in hundreds of dollars for Ronnie's Roller Rink in Houston, Texas.

1990

J	F	M	A	M	J	J	A	S	O	N	D
18.0	18.5	18.9	18.7	18.5	17.5	17	17	18.9	19	19.9	21

1991

J	F	M	A	M	J	J	A	S	O	N	D
20.5	21.5	22	22.5	23	23.5	23	22	21	22	23	24.5

a. Calculate the seasonal (monthly) indexes.
b. Calculate the deseasonalized values.
c. Compute the trend line and forecast sales in May 1992.
25. John Wolf feels that exponential smoothing with an α-value of 0.8 can best forecast September inventories of his medical supply firm. His brother and business partner thinks an α of 0.4 should be used. What is the forecast in each case, and who is correct based on these values for inventories per month?

Inventories	J	F	M	A	M	J	J	A
($100)	41	48	37	32	45	43	49	38

26. CNN News reported that employee thefts have been on the rise. Figures for Livingston Plastics are shown here. Livingston is considering a security system which should reduce thefts to virtually zero by August 1992. The security system will cost approximately $1,500 per month. Basing your decision on potential savings by August 1992, should the security system be implemented?

1991	Thefts ($100)
Jan	
Feb	10.1
March	12.3
April	11.7
May	12.2
June	13.7
July	13.5
Aug	14.1
Sept	14.9
Oct	15.6
Nov	15.1
Dec	16.2
1992	
Jan	16.5
Feb	16.5
March	17.1

27. How well does the linear model in the previous problem describe the trend in employee thefts?
28. An economist for the president's task force on health care claims that costs have risen dramatically, as shown by these data. The projection for the year 2000 is $1,500 billion.

Year	Cost in Billions
1950	$ 13
1960	27
1970	75
1980	248
1990	510

   a. Graph the data. Does it appear a linear model will forecast accurately? If not, what type of logarithmic transformation is necessary?
   b. Develop the trend model and project costs for the year 2000.
29. By about what percentage are health costs increasing each decade according to the previous problem?
30. What is the strength of the relationship between time and health care costs based on the logarithmic model developed in Problem 28?
31. Calculate a linear model using the earlier data for health care costs. How does it compare in its ability to explain costs compared with the logarithmic model? Plot the original data along with the predicted values based on both models. Comment.

32. The chief economist for the U.S. Department of Commerce reported these seasonally adjusted values for the consumption of durable goods for 1989. Values are in billions of dollars.

Durable Goods

J	F	M	A	M	J	J	A	S	O	N	D
129	124	126	131	123	125	122	127	126	125	131	134

a. Calculate the linear trend model. Does it appear to be a good fit based on the r^2-value?
b. Plot the original data and the expected values based on the model. Comment on the results.

33. Three Finger Louie, the town's only butcher, is concerned about the volume of customers' bad debt he must write off as uncollectable each month. Dollar amounts in hundreds are shown here for the past three years.

1991

| 14.1 | 13.7 | 12.1 | 13.1 | 13.5 | 9.1 | 7.2 | 6.1 | 8.7 | 10.1 | 11.8 | 12.2 |

1992

| 15.2 | 14.1 | 13.2 | 13.9 | 14.0 | 9.5 | 7.2 | 6.5 | 9.1 | 11.5 | 12.2 | 13.4 |

1993

| 13.7 | 12.5 | 11.8 | 12.0 | 13.0 | 8.7 | 6.3 | 6.0 | 8.2 | 9.8 | 10.9 | 11.8 |

a. Plot the data. Does a seasonal factor seem to exist? (Consider a "season" to be one month.)
b. Use a 12-period moving average to smooth out the seasonal variation.
c. Calculate seasonal indexes.
d. Deseasonalize the data.
e. Plot the original data and the deseasonalized data.

34. Payroll taxes for ABL, Inc., have shown the progression recorded here in hundreds of dollars.

J	F	M	A	M	J	J	A
20.1	30.15	45.23	67.84	101.76	152.63	228.95	343.43

a. Plot the data.
b. Compute the trend model.
c. How well does the model explain taxes?
d. What are projected taxes in December?

35. What is the instantaneous rate of growth in taxes in the previous problem?

36. Packer Industries is concerned that sales may fall below $100,000 in December. Using these data, in thousands of dollars, what is your projection? Plot the data first.

Jan	Feb	Mar	Apr	May	June	July	Aug
42.7	57.3	68.3	76.8	84	88.1	90	90.1

37. *U.S. News and World Report* stated that projections by the U.S. Department of Commerce for median earnings of full-time workers were

Year	Earnings ($1,000)
1990	24.28
1995	30.26
2000	37.71
2005	47.00
2010	58.56
2015	73.00
2020	90.94
2025	113.33
2030	171.23
2035	176.00
2040	219.33

a. Plot the data.
b. Compute the trend model.
c. What is the projection for the year 2050?

38. How well does the model in the previous problem explain earnings?

39. Starting in July 1992, workers at the local plant unionized. Hourly wages prior to that time are shown here along with the trend in bonuses following unionization. Use trend analysis to determine if wages would be any different in December 1993 had the plant not unionized. Graph the data first.

Time Period	Hourly Wages
1992 Jan	10.12
Feb	10.57
March	11.05
April	11.65
May	12.01
June	12.50
July	16.25
Aug	20.00
Sept	26.50
Oct	34.70
Nov	45.00
Dec	58.10

40. Milles Products recorded the profits in the table.
    a. Use exponential smoothing to forecast future profits. First, set $\alpha = 0.2$, then 0.9.
    b. Which α-value produces a more reliable estimate?
    c. How could you have known this beforehand?

Week	1	2	3	4	5	6	7
Profits ($1,000)	10	25	3	15	2	27	5

41. *Fortune* magazine reported the vacancy rates for office space in Houston as shown here.

	1988	1989	1990
Jan	22.2%	18.8%	17.5%
Feb	21.7	18.3	17.7
March	20.2	18.6	17.1
April	21.5	18.5	17.1
May	20.1	18.0	17.0
June	19.7	18.6	17.3
July	20.5	17.5	17.5
Aug	19.2	17.9	17.4
Sept	19.1	17.8	17.9
Oct	19.1	17.8	17.8
Nov	20.5	17.8	17.1
Dec	19.0	17.5	17.4

    a. Harry uses a three-period moving average to forecast for April 1991. What answer does he get? Is it a good idea to use a moving average technique in this case? Explain.
    b. Deseasonalize the data and calculate the values.
42. *The Journal of Real Estate Appraisal and Economics* reported the rates of return on national real estate investment trusts (REIT) for 1991 to be

Jan	4.2	May	3.9	Sept	4.1
Feb	3.7	June	3.9	Oct	4.0
March	4.5	July	4.0	Nov	3.9
April	4.4	Aug	3.8	Dec	4.0

    a. Forecast January 1992 with a three-period moving average.
    b. Forecast January 1992 using exponential smoothing. Set α at 0.8.

43. Willie Wiener sells hot dogs in Central Park. His quarterly revenues are as shown here in hundred of dollars.

	1989	1990	1991
I	47	59	61
II	52	64	64
III	57	63	69
IV	56	60	72

Develop the trend model for Willie. Forecast his revenue for March of 1992.

44. Using the data from the previous problem, calculate the cyclical component.

CASE APPLICATIONS

45. In 1990, Senator Daniel Moynihan proposed changes in the payroll tax. Shown here are the median earnings of full-time workers, along with the taxes paid under the existing system and those required by the Moynihan plan.

   In considering the relative impact of the two tax systems, congressional committees must examine the level of taxes workers would be required to pay well into the future. Provide the necessary estimates of incomes and taxes, and discuss the relative merits of the two tax systems. Which tax system calls for a higher rate of growth in taxes paid? What is the rate at which income is growing?

   Senator Moynihan's plan would lower payroll tax rates for the next 25 years but boost them substantially after that.

1990	$ 24,280	$ 1,857	$ 1,823	$ 34
1995	30,258	2,315	1,982	333
2000	37,708	2,885	2,470	415
2005	46,991	3,595	3,078	517
2010	58,560	4,480	3,836	644
2015	72,977	5,583	5,583	0
2020	90,943	6,957	7,594	−637
2025	113,331	8,670	10,483	−1,813
2030	141,231	10,804	13,064	−2,260
2035	175,999	13,464	16,280	−2,816
2040	219,327	16,779	20,280	−3,509

Note: Earnings are estimates for an employee working at least 35 hours per week, 50 hours a year with an annual 4.5 percent increase. Under existing law, wages up to a mandated cutoff (or wage base) are now taxed at a rate of 7.65 percent. Estimates are in current, not constant, dollars. *USN&WR*-Basic data: U.S. Dept of Commerce. *USN&WR* estimates.

COMPUTER EXERCISES

1. Access the file TREND. It contains 18 months of data for unemployment rates in the Midwest. Develop the trend model and forecast the unemployment rate for month 20.

2. Access the file SMOOTH. It contains data for monthly revenues of McNeese, Inc., a small manufacturing firm in Chicago. Using a four-period moving average, forecast revenues in the next month. Compare this result to the forecast you get using exponential smoothing, setting α at 0.2 and at 0.9.

CHAPTER SEVENTEEN

INDEX NUMBERS

A PREVIEW OF THINGS TO LOOK FOR

1 The difference between a simple index, a composite index, and a weighted index.

2 How the base period is used in calculating index numbers.

3 The proper interpretation of an index number.

4 How an index number can be used to deflate values and determine real income.

CHAPTER BLUEPRINT

Many uses are found for price indexes in the analysis of business and economic data. Many facts and conditions can be discovered only through the application of index numbers to data bases containing economic variables. This chapter examines the way in which index numbers are used in the analysis of many business problems.

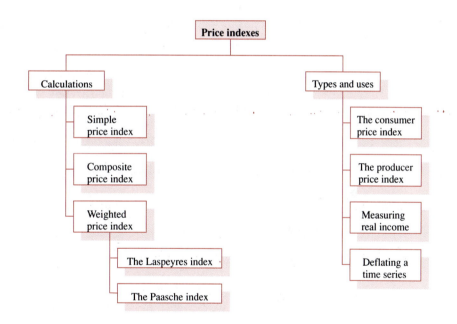

Statistics show that 22% of all females and 68% of all males like the way they look in the nude.

17.1   INTRODUCTION

Business and economic conditions tend to fluctuate widely over time. These vacillations make it difficult to analyze essential business data or to properly interpret economic variables. Comparisons from one time period to the next often become misleading.

The use of index numbers can alleviate many of these problems. Decision makers obtain a more accurate picture of the behavior of economic variables and the relationships which exist among these variables. An index number relates a value in one time period, called the **base period,** to another value in a different time period, called the **reference** (or **current**) **period**. The use of index numbers has become prevalent within our business and economic community over the last several years.

Index numbers are very important to many private business decisions and are crucial in measuring the impact of many government socioeconomic programs. We will investigate different types of indexes and the way in which they relate to business and economic matters. Our analysis of index numbers will be restricted primarily to the prices of commodities.

Our description of the role of index numbers covers

- Simple price index.
- Composite price index.
- Weighted price indexes:
  - The Laspeyres index.
  - The Paasche index.
- Relative indexes.
- How the base period can be changed.
- Specific types of indexes such as the consumer price index (CPI).

17.2   A SIMPLE PRICE INDEX

A **simple price index** characterizes the relationship between the price of a good or service at one point in time, called the *base period,* to the price of that same good or service at a different point in time, called the *reference period*.

> **Simple Price Index**
> The simple price index measures the relative change in the price of a simple good or service from the base period to the reference period.

To calculate a simple index, you merely divide the price of the commodity in the reference period by its price in the base period and multiply by 100. For example, if you wished to determine the price index for the reference period 1990 and chose 1985 as the base period, you would have

$$PI_R = \frac{P_R}{P_B} \times 100 \qquad (17.1)$$

$$PI_{1990} = \frac{P_{1990}}{P_{1985}} \times 100$$

where PI is the price index and P is the price in the respective years.

Jack Nipp and his partner, Harry Tuck, own a meat packing plant in Duluth. Data for their three most popular items are shown in Table 17-1. Nipp tells Tuck to compute a simple price index for each product with 1990 as the base period. Using Formula (17.1), Tuck finds that the price indexes for beef in each of the three years are

$$PI_{1990} = \frac{P_{1990}}{P_{1990}} \times 100 = \frac{3.00}{3.00} \times 100$$

$$= 100$$

$$PI_{1991} = \frac{P_{1991}}{P_{1990}} \times 100 = \frac{3.30}{3.00} \times 100$$

$$= 110$$

$$PI_{1992} = \frac{P_{1992}}{P_{1990}} \times 100 = \frac{4.50}{3.00} \times 100$$

$$= 150$$

TABLE 17-1   Data for Nipp and Tuck, Inc.

		Price/Unit		
Item	**Unit**	**1990**	**1991**	**1992**
Beef	1 pound	3.00	3.30	4.50
Pork	1 pound	2.00	2.20	2.10
Veal	1 pound	4.00	4.50	3.64

From the base year of 1990 to 1991, the price index rose from 100 to 110. Tuck can therefore conclude that the price of beef increased by 10 percent. This is calculated as the difference between the two index numbers divided by the base number.

That is,

$$\frac{PI_{1991} - PI_{1990}}{PI_{1990}} = \frac{110 - 100}{100}$$

$$= 10\%$$

Similarly, it can be concluded that a 50 percent increase occurred from 1990 to 1992:

$$\frac{PI_{1992} - PI_{1990}}{PI_{1990}} = \frac{150 - 100}{100}$$

$$= 50\%$$

You might want to conclude that a 40 percent increase in price occurred from 1991 to 1992 since the price index increased by 40. However, this is *not* the case. The percentage increase from 1991 to 1992 is

$$\frac{PI_{1992} - PI_{1991}}{PI_{1991}} = \frac{150 - 110}{110}$$

$$= 36.4\%$$

The 40 percent difference between the index numbers in 1991 and 1992 is called the *percentage point* increase, not the percentage increase.

Notice that the price index in the base year is always 100. This will always be the case since the price in the base year is, of course, 100 percent of itself.

The indexes for pork and veal are calculated in similar fashion and are shown in Table 17-2. Notice that the 1992 index for veal is less than 100. This reflects the fact that veal prices in 1992 were lower than they were in the base year of 1990. Specifically, prices for veal went down by $100 - 91/100 = 9$ percent from 1990 to 1992.

TABLE 17-2   Price Indexes for Nipp and Tuck, Inc. (1990 = 100)

Item	1990	1991	1992
Beef	$\frac{3.00}{3.00} \times 100 = 100$	$\frac{3.30}{3.00} \times 100 = 110$	$\frac{4.50}{3.00} \times 100 = 150$
Pork	$\frac{2.00}{2.00} \times 100 = 100$	$\frac{2.20}{2.00} \times 100 = 110$	$\frac{2.10}{2.00} \times 100 = 105$
Veal	$\frac{4.00}{4.00} \times 100 = 100$	$\frac{4.50}{4.00} \times 100 = 112$	$\frac{3.64}{4.00} \times 100 = 91$

EXAMPLE 17-1 Price Indexes for Gasoline

Monthly prices for a gallon of gasoline are shown here. Using March as the base period, calculate the price indexes. What was the percentage increase from March to May and from May to June? What is the percentage point increase from May to June?

Jan	Feb	Mar	Apr	May	June	July
1.79	1.82	1.96	2.01	2.10	2.25	2.15

SOLUTION:

Price Indexes (March = 100)

Month	Index	Month	Index
Jan	$\frac{1.79}{1.96}(100) = 91.3$	May	$\frac{2.10}{1.96}(100) = 107.1$
Feb	$\frac{1.82}{1.96}(100) = 92.9$	June	$\frac{2.25}{1.96}(100) = 114.8$
March	$\frac{1.96}{1.96}(100) = 100$	July	$\frac{2.15}{1.96}(100) = 109.7$
April	$\frac{2.01}{1.96}(100) = 102.6$		

The percentage increase from March to May is

$$\frac{107.1 - 100.0}{100.0} = 7.1\%$$

From May to June, the percentage increase is

$$\frac{114.8 - 107.1}{107.1} = 7.2\%$$

and the percentage point increase is $114.8 - 107.1 = 7.7\%$.

STATISTICAL INTERPRETATION:
The base period will always report an index of 100. Periods in which the values are less than the base year will have an index less than 100, and periods with values in excess of that in the base year will have an index above 100.

If more than one time period is used as the base, the average of the values for those periods becomes the base. If Nipp and Tuck were to use the years 1990–1991 as the base period for beef, the base value is ($3.00 + $3.30)/2 = 3.15. The index numbers are then

$$1990 = (3/3.15)(100) = 95.2$$

$$1991 = (3.3/3.15)(100) = 104.8$$

$$1992 = (4.5/3.15)(100) = 142.9$$

17.3 COMPOSITE PRICE INDEXES

Often we want to calculate a price index for several goods. This is called a **composite price index.** Firms that produce two or more products are usually interested in a composite index. So are many government agencies who chart consumer behavior. The U.S. Department of Labor compiles the consumer price index, which measures relative prices for a typical "market basket" of goods and services consumed by the general public.

The composite index is computed by adding the price of the individual commodities in the reference year and dividing by the summation of those prices in the base year. The result is then multiplied by 100.

$$PI_R = \frac{\Sigma P_R}{\Sigma P_B} \times 100 \qquad (17.2)$$

Using the data for Nipp and Tuck, we find that the 1990 composite index for all three products, retaining 1990 as the base period, is

$$PI_{1990} = \frac{3.00 + 2.00 + 4.00}{3.00 + 2.00 + 4.00}(100) = 100.0$$

The index for 1991 is

$$PI_{1991} = \frac{3.30 + 2.20 + 4.50}{3.00 + 2.00 + 4.00}(100) = 111.1$$

And 1992 produces

$$PI_{1992} = \frac{4.50 + 2.10 + 3.64}{3.00 + 2.00 + 4.00}(100) = 113.8$$

This means that in 1992 it would take $113.80 to buy what $100 would buy in 1990.

QUICK CHECK 17.3.1

○○○○

The retail prices for fish and chips for 1985 through 1990 were $3.12, $3.40, $3.90, $3.80, $4.10, and $3.00 for fish, and $0.97, $1.01, $1.45, $1.35, $1.10, and $0.90 for chips. Calculate the index for fish with 1985 as the base, and the composite for both goods with 1985 as the base.

Answer:

	1985	1986	1987	1988	1989	1990
Fish	100	109	125	121.8	131.4	96.2
Composite	100	107.8	130.8	125.9	127.1	95.4

17.4 WEIGHTED COMPOSITED PRICE INDEXES

At least two problems arise with the use of composite price indexes. The first concerns the arbitrary nature in which the units are expressed. Had Nipp and Tuck priced beef at $1.50 per half pound instead of $3.00 per pound, the price index would have been entirely different. Second, the composite indexes as computed do not take into account the fact that some goods sell in larger quantities than do other, less popular, products. No consideration is given to the respective amounts of each product that are sold.

For example, in the composite index calculated for Nipp and Tuck, the same importance, or weight, is given to beef as to pork, even though twice as much of the former may have been purchased by the consumers. It is for these reasons that we may want to compute a **weighted price index.** Such a calculation assigns different weights to individual prices. These weights are established so as to measure the amounts sold of each product. This provides a more accurate reflection of the true cost of the consumer's market basket of goods.

The quantities selected as weights can be taken from the number of units sold in the (1) base period or (2) reference period. Two common indexes are the Laspeyres index and the Paasche index. The Laspeyres index uses quantities sold in the base year as weights; the Paasche index relies on quantities sold in the reference year as weights. Each procedure has its own advantages and disadvantages.

The **Laspeyres index** uses **base period** weights (quantities) in its calculation. The rationale is that these quantities will not change from one calculation to the next, thereby permitting more meaningful comparisons over time.

Laspeyres Index
This weighted composite price index uses quantities sold in the base period as the weight factor.

To illustrate, consider the data for Nipp and Tuck in Table 17-3, which also includes the amounts sold for each product. The Laspeyres index is

$$L = \frac{\Sigma(P_R \times Q_B)}{\Sigma(P_B \times Q_B)} \times 100 \qquad (17.3)$$

where P_R is the price in the reference period, and P_B and Q_B are the price and quantities sold in the period selected as the base period.

The numerator uses Q_B, the quantities of each item in the base year. Computations necessary for the Laspeyres index using 1990 as the base year are shown in Table 17-4. The numerator for L is figured by first multiplying each price by the

TABLE 17-3   Nipp and Tuck, Inc.

Item	Unit	Price/Unit			Quantity Sold (100's lb)		
		1990	1991	1992	1990	1991	1992
Beef	1 pound	3.00	3.30	4.50	250	320	350
Pork	1 pound	2.00	2.20	2.10	150	200	225
Veal	1 pound	4.00	4.50	3.64	80	90	70

TABLE 17-4   The Laspeyres Index for Nipp and Tuck (1990 = 100)

Item	Prices			Quantities in 1990	$P_R \times Q_B$		
	1990	1991	1992		$P_{90}Q_{90}$	$P_{91}Q_{90}$	$P_{92}Q_{90}$
Beef	3.00	3.30	4.50	250	750	825	1,125.0
Pork	2.00	2.20	2.10	150	300	330	315.0
Veal	4.00	4.50	3.64	80	320	360	291.2
					1,370	1,515	1,731.2

quantities sold in the base period of 1990. The denominator is then determined by multiplying the price in the base year by the quantity in the base year. The index for 1990 is

$$L_{1990} = \frac{\Sigma(P_{1990} \times Q_{1990})}{\Sigma(P_{1990} \times Q_{1990})}(100)$$

$$= \frac{1,370}{1,370}(100) = 100$$

The index for 1991 uses the prices in the reference year (1991) and the quantities in the base year (1990) for the numerator:

$$L_{1991} = \frac{\Sigma(P_{1991} \times Q_{1990})}{\Sigma(P_{1990} \times Q_{1990})}(100)$$

$$= \frac{1,515}{1,370}(100)$$

$$= 110.58$$

The numerator for 1992 uses prices in 1992 and quantities in 1990:

$$L_{1992} = \frac{\Sigma(P_{1992} \times Q_{1990})}{\Sigma(P_{1990} \times Q_{1990})}(100)$$

$$= \frac{1,731.2}{1,370}(100)$$

$$= 126.38$$

The interpretation of the Laspeyres index is like that for our earlier indexes. From 1990 to 1992, the price of the market basket for these three meat items increased by 26.38 percent. It would take $126.38 in 1992 to buy what $100 did in 1990. Or, alternatively, it would require $1.26 in 1992 to buy what $1.00 did in 1990.

Notice that the denominator is the same in all three years since the Laspeyres index always uses quantities in the base period.

The **Paasche index,** on the other hand, uses as weights the quantities sold in each of the various reference years. This has the advantage of basing the index on current consumer behavior patterns. As consumers change their buying habits, these changes in consumer tastes are reflected by the index. Commodities which no longer attract consumers' interest, such as buggy whips and top hats, do not receive as much consideration.

> **Paasche Index**
> This weighted composite price index uses quantities sold in the reference period as the weight factor.

Its calculation is a bit more involved than the Laspeyres:

$$P = \frac{\Sigma(P_R \times Q_R)}{\Sigma(P_B \times Q_R)} \times 100 \qquad (17.4)$$

The quantities for the reference years appear in both the numerator and denominator. Table 17-5 provides the computation necessary for the Paasche, using the Nipp and Tuck data with 1990 as the base. We must first multiply prices and quantities for all three years to get $P_R \times Q_R$, which is used in the numerator. We also need the

TABLE 17-5   Paasche Index for Nipp and Tuck (1990 = 100)

	1990		1991		1992	
Item	**P**	**Q**	**P**	**Q**	**P**	**Q**
Beef	3.00	250	3.30	320	4.50	350
Pork	2.00	150	2.20	200	2.10	225
Veal	4.00	80	4.50	90	3.64	70
	$P_{90}Q_{90}$	$P_{91}Q_{91}$	$P_{92}Q_{92}$	$P_{90}Q_{91}$	$P_{90}Q_{92}$	
	750	1,056	1,575.0	960	1,050	
	300	440	472.5	400	450	
	320	405	254.8	360	280	
	1,370	1,901	2,302.3	1,720	1,780	

value for price in the base year, 1990, times the quantity for each reference year to get $P_B \times Q_R$, which is used in the denominator. The Paasche index for 1990 is

$$P_{1990} = \frac{\Sigma(P_{90} \times Q_{90})}{\Sigma(P_{90} \times Q_{90})}(100)$$

$$= \frac{1,370}{1,370}(100) = 100$$

For 1991, it is

$$P_{1991} = \frac{\Sigma(P_{91} \times Q_{91})}{\Sigma(P_{90} \times Q_{91})}(100)$$

$$= \frac{1,901}{1,720}(100) = 110.5$$

For 1992, it is

$$P_{1992} = \frac{\Sigma(P_{92} \times Q_{92})}{\Sigma(P_{90} \times Q_{92})}(100)$$

$$= \frac{2,302.3}{1,780}(100) = 129.3$$

The usual interpretation applies.

The Laspeyres index requires quantity data for only one year and is easier to compute. Therefore, it is used more frequently than the Paasche. Since the base period quantities are always used, more meaningful comparisons over time are permitted.

However, the Laspeyres tends to overweigh goods whose prices increase. This occurs because the increase in price will decrease quantities sold, but the lower quantity will not be reflected by the Laspeyres index because it uses quantities from the base year.

EXAMPLE 17-2 Hair Today

The Dippy Do Hair Salon is considering price adjustments in their services. Harriet Follicle, manager of Dippy Doo, wants to calculate Laspeyres and Paasche indexes, using these data for prices and the number of services rendered. January is taken as the base period.

	Price			Quantity		
	Jan	Feb	Mar	Jan	Feb	Mar
Shampoo	$10	$12.00	$16.50	20	22	25
Trim	8	10.50	9.50	25	20	25
Style	12	13.50	14.00	30	31	33

SOLUTION:

The Laspeyres is based on the following table:

	Price			Quantity in Jan	$P_R \times Q_{Jan}$		
	Jan	Feb	Mar		Jan	Feb	Mar
Shampoo	$10	$12.00	$16.50	20	200	240	330
Trim	8	10.50	9.50	25	200	262.5	237.5
Style	12	13.50	14.00	30	360	405	420
					760	907.5	987.5

$$L_{Jan} = \frac{\Sigma(P_{Jan} \times Q_{Jan})}{\Sigma(P_{Jan} \times Q_{Jan})}(100)$$

$$= \frac{760}{760}(100)$$

$$= 100$$

$$L_{Feb} = \frac{\Sigma(P_{Feb} \times Q_{Jan})}{\Sigma(P_{Jan} \times Q_{Jan})}(100)$$

$$= \frac{907.5}{760}(100)$$

$$= 119.4$$

$$L_{Mar} = \frac{\Sigma(P_{Mar} \times Q_{Jan})}{\Sigma(P_{Jan} \times Q_{Jan})}(100)$$

$$= \frac{987.5}{760}(100)$$

$$= 129.9$$

The Paasche index requires another set of calculations.

	Jan		Feb		Mar	
	P	Q	P	Q	P	Q
Shampoo	10	20	12.00	22	16.50	25
Trim	8	25	10.50	20	9.50	25
Style	12	30	13.50	31	14.00	33

Price × Quantity

$P_{Jan} Q_{Jan}$	$P_{Feb} Q_{Feb}$	$P_{Mar} Q_{Mar}$	$P_{Jan} Q_{Feb}$	$P_{Jan} Q_{Mar}$
200	264	412.5	220	250
200	210	237.5	160	200
360	418.5	462	372	396
760	892.5	1,112	752	846

$$P_{Jan} = \frac{\Sigma(P_{Jan} \times Q_{Jan})}{\Sigma(P_{Jan} \times Q_{Jan})}(100)$$

$$= \frac{760}{760}(100)$$

$$= 100$$

$$P_{Feb} = \frac{\Sigma(P_{Feb} \times Q_{Feb})}{\Sigma(P_{Jan} \times Q_{Feb})}(100)$$

$$= \frac{892.5}{752}(100)$$

$$= 118.7$$

$$P_{Mar} = \frac{\Sigma(P_{Mar} \times Q_{Mar})}{\Sigma(P_{Mar} \times Q_{Mar})}(100)$$

$$= \frac{1,112}{846}(100)$$

$$= 131.4$$

STATISTICAL INTERPRETATION:

The two indexes produce different results. They are based on different weighting systems. However, it is clear that an increase in prices by Dippy Doo is unwise. Prices have risen by 29.9 percent according to the Laspeyres index in only three months.

As noted, the Laspeyres tends to overweigh goods whose prices rise, because this price increase is accompanied by a reduction in quantity which is not reflected in the Laspeyres, since it uses fixed-base quantities as the weight. The Paasche, on the other hand, tends to overweigh goods whose prices go down. In an effort to offset these shortcomings, **Fisher's ideal index** is sometimes suggested. This index combines the Laspeyres and the Paasche by finding the square root of their product:

$$F = \sqrt{L \times P}$$

The interpretation of the Fisher index is, however, subject to some dispute. For this reason, it is not widely used.

17.5   AVERAGE OF RELATIVES METHOD

Another type of composite index is the **average of relatives index.** As the name suggests, this index finds the average of several relative indexes. Formula (17.5) illustrates. The price of each good in a given reference period is divided by its price in the base period and multiplied by 100. The results are summed and averaged over the number of goods N.

$$AR = \frac{\Sigma[(P_R/P_B)(100)]}{N} \qquad (17.5)$$

Consider again the data for Nipp and Tuck. With 1990 as the base period, the average of relatives index for 1991 is found by dividing the price of each good in the reference year, 1991, by its price in the base year and multiplying by 100. This is done for all three goods. The results are added and divided by 3 to get the average. Thus, the average of relatives index for 1991 is

For beef: $\dfrac{P_{91}}{P_{90}}(100) = \dfrac{3.30}{3.00}(100) = 110$

For pork: $\dfrac{P_{91}}{P_{90}}(100) = \dfrac{2.20}{2.00}(100) = 110$

For veal: $\dfrac{P_{91}}{P_{90}}(100) = \dfrac{4.50}{4.00}(100) = 112.5$

Then

$$AR_{91} = \frac{110 + 110 + 112.5}{3} = 110.83$$

Table 17.6 shows the full set of computations.

TABLE 17-6   The Average of Relatives Index for Nipp and Tuck (1990 = 100)

	1990	1991	1992
Beef	$\dfrac{3.00}{3.00}(100) = 100$	$\dfrac{3.30}{3.00}(100) = 110.0$	$\dfrac{4.50}{3.00}(100) = 150.00$
Pork	$\dfrac{2.00}{2.00}(100) = 100$	$\dfrac{2.20}{2.00}(100) = 110.0$	$\dfrac{2.10}{2.00}(100) = 105.00$
Veal	$\dfrac{4.00}{4.00}(100) = 100$	$\dfrac{4.50}{4.00}(100) = 112.5$	$\dfrac{3.64}{4.00}(100) = 91.00$
	300	332.5	346.00
÷ 3			
AR	100	110.8	115.3

On the average, prices rose by 10.8 percent from 1990 to 1991 and by 15.3 percent from 1990 to 1992. What $100 would buy in 1990 would cost $115.30 in 1992.

An obvious drawback of this method is its failure to account for weights. Although in 1990, consumers bought more beef than either of the other two products, the price of beef is given the same importance as the prices of pork and veal in calculating the index.

This deficiency is corrected by calculating a **weighted average of relatives index,** which accounts for different quantities. This is precisely what the Laspeyres and Paasche indexes do. That is, the Laspeyres and Paasche indexes are weighted average of relatives indexes.

17.6   SELECTION OF THE BASE PERIOD

Choosing an appropriate base period is critical. You must use a time period that is "representative" of the prevailing economic life-style. However, determining what is representative is quite subjective and often difficult. Time periods containing wars or major depressions should obviously be avoided.

There often arises the need to change the base period. In order to modernize the index or better reflect current trends and conditions, it may become desirable to shift the base to a different time period. This is accomplished by dividing the existing index numbers by the index number in the new base period and multiplying by 100. Table 17-7 shifts the base period from 1983 to 1985. Each of the index numbers based on 1983 are divided by 118, the index number of 1985. This produces the index numbers with 1985 as the base period.

TABLE 17-7   Shifting the Base from 1980 to 1985

Year	Index (1983 = 100)	Index (1985 = 100)
1981	89	$(89/118)(100)$ = 75
1982	95	$(95/118)(100)$ = 81
1983	100	$(100/118)(100)$ = 85
1984	110	$(110/118)(100)$ = 93
1985	118	$(118/118)(100)$ = 100
1986	121	$(121/118)(100)$ = 103
1987	125	$(125/118)(100)$ = 106
1988	131	$(131/118)(100)$ = 111
1989	132	$(132/118)(100)$ = 112
1990	138	$(138/118)(100)$ = 117

If two indexes with different base periods are to be compared, it is advisable to shift the base period of one index to that of the other index. Comparisons are thereby more meaningful.

Furthermore, it frequently becomes necessary to combine two indexes with different base periods. This is particularly true if, in conducting a study, we find that our time frame includes the period in which the series was rebased. We must then **splice** the two series together.

Notice from Table 17-8 that the index for producer prices is given for years 1984 to 1987 with 1975 = 100, and for 1987 to 1990 with the base of 1979 = 100.

TABLE 17-8   Splicing Indexes for Producer Prices

Year	Index (1975 = 100)	Index (1979 = 100)	Spliced Index (1979 = 100)
1984	142		98.19
1985	147		101.65
1986	153		105.80
1987	162	112	112.00
1988		114	114.00
1989		121	121.00
1990		130	130.00

In order to splice, you must have at least one time period (1987 in this case) in which the index number is given for both series. Splicing is accomplished by starting at 1986 and working backwards (1985, 1984, etc.). The spliced value for 1986 is found by dividing the 1986 value by the 1987 value in the 1975 series, and multiplying by the 1987 value in the 1979 series.

That is,

$$\frac{153}{162}(112) = 105.8$$

The 105.8 is the first value we find for the spliced series. The spliced value for 1985 is found similarly to be

$$\frac{147}{153}(105.8) = 101.65$$

The value for 1984 is

$$\frac{142}{147}(101.65) = 98.19$$

17.7   SPECIFIC TYPES OF INDEXES

Numerous governmental agencies as well as the Federal Reserve System (which is not part of the federal government) and private businesses compile different indexes for a variety of purposes. The use to which a specific index may be put depends on who is compiling it and what factors go into its formulation. Perhaps the best-known index series is the **consumer price index.**

A.   CONSUMER PRICE INDEX

The consumer price index (CPI) is reported monthly by the Bureau of Labor Statistics (BLS) of the U.S. Department of Labor. It was first reported in 1914 as a means to determine if the wages of industrial workers were keeping pace with the inflation pressures brought on by World War I. Prior to 1978, there was only one CPI. This traditional measure reflected changes in prices of a fixed market basket of about 400 goods and services commonly purchased by "typical" urban and clerical workers. It encompassed about 40 percent of the nation's total population.

In January 1978, the BLS began reporting a more comprehensive index, the consumer price index for all urban consumers. It is called CPI-U, and the older index was designated CPI-W. The newer CPI-U covers about 80 percent of the population and includes around 3,000 consumer products ranging from basic necessities, such as food, clothing, and housing, to allowances for educational and entertainment expenses. In 1988 both CPI series were rebased from 1967 to 1982–1984.

Both the CPI-W and the CPI-U employ a weighting system for the types of goods and services purchased by consumers. Food, for example, is assigned a weight, or measure of relative importance, of about 18, while housing is given a weight of about 43. Medical care and entertainment each receive a weight of 5. The total weights for all commodities sum to 100. The weights on these products are adjusted about every 10 years. In this manner, the CPI-W and the CPI-U are similar to the Laspeyres index. Technically, the CPI differs slightly from a true Laspeyres because the weighting system used by the CPI is not revised at the same time that the index is rebased. The CPI is therefore sometimes referred to as a *fixed-weight aggregate price index*.

The CPI is highly useful in gauging inflation, measuring "real" changes in monetary values by removing the impact of price changes, and, to a limited extent, serving as a cost-of-living index. It is even instrumental in determining raises in Social Security benefits and negotiated wage settlements in labor contracts. Its many uses will be more fully examined in the next section.

B.   OTHER INDEXES

The **producer price index** (formerly, the wholesale price index) is also published monthly by the BLS. It measures changes in the prices of goods in primary markets for raw materials used in manufacturing. It, too, is similar to the Laspeyres index and covers almost 3,000 producer goods.

The **industrial production index** is reported by the Federal Reserve System. It is not a monetary measurement, but tracks changes in the volume of industrial output in the nation. The base period is currently 1977.

There are numerous stock market indexes. Perhaps the most well known is the **Dow-Jones industrial average.** This index covers 30 selected industrial stocks to represent the almost 1,800 stocks traded in the New York Stock Exchange. **Standard and Poor's composite index** of 500 industrial stocks is also highly watched.

17.8   USES FOR THE CPI

Movements in the CPI have a major impact on many business conditions and economic considerations. As noted, the CPI is often viewed as a measure of inflation in the economy. Annual rates of inflation are measured by the percentage change in the CPI from one year to the next. The inflation rate from year to year is

$$\frac{\text{CPI}_t - \text{CPI}_{t-1}}{\text{CPI}_{t-1}} \times 100$$

where CPI_t is the CPI in time period t, and CPI_{t-1} is the CPI in the previous time period.

Table 17-9 shows the CPI for 1986 to 1989 using 1982–1984 as the base. The figures were taken from the *Federal Reserve Bulletin,* published monthly by the Board of Governors of the Federal Reserve System. The inflation rate for 1987, for example, is

$$\frac{113.6 - 109.6}{109.6}(100) = 3.6\%$$

TABLE 17-9   CPI and Inflation Rates for Selected Years

Year	CPI	Inflation Rate (%)
1986	109.6	
1987	113.6	3.6
1988	118.3	4.1
1989	124.3	5.1
1990	127.2	2.3

Changes in the CPI are also often taken as a measure of the cost of living. It is argued, however, that such a practice is questionable. The CPI does not reflect certain costs or expenditures such as taxes, nor does it account for changes in the quality of goods available. Further, the CPI fails to measure other valued items in our economic structure, such as increased leisure time by the average worker or improvements in the variety of commodities from which consumers can choose. Nevertheless, the CPI is often cited in the popular press as a measure of the cost of living.

The CPI is often the basis for adjustments in wage rates, Social Security payments, and even rental and lease agreements. Many labor contracts contain cost-of-living adjustments (COLAs) which stipulate that an increase in the CPI of an agreed-upon amount will automatically trigger a rise in the workers' wage levels.

The CPI can also be used to **deflate** a time series. Deflating a series removes the effect of price changes and expresses the series in *constant* dollars. Economists often distinguish between nominal (or current) dollars and real (or constant) dollars.

Regarding a recent labor dispute over pay levels, an article in *The Wall Street Journal* illustrated how price indexes can be used to adjust wages. A local chapter of the United Mine Workers had agreed to a specific wage increase, but the miners were still concerned that inflation might erode their hard-earned wage gains. They refused to enter the mines until some assurance was provided that their incomes would be protected from rising prices.

It was finally agreed that wages would be increased by 1 percent for every 3 percent increase in the CPI. This was in addition to other wage increases labor had already gained.

If a time series, such as your annual income over several years, is expressed in terms of 1982 dollars, that income is said to be real income. Assume your money (nominal) income was as shown in Table 17-10. In 1986, for example, you actually earned $42,110. It would seem that you are doing quite well financially. Your income increased from $42,100 to $53,300 over that time period. However, prices have been going up also. To obtain a measure of how much your income has really increased, in real terms, you must deflate your income stream. This is done by dividing your money income by the CPI and multiplying by 100. The result is your real income expressed in constant (real) dollars of a given base year.

TABLE 17-10   Money and Real Incomes for Selected Years

Year	Money Income	CPI (1982–84 = 100)	Real Income	Purchasing Power of a Dollar
1986	$42,110	109.6	$38,421	0.91
1987	46,000	113.6	40,493	0.88
1988	49,800	118.3	42,096	0.85
1989	53,500	124.3	43,041	0.80

Real Income
Real income is the purchasing power of your money income.

$$\text{Real income} = \frac{\text{Money income}}{\text{CPI}} \times 100$$

You earned $42,110 in 1986, but it was worth only $38,421 in 1982–84 prices. That is, keeping prices constant at the 1982–84 level, you are earning an equivalent of only $38,421. Your constant (real) income based on 1982–84 price levels is $38,421. The difference between $42,110 and $38,421 was consumed by rising prices from

○○○○   DECISION MAKING THROUGH PROBLEM SOLVING   ○○○○
ILLUSTRATION 17-2

The local newspaper in Huntington, West Virginia, carried a story about a water company that had requested a rate hike from the state Public Utilities Commission (PUC). The government denied the water company's request for a rate hike, arguing that they had just raised rates to consumers the past year. The water company acknowledged the recent hike in rates, but argued that inflationary pressures made another one mandatory. The company used price indexes to show that the real cost of water had actually gone down when measured against overall inflationary rates. On this basis, the government reversed its earlier decision and granted the water company its request for another rate hike.

1982–84 to 1986. Your money income rose by $53,500 − $42,110 = $11,390, but your real income went up by only $43,041 − $38,421 = $4,620. If prices had gone up faster than your money income, your real income would have actually decreased.

The purchasing power of your dollar is found to be 100/CPI. For 1986, we have 100/109.6 = 0.91. This means that $1.00 in 1986 would buy what $0.91 would purchase in 1982–84.

Economists commonly deflate gross national product (GNP) to obtain a measurement of the increase in our nation's real output. **Gross national product** is the monetary value of all final goods and services produced in our economy. By deflating GNP over time, economists eliminate any increase due to price inflation, and arrive at a measure of the actual increase in the production of goods and services available for consumption. Table 17-11 illustrates that real GNP is found by dividing nominal (or current) GNP by the CPI and multiplying by 100.

TABLE 17-11   Nominal and Real GNP (in $ billions)

Year	Nominal GNP	CPI	Real GNP
1986	4,140.3	109.6	3,777.6
1987	4,526.7	113.6	3,984.8
1988	4,864.3	118.3	4,111.8
1989	5,116.8	124.3	4,116.5

Real GNP
Real GNP measures the value of our nation's output in constant dollars in some base period. It omits any fluctuation due to changing prices.

$$\text{Real GNP} = \frac{\text{Nominal GNP}}{\text{CPI}} \times 100$$

○○○○   **DECISION MAKING THROUGH PROBLEM SOLVING**   ○○○○
ILLUSTRATION 17-3

According to *Business Week,* Eastman Kodak Company was experiencing a problem maintaining accurate records on the amount of exports they sold to European and Eastern markets. Persistent fluctuations in prices and exchange rates made comparisons over time almost meaningless. It was impossible to determine if movements in export levels were due to a change in the actual volume of business or simply a result of instability in the financial world. This inability to gain a full appreciation of their international market made planning and decision making quite tenuous.

It was finally decided to index export levels, using prices and exchange rates in a selected base period. In this manner, it was possible for Kodak to get a more realistic picture of their true market position.

Values for CPI-U taken from the *Handbook of Labor Statistics* are shown in Table 17-12.

TABLE 17-12   CPI for Selected Years

Year	CPI	Year	CPI	Year	CPI
1975	53.8	1980	82.4	1985	107.6
1976	56.9	1981	90.9	1986	109.6
1977	60.6	1982	96.5	1987	113.6
1978	65.2	1983	99.6	1988	118.3
1979	72.6	1984	103.9	1989	123.5
				1990	127.2

17.9   SOLVED PROBLEMS

1. **Stock Price Indexes** As an economic analyst for your firm, you must examine the behavior of the price of your stock sold on the New York Stock Exchange. The average daily prices for each month are shown for the common stock and the preferred stock of your firm.

Month	Common Stock Price	Preferred Stock Price
January	5.12	10.15
February	6.14	11.12
March	7.52	12.11
April	7.22	15.01
May	8.15	14.12
June	8.90	15.17
July	8.70	15.90

a. Develop a simple price index for each stock, with March as the base period.

Month	Common Stock Index	Preferred Stock Index
January	68.1	83.8
February	81.6	91.8
March	100.0	100.0
April	96.0	123.9
May	108.4	116.6
June	118.4	125.3
July	115.7	131.3

b. Develop a composite index for both stocks (March = 100).

Month	Composite Index
January	77.8
February	87.9
March	100.0
April	113.2
May	113.4
June	122.6
July	125.3

c. Develop a simple price index for the common stock, with March–May as the base. The base value is $(7.52 + 7.22 + 8.15)/3 = 7.63$. Then

Month	Index (March–May = 100)
January	$(5.12/7.63) \times 100 = 67.1$
February	$(6.14/7.63) \times 100 = 80.5$
March	98.6
April	94.6
May	106.8
June	116.6
July	114.0

2. A Gross Report by the President According to the 1991 *Economic Report of the President*, gross national product in billions of current dollars is as shown here. Use the CPI-U to obtain real (or constant) GNP in 1982–84 dollars.

Year	Money GNP	CPI (82–84 = 100)	Real GNP
1985	4,010.3	107.6	3,727.0
1986	4,231.6	109.6	3,860.9
1987	4,524.3	113.6	3,982.7
1988	4,880.6	118.3	4,125.6
1989	5,348	121.3	4,408.9

3. **The Laspeyres and Paasche Indexes** Your firm manufacturers three grades of lubricant. The prices and quantities sold for each are as follows:

Grade	Prices			Quantities		
	Oct	Nov	Dec	Oct	Nov	Dec
A	$3.00	$3.30	$4.50	250	320	350
B	2.00	2.20	2.10	150	200	225
C	4.00	4.50	3.64	80	90	70

a. Calculate the Laspeyres index with October as the base.

$P_{Oct} Q_{Oct}$	$P_{Nov} Q_{Oct}$	$P_{Dec} Q_{Oct}$
750	825	1,125.0
300	330	315.0
320	360	291.2
1,370	1,515	1,731.2

$$L = \frac{\Sigma(P_R \times Q_B)}{\Sigma(P_B \times Q_B)}(100)$$

October:

$$L_{Oct} = \frac{1,370}{1,370}(100) = 100$$

November:

$$L_{Nov} = \frac{1,515}{1,370}(100) = 110.58$$

December:

$$L_{Dec} = \frac{1,731.2}{1,370}(100) = 126.4$$

b. Calculate the Paasche index with October as the base.

$P_{Dec} \times Q_{Oct}$	$P_{Nov} \times Q_{Nov}$	$P_{Dec} \times Q_{Dec}$	$P_{Dec} \times Q_{Nov}$	$P_{Oct} \times Q_{Dec}$
750	1,056	1,575.0	960	1,050
300	440	472.5	400	450
320	405	254.8	360	280
1,370	1,901	2,302.3	1,720	1,780

$$P = \frac{\Sigma(P_R \times Q_R)}{\Sigma(P_B \times Q_R)}(100)$$

October:

$$P_{\text{Oct}} = \frac{1,370}{1,370}(100) = 100$$

November:

$$P_{\text{Nov}} = \frac{1,901}{1,720}(100) = 110.52$$

December:

$$P_{\text{Dec}} = \frac{2,302.3}{1,780}(100) = 129.34$$

17.10 WHAT YOU SHOULD HAVE LEARNED FROM THIS CHAPTER

Index numbers are essential for expressing value in constant terms over time. They permit comparisons among different time periods, which would otherwise be impossible or, at best, meaningless.

In addition, certain price indexes, such as the CPI, permit us to deflate a time series and thereby express values in constant terms which discount the effect of price changes.

LIST OF FORMULAS

$$PI_R = \frac{P_R}{P_B} \times 100 \tag{17.1}$$

Used to calculate a simple index.

$$PI_R = \frac{\Sigma P_R}{\Sigma P_B}(100) \tag{17.2}$$

Used to calculate a composite index.

$$L = \frac{\Sigma(P_R \times Q_B)}{\Sigma(P_B \times Q_B)}(100) \tag{17.3}$$

Used to calculate the Laspeyres index.

$$P = \frac{\Sigma(P_R \times Q_R)}{\Sigma(P_B \times Q_R)}(100) \tag{17.4}$$

Used to calculate the Paasche index.

$$AR = \frac{\Sigma[(P_R/P_B)(100)]}{N} \tag{17.5}$$

Used to calculate the average of relatives index.

CHAPTER EXERCISES

YOU MAKE THE DECISION

1. You have just been hired as a marketing specialist for the Jensu Japanese Knife Company. Your boss wants you to explain how index numbers can be used to aid in marketing decisions. How do you respond? What is an index number? What is the difference between a simple index, a composite index, and a weighted composite index?

2. While developing the index numbers in the previous problem, you are asked to explain the difference between money (current) income and real (constant) income.

3. You have just been promoted to chief accountant for the Doit and Quick Accounting firm in Crab Apple Cove, Maine. Your new job duties require that you deflate a time series. What does it mean to deflate a time series, and what is the purpose in doing so?

4. The local chamber of commerce wants you to explain the relationship between income and changes in prices. Specifically, you must explain the following: If prices were falling, what would happen to real income if money income remained constant, went up, or went down?

5. The chamber of commerce also wants you to answer the following question: "If prices increase more rapidly than money income, what happens to real income?" How would you respond?

6. The statistical analyst for your firm is on maternity leave. The manager of the finance division wants you to develop an index for the firm's sales over the past several years. Under what conditions might you use a Paasche index? a Laspeyres index? What is the difference between them? What are their advantages?

PROBLEMS

7. Mr. Mom has kept this record of his food costs over the past five years:

	1987	1988	1989	1990	1991
Kumquats	$1.15	$1.25	$1.31	$1.29	$1.45
Bean sprouts	0.79	0.63	0.82	0.97	0.99
Guava	2.79	3.10	5.17	4.89	5.20

 a. Develop a simple price index for kumquats, with 1988 as the base.
 b. Determine the composite index with 1988 as the base.
 c. Calculate the average of relative indexes (1988 = 100).

8. Assume Mr. Mom bought the quantities shown:

	1987	1988	1989	1990	1991
Kumquats	40	52	47	0	10
Bean sprouts	20	32	52	50	45
Guava	17	18	23	17	20

 a. Calculate the weighted composite index which uses fixed-base weights (1988 = 100).
 b. Calculate the weighted composite index using weights from the reference period.

9. Based on the Paasche index from the previous problem, what was the percentage increase in prices from
   a. 1988 to 1989?
   b. 1988 to 1990?
   c. 1989 to 1990?

10. In the table are indexes for the CPI for selected years with different bases.
   a. Splice them.
   b. Rebase the spliced series to 1985 = 100.

Year	CPI (1967 = 100)	CPI (1982–84 = 100)
1980	246.8	
1981	272.4	
1982	289.1	
1983	298.4	
1984	311.1	103.9
1985		107.6
1986		109.6
1987		113.6

11. Here are values for GNP in current dollars taken from the *Economic Report of the President*. Use the data in Table 17-12 to find GNP in constant (real) dollars. Interpret the deflated series. (Data are in billions of dollars.)

Year	GNP	Year	GNP	Year	GNP
1975	1,598.4	1980	2,732.0	1985	4,014.9
1976	1,782.8	1981	3,052.6	1986	4,231.6
1977	1,990.5	1982	3,166.0	1987	4,524.3
1978	2,249.7	1983	3,405.7	1988	4,880.6
1979	2,508.2	1984	3,772.2	1989	5,348.2

12. Jamie's money income over the past several years is shown here. His income has risen over $4,000, and he feels good about that. Should he?

Year	Money Income	Year	Money Income
1984	$42,111	1987	$44,670
1985	42,953	1988	45,573
1986	43,815	1989	46,540

13. A COLA provision in a labor contract calls for a 25-cent adjustment in the wage rate if the CPI increases by at least 9 percent from 1987 to 1989. Using the information in Table 17-12, should the adjustment be made?

14. The average weekly wages for employees shown here are taken from the *Monthly Labor Review* published by the Bureau of Labor Statistics of the U.S. Department of Labor.
   a. Does it appear that wages are keeping up with inflation?
   b. What wage level would be necessary to give the workers the same real income in 1987 that they had in 1984? (You will need the data in Table 17-12.)

Year	Median Weekly Earnings in Current Dollars
1984	499
1985	522
1986	543
1987	572

15. A labor agreement states that if annual inflation exceeds 3 percent, wages will increase by an amount equal to the difference between the inflation rate and 3 percent. From 1984 to 1987, how much will wages increase each year? Consult Table 17-12.

16. According to the *Statistical Abstract of the United States,* monthly salaries for new accounting graduates were as follows:

1985	1,697
1986	1,789
1987	1,812
1988	2,010
1989	2,215

   a. What are the salaries in real terms?
   b. Interpret the value in part (a).

17. What salary was necessary in 1989 to ensure the same real income as in 1985?

18. How much is $1 worth in 1987 in terms of 1982–84 values? Consult Table 17-12.

19. A recent college graduate is offered a job at a starting salary of $1,912 per month in New York, and another job at $1,792 per month in Kansas City. She consults the *Monthly Labor Review* and finds costs-of-living indexes for each city to be 126.5 for New York and 114.2 for Kansas City. Where would she be better off financially?

20. Your real income in 1985 was $30,112 in 1982–84 dollars, and in 1989 it was $45,010 in 1982–84 dollars. By how much did your money income increase from 1985 to 1989?

21. You purchased a home in 1985 at $80,000. It is now 1990 and you wish to sell the home, but are puzzled as to the asking price. You find in the *Statistical Abstract of the United States* that the construction cost index was 108.4 (1982 = 100) for 1985 and 119.2 in 1990. How might that help in setting a price?

22. Pam McGuire, the director of operations for Columbia Records, compiled the following data on recording costs and the number of times each item was used over the last three years for three items commonly used in the recording business.

	Cost per Usage			Usage Frequency		
	1989	**1990**	**1991**	**1989**	**1990**	**1991**
Studio costs	$120	$145	$165	30	35	37
Recording equipment	420	530	620	40	43	46
Backup singers	300	250	200	50	63	72

Sam O'Donnell, the director of statistical procedures, must calculate a Laspeyres index and a Paasche index, using 1989 as the base, and then determine the rate at which costs have risen each year under both indexes, as well as the rate of inflation over all three years.

23. From Problem 22, which index is probably a better measure of Columbia's rise in costs? Why? Support your choice.

24. Indexed living costs shown here were taken from the *Monthly Labor Review.* What are the average of relatives indexes for all three years? (1982 = 100)

Region	**1989**	**1990**	**1991**
East	126.1	132.8	139.7
South	117.3	121.2	124.6
Midwest	112.7	119.3	121.2
West	119.2	123.4	125.2

25. From the data in Problem 24, which region has the lowest average of relatives index over the three-year period?

26. In 1989, Bob's starting salary was $28,800. In 1984, Bob's sister, Martha, earned a starting salary of $25,000. Bob belittled his sister's low starting salary. What might Martha's response be?

27. The federal government's 1990 fiscal expenditure on national defense was $296.3 billion. President Bush budgeted $303.3 billion for 1991, and thereby caused a protest from those who objected to the increase. Based on a 1991 projected CPI of 131.2, the president's advisors argued that defense spending decreased. How is this so?

28. Red Wing Enterprises markets sweaters of wool, cotton, and cashmere. Prices and volumes are shown here. Using 1989 as the base year, develop Laspeyres and Paasche indexes.

	Prices			Quantities		
	Wool	**Cotton**	**Cashmere**	**Wool**	**Cotton**	**Cashmere**
1989	45	37	85	14	18	12
1990	52	41	105	18	22	10
1991	54	39	90	22	25	18
1992	56	44	110	25	20	19

29. Just Pizza bought the amounts of ingredients at the prices shown in the table. Janet Jackson, manager of Just Pizza, is worried about rising prices. Develop Laspeyres and Paasche indexes for her, using January as the base.

	Price/Pound				Pounds Used (100's)			
	Jan	**Feb**	**Mar**	**Apr**	**Jan**	**Feb**	**Mar**	**Apr**
Cheese	2.10	2.15	2.20	2.25	10	12	15	12
Pepperoni	1.18	1.20	1.25	1.31	8	10	8	10
Sausage	1.25	1.31	1.35	1.42	7	6	7	7

30. Using Janet's data from the previous problem, does the Paasche index show that the rate at which prices are going up is increasing or decreasing?

31. In a recent issue of *Business Week,* Manuel Johnson, then vice-chairman of the Federal Reserve System, commented on the advisability of maintaining the stock of monetary reserves at a constant real level. The money stock (M1) in 1987 was $742 billion. What level is needed in 1990 to achieve the same real stock of money reserves?

CASE APPLICATIONS

32. Caterpillar, Inc., maintains worldwide sales forces in New York and its headquarters in Peoria, Illinois. Recent personnel changes, coupled with drastic conditions in the agricultural economy in the late 1980s, created significant problems for Caterpillar.

    Competition developed between the New York and Peoria offices to hold down labor costs. It was decided that each office should receive the same money per employee in real terms based on local price indexes.

    In 1989, company records showed that Peoria was to receive, in thousands of dollars, prior to the necessary cutback, 42.7, 42.0, 38.9, and 45.7 during the years 1989–1992. The price indexes for central Illinois during those years were 104.1, 107.2, 107.9, and 110.3. Indexes for New York were 127.1, 131.4, 137.2, and 141.2.

    How much money must Caterpillar allocate for New York each year to ensure both locations got equal labor expenditures measured in real terms?

TECHNIQUES OF QUALITY CONTROL

A PREVIEW OF THINGS TO LOOK FOR

1 The difference between chance variation and assignable cause variation.

2 How control charts can be used to maintain quality.

3 The principle and purpose of acceptance sampling.

4 The relationship between producer risk and consumer risk.

5 The impact of changes in the acceptance number.

6 The use of operating characteristic curves.

CHAPTER BLUEPRINT

As competition for the consumer dollar intensifies worldwide, the importance that a firm attaches to improving the quality of its product grows proportionately. More and more effort and resources are expended by businesses to increase their competitive position. It is increasingly apparent that a firm cannot prosper without ensuring that its products meet minimum standards. This chapter explores the tests that firms may conduct to implement a quality control program designed to promote reliability and expand its competitive position in the market.

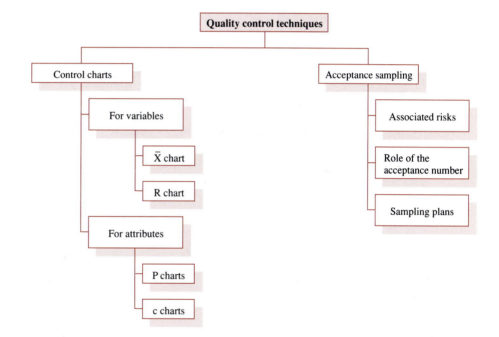

18.1   INTRODUCTION

Over the past several years the level of domestic and foreign competition has inten-
sified considerably. This increased level of rivalry among business firms has created
an ever-pressing need to monitor and maintain the quality of their products. As
competition stiffens, it becomes increasingly difficult to acquire and retain a share
of the market sufficient to permit economic survival. A 1990 issue of *Fortune* discusses the topic of increased competition worldwide. Citing an emerging central
Europe as an economic force and the strength of the Japanese economy, the article
states that "industrial competition has grown from merely harsh to downright bru-
tal." Without careful measures to ensure that its product meets certain minimum
specifications, a business is even less likely to endure the harsh competitive conditions of today's marketplace.

This chapter examines the numerous statistical tools that firms can use to ad-
minister an effective program to regulate the overall quality of their products and
thereby make them more competitive. A quality control program of this nature usually relies quite heavily on techniques such as

- Control charts for variables:
  - $\overline{X}$-chart.
  - R-chart.
- Control charts for attributes:
  - p-charts.
  - c-charts.
- Operating characteristic curves.
- Acceptance sampling.

18.2   CONTROL CHARTS FOR VARIABLES

Control charts are commonly used to monitor the quality of a product in an ongoing
manufacturing process. It allows the quality control expert to closely observe any
variation in the process, and alerts the manufacturers to changes in the nature of
the product. This aids in the assurance that the product meets certain manufacturing specifications and quality standards.

Eastman-Kodak manufactures a shutter release for its cameras which must meet
precise production specifications. The device must measure 0.94 centimeters (cm),
with an allowable tolerance of 0.03 cm. That is, its acceptable range is from 0.91 to
0.97 cm. Measurements are periodically taken, and the results are recorded in a

control chart. It can then quickly be determined if the release mechanism fails to meet production standards.

Almost all manufacturing firms pursue similar quality control programs. The purpose is to detect as soon as possible any variation in an important characteristic of a product such as its size, weight, color tone, or, in the case of containers, fill level. Such variation has two sources: (1) chance (or common) variation, and (2) assignable cause variation. **Chance variation** occurs simply because, like snowflakes, no two items are identical. Natural differences are to be expected, and cause no real problems in terms of controlling a product's quality level. Every product contains some slight inherent variation.

Chance Variation
Small variations in the product or production process are to be expected due to the inherent dissimilarity in productive inputs used in the production process.

An **assignable cause variation,** however, is a variation in excess of any natural difference. It is due to some specific cause which can (and must) be identified and corrected. An assignable cause variation results in defective products and is cause for alarm. It is due to human error, a faulty mechanical device used in the production process, or other improper procedure.

Assignable Cause Variation
Assignable cause variation in the product or production process signals that the process is out of control and corrective efforts are required.

If an assignable cause variation is detected, the production process is said to be *out of control,* and corrective steps must be taken.

Control charts aid in the detection of assignable cause variation. Control charts are formed for at least two variables. The first, often called an $\overline{X}$-chart, is designed to measure the variation in sample means. The second type of control chart measures variation in the range of samples. Logically, it is called an R-chart. A discussion of both types of control charts follows.

A. THE $\overline{X}$-CHART

The typical $\overline{X}$-chart is used to measure the variation of sample means around some generally accepted level. As Figure 18-1 shows, an upper control limit ($UCL_{\overline{x}}$) and a lower control limit ($LCL_{\overline{x}}$) are established around an acceptable measure, which is determined as the grand mean, $\overline{\overline{X}}$, of several sample means. The value $\overline{\overline{X}}$ serves as our estimate of μ.

FIGURE 18-1   An $\overline{X}$-Chart

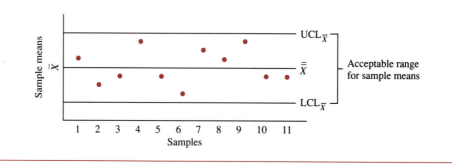

If the sample means fall within the acceptable range, as shown in Figure 18-1, only chance variation is said to occur. However, if the sample means exceed the $\text{UCL}_{\overline{x}}$ or fall below the $\text{LCL}_{\overline{x}}$, the quality control process has detected an assignable cause variation, and the production process is out of control. The cause for this excessive variation must be determined and corrected.

It is customary in quality control procedures to set the $\text{UCL}_{\overline{x}}$ and the $\text{LCL}_{\overline{x}}$ three standard errors above and below $\overline{X}$. This custom results from the empirical rule which states that 99.7 percent of all observations in a normal distribution will be within that range.

Thus,

$$\text{UCL} = \overline{\overline{X}} + 3\sigma_{\overline{x}} \tag{18.1}$$

and

$$\text{LCL} = \overline{\overline{X}} - 3\sigma_{\overline{x}} \tag{18.2}$$

However, in practice, $3\sigma_{\bar{x}}$ is estimated as $A_2\bar{R}$, where $\bar{R}$ is the mean range of several samples, and A_2 is a constant based on the sample size. Values for A_2 can be found in Table O. The process of substituting $A_2\bar{R}$ for $3\sigma_{\bar{x}}$ produces similar results and is considerably easier. We then find

$$\text{UCL} = \bar{\bar{X}} + A_2\bar{R} \qquad (18.3)$$

and

$$\text{LCL} = \bar{\bar{X}} - A_2\bar{R} \qquad (18.4)$$

Consider the problem faced by Janet Lugg, director of quality control measures for AT&T. Her plant produces frames for desktop computers which must meet certain size specifications. To ensure these standards are met, Janet collects $K = 10$ different samples of size $n = 12$ and measures their width. The results are reported in Table 18-1.

TABLE 18-1 Measurements (in centimeters) of AT&T Desktop Computers ($K = 10$, $n = 12$)

Sample	\multicolumn{12}{c}{Frames}											$\bar{X}$	R
	1	2	3	4	5	6	7	8	9	10	11	12		
1	16.2	17.1	15.9	15.8	17.2	16.9	16.8	17.1	17.2	16.5	16.4	16.3	16.6	1.4
2	17.3	16.5	15.1	15.9	16.2	16.2	16.8	17.5	17.1	16.2	16.3	16.4	16.5	2.4
3	17.1	16.5	16.5	15.8	15.7	15.7	15.8	16.2	17.2	15.3	16.1	16.4	16.2	1.9
4	17.3	16.2	17.1	17.1	15.8	15.9	15.9	16.2	17.1	17.0	17.1	15.2	16.5	2.1
5	16.2	15.1	15.3	16.1	17.3	17.1	17.0	16.0	15.3	15.1	16.1	17.1	16.1	2.2
6	17.1	17.0	16.0	15.3	17.5	17.3	17.1	17.2	17.2	16.9	16.1	16.5	16.8	2.2
7	17.0	17.1	16.2	16.2	16.3	15.8	17.1	16.0	15.3	16.9	16.5	17.3	16.5	2.0
8	17.5	15.2	17.3	16.3	16.3	15.1	15.9	15.8	17.1	17.1	16.9	16.3	16.4	2.4
9	17.3	17.2	16.3	16.1	16.5	15.6	15.7	15.6	15.8	16.1	17.1	17.1	16.4	1.7
10	17.1	15.2	15.3	15.3	15.5	16.1	17.1	17.3	17.1	17.2	17.2	17.2	16.5	2.1
													164.5	20.4

$$\bar{\bar{X}} = 16.45$$
$$\bar{R} = 2.04$$

The mean and range for each sample is shown in the last two columns of the table. The grand mean and the mean range are computed. With this information,

○○○○   **DECISION MAKING THROUGH PROBLEM SOLVING**   ○○○○
                              ILLUSTRATION 18-2´

Business Week announced renewed efforts by Rolls-Royce Motor Cars, Inc. to improve the quality image maintained by its Bently Turbo R sedan. An integral part of this quality control program, based on an elaborate computerized system, is designed to ensure that the mean time required for the automobile to respond to changes in the road conditions does not exceed 3/100 of a second.

the UCL and LCL for $\overline{X}$ can be determined. Since each sample size is $n = 12$, Table O reveals A_2 to be 0.266. Then

$$\text{UCL}_{\overline{x}} = \overline{\overline{X}} + A_2\overline{R}$$

$$= 16.45 + 0.266(2.04)$$

$$= 16.99$$

$$\text{LCL}_{\overline{x}} = \overline{\overline{X}} - A_2 R$$

$$= 15.91$$

Figure 18-2 is Janet's control chart for the computers. The means of all 10 samples are seen to be within the UCL and the LCL. The process is not out of control, and quality is being maintained with respect to the width of the computer.

FIGURE 18-2   An $\overline{X}$-Control Chart for Janet Lugg

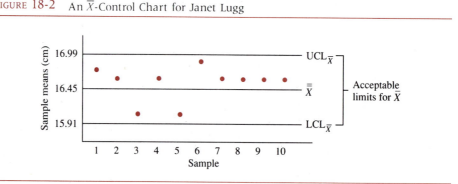

At this point, Ms. Lugg might find it useful to conduct the runs test for randomness that we discussed in Chapter 15. The test should be designed to determine if there is randomness in the values of $\overline{X}$ above and below $\overline{\overline{X}}$. If the null is rejected, this might suggest a problem in control factors.

B. THE *R*-CHART

In addition to monitoring changes in the mean, it is also useful to closely scrutinize variation in the dispersion within a process. Although the standard deviation is a dependable measure of dispersion, quality control techniques usually rely on the range as an indication in the variability of the process. The range is easier to compute and more readily understood by those without a sufficient statistical background.

A lower control limit (LCL_R) and upper control limit (UCL_R) for the range are calculated which, like those for the $\overline{X}$-chart, are three standard errors above and below the mean. In principle, they are determined as follows:

$$UCL_R = \overline{R} + 3s_R \qquad (18.5)$$

and

$$LCL_R = \overline{R} - 3s_R \qquad (18.6)$$

where s_R is the standard deviation in the sample ranges. However, in practice, it is simpler to use

$$UCL_R = D_4\overline{R} \qquad (18.7)$$

and

$$LCL_R = D_3\overline{R} \qquad (18.8)$$

Values for D_4 and D_3 are taken from Table O.

Using Lugg's data from Table 18-1, we find

$$UCL_R = 1.716(2.04) = 3.50$$
$$LCL_R = 0.284(2.04) = 0.579$$

The R-chart is shown in Figure 18-3.

FIGURE 18-3   An R-Chart for Janet Lugg

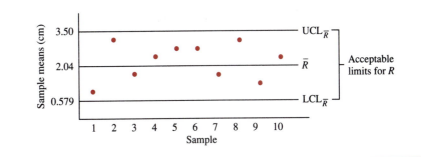

By examining the $\bar{X}$- and R-charts, Janet can clearly see that quality specifications are being maintained. Had some of the $\bar{X}$'s or sample ranges been outside their control limits, Janet might undertake a search effort to determine the cause for the excessive variation.

EXAMPLE 18-1 The Guppy and the Whale

In December 1990, GTW Electronics, a small manufacturing firm in New Jersey, announced its intention to compete directly with General Electric in the manufacturing of certain electrical components. The CEO for GTW called for quality control checks designed to measure the variation in the weight of one of the components. Samples of size $n = 6$ were taken each hour for $K = 5$ hours. The results, in ounces, are tabulated.

Hour (A.M.)	1	2	3	4	5	6	$\bar{X}$	R
8:00	4.9	4.8	4.8	5.1	6.6	5.2	5.23	1.8
9:00	6.8	5.1	5.2	7.1	5.3	5.2	5.78	2.0
10:00	7.1	6.9	5.9	6.2	6.9	6.9	6.65	1.2
11:00	6.8	6.2	6.5	7.1	7.6	6.8	6.83	1.4
12:00	6.0	4.6	4.5	4.5	4.3	5.2	4.85	1.7
							29.34	8.1

$\bar{\bar{X}} = 5.87$
$\bar{R} = 1.62$

The director of quality operations must prepare an $\bar{X}$-chart and an R-chart.

SOLUTION:

$$\text{UCL}_{\bar{x}} = \bar{\bar{X}} + A_2\bar{R}$$

$$= 5.87 + (0.483)(1.62)$$

$$= 6.64$$

$$\text{LCL}_{\bar{x}} = \bar{\bar{X}} - A_2\bar{R}$$

$$= 5.08$$

$$\text{UCL}_R = D_4\bar{R}$$

$$= (2.004)(1.62)$$

$$= 3.25$$

$$\text{LCL}_R = D_3\bar{R}$$

$$= (0)(1.62)$$

$$= 0$$

The LCL_R for all samples of $n \leq 6$ will always be zero.

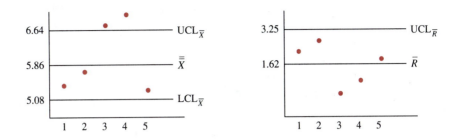

STATISTICAL INTERPRETATION:

The mean size of the electrical component was found to be out of control. Management halted production to identify the assignable cause. It was determined to be a worn machine part which would not hold a precise calibration. The part was replaced and production was continued.

In this example the mean went out of control while the range remained in control. Figure 18-4 shows the situation in which the range goes out of control while the mean remains in control. Notice that the mean has changed very little from its original position, yet the distribution is much more dispersed in Figure 18-4(b), indicating a much higher range.

FIGURE 18-4   Range is out of Control

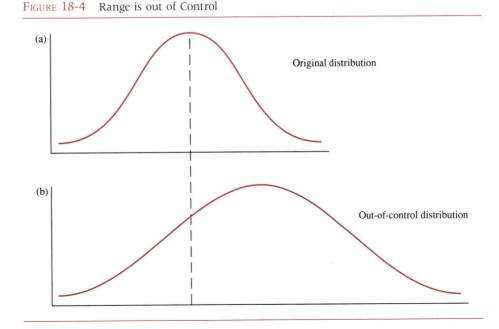

Samples of size $n = 7$ are taken for the time required to complete a task. The means and ranges for each sample, in minutes, are shown here. What are the control limits for $\overline{X}$ and R?

$\overline{X}_1 = 6.2$, $R_1 = 1.5$; $\overline{X}_2 = 7.3$, $R_2 = 1.7$; $\overline{X}_3 = 8.1$, $R_3 = 1.9$; $\overline{X}_4 = 7.2$, $R_4 = 1.2$; $\overline{X}_5 = 6.3$, $R_5 = 1.1$.

Answer: $\text{UCL}_{\overline{x}} = 7.64$, $\text{LCL}_{\overline{x}} = 6.40$; $\text{UCL}_R = 2.89$, $\text{LCL}_R = 0.11$

18.3 CONTROL CHARTS FOR ATTRIBUTES

The control charts for $\overline{X}$ and R are designed to monitor quantitative data in a process. In many cases it is necessary or desirable to measure the quality of a process, or the output of that process, based on the attribute of acceptability. This statistical procedure determines whether a process is acceptable based on the proportion and number of defects. Two common types of control charts focus on acceptability. **p-charts** measure the proportion of defects, and **c-charts** record the number of defects per item.

A. p-CHARTS

In constructing p-charts, we simply take note of the proportion of defective items in a sample. This proportion, p, is

$$p = \frac{\text{Number of defects in a sample}}{\text{Sample size}}$$

As with control charts for variables, several samples are taken, yielding several values for p. The mean proportion of defects for these several samples, $\overline{p}$, is then calculated as

$$\overline{p} = \frac{\text{Total number of defects in all samples}}{\text{Total number of all items inspected}}$$

The value of $\overline{p}$ serves as our estimate of π, the population proportion of defects, in the event π is unknown.

The standard deviation of the proportion of defects is

$$\sigma_p = \sqrt{\frac{\pi(1 - \pi)}{n}} \qquad (18.9)$$

If π is unknown, σ_p is estimated by s_p, where

$$s_p = \sqrt{\frac{\bar{p}(1 - \bar{p})}{n}} \tag{18.10}$$

Recall from our discussion of the binomial distribution that the detection of defects is based on the Bernoulli processes.

Upper control limits (UCL_p) and lower control limits (LCL_p) are formed three standard deviations above and below the population proportion of defects. If π is known,

$$\begin{aligned} UCL_p &= \pi + 3\sigma_p \\ &= \pi + 3\sqrt{\frac{\pi(1 - \pi)}{n}} \end{aligned} \tag{18.11}$$

and

$$\begin{aligned} LCL_p &= \pi - 3\sigma_p \\ &= \pi - 3\sqrt{\frac{\pi(1 - \pi)}{n}} \end{aligned} \tag{18.12}$$

If π is unknown,

$$\begin{aligned} UCL_p &= \bar{p} + 3s_p \\ &= \bar{p} + 3\sqrt{\frac{\bar{p}(1 - \bar{p})}{n}} \end{aligned} \tag{18.13}$$

and

$$\begin{aligned} LCL_p &= \bar{p} - 3s_p \\ &= \bar{p} - 3\sqrt{\frac{\bar{p}(1 - \bar{p})}{n}} \end{aligned} \tag{18.14}$$

Opus, Inc. makes electric guitars and other musical instruments. A quality control procedure to detect defects in their Auditory Annihilator model 1000 guitar entailed the selection of $K = 15$ different samples of size $n = 40$. The number of defects in each sample is shown in Table 18-2. A total of $(15)(40) = 600$ guitars is inspected.

TABLE 18-2   Defects in $K = 15$ Samples of Size $n = 40$

Sample	Number of Defects	p	Sample	Number of Defects	p
1	10	0.25	9	13	0.33
2	12	0.30	10	15	0.38
3	9	0.23	11	17	0.43
4	15	0.38	12	3	0.08
5	27	0.68	13	25	0.63
6	8	0.20	14	18	0.45
7	11	0.28	15	17	0.43
8	11	0.28		$\overline{211}$	

With these data, a quality control specialist for Opus finds

$$\bar{p} = \frac{211}{600}$$

$$= 0.35$$

Then

$$\text{UCL}_p = \bar{p} + 3\sqrt{\frac{\bar{p}(1 - \bar{p})}{n}}$$

$$= 0.35 + 3\sqrt{\frac{(0.35)(0.65)}{40}}$$

$$= 0.58$$

$$\text{LCL}_p = \bar{p} - 3\sqrt{\frac{\bar{p}(1 - \bar{p})}{n}}$$

$$= 0.12$$

A **preliminary** control chart is formed from these findings, as in Figure 18-5.

Samples 5 ($p = 0.68$), 12 ($p = 0.08$), and 13 ($p = 0.63$) are clearly out of control. The search for the assignable causes revealed that sample 5 was taken during a time when certain key personnel were on vacation, and less skilled employees were forced to fill in. The unusually low proportion of defects for sample 12 resulted from a one-time use of superior raw materials when the regular supplier was unable to provide Opus with the usual materials. Sample 13 was taken when new construction

FIGURE 18-5 Opus's Control Chart for p

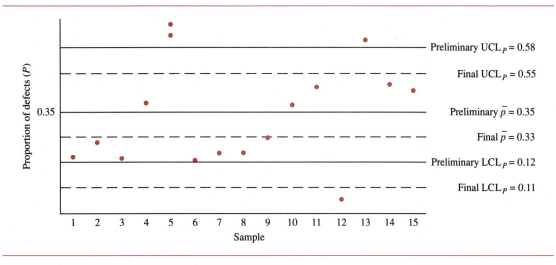

at the plant temporarily interrupted electric power, thus disallowing the use of computerized production methods.

The assignable cause has been identified for each anomaly. If desired, action can be taken to prevent their reoccurrence. Opus may, for example, ensure that in the future key personnel stagger their vacations to prevent a repeat of sample 5.

Furthermore, it is suggested that all sample values which fall outside the preliminary control limits be eliminated, and final limits be calculated on this reduced sample, which are then used to monitor production in the future. Alternatively, you may choose to eliminate *only* those values from the preliminary data set for which assignable causes can be found. We will follow the practice of removing all anomalies in calculating final limits whether or not assignable cause has been determined. (With Opus it would make no difference which rule was followed since an assignable cause for all three anomalies was determined.)

Eliminating samples 5, 12, and 13 yields

$$\bar{p} = \frac{156}{480}$$

$$= 0.33$$

$$\text{UCL}_p = 0.33 + 3\sqrt{\frac{(0.33)\,(0.67)}{40}}$$

$$= 0.55$$

$$\text{LCL}_p = 0.33 - 3\sqrt{\frac{(0.33)\,(0.67)}{40}}$$

$$= 0.11$$

The final limits are also shown in Figure 18-5.

You might presume that an LCL_p should not be a concern since low rates of defects are desirable. However, unusually low values for p might aid in identifying ways in which defects can be minimized. For example, Opus may want to consider regular use of the superior raw materials obtained in sample 12 if they are not cost-prohibitive. Perhaps a study should be done to compare the effect on profits of using the higher-grade raw materials. Furthermore, exceptionally low p-values may indicate a problem in that the quality control program is simply not effectively detecting defects.

B.   *c*-Charts

A second type of attribute control chart is the *c*-chart, which is designed to detect the number of defects in a single unit. In developing a *p*-chart, an entire unit was deemed either defective or not defective. In many instances, however, the presence of one or more defects may not render the unit unacceptable. A manufacturer of furniture may find several minor defects in a sofa and yet not consider it unacceptable. If the defects per 100 square yards of floor covering were few and minor, the manufacturer may decide to sell it despite the flaws. A *c*-chart is used to analyze the number of flaws per unit of output.

The *c*-chart is concerned with the number of occurrences (defects) per unit (per sofa or per 100 square yards). This consideration fits a Poisson distribution.

Control limits are established around the number of defects in the population, c. In the likely event c is unknown, it is estimated by $\bar{c}$, the mean number of defects in the units.

A unit may consist of a single item, such as a sofa or a 100-square-yard piece of carpet, or it might contain, for example, a shipment of 50 printed pages in which typos are detected. The unit must be consistent in size, number, or area. Earlier we defined the standard deviation of the number of occurrences as the square root of the mean number of occurrences. Thus,

$$s_{\bar{c}} = \sqrt{\bar{c}} \qquad (18.15)$$

The control limits are three standard deviations above and below $\bar{c}$.

$$UCL_c = \bar{c} + 3s_{\bar{c}} \qquad (18.16)$$

and

$$LCL_c = \bar{c} - 3s_{\bar{c}} \qquad (18.17)$$

TABLE 18-3   Number of Defects in 20 Pieces of Gift Wrap

Sheet	Number of Defects	Sheet	Number of Defects
1	5	11	3
2	4	12	15
3	3	13	10
4	5	14	8
5	16	15	4
6	1	16	2
7	8	17	10
8	9	18	12
9	9	19	7
10	4	20	17
			152

International Paper inspected 20 sheets of a new type of gift wrap for defects. The results are shown in Table 18-3. A c-chart is to be constructed.

$$\bar{c} = \frac{152}{20}$$

$$= 7.6$$

$$s_{\bar{c}} = \sqrt{7.6}$$

$$= 2.76$$

$$\text{UCL}_c = \bar{c} + 3s_{\bar{c}}$$

$$= 7.6 + 3(2.76)$$

$$= 15.88$$

$$\text{LCL}_c = \bar{c} - 3s_{\bar{c}}$$

$$= 0.68$$

Figure 18-6 contains the c-chart.

Units 5, 6, and 12 indicate the process is out of control, and the assignable cause(s) should be determined. If $\text{LCL}_c < 0$, it is set equal to zero since a negative number of defects is impossible.

QUICK CHECK 18.3.1

Forty cameras of a newly produced model were inspected and 117 defects were found. Determine UCL_c and LCL_c.

Answer: $\text{UCL}_c = 8$, $\text{LCL}_c = 0$

FIGURE 18-6   *c*-Chart for International Paper

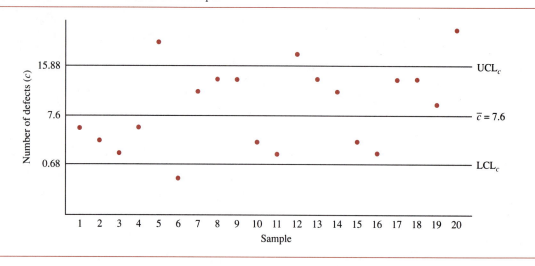

18.4   ACCEPTANCE SAMPLING

Decisions must often be made regarding the acceptability of an entire lot or shipment of goods. A firm may purchase raw materials from its supplier without complete knowledge of the quality of those materials. It must then test the shipment to determine if the materials meet certain minimum specifications. Rarely does a firm examine every item in a shipment. Such a process would be too time-consuming and costly. Instead, a sample is selected to determine whether the entire shipment should be accepted or returned to the supplier.

During production a manufacturing firm often inspects several unfinished units to determine if production should continue or if the semifinished units should be scrapped and procedures reviewed to determine the cause for excessive defects. This decision also involves the use of samples in deciding if minimum standards are being met. This practice is called **acceptance sampling.**

> **Acceptance Sampling**
> A sample of a shipment or production lot is examined to determine if it meets certain minimum quality specifications and is therefore acceptable.

Acceptance sampling is an important and integral part of quality control measures. Decisions regarding the acceptability of materials have a significant bearing on the firm's revenue and cost structure.

Ensuring that a part fits production standards is crucial to the overall manufacturing process. Whether the manufacturing firm produces the part or obtains it from a supplier, specific production standards must be met. If a manufacturer of compact disk systems uses a part that is too small, the entire system is likely not to function properly. If an aircraft assemblage company relies on a metal that is too heavy or unable to withstand minimum stress, a serious consequence is likely. Obviously, quality control decisions concerning production specifications are critical.

Consider a firm making cellular telephones. It obtains a critical part for each phone from a supplier in Chicago. The parts are shipped in lots of several hundred. The firm cannot test each part received, so acceptance sampling is necessary. The firm is willing to accept a maximum of 5 percent defective parts in each shipment. This number is called the **acceptance quality level** (AQL). The firm also limits to 1 percent those shipments that meet the AQL but are mistakenly rejected. This has the effect of constraining the number of nondefective shipments that are discarded.

In common practice, decisions regarding these percentages are most often determined on the basis of company policy, often in agreement with the supplier. If a less judgmental approach is desired in arriving at proper percentages, the *Military Standard Sampling Procedures and Tables for Inspection by Attributes* (MIL-STD-105D) can be used. These tables specify the proper sample size and number of defects necessary to reject the shipment.

Since sampling is involved, it is possible that an error is made in deciding whether to accept or reject a shipment. A shipment that meets the minimum specifications might be rejected. This is a Type I error, and is called **producer risk,** because producers run the risk of having a good shipment returned to them.

Producer Risk
The probability that sampling error will cause a buyer to mistakenly reject a shipment and return it to the seller is a producer risk. This is called a Type I error.

A Type II error occurs when a bad shipment is accepted. Accepting a bad shipment is called **consumer risk,** since the buyer would unknowingly retain a shipment with an excessive number of defects.

Consumer Risk
The probability that sampling error will lead the buyer to retain a shipment that contains a disproportionate number of defects is a consumer risk. This is called a Type II error.

A Type I error is called the α-level, and the probability of a Type II error is called β.

Consider again the cellular phone company. It was stated that a shipment containing more than 5 percent defects should be rejected (AQL = 5 percent), and only 1 percent of the good shipments would be erroneously returned (α = 1 percent).

This 1 percent is the value of the producer's risk. Its purpose is to protect the firm's suppliers from unwarranted rejection of a good lot or shipment.

Recall from our earlier discussion of probability distributions that a hypergeometric distribution could be used to determine the probability that a certain number of defects would be found in a shipment. However, in practice, the binomial distribution, due to its simplicity, is often used to provide an accurate approximation.

Assume that from several hundred parts received by the cellular phone company, a sample of $n = 50$ is taken. Given that the firm agrees to an AQL of 5 percent, π is set at 0.05. It is then necessary to determine what number of defects ensure that no more than 1 percent of the good shipments are rejected. That is, what number of defects will ensure that at least 99 percent of the good shipments containing 95 percent $(1.00 - AQL)$ nondefects are accepted. This number of defects upon which the decision to accept the shipment is called the **acceptance number.**

Acceptance Number
The acceptance number is the maximum number of defects out of a sample that can occur without rejection of the shipment. It ensures that the AQL is maintained without rejecting more than some prescribed percentage of good shipments.

The maximum number of defects, C, can then be found in the extension to Table C. For $n = 50$, move down the column headed by $\pi = 0.05$ until you find the first value that exceeds $1.00 -$ producer's risk, here $1.00 - 0.01 = 0.99$. This value is 0.9968, which is associated with $C = 7$. The closest probability not exceeding 1 percent defects is $1.00 - 0.9968 = 0.0032 < 0.01$. If there are more than $C = 7$ defects out of a sample of $n = 50$, the entire lot should be returned.

EXAMPLE 18-2 Claude and Carol's Dilemma

Claude Vaughan is director of quality control at the Pepsico bottling plant in Cincinnati. Data on production levels show that an inordinate number of bottles are underfilled. Fearing that shipment of the bottles could drive away customers, Claude proposes an acceptance sampling plan to minimize underfill shipments without causing too many bottles that are properly filled to be discarded.

He agrees with the production supervisor, Carol Henning, that they can ship a maximum of 1 percent underfills. This represents the acceptable level of defects, so AQL = 1 percent. Carol insists that not more than 10 percent of the acceptable production lots should be rejected. That is, the producer's risk should be limited to 10 percent. If samples of 100 are taken from a production run, what is the acceptance number of underfills Claude and Carol can tolerate before the entire run must be rejected?

SOLUTION:
Using the extension of the cumulative binomial table, π is set equal to the AQL of 1 percent. Claude and Carol must find the number of underfills that would not result

in the rejection of more than 10 percent of the good production runs. They select a sample of 100 bottles from the most recent run. Given $\pi = 0.01$, the number of underfills that ensures that no more than 10 percent of the good runs are rejected is that value of C with a probability that exceeds $1.00 -$ producer's risk, or $1.00 - 0.10 = 0.90$. In the table under $n = 100$, find the column headed $\pi = 0.01$. Travel down the column until you find a probability in excess of 0.90. This value is 0.9206, which carries an acceptance number of $C = 2$.

STATISTICAL INTERPRETATION:

By rejecting all production runs from which samples of $n = 100$ were taken that contain more than two underfills, Claude and Carol will ensure that, over the long run, production runs will not contain more then 1 percent underfills and that runs with less than 1 percent underfills will be rejected no more than 10 percent of the time.

A.   DIFFERENT SAMPLING PLANS

Acceptance sampling assumes only one sample is taken. This, logically, is referred to as a single-sample plan. However, two or more samples can be taken. Such plans are termed **multiple**, or **sequential**, sampling plans.

A **double-sampling** plan involves selection of a primary sample. On the basis of the results of this first sample, the plan may then call for one of three actions: (1) the lot may be rejected; (2) the lot may be accepted; or (3) a second sample may be taken. Two values of C are specified, where C_1 is the acceptance number for the first sample, and C_2 is the acceptance number for both samples.

To illustrate, assume a double-sampling plan stipulates $n_1 = 100$, $n_2 = 100$, $C_1 = 3$, $C_2 = 8$. A preliminary sample of 100 is selected. If three or fewer defects are found, the lot is accepted. If 11 $(3 + 8)$ or more are found, the lot is rejected. If the first sample contains 4 to 10 defects, a second sample of $n_2 = 100$ is taken. If the total defects in both samples exceed 11, the lot is rejected.

Sequential plans tend to be more efficient than single-sampling plans in that fewer observations are needed to ensure the same degree of accuracy. Sequential plans are often used when testing requires the destruction of each unit.

As competition stiffens in the world market, a firm must ensure that its product or service meets minimum standards if it expects to stay in business. Hence, quality control measures are vital.

B.   OPERATING CHARACTERISTIC CURVES

Those involved with quality control plans often find it convenient to construct operating characteristic (OC) curves when making determinations regarding the acceptance of a lot. These curves display the probability of acceptance under a variety of conditions. Specifically, an OC curve can allow the quality control specialist to ascertain, given different values for the proportion of defects π, the likelihood of accepting a lot given (1) the size of the sample n and (2) the maximum number of allowable defects, C.

To illustrate, a sampling plan may be devised in which $n = 10$ units are routinely chosen from each shipment on a random basis. It is determined that if $C = 3$ or fewer units are defective, the entire lot will be accepted. Under this scheme, it is possible to calculate the probability of acceptance for different values of π. For example, if, typically, $\pi = 5$ percent of the units are defective, what is the probability that a given lot will be accepted? This question can, of course, be answered with the use of the cumulative binomial distribution. From the cumulative binomial table, it can be seen that the probability of acceptance $= P(C \leq 3 \,|\, n = 10, \pi = 0.05) = 0.9990$. If, on the other hand, the proportion of defects in the past has proven to be 10 percent, the probability of acceptance becomes $P(C \leq 3 \,|\, n = 10, \pi = 0.10) = 0.9872$. Notice, logically, that the higher the value for π, the less likely it is that the shipment will be accepted. If other possible values for π are selected, the relationship between π and the probability of acceptance can be determined and depicted by an OC curve as shown in Figure 18-7.

FIGURE 18-7   An Operating Characteristic Curve for $n = 10$, $C = 3$

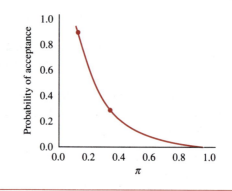

The shape of the OC is determined by the π-value, but other factors also affect it. If, for example, C is increased, the probability of acceptance goes up for any value of π. Thus, the entire OC curve would shift upward.

If the sample size n were increased, the entire curve shifts downward. We have $P(C \leq 3 \,|\, n = 10,\ \pi = 0.08) = 0.9872$, but $P(C \leq 3 \,|\, n = 15,\ \pi = 0.10) = 0.9444$. The likelihood that a larger sample will result in acceptance, given values for C and π, is smaller than that for a smaller sample with corresponding values for C and π. In this manner an OC curve can be used to tailor a quality control plan to the specific needs of any business operation.

18.5   SOLVED PROBLEMS

1. **Finding the Fault for Defaults** *Business Week* described the problem a major bank in Chicago had with loan defaults. Assume that samples of size 5 for seven officials were selected, and the results tabulated. Develop an $\overline{X}$-chart and an R-chart for the bank.

Loan Amount (in $1,000's)

Official	1	2	3	4	5	$\overline{X}$	R
1	14.2	9.2	7.1	6.8	6.0	8.7	8.2
2	45.5	65.5	45.2	55.2	55.1	53.3	20.3
3	23.4	31.2	36.3	31.5	32.6	31.0	12.9
4	32.3	31.2	29.1	27.8	28.1	29.7	4.5
5	56.7	65.3	45.2	55.5	58.2	56.2	20.1
6	89.7	90.2	84.2	85.5	89.2	87.8	6.0
7	112.0	99.2	115.3	98.5	153.2	115.6	54.7
$\overline{\overline{X}}$						54.6	
$\overline{R}$							18.1

$$\text{UCL}_{\overline{X}} = \overline{\overline{X}} + A_2\overline{R}$$

$$= 54.6 + (0.577)(18.1)$$

$$= 65.05$$

$$\text{LCL}_{\overline{X}} = \overline{\overline{X}} - A_2\overline{R}$$

$$= 44.17$$

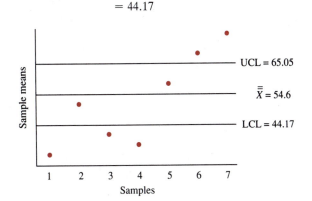

There is apparent inconsistency in the size of loans granted by the seven bank officers. Perhaps some effort should be made to find an explanation for the disparity in the officers' practices. The first, third, and fourth officers are granting unusually small loans, and the last officer seems to extend exceedingly large loans.

The R-chart is found as

$$\text{UCL}_R = D_4 \overline{R}$$

$$= (2.115)(18.1)$$

$$= 38.3$$

$$\text{LCL}_R = D_3 \overline{R}$$

$$= (0)(18.1)$$

$$= 0$$

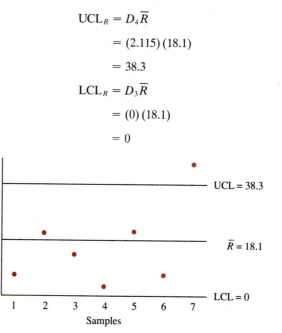

Only one officer seems to violate the control limits for the range. Again, the pattern of the seventh officer stands out from the rest, suggesting his or her practices should be reviewed.

2. **A Comparison of Each Officer** Considering the disparity in the officers' performances, it might be wise to use a p-chart to compare each officer. Samples of 10 loans by each officer are selected, and the proportion of loan defaults for each is recorded.

Officer	Number of Defects (defaults), c	Proportion of Defects, p
1	4	0.4
2	3	0.3
3	3	0.3
4	2	0.2
5	0	0.0
6	3	0.3
7	8	0.8
	23	

$$\overline{p} = \frac{23}{70} = 0.33$$

$$UCL_p = \bar{p} + 3\sqrt{\frac{\bar{p}(1 - \bar{p})}{n}}$$

$$= 0.33 + 3(0.056)$$

$$= 0.498$$

$$LCL_p = \bar{p} - 3\sqrt{\frac{\bar{p}(1 - \bar{p})}{n}}$$

$$= 0.162$$

We find that 0.498 and 0.162 are the preliminary limits for p and are shown on the p-chart. The last officer is again differentiated from the rest. His or her rate of default is excessive. Further, the fact that the fifth officer had no defaults might also indicate a trouble spot. He or she is perhaps being too conservative in extending loans, and a greater degree of aggressiveness might be called for.

By eliminating the fifth and seventh samples, we can determine final limits. These are $UCL_p = 0.495$ and $LCL_p = 0.105$.

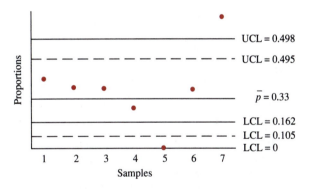

A further examination of the loan process might involve the use of c-charts to control for the number of errors (defects) made in each loan application (unit). In this effort, $n = 12$ loans are randomly selected, and the number of violations of bank policy for each loan application is tallied.

Loan	Violations (defects), c	Loan	Violations (defects), c
1	3	7	2
2	4	8	0
3	2	9	3
4	3	10	4
5	10	11	2
6	1	12	3
			37

In 37 instances bank policy was not followed when extending the 12 loans. Thus,

$$\bar{c} = \frac{37}{12} = 3.08$$

$$s_{\bar{c}} = \sqrt{3.08}$$

$$= 1.75$$

Then

$$UCL_c = \bar{c} + 3s_{\bar{c}}$$

$$= 8.33$$

$$LCL_c = c - 3s_{\bar{c}}$$

$$= -2.3, \text{ and is set equal to } 0$$

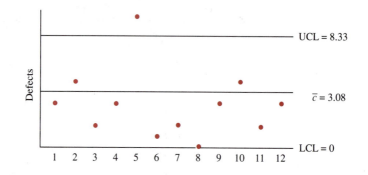

Only the fifth loan in the sample suggests a problem. It should be determined who approved that loan, and action can then be taken to reduce the number of loan defaults.

3. **Three Scoops or You're Out** Crisp-O Raisin Bran, a major cereal manufacturer, promises three scoops of raisins in every box. A box with fewer raisins is considered defective. A customer of Crisp-O will accept a maximum of only 1 percent defective boxes. Crisp-O agrees to this quality check, but insists on limiting its producer's risk to 5 percent. That is, no more than 5 percent of the shipments that meet this restriction of containing at least 99 percent of boxes with three scoops must be rejected. Thus, at least 95 percent of the good shipments must be accepted. From a sample of 100 boxes selected from a large shipment, what is the acceptance number of defects that will result in rejection of that shipment?

Since the customer will accept no more than 1 percent defects, the AQL is set at 1 percent. From the extension to the binomial table, we must find a number C that will not cause the rejection of more than 5 percent of the good shipments (a good shipment is one that contains at least 99 percent of the boxes with three scoops). The value of π is set equal to 1 percent. Moving down the column headed by $\pi = 0.01$ with $n = 100$, we find the first number to exceed $1.00 -$ producer's risk, or $1.00 - 0.05 = 0.95$, is 0.9816, which is associated with $C = 3$. Thus, if a sample of $n = 100$ is taken from a large shipment, and more than three boxes out of the 100 examined contain less than three scoops, the entire shipment should be returned to Crisp-O.

18.6 WHAT YOU SHOULD HAVE LEARNED FROM THIS CHAPTER

Quality control is an essential feature of any ongoing process. To ensure that quality is maintained and to guard against decreased efficiency and productivity, the measures of quality control discussed in this chapter should be applied.

These tools designed to preserve product integrity include the formulation of different types of charts which monitor and detect any significant departures from the norm. Such departures are often cause for alarm, and certainly should receive the attention of those personnel concerned with quality maintenance.

The practice of acceptance sampling is increasingly common in a commercial setting. Businesses are learning how improvements in products and services can arise as a result of the application of this simple and advantageous practice.

LIST OF FORMULAS

$$UCL = \overline{\overline{X}} + 3\sigma_{\overline{X}} \tag{18.1}$$

The upper control limit for $\overline{X}$.

$$LCL = \overline{\overline{X}} - 3\sigma_{\overline{X}} \tag{18.2}$$

The lower control limit for $\overline{X}$.

$$UCL = \overline{\overline{X}} + A_2\overline{R} \tag{18.3}$$

A practical calculation of the upper control limit for $\overline{X}$.

$$LCL = \overline{\overline{X}} - A_2\overline{R} \tag{18.4}$$

A practical calculation of the lower control limit for $\overline{X}$.

$$UCL_R = \overline{R} + 3s_R \tag{18.5}$$

The upper control limit for the range.

$$LCL_R = \overline{R} - 3s_R \tag{18.6}$$

The lower control limit for the range.

$$UCL_R = D_4\overline{R} \tag{18.7}$$

A practical calculation for the upper control limit for the range.

$$LCL_R = D_3\overline{R} \tag{18.8}$$

A practical calculation for the lower control limit for the range.

$$\sigma_p = \sqrt{\frac{\pi(1 - \pi)}{n}} \tag{18.9}$$

Standard deviation of the proportion of defects.

$$s_p = \sqrt{\frac{\bar{p}(1 - \bar{p})}{n}}$$ (18.10)

Estimate of σ_p when π is unknown.

$$\text{UCL}_p = \pi + 3\sqrt{\frac{\pi(1 - \pi)}{n}}$$ (18.11)

The upper control limit for the proportion of defects when π is known.

$$\text{LCL}_p = \pi - 3\sqrt{\frac{\pi(1 - \pi)}{n}}$$ (18.12)

The lower control limit for the proportion of defects when π is known.

$$\text{UCL}_p = \bar{p} + 3\sqrt{\frac{\bar{p}(1 - \bar{p})}{n}}$$ (18.13)

The upper control limit for the proportion of defects when π is unknown.

$$\text{LCL}_p = \bar{p} - 3\sqrt{\frac{\bar{p}(1 - \bar{p})}{n}}$$ (18.14)

The lower control limit for the proportion of defects when π is unknown.

$$s_{\bar{c}} = \sqrt{\bar{c}}$$ (18.15)

The standard deviation of the number of occurrences.

$$\text{UCL}_c = \bar{c} + 3s_{\bar{c}}$$ (18.16)

The upper control limit for the number of occurrences.

$$\text{LCL}_c = \bar{c} - 3s_{\bar{c}}$$ (18.17)

The lower control limit for the number of occurrences.

CHAPTER EXERCISES

CONCEPTUAL QUESTIONS

1. The director of your division at your firm happens by your desk and notices that you are working with something called a control chart. Since he got his job because he is the boss's son-in-law and knows nothing about control charts or quality control, he wants you to describe what you are doing and why you are doing it. Describe in your own words the purpose and function of $\overline{X}$-, R-, c-, and p-control charts.

2. Define the acceptance number and the acceptance quality level as used in acceptance sampling. If AQL is 5 percent and producer's risk is 1 percent, how would you describe the acceptance number in terms of these two percentages?

PROBLEMS

3. Acme Salt Mine, where you work as a go-fer trainee, has asked you to record the number of miles the sales staff drives in making sales calls. Using these data, samples are taken over five consecutive days. From the results shown, construct $\overline{X}$- and R-charts. Does the system appear out of control?

	Miles Driven					
Sample						
1	112	132	145	117	125	189
2	214	252	274	189	236	203
3	198	205	185	214	236	199
4	236	250	245	210	210	259
5	109	111	125	132	145	152

4. An accountant for the IRS notices what she feels are abnormalities in the amounts of tax returns to people in New York. She selects six samples of returns. Does an $\overline{X}$- or R-chart suggest that her suspicions are valid?

	Amount of Return				
Sample					
1	412	396	385	396	399
2	812	789	799	825	801
3	855	321	541	652	845
4	117	101	123	134	112
5	512	523	489	478	501
6	612	589	578	604	598

5. The IRS accountant from the previous problem is concerned that too many mistakes are occurring on tax returns. She collects samples of size $n = 50$ and finds the numbers of improperly completed returns in each sample to be 10, 12, 10, 9, 8, 5, 21, 25, 11, and 13. Does a p-chart indicate a problem?

6. TeleMarketing takes $k = 12$ samples, each on a different day, of size $n = 25$ of the cost of long-distance calls over the past several months. The sample means and ranges are tabulated. Does it appear that the calling process is out of control?

Sample	Mean	Range	Sample	Mean	Range
1	$23.10	$1.12	7	$12.89	$12.12
2	21.45	2.89	8	15.67	19.89
3	19.01	2.98	9	29.78	10.98
4	17.45	1.12	10	18.38	20.87
5	8.90	2.98	11	19.89	19.78
6	11.21	3.45	12	17.89	11.67

7. If it were determined that on the seventh day TeleMarketing (see previous problem) changed its long-distance carrier, what might you conclude?

8. A clothing manufacturer inspects 15 garments and finds the number of defects in each to be 5, 4, 7, 2, 0, 1, 5, 12, 4, 3, 3, 4, 6, 7, and 7. Does a c-chart suggest a problem?

9. To minimize printing errors, a publishing company finds 2,112 mistakes in 1,000 pages of printed material. If a single page is taken as a sample, construct a c-chart which could be used to determine if the printing process is out of control.

10. The publishing company has established a policy in which it will allow only 1 percent of the pages to contain errors. If a printing exceeds that limit, the entire manuscript must be reprinted. However, it cannot proofread every page. The company decides that 5 percent of those manuscripts that have less than 1 percent errors will mistakenly be reprinted. What is the maximum number of errors a sample of 100 pages can contain before it must be rejected and a reprint order issued?

11. If the actual but unknown percentage of pages with errors in Problem 10 is 10 percent, what is the probability that the manuscript will be accepted?

12. The AllRight Insurance Company of Buffalo, New York, collects five samples of size 12 each of claims filed against them for auto damage. The means and ranges are given here. Construct $\overline{X}$- and R-charts, and comment.

Sample	Mean	Range
Jan	$812	$54
Feb	234	23
Mar	321	27
Apr	250	29
May	276	20

13. In Problem 12 what would a heavy snow storm in January constitute?

14. A large auto parts store in Little Rock refuses to accept a shipment of distributor caps if more than 5 percent are defective. They agree, to protect their suppliers, that in sampling shipments they will not return more than 20 percent of all shipments that meet the 5 percent requirement. If samples of 50 are taken, what is the acceptance number?

15. For Problem 14 what is the acceptance number if samples of 20 are taken?

16. In Problem 14 if the actual percentage of defective caps is 10 percent, what is the probability a shipment will be accepted if a sample of 50 caps is taken?

17. From Problems 14 and 16, if the true percentage of defects is 1 percent, what is the probability that the shipment will be accepted? Comment on the difference in your answers in this problem and Problem 16.

18. K mart sells radar detector units used by motorists. Company policy is to accept a maximum of 5 percent defective units. Only 10 percent of those shipments that contain fewer than 5 percent defects will be sent back to the supplier. What is the maximum number of defective detectors that can occur in a sample of 50?

19. If producer risk is reduced to 1 percent in Problem 18, what is the acceptance number? Comment on the difference in your answer from Problem 18.

20. *Nation's Business* cites William M. Kizer, CEO of the Wellness Council of America in Omaha, Nebraska, as saying that employee wellness programs can drastically reduce the cost of medical coverage to the nation's workers. Samples of size 20 for the claims by

employees in wellness programs provided these means and ranges. Compute and comment on the $\overline{X}$- and R-charts.

Sample	Mean	Range
1	$401	$67
2	405	74
3	422	84
4	420	60
5	423	53
6	420	49
7	417	54

21. Samples of claims from employees without wellness programs as in Problem 20 yielded these values. Calculate and comment on the $\overline{X}$- and R-charts.

Sample	Mean	Range
1	$512	$34
2	436	54
3	365	47
4	265	51
5	378	38
6	542	37

22. TCBY Yogurt tested the stability of its franchise operation by taking samples of 25 each in six states. The numbers of failed franchises were 4, 7, 2, 6, 8, and 12. Develop a p-chart to help TCBY monitor its outlets.

23. Bradley University uses two word processing packages: Professional Write and WordPerfect. In a comparison of their relative merits, samples of size 18 are taken for the time required for faculty and staff to master each package. The results are shown here. Prepare $\overline{X}$- and R-charts for use in evaluating each package. What are your conclusions?

Professional Write v.2.0

Sample	Mean (hours)	Range (hours)
1	3.2	1.2
2	3.9	0.9
3	3.9	1.5
4	3.7	1.5
5	3.6	1.1
6	3.3	1.9
7	2.5	1.8
8	3.6	1.7

WordPerfect v.5.1

Sample	Mean (hours)	Range (hours)
1	78.5	10.2
2	79.5	8.7
3	55.6	6.8
4	78.6	7.8
5	58.9	11.3
6	72.8	10.6
7	86.9	12.3

24. In a continued review (see Problem 23) of the word processing packages, personnel at Bradley University took four samples (actually, the number of samples was much greater) of 50 pages each typed by WordPerfect and found

   10 pages with a total of 12 errors.
   12 pages with a total of 18 errors.
   8 pages with a total of 15 errors.
   17 pages with a total of 13 errors.

   Four samples of 50 pages each typed by Professional Write revealed

   2 pages with a total of 2 errors.
   0 pages with errors.
   1 page with a total of 1 error.
   3 pages with a total of 3 errors.

   Prepare a *p*-chart and a *c*-chart for these data.

25. *Up Your Cash Flow* (Granville Publications), by Harvey Goldstein, CPA, discusses various computer spreadsheets and the speed with which they can forecast budgets. Lilly Paper Products applied some of the principles found in the book. They discovered that 10 samples of size 15 of the number of days it took local offices to prepare their quarterly budgets yielded means and ranges of

Sample	Mean	Range	Sample	Mean	Range
1	32.4	23.4	6	45.7	34.6
2	68.7	45.3	7	56.7	17.5
3	45.6	18.6	8	13.2	12.2
4	67.6	45.6	9	34.5	29.8
5	23.8	18.3	10	76.7	67.9

   Construct $\overline{X}$- and *R*-charts. What can you conclude?

26. *Nation's Business* reported that Harvey Mackay's new book, *Beware the Naked Man Who Offers You His Shirt* (Morrow), tells business executives, among other things, how to select a lawyer. A large law firm chooses one sample of size 30 each month over the last

15 months of the number of legal cases it handled. Recorded are the numbers of those cases that the firm lost: 5, 4, 12, 0, 19, 21, 4, 23, 8, 12, 19, 12, 23, 6, and 10. Construct a p-chart to determine if the process is in control.

27. A large bank in Chicago monitors the time it takes for checks to clear the Federal Reserve System. Daily samples of 25 checks are taken for eight days, producing these means and ranges.

Sample	Mean	Range	Sample	Mean	Range
1	2.2	2.1	5	3.2	2.9
2	2.5	2.3	6	2.1	2.5
3	3.1	2.2	7	2.2	2.6
4	2.7	2.1	8	2.5	2.4

Construct $\overline{X}$- and R-charts.

28. A firm which prepares tax returns tries to double-check all forms it completes. However, from January to April 15, this is often impossible. The firm's policy is to allow a maximum of 1 percent of the returns to contain errors. If more errors are suspected, the entire batch must be redone. However, the firm does not want to redo a batch of returns if fewer than 1 percent contain errors, if this can be avoided. It decides to set a limit on recalculating a good batch to only 5 percent of the time. A sample of 20 taken from a large batch reveals five returns have mistakes. Should the entire batch be reworked?

29. Mother's Best sells doughnut holes retail. From a truckload, a sample of 100 is selected, and 8 holes are found to be defective. If Mother's Best is willing to accept a maximum of 10 percent defects, and its suppliers want to restrict their risk to 20 percent, should this shipment be sent back?

30. Yakov Smirnoff, a Russian-American comedian, advertises that Best Western has economical rooms for travelers. The cost of a night's lodging for 15 nights ($n = 15$) was averaged 20 times ($k = 20$ samples). The mean of those 20 sample means proved to be $45.12, with a mean range of $12.34. What are the values for $\overline{X}$- and R-charts?

31. Budget Rental, a nationwide car rental firm, practices a policy in which each car is put through a checklist before it is given to a customer. A recent assessment of 20 cars found the following number of checkpoints had been neglected: 3, 5, 7, 2, 6, 8, 10, 4, 9, 12, 7, 3, 6, 13, 12, 4, 15, 4, 5, and 9. Does it appear the checklist system is in control?

32. Bids by a construction firm for a job are monitored to determine if it might increase the number of bids the firm wins over its competitors. Samples of size 40 bids are taken, yielding means and ranges shown here in thousands of dollars. Is the bidding process out of control?

Sample	Mean	Range
1	7.5	5.4
2	8.6	4.5
3	4.5	3.4
4	5.6	2.5
5	8.9	3.2

33. Suspicious that My Mother's Catch, a fishing boat in the Bering Sea, is using illegal means to augment its daily catch, the U.S. Coast Guard takes samples of the five boats' hauls for six days over the past month. Could unlawful tactics be a possible assignable cause?

Boat	Mean Haul (tons)	Range
My Mother's Catch	39.4	12.2
Neptune's Spear	18.6	18.2
Salty Dog	19.6	21.2
Wind Ablow	38.8	22.5
Deep 6	21.2	19.2

34. Fox Pictures distributes many films to its movie theaters throughout the country. It decides to sample batches of a particular film to determine if copies were reproduced without flaws. If the sampling process suggests that no more than 5 percent of the copies have a flaw, the entire lot will be distributed to the movie houses. Officials wish to reject good lots no more than 10 percent of the time. If they screen 20 copies of a film and find 7 with flaws, should the entire lot be destroyed?

35. In the 20 films Fox screened in Problem 34, they find the following number of flaws in each film: 6, 7, 2, 12, 19, 10, 2, 2, 22, 21, 0, 1, 19, 0, 15, 3, 12, 21, 2, and 5. Does it appear that the reproduction process is out of control?

36. Labor, Inc. selects several samples of size 50 employees for whom it has recently found jobs, and finds that the number in each sample who still have the same job one year later is 10, 12, 4, 17, 2, 21, 34, 32, 43, 12, 5, and 5. Is the placement system out of control?

37. Calculate the final control limits in Problem 36.

38. The new IBM 4019 laser printer produces almost 10 pages per minute on the average. Of 1,200 pages printed, 100 are selected at random and examined for errors. Twelve pages are found to have an average of 2.3 errors. Should the entire 1,200 pages be reprinted if AQL = 5 percent and producer risk is set at 15 percent?

39. Determine the control limits for a c-chart in problem 38.

40. Temperatures in refrigeration boxes are monitored over a 10-day period, in which the temperature is registered every hour for eight hours. The resulting means and ranges are shown. Does it appear that something should be done about the refrigeration process?

Sample	Mean (°F)	Range	Sample	Mean (°F)	Range
1	32	29	6	23	21
2	45	21	7	57	34
3	12	45	8	13	45
4	54	34	9	31	12
5	17	24	10	47	2

41. Federal Express takes eight samples of size 25 for the number of hours it took to deliver packages. The results of that survey are shown here. Need corrective action be taken?

Sample	Mean	Range	Sample	Mean	Range
1	22.2	3.2	5	24.6	3.3
2	17.5	3.4	6	23.3	2.4
3	18.0	2.9	7	21.5	2.4
4	23.4	2.5	8	19.8	3.1

42. Assume that the ranges from Problem 41 are 6.7, 6.8, 5.6, 7.6, 8.1, 7.4, 7.8, and 9.1. Without working the problem, what do you think the control limits for $\overline{X}$ would be relative to those you calculated before? Explain your response. Now work the problem with these new ranges and see if you were right.

CASE APPLICATIONS

43. Melvin Poe and his wife Judy own a painting contract business in Peoria, Illinois. They have 30 employees who work in six crews of five painters. Each crew is named after one of Judy's favorite colors: blue, taupe, topaz, yellow, orange, and cerise.

   Poes' Painting has recently signed a contract with a large apartment complex to paint all of its apartment units in the city. To evaluate the work thus far, the Poes collect a variety of data on the performances of their employees. Melvin personally inspects 20 of the 100 apartments recently painted by the blue crew, one of the less experienced crews. His intention is to determine if any of the apartments must be repainted. Melvin is willing to allow 5 percent of all the apartments this crew paints to contain some defects, as long as he does not make the mistake of repainting more than 20 percent of the units when they don't really need to be repainted. His inspection reveals that three of the apartment units contained unacceptable paint jobs. Each apartment had seven, five, and eight major painting blemishes, respectively.

   Judy attempts to control the time required by the crews to paint each unit. She collects sample data, in hours, on how long it took for each crew to paint eight apartments. All of the apartments were of the same size.

Crew	Apartments							
	1	2	3	4	5	6	7	8
Blue	22.2	14.3	15.7	18.9	19.2	28.9	32.2	25.5
Tope	8.7	10.5	10.9	11.2	11.4	8.8	10.7	11.2
Topaz	7.6	11.2	8.8	10.9	10.2	8.9	11.1	11.2
Yellow	10.1	9.9	8.9	10.0	10.5	9.5	10.0	9.3
Orange	8.7	9.8	10.9	10.8	9.4	9.8	10.4	10.6
Cerise	10.1	9.5	9.3	11.1	10.4	8.7	7.8	9.9

   Fearing that the blue crew needs additional scrutiny, Judy also obtains information on eight samples of 36 apartments each that it painted. She finds that in each sample, the number of apartments containing at least one flaw are 3, 26, 2, 32, 5, 6, 17, and 28.

   Using this information, assist Mel and Judy in evaluating the quality of their job so far.

APPENDIXES

STATISTICAL TABLES

TABLE A   Random Numbers

	00–04	05–09	10–14	15–19	20–24	25–29	30–34	35–39	40–44	45–49
00	49317	61129	89131	29072	80328	28430	78219	60095	04875	30641
01	07046	86793	60292	56275	32920	27352	55677	34884	87794	22116
02	56428	89199	96669	95523	00874	01737	08316	00882	56108	34900
03	68900	32909	98886	85352	20112	46277	62505	69155	07346	92641
04	65662	92876	33167	85630	60153	25658	04163	81487	59085	33576
05	30626	89793	89030	39186	62672	34096	79259	15484	82961	86128
06	08944	92260	71141	63269	05390	42740	02812	98612	58029	78535
07	53490	30321	64325	57140	95602	92005	05120	24503	74878	21816
08	33484	23794	22548	16752	78833	64716	14800	69177	26377	02784
09	16467	95532	29912	12393	74101	24446	45482	55675	59413	91906
10	35648	85681	27823	00756	75951	51803	04182	35073	89864	78820
11	73724	25186	66154	26528	02112	53109	15320	44726	02152	14321
12	61085	53289	05080	77312	79142	58556	45233	37393	60769	37304
13	23284	89012	94167	81623	59675	85151	78454	84486	31295	94858
14	81334	97145	27866	93469	02050	99518	30914	79136	89952	51563
15	70229	95039	36517	04863	14328	71347	16221	92383	90054	08118
16	84379	45707	36649	43629	61046	93738	36678	57640	90478	50696
17	91202	42142	73277	70202	61335	18636	27563	02650	45680	24077
18	69071	10757	67521	59631	22410	24987	37794	12790	97416	19615
19	42822	63339	34940	43796	83207	39270	98714	70333	82408	52589
20	86633	11146	47855	13344	43564	53166	42681	00803	37026	44351
21	61596	11753	08231	18109	94006	35433	01043	39224	38726	13111
22	86215	20972	18304	21153	17059	12093	69457	56257	84432	05259
23	98688	73108	70887	75456	83201	93243	38804	66203	59053	90063
24	32796	91274	53344	24202	18083	07536	04096	55453	15316	11471
25	15977	05506	18654	22614	91478	64332	51332	63110	76297	19613
26	17925	59081	74018	14369	24886	19808	61363	19310	58818	99851
27	67049	15491	35555	35341	35698	97895	39569	07110	49428	50891
28	75900	74079	27038	77422	29686	24769	88667	16058	21021	04819
29	48659	92532	93316	11508	82066	12347	35076	23829	11305	48093
30	23159	60432	40676	89822	36698	69157	38945	01148	44429	78018
31	37587	46602	28947	12981	14217	76012	04095	04679	23535	31867
32	09754	64860	72470	18049	67372	37792	85406	05552	06024	27259
33	89173	97364	23088	43273	31372	23748	50282	89728	03484	80002
34	34997	55750	50195	60033	87970	94694	98383	47484	77607	53880
35	68498	33841	10761	73957	29175	19068	76619	60242	12495	44883
36	99127	03990	54471	01563	50411	63460	85032	53959	74689	78264
37	44161	42863	30138	21892	91664	93233	07974	44475	52732	21112
38	15269	95676	29448	72868	62829	44748	67316	21874	31629	92205
39	98973	40380	26128	53541	02008	12446	44222	22946	05278	12020

TABLE A   Random Numbers (*concluded*)

	50–54	55–59	60–64	65–69	70–74	75–79	80–84	85–89	90–94	95–99
00	03424	74864	11746	77342	24970	15430	76369	08232	05402	66087
01	01677	84988	35246	15095	08838	31175	20982	30309	18096	84899
02	57939	08859	48441	57896	84319	83283	14811	97076	89291	35910
03	27552	57307	58843	38377	02136	59389	82338	26309	28637	68452
04	97565	86873	98942	00360	64645	46932	71799	09485	09314	51819
05	84800	50323	33396	46177	09149	02865	00588	46994	99550	40506
06	52914	13681	23381	38797	28428	48170	03086	32809	75236	00058
07	54951	66790	09596	29427	05105	92584	45968	12386	07806	40655
08	80362	43955	61191	47628	11426	99325	69607	28305	73922	89271
09	62421	70476	37258	31697	61109	18333	91701	95563	46201	12514
10	33012	34971	29595	09899	95259	51098	16799	89517	09909	48352
11	93937	10140	85341	57364	65055	85239	68144	72578	85758	20926
12	47343	53008	64554	77142	54813	94272	13220	93276	12028	05842
13	36728	89534	32162	58174	07438	49352	68648	65773	47769	73026
14	54192	52552	94695	93188	69058	53322	86416	18973	95293	10967
15	73243	63347	17348	17122	59731	57994	34753	97620	20537	42766
16	38748	95561	20099	98539	36899	30760	28145	60312	83863	96312
17	95047	14426	44302	54731	18933	19080	72952	57627	56855	34859
18	77174	73993	06339	33863	27247	70802	72386	35801	43204	07923
19	75687	63671	09641	21688	19629	77186	34847	76911	77754	74082
20	65318	93663	57336	82518	72106	38375	45361	17294	32214	77321
21	39689	65062	26294	06957	28051	32978	04044	19522	00154	07399
22	86917	30252	02536	28503	08677	89051	37121	30540	24812	33251
23	87081	02290	11567	64665	52242	44974	06450	82159	86458	35857
24	20029	12125	22239	70058	66242	78416	53416	76656	37235	37497
25	41343	01619	68185	65843	30455	16122	43529	99837	08684	56947
26	48802	86690	70360	61800	96292	54364	27178	39817	58175	64075
27	00201	53674	62822	14069	80581	45643	92836	46278	82670	37519
28	96157	13631	45042	85158	13973	67170	14192	72897	13882	68487
29	66903	83523	64279	09547	78335	40315	74289	05578	98707	68894
30	77037	12096	69134	13504	00181	31991	79227	67942	70880	37872
31	07666	49845	86053	94798	83079	50421	68467	76689	02028	55555
32	60628	11373	54477	41349	96997	02999	16166	57749	13288	05359
33	08193	10440	76553	44186	83076	05119	31491	82985	61346	08473
34	64368	14947	82460	06619	79026	51058	65457	59765	09322	71875
35	17654	34052	30839	63725	84414	76157	74516	53829	88846	77860
36	73333	12388	33682	35931	08861	84952	54744	06407	28523	22183
37	71375	07499	20422	92949	04918	90317	23064	83117	82547	17584
38	46163	11272	64918	50711	54539	23970	17133	55776	16550	91313
39	49910	95947	81477	20980	47258	33546	64109	68526	73100	49610

TABLE B   Binomial Distribution

n	X	0.05	0.10	0.15	0.20	π 0.25	0.30	0.35	0.40	0.45	0.50
1	0	0.9500	0.9000	0.8500	0.8000	0.7500	0.7000	0.6500	0.6000	0.5500	0.5000
	1	0.0500	0.1000	0.1500	0.2000	0.2500	0.3000	0.3500	0.4000	0.4500	0.5000
2	0	0.9025	0.8100	0.7225	0.6400	0.5625	0.4900	0.4225	0.3600	0.3025	0.2500
	1	0.0950	0.1800	0.2550	0.3200	0.3750	0.4200	0.4550	0.4800	0.4950	0.5000
	2	0.0025	0.0100	0.0225	0.0400	0.0625	0.0900	0.1225	0.1600	0.2025	0.2500
3	0	0.8574	0.7290	0.6141	0.5120	0.4219	0.3430	0.2746	0.2160	0.1664	0.1250
	1	0.1354	0.2430	0.3251	0.3840	0.4219	0.4410	0.4436	0.4320	0.4084	0.3750
	2	0.0071	0.0270	0.0574	0.0960	0.1406	0.1890	0.2389	0.2880	0.3341	0.3750
	3	0.0001	0.0010	0.0034	0.0080	0.0156	0.0270	0.0429	0.0640	0.0911	0.1250
4	0	0.8145	0.6561	0.5220	0.4096	0.3164	0.2401	0.1785	0.1296	0.0915	0.0625
	1	0.1715	0.2916	0.3685	0.4096	0.4219	0.4116	0.3845	0.3456	0.2995	0.2500
	2	0.0135	0.0486	0.0975	0.1536	0.2109	0.2646	0.3105	0.3456	0.3675	0.3750
	3	0.0005	0.0036	0.0115	0.0256	0.0469	0.0756	0.1115	0.1536	0.2005	0.2500
	4	0.0000	0.0001	0.0005	0.0016	0.0039	0.0081	0.0150	0.0256	0.0410	0.0625
5	0	0.7738	0.5905	0.4437	0.3277	0.2373	0.1681	0.1160	0.0778	0.0503	0.0313
	1	0.2036	0.3281	0.3915	0.4096	0.3955	0.3602	0.3124	0.2592	0.2059	0.1563
	2	0.0214	0.0729	0.1382	0.2048	0.2637	0.3087	0.3364	0.3456	0.3369	0.3125
	3	0.0011	0.0081	0.0244	0.0512	0.0879	0.1323	0.1811	0.2304	0.2757	0.3125
	4	0.0000	0.0005	0.0022	0.0064	0.0146	0.0284	0.0488	0.0768	0.1128	0.1563
	5	0.0000	0.0000	0.0001	0.0003	0.0010	0.0024	0.0053	0.0102	0.0185	0.0313
6	0	0.7351	0.5314	0.3771	0.2621	0.1780	0.1176	0.0754	0.0467	0.0277	0.0156
	1	0.2321	0.3543	0.3993	0.3932	0.3560	0.3025	0.2437	0.1866	0.1359	0.0938
	2	0.0305	0.0984	0.1762	0.2458	0.2966	0.3241	0.3280	0.3110	0.2780	0.2344
	3	0.0021	0.0146	0.0415	0.0819	0.1318	0.1852	0.2355	0.2765	0.3032	0.3125
	4	0.0001	0.0012	0.0055	0.0154	0.0330	0.0595	0.0951	0.1382	0.1861	0.2344
	5	0.0000	0.0001	0.0004	0.0015	0.0044	0.0102	0.0205	0.0369	0.0609	0.0938
	6	0.0000	0.0000	0.0000	0.0001	0.0002	0.0007	0.0018	0.0041	0.0083	0.0156
7	0	0.6983	0.4783	0.3206	0.2097	0.1335	0.0824	0.0490	0.0280	0.0152	0.0078
	1	0.2573	0.3720	0.3960	0.3670	0.3115	0.2471	0.1848	0.1306	0.0872	0.0547
	2	0.0406	0.1240	0.2097	0.2753	0.3115	0.3177	0.2985	0.2613	0.2140	0.1641
	3	0.0036	0.0230	0.0617	0.1147	0.1730	0.2269	0.2679	0.2903	0.2918	0.2734
	4	0.0002	0.0026	0.0109	0.0287	0.0577	0.0972	0.1442	0.1935	0.2388	0.2734
	5	0.0000	0.0002	0.0012	0.0043	0.0115	0.0250	0.0466	0.0774	0.1172	0.1641
	6	0.0000	0.0000	0.0001	0.0004	0.0013	0.0036	0.0084	0.0172	0.0320	0.0547
	7	0.0000	0.0000	0.0000	0.0000	0.0001	0.0002	0.0006	0.0016	0.0037	0.0078

TABLE B   Binomial Distribution (*continued*)

n	X	0.05	0.10	0.15	0.20	π 0.25	0.30	0.35	0.40	0.45	0.50
8	0	0.6634	0.4305	0.2725	0.1678	0.1001	0.0576	0.0319	0.0168	0.0084	0.0039
	1	0.2793	0.3826	0.3847	0.3355	0.2670	0.1977	0.1373	0.0896	0.0548	0.0313
	2	0.0515	0.1488	0.2376	0.2936	0.3115	0.2965	0.2587	0.2090	0.1569	0.1094
	3	0.0054	0.0331	0.0839	0.1468	0.2076	0.2541	0.2786	0.2787	0.2568	0.2188
	4	0.0004	0.0046	0.0185	0.0459	0.0865	0.1361	0.1875	0.2322	0.2627	0.2734
	5	0.0000	0.0004	0.0026	0.0092	0.0231	0.0467	0.0808	0.1239	0.1719	0.2188
	6	0.0000	0.0000	0.0002	0.0011	0.0038	0.0100	0.0217	0.0413	0.0703	0.1094
	7	0.0000	0.0000	0.0000	0.0001	0.0004	0.0012	0.0033	0.0079	0.0164	0.0313
	8	0.0000	0.0000	0.0000	0.0000	0.0000	0.0001	0.0002	0.0007	0.0017	0.0039
9	0	0.6302	0.3874	0.2316	0.1342	0.0751	0.0404	0.0207	0.0101	0.0046	0.0020
	1	0.2985	0.3874	0.3679	0.3020	0.2253	0.1556	0.1004	0.0605	0.0339	0.0176
	2	0.0629	0.1722	0.2597	0.3020	0.3003	0.2668	0.2162	0.1612	0.1110	0.0703
	3	0.0077	0.0446	0.1069	0.1762	0.2336	0.2668	0.2716	0.2508	0.2119	0.1641
	4	0.0006	0.0074	0.0283	0.0661	0.1168	0.1715	0.2194	0.2508	0.2600	0.2461
	5	0.0000	0.0008	0.0050	0.0165	0.0389	0.0735	0.1181	0.1672	0.2128	0.2461
	6	0.0000	0.0001	0.0006	0.0028	0.0087	0.0210	0.0424	0.0743	0.1160	0.1641
	7	0.0000	0.0000	0.0000	0.0003	0.0012	0.0039	0.0098	0.0212	0.0407	0.0703
	8	0.0000	0.0000	0.0000	0.0000	0.0001	0.0004	0.0013	0.0035	0.0083	0.0176
	9	0.0000	0.0000	0.0000	0.0000	0.0000	0.0000	0.0001	0.0003	0.0008	0.0020
10	0	0.5987	0.3487	0.1969	0.1074	0.0563	0.0282	0.0135	0.0060	0.0025	0.0010
	1	0.3151	0.3874	0.3474	0.2684	0.1877	0.1211	0.0725	0.0403	0.0207	0.0098
	2	0.0746	0.1937	0.2759	0.3020	0.2816	0.2335	0.1757	0.1209	0.0763	0.0439
	3	0.0105	0.0574	0.1298	0.2013	0.2503	0.2668	0.2522	0.2150	0.1665	0.1172
	4	0.0010	0.0112	0.0401	0.0881	0.1460	0.2001	0.2377	0.2508	0.2384	0.2051
	5	0.0001	0.0015	0.0085	0.0264	0.0584	0.1029	0.1536	0.2007	0.2340	0.2461
	6	0.0000	0.0001	0.0012	0.0055	0.0162	0.0368	0.0689	0.1115	0.1596	0.2051
	7	0.0000	0.0000	0.0001	0.0008	0.0031	0.0090	0.0212	0.0425	0.0746	0.1172
	8	0.0000	0.0000	0.0000	0.0001	0.0004	0.0014	0.0043	0.0106	0.0229	0.0439
	9	0.0000	0.0000	0.0000	0.0000	0.0000	0.0001	0.0005	0.0016	0.0042	0.0098
	10	0.0000	0.0000	0.0000	0.0000	0.0000	0.0000	0.0000	0.0001	0.0003	0.0010
11	0	0.5688	0.3138	0.1673	0.0859	0.0422	0.0198	0.0088	0.0036	0.0014	0.0005
	1	0.3293	0.3835	0.3248	0.2362	0.1549	0.0932	0.0518	0.0266	0.0125	0.0054
	2	0.0867	0.2131	0.2866	0.2953	0.2581	0.1998	0.1395	0.0887	0.0513	0.0269
	3	0.0137	0.0710	0.1517	0.2215	0.2581	0.2568	0.2254	0.1774	0.1259	0.0806
	4	0.0014	0.0158	0.0536	0.1107	0.1721	0.2201	0.2428	0.2365	0.2060	0.1611
	5	0.0001	0.0025	0.0132	0.0388	0.0803	0.1321	0.1830	0.2207	0.2360	0.2256
	6	0.0000	0.0003	0.0023	0.0097	0.0268	0.0566	0.0985	0.1471	0.1931	0.2256
	7	0.0000	0.0000	0.0003	0.0017	0.0064	0.0173	0.0379	0.0701	0.1128	0.1611
	8	0.0000	0.0000	0.0000	0.0002	0.0011	0.0037	0.0102	0.0234	0.0462	0.0806

TABLE B   Binomial Distribution (*continued*)

n	X	0.05	0.10	0.15	0.20	0.25	0.30	0.35	0.40	0.45	0.50
11	9	0.0000	0.0000	0.0000	0.0000	0.0001	0.0005	0.0018	0.0052	0.0126	0.0269
	10	0.0000	0.0000	0.0000	0.0000	0.0000	0.0000	0.0002	0.0007	0.0021	0.0054
	11	0.0000	0.0000	0.0000	0.0000	0.0000	0.0000	0.0000	0.0000	0.0002	0.0005
12	0	0.5404	0.2824	0.1422	0.0687	0.0317	0.0138	0.0057	0.0022	0.0008	0.0002
	1	0.3413	0.3766	0.3012	0.2062	0.1267	0.0712	0.0368	0.0174	0.0075	0.0029
	2	0.0988	0.2301	0.2924	0.2835	0.2323	0.1678	0.1088	0.0639	0.0339	0.0161
	3	0.0173	0.0852	0.1720	0.2362	0.2581	0.2397	0.1954	0.1419	0.0923	0.0537
	4	0.0021	0.0213	0.0683	0.1329	0.1936	0.2311	0.2367	0.2128	0.1700	0.1208
	5	0.0002	0.0038	0.0193	0.0532	0.1032	0.1585	0.2039	0.2270	0.2225	0.1934
	6	0.0000	0.0005	0.0040	0.0155	0.0401	0.0792	0.1281	0.1766	0.2124	0.2256
	7	0.0000	0.0000	0.0006	0.0033	0.0115	0.0291	0.0591	0.1009	0.1489	0.1934
	8	0.0000	0.0000	0.0001	0.0005	0.0024	0.0078	0.0199	0.0420	0.0762	0.1208
	9	0.0000	0.0000	0.0000	0.0001	0.0004	0.0015	0.0048	0.0125	0.0277	0.0537
	10	0.0000	0.0000	0.0000	0.0000	0.0000	0.0002	0.0008	0.0025	0.0068	0.0161
	11	0.0000	0.0000	0.0000	0.0000	0.0000	0.0000	0.0001	0.0003	0.0010	0.0029
	12	0.0000	0.0000	0.0000	0.0000	0.0000	0.0000	0.0000	0.0000	0.0001	0.0002
13	0	0.5133	0.2542	0.1209	0.0550	0.0238	0.0097	0.0037	0.0013	0.0004	0.0001
	1	0.3512	0.3672	0.2774	0.1787	0.1029	0.0540	0.0259	0.0113	0.0045	0.0016
	2	0.1109	0.2448	0.2937	0.2680	0.2059	0.1388	0.0836	0.0453	0.0220	0.0095
	3	0.0214	0.0997	0.1900	0.2457	0.2517	0.2181	0.1651	0.1107	0.0660	0.0349
	4	0.0028	0.0277	0.0838	0.1535	0.2097	0.2337	0.2222	0.1845	0.1350	0.0873
	5	0.0003	0.0055	0.0266	0.0691	0.1258	0.1803	0.2154	0.2214	0.1989	0.1571
	6	0.0000	0.0008	0.0063	0.0230	0.0559	0.1030	0.1546	0.1968	0.2169	0.2095
	7	0.0000	0.0001	0.0011	0.0058	0.0186	0.0442	0.0833	0.1312	0.1775	0.2095
	8	0.0000	0.0000	0.0001	0.0011	0.0047	0.0142	0.0336	0.0656	0.1089	0.1571
	9	0.0000	0.0000	0.0000	0.0001	0.0009	0.0034	0.0101	0.0243	0.0495	0.0873
	10	0.0000	0.0000	0.0000	0.0000	0.0001	0.0006	0.0022	0.0065	0.0162	0.0349
	11	0.0000	0.0000	0.0000	0.0000	0.0000	0.0001	0.0003	0.0012	0.0036	0.0095
	12	0.0000	0.0000	0.0000	0.0000	0.0000	0.0000	0.0000	0.0001	0.0005	0.0016
	13	0.0000	0.0000	0.0000	0.0000	0.0000	0.0000	0.0000	0.0000	0.0000	0.0001
14	0	0.4877	0.2288	0.1028	0.0440	0.0178	0.0068	0.0024	0.0008	0.0002	0.0001
	1	0.3593	0.3559	0.2539	0.1539	0.0832	0.0407	0.0181	0.0073	0.0027	0.0009
	2	0.1229	0.2570	0.2912	0.2501	0.1802	0.1134	0.0634	0.0317	0.0141	0.0056
	3	0.0259	0.1142	0.2056	0.2501	0.2402	0.1943	0.1366	0.0845	0.0462	0.0222
	4	0.0037	0.0349	0.0998	0.1720	0.2202	0.2290	0.2022	0.1549	0.1040	0.0611
	5	0.0004	0.0078	0.0352	0.0860	0.1468	0.1963	0.2178	0.2066	0.1701	0.1222
	6	0.0000	0.0013	0.0093	0.0322	0.0734	0.1262	0.1759	0.2066	0.2088	0.1833
	7	0.0000	0.0002	0.0019	0.0092	0.0280	0.0618	0.1082	0.1574	0.1952	0.2095
	8	0.0000	0.0000	0.0003	0.0020	0.0082	0.0232	0.0510	0.0918	0.1398	0.1833

TABLE B   Binomial Distribution (*continued*)

n	X	0.05	0.10	0.15	0.20	π 0.25	0.30	0.35	0.40	0.45	0.50
14	9	0.0000	0.0000	0.0000	0.0003	0.0018	0.0066	0.0183	0.0408	0.0762	0.1222
	10	0.0000	0.0000	0.0000	0.0000	0.0003	0.0014	0.0049	0.0136	0.0312	0.0611
	11	0.0000	0.0000	0.0000	0.0000	0.0000	0.0002	0.0010	0.0033	0.0093	0.0222
	12	0.0000	0.0000	0.0000	0.0000	0.0000	0.0000	0.0001	0.0005	0.0019	0.0056
	13	0.0000	0.0000	0.0000	0.0000	0.0000	0.0000	0.0000	0.0001	0.0002	0.0009
	14	0.0000	0.0000	0.0000	0.0000	0.0000	0.0000	0.0000	0.0000	0.0000	0.0001
15	0	0.4633	0.2059	0.0874	0.0352	0.0134	0.0047	0.0016	0.0005	0.0001	0.0000
	1	0.3658	0.3432	0.2312	0.1319	0.0668	0.0305	0.0126	0.0047	0.0016	0.0005
	2	0.1348	0.2669	0.2856	0.2309	0.1559	0.0916	0.0476	0.0219	0.0090	0.0032
	3	0.0307	0.1285	0.2184	0.2501	0.2252	0.1700	0.1110	0.0634	0.0318	0.0139
	4	0.0049	0.0428	0.1156	0.1876	0.2252	0.2186	0.1792	0.1268	0.0780	0.0417
	5	0.0006	0.0105	0.0449	0.1032	0.1651	0.2061	0.2123	0.1859	0.1404	0.0916
	6	0.0000	0.0019	0.0132	0.0430	0.0917	0.1472	0.1906	0.2066	0.1914	0.1527
	7	0.0000	0.0003	0.0030	0.0138	0.0393	0.0811	0.1319	0.1771	0.2013	0.1964
	8	0.0000	0.0000	0.0005	0.0035	0.0131	0.0348	0.0710	0.1181	0.1647	0.1964
	9	0.0000	0.0000	0.0001	0.0007	0.0034	0.0116	0.0298	0.0612	0.1048	0.1527
	10	0.0000	0.0000	0.0000	0.0001	0.0007	0.0030	0.0096	0.0245	0.0515	0.0916
	11	0.0000	0.0000	0.0000	0.0000	0.0001	0.0006	0.0024	0.0074	0.0191	0.0417
	12	0.0000	0.0000	0.0000	0.0000	0.0000	0.0001	0.0004	0.0016	0.0052	0.0139
	13	0.0000	0.0000	0.0000	0.0000	0.0000	0.0000	0.0001	0.0003	0.0010	0.0032
	14	0.0000	0.0000	0.0000	0.0000	0.0000	0.0000	0.0000	0.0000	0.0001	0.0005
	15	0.0000	0.0000	0.0000	0.0000	0.0000	0.0000	0.0000	0.0000	0.0000	0.0000
16	0	0.4401	0.1853	0.0743	0.0281	0.0100	0.0033	0.0010	0.0003	0.0001	0.0000
	1	0.3706	0.3294	0.2097	0.1126	0.0535	0.0228	0.0087	0.0030	0.0009	0.0002
	2	0.1463	0.2745	0.2775	0.2111	0.1336	0.0732	0.0353	0.0150	0.0056	0.0018
	3	0.0359	0.1423	0.2285	0.2463	0.2079	0.1465	0.0888	0.0468	0.0215	0.0085
	4	0.0061	0.0514	0.1311	0.2001	0.2252	0.2040	0.1553	0.1014	0.0572	0.0278
	5	0.0008	0.0137	0.0555	0.1201	0.1802	0.2099	0.2008	0.1623	0.1123	0.0667
	6	0.0001	0.0028	0.0180	0.0550	0.1101	0.1649	0.1982	0.1983	0.1684	0.1222
	7	0.0000	0.0004	0.0045	0.0197	0.0524	0.1010	0.1524	0.1889	0.1969	0.1746
	8	0.0000	0.0001	0.0009	0.0055	0.0197	0.0487	0.0923	0.1417	0.1812	0.1964
	9	0.0000	0.0000	0.0001	0.0012	0.0058	0.0185	0.0442	0.0840	0.1318	0.1746
	10	0.0000	0.0000	0.0000	0.0002	0.0014	0.0056	0.0167	0.0392	0.0755	0.1222
	11	0.0000	0.0000	0.0000	0.0000	0.0002	0.0013	0.0049	0.0142	0.0337	0.0667
	12	0.0000	0.0000	0.0000	0.0000	0.0000	0.0002	0.0011	0.0040	0.0115	0.0278
	13	0.0000	0.0000	0.0000	0.0000	0.0000	0.0000	0.0002	0.0008	0.0029	0.0085
	14	0.0000	0.0000	0.0000	0.0000	0.0000	0.0000	0.0000	0.0001	0.0005	0.0018
	15	0.0000	0.0000	0.0000	0.0000	0.0000	0.0000	0.0000	0.0000	0.0001	0.0002
	16	0.0000	0.0000	0.0000	0.0000	0.0000	0.0000	0.0000	0.0000	0.0000	0.0000

TABLE B   Binomial Distribution (*continued*)

n	X	0.05	0.10	0.15	0.20	0.25	0.30	0.35	0.40	0.45	0.50
17	0	0.4181	0.1668	0.0631	0.0225	0.0075	0.0023	0.0007	0.0002	0.0000	0.0000
	1	0.3741	0.3150	0.1893	0.0957	0.0426	0.0169	0.0060	0.0019	0.0005	0.0001
	2	0.1575	0.2800	0.2673	0.1914	0.1136	0.0581	0.0260	0.0102	0.0035	0.0010
	3	0.0415	0.1556	0.2359	0.2393	0.1893	0.1245	0.0701	0.0341	0.0144	0.0052
	4	0.0076	0.0605	0.1457	0.2093	0.2209	0.1868	0.1320	0.0796	0.0411	0.0182
	5	0.0010	0.0175	0.0668	0.1361	0.1914	0.2081	0.1849	0.1379	0.0875	0.0472
	6	0.0001	0.0039	0.0236	0.0680	0.1276	0.1784	0.1991	0.1839	0.1432	0.0944
	7	0.0000	0.0007	0.0065	0.0267	0.0668	0.1201	0.1685	0.1927	0.1841	0.1484
	8	0.0000	0.0001	0.0014	0.0084	0.0279	0.0644	0.1134	0.1606	0.1883	0.1855
	9	0.0000	0.0000	0.0003	0.0021	0.0093	0.0276	0.0611	0.1070	0.1540	0.1855
	10	0.0000	0.0000	0.0000	0.0004	0.0025	0.0095	0.0263	0.0571	0.1008	0.1484
	11	0.0000	0.0000	0.0000	0.0001	0.0005	0.0026	0.0090	0.0242	0.0525	0.0944
	12	0.0000	0.0000	0.0000	0.0000	0.0001	0.0006	0.0024	0.0081	0.0215	0.0472
	13	0.0000	0.0000	0.0000	0.0000	0.0000	0.0001	0.0005	0.0021	0.0068	0.0182
	14	0.0000	0.0000	0.0000	0.0000	0.0000	0.0000	0.0001	0.0004	0.0016	0.0052
	15	0.0000	0.0000	0.0000	0.0000	0.0000	0.0000	0.0000	0.0001	0.0003	0.0010
	16	0.0000	0.0000	0.0000	0.0000	0.0000	0.0000	0.0000	0.0000	0.0000	0.0001
	17	0.0000	0.0000	0.0000	0.0000	0.0000	0.0000	0.0000	0.0000	0.0000	0.0000
18	0	0.3972	0.1501	0.0536	0.0180	0.0056	0.0016	0.0004	0.0001	0.0000	0.0000
	1	0.3763	0.3002	0.1704	0.0811	0.0338	0.0126	0.0042	0.0012	0.0003	0.0001
	2	0.1683	0.2835	0.2556	0.1723	0.0958	0.0458	0.0190	0.0069	0.0022	0.0006
	3	0.0473	0.1680	0.2406	0.2297	0.1704	0.1046	0.0547	0.0246	0.0095	0.0031
	4	0.0093	0.0700	0.1592	0.2153	0.2130	0.1681	0.1104	0.0614	0.0291	0.0117
	5	0.0014	0.0218	0.0787	0.1507	0.1988	0.2017	0.1664	0.1146	0.0666	0.0327
	6	0.0002	0.0052	0.0301	0.0816	0.1436	0.1873	0.1941	0.1655	0.1181	0.0708
	7	0.0000	0.0010	0.0091	0.0350	0.0820	0.1376	0.1792	0.1892	0.1657	0.1214
	8	0.0000	0.0002	0.0022	0.0120	0.0376	0.0811	0.1327	0.1734	0.1864	0.1669
	9	0.0000	0.0000	0.0004	0.0033	0.0139	0.0386	0.0794	0.1284	0.1694	0.1855
	10	0.0000	0.0000	0.0001	0.0008	0.0042	0.0149	0.0385	0.0771	0.1248	0.1669
	11	0.0000	0.0000	0.0000	0.0001	0.0010	0.0046	0.0151	0.0374	0.0742	0.1214
	12	0.0000	0.0000	0.0000	0.0000	0.0002	0.0012	0.0047	0.0145	0.0354	0.0708
	13	0.0000	0.0000	0.0000	0.0000	0.0000	0.0002	0.0012	0.0045	0.0134	0.0327
	14	0.0000	0.0000	0.0000	0.0000	0.0000	0.0000	0.0002	0.0011	0.0039	0.0117
	15	0.0000	0.0000	0.0000	0.0000	0.0000	0.0000	0.0000	0.0002	0.0009	0.0031
	16	0.0000	0.0000	0.0000	0.0000	0.0000	0.0000	0.0000	0.0000	0.0001	0.0006
	17	0.0000	0.0000	0.0000	0.0000	0.0000	0.0000	0.0000	0.0000	0.0000	0.0001
	18	0.0000	0.0000	0.0000	0.0000	0.0000	0.0000	0.0000	0.0000	0.0000	0.0000
19	0	0.3774	0.1351	0.0456	0.0144	0.0042	0.0011	0.0003	0.0001	0.0000	0.0000
	1	0.3774	0.2852	0.1529	0.0685	0.0268	0.0093	0.0029	0.0008	0.0002	0.0000

Table B   Binomial Distribution (*concluded*)

n	X	0.05	0.10	0.15	0.20	π 0.25	0.30	0.35	0.40	0.45	0.50
19	2	0.1787	0.2852	0.2428	0.1540	0.0803	0.0358	0.0138	0.0046	0.0013	0.0003
	3	0.0533	0.1796	0.2428	0.2182	0.1517	0.0869	0.0422	0.0175	0.0062	0.0018
	4	0.0112	0.0798	0.1714	0.2182	0.2023	0.1491	0.0909	0.0467	0.0203	0.0074
	5	0.0018	0.0266	0.0907	0.1636	0.2023	0.1916	0.1468	0.0933	0.0497	0.0222
	6	0.0002	0.0069	0.0374	0.0955	0.1574	0.1916	0.1844	0.1451	0.0949	0.0518
	7	0.0000	0.0014	0.0122	0.0443	0.0974	0.1525	0.1844	0.1797	0.1443	0.0961
	8	0.0000	0.0002	0.0032	0.0166	0.0487	0.0981	0.1489	0.1797	0.1771	0.1442
	9	0.0000	0.0000	0.0007	0.0051	0.0198	0.0514	0.0980	0.1464	0.1771	0.1762
	10	0.0000	0.0000	0.0001	0.0013	0.0066	0.0220	0.0528	0.0976	0.1449	0.1762
	11	0.0000	0.0000	0.0000	0.0003	0.0018	0.0077	0.0233	0.0532	0.0970	0.1442
	12	0.0000	0.0000	0.0000	0.0000	0.0004	0.0022	0.0083	0.0237	0.0529	0.0961
	13	0.0000	0.0000	0.0000	0.0000	0.0001	0.0005	0.0024	0.0085	0.0233	0.0518
	14	0.0000	0.0000	0.0000	0.0000	0.0000	0.0001	0.0006	0.0024	0.0082	0.0222
	15	0.0000	0.0000	0.0000	0.0000	0.0000	0.0000	0.0001	0.0005	0.0022	0.0074
	16	0.0000	0.0000	0.0000	0.0000	0.0000	0.0000	0.0000	0.0001	0.0005	0.0018
	17	0.0000	0.0000	0.0000	0.0000	0.0000	0.0000	0.0000	0.0000	0.0001	0.0003
	18	0.0000	0.0000	0.0000	0.0000	0.0000	0.0000	0.0000	0.0000	0.0000	0.0000
	19	0.0000	0.0000	0.0000	0.0000	0.0000	0.0000	0.0000	0.0000	0.0000	0.0000
20	0	0.3585	0.1216	0.0388	0.0115	0.0032	0.0008	0.0002	0.0000	0.0000	0.0000
	1	0.3774	0.2702	0.1368	0.0576	0.0211	0.0068	0.0020	0.0005	0.0001	0.0000
	2	0.1887	0.2852	0.2293	0.1369	0.0669	0.0278	0.0100	0.0031	0.0008	0.0002
	3	0.0596	0.1901	0.2428	0.2054	0.1339	0.0716	0.0323	0.0123	0.0040	0.0011
	4	0.0133	0.0898	0.1821	0.2182	0.1897	0.1304	0.0738	0.0350	0.0139	0.0046
	5	0.0022	0.0319	0.1028	0.1746	0.2023	0.1789	0.1272	0.0746	0.0365	0.0148
	6	0.0003	0.0089	0.0454	0.1091	0.1686	0.1916	0.1712	0.1244	0.0746	0.0370
	7	0.0000	0.0020	0.0160	0.0545	0.1124	0.1643	0.1844	0.1659	0.1221	0.0739
	8	0.0000	0.0004	0.0046	0.0222	0.0609	0.1144	0.1614	0.1797	0.1623	0.1201
	9	0.0000	0.0001	0.0011	0.0074	0.0271	0.0654	0.1158	0.1597	0.1771	0.1602
	10	0.0000	0.0000	0.0002	0.0020	0.0099	0.0308	0.0686	0.1171	0.1593	0.1762
	11	0.0000	0.0000	0.0000	0.0005	0.0030	0.0120	0.0336	0.0710	0.1185	0.1602
	12	0.0000	0.0000	0.0000	0.0001	0.0008	0.0039	0.0136	0.0355	0.0727	0.1201
	13	0.0000	0.0000	0.0000	0.0000	0.0002	0.0010	0.0045	0.0146	0.0366	0.0739
	14	0.0000	0.0000	0.0000	0.0000	0.0000	0.0002	0.0012	0.0049	0.0150	0.0370
	15	0.0000	0.0000	0.0000	0.0000	0.0000	0.0000	0.0003	0.0013	0.0049	0.0148
	16	0.0000	0.0000	0.0000	0.0000	0.0000	0.0000	0.0000	0.0003	0.0013	0.0046
	17	0.0000	0.0000	0.0000	0.0000	0.0000	0.0000	0.0000	0.0000	0.0002	0.0011
	18	0.0000	0.0000	0.0000	0.0000	0.0000	0.0000	0.0000	0.0000	0.0000	0.0002
	19	0.0000	0.0000	0.0000	0.0000	0.0000	0.0000	0.0000	0.0000	0.0000	0.0000

TABLE C   Cumulative Binomial Distribution

							π					
n	X	0.01	0.05	0.10	0.15	0.20	0.25	0.30	0.35	0.40	0.45	0.50
2	0	0.9801	0.9025	0.8100	0.7225	0.6400	0.5625	0.4900	0.4225	0.3600	0.3025	0.2500
	1	0.9999	0.9975	0.9900	0.9775	0.9600	0.9375	0.9100	0.8775	0.8400	0.7975	0.7500
3	0	0.9703	0.8574	0.7290	0.6141	0.5120	0.4219	0.3430	0.2746	0.2160	0.1664	0.1250
	1	0.9997	0.9928	0.9720	0.9393	0.8960	0.8438	0.7840	0.7183	0.6480	0.5748	0.5000
	2	1.0000	0.9999	0.9990	0.9966	0.9920	0.9844	0.9730	0.9571	0.9360	0.9089	0.8750
4	0	0.9606	0.8145	0.6561	0.5220	0.4096	0.3164	0.2401	0.1785	0.1296	0.0915	0.0625
	1	0.9994	0.9860	0.9477	0.8905	0.8192	0.7383	0.6517	0.5630	0.4752	0.3910	0.3125
	2	1.0000	0.9995	0.9963	0.9880	0.9728	0.9492	0.9163	0.8735	0.8208	0.7585	0.6875
	3	1.0000	1.0000	0.9999	0.9995	0.9984	0.9961	0.9919	0.9850	0.9744	0.9590	0.9375
5	0	0.9510	0.7738	0.5905	0.4437	0.3277	0.2373	0.1681	0.1160	0.0778	0.0503	0.0313
	1	0.9990	0.9774	0.9185	0.8352	0.7373	0.6328	0.5282	0.4284	0.3370	0.2562	0.1875
	2	1.0000	0.9988	0.9914	0.9734	0.9421	0.8965	0.8369	0.7648	0.6826	0.5931	0.5000
	3	1.0000	1.0000	0.9995	0.9978	0.9933	0.9844	0.9692	0.9460	0.9130	0.8688	0.8125
	4	1.0000	1.0000	1.0000	0.9999	0.9997	0.9990	0.9976	0.9947	0.9898	0.9815	0.9688
6	0	0.9415	0.7351	0.5314	0.3771	0.2621	0.1780	0.1176	0.0754	0.0467	0.0277	0.0156
	1	0.9985	0.9672	0.8857	0.7765	0.6554	0.5339	0.4202	0.3191	0.2333	0.1636	0.1094
	2	1.0000	0.9978	0.9842	0.9527	0.9011	0.8306	0.7443	0.6471	0.5443	0.4415	0.3438
	3	1.0000	0.9999	0.9987	0.9941	0.9830	0.9624	0.9295	0.8826	0.8208	0.7447	0.6563
	4	1.0000	1.0000	0.9999	0.9996	0.9984	0.9954	0.9891	0.9777	0.9590	0.9308	0.8906
	5	1.0000	1.0000	1.0000	1.0000	0.9999	0.9998	0.9993	0.9982	0.9959	0.9917	0.9844
7	0	0.9321	0.6983	0.4783	0.3206	0.2097	0.1335	0.0824	0.0490	0.0280	0.0152	0.0078
	1	0.9980	0.9556	0.8503	0.7166	0.5767	0.4449	0.3294	0.2338	0.1586	0.1024	0.0625
	2	1.0000	0.9962	0.9743	0.9262	0.8520	0.7564	0.6471	0.5323	0.4199	0.3164	0.2266
	3	1.0000	0.9998	0.9973	0.9879	0.9667	0.9294	0.8740	0.8002	0.7102	0.6083	0.5000
	4	1.0000	1.0000	0.9998	0.9988	0.9953	0.9871	0.9712	0.9444	0.9037	0.8471	0.7734
	5	1.0000	1.0000	1.0000	0.9999	0.9996	0.9987	0.9962	0.9910	0.9812	0.9643	0.9375
	6	1.0000	1.0000	1.0000	1.0000	1.0000	0.9999	0.9998	0.9994	0.9984	0.9963	0.9922
8	0	0.9227	0.6634	0.4305	0.2725	0.1678	0.1001	0.0576	0.0319	0.0168	0.0084	0.0039
	1	0.9973	0.9428	0.8131	0.6572	0.5033	0.3671	0.2553	0.1691	0.1064	0.0632	0.0352
	2	0.9999	0.9942	0.9619	0.8948	0.7969	0.6785	0.5518	0.4278	0.3154	0.2201	0.1445
	3	1.0000	0.9996	0.9950	0.9786	0.9437	0.8862	0.8059	0.7064	0.5941	0.4770	0.3633
	4	1.0000	1.0000	0.9996	0.9971	0.9896	0.9727	0.9420	0.8939	0.8263	0.7396	0.6367

TABLE C   Cumulative Binomial Distribution (*continued*)

n	X	0.01	0.05	0.10	0.15	0.20	0.25	0.30	0.35	0.40	0.45	0.50
8	5	1.0000	1.0000	1.0000	0.9998	0.9988	0.9958	0.9887	0.9747	0.9502	0.9115	0.8555
	6	1.0000	1.0000	1.0000	1.0000	0.9999	0.9996	0.9987	0.9964	0.9915	0.9819	0.9648
	7	1.0000	1.0000	1.0000	1.0000	1.0000	1.0000	0.9999	0.9998	0.9993	0.9983	0.9961
9	0	0.9135	0.6302	0.3874	0.2316	0.1342	0.0751	0.0404	0.0207	0.0101	0.0046	0.0020
	1	0.9966	0.9288	0.7748	0.5995	0.4362	0.3003	0.1960	0.1211	0.0705	0.0385	0.0195
	2	0.9999	0.9916	0.9470	0.8591	0.7382	0.6007	0.4628	0.3373	0.2318	0.1495	0.0898
	3	1.0000	0.9994	0.9917	0.9661	0.9144	0.8343	0.7297	0.6089	0.4826	0.3614	0.2539
	4	1.0000	1.0000	0.9991	0.9944	0.9804	0.9511	0.9012	0.8283	0.7334	0.6214	0.5000
	5	1.0000	1.0000	0.9999	0.9994	0.9969	0.9900	0.9747	0.9464	0.9006	0.8342	0.7461
	6	1.0000	1.0000	1.0000	1.0000	0.9997	0.9987	0.9957	0.9888	0.9750	0.9502	0.9102
	7	1.0000	1.0000	1.0000	1.0000	1.0000	0.9999	0.9996	0.9986	0.9962	0.9909	0.9805
	8	1.0000	1.0000	1.0000	1.0000	1.0000	1.0000	1.0000	0.9999	0.9997	0.9992	0.9980
10	0	0.9044	0.5987	0.3487	0.1969	0.1074	0.0563	0.0282	0.0135	0.0060	0.0025	0.0010
	1	0.9957	0.9139	0.7361	0.5443	0.3758	0.2440	0.1493	0.0860	0.0464	0.0233	0.0107
	2	0.9999	0.9885	0.9298	0.8202	0.6778	0.5256	0.3828	0.2616	0.1673	0.0996	0.0547
	3	1.0000	0.9990	0.9872	0.9500	0.8791	0.7759	0.6496	0.5138	0.3823	0.2660	0.1719
	4	1.0000	0.9999	0.9984	0.9901	0.9672	0.9219	0.8497	0.7515	0.6331	0.5044	0.3770
	5	1.0000	1.0000	0.9999	0.9986	0.9936	0.9803	0.9527	0.9051	0.8338	0.7384	0.6230
	6	1.0000	1.0000	1.0000	0.9999	0.9991	0.9965	0.9894	0.9740	0.9452	0.8980	0.8281
	7	1.0000	1.0000	1.0000	1.0000	0.9999	0.9996	0.9984	0.9952	0.9877	0.9726	0.9453
	8	1.0000	1.0000	1.0000	1.0000	1.0000	1.0000	0.9999	0.9995	0.9983	0.9955	0.9893
	9	1.0000	1.0000	1.0000	1.0000	1.0000	1.0000	1.0000	1.0000	0.9999	0.9997	0.9990
11	0	0.8953	0.5688	0.3138	0.1673	0.0859	0.0422	0.0198	0.0088	0.0036	0.0014	0.0005
	1	0.9948	0.8981	0.6974	0.4922	0.3221	0.1971	0.1130	0.0606	0.0302	0.0139	0.0059
	2	0.9998	0.9848	0.9104	0.7788	0.6174	0.4552	0.3127	0.2001	0.1189	0.0652	0.0327
	3	1.0000	0.9984	0.9815	0.9306	0.8389	0.7133	0.5696	0.4256	0.2963	0.1911	0.1133
	4	1.0000	0.9999	0.9972	0.9841	0.9496	0.8854	0.7897	0.6683	0.5328	0.3971	0.2744
	5	1.0000	1.0000	0.9997	0.9973	0.9883	0.9657	0.9218	0.8513	0.7535	0.6331	0.5000
	6	1.0000	1.0000	1.0000	0.9997	0.9980	0.9924	0.9784	0.9499	0.9006	0.8262	0.7256
	7	1.0000	1.0000	1.0000	1.0000	0.9998	0.9988	0.9957	0.9878	0.9707	0.9390	0.8867
	8	1.0000	1.0000	1.0000	1.0000	1.0000	0.9999	0.9994	0.9980	0.9941	0.9852	0.9673
	9	1.0000	1.0000	1.0000	1.0000	1.0000	1.0000	1.0000	0.9998	0.9993	0.9978	0.9941
	10	1.0000	1.0000	1.0000	1.0000	1.0000	1.0000	1.0000	1.0000	1.0000	0.9998	0.9995
12	0	0.8864	0.5404	0.2824	0.1422	0.0687	0.0317	0.0138	0.0057	0.0022	0.0008	0.0002
	1	0.9938	0.8816	0.6590	0.4435	0.2749	0.1584	0.0850	0.0424	0.0196	0.0083	0.0032
	2	0.9998	0.9804	0.8891	0.7358	0.5583	0.3907	0.2528	0.1513	0.0834	0.0421	0.0193

TABLE C   Cumulative Binomial Distribution (*continued*)

n	X	0.01	0.05	0.10	0.15	0.20	0.25	0.30	0.35	0.40	0.45	0.50
							π					
12	3	1.0000	0.9978	0.9744	0.9078	0.7946	0.6488	0.4925	0.3467	0.2253	0.1345	0.0730
	4	1.0000	0.9998	0.9957	0.9761	0.9274	0.8424	0.7237	0.5833	0.4382	0.3044	0.1938
	5	1.0000	1.0000	0.9995	0.9954	0.9806	0.9456	0.8822	0.7873	0.6652	0.5269	0.3872
	6	1.0000	1.0000	0.9999	0.9993	0.9961	0.9857	0.9614	0.9154	0.8418	0.7393	0.6128
	7	1.0000	1.0000	1.0000	0.9999	0.9994	0.9972	0.9905	0.9745	0.9427	0.8883	0.8062
	8	1.0000	1.0000	1.0000	1.0000	0.9999	0.9996	0.9983	0.9944	0.9847	0.9644	0.9270
	9	1.0000	1.0000	1.0000	1.0000	1.0000	1.0000	0.9998	0.9992	0.9972	0.9921	0.9807
	10	1.0000	1.0000	1.0000	1.0000	1.0000	1.0000	1.0000	0.9999	0.9997	0.9989	0.9968
	11	1.0000	1.0000	1.0000	1.0000	1.0000	1.0000	1.0000	1.0000	1.0000	0.9999	0.9998
13	0	0.8775	0.5133	0.2542	0.1209	0.0550	0.0238	0.0097	0.0037	0.0013	0.0004	0.0001
	1	0.9928	0.8646	0.6213	0.3983	0.2336	0.1267	0.0637	0.0296	0.0126	0.0049	0.0017
	2	0.9997	0.9755	0.8661	0.6920	0.5017	0.3326	0.2025	0.1132	0.0579	0.0269	0.0112
	3	1.0000	0.9969	0.9658	0.8820	0.7473	0.5843	0.4206	0.2783	0.1686	0.0929	0.0461
	4	1.0000	0.9997	0.9935	0.9658	0.9009	0.7940	0.6543	0.5005	0.3530	0.2279	0.1334
	5	1.0000	1.0000	0.9991	0.9925	0.9700	0.9198	0.8346	0.7159	0.5744	0.4268	0.2905
	6	1.0000	1.0000	0.9999	0.9987	0.9930	0.9757	0.9376	0.8705	0.7712	0.6437	0.5000
	7	1.0000	1.0000	1.0000	0.9998	0.9988	0.9944	0.9818	0.9538	0.9023	0.8212	0.7095
	8	1.0000	1.0000	1.0000	1.0000	0.9998	0.9990	0.9960	0.9874	0.9679	0.9302	0.8666
	9	1.0000	1.0000	1.0000	1.0000	1.0000	0.9999	0.9993	0.9975	0.9922	0.9797	0.9539
	10	1.0000	1.0000	1.0000	1.0000	1.0000	1.0000	0.9999	0.9997	0.9987	0.9959	0.9888
	11	1.0000	1.0000	1.0000	1.0000	1.0000	1.0000	1.0000	1.0000	0.9999	0.9995	0.9983
	12	1.0000	1.0000	1.0000	1.0000	1.0000	1.0000	1.0000	1.0000	1.0000	1.0000	0.9999
14	0	0.8687	0.4877	0.2288	0.1028	0.0440	0.0178	0.0068	0.0024	0.0008	0.0002	0.0001
	1	0.9916	0.8470	0.5846	0.3567	0.1979	0.1010	0.0475	0.0205	0.0081	0.0029	0.0009
	2	0.9997	0.9699	0.8416	0.6479	0.4481	0.2811	0.1608	0.0839	0.0398	0.0170	0.0065
	3	1.0000	0.9958	0.9559	0.8535	0.6982	0.5213	0.3552	0.2205	0.1243	0.0632	0.0287
	4	1.0000	0.9996	0.9908	0.9533	0.8702	0.7415	0.5842	0.4227	0.2793	0.1672	0.0898
	5	1.0000	1.0000	0.9985	0.9885	0.9561	0.8883	0.7805	0.6405	0.4859	0.3373	0.2120
	6	1.0000	1.0000	0.9998	0.9978	0.9884	0.9617	0.9067	0.8164	0.6925	0.5461	0.3953
	7	1.0000	1.0000	1.0000	0.9997	0.9976	0.9897	0.9685	0.9247	0.8499	0.7414	0.6047
	8	1.0000	1.0000	1.0000	1.0000	0.9996	0.9978	0.9917	0.9757	0.9417	0.8811	0.7880
	9	1.0000	1.0000	1.0000	1.0000	1.0000	0.9997	0.9983	0.9940	0.9825	0.9574	0.9102
	10	1.0000	1.0000	1.0000	1.0000	1.0000	1.0000	0.9998	0.9989	0.9961	0.9886	0.9713
	11	1.0000	1.0000	1.0000	1.0000	1.0000	1.0000	1.0000	0.9999	0.9994	0.9978	0.9935
	12	1.0000	1.0000	1.0000	1.0000	1.0000	1.0000	1.0000	1.0000	0.9999	0.9997	0.9991
	13	1.0000	1.0000	1.0000	1.0000	1.0000	1.0000	1.0000	1.0000	1.0000	1.0000	0.9999

TABLE C   Cumulative Binomial Distribution (*continued*)

n	X	0.01	0.05	0.10	0.15	0.20	0.25	0.30	0.35	0.40	0.45	0.50
							π					
15	0	0.8601	0.4633	0.2059	0.0874	0.0352	0.0134	0.0047	0.0016	0.0005	0.0001	0.0000
	1	0.9904	0.8290	0.5490	0.3186	0.1671	0.0802	0.0353	0.0142	0.0052	0.0017	0.0005
	2	0.9996	0.9638	0.8159	0.6042	0.3980	0.2361	0.1268	0.0617	0.0271	0.0107	0.0037
	3	1.0000	0.9945	0.9444	0.8227	0.6482	0.4613	0.2969	0.1727	0.0905	0.0424	0.0176
	4	1.0000	0.9994	0.9873	0.9383	0.8358	0.6865	0.5155	0.3519	0.2173	0.1204	0.0592
	5	1.0000	0.9999	0.9978	0.9832	0.9389	0.8516	0.7216	0.5643	0.4032	0.2608	0.1509
	6	1.0000	1.0000	0.9997	0.9964	0.9819	0.9434	0.8689	0.7548	0.6098	0.4522	0.3036
	7	1.0000	1.0000	1.0000	0.9994	0.9958	0.9827	0.9500	0.8868	0.7869	0.6535	0.5000
	8	1.0000	1.0000	1.0000	0.9999	0.9992	0.9958	0.9848	0.9578	0.9050	0.8182	0.6964
	9	1.0000	1.0000	1.0000	1.0000	0.9999	0.9992	0.9963	0.9876	0.9662	0.9231	0.8491
	10	1.0000	1.0000	1.0000	1.0000	1.0000	0.9999	0.9993	0.9972	0.9907	0.9745	0.9408
	11	1.0000	1.0000	1.0000	1.0000	1.0000	1.0000	0.9999	0.9995	0.9981	0.9937	0.9824
	12	1.0000	1.0000	1.0000	1.0000	1.0000	1.0000	1.0000	0.9999	0.9997	0.9989	0.9963
	13	1.0000	1.0000	1.0000	1.0000	1.0000	1.0000	1.0000	1.0000	1.0000	0.9999	0.9995
	14	1.0000	1.0000	1.0000	1.0000	1.0000	1.0000	1.0000	1.0000	1.0000	1.0000	1.0000
16	0	0.8515	0.4401	0.1853	0.0743	0.0281	0.0100	0.0033	0.0010	0.0003	0.0001	0.0000
	1	0.9891	0.8108	0.5147	0.2839	0.1407	0.0635	0.0261	0.0098	0.0033	0.0010	0.0003
	2	0.9995	0.9571	0.7892	0.5614	0.3518	0.1971	0.0994	0.0451	0.0183	0.0066	0.0021
	3	1.0000	0.9930	0.9316	0.7899	0.5981	0.4050	0.2459	0.1339	0.0651	0.0281	0.0106
	4	1.0000	0.9991	0.9830	0.9209	0.7982	0.6302	0.4499	0.2892	0.1666	0.0853	0.0384
	5	1.0000	0.9999	0.9967	0.9765	0.9183	0.8103	0.6598	0.4900	0.3288	0.1976	0.1051
	6	1.0000	1.0000	0.9995	0.9944	0.9733	0.9204	0.8247	0.6881	0.5272	0.3660	0.2272
	7	1.0000	1.0000	0.9999	0.9989	0.9930	0.9729	0.9256	0.8406	0.7161	0.5629	0.4018
	8	1.0000	1.0000	1.0000	0.9998	0.9985	0.9925	0.9743	0.9329	0.8577	0.7441	0.5982
	9	1.0000	1.0000	1.0000	1.0000	0.9998	0.9984	0.9929	0.9771	0.9417	0.8759	0.7728
	10	1.0000	1.0000	1.0000	1.0000	1.0000	0.9997	0.9984	0.9938	0.9809	0.9514	0.8949
	11	1.0000	1.0000	1.0000	1.0000	1.0000	1.0000	0.9997	0.9987	0.9951	0.9851	0.9616
	12	1.0000	1.0000	1.0000	1.0000	1.0000	1.0000	1.0000	0.9998	0.9991	0.9965	0.9894
	13	1.0000	1.0000	1.0000	1.0000	1.0000	1.0000	1.0000	1.0000	0.9999	0.9994	0.9979
	14	1.0000	1.0000	1.0000	1.0000	1.0000	1.0000	1.0000	1.0000	1.0000	0.9999	0.9997
	15	1.0000	1.0000	1.0000	1.0000	1.0000	1.0000	1.0000	1.0000	1.0000	1.0000	1.0000
17	0	0.8429	0.4181	0.1668	0.0631	0.0225	0.0075	0.0023	0.0007	0.0002	0.0000	0.0000
	1	0.9877	0.7922	0.4818	0.2525	0.1182	0.0501	0.0193	0.0067	0.0021	0.0006	0.0001
	2	0.9994	0.9497	0.7618	0.5198	0.3096	0.1637	0.0774	0.0327	0.0123	0.0041	0.0012
	3	1.0000	0.9912	0.9174	0.7556	0.5489	0.3530	0.2019	0.1028	0.0464	0.0184	0.0064
	4	1.0000	0.9988	0.9779	0.9013	0.7582	0.5739	0.3887	0.2348	0.1260	0.0596	0.0245
	5	1.0000	0.9999	0.9953	0.9681	0.8943	0.7653	0.5968	0.4197	0.2639	0.1471	0.0717

TABLE C   Cumulative Binomial Distribution (*continued*)

n	X	0.01	0.05	0.10	0.15	0.20	0.25	0.30	0.35	0.40	0.45	0.50
							π					
17	6	1.0000	1.0000	0.9992	0.9917	0.9623	0.8929	0.7752	0.6188	0.4478	0.2902	0.1662
	7	1.0000	1.0000	0.9999	0.9983	0.9891	0.9598	0.8954	0.7872	0.6405	0.4743	0.3145
	8	1.0000	1.0000	1.0000	0.9997	0.9974	0.9876	0.9597	0.9006	0.8011	0.6626	0.5000
	9	1.0000	1.0000	1.0000	1.0000	0.9995	0.9969	0.9873	0.9617	0.9081	0.8166	0.6855
	10	1.0000	1.0000	1.0000	1.0000	0.9999	0.9994	0.9968	0.9880	0.9652	0.9174	0.8338
	11	1.0000	1.0000	1.0000	1.0000	1.0000	0.9999	0.9993	0.9970	0.9894	0.9699	0.9283
	12	1.0000	1.0000	1.0000	1.0000	1.0000	1.0000	0.9999	0.9994	0.9975	0.9914	0.9755
	13	1.0000	1.0000	1.0000	1.0000	1.0000	1.0000	1.0000	0.9999	0.9995	0.9981	0.9936
	14	1.0000	1.0000	1.0000	1.0000	1.0000	1.0000	1.0000	1.0000	0.9999	0.9997	0.9988
	15	1.0000	1.0000	1.0000	1.0000	1.0000	1.0000	1.0000	1.0000	1.0000	1.0000	0.9999
	16	1.0000	1.0000	1.0000	1.0000	1.0000	1.0000	1.0000	1.0000	1.0000	1.0000	1.0000
18	0	0.8345	0.3972	0.1501	0.0536	0.0180	0.0056	0.0016	0.0004	0.0001	0.0000	0.0000
	1	0.9862	0.7735	0.4503	0.2241	0.0991	0.0395	0.0142	0.0046	0.0013	0.0003	0.0001
	2	0.9993	0.9419	0.7338	0.4797	0.2713	0.1353	0.0600	0.0236	0.0082	0.0025	0.0007
	3	1.0000	0.9891	0.9018	0.7202	0.5010	0.3057	0.1646	0.0783	0.0328	0.0120	0.0038
	4	1.0000	0.9985	0.9718	0.8794	0.7164	0.5187	0.3327	0.1886	0.0942	0.0411	0.0154
	5	1.0000	0.9998	0.9936	0.9581	0.8671	0.7175	0.5344	0.3550	0.2088	0.1077	0.0481
	6	1.0000	1.0000	0.9988	0.9882	0.9487	0.8610	0.7217	0.5491	0.3743	0.2258	0.1189
	7	1.0000	1.0000	0.9998	0.9973	0.9837	0.9431	0.8593	0.7283	0.5634	0.3915	0.2403
	8	1.0000	1.0000	1.0000	0.9995	0.9957	0.9807	0.9404	0.8609	0.7368	0.5778	0.4073
	9	1.0000	1.0000	1.0000	0.9999	0.9991	0.9946	0.9790	0.9403	0.8653	0.7473	0.5927
	10	1.0000	1.0000	1.0000	1.0000	0.9998	0.9988	0.9939	0.9788	0.9424	0.8720	0.7597
	11	1.0000	1.0000	1.0000	1.0000	1.0000	0.9998	0.9986	0.9938	0.9797	0.9463	0.8811
	12	1.0000	1.0000	1.0000	1.0000	1.0000	1.0000	0.9997	0.9986	0.9942	0.9817	0.9519
	13	1.0000	1.0000	1.0000	1.0000	1.0000	1.0000	1.0000	0.9997	0.9987	0.9951	0.9846
	14	1.0000	1.0000	1.0000	1.0000	1.0000	1.0000	1.0000	1.0000	0.9998	0.9990	0.9962
	15	1.0000	1.0000	1.0000	1.0000	1.0000	1.0000	1.0000	1.0000	1.0000	0.9999	0.9993
	16	1.0000	1.0000	1.0000	1.0000	1.0000	1.0000	1.0000	1.0000	1.0000	1.0000	0.9999
	17	1.0000	1.0000	1.0000	1.0000	1.0000	1.0000	1.0000	1.0000	1.0000	1.0000	1.0000
19	0	0.8262	0.3774	0.1351	0.0456	0.0144	0.0042	0.0011	0.0003	0.0001	0.0000	0.0000
	1	0.9847	0.7547	0.4203	0.1985	0.0829	0.0310	0.0104	0.0031	0.0008	0.0002	0.0000
	2	0.9991	0.9335	0.7054	0.4413	0.2369	0.1113	0.0462	0.0170	0.0055	0.0015	0.0004
	3	1.0000	0.9868	0.8850	0.6841	0.4551	0.2631	0.1332	0.0591	0.0230	0.0077	0.0022
	4	1.0000	0.9980	0.9648	0.8556	0.6733	0.4654	0.2822	0.1500	0.0696	0.0280	0.0096
	5	1.0000	0.9998	0.9914	0.9463	0.8369	0.6678	0.4739	0.2968	0.1629	0.0777	0.0318
	6	1.0000	1.0000	0.9983	0.9837	0.9324	0.8251	0.6655	0.4812	0.3081	0.1727	0.0835
	7	1.0000	1.0000	0.9997	0.9959	0.9767	0.9225	0.8180	0.6656	0.4878	0.3169	0.1796

TABLE C   Cumulative Binomial Distribution (*continued*)

n	X	0.01	0.05	0.10	0.15	0.20	0.25	0.30	0.35	0.40	0.45	0.50
19	8	1.0000	1.0000	1.0000	0.9992	0.9933	0.9713	0.9161	0.8145	0.6675	0.4940	0.3238
	9	1.0000	1.0000	1.0000	0.9999	0.9984	0.9911	0.9674	0.9125	0.8139	0.6710	0.5000
	10	1.0000	1.0000	1.0000	1.0000	0.9997	0.9977	0.9895	0.9653	0.9115	0.8159	0.6762
	11	1.0000	1.0000	1.0000	1.0000	1.0000	0.9995	0.9972	0.9886	0.9648	0.9129	0.8204
	12	1.0000	1.0000	1.0000	1.0000	1.0000	0.9999	0.9994	0.9969	0.9884	0.9658	0.9165
	13	1.0000	1.0000	1.0000	1.0000	1.0000	1.0000	0.9999	0.9993	0.9969	0.9891	0.9682
	14	1.0000	1.0000	1.0000	1.0000	1.0000	1.0000	1.0000	0.9999	0.9994	0.9972	0.9904
	15	1.0000	1.0000	1.0000	1.0000	1.0000	1.0000	1.0000	1.0000	0.9999	0.9995	0.9978
	16	1.0000	1.0000	1.0000	1.0000	1.0000	1.0000	1.0000	1.0000	1.0000	0.9999	0.9996
	17	1.0000	1.0000	1.0000	1.0000	1.0000	1.0000	1.0000	1.0000	1.0000	1.0000	1.0000
20	0	0.8179	0.3585	0.1216	0.0388	0.0115	0.0032	0.0008	0.0002	0.0000	0.0000	0.0000
	1	0.9831	0.7358	0.3917	0.1756	0.0692	0.0243	0.0076	0.0021	0.0005	0.0001	0.0000
	2	0.9990	0.9245	0.6769	0.4049	0.2061	0.0913	0.0355	0.0121	0.0036	0.0009	0.0002
	3	1.0000	0.9841	0.8670	0.6477	0.4114	0.2252	0.1071	0.0444	0.0160	0.0049	0.0013
	4	1.0000	0.9974	0.9568	0.8298	0.6296	0.4148	0.2375	0.1182	0.0510	0.0189	0.0059
	5	1.0000	0.9997	0.9887	0.9327	0.8042	0.6172	0.4164	0.2454	0.1256	0.0553	0.0207
	6	1.0000	1.0000	0.9976	0.9781	0.9133	0.7858	0.6080	0.4166	0.2500	0.1299	0.0577
	7	1.0000	1.0000	0.9996	0.9941	0.9679	0.8982	0.7723	0.6010	0.4159	0.2520	0.1316
	8	1.0000	1.0000	0.9999	0.9987	0.9900	0.9591	0.8867	0.7624	0.5956	0.4143	0.2517
	9	1.0000	1.0000	1.0000	0.9998	0.9974	0.9861	0.9520	0.8782	0.7553	0.5914	0.4119
	10	1.0000	1.0000	1.0000	1.0000	0.9994	0.9961	0.9829	0.9468	0.8725	0.7507	0.5881
	11	1.0000	1.0000	1.0000	1.0000	0.9999	0.9991	0.9949	0.9804	0.9435	0.8692	0.7483
	12	1.0000	1.0000	1.0000	1.0000	1.0000	0.9998	0.9987	0.9940	0.9790	0.9420	0.8684
	13	1.0000	1.0000	1.0000	1.0000	1.0000	1.0000	0.9997	0.9985	0.9935	0.9786	0.9423
	14	1.0000	1.0000	1.0000	1.0000	1.0000	1.0000	1.0000	0.9997	0.9984	0.9936	0.9793
	15	1.0000	1.0000	1.0000	1.0000	1.0000	1.0000	1.0000	1.0000	0.9997	0.9985	0.9941
	16	1.0000	1.0000	1.0000	1.0000	1.0000	1.0000	1.0000	1.0000	1.0000	0.9997	0.9987
	17	1.0000	1.0000	1.0000	1.0000	1.0000	1.0000	1.0000	1.0000	1.0000	1.0000	0.9998
	18	1.0000	1.0000	1.0000	1.0000	1.0000	1.0000	1.0000	1.0000	1.0000	1.0000	1.0000
21	0	0.8097	0.3406	0.1094	0.0329	0.0092	0.0024	0.0006	0.0001	0.0000	0.0000	0.0000
	1	0.9815	0.7170	0.3647	0.1550	0.0576	0.0190	0.0056	0.0014	0.0003	0.0001	0.0000
	2	0.9988	0.9151	0.6484	0.3705	0.1787	0.0745	0.0271	0.0086	0.0024	0.0006	0.0001
	3	0.9999	0.9811	0.8480	0.6113	0.3704	0.1917	0.0856	0.0331	0.0110	0.0031	0.0007
	4	1.0000	0.9968	0.9478	0.8025	0.5860	0.3674	0.1984	0.0924	0.0370	0.0126	0.0036
	5	1.0000	0.9996	0.9856	0.9173	0.7693	0.5666	0.3627	0.2009	0.0957	0.0389	0.0133
	6	1.0000	1.0000	0.9967	0.9713	0.8915	0.7436	0.5505	0.3567	0.2002	0.0964	0.0392
	7	1.0000	1.0000	0.9994	0.9917	0.9569	0.8701	0.7230	0.5365	0.3495	0.1971	0.0946

TABLE C   Cumulative Binomial Distribution (*continued*)

n	X	0.01	0.05	0.10	0.15	0.20	0.25	0.30	0.35	0.40	0.45	0.50
21	8	1.0000	1.0000	0.9999	0.9980	0.9856	0.9439	0.8523	0.7059	0.5237	0.3413	0.1917
	9	1.0000	1.0000	1.0000	0.9996	0.9959	0.9794	0.9324	0.8377	0.6914	0.5117	0.3318
	10	1.0000	1.0000	1.0000	0.9999	0.9990	0.9936	0.9736	0.9228	0.8256	0.6790	0.5000
	11	1.0000	1.0000	1.0000	1.0000	0.9998	0.9983	0.9913	0.9687	0.9151	0.8159	0.6682
	12	1.0000	1.0000	1.0000	1.0000	1.0000	0.9996	0.9976	0.9892	0.9648	0.9092	0.8083
	13	1.0000	1.0000	1.0000	1.0000	1.0000	0.9999	0.9994	0.9969	0.9877	0.9621	0.9054
	14	1.0000	1.0000	1.0000	1.0000	1.0000	1.0000	0.9999	0.9993	0.9964	0.9868	0.9608
	15	1.0000	1.0000	1.0000	1.0000	1.0000	1.0000	1.0000	0.9999	0.9992	0.9963	0.9867
	16	1.0000	1.0000	1.0000	1.0000	1.0000	1.0000	1.0000	1.0000	0.9998	0.9992	0.9964
	17	1.0000	1.0000	1.0000	1.0000	1.0000	1.0000	1.0000	1.0000	1.0000	0.9999	0.9993
	18	1.0000	1.0000	1.0000	1.0000	1.0000	1.0000	1.0000	1.0000	1.0000	1.0000	0.9999
	19	1.0000	1.0000	1.0000	1.0000	1.0000	1.0000	1.0000	1.0000	1.0000	1.0000	1.0000
22	0	0.8016	0.3235	0.0985	0.0280	0.0074	0.0018	0.0004	0.0001	0.0000	0.0000	0.0000
	1	0.9798	0.6982	0.3392	0.1367	0.0480	0.0149	0.0041	0.0010	0.0002	0.0000	0.0000
	2	0.9987	0.9052	0.6200	0.3382	0.1545	0.0606	0.0207	0.0061	0.0016	0.0003	0.0001
	3	0.9999	0.9778	0.8281	0.5752	0.3320	0.1624	0.0681	0.0245	0.0076	0.0020	0.0004
	4	1.0000	0.9960	0.9379	0.7738	0.5429	0.3235	0.1645	0.0716	0.0266	0.0083	0.0022
	5	1.0000	0.9994	0.9818	0.9001	0.7326	0.5168	0.3134	0.1629	0.0722	0.0271	0.0085
	6	1.0000	0.9999	0.9956	0.9632	0.8670	0.6994	0.4942	0.3022	0.1584	0.0705	0.0262
	7	1.0000	1.0000	0.9991	0.9886	0.9439	0.8385	0.6713	0.4736	0.2898	0.1518	0.0669
	8	1.0000	1.0000	0.9999	0.9970	0.9799	0.9254	0.8135	0.6466	0.4540	0.2764	0.1431
	9	1.0000	1.0000	1.0000	0.9993	0.9939	0.9705	0.9084	0.7916	0.6244	0.4350	0.2617
	10	1.0000	1.0000	1.0000	0.9999	0.9984	0.9900	0.9613	0.8930	0.7720	0.6037	0.4159
	11	1.0000	1.0000	1.0000	1.0000	0.9997	0.9971	0.9860	0.9526	0.8793	0.7543	0.5841
	12	1.0000	1.0000	1.0000	1.0000	0.9999	0.9993	0.9957	0.9820	0.9449	0.8672	0.7383
	13	1.0000	1.0000	1.0000	1.0000	1.0000	0.9999	0.9989	0.9942	0.9785	0.9383	0.8569
	14	1.0000	1.0000	1.0000	1.0000	1.0000	1.0000	0.9998	0.9984	0.9930	0.9757	0.9331
	15	1.0000	1.0000	1.0000	1.0000	1.0000	1.0000	1.0000	0.9997	0.9981	0.9920	0.9738
	16	1.0000	1.0000	1.0000	1.0000	1.0000	1.0000	1.0000	0.9999	0.9996	0.9979	0.9915
	17	1.0000	1.0000	1.0000	1.0000	1.0000	1.0000	1.0000	1.0000	0.9999	0.9995	0.9978
	18	1.0000	1.0000	1.0000	1.0000	1.0000	1.0000	1.0000	1.0000	1.0000	0.9999	0.9996
	19	1.0000	1.0000	1.0000	1.0000	1.0000	1.0000	1.0000	1.0000	1.0000	1.0000	0.9999
	20	1.0000	1.0000	1.0000	1.0000	1.0000	1.0000	1.0000	1.0000	1.0000	1.0000	1.0000
23	0	0.7936	0.3074	0.0886	0.0238	0.0059	0.0013	0.0003	0.0000	0.0000	0.0000	0.0000
	1	0.9780	0.6794	0.3151	0.1204	0.0398	0.0116	0.0030	0.0007	0.0001	0.0000	0.0000
	2	0.9985	0.8948	0.5920	0.3080	0.1332	0.0492	0.0157	0.0043	0.0010	0.0002	0.0000
	3	0.9999	0.9742	0.8073	0.5396	0.2965	0.1370	0.0538	0.0181	0.0052	0.0012	0.0002

TABLE C   Cumulative Binomial Distribution (*continued*)

n	X	0.01	0.05	0.10	0.15	0.20	0.25	0.30	0.35	0.40	0.45	0.50
23	4	1.0000	0.9951	0.9269	0.7440	0.5007	0.2832	0.1356	0.0551	0.0190	0.0055	0.0013
	5	1.0000	0.9992	0.9774	0.8811	0.6947	0.4685	0.2688	0.1309	0.0540	0.0186	0.0053
	6	1.0000	0.9999	0.9942	0.9537	0.8402	0.6537	0.4399	0.2534	0.1240	0.0510	0.0173
	7	1.0000	1.0000	0.9988	0.9848	0.9285	0.8037	0.6181	0.4136	0.2373	0.1152	0.0466
	8	1.0000	1.0000	0.9998	0.9958	0.9727	0.9037	0.7709	0.5860	0.3884	0.2203	0.1050
	9	1.0000	1.0000	1.0000	0.9990	0.9911	0.9592	0.8799	0.7408	0.5562	0.3636	0.2024
	10	1.0000	1.0000	1.0000	0.9998	0.9975	0.9851	0.9454	0.8575	0.7129	0.5278	0.3388
	11	1.0000	1.0000	1.0000	1.0000	0.9994	0.9954	0.9786	0.9318	0.8364	0.6865	0.5000
	12	1.0000	1.0000	1.0000	1.0000	0.9999	0.9988	0.9928	0.9717	0.9187	0.8164	0.6612
	13	1.0000	1.0000	1.0000	1.0000	1.0000	0.9997	0.9979	0.9900	0.9651	0.9063	0.7976
	14	1.0000	1.0000	1.0000	1.0000	1.0000	0.9999	0.9995	0.9970	0.9872	0.9589	0.8950
	15	1.0000	1.0000	1.0000	1.0000	1.0000	1.0000	0.9999	0.9992	0.9960	0.9847	0.9534
	16	1.0000	1.0000	1.0000	1.0000	1.0000	1.0000	1.0000	0.9998	0.9990	0.9952	0.9827
	17	1.0000	1.0000	1.0000	1.0000	1.0000	1.0000	1.0000	1.0000	0.9998	0.9988	0.9947
	18	1.0000	1.0000	1.0000	1.0000	1.0000	1.0000	1.0000	1.0000	1.0000	0.9998	0.9987
	19	1.0000	1.0000	1.0000	1.0000	1.0000	1.0000	1.0000	1.0000	1.0000	1.0000	0.9998
	20	1.0000	1.0000	1.0000	1.0000	1.0000	1.0000	1.0000	1.0000	1.0000	1.0000	1.0000
24	0	0.7857	0.2920	0.0798	0.0202	0.0047	0.0010	0.0002	0.0000	0.0000	0.0000	0.0000
	1	0.9761	0.6608	0.2925	0.1059	0.0331	0.0090	0.0022	0.0005	0.0001	0.0000	0.0000
	2	0.9983	0.8841	0.5643	0.2798	0.1145	0.0398	0.0119	0.0030	0.0007	0.0001	0.0000
	3	0.9999	0.9702	0.7857	0.5049	0.2639	0.1150	0.0424	0.0133	0.0035	0.0008	0.0001
	4	1.0000	0.9940	0.9149	0.7134	0.4599	0.2466	0.1111	0.0422	0.0134	0.0036	0.0008
	5	1.0000	0.9990	0.9723	0.8606	0.6559	0.4222	0.2288	0.1044	0.0400	0.0127	0.0033
	6	1.0000	0.9999	0.9925	0.9428	0.8111	0.6074	0.3886	0.2106	0.0960	0.0364	0.0113
	7	1.0000	1.0000	0.9983	0.9801	0.9108	0.7662	0.5647	0.3575	0.1919	0.0863	0.0320
	8	1.0000	1.0000	0.9997	0.9941	0.9638	0.8787	0.7250	0.5257	0.3279	0.1730	0.0758
	9	1.0000	1.0000	0.9999	0.9985	0.9874	0.9453	0.8472	0.6866	0.4891	0.2991	0.1537
	10	1.0000	1.0000	1.0000	0.9997	0.9962	0.9787	0.9258	0.8167	0.6502	0.4539	0.2706
	11	1.0000	1.0000	1.0000	0.9999	0.9990	0.9928	0.9686	0.9058	0.7870	0.6151	0.4194
	12	1.0000	1.0000	1.0000	1.0000	0.9998	0.9979	0.9885	0.9577	0.8857	0.7580	0.5806
	13	1.0000	1.0000	1.0000	1.0000	1.0000	0.9995	0.9964	0.9836	0.9465	0.8659	0.7294
	14	1.0000	1.0000	1.0000	1.0000	1.0000	0.9999	0.9990	0.9945	0.9783	0.9352	0.8463
	15	1.0000	1.0000	1.0000	1.0000	1.0000	1.0000	0.9998	0.9984	0.9925	0.9731	0.9242
	16	1.0000	1.0000	1.0000	1.0000	1.0000	1.0000	1.0000	0.9996	0.9978	0.9905	0.9680
	17	1.0000	1.0000	1.0000	1.0000	1.0000	1.0000	1.0000	0.9999	0.9995	0.9972	0.9887
	18	1.0000	1.0000	1.0000	1.0000	1.0000	1.0000	1.0000	1.0000	0.9999	0.9993	0.9967
	19	1.0000	1.0000	1.0000	1.0000	1.0000	1.0000	1.0000	1.0000	1.0000	0.9999	0.9992

TABLE C   Cumulative Binomial Distribution (*continued*)

n	X	0.01	0.05	0.10	0.15	0.20	0.25	0.30	0.35	0.40	0.45	0.50
							π					
24	20	1.0000	1.0000	1.0000	1.0000	1.0000	1.0000	1.0000	1.0000	1.0000	1.0000	0.9999
	21	1.0000	1.0000	1.0000	1.0000	1.0000	1.0000	1.0000	1.0000	1.0000	1.0000	1.0000
25	0	0.7778	0.2774	0.0718	0.0172	0.0038	0.0008	0.0001	0.0000	0.0000	0.0000	0.0000
	1	0.9742	0.6424	0.2712	0.0931	0.0274	0.0070	0.0016	0.0003	0.0001	0.0000	0.0000
	2	0.9980	0.8729	0.5371	0.2537	0.0982	0.0321	0.0090	0.0021	0.0004	0.0001	0.0000
	3	0.9999	0.9659	0.7636	0.4711	0.2340	0.0962	0.0332	0.0097	0.0024	0.0005	0.0001
	4	1.0000	0.9928	0.9020	0.6821	0.4207	0.2137	0.0905	0.0320	0.0095	0.0023	0.0005
	5	1.0000	0.9988	0.9666	0.8385	0.6167	0.3783	0.1935	0.0826	0.0294	0.0086	0.0020
	6	1.0000	0.9998	0.9905	0.9305	0.7800	0.5611	0.3407	0.1734	0.0736	0.0258	0.0073
	7	1.0000	1.0000	0.9977	0.9745	0.8909	0.7265	0.5118	0.3061	0.1536	0.0639	0.0216
	8	1.0000	1.0000	0.9995	0.9920	0.9532	0.8506	0.6769	0.4668	0.2735	0.1340	0.0539
	9	1.0000	1.0000	0.9999	0.9979	0.9827	0.9287	0.8106	0.6303	0.4246	0.2424	0.1148
	10	1.0000	1.0000	1.0000	0.9995	0.9944	0.9703	0.9022	0.7712	0.5858	0.3843	0.2122
	11	1.0000	1.0000	1.0000	0.9999	0.9985	0.9893	0.9558	0.8746	0.7323	0.5426	0.3450
	12	1.0000	1.0000	1.0000	1.0000	0.9996	0.9966	0.9825	0.9396	0.8462	0.6937	0.5000
	13	1.0000	1.0000	1.0000	1.0000	0.9999	0.9991	0.9940	0.9745	0.9222	0.8173	0.6550
	14	1.0000	1.0000	1.0000	1.0000	1.0000	0.9998	0.9982	0.9907	0.9656	0.9040	0.7878
	15	1.0000	1.0000	1.0000	1.0000	1.0000	1.0000	0.9995	0.9971	0.9868	0.9560	0.8852
	16	1.0000	1.0000	1.0000	1.0000	1.0000	1.0000	0.9999	0.9992	0.9957	0.9826	0.9461
	17	1.0000	1.0000	1.0000	1.0000	1.0000	1.0000	1.0000	0.9998	0.9988	0.9942	0.9784
	18	1.0000	1.0000	1.0000	1.0000	1.0000	1.0000	1.0000	1.0000	0.9997	0.9984	0.9927
	19	1.0000	1.0000	1.0000	1.0000	1.0000	1.0000	1.0000	1.0000	0.9999	0.9996	0.9980
	20	1.0000	1.0000	1.0000	1.0000	1.0000	1.0000	1.0000	1.0000	1.0000	0.9999	0.9995
	21	1.0000	1.0000	1.0000	1.0000	1.0000	1.0000	1.0000	1.0000	1.0000	1.0000	0.9999
	22	1.0000	1.0000	1.0000	1.0000	1.0000	1.0000	1.0000	1.0000	1.0000	1.0000	1.0000
50	0	0.6050	0.0769	0.0052	0.0003	0.0000	0.0000	0.0000	0.0000	0.0000	0.0000	0.0000
	1	0.9106	0.2794	0.0338	0.0029	0.0002	0.0000	0.0000	0.0000	0.0000	0.0000	0.0000
	2	0.9862	0.5405	0.1117	0.0142	0.0013	0.0001	0.0000	0.0000	0.0000	0.0000	0.0000
	3	0.9984	0.7604	0.2503	0.0460	0.0057	0.0005	0.0000	0.0000	0.0000	0.0000	0.0000
	4	0.9999	0.8964	0.4312	0.1121	0.0185	0.0021	0.0002	0.0000	0.0000	0.0000	0.0000
	5	1.0000	0.9622	0.6161	0.2194	0.0480	0.0070	0.0007	0.0001	0.0000	0.0000	0.0000
	6	1.0000	0.9882	0.7702	0.3613	0.1034	0.0194	0.0025	0.0002	0.0000	0.0000	0.0000
	7	1.0000	0.9968	0.8779	0.5188	0.1904	0.0453	0.0073	0.0008	0.0001	0.0000	0.0000
	8	1.0000	0.9992	0.9421	0.6681	0.3073	0.0916	0.0183	0.0025	0.0002	0.0000	0.0000
	9	1.0000	0.9998	0.9755	0.7911	0.4437	0.1637	0.0402	0.0067	0.0008	0.0001	0.0000
	10	1.0000	1.0000	0.9906	0.8801	0.5836	0.2622	0.0789	0.0160	0.0022	0.0002	0.0000
	11	1.0000	1.0000	0.9968	0.9372	0.7107	0.3816	0.1390	0.0342	0.0057	0.0006	0.0000

TABLE C   Cumulative Binomial Distribution (*continued*)

n	X	0.01	0.05	0.10	0.15	0.20	0.25	0.30	0.35	0.40	0.45	0.50
50	12	1.0000	1.0000	0.9990	0.9699	0.8139	0.5110	0.2229	0.0661	0.0133	0.0018	0.0002
	13	1.0000	1.0000	0.9997	0.9868	0.8894	0.6370	0.3279	0.1163	0.0280	0.0045	0.0005
	14	1.0000	1.0000	0.9999	0.9947	0.9393	0.7481	0.4468	0.1878	0.0540	0.0104	0.0013
	15	1.0000	1.0000	1.0000	0.9981	0.9692	0.8369	0.5692	0.2801	0.0955	0.0220	0.0033
	16	1.0000	1.0000	1.0000	0.9993	0.9856	0.9017	0.6839	0.3889	0.1561	0.0427	0.0077
	17	1.0000	1.0000	1.0000	0.9998	0.9937	0.9449	0.7822	0.5060	0.2369	0.0765	0.0164
	18	1.0000	1.0000	1.0000	0.9999	0.9975	0.9713	0.8594	0.6216	0.3356	0.1273	0.0325
	19	1.0000	1.0000	1.0000	1.0000	0.9991	0.9861	0.9152	0.7264	0.4465	0.1974	0.0595
	20	1.0000	1.0000	1.0000	1.0000	0.9997	0.9937	0.9522	0.8139	0.5610	0.2862	0.1013
	21	1.0000	1.0000	1.0000	1.0000	0.9999	0.9974	0.9749	0.8813	0.6701	0.3900	0.1611
	22	1.0000	1.0000	1.0000	1.0000	1.0000	0.9990	0.9877	0.9290	0.7660	0.5019	0.2399
	23	1.0000	1.0000	1.0000	1.0000	1.0000	0.9996	0.9944	0.9604	0.8438	0.6134	0.3359
	24	1.0000	1.0000	1.0000	1.0000	1.0000	0.9999	0.9976	0.9793	0.9022	0.7160	0.4439
	25	1.0000	1.0000	1.0000	1.0000	1.0000	1.0000	0.9991	0.9900	0.9427	0.8034	0.5561
	26	1.0000	1.0000	1.0000	1.0000	1.0000	1.0000	0.9997	0.9955	0.9686	0.8721	0.6641
	27	1.0000	1.0000	1.0000	1.0000	1.0000	1.0000	0.9999	0.9981	0.9840	0.9220	0.7601
	28	1.0000	1.0000	1.0000	1.0000	1.0000	1.0000	1.0000	0.9993	0.9924	0.9556	0.8389
	29	1.0000	1.0000	1.0000	1.0000	1.0000	1.0000	1.0000	0.9997	0.9966	0.9765	0.8987
	30	1.0000	1.0000	1.0000	1.0000	1.0000	1.0000	1.0000	0.9999	0.9986	0.9884	0.9405
	31	1.0000	1.0000	1.0000	1.0000	1.0000	1.0000	1.0000	1.0000	0.9995	0.9947	0.9675
	32	1.0000	1.0000	1.0000	1.0000	1.0000	1.0000	1.0000	1.0000	0.9998	0.9978	0.9836
	33	1.0000	1.0000	1.0000	1.0000	1.0000	1.0000	1.0000	1.0000	0.9999	0.9991	0.9923
	34	1.0000	1.0000	1.0000	1.0000	1.0000	1.0000	1.0000	1.0000	1.0000	0.9997	0.9967
	35	1.0000	1.0000	1.0000	1.0000	1.0000	1.0000	1.0000	1.0000	1.0000	0.9999	0.9987
	36	1.0000	1.0000	1.0000	1.0000	1.0000	1.0000	1.0000	1.0000	1.0000	1.0000	0.9995
	37	1.0000	1.0000	1.0000	1.0000	1.0000	1.0000	1.0000	1.0000	1.0000	1.0000	0.9998
	38	1.0000	1.0000	1.0000	1.0000	1.0000	1.0000	1.0000	1.0000	1.0000	1.0000	1.0000
100	0	0.3660	0.0059	0.0000	0.0000	0.0000	0.0000	0.0000	0.0000	0.0000	0.0000	0.0000
	1	0.7358	0.0371	0.0003	0.0000	0.0000	0.0000	0.0000	0.0000	0.0000	0.0000	0.0000
	2	0.9206	0.1183	0.0019	0.0000	0.0000	0.0000	0.0000	0.0000	0.0000	0.0000	0.0000
	3	0.9816	0.2578	0.0078	0.0001	0.0000	0.0000	0.0000	0.0000	0.0000	0.0000	0.0000
	4	0.9966	0.4360	0.0237	0.0004	0.0000	0.0000	0.0000	0.0000	0.0000	0.0000	0.0000
	5	0.9995	0.6160	0.0576	0.0016	0.0000	0.0000	0.0000	0.0000	0.0000	0.0000	0.0000
	6	0.9999	0.7660	0.1172	0.0047	0.0001	0.0000	0.0000	0.0000	0.0000	0.0000	0.0000
	7	1.0000	0.8720	0.2061	0.0122	0.0003	0.0000	0.0000	0.0000	0.0000	0.0000	0.0000
	8	1.0000	0.9369	0.3209	0.0275	0.0009	0.0000	0.0000	0.0000	0.0000	0.0000	0.0000
	9	1.0000	0.9718	0.4513	0.0551	0.0023	0.0000	0.0000	0.0000	0.0000	0.0000	0.0000
	10	1.0000	0.9885	0.5832	0.0994	0.0057	0.0001	0.0000	0.0000	0.0000	0.0000	0.0000

TABLE C   Cumulative Binomial Distribution (*continued*)

							π					
n	*X*	0.01	0.05	0.10	0.15	0.20	0.25	0.30	0.35	0.40	0.45	0.50
100	11	1.0000	0.9957	0.7030	0.1635	0.0126	0.0004	0.0000	0.0000	0.0000	0.0000	0.0000
	12	1.0000	0.9985	0.8018	0.2473	0.0253	0.0010	0.0000	0.0000	0.0000	0.0000	0.0000
	13	1.0000	0.9995	0.8761	0.3474	0.0469	0.0025	0.0001	0.0000	0.0000	0.0000	0.0000
	14	1.0000	0.9999	0.9274	0.4572	0.0804	0.0054	0.0002	0.0000	0.0000	0.0000	0.0000
	15	1.0000	1.0000	0.9601	0.5683	0.1285	0.0111	0.0004	0.0000	0.0000	0.0000	0.0000
	16	1.0000	1.0000	0.9794	0.6725	0.1923	0.0211	0.0010	0.0000	0.0000	0.0000	0.0000
	17	1.0000	1.0000	0.9900	0.7633	0.2712	0.0376	0.0022	0.0001	0.0000	0.0000	0.0000
	18	1.0000	1.0000	0.9954	0.8372	0.3621	0.0630	0.0045	0.0001	0.0000	0.0000	0.0000
	19	1.0000	1.0000	0.9980	0.8935	0.4602	0.0995	0.0089	0.0003	0.0000	0.0000	0.0000
	20	1.0000	1.0000	0.9992	0.9337	0.5595	0.1488	0.0165	0.0008	0.0000	0.0000	0.0000
	21	1.0000	1.0000	0.9997	0.9607	0.6540	0.2114	0.0288	0.0017	0.0000	0.0000	0.0000
	22	1.0000	1.0000	0.9999	0.9779	0.7389	0.2864	0.0479	0.0034	0.0001	0.0000	0.0000
	23	1.0000	1.0000	1.0000	0.9881	0.8109	0.3711	0.0755	0.0066	0.0003	0.0000	0.0000
	24	1.0000	1.0000	1.0000	0.9939	0.8686	0.4617	0.1136	0.0121	0.0006	0.0000	0.0000
	25	1.0000	1.0000	1.0000	0.9970	0.9125	0.5535	0.1631	0.0211	0.0012	0.0000	0.0000
	26	1.0000	1.0000	1.0000	0.9986	0.9442	0.6417	0.2244	0.0351	0.0024	0.0001	0.0000
	27	1.0000	1.0000	1.0000	0.9994	0.9658	0.7224	0.2964	0.0558	0.0046	0.0002	0.0000
	28	1.0000	1.0000	1.0000	0.9997	0.9800	0.7925	0.3768	0.0848	0.0084	0.0004	0.0000
	29	1.0000	1.0000	1.0000	0.9999	0.9888	0.8505	0.4623	0.1236	0.0148	0.0008	0.0000
	30	1.0000	1.0000	1.0000	1.0000	0.9939	0.8962	0.5491	0.1730	0.0248	0.0015	0.0000
	31	1.0000	1.0000	1.0000	1.0000	0.9969	0.9307	0.6331	0.2331	0.0398	0.0030	0.0001
	32	1.0000	1.0000	1.0000	1.0000	0.9984	0.9554	0.7107	0.3029	0.0615	0.0055	0.0002
	33	1.0000	1.0000	1.0000	1.0000	0.9993	0.9724	0.7793	0.3803	0.0913	0.0098	0.0004
	34	1.0000	1.0000	1.0000	1.0000	0.9997	0.9836	0.8371	0.4624	0.1303	0.0166	0.0009
	35	1.0000	1.0000	1.0000	1.0000	0.9999	0.9906	0.8839	0.5458	0.1795	0.0272	0.0018
	36	1.0000	1.0000	1.0000	1.0000	0.9999	0.9948	0.9201	0.6269	0.2386	0.0429	0.0033
	37	1.0000	1.0000	1.0000	1.0000	1.0000	0.9973	0.9470	0.7024	0.3068	0.0651	0.0060
	38	1.0000	1.0000	1.0000	1.0000	1.0000	0.9986	0.9660	0.7699	0.3822	0.0951	0.0105
	39	1.0000	1.0000	1.0000	1.0000	1.0000	0.9993	0.9790	0.8276	0.4621	0.1343	0.0176
	40	1.0000	1.0000	1.0000	1.0000	1.0000	0.9997	0.9875	0.8750	0.5433	0.1831	0.0284
	41	1.0000	1.0000	1.0000	1.0000	1.0000	0.9999	0.9928	0.9123	0.6225	0.2415	0.0443
	42	1.0000	1.0000	1.0000	1.0000	1.0000	0.9999	0.9960	0.9406	0.6967	0.3087	0.0666
	43	1.0000	1.0000	1.0000	1.0000	1.0000	1.0000	0.9979	0.9611	0.7635	0.3828	0.0967
	44	1.0000	1.0000	1.0000	1.0000	1.0000	1.0000	0.9989	0.9754	0.8211	0.4613	0.1356
	45	1.0000	1.0000	1.0000	1.0000	1.0000	1.0000	0.9995	0.9850	0.8689	0.5413	0.1841
	46	1.0000	1.0000	1.0000	1.0000	1.0000	1.0000	0.9997	0.9912	0.9070	0.6196	0.2421
	47	1.0000	1.0000	1.0000	1.0000	1.0000	1.0000	0.9999	0.9950	0.9362	0.6931	0.3086
	48	1.0000	1.0000	1.0000	1.0000	1.0000	1.0000	0.9999	0.9973	0.9577	0.7596	0.3822
	49	1.0000	1.0000	1.0000	1.0000	1.0000	1.0000	1.0000	0.9985	0.9729	0.8173	0.4602

TABLE C   Cumulative Binomial Distribution (*concluded*)

							π					
n	*X*	0.01	0.05	0.10	0.15	0.20	0.25	0.30	0.35	0.40	0.45	0.50
100	50	1.0000	1.0000	1.0000	1.0000	1.0000	1.0000	1.0000	0.9993	0.9832	0.8654	0.5398
	51	1.0000	1.0000	1.0000	1.0000	1.0000	1.0000	1.0000	0.9996	0.9900	0.9040	0.6178
	52	1.0000	1.0000	1.0000	1.0000	1.0000	1.0000	1.0000	0.9998	0.9942	0.9338	0.6914
	53	1.0000	1.0000	1.0000	1.0000	1.0000	1.0000	1.0000	0.9999	0.9968	0.9559	0.7579
	54	1.0000	1.0000	1.0000	1.0000	1.0000	1.0000	1.0000	1.0000	0.9983	0.9716	0.8159
	55	1.0000	1.0000	1.0000	1.0000	1.0000	1.0000	1.0000	1.0000	0.9991	0.9824	0.8644
	56	1.0000	1.0000	1.0000	1.0000	1.0000	1.0000	1.0000	1.0000	0.9996	0.9894	0.9033
	57	1.0000	1.0000	1.0000	1.0000	1.0000	1.0000	1.0000	1.0000	0.9998	0.9939	0.9334
	58	1.0000	1.0000	1.0000	1.0000	1.0000	1.0000	1.0000	1.0000	0.9999	0.9966	0.9557
	59	1.0000	1.0000	1.0000	1.0000	1.0000	1.0000	1.0000	1.0000	1.0000	0.9982	0.9716
	60	1.0000	1.0000	1.0000	1.0000	1.0000	1.0000	1.0000	1.0000	1.0000	0.9991	0.9824
	61	1.0000	1.0000	1.0000	1.0000	1.0000	1.0000	1.0000	1.0000	1.0000	0.9995	0.9895
	62	1.0000	1.0000	1.0000	1.0000	1.0000	1.0000	1.0000	1.0000	1.0000	0.9998	0.9940
	63	1.0000	1.0000	1.0000	1.0000	1.0000	1.0000	1.0000	1.0000	1.0000	0.9999	0.9967
	64	1.0000	1.0000	1.0000	1.0000	1.0000	1.0000	1.0000	1.0000	1.0000	1.0000	0.9982
	65	1.0000	1.0000	1.0000	1.0000	1.0000	1.0000	1.0000	1.0000	1.0000	1.0000	0.9991
	66	1.0000	1.0000	1.0000	1.0000	1.0000	1.0000	1.0000	1.0000	1.0000	1.0000	0.9996
	67	1.0000	1.0000	1.0000	1.0000	1.0000	1.0000	1.0000	1.0000	1.0000	1.0000	0.9998
	68	1.0000	1.0000	1.0000	1.0000	1.0000	1.0000	1.0000	1.0000	1.0000	1.0000	0.9999
	69	1.0000	1.0000	1.0000	1.0000	1.0000	1.0000	1.0000	1.0000	1.0000	1.0000	1.0000

TABLE D   Poisson Distribution

x	0.1	0.2	0.3	0.4	μ 0.5	0.6	0.7	0.8	0.9	1.0
0	0.9048	0.8187	0.7408	0.6703	0.6065	0.5488	0.4966	0.4493	0.4066	0.3679
1	0.0905	0.1637	0.2222	0.2681	0.3033	0.3293	0.3476	0.3595	0.3659	0.3679
2	0.0045	0.0164	0.0333	0.0536	0.0758	0.0988	0.1217	0.1438	0.1647	0.1839
3	0.0002	0.0011	0.0033	0.0072	0.0126	0.0198	0.0284	0.0383	0.0494	0.0613
4	0.0000	0.0001	0.0003	0.0007	0.0016	0.0030	0.0050	0.0077	0.0111	0.0153
5	0.0000	0.0000	0.0000	0.0001	0.0002	0.0004	0.0007	0.0012	0.0020	0.0031
6	0.0000	0.0000	0.0000	0.0000	0.0000	0.0000	0.0001	0.0002	0.0003	0.0005
7	0.0000	0.0000	0.0000	0.0000	0.0000	0.0000	0.0000	0.0000	0.0000	0.0001

x	1.1	1.2	1.3	1.4	μ 1.5	1.6	1.7	1.8	1.9	2.0
0	0.3329	0.3012	0.2725	0.2466	0.2231	0.2019	0.1827	0.1653	0.1496	0.1353
1	0.3662	0.3614	0.3543	0.3452	0.3347	0.3230	0.3106	0.2975	0.2842	0.2707
2	0.2014	0.2169	0.2303	0.2417	0.2510	0.2584	0.2640	0.2678	0.2700	0.2707
3	0.0738	0.0867	0.0998	0.1128	0.1255	0.1378	0.1496	0.1607	0.1710	0.1804
4	0.0203	0.0260	0.0324	0.0395	0.0471	0.0551	0.0636	0.0723	0.0812	0.0902
5	0.0045	0.0062	0.0084	0.0111	0.0141	0.0176	0.0216	0.0260	0.0309	0.0361
6	0.0008	0.0012	0.0018	0.0026	0.0035	0.0047	0.0061	0.0078	0.0098	0.0120
7	0.0001	0.0002	0.0003	0.0005	0.0008	0.0011	0.0015	0.0020	0.0027	0.0034
8	0.0000	0.0000	0.0001	0.0001	0.0001	0.0002	0.0003	0.0005	0.0006	0.0009

x	2.1	2.2	2.3	2.4	μ 2.5	2.6	2.7	2.8	2.9	3.0
0	0.1225	0.1108	0.1003	0.0907	0.0821	0.0743	0.0672	0.0608	0.0550	0.0498
1	0.2572	0.2438	0.2306	0.2177	0.2052	0.1931	0.1815	0.1703	0.1596	0.1494
2	0.2700	0.2681	0.2652	0.2613	0.2565	0.2510	0.2450	0.2384	0.2314	0.2240
3	0.1890	0.1966	0.2033	0.2090	0.2138	0.2176	0.2205	0.2225	0.2237	0.2240
4	0.0992	0.1082	0.1169	0.1254	0.1336	0.1414	0.1488	0.1557	0.1622	0.1680
5	0.0417	0.0476	0.0538	0.0602	0.0668	0.0735	0.0804	0.0872	0.0940	0.1008
6	0.0146	0.0174	0.0206	0.0241	0.0278	0.0319	0.0362	0.0407	0.0455	0.0504
7	0.0044	0.0055	0.0068	0.0083	0.0099	0.0118	0.0139	0.0163	0.0188	0.0216
8	0.0011	0.0015	0.0019	0.0025	0.0031	0.0038	0.0047	0.0057	0.0068	0.0081
9	0.0003	0.0004	0.0005	0.0007	0.0009	0.0011	0.0014	0.0018	0.0022	0.0027
10	0.0001	0.0001	0.0001	0.0002	0.0002	0.0003	0.0004	0.0005	0.0006	0.0008
11	0.0000	0.0000	0.0000	0.0000	0.0000	0.0001	0.0001	0.0001	0.0002	0.0002
12	0.0000	0.0000	0.0000	0.0000	0.0000	0.0000	0.0000	0.0000	0.0000	0.0001

TABLE D Poisson Distribution (*continued*)

x	3.1	3.2	3.3	3.4	μ 3.5	3.6	3.7	3.8	3.9	4.0
0	0.0450	0.0408	0.0369	0.0334	0.0302	0.0273	0.0247	0.0224	0.0202	0.0183
1	0.1397	0.1304	0.1217	0.1135	0.1057	0.0984	0.0915	0.0850	0.0789	0.0733
2	0.2165	0.2087	0.2008	0.1929	0.1850	0.1771	0.1692	0.1615	0.1539	0.1465
3	0.2237	0.2226	0.2209	0.2186	0.2158	0.2125	0.2087	0.2046	0.2001	0.1954
4	0.1733	0.1781	0.1823	0.1858	0.1888	0.1912	0.1931	0.1944	0.1951	0.1954
5	0.1075	0.1140	0.1203	0.1264	0.1322	0.1377	0.1429	0.1477	0.1522	0.1563
6	0.0555	0.0608	0.0662	0.0716	0.0771	0.0826	0.0881	0.0936	0.0989	0.1042
7	0.0246	0.0278	0.0312	0.0348	0.0385	0.0425	0.0466	0.0508	0.0551	0.0595
8	0.0095	0.0111	0.0129	0.0148	0.0169	0.0191	0.0215	0.0241	0.0269	0.0298
9	0.0033	0.0040	0.0047	0.0056	0.0066	0.0076	0.0089	0.0102	0.0116	0.0132
10	0.0010	0.0013	0.0016	0.0019	0.0023	0.0028	0.0033	0.0039	0.0045	0.0053
11	0.0003	0.0004	0.0005	0.0006	0.0007	0.0009	0.0011	0.0013	0.0016	0.0019
12	0.0001	0.0001	0.0001	0.0002	0.0002	0.0003	0.0003	0.0004	0.0005	0.0006
13	0.0000	0.0000	0.0000	0.0000	0.0001	0.0001	0.0001	0.0001	0.0002	0.0002
14	0.0000	0.0000	0.0000	0.0000	0.0000	0.0000	0.0000	0.0000	0.0000	0.0001

x	4.1	4.2	4.3	4.4	μ 4.5	4.6	4.7	4.8	4.9	5.0
0	0.0166	0.0150	0.0136	0.0123	0.0111	0.0101	0.0091	0.0082	0.0074	0.0067
1	0.0679	0.0630	0.0583	0.0540	0.0500	0.0462	0.0427	0.0395	0.0365	0.0337
2	0.1393	0.1323	0.1254	0.1188	0.1125	0.1063	0.1005	0.0948	0.0894	0.0842
3	0.1904	0.1852	0.1798	0.1743	0.1687	0.1631	0.1574	0.1517	0.1460	0.1404
4	0.1951	0.1944	0.1933	0.1917	0.1898	0.1875	0.1849	0.1820	0.1789	0.1755
5	0.1600	0.1633	0.1662	0.1687	0.1708	0.1725	0.1738	0.1747	0.1753	0.1755
6	0.1093	0.1143	0.1191	0.1237	0.1281	0.1323	0.1362	0.1398	0.1432	0.1462
7	0.0640	0.0686	0.0732	0.0778	0.0824	0.0869	0.0914	0.0959	0.1002	0.1044
8	0.0328	0.0360	0.0393	0.0428	0.0463	0.0500	0.0537	0.0575	0.0614	0.0653
9	0.0150	0.0168	0.0188	0.0209	0.0232	0.0255	0.0281	0.0307	0.0334	0.0363
10	0.0061	0.0071	0.0081	0.0092	0.0104	0.0118	0.0132	0.0147	0.0164	0.0181
11	0.0023	0.0027	0.0032	0.0037	0.0043	0.0049	0.0056	0.0064	0.0073	0.0082
12	0.0008	0.0009	0.0011	0.0013	0.0016	0.0019	0.0022	0.0026	0.0030	0.0034
13	0.0002	0.0003	0.0004	0.0005	0.0006	0.0007	0.0008	0.0009	0.0011	0.0013
14	0.0001	0.0001	0.0001	0.0001	0.0002	0.0002	0.0003	0.0003	0.0004	0.0005
15	0.0000	0.0000	0.0000	0.0000	0.0001	0.0001	0.0001	0.0001	0.0001	0.0002

x	5.1	5.2	5.3	5.4	μ 5.5	5.6	5.7	5.8	5.9	6.0
0	0.0061	0.0055	0.0050	0.0045	0.0041	0.0037	0.0033	0.0030	0.0027	0.0025
1	0.0311	0.0287	0.0265	0.0244	0.0225	0.0207	0.0191	0.0176	0.0162	0.0149

TABLE D   Poisson Distribution (*continued*)

x	5.1	5.2	5.3	5.4	μ 5.5	5.6	5.7	5.8	5.9	6.0
2	0.0793	0.0746	0.0701	0.0659	0.0618	0.0580	0.0544	0.0509	0.0477	0.0446
3	0.1348	0.1293	0.1239	0.1185	0.1133	0.1082	0.1033	0.0985	0.0938	0.0892
4	0.1719	0.1681	0.1641	0.1600	0.1558	0.1515	0.1472	0.1428	0.1383	0.1339
5	0.1753	0.1748	0.1740	0.1728	0.1714	0.1697	0.1678	0.1656	0.1632	0.1606
6	0.1490	0.1515	0.1537	0.1555	0.1571	0.1584	0.1594	0.1601	0.1605	0.1606
7	0.1086	0.1125	0.1163	0.1200	0.1234	0.1267	0.1298	0.1326	0.1353	0.1377
8	0.0692	0.0731	0.0771	0.0810	0.0849	0.0887	0.0925	0.0962	0.0998	0.1033
9	0.0392	0.0423	0.0454	0.0486	0.0519	0.0552	0.0586	0.0620	0.0654	0.0688
10	0.0200	0.0220	0.0241	0.0262	0.0285	0.0309	0.0334	0.0359	0.0386	0.0413
11	0.0093	0.0104	0.0116	0.0129	0.0143	0.0157	0.0173	0.0190	0.0207	0.0225
12	0.0039	0.0045	0.0051	0.0058	0.0065	0.0073	0.0082	0.0092	0.0102	0.0113
13	0.0015	0.0018	0.0021	0.0024	0.0028	0.0032	0.0036	0.0041	0.0046	0.0052
14	0.0006	0.0007	0.0008	0.0009	0.0011	0.0013	0.0015	0.0017	0.0019	0.0022
15	0.0002	0.0002	0.0003	0.0003	0.0004	0.0005	0.0006	0.0007	0.0008	0.0009
16	0.0001	0.0001	0.0001	0.0001	0.0001	0.0002	0.0002	0.0002	0.0003	0.0003
17	0.0000	0.0000	0.0000	0.0000	0.0000	0.0001	0.0001	0.0001	0.0001	0.0001

x	6.1	6.2	6.3	6.4	μ 6.5	6.6	6.7	6.8	6.9	7.0
0	0.0022	0.0020	0.0018	0.0017	0.0015	0.0014	0.0012	0.0011	0.0010	0.0009
1	0.0137	0.0126	0.0116	0.0106	0.0098	0.0090	0.0082	0.0076	0.0070	0.0064
2	0.0417	0.0390	0.0364	0.0340	0.0318	0.0296	0.0276	0.0258	0.0240	0.0223
3	0.0848	0.0806	0.0765	0.0726	0.0688	0.0652	0.0617	0.0584	0.0552	0.0521
4	0.1294	0.1249	0.1205	0.1162	0.1118	0.1076	0.1034	0.0992	0.0952	0.0912
5	0.1579	0.1549	0.1519	0.1487	0.1454	0.1420	0.1385	0.1349	0.1314	0.1277
6	0.1605	0.1601	0.1595	0.1586	0.1575	0.1562	0.1546	0.1529	0.1511	0.1490
7	0.1399	0.1418	0.1435	0.1450	0.1462	0.1472	0.1480	0.1486	0.1489	0.1490
8	0.1066	0.1099	0.1130	0.1160	0.1188	0.1215	0.1240	0.1263	0.1284	0.1304
9	0.0723	0.0757	0.0791	0.0825	0.0858	0.0891	0.0923	0.0954	0.0985	0.1014
10	0.0441	0.0469	0.0498	0.0528	0.0558	0.0588	0.0618	0.0649	0.0679	0.0710
11	0.0244	0.0265	0.0285	0.0307	0.0330	0.0353	0.0377	0.0401	0.0426	0.0452
12	0.0124	0.0137	0.0150	0.0164	0.0179	0.0194	0.0210	0.0227	0.0245	0.0263
13	0.0058	0.0065	0.0073	0.0081	0.0089	0.0099	0.0108	0.0119	0.0130	0.0142
14	0.0025	0.0029	0.0033	0.0037	0.0041	0.0046	0.0052	0.0058	0.0064	0.0071
15	0.0010	0.0012	0.0014	0.0016	0.0018	0.0020	0.0023	0.0026	0.0029	0.0033
16	0.0004	0.0005	0.0005	0.0006	0.0007	0.0008	0.0010	0.0011	0.0013	0.0014
17	0.0001	0.0002	0.0002	0.0002	0.0003	0.0003	0.0004	0.0004	0.0005	0.0006
18	0.0000	0.0001	0.0001	0.0001	0.0001	0.0001	0.0001	0.0002	0.0002	0.0002
19	0.0000	0.0000	0.0000	0.0000	0.0000	0.0000	0.0001	0.0001	0.0001	0.0001

TABLE D   Poisson Distribution (*continued*)

x	7.1	7.2	7.3	7.4	7.5	7.6	7.7	7.8	7.9	8.0
0	0.0008	0.0007	0.0007	0.0006	0.0006	0.0005	0.0005	0.0004	0.0004	0.0003
1	0.0059	0.0054	0.0049	0.0045	0.0041	0.0038	0.0035	0.0032	0.0029	0.0027
2	0.0208	0.0194	0.0180	0.0167	0.0156	0.0145	0.0134	0.0125	0.0116	0.0107
3	0.0492	0.0464	0.0438	0.0413	0.0389	0.0366	0.0345	0.0324	0.0305	0.0286
4	0.0874	0.0836	0.0799	0.0764	0.0729	0.0696	0.0663	0.0632	0.0602	0.0573
5	0.1241	0.1204	0.1167	0.1130	0.1094	0.1057	0.1021	0.0986	0.0951	0.0916
6	0.1468	0.1445	0.1420	0.1394	0.1367	0.1339	0.1311	0.1282	0.1252	0.1221
7	0.1489	0.1486	0.1481	0.1474	0.1465	0.1454	0.1442	0.1428	0.1413	0.1396
8	0.1321	0.1337	0.1351	0.1363	0.1373	0.1381	0.1388	0.1392	0.1395	0.1396
9	0.1042	0.1070	0.1096	0.1121	0.1144	0.1167	0.1187	0.1207	0.1224	0.1241
10	0.0740	0.0770	0.0800	0.0829	0.0858	0.0887	0.0914	0.0941	0.0967	0.0993
11	0.0478	0.0504	0.0531	0.0558	0.0585	0.0613	0.0640	0.0667	0.0695	0.0722
12	0.0283	0.0303	0.0323	0.0344	0.0366	0.0388	0.0411	0.0434	0.0457	0.0481
13	0.0154	0.0168	0.0181	0.0196	0.0211	0.0227	0.0243	0.0260	0.0278	0.0296
14	0.0078	0.0086	0.0095	0.0104	0.0113	0.0123	0.0134	0.0145	0.0157	0.0169
15	0.0037	0.0041	0.0046	0.0051	0.0057	0.0062	0.0069	0.0075	0.0083	0.0090
16	0.0016	0.0019	0.0021	0.0024	0.0026	0.0030	0.0033	0.0037	0.0041	0.0045
17	0.0007	0.0008	0.0009	0.0010	0.0012	0.0013	0.0015	0.0017	0.0019	0.0021
18	0.0003	0.0003	0.0004	0.0004	0.0005	0.0006	0.0006	0.0007	0.0008	0.0009
19	0.0001	0.0001	0.0001	0.0002	0.0002	0.0002	0.0003	0.0003	0.0003	0.0004
20	0.0000	0.0000	0.0001	0.0001	0.0001	0.0001	0.0001	0.0001	0.0001	0.0002
21	0.0000	0.0000	0.0000	0.0000	0.0000	0.0000	0.0000	0.0000	0.0001	0.0001

x	8.1	8.2	8.3	8.4	8.5	8.6	8.7	8.8	8.9	9.0
0	0.0003	0.0003	0.0002	0.0002	0.0002	0.0002	0.0002	0.0002	0.0001	0.0001
1	0.0025	0.0023	0.0021	0.0019	0.0017	0.0016	0.0014	0.0013	0.0012	0.0011
2	0.0100	0.0092	0.0086	0.0079	0.0074	0.0068	0.0063	0.0058	0.0054	0.0050
3	0.0269	0.0252	0.0237	0.0222	0.0208	0.0195	0.0183	0.0171	0.0160	0.0150
4	0.0544	0.0517	0.0491	0.0466	0.0443	0.0420	0.0398	0.0377	0.0357	0.0337
5	0.0882	0.0849	0.0816	0.0784	0.0752	0.0722	0.0692	0.0663	0.0635	0.0607
6	0.1191	0.1160	0.1128	0.1097	0.1066	0.1034	0.1003	0.0972	0.0941	0.0911
7	0.1378	0.1358	0.1338	0.1317	0.1294	0.1271	0.1247	0.1222	0.1197	0.1171
8	0.1395	0.1392	0.1388	0.1382	0.1375	0.1366	0.1356	0.1344	0.1332	0.1318
9	0.1256	0.1269	0.1280	0.1290	0.1299	0.1306	0.1311	0.1315	0.1317	0.1318
10	0.1017	0.1040	0.1063	0.1084	0.1104	0.1123	0.1140	0.1157	0.1172	0.1186
11	0.0749	0.0776	0.0802	0.0828	0.0853	0.0878	0.0902	0.0925	0.0948	0.0970
12	0.0505	0.0530	0.0555	0.0579	0.0604	0.0629	0.0654	0.0679	0.0703	0.0728
13	0.0315	0.0334	0.0354	0.0374	0.0395	0.0416	0.0438	0.0459	0.0481	0.0504

TABLE D   Poisson Distribution (*continued*)

					μ					
x	8.1	8.2	8.3	8.4	8.5	8.6	8.7	8.8	8.9	9.0
14	0.0182	0.0196	0.0210	0.0225	0.0240	0.0256	0.0272	0.0289	0.0306	0.0324
15	0.0098	0.0107	0.0116	0.0126	0.0136	0.0147	0.0158	0.0169	0.0182	0.0194
16	0.0050	0.0055	0.0060	0.0066	0.0072	0.0079	0.0086	0.0093	0.0101	0.0109
17	0.0024	0.0026	0.0029	0.0033	0.0036	0.0040	0.0044	0.0048	0.0053	0.0058
18	0.0011	0.0012	0.0014	0.0015	0.0017	0.0019	0.0021	0.0024	0.0026	0.0029
19	0.0005	0.0005	0.0006	0.0007	0.0008	0.0009	0.0010	0.0011	0.0012	0.0014
20	0.0002	0.0002	0.0002	0.0003	0.0003	0.0004	0.0004	0.0005	0.0005	0.0006
21	0.0001	0.0001	0.0001	0.0001	0.0001	0.0002	0.0002	0.0002	0.0002	0.0003
22	0.0000	0.0000	0.0000	0.0000	0.0001	0.0001	0.0001	0.0001	0.0001	0.0001

					μ					
x	9.1	9.2	9.3	9.4	9.5	9.6	9.7	9.8	9.9	10.0
0	0.0001	0.0001	0.0001	0.0001	0.0001	0.0001	0.0001	0.0001	0.0001	0.0000
1	0.0010	0.0009	0.0009	0.0008	0.0007	0.0007	0.0006	0.0005	0.0005	0.0005
2	0.0046	0.0043	0.0040	0.0037	0.0034	0.0031	0.0029	0.0027	0.0025	0.0023
3	0.0140	0.0131	0.0123	0.0115	0.0107	0.0100	0.0093	0.0087	0.0081	0.0076
4	0.0319	0.0302	0.0285	0.0269	0.0254	0.0240	0.0226	0.0213	0.0201	0.0189
5	0.0581	0.0555	0.0530	0.0506	0.0483	0.0460	0.0439	0.0418	0.0398	0.0378
6	0.0881	0.0851	0.0822	0.0793	0.0764	0.0736	0.0709	0.0682	0.0656	0.0631
7	0.1145	0.1118	0.1091	0.1064	0.1037	0.1010	0.0982	0.0955	0.0928	0.0901
8	0.1302	0.1286	0.1269	0.1251	0.1232	0.1212	0.1191	0.1170	0.1148	0.1126
9	0.1317	0.1315	0.1311	0.1306	0.1300	0.1293	0.1284	0.1274	0.1263	0.1251
10	0.1198	0.1210	0.1219	0.1228	0.1235	0.1241	0.1245	0.1249	0.1250	0.1251
11	0.0991	0.1012	0.1031	0.1049	0.1067	0.1083	0.1098	0.1112	0.1125	0.1137
12	0.0752	0.0776	0.0799	0.0822	0.0844	0.0866	0.0888	0.0908	0.0928	0.0948
13	0.0526	0.0549	0.0572	0.0594	0.0617	0.0640	0.0662	0.0685	0.0707	0.0729
14	0.0342	0.0361	0.0380	0.0399	0.0419	0.0439	0.0459	0.0479	0.0500	0.0521
15	0.0208	0.0221	0.0235	0.0250	0.0265	0.0281	0.0297	0.0313	0.0330	0.0347
16	0.0118	0.0127	0.0137	0.0147	0.0157	0.0168	0.0180	0.0192	0.0204	0.0217
17	0.0063	0.0069	0.0075	0.0081	0.0088	0.0095	0.0103	0.0111	0.0119	0.0128
18	0.0032	0.0035	0.0039	0.0042	0.0046	0.0051	0.0055	0.0060	0.0065	0.0071
19	0.0015	0.0017	0.0019	0.0021	0.0023	0.0026	0.0028	0.0031	0.0034	0.0037
20	0.0007	0.0008	0.0009	0.0010	0.0011	0.0012	0.0014	0.0015	0.0017	0.0019
21	0.0003	0.0003	0.0004	0.0004	0.0005	0.0006	0.0006	0.0007	0.0008	0.0009
22	0.0001	0.0001	0.0002	0.0002	0.0002	0.0002	0.0003	0.0003	0.0004	0.0004
23	0.0000	0.0001	0.0001	0.0001	0.0001	0.0001	0.0001	0.0001	0.0002	0.0002
24	0.0000	0.0000	0.0000	0.0000	0.0000	0.0000	0.0000	0.0001	0.0001	0.0001

TABLE D   Poisson Distribution (*concluded*)

x	11	12	13	14	μ 15	16	17	18	19	20
0	0.0000	0.0000	0.0000	0.0000	0.0000	0.0000	0.0000	0.0000	0.0000	0.0000
1	0.0002	0.0001	0.0000	0.0000	0.0000	0.0000	0.0000	0.0000	0.0000	0.0000
2	0.0010	0.0004	0.0002	0.0001	0.0000	0.0000	0.0000	0.0000	0.0000	0.0000
3	0.0037	0.0018	0.0008	0.0004	0.0002	0.0001	0.0000	0.0000	0.0000	0.0000
4	0.0102	0.0053	0.0027	0.0013	0.0006	0.0003	0.0001	0.0001	0.0000	0.0000
5	0.0224	0.0127	0.0070	0.0037	0.0019	0.0010	0.0005	0.0002	0.0001	0.0001
6	0.0411	0.0255	0.0152	0.0087	0.0048	0.0026	0.0014	0.0007	0.0004	0.0002
7	0.0646	0.0437	0.0281	0.0174	0.0104	0.0060	0.0034	0.0019	0.0010	0.0005
8	0.0888	0.0655	0.0457	0.0304	0.0194	0.0120	0.0072	0.0042	0.0024	0.0013
9	0.1085	0.0874	0.0661	0.0473	0.0324	0.0213	0.0135	0.0083	0.0050	0.0029
10	0.1194	0.1048	0.0859	0.0663	0.0486	0.0341	0.0230	0.0150	0.0095	0.0058
11	0.1194	0.1144	0.1015	0.0844	0.0663	0.0496	0.0355	0.0245	0.0164	0.0106
12	0.1094	0.1144	0.1099	0.0984	0.0829	0.0661	0.0504	0.0368	0.0259	0.0176
13	0.0926	0.1056	0.1099	0.1060	0.0956	0.0814	0.0658	0.0509	0.0378	0.0271
14	0.0728	0.0905	0.1021	0.1060	0.1024	0.0930	0.0800	0.0655	0.0514	0.0387
15	0.0534	0.0724	0.0885	0.0989	0.1024	0.0992	0.0906	0.0786	0.0650	0.0516
16	0.0367	0.0543	0.0719	0.0866	0.0960	0.0992	0.0963	0.0884	0.0772	0.0646
17	0.0237	0.0383	0.0550	0.0713	0.0847	0.0934	0.0963	0.0936	0.0863	0.0760
18	0.0145	0.0255	0.0397	0.0554	0.0706	0.0830	0.0909	0.0936	0.0911	0.0844
19	0.0084	0.0161	0.0272	0.0409	0.0557	0.0699	0.0814	0.0887	0.0911	0.0888
20	0.0046	0.0097	0.0177	0.0286	0.0418	0.0559	0.0692	0.0798	0.0866	0.0888
21	0.0024	0.0055	0.0109	0.0191	0.0299	0.0426	0.0560	0.0684	0.0783	0.0846
22	0.0012	0.0030	0.0065	0.0121	0.0204	0.0310	0.0433	0.0560	0.0676	0.0769
23	0.0006	0.0016	0.0037	0.0074	0.0133	0.0216	0.0320	0.0438	0.0559	0.0669
24	0.0003	0.0008	0.0020	0.0043	0.0083	0.0144	0.0226	0.0328	0.0442	0.0557
25	0.0001	0.0004	0.0010	0.0024	0.0050	0.0092	0.0154	0.0237	0.0336	0.0446
26	0.0000	0.0002	0.0005	0.0013	0.0029	0.0057	0.0101	0.0164	0.0246	0.0343
27	0.0000	0.0001	0.0002	0.0007	0.0016	0.0034	0.0063	0.0109	0.0173	0.0254
28	0.0000	0.0000	0.0001	0.0003	0.0009	0.0019	0.0038	0.0070	0.0117	0.0181
29	0.0000	0.0000	0.0001	0.0002	0.0004	0.0011	0.0023	0.0044	0.0077	0.0125
30	0.0000	0.0000	0.0000	0.0001	0.0002	0.0006	0.0013	0.0026	0.0049	0.0083
31	0.0000	0.0000	0.0000	0.0000	0.0001	0.0003	0.0007	0.0015	0.0030	0.0054
32	0.0000	0.0000	0.0000	0.0000	0.0001	0.0001	0.0004	0.0009	0.0018	0.0034
33	0.0000	0.0000	0.0000	0.0000	0.0000	0.0001	0.0002	0.0005	0.0010	0.0020
34	0.0000	0.0000	0.0000	0.0000	0.0000	0.0000	0.0001	0.0002	0.0006	0.0012
35	0.0000	0.0000	0.0000	0.0000	0.0000	0.0000	0.0000	0.0001	0.0003	0.0007
36	0.0000	0.0000	0.0000	0.0000	0.0000	0.0000	0.0000	0.0001	0.0002	0.0004
37	0.0000	0.0000	0.0000	0.0000	0.0000	0.0000	0.0000	0.0000	0.0001	0.0002
38	0.0000	0.0000	0.0000	0.0000	0.0000	0.0000	0.0000	0.0000	0.0000	0.0001
39	0.0000	0.0000	0.0000	0.0000	0.0000	0.0000	0.0000	0.0000	0.0000	0.0001

TABLE E The Normal Distribution

Z	0.00	0.01	0.02	0.03	0.04	0.05	0.06	0.07	0.08	0.09
0.0	0.0000	0.0040	0.0080	0.0120	0.0160	0.0199	0.0239	0.0279	0.0319	0.0359
0.1	0.0398	0.0438	0.0478	0.0517	0.0557	0.0596	0.0636	0.0675	0.0714	0.0753
0.2	0.0793	0.0832	0.0871	0.0910	0.0948	0.0987	0.1026	0.1064	0.1103	0.1141
0.3	0.1179	0.1217	0.1255	0.1293	0.1331	0.1368	0.1406	0.1443	0.1480	0.1517
0.4	0.1554	0.1591	0.1628	0.1664	0.1700	0.1736	0.1772	0.1808	0.1844	0.1879
0.5	0.1915	0.1950	0.1985	0.2019	0.2054	0.2088	0.2123	0.2157	0.2190	0.2224
0.6	0.2257	0.2291	0.2324	0.2357	0.2389	0.2422	0.2454	0.2486	0.2517	0.2549
0.7	0.2580	0.2611	0.2642	0.2673	0.2704	0.2734	0.2764	0.2794	0.2823	0.2852
0.8	0.2881	0.2910	0.2939	0.2967	0.2995	0.3023	0.3051	0.3078	0.3106	0.3133
0.9	0.3159	0.3186	0.3212	0.3238	0.3264	0.3289	0.3315	0.3340	0.3365	0.3389
1.0	0.3413	0.3438	0.3461	0.3485	0.3508	0.3531	0.3554	0.3577	0.3599	0.3621
1.1	0.3643	0.3665	0.3686	0.3708	0.3729	0.3749	0.3770	0.3790	0.3810	0.3830
1.2	0.3849	0.3869	0.3888	0.3907	0.3925	0.3944	0.3962	0.3980	0.3997	0.4015
1.3	0.4032	0.4049	0.4066	0.4082	0.4099	0.4115	0.4131	0.4147	0.4162	0.4177
1.4	0.4192	0.4207	0.4222	0.4236	0.4251	0.4265	0.4279	0.4292	0.4306	0.4319
1.5	0.4332	0.4345	0.4357	0.4370	0.4382	0.4394	0.4406	0.4418	0.4429	0.4441
1.6	0.4452	0.4463	0.4474	0.4484	0.4495	0.4505	0.4515	0.4525	0.4535	0.4545
1.7	0.4554	0.4564	0.4573	0.4582	0.4591	0.4599	0.4608	0.4616	0.4625	0.4633
1.8	0.4641	0.4649	0.4656	0.4664	0.4671	0.4678	0.4686	0.4693	0.4699	0.4706
1.9	0.4713	0.4719	0.4726	0.4732	0.4738	0.4744	0.4750	0.4756	0.4761	0.4767
2.0	0.4772	0.4778	0.4783	0.4788	0.4793	0.4798	0.4803	0.4808	0.4812	0.4817
2.1	0.4821	0.4826	0.4830	0.4834	0.4838	0.4842	0.4846	0.4850	0.4854	0.4857
2.2	0.4861	0.4864	0.4868	0.4871	0.4875	0.4878	0.4881	0.4884	0.4887	0.4890
2.3	0.4893	0.4896	0.4898	0.4901	0.4904	0.4906	0.4909	0.4911	0.4913	0.4916
2.4	0.4918	0.4920	0.4922	0.4925	0.4927	0.4929	0.4931	0.4932	0.4934	0.4936
2.5	0.4938	0.4940	0.4941	0.4943	0.4945	0.4946	0.4948	0.4949	0.4951	0.4952
2.6	0.4953	0.4955	0.4956	0.4957	0.4959	0.4960	0.4961	0.4962	0.4963	0.4964
2.7	0.4965	0.4966	0.4967	0.4968	0.4969	0.4970	0.4971	0.4972	0.4973	0.4974
2.8	0.4974	0.4975	0.4976	0.4977	0.4977	0.4978	0.4979	0.4979	0.4980	0.4981
2.9	0.4981	0.4982	0.4982	0.4983	0.4984	0.4984	0.4985	0.4985	0.4986	0.4986
3.0	0.4987	0.4987	0.4987	0.4988	0.4988	0.4989	0.4989	0.4989	0.4990	0.4990
3.1	0.4990	0.4991	0.4991	0.4991	0.4992	0.4992	0.4992	0.4992	0.4993	0.4993
3.2	0.4993	0.4993	0.4994	0.4994	0.4994	0.4994	0.4994	0.4995	0.4995	0.4995
3.3	0.4995	0.4995	0.4995	0.4996	0.4996	0.4996	0.4996	0.4996	0.4996	0.4997
3.4	0.4997	0.4997	0.4997	0.4997	0.4997	0.4997	0.4997	0.4997	0.4997	0.4998
3.5	0.4998	0.4998	0.4998	0.4998	0.4998	0.4998	0.4998	0.4998	0.4998	0.4998
3.6	0.4998	0.4998	0.4999	0.4999	0.4999	0.4999	0.4999	0.4999	0.4999	0.4999
3.7	0.4999	0.4999	0.4999	0.4999	0.4999	0.4999	0.4999	0.4999	0.4999	0.4999
3.8	0.4999	0.4999	0.4999	0.4999	0.4999	0.4999	0.4999	0.4999	0.4999	0.4999
3.9	0.5000	0.5000	0.5000	0.5000	0.5000	0.5000	0.5000	0.5000	0.5000	0.5000

TABLE F   The *t*-Distribution

d.f.	0.900 0.100	0.700 0.300	0.500 0.500	0.300 0.700	0.200 0.800	0.100 0.900	0.050 0.950	0.020 0.980	0.010 0.990	α value CL	two tailed-test
	0.450 0.550	0.350 0.650	0.250 0.750	0.150 0.850	0.100 0.900	0.050 0.950	0.025 0.975	0.010 0.990	0.005 0.995	α value CL	one tailed-test

d.f.					Values of *t*				
1	0.158	0.510	1.000	1.963	3.078	6.314	12.706	31.821	63.657
2	0.142	0.445	0.816	1.386	1.886	2.920	4.303	6.965	9.925
3	0.137	0.424	0.765	1.250	1.638	2.353	3.182	4.541	5.841
4	0.134	0.414	0.741	1.190	1.533	2.132	2.776	3.747	4.604
5	0.132	0.408	0.727	1.156	1.476	2.015	2.571	3.365	4.032
6	0.131	0.404	0.718	1.134	1.440	1.943	2.447	3.143	3.707
7	0.130	0.402	0.711	1.119	1.415	1.895	2.365	2.998	3.499
8	0.130	0.399	0.706	1.108	1.397	1.860	2.306	2.896	3.355
9	0.129	0.398	0.703	1.100	1.383	1.833	2.262	2.821	3.250
10	0.129	0.397	0.700	1.093	1.372	1.812	2.228	2.764	3.169
11	0.129	0.396	0.697	1.088	1.363	1.796	2.201	2.718	3.106
12	0.128	0.395	0.695	1.083	1.356	1.782	2.179	2.681	3.055
13	0.128	0.394	0.694	1.079	1.350	1.771	2.160	2.650	3.012
14	0.128	0.393	0.692	1.076	1.345	1.761	2.145	2.624	2.977
15	0.128	0.393	0.691	1.074	1.341	1.753	2.131	2.602	2.947
16	0.128	0.392	0.690	1.071	1.337	1.746	2.120	2.583	2.921
17	0.128	0.392	0.689	1.069	1.333	1.740	2.110	2.567	2.898
18	0.127	0.392	0.688	1.067	1.330	1.734	2.101	2.552	2.878
19	0.127	0.391	0.688	1.066	1.328	1.729	**2.093**	2.539	2.861
20	0.127	0.391	0.687	1.064	1.325	1.725	2.086	2.528	2.845
21	0.127	0.391	0.686	1.063	1.323	1.721	2.080	2.518	2.831
22	0.127	0.390	0.686	1.061	1.321	1.717	2.074	2.508	2.819
23	0.127	0.390	0.685	1.060	1.319	1.714	2.069	2.500	2.807
24	0.127	0.390	0.685	1.059	1.318	1.711	2.064	2.492	2.797
25	0.127	0.390	0.684	1.058	1.316	1.708	2.060	2.485	2.787
26	0.127	0.390	0.684	1.058	1.315	1.706	2.056	2.479	2.779
27	0.127	0.389	0.684	1.057	1.314	1.703	2.052	2.473	2.771
28	0.127	0.389	0.683	1.056	1.313	1.701	2.048	2.467	2.763
29	0.127	0.389	0.683	1.055	1.311	1.699	2.045	2.462	2.756
30	0.127	0.389	0.683	1.055	1.310	1.697	2.042	2.457	2.750
40	0.126	0.388	0.681	1.050	1.303	1.684	2.021	2.423	2.704
60	0.126	0.387	0.679	1.045	1.296	1.671	2.000	2.390	2.660
120	0.126	0.386	0.677	1.041	1.289	1.658	1.980	2.358	2.617
∞	0.126	0.385	0.674	1.036	1.282	1.645	1.960	2.326	2.576

TABLE G   The *F*-Distribution

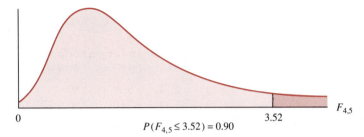

$P(F_{4,5} \leq 3.52) = 0.90$

	$F_{0.90}; \alpha = 0.10$								
Denominator degrees of freedom	Numerator degrees of freedom								
	1	2	3	4	5	6	7	8	9
1	39.86	49.50	53.59	55.83	57.24	58.20	58.91	59.44	59.86
2	8.53	9.00	9.16	9.24	9.29	9.33	9.35	9.37	9.38
3	5.54	5.46	5.39	5.34	5.31	5.28	5.27	5.25	5.24
4	4.54	4.32	4.19	4.11	4.05	4.01	3.98	3.95	3.94
5	4.06	3.78	3.62	3.52	3.45	3.40	3.37	3.34	3.32
6	3.78	3.46	3.29	3.18	3.11	3.05	3.01	2.98	2.96
7	3.59	3.26	3.07	2.96	2.88	2.83	2.78	2.75	2.72
8	3.46	3.11	2.92	2.81	2.73	2.67	2.62	2.59	2.56
9	3.36	3.01	2.81	2.69	2.61	2.55	2.51	2.47	2.44
10	3.29	2.92	2.73	2.61	2.52	2.46	2.41	2.38	2.35
11	3.23	2.86	2.66	2.54	2.45	2.39	2.34	2.30	2.27
12	3.18	2.81	2.61	2.48	2.39	2.33	2.28	2.24	2.21
13	3.14	2.76	2.56	2.43	2.35	2.28	2.23	2.20	2.16
14	3.10	2.73	2.52	2.39	2.31	2.24	2.19	2.15	2.12
15	3.07	2.70	2.49	2.36	2.27	2.21	2.16	2.12	2.09
16	3.05	2.67	2.46	2.33	2.24	2.18	2.13	2.09	2.06
17	3.03	2.64	2.44	2.31	2.22	2.15	2.10	2.06	2.03
18	3.01	2.62	2.42	2.29	2.20	2.13	2.08	2.04	2.00
19	2.99	2.61	2.40	2.27	2.18	2.11	2.06	2.02	1.98
20	2.97	2.59	2.38	2.25	2.16	2.09	2.04	2.00	1.96
21	2.96	2.57	2.36	2.23	2.14	2.08	2.02	1.98	1.95
22	2.95	2.56	2.35	2.22	2.13	2.06	2.01	1.97	1.93
23	2.94	2.55	2.34	2.21	2.11	2.05	1.99	1.95	1.92
24	2.93	2.54	2.33	2.19	2.10	2.04	1.98	1.94	1.91
25	2.92	2.53	2.32	2.18	2.09	2.02	1.97	1.93	1.89
26	2.91	2.52	2.31	2.17	2.08	2.01	1.96	1.92	1.88
27	2.90	2.51	2.30	2.17	2.07	2.00	1.95	1.91	1.87
28	2.89	2.50	2.29	2.16	2.06	2.00	1.94	1.90	1.87
29	2.89	2.50	2.28	2.15	2.06	1.99	1.93	1.89	1.86

TABLE G   The *F*-Distribution (*continued*)

Denominator degrees of freedom	$F_{0.90}$; $\alpha = 0.10$								
	Numerator degrees of freedom								
	1	2	3	4	5	6	7	8	9
30	2.88	2.49	2.28	2.14	2.05	1.98	1.93	1.88	1.85
40	2.84	2.44	2.23	2.09	2.00	1.93	1.87	1.83	1.79
60	2.79	2.39	2.18	2.04	1.95	1.87	1.82	1.77	1.74
120	2.75	2.35	2.13	1.99	1.90	1.82	1.77	1.72	1.68
∞	2.71	2.30	2.08	1.95	1.85	1.77	1.72	1.67	1.63

Denominator degrees of freedom	$F_{0.90}$; $\alpha = 0.10$									
	Numerator degrees of freedom									
	10	12	15	20	24	30	40	60	120	∞
1	60.19	60.71	61.22	61.74	62.00	62.26	62.53	62.79	63.06	63.33
2	9.39	9.41	9.42	9.44	9.45	9.46	9.47	9.47	9.48	9.49
3	5.23	5.22	5.20	5.18	5.18	5.17	5.16	5.15	5.14	5.13
4	3.92	3.90	3.87	3.84	3.83	3.82	3.80	3.79	3.78	3.76
5	3.30	3.27	3.24	3.21	3.19	3.17	3.16	3.14	3.12	3.11
6	2.94	2.90	2.87	2.84	2.82	2.80	2.78	2.76	2.74	2.72
7	2.70	2.67	2.63	2.59	2.58	2.56	2.54	2.51	2.49	2.47
8	2.54	2.50	2.46	2.42	2.40	2.38	2.36	2.34	2.32	2.29
9	2.42	2.38	2.34	2.30	2.28	2.25	2.23	2.21	2.18	2.16
10	2.32	2.28	2.24	2.20	2.18	2.16	2.13	2.11	2.08	2.06
11	2.25	2.21	2.17	2.12	2.10	2.08	2.05	2.03	2.00	1.97
12	2.19	2.15	2.10	2.06	2.04	2.01	1.99	1.96	1.93	1.90
13	2.14	2.10	2.05	2.01	1.98	1.96	1.93	1.90	1.88	1.85
14	2.10	2.05	2.01	1.96	1.94	1.91	1.89	1.86	1.83	1.80
15	2.06	2.02	1.97	1.92	1.90	1.87	1.85	1.82	1.79	1.76
16	2.03	1.99	1.94	1.89	1.87	1.84	1.81	1.78	1.75	1.72
17	2.00	1.96	1.91	1.86	1.84	1.81	1.78	1.75	1.72	1.69
18	1.98	1.93	1.89	1.84	1.81	1.78	1.75	1.72	1.69	1.66
19	1.96	1.91	1.86	1.81	1.79	1.76	1.73	1.70	1.67	1.63
20	1.94	1.89	1.84	1.79	1.77	1.74	1.71	1.68	1.64	1.61
21	1.92	1.87	1.83	1.78	1.75	1.72	1.69	1.66	1.62	1.59
22	1.90	1.86	1.81	1.76	1.73	1.70	1.67	1.64	1.60	1.57
23	1.89	1.84	1.80	1.74	1.72	1.69	1.66	1.62	1.59	1.55
24	1.88	1.83	1.78	1.73	1.70	1.67	1.64	1.61	1.57	1.53
25	1.87	1.82	1.77	1.72	1.69	1.66	1.63	1.59	1.56	1.52
26	1.86	1.81	1.76	1.71	1.68	1.65	1.61	1.58	1.54	1.50
27	1.85	1.80	1.75	1.70	1.67	1.64	1.60	1.57	1.53	1.49

TABLE G   The *F*-Distribution (*continued*)

| | $F_{0.90}$; $\alpha = 0.10$ | | | | | | | | | |

Denominator degrees of freedom	Numerator degrees of freedom									
	10	12	15	20	24	30	40	60	120	∞
28	1.84	1.79	1.74	1.69	1.66	1.63	1.59	1.56	1.52	1.48
29	1.83	1.78	1.73	1.68	1.65	1.62	1.58	1.55	1.51	1.47
30	1.82	1.77	1.72	1.67	1.64	1.61	1.57	1.54	1.50	1.46
40	1.76	1.71	1.66	1.61	1.57	1.54	1.51	1.47	1.42	1.38
60	1.71	1.66	1.60	1.54	1.51	1.48	1.44	1.40	1.35	1.29
120	1.65	1.60	1.55	1.48	1.45	1.41	1.37	1.32	1.26	1.19
∞	1.60	1.55	1.49	1.42	1.38	1.34	1.30	1.24	1.17	1.00

| | $F_{0.95}$; $\alpha = 0.05$ | | | | | | | | |

Denominator degrees of freedom	Numerator degrees of freedom								
	1	2	3	4	5	6	7	8	9
1	161.45	199.50	215.71	224.58	230.16	233.99	236.77	238.88	240.54
2	18.51	19.00	19.16	19.25	19.30	19.33	19.35	19.37	19.38
3	10.13	9.55	9.28	9.12	9.01	8.94	8.89	8.85	8.81
4	7.71	6.94	6.59	6.39	6.26	6.16	6.09	6.04	6.00
5	6.61	5.79	5.41	5.19	5.05	4.95	4.88	4.82	4.77
6	5.99	5.14	4.76	4.53	4.39	4.28	4.21	4.15	4.10
7	5.59	4.74	4.35	4.12	3.97	3.87	3.79	3.73	3.68
8	5.32	4.46	4.07	3.84	3.69	3.58	3.50	3.44	3.39
9	5.12	4.26	3.86	3.63	3.48	3.37	3.29	3.23	3.18
10	4.96	4.10	3.71	3.48	3.33	3.22	3.14	3.07	3.02
11	4.84	3.98	3.59	3.36	3.20	3.09	3.01	2.95	2.90
12	4.75	3.89	3.49	3.26	3.11	3.00	2.91	2.85	2.80
13	4.67	3.81	3.41	3.18	3.03	2.92	2.83	2.77	2.71
14	4.60	3.74	3.34	3.11	2.96	2.85	2.76	2.70	2.65
15	4.54	3.68	3.29	3.06	2.90	2.79	2.71	2.64	2.59
16	4.49	3.63	3.24	3.01	2.85	2.74	2.66	2.59	2.54
17	4.45	3.59	3.20	2.96	2.81	2.70	2.61	2.55	2.49
18	4.41	3.55	3.16	2.93	2.77	2.66	2.58	2.51	2.46
19	4.38	3.52	3.13	2.90	2.74	2.63	2.54	2.48	2.42
20	4.35	3.49	3.10	2.87	2.71	2.60	2.51	2.45	2.39
21	4.32	3.47	3.07	2.84	2.68	2.57	2.49	2.42	2.37
22	4.30	3.44	3.05	2.82	2.66	2.55	2.46	2.40	2.34
23	4.28	3.42	3.03	2.80	2.64	2.53	2.44	2.37	2.32
24	4.26	3.40	3.01	2.78	2.62	2.51	2.42	2.36	2.30

TABLE G   The *F*-Distribution (*continued*)

$F_{0.95}; \alpha = 0.05$

Denominator degrees of freedom	Numerator degrees of freedom								
	1	2	3	4	5	6	7	8	9
25	4.24	3.39	2.99	2.76	2.60	2.49	2.40	2.34	2.28
26	4.23	3.37	2.98	2.74	2.59	2.47	2.39	2.32	2.27
27	4.21	3.35	2.96	2.73	2.57	2.46	2.37	2.31	2.25
28	4.20	3.34	2.95	2.71	2.56	2.45	2.36	2.29	2.24
29	4.18	3.33	2.93	2.70	2.55	2.43	2.35	2.28	2.22
30	4.17	3.32	2.92	2.69	2.53	2.42	2.33	2.27	2.21
40	4.08	3.23	2.84	2.61	2.45	2.34	2.25	2.18	2.12
60	4.00	3.15	2.76	2.53	2.37	2.25	2.17	2.10	2.04
120	3.92	3.07	2.68	2.45	2.29	2.18	2.09	2.02	1.96
∞	3.84	3.00	2.61	2.37	2.21	2.10	2.01	1.94	1.88

$F_{0.95}; \alpha = 0.05$

Denominator degrees of freedom	Numerator degrees of freedom									
	10	12	15	20	24	30	40	60	120	∞
1	241.88	243.91	245.95	248.01	249.05	250.10	251.14	252.20	253.25	254.31
2	19.40	19.41	19.43	19.45	19.45	19.46	19.47	19.48	19.49	19.50
3	8.79	8.74	8.70	8.66	8.64	8.62	8.59	8.57	8.55	8.53
4	5.96	5.91	5.86	5.80	5.77	5.75	5.72	5.69	5.66	5.63
5	4.74	4.68	4.62	4.56	4.53	4.50	4.46	4.43	4.40	4.37
6	4.06	4.00	3.94	3.87	3.84	3.81	3.77	3.74	3.70	3.67
7	3.64	3.57	3.51	3.44	3.41	3.38	3.34	3.30	3.27	3.23
8	3.35	3.28	3.22	3.15	3.12	3.08	3.04	3.01	2.97	2.93
9	3.14	3.07	3.01	2.94	2.90	2.86	2.83	2.79	2.75	2.71
10	2.98	2.91	2.85	2.77	2.74	2.70	2.66	2.62	2.58	2.54
11	2.85	2.79	2.72	2.65	2.61	2.57	2.53	2.49	2.45	2.40
12	2.75	2.69	2.62	2.54	2.51	2.47	2.43	2.38	2.34	2.30
13	2.67	2.60	2.53	2.46	2.42	2.38	2.34	2.30	2.25	2.21
14	2.60	2.53	2.46	2.39	2.35	2.31	2.27	2.22	2.18	2.13
15	2.54	2.48	2.40	2.33	2.29	2.25	2.20	2.16	2.11	2.07
16	2.49	2.42	2.35	2.28	2.24	2.19	2.15	2.11	2.06	2.01
17	2.45	2.38	2.31	2.23	2.19	2.15	2.10	2.06	2.01	1.96
18	2.41	2.34	2.27	2.19	2.15	2.11	2.06	2.02	1.97	1.92
19	2.38	2.31	2.23	2.16	2.11	2.07	2.03	1.98	1.93	1.88
20	2.35	2.28	2.20	2.12	2.08	2.04	1.99	1.95	1.90	1.84
21	2.32	2.25	2.18	2.10	2.05	2.01	1.96	1.92	1.87	1.81
22	2.30	2.23	2.15	2.07	2.03	1.98	1.94	1.89	1.84	1.78

TABLE G The *F*-Distribution (*continued*)

				$F_{0.95}$; $\alpha = 0.05$						
Denominator degrees of freedom	Numerator degrees of freedom									
	10	12	15	20	24	30	40	60	120	∞
23	2.27	2.20	2.13	2.05	2.01	1.96	1.91	1.86	1.81	1.76
24	2.25	2.18	2.11	2.03	1.98	1.94	1.89	1.84	1.79	1.73
25	2.24	2.16	2.09	2.01	1.96	1.92	1.87	1.82	1.77	1.71
26	2.22	2.15	2.07	1.99	1.95	1.90	1.85	1.80	1.75	1.69
27	2.20	2.13	2.06	1.97	1.93	1.88	1.84	1.79	1.73	1.67
28	2.19	2.12	2.04	1.96	1.91	1.87	1.82	1.77	1.71	1.65
29	2.18	2.10	2.03	1.94	1.90	1.85	1.81	1.75	1.70	1.64
30	2.16	2.09	2.01	1.93	1.89	1.84	1.79	1.74	1.68	1.62
40	2.08	2.00	1.92	1.84	1.79	1.74	1.69	1.64	1.58	1.51
60	1.99	1.92	1.84	1.75	1.70	1.65	1.59	1.53	1.47	1.39
120	1.91	1.83	1.75	1.66	1.61	1.55	1.50	1.43	1.35	1.25
∞	1.83	1.75	1.67	1.57	1.52	1.46	1.39	1.32	1.22	1.00

				$F_{0.975}$; $\alpha = 0.025$					
Denominator degrees of freedom	Numerator degrees of freedom								
	1	2	3	4	5	6	7	8	9
1	647.8	799.5	864.2	899.6	921.8	937.1	948.2	956.7	963.3
2	38.51	39.00	39.17	39.25	39.30	39.33	39.36	39.37	39.39
3	17.44	16.04	15.44	15.10	14.88	14.73	14.62	14.54	14.47
4	12.22	10.65	9.98	9.60	9.36	9.20	9.07	8.98	8.90
5	10.01	8.43	7.76	7.39	7.15	6.98	6.85	6.76	6.68
6	8.81	7.26	6.60	6.23	5.99	5.82	5.70	5.60	5.52
7	8.07	6.54	5.89	5.52	5.29	5.12	4.99	4.90	4.82
8	7.57	6.06	5.42	5.05	4.82	4.65	4.53	4.43	4.36
9	7.21	5.71	5.08	4.72	4.48	4.32	4.20	4.10	4.03
10	6.94	5.46	4.83	4.47	4.24	4.07	3.95	3.85	3.78
11	6.72	5.26	4.63	4.28	4.04	3.88	3.76	3.66	3.59
12	6.55	5.10	4.47	4.12	3.89	3.73	3.61	3.51	3.44
13	6.41	4.97	4.35	4.00	3.77	3.60	3.48	3.39	3.31
14	6.30	4.86	4.24	3.89	3.66	3.50	3.38	3.29	3.21
15	6.20	4.77	4.15	3.80	3.58	3.41	3.29	3.20	3.12
16	6.12	4.69	4.08	3.73	3.50	3.34	3.22	3.12	3.05
17	6.04	4.62	4.01	3.66	3.44	3.28	3.16	3.06	2.98
18	5.98	4.56	3.95	3.61	3.38	3.22	3.10	3.01	2.93
19	5.92	4.51	3.90	3.56	3.33	3.17	3.05	2.96	2.88

TABLE G   The *F*-Distribution (*continued*)

$F_{0.975}$; $\alpha = 0.025$

Denominator degrees of freedom	Numerator degrees of freedom								
	1	2	3	4	5	6	7	8	9
20	5.87	4.46	3.86	3.51	3.29	3.13	3.01	2.91	2.84
21	5.83	4.42	3.82	3.48	3.25	3.09	2.97	2.87	2.80
22	5.79	4.38	3.78	3.44	3.22	3.05	2.93	2.84	2.76
23	5.75	4.35	3.75	3.41	3.18	3.02	2.90	2.81	2.73
24	5.72	4.32	3.72	3.38	3.15	2.99	2.87	2.78	2.70
25	5.69	4.29	3.69	3.35	3.13	2.97	2.85	2.75	2.68
26	5.66	4.27	3.67	3.33	3.10	2.94	2.82	2.73	2.65
27	5.63	4.24	3.65	3.31	3.08	2.92	2.80	2.71	2.63
28	5.61	4.22	3.63	3.29	3.06	2.90	2.78	2.69	2.61
29	5.59	4.20	3.61	3.27	3.04	2.88	2.76	2.67	2.59
30	5.57	4.18	3.59	3.25	3.03	2.87	2.75	2.65	2.57
40	5.42	4.05	3.46	3.13	2.90	2.74	2.62	2.53	2.45
60	5.29	3.93	3.34	3.01	2.79	2.63	2.51	2.41	2.33
120	5.15	3.80	3.23	2.89	2.67	2.52	2.39	2.30	2.22
∞	5.02	3.69	3.12	2.79	2.57	2.41	2.29	2.19	2.11

$F_{0.975}$; $\alpha = 0.025$

Denominator degrees of freedom	Numerator degrees of freedom									
	10	12	15	20	24	30	40	60	120	∞
1	968.6	976.7	984.9	993.1	997.2	1001.4	1005.6	1009.8	1014.0	1018.2
2	39.40	39.41	39.43	39.45	39.46	39.46	39.47	39.48	39.49	39.50
3	14.42	14.34	14.25	14.17	14.12	14.08	14.04	13.99	13.95	13.90
4	8.84	8.75	8.66	8.56	8.51	8.46	8.41	8.36	8.31	8.26
5	6.62	6.52	6.43	6.33	6.28	6.23	6.18	6.12	6.07	6.02
6	5.46	5.37	5.27	5.17	5.12	5.07	5.01	4.96	4.90	4.85
7	4.76	4.67	4.57	4.47	4.41	4.36	4.31	4.25	4.20	4.14
8	4.30	4.20	4.10	4.00	3.95	3.89	3.84	3.78	3.73	3.67
9	3.96	3.87	3.77	3.67	3.61	3.56	3.51	3.45	3.39	3.33
10	3.72	3.62	3.52	3.42	3.37	3.31	3.26	3.20	3.14	3.08
11	3.53	3.43	3.33	3.23	3.17	3.12	3.06	3.00	2.94	2.88
12	3.37	3.28	3.18	3.07	3.02	2.96	2.91	2.85	2.79	2.73
13	3.25	3.15	3.05	2.95	2.89	2.84	2.78	2.72	2.66	2.60
14	3.15	3.05	2.95	2.84	2.79	2.73	2.67	2.61	2.55	2.49
15	3.06	2.96	2.86	2.76	2.70	2.64	2.59	2.52	2.46	2.40
16	2.99	2.89	2.79	2.68	2.63	2.57	2.51	2.45	2.38	2.32
17	2.92	2.82	2.72	2.62	2.56	2.50	2.44	2.38	2.32	2.25

TABLE G The F-Distribution (*continued*)

	$F_{0.975}$; $\alpha = 0.025$									
Denominator degrees of freedom	Numerator degrees of freedom									
	10	12	15	20	24	30	40	60	120	∞
18	2.87	2.77	2.67	2.56	2.50	2.44	2.38	2.32	2.26	2.19
19	2.82	2.72	2.62	2.51	2.45	2.39	2.33	2.27	2.20	2.13
20	2.77	2.68	2.57	2.46	2.41	2.35	2.29	2.22	2.16	2.09
21	2.73	2.64	2.53	2.42	2.37	2.31	2.25	2.18	2.11	2.04
22	2.70	2.60	2.50	2.39	2.33	2.27	2.21	2.14	2.08	2.00
23	2.67	2.57	2.47	2.36	2.30	2.24	2.18	2.11	2.04	1.97
24	2.64	2.54	2.44	2.33	2.27	2.21	2.15	2.08	2.01	1.94
25	2.61	2.51	2.41	2.30	2.24	2.18	2.12	2.05	1.98	1.91
26	2.59	2.49	2.39	2.28	2.22	2.16	2.09	2.03	1.95	1.88
27	2.57	2.47	2.36	2.25	2.19	2.13	2.07	2.00	1.93	1.85
28	2.55	2.45	2.34	2.23	2.17	2.11	2.05	1.98	1.91	1.83
29	2.53	2.43	2.32	2.21	2.15	2.09	2.03	1.96	1.89	1.81
30	2.51	2.41	2.31	2.20	2.14	2.07	2.01	1.94	1.87	1.79
40	2.39	2.29	2.18	2.07	2.01	1.94	1.88	1.80	1.72	1.64
60	2.27	2.17	2.06	1.94	1.88	1.82	1.74	1.67	1.58	1.48
120	2.16	2.05	1.94	1.82	1.76	1.69	1.61	1.53	1.43	1.31
∞	2.05	1.95	1.83	1.71	1.64	1.57	1.48	1.39	1.27	1.00

	$F_{0.99}$; $\alpha = 0.01$								
Denominator degrees of freedom	Numerator degrees of freedom								
	1	2	3	4	5	6	7	8	9
1	4052.2	4999.5	5403.4	5624.6	5763.6	5859.0	5928.4	5981.1	6022.5
2	98.50	99.00	99.17	99.25	99.30	99.33	99.36	99.37	99.39
3	34.12	30.82	29.46	28.71	28.24	27.91	27.67	27.49	27.35
4	21.20	18.00	16.69	15.98	15.52	15.21	14.98	14.80	14.66
5	16.26	13.27	12.06	11.39	10.97	10.67	10.46	10.29	10.16
6	13.75	10.92	9.78	9.15	8.75	8.47	8.26	8.10	7.98
7	12.25	9.55	8.45	7.85	7.46	7.19	6.99	6.84	6.72
8	11.26	8.65	7.59	7.01	6.63	6.37	6.18	6.03	5.91
9	10.56	8.02	6.99	6.42	6.06	5.80	5.61	5.47	5.35
10	10.04	7.56	6.55	5.99	5.64	5.39	5.20	5.06	4.94
11	9.65	7.21	6.22	5.67	5.32	5.07	4.89	4.74	4.63
12	9.33	6.93	5.95	5.41	5.06	4.82	4.64	4.50	4.39
13	9.07	6.70	5.74	5.21	4.86	4.62	4.44	4.30	4.19
14	8.86	6.51	5.56	5.04	4.69	4.46	4.28	4.14	4.03

TABLE G   The *F*-Distribution (*continued*)

	$F_{0.99};\ \alpha = 0.01$								
Denominator degrees of freedom	Numerator degrees of freedom								
	1	2	3	4	5	6	7	8	9
15	8.68	6.36	5.42	4.89	4.56	4.32	4.14	4.00	3.89
16	8.53	6.23	5.29	4.77	4.44	4.20	4.03	3.89	3.78
17	8.40	6.11	5.18	4.67	4.34	4.10	3.93	3.79	3.68
18	8.29	6.01	5.09	4.58	4.25	4.01	3.84	3.71	3.60
19	8.18	5.93	5.01	4.50	4.17	3.94	3.77	3.63	3.52
20	8.10	5.85	4.94	4.43	4.10	3.87	3.70	3.56	3.46
21	8.02	5.78	4.87	4.37	4.04	3.81	3.64	3.51	3.40
22	7.95	5.72	4.82	4.31	3.99	3.76	3.59	3.45	3.35
23	7.88	5.66	4.76	4.26	3.94	3.71	3.54	3.41	3.30
24	7.82	5.61	4.72	4.22	3.90	3.67	3.50	3.36	3.26
25	7.77	5.57	4.68	4.18	3.85	3.63	3.46	3.32	3.22
26	7.72	5.53	4.64	4.14	3.82	3.59	3.42	3.29	3.18
27	7.68	5.49	4.60	4.11	3.78	3.56	3.39	3.26	3.15
28	7.64	5.45	4.57	4.07	3.75	3.53	3.36	3.23	3.12
29	7.60	5.42	4.54	4.04	3.73	3.50	3.33	3.20	3.09
30	7.56	5.39	4.51	4.02	3.70	3.47	3.30	3.17	3.07
40	7.31	5.18	4.31	3.83	3.51	3.29	3.12	2.99	2.89
60	7.08	4.98	4.13	3.65	3.34	3.12	2.95	2.82	2.72
120	6.85	4.79	3.95	3.48	3.17	2.96	2.79	2.66	2.56
∞	6.64	4.61	3.78	3.32	3.02	2.80	2.64	2.51	2.41

	$F_{0.99};\ \alpha = 0.01$									
Denominator degrees of freedom	Numerator degrees of freedom									
	10	12	15	20	24	30	40	60	120	∞
1	6055.8	6106.3	6157.3	6208.7	6234.6	6260.6	6286.8	6313.0	6339.4	6365.8
2	99.40	99.42	99.43	99.45	99.46	99.47	99.47	99.48	99.49	99.50
3	27.23	27.05	26.87	26.69	26.60	26.50	26.41	26.32	26.22	26.13
4	14.55	14.37	14.20	14.02	13.93	13.84	13.75	13.65	13.56	13.46
5	10.05	9.89	9.72	9.55	9.47	9.38	9.29	9.20	9.11	9.02
6	7.87	7.72	7.56	7.40	7.31	7.23	7.14	7.06	6.97	6.88
7	6.62	6.47	6.31	6.16	6.07	5.99	5.91	5.82	5.74	5.65
8	5.81	5.67	5.52	5.36	5.28	5.20	5.12	5.03	4.95	4.86
9	5.26	5.11	4.96	4.81	4.73	4.65	4.57	4.48	4.40	4.31
10	4.85	4.71	4.56	4.41	4.33	4.25	4.17	4.08	4.00	3.91
11	4.54	4.40	4.25	4.10	4.02	3.94	3.86	3.78	3.69	3.60
12	4.30	4.16	4.01	3.86	3.78	3.70	3.62	3.54	3.45	3.36

TABLE G   The *F*-Distribution (*continued*)

$$F_{0.99}; \alpha = 0.01$$

Denominator degrees of freedom	Numerator degrees of freedom									
	10	12	15	20	24	30	40	60	120	∞
13	4.10	3.96	3.82	3.66	3.59	3.51	3.43	3.34	3.25	3.17
14	3.94	3.80	3.66	3.51	3.43	3.35	3.27	3.18	3.09	3.00
15	3.80	3.67	3.52	3.37	3.29	3.21	3.13	3.05	2.96	2.87
16	3.69	3.55	3.41	3.26	3.18	3.10	3.02	2.93	2.84	2.75
17	3.59	3.46	3.31	3.16	3.08	3.00	2.92	2.83	2.75	2.65
18	3.51	3.37	3.23	3.08	3.00	2.92	2.84	2.75	2.66	2.57
19	3.43	3.30	3.15	3.00	2.92	2.84	2.76	2.67	2.58	2.49
20	3.37	3.23	3.09	2.94	2.86	2.78	2.69	2.61	2.52	2.42
21	3.31	3.17	3.03	2.88	2.80	2.72	2.64	2.55	2.46	2.36
22	3.26	3.12	2.98	2.83	2.75	2.67	2.58	2.50	2.40	2.31
23	3.21	3.07	2.93	2.78	2.70	2.62	2.54	2.45	2.35	2.26
24	3.17	3.03	2.89	2.74	2.66	2.58	2.49	2.40	2.31	2.21
25	3.13	2.99	2.85	2.70	2.62	2.54	2.45	2.36	2.27	2.17
26	3.09	2.96	2.81	2.66	2.58	2.50	2.42	2.33	2.23	2.13
27	3.06	2.93	2.78	2.63	2.55	2.47	2.38	2.29	2.20	2.10
28	3.03	2.90	2.75	2.60	2.52	2.44	2.35	2.26	2.17	2.06
29	3.00	2.87	2.73	2.57	2.49	2.41	2.33	2.23	2.14	2.03
30	2.98	2.84	2.70	2.55	2.47	2.39	2.30	2.21	2.11	2.01
40	2.80	2.66	2.52	2.37	2.29	2.20	2.11	2.02	1.92	1.81
60	2.63	2.50	2.35	2.20	2.12	2.03	1.94	1.84	1.73	1.60
120	2.47	2.34	2.19	2.03	1.95	1.86	1.76	1.66	1.53	1.38
∞	2.32	2.19	2.04	1.88	1.79	1.70	1.59	1.47	1.33	1.00

$$F_{0.995}; \alpha = 0.005$$

Denominator degrees of freedom	Numerator degrees of freedom								
	1	2	3	4	5	6	7	8	9
1	16211	20000	21615	22500	23056	23437	23715	23925	24091
2	198.50	199.00	199.17	199.25	199.30	199.33	199.36	199.37	199.39
3	55.55	49.80	47.47	46.19	45.39	44.84	44.43	44.13	43.88
4	31.33	26.28	24.26	23.15	22.46	21.97	21.62	21.35	21.14
5	22.78	18.31	16.53	15.56	14.94	14.51	14.20	13.96	13.77
6	18.63	14.54	12.92	12.03	11.46	11.07	10.79	10.57	10.39
7	16.24	12.40	10.88	10.05	9.52	9.16	8.89	8.68	8.51
8	14.69	11.04	9.60	8.81	8.30	7.95	7.69	7.50	7.34
9	13.61	10.11	8.72	7.96	7.47	7.13	6.88	6.69	6.54

TABLE G   The *F*-Distribution (*continued*)

	$F_{0.995}$; $\alpha = 0.005$								
Denominator degrees of freedom	Numerator degrees of freedom								
	1	2	3	4	5	6	7	8	9
10	12.83	9.43	8.08	7.34	6.87	6.54	6.30	6.12	5.97
11	12.23	8.91	7.60	6.88	6.42	6.10	5.86	5.68	5.54
12	11.75	8.51	7.23	6.52	6.07	5.76	5.52	5.35	5.20
13	11.37	8.19	6.93	6.23	5.79	5.48	5.25	5.08	4.94
14	11.06	7.92	6.68	6.00	5.56	5.26	5.03	4.86	4.72
15	10.80	7.70	6.48	5.80	5.37	5.07	4.85	4.67	4.54
16	10.58	7.51	6.30	5.64	5.21	4.91	4.69	4.52	4.38
17	10.38	7.35	6.16	5.50	5.07	4.78	4.56	4.39	4.25
18	10.22	7.21	6.03	5.37	4.96	4.66	4.44	4.28	4.14
19	10.07	7.09	5.92	5.27	4.85	4.56	4.34	4.18	4.04
20	9.94	6.99	5.82	5.17	4.76	4.47	4.26	4.09	3.96
21	9.83	6.89	5.73	5.09	4.68	4.39	4.18	4.01	3.88
22	9.73	6.81	5.65	5.02	4.61	4.32	4.11	3.94	3.81
23	9.63	6.73	5.58	4.95	4.54	4.26	4.05	3.88	3.75
24	9.55	6.66	5.52	4.89	4.49	4.20	3.99	3.83	3.69
25	9.48	6.60	5.46	4.84	4.43	4.15	3.94	3.78	3.64
26	9.41	6.54	5.41	4.79	4.38	4.10	3.89	3.73	3.60
27	9.34	6.49	5.36	4.74	4.34	4.06	3.85	3.69	3.56
28	9.28	6.44	5.32	4.70	4.30	4.02	3.81	3.65	3.52
29	9.23	6.40	5.28	4.66	4.26	3.98	3.77	3.61	3.48
30	9.18	6.35	5.24	4.62	4.23	3.95	3.74	3.58	3.45
40	8.83	6.07	4.98	4.37	3.99	3.71	3.51	3.35	3.22
60	8.49	5.79	4.73	4.14	3.76	3.49	3.29	3.13	3.01
120	8.18	5.54	4.50	3.92	3.55	3.28	3.09	2.93	2.81
∞	7.88	5.30	4.28	3.72	3.35	3.09	2.90	2.75	2.62

	$F_{0.995}$; $\alpha = 0.005$									
Denominator degrees of freedom	Numerator degrees of freedom									
	10	12	15	20	24	30	40	60	120	∞
1	24224	24426	24630	24836	24940	25044	25148	25253	25359	25464
2	199.40	199.42	199.43	199.45	199.46	199.47	199.47	199.48	199.49	199.50
3	43.69	43.39	43.08	42.78	42.62	42.47	42.31	42.15	41.99	41.83
4	20.97	20.70	20.44	20.17	20.03	19.89	19.75	19.61	19.47	19.33
5	13.62	13.38	13.15	12.90	12.78	12.66	12.53	12.40	12.27	12.14
6	10.25	10.03	9.81	9.59	9.47	9.36	9.24	9.12	9.00	8.88
7	8.38	8.18	7.97	7.75	7.64	7.53	7.42	7.31	7.19	7.08

TABLE G The *F*-Distribution (*concluded*)

Denominator degrees of freedom	Numerator degrees of freedom									
$F_{0.995}; \alpha = 0.005$	10	12	15	20	24	30	40	60	120	∞
8	7.21	7.01	6.81	6.61	6.50	6.40	6.29	6.18	6.06	5.95
9	6.42	6.23	6.03	5.83	5.73	5.62	5.52	5.41	5.30	5.19
10	5.85	5.66	5.47	5.27	5.17	5.07	4.97	4.86	4.75	4.64
11	5.42	5.24	5.05	4.86	4.76	4.65	4.55	4.45	4.34	4.23
12	5.09	4.91	4.72	4.53	4.43	4.33	4.23	4.12	4.01	3.90
13	4.82	4.64	4.46	4.27	4.17	4.07	3.97	3.87	3.76	3.65
14	4.60	4.43	4.25	4.06	3.96	3.86	3.76	3.66	3.55	3.44
15	4.42	4.25	4.07	3.88	3.79	3.69	3.58	3.48	3.37	3.26
16	4.27	4.10	3.92	3.73	3.64	3.54	3.44	3.33	3.22	3.11
17	4.14	3.97	3.79	3.61	3.51	3.41	3.31	3.21	3.10	2.98
18	4.03	3.86	3.68	3.50	3.40	3.30	3.20	3.10	2.99	2.87
19	3.93	3.76	3.59	3.40	3.31	3.21	3.11	3.00	2.89	2.78
20	3.85	3.68	3.50	3.32	3.22	3.12	3.02	2.92	2.81	2.69
21	3.77	3.60	3.43	3.24	3.15	3.05	2.95	2.84	2.73	2.61
22	3.70	3.54	3.36	3.18	3.08	2.98	2.88	2.77	2.66	2.55
23	3.64	3.47	3.30	3.12	3.02	2.92	2.82	2.71	2.60	2.48
24	3.59	3.42	3.25	3.06	2.97	2.87	2.77	2.66	2.55	2.43
25	3.54	3.37	3.20	3.01	2.92	2.82	2.72	2.61	2.50	2.38
26	3.49	3.33	3.15	2.97	2.87	2.77	2.67	2.56	2.45	2.33
27	3.45	3.28	3.11	2.93	2.83	2.73	2.63	2.52	2.41	2.29
28	3.41	3.25	3.07	2.89	2.79	2.69	2.59	2.48	2.37	2.25
29	3.38	3.21	3.04	2.86	2.76	2.66	2.56	2.45	2.33	2.21
30	3.34	3.18	3.01	2.82	2.73	2.63	2.52	2.42	2.30	2.18
40	3.12	2.95	2.78	2.60	2.50	2.40	2.30	2.18	2.06	1.93
60	2.90	2.74	2.57	2.39	2.29	2.19	2.08	1.96	1.83	1.69
120	2.71	2.54	2.37	2.19	2.09	1.98	1.87	1.75	1.61	1.43
∞	2.52	2.36	2.19	2.00	1.90	1.79	1.67	1.53	1.36	1.00

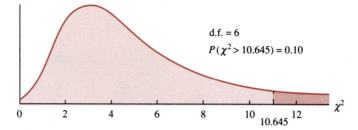

$$\text{d.f.} = 6$$
$$P(\chi^2 > 10.645) = 0.10$$

TABLE H Chi-Square Distribution

d.f.	$\chi^2_{0.995}$	$\chi^2_{0.990}$	$\chi^2_{0.975}$	$\chi^2_{0.950}$	$\chi^2_{0.900}$	$\chi^2_{0.700}$	$\chi^2_{0.500}$	$\chi^2_{0.300}$	$\chi^2_{0.200}$	$\chi^2_{0.100}$	$\chi^2_{0.050}$	$\chi^2_{0.020}$	$\chi^2_{0.010}$
1	0.000	0.000	0.001	0.004	0.016	0.148	0.455	1.074	1.642	2.706	3.841	5.412	6.635
2	0.010	0.020	0.051	0.103	0.211	0.713	1.386	2.408	3.219	4.605	5.991	7.824	9.210
3	0.072	0.115	0.216	0.352	0.584	1.424	2.366	3.665	4.642	6.251	7.815	9.837	11.345
4	0.207	0.297	0.484	0.711	1.064	2.195	3.357	4.878	5.989	7.779	9.488	11.668	13.277
5	0.412	0.554	0.831	1.145	1.610	3.000	4.351	6.064	7.289	9.236	11.070	13.388	15.086
6	0.676	0.872	1.237	1.635	2.204	3.828	5.348	7.231	8.558	10.645	12.592	15.033	16.812
7	0.989	1.239	1.690	2.167	2.833	4.671	6.346	8.383	9.803	12.017	14.067	16.622	18.475
8	1.344	1.646	2.180	2.733	3.490	5.527	7.344	9.524	11.030	13.362	15.507	18.168	20.090
9	1.735	2.088	2.700	3.325	4.168	6.393	8.343	10.656	12.242	14.684	16.919	19.679	21.666
10	2.156	2.558	3.247	3.940	4.865	7.267	9.342	11.781	13.442	15.987	18.307	21.161	23.209
11	2.603	3.053	3.816	4.575	5.578	8.148	10.341	12.899	14.631	17.275	19.675	22.618	24.725
12	3.074	3.571	4.404	5.226	6.304	9.034	11.340	14.011	15.812	18.549	21.026	24.054	26.217
13	3.565	4.107	5.009	5.892	7.042	9.926	12.340	15.119	16.985	19.812	22.362	25.472	27.688
14	4.075	4.660	5.629	6.571	7.790	10.821	13.339	16.222	18.151	21.064	23.685	26.873	29.141
15	4.601	5.229	6.262	7.261	8.547	11.721	14.339	17.322	19.311	22.307	24.996	28.259	30.578
16	5.142	5.812	6.908	7.962	9.312	12.624	15.338	18.418	20.465	23.542	26.296	29.633	32.000
17	5.697	6.408	7.564	8.672	10.085	13.531	16.338	19.511	21.615	24.769	27.587	30.995	33.409
18	6.265	7.015	8.231	9.390	10.865	14.440	17.338	20.601	22.760	25.989	28.869	32.346	34.805
19	6.844	7.633	8.907	10.117	11.651	15.352	18.338	21.689	23.900	27.204	30.144	33.687	36.191
20	7.434	8.260	9.591	10.851	12.443	16.266	19.337	22.775	25.038	28.412	31.410	35.020	37.566
21	8.034	8.897	10.283	11.591	13.240	17.182	20.337	23.858	26.171	29.615	32.671	36.343	38.932
22	8.643	9.542	10.982	12.338	14.041	18.101	21.337	24.939	27.301	30.813	33.924	37.659	40.289
23	9.260	10.196	11.689	13.091	14.848	19.021	22.337	26.018	28.429	32.007	35.172	38.968	41.638
24	9.886	10.856	12.401	13.848	15.659	19.943	23.337	27.096	29.553	33.196	36.415	40.270	42.980
25	10.520	11.524	13.120	14.611	16.473	20.867	24.337	28.172	30.675	34.382	37.652	41.566	44.314
26	11.160	12.198	13.844	15.379	17.292	21.792	25.336	29.246	31.795	35.563	38.885	42.856	45.642
27	11.808	12.879	14.573	16.151	18.114	22.719	26.336	30.319	32.912	36.741	40.113	44.140	46.963
28	12.461	13.565	15.308	16.928	18.939	23.647	27.336	31.391	34.027	37.916	41.337	45.419	48.278
29	13.121	14.256	16.047	17.708	19.768	24.577	28.336	32.461	35.139	39.087	42.557	46.693	49.588
30	13.787	14.953	16.791	18.493	20.599	25.508	29.336	33.530	36.250	40.256	43.773	47.962	50.892
40	20.707	22.164	24.433	26.509	29.051	34.872	39.335	44.165	47.269	51.805	55.758	60.436	63.691
50	27.991	29.707	32.357	34.764	37.689	44.313	49.335	54.723	58.164	63.167	67.505	72.613	76.154
60	35.534	37.485	40.482	43.188	46.459	53.809	59.335	65.227	68.972	74.397	79.082	84.580	88.379
70	43.275	45.442	48.758	51.739	55.329	63.346	69.334	75.689	79.715	85.527	90.531	96.388	100.425
80	51.172	53.540	57.153	60.391	64.278	72.915	79.334	86.120	90.405	96.578	101.879	108.069	112.329
90	59.196	61.754	65.647	69.126	73.291	82.511	89.334	96.524	101.054	107.565	113.145	119.648	124.116
100	67.328	70.065	74.222	77.929	82.358	92.129	99.334	106.906	111.667	118.498	124.342	131.142	135.807

TABLE I   Common Logarithms

	0.0	0.1	0.2	0.3	0.4	0.5	0.6	0.7	0.8	0.9
1	0.0000	0.0414	0.0792	0.1139	0.1461	0.1761	0.2041	0.2304	0.2553	0.2788
2	0.3010	0.3222	0.3424	0.3617	0.3802	0.3979	0.4150	0.4314	0.4472	0.4624
3	0.4771	0.4914	0.5051	0.5185	0.5315	0.5441	0.5563	0.5682	0.5798	0.5911
4	0.6021	0.6128	0.6232	0.6335	0.6435	0.6532	0.6628	0.6721	0.6812	0.6902
5	0.6990	0.7076	0.7160	0.7243	0.7324	0.7404	0.7482	0.7559	0.7634	0.7709
6	0.7782	0.7853	0.7924	0.7993	0.8062	0.8129	0.8195	0.8261	0.8325	0.8388
7	0.8451	0.8513	0.8573	0.8633	0.8692	0.8751	0.8808	0.8865	0.8921	0.8976
8	0.9031	0.9085	0.9138	0.9191	0.9243	0.9294	0.9345	0.9395	0.9445	0.9494
9	0.9542	0.9590	0.9638	0.9685	0.9731	0.9777	0.9823	0.9868	0.9912	0.9956
10	1.0000	1.0043	1.0086	1.0128	1.0170	1.0212	1.0253	1.0294	1.0334	1.0374
11	1.0414	1.0453	1.0492	1.0531	1.0569	1.0607	1.0645	1.0682	1.0719	1.0755
12	1.0792	1.0828	1.0864	1.0899	1.0934	1.0969	1.1004	1.1038	1.1072	1.1106
13	1.1139	1.1173	1.1206	1.1239	1.1271	1.1303	1.1335	1.1367	1.1399	1.1430
14	1.1461	1.1492	1.1523	1.1553	1.1584	1.1614	1.1644	1.1673	1.1703	1.1732
15	1.1761	1.1790	1.1818	1.1847	1.1875	1.1903	1.1931	1.1959	1.1987	1.2014
16	1.2041	1.2068	1.2095	1.2122	1.2148	1.2175	1.2201	1.2227	1.2253	1.2279
17	1.2304	1.2330	1.2355	1.2380	1.2405	1.2430	1.2455	1.2480	1.2504	1.2529
18	1.2553	1.2577	1.2601	1.2625	1.2648	1.2672	1.2695	1.2718	1.2742	1.2765
19	1.2788	1.2810	1.2833	1.2856	1.2878	1.2900	1.2923	1.2945	1.2967	1.2989
20	1.3010	1.3032	1.3054	1.3075	1.3096	1.3118	1.3139	1.3160	1.3181	1.3201
21	1.3222	1.3243	1.3263	1.3284	1.3304	1.3324	1.3345	1.3365	1.3385	1.3404
22	1.3424	1.3444	1.3464	1.3483	1.3502	1.3522	1.3541	1.3560	1.3579	1.3598
23	1.3617	1.3636	1.3655	1.3674	1.3692	1.3711	1.3729	1.3747	1.3766	1.3784
24	1.3802	1.3820	1.3838	1.3856	1.3874	1.3892	1.3909	1.3927	1.3945	1.3962
25	1.3979	1.3997	1.4014	1.4031	1.4048	1.4065	1.4082	1.4099	1.4116	1.4133
26	1.4150	1.4166	1.4183	1.4200	1.4216	1.4232	1.4249	1.4265	1.4281	1.4298
27	1.4314	1.4330	1.4346	1.4362	1.4378	1.4393	1.4409	1.4425	1.4440	1.4456
28	1.4472	1.4487	1.4502	1.4518	1.4533	1.4548	1.4564	1.4579	1.4594	1.4609
29	1.4624	1.4639	1.4654	1.4669	1.4683	1.4698	1.4713	1.4728	1.4742	1.4757
30	1.4771	1.4786	1.4800	1.4814	1.4829	1.4843	1.4857	1.4871	1.4886	1.4900
31	1.4914	1.4928	1.4942	1.4955	1.4969	1.4983	1.4997	1.5011	1.5024	1.5038
32	1.5051	1.5065	1.5079	1.5092	1.5105	1.5119	1.5132	1.5145	1.5159	1.5172
33	1.5185	1.5198	1.5211	1.5224	1.5237	1.5250	1.5263	1.5276	1.5289	1.5302
34	1.5315	1.5328	1.5340	1.5353	1.5366	1.5378	1.5391	1.5403	1.5416	1.5428
35	1.5441	1.5453	1.5465	1.5478	1.5490	1.5502	1.5514	1.5527	1.5539	1.5551

Table I   Common Logarithms (*continued*)

	0.0	0.1	0.2	0.3	0.4	0.5	0.6	0.7	0.8	0.9
36	1.5563	1.5575	1.5587	1.5599	1.5611	1.5623	1.5635	1.5647	1.5658	1.5670
37	1.5682	1.5694	1.5705	1.5717	1.5729	1.5740	1.5752	1.5763	1.5775	1.5786
38	1.5798	1.5809	1.5821	1.5832	1.5843	1.5855	1.5866	1.5877	1.5888	1.5899
39	1.5911	1.5922	1.5933	1.5944	1.5955	1.5966	1.5977	1.5988	1.5999	1.6010
40	1.6021	1.6031	1.6042	1.6053	1.6064	1.6075	1.6085	1.6096	1.6107	1.6117
41	1.6128	1.6138	1.6149	1.6160	1.6170	1.6180	1.6191	1.6201	1.6212	1.6222
42	1.6232	1.6243	1.6253	1.6263	1.6274	1.6284	1.6294	1.6304	1.6314	1.6325
43	1.6335	1.6345	1.6355	1.6365	1.6375	1.6385	1.6395	1.6405	1.6415	1.6425
44	1.6435	1.6444	1.6454	1.6464	1.6474	1.6484	1.6493	1.6503	1.6513	1.6522
45	1.6532	1.6542	1.6551	1.6561	1.6571	1.6580	1.6590	1.6599	1.6609	1.6618
46	1.6628	1.6637	1.6646	1.6656	1.6665	1.6675	1.6684	1.6693	1.6702	1.6712
47	1.6721	1.6730	1.6739	1.6749	1.6758	1.6767	1.6776	1.6785	1.6794	1.6803
48	1.6812	1.6821	1.6830	1.6839	1.6848	1.6857	1.6866	1.6875	1.6884	1.6893
49	1.6902	1.6911	1.6920	1.6928	1.6937	1.6946	1.6955	1.6964	1.6972	1.6981
50	1.6990	1.6998	1.7007	1.7016	1.7024	1.7033	1.7042	1.7050	1.7059	1.7067
51	1.7076	1.7084	1.7093	1.7101	1.7110	1.7118	1.7126	1.7135	1.7143	1.7152
52	1.7160	1.7168	1.7177	1.7185	1.7193	1.7202	1.7210	1.7218	1.7226	1.7235
53	1.7243	1.7251	1.7259	1.7267	1.7275	1.7284	1.7292	1.7300	1.7308	1.7316
54	1.7324	1.7332	1.7340	1.7348	1.7356	1.7364	1.7372	1.7380	1.7388	1.7396
55	1.7404	1.7412	1.7419	1.7427	1.7435	1.7443	1.7451	1.7459	1.7466	1.7474
56	1.7482	1.7490	1.7497	1.7505	1.7513	1.7520	1.7528	1.7536	1.7543	1.7551
57	1.7559	1.7566	1.7574	1.7582	1.7589	1.7597	1.7604	1.7612	1.7619	1.7627
58	1.7634	1.7642	1.7649	1.7657	1.7664	1.7672	1.7679	1.7686	1.7694	1.7701
59	1.7709	1.7716	1.7723	1.7731	1.7738	1.7745	1.7752	1.7760	1.7767	1.7774
60	1.7782	1.7789	1.7796	1.7803	1.7810	1.7818	1.7825	1.7832	1.7839	1.7846
61	1.7853	1.7860	1.7868	1.7875	1.7882	1.7889	1.7896	1.7903	1.7910	1.7917
62	1.7924	1.7931	1.7938	1.7945	1.7952	1.7959	1.7966	1.7973	1.7980	1.7987
63	1.7993	1.8000	1.8007	1.8014	1.8021	1.8028	1.8035	1.8041	1.8048	1.8055
64	1.8062	1.8069	1.8075	1.8082	1.8089	1.8096	1.8102	1.8109	1.8116	1.8122
65	1.8129	1.8136	1.8142	1.8149	1.8156	1.8162	1.8169	1.8176	1.8182	1.8189
66	1.8195	1.8202	1.8209	1.8215	1.8222	1.8228	1.8235	1.8241	1.8248	1.8254
67	1.8261	1.8267	1.8274	1.8280	1.8287	1.8293	1.8299	1.8306	1.8312	1.8319
68	1.8325	1.8331	1.8338	1.8344	1.8351	1.8357	1.8363	1.8370	1.8376	1.8382
69	1.8388	1.8395	1.8401	1.8407	1.8414	1.8420	1.8426	1.8432	1.8439	1.8445
70	1.8451	1.8457	1.8463	1.8470	1.8476	1.8482	1.8488	1.8494	1.8500	1.8506
71	1.8513	1.8519	1.8525	1.8531	1.8537	1.8543	1.8549	1.8555	1.8561	1.8567
72	1.8573	1.8579	1.8585	1.8591	1.8597	1.8603	1.8609	1.8615	1.8621	1.8627
73	1.8633	1.8639	1.8645	1.8651	1.8657	1.8663	1.8669	1.8675	1.8681	1.8686
74	1.8692	1.8698	1.8704	1.8710	1.8716	1.8722	1.8727	1.8733	1.8739	1.8745
75	1.8751	1.8756	1.8762	1.8768	1.8774	1.8779	1.8785	1.8791	1.8797	1.8802

TABLE I Common Logarithms (*concluded*)

	0.0	0.1	0.2	0.3	0.4	0.5	0.6	0.7	0.8	0.9
76	1.8808	1.8814	1.8820	1.8825	1.8831	1.8837	1.8842	1.8848	1.8854	1.8859
77	1.8865	1.8871	1.8876	1.8882	1.8887	1.8893	1.8899	1.8904	1.8910	1.8915
78	1.8921	1.8927	1.8932	1.8938	1.8943	1.8949	1.8954	1.8960	1.8965	1.8971
79	1.8976	1.8982	1.8987	1.8993	1.8998	1.9004	1.9009	1.9015	1.9020	1.9025
80	1.9031	1.9036	1.9042	1.9047	1.9053	1.9058	1.9063	1.9069	1.9074	1.9079
81	1.9085	1.9090	1.9096	1.9101	1.9106	1.9112	1.9117	1.9122	1.9128	1.9133
82	1.9138	1.9143	1.9149	1.9154	1.9159	1.9165	1.9170	1.9175	1.9180	1.9186
83	1.9191	1.9196	1.9201	1.9206	1.9212	1.9217	1.9222	1.9227	1.9232	1.9238
84	1.9243	1.9248	1.9253	1.9258	1.9263	1.9269	1.9274	1.9279	1.9284	1.9289
85	1.9294	1.9299	1.9304	1.9309	1.9315	1.9320	1.9325	1.9330	1.9335	1.9340
86	1.9345	1.9350	1.9355	1.9360	1.9365	1.9370	1.9375	1.9380	1.9385	1.9390
87	1.9395	1.9400	1.9405	1.9410	1.9415	1.9420	1.9425	1.9430	1.9435	1.9440
88	1.9445	1.9450	1.9455	1.9460	1.9465	1.9469	1.9474	1.9479	1.9484	1.9489
89	1.9494	1.9499	1.9504	1.9509	1.9513	1.9518	1.9523	1.9528	1.9533	1.9538
90	1.9542	1.9547	1.9552	1.9557	1.9562	1.9566	1.9571	1.9576	1.9581	1.9586
91	1.9590	1.9595	1.9600	1.9605	1.9609	1.9614	1.9619	1.9624	1.9628	1.9633
92	1.9638	1.9643	1.9647	1.9652	1.9657	1.9661	1.9666	1.9671	1.9675	1.9680
93	1.9685	1.9689	1.9694	1.9699	1.9703	1.9708	1.9713	1.9717	1.9722	1.9727
94	1.9731	1.9736	1.9741	1.9745	1.9750	1.9754	1.9759	1.9763	1.9768	1.9773
95	1.9777	1.9782	1.9786	1.9791	1.9795	1.9800	1.9805	1.9809	1.9814	1.9818
96	1.9823	1.9827	1.9832	1.9836	1.9841	1.9845	1.9850	1.9854	1.9859	1.9863
97	1.9868	1.9872	1.9877	1.9881	1.9886	1.9890	1.9894	1.9899	1.9903	1.9908
98	1.9912	1.9917	1.9921	1.9926	1.9930	1.9934	1.9939	1.9943	1.9948	1.9952
99	1.9956	1.9961	1.9965	1.9969	1.9974	1.9978	1.9983	1.9987	1.9991	1.9996

TABLE J   The Greek Alphabet

A	α	alpha	N	ν	nu
B	β	beta	Ξ	ξ	xi
Γ	γ	gamma	O	o	omicron
Δ	δ	delta	Π	π	pi
E	ε	epsilon	P	ρ	rho
Z	ζ	zeta	Σ	σ	sigma
H	η	eta	T	τ	tau
Θ	θ	theta	Υ	υ	upsilon
I	ι	iota	Φ	ϕ	phi
K	κ	kappa	X	χ	chi
Λ	λ	lambda	Ψ	ψ	psi
M	μ	mu	Ω	ω	omega

TABLE K[1] Durbin-Watson Statistic (d). Significance Points of d_L and d_U (1 percent)

n	$k = 1$		$k = 2$		$k = 3$		$k = 4$		$k = 5$	
	d_L	d_U	d_L	d_U	d_L	d_U	d_L	d_U	d_L	d_U
15	0.81	1.07	0.70	1.25	0.59	1.46	0.49	1.70	0.39	1.96
16	0.84	1.09	0.74	1.25	0.63	1.44	0.53	1.66	0.44	1.90
17	0.87	1.10	0.77	1.25	0.67	1.43	0.57	1.63	0.48	1.85
18	0.90	1.12	0.80	1.26	0.71	1.42	0.61	1.60	0.52	1.80
19	0.93	1.13	0.83	1.26	0.74	1.41	0.65	1.58	0.56	1.77
20	0.95	1.15	0.86	1.27	0.77	1.41	0.68	1.57	0.60	1.74
21	0.97	1.16	0.89	1.27	0.80	1.41	0.72	1.55	0.63	1.71
22	1.00	1.17	0.91	1.28	0.83	1.40	0.75	1.54	0.66	1.69
23	1.02	1.19	0.94	1.29	0.86	1.40	0.77	1.53	0.70	1.67
24	1.04	1.20	0.96	1.30	0.88	1.41	0.80	1.53	0.72	1.66
25	1.05	1.21	0.98	1.30	0.90	1.41	0.83	1.52	0.75	1.65
26	1.07	1.22	1.00	1.31	0.93	1.41	0.85	1.52	0.78	1.64
27	1.09	1.23	1.02	1.32	0.95	1.41	0.88	1.51	0.81	1.63
28	1.10	1.24	1.04	1.32	0.97	1.41	0.90	1.51	0.83	1.62
29	1.12	1.25	1.05	1.33	0.99	1.42	0.92	1.51	0.85	1.61
30	1.13	1.26	1.07	1.34	1.01	1.42	0.94	1.51	0.88	1.61
31	1.15	1.27	1.08	1.34	1.02	1.42	0.96	1.51	0.90	1.60
32	1.16	1.28	1.10	1.35	1.04	1.43	0.98	1.51	0.92	1.60
33	1.17	1.29	1.11	1.36	1.05	1.43	1.00	1.51	0.94	1.59
34	1.18	1.30	1.13	1.36	1.07	1.43	1.01	1.51	0.95	1.59
35	1.19	1.31	1.14	1.37	1.08	1.44	1.03	1.51	0.97	1.59
36	1.21	1.32	1.15	1.38	1.10	1.44	1.04	1.51	0.99	1.59
37	1.22	1.32	1.16	1.38	1.11	1.45	1.06	1.51	1.00	1.59
38	1.23	1.33	1.18	1.39	1.12	1.45	1.07	1.52	1.02	1.58
39	1.24	1.34	1.19	1.39	1.14	1.45	1.09	1.52	1.03	1.58
40	1.25	1.34	1.20	1.40	1.15	1.46	1.10	1.52	1.05	1.58
45	1.29	1.38	1.24	1.42	1.20	1.48	1.16	1.53	1.11	1.58
50	1.32	1.40	1.28	1.45	1.24	1.49	1.20	1.54	1.16	1.59
55	1.36	1.43	1.32	1.47	1.28	1.51	1.25	1.55	1.21	1.59
60	1.38	1.45	1.35	1.48	1.32	1.52	1.28	1.56	1.25	1.60
65	1.41	1.47	1.38	1.50	1.35	1.53	1.31	1.57	1.28	1.61
70	1.43	1.49	1.40	1.52	1.37	1.55	1.34	1.58	1.31	1.61
75	1.45	1.50	1.42	1.53	1.39	1.56	1.37	1.59	1.34	1.62
80	1.47	1.52	1.44	1.54	1.42	1.57	1.39	1.60	1.36	1.62
85	1.48	1.53	1.46	1.55	1.43	1.58	1.41	1.60	1.39	1.63
90	1.50	1.54	1.47	1.56	1.45	1.59	1.43	1.61	1.41	1.64
95	1.51	1.55	1.49	1.57	1.47	1.60	1.45	1.62	1.42	1.64
100	1.52	1.56	1.50	1.58	1.48	1.60	1.46	1.63	1.44	1.65

n = number of observations.
k = number of explanatory variables.
[1]This table is reproduced from *Biometrika*, vol. 41, 1951, p. 175, with the permission of the trustees.

TABLE K[1]   Durbin-Watson Statistic (d). Significance Points of d_L and d_U (5 percent)

n	$k = 1$		$k = 2$		$k = 3$		$k = 4$		$k = 5$	
	d_L	d_U	d_L	d_U	d_L	d_U	d_L	d_U	d_L	d_U
15	1.08	1.36	0.95	1.54	0.82	1.75	0.69	1.97	0.56	2.21
16	1.10	1.37	0.98	1.54	0.86	1.73	0.74	1.93	0.62	2.15
17	1.13	1.38	1.02	1.54	0.90	1.71	0.78	1.90	0.67	2.10
18	1.16	1.39	1.05	1.53	0.93	1.69	0.82	1.87	0.71	2.06
19	1.18	1.40	1.08	1.53	0.97	1.68	0.86	1.85	0.75	2.02
20	1.20	1.41	1.10	1.54	1.00	1.68	0.90	1.83	0.79	1.99
21	1.22	1.42	1.13	1.54	1.03	1.67	0.93	1.81	0.83	1.96
22	1.24	1.43	1.15	1.54	1.05	1.66	0.96	1.80	0.86	1.94
23	1.26	1.44	1.17	1.54	1.08	1.66	0.99	1.79	0.90	1.92
24	1.27	1.45	1.19	1.55	1.10	1.66	1.01	1.78	0.93	1.90
25	1.29	1.45	1.21	1.55	1.12	1.66	1.04	1.77	0.95	1.89
26	1.30	1.46	1.22	1.55	1.14	1.65	1.06	1.76	0.98	1.88
27	1.32	1.47	1.24	1.56	1.16	1.65	1.08	1.76	1.01	1.86
28	1.33	1.48	1.26	1.56	1.18	1.65	1.10	1.75	1.03	1.85
29	1.34	1.48	1.27	1.56	1.20	1.65	1.12	1.74	1.05	1.84
30	1.35	1.49	1.28	1.57	1.21	1.65	1.14	1.74	1.07	1.83
31	1.36	1.50	1.30	1.57	1.23	1.65	1.16	1.74	1.09	1.83
32	1.37	1.50	1.31	1.57	1.24	1.65	1.18	1.73	1.11	1.82
33	1.38	1.51	1.32	1.58	1.26	1.65	1.19	1.73	1.13	1.81
34	1.39	1.51	1.33	1.58	1.27	1.65	1.21	1.73	1.15	1.81
35	1.40	1.52	1.34	1.58	1.28	1.65	1.22	1.73	1.16	1.80
36	1.41	1.52	1.35	1.59	1.29	1.65	1.24	1.73	1.18	1.80
37	1.42	1.53	1.36	1.59	1.31	1.66	1.25	1.72	1.19	1.80
38	1.43	1.54	1.37	1.59	1.32	1.66	1.26	1.72	1.21	1.79
39	1.43	1.54	1.38	1.60	1.33	1.66	1.27	1.72	1.22	1.79
40	1.44	1.54	1.39	1.60	1.34	1.66	1.29	1.72	1.23	1.79
45	1.48	1.57	1.43	1.62	1.38	1.67	1.34	1.72	1.29	1.78
50	1.50	1.59	1.46	1.63	1.42	1.67	1.38	1.72	1.34	1.77
55	1.53	1.60	1.49	1.64	1.45	1.68	1.41	1.72	1.38	1.77
60	1.55	1.62	1.51	1.65	1.48	1.69	1.44	1.73	1.41	1.77
65	1.57	1.63	1.54	1.66	1.50	1.70	1.47	1.73	1.44	1.77
70	1.58	1.64	1.55	1.67	1.52	1.70	1.49	1.74	1.46	1.77
75	1.60	1.65	1.57	1.68	1.54	1.71	1.51	1.74	1.49	1.77
80	1.61	1.66	1.59	1.69	1.56	1.72	1.53	1.74	1.51	1.77
85	1.62	1.67	1.60	1.70	1.57	1.72	1.55	1.75	1.52	1.77
90	1.63	1.68	1.61	1.70	1.59	1.73	1.57	1.75	1.54	1.78
95	1.64	1.69	1.62	1.71	1.60	1.73	1.58	1.75	1.56	1.78
100	1.65	1.69	1.63	1.72	1.61	1.74	1.59	1.76	1.57	1.78

n = number of observations.
k = number of explanatory variables.
[1]This table is reproduced from *Biometrika,* vol. 41, 1951, p. 173, with the permission of the trustees.

TABLE L   Critical Values of the Studentized Range Distribution for $\alpha = 0.05$

$n-c$												c								
	2	3	4	5	6	7	8	9	10	11	12	13	14	15	16	17	18	19	20
1	18.0	27.0	32.8	37.1	40.4	43.1	45.4	47.4	49.1	50.6	52.0	53.2	54.3	55.4	56.3	57.2	58.0	58.8	59.6
2	6.08	8.33	9.80	10.9	11.7	12.4	13.0	13.5	14.0	14.4	14.7	15.1	15.4	15.7	15.9	16.1	16.4	16.6	16.8
3	4.50	5.91	6.82	7.50	8.04	8.48	8.85	9.18	9.46	9.72	9.95	10.2	10.3	10.5	10.7	10.8	11.0	11.1	11.2
4	3.93	5.04	5.76	6.29	6.71	7.05	7.35	7.60	7.83	8.03	8.21	8.37	8.52	8.66	8.79	8.91	9.03	9.13	9.23
5	3.64	4.60	5.22	5.67	6.03	6.33	6.58	6.80	6.99	7.17	7.32	7.47	7.60	7.72	7.83	7.93	8.03	8.12	8.21
6	3.46	4.34	4.90	5.30	5.63	5.90	6.12	6.32	6.49	6.65	6.79	6.92	7.03	7.14	7.24	7.34	7.43	7.51	7.59
7	3.34	4.16	4.68	5.06	5.36	5.61	5.82	6.00	6.16	6.30	6.43	6.55	6.66	6.76	6.85	6.94	7.02	7.10	7.17
8	3.26	4.04	4.53	4.89	5.17	5.40	5.60	5.77	5.92	6.05	6.18	6.29	6.39	6.48	6.57	6.65	6.73	6.80	6.87
9	3.20	3.95	4.41	4.76	5.02	5.24	5.43	5.59	5.74	5.87	5.98	6.09	6.19	6.28	6.36	6.44	6.51	6.58	6.64
10	3.15	3.88	4.33	4.65	4.91	5.12	5.30	5.46	5.60	5.72	5.83	5.93	6.03	6.11	6.19	6.27	6.34	6.40	6.47
11	3.11	3.82	4.26	4.57	4.82	5.03	5.20	5.35	5.49	5.61	5.71	5.81	5.90	5.98	6.06	6.13	6.20	6.27	6.33
12	3.08	3.77	4.20	4.51	4.75	4.95	5.12	5.27	5.39	5.51	5.61	5.71	5.80	5.88	5.95	6.02	6.09	6.15	6.21
13	3.06	3.73	4.15	4.45	4.69	4.88	5.05	5.19	5.32	5.43	5.53	5.63	5.71	5.79	5.86	5.93	5.99	6.05	6.11
14	3.03	3.70	4.11	4.41	4.64	4.83	4.99	5.13	5.25	5.36	5.46	5.55	5.64	5.71	5.79	5.85	5.91	5.97	6.03
15	3.01	3.67	4.08	4.37	4.59	4.78	4.94	5.08	5.20	5.31	5.40	5.49	5.57	5.65	5.72	5.78	5.85	5.90	5.96
16	3.00	3.65	4.05	4.33	4.56	4.74	4.90	5.03	5.15	5.26	5.35	5.44	5.52	5.59	5.66	5.73	5.79	5.84	5.90
17	2.98	3.63	4.02	4.30	4.52	4.70	4.86	4.99	5.11	5.21	5.31	5.39	5.47	5.54	5.61	5.67	5.73	5.79	5.84
18	2.97	3.61	4.00	4.28	4.49	4.67	4.82	4.96	5.07	5.17	5.27	5.35	5.43	5.50	5.57	5.63	5.69	5.74	5.79
19	2.96	3.59	3.98	4.25	4.47	4.65	4.79	4.92	5.04	5.14	5.23	5.31	5.39	5.46	5.53	5.59	5.65	5.70	5.75
20	2.95	3.58	3.96	4.23	4.45	4.62	4.77	4.90	5.01	5.11	5.20	5.28	5.36	5.43	5.49	5.55	5.61	5.66	5.71
24	2.92	3.53	3.90	4.17	4.37	4.54	4.68	4.81	4.92	5.01	5.10	5.18	5.25	5.32	5.38	5.44	5.49	5.55	5.59
30	2.89	3.49	3.85	4.10	4.30	4.46	4.60	4.72	4.82	4.92	5.00	5.08	5.15	5.21	5.27	5.33	5.38	5.43	5.47
40	2.86	3.44	3.79	4.04	4.23	4.39	4.52	4.63	4.73	4.82	4.90	4.98	5.04	5.11	5.16	5.22	5.27	5.31	5.36
60	2.83	3.40	3.74	3.98	4.16	4.31	4.44	4.55	4.65	4.73	4.81	4.88	4.94	5.00	5.06	5.11	5.15	5.20	5.24
120	2.80	3.36	3.68	3.92	4.10	4.24	4.36	4.47	4.56	4.64	4.71	4.78	4.84	4.90	4.95	5.00	5.04	5.09	5.13
α	2.77	3.31	3.63	3.86	4.03	4.17	4.29	4.39	4.47	4.55	4.62	4.68	4.74	4.80	4.85	4.89	4.93	4.97	5.01

Reprinted by permission of the *Biometrika* trustees from E. S. Pearson and H. O. Hartley, eds., *Biometrika Tables for Statisticians*, vol. 1, 3rd ed. (Cambridge University Press, 1966).

TABLE L. Critical Values of the Studentized Range Distribution for $\alpha = 0.01$ (concluded)

$n-c$										c									
	2	3	4	5	6	7	8	9	10	11	12	13	14	15	16	17	18	19	20
1	90.0	135	164	186	202	216	227	237	246	253	260	266	272	277	282	286	290	294	298
2	14.0	19.0	22.3	24.7	26.6	28.2	29.5	30.7	31.7	32.6	33.4	34.1	34.8	35.4	36.0	36.5	37.0	37.5	37.9
3	8.26	10.6	12.2	13.3	14.2	15.0	15.6	16.2	16.7	17.1	17.5	17.9	18.2	18.5	18.8	19.1	19.3	19.5	19.8
4	6.51	8.12	9.17	9.96	10.6	11.1	11.5	11.9	12.3	12.6	12.8	13.1	13.3	13.5	13.7	13.9	14.1	14.2	14.4
5	5.70	6.97	7.80	8.42	8.91	9.32	9.67	9.97	10.2	10.5	10.7	10.9	11.1	11.2	11.4	11.6	11.7	11.8	11.9
6	5.24	6.33	7.03	7.56	7.97	8.32	8.61	8.87	9.10	9.30	9.49	9.65	9.81	9.95	10.1	10.2	10.3	10.4	10.5
7	4.95	5.92	6.54	7.01	7.37	7.68	7.94	8.17	8.37	8.55	8.71	8.86	9.00	9.12	9.24	9.35	9.46	9.55	9.65
8	4.74	5.63	6.20	6.63	6.96	7.24	7.47	7.68	7.87	8.03	8.18	8.31	8.44	8.55	8.66	8.76	8.85	8.94	9.03
9	4.60	5.43	5.96	6.35	6.66	6.91	7.13	7.32	7.49	7.65	7.78	7.91	8.03	8.13	8.23	8.32	8.41	8.49	8.57
10	4.48	5.27	5.77	6.14	6.43	6.67	6.87	7.05	7.21	7.36	7.48	7.60	7.71	7.81	7.91	7.99	8.07	8.15	8.22
11	4.39	5.14	5.62	5.97	6.25	6.48	6.67	6.84	6.99	7.13	7.25	7.36	7.46	7.56	7.65	7.73	7.81	7.88	7.95
12	4.32	5.04	5.50	5.84	6.10	6.32	6.51	6.67	6.81	6.94	7.06	7.17	7.26	7.36	7.44	7.52	7.59	7.66	7.73
13	4.26	4.96	5.40	5.73	5.98	6.19	6.37	6.53	6.67	6.79	6.90	7.01	7.10	7.19	7.27	7.34	7.42	7.48	7.55
14	4.21	4.89	5.32	5.63	5.88	6.08	6.26	6.41	6.54	6.66	6.77	6.87	6.96	7.05	7.12	7.20	7.27	7.33	7.39
15	4.17	4.83	5.25	5.56	5.80	5.99	6.16	6.31	6.44	6.55	6.66	6.76	6.84	6.93	7.00	7.07	7.14	7.20	7.26
16	4.13	4.78	5.19	5.49	5.72	5.92	6.08	6.22	6.35	6.46	6.56	6.66	6.74	6.82	6.90	6.97	7.03	7.09	7.15
17	4.10	4.74	5.14	5.43	5.66	5.85	6.01	6.15	6.27	6.38	6.48	6.57	6.66	6.73	6.80	6.87	6.94	7.00	7.05
18	4.07	4.70	5.09	5.38	5.60	5.79	5.94	6.08	6.20	6.31	6.41	6.50	6.58	6.65	6.72	6.79	6.85	6.91	6.96
19	4.05	4.67	5.05	5.33	5.55	5.73	5.89	6.02	6.14	6.25	6.34	6.43	6.51	6.58	6.65	6.72	6.78	6.84	6.89
20	4.02	4.64	5.02	5.29	5.51	5.69	5.84	5.97	6.09	6.19	6.29	6.37	6.45	6.52	6.59	6.65	6.71	6.76	6.82
24	3.96	4.54	4.91	5.17	5.37	5.54	5.69	5.81	5.92	6.02	6.11	6.19	6.26	6.33	6.39	6.45	6.51	6.56	6.61
30	3.89	4.45	4.80	5.05	5.24	5.40	5.54	5.65	5.76	5.85	5.93	6.01	6.08	6.14	6.20	6.26	6.31	6.36	6.41
40	3.82	4.37	4.70	4.93	5.11	5.27	5.39	5.50	5.60	5.69	5.77	5.84	5.90	5.96	6.02	6.07	6.12	6.17	6.21
60	3.76	4.28	4.60	4.82	4.99	5.13	5.25	5.36	5.45	5.53	5.60	5.67	5.73	5.79	5.84	5.89	5.93	5.98	6.02
120	3.70	4.20	4.50	4.71	4.87	5.01	5.12	5.21	5.30	5.38	5.44	5.51	5.56	5.61	5.66	5.71	5.75	5.79	5.83
α	3.64	4.12	4.40	4.60	4.76	4.88	4.99	5.08	5.16	5.23	5.29	5.35	5.40	5.45	5.49	5.54	5.57	5.61	5.65

TABLE M   Critical Values of *r* in the Runs Test

Table M1 and Table M2 contain various critical values of *r* for various values of n_1 and n_2. For the one-sample runs test, any value of *r* that is equal to or smaller than that shown in Table M1 or equal to or larger than that shown in Table M2 is significant at the 0.05 level.

Table M1

n_1 \ n_2	2	3	4	5	6	7	8	9	10	11	12	13	14	15	16	17	18	19	20
2											2	2	2	2	2	2	2	2	2
3			2	2	2	2	2	2	2	2	2	2	2	3	3	3	3	3	3
4			2	2	2	3	3	3	3	3	3	3	3	3	4	4	4	4	4
5		2	2	3	3	3	3	3	4	4	4	4	4	4	4	4	5	5	5
6		2	2	3	3	3	3	4	4	4	4	5	5	5	5	5	5	6	6
7		2	2	3	3	3	4	4	5	5	5	5	5	6	6	6	6	6	6
8		2	3	3	3	4	4	5	5	5	6	6	6	6	6	7	7	7	7
9		2	3	3	4	4	5	5	5	6	6	6	7	7	7	7	8	8	8
10		2	3	3	4	5	5	5	6	6	7	7	7	7	8	8	8	8	9
11		2	3	4	4	5	5	6	6	7	7	7	8	8	8	9	9	9	9
12	2	2	3	4	4	5	6	6	7	7	7	8	8	8	9	9	9	10	10
13	2	2	3	4	5	5	6	6	7	7	8	8	9	9	9	10	10	10	10
14	2	2	3	4	5	5	6	7	7	8	8	9	9	9	10	10	10	11	11
15	2	3	3	4	5	6	6	7	7	8	8	9	9	10	10	11	11	11	12
16	2	3	4	4	5	6	6	7	8	8	9	9	10	10	11	11	11	12	12
17	2	3	4	4	5	6	7	7	8	9	9	10	10	11	11	11	12	12	13
18	2	3	4	5	5	6	7	8	8	9	9	10	10	11	11	12	12	13	13
19	2	3	4	5	6	6	7	8	8	9	10	10	11	11	12	12	13	13	13
20	2	3	4	5	6	6	7	8	9	9	10	10	11	12	12	13	13	13	14

Table M2

n_1 \ n_2	2	3	4	5	6	7	8	9	10	11	12	13	14	15	16	17	18	19	20
2																			
3																			
4				9	9														
5			9	10	10	11	11												
6			9	10	11	12	12	13	13	13	13								
7				11	12	13	13	14	14	14	14	15	15	15					
8				11	12	13	14	14	15	15	16	16	16	16	17	17	17	17	17
9					13	14	14	15	16	16	16	17	17	18	18	18	18	18	18
10					13	14	15	16	16	17	17	18	18	18	19	19	19	20	20
11					13	14	15	16	17	17	18	19	19	19	20	20	20	21	21
12					13	14	16	16	17	18	19	19	20	20	21	21	21	22	22
13						15	16	17	18	19	19	20	20	21	21	22	22	23	23
14						15	16	17	18	19	20	20	21	22	22	23	23	23	24
15						15	16	18	18	19	20	21	22	22	23	23	24	24	25
16							17	18	19	20	21	21	22	23	23	24	25	25	25
17							17	18	19	20	21	22	23	23	24	25	25	26	26
18							17	18	19	20	21	22	23	24	25	25	26	26	27
19							17	18	20	21	22	23	23	24	25	26	26	27	27
20							17	18	20	21	22	23	24	25	25	26	27	27	28

Adapted from Frieda S. Swed and C. Eisenhart, "Tables for Testing Randomness of Grouping in a Sequence of Alternatives," *Annals of Mathematical Statistics* 14, 1943, pp. 66–87. Used by permission.

TABLE N Spearman's Rank Correlation, Combined Areas in Both Tails

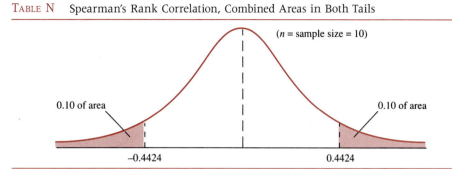

Example: For a two-tailed test of significance at the 0.20 level, with $n = 10$, the appropriate value for r_s can be found by looking under the 0.20 column and proceeding down to the 10; there we find the appropriate r_s value to be 0.4424.

n	0.20	0.10	0.05	0.02	0.01	0.002
4	0.8000	0.8000				
5	0.7000	0.8000	0.9000	0.9000		
6	0.6000	0.7714	0.8286	0.8857	0.9429	
7	0.5357	0.6786	0.7450	0.8571	0.8929	0.9643
8	0.5000	0.6190	0.7143	0.8095	0.8571	0.9286
9	0.4667	0.5833	0.6833	0.7667	0.8167	0.9000
10	0.4424	0.5515	0.6364	0.7333	0.7818	0.8667
11	0.4182	0.5273	0.6091	0.7000	0.7455	0.8364
12	0.3986	0.4965	0.5804	0.6713	0.7273	0.8182
13	0.3791	0.4780	0.5549	0.6429	0.6978	0.7912
14	0.3626	0.4593	0.5341	0.6220	0.6747	0.7670
15	0.3500	0.4429	0.5179	0.6000	0.6536	0.7464
16	0.3382	0.4265	0.5000	0.5824	0.6324	0.7265
17	0.3260	0.4118	0.4853	0.5637	0.6152	0.7083
18	0.3148	0.3994	0.4716	0.5480	0.5975	0.6904
19	0.3070	0.3895	0.4579	0.5333	0.5825	0.6737
20	0.2977	0.3789	0.4451	0.5203	0.5684	0.6586
21	0.2909	0.3688	0.4351	0.5078	0.5545	0.6455
22	0.2829	0.3597	0.4241	0.4963	0.5426	0.6318
23	0.2767	0.3518	0.4150	0.4852	0.5306	0.6186
24	0.2704	0.3435	0.4061	0.4748	0.5200	0.6070
25	0.2646	0.3362	0.3977	0.4654	0.5100	0.5962
26	0.2588	0.3299	0.3894	0.4564	0.5002	0.5856
27	0.2540	0.3236	0.3822	0.4481	0.4915	0.5757
28	0.2490	0.3175	0.3749	0.4401	0.4828	0.5660
29	0.2443	0.3113	0.3685	0.4320	0.4744	0.5567
30	0.2400	0.3059	0.3620	0.4251	0.4665	0.5479

Adapted from Glasser and Winter, *Biometrika*, 1961, with the permission of the *Biometrika* trustees.

TABLE O   Critical Factors for Control Charts

n	**Chart for averages** Factor for control limit A_2	**Chart for ranges** Factor for central line d_2	**Chart for ranges** Factors for control limits D_3	D_4	d_3
2	1.880	1.128	0	3.267	0.8525
3	1.023	1.693	0	2.575	0.8884
4	0.729	2.059	0	2.282	0.8798
5	0.577	2.326	0	2.115	0.8641
6	0.483	2.534	0	2.004	0.8480
7	0.419	2.704	0.076	1.924	0.833
8	0.373	2.847	0.136	1.864	0.820
9	0.337	2.970	0.184	1.816	0.808
10	0.308	3.078	0.223	1.777	0.797
11	0.285	3.173	0.256	1.744	0.787
12	0.266	3.258	0.284	1.716	0.778
13	0.249	3.336	0.308	1.692	0.770
14	0.235	3.407	0.329	1.671	0.762
15	0.223	3.472	0.348	1.652	0.755
16	0.212	3.532	0.364	1.636	0.749
17	0.203	3.588	0.379	1.621	0.743
18	0.194	3.640	0.392	1.608	0.738
19	0.187	3.689	0.404	1.596	0.733
20	0.180	3.735	0.414	1.586	0.729
21	0.173	3.778	0.425	1.575	0.724
22	0.167	3.819	0.434	1.566	0.720
23	0.162	3.858	0.443	1.557	0.716
24	0.157	3.895	0.452	1.548	0.712
25	0.153	3.931	0.459	1.541	0.709

Values of d_2 and d_3 are from E. S. Pearson, "The Percentage Limits for the Distribution of Range in Samples from a Normal Population," *Biometrika 24,* 1932, p. 416. Used by permission of the *Biometrika* trustees.
$A_2 = 3/(d_2 \sqrt{n})$, $D_3 = 1 - 3(d_3/d_2)$, $D_4 = 1 + 3(d_3/d_2)$.

TABLE P   Combinatorials

n	$_nC_0$	$_nC_1$	$_nC_2$	$_nC_3$	$_nC_4$	$_nC_5$	$_nC_6$	$_nC_7$	$_nC_8$	$_nC_9$	$_nC_{10}$
0	1										
1	1	1									
2	1	2	1								
3	1	3	3	1							
4	1	4	6	4	1						
5	1	5	10	10	5	1					
6	1	6	15	20	15	6	1				
7	1	7	21	35	35	21	7	1			
8	1	8	28	56	70	56	28	8	1		
9	1	9	36	84	126	126	84	36	9	1	
10	1	10	45	120	210	252	210	120	45	10	1
11	1	11	55	165	330	462	462	330	165	55	11
12	1	12	66	220	495	792	924	792	495	220	66
13	1	13	78	286	715	1287	1716	1716	1287	715	286
14	1	14	91	364	1001	2002	3003	3432	3003	2002'	1001
15	1	15	105	455	1365	3003	5005	6435	6435	5005	3003
16	1	16	120	560	1820	4368	8008	11440	12870	11440	8008
17	1	17	136	680	2380	6188	12376	19448	24310	24310	19448
18	1	18	153	816	3060	8568	18564	31824	43758	48620	43758
19	1	19	171	969	3876	11628	27132	50388	75582	92378	92378
20	1	20	190	1140	4845	15504	38760	77520	125970	167960	184756

ANSWERS TO SELECTED EVEN-NUMBERED PROBLEMS

Chapter 2

10. 7

12. $CI = 120,000$

14.

Relative Frequency Table

Classes	Relative Class Frequency
100 and under 315	$6/40 = 0.150$
315 and under 530	$5/40 = 0.125$
530 and under 745	$6/40 = 0.150$
745 and under 960	$7/40 = 0.175$
960 and under 1,175	$4/40 = 0.100$
1,175 and under 1,390	$6/40 = 0.150$
1,390 and under 1,605	$6/40 = 0.150$

Cumulative Relative Frequency Table (more than)

$40/40 = 1.000$
$34/40 = 0.850$
$29/40 = 0.725$
$23/40 = 0.575$
$16/40 = 0.400$
$12/40 = 0.300$
$6/40 = 0.150$
$0/40 = 0.000$

Cumulative Relative Frequency Table (less than)

$0/40 = 0.000$
$6/40 = 0.150$
$11/40 = 0.275$
$17/40 = 0.425$
$24/40 = 0.600$
$28/40 = 0.700$
$34/40 = 0.850$
$40/40 = 1.000$

16. The bars should reflect the intervals and the percentages shown in the answer to Problem 14.

18. *a.*

Stem	Leaf
35	0, 2, 5, 8, 9, 9, 9
36	1, 3, 7, 9, 9
37	3, 4, 9
38	2, 2, 3, 7, 9, 9
39	2, 7, 9
40	1, 1, 2, 7, 9
41	1, 1, 2, 5, 7
42	5, 5, 8
43	1, 3, 5, 7, 9
44	1, 2, 4, 5, 5, 7
45	0, 3, 8
46	0, 2, 5, 7
47	3, 3, 3, 5
48	2, 2, 9, 9
49	1, 3, 5, 7, 7, 9, 9
50	0, 2, 3, 7
51	1, 2, 3, 3, 7, 7, 9
52	0, 1, 2, 3, 5, 7, 8, 8, 9
53	7, 9
54	0, 1, 1, 2, 3, 4, 5
56	4

b. $2^c \geq 100 = 7$

$$CI = \frac{56.4 - 35}{7} = 3.1 \approx 3.0 \,(\text{produces } 8 \text{ classes})$$

Cumulative Frequency Distribution (more than)

Classes	Cumulative Frequency
35 or more	100
38 or more	85
41 or more	71
44 or more	58
47 or more	45
50 or more	30
53 or more	10
56 or more	1
59 or more	0

**Cumulative Frequency Distribution
(less than)**

Classes	Cumulative Frequency
Less than 35	0
Less than 38	15
Less than 41	29
Less than 44	42
Less than 47	55
Less than 50	70
Less than 53	90
Less than 56	99
Less than 59	100

**Cumulative Relative Frequency Distribution
(more than)**

Classes	Cumulative Relative Frequency
35 or more	$100/100 = 1.00$
38 or more	$85/100 = 0.85$
41 or more	$71/100 = 0.71$
44 or more	$58/100 = 0.58$
47 or more	$45/100 = 0.45$
50 or more	$30/100 = 0.30$
53 or more	$10/100 = 0.10$
56 or more	$1/100 = 0.01$
59 or more	$0/100 = 0.00$

c.

Relative Frequency Distribution

Classes	Relative Frequency
35 and under 38	$15/100 = 0.15$
38 and under 41	$14/100 = 0.14$
41 and under 44	$13/100 = 0.13$
44 and under 47	$13/100 = 0.13$
47 and under 50	$15/100 = 0.15$
50 and under 53	$20/100 = 0.20$
53 and under 56	$9/100 = 0.09$
56 and under 59	$1/100 = 0.01$

d. **Cumulative Relative Frequency Distribution
(less than)**

Classes	Cumulative Relative Frequency
Less than 35	$0/100 = 0.00$
Less than 38	$15/100 = 0.15$
Less than 41	$29/100 = 0.29$
Less than 44	$42/100 = 0.42$
Less than 47	$55/100 = 0.55$
Less than 50	$70/100 = 0.70$
Less than 53	$90/100 = 0.90$
Less than 56	$99/100 = 0.99$
Less than 59	$100/100 = 1.00$

20. a.

Stem	Leaf
5	1, 5, 9
6	5, 8
7	0, 2, 3
8	3, 4, 5, 5, 7, 8
9	1, 1, 3, 8, 9
10	0, 2, 3
11	0, 5, 7
12	3, 7
13	2, 4, 7
14	2, 3
15	0, 2, 3
16	0, 3, 3, 7
17	0, 3, 5

c. $2^c > 42 = 6$

$$CI = \frac{17.5 - 5.1}{6} = 2.06 \approx 2.00$$

Class	Frequency	M	Relative Frequency
5 and under 7	5	6	$5/42 = 0.119$
7 and under 9	9	8	$9/42 = 0.214$
9 and under 11	8	10	$8/42 = 0.190$
11 and under 13	5	12	$5/42 = 0.119$
13 and under 15	5	14	$5/42 = 0.119$
15 and under 17	7	16	$7/42 = 0.167$
17 and under 19	3	18	$3/42 = 0.071$
	42		1.00

More Than Cumulative Frequency Distribution

Class	Cumulative Frequency
5 or more	42
7 or more	37
9 or more	28
11 or more	20
13 or more	15
15 or more	10
17 or more	3
19 or more	0

28.

Status	Range: $0 to 4,999	$5,000 to 9,999	$10,000 to 14,999	$15,000 and up	Total
Due	10 (0.083)	15 (0.125)	11 (0.092)	5 (0.042)	41 (0.342)
Overdue	5 (0.042)	10 (0.083)	10 (0.083)	7 (0.058)	32 (0.267)
Delinquent	10 (0.083)	12 (0.10)	18 (0.15)	7 (0.058)	47 (0.392)
Totals	25 (0.208)	37 (0.308)	39 (0.325)	19 (0.158)	120 (1.00)

30. One possibility is

Stem	Leaf
5	0.00, 1.02, 7.03, 8.73, 9.99
6	0.00, 0.00, 1.11, 3.09, 5.72, 9.99, 9.99
7	0.00, 1.11, 2.14, 3.99, 7.77, 9.82, 9.99
8	0.00, 0.00, 1.00, 2.22, 3.21, 9.49, 9.89, 9.99
9	0.00, 2.29, 9.99

OR

Stem	Leaf (rounded to nearest dollar)
5	0, 1, 7, 9
6	0, 0, 0, 1, 3, 6
7	0, 0, 0, 1, 2, 4, 8
8	0, 0, 0, 0, 1, 2, 3, 9
9	0, 0, 0, 2
10	0

38. $11,258 ≈ $11,250
40. 5

42. If CI = 6.5, yields 6 classes instead of 5.

Class	Frequency
37.0 and under 43.5	9
43.5 and under 50.0	2
50.0 and under 56.5	5
56.5 and under 63.0	3
63.0 and under 69.5	8
69.5 and under 76.0	3
	30

44. **Less Than Cumulative Distribution**

Class	Cumulative Frequency
Less than 37.0	0
Less than 43.5	9
Less than 50.0	11
Less than 56.5	15
Less than 63.0	17
Less than 69.5	22
Less than 76.0	30

46.

Class	Cumulative Relative Distribution
37.0 or more	30/30 = 1.00
43.5 or more	21/30 = 0.70
50.0 or more	19/30 = 0.63
56.5 or more	14/30 = 0.47
63.0 or more	11/30 = 0.37
69.5 or more	3/30 = 0.10
76.0 or more	0/30 = 0.00

54.

Stem	Leaf
4	3, 7
5	3, 4, 5, 5, 6, 7, 7
6	1, 5, 8
7	0, 1, 2

Chapter 3

10. $\overline{X}_w = 10.18$
    median = 10
    mode = 9.5
12. mean = 1.25
    median = 1
    mode: none
14. Depends on which average is used.
    $\overline{X} = 5.47\%$; median = 5.75; mode = 4.5
16. a. 7.7%
    b. \$4036.31 billion
18. median \$19,750
20. John: 7.22%; Lars: 6.938%
22. 9.43%
24. GM = 18.6%; yes
26. a. 87.3
    b. $s = 16.42$
    c. $P_{25} = 74.5$; $P_{50} = 86.67$; $P_{75} = 100.00$
28. $s_1 = 0.348$ inches; $CV_1 = 2.9\%$
    $s_2 = 0.251$ inches; $CV_2 = 2.1\%$
    Use the second machine.
30. $\overline{X} = 6.2$; median = 5.5; mode = 5
32. a. $s^2 = 3.17$; $s = 1.78$
    b. The data tend to be dispersed around their mean
        of \$0.82 by 1.78.
34. a. 110.88 miles
    b. 109.25 miles
    c. $s^2 = 161.41$ miles, squared; $s = 12.7$ miles
36. a. 42 hours
    b. 267.43 hours, squared
    c. 16.35 hours
    d. MAD = 12.875. It does not lend itself to fur-
        ther calculations.

e. $P_{25} = 20.5$
f. Same as e.
g. IQR = 30.5

38.

	Kays	Kroc
$\overline{X}_g$	22	19.25
median	23	19.57
mode	24.5	20.00
s	8.09	8.21

40. a. $\overline{X}_g = 18.56$
        median = 20.26
        mode = 23.46
        Pam's averages exceed that of other offices.
    b. $s^2 = 55.03$
        $s = 7.42$
42. $s = 3.96$ minutes
44. a. $\overline{X}_g = \$87.5$ thousand
        median = \$92.22 thousand
        mode = \$111.82 thousand
    b. $s = \$35.53$ thousand
46. $s^2 = 410.98$ dollars, squared
    $s = \$20.27$

48.

	Production Worker	Office Workers
$\overline{X}$	\$17.17	\$17.82
s	\$ 2.32	\$ 1.52
CV	13.51%	8.53%

50. a.

	UCLA	Notre Dame
CV	12.45%	14.46%

    b. UCLA: $\mu + 3s = 353$; N.D. $\mu + 3s = 347$
        UCLA probably has the larger players.
52. $CV_1 = 12\%$
    $CV_2 = 25\%$
54. a. $\overline{X} = 7.34\%$
        $s = 1.55\%$
    b. 22.5
    c. 4.24 to 10.44; all but one
56. a. $P_{60} = 23.0$ or \$2,300
        $P_{25} = 14.29$
        $P_{50} = 20.5$
        $P_{75} = 26.25$
    b. $P_{10} = 10$
        $P_{90} = 31.67$

58. *a.* 82.8; 88; 88
    b. 66.3; 70; 73 and 75
60. $c = 6$; $CI = 0.5$
    $\overline{X}_g = 2.43$; median = 2.57; mode = 3.22
62. $P_{25} = 12$; $P_{75} = 31$; IQR is PepsiCo through Dupont
64. $s = 7.79$
66. *a.* 6,880
    b. 9,550
    c. 15 below 36 and 15 above 69
68. Only 68.8% are within the range 34 to 38. Less in narrower range of 35.5 to 36.5. CEO not supported.

CHAPTER 4

8. 5/6
10. *a.* 1/6
    b. 1/2
    c. 13/52 = 1/4
    d. 4/52 = 1/13
12. *a.* 52/312 = 1/6
    b. 1/8
    c. 4/208 = 1/52
14. Both equal 3/6
16. 4/36 = 1/9

18.

Stockholder Wealth

Method	Maxed	Not Maxed	Total
NPV	0.54	0.10	0.64
IRR	0.14	0.22	0.36
Total	0.68	0.32	1.00

20. *a.* 6/22
    b. 2/22
    c. 14/22
    d. 12/22
    e. 4/22
22. No. Compare different probabilities to see.
26. *a.* 0.31
    b. 0.24
    c. 0.50
28. *a.* 132/812
    b. 204/812
    c. 408/812
30. $P(D \ \& \ I) \neq 0$. The two sets, *D* & *I*, have an intersection.
32. 0.30
34. 0.0000014

36. *a.* 312/414
    b. 306/586
    c. No. Compare the proper probabilities to reach this conclusion.
38. 1/2
40. 0.32
42. 1/10,000
44. 96
46. *a.* 12
    b. 31
48. Houston
50. Yes. 63 > 50
52. 10,000
54. No; 10,000 < 10,001
56. 140

CHAPTER 5

2.

Managers (X)	Relative Frequency $P(X = x)$	Cumulative Frequency $P(X \leq x)$
2	0.190	0.190
3	0.231	0.421
4	0.308	0.729
5	0.269	$0.998 \approx 1.00$

4. *a.* $60 for gold; $40 for mutuals
   b. Gold: 646.35%; mutuals: 207.68%
      Mutuals are safer.
6. $\mu = \$12.10$; $\sigma = \$13.42$
8. *a.* 0.1032
   b. 0.9389
   c. 0.1642
   d. 0.5839
10. *a.* 0.0015
    b. 0.0038
    c. 0.0319
12. $\mu = 6$; $\sigma = 1.22$
14. *a.* 0.0510
    b. 0.8215
    c. 0.4044
16. *a.* 0.2669
    b. 0.8159
    c. 0.0428
    d. 0.0556
18. *a.* 0.2269
    b. 0.3491
    c. 0.6471
    d. 0.0288

20. One
22. 60.84____79.16
24. *a.* 0.2001   *e.* 0.6172
    b. 0.0000   *f.* 0.0106
    c. 0.0000   *g.* 0.8491
    d. 0.9526   *h.* 0.6170
26. 0.1167
28. 0.9298
30. 0.1551
32. 0.0065
34. 0.1167
36. 0.6703
38. 4
40. *a.* 0.0710   *d.* 0.4242
    b. 0.1410   *e.* 0.8490
    c. 0.1410
42. 0.0895
44. No; $P(X = 3)$ if $r = 3$ is only 0.061
46. *a.* 86.5 minutes
    b. 57%
48. 53%
50. 0.7769
52. *a.* $L = 5$; No, space is not sufficient.
    b. 0.0970
    c. $W = 0.5$ hours
        $L_q = 4.17$ cars
        $W_q = 0.417$ hours

Chapter 6

4. *a.* 0.3446
   b. 0.9452
   c. 0.2384
   d. 0.4514
6. $P(X < 300) = 0.1038$; not likely
8. *a.* 0.7486
   b. 0.8665
   c. 0.1940
   d. 0.8686
10. *a.* 0.2296
    b. 0.2296
12. $X = \$1,548.16 < 2,250$; yes, you get the day off
14. 0.1894
16. 2,143.75 to 3,316.25 pounds
18. 23.27, or 24 days
20. 0.58
22. 0.0000
24. 442.8 or 443 pants
26. *a.* 0.5636
    b. 0.6331
    c. 0.1967
28. 0.3897
30. 0.2483
32. $P(\text{sued}) = 0.2981 < 0.30$; yes, take the job
34. 0.4602
36. 0.4562

Chapter 7

4. *a.* 8.64
   c. 5.29
   d. 32.4
   e. 32.4
6. $\overline{\overline{X}} = 2.7$; $\sigma_{\bar{x}} = 0.156$
10. $P(X \geq 50) = 0.0122$ for K.C.
    $P(X \geq 50) = 0.0062$ for Dallas
    Use K.C.
12. *a.* 0.4443
    b. 0.1379
    c. $\sigma_{\bar{x}} < \sigma$
14. *a.* 0.5319
    b. 0.7881
    c. 0.8708
16. 0.9582
18. $\overline{X} = \$21.15$; $\sigma_{\bar{x}} = 0.52$
20. 0.9370
22. 0.4834
24. It would decrease because the standard error would go up.
26. No. $P(\overline{X} \leq 9.6)$ if $\mu = 10.2$ is only 0.0516
28. No; $P(\overline{X} \geq 4.6)$ if $\mu = 4.2$ is only 0.59%
30. $P(\overline{X} \leq 41,000)$ if $\mu = 42,550$ is only 2.5%, even less than in Problem 29.
32. *a.* 0.9251
    b. 0.3594
34. *a.* $P(\overline{X} > \mu + 4) = 0.1151$
        $P(\overline{X} < \mu - 1) = 0.3821$
36. *a.* 1.88 mph
    b. 0.37 mph
38. 0.9930
40. 0.8132
42. 0.0436
44. 0.9699
46. Yes; $P(p \leq .27)$ if $\pi = 0.85$ is 0.00%. This supplier is unreliable.
48. 0.0062; Yes
50. 0.8365

Chapter 8

6. $0.4799 \leq \mu \leq 0.560$
8. $3.71 \leq \mu \leq 4.69$
10. Not correct
12. $3.49 \leq \mu \leq 4.12$; yes
14. $1.73 \leq \mu \leq 1.85$
16. $13.3 \leq \mu \leq 14.9$; avoid supplier
18. $14.9 \leq \mu \leq 15.7$
20. *a.* Interval is wider, since standard error increases.
    b. $14.712 \leq \mu \leq 15.888$
22. 95%
24. $\$11,530 \leq \mu \leq \$14,310$
26. $\$9.91 \leq \mu \leq \$12.27$ million
28. *a.* $0.013 \leq \mu_d \leq 0.32$ hours
    b. The differences in times are normal.

30. $1.32 \leq \mu_d \leq 2.52$
32. $78.82 \leq \mu \leq 87.58$
34. $-\$10.64 \leq \mu_1 - \mu_2 \leq \$50.3$ thousand; yes
36. $-1961 \leq \mu_1 - \mu_2 \leq -437$
38. $\$5.56 \leq \mu_1 - \mu_2 \leq \$11.04$
40. $6.95 \leq \mu_1 - \mu_2 \leq 39.05$
42. $-\$388.07 \leq \mu_1 - \mu_2 \leq -\$61.93$
44. $106.6 \leq \mu_1 - \mu_2 \leq 176.16$
46. $-1.48 \leq \mu_1 - \mu_2 \leq 1.54$ inches
48. $-102.04 \leq \mu_1 - \mu_2 \leq 78.44$
50. $14.87 \leq \mu_1 - \mu_2 \leq 20.73$
52. $-5.75 \leq \mu_u - \mu_2 \leq -2.23$; yes
54. $-4.52 \leq \mu_m - \mu_n \leq 34.7$; No
56. $0.787 \leq \pi \leq 0.853$
58. $0.77 \leq \pi \leq 0.95$
60. $0.53 \leq \pi \leq 0.77$
62. $0.12 \leq \pi \leq 0.24$; yes
64. $0.11 \leq \pi_1 - \pi_2 \leq 0.23$
66. $0.13 \leq \pi_f - \pi_m \leq 0.23$
68. $0.01 \leq \pi_s - \pi_e \leq 0.09$
70. $0.37 \leq \pi_1 - \pi_2 \leq 0.45$
72. 426
74. 2
76. 16,641
78. 2,089

Chapter 9

8. $\bar{X}_c = 15.7$ and 16.3; DNR
10. $\bar{X}_c = 49.09$ and 50.91; reject
12. $\bar{X}_c = 17.59$ and 18.41; reject
14. $\bar{X}_c = 111,090$ and $118,910$; DNR
16. $\bar{X}_c = 12.17$ and 13.83; DNR and approve the drug
18. $\bar{X}_c = 1.85$ and 2.15; reject and impose restriction
20. $\bar{X}_c = 24.62$ and 29.38; DNR
22. $P_c = 0.23$ and 0.27; reject
24. $P_c = 0.26$ and 0.34; DNR
26. $P_c = 0.17$ and 0.23; reject null and reverse promotion process
28. $P_c = 0.15$ and 0.25; DNR
30. $\bar{X}_c = 11,750$; DNR and open the store
32. $\bar{X}_c = \$44,183$; reject null. Article is supported.
34. $\bar{X}_c = 2.49$; DNR. Senator Kennedy's claim is not supported.
36. $\bar{X}_c = 3.88$; reject null and do not buy the machine.
38. $\bar{X}_c = 812.51$; reject null. Claim is supported.
40. $P_c = 0.17$; DNR. Keep plant open.
42. $P_c = 0.69$; reject null
44. $P_c = 0.90$; DNR. At least 95% are on time.
46. $P_c = 0.565$; DNR. Money not well spent.
48. $P_c = 0.12$ and 0.38; DNR. Agreement is met.
50. *a.* $Z_{\text{test}} = 0.61$; DNR
    b. p-value $= 0.2709$
52. *a.* $\bar{X}_c = 511.74$; DNR
    b. 0.8264

Chapter 10

4. $d_c = \pm0.23$; DNR. Further consideration not warranted.
6. $d_c = \pm1.16$; reject. It appears to make a difference which chain you select.
8. $d_c = \pm0.31$; reject null. Use method 1.
10. $d_c = \pm0.035$; reject. There appears to be a difference in times.
12. $d_c \pm 3.76$; reject null
14. $d_c \pm \$4,331$; reject null
16. $d_c = 7.82$ pounds; DNR
18. $d_c \pm 1.93$; reject null. Union elves not as productive.
20. $d_c = -4.66$; DNR. CEO is not correct.
22. $d_c = 117$; DNR. Manager is incorrect.
24. $d_c = 1034$; reject null. Director is correct.
26. $d_c = \pm9.52$; DNR
28. $d_c = \pm10.55$; DNR
30. $d_c = 7.25$; reject null. Skinner is supported.
32. $d_c = \pm1.72$; DNR
34. $d_c = \pm4.53$; reject null. Fixed salaries tend to promote satisfaction.
36. $d_c = -1.28$; reject null
38. $d_c = 49.23$; reject null. Decrease in 1990 was significant.
40. $d_c = \pm5.38$; DNR
42. $d_c = 2.57$; reject null. Training increases output.
44. $d_c = \pm0.143$; DNR
46. $d_c = -0.09$; DNR
48. $d_c = -0.031$; reject null
50. $d_c = 0.05$; reject null
52. $d_c = 0.11$; DNR
54. $2.02 \leq \mu_1 - \mu_2 \leq 11.98$
56. $-4.15 \leq \mu_1 - \mu_2 \leq -1.15$

Chapter 11

4. Chi-square $= 27 < 32.671$; DNR
8. Chi-square $= 6.82 > 4.168$; DNR. Buy the lease.
10. Chi-square $= 11.88 > 7.042$; DNR
12. $24.85 \leq \sigma \leq 42.88$ thousand
14. $F = 1.22 < 4.1$; DNR
16. $F = 12.86 > 3.50$; reject null
18. Chi-square $= 10.84 > 7.79$; DNR
20. $F = 2.38 < 2.01$; reject null
22. $F = 2.51$; DNR
24. $T = 1.75$
    $LSD = 1.31$
26. $F = 5.52 > 3.55$; reject null
28. $F = 1.26 < 2.70$; DNR
30. $F = 3.83 < 3.89$; DNR
32. $F = 184.71 > 6.93$; reject null
34. $T = 224$; $LSD = 167$
36. $F = 3.94 > 3.10$; reject null
    $T = 2.35$
    $LSD = 1.75$
38. $LSD = 1.98$; $T = 2.37$

40. F for between block is $25.00 > 7.01$; reject null
F for between samples is $14.88 > 8.65$; reject null

42. F for between block is $4.09 > 3.84$; reject null
F for between samples is $20.04 > 4.46$; reject null
$LSD = 5.39$
$T = 6.59$

44. F for between blocks is $4.85 > 4.76$; reject null
F for between samples is $0.163 < 5.14$; DNR

46. F for between block is $0.88 < 7.01$; DNR
$F = 0.23 < 6.93$; DNR

CHAPTER 12

6. *a.* Cost is the dependent variable.
   c. $\hat{C} = -0.611 + 1.185$ (out)
   e. $\hat{C} = \$1,302.89$
   Cost was actually \$1,300. Difference is due to sampling error and explanatory variables other than output which are not included in your model. Improve prediction by increasing sample size and searching for additional explanatory models.

8. *a.* $\hat{R} = 1.38 + 1.125$ (out)
   b. Profits $= -\$64.01$

10. $Se = 2.09199$

12. $r^2 = 0.35268$

14. $Se = 0.19792$

16. $t = -2.0869 < -1.860$; reject null

18. *a.* Investment is the dependent variable.
    b. Invest $= 2.24 + 0.093$ (Income)
    $r^2 = 0.868$
    c. Cross-sectional

20. *a.* Dow Jones Index is dependent variable.
    b. $\hat{DJ} = 2885.21 - 120.93$ (FFR)
    $r^2 = 0.84$
    Financial theory is corroborated as evidenced by the negative coefficient for FFR.

22. Return $= 0.4902 + 3.39$ (Beta)
    $r^2 = 0.80457$
    $r = 0.89698$
    Both b_1 and r are positive. The financial theory of a direct relationship is supported.

24. *a.* $t = 6.416 > 2.228$; reject null
    b. $t = 6.416 > 2.228$; reject null

26. *a.* $\hat{GPA} = 1.055 + 0.026(50) = 2.36$
    b. $r^2 = 0.5046$

28. *a.* $\hat{CI} = 32.57 - 2.25$ (IR)
    b. Yes. Line has negative slope.
    c. Yes

30. 12.26 would since it has the larger Se.

32. *a.* Salary is the dependent variable.
    b. $\hat{S} = 4.2216 + 1.990R$
    c. $r^2 = 0.98666$
    $Se = 4.39$
    d. $101.50 \le \mu_{y|x} \le 105.98$

e. $95.99 \le Y_x \le 111.76$
f. Individual values have a greater dispersion and are therefore harder to predict.

34. *a.* $t = 31.04 > 2.160$; reject null
    b. $t = 30.99 > 2.160$; reject null

36. *a.* $\hat{Y} = 9.766 + 2.007X$
    $= 25.88$
    b. $Se = 1.687$

38. $26.957 \le Y_x \le 32.72$

40. *a.* $1.821 < \beta_1 < 2.193$
    b. $0.92 < Rho < 0.98$

42. $19.42 \le \mu_{y|x} \le 21.35$
    Since 30 is not in the interval, he should not proceed.

44. *a.* For each additional hour in OJT, efficiency increases by 1.68 points.
    b. $t = 20.28 > 1.65$. There is a relationship at the population level.

46. $r^2 = 0.461$

48. $t = 6.411 > 2.58$; reject null

52. *a.* Delivery time is the dependent variable.
    b. $\hat{Y} = 6.4366 - 2.032X$
    c. $r = -0.955$

CHAPTER 13

6.

	P	D	G
P	1.00		
D	.99748	1.00	
G	.75995	.72443	1.00

8. *a.*

	Y	X_1	X_2
Y	1.00		
X_1	.47	1.00	
X_2	.53	.63	1.00

b. $t = 3.89 > 1.714$; reject null
c. $VIF_{x_1} = VIF_{x_2} = 1.658$

12. *a.* Increase by \$7,400
    b. $H_0: \beta_1 = \beta_2 = \beta_3 = 0$
    H_a: At least one β is not zero.
    DNR if $F < F_{.05, 3, 21} = 3.07$; reject otherwise
    $F = 5.97 > 3.07$; reject null
    c. $H_0: \beta_i = 0$
    $H_a: \beta_i \neq 0$
    DNR if t between $\pm t_{.05, 21} = 1.721$; reject otherwise
    Conclusion: reject null in all cases.
    d. $\overline{R}^2 = 0.6229$

14. Nothing

16. *a.* No. r should carry a negative sign.
    b. $F = 296.60 > F_{.01, 2, 9} = 8.02$; reject null

18. $R^2 = 0.985$

20. $F = 2.99 < F_{.05, 3, 4} = 6.59$; only RY significant at 10% multicollinearity possible

22. *a.* $\hat{Y} = -39.6 + 0.144X_1 + 1.25X_2 + 0.683X_3$
    $F = 14.29 > F_{.05,3,11} = 3.59$
    b. $t_1 = 0.72 < t_{.05,11} = 2.201$; DNR
    $t_2 = 2.53 > 2.201$; reject
    $t_3 = 1.55 < 2.201$; DNR
24. $VIF_1 = 1.1$
    $VIF_2 = 2.7$
    $VIF_3 = 2.6$
26. *a.* $\hat{Y} = 88.8 + 0.289X_1 - 57.2X_2$
    $F = 24.26 > F_{.01,2,9} = 8.02$
    b. $t_1 = 1.86 < t_{.01,9} = 3.25$; DNR
    $t_2 = -1.87 > t_{.01,9} = 3.25$; DNR
    c. Yes
28. $VIF = 3.7$; No
30. It will be $114.40 higher.
32. $\hat{Y} = -110.95 + 0.19$ SQFT $+ 6.69$ Lux
    $R^2 = 94.7\%$ $F = 80.67$
34. $\hat{c} = 1.25 + 0.747$ Perm
    $\hat{c} = 0.39 + 0.674$ Peak
36. *a.* $\hat{P} = -0.48 + 3.37D + 10.7DR - 0.097SO$
    b. Go up by $3.37
    c. Go down by $53.50
    d. Go down by $0.049
38. *a.* $\hat{D} = 9.04 + 7.56E + 10.61T$
    $R^2 = 99.7\%$; $F = 725.77$
    Signs are as expected.
    b. Increase by 15.12
    c. Increase by 5.3
40. The customer with more experience

CHAPTER 14

6. $d = 2.21$
   At 5%, $d_L = 0.95$, $d_u = 1.54$; $4 - d_u = 2.46$;
   $4 - d_L = 3.05$, if use $n = 15$.
8. Two dummy variables are needed. One possible approach:
   $X_1 = 1$ if Republican, 0 otherwise, and
   $X_2 = 1$ if Democrat, 0 otherwise
10. Assuming the CPA is helpful and reduces time spent on audit, $b_2 < 0$.
12. $\hat{Y} = 95.29$ in district with office
    $Y = 78.09$ in district without office
14. *a.* Three variables are necessary for education level and two for race.
    b. $X_1 = 1$ for no high school; 0 otherwise
    $X_2 = 1$ for no undergraduate degree; 0 otherwise
    $X_3 = 1$ for no master's; 0 otherwise
    $X_4 = 1$ for degree above master's; 0 otherwise
16. $\hat{Y}$ would equal the intercept term. There would be no regression line.
18. *a.* One possibility: $X_2 = 1$ if N, 0 otherwise
    $X_3 = 1$ if S, 0 otherwise
    $X_4 = 1$ if M, 0 otherwise
    b. $\hat{Y} = 768 - 143X_1 - 263X_2 + 6.5X_3 + 91.9X_4$

c. $\hat{Y} = 505 - 143X_1$ for N
    $= 775 - 143X_1$ for S
    $= 859.9 - 143X_1$ for M
    $= 768 - 143X_1$ for W
d. $d = 1.94$
20. $nR^2 = 8.67$
    Chi-square $= 15.507 > 8.67$; DNR. Assume heteroscadasticity does not exist.

CHAPTER 15

2. *a.* DNR if $\chi^2 < \chi^2_{.01,5} = 15.086$
   b. $\chi^2 = 20.52 > 15.086$; reject null
4. $\chi^2 = 8.83 > \chi^2_{.05,7} = 14.067$; reject null
6. $\chi^2 = 5.1 < \chi^2_{.05,3} = 7.815$; DNR null. Do not adjust pattern.
8. $\chi^2 = 0.12 < \chi^2_{.05,3} = 7.815$; DNR null
10. $\chi^2 = 8.85 < \chi^2_{.05,3} = 7.815$; DNR null
12. $\chi^2 = 30.76 > \chi^2_{.01,4} = 13.277$; reject null
14. $\chi^2 = 21.24 > \chi^2_{.05,12} = 21.026$; reject null
16. $\chi^2 = 0.954 < \chi^2_{.10,4} = 7.779$
18. $P(p \le 6 | n = 9, \pi = 0.5) = 0.9103$; DNR
20. $P(m \ge 6 | n = 6, \pi = 0.5) = 0.0156 < .05$;   Reject null. CEO is correct.
22. $P(p \ge 6 | n = 9, \pi = 0.5) = 0.2540 > 0.10$;   DNR; argument supported.
24. $P(p \le 6 | n = 14, \pi = 0.5) = 0.3954 > 0.10/2 = 0.05$; DNR null
26. $Z = 1.17 < 1.65$; DNR
28. Critical values are 3 and 12; DNR null
30. $Z = 1.39$; DNR
32. $Z = -3.14$; reject null
34. $Z = 2.82$; reject null
36. $Z = -2.01$; reject null
38. $K = 1.85$; $K' = 1.86$; DNR
40. $K = 12.989$; $K' = 13.067$; reject null
42. $K = 9.66$; $K' = 9.73$; reject null
44. $K = 0.4886$; DNR

CHAPTER 16

10.	1991	July	21.12
		Aug	21.18
		Sept -	21.23
		Oct	21.30
		Nov	21.37
		Dec	21.45
	1992	Jan	21.50
		Feb	21.51
		Mar .	21.57
		Apr	21.55
		May	21.37
		June	21.16
		July	21.00
		Aug	20.85
		Sept	20.69

	Oct	20.57
	Nov	20.48
	Dec	20.45
1993	Jan	20.41
	Feb	20.31
	Mar	20.25
	Apr	20.22
	May	20.25
	June	20.27

12.

	Actual Sales	**Seasonally Adjusted Sales**
July	22.7	19.9
Aug	25.0	20.3
Sept	21.9	21.3
Oct	17.3	19.5
Nov	21.2	21.0
Dec	16.2	18.6

14. $\hat{Y} = 0.715 + 0.061t$
$\quad = 1.14$
$\quad r^2 = 0.877$

16. *a.*

	P/E	**MA**	**Centered MA**
1985	11		
1986	16	13.5	15.50
1987	19	17.5	17.00
1988	14	16.5	15.00
1989	13	13.5	13.75
1990	15	14.0	

b. $F_{1991} = 13.75$
c. $MSE_{.20} = 15.43$
$\quad MSE_{.90} = 12.89$

18. *a.* Both a strong cyclical component and a trend component appear.
b. $\hat{Y} = 3.78 + 0.3395t$
$\quad = 9.2 < 10.5$

c.

Quarter	**Seasonal Index**
I	0.9952
II	0.9385
III	1.0083
IV	1.0713

Deseasonalized Values

	1989	**1990**	**1991**
I	4.22	5.93	6.53
II	4.11	5.62	7.57
III	4.86	6.25	7.44
IV	5.41	6.35	7.47

20. $\hat{Y} = 17.85 - 0.032t$
In April, $\hat{Y} = 8.89 < 9.00$
22. $r^2 = 0.938$

24. *a.*

Month	**Index**
Jan	0.9900
Feb	1.0159
Mar	1.0252
Apr	1.0382
May	1.0490
June	1.0586
July	0.9113
Aug	0.9003
Sept	0.9876
Oct	0.9781
Nov	1.0066
Dec	1.0392

b.

1990	Jan	18.1811	1991	Jan	20.7062
	Feb	18.2109		Feb	21.1639
	Mar	18.4356		Mar	21.4594
	Apr	18.0115		Apr	21.6716
	May	17.6357		May	21.9255
	June	16.5320		June	22.2001
	July	18.6548		July	25.2388
	Aug	18.8836		Aug	24.4376
	Sept	19.1375		Sept	21.2638
	Oct	19.4246		Oct	22.4916
	Nov	19.7699		Nov	22.8497
	Dec	20.2069		Dec	23.5747

c. $\hat{Y} = 17.02 + 0.277(29) = 25.05$
26. $\hat{Y} = 10.58 + 0.489(19) = 19.87 = \$1,987$ in thefts
Since $\$1,987 > \$1,500$, purchase system.
28. *a.* Data not linear; $\log \hat{Y} = \log a + \log b(t)$ is required.
b. $\hat{Y} = \$1,409$ billion
30. $r^2 = 0.993$
32. *a.* $\hat{Y} = 124.76 + 0.332(t)$
$\quad r^2 = 0.109$
$\quad$ Very poor fit.

b.

Y	$\hat{Y}$	Y	$\hat{Y}$
129	125.09	127	127.41
124	125.42	126	127.75
126	125.75	125	128.08
131	126.09	131	128.41
123	126.42	134	128.74
125	126.75		
122	127.08		

The two data series do not fit well. The linear data miss the highs and lows of the original data.

34. *a.* Non-linear
    b. $\log \hat{Y} = 1.13 + 0.175t$
    c. $r^2 = 0.999$
    d. $Y_{Dec} = 1698.24$
36. $\hat{Y} = 103.1$
38. $r^2 = 0.999$
40. *b.* $MSE_{.20} = 133.32$ $MSE_{.90} = 306.15$.
    c. The high volatility of the data requires a low value for alpha.

CHAPTER 17

8. *a.* $L_{1987} = 96.0$
       $L_{1988} = 100.0$
       $L_{1989} = 133.0$
       $L_{1990} = 132.1$
       $L_{1991} = 142.4$
   b. $P_{1987} = 94.7$
       $P_{1988} = 100.0$
       $P_{1989} = 137.0$
       $P_{1990} = 156.3$
       $P_{1991} = 158.5$

10.

Year	Spliced Series (1982–84 = 100)	Rebased Series (1985 = 100)
1980	82.4	76.6
1981	91.0	84.6
1982	96.6	89.8
1983	99.7	92.7
1984	103.9	96.6
1985	107.6	100.0
1986	109.6	101.9
1987	113.6	105.6

12. Use CPI to deflate income.

Year	Real Income	Year	Real Income
1984	$40,530	1987	$39,322
1985	39,919	1988	38,523
1986	39,974	1989	37,684

14. *a.* **Real Income**

    1984 = $480
    1985 = $485
    1986 = $495
    1987 = $504

    b. $X = \$545.59$

16. *a.*

1985	$1,577	1988	$1,699
1986	1,632	1989	1,794
1987	1,595		

    b. The values measure the purchasing power of the money incomes.

18. 0.88
20. 1985: $23,187
    1989: $55,587
22. $L_{89} = 100$
    $L_{90} = 107.49$
    $L_{91} = 112.29$
    $P_{89} = 100$
    $P_{90} = 105.96$
    $P_{91} = 108.08$
    Inflation:

Laspeyres	Paasche
89–90: 7.49%	89–90: 5.96%
90–91: 4.46%	90–91: 2.00%
89–91: 12.29%	91–92 8.08%

24. 1989: 118.8; 1990: 124.18; 1991: 127.68
26. Martha's real income is higher: $23,300 < 24,062$
28. $L_{89} = 100$ $P_{89} = 100$
    $L_{90} = 117.7$ $P_{90} = 116.73$
    $L_{91} = 109.6$ $P_{91} = 109.2$
    $L_{92} = 125.0$ $P_{92} = 125.6$
30. The increase from January to February is 2.6%.
    The increase from February to March is 2.9%.
    The increase from March to April is 3.6%.

CHAPTER 18

4. Only $\overline{X}_5$ is in control.
   R_3 is out of control.
6. $\overline{X}$ and R charts show system is out of control.
8. Only one sample, $C = 12$, suggests a problem.
10. $C = 3$
12. The process is out of control, especially with regard to $\overline{X}$.
14. $C = 4$
16. 0.4312
18. $C = 5$
20. $\text{UCL}_{\bar{x}} = 441.83$ $\text{UCL}_R = 121.21$
    $\text{LCL}_{\bar{x}} = 389.03$ $\text{LCL}_R = 4.79$
22. $\text{UCL}_P = 0.524$ $\text{LCL}_p = 0$
24. For WordPerfect:
    $\text{UCL}_p = 0.48$; $\text{LCL}_p = 0.098$
    $\text{UCL}_c = 1.9$; $\text{LCL}_c = 0$

For Professional Write
    $\text{UCL}_p = 0.09$; $\text{LCL}_p = 0$
    $\text{UCL}_c = 0.55$; $\text{LCL}_c = 0$
26. $\text{UCL}_p = 0.66$; $\text{LCL}_p = 0.12$
28. $C = 1$
30. $\text{UCL}_{\bar{x}} = \$47.87$; $\text{LCL}_{\bar{x}} = \$42.37$
    $\text{UCL}_R = 20.39$; $\text{LCL}_R = 4.29$
32. $\text{UCL}_{\bar{x}} = 7.6$; $\text{LCL}_{\bar{x}} = 6.4$
    $\text{UCL}_R = 5.9$; $\text{LCL}_R = 1.7$
34. $C = 2 < 7$; yes
36. $\text{UCL}_p = 0.54$; $\text{LCL}_p = 0.12$
38. $C = 7 < 12$; yes
40. $\text{UCL}_{\bar{x}} = 43.1$; $\text{LCL}_{\bar{x}} = 23.1$
    $\text{UCL}_R = 49.8$; $\text{LCL}_R = 3.63$
42. $\text{UCL}_{\bar{x}} = 22.4$; $\text{LCL}_{\bar{x}} = 20.2$

INDEX